Collins
Italian
Dictionary

HarperCollins Publishers
Westerhill Road
Bishopbriggs
Glasgow G64 2QT
Great Britain

Sixth Edition 2005

© William Collins Sons & Co. Ltd.
1982, 1989
© HarperCollins Publishers 1993,
1998, 2001, 2005

ISBN 0-00-712624-7

Collins Gem ® is a registered
trademark of HarperCollins
Publishers Limited

www.collins.co.uk

A catalogue record for this book
is available from the British
Library

Typeset by Thomas Callan

Printed in Italy by Legoprint
S.P.A.

Acknowledgements
We would like to acknowledge the
assistance of the many hundreds of
individuals and companies who
have kindly given permission for
copyright material to be used in the
Collins Word Web. The written
sources include many national and
regional newspapers in Britain and
overseas; magazine and periodical
publishers; and book publishers in
Britain, the United States and
Australia. Extensive spoken data
have been provided by radio and
television broadcasting companies;
research workers at many
universities and other institutions;
and numerous individual contributors. We are grateful to them all.

CONTRIBUTORS
G. Bacchelli, M Clari,
J. Littlejohn, M. Noble, L. Riu

BASED ON THE FIRST EDITION BY
Catherine E. Love
P. L. Rossi, D. M. Chaplin,
F. Villa, E. Bilucaglia

INDICE		CONTENTS

I marchi registrati

I termini che a nostro parere costituiscono un marchio registrato sono stati designati come tali. In ogni caso, né la presenza né l'assenza di tale designazione implicano alcuna valutazione del loro reale stato giuridico.

Note on trademarks

Entered words that we have reason to believe constitute trademarks have been designated as such. However, neither the presence nor the absence of such designation should be regarded as affecting the legal status of any trademark.

INTRODUZIONE

Vi ringraziamo di aver scelto il Dizionario inglese Collins Gem e ci auguriamo che esso si riveli uno strumento utile e piacevole da usare nello studio, in vacanza e sul lavoro.

In questa introduzione troverete alcuni suggerimenti per aiutarvi a trarre il massimo beneficio dal vostro nuovo dizionario, ricco non solo per il suo ampio lemmario ma anche per il gran numero di informazioni contenute in ciascuna voce.

All'inizio del dizionario troverete l'elenco delle abbreviazioni usate nel testo e una guida alla pronuncia. Troverete inoltre un utile elenco delle forme dei verbi irregolari inglesi e italiani, seguito da una sezione finale con i numeri, l'ora e la data.

Come usare il dizionario Collins Gem

Per imparare ad usare in modo efficace il dizionario è importante comprendere la funzione delle differenziazioni tipografiche, dei simboli e delle abbreviazioni usati nel testo. Vi forniamo pertanto qui di seguito alcuni chiarimenti in merito a tali convenzioni.

I lemmi

Sono le parole in **neretto** elencate in ordine alfabetico. Il primo e l'ultimo lemma di ciascuna pagina appaiono al margine superiore.

Dove opportuno, informazioni sull'ambito d'uso o il livello di formalità di certe parole vengono fornite tra parentesi in corsivo e spesso in forma abbreviata dopo l'indicazione della categoria grammaticale (es. (*Comm*), (*inf*)).

In certi casi più parole con radice comune sono raggruppate sotto lo stesso lemma. Tali parole appaiono in neretto ma in un carattere leggermente ridotto (es. **acceptance**).

Esempi d'uso del lemma sono a loro volta in neretto ma in un carattere diverso dal lemma (es. **to be cold**).

La trascrizione fonetica

La trascrizione fonetica che illustra la corretta pronuncia del lemma è tra parentesi quadre e segue immediatamente il lemma (es. **knee** [niː]). L'elenco dei simboli fonetici è alle pagine xii-xiii.

Le traduzioni

Le traduzioni sono in carattere tondo e, quando il lemma ha più di un significato, le traduzioni sono separate da un punto e virgola. Spesso diverse traduzioni di un lemma sono introdotte da una o più parole in corsivo tra parentesi tonde: la loro funzione è di chiarire a quale significato del lemma si riferisce la traduzione. Possono essere sinonimi, indicazioni di ambito d'uso o di registro del lemma (es. **party** *(Pol)*, *(team)*, *(celebration)*; **laid back** *(inf)* ecc.).

Le 'parole chiave' ⚪

Un trattamento particolare è stato riservato a quelle parole che, per frequenza d'uso o complessità, necessitano una strutturazione più chiara ed esauriente (es. **da, di, avere** in italiano, **at, to, be, this** in inglese). Frecce e numeri vi guidano attraverso le varie distinzioni grammaticali e di significato; ulteriori informazioni sono fornite in corsivo tra parentesi.

Informazioni grammaticali

Le parti del discorso (noun, adjective ecc.) sono espresse da abbreviazioni convenzionali in corsivo *(n, adj* ecc.) e seguono la trascrizione fonetica del lemma.

Eventuali ulteriori informazioni grammaticali, come ad esempio le forme di un verbo irregolare o il plurale irregolare di un sostantivo, precedono tra parentesi la parte del discorso (es. **give** *(pt* **gave**, *pp* **given)** *vt;* **man** [...] *(pl* **men)** *n).*

INTRODUCTION

We are delighted that you have decided to buy the Collins Gem Italian Dictionary and hope you will enjoy and benefit from using it at school, at home, on holiday or at work.

This introduction gives you a few tips on how to get the most out of your dictionary – not simply from its comprehensive wordlist but also from the information provided in each entry. This will help you to read and understand modern Italian, as well as communicate and express yourself in the language.

The dictionary begins by listing the abbreviations used in the text and illustrating the sounds shown by the phonetic symbols. You will also find Italian and English verb tables, followed by a section on numbers and time expressions.

Using your Collins Gem dictionary

A wealth of information is presented in the dictionary, using various typefaces, sizes of type, symbols, abbreviations and brackets. The various conventions and symbols used are explained in the following sections.

Headwords

The words you look up in a dictionary – "headwords" – are listed alphabetically. They are printed in **bold type** for rapid identification. The two headwords appearing at the top of each page indicate the first and last word dealt with on the page in question.

Information about the usage or form of certain headwords is given in brackets after the part of speech. This usually appears in abbreviated form and in italics (e.g. (*fam*), (*Comm*)).

Where appropriate, words related to headwords are grouped in the same entry (e.g. **illustrare, illustrazione**) in a slightly smaller bold type than the headword.

Common expressions in which the headword appears are shown in a different bold roman type (e.g. **aver freddo**).

Phonetic spellings

Where the phonetic spelling of headwords (indicating their pronunciation) is given, it will appear in square brackets immediately after the headword (e.g. **calza** ['kaltsa]). A list of these symbols is given on pages xii-xiii.

Translations

Headword translations are given in ordinary type and, where more than one meaning or usage exists, these are separated by a semicolon. You will often find other words in italics in brackets before the translations. These offer suggested contexts in which the headword might appear (e.g. **duro** (*pietra*) or (*lavoro*)) or provide synonyms (e.g. **duro** (*ostinato*)).

"Key" words ○

Special status is given to certain Italian and English words which are considered as "key" words in each language. They may, for example, occur very frequently or have several types of usage (e.g. **da, di, avere** in Italian, **at, to, be, this** in English). A combination of arrows and numbers helps you to distinguish different parts of speech and different meanings. Further helpful information is provided in brackets and italics.

Grammatical information

Parts of speech are given in abbreviated form in italics after the phonetic spellings of headwords (e.g. *vt, av, cong*).

Genders of Italian nouns are indicated as follows: *sm* for a masculine and *sf* for a feminine noun. Feminine and irregular plural forms of nouns are also shown (e.g. **uovo**, (*pl(f)* **uova**); **dottore, essa**).

Feminine adjective endings are given, as are plural forms (e.g. **opaco, a, chi, che**).

ABBREVIAZIONI		ABBREVIATIONS
abbreviazione	abbr	abbreviation
aggettivo	adj	adjective
amministrazione	Admin	administration
avverbio	adv	adverb
aeronautica, viaggi aerei	Aer	flying, air travel
aggettivo	ag	adjective
agricoltura	Agr	agriculture
amministrazione	Amm	administration
anatomia	Anat	anatomy
architettura	Archit	architecture
articolo determinativo	art def	definite article
articolo indeterminativo	art indef	indefinite article
attributivo	attrib	attributive
ausiliare	aus, aux	auxiliary
automobile	Aut	motor car and motoring
avverbio	av	adverb
aeronautica, viaggi aerei	Aviat	flying, air travel
biologia	Biol	biology
botanica	Bot	botany
inglese britannico	BRIT	British English
consonante	C	consonant
chimica	Chim, Chem	chemistry
commercio, finanza	Comm	commerce, finance
comparativo	compar	comparative
informatica	Comput	computing
congiunzione	cong, conj	conjunction
edilizia	Constr	building
sostantivo usato come aggettivo, ma mai con funzione predicativa	cpd	compound element: noun used as adjective and which cannot follow the noun it qualifies
cucina	Cuc, Culin	cookery
davanti a	dav	before

ABBREVIAZIONI		ABBREVIATIONS
articolo determinativo	*def art*	definite article
determinativo; articolo, aggettivo dimostrativo o indefinito ecc	*det*	determiner: article, demonstrative etc
diminutivo	*dimin*	diminutive
diritto	*Dir*	law
economia	*Econ*	economics
edilizia	*Edil*	building
elettricità, elettronica	*Elettr, Elec*	electricity, electronics
esclamazione	*escl, excl*	exclamation
femminile	*f*	feminine
familiare (! da evitare)	*fam(!)*	colloquial usage (! particularly offensive)
ferrovia	*Ferr*	railways
senso figurato	*fig*	figurative use
fisiologia	*Fisiol*	physiology
fotografia	*Fot*	photography
verbo inglese la cui particella è inseparabile dal verbo	*fus*	(phrasal verb) where the particle cannot be separated from the main verb
nella maggior parte dei sensi; generalmente	*gen*	in most or all senses; generally
geografia, geologia	*Geo*	geography, geology
geometria	*Geom*	geometry
storia, storico	*Hist*	history, historical
impersonale	*impers*	impersonal
articolo indeterminativo	*indef art*	indefinite article
familiare (! da evitare)	*inf(!)*	colloquial usage (! particularly offensive)
infinito	*infin*	infinitive
informatica	*Inform*	computing

ABBREVIAZIONI		ABBREVIATIONS
insegnamento, sistema scolastico e universitario	*Ins*	schooling, schools and universities
invariabile	*inv*	invariable
irregolare	*irreg*	irregular
grammatica, linguistica	*Ling*	grammar, linguistics
maschile	*m*	masculine
matematica	*Mat(h)*	mathematics
termine medico, medicina	*Med*	medical term, medicine
il tempo, meteorologia	*Meteor*	the weather, meteorology
maschile o femminile	*m/f*	masculine or feminine
esercito, linguaggio militare	*Mil*	military matters
musica	*Mus*	music
sostantivo	*n*	noun
nautica	*Naut*	sailing, navigation
numerale (aggettivo, sostantivo)	*num*	numeral adjective or noun
	o.s.	oneself
peggiorativo	*peg, pej*	derogatory, pejorative
fotografia	*Phot*	photography
fisiologia	*Physiol*	physiology
plurale	*pl*	plural
politica	*Pol*	politics
participio passato	*pp*	past participle
preposizione	*prep*	preposition
pronome	*pron*	pronoun
psicologia, psichiatria	*Psic, Psych*	psychology, psychiatry
tempo passato	*pt*	past tense
qualcosa	*qc*	
qualcuno	*qn*	
religione, liturgia	*Rel*	religions, church service
sostantivo	*s*	noun
	sb	somebody

ABBREVIAZIONI		ABBREVIATIONS
insegnamento, sistema scolastico e universitario	Scol	schooling, schools and universities
singolare	sg	singular
soggetto (grammaticale)	sog	(grammatical) subject
	sth	something
congiuntivo	sub	subjunctive
soggetto (grammaticale)	subj	(grammatical) subject
superlativo	superl	superlative
termine tecnico, tecnologia	Tecn, Tech	technical term, technology
telecomunicazioni	Tel	telecommunications
tipografia	Tip	typography, printing
televisione	TV	television
tipografia	Typ	typography, printing
università	Univ	university
inglese americano	US	American English
vocale	V	vowel
verbo	vb	verb
verbo o gruppo verbale con funzione intransitiva	vi	verb or phrasal verb used intransitively
verbo pronominale o riflessivo	vpr	pronominal or reflexive verb
verbo o gruppo verbale con funzione transitiva	vt	verb or phrasal verb used transitively
zoologia	Zool	zoology
marchio registrato	®	registered trademark
introduce un'equivalenza culturale	≈	introduces a cultural equivalent

TRASCRIZIONE FONETICA

Consonanti		Consonants

NB **p, b, t, d, k, g** sono seguite da un'aspirazione in inglese.

NB **p, b, t, d, k, g** are not aspirated in Italian.

padre	p	puppy
bambino	b	baby
/tutto	t	tent
dado	d	daddy
cane che	k	cork kiss chord
gola ghiro	g	gag guess
sano	s	so rice kiss
svago esame	z	cousin buzz
scena	∫	sheep sugar
	ʒ	pleasure beige
pece lanciare	t∫	church
giro gioco	dʒ	judge general
afa faro	f	farm raffle
vero bravo	v	very rev
	θ	thin maths
	ð	that other
letto ala	l	little ball
gli	ʎ	million
rete arco	r	rat rare
ramo madre	m	mummy comb
no fumante	n	no ran
gnomo	ɲ	canyon
	ŋ	singing bank
	h	hat reheat
buio piacere	j	yet
uomo guaio	w	wall bewail
	x	loch

Varie		Miscellaneous
per l'inglese: la "r" finale viene pronunciata se seguita da una vocale	r	
precede la sillaba accentata	'	precedes the stressed syllable

PHONETIC TRANSCRIPTION

Vocali		Vowels

NB La messa in equivalenza di certi suoni indica solo una rassomiglianza approssimativa.

NB The pairing of some vowel sounds only indicates approximate equivalence.

vino idea	i i:	heel bead
	ɪ	hit pity
stella edera	e	
epoca eccetto	ɛ	set tent
mamma amore	a æ	bat apple
	ɑ:	after car calm
	ã	fiancé
	ʌ	fun cousin
müsli	y	
	ə	over above
	ə:	urn fern work
rosa occhio	ɔ	wash pot
	ɔ:	born cork
ponte ognuno	o	
föhn	ø	
utile zucca	u	full soot
	u:	boon lewd

Dittonghi

Diphthongs

ɪə	beer tier
ɛə	tear fair there
eɪ	date plaice day
aɪ	life buy cry
au	owl foul now
əu	low no
ɔɪ	boil boy oily
uə	poor tour

xiii

ITALIAN PRONUNCIATION

Vowels

Where the vowel **e** or the vowel **o** appears in a stressed syllable it can be either open [ɛ], [ɔ] or closed [e], [o]. As the open or closed pronunciation of these vowels is subject to regional variation, the distinction is of little importance to the user of this dictionary. Phonetic transcription for headwords containing these vowels will therefore only appear where other pronunciation difficulties are present.

Consonants

c before "e" or "i" is pronounced like the *"tch"* in match.
ch is pronounced like the "k" in "kit".
g before "e" or "i" is pronounced like the *"j"* in "jet".
gh is pronounced like the "g" in "get".
gl before "e" or "i" is normally pronounced like the *"lli"* in "million", and in a few cases only like the *"gl"* in "glove".
gn is pronounced like the *"ny"* in "canyon"
sc before "e" or "i" is pronounced "sh".
z is pronounced like the *"ts"* in "stetson", or like the *"d's"* in "bird's-eye".

Headwords containing the above consonants and consonantal groups have been given full phonetic transcription in this dictionary.

NB All double written consonants in Italian are fully sounded: e.g. the *tt* in "tutto" is pronounced as in "hat trick".

ITALIAN VERB FORMS

1 Gerundio **2** Participio passato **3** Presente **4** Imperfetto **5** Passato remoto **6** Futuro **7** Condizionale **8** Congiuntivo presente **9** Congiuntivo passato **10** Imperativo

andare 3 vado, vai, va, andiamo, andate, vanno **6** andrò *ecc.* **8** vada **10** va'!, vada!, andate!, vadano!

apparire 2 apparso **3** appaio, appari *o* apparisci, appare *o* apparisce, appaiono *o* appariscono **5** apparvi *o* apparsi, apparisti, apparve *o* apparì *o* apparse, apparvero *o* apparirono *o* apparsero **8** appaia *o* apparisca

aprire 2 aperto **3** apro **5** aprii, apristi **8** apra

AVERE 3 ho, hai, ha, abbiamo, avete, hanno **5** ebbi, avesti, ebbe, avemmo, aveste, ebbero **6** avrò *ecc.* **8** abbia *ecc.* **10** abbi!, abbia!, abbiate!, abbiano!

bere 1 bevendo **2** bevuto **3** bevo *ecc.* **4** bevevo *ecc.* **5** bevvi *o* bevetti, bevesti **6** berrò *ecc.* **8** beva *ecc.* **9** bevessi *ecc.*

cadere 5 caddi, cadesti **6** cadrò *ecc.*

cogliere 2 colto **3** colgo, colgono **5** colsi, cogliesti **8** colga

correre 2 corso **5** corsi, corresti

cuocere 2 cotto **3** cuocio, cociamo, cuociono **5** cossi, cocesti

dare 3 do, dai, dà, diamo, date, danno **5** diedi *o* detti, desti **6** darò *ecc.* **9** dessi *ecc.* **10** da'!, dai!, date! diano!

dire 1 dicendo **2** detto **3** dico, dici, dice, diciamo, dite, dicono **4** dicevo *ecc.* **5** dissi, dicesti **6** dirò *ecc.* **8** dica, diciamo, diciate, dicano **9** dicessi *ecc.* **10** di'!, dica!, dite!, dicano!

dolere 3 dolgo, duoli, duole, dolgono **5** dolsi, dolesti **6** dorrò *ecc.* **8** dolga

dovere 3 devo *o* debbo, devi, deve, dobbiamo, dovete, devono *o* debbono **6** dovrò *ecc.* **8** debba, dobbiamo, dobbiate, devano *o* debbano

ESSERE 2 stato **3** sono, sei, è, siamo, siete, sono **4** ero, eri, era, eravamo, eravate, erano **5** fui, fosti, fu, fummo, foste, furono **6** sarò *ecc.* **8** sia *ecc.* **9** fossi, fossi, fosse, fossimo, foste, fossero **10** sii!, sia!, siate!, siano!

fare 1 facendo **2** fatto **3** faccio, fai, fa, facciamo, fate, fanno **4** facevo *ecc.* **5** feci, facesti **6** farò *ecc.* **8** faccia *ecc.* **9** facessi *ecc.* **10** fa'!, faccia!, fate!, facciano!

FINIRE 1 finendo **2** finito **3** finisco, finisci, finisce, finiamo, finite, finiscono **4** finivo, finivi, finiva, finivamo, finivate, finivano **5** finii, finisti, finì, finimmo, finiste, finirono **6** finirò, finirai, finirà, finiremo, finirete, finiranno **7** finirei, finiresti, finirebbe, finiremmo, finireste, finirebbero **8** finisca, finisca, finisca, finiamo, finiate, finiscano **9** finissi, finissi, finisse, finissimo, finiste, finissero **10** finisci!, finisca!, finite!, finiscano!

giungere 2 giunto **5** giunsi, giungesti

leggere 2 letto **5** lessi, leggesti

mettere 2 messo **5** misi, mettesti

morire 2 morto **3** muoio, muori, muore, moriamo, morite, muoiono **6** morirò *o* morrò *ecc.* **8** muoia

muovere 2 mosso **5** mossi, movesti

nascere 2 nato **5** nacqui, nascesti

nuocere 2 nuociuto **3** nuoccio, nuoci, nuoce, nociamo *o* nuociamo, nuocete, nuocciono *o* nuociono *ecc.* **5** nocqui, nuocesti **6** nuocerò *ecc.* **7** nuoccia

offrire 2 offerto **3** offro **5** offersi *o* offrii, offristi **8** offra

parere 2 parso **3** paio, paiamo, paiono **5** parvi *o* parsi, paresti **6** parrò *ecc.* **8** paia, paiamo, paiate, paiano

PARLARE 1 parlando 2 parlato 3 parlo, parli, parla, parliamo, parlate, parlano 4 parlavo, parlavi, parlava, parlavamo, parlavate, parlavano 5 parlai, parlasti, parlò, parlammo, parlaste, parlarono 6 parlerò, parlerai, parlerà, parleremo, parlerete, parleranno 7 parlerei, parleresti, parlerebbe, parleremmo, parlereste, parlerebbero 8 parli, parli, parli, parliamo, parliate, parlino 9 parlassi, parlassi, parlasse, parlassimo, parlaste, parlassero 10 parla!, parli!, parlate!, parlino!

piacere 2 piaciuto 3 piaccio, piacciamo, piacciono 5 piacqui, piacesti 8 piaccia ecc.

porre 1 ponendo 2 posto 3 pongo, poni, pone, poniamo, ponete, pongono 4 ponevo ecc. 5 posi, ponesti 6 porrò ecc. 8 ponga, poniamo, poniate, pongano 9 ponessi ecc.

potere 3 posso, puoi, può, possiamo, potete, possono 6 potrò ecc. 8 possa, possiamo, possiate, possano

prendere 2 preso 5 presi, prendesti

ridurre 1 riducendo 2 ridotto 3 riduco ecc. 4 riducevo ecc. 5 ridussi, riducesti 6 ridurrò ecc. 8 riduca ecc. 9 riducessi ecc.

riempire 1 riempiendo 3 riempio, riempi, riempie, riempiono

rimanere 2 rimasto 3 rimango, rimangono 5 rimasi, rimanesti 6 rimarrò ecc. 8 rimanga

rispondere 2 risposto 5 risposi, rispondesti

salire 3 salgo, sali, salgono 8 salga

sapere 3 so, sai, sa, sappiamo, sapete, sanno 5 seppi, sapesti 6 saprò ecc. 8 sappia ecc. 10 sappi!, sappia!, sappiate!, sappiano!

scrivere 2 scritto 5 scrissi, scrivesti

sedere 3 siedo, siedi, siede, siedono 8 sieda

spegnere 2 spento 3 spengo, spengono 5 spensi, spegnesti 8 spenga

stare 2 stato 3 sto, stai, sta, stiamo, state, stanno 5 stetti, stesti 6 starò ecc. 8 stia ecc. 9 stessi ecc. 10 sta'!, stia!, state!, stiano!

tacere 2 taciuto 3 taccio, tacciono 5 tacqui, tacesti 8 taccia

tenere 3 tengo, tieni, tiene, tengono 5 tenni, tenesti 6 terrò ecc. 8 tenga

trarre 1 traendo 2 tratto 3 traggo, trai, trae, traiamo, traete, traggono 4 traevo ecc. 5 trassi, traesti 6 trarrò ecc. 8 tragga 9 traessi ecc.

udire 3 odo, odi, ode, odono 8 oda

uscire 3 esco, esci, esce, escono 8 esca

valere 2 valso 3 valgo, valgono 5 valsi, valesti 6 varrò ecc. 8 valga

VENDERE 1 vendendo 2 venduto 3 vendo, vendi, vende, vendiamo, vendete, vendono 4 vendevo, vendevi, vendeva, vendevamo, vendevate, vendevano 5 vendei o vendetti, vendesti, vendé o vendette, vendemmo, vendeste, venderono o vendettero 6 venderò, venderai, venderà, venderemo, venderete, venderanno 7 venderei, venderesti, venderebbe, venderemmo, vendereste, venderebbero 8 venda, venda, venda, vendiamo, vendiate, vendano 9 vendessi, vendessi, vendesse, vendessimo, vendeste, vendessero 10 vendi!, venda!, vendete!, vendano!

venire 2 venuto 3 vengo, vieni, viene, vengono 5 venni, venisti 6 verrò ecc. 8 venga

vivere 2 vissuto 3 vivo, vissi, vivesti

volere 3 voglio, vuoi, vuole, vogliamo, volete, vogliono 5 volli, volesti 6 vorrò ecc. 8 voglia ecc. 10 vogli!, voglia!, vogliate!, vogliano!

ENGLISH VERB FORMS

present	*pt*	*pp*	*present*	*pt*	*pp*
arise	arose	arisen	feed	fed	fed
awake	awoke	awoken	feel	felt	felt
be(am, is, are; being)	was, were	been	fight	fought	fought
bear	bore	born(e)	find	found	found
beat	beat	beaten	flee	fled	fled
become	became	become	fling	flung	flung
begin	began	begun	fly	flew	flown
bend	bent	bent	forbid	forbade	forbidden
bet	bet, betted	bet, betted	forecast	forecast	forecast
bid (at auction, cards)	bid	bid	forget	forgot	forgotten
bid (say)	bade	bidden	forgive	forgave	forgiven
bind	bound	bound	forsake	forsook	forsaken
bite	bit	bitten	freeze	froze	frozen
bleed	bled	bled	get	got	got, (US) gotten
blow	blew	blown	give	gave	given
break	broke	broken	go (goes)	went	gone
breed	bred	bred	grind	ground	ground
bring	brought	brought	grow	grew	grown
build	built	built	hang	hung	hung
burn	burnt, burned	burnt, burned	hang (execute)	hanged	hanged
burst	burst	burst	have (has; having)	had	had
buy	bought	bought	hear	heard	heard
can	could	(been able)	hide	hid	hidden
cast	cast	cast	hit	hit	hit
catch	caught	caught	hold	held	held
choose	chose	chosen	hurt	hurt	hurt
cling	clung	clung	keep	kept	kept
come	came	come	kneel	knelt, kneeled	knelt, kneeled
cost	cost	cost	know	knew	known
cost (work out price of)	costed	costed	lay	laid	laid
creep	crept	crept	lead	led	led
cut	cut	cut	lean	leant, leaned	leant, leaned
deal	dealt	dealt	leap	leapt, leaped	leapt, leaped
dig	dug	dug	learn	learnt, learned	learnt, learned
do (does)	did	done	leave	left	left
draw	drew	drawn	lend	lent	lent
dream	dreamed, dreamt	dreamed, dreamt	let	let	let
drink	drank	drunk	lie (lying)	lay	lain
drive	drove	driven	light	lit, lighted	lit, lighted
dwell	dwelt	dwelt	lose	lost	lost
eat	ate	eaten	make	made	made
fall	fell	fallen			

present	pt	pp	present	pt	pp
may	might	—	spell	spelt, spelled	spelt, spelled
mean	meant	meant			
meet	met	met	spend	spent	spent
mistake	mistook	mistaken	spill	spilt, spilled	spilt, spilled
mow	mowed	mown, mowed			
			spin	spun	spun
must	(had to)	(had to)	spit	spat	spat
pay	paid	paid	split	split	split
put	put	put	spoil	spoiled, spoilt	spoiled, spoilt
quit	quit, quitted	quit, quitted			
			spread	spread	spread
read	read	read	spring	sprang	sprung
rid	rid	rid	stand	stood	stood
ride	rode	ridden	steal	stole	stolen
ring	rang	rung	stick	stuck	stuck
rise	rose	risen	sting	stung	stung
run	ran	run	stink	stank	stunk
saw	sawed	sawed, sawn	stride	strode	stridden
say	said	said	strike	struck	struck, stricken
see	saw	seen			
seek	sought	sought	strive	strove	striven
sell	sold	sold	swear	swore	sworn
send	sent	sent	sweep	swept	swept
set	set	set	swell	swelled	swollen, swelled
sew	sewed	sewn			
shake	shook	shaken	swim	swam	swum
shear	sheared	shorn, sheared	swing	swung	swung
			take	took	taken
shed	shed	shed	teach	taught	taught
shine	shone	shone	tear	tore	torn
shoot	shot	shot	tell	told	told
show	showed	shown	think	thought	thought
shrink	shrank	shrunk	throw	threw	thrown
shut	shut	shut	thrust	thrust	thrust
sing	sang	sung	tread	trod	trodden
sink	sank	sunk	wake	woke, waked	woken, waked
sit	sat	sat			
slay	slew	slain	wear	wore	worn
sleep	slept	slept	weave	wove, weaved	woven, weaved
slide	slid	slid			
sling	slung	slung	wed	wedded, wed	wedded, wed
slit	slit	slit			
smell	smelt, smelled	smelt, smelled	weep	wept	wept
			win	won	won
sow	sowed	sown, sowed	wind	wound	wound
			wring	wrung	wrung
speak	spoke	spoken	write	wrote	written
speed	sped, speeded	sped, speeded			

I NUMERI		NUMBERS
uno(a)	1	one
due	2	two
tre	3	three
quattro	4	four
cinque	5	five
sei	6	six
sette	7	seven
otto	8	eight
nove	9	nine
dieci	10	ten
undici	11	eleven
dodici	12	twelve
tredici	13	thirteen
quattordici	14	fourteen
quindici	15	fifteen
sedici	16	sixteen
diciassette	17	seventeen
diciotto	18	eighteen
diciannove	19	nineteen
venti	20	twenty
ventuno	21	twenty-one
ventidue	22	twenty-two
ventitré	23	twenty-three
ventotto	28	twenty-eight
trenta	30	thirty
quaranta	40	forty
cinquanta	50	fifty
sessanta	60	sixty
settanta	70	seventy
ottanta	80	eighty
novanta	90	ninety
cento	100	a hundred
cento uno	101	a hundred and one
duecento	200	two hundred
mille	1 000	a thousand
milleduecentodue	1 202	one thousand two hundred and two
cinquemila	5000	five thousand
un milione	1 000 000	a million

I NUMERI	NUMBERS
primo(a)	first, 1st
secondo(a)	second, 2nd
terzo(a)	third, 3rd
quarto(a)	fourth, 4th
quinto(a)	fifth, 5th
sesto(a)	sixth, 6th
settimo(a)	seventh
ottavo(a)	eighth
nono(a)	ninth
decimo(a)	tenth
undicesimo(a)	eleventh
dodicesimo(a)	twelfth
tredicesimo(a)	thirteenth
quattordicesimo(a)	fourteenth
quindicesimo(a)	fifteenth
sedicesimo(a)	sixteenth
diciassettesimo(a)	seventeenth
diciottesimo(a)	eighteenth
diciannovesimo(a)	nineteenth
ventesimo(a)	twentieth
ventunesimo(a)	twenty-first
ventiduesimo(a)	twenty-second
ventitreesimo(a)	twenty-third
ventottesimo(a)	twenty-eighth
trentesimo(a)	thirtieth
centesimo(a)	hundredth
centunesimo(a)	hundred-and-first
millesimo(a)	thousandth
milionesimo(a)	millionth

Frazioni

mezzo
terzo
due terzi
quarto
quinto
zero virgola cinque, 0,5
tre virgola quattro, 3,4
dieci per cento
cento per cento

Esempi

abita al numero dieci
si trova nel capitolo sette,
  a pagina sette
abita al terzo piano
arrivò quarto
scala uno a venticinquemila

Fractions

half
third
two thirds
quarter
fifth
(nought) point five, 0.5
three point four, 3.4
ten per cent
a hundred per cent

Examples

he lives at number 10
it's in chapter 7, on page 7

he lives on the 3rd floor
he came in 4th
scale 1:25,000

L'ORA

che ora è?, che ore sono?

è ..., sono ...

mezzanotte
l'una (di notte)

le tre del mattino

l'una e cinque
l'una e dieci
l'una e un quarto, l'una e quindici

l'una e venticinque

l'una e mezzo *or* mezza, l'una e
  trenta
le due meno venticinque, l'una
  e trentacinque
le due meno venti, l'una e
  quaranta
le due meno un quarto, l'una e
  tre quarti
le due meno dieci, l'una e cinquanta
le dodici, mezzogiorno

l'una, le tredici

le sette (di sera), le diciannove

a che ora?

a mezzanotte
all'una, alle tredici
fra venti minuti
venti minuti fa

THE TIME

what time is it?

it's ...

midnight
one o'clock (in the
  morning), one (a.m.)
three o'clock (in the
  morning), three (a.m.)
five past one
ten past one
a quarter past one,
  one fifteen
twenty-five past one,
  one twenty-five
half past one, one thirty

twenty-five to two,
  one thirty-five
twenty to two, one forty

a quarter to two, one
  forty-five
ten to two, one fifty
twelve o'clock, midday,
  noon
one o'clock (in the
  afternoon), one (p.m.)
seven o'clock (in the
  evening), seven (p.m.)

at what time?

at midnight
at one o'clock
in twenty minutes
twenty minutes ago

LA DATA	DATES
oggi	today
ogni giorno, tutti i giorni	every day
ieri	yesterday
stamattina	this morning
domani notte; domani sera	tomorrow night
l'altroieri notte; l'altroieri sera	the night before last
l'altroieri	the day before yesterday
ieri notte; ieri sera	last night
due giorni/sei anni fa	two days/six years ago
domani pomeriggio	tomorrow afternoon
dopodomani	the day after tomorrow
tutti i giovedì, di or il giovedì	every Thursday, on Thursdays
ci va di or il venerdì	he goes on Fridays
"chiuso il mercoledì"	"closed on Wednesdays"
dal lunedì al venerdì	from Monday to Friday
per giovedì, entro giovedì	by Thursday
un sabato di marzo	one Saturday in March
tra una settimana	in a week's time
martedì a otto	a week next or on Tuesday
questa/la prossima/la scorsa settimana	this/next/last week
tra due settimane, tra quindici giorni	in two weeks or a fortnight
lunedì a quindici	two weeks on Monday
il primo/l'ultimo venerdì del mese	the first/last Friday of the month
il mese prossimo	next month
l'anno scorso	last year
il primo giugno	the 1st of June, June first
il due ottobre	the 2nd of October or October 2nd
sono nato nel 1987	I was born in 1987
il suo compleanno è il 5 giugno	his birthday is on June 5th (BRIT) or 5th June (US)
il 18 agosto	on 18th August (BRIT) or August 18 (US)
nel '96	in '96
nella primavera del '94	in the Spring of '94
dal 19 al 3	from the 19th to the 3rd
quanti ne abbiamo oggi?	what's the date? or what date is it today?

oggi è il 15	today's date is the 15th *or* today is the 15th
1988 - millenovecentottantotto	1988 - nineteen eighty-eight
2005 - duemilacinque	2005 - two thousand and five
10 anni esatti	10 years to the day
alla fine del mese	at the end of the month
la settimana del 30/7	week ending 30/7
giornalmente *or* al giorno	daily
settimanalmente *or* alla settimana	weekly
mensilmente, al mese	monthly
annualmente *or* all'anno	annually
due volte alla settimana/al mese/ all'anno	twice a week/month/year
bimestralmente	bi-monthly
nel 4 a.C.	in 4 B.C. *or* B.C. 4
nel 79 d.C.	in 79 A.D *or* A.D. 79
nel tredicesimo secolo	in the 13th century
negli anni '80	in *or* during the 80s
nel 1990 e rotti	in 1990 something

La data nelle lettere

Headings of letters

9 ottobre 2004	9th October 2004 *or* 9 October 2004

ITALIANO - INGLESE
ITALIAN - ENGLISH

a

A abbr (= autostrada) ≈ M (motorway)

a (a + il = **al**, a + lo = **allo**, a + l' = **all'**, a + la = **alla**, a + i = **ai**, a + gli = **agli**, a + le = **alle**) prep

1 (stato in luogo) at; (: in) in; **essere alla stazione** to be at the station; **essere a casa/a scuola/a Roma** to be at home/ at school/in Rome; **è a 10 km da qui** it's 10 km from here, it's 10 km away

2 (moto a luogo) to; **andare a casa/a scuola** to go home/to school

3 (tempo): (all'epoca, stagione) in; **alle cinque** at five (o'clock); **a mezzanotte/Natale** at midnight/ Christmas; **al mattino** in the morning; **a maggio/primavera** in May/spring; **a cinquant'anni** at fifty (years of age); **a domani!** see you tomorrow!

4 (complemento di termine) to; **dare qc a qn** to give sth to sb

5 (mezzo, modo) with, by; **a piedi/ cavallo** on foot/horseback; **fatto a mano** made by hand, handmade; **una barca a motore** a motorboat; **a uno a uno** one by one; **all'italiana** the Italian way, in the Italian fashion

6 (rapporto) a, per; (: con prezzi) at; **prendo 850 euro al mese** I get 850 euros a o per month; **pagato a ore** paid by the hour; **vendere qc a 2 euro il chilo** to sell sth at 2 euros a o per kilo

abbagli'ante [abbaʎˈʎante] ag dazzling; **abbaglianti** smpl (Aut):

accendere gli abbaglianti to put one's headlights on full (BRIT) o high (US) beam

abbagli'are [abbaʎˈʎare] vt to dazzle; (illudere) to delude

abbai'are vi to bark

abbando'nare vt to leave, abandon, desert; (trascurare) to neglect; (rinunciare a) to abandon, give up; **abbandonarsi** vpr to let o.s. go; **abbandonarsi a** (ricordi, vizio) to give o.s. up to

abbas'sare vt to lower; (radio) to turn down; **abbassarsi** vpr (chinarsi) to stoop; (livello, sole) to go down; (fig: umiliarsi) to demean o.s.; **~ i fari** (Aut) to dip o dim (US) one's lights

ab'basso escl **~ il re!** down with the king!

abbas'tanza [abbasˈtantsa] av (a sufficienza) enough; (alquanto) quite, rather, fairly; **non è ~ furbo** he's not shrewd enough; **un vino ~ dolce** quite a sweet wine; **averne ~ di qn/qc** to have had enough of sb/sth

ab'battere vt (muro, casa) to pull down; (ostacolo) to knock down; (albero) to fell; (: vento) to bring down; (bestie da macello) to slaughter; (cane, cavallo) to destroy, put down; (selvaggina, aereo) to shoot down; (fig: malattia, disgrazia) to lay low; **abbattersi** vpr (avvilirsi) to lose heart; **abbat'tuto, -a** ag (fig) depressed

abba'zia [abbatˈtsia] sf abbey

'abbia vb vedi **avere**

abbi'ente ag well-to-do, well-off; **abbienti** smpl **gli abbienti** the well-to-do

abbiglia'mento [abbiʎʎaˈmento] sm dress no pl; (indumenti) clothes pl; (industria) clothing industry

abbi'nare vt ~ (a) to combine (with)

abboc'care vi (pesce) to bite; (tubi) to join; **~ (all'amo)** (fig) to swallow the bait

abbona'mento sm subscription; (alle ferrovie ecc) season ticket; **fare l'~** to take out a subscription (o season ticket)

abbo'narsi vpr **~ a un giornale** to take out a subscription to a newspaper; **~ al teatro/alle ferrovie** to take out a season ticket for the theatre/the train

abbon'dante ag abundant, plentiful; (giacca) roomy

abbon'danza [abbon'dantsa] sf abundance; plenty

abbor'dabile ag (persona) approachable; (prezzo) reasonable

abbot'tonare vt to button up, do up

abbracci'are [abbrat't∫are] vt to embrace; (persona) to hug, embrace; (professione) to take up; (contenere) to include; **abbracciarsi** vpr to hug o embrace (one another); **ab'braccio** sm hug, embrace

abbrevi'are vt to shorten; (parola) to abbreviate

abbreviazi'one [abbrevjat'tsjone] sf abbreviation

abbron'zante [abbron'dzante] ag tanning, sun cpd

abbronzarsi vpr to tan, get a tan

abbron'zato, -a [abbron'dzato] ag (sun)tanned

abbrusto'lire vt (pane) to toast; (caffè) to roast; **abbrustolirsi** vpr to toast; (fig: al sole) to soak up the sun

abbuf'farsi vpr (fam): **~ (di qc)** to stuff o.s. (with sth)

abdi'care vi to abdicate; **~ a** to give up, renounce

a'bete sm fir (tree); **abete rosso** spruce

'abile ag (idoneo): **~ (a qc/a fare qc)** fit (for sth/to do sth); (capace) able; (astuto) clever; (accorto) skilful; **~ al servizio militare** fit for military

service; **abilità** sf inv ability; cleverness; skill

a'bisso sm abyss, gulf

abi'tante sm/f inhabitant

abi'tare vt to live in, dwell in ▶ vi **~ in campagna/a Roma** to live in the country/in Rome; **dove abita?** where do you live?; **abitazi'one** sf residence; house

'abito sm dress no pl; (da uomo) suit; (da donna) dress; (abitudine, disposizione, Rel) habit; **abiti** smpl (vestiti) clothes; **in ~ da sera** in evening dress

abitu'ale ag usual, habitual; (cliente) regular

abitual'mente av usually, normally

abitu'are vt **~ qn a** to get sb used o accustomed to; **abituarsi a** to get used to, accustom o.s. to

abitudi'nario, -a ag of fixed habits ▶ sm/f regular customer

abi'tudine sf habit; **aver l'~ di fare qc** to be in the habit of doing sth; **d'~** usually; **per ~** from o out of habit

abo'lire vt to abolish; (Dir) to repeal

abor'tire vi (Med) to miscarry, have a miscarriage; (: deliberatamente) to have an abortion; (fig) to miscarry, fail; **a'borto** sm miscarriage; abortion

ABS [abi'esse] sigla m (= Anti-Blockier System) ABS

'abside sf apse

abu'sare vi to abuse, misuse; (alcool) to take to excess; (approfittare, violare) to take advantage of

abu'sivo, -a ag unauthorized, unlawful; (occupante) ~ (di una casa) squatter

⚠️ Attenzione! In inglese esiste la parola abusive che però vuol dire ingiurioso.

a.C. av abbr (= avanti Cristo) B.C.

a'cacia, -cie [a'kat∫a] sf (Bot) acacia

ac'cadde vb vedi **accadere**

acca'demia sf (società) learned society; (scuola: d'arte, militare) academy

acca'dere vb impers to happen, occur

accal'dato ag hot

accalo'rarsi vpr (fig) to get excited

accampa'mento sm camp

accam'parsi vpr to camp

acca'nirsi vpr (infierire) to rage; (ostinarsi) to persist; **acca'nito, -a** ag (odio, gelosia) fierce, bitter; (lavoratore) assiduous, dogged; (fumatore) inveterate

ac'canto av near, nearby; **~ a** prep near, beside, close to

accan'tonare vt (problema) to shelve; (somma) to set aside

accappa'toio sm bathrobe

accarez'zare [akkaret'tsare] vt to caress, stroke, fondle; (fig) to toy with

acca'sarsi vpr to set up house; to get married

accasci'arsi [akkaʃ'ʃarsi] vpr to collapse; (fig) to lose heart

accat'tone, -a sm/f beggar

accaval'lare vt (gambe) to cross

acce'care [attʃe'kare] vt to blind ▶ vi to go blind

ac'cedere [at'tʃedere] vi **~ a** to enter; (richiesta) to grant, accede to

accele'rare [attʃele'rare] vt to speed up ▶ vi (Aut) to accelerate; **~ il passo** to quicken one's pace; **accelera'tore** sm (Aut) accelerator

ac'cendere [at'tʃɛndere] vt (fuoco, sigaretta) to light; (luce, televisione) to put on, switch on, turn on; (Aut: motore) to switch on; (Comm: conto) to open; (fig: suscitare) to inflame, stir up; **ha da ~?** have you got a light?; **non riesco ad ~ il riscaldamento** I can't turn the heating on; **accen'dino, accendi'sigaro** sm (cigarette) lighter

accen'nare [attʃen'nare] vt (Mus) to pick out the notes of; to hum ▶ vi **~ a**

(fig: alludere a) to hint at; (: far atto di) to make as if; **~ un saluto** (con la mano) to make as if to wave; (col capo) to half nod; **accenna a piovere** it looks as if it's going to rain

ac'cenno [at'tʃenno] sm (cenno) sign; nod; (allusione) hint

accensi'one [attʃen'sjone] sf (vedi verbo) lighting; switching on; opening; (Aut) ignition

ac'cento [at'tʃento] sm accent; (Fonetica, fig) stress; (inflessione) tone (of voice)

accentu'are [attʃentu'are] vt to stress, emphasize; **accentuarsi** vpr to become more noticeable

accerchi'are [attʃer'kjare] vt to surround, encircle

accerta'mento [attʃerta'mento] sm check; assessment

accer'tare [attʃer'tare] vt to ascertain; (verificare) to check; (reddito) to assess; **accertarsi** vpr **accertarsi (di)** to make sure (of)

ac'ceso, -a [at'tʃeso] pp di **accendere** ▶ ag lit; on; open; (colore) bright

acces'sibile [attʃes'sibile] ag (luogo) accessible; (persona) approachable; (prezzo) reasonable

ac'cesso [at'tʃesso] sm (anche Inform) access; (Med) attack, fit; (impulso violento) fit, outburst

accessori smpl accessories

ac'cetta [at'tʃetta] sf hatchet

accet'tabile [attʃet'tabile] ag acceptable

accet'tare [attʃet'tare] vt to accept; **accettate carte di credito?** do you accept credit cards?; **~ di fare qc** to agree to do sth; **accettazi'one** sf acceptance; (locale o servizio pubblico) reception; **accettazione bagagli** (Aer) check-in (desk)

acchiap'pare [akkjap'pare] vt to catch

acciaie'ria [attʃaje'ria] *sf* steelworks *sg*

acci'aio [at'tʃajo] *sm* steel

acciden'tato, -a [attʃiden'tato] *ag* (*terreno ecc*) uneven

acci'gliato, -a [attʃiʎ'ʎato] *ag* frowning

ac'cingersi [at'tʃindʒersi] *vpr* ~ **a fare qc** to be about to do sth

acciuf'fare [attʃuf'fare] *vt* to seize, catch

acci'uga, -ghe [at'tʃuga] *sf* anchovy

ac'cludere *vt* to enclose

accoc'co'larsi *vpr* to crouch

accogli'ente [akkoʎ'ʎɛnte] *ag* welcoming, friendly

ac'cogliere [ak'kɔʎʎere] *vt* (*ricevere*) to receive; (*dare il benvenuto*) to welcome; (*approvare*) to agree to, accept; (*contenere*) to hold, accommodate

ac'colgo *ecc vb vedi* **accogliere**

ac'colsi *ecc vb vedi* **accogliere**

accoltel'lare *vt* to knife, stab

accomoda'mento *sm* agreement, settlement

accomo'dante *ag* accommodating

accomo'darsi *vpr* (*sedersi*) to sit down; (*entrare*) to come in; **s'accomodi!** (*venga avanti*) come in!; (*si sieda*) take a seat!

accompagna'mento [akkompaɲɲa'mento] *sm* (*Mus*) accompaniment

accompa'gnare [akkompaɲ'ɲare] *vt* to accompany, come o go with; (*Mus*) to accompany; (*unire*) to couple; **~ la porta** to close the door gently

accompagna'tore, -trice *sm/f* companion; **~ turistico** courier

acconcia'tura [akkontʃa'tura] *sf* hairstyle

accondiscen'dente [akkondiʃʃen'dɛnte] *ag* affable

acconsen'tire *vi* ~ **(a)** to agree o consent (to)

accon'tentare *vt* to satisfy; **accontentarsi** *vpr* **accontentarsi di** to be satisfied with, content o.s. with

ac'conto *sm* part payment; **pagare una somma in ~** to pay a sum of money as a deposit

acco'rato, -a *ag* heartfelt

accorci'are [akkor'tʃare] *vt* to shorten; **accorciarsi** *vpr* to become shorter

accor'dare *vt* to reconcile; (*colori*) to match; (*Mus*) to tune; (*Ling*): **~ qc con qc** to make sth agree with sth; (*Dir*) to grant; **accordarsi** *vpr* to agree, come to an agreement; (*colori*) to match

ac'cordo *sm* agreement; (*armonia*) harmony; (*Mus*) chord; **essere d'~** to agree; **andare d'~** to get on well together; **d'~!** all right!, agreed!; **accordo commerciale** trade agreement

ac'corgersi [ak'kordʒersi] *vpr* ~ **di** to notice; (*fig*) to realize

ac'correre *vi* to run up

ac'corto, -a *pp di* **accorgersi** ▶ *ag* shrewd; **stare** ~ to be on one's guard

accos'tare *vt* (*avvicinare*): **~ qc a** to bring sth near to, put sth near to; (*avvicinarsi a*) to approach; (*socchiudere: imposte*) to half-close; (: *porta*) to leave ajar ▶ *vi* (*Naut*) to come alongside; **accostarsi** *vpr* **accostarsi a** to draw near, approach; (*fig*) to support

accredi'tare *vt* (*notizia*) to confirm the truth of; (*Comm*) to credit; (*diplomatico*) to accredit

ac'credito *sm* (*Comm: atto*) crediting; (: *effetto*) credit

accucci'arsi [akkut'tʃarsi] *vpr* (*cane*) to lie down

accu'dire *vi* (*anche: vi* ~ **a**) to attend to

accumu'lare *vt* to accumulate; **accumularsi** *vpr* to accumulate; (*Finanza*) to accrue

accu'rato, -a ag (diligente) careful; (preciso) accurate

ac'cusa sf accusation; (Dir) charge; **la pubblica ~** the prosecution

accu'sare vt **~ qn di qc** to accuse sb of sth; (Dir) to charge sb with sth; **~ ricevuta di** (Comm) to acknowledge receipt of

accusa'tore, -'trice sm/f accuser ▶ sm (Dir) prosecutor

a'cerbo, -a [a'tʃɛrbo] ag bitter; (frutta) sour, unripe; (persona) immature

'acero ['atʃero] sm maple

a'cerrimo, -a [a'tʃɛrrimo] ag very fierce

a'ceto [a'tʃeto] sm vinegar

ace'tone [atʃe'tone] sm nail varnish remover

A.C.I. ['atʃi] sigla m = **Automobile Club d'Italia**

'acido, -a ['atʃido] ag (sapore) acid, sour; (Chim) acid ▶ sm (Chim) acid

'acino ['atʃino] sm berry; **acino d'uva** grape

'acne sf acne

'acqua sf water; (pioggia) rain; **acque** sfpl (di mare, fiume ecc) waters; **fare ~** (Naut) to leak, take in water; **~ in bocca!** mum's the word!; **acqua corrente** running water; **acqua dolce/salata** fresh/salt water; **acqua minerale/potabile/tonica** mineral/drinking/tonic water; **acque termali** thermal waters

a'cquaio sm sink

acqua'ragia [akkwa'radʒa] sf turpentine

a'cquario sm aquarium; (dello zodiaco): **A~** Aquarius

acquascooter [akkwas'kuter] sm inv Jet Ski®

ac'quatico, -a, -ci, -che ag aquatic; (Sport, Scienza) water cpd

acqua'vite sf brandy

acquaz'zone [akkwat'tsone] sm

cloudburst, heavy shower

acque'dotto sm aqueduct; waterworks pl, water system

acque'rello sm watercolour

acqui'rente sm/f purchaser, buyer

acquis'tare vt to purchase, buy; (fig) to gain; **a'quisto** sm purchase; **fare acquisti** to go shopping

acquo'lina sf far venire l'~ **in bocca a qn** to make sb's mouth water

a'crobata, -i, -e sm/f acrobat

'aculeo sm (Zool) sting; (Bot) prickle

a'cume sm acumen, perspicacity

a'custico, -a, ci, che ag acoustic ▶ sf (scienza) acoustics sg; (di una sala) acoustics pl; **cornetto ~** ear trumpet; **apparecchio ~** hearing aid

a'cuto, -a ag (appuntito) sharp, pointed; (suono, voce) shrill, piercing; (Mat, Ling, Med) acute; (Mus) high-pitched; (fig: dolore, desiderio) intense; (: perspicace) acute, keen

a'dagio [a'dadʒo] av slowly ▶ sm (Mus) adagio; (proverbio) adage, saying

adatta'mento sm adaptation

adat'tare vt to adapt; (sistemare) to fit; **adattarsi** vpr adattarsi (a) (ambiente, tempi) to adapt (to); (essere adatto) to be suitable (for)

a'datto, -a ag ~ (a) suitable (for), right (for)

addebi'tare vt **~ qc a qn** to debit sb with sth

ad'debito sm (Comm) debit

adden'tare vt to bite into

adden'trarsi vpr **~ in** to penetrate, go into

addestra'mento sm training

addes'trare vt to train

ad'detto, -a ag **~ a** (persona) assigned to; (oggetto) intended for ▶ sm employee; (funzionario) attaché; **gli addetti ai lavori** authorized personnel; (fig) those in the know; **addetto commerciale** commercial attaché; **addetto stampa** press attaché

ad'dio sm, escl goodbye, farewell

addirit'tura av (veramente) really, absolutely; (perfino) even; (direttamente) directly, right away

addi'tare vt to point out; (fig) to expose

addi'tivo sm additive

addizi'one sf addition

addob'bare vt to decorate; **ad'dobbo** sm decoration

addolo'rare vt to pain, grieve; **addolorarsi (per)** to be distressed (by)

addolo'rato, -a ag distressed, upset; **l'Addolorata** (Rel) Our Lady of Sorrows

ad'dome sm abdomen

addomesti'care vt to tame

addomi'nale ag abdominal; **(muscoli mpl) addominali** stomach muscles

addormen'tare vt to put to sleep; **addormentarsi** vpr to fall asleep, go to sleep

ad'dosso av on; **mettersi ~ il cappotto** to put one's coat on; **~ a** (sopra) on; (molto vicino) right next to; **stare ~ a qn** (fig) to breathe down sb's neck; **dare ~ a qn** (fig) to attack sb

adeguarsi vpr to adapt

adegu'ato, -a ag adequate; (conveniente) suitable; (equo) fair

a'dempiere vt to fulfil, carry out

ade'rente ag adhesive; (vestito) close-fitting ▶ sm/f follower

ade'rire vi (stare attaccato) to adhere, stick; **~ a** to adhere to, stick to; (fig: società, partito) to join; (: opinione) to support; (richiesta) to agree to

adesi'one sf adhesion; (fig) agreement, acceptance; **ade'sivo, -a** ag, sm adhesive

a'desso av (ora) now; (or ora, poco fa) just now; (tra poco) any moment now

adia'cente [adja'tʃɛnte] ag adjacent

adi'bire vt (usare): **~ qc a** to turn sth into

adole'scente [adoleʃ'ʃɛnte] ag, sm/f adolescent

adope'rare vt to use

ado'rare vt to adore; (Rel) to adore, worship

adot'tare vt to adopt; (decisione, provvedimenti) to pass; **adot'tivo, -a** ag (genitori) adoptive; (figlio, patria) adopted; **adozi'one** sf adoption; **adozione a distanza** child sponsorship

adri'atico, -a, -ci, -che ag Adriatic ▶ sm l'A~, il mare A~ the Adriatic, the Adriatic Sea

adu'lare vt to adulate, flatter

a'dultero, -a ag adulterous ▶ sm/f adulterer (adulteress)

a'dulto, -a ag adult; (fig) mature ▶ sm adult, grown-up

a'ereo, -a ag air cpd; (radice) aerial ▶ sm aerial; (aeroplano) plane; **aereo da caccia** fighter (plane); **aereo di linea** airliner; **aereo a reazione** jet (plane); **ae'robica** sf aerobics sg; **aero'nautica** sf (scienza) aeronautics sg; **aeronautica militare** air force

aero'porto sm airport; **all'~ per favore** to the airport, please

aero'sol sm inv aerosol

'afa sf sultriness

af'fabile ag affable

affaccen'dato, -a [affattʃen'dato] ag (persona) busy

affacci'arsi [affat'tʃarsi] vpr to appear (at)

affa'mato, -a ag starving; (fig): **~ (di)** eager (for)

affan'noso, -a ag (respiro) difficult; (fig) troubled, anxious

af'fare sm (faccenda) matter, affair; (Comm) piece of business, (business) deal; (occasione) bargain; (Dir) case;

(*fam*: *cosa*) thing; **affari** *smpl* (*Comm*) business *sg*; **Ministro degli Affari esteri** Foreign Secretary (*BRIT*), Secretary of State (*US*)

affasci'nante [affaʃʃi'nante] *ag* fascinating

affasci'nare [affaʃʃi'nare] *vt* to bewitch; (*fig*) to charm, fascinate

affati'care *vt* to tire; **affaticarsi** *vpr* (*durar fatica*) to tire o.s. out;
affati'cato, -a *ag* tired

af'fatto *av* completely; **non ... ~** not ... at all; **niente ~** not at all

affer'mare *vt* (*dichiarare*) to maintain, affirm; **affermarsi** *vpr* to assert o.s., make one's name known;
affer'mato, -a *ag* established, well-known; **affermazi'one** *sf* affirmation, assertion; (*successo*) achievement

affer'rare *vt* to seize, grasp; (*fig*: *idea*) to grasp; **afferrarsi** *vpr* **afferrarsi a** to cling to

affet'tare *vt* (*tagliare a fette*) to slice; (*ostentare*) to affect

affetta'trice [affetta'tritʃe] *sf* meat slicer

affet'tivo, -a *ag* emotional, affective

af'fetto *sm* affection; **affettu'oso, -a** *ag* affectionate

affezio'narsi [affettsjo'narsi] *vpr* **~ a** to grow fond of

affezio'nato, -a [affettsjo'nato] *ag* **~ a qn/qc** fond of sb/sth; (*attaccato*) attached to sb/sth

affia'tato, -a *ag* **essere molto affiatati** to get on very well

affib'biare *vt* (*fig*: *dare*) to give

affi'dabile *ag* reliable

affida'mento *sm* (*Dir*: *di bambino*) custody; (*fiducia*) **fare ~ su qn** to rely on sb; **non dà nessun ~** he's not to be trusted

affi'dare *vt* **~ qc o qn a qn** to entrust sth o sb to sb; **affidarsi** *vpr* **affidarsi a**

to place one's trust in

affi'lare *vt* to sharpen

affi'lato, -a *ag* (*gen*) sharp; (*volto*, *naso*) thin

affinché [affin'ke] *cong* in order that, so that

affit'tare *vt* (*dare in affitto*) to let, rent (out); (*prendere in affitto*) to rent; **af'fitto** *sm* rent; (*contratto*) lease

af'fliggere [af'fliddʒere] *vt* to torment; **affliggersi** *vpr* to grieve

af'flissi *ecc vb vedi* **affliggere**

afflosci'arsi [afflo'ʃarsi] *vpr* to go limp

afflu'ente *sm* tributary

affo'gare *vt, vi* to drown

affol'lare *vt* to crowd; **affollarsi** *vpr* to crowd; **affol'lato, -a** *ag* crowded

affon'dare *vt* to sink

affran'care *vt* to free, liberate; (*Amm*) to redeem; (*lettera*) to stamp; (: *meccanicamente*) to frank (*BRIT*), meter (*US*)

af'fresco, -schi *sm* fresco

affrettarsi *vpr* to hurry; **~ a fare qc** to hurry o hasten to do sth

affret'tato, -a *ag* (*veloce*: *passo*, *ritmo*) quick, fast; (*frettoloso*: *decisione*) hurried, hasty; (: *lavoro*) rushed

affron'tare *vt* (*pericolo ecc*) to face; (*nemico*) to confront; **affrontarsi** *vpr* (*reciproco*) to come to blows

affumi'cato, -a *ag* (*prosciutto*, *aringa ecc*) smoked

affuso'lato, -a *ag* tapering

Af'ganistan *sm* l'~ Afghanistan

a'foso, -a *ag* sultry, close

'Africa *sf* l'~ Africa; **afri'cano, -a** *ag*, *sm/f* African

a'genda [a'dʒɛnda] *sf* diary
Attenzione! In inglese esiste la parola agenda che però vuol dire ordine del giorno.

a'gente [a'dʒɛnte] *sm* agent; **agente di cambio** stockbroker; **agente**

di polizia police officer; **agente segreto** secret agent; **agen'zia** sf agency; (*succursale*) branch; **agenzia immobiliare** estate agent's (office) (BRIT), real estate office (US); **agenzia di collocamento/stampa** employment/press agency; **agenzia viaggi** travel agency

agevo'lare [adʒevoˈlare] vt to facilitate, make easy

agevolazi'one [adʒevolatˈtsjone] sf (*facilitazione economica*) facility; **agevolazione di pagamento** payment on easy terms; **agevolazioni creditizie** credit facilities; **agevolazioni fiscali** tax concessions

a'gevole [aˈdʒevole] ag easy; (*strada*) smooth

agganci'are [agganˈtʃare] vt to hook up; (*Ferr*) to couple

ag'geggio [adˈdʒeddʒo] sm gadget, contraption

agget'tivo [addʒetˈtivo] sm adjective

agghiacci'ante [aggjatˈtʃante] ag chilling

aggior'nare [addʒorˈnare] vt (*opera, manuale*) to bring up-to-date; (*seduta ecc*) to postpone; **aggiornarsi** vpr to bring (*o keep*) o.s. up-to-date; **aggior'nato, -a** ag up-to-date

aggi'rare [addʒiˈrare] vt to go round; (*fig: ingannare*) to trick; **aggirarsi** vpr to wander about; **il prezzo s'aggira sul milione** the price is around the million mark

aggi'ungere [adˈdʒundʒere] vt to add

aggi'unsi ecc [adˈdʒunsi] vb vedi **aggiungere**

aggius'tare [addʒusˈtare] vt (*accomodare*) to mend, repair; (*riassettare*) to adjust; (*fig: lite*) to settle

aggrap'parsi vpr **~ a** to cling to

aggra'vare vt (*aumentare*) to increase;

(*appesantire: anche fig*) to weigh down, make heavy; (*pena*) to make worse; **aggravarsi** vpr to worsen, become worse

aggre'dire vt to attack, assault

aggressi'one sf aggression; (*atto*) attack, assault

aggres'sivo, -a ag aggressive

aggres'sore sm aggressor, attacker

aggrot'tare vt **~ le sopracciglia** to frown

aggrovigli'arsi vpr (*fig*) to become complicated

aggu'ato sm trap; (*imboscata*) ambush; **tendere un ~ a qn** to set a trap for sb

agguer'rito, -a ag fierce

agi'ato, -a [aˈdʒato] ag (*vita*) easy; (*persona*) well-off, well-to-do

'agile [ˈadʒile] ag agile, nimble

'agio [ˈadʒo] sm ease, comfort; **mettersi a proprio ~** to make o.s. at home *o* comfortable; **agi** smpl comforts; **mettersi a proprio ~** to make o.s. at home *o* comfortable; **dare ~ a qn di fare qc** to give sb the chance of doing sth

a'gire [aˈdʒire] vi to act; (*esercitare un'azione*) to take effect; (*Tecn*) to work, function; **~ contro qn** (*Dir*) to take action against sb

agi'tare [adʒiˈtare] vt (*bottiglia*) to shake; (*mano, fazzoletto*) to wave; (*fig: turbare*) to disturb; (*: incitare*) to stir (up); (*: dibattere*) to discuss; **agitarsi** vpr (*mare*) to be rough; (*malato, dormitore*) to toss and turn; (*bambino*) to fidget; (*emozionarsi*) to get upset; (*Pol*) to become agitated; **agi'tato, -a** ag rough; restless; fidgety; upset, perturbed

'aglio [ˈaʎʎo] sm garlic

a'gnello [aɲˈɲɛllo] sm lamb

'ago (*pl* 'aghi) sm needle

ago'nistico, -a, -ci, -che ag athletic; (*fig*) competitive

agopun'tura sf acupuncture

a'gosto sm August

a'grario, -a ag agrarian, agricultural; (riforma) land cpd

a'gricolo, -a ag agricultural, farm cpd; **agricol'tore** sm farmer; **agricol'tura** sf agriculture, farming

agri'foglio [agri'fɔʎʎo] sm holly

agritu'rismo sm farm holidays pl

agrodolce ag bittersweet; (salsa) sweet and sour

a'grume sm (spesso al pl: pianta) citrus; (: frutto) citrus fruit

a'guzzo, -a [a'guttso] ag sharp

'ahi escl (dolore) ouch!

'Aia sf l'~ the Hague

'aids abbr m o f Aids

airbag sm inv air bag

ai'rone sm heron

aiu'ola sf flower bed

aiu'tante sm/f assistant ▸ sm (Mil) adjutant; (Naut) master-at-arms; **aiutante di campo** aide-de-camp

aiu'tare vt to help; ~ **qn (a fare)** to help sb (to do); **aiutarsi** vpr to help each other; ~ **qn in qc/a fare qc** to help sb with sth/to do sth; **può aiutarmi?** can you help me?

ai'uto sm help, assistance, aid; (aiutante) assistant; **venire in ~ di qn** to come to sb's aid; **aiuto chirurgo** assistant surgeon

'ala (pl 'ali) sf wing; **fare ~** to fall back, make way; **ala destra/sinistra** (Sport) right/left wing

ala'bastro sm alabaster

a'lano sm Great Dane

'alba sf dawn

alba'nese ag, sm/f, sm Albanian

Alba'nia sf l'~ Albania

albe'rato, -a ag (viale, piazza) lined with trees, tree-lined

al'bergo, -ghi sm hotel; **albergo della gioventù** youth hostel

'albero sm tree; (Naut) mast; (Tecn) shaft; **albero genealogico** family tree; **albero a gomiti** crankshaft; **albero maestro** mainmast; **albero di Natale** Christmas tree; **albero di trasmissione** transmission shaft

albi'cocca, -che sf apricot

'album sm album; **album da disegno** sketch book

al'bume sm albumen

'alce ['altʃe] sm elk

'alcol sm inv = **alcool**

al'colico, -a, -ci, -che ag alcoholic ▸ sm alcoholic drink

alcoliz'zato, -a [alkolid'dzato] sm/f alcoholic

'alcool sm inv alcohol

al'cuno, -a (det: dav sm: **alcun** + C, V, **alcuno** + s impura, gn, pn, ps, x, z; dav sf: **alcuna** + C, **alcun'** + V) det (nessuno): **non ... ~** no, not any; **alcuni, e** det pl some, a few; **non c'è alcuna fretta** there's no hurry, there isn't any hurry; **senza alcun riguardo** without any consideration ▸ pron pl **alcuni, e** some, a few

alfa'betico, -a, ci, che ag alphabetical

alfa'beto sm alphabet

'alga, -ghe sf seaweed no pl, alga

'algebra ['aldʒebra] sf algebra

Alge'ria [aldʒe'ria] sf l'~ Algeria

alge'rino, -a [aldʒe'rino] ag, sm/f Algerian

ali'ante sm (Aer) glider

'alibi sm inv alibi

a'lice [a'litʃe] sf anchovy

ali'eno, -a ag (avverso): ~ **(da)** opposed (to), averse (to) ▸ sm/f alien

alimen'tare vt to feed; (Tecn) to feed; to supply; (fig) to sustain ▸ ag food cpd; **alimentari** smpl foodstuffs; (anche: **negozio di alimentari**) grocer's shop; **alimentazi'one** sf feeding; supplying; sustaining; (gli alimenti) diet

a'liquota sf share; (d'imposta) rate; **aliquota d'imposta** tax rate

alis'cafo sm hydrofoil

'alito sm breath

all. abbr (= allegato) encl.

allaccia'mento [allattʃa'mento] sm (Tecn) connection

allacci'are [allat'tʃare] vt (scarpe) to tie, lace (up); (cintura) to do up, fasten; (luce, gas) to connect; (amicizia) to form

allaccia'tura [allattʃa'tura] sf fastening

alla'gare vt to flood; **allagarsi** vpr to flood

allar'gare vt to widen; (vestito) to let out; (aprire) to open; (fig: dilatare) to extend; **allargarsi** vpr (gen) to widen; (scarpe, pantaloni) to stretch; (fig: problema, fenomeno) to spread

allar'mare vt to alarm

al'larme sm alarm; **allarme aereo** air-raid warning

allat'tare vt to feed

alle'anza [alle'antsa] sf alliance

alle'arsi vr to form an alliance; **alle'ato, -a** ag allied ▸ sm/f ally

alle'gare vt (accludere) to enclose; (Dir: citare) to cite, adduce; (denti) to set on edge; **alle'gato, -a** ag enclosed ▸ sm enclosure; (di e-mail) attachment; **in allegato** enclosed

alleg'gerire [alleddʒe'rire] vt to lighten, make lighter; (fig: lavoro, tasse) to reduce

alle'gria sf gaiety, cheerfulness

al'legro, -a ag cheerful, merry; (un po' brillo) merry, tipsy; (vivace: colore) bright ▸ sm (Mus) allegro

allena'mento sm training

alle'nare vt to train; **allenarsi** vpr to train; **allena'tore** sm (Sport) trainer, coach

allen'tare vt to slacken; (disciplina) to relax; **allentarsi** vpr to become slack;

(ingranaggio) to work loose

aller'gia, -'gie [aller'dʒia] sf allergy; **al'lergico, -a, -ci, -che** ag allergic; **sono allergico alla penicillina** I'm allergic to penicillin

alles'tire vt (cena) to prepare; (esercito, nave) to equip, fit out; (spettacolo) to stage

allet'tante ag attractive, alluring

alle'vare vt (animale) to breed, rear; (bambino) to bring up

allevi'are vt to alleviate

alli'bito, -a ag astounded

alli'evo sm/f (apprendista) apprentice; (Mil) cadet

alliga'tore sm alligator

alline'are vt (persone, cose) to line up; (Tip) to align; (fig: economia, salari) to adjust, align; **allinearsi** vpr to line up; (fig: a idee): **allinearsi a** to come into line with

al'lodola sf (sky)lark

alloggi'are [allod'dʒare] vt to accommodate ▸ vi to live; **al'loggio** sm lodging, accommodation (BRIT), accommodations (US)

allonta'nare vt to send away, send off; (impiegato) to dismiss; (pericolo) to avert, remove; (estraniare) to alienate; **allontanarsi** vpr allontanarsi (da) to go away (from); (estraniarsi) to become estranged (from)

al'lora av (in quel momento) then ▸ cong (in questo caso) well then; (dunque) well then, so; **la gente d'~** people then o in those days; **da ~ in poi** from then on

al'loro sm laurel

al'luce ['allutʃe] sm big toe

alluci'nante [allutʃi'nante] ag awful; (fam) amazing

allucinazi'one [allutʃinat'tsjone] sf hallucination

al'ludere vi **-a** to allude to, hint at

allu'minio sm aluminium (BRIT), aluminum (US)

allun'gare vt to lengthen; (*distendere*) to prolong; extend; (*diluire*) to water down; **allungarsi** vpr to lengthen; (*ragazzo*) to stretch, grow taller; (*sdraiarsi*) to lie down, stretch out

al'lusi ecc vb vedi **alludere**

allusi'one sf hint, allusion

alluvi'one sf flood

al'meno av at least ▸ cong (**se**) ~ if only; (**se**) ~ **piovesse!** if only it would rain!

a'logeno, -a [a'lɔdʒeno] ag **lampada alogena** halogen lamp

a'lone sm halo

'Alpi sfpl **le** ~ the Alps

alpi'nismo sm mountaineering, climbing; **alpi'nista, -i, -e** sm/f mountaineer, climber

al'pino, -a ag Alpine; mountain cpd; **alpini** smpl (Mil) Italian Alpine troops

alt escl halt!, stop!

alta'lena sf (a funi) swing; (in bilico) seesaw

al'tare sm altar

alter'nare vt to alternate; **alternarsi** vpr to alternate; **alterna'tiva** sf alternative; **alterna'tivo, -a** ag alternative

al'terno, -a ag alternate; **a giorni alterni** on alternate days, every other day

al'tero, -a ag proud

al'tezza [al'tettsa] sf height; width; breadth; depth; pitch; (Geo) latitude; (titolo) highness; (fig: nobiltà) greatness; **essere all'~ di** to be on a level with; (fig) to be up to o equal to

al'ticcio, -a, -ci, -ce [al'tittʃo] ag tipsy

alti'tudine sf altitude

'alto, -a ag high; (persona) tall; (tessuto) wide, broad; (suono, acque) deep; (suono) high(-pitched); (Geo) upper; (settentrionale) northern ▸ sm top (part) ▸ av high; (parlare) aloud,

loudly; **il palazzo è ~ 20 metri** the building is 20 metres high; **ad alta voce** aloud; **a notte alta** in the dead of night; **in ~** up, upwards; at the top; **dall'~ in o al basso** up and down; **degli alti e bassi** (fig) ups and downs; **alta fedeltà** high fidelity, hi-fi; **alta finanza/società** high finance/society; **alta moda** haute couture

altopar'lante sm loudspeaker

altopi'ano (pl altipi'ani) sm plateau, upland plain

altret'tanto, -a ag, pron as much; (pl) as many ▸ av equally; **tanti auguri! — grazie, ~** all the best! — thank you, the same to you

altri'menti av otherwise

⬤ **'altro, -a**
det

1 (diverso) other, different; **questa è un'altra cosa** that's another o a different thing

2 (supplementare) other; **prendi un altro cioccolatino** have another chocolate; **hai avuto altre notizie?** have you had any more o any other news?

3 (nel tempo): **l'altro giorno** the other day; **l'altr'anno** last year; **l'altro ieri** the day before yesterday; **domani l'altro** the day after tomorrow; **quest'altro mese** next month

4: **d'altra parte** on the other hand ▸ pron

1 (persona, cosa diversa o supplementare): **un altro, un'altra** another (one); **lo farà un altro** someone else will do it; **altri, e** others; **gli altri** (la gente) others, other people; **l'uno e l'altro** both (of them); **aiutarsi l'un l'altro** to help one another; **da un giorno all'altro** from day to day; (nel giro di) from one day to the next; (da un momento all'altro) any day now

2 (sostantivato: solo maschile)

something else; (: *in espressioni interrogative*) anything else; **non ho altro da dire** I have nothing else to do I don't have anything else to say; **più che altro** above all; **se non altro** at least; **tra l'altro** among other things; **ci mancherebbe altro!** that's all we need!; **non faccio altro che lavorare** I do nothing but work; **contento?** —**altro che!** are you pleased? — and how!; *vedi* **senza**; **noialtri**; **voialtri**; **tutto**

al'trove *av* elsewhere, somewhere else

altru'ista, -i, -e *ag* altruistic

a'lunno, -a *sm/f* pupil

alve'are *sm* hive

al'zare [al'tsare] *vt* to raise, lift; (*issare*) to hoist; (*costruire*) to build, erect; **alzarsi** *vpr* to rise; (*dal letto*) to get up; (*crescere*) to grow tall (o taller); ~ **le spalle** to shrug one's shoulders; **alzarsi in piedi** to stand up, to get to one's feet

a'maca, -che *sf* hammock

amalga'mare *vt* to amalgamate; **amalgamarsi** *vpr* to amalgamate

a'mante *ag* ~ **di** (*musica ecc*) fond of ▶ *sm/f* lover/mistress

a'mare *vt* to love; (*amico, musica, sport*) to like; **amarsi** *vpr* to love each other

amareggi'ato, -a [amared'dʒato] *ag* upset, saddened

ama'rena *sf* sour black cherry

ama'rezza [ama'rettsa] *sf* bitterness

a'maro, -a *ag* bitter ▶ *sm* bitterness; (*liquore*) bitters *pl*

amaz'zonico, -a, -ci, -che [amad'dzɔniko] *ag* Amazonian; Amazon *cpd*

ambasci'ata [ambaʃʃata] *sf* embassy; (*messaggio*) message; **ambascia'tore, -'trice** *sm/f* ambassador/ambassadress

ambe'due *ag inv* ~ **i ragazzi** both boys

▶ *pron inv* both

ambienta'lista, -i, e *ag* environmental ▶ *sm/f* environmentalist

ambien'tare *vt* to acclimatize; (*romanzo, film*) to set; **ambientarsi** *vpr* to get used to one's surroundings

ambi'ente *sm* environment; (*fig: insieme di persone*) milieu; (*stanza*) room

am'biguo, -a *ag* ambiguous

ambizi'one [ambit'tsjone] *sf* ambition; **ambizi'oso, -a** *ag* ambitious

'ambo *ag inv* both ▶ *sm* (*al gioco*) double

'ambra *sf* amber; **ambra grigia** ambergris

ambu'lante *ag* itinerant ▶ *sm* peddler

ambu'lanza [ambu'lantsa] *sf* ambulance; **chiamate un ~** call an ambulance

ambula'torio *sm* (*studio medico*) surgery

A'merica *sf* l'~ America; l'~ **latina** Latin America; **ameri'cano, -a** *ag, sm/f* American

ami'anto *sm* asbestos

ami'chevole [ami'kevole] *ag* friendly

ami'cizia [ami'tʃittsja] *sf* friendship; **amicizie** *sfpl* (*amici*) friends

a'mico, -a, -ci, -che *sm/f* friend; (*fidanzato*) boyfriend/girlfriend; **amico del cuore** bosom friend

'amido *sm* starch

ammac'care *vt* (*pentola*) to dent; (*persona*) to bruise

ammacca'tura *sf* dent; bruise

ammaes'trare *vt* (*animale*) to train

ammai'nare *vt* to lower, haul down

amma'larsi *vpr* to fall ill; **amma'lato, -a** *ag* ill, sick ▶ *sm/f* sick person; (*paziente*) patient

ammanet'tare *vt* to handcuff

ammas'sare *vt* (*ammucchiare*)

to amass; (*raccogliere*) to gather together; **ammassarsi** *vpr* to pile up; to gather

ammat'tire *vi* to go mad

ammaz'zare [ammat'tsare] *vt* to kill; **ammazzarsi** *vpr* (*uccidersi*) to kill o.s.; (*rimanere ucciso*) to be killed; **ammazzarsi di lavoro** to work o.s. to death

am'mettere *vt* to admit; (*riconoscere: fatto*) to acknowledge, admit; (*permettere*) to allow, accept; (*supporre*) to suppose

amminis'trare *vt* to run, manage; (*Rel, Dir*) to administer; **amministra'tore** *sm* administrator; (*di condominio*) flats manager; **amministratore delegato** managing director; **amministrazi'one** *sf* management; administration

ammi'raglio [ammi'raʎʎo] *sm* admiral

ammi'rare *vt* to admire; **ammirazi'one** *sf* admiration

am'misi *ecc vb vedi* **ammettere**

ammobili'ato, -a *ag* furnished

am'mollo *sm* **lasciare in ~** to leave to soak

ammo'niaca *sf* ammonia

ammo'nire *vt* (*avvertire*) to warn; (*rimproverare*) to admonish; (*Dir*) to caution

ammonizi'one [ammonit'tsjone] *sf* (*monito: anche Sport*) warning; (*rimprovero*) reprimand; (*Dir*) caution

ammon'tare *vi* **~ a** to amount to ▶ *sm* (*totale*) amount

ammorbi'dente *sm* fabric conditioner

ammorbi'dire *vt* to soften

ammortizza'tore *sm* (*Aut, Tecn*) shock-absorber

ammucchi'are [ammuk'kjare] *vt* to pile up, accumulate

ammuf'fire *vi* to go mouldy (BRIT) *o* moldy (US)

ammuto'lire *vi* to be struck dumb

amne'sia *sf* amnesia

amnis'tia *sf* amnesty

'amo *sm* (*Pesca*) hook; (*fig*) bait

a'more *sm* love; **amori** *smpl* love affairs; **il tuo bambino è un ~** your baby's a darling; **fare l'~ o all'~** to make love; **per ~ o per forza** by hook or by crook; **amor proprio** self-esteem, pride

amo'roso, -a *ag* (*affettuoso*) loving, affectionate; (*d'amore: sguardo*) amorous; (: *poesia, relazione*) love *cpd*

'ampio, -a *ag* wide, broad; (*spazioso*) spacious; (*abbondante: vestito*) loose; (: *gonna*) full; (: *spiegazione*) ample, full

am'plesso *sm* intercourse

ampli'are *vt* (*ingrandire*) to enlarge; (*allargare*) to widen; **ampliarsi** *vpr* to grow, increase

amplifica'tore *sm* (*Tecn, Mus*) amplifier

ampu'tare *vt* (*Med*) to amputate

A.N. *sigla f* (= *Alleanza Nazionale*) *Italian right-wing party*

anabbaglianti *smpl* dipped (BRIT) *o* dimmed (US) headlights

anaboliz'zante *ag* anabolic ▶ *sm* anabolic steroid

anal'colico, -a, -ci, -che *ag* non-alcoholic ▶ *sm* soft drink

analfa'beta, -i, -e *ag, sm/f* illiterate

anal'gesico, -a, -ci, -che [anal'dʒɛziko] *ag, sm* analgesic

a'nalisi *sf inv* analysis; (*Med: esame*) test; **analisi del sangue** blood test *sg*

analiz'zare [analid'dzare] *vt* to analyse; (*Med*) to test

a'nalogo, -a, -ghi, -ghe *ag* analogous

'ananas *sm inv* pineapple

anar'chia [anar'kia] *sf* anarchy;

a'narchico, -a, -ci, -che ag anarchic(al) ▸ sm/f anarchist

anarco-insurreziona'lista ag anarcho-revolutionary

'A.N.A.S. sigla f (= Azienda Nazionale Autonoma delle Strade) national roads department

anato'mia sf anatomy

'anatra sf duck

'anca, -che sf (Anat) hip

'anche ['anke] cong (inoltre, pure) also, too; (perfino) even; **vengo anch'io** I'm coming too; **~ se** even if

an'cora av still; (di nuovo) again; (di più) some more; (persino): **~ più forte** even stronger; **non ~** not yet; **una volta** once more, once again; **~ un po'** a little more; (di tempo) a little longer

▸ **an'dare** sm a lungo — in the long run ▸ vi to go; (essere adatto): **~ a** to suit; (piacere): **il suo comportamento non mi va** I don't like the way he behaves; **ti va di ~ al cinema?** do you feel like going to the cinema?; **andarsene** to go away; **questa camicia va lavata** this shirt needs a wash o should be washed; **~ a cavallo** to ride; **~ in macchina/aereo** to go by car/plane; **~ a fare qc** to go and do sth; **~ a pescare/sciare** to go fishing/skiing; **~ a male** to go bad; **come va?** (lavoro, progetto) how are things?; **come va?** — **bene, grazie!** how are you? — fine, thanks!; **va fatto entro oggi** it's got to be done today; **ne va della nostra vita** our lives are at stake; **an'data** sf going; (viaggio) outward journey; **biglietto di sola andata** single (BRIT) o one-way ticket; **biglietto di andata e ritorno** (BRIT) o round-trip (US) ticket

andrò ecc vb vedi **andare**

a'neddoto sm anecdote

a'nello sm ring; (di catena) link; **anelli** smpl (Ginnastica) rings

a'nemico, -a, -ci, -che ag anaemic

aneste'sia sf anaesthesia

'angelo ['andʒelo] sm angel; **angelo custode** guardian angel

anghe'ria [ange'ria] sf vexation

angli'cano, -a ag Anglican

anglo'sassone ag Anglo-Saxon

'angolo sm corner; (Mat) angle; **angolo cottura** (di appartamento ecc) cooking area

an'goscia, -sce [an'gɔʃʃa] sf deep anxiety, anguish **no pl**

angu'illa sf eel

an'guria sf watermelon

'anice ['anitʃe] sm (Cuc) aniseed; (Bot) anise

'anima sf soul; (abitante) inhabitant; **non c'era ~ viva** there wasn't a living soul; **anima gemella** soul mate

ani'male sm, ag animal; **animale domestico** pet

anna'cquare vt to water down, dilute

annaffi'are vt to water; **annaffia'toio** sm watering can

an'nata sf year; (importo annuo) annual amount; **vino d'~** vintage wine

anne'gare vt, vi to drown

anne'rire vt to blacken ▸ vi to become black

annien'tare vt to annihilate, destroy

anniver'sario sm anniversary; **anniversario di matrimonio** wedding anniversary

'anno sm year; **ha 8 anni** he's 8 (years old)

anno'dare vt to knot, tie; (fig: rapporto) to form

annoi'are vt to bore; **annoiarsi** vpr to be bored

Attenzione! In inglese esiste il verbo to annoy che però vuol dire dare fastidio a.

anno'tare vt (registrare) to note, note down; (commentare) to annotate

annu'ale *ag* annual

annu'ire *vi* to nod; (*acconsentire*) to agree

annul'lare *vt* to annihilate, destroy; (*contratto, francobollo*) to cancel; (*matrimonio*) to annul; (*sentenza*) to quash; (*risultati*) to declare void

annunci'are [annun'tʃare] *vt* to announce; (*dar segni rivelatori*) to herald

an'nuncio [an'nuntʃo] *sm* announcement; (*fig*) sign; **annunci economici** classified advertisements, small ads; **annunci mortuari** (*colonna*) obituary column; **annuncio pubblicitario** advertisement

'annuo, -a *ag* annual, yearly

annu'sare *vt* to sniff, smell; **~ tabacco** to take snuff

a'nomalo, -a *ag* anomalous

a'nonimo, -a *ag* anonymous ▶ *sm* (*autore*) anonymous writer (*o painter ecc*); **società anonima** (*Comm*) joint stock company

anores'sia *sf* anorexia

ano'ressico, -a, ci, che *ag* anorexic

anor'male *ag* abnormal ▶ *sm/f* subnormal person

ANSA *sigla f* (= *Agenzia Nazionale Stampa Associata*) press agency

'ansia *sf* anxiety

ansi'mare *vi* to pant

ansi'oso, -a *ag* anxious

'anta *sf* (*di finestra*) shutter; (*di armadio*) door

An'tartide *sf* **l'~** Antarctica

an'tenna *sf* (*Radio, TV*) aerial; (*Zool*) antenna, feeler; (*Naut*) yard; **antenna parabolica** satellite dish

ante'prima *sf* preview; **anteprima di stampa** (*Inform*) print preview

anteri'ore *ag* (*ruota, zampa*) front; (*fatti*) previous, preceding

antiade'rente *ag* non-stick

antibi'otico, -a, -ci, -che *ag, sm* antibiotic

anti'camera *sf* anteroom; **fare ~** to wait (for an audience)

antici'pare [antitʃi'pare] *vt* (*consegna, visita*) to bring forward, anticipate; (*somma di denaro*) to pay in advance; (*notizia*) to disclose ▶ *vi* to be ahead of time; **an'ticipo** *sm* anticipation; (*di denaro*) advance; **in anticipo** early, in advance; **occorre che prenoti in anticipo?** do I need to book in advance?

an'tico, -a, -chi, -che *ag* (*quadro, mobili*) antique; (*dell'antichità*) ancient; **all'antica** old-fashioned

anticoncezio'nale [antikontʃettsjo'nale] *sm* contraceptive

anticonfor'mista, -i, -e *ag, sm/f* nonconformist

anti'corpo *sm* antibody

antido'rifico, -ci *sm* painkiller

anti'doping *sm* drug testing ▶ *ag inv* test ~ drugs (*BRIT*) *o* drug (*US*) test

an'tifona *sf* (*Mus, Rel*) antiphon; **capire l'~** (*fig*) to take the hint

anti'forfora *ag inv* anti-dandruff

anti'furto *sm* anti-theft device

anti'gelo [anti'dʒelo] *ag* (*liquido*) ~ (*per motore*) antifreeze; (*per cristalli*) de-icer

antiglobalizzazione [antiglobalidd zat'tsjone] *ag inv* **movimento ~** anti-globalization movement

An'tille *sfpl* **le ~** the West Indies

antin'cendio [antin'tʃendjo] *ag inv* fire *cpd*

anti'nebbia *sm inv* (*anche:* **faro ~:** *Aut*) fog lamp

antinfiamma'torio, -a *ag, sm* anti-inflammatory

antio'rario [antio'rarjo] *ag* **in senso ~** anticlockwise

anti'pasto *sm* hors d'œuvre

antipa'tia sf antipathy, dislike; **anti'patico, -a, -ci, -che** ag unpleasant, disagreeable

antiproi'ettile ag inv bulletproof

antiquari'ato sm antique trade; **un oggetto d'~** an antique

anti'quario sm antique dealer

anti'quato, -a ag antiquated, old-fashioned

anti'rughe ag inv (crema, prodotto) anti-wrinkle

antitraspi'rante ag antiperspirant

anti'vipera ag inv siero ~ remedy for snake bites

antivirus [anti'virus] sm inv antivirus software no pl ▶ ag inv antivirus

antolo'gia, -'gie [antolo'dʒia] sf anthology

anu'lare ag ring cpd ▶ sm third finger

'anzi ['antsi] av (invece) on the contrary; (o meglio) or rather, or better still

anzi'ano, -a [an'tsjano] ag old; (Amm) senior ▶ sm/f old person; senior member

anziché [antsi'ke] cong rather than

a'patico, -a, -ci, -che ag apathetic

'ape sf bee

aperi'tivo sm apéritif

aperta'mente av openly

a'perto, -a pp di **aprire** ▶ ag open; all'~ in the open (air); è ~ al pubblico? is it open to the public?; **quando è ~ il museo?** when is the museum open?

aper'tura sf opening; (ampiezza) width; (Fot) aperture; **apertura alare** wing span; **apertura mentale** open-mindedness

ap'nea sf immergersi in ~ to dive without breathing apparatus

a'postrofo sm apostrophe

ap'paio ecc vb vedi **apparire**

ap'palto sm (Comm) contract; **dare/prendere in ~ un lavoro** to let out/undertake a job on contract

appannarsi vpr to mist over; to grow dim

apparecchi'are [apparek'kjare] vt to prepare; (tavola) to set ▶ vi to set the table

appa'recchio [appa'rekkjo] sm piece of apparatus, device; (aeroplano) aircraft inv; **apparecchio acustico** hearing aid; **apparecchio telefonico** telephone; **apparecchio televisivo** television set

appa'rente ag apparent

appa'rire vi to appear; (sembrare) to seem, appear

apparta'mento sm flat (BRIT), apartment (US)

appar'tarsi vpr to withdraw

appar'nere vi ~ a to belong to

ap'parvi ecc vb vedi **apparire**

appassio'nare vt to thrill; (commuovere) to move; **appassionarsi** vpr **appassionarsi a qc** to take a great interest in sth; **appassio'nato, -a** ag passionate; (entusiasta): **appassionato (di)** keen (on)

appas'sire vi to wither

appas'sito, -a ag dead

ap'pello sm roll-call; (implorazione, Dir) appeal; **fare ~ a** to appeal to

ap'pena av (a stento) hardly, scarcely; (solamente, da poco) just ▶ cong as soon as; **(non) ~ furono arrivati ... as soon as they had arrived ...; ~ ...che** no sooner ... than

ap'pendere vt to hang (up)

appen'dice [appen'ditʃe] sf appendix; **romanzo d'~** popular serial

appendi'cite [appendi'tʃite] sf appendicitis

Appen'nini smpl gli ~ the Apennines

appesan'tire vt to make heavy; **appesantirsi** vpr to grow stout

appe'tito sm appetite

appic'care vt ~ il fuoco a to set fire to, set on fire

appicci'care [appittʃi'kare] vt to stick; **appiccicarsi** vpr to stick; (fig: persona) to cling

appiso'larsi vpr to doze off

applau'dire vt, vi to applaud; **ap'plauso** sm applause

appli'care vt to apply; (regolamento) to enforce; **applicarsi** vpr to apply o.s.

appoggi'are [appod'dʒare] vt (mettere contro): ~ qc a qc to lean o rest sth against sth; (fig: sostenere) to support; **appoggiarsi** vpr **appoggiarsi a** to lean against; (fig) to rely upon; **ap'poggio** sm support

apposita'mente av specially; (apposta) on purpose

ap'posito, -a ag appropriate

ap'posta av on purpose, deliberately

appos'tarsi vpr to lie in wait

ap'prendere vt (imparare) to learn

appren'dista, -i, -e smf apprentice

apprensi'one sf apprehension

apprez'zare [appret'tsare] vt to appreciate

appro'dare vi (Naut) to land; (fig): non ~ a nulla to come to nothing

approfit'tare vi ~ di to make the most of; (peg) to take advantage of

approfon'dire vt to deepen; (fig) to study in depth

appropri'ato, -a ag appropriate

approssima'tivo, -a ag approximate, rough; (impreciso) inexact, imprecise

appro'vare vt (condotta, azione) to approve of; (candidato) to pass; (progetto di legge) to approve

appunta'mento sm appointment; (amoroso) date; **darsi** ~ to arrange to meet (one another); **ho un** ~ **con...** I have an appointment with...; **vorrei prendere un** ~ I'd like to make an appointment

ap'punto sm note; (rimprovero) reproach ▶ av (proprio) exactly, just;

per l'~!, ~! exactly!

apribot'tiglie [apribot'tiʎʎe] sm inv bottle opener

a'prile sm April

a'prire vt to open; (via, cadavere) to open up; (gas, luce, acqua) to turn on ▶ vi to open; **aprirsi** vpr to open; **aprirsi a qn** to confide in sb, open one's heart to sb; **a che ora aprite?** what time do you open?

apris'catole sm inv tin (BRIT) o can opener

APT sigla f (= Azienda di Promozione) ≈ tourist board

aquagym [akkwa'dʒim] sf aquaerobics

'aquila sf (Zool) eagle; (fig) genius

aqui'lone sm (giocattolo) kite; (vento) North wind

A/R abbr = andata e ritorno (biglietto) return ticket (BRIT), round-trip ticket (US)

A'rabia Sau'dita sf l'~ Saudi Arabia

'arabo, -a ag, sm/f Arab ▶ sm (Ling) Arabic

a'rachide [a'rakide] sf peanut

ara'gosta sf crayfish; lobster

a'rancia, -ce [a'rantʃa] sf orange; **aranci'ata** sf orangeade; **aranci'one** ag inv (color) arancione bright orange

a'rare vt to plough (BRIT), plow (US)

a'ratro sm plough (BRIT), plow (US)

a'razzo [a'rattso] sm tapestry

arbi'trare vt (Sport) to referee; to umpire; (Dir) to arbitrate

arbi'trario, -a ag arbitrary

'arbitro sm arbiter, judge; (Dir) arbitrator; (Sport) referee; (: Tennis, Cricket) umpire

ar'busto sm shrub

archeolo'gia [arkeolo'dʒia] sf arch(a)eology; **arche'ologo, -a, -gi, -ghe** sm/f arch(a)eologist

architet'tare [arkitet'tare] vt (fig: ideare) to devise; (: macchinare) to plan, concoct

archi'tetto [arki'tetto] sm architect;
architet'tura sf architecture

ar'chivio [ar'kivjo] sm archives pl;
(Inform) file

'arco sm (arma, Mus) bow; (Archit) arch;
(Mat) arc

arcoba'leno sm rainbow

arcu'ato, -a ag curved, bent

'ardere vt, vi to burn

ar'desia sf slate

'area sf area; (Edil) land, ground; **area
di rigore** (Sport) penalty area; **area di
servizio** (Aut) service area

a'rena sf arena; (per corride) bullring;
(sabbia) sand

are'narsi vpr to run aground

argente'ria [ardʒente'ria] sf
silverware, silver

Argen'tina [ardʒen'tina] sf l'~
Argentina; **argen'tino, -a** ag, sm/f
Argentinian

ar'gento [ar'dʒento] sm silver;
argento vivo quicksilver

ar'gilla [ar'dʒilla] sf clay

'argine [ardʒine] sm embankment,
bank; (diga) dyke, dike

argo'mento sm argument; (motivo)
motive; (materia, tema) subject

'aria sf air; (espressione, aspetto) air,
look; (Mus: melodia) tune; (di opera)
aria; **mandare all'~** qc to ruin o upset
sth; **all'~ aperta** in the open (air)

'arido, -a ag arid

arieggi'are [arjed'dʒare] vt (cambiare
aria) to air; (imitare) to imitate

ari'ete sm ram; (Mil) battering ram;
(dello zodiaco): **A~** Aries

a'ringa, -ghe sf herring inv

arit'metica sf arithmetic

'arma, -i sf weapon, arm; (parte
dell'esercito) arm; **chiamare alle armi**
to call up (BRIT), draft (US); **sotto le
armi** in the army (o forces); **alle armi!**
to arms!; **arma atomica/nucleare**

atomic/nuclear weapon; **arma da
fuoco** firearm; **armi di distruzione
di massa** weapons of mass
destruction

arma'dietto sm (di medicinali)
medicine cabinet; (in palestra ecc)
locker; (in cucina) (kitchen) cupboard

ar'madio sm cupboard; (per abiti)
wardrobe; **armadio a muro** built-in
cupboard

ar'mato, -a ag ~ (di) (anche fig)
armed (with) ▶ sf (Mil) army; (Naut)
fleet; **rapina a mano armata** armed
robbery

arma'tura sf (struttura di sostegno)
framework; (impalcatura) scaffolding;
(Storia) armour no pl, suit of armour

armis'tizio [armis'tittsjo] sm
armistice

armo'nia sf harmony

ar'nese sm tool, implement; (oggetto
indeterminato) thing, contraption;
male in ~ (malvestito) badly dressed;
(di salute malferma) in poor health;
(povero) down-at-heel

'arnia sf hive

a'roma, -i sm aroma; fragrance;
aromi smpl (Cuc) herbs and spices;
aromatera'pia sf aromatherapy

'arpa sf (Mus) harp

arrabbi'are vi (cane) to be affected
with rabies; **arrabbi'arsi** vpr (essere
preso dall'ira) to get angry, fly into a
rage; **arrabbi'ato, -a** ag rabid, with
rabies; furious, angry

arrampi'carsi vpr to climb (up)

arrangi'arsi vpr to manage, do the
best one can

arreda'mento sm (studio) interior
design; (mobili ecc) furnishings pl

arre'dare vt to furnish

ar'rendersi vpr to surrender

arres'tare vt (fermare) to stop, halt;
(catturare) to arrest; **arrestarsi**
vpr (fermarsi) to stop; **ar'resto** sm

(cessazione) stopping; *(fermata)* stop; *(cattura, Med)* arrest; **subire un arresto** to come to a stop o standstill; **mettere agli arresti** to place under arrest; **arresti domiciliari** house arrest sg

arre'trare vt, vi to withdraw; **arre'trato, -a** ag *(lavoro)* behind schedule; *(paese, bambino)* backward; *(numero di giornale)* back cpd; **arretrati** smpl arrears

arric'chire [arrik'kire] vt to enrich; **arricchirsi** vpr to become rich

arri'vare vi to arrive; *(accadere)* to happen, occur; **~ a** *(livello, grado ecc)* to reach; **a che ora arriva il treno da Londra?** what time does the train from London arrive?; **non ci arrivo** I can't reach it; *(fig: non capisco)* I can't understand it

arrive'derci [arrive'dertʃi] escl goodbye!

arri'vista, -i, -e sm/f go-getter

ar'rivo sm arrival; *(Sport)* finish, finishing line

arro'gante ag arrogant

arros'sire vi *(per vergogna, timidezza)* to blush, flush; *(per gioia, rabbia)* to flush

arros'tire vt to roast; *(pane)* to toast; *(ai ferri)* to grill

ar'rosto sm, ag inv roast

arroto'lare vt to roll up

arroton'dare vt *(forma, oggetto)* to round; *(stipendio)* to add to; *(somma)* to round off

arruggi'nito, -a [arrudd ʒi'nito] ag rusty

'arsi vb vedi ardere

'arte sf art; *(abilità)* skill

ar'teria sf artery; **arteria stradale** main road

'artico, -a, -ci, -che ag Arctic

articolazi'one sf articulation; *(Anat, Tecn)* joint

ar'ticolo sm article; **articolo di fondo** *(Stampa)* leader, leading article

artifici'ale [artifi'tʃale] ag artificial

artigia'nato [artidʒa'nato] sm craftsmanship; craftsmen pl

artigi'ano, -a [arti'dʒano] sm/f craftsman/woman

ar'tista, -i, -e sm/f artist; **ar'tistico, -a, -ci, -che** ag artistic

ar'trite sf *(Med)* arthritis

a'scella [aʃʃella] sf *(Anat)* armpit

ascen'dente [aʃʃen'dɛnte] sm ancestor; *(fig)* ascendancy; *(Astr)* ascendant

ascen'sore [aʃʃen'sore] sm lift

a'scesso [aʃʃesso] sm *(Med)* abscess

asciuga'pelli [aʃʃugaka'pelli] sm hair-drier

asciuga'mano [aʃʃuga'mano] sm towel

asciu'gare [aʃʃu'gare] vt to dry; **asciugarsi** vpr to dry o.s.; *(diventare asciutto)* to dry

asci'utto, -a [aʃʃutto] ag dry; *(fig: magro)* lean; *(: burbero)* curt; **restare a bocca asciutta** *(fig)* to be disappointed

ascol'tare vt to listen to

as'falto sm asphalt

'Asia sf l' ~ Asia; **asi'atico, -a, -ci, -che** ag, sm/f Asiatic, Asian

a'silo sm refuge, sanctuary; **~ (d'infanzia)** nursery(-school); **asilo nido** crèche; **asilo politico** political asylum

'asino sm donkey, ass

ASL sigla f (= Azienda Sanitaria Locale) local health centre

'asma sf asthma

as'parago, -gi sm asparagus no pl

aspet'tare vt to wait for; *(anche Comm)* to await; *(aspettarsi)* to expect ▸ vi to wait; **aspettami, per favore** wait for me, please

as'petto sm *(apparenza)* aspect, appearance; look; *(punto di vista)* point of view; **di bell'~** good-looking

aspira'polvere sm inv vacuum cleaner

aspi'rare vt (respirare) to breathe in, inhale; (apparecchio) to suck (up) ▶ vi: **~ a** to aspire to

aspi'rina sf aspirin

'aspro, -a ag (sapore) sour, tart; (odore) acrid, pungent; (voce, clima, fig) harsh; (superficie) rough; (paesaggio) rugged

assaggi'are [assad'dʒare] vt to taste; **posso assaggiarlo?** can I have a taste?; **assaggio** [assad'dʒino] sm

assaggini [assad'dʒini] smpl (Cuc) selection of first courses; **solo un assaggino** just a little

as'sai av (molto) a lot, much; (: con ag) very; (a sufficienza) enough ▶ ag inv (quantità) a lot of, much; (numero) a lot of, many; **~ contento** very pleased

as'salgo ecc vb vedi **assalire**

assa'lire vt to attack, assail

assal'tare vt (Mil) to storm; (banca) to raid; (treno, diligenza) to hold up

as'salto sm attack, assault

assassi'nare vt to murder; to assassinate; (fig) to ruin; **assas'sino, -a** ag murderous ▶ sm/f murderer; assassin

'asse sm (Tecn) axle; (Mat) axis ▶ sf board; **asse** sf **da stiro** ironing board

assedi'are vt to besiege

asse'gnare [assen'nare] vt to assign, allot; (premio) to award

as'segno [as'senno] sm allowance; (anche: **~ bancario**) cheque (BRIT), check (US); **contro ~** cash on delivery; **posso pagare con un ~?** can I pay by cheque?; **assegno circolare** bank draft; **assegni familiari** = child benefit no pl; **assegno sbarrato** crossed cheque; **assegno di viaggio** traveller's cheque; **assegno a vuoto** dud cheque; **assegno di malattia/di invalidità** sick pay/disability benefit

assem'blea sf assembly

assen'tarsi vpr to go out

as'sente ag absent; (fig) faraway, vacant; **as'senza** sf absence

asse'tato, -a ag thirsty, parched

assicu'rare vt (accertare) to ensure; (infondere certezza) to assure; (fermare, legare) to make fast, secure; (fare un contratto di assicurazione) to insure; **assicurarsi** vpr (accertarsi): **assicurarsi (di)** to make sure (of); (contro il furto ecc): **assicurarsi (contro)** to insure o.s. (against); **assicurazi'one** sf assurance; insurance

assi'eme av (insieme) together; **~ a** (together) with

assil'lare vt to pester, torment

assis'tente sm/f assistant; **assistente sociale** social worker; **assistente di volo** (Aer) steward/ stewardess

assis'tenza [assis'tɛntsa] sf assistance; **~ ospedaliera** free hospital treatment; **~ sociale** welfare services pl; **assistenza sanitaria** health service

as'sistere vt (aiutare) to assist, help; (curare) to treat ▶ vi: **~ (a qc)** (essere presente) to be present (at sth), to attend (sth)

'asso sm ace; **piantare qn in ~** to leave sb in the lurch

associ'are [asso'tʃare] vt to associate; **associarsi** vpr to enter into partnership; **associarsi a** to become a member of, join; (dolori, gioie) to share in; **~ qn alle carceri** to take sb to prison

associazi'one [assotʃat'tsjone] sf association; (Comm) association, society; **~ a delinquere** (Dir) criminal association

as'solsi ecc vb vedi **assolvere**

assoluta'mente av absolutely

asso'luto, -a ag absolute

assoluzi'one [assolut'tsjone] sf (Dir) acquittal; (Rel) absolution

as'solvere vt (Dir) to acquit; (Rel) to absolve; (adempiere) to carry out, perform

assomigli'are [assomiʎ'ʎare] vi ~ a to resemble, look like; **assomigliarsi** vpr to look alike; (nel carattere) to be alike

asson'nato, -a ag sleepy

asso'pirsi vpr to doze off

assor'bente ag absorbent ▶ sm: **assorbente interno** tampon; **assorbente esterno/igienico** sanitary towel

assor'bire vt to absorb

assor'dare vt to deafen

assorti'mento sm assortment

assor'tito, -a ag assorted; matched, matching

assuefazi'one [assuefat'tsjone] sf (Med) addiction

as'sumere vt (impiegato) to take on, engage; (responsabilità) to assume, take upon o.s.; (contegno, espressione) to assume, put on; (droga) to consume

as'sunsi ecc vb vedi **assumere**

assurdità sf inv absurdity; **dire delle ~** to talk nonsense

as'surdo, -a ag absurd

'asta sf pole; (vendita) auction

as'temio, -a ag teetotal ▶ sm/f teetotaller

▌ Attenzione! In inglese esiste la parola abstemious che però vuol dire moderato.

aste'nersi vpr ~ (da) to abstain (from), refrain (from); (Pol) to abstain (from)

aste'risco, -schi sm asterisk

'astice ['astitʃe] sm lobster

astig'matico, -a, ci, che ag astigmatic

asti'nenza [asti'nɛntsa] sf abstinence; **essere in crisi di ~** to suffer from withdrawal symptoms

as'tratto, -a ag abstract

'astro... prefisso; **astrolo'gia** [astrolo'dʒia] sf astrology; **astro'nauta, -i, -e** sm/f astronaut; **astro'nave** sf space ship; **astrono'mia** sf astronomy; **astro'nomico, -a, -ci, -che** ag astronomic(al)

as'tuccio [as'tuttʃo] sm case, box, holder

as'tuto, -a ag astute, cunning, shrewd

A'tene sf Athens

'ateo, -a ag, sm/f atheist

at'lante sm atlas

at'lantico, -a, -ci, -che ag Atlantic ▶ sm l'A~, l'Oceano A~ the Atlantic, the Atlantic Ocean

at'leta, -i, -e sm/f athlete; **at'letica** sf athletics sg; **atletica leggera** track and field events pl; **atletica pesante** weightlifting and wrestling

atmos'fera sf atmosphere

a'tomico, -a, -ci, -che ag atomic; (nucleare) atomic, atom cpd, nuclear

'atomo sm atom

'atrio sm entrance hall, lobby

a'troce [a'trotʃe] ag (che provoca orrore) dreadful; (terribile) atrocious

attac'cante sm/f (Sport) forward

attacca'panni sm hook, peg; (mobile) hall stand

attac'care vt (unire) to attach; (cucendo) to sew on; (far aderire) to stick (on); (appendere) to hang (up); (assalire: anche fig) to attack; (iniziare) to begin, start; (fig: contagiare) to pass on ▶ vi to stick, adhere; **attaccarsi** vpr to stick, adhere; (trasmettersi per contagio) to be contagious; (afferrarsi): **attaccarsi (a)** to cling (to); (fig: affezionarsi): **attaccarsi (a)** to become attached (to); **~ discorso** to start a conversation; **at'tacco, -chi** sm (azione offensiva: anche fig) attack; (Med) attack, fit; (Sci) binding; (Elettr) socket

atteggia'mento [atteddʒa'mento] *sm* attitude

at'tendere *vt* to wait for, await ▶ *vi* ~ **a** to attend to

atten'dibile *ag* (*storia*) credible; (*testimone*) reliable

atten'tato *sm* attack; ~ **alla vita di qn** attempt on sb's life

at'tento, -a *ag* attentive; (*accurato*) careful, thorough; **stare ~ a qc** to pay attention to sth; **~! be careful!**

attenzi'one [atten'tsjone] *sf* attention; **~! watch out!, be careful!**; **attenzioni** *sfpl* (*premure*) attentions; **fare ~ a** to watch out for; **coprire qn di attenzioni** to lavish attentions on sb

atter'raggio [atter'raddʒo] *sm* landing

atter'rare *vt* to bring down ▶ *vi* to land

at'tesa *sf* waiting; (*tempo trascorso aspettando*) wait; **essere in ~ di qc** to be waiting for sth

at'tesi *ecc vb vedi* **attendere**

at'teso, -a *pp di* **attendere**

'attico, -ci *sm* attic

attil'lato, -a *ag* (*vestito*) close-fitting

'attimo *sm* moment; **in un ~** in a moment

atti'rare *vt* to attract

atti'tudine *sf* (*disposizione*) aptitude; (*atteggiamento*) attitude

attività *sf inv* activity; (*Comm*) assets *pl*

at'tivo, -a *ag* active; (*Comm*) profit-making, credit *cpd* ▶ *sm* (*Comm*) assets *pl*; **in ~** in credit

'atto *sm* act; (*azione, gesto*) action, act, deed; (*Dir: documento*) deed, document; **atti** *smpl* (*di congressi ecc*) proceedings; **mettere in ~** to put into action; **fare ~ di fare qc** to make as if to do sth; **atto di morte/di nascita** death/birth certificate

at'tore, -'trice *sm/f* actor/actress

at'torno *av* round, around, about; **~ a** round, around, about

attrac'care *vt, vi* (*Naut*) to dock, berth

at'tracco, -chi *sm* (*Naut*) docking *no pl*; berth

at'trae *ecc vb vedi* **attrarre**

attra'ente *ag* attractive

at'traggo *ecc vb vedi* **attrarre**

at'trarre *vt* to attract

at'trassi *ecc vb vedi* **attrarre**

attraver'sare *vt* to cross; (*città, bosco, fig: periodo*) to go through; (*fiume*) to run through

attra'verso *prep* through; (*da una parte all'altra*) across

attrazi'one [attrat'tsjone] *sf* attraction

at'trezzo *sm* tool, instrument; (*Sport*) piece of equipment

at'trice [at'tritʃe] *sf vedi* **attore**

attu'ale *ag* (*presente*) present; (*di attualità*) topical; **attualità** *sf inv* topicality; (*avvenimento*) current event; **attual'mente** *av* at the moment, at present

> Attenzione! In inglese esiste la parola *actual* che però vuol dire *effettivo*.
>
> Attenzione! In inglese esiste la parola *actually* che però vuol dire *effettivamente* oppure *veramente*.

attu'are *vt* to carry out

attu'tire *vt* to deaden, reduce

'audio *sm* (*TV, Radio, Cine*) sound

audiovi'sivo, -a *ag* audiovisual

audizi'one [audit'tsjone] *sf* hearing; (*Mus*) audition

augu'rare *vt* to wish; **augurarsi qc** to hope for sth

au'guri *smpl* best wishes; **fare gli ~ a qn** to give sb one's best wishes; **tanti ~!** best wishes!; (*per compleanno*) happy birthday!

'aula *sf* (*scolastica*) classroom;

(*universitaria*) lecture theatre; (*di edificio pubblico*) hall

aumen'tare *vt, vi* to increase; **au'mento** *sm* increase

au'rora *sf* dawn

ausili'are *ag, sm, sm/f* auxiliary

Aus'tralia *sf l* ~ Australia; **australi'ano, -a** *ag, sm/f* Australian

'Austria *sf l* ~ Austria; **aus'triaco, -a, -ci, -che** *ag, sm/f* Austrian

au'tentico, -a, -ci, -che *ag* authentic, genuine

au'tista, -i *sm* driver

'auto *sf inv* car

autoabbron'zante *sm, ag* self-tan

autoade'sivo, -a *ag* self-adhesive ▶ *sm* sticker

autobio'grafico, -a, ci, che *ag* autobiographic(al)

'autobus *sm inv* bus

auto'carro *sm* lorry (BRIT), truck

autocertificazi'one [autotʃertifikat'tsjone] *sf* self-declaration

autodistrut'tivo, -a *ag* self-destructive

auto'gol *sm inv* own goal

au'tografo, -a *ag, sm* autograph

auto'grill® *sm inv* motorway restaurant

auto'matico, -a, -ci, -che *ag* automatic ▶ *sm* (*bottone*) snap fastener; (*fucile*) automatic

auto'mobile *sf* (motor) car

automobi'lista, -i, -e *sm/f* motorist

auto'noleggio *sm* car hire

autono'mia *sf* autonomy; (*di volo*) range

au'tonomo, -a *ag* autonomous, independent

autop'sia *sf* post-mortem, autopsy

auto'radio *sf inv* (*apparecchio*) car radio; (*autoveicolo*) radio car

au'tore, -'trice *sm/f* author

autoreggente [autored'dʒente] *ag*

calze autoreggenti hold ups

auto'revole *ag* authoritative; (*persona*) influential

autoricari'cabile *ag* **scheda ~** top-up card

autori'messa *sf* garage

autorità *sf inv* authority

autoriz'zare [autorid'dzare] *vt* (*permettere*) to authorize; (*giustificare*) to allow, sanction

autos'contro *sm* dodgem car (BRIT), bumper car (US)

autoscu'ola *sf* driving school

autos'tima *sf* self-esteem

autos'top *sm* hitchhiking; **autostop'pista, -i, -e** *sm/f* hitchhiker

autos'trada *sf* motorway (BRIT), highway (US); **autostrada informatica** information superhighway

- **autostrade**
- You have to pay to use Italian
- motorways. They are indicated by an
- "A" followed by a number on a green
- sign. The speed limit on Italian
- motorways is 130 kph.

auto'velox® *sm inv* (police) speed camera

autovet'tura *sf* (motor) car

au'tunno *sm* autumn

avam'braccio [avam'brattʃo] (*pl* (*f*) **-cia**) *sm* forearm

avan'guardia *sf* vanguard

a'vanti *av* (*stato in luogo*) in front; (*moto: andare, venire*) forward; (*tempo: prima*) before ▶ *prep* (*luogo*): **~ a** before, in front of; (*tempo*): **~ Cristo** before Christ ▶ *escl* (*entrate*) come (o go) in!; (*Mil*) forward!; (*coraggio*) come on! ▶ *sm inv* (*Sport*) forward; **~ e indietro** backwards and forwards; **andare ~** to go forward; (*continuare*) to go on; (*precedere*) to go (o go) ahead; (*orologio*) to be fast; **essere ~ negli studi** to be well advanced with one's studies

avan'zare [avan'tsare] vt (spostare in avanti) to move forward, advance; (domanda) to put forward; (promuovere) to promote; (essere creditore): ~ **qc a qn** to be owed sth by sb ▶ vi (andare avanti) to move forward, advance; (progredire) to make progress; (essere d'avanzo) to be left, remain

ava'ria sf (guasto) damage; (: meccanico) breakdown

a'varo, -a ag avaricious, miserly
▶ sm miser

a've ⊙ sm (Comm) credit; **gli averi** (ricchezze) wealth sg
▶ vt

1 (possedere) to have; **ha due bambini/una bella casa** she has (got) two children/a lovely house; **ha i capelli lunghi** he has (got) long hair; **non ho da mangiare/bere** I've (got) nothing to eat/drink, I don't have anything to eat/drink

2 (indossare) to wear, have on; **aveva una maglietta rossa** he was wearing o he had on a red tee-shirt; **ha gli occhiali** he wears o has glasses

3 (ricevere) to get; **hai avuto l'assegno?** did you get o have you had the cheque?

4 (età, dimensione) to be; **ha 9 anni** he is 9 (years old); **la stanza ha 3 metri di lunghezza** the room is 3 metres in length; vedi **fame**; **paura** ecc

5 (tempo): **quanti ne abbiamo oggi?** what's the date today?; **ne hai per molto?** will you be long?

6 (fraseologia): **avercela con qn** to be angry with sb; **cos'hai?** what's wrong o what's the matter (with you)?; **non ha niente a che vedere o fare con me** it's got nothing to do with me
▶ vb aus

1 to have; **aver bevuto/mangiato** to have drunk/eaten

2 (+ da + infinito): **avere da fare qc** to have to do sth; **non hai che da chiederlo** you only have to ask him

aviazi'one [avjat'tsjone] sf aviation; (Mil) air force

'avido, -a ag eager; (peg) greedy

avo'cado sm avocado

a'vorio sm ivory

Avv. abbr = **avvocato**

avvantaggi'are [avvantad'dʒare] vt to favour; **avvantaggiarsi** vpr **avvantaggiarsi negli affari/sui concorrenti** to get ahead in business/of one's competitors

avvele'nare vt to poison

av'vengo ecc vb vedi **avvenire**

avveni'mento sm event

avve'nire vi, vb impers to happen, occur ▶ sm future

av'venni ecc vb vedi **avvenire**

avven'tato, -a ag rash, reckless

avven'tura sf adventure; (amorosa) affair

avventu'rarsi vpr to venture

avventu'roso, -a ag adventurous

avve'rarsi vpr to come true

av'verbio sm adverb

avverrò ecc vb vedi **avvenire**

avver'sario, -a ag opposing ▶ sm opponent, adversary

avver'tenza [avver'tentsa] sf (ammonimento) warning; (cautela) care; (premessa) foreword; **avvertenze** sfpl (istruzioni per l'uso) instructions

avverti'mento sm warning

avver'tire vt (avvisare) to warn; (rendere consapevole) to inform, notify; (percepire) to feel

avvi'are vt (mettere sul cammino) to direct; (impresa, trattative) to begin, start; (motore) to start; **avviarsi** vpr to set off, set out

avvici'nare [avvitʃi'nare] vt to bring near; (trattare con: persona) to approach; **avvicinarsi** vpr **avvicinarsi (a qn/qc)** to approach (sb/sth), draw near (to sb/sth)

avvi'lito, -a ag discouraged

avvin'cente ag captivating

avvi'sare vt (far sapere) to inform; (mettere in guardia) to warn;

av'viso sm warning; (annuncio) announcement; (: affisso) notice; (inserzione pubblicitaria) advertisement; **a mio avviso** in my opinion; **avviso di chiamata** (servizio) call waiting; (segnale) call waiting signal; **avviso di garanzia** (Dir) notification (of impending investigation and of the right to name a defence lawyer)

> Attenzione! In inglese esiste la parola *advice* che però vuol dire *consiglio*.

avvis'tare vt to sight

avvi'tare vt to screw down (o in)

avvo'cato, -'essa sm/f (Dir) barrister (BRIT), lawyer; (fig) defender, advocate

av'volgere [av'vɔldʒere] vt to roll up; (avviluppare) to wrap up; **avvolgersi** vpr (avvilupparsi) to wrap o.s. up;

avvol'gibile sm roller blind (BRIT), blind

av'volsi ecc vb vedi **avvolgere**

avvol'toio sm vulture

aza'lea [addza'lɛa] sf azalea

azi'enda [ad'dzjɛnda] sf business, firm, concern; **azienda agricola** farm

azi'one [at'tsjone] sf action; (Comm) share

a'zoto [ad'dzɔto] sm nitrogen

azzar'dare [addzar'dare] vt (soldi, vita) to risk, hazard; (domanda, ipotesi) to hazard, venture; **azzardarsi** vpr **azzardarsi a fare** to dare (to) do

az'zardo [ad'dzardo] sm risk

azzec'care [attsek'kare] vt (risposta ecc) to get right

azzuf'farsi [attsuf'farsi] vpr to come to blows

az'zurro, -a [ad'dzurro] ag blue ▶ sm (colore) blue; **gli azzurri** (Sport) the Italian national team

b

'babbo sm (fam) dad, daddy; **Babbo Natale** Father Christmas

baby-sitter ['beɪbɪsɪtə'] sm/f inv baby-sitter

'bacca, -che sf berry

baccalà sm dried salted cod; (fig: peg) dummy

bac'chetta [bak'ketta] sf (verga) stick, rod; (di direttore d'orchestra) baton; (di tamburo) drumstick; ~ **magica** magic wand

ba'checa, -che [ba'kɛka] sf (mobile) showcase, display case; (Univ, in ufficio) notice board (BRIT), bulletin board (US)

baci'are [ba'tʃare] vt to kiss; **baciarsi** vpr to kiss (one another)

baci'nella [batʃi'nɛlla] sf basin

ba'cino [ba'tʃino] sm basin; (Mineralogia) field, bed; (Anat) pelvis; (Naut) dock

'bacio ['batʃo] sm kiss

'baco, -chi sm worm; **baco da seta** silkworm

ba'dare vi (fare attenzione) to take care,

be careful; (occuparsi di): **~ a** to look after, take care of; (dar ascolto): **~ a** to pay attention to; **bada ai fatti tuoi!** mind your own business!

'baffi smpl moustache sg; (di animale) whiskers; **ridere sotto i ~** to laugh up one's sleeve; **leccarsi i ~** to lick one's lips

bagagli'aio [bagaʎˈʎajo] sm luggage van (BRIT) or car (US); (Aut) boot (BRIT), trunk (US)

ba'gaglio [baˈgaʎʎo] sm luggage no pl, baggage no pl; **fare/disfare i bagagli** to pack/unpack; **i nostri bagagli non sono arrivati** our luggage has not arrived; **può mandare qualcuno a prendere i nostri bagagli?** could you send someone to collect our luggage?; **bagaglio a mano** hand luggage

bagli'ore [baʎˈʎore] sm flash, dazzling light; **un ~ di speranza** a ray of hope

ba'gnante [baɲˈɲante] sm/f bather

ba'gnare [baɲˈɲare] vt to wet; (inzuppare) to soak; (innaffiare) to water; (fiume) to flow through; (: mare) to wash, bathe; **bagnarsi** vpr to get wet; (al mare) to go swimming o bathing; (in vasca) to have a bath

ba'gnato, -a [baɲˈɲato] ag wet

ba'gnino [baɲˈɲino] sm lifeguard

'bagno [ˈbaɲɲo] sm bath; (stanza) bathroom; (toilette) toilet; **bagni** smpl (stabilimento) baths; **fare il ~** to have a bath; (nel mare) to go swimming o bathing; **dov'è il ~?** where's the toilet?; **fare il ~ a qn** to give sb a bath; **mettere a ~** to soak; **~ schiuma** bubble bath

bagnoma'ria [baɲɲomaˈria] sm **cuocere a ~** to cook in a double saucepan

bagnoschi'uma [baɲɲoskjˈuma] sm inv bubble bath

'baia sf bay

balbet'tare vi to stutter, stammer; (bimbo) to babble ▶ vt to stammer out

bal'canico, -a, ci, che ag Balkan

bal'cone sm balcony; **avete una camera con ~?** do you have a room with a balcony?

bal'doria sf **fare ~** to have a riotous time

ba'lena sf whale

ba'leno sm flash of lightning; **in un ~** in a flash

bal'lare vt, vi to dance

balle'rina sf dancer; ballet dancer; (scarpa) ballet shoe

balle'rino sm dancer; ballet dancer

bal'letto sm ballet

'ballo sm dance; (azione) dancing no pl; **essere in ~** (fig: persona) to be involved; (: cosa) to be at stake

balne'are sf seaside cpd; (stagione) bathing

'balsamo sm (aroma) balsam; (lenimento, fig) balm

bal'zare [balˈtsare] vi to bounce; (lanciarsi) to jump, leap; **'balzo** sm bounce; jump, leap; (del terreno) crag

bam'bina ag, sf vedi **bambino**

bam'bino, -a sm/f child

'bambola sf doll

bambù sm bamboo

ba'nale ag banal, commonplace

ba'nana sf banana

'banca, -che sf bank; **banca dati** data bank

banca'rella sf stall

banca'rotta sf bankruptcy; **fare ~** to go bankrupt

ban'chetto [banˈketto] sm banquet

banchi'ere [banˈkjere] sm banker

ban'china [banˈkina] sf (di porto) quay; (per pedoni, ciclisti) path; (di stazione) platform; (di strada): **~ cedevole** (Aut) soft verge (BRIT) o shoulder (US)

'banco, -chi sm bench; (di negozio) counter; (di mercato) stall; (di officina) (work-)bench; (*Geo, banca*) bank; **banco di corallo** coral reef; **banco degli imputati** dock; **banco di prova** (*fig*) testing ground; **banco dei testimoni** witness box; **banco dei pegni** pawnshop; **banco di nebbia** bank of fog

'Bancomat® *sm inv* automated banking; (*tessera*) cash card

banco'nota *sf* banknote

'banda *sf* band; (*di stoffa*) band, stripe; (*lato, parte*) side; **~ perforata** punch tape

bandi'era *sf* flag, banner

ban'dito *sm* outlaw, bandit

'bando *sm* proclamation; (*esilio*) exile, banishment; **~ alle chiacchiere!** that's enough talk!; **bando di concorso** announcement of a competition

bar *sm inv* bar

'bara *sf* coffin

ba'racca, -che *sf* shed, hut; (*peg*) hovel; **mandare avanti la ~** to keep things going

ba'rare *vi* to cheat

ba'ratro *sm* abyss

ba'ratto *sm* barter

ba'rattolo *sm* (*di latta*) tin; (*di vetro*) jar; (*di coccio*) pot

'barba *sf* beard; **farsi la ~** to shave; **farla in ~ a qn** (*fig*) to do sth to sb's face; **che ~!** what a bore!

barbabi'etola *sf* beetroot (*BRIT*), beet (*US*); **barbabietola da zucchero** sugar beet

barbi'ere *sm* barber

bar'bone *sm* (*cane*) poodle; (*vagabondo*) tramp

'barca, -che *sf* boat; **barca a motore** motorboat; **barca a remi** rowing boat; **barca a vela** sail(ing) boat

barcol'lare *vi* to stagger

ba'rella *sf* (*lettiga*) stretcher

ba'rile *sm* barrel, cask

ba'rista, -i, -e *sm/f* barman/maid; (*proprietario*) bar owner

ba'rocco, -a, -chi, -che *ag, sm* baroque

ba'rometro *sm* barometer

ba'rone *sm* baron; **baro'nessa** *sf* baroness

'barra *sf* bar; (*Naut*) helm; (*linea grafica*) line, stroke

bar'rare *vt* to bar

barri'carsi *vpr* to barricade o.s.

barri'era *sf* barrier; (*Geo*) reef

ba'ruffa *sf* scuffle

barzel'letta [bardzel'letta] *sf* joke, funny story

ba'sare *vt* to base, found; **basarsi** *vpr* **basarsi su** (*fatti, prove*) to be based o founded on; (: *persona*) to base one's arguments on

'basco, -a, -schi, -sche *ag* Basque ▶ *sm* (*copricapo*) beret

'base *sf* base; (*fig: fondamento*) basis; (*Pol*) rank and file; **di ~** basic; **in ~ a** on the basis of, according to; **a ~ di caffè** coffee-based

'baseball ['beisbo:l] *sm* baseball

ba'sette *sfpl* sideburns

ba'silica, -che *sf* basilica

ba'silico *sm* basil

basket ['basket] *sm* basketball

bas'sista, -i, -e *sm/f* bass player

'basso, -a *ag* low; (*di statura*) short; (*meridionale*) southern ▶ *sm* bottom, lower part; (*Mus*) bass; **la bassa Italia** southern Italy

bassorili'evo *sm* bas-relief

bas'sotto, -a *ag* squat ▶ *sm* (*cane*) dachshund

'basta *escl* (that's) enough!, that will do!

bas'tardo, -a *ag* (*animale, pianta*) hybrid, crossbreed; (*persona*) illegitimate, bastard; (*peg*) ▶ *sm/f* illegitimate child, bastard (*peg*)

bas'tare *vi, vb impers* to be enough,

be sufficient; **~ a qn** to be enough for sb; **basta chiedere o che chieda a un vigile** you have only to o need only ask a policeman; **basta così, grazie** that's enough, thanks

basto'nare vt beat, thrash

baston'cino [baston'tʃino] sm (Sci) ski pole; **bastoncini di pesce** fish fingers

bas'tone sm stick; **~ da passeggio** walking stick

bat'taglia [bat'taʎʎa] sf battle; fight

bat'tello sm boat

bat'tente sm (imposta: di porta) wing, flap; (: di finestra) shutter; (batacchio: di porta) knocker; (: di orologio) hammer; **chiudere i battenti** (fig) to shut up shop

'battere vt to beat; (grano) to thresh; (percorrere) to scour ▶ vi (bussare) to knock; (urtare): **~ contro** to hit o strike against; (pioggia, sole) to beat down; (cuore) to beat; (Tennis) to serve; **battersi** vpr to fight; **~ le mani** to clap; **~ i piedi** to stamp one's feet; **~ a macchina** to type; **bandiera italiana** to fly the Italian flag; **~ in testa** (Aut) to knock; **in un batter d'occhio** in the twinkling of an eye

batte'ria sf battery; (Mus) drums pl

bat'terio sm bacterium

batte'rista, -i, -e sm/f drummer

bat'tesimo sm (rito) baptism; christening

battez'zare [batted'dzare] vt to baptize; to christen

batti'panni sm inv carpet-beater

battis'trada sm inv (di pneumatico) tread; (di gara) pacemaker

'battito sm beat, throb; **battito cardiaco** heartbeat

bat'tuta sf blow; (di macchina da scrivere) stroke; (Mus) bar; beat; (Teatro) cue; (frase spiritosa) witty remark; (di caccia) beating; (Polizia) combing, scouring; (Tennis) service

ba'tuffolo sm wad

ba'ule sm trunk; (Aut) boot (BRIT), trunk (US)

'bava sf (di animale) slaver, slobber; (di lumaca) slime; (di vento) breath

bava'glino [bavaʎ'ʎino] sm bib

ba'vaglio [ba'vaʎʎo] sm gag

'bavero sm collar

ba'zar [bad'dzar] sm inv bazaar

BCE sigla f (= Banca centrale europea) ECB

be'ato, -a ag blessed; (fig) happy; **~ te!** lucky you!

bec'care vt to peck; (fig: raffreddore) to catch; **beccarsi** vpr (fig) to squabble; **beccarsi qc** to catch sth

beccherò ecc [bekke'rɔ] vb vedi **beccare**

'becco, -chi sm beak, bill; (di caffettiera ecc) spout; lip

be'fana sf hag, witch; **la B~** old woman who, according to legend, brings children their presents at the Epiphany; (Epifania) Epiphany

● **Befana**

● The **Befana** is a national holiday on
● the feast of the Epiphany. It takes
● its name from **la Befana**, the old
● woman who, according to Italian
● legend comes down the chimney
● during the night leaving gifts for
● children who have been good, and
● coal for those who have not.

bef'fardo, -a ag scornful, mocking

'begli ['beʎʎi] ag vedi **bello**

'bei ag vedi **bello**

beige [bεʒ] ag inv beige

bel ag vedi **bello**

be'lare vi to bleat

'belga, -gi, -ghe ag, sm/f Belgian

'Belgio ['bεldʒo] sm il ~ Belgium

'bella sf (Sport) decider; vedi anche **bello**

bel'lezza [bel'lettsa] sf beauty

○ **'bello, -a**
(ag: dav sm **bel** + C, **bell'** +V, **bello** + s impura, gn, pn, ps, x, z, pl **bei** + C, **begli** +

s impura ecc oV) ag

1 (*oggetto, donna, paesaggio*) beautiful, lovely; (*uomo*) handsome; (*tempo*) beautiful, fine, lovely; **le belle arti** fine arts

2 (*quantità*): **una bella cifra** a considerable sum of money; **un bel niente** absolutely nothing

3 (*rafforzativo*): **è una truffa bella e buona!** it's a real fraud!; **è bell'e finito** it's already finished

▶ *sm*

1 (*bellezza*) beauty; (*tempo*) fine weather

2: **adesso viene il bello** now comes the best bit; **sul più bello** at the crucial point; **cosa fai di bello?** are you doing anything interesting?

▶ *av* **fa bello** the weather is fine, it's fine

'belva *sf* wild animal

belve'dere *sm inv* panoramic viewpoint

benché [ben'ke] *cong* although

'benda *sf* bandage; (*per gli occhi*) blindfold; **ben'dare** *vt* to bandage; to blindfold

'bene *av* well; (*completamente, affatto*): **è ben difficile** it's very difficult ▶ *ag inv* **gente ~** well-to-do people ▶ *sm* good; **beni** *smpl* (*averi*) property *sg*, estate *sg*; **io sto ~/poco ~** I'm well/not very well; **va ~** all right; **volere un ~ dell'anima a qn** to love sb very much; **un uomo per ~** a respectable man; **fare ~** to do the right thing; **fare ~ a** (*salute*) to be good for; **fare del ~ a qn** to do sb a good turn; **beni di consumo** consumer goods

bene'detto, -a *pp di* **benedire** ▶ *ag* blessed, holy

bene'dire *vt* to bless; to consecrate

benedu'cato, -a *ag* well-mannered

benefi'cenza [benefi'ʃentsa] *sf* charity

benefi'cio [bene'fiʧo] *sm* benefit; **con**

~ d'inventario (*fig*) with reservations

be'nessere *sm* well-being

benes'tante *ag* well-to-do

be'nigno, -a [be'niɲɲo] *ag* kind, kindly; (*critica ecc*) favourable; (*Med*) benign

benve'nuto, -a *ag, sm* welcome; **dare il ~ a qn** to welcome sb

ben'zina [ben'dzina] *sf* petrol (*BRIT*), gas (*US*); **fare ~** to get petrol (*BRIT*) o gas (*US*); **sono rimasto senza ~** I have run out of petrol (*BRIT*) o gas (*US*); **benzina verde** unleaded (petrol); **benzi'naio** *sm* petrol (*BRIT*) o gas (*US*) pump attendant

'bere *vt* to drink; (*assorbire*) to soak up; **darla a ~ a qn** (*fig*) to fool sb; **vuoi qualcosa da ~?** would you like a drink?

ber'lina *sf* (*Aut*) saloon (car) (*BRIT*), sedan (*US*)

Ber'lino *sf* Berlin

ber'muda *smpl* (*calzoncini*) Bermuda shorts

ber'noccolo *sm* bump; (*inclinazione*) flair

ber'retto *sm* cap

berrò *ecc vb vedi* **bere**

ber'saglio [ber'saʎʎo] *sm* target

besciamella [beʃʃa'mɛlla] *sf* béchamel sauce

bes'temmia *sf* curse; (*Rel*) blasphemy

bestemmi'are *vi* to curse, swear; to blaspheme ▶ *vt* to curse, swear at; to blaspheme

'bestia *sf* animal; **andare in ~** (*fig*) to fly into a rage; **besti'ale** *ag* beastly; animal *cpd*; (*fam*): **fa un freddo bestiale** it's bitterly cold; **besti'ame** *sm* livestock; (*bovino*) cattle *pl*

be'tulla *sf* birch

be'vanda *sf* drink, beverage

'bevo *ecc vb vedi* **bere**

be'vuto, -a *pp di* **bere**

'bevvi *ecc vb vedi* **bere**

bianche'ria [bjanke'ria] *sf* linen; **~ da**

donna ladies' underwear, lingerie; **biancheria femminile** lingerie; **biancheria intima** underwear

bi'anco, -a, -chi, -che *ag* white; (*non scritto*) blank ▶ *sm* white; (*intonaco*) whitewash ▶ *sm/f* white (white man/woman; (**in ~** (*foglio, assegno*) blank; (*notte*) sleepless; **in ~ e nero** (*TV, Fot*) black and white; **mangiare in ~** to follow a bland diet; **pesce in ~** boiled fish; **andare in ~** (*non riuscire*) to fail; **bianco dell'uovo** egg-white

biasi'mare *vt* to disapprove of, censure

'Bibbia *sf* (*anche fig*) bible

bibe'ron *sm inv* feeding bottle

'bibita *sf* (soft) drink

biblio'teca, -che *sf* library; (*mobile*) bookcase

bicarbo'nato *sm* ~ (**di sodio**) bicarbonate (of soda)

bicchi'ere [bik'kjɛre] *sm* glass

bici'cletta [bitʃi'kletta] *sf* bicycle; **andare in ~** to cycle

bidè *sm inv* bidet

bi'dello, -a *sm/f* (*Ins*) janitor

bi'done *sm* drum, can; (*anche:* **~ dell'immondizia**) (dust)bin; (*fam: truffa*) swindle; **fare un ~ a qn** (*fam*) to let sb down; to cheat sb

bien'nale *ag* biennial

■ **Biennale di Venezia**
▪ The Biennale di Venezia is an
▪ international contemporary art
▪ festival, which takes place every
▪ two years at Giardini in Venice. In
▪ its current form, it includes exhibits
▪ by artists from the many countries
▪ taking part, a thematic exhibition
▪ and a section for young artists.

bifami'liare *sf* = semi-detached house

bifor'carsi *vpr* to fork

bigiotte'ria [bidʒotte'ria] *sf* costume jewellery; (*negozio*) jeweller's (selling

only costume jewellery)

bigliet'taio, -a *sm/f* (*in treno*) ticket inspector; (*in autobus*) conductor

bigliette'ria [biʎʎette'ria] *sf* (*di stazione*) ticket office; booking office; (*di teatro*) box office

bigli'etto [biʎ'ʎetto] *sm* (*per viaggi, spettacoli ecc*) ticket; (*cartoncino*) card; (*anche:* **~ di banca**) (bank)note; **biglietto d'auguri** greetings card; **biglietto da visita** visiting card; **biglietto d'andata e ritorno** return (ticket), round-trip ticket (US); **biglietto di sola andata** single (ticket)

bignè [biɲ'ɲe] *sm inv* cream puff

bigo'dino *sm* roller, curler

bi'gotto, -a *ag* over-pious ▶ *sm/f* church fiend

bi'kini *sm inv* bikini

bi'lancia, -ce [bi'lantʃa] *sf* (*pesa*) scales *pl*; (*: di precisione*) balance; (*dello zodiaco*): **B~** Libra; **bilancia commerciale** balance of trade; **bilancia dei pagamenti** balance of payments

bi'lancio [bi'lantʃo] *sm* (*Comm*) balance(-sheet); (*statale*) budget; **fare il ~ di** (*fig*) to assess; **bilancio consuntivo** (final) balance; **bilancio preventivo** budget

bili'ardo *sm* billiards *sg*; billiard table

bi'lingue *ag* bilingual

bilo'cale *sm* two-room flat (*Brit*) or apartment (*US*)

bi'nario, -a *ag* (*sistema*) binary ▶ *ag* (*railway*) track o line; (*piattaforma*) platform; **da che ~ parte il treno per Londra?** which platform does the train for London go from?; **binario morto** dead-end track

bi'nocolo *sm* binoculars *pl*

bio... *prefisso*: **biodegra'dabile** *ag* biodegradable; **biodi'namico, -a, -ci, -che** *ag* biodynamic; **biogra'fia** *sf* biography; **biolo'gia** sf biology

bio'logico, -a, -ci, -che ag (scienze, fenomeni ecc)) biological; (agricoltura, prodotti) organic; **guerra biologica** biological warfare

bi'ondo, -a ag blond, fair

biotecnologia [biotekno'lo:dʒia] sf biotechnology

biri'chino, -a [biri'kino] ag mischievous ▶ sm/f scamp, little rascal

bi'rillo sm skittle (BRIT), pin (US)

'biro® sf inv biro®

birra sf beer; **a tutta ~** (fig) at top speed; **birra chiara/scura** ≈ lager/stout; **birra'ria** sf = bierkeller

bis escl, sm inv encore

bis'betico, -a, -ci, -che ag ill-tempered, crabby

bisbigli'are [bisbiʎ'ʎare] vt, vi to whisper

'bisca, -sche sf gambling-house

'biscia, -sce ['biʃʃa] sf snake; **biscia d'acqua** grass snake

biscot'tato, -a ag crisp; **fette biscottate** rusks

bis'cotto sm biscuit

bisessu'ale ag, sm/f bisexual

bises'tile ag **anno ~** leap year

bis'nonno, -a sm/f great grandfather/grandmother

biso'gnare [bizoɲ'ɲare] vb impers **bisogna che tu parta/lo faccia** you'll have to go/do it; **bisogna parlargli** we'll (o I'll) have to talk to him

bi'sogno [bi'zoɲɲo] sm need; **ha ~ di qualcosa?** do you need anything?

bis'tecca, -che sf steak, beefsteak

bisticci'are [bistit'tʃare] vi to quarrel, bicker; **bisticciarsi** vpr to quarrel, bicker

'bisturi sm scalpel

'bivio sm fork; (fig) dilemma

biz'zarro, -a [bid'dzarro] ag bizarre, strange

blate'rare vi to chatter

blin'dato, -a ag armoured

bloc'care vt to block; (isolare) to isolate, cut off; (porto) to blockade; (prezzi, beni) to freeze; (meccanismo) to jam; **bloccarsi** vpr (motore) to stall; (freni, porta) to jam, stick; (ascensore) to stop, get stuck

bloccherò ecc [blokke'rɔ] vb vedi **bloccare**

bloc'chetto [blok'ketto] sm notebook; (di biglietti) book

'blocco, -chi sm block; (Mil) blockade; (dei fitti) restriction; (quadernetto) pad; (fig: unione) coalition; (il bloccare) blocking; isolating, cutting-off; blockading; freezing; jamming; **in ~** (nell'insieme) as a whole; (Comm) in bulk; **blocco cardiaco** cardiac arrest; **blocco stradale** road block

blu ag inv, sm dark blue

'blusa sf (camiciotto) smock; (camicetta) blouse

'boa sm inv (Zool) boa constrictor; (sciarpa) feather boa ▶ sf buoy

bo'ato sm rumble, roar

bob [bɔb] sm inv bobsleigh

'bocca, -che sf mouth; **in ~ al lupo!** good luck!

boc'caccia, -ce [bok'kattʃa] sf (malalingua) gossip; **fare le boccacce** to pull faces

boc'cale sm jug; **boccale da birra** tankard

boc'cetta [bot'tʃetta] sf small bottle

'boccia, -ce ['bottʃa] sf bottle; (da vino) decanter, carafe; (palla) bowl; **gioco delle bocce** bowls sg

bocci'are [bot'tʃare] vt (proposta, progetto) to reject; (Ins) to fail; (Bocce) to hit

bocci'olo [bot'tʃɔlo] sm bud

boc'cone sm mouthful, morsel

boicot'tare vt to boycott

'bolla sf bubble; (Med) blister; **bolla**

di consegna (*Comm*) delivery note; **bolla papale** papal bull

bol'lente *ag* boiling; boiling hot

bol'letta *sf* bill; (*ricevuta*) receipt; **essere in ~** to be hard up

bollet'tino *sm* bulletin; (*Comm*) note; **bollettino meteorologico** weather report; **bollettino di spedizione** consignment note

bollicina [bolli'tʃina] *sf* bubble

bol'lire *vt*, *vi* to boil

bolli'tore *sm* (*Cuc*) kettle; (*per riscaldamento*) boiler

'bollo *sm* stamp; **bollo per patente** driving licence tax; **bollo postale** postmark

'bomba *sf* bomb; **bomba atomica** atom bomb; **bomba a mano** hand grenade; **bomba ad orologeria** time bomb

bombarda'mento *sm* bombardment; bombing

bombar'dare *vt* to bombard; (*da aereo*) to bomb

'bombola *sf* cylinder

bombo'letta *sf* aerosol

bomboni'era *sf* box of sweets (*as souvenir at weddings, first communions etc*)

bo'nifico, -ci *sm* (*riduzione, abbuono*) discount; (*versamento a terzi*) credit transfer

bontà *sf* goodness; (*cortesia*) kindness; **aver la ~ di fare qc** to be good *o* kind enough to do sth

borbot'tare *vi* to mumble

'borchia ['borkja] *sf* stud

bor'deaux [bor'dɔ] *ag inv*, *sm inv* maroon

'bordo *sm* (*Naut*) ship's side; (*orlo*) edge; (*striscia di guarnizione*) border, trim; **a ~ di** (*nave, aereo*) aboard, on board; (*macchina*) in

bor'ghese [bor'geze] *ag* (*spesso peg*) middle-class; bourgeois; **abito ~** civilian dress

'borgo, -ghi *sm* (*paesino*) village; (*quartiere*) district; (*sobborgo*) suburb

boro'talco *sm* talcum powder

bor'raccia, -ce [bor'rattʃa] *sf* canteen, water-bottle

'borsa *sf* bag; (*anche*: **~ da signora**) handbag; (*Econ*): **la B~ (valori)** the Stock Exchange; **borsa dell'acqua calda** hot-water bottle; **borsa nera** black market; **borsa della spesa** shopping bag; **borsa di studio** grant; **borsel'lino** *sm* purse; **bor'setta** *sf* handbag

'bosco, -schi *sm* wood

bos'niaco, -a, ci, che *ag*, *sm/f* Bosnian

'Bosnia Erze'govina ['bɔsnja erdze'govina] *sf* la ~ Bosnia Herzegovina

Bot, bot *sigla m inv* (= *buono ordinario del Tesoro*) short-term Treasury bond

bo'tanica *sf* botany

bo'tanico, -a, -ci, -che *ag* botanical ▶ *sm* botanist

'botola *sf* trap door

'botta *sf* blow; (*rumore*) bang

'botte *sf* barrel, cask

bot'tega, -ghe *sf* shop; (*officina*) workshop

bot'tiglia [bot'tiʎʎa] *sf* bottle; **bottiglie'ria** *sf* wine shop

bot'tino *sm* (*di guerra*) booty; (*di rapina, furto*) loot

'botto *sm* bang; crash; **di ~** suddenly

bot'tone *sm* button; **attaccare ~ a qn** (*fig*) to buttonhole sb

bo'vino, -a *ag* bovine; **bovini** *smpl* cattle

box [bɔks] *sm inv* (*per cavalli*) horsebox; (*per macchina*) lock-up; (*per macchina da corsa*) pit; (*per bambini*) playpen

boxe [bɔks] *sf* boxing

'boxer ['bɔkser] *sm inv* (*cane*) boxer ▶ *smpl* (*mutande*): **un paio di ~** a pair of boxer shorts

BR *sigla fpl* = **Brigate Rosse**

brac'cetto [brat'tʃetto] *sm* a ~ arm in arm

braccia'letto *sm* bracelet, bangle

bracci'ata [brat'tʃata] *sf* (*nel nuoto*) stroke

'braccio ['brattʃo] (*pl(f)* **braccia**) *sm* (*Anat*) arm; (*pl(m)* **bracci**: *di gru, fiume*) arm; (: *di edificio*) wing; **braccio di mare** sound; **bracci'olo** *sm* (*appoggio*) arm

'bracco, -chi *sm* hound

'brace ['bratʃe] *sf* embers *pl*

braci'ola [bra'tʃɔla] *sf* (*Cuc*) chop

'branca, -che *sf* branch

'branchia ['brankja] *sf* (*Zool*) gill

'branco, -chi *sm* (*di cani, lupi*) pack; (*di pecore*) flock; (*peg: di persone*) gang, pack

bran'dina *sf* camp bed (BRIT), cot (US)

'brano *sm* piece; (*di libro*) passage

Bra'sile *sm* il ~ Brazil; **brasili'ano, -a** *ag, sm/f* Brazilian

'bravo, -a *ag* (*abile*) clever, capable, skilful; (*buono*) good, honest; (: *bambino*) good; (*coraggioso*) brave; ~! well done!; (*a teatro*) bravo!

bra'vura *sf* cleverness, skill

Bre'tagna [bre'taɲɲa] *sf* la ~ Brittany

bre'tella [bre'tella] *sf* (*Aut*) link; **bretelle** *sfpl* (*di calzoni*) braces

'bretone *ag, sm/f* Breton

'breve *ag* brief, short; **in ~** in short

brevet'tare *vt* to patent

bre'vetto *sm* patent; **brevetto di pilotaggio** pilot's licence (BRIT) o license (US)

'bricco, -chi *sm* jug; **bricco del caffè** coffeepot

brici'ola ['britʃola] *sf* crumb

bricio'lo ['britʃolo] *sm* (*specie fig*) bit

'briga, -ghe *sf* (*fastidio*) trouble, bother; **pigliarsi la ~ di fare qc** to take the trouble to do sth

bri'gata *sf* (*Mil*) brigade; (*gruppo*) group, party; **Brigate Rosse** (*Pol*) Red Brigades

'briglia ['briʎʎa] *sf* rein; **a ~ sciolta** at full gallop; (*fig*) at full speed

bril'lante *ag* bright; (*anche fig*) brilliant; (*che luccica*) shining ▶ *sm* diamond

bril'lare *vi* to shine; (*mina*) to blow up ▶ *vt* (*mina*) to set off

'brillo, -a *ag* merry, tipsy

'brina *sf* hoarfrost

brin'dare *vi* ~ a qn/qc to drink to o toast sb/sth

'brindisi *sm inv* toast

bri'oche [bri'ɔʃ] *sf inv* brioche

bri'tannico, -a, -ci, -che *ag* British

'brivido *sm* shiver; (*di ribrezzo*) shudder; (*fig*) thrill

brizzo'lato, -a [brittso'lato] *ag* (*persona*) going grey; (*barba, capelli*) greying

'brocca, -che *sf* jug

'broccoli *smpl* broccoli *sg*

'brodo *sm* broth; (*per cucinare*) stock; **brodo ristretto** consommé

bron'chite [bron'kite] *sf* (*Med*) bronchitis

bronto'lare *vi* to grumble; (*tuono, stomaco*) to rumble

'bronzo ['brondzo] *sm* bronze

'browser ['brauzer] *sm inv* (*Inform*) browser

brucia'pelo [brutʃa'pelo] *sm* a ~ *av* point-blank

bruci'are [bru'tʃare] *vt* to burn; (*scottare*) to scald ▶ *vi* to burn; **bruciarsi** *vpr* to burn o.s.; (*fallire*) to ruin one's chances; ~ **le tappe** (*fig*) to shoot ahead; **bruciarsi la carriera** to ruin one's career

'bruco, -chi *sm* caterpillar; grub

bru'folo *sm* pimple, spot

'brullo, -a *ag* bare, bleak

'bruno, -a *ag* brown, dark; (*persona*)

dark(-haired)

brusco, -a, -schi, -sche ag (sapore) sharp; (modi, persona) brusque, abrupt; (movimento) abrupt, sudden

bru'sio sm buzz, buzzing

bru'tale ag brutal

brutto, -a ag ugly; (cattivo) bad; (malattia, strada, affare) nasty, bad; ~ **tempo** bad weather

Bru'xelles [bry'sɛl] sf Brussels

BSE [biɛsse] sigla f (= encefalopatia spongiforme bovina) BSE

buca, -che sf hole; (avvallamento) hollow; **buca delle lettere** letterbox

buca'neve sm inv snowdrop

bu'care vt (forare) to make a hole (o holes) in; (pungere) to pierce; (biglietto) to punch; **bucarsi** vpr (di eroina) to mainline; ~ **una gomma** to have a puncture

bu'cato sm (operazione) washing; (panni) wash, washing

buccia, -ce ['buttʃa] sf skin, peel

bucherò ecc [buke'rɔ] vb vedi **bucare**

buco, -chi sm hole

bud'dismo sm Buddhism

bu'dino sm pudding

bue sm ox; **carne di ~** beef

bu'fera sf storm

buffo, -a ag funny; (Teatro) comic

bu'gia, -gie [bu'dʒia] sf lie; **dire una ~** to tell a lie; **bugi'ardo, -a** ag lying, deceitful ▶ sm/f liar

buio, -a ag dark ▶ sm dark, darkness

bulbo sm (Bot) bulb; **bulbo oculare** eyeball

Bulga'ria sf la ~ Bulgaria

bulgaro, -a ag, sm/f, sm Bulgarian

buli'mia sf bulimia; **bu'limico, -a, -ci, -che** ag bulimic

bul'lone sm bolt

buona'notte escl good night! ▶ sf **dare la ~ a** to say good night to

buona'sera escl good evening!

buongi'orno [bwon'dʒorno] escl good

morning (o afternoon)!

buongu'staio, -a sm/f gourmet

bu'ono, -a
(ag: dav sm **buon** + C o V, buono + s impura, gn, pn, ps, x, z; dav sf **buon'** + V)
1 (gen) good; **un buon pranzo/ristorante** a good lunch/restaurant; (stai) **buono!** behave!
2 (benevolo): **buono (con)** good (to), kind (to)
3 (giusto, valido) right; **al momento buono** at the right moment
4 (adatto): **buono a/da** fit for/to; **essere buono a nulla** to be no good o use at anything
5 (auguri): **buon anno!** happy New Year!; **buon appetito!** enjoy your meal!; **buon compleanno!** happy birthday!; **buon divertimento!** have a nice time!; **buona fortuna!** good luck!; **buon riposo!** sleep well!; **buon viaggio!** bon voyage!, have a good trip!
6: **a buon mercato** cheap; **di buon'ora** early; **buon senso** common sense; **alla buona** ag simple
▶ av in a simple way, without any fuss
▶ sm
1 (bontà) goodness, good
2 (Comm) voucher, coupon; **buono di cassa** cash voucher; **buono di consegna** delivery note; **buono del Tesoro** Treasury bill

buon'senso sm = **buon senso**

burat'tino sm puppet

burbero, -a ag surly, gruff

buro'cratico, -a, -ci, -che ag bureaucratic

burocra'zia [burokrat'tsia] sf bureaucracy

bur'rasca, -sche sf storm

burro sm butter

bur'rone sm ravine

bus'sare vi to knock

bussola sf compass

busta sf (da lettera) envelope;

(astuccio) case; **in ~ aperta/chiusa** in an unsealed/sealed envelope; **busta paga** pay packet

bus'trella *sf* bribe, backhander

bus'tina *sf* (piccola busta) envelope; (di cibi, farmaci) sachet; (Mil) forage cap; **bustina di tè** tea bag

'busto *sm* bust; (indumento) corset, girdle; **a mezzo ~** (foto) half-length

but'tare *vt* to throw; (anche: **~ via**) to throw away; **~ giù** (scritto) to scribble down; (cibo) to gulp down; (edificio) to pull down, demolish; (pasta, verdura) to put into boiling water; **buttarsi** *vpr* (saltare) to jump; **buttarsi dalla finestra** to jump out of the window

byte ['bait] *sm inv* byte

C

ca'bina *sf* (di nave) cabin; (da spiaggia) beach hut; (di autocarro, treno) cab; (di aereo) cockpit; (di ascensore) cage; **cabi'nato** *sm* cabin cruiser; **cabina di pilotaggio** cockpit; **cabina telefonica** call o (tele)phone box

ca'cao *sm* cocoa

'caccia ['kattʃa] *sf* hunting; (con fucile) shooting; (inseguimento) chase; (cacciagione) game ▶ *sm inv* (aereo) fighter; (nave) destroyer; **caccia grossa** big-game hunting; **caccia all'uomo** manhunt

cacci'are [kat'tʃare] *vt* to hunt; (mandar via) to chase away; (ficcare) to shove, stick ▶ *vi* to hunt; **cacciarsi** *vpr* dove s'è cacciata la mia borsa? where has my bag got to?; **cacciarsi nei guai** to get into trouble; **~ fuori** *qc* to whip o pull sth out; **~ un urlo** to let out a yell; **caccia'tore** *sm* hunter; **cacciatore di frodo** poacher

caccia'vite [kattʃa'vite] *sm inv* screwdriver

'cactus *sm inv* cactus

ca'davere *sm* (dead) body, corpse

'caddi *ecc vb vedi* **cadere**

ca'denza [ka'dɛntsa] *sf* cadence; (ritmo) rhythm; (Mus) cadenza

ca'dere *vi* to fall; (denti, capelli) to fall out; (tetto) to fall in; **questa gonna cade bene** this skirt hangs well; **lasciar ~** (anche fig) to drop; (anche: **~ dal sonno**) to be falling asleep on one's feet; **~ dalle nuvole** (fig) to be taken aback

cadrò *ecc vb vedi* **cadere**

ca'duta *sf* fall; **la ~ dei capelli** hair loss

caffè *sm inv* coffee; (locale) café; **caffè corretto** espresso coffee with a shot of spirits; **caffè macchiato** coffee with a dash of milk; **caffè macinato** ground coffee

caffel'latte *sm inv* white coffee

caffet'tiera *sf* coffeepot

'cagna ['kaɲɲa] *sf* (Zool, peg) bitch

CAI *sigla m* = Club Alpino Italiano

cala'brone *sm* hornet

cala'maro *sm* squid

cala'mita *sf* magnet

calamità *sf inv* calamity, disaster

ca'lare *vt* (far discendere) to lower; (Maglia) to decrease ▶ *vi* (discendere) to go (o come) down; (tramontare) to set, go down; **~ di peso** to lose weight

cal'cagno [kal'kaɲɲo] *sm* heel

cal'care *sm* (incrostazione) (lime)scale

'calce ['kaltʃe] *sm* **in ~** at the foot of the

page ▸ *sf* lime; **calce viva** quicklime
calci'are [kal'tʃare] *vt*, *vi* to kick;
calcia'tore *sm* footballer
'calcio ['kaltʃo] *sm* (*pedata*) kick;
(*sport*) football, soccer; (*di pistola*,
fucile) butt; (*Chim*) calcium; **calcio
d'angolo** (*Sport*) corner (kick); **calcio
di punizione** (*Sport*) free kick; **calcio
di rigore** penalty
calco'lare *vt* to calculate, work out,
reckon; (*ponderare*) to weigh (up);
calcola'tore, -'trice *ag* calculating
▸ *sm* calculator; (*fig*) calculating
person; **calcolatore elettronico**
computer; **calcola'trice** *sf* calculator
'calcolo *sm* (*anche Mat*) calculation;
(*infinitesimale ecc*) calculus; (*Med*)
stone; **fare i propri calcoli** (*fig*) to
weigh the pros and cons; **per ~** out of
self-interest
cal'daia *sf* boiler
'caldo, -a *ag* warm; (*molto caldo*) hot;
(*fig*: *appassionato*) keen; hearty ▸ *sm*
heat; **ho ~** I'm warm; I'm hot; **fa ~** it's
warm; it's hot
caleidos'copio *sm* kaleidoscope
calen'dario *sm* calendar
'calibro *sm* (*di arma*) calibre, bore;
(*Tecn*) callipers *pl*; (*fig*) calibre; **di
grosso ~** (*fig*) prominent
'calice ['kalitʃe] *sm* goblet; (*Rel*) chalice
Cali'fornia *sf* California
californi'ano, -a *ag* Californian
calligra'fia *sf* (*scrittura*) handwriting;
(*arte*) calligraphy
'callo *sm* callus; (*ai piedi*) corn
'calma *sf* calm
cal'mante *sm* tranquillizer
cal'mare *vt* to calm; (*lenire*) to soothe;
calmarsi *vpr* to grow calm, calm
down; (*vento*) to abate; (*dolori*) to ease
'calmo, -a *ag* calm, quiet
'calo *sm* (*Comm*: *di prezzi*) fall; (: *di
volume*) shrinkage; (: *di peso*) loss
ca'lore *sm* warmth; heat; **in ~** (*Zool*)

on heat
calo'ria *sf* calorie
calo'rifero *sm* radiator
calo'roso, -a *ag* warm
calpes'tare *vt* to tread on, trample
on; **"è vietato ~ l'erba"** "keep off
the grass"
ca'lunnia *sf* slander; (*scritta*) libel
cal'vizie [kal'vittsje] *sf* baldness
'calvo, -a *ag* bald
'calza ['kaltsa] *sf* (*da donna*) stocking;
(*da uomo*) sock; **fare la ~** to knit; **calze
di nailon** nylons, (nylon) stockings
calza'maglia [kaltsa'maʎʎa] *sf* tights
pl; (*per danza*, *ginnastica*) leotard
calzet'tone [kaltset'tone] *sm* heavy
knee-length sock
cal'zino [kal'tsino] *sm* sock
calzo'laio [kaltso'lajo] *sm* shoemaker;
(*che ripara scarpe*) cobbler
calzon'cini [kaltson'tʃini] *smpl*
shorts; **calzoncini da bagno**
(swimming) trunks
cal'zone [kal'tsone] *sm* trouser
leg; (*Cuc*) savoury turnover made with
pizza dough; **calzoni** *smpl* (*pantaloni*)
trousers (BRIT), pants (US)
camale'onte *sm* chameleon
cambia'mento *sm* change
cambi'are *vt* to change; (*modificare*)
to alter, change; (*barattare*): **~ qc con
qn/qc** to exchange (sth with sb/for
sth) ▸ *vi* to change, alter; **cambiarsi**
vpr (*d'abito*) to change; **~ casa** to
move (house); **~ idea** to change one's
mind; **~ treno** to change trains; **dove
posso ~ dei soldi?** where can I change
some money?; **ha da ~?** have you got
any change?; **posso cambiarlo, per
favore?** could I exchange this, please?
cambia'lute *vt inv* exchange
office
'cambio *sm* change; (*modifica*)
alteration, change; (*scambio*, *Comm*)
exchange; (*corso dei cambi*) rate (of

exchange); (*Tecn,Aut*) gears *pl*; **in ~ di** in exchange for; **dare il ~ a qn** to take over from sb

'**camera** *sf* room; (*anche*: **~ da letto**) bedroom; (*Pol*) chamber, house; **camera ardente** mortuary chapel; **camera d'aria** inner tube; (*di pallone*) bladder; **camera di commercio** Chamber of Commerce; **Camera dei Deputati** Chamber of Deputies, ≈ House of Commons (*BRIT*), ≈ House of Representatives (*US*); **camera a gas** gas chamber; **camera a un letto/due letti** single/twin-bedded room; **camera matrimoniale** double room; **camera oscura** (*Fot*) dark room

> Attenzione! In inglese esiste la parola *camera*, che però significa *macchina fotografica*.

came'rata, **-i**, **-e** *sm/f* companion, mate ▶ *sf* dormitory

cameri'era *sf* (*domestica*) maid; (*che serve a tavola*) waitress; (*che fa le camere*) chambermaid

cameri'ere *sm* (*man*)servant; (*di ristorante*) waiter

came'rino *sm* (*Teatro*) dressing room

ca'mice ['kamitʃe] *sm* (*Rel*) alb; (*per medici ecc*) white coat

cami'cetta [kami'tʃetta] *sf* blouse

ca'micia, **-cie** [ka'mitʃa] *sf* (*da uomo*) shirt; (*da donna*) blouse; **camicia di forza** straitjacket; **camicia da notte** (*da donna*) nightdress; (*da uomo*) nightshirt

cami'netto *sm* hearth, fireplace

ca'mino *sm* chimney; (*focolare*) fireplace, hearth

'camion *sm inv* lorry (*BRIT*), truck (*US*)

camio'nista, **-i** *sm* lorry driver (*BRIT*), truck driver (*US*)

cam'mello *sm* (*Zool*) camel; (*tessuto*) camel hair

cammi'nare *vi* to walk; (*funzionare*)

to work, go

cam'mino *sm* walk; (*sentiero*) path; (*itinerario, direzione, tragitto*) way; **mettersi in ~** to set o start off

camo'milla *sf* camomile; (*infuso*) camomile tea

ca'moscio [ka'mɔʃʃo] *sm* chamois; **di ~** (*scarpe, borsa*) suede *cpd*

cam'pagna [kam'paɲɲa] *sf* country, countryside; (*Pol, Comm, Mil*) campaign; **in ~** in the country; **andare in ~** to go to the country; **fare una ~** to campaign; **campagna pubblicitaria** advertising campaign

cam'pana *sf* bell; (*anche*: **~ di vetro**) bell jar; **campa'nello** *sm* (*all'uscio, da tavola*) bell

campa'nile *sm* bell tower, belfry

cam'peggio *sm* camping; (*terreno*) camp site; **fare (del) ~** to go camping

camper ['kamper] *sm inv* motor caravan (*BRIT*), motor home (*US*)

campio'nario, **-a** *ag* **fiera campionaria** trade fair ▶ *sm* collection of samples

campio'nato *sm* championship

campio'ne, **-'essa** *sm/f* (*Sport*) champion ▶ *sm* (*Comm*) sample

'**campo** *sm* field; (*Mil*) field; (*accampamento*) camp; (*spazio delimitato: sportivo ecc*) ground; field; (*di quadro*) background; **i campi** (*campagna*) the countryside; **campo di aviazione** airfield; **campo di battaglia** (*Mil, fig*) battlefield; **campo di concentramento** concentration camp; **campo da golf** golf course; **campo profughi** refugee camp; **campo sportivo** sports ground; **campo da tennis** tennis court; **campo visivo** field of vision

'**Canada** *sm* **il ~** Canada; **cana'dese** *ag, sm/f* Canadian ▶ *sf* (*anche*: **tenda canadese**) ridge tent

ca'naglia [ka'naʎʎa] *sf* rabble, mob;

(persona) scoundrel, rogue

ca'nale *sm (anche fig)* channel; *(artificiale)* canal

'canapa *sf* hemp; **canapa indiana** *(droga)* cannabis

cana'rino *sm* canary

cancel'lare [kantʃel'lare] *vt (con la gomma)* to rub out, erase; *(con la penna)* to strike out; *(annullare)* to annul, cancel; *(disdire)* to cancel

cancelle'ria [kantʃelle'ria] *sf* chancery; *(materiale per scrivere)* stationery

can'cello [kan'tʃello] *sm* gate

'cancro *sm (Med)* cancer; *(dello zodiaco)*: **C~** Cancer

candeg'gina [kanded'dʒina] *sf* bleach

can'dela *sf* candle; **candela (di accensione)** *(Aut)* spark(ing) plug

cande'labro *sm* candelabra

candeli'ere *sm* candlestick

candi'dare *vt* to present as candidate; **candidarsi** *vpr* to present o.s. as candidate

candi'dato, -a *sm/f* candidate; *(aspirante a una carica)* applicant

'candido, -a *ag* white as snow; *(puro)* pure; *(sincero)* sincere, candid

can'dito, -a *ag* candied

'cane *sm* dog; *(di pistola, fucile)* cock; **fa un freddo ~** it's bitterly cold; **non c'era un ~** there wasn't a soul; **cane da caccia/da guardia** hunting/guard dog; **cane lupo** Alsatian; **cane pastore** sheepdog

ca'nestro *sm* basket

can'guro *sm* kangaroo

ca'nile *sm* kennel; *(di allevamento)* kennels *pl*; **canile municipale** dog pound

'canna *sf (pianta)* reed; (: *indica, da zucchero)* cane; *(bastone)* stick, cane; *(di fucile)* barrel; *(di organo)* pipe; *(fam: droga)* joint; **canna fumaria** chimney

flue; **canna da pesca** (fishing) rod; **canna da zucchero** sugar cane

cannel'loni *smpl* pasta tubes stuffed with sauce and baked

cannocchi'ale [kannok'kjale] *sm* telescope

can'none *sm (Mil)* gun; *(Storia)* cannon; *(tubo)* pipe, tube; *(piega)* box pleat; *(fig)* ace

can'nuccia, -ce [kan'nuttʃa] *sf* (drinking) straw

ca'noa *sf* canoe

'canone *sm* canon, criterion; *(mensile, annuo)* rent; fee

canot'taggio [kanot'taddʒo] *sm* rowing

canotti'era *sf* vest

ca'notto *sm* small boat, dinghy; canoe

can'tante *sm/f* singer

can'tare *vt, vi* to sing; **cantau'tore, -'trice** *sm/f* singer-composer

canti'ere *sm (Edil)* (building) site; *(cantiere navale)* shipyard

can'tina *sf* cellar; *(bottega)* wine shop; **cantina sociale** cooperative winegrowers' association

▌ Attenzione! In inglese esiste la parola canteen, che però significa mensa.

'canto *sm* song; *(arte)* singing; *(Rel)* chant; chanting; *(poesia)* poem, lyric; *(parte di una poesia)* canto; *(parte, lato)*: **da un ~** on the one hand; **d'altro ~** on the other hand

canzo'nare [kantso'nare] *vt* to tease

can'zone [kan'tsone] *sf* song; *(Poesia)* canzone

'caos *sm inv* chaos; **ca'otico, -a, -ci, -che** *ag* chaotic

CAP *sigla m* = **codice di avviamento postale**

ca'pace [ka'patʃe] *ag* able, capable; *(ampio, vasto)* large, capacious; **sei ~ di farlo?** can you o are you able to do it?; **capacità** sf inv ability; (Dir, di recipiente) capacity

ca'panna sf hut

capan'none sm (Agr) barn; (fabbricato industriale) (factory) shed

ca'parbio, -a ag stubborn

ca'parra sf deposit, down payment

ca'pello sm hair; **capelli** smpl (capigliatura) hair sg

ca'pezzolo [ka'pettsolo] sm nipple

ca'pire vt to understand; **non capisco** I don't understand

capi'tale ag (mortale) capital; (fondamentale) main, chief ▶ sf (città) capital ▶ sm (Econ) capital

capi'tano sm captain

capi'tare vi (giungere casualmente) to happen to go, find o.s.; (accadere) to happen; (presentarsi: cosa) to turn up, present itself ▶ vb impers to happen; **mi è capitato un guaio** I've had a spot of trouble

capi'tello sm (Archit) capital

ca'pitolo sm chapter

capi'tombolo sm headlong fall, tumble

'capo sm head; (persona) head, leader; (: in ufficio) boss, chief; (: in tribù) chief; (di oggetti) head; top; end; (Geo) cape; **andare a ~** to start a new paragraph; **da ~** over again; **capo di bestiame** head inv of cattle; **capo di vestiario** item of clothing; **Capo'danno** sm New Year; **capo'giro** sm dizziness no pl; **capola'voro, -i** sm masterpiece; **capo'linea** (pl **capi'linea**) sm terminus; **capostazi'one** (pl **capistazi'oni**) sm station master

capo'tavola (pl(m) **capi'tavola**) pl(f) inv sm/f (persona) head of the table; **sedere a ~** to sit at the head of the table

capo'volgere [kapo'voldʒere] vt to overturn; (fig) to reverse; (barca)

to capsize; (fig) to be reversed

capovolgersi vpr to overturn; (barca)

'cappa sf (mantello) cape, cloak; (del camino) hood

cap'pella sf (Rel) chapel

cap'pello sm hat

'cappero sm caper

cap'pone sm capon

cap'potto sm (over)coat

cappuc'cino [kapput'tʃino] sm (frate) Capuchin monk; (bevanda) cappuccino, frothy white coffee

cap'puccio [kap'puttʃo] sm (copricapo) hood; (della biro) cap

'capra sf (she-)goat

ca'priccio [ka'prittʃo] sm caprice, whim; (bizza) tantrum; **fare i capricci** to be very naughty; **capricci'oso, -a** ag capricious, whimsical; naughty

Capri'corno sm Capricorn

capri'ola sf somersault

capri'olo sm roe deer

'capro sm ~ **espiatorio** scapegoat

ca'prone sm billy-goat

'capsula sf capsule; (di arma, per bottiglie) cap

cap'tare vt (Radio, TV) to pick up; (cattivarsi) to gain, win

carabini'ere sm member of Italian military police force

- **carabinieri**
- Originally part of the armed forces,
- the **carabinieri** are police who
- perform both military and civil
- duties. They include paratroopers
- and mounted divisions.

ca'raffa sf carafe

Ca'raibi smpl **il mar dei ~** the Caribbean (Sea)

cara'mella sf sweet

ca'rattere sm character; (caratteristica) characteristic, trait; **avere un buon ~** to be good-natured; **carattere jolly** wild card; **caratte'ristica, -che** sf characteristic, trait, peculiarity;

caratte'ristico, -a, -ci, -che *ag* characteristic

car'bone *sm* coal

carbu'rante *sm* (motor) fuel

carbura'tore *sm* carburettor

carce'rato, -a [kartʃe'rato] *sm/f* prisoner

'carcere ['kartʃere] *sm* prison; (*pena*) imprisonment

carci'ofo [kar'tʃɔfo] *sm* artichoke

cardel'lino *sm* goldfinch

car'diaco, -a, -ci, -che *ag* cardiac, heart *cpd*

cardi'nale *ag, sm* cardinal

'cardine *sm* hinge

'cardo *sm* thistle

ca'rente *ag* ~ **di** lacking in

cares'tia *sf* famine; (*penuria*) scarcity, dearth

ca'rezza [ka'rettsa] *sf* caress

'carica, -che *sf* (*mansione ufficiale*) office, position; (*Mil, Tecn, Elettr*) charge; **ha una forte ~ di simpatia** he's very likeable; *vedi anche* **carico**

caricabatte'ria *sm inv* battery charger

cari'care *vt* (*merce, Inform*) to load; (*orologio*) to wind up; (*batteria, Mil*) to charge

'carico, -a, -chi, -che *ag* (*che porta un peso*): ~ **di** loaded o laden with; (*fucile*) loaded; (*orologio*) wound up; (*batteria*) charged; (*colore*) deep; (*caffè, tè*) strong ▸ *sm* (*il caricare*) loading; (*ciò che si carica*) load; (*fig: peso*) burden, weight; **persona a ~** dependent; **essere a ~ di qn** (*spese ecc*) to be charged to sb

'carie *sf* (*dentaria*) decay

ca'rino, -a *ag* (*grazioso*) lovely, pretty, nice; (*riferito a uomo, anche simpatico*) nice

carità *sf* charity; **per ~!** (*escl di rifiuto*) good heavens, no!

carnagi'one [karna'dʒone] *sf* complexion

'carne *sf* flesh; (*bovina, ovina ecc*) meat; **non mangio ~** I don't eat meat; **carne di maiale/manzo/pecora** pork/beef/mutton; **carne in scatola** tinned o canned meat; **carne tritata** o **macinata** mince (*BRIT*), hamburger meat (*US*), minced (*BRIT*) o ground (*US*) meat

carne'vale *sm* carnival

● **carnevale**
● Carnevale is the period between
● Epiphany (Jan. 6th) and the
● beginning of Lent. People wear
● fancy dress, and there are parties,
● processions of floats and bonfires. It
● culminates immediately before Lent
● in the festivities of **martedì grasso**
● (Shrove Tuesday).

'caro, -a *ag* (*amato*) dear; (*costoso*) dear, expensive; **è troppo ~** it's too expensive

ca'rogna [ka'roɲɲa] *sf* carrion; (*anche: fig: man*) swine

ca'rota *sf* carrot

caro'vana *sf* caravan

car'poni *av* on all fours

car'rabile *ag* suitable for vehicles; "**passo ~**" "keep clear"

carreggi'ata [karred'dʒata] *sf* carriageway (*BRIT*), (road)way

car'rello *sm* trolley; (*Aer*) undercarriage; (*Cinema*) dolly; (*di macchina da scrivere*) carriage

carri'era *sf* career; **fare ~** to get on; **a gran ~** at full speed

carri'ola *sf* wheelbarrow

'carro *sm* cart, wagon; **carro armato** tank; **carro attrezzi** breakdown van

car'rozza [kar'rɔttsa] *sf* carriage, coach

carrozze'ria [karrottse'ria] *sf* body, coachwork (*BRIT*); (*officina*) coachbuilder's workshop (*BRIT*), body shop

carroz'zina [karrot'tsina] *sf* pram (BRIT), baby carriage (US)

'**carta** *sf* paper; (al ristorante) menu; (Geo) map; plan; (documento) card; (costituzione) charter; **carte** *sfpl* (documenti) papers, documents; **alla ~** (al ristorante) à la carte; **carta assegni** bank card; **carta assorbente** blotting paper; **carta bollata** o **da bollo** official stamped paper; **carta (da gioco)** playing card; **carta di credito** credit card; **carta (geografica)** map; **carta d'identità** identity card; **carta igienica** toilet paper; **carta d'imbarco** (Aer, Naut) boarding card; **carta da lettere** writing paper; **carta per pacchi** wrapping paper; **carta da parati** wallpaper; **carta libera** (Amm) unstamped paper; **carta stradale** road map; **carta verde** (Aut) green card; **carta vetrata** sandpaper; **carta da visita** visiting card

car'taccia, -ce [kar'tattʃa] *sf* waste paper

carta'pesta *sf* papier-mâché

car'tella *sf* (scheda) card; (Inform, custodia: di cartone) folder; (: di uomo d'affari ecc) briefcase; (: di scolaro) schoolbag, satchel; **cartella clinica** (Med) case sheet

cartel'lino *sm* (etichetta) label; (su porta) notice; (scheda) card; **timbrare il ~** (all'entrata) to clock in; (all'uscita) to clock out; **cartellino di presenza** clock card, timecard

car'tello *sm* sign; (pubblicitario) poster; (stradale) sign, signpost; (Econ) cartel; (in dimostrazioni) placard; **cartello stradale** road sign; **cartel'lone** *sm* (della tombola) scoring frame; (Teatro) playbill; **tenere il cartellone** (spettacolo) to have a long run; **cartellone pubblicitario** advertising poster

car'tina *sf* (Aut, Geo) map; **può indicarmelo sulla ~?** can you show it to me on the map?

car'toccio [kar'tottʃo] *sm* paper bag

carto'leria *sf* stationer's (shop)

carto'lina *sf* postcard; **cartolina postale** ready-stamped postcard

car'tone *sm* cardboard; (Arte) cartoon; **cartoni animati** (Cinema) cartoons

car'tuccia, -ce [kar'tuttʃa] *sf* cartridge

'**casa** *sf* house; (in senso astratto) home; (Comm) firm, house; **essere a ~** to be at home; **vado a ~ mia/tua** I'm going home/to your house; **vino della ~** house wine; **casa di cura** nursing home; **casa editrice** publishing house; **Casa delle Libertà** centre-right coalition; **casa di riposo** (old people's) home, care home; **case popolari** ≈ council houses (o flats) (BRIT), ≈ public housing units (US); **casa dello studente** student hostel

ca'sacca, -che *sf* military coat; (di fantino) blouse

casa'linga, -ghe *sf* housewife

casa'lingo, -a, -ghi, -ghe *ag* household, domestic; (fatto a casa) home-made; (semplice) homely; (amante della casa) home-loving

cas'care *vi* to fall; **cas'cata** *sf* fall; (d'acqua) cascade, waterfall

cascherò [kaske'rɔ] *vb vedi* cascare

'**casco, -schi** *sm* helmet; (del parrucchiere) hair-drier; (di banane) bunch; **casco blu** (Mil) blue helmet (UN soldier)

casei'ficio [kazei'fitʃo] *sm* creamery

ca'sella *sf* pigeon-hole; **casella postale** post office box

ca'sello *sm* (di autostrada) toll-house

ca'serma *sf* barracks *pl*

ca'sino (fam) *sm* brothel; (confusione)

row, racket

casinò sm inv casino

'caso sm chance; (fatto, vicenda) event, incident; (possibilità) possibility; (Med, Ling) case; **a ~** at random; **per ~** by chance, by accident; **in ogni ~, in tutti i casi** in any case, at any rate; **al ~ should** the opportunity arise; **nel ~ che** in case; **~ mai** if by chance; **caso limite** borderline case

caso'lare sm cottage

'caspita escl (di sorpresa) good heavens!; (di impazienza) for goodness' sake!

'cassa sf case, crate, box; (bara) coffin; (mobile) chest; (involucro: di orologio ecc) case; (macchina) cash register, till; (luogo di pagamento) checkout (counter); (fondo) fund; (istituto bancario) bank; **cassa automatica prelievi** cash dispenser; **cassa continua** night safe; **cassa mutua** o **malattia** health insurance scheme; **cassa integrazione: mettere in cassa integrazione** ≈ to lay off; **cassa di risparmio** savings bank; **cassa toracica** (Anat) chest

cassa'forte (pl **casse'forti**) sf safe; **lo potrebbe mettere nella ~?** could you put this in the safe, please?

cassa'panca (pl **cassa'panche** o **casse'panche**) sf settle

casseru'ola sf saucepan

cas'setta sf box; (per registratore) cassette; (Cinema, Teatro) box-office takings pl; **film di ~** box-office draw; **cassetta di sicurezza** strongbox; **cassetta delle lettere** letterbox

cas'setto sm drawer

cassi'ere, -a sm/f cashier; (di banca) teller

casso'netto sm wheelie-bin

cas'tagna [kas'taɲɲa] sf chestnut

cas'tagno [kas'taɲɲo] sm chestnut (tree)

cas'tano, -a ag chestnut (brown)

cas'tello sm castle; (Tecn) scaffolding

casti'gare vt to punish; **cas'tigo, -ghi** sm punishment

cas'toro sm beaver

casu'ale ag chance cpd; (Inform) random cpd

catalizza'tore [kataliddza'tore] sm (anche fig) catalyst; (Aut) catalytic converter

ca'talogo, -ghi sm catalogue

catarifran'gente [katarifran'dʒɛnte] sm (Aut) reflector

ca'tarro sm catarrh

ca'tastrofe sf catastrophe, disaster

catego'ria sf category

ca'tena sf chain; **catena di montaggio** assembly line; **catene da neve** (Aut) snow chains; **cate'nina** sf (gioiello) (thin) chain

cate'ratta sf cataract; (chiusa) sluice-gate

ca'tino sm basin

ca'trame sm tar

'cattedra sf teacher's desk; (di docente) chair

catte'drale sf cathedral

catti'veria sf malice, spite; naughtiness; (atto) spiteful act; (parole) malicious o spiteful remark

cat'tivo, -a ag (malvagio) bad, wicked; (turbolento: bambino) bad, naughty; (: mare) rough; (odore, sapore) nasty, bad

cat'tolico, -a, -ci, -che ag, sm/f (Roman) Catholic

cattu'rare vt to capture

'causa sf cause; (Dir) lawsuit, case, action; **a ~ di, per ~ di** because of; **fare** o **muovere ~ a qn** to take legal action against sb

cau'sare vt to cause

cau'tela sf caution, prudence

'cauto, -a ag cautious, prudent

cauzi'one [kaut'tsjone] sf security;

(Dir) bail

'cava sf quarry

caval'care vt (cavallo) to ride; (muro) to sit astride; (ponte) to span; **caval'cata** sf ride; (gruppo di persone) riding party

cavalca'via sm inv flyover

cavalci'oni [kaval'tʃoni]: **a ~ di** prep astride

cavali'ere sm rider; (feudale, titolo) knight; (soldato) cavalryman; (al ballo) partner

caval'letta sf grasshopper

caval'letto sm (Fot) tripod; (da pittore) easel

ca'vallo sm (anche: Scacchi) knight; (Aut: anche: ~ vapore) horsepower; (dei pantaloni) crotch; **a ~** on horseback; **a ~ di** astride, straddling; **cavallo di battaglia** (fig) hobby-horse; **cavallo da corsa** racehorse; **cavallo a dondolo** rocking horse

ca'vare vt (togliere) to draw out, extract, take out; (: giacca, scarpe) to take off; (: fame, sete, voglia) to satisfy; **cavarsela** to manage, get on all right; (scamparla) to get away with it

cava'tappi sm inv corkscrew

ca'verna sf cave

'cavia sf guinea pig

cavi'ale sm caviar

ca'viglia [ka'viʎʎa] sf ankle

'cavo, -a ag hollow ♦ sm (Anat) cavity; (corda, Elettr, Tel) cable

cavo'letto sm **~ di Bruxelles** Brussels sprout

cavolfi'ore sm cauliflower

'cavolo sm cabbage; (fam): **non m'importa un ~** I don't give a damn

'cazzo ['kattso] sm (fam!: pene) prick (!); **non gliene importa un ~** (fig fam!) he doesn't give a damn about it; **fatti i cazzi tuoi** (fig fam!) mind your own damn business

C.C.D. sigla m (= Centro Cristiano Democratico) Italian political party of the centre

CD sm inv CD; (lettore) CD player

CD-Rom ['tʃidi'rom] sm inv CD-ROM

C.D.U. sigla m (= Cristiano Democratici Uniti) Italian centre-right political party

ce [tʃe] pron, av vedi **ci**

Ce'cenia [tʃe'tʃenia] sf la ~ Chechnya

ce'ceno, -a [tʃe'tʃeno] sm/f, ag Chechen

'ceco, -a, -chi, -che ['tʃɛko] ag, sm/f Czech; **la Repubblica Ceca** the Czech Republic

'cedere vt (concedere posto) to give up; (Dir) to transfer, make over ♦ vi (cadere) to give way, subside; **~ (a)** to surrender (to), yield (to), give in (to)

'cedola ['tʃɛdola] sf (Comm) coupon, voucher

'ceffo (peg) sm ugly mug

cef'fone [tʃef'fone] sm slap, smack

cele'brare [tʃele'brare] vt to celebrate

'celebre ['tʃelebre] ag famous, celebrated

ce'leste [tʃe'leste] ag celestial; heavenly; (colore) sky-blue

'celibe ['tʃelibe] ag single, unmarried

'cella ['tʃɛlla] sf cell; **cella frigorifera** cold store

'cellula ['tʃellula] sf (Biol, Elettr, Pol) cell; **cellu'lare** sm cellphone

cellu'lite [tʃellu'lite] sf cellulite

cemen'tare [tʃemen'tare] vt (anche fig) to cement

ce'mento [tʃe'mento] sm cement; **cemento armato** reinforced concrete

'cena ['tʃena] sf dinner; (leggera) supper

ce'nare [tʃe'nare] vi to dine, have dinner

'cenere ['tʃenere] sf ash

'cenno ['tʃenno] sm (segno) sign, signal; (gesto) gesture; (col capo) nod;

(con la mano) wave; (allusione) hint, mention; (breve esposizione) short account; **far ~ di sì/no** to nod (one's head)/shake one's head

censi'mento [tʃensi'mento] *sm* census

cen'sura [tʃen'sura] *sf* censorship; censor's office; (*fig*) censure

cente'nario, -a [tʃente'narjo] *ag* (*che ha cento anni*) hundred-year-old; (*che ricorre ogni cento anni*) centennial, centenary *cpd* ▸ *sm/f* centenarian ▸ *sm* centenary

cen'tesimo, -a [tʃen'tezimo] *ag, sm* hundredth; (*di euro, dollaro*) cent

cen'tigrado, -a [tʃen'tigrado] *ag* centigrade; **20 gradi centigradi** 20 degrees centigrade

cen'timetro [tʃen'timetro] *sm* centimetre

centi'naio [tʃenti'najo] (*pl(f)* -**aia**) *sm* **un ~ (di)** a hundred; about a hundred

'cento ['tʃento] *num* a hundred, one hundred

cento'mila [tʃento'mila] *num* a o one hundred thousand; **te l'ho detto ~ volte** (*fig*) I've told you a thousand times

cen'trale [tʃen'trale] *ag* central ▸ *sf*; **centrale telefonica** (telephone) exchange; **centrale elettrica** electric power station; **centrali'nista** *sm/f* operator; **centra'lino** *sm* (*di albergo ecc*) (telephone) exchange; (*di albergo ecc*) switchboard; **centralizzato, -a** [tʃentralid'dzato] *ag* central

cen'trare [tʃen'trare] *vt* to hit the centre of; (*Tecn*) to centre

cen'trifuga [tʃen'trifuga] *sf* spin-drier

'centro ['tʃentro] *sm* centre; **centro civico** civic centre; **centro commerciale** shopping centre; (*città*) commercial centre

'ceppo ['tʃeppo] *sm* (*di albero*) stump; (*pezzo di legno*) log

'cera ['tʃera] *sf* wax; (*aspetto*) appearance

ce'ramica, -che [tʃe'ramika] *sf* ceramic; (*Arte*) ceramics *sg*

cerbi'atto [tʃer'bjatto] *sm* (*Zool*) fawn

cer'care [tʃer'kare] *vt* to look for, search for ▸ *vi* ~ **di fare qc** to try to do sth; **stiamo cercando un albergo/ristorante** we're looking for a hotel/restaurant

cerche'rò *ecc* [tʃerke'rɔ] *vb vedi* **cercare**

'cerchia ['tʃerkja] *sf* circle

cerchi'etto [tʃer'kjetto] *sm* (*per capelli*) hairband

'cerchio ['tʃerkjo] *sm* circle; (*giocattolo, di botte*) hoop

cere'ali [tʃere'ali] *smpl* cereal *sg*

ceri'monia [tʃeri'mɔnja] *sf* ceremony

ce'rino [tʃe'rino] *sm* wax match

'cernia ['tʃɛrnja] *sf* (*Zool*) stone bass

cerni'era [tʃer'njɛra] *sf* hinge; **cerniera lampo** zip (fastener) (BRIT), zipper (US)

'cero ['tʃero] *sm* (church) candle

ce'rotto [tʃe'rotto] *sm* sticking plaster

certa'mente [tʃerta'mente] *av* certainly

certifi'cato [tʃertifi'kato] *sm* certificate; **certificato medico** medical certificate; **certificato di nascita/di morte** birth/death certificate

○ **'certo, -a**
['tʃɛrto] *ag* (*sicuro*): **certo (di/che)** certain o sure (of/that)
▸ *det*

1 (*tale*) certain; **un certo signor Smith** a (certain) Mr Smith

2 (*qualche: con valore intensivo*) some; **dopo un certo tempo** after some time; **un fatto di una certa importanza** a matter of some importance; **di una certa età** past one's prime, not so young

▸ *pron* **certi, e** *pl* some

▸ *av* (*certamente*) certainly; (*senz'altro*)

of course; **di certo** certainly; **no (di) certo!, certo che no!** certainly not!; **sì certo** yes indeed, certainly

cer'vello [tʃer'vello] (Anat) (pl(f) -a) sm brain; **cervello elettronico** computer

'cervo, -a ['tʃervo] sm/f stag/doe ▶ sm deer; **cervo volante** stag beetle

ces'puglio [tʃes'puʎʎo] sm bush

ces'sare [tʃes'sare] vi, vt to stop, cease; **~ di fare qc** to stop doing sth

ces'tino [tʃes'tino] sm basket; (per la carta straccia) wastepaper basket; **cestino da viaggio** (Ferr) packed lunch (o dinner)

'cesto ['tʃesto] sm basket

'ceto ['tʃeto] sm (social) class

cetrio'lino [tʃetrio'lino] sm gherkin

cetri'olo [tʃetri'ɔlo] sm cucumber

Cfr. abbr (= confronta) cf

CGIL sigla f (= Confederazione Generale Italiana del Lavoro) trades union organization

chat line [tʃæt'laen] sf inv chat room

chattare [tʃat'tare] vi (Inform) to chat online

che
[ke] pron
1 (relativo: persona: soggetto) who; (: oggetto) whom, that; (: cosa, animale) which, that; **il ragazzo che è venuto** the boy who came; **l'uomo che io vedo** the man (whom) I see; **il libro che è sul tavolo** the book which o that is on the table; **il libro che vedi** the book (which o that) you see; **la sera che ti ho visto** the evening I saw you
2 (interrogativo, esclamativo) what; **che (cosa) fai?** what are you doing?; **a che (cosa) pensi?** what are you thinking about?; **non sa che (cosa) fare** he doesn't know what to do; **ma che dici!** what are you saying!
3 (indefinito): **quell'uomo ha un che di losco** there's something suspicious

about that man; **un certo non so che** an indefinable something
▶ det
1 (interrogativo: tra tanti) what; (: tra pochi) which; **che tipo di film preferisci?** what sort of film do you prefer?; **che vestito ti vuoi mettere?** what (o which) dress do you want to put on?
2 (esclamativo: seguito da aggettivo) how; (: seguito da sostantivo) what; **che buono!** how delicious!; **che bel vestito!** what a lovely dress!
▶ cong
1 (con proposizioni subordinate) that; **credo che verrà** I think he'll come; **voglio che tu studi** I want you to study; **so che tu c'eri** I know (that) you were there; **non che sia sbagliato, ma ...** not that it's wrong, but ...
2 (finale) so that; **vieni qua, che ti veda** come here, so (that) I can see you
3 (temporale): **arrivai che eri già partito** you had already left when I arrived; **sono anni che non lo vedo** I haven't seen him for years
4 (in frasi imperative, concessive): **che venga pure!** let him come by all means!; **che tu sia benedetto!** may God bless you!
5 (comparativo: con più, meno) than; vedi anche **più; meno; così ecc**

chemioterapia [kemjotera'pia] sf chemotherapy

chero'sene [kero'zɛne] sm kerosene

chi
[ki] pron
1 (interrogativo: soggetto) who; (: oggetto) who, whom; **chi è?** who is it?; **di chi è questo libro?** whose book is this?, whose is this book?; **con chi parli?** who are you talking to?; **a chi pensi?** who are you thinking about?; **chi di voi?** which of you?; **non so a chi**

rivolgermi I don't know who to ask **2** (*relativo*) whoever, anyone who; **dillo a chi vuoi** tell whoever you like **3** (*indefinito*): **chi ... chi ...** some ... others ...; **chi dice una cosa, chi dice un'altra** some say one thing, others say another

chiacchie'rare [kjakkje'rare] *vi* to chat; (*discorrere futilmente*) to chatter; (*far pettegolezzi*) to gossip; **chi'acchiere** *sfpl* **fare due o quattro chiacchiere** to have a chat

chia'mare [kja'mare] *vt* to call; (*rivolgersi a qn*) to call (on), send for; **chiamarsi** *vpr* (*aver nome*) to be called; **come ti chiami?** what's your name?; **mi chiamo Paolo** my name is Paolo, I'm called Paolo; ~ **alle armi** to call up; ~ **in giudizio** to summon; **chia'mata** *sf* (*Tel*) call; (*Mil*) call-up

chia'rezza [kja'rettsa] *sf* clearness, clarity

chia'rire [kja'rire] *vt* to make clear; (*fig: spiegare*) to clear up, explain

chi'aro, -a [kjaro] *ag* clear; (*luminoso*) clear, bright; (*colore*) pale, light

chi'asso [kjasso] *sm* uproar, row

chi'ave [kjave] *sf* key ▶ *ag inv* key *cpd*: **posso avere la mia ~?** can I have my key?; **chiave d'accensione** (*Aut*) ignition key; **chiave di volta** keystone; **chiave inglese** monkey wrench

chi'azza [kjattsa] *sf* stain; splash

'chicco, -chi ['kikko] *sm* grain; (*di caffè*) bean; **chicco d'uva** grape

chi'edere [kjɛdere] *vt* (*per sapere*) to ask; (*per avere*) to ask for ▶ *vi* ~ **di qn** to ask after sb; (*al telefono*) to ask for o want sb; ~ **qc a qn** to ask sb sth; to ask sb per sth; **chiedersi** *vpr* **chiedersi (se)** to wonder (whether)

chi'esa [kjɛza] *sf* church

chi'esi *ecc* ['kjɛzi] *vb vedi* **chiedere**

chi'glia ['kiʎʎa] *sf* keel

'chilo ['kilo] *sm* kilo; **chi'lometro** *sm* kilometre

'chimica ['kimika] *sf* chemistry

'chimico, -a, -ci, -che ['kimiko] *ag* chemical ▶ *sm/f* chemist

chi'nare [ki'nare] *vt* to lower, bend; **chinarsi** *vpr* to stoop, bend

chi'occiola ['kjɔttʃola] *sf* snail; (*di indirizzo e-mail*) at sign, @; **scala a ~** spiral staircase

chi'odo ['kjɔdo] *sm* nail; (*fig*) obsession; **chiodo di garofano** (*Cuc*) clove

chi'osco, -schi ['kjɔsko] *sm* kiosk, stall

chi'ostro ['kjɔstro] *sm* cloister

chiro'mante [kiro'mante] *sm/f* palmist

chirur'gia [kirur'dʒia] *sf* surgery; **chirurgia estetica** cosmetic surgery; **chi'rurgo, -ghi o gi** *sm* surgeon

chissà [kis'sa] *av* who knows, I wonder

chi'tarra [ki'tarra] *sf* guitar; **chitar'rista, -i, e** [kitar'rista] *sm/f* guitarist, guitar player

chi'udere ['kjudere] *vt* to close, shut; (*luce, acqua*) to put off, turn off; (*definitivamente: fabbrica*) to close down, shut down; (*strada*) to close; (*recingere*) to enclose; (*porre termine a*) to end ▶ *vi* to close, shut; to close down, shut down; to end; **chiudersi** *vpr* to shut, close; (*ritirarsi: anche fig*) to shut o.s. away; (*ferita*) to close up; **a che ora chiudete?** what time do you close?

chi'unque [ki'unkwe] *pron* (*relativo*) whoever; (*indefinito*) anyone, anybody; ~ **sia** whoever it is

'chiusi *ecc* ['kjusi] *vb vedi* **chiudere**

chi'uso, -a ['kjuso] *pp di* **chiudere** ▶ *sf* (*di corso d'acqua*) sluice, lock; (*recinto*) enclosure; (*di discorso ecc*) conclusion, ending; **chiu'sura** *sf* (*vedi*

chiudere [tʃu'dere] closing; shutting; closing o shutting down; enclosing; putting o turning off; ending; (dispositivo) catch; fastening; fastener; **chiusura lampo®** zip (fastener) (BRIT), zipper (US)

C.I. abbr = **carta d'identità**

ci [tʃi] (dav lo, la, li, le, ne diventa ce) pron

1 (personale: complemento oggetto) us; (: a noi: complemento di termine) (to) us; (: riflessivo) ourselves; (: reciproco) each other, one another; (: impersonale): **ci siveste** we get dressed; **ci ha visti** he's seen us; **non ci ha dato niente** he gave us nothing; **ci vestiamo** we get dressed; **ci amiamo** we love one another o each other

2 (dimostrativo: di ciò, su ciò, in ciò ecc) about (o on o of) it; **non so cosa farci** I don't know what to do about it; **che c'entro io?** what have I got to do with it?

▶ av (qui) here; (lì) there; (moto attraverso luogo): **ci passa sopra un ponte** a bridge passes over it; **non ci passa più nessuno** nobody comes this way any more; **esserci** vedi **essere**

cia'batta [tʃa'batta] sf slipper; (pane) ciabatta

ciam'bella [tʃam'bɛlla] sf (Cuc) ring-shaped cake; (salvagente) rubber ring

ci'ao [tʃao] escl (all'arrivo) hello!; (alla partenza) cheerio! (BRIT), bye!

cias'cuno, -a [tʃas'kuno] (det: dav sm ciascun +C, V, ciascuno +s impura, gn, pn, ps, x, z; dav sf: ciascuna +C, ciascun' +V) det every, each; (ogni) every ▶ pron each (one); (tutti) everyone, everybody

ci'barie [tʃi'barje] sfpl foodstuffs

ciber'nauta, -i, -e [tʃiber'nauta] sm/f Internet surfer

ciberspazio [tʃiber'spattsjo] sm cyberspace

'cibo [tʃibo] sm food

ci'cala [tʃi'kala] sf cicada

cica'trice [tʃika'tritʃe] sf scar

'cicca [tʃikka] sf cigarette end

'ciccia [tʃittʃa] (fam) sf fat

cicci'one, -a [tʃit'tʃone] sm/f (fam) fatty

cicla'mino [tʃikla'mino] sm cyclamen

ci'clismo [tʃi'klizmo] sm cycling; **ci'clista, -i, -e** sm/f cyclist

'ciclo [tʃiklo] sm cycle; (di malattia) course

ciclomo'tore [tʃiklomo'tore] sm moped

ci'clone [tʃi'klone] sm cyclone

ci'cogna [tʃi'koɲɲa] sf stork

ci'eco, -a, -chi, -che [tʃɛko] ag blind ▶ sm/f blind man/woman

ci'elo [tʃɛlo] sm sky; (Rel) heaven

'cifra [tʃifra] sf (numero) figure; numeral; (somma di denaro) sum, figure; (monogramma) monogram, initials pl; (codice) code, cipher

'ciglio, -i [tʃiʎʎo] (delle palpebre) (pl(f) ciglia) sm (margine) edge, verge; (eye)lash; (eye)lid; (sopracciglio) eyebrow

'cigno [tʃiɲɲo] sm swan

cigo'lare [tʃigo'lare] vi to squeak, creak

'Cile [tʃile] sm il ~ Chile

ci'leno, -a [tʃi'lɛno] ag, sm/f Chilean

cili'egia, -gie o ge [tʃi'ljɛdʒa] sf cherry

cilie'gina [tʃilje'dʒina] sf glacé cherry

cilin'drata [tʃilin'drata] sf (Aut) (cubic) capacity; **una macchina di grossa ~** a big-engined car

ci'lindro [tʃi'lindro] sm cylinder; (cappello) top hat

'cima [tʃima] sf (sommità) top; (di monte) top, summit; (estremità) end; **in ~ a** at the top of; **da ~ a fondo** from top to bottom; (fig) from beginning to end

'cimice ['tʃimitʃe] sf (Zool) bug; (puntina) drawing pin (BRIT), thumbtack (US)

cimin'iera [tʃimin'jɛra] sf chimney; (di nave) funnel

cimi'tero [tʃimi'tero] sm cemetery

'Cina ['tʃina] sf la ~ China

cin'cin [tʃin'tʃin] escl cheers!

'cinema ['tʃinema] sm inv cinema

ci'nese [tʃi'nese] ag, sm/f, sm Chinese inv

'cinghia ['tʃingja] sf strap; (cintura, Tecn) belt

cinghi'ale [tʃin'gjale] sm wild boar

cinguet'tare [tʃingwet'tare] vi to twitter

'cinico, -a, -ci, -che ['tʃiniko] ag cynical ▶ sm/f cynic

cin'quanta [tʃin'kwanta] num fifty; **cinquan'tesimo, -a** num fiftieth

cinquan'tina [tʃinkwan'tina] sf (serie): **una ~ (di)** about fifty; (età): **essere sulla ~** to be about fifty

'cinque ['tʃinkwe] num five; **avere ~ anni** to be five (years old); **il ~ dicembre 1998** the fifth of December 1998; **alle ~ (ora)** at five (o'clock)

cinque'cento [tʃinkwe'tʃento] num five hundred ▶ sm **il C~** the sixteenth century

cin'tura [tʃin'tura] sf belt; **cintura di salvataggio** lifebelt (BRIT), life preserver (US); **cintura di sicurezza** (Aut, Aer) safety o seat belt

cintu'rino [tʃintu'rino] sm strap; ~ **dell'orologio** watch strap

ciò [tʃɔ] pron this; that; ~ **che** what; ~ **nonostante** o **nondimeno** nevertheless, in spite of that

ci'occa, -che ['tʃɔkka] sf (di capelli) lock

ciocco'lata [tʃokko'lata] sf chocolate; (bevanda) (hot) chocolate; **cioccola'tino** sm chocolate

cioè [tʃo'ɛ] av that is (to say)

ci'otola ['tʃɔtola] sf bowl

ci'ottolo ['tʃɔttolo] sm pebble; (di strada) cobble(stone)

ci'polla [tʃi'polla] sf onion; (di tulipano ecc) bulb

cipol'lina [tʃipol'lina] sf **cipolline sottaceto** pickled onions

ci'presso [tʃi'presso] sm cypress (tree)

'cipria ['tʃiprja] sf (face) powder

'Cipro ['tʃipro] sf Cyprus

'circa ['tʃirka] av about, roughly ▶ prep about, concerning; **a mezzogiorno ~** about midday

'circo, -chi ['tʃirko] sm circus

circo'lare [tʃirko'lare] vi to circulate; (Aut) to drive (along), move (along) ▶ ag circular; (di Amm) circular; (di autobus) circle (line)

'circolo ['tʃirkolo] sm circle

circon'dare [tʃirkon'dare] vt to surround; **circondarsi** vpr **circondarsi di** to surround o.s. with

circonvallazi'one [tʃirkonvallat'tsjone] sf ring road (BRIT), beltway (US); (per evitare una città) by-pass

circos'petto, -a [tʃirkos'petto] ag circumspect, cautious

circos'tante [tʃirkos'tante] ag surrounding, neighbouring

circos'tanza [tʃirkos'tantsa] sf circumstance; (occasione) occasion

cir'cuito [tʃir'kuito] sm circuit

CISL sigla f (= Confederazione Italiana Sindacati Lavoratori) trades union organization

cis'terna [tʃis'tɛrna] sf tank, cistern

'cisti ['tʃisti] sf cyst

cis'tite [tʃis'tite] sf cystitis

ci'tare [tʃi'tare] vt (Dir) to summon; (autore) to quote; (a esempio, modello) to cite

ci'tofono [tʃi'tɔfono] sm entry phone; (in uffici) intercom

città [tʃit'ta] sf inv town; (importante)

city; **città universitaria** university campus

cittadi'nanza [tʃittadi'nantsa] *sf* citizens *pl*; (*Dir*) citizenship

citta'dino, -a [tʃitta'dino] *ag* town *cpd*; city *cpd* ▸ *sm/f (di uno Stato)* citizen; (*abitante di città*) townsman, city dweller

ci'uccio ['tʃuttʃo] *sm* (*fam*) comforter, dummy (*BRIT*), pacifier (*US*)

ci'uffo ['tʃuffo] *sm* tuft

ci'vetta [tʃi'vetta] *sf* (*Zool*) owl; (*fig: donna*) coquette, flirt ▸ *ag inv* auto/nave~ decoy car/ship

'civico, -a, -ci, -che ['tʃivico] *ag* civic; (*museo*) municipal, town *cpd*; (*Dir*) city *cpd*

ci'vile [tʃi'vile] *ag* civil; (*non militare*) civilian; (*nazione*) civilized ▸ *sm* civilian

civiltà [tʃivil'ta] *sf* civilization; (*cortesia*) civility

'clacson *sm inv* (*Aut*) horn

clandes'tino, -a *ag* clandestine; (*Pol*) underground, clandestine; (*immigrato*) illegal ▸ *sm/f* stowaway; (*anche*: **immigrato~**) illegal immigrant

'classe *sf* class; **di ~** (*fig*) with class; of excellent quality; **classe operaia** working class; **classe turistica** (*Aer*) economy class

'classico, -a, -ci, -che *ag* classical; (*tradizionale: moda*) classic(al) ▸ *sm* classic; classical author

clas'sifica *sf* classification; (*Sport*) placings *pl*

classifi'care *vt* to classify; (*candidato, compito*) to grade; **classificarsi** *vpr* to be placed

'clausola *sf* (*Dir*) clause

clavi'cembalo [klavi'tʃembalo] *sm* harpsichord

cla'vicola *sf* (*Anat*) collar bone

clic'care *vi* (*Inform*): **~ su** to click on

cli'ente *sm/f* customer, client

'clima, -i *sm* climate; **climatizzatore** *sm* air conditioning system

'clinica, -che *sf* (*scienza*) clinical medicine; (*casa di cura*) clinic, nursing home; (*settore d'ospedale*) clinic

clo'nare *vt* to clone; **clonazione** [klona'tsjone] *sf* cloning

'cloro *sm* chlorine

club *sm inv* club

c.m. *abbr* = **corrente mese**

cm *abbr* (= *centimetro*) cm

coali'zione [koalit'tsjone] *sf* coalition

'COBAS *sigla mpl* (= *Comitati di base*) independent trades unions

'coca *sf* (*bibita*) Coke®; (*droga*) cocaine

coca'ina *sf* cocaine

cocci'nella [kottʃi'nella] *sf* ladybird (*BRIT*), ladybug (*US*)

cocci'uto, -a [kot'tʃuto] *ag* stubborn, pigheaded

'cocco, -chi *sm* (*pianta*) coconut palm; (*frutto*): **noce di ~** coconut ▸ *sm/f* (*fam*) darling

cocco'drillo *sm* crocodile

cocco'lare *vt* to cuddle, fondle

cocerò *ecc* [kotʃe'rɔ] *vb vedi* **cuocere**

co'comero *sm* watermelon

'coda *sf* tag; (*fila di persone, auto*) queue (*BRIT*), line (*US*); (*di abiti*) train; **con la ~ dell'occhio** out of the corner of one's eye; **mettersi in ~** to queue (up) (*BRIT*), line up (*US*); to join the queue (*BRIT*) o line (*US*); **coda di cavallo** (*acconciatura*) ponytail

co'dardo, -a *ag* cowardly ▸ *sm/f* coward

'codice ['kɔditʃe] *sm* code; **codice di avviamento postale** postcode (*BRIT*), zip code (*US*); **codice a barre** bar code; **codice civile** civil code; **codice fiscale** tax code; **codice penale** penal code; **codice segreto** (*di tessera magnetica*) PIN (number); **codice della strada** highway code

coe'rente *ag* coherent

coe'taneo, -a *ag, sm/f* contemporary

'cofano *sm* (Aut) bonnet (BRIT), hood (US); (forziere) chest

'cogliere ['kɔʎʎere] *vt* (fiore: frutto) to pick, gather; (sorprendere) to catch, surprise; (bersaglio) to hit; (fig: momento opportuno ecc) to grasp, seize, take; (: capire) to grasp; ~ qn in flagrante o in fallo to catch sb red-handed

co'gnato, -a [koɲ'ɲato] *sm/f* brother-/sister-in-law

co'gnome [koɲ'ɲome] *sm* surname

coinci'denza [kointʃi'dɛntsa] *sf* coincidence; (Ferr, Aer, di autobus) connection

coin'cidere [koin'tʃidere] *vi* to coincide

coin'volgere [koin'vɔldʒere] *vt* ~ in to involve in

cola'pasta *sm inv* colander

co'lare *vt* (liquido) to strain; (pasta) to drain; (oro fuso) to pour ▶ *vi* (sudore) to drip; (botte) to leak; (cera) to melt; ~ a picco *vt, vi* (nave) to sink

colazi'one [kolat'tsjone] *sf* breakfast; fare ~ to have breakfast; a che ora è servita la ~? what time is breakfast?

co'lera *sm* (Med) cholera

'colgo *ecc vb vedi* cogliere

'colica *sf* (Med) colic

co'lino *sm* strainer

'colla *sf* glue; (di farina) paste

collabo'rare *vi* to collaborate; ~ a to collaborate on; (giornale) to contribute to; collabora'tore, -'trice *sm/f* collaborator; contributor; collaboratore esterno freelance; collaboratrice familiare home help

col'lana *sf* necklace; (collezione) collection, series

col'lant [kɔ'lɑ̃] *sm inv* tights *pl*

col'lare *sm* collar

col'lasso *sm* (Med) collapse

collau'dare *vt* to test, try out

col'lega, -ghi, -ghe *sm/f* colleague

collega'mento *sm* connection; (Mil) liaison

colle'gare *vt* to connect, join, link; collegarsi *vpr* (Radio, TV) to link up; collegarsi con (Tel) to get through to

col'legio [kol'lɛdʒo] *sm* college; (convitto) boarding school; collegio elettorale (Pol) constituency

'collera *sf* anger

col'lerico, -a, -ci, -che *ag* quick-tempered, irascible

col'letta *sf* collection

col'letto *sm* collar

collezio'nare [kollettsjo'nare] *vt* to collect

collezi'one [kollet'tsjone] *sf* collection

col'lina *sf* hill

col'lirio *sm* eyewash

'collo *sm* neck; (di abito) neck, collar; (pacco) parcel; collo del piede instep

colloca'mento *sm* (impiego) employment; (disposizione) placing, arrangement

collo'care *vt* (libri, mobili) to place; (Comm: merce) to find a market for

collocazi'one [kollokat'tsjone] *sf* placing; (di libro) classification

col'loquio *sm* conversation, talk; (ufficiale, per un lavoro) interview; (Ins) preliminary oral exam

col'mare *vt* ~ di (anche fig) to fill with; (dare in abbondanza) to load o overwhelm with

co'lombo, -a *sm/f* dove; pigeon

co'lonia *sf* colony; (per bambini) holiday camp; (acqua di) ~ (eau de) cologne

co'lonna *sf* column; colonna sonora (Cinema) sound track; colonna vertebrale spine, spinal column

colon'nello *sm* colonel

colo'rante *sm* colouring

colo'rare vt to colour; (disegno) to colour in

co'lore sm colour; **a colori** in colour, colour cpd; **farne di tutti i colori** to get up to all sorts of mischief; **vorrei un ~ diverso** I'd like a different colour

colo'rito, -a ag coloured; (viso) rosy, pink; (linguaggio) colourful ▶ sm (tinta) colour; (carnagione) complexion

'colpa sf fault; (biasimo) blame; (colpevolezza) guilt; (azione colpevole) offence; (peccato) sin; **di chi è la ~?** whose fault is it?; **è ~ sua** it's his fault; **per ~ di** through, owing to; **col'pevole** ag guilty

col'pire vt to hit, strike; (fig) to strike; **rimanere colpito da qc** to be amazed o struck by sth

'colpo sm (urto) knock; (: affettivo) blow, shock; (: aggressivo) blow; (di pistola) shot; (Med) stroke; (rapina) raid; **di ~** suddenly; **fare un ~** to make a strong impression; **colpo d'aria** chill; **colpo in banca** bank job o raid; **colpo basso** (Pugilato, fig) punch below the belt; **colpo di fulmine** love at first sight; **colpo di grazia** coup de grâce; **colpo di scena** (Teatro) coup de théâtre; (fig) dramatic turn of events; **colpo di sole** sunstroke; **colpo di Stato** coup d'état; **colpo di telefono** phone call; **colpo di testa** (sudden) impulse o whim; **colpo di vento** gust (of wind); **colpi di sole** (nei capelli) highlights

'colsi ecc vb vedi **cogliere**

coltel'lata sf stab

col'tello sm knife; **coltello a serramanico** clasp knife

colti'vare vt to cultivate; (verdura) to grow, cultivate

'colto, -a pp di **cogliere** ▶ ag (istruito) cultured, educated

'coma sm inv coma

comanda'mento sm (Rel)

commandment

coman'dante sm (Mil) commander, commandant; (di reggimento) commanding officer; (Naut, Aer) captain

coman'dare vi to be in command ▶ vt to command; (imporre) to order, command; **~ a qn di fare** to order sb to do

combaci'are [komba'tʃare] vi to meet; (fig: coincidere) to coincide

com'battere vt, vi to fight

combi'nare vt to combine; (organizzare) to arrange; (fam: fare) to make, cause; **combinazi'one** sf combination; (caso fortuito) coincidence; **per combinazione** by chance

combus'tibile ag combustible ▶ sm fuel

O 'come
av

1 (alla maniera di) like; **ti comporti come lui** you behave like him o like he does; **bianco come la neve** (as) white as snow; **come se** as if, as though

2 (in qualità di) as a; **lavora come autista** he works as a driver

3 (interrogativo) how; **come ti chiami?** what's your name?; **come sta?** how are you?; **com'è il tuo amico?** what's your friend like?; **come?** (prego?) pardon?, sorry?; **come mai?** how come?; **come mai non ci hai avvertiti?** why on earth didn't you warn us?

4 (esclamativo) **come sei bravo!** how clever you are!; **come mi dispiace!** I'm terribly sorry!

▶ cong

1 (in che modo) how; **mi ha spiegato come l'ha conosciuto** he told me how he met him

2 (correlativo) as; (con comparativi di maggioranza) than; **non è bravo come pensavo** he isn't as clever as I thought;

è meglio di come pensassi it's better than I thought

3 (*appena che, quando*) as soon as; **come arrivò, iniziò a lavorare** as soon as he arrived, he set to work; *vedi* **così**; **tanto**

'**comico, -a, -ci, -che** ag (*Teatro*) comic; (*buffo*) comical ▶ sm (*attore*) comedian, comic actor

cominci'are [komin'tʃare] vt, vi to begin, start; ~ **a fare/col fare** to begin to do/by doing; **a che ora comincia il film?** when does the film start?

comi'tato sm committee

comi'tiva sf party, group

co'mizio [ko'mittsjo] sm (*Pol*) meeting, assembly

com'media sf comedy; (*opera teatrale*) play; (*: che fa ridere*) comedy; (*fig*) playacting no pl

commemo'rare vt to commemorate

commen'tare vt to comment on; (*testo*) to annotate; (*Radio, TV*) to give a commentary on

commerci'ale [kommer'tʃale] ag commercial, trading; (*peg*) commercial

commercia'lista, -i, e [kommertʃa'lista] sm/f (*laureato*) graduate in economics and commerce; (*consulente*) business consultant

commerci'ante [kommer'tʃante] sm/f trader, dealer; (*negoziante*) shopkeeper

commerci'are [kommer'tʃare] vt, vi ~ **in** to deal o trade in

com'mercio [kom'mertʃo] sm trade, commerce; **essere in** ~ (*prodotto*) to be on the market o on sale; **essere nel** ~ (*persona*) to be in business; **commercio al dettaglio/all'ingrosso** retail/wholesale trade; **commercio elettronico** e-commerce

com'messo, -a pp di **commettere** ▶ sm/f shop assistant (*BRIT*), sales clerk (*US*) ▶ sm (*impiegato*) clerk; **commesso viaggiatore** commercial traveller

commes'tibile ag edible

com'mettere vt to commit

com'misi ecc vb vedi **commettere**

commissari'ato sm (*Amm*) commissionership; (*: sede*) commissioner's office

commissariato di polizia police station

commis'sario sm commissioner; (*di pubblica sicurezza*) ≈ (police) superintendent (*BRIT*), ≈ (police) captain (*US*); (*Sport*) steward; (*membro di commissione*) member of a committee o board

commissi'one sf (*incarico*) errand; (*comitato, percentuale*) commission; (*Comm: ordinazione*) order; **commissioni** sfpl (*acquisti*) shopping sg; **commissioni bancarie** bank charges; **commissione d'esame** examining board

com'mosso, -a pp di **commuovere**

commo'vente ag moving

commozi'one [kommot'tsjone] sf emotion, deep feeling; **commozione cerebrale** (*Med*) concussion

commu'overe vt to move, affect; **commuoversi** vpr to be moved

como'dino sm bedside table

comodità sf inv comfort; convenience

'**comodo, -a** ag comfortable; (*facile*) easy; (*conveniente*) convenient; (*utile*) useful, handy ▶ sm comfort; convenience; **con** ~ at one's convenience o leisure; **fare il proprio** ~ to do as one pleases; **far** ~ to be useful o handy

compa'gnia [kompaɲ'ɲia] sf company; (*gruppo*) gathering

com'pagno, -a [kom'paɲɲo]

sm/f (di classe, gioco) companion; (Pol) comrade

com'paio ecc vb vedi **comparire**

compa'rare vt to compare

compara'tivo, -a ag, sm comparative

compa'rire vi to appear

com'parvi ecc vb vedi **comparire**

compassi'one sf compassion, pity; **avere ~ di qn** to feel sorry for sb, to pity sb

com'passo sm (pair of) compasses pl; callipers pl

compa'tibile ag (scusabile) excusable; (conciliabile, Inform) compatible

compa'tire vt (aver compassione di) to sympathize with, feel sorry for; (scusare) to make allowances for

com'patto, -a ag compact; (roccia) solid; (folla) dense; (fig: gruppo, partito) united

compen'sare vt (equilibrare) to compensate for, make up for; **~ qn di** (rimunerare) to pay o remunerate sb for; (risarcire) to pay compensation to sb for; (fig: fatiche, dolori) to reward sb for; **com'penso** sm compensation payment, remuneration; reward; **in compenso** (d'altra parte) on the other hand

compe'rare vt = **comprare**

'compere sfpl **fare ~** to do the shopping

compe'tente ag competent; (mancia) apt, suitable

com'petere vi to compete, vie; (Dir: spettare): **~ a** to lie within the competence of; **competizi'one** sf competition

compi'angere [kom'pjandʒere] vt to sympathize with, feel sorry for

'compiere vt (concludere) to finish, complete; (adempiere) to carry out, fulfil; **compiersi** vpr (avverarsi) to be fulfilled, come true; **~ gli anni** to have one's birthday

compi'lare vt (modulo) to fill in; (dizionario, elenco) to compile

'compito sm (incarico) task, duty; (dovere) duty; (Ins) exercise; (: a casa) piece of homework; **fare i compiti** to do one's homework

comple'anno sm birthday

complessità sf complexity

comples'sivo, -a ag (globale) comprehensive, overall; (totale: cifra) total

com'plesso, -a ag complex ▶ sm (Psic, Edil) complex; (Mus: corale) ensemble; (: orchestrina) band; (: di musica pop) group; **in no nel ~** on the whole; **complesso alberghiero** hotel complex; **complesso edilizio** building complex; **complesso vitaminico** vitamin complex

completa'mente av completely

comple'tare vt to complete

com'pleto, -a ag complete; (teatro, autobus) full ▶ sm suit; **al ~** full; (tutti presenti) all present; **completo da sci** ski suit

compli'care vt to complicate; **complicarsi** vpr to become complicated

'complice ['komplitʃe] sm/f accomplice

complicità [komplitʃi'ta] sf inv complicity; **un sorriso/uno sguardo di ~** a knowing smile/look

complimen'tarsi vpr **~ con** to congratulate

compli'mento sm compliment; **complimenti** smpl (cortesia eccessiva) ceremony sg; (ossequi) regards, compliments; **complimenti!** congratulations!; **senza complimenti!** don't stand on ceremony!; make yourself at home!; help yourself!

complot'tare vi to plot, conspire

com'plotto sm plot, conspiracy

com'pone ecc vb vedi **comporre**

compo'nente sm/f member ▶ sf component

com'pongo ecc vb vedi **comporre**

componi'mento sm (Dir) settlement; (Ins) composition; (poetico, teatrale) work

com'porre vt (musica, testo) to compose; (mettere in ordine) to arrange; (Dir: lite) to settle; (Tip) to set; (Tel) to dial; **comporsi** vpr **comporsi di** to consist of, be composed of

comporta'mento sm behaviour

compor'tare vt (implicare) to involve; **comportarsi** vpr to behave

com'posi ecc vb vedi **comporre**

composi'tore, -'trice sm/f composer; (Tip) compositor, typesetter

com'posto, -a pp di **comporre** ▶ ag (persona) composed, self-possessed; (: decoroso) dignified; (formato da più elementi) compound cpd ▶ sm compound

com'prare vt to buy; **dove posso ~ delle cartoline?** where can I buy some postcards?

com'prendere vt (contenere) to comprise, consist of; (capire) to understand

compren'sibile ag understandable

comprensi'one sf understanding

compren'sivo, -a ag (prezzo): **~ di** inclusive of; (indulgente) understanding

> Attenzione! In inglese esiste la parola comprehensive, che però in genere significa completo.

com'preso, -a pp di **comprendere** ▶ ag (incluso) included; **il servizio è ~?** is service included?

com'pressa sf (Med: garza) compress; (: pastiglia) tablet; vedi anche **compresso**

com'primere vt (premere) to press;

(Fisica) to compress; (fig) to repress

compro'messo, -a pp di **compromettere** ▶ sm compromise

compro'mettere vt to compromise; **compromettersi** vpr to compromise o.s.

com'puter sm inv computer

comu'nale ag municipal, town cpd, ≈ borough cpd

co'mune ag common; (consueto) common, everyday; (di livello medio) average; (ordinario) ordinary ▶ sm (Amm) town council; (: sede) town hall ▶ sf (di persone) commune; **fuori del ~** out of the ordinary; **avere in ~** to have in common, share; **mettere in ~** to share

comuni'care vt (notizia) to pass on, convey; (malattia) to pass on; (ansia ecc) to communicate; (trasmettere: calore ecc) to transmit, communicate; (Rel) to administer communion to ▶ vi to communicate

comuni'cato sm communiqué; **comunicato stampa** press release

comunicazi'one [komunikat'tsjone] sf communication; (annuncio) announcement; (Tel): **dare la ~ a qn** to put sb through; **ottenere la ~** to get through; **comunicazione (telefonica)** (telephone) call

comuni'one sf communion; **comunione di beni** (Dir) joint ownership of property

comu'nismo sm communism

comu'nità sf inv community; **Comunità Europea** European Community

co'munque cong however, no matter how ▶ av (in ogni modo) in any case; (tuttavia) however, nevertheless

con prep with; **partire col treno** to leave by train; **~ mio grande stupore** to my great astonishment; **~ tutto ciò** for all that

con'cedere [kon'tʃedere] vt (accordare) to grant; (ammettere) to admit, concede; **concedersi qc** to treat o.s. to sth, to allow o.s. sth

concentrarsi vpr to concentrate

concentrazi'one sf concentration

conce'pire [kontʃe'pire] vt (bambino) to conceive; (progetto, idea) to conceive (of); (metodo, piano) to devise

con'certo [kon'tʃerto] sm (Mus) concert; (: componimento) concerto

con'cessi ecc [kon'tʃessi] vb vedi **concedere**

con'cetto [kon'tʃetto] sm (pensiero, idea) concept; (opinione) opinion

concezi'one [kontʃet'tsjone] sf conception

con'chiglia [kon'kiʎʎa] sf shell

conci'are [kon'tʃare] vt (pelli) to tan; (tabacco) to cure; (fig: ridurre in cattivo stato) to beat up; **conciarsi** vpr (sporcarsi) to get in a mess; (vestirsi male) to dress badly

concili'are [kontʃi'ljare] vt to reconcile; (contravvenzione) to pay on the spot; (sonno) to be conducive to, induce; **conciliarsi qc** to gain o win sth (for o.s.); **conciliarsi qn** to win sb over; **conciliarsi con** to be reconciled with

con'cime [kon'tʃime] sm manure; (chimico) fertilizer

con'ciso, -a [kon'tʃizo] ag concise, succinct

concitta'dino, -a [kontʃitta'dino] sm/f fellow citizen

con'cludere vt to conclude; (portare a compimento) to conclude, finish, bring to an end; (operare positivamente) to achieve ▶ vi (essere convincente) to be conclusive; **concludersi** vpr to come to an end, close

concor'dare vt (tregua, prezzo) to agree on; (Ling) to make agree ▶ vi to agree

con'corde ag (d'accordo) in agreement; (simultaneo) simultaneous

concor'rente sm/f competitor; (Ins) candidate; **concor'renza** sf competition

concorrenzi'ale [konkorren'tsjale] ag competitive

con'correre vi ~ (in) (Mat) to converge o meet (in); ~ **(a)** (competere) to compete (for); (: Ins: a una cattedra) to apply (for); (partecipare: a un'impresa) to take part in), contribute (to); **con'corso, -a** pp di **concorrere** ▶ sm competition; (Ins) competitive examination; **concorso di colpa** (Dir) contributory negligence

con'creto, -a ag concrete

con'danna sf sentence; conviction; condemnation

condan'nare vt (Dir) ~ **a** to sentence to; ~ **per** to convict of; (disapprovare) to condemn

conden'sare vt to condense

condi'mento sm seasoning; dressing

con'dire vt to season; (insalata) to dress

condi'videre vt to share

condizio'nale [kondittsjo'nale] ag conditional ▶ sm (Ling) conditional ▶ sf (Dir) suspended sentence

condizio'nare [kondittsjo'nare] vt to condition; **ad aria condizionata** air-conditioned; **condiziona'tore** sm air conditioner

condizi'one [kondit'tsjone] sf condition

condogli'anze [kondoʎ'ʎantse] sfpl condolences

condo'minio sm joint ownership; (edificio) jointly-owned building

con'dotta sf (modo di comportarsi) conduct, behaviour; (di un affare ecc) handling; (di acqua) piping; (incarico sanitario) country medical practice controlled by a local authority

condu'cente [kondu'tʃɛnte] *sm* driver
con'duco *ecc vb vedi* **condurre**
con'durre *vt* to conduct; *(azienda)* to manage; *(accompagnare: bambino)* to take; *(automobile)* to drive; *(trasportare: acqua, gas)* to convey, conduct; *(fig)* to lead ▶ *vi* to lead
con'dussi *ecc vb vedi* **condurre**
confe'renza [konfe'rɛntsa] *sf (discorso)* lecture; *(riunione)* conference; **conferenza stampa** press conference
con'ferma *sf* confirmation
confer'mare *vt* to confirm
confes'sare *vt* to confess; **confessarsi** *vpr* to confess; **andare a confessarsi** *(Rel)* to go to confession
con'fetto *sm* sugared almond; *(Med)* pill

> Attenzione! In inglese esiste la parola *confetti*, che però significa *coriandoli*.

confet'tura *sf (gen)* jam; *(di arance)* marmalade
confezio'nare [konfettsjo'nare] *vt (vestito)* to make (up); *(merci, pacchi)* to package
confezi'one [konfet'tsjone] *sf (di abiti: da uomo)* tailoring; (*: da donna)* dressmaking; *(imballaggio)* packaging; **confezioni per signora** ladies' wear; **confezioni da uomo** menswear; **confezione regalo** gift pack
confic'care *vt* ~ **qc in** to hammer *o* drive sth into; **conficcarsi** *vpr* to stick
confi'dare *vi* ~ **in** to confide in, rely on ▶ *vt* to confide; **confidarsi con qn** to confide in sb
configu'rare *vt (Inform)* to set
configurazi'one [konfigurat'tsjone] *sf* configuration; *(Inform)* setting
confi'nare *vi* ~ **con** to border on ▶ *vt (Pol)* to intern; *(fig)* to confine
Confin'dustria *sigla f* (= Confederazione

Generale dell'Industria Italiana) employers' association, ≈ CBI (BRIT)
con'fine *sm* boundary; *(di paese)* border, frontier
confis'care *vt* to confiscate
con'flitto *sm* conflict
conflu'enza [konflu'ɛntsa] *sf (di fiumi)* confluence; *(di strade)* junction
con'fondere *vt* to mix up, confuse; *(imbarazzare)* to embarrass; **confondersi** *vpr (mescolarsi)* to mingle; *(turbarsi)* to be confused; *(sbagliare)* to get mixed up
confor'tare *vt* to comfort, console
confron'tare *vt* to compare
con'fronto *sm* comparison; **in o a ~ di** in comparison with, compared to; **nei miei** (*o tuoi ecc*) **confronti** towards me (*o you ecc*)
con'fusi *ecc vb vedi* **confondere**
confusi'one *sf* confusion; *(chiasso)* racket, noise; *(imbarazzo)* embarrassment
con'fuso, -a *pp di* **confondere** ▶ *ag (vedi* **confondere***)* confused; embarrassed
conge'dare [kondʒe'dare] *vt* to dismiss; *(Mil)* to demobilize; **congedarsi** *vpr* to take one's leave
con'gegno *sm* device, mechanism
conge'lare [kondʒe'lare] *vt* to freeze; **congelarsi** *vpr* to freeze; **congela'tore** *sm* freezer
congesti'one [kondʒes'tjone] *sf* congestion
conget'tura [kondʒet'tura] *sf* conjecture
con'giungere [kon'dʒundʒere] *vt* to join (together); **congiungersi** *vpr* to join (together)
congiun'tivite [kondʒunti'vite] *sf* conjunctivitis
congiun'tivo [kondʒun'tivo] *sm (Ling)* subjunctive
congi'unto, -a [kon'dʒunto] *pp di*

congiungere ▶ *ag (unito)* joined
▶ *sm/f* relative
congiunzi'one [kondʒun'tsjone] *sf*
(*Ling*) conjunction
congi'ura [kon'dʒura] *sf* conspiracy
congratu'larsi *vpr* ~ **con qn per qc** to
congratulate sb on sth
congratulazi'oni
[kongratulat'tsjoni] *sfpl*
congratulations
con'gresso *sm* congress
C.O.N.I. *sigla m* (= *Comitato Olimpico
Nazionale Italiano*) Italian Olympic
Games Committee
coni'are *vt* to mint, coin; (*fig*) to coin
co'niglio [ko'niʎʎo] *sm* rabbit
coniu'gare *vt* (*Ling*) to conjugate;
coniugarsi *vpr* to get married
'coniuge ['konjudʒe] *sm/f* spouse
connazio'nale [konnattsjo'nale]
sm/f fellow-countryman/woman
connessi'one *sf* connection
con'nettere *vt* to connect, join ▶ *vi*
(*fig*) to think straight
'cono *sm* cone; **cono gelato** ice-
cream cone
co'nobbi *ecc vb vedi* **conoscere**
cono'scente [konoʃ'ʃente] *sm/f*
acquaintance
cono'scenza [konoʃ'ʃentsa] *sf* (*il
sapere*) knowledge *no pl*; (*persona*)
acquaintance; (*facoltà sensoriale*)
consciousness *no pl*; **perdere** ~ to lose
consciousness
co'noscere [ko'noʃʃere] *vt* to know; **ci
siamo conosciuti a Firenze** we (first)
met in Florence; **conoscersi** *vpr* to
know o.s.; (*reciproco*) to know each
other; (*incontrarsi*) to meet; ~ **qn di
vista** to know sb by sight; **farsi** ~ (*fig*)
to make a name for o.s.; **conosci'uto,
-a** *pp di* **conoscere** ▶ *ag* well-known
con'quista *sf* conquest
conquis'tare *vt* to conquer; (*fig*) to
gain, win

consa'pevole *ag* ~ **di** aware *o*
conscious of
'conscio, -a, -sci, -sce ['konʃo] *ag* ~ **di**
aware *o* conscious of
consecu'tivo, -a *ag* consecutive;
(*successivo: giorno*) following, next
con'segna [kon'seɲɲa] *sf* delivery;
(*merce consegnata*) consignment;
(*custodia*) care, custody; (*Mil: ordine*)
orders *pl*; (*: punizione*) confinement to
barracks; **pagamento alla** ~ cash on
delivery; **dare qc in** ~ **a qn** to entrust
sth to sb
conse'gnare [konseɲ'ɲare] *vt* to
deliver; (*affidare*) to entrust, hand
over; (*Mil*) to confine to barracks
consegu'enza [konse'gwentsa] *sf*
consequence; **per** *o* **di** ~ consequently
consen'tire *vi* ~ **a** to consent *o* agree
to ▶ *vt* to allow, permit
con'senso *sm* approval, consent;
consenso informato informed
consent
con'serva *sf* (*Cuc*) preserve;
conserva di frutta jam; **conserva di
pomodoro** tomato purée
conser'vante *sm* (*per alimenti*)
preservative
conser'vare *vt* (*Cuc*) to preserve;
(*custodire*) to keep; (*: dalla distruzione
ecc*) to preserve, conserve
conserva'tore, -'trice *sm/f* (*Pol*)
conservative
conserva'torio *sm* (*di musica*)
conservatory
conservazi'one [konservat'tsjone] *sf*
preservation; conservation
conside'rare *vt* to consider; (*reputare*)
to consider, regard; **considerarsi** *vpr*
to consider o.s.
consigli'are [konsiʎ'ʎare] *vt*
(*persona*) to advise; (*metodo, azione*)
to recommend, advise, suggest; **mi
può** ~ **un buon ristorante?** can you
recommend a good restaurant?;

con'siglio sm (suggerimento) advice no pl, piece of advice; (assemblea) council; **consiglio d'amministrazione** board; **Consiglio d'Europa** Council of Europe; **Consiglio dei Ministri** (Pol): **il Consiglio dei Ministri** ≈ the Cabinet

consis'tente ag thick; solid; (fig) sound, valid

con'sistere vi ~ **in** to consist of

conso'lare ag consular ▶ vt (confortare) to console, comfort; (rallegrare) to cheer up; **consolarsi** vpr to be comforted; to cheer up

conso'lato sm consulate

consolazi'one [konsolat'tsjone] sf consolation, comfort

'console sm consul

conso'nante sf consonant

'consono, -a ag ~ **a** consistent with, consonant with

con'sorte sm/f consort

consta'tare vt to establish, verify

consu'eto, -a ag habitual, usual

consu'lente sm/f consultant

consul'tare vt to consult; **consultarsi** vpr **consultarsi con qn** to seek the advice of sb

consul'torio sm ~ **familiare** family planning clinic

consu'mare vt (logorare: abiti, scarpe) to wear out; (usare) to consume, use up; (mangiare, bere) to consume; (Dir) to consummate; **consumarsi** vpr to wear out; to be used up; (anche fig) to be consumed; (combustibile) to burn out

con'tabile ag accounts cpd, accounting ▶ sm/f accountant

contachi'lometri [kontaki'lometri] sm inv ≈ mileometer

conta'dino, -a sm/f countryman/ woman, farm worker; (peg) peasant

contagi'are [konta'dʒare] vt to infect

contagi'oso, -a ag infectious;

contagious

conta'gocce [konta'gottʃe] sm inv (Med) dropper

contami'nare vt to contaminate

con'tante sm cash; **pagare in contanti** to pay cash; **non ho contanti** I haven't got any cash

con'tare vt to count; (considerare) to consider ▶ vi to count, be of importance; ~ **su qn** to count o rely on sb; ~ **di fare qc** to intend to do sth; **conta'tore** sm meter

contat'tare vt to contact

con'tatto sm contact

'conte sm count

conteggi'are [konted'dʒare] vt to charge, put on the bill

con'tegno [kon'teɲno] sm (comportamento) behaviour; (atteggiamento) attitude; **darsi un ~** to act nonchalant; to pull o.s. together

contemporanea'mente av simultaneously; at the same time

contempo'raneo, -a ag, sm/f contemporary

conten'dente sm/f opponent, adversary

conte'nere vt to contain; **conteni'tore** sm container

conten'tezza [konten'tettsa] sf contentment

con'tento, -a ag pleased, glad; ~ **di** pleased with

conte'nuto sm contents pl; (argomento) content

con'tessa sf countess

contes'tare vt (Dir) to notify; (fig) to dispute

con'testo sm context

continen'tale ag, sm/f continental

conti'nente ag continent ▶ sm (Geo) continent; (: terra ferma) mainland

contin'gente [kontin'dʒente] ag contingent ▶ sm (Comm) quota; (Mil) contingent

continua'mente av (senza interruzione) continuously, nonstop; (ripetutamente) continually

continu'are vt to continue (with), go on with ▶ vi to continue, go on; **~ a fare qc** to go on o continue doing sth

continuità sf continuity

con'tinuo, -a ag (numerazione) continuous; (pioggia) continual, constant; (Elettr): **corrente continua** direct current; **di ~** continually

'**conto** sm (calcolo) calculation; (Comm, Econ) account; (di ristorante, albergo) bill; (fig: stima) consideration, esteem; **il ~, per favore** can I have the bill, please?; **lo metta sul mio ~** put it on my bill; **fare i conti con qn** to settle one's account with sb; **fare ~ su qn/qc** to count o rely on sb; **rendere ~ a qn di qc** to be accountable to sb for sth; **tener ~ di qn/qc** to take sb/sth into account; **per ~ di** on behalf of; **per ~ mio** as far as I'm concerned; **a conti fatti, in fin dei conti** all things considered; **conto corrente** current account; **conto alla rovescia** countdown

con'torno sm (linea) outline, contour; (ornamento) border; (Cuc) vegetables pl

con'torto, -a pp di **contorcere**

contrabbandi'ere, -a sm/f smuggler

contrab'bando sm smuggling, contraband; **merce di ~** contraband, smuggled goods pl

contrab'basso sm (Mus) (double) bass

contraccambi'are vt (favore ecc) to return

contraccet'tivo [kontrattʃet'tivo] ag, sm contraceptive

contrac'colpo sm rebound; (di arma da fuoco) recoil; (fig) repercussion

contrad'dire vt to contradict; **contraddirsi** vpr to contradict o.s.; (uso reciproco: persone) to contradict

each other o one another; (: testimonianze ecc) to be contradictory

contraf'fare vt (persona) to mimic; (alterare: voce) to disguise; (firma) to forge, counterfeit

contraria'mente av **~ a** contrary to

contrari'are vt (contrastare) to thwart, oppose; (irritare) to annoy, bother

con'trario, -a ag opposite; (sfavorevole) unfavourable ▶ sm opposite; **essere ~ a qc** (persona) to be against sth; **in caso ~** otherwise; **avere qc in ~** to have some objection; **al ~** on the contrary

contrasse'gnare [kontrasseɲ'ɲare] vt to mark

contras'tare vt (avversare) to oppose; (impedire) to bar; (negare: diritto) to contest, dispute ▶ vi **~ (con)** (essere in disaccordo) to contrast (with); (lottare) to struggle (with)

contrat'tacco sm counterattack

contrat'tare vt, vi to negotiate

contrat'tempo sm hitch

con'tratto, -a pp di **contrarre** ▶ sm contract

contravvenzi'one [kontravven'tsjone] sf contravention; (ammenda) fine

contrazi'one [kontrat'tsjone] sf contraction; (di prezzi ecc) reduction

contribu'ente sm/f taxpayer; ratepayer (BRIT), property tax payer (US)

contribu'ire vi to contribute

'**contro** prep against; **~ di me/lui** against me/him; **pastiglie ~ la tosse** throat lozenges; **~ pagamento** (Comm) on payment ▶ pref **contro-**

controfi'gura sf (Cinema) double

control'lare vt (accertare) to check; (sorvegliare) to watch, control; (tenere nel proprio potere, fig: dominare) to control; **controllarsi** vpr to control o.s.; **con'trollo** sm check; watch; control; **controllo delle nascite** birth control; **control'lore** sm (Ferr, Autobus) (ticket) inspector

contro'luce [kontro'lutʃe] sf inv (Fot) backlit shot ▶ av (in) ~ against the light; (fotografare) into the light

contro'mano av guidare ~ to drive on the wrong side of the road; (in un senso unico) to drive the wrong way up a one-way street

controprodu'cente [kontroprodu'tʃɛnte] ag counterproductive

contro'senso sm (contraddizione) contradiction in terms; (assurdità) nonsense

controspio'naggio [kontrospio'naddʒo] sm counterespionage

contro'versia sf (Dir) controversy; (Dir) dispute

contro'verso, -a ag controversial

contro'voglia [kontro'vɔʎʎa] av unwillingly

contusi'one sf (Med) bruise

convale'scente [konvaleʃ'ʃɛnte] ag, sm/f convalescent

convali'dare vt (Amm) to validate; (fig: sospetto, dubbio) to confirm

con'vegno [kon'veɲɲo] sm (incontro) meeting; (congresso) convention, congress; (luogo) meeting place

conve'nevoli smpl civilities

conveni'ente ag suitable; (vantaggioso) profitable; (: prezzo) cheap

> Attenzione! In inglese esiste la parola *convenient*, che però significa *comodo*.

conve'nire vi (riunirsi) to gather, assemble; (concordare) to agree; (tornare utile) to be worthwhile ▶ vb impers conviene fare questo it is advisable to do this; **conviene**

andarsene we should go; **ne convengo** I agree

con'vento sm (di frati) monastery; (di suore) convent

convenzio'nale [konventsjo'nale] ag conventional

convenzi'one [konven'tsjone] sf (Dir) agreement; (nella società) convention

conver'sare vi to have a conversation, converse

conversazi'one [konversat'tsjone] sf conversation; **fare** ~ to chat, have a chat

conversi'one sf conversion; **conversione ad U** (Aut) U-turn

conver'tire vt (trasformare) to change; (Pol, Rel) to convert; **convertirsi** vpr **convertirsi (a)** to be converted (to)

con'vesso, -a ag convex

convin'cente [konvin'tʃɛnte] ag convincing

con'vincere [kon'vintʃere] vt to convince; ~ **qn di qc** to convince sb of sth; ~ **qn a fare qc** to persuade sb to do sth; **convincersi** vpr **convincersi (di qc)** to convince o.s. (of sth); ~ **qn di qc** to convince sb of sth; ~ **qn a fare qc** to convince sb to do sth

convi'vente sm/f common-law husband/wife

con'vivere vi to live together

convo'care vt to call, convene; (Dir) to summon

convulsi'one sf convulsion

coope'rare vi ~ **(a)** to cooperate (in); **coopera'tiva** sf cooperative

coordi'nare vt to coordinate

co'perchio [ko'perkjo] sm cover; (di pentola) lid

co'perta sf cover; (di lana) blanket; (da viaggio) rug; (Naut) deck

coper'tina sf (Stampa) cover, jacket

co'perto, -a pp di **coprire** ▶ ag covered; (cielo) overcast ▶ sm place setting; (posto a tavola) place; (al *ristorante*) cover charge; **~ di** covered in o with

coper'tone *sm* (Aut) rubber tyre

coper'tura *sf* (*anche Econ, Mil*) cover; (*di edificio*) roofing

'copia *sf* copy; **brutta/bella ~** rough/ final copy

copi'are *vt* to copy

copi'one *sm* (*Cinema, Teatro*) script

'coppa *sf* (*bicchiere*) goblet; (*per frutta, gelato*) dish; (*trofeo*) cup, trophy; **coppa dell'olio** oil sump (BRIT) o pan (US)

'coppia *sf* (*di persone*) couple; (*di animali, Sport*) pair

coprifu'oco, -chi *sm* curfew

copri'letto *sm* bedspread

copripiu'mino *sm* duvet cover

co'prire *vt* to cover; (*occupare: carica, posto*) to hold; **coprirsi** *vpr* (*cielo*) to cloud over; (*vestirsi*) to wrap up, cover up; (*Econ*) to cover o.s.; **coprirsi di** (*macchie, muffa*) to become covered in

coque [kɔk] *sf* **uovo alla ~** boiled egg

co'raggio [ko'raddʒo] *sm* courage, bravery; **~!** (*forza!*) come on!; (*animo!*) cheer up!

co'rallo *sm* coral

Co'rano *sm* (*Rel*) Koran

co'razza [ko'rattsa] *sf* armour; (*di animali*) carapace, shell; (*Mil*) armour(-plating)

cordi'ale *ag* cordial, warm ▶ *sm* (*bevanda*) cordial

'cordless ['kɔːdlɪs] *sm inv* cordless phone

cor'done *sm* cord, string; (*linea: di polizia*) cordon; **cordone ombelicale** umbilical cord

Co'rea *sf* **la ~** Korea

coreogra'fia *sf* choreography

cori'andolo *sm* (*Bot*) coriander; **coriandoli** *smpl* confetti *sg*

cor'nacchia [kor'nakkja] *sf* crow

corna'musa *sf* bagpipes *pl*

cor'netta *sf* (*Mus*) cornet; (*Tel*) receiver

cor'netto *sm* (*Cuc*) croissant; (*gelato*) cone

cor'nice [kor'niʧe] *sf* frame; (*fig*) setting, background

cornici'one [korni'ʧone] *sm* (*di edificio*) ledge; (*Archit*) cornice

'corno (*pl(f)-a*) *sm* (*Zool*) horn; (*pl(m) -i: Mus*) horn; **fare le corna a qn** to be unfaithful to sb

Corno'vaglia [korno'vaʎʎa] *sf* **la ~** Cornwall

cor'nuto, -a *ag* (*con corna*) horned; (*fam!: marito*) cuckolded ▶ *sm* (*fam!*) cuckold; (: *insulto*) bastard (!)

'coro *sm* chorus; (*Rel*) choir

co'rona *sf* crown; (*di fiori*) wreath

'corpo *sm* body; (*militare, diplomatico*) corps *inv*; **prendere ~** to take shape; **a ~ a ~** hand-to-hand; **corpo di ballo** corps de ballet; **corpo insegnante** teaching staff

corpora'tura *sf* build, physique

cor'reggere [kor'reddʒere] *vt* to correct; (*compiti*) to correct, mark

cor'rente *ag* (*acqua: di fiume*) flowing; (: *di rubinetto*) running; (*moneta, prezzo*) current; (*comune*) everyday ▶ *sm* **essere al ~ (di)** to be well-informed (about); **mettere al ~ (di)** to inform (of) ▶ *sf* (*d'acqua*) current, stream; (*spiffero*) draught; (*Elettr, Meteor*) current; (*fig*) trend, tendency; **la vostra lettera del 5 ~ mese** (*Comm*) your letter of the 5th of this month; **corrente alternata/ continua** alternate/direct current; **corrente'mente** *av* commonly;

parlare una lingua correntemente to speak a language fluently

'correre vi to run; (precipitarsi) to rush; (partecipare a una gara) to race, run; (fig: diffondersi) to go round ▶ vt (Sport: gara) to compete in; (rischio) to run; (pericolo) to face; ~ **dietro a qn** to run after sb; **corre voce che ...** it is rumoured that ...

cor'ressi ecc vb vedi **correggere**

correzi'one [korret'tsjone] sf correction; marking; **correzione di bozze** proofreading

corri'doio sm corridor; (in aereo, al cinema) aisle; **vorrei un posto sul ~ I** like an aisle seat

corri'dore sm (Sport) runner; (: su veicolo) racer

corri'era sf coach (BRIT), bus

corri'ere sm (diplomatico, di guerra, postale) courier; (Comm) carrier

corri'mano sm handrail

corrispon'dente ag corresponding ▶ sm/f correspondent

corrispon'denza [korrispon'dɛntsa] sf correspondence

corris'pondere vi (equivalere): ~ **(a)** to correspond (to) ▶ vt (stipendio) to pay; (fig: amore) to return

cor'rodere vt to corrode

cor'rompere vt to corrupt; (comprare) to bribe

cor'roso, -a pp di **corrodere**

cor'rotto, -a pp di **corrompere** ▶ ag corrupt

corru'gare vt to wrinkle; ~ **la fronte** to knit one's brows

cor'ruppi ecc vb vedi **corrompere**

corruzi'one [korrut'tsjone] sf corruption; bribery

'corsa sf running no pl; (gara) race; (di autobus, taxi) journey, trip; **fare una** ~ to run, dash; (Sport) to run a race; **corsa campestre** cross-country race

'corsi ecc vb vedi **correre**

cor'sia sf (Aut, Sport) lane; (di ospedale) ward

'Corsica sf **la ~ Corsica**

cor'sivo sm cursive (writing); (Tip) italics pl

'corso, -a pp di **correre** ▶ sm course; (strada cittadina) main street; (di unità monetaria) circulation; (di titoli, valori) rate, price; **in ~** in progress, under way; (annata) current; **corso d'acqua** river, stream; (artificiale) waterway; **corso d'aggiornamento** refresher course; **corso serale** evening class

'corte sf (cortile) (court)yard; (Dir, regale) court; **fare la ~ a qn** to court sb; **corte marziale** court-martial

cor'teccia, -ce [kor'tettʃa] sf bark

corteggi'are [korted'dʒare] vt to court

cor'teo sm procession

cor'tese ag courteous; **corte'sia** sf courtesy; **per cortesia ...** excuse me, please ...

cor'tile sm (court)yard

cor'tina sf curtain; (anche fig) screen

'corto, -a ag short; **essere a ~ di qc** to be short of sth; **corto circuito** short-circuit

'corvo sm raven

'cosa sf thing; (faccenda) affair, matter, business no pl; (che) ~? what?; (che) **cos'è?** what is it?; **a ~ pensi?** what are you thinking about?

'coscia, -sce ['kɔʃʃa] sf thigh; **coscia di pollo** (Cuc) chicken leg

cosci'ente [koʃ'ʃɛnte] ag conscious; ~ **di** conscious o aware of

 così
av

1 (in questo modo) like this, (in) this way; (in tal modo) so; **le cose stanno così** this is the way things stand; **non ho detto così** I didn't say that!; **come stai? — (e) così** how are you? — so-so; **e così via** and so on; **per così dire** so to speak

2 (tanto) so; **così lontano** so far away; **un ragazzo così intelligente** such an intelligent boy

▶ ag inv (tale): **non ho mai visto un film così** I've never seen such a film

▶ cong

1 (perciò) so, therefore

2: **così ... come** as ... as; **non è così bravo come te** he's not as good as you; **così ... che** so ... that

cosid'detto, -a ag so-called

cos'metico, -a, -ci, -che ag, sm cosmetic

cos'pargere [kos'pardʒere] vt ~ di to sprinkle with

cos'picuo, -a ag considerable, large

cospi'rare vi to conspire

'cossi ecc vb vedi **cuocere**

'costa sf (tra terra e mare) coast(line); (litorale) shore; (Anat) rib; **la C~ Azzurra** the French Riviera

cos'tante ag constant; (persona) steadfast ▶ sf constant

cos'tare vi, vt to cost; **quanto costa?** how much does it cost?; ~ **caro** to be expensive, cost a lot

cos'tata sf (Cuc) large chop

costeggi'are [kosted'dʒare] vt to be close to; to run alongside

cos'tiero, -a ag coastal, coast cpd

costitu'ire vt (comitato, gruppo) to set up, form; (elementi, parti: comporre) to make up, constitute; (rappresentare) to constitute; (Dir) to appoint; **costituirsi** vpr **costituirsi alla polizia** to give o.s. up to the police

costituzi'one [kostitu'tsjone] sf setting up; building up; constitution

'costo sm cost; **a ogni o qualunque ~, a tutti i costi** at all costs

'costola sf (Anat) rib

cos'toso, -a ag expensive, costly

cos'tringere [kos'trindʒere] vt ~ **qn a fare qc** to force sb to do sth

costru'ire vt to construct, build; **costruzi'one** sf construction, building

cos'tume sm (uso) custom; (foggia di vestire, indumento) costume; **costume da bagno** bathing o swimming costume (BRIT), swimsuit; (da uomo) bathing o swimming trunks pl

co'tenna sf bacon rind

coto'letta sf (di maiale, montone) chop; (di vitello, agnello) cutlet

co'tone sm cotton; **cotone idrofilo** cotton wool (BRIT), absorbent cotton (US)

'cotta sf (fam: innamoramento) crush

'cottimo sm **lavorare a ~** to do piecework

'cotto, -a pp di **cuocere** ▶ ag cooked; (fam: innamorato) head-over-heels in love; **ben ~** (carne) well done

cot'tura sf cooking; (in forno) baking; (in umido) stewing

co'vare vt to hatch; (fig: malattia) to be sickening for; (: odio, rancore) to nurse ▶ vi (fuoco, fig) to smoulder

'covo sm den

co'vone sm sheaf

'cozza ['kɔttsa] sf mussel

coz'zare [kot'tsare] vi ~ **contro** to bang into, collide with

'crampo sm cramp; **ho un ~ alla gamba** I've got cramp in my leg

'cranio sm skull

cra'tere sm crater

cra'vatta sf tie

cre'are vt to create

'crebbi ecc vb vedi **crescere**

cre'dente sm/f (Rel) believer

cre'denza [kre'dɛntsa] sf belief; (armadio) sideboard

'credere vt to believe ▶ vi ~ **in, ~ a** to believe in; ~ **qn onesto** to believe sb (to be) honest; ~ **che** to believe o think that; **credersi furbo** to think one is clever '**credito** sm (anche Comm) credit; (reputazione) esteem, repute; **comprare a ~** to buy on credit

'**crema** sf cream; (con uova, zucchero ecc) custard; **crema pasticcera** confectioner's custard; **crema solare** sun cream

cre'**mare** vt to cremate

'**crepa** sf crack

cre'**paccio** [kre'pattʃo] sm large crack, fissure; (di ghiacciaio) crevasse

crepacu'**ore** sm broken heart

cre'**pare** vi (fam: morire) to snuff it, kick the bucket; **~ dalle risa** to split one's sides laughing

crêpe [krɛp] sf inv pancake

cre'**puscolo** sm twilight, dusk

'**crescere** ['kreʃʃere] vi to grow ▶ vt (figli) to raise

cre'**sima** sf (Rel) confirmation

'**crespo, -a** ag (capelli) frizzy; (tessuto) puckered ▶ sm crêpe

'**cresta** sf crest; (di polli, uccelli) crest, comb

'**creta** sf chalk; clay

creti'**nata** sf (fam): **dire/fare una ~** to say/do a stupid thing

cre'**tino, -a** ag stupid ▶ sm/f idiot, fool

CRI sigla f = Croce Rossa Italiana

cric sm inv (Tecn) jack

cri'**ceto** [kri'tʃeto] sm hamster

crimi'**nale** ag, sm/f criminal

criminali'**tà** sf crime; **criminalità organizzata** organized crime

'**crimine** sm (Dir) crime

crip'**tare** vt (TV: programma) to encrypt

crisan'**temo** sm chrysanthemum

'**crisi** sf inv crisis; (Med) attack, fit; **crisi di nervi** attack o fit of nerves

cris'**tallo** sm crystal; **cristalli liquidi** liquid crystals

cristia'**nesimo** sm Christianity

cristi'**ano, -a** ag, sm/f Christian

'**Cristo** sm Christ

cri'**terio** sm criterion; (buon senso) (common) sense

'**critica, -che** sf criticism; **la ~** (attività) criticism; (persone) the critics pl; vedi anche **critico**

criti'**care** vt to criticize

'**critico, -a, -ci, -che** ag critical ▶ sm critic

cro'**ato, -a** ag, sm/f Croatian, Croat

Croa'**zia** [kroa'ttsja] sf Croatia

croc'**cante** ag crisp, crunchy

'**croce** ['krotʃe] sf cross; **in ~** (di traverso) crosswise; (fig) on tenterhooks; **Croce Rossa** Red Cross

croci'**ata** [kro'tʃata] sf crusade

croci'**era** [kro'tʃera] sf (viaggio) cruise; (Archit) transept

croci'**fisso, -a** pp di crocifiggere

crol'**lare** vi to collapse; '**crollo** sm collapse; (di prezzi) slump, sudden fall; **crollo in Borsa** slump in prices on the Stock Exchange

cro'**mato, -a** ag chromium-plated

'**cromo** sm chrome, chromium

'**cronaca, -che** sf (Stampa) news sg; (: rubrica) column; (TV, Radio) commentary; **fatto o episodio di ~** news item; **cronaca nera** crime news sg; crime column

'**cronico, -a, -ci, -che** ag chronic

cro'**nista, -i** sm (Stampa) reporter

cro'**nometro** sm chronometer; (a scatto) stopwatch

'**crosta** sf crust

cros'**tacei** [kros'tatʃei] smpl shellfish

cros'**tata** sf (Cuc) tart

cros'**tino** sm (Cuc) crouton; (: da antipasto) canapé

cruci'**ale** [kru'tʃale] ag crucial

cruci'**verba** sm inv crossword (puzzle)

cru'**dele** ag cruel

'**crudo, -a** ag (non cotto) raw; (aspro) harsh, severe

cru'**miro** (peg) sm blackleg (BRIT), scab

'**crusca** sf bran

crus'**cotto** sm (Aut) dashboard

CSI sigla f inv (= Comunità Stati Indipendenti) CIS

CSM [tʃiesse'emme] sigla m (= consiglio superiore della magistratura) Magistrates' Board of Supervisors

'Cuba sf Cuba

cu'bano, -a ag, sm/f Cuban

cu'betto sm: **cubetto di ghiaccio** ice cube

'cubico, -a, -ci, -che ag cubic

cu'bista, -i, -e ag (Arte) Cubist ▸ sf (in discoteca) podium dancer

'cubo, -a ag cubic ▸ sm cube; **elevare al ~** (Mat) to cube

cuc'cagna [kuk'kaŋŋa] sf **paese della ~** land of plenty; **albero della ~** greasy pole (fig)

cuc'cetta [kut'tʃetta] sf (Ferr) couchette; (Naut) berth

cucchia'iata [kukkja'jata] sf spoonful

cucchia'ino [kukkja'ino] sm teaspoon; **coffee spoon**

cucchi'aio [kuk'kjajo] sm spoon

'cuccia, -ce ['kuttʃa] sf dog's bed; **a ~!** down!

'cucciolo ['kuttʃolo] sm cub; (di cane) puppy

cu'cina [ku'tʃina] sf (locale) kitchen; (arte culinaria) cooking, cookery; (le vivande) food, cooking; (apparecchio) cooker; **cucina componibile** fitted kitchen; **cuci'nare** vt to cook

cu'cire [ku'tʃire] vt to sew, stitch; **cuci'trice** sf stapler

cucù sm inv cuckoo

'cuffia sf bonnet, cap; (da infermiera) cap; (da bagno) (bathing) cap; (per ascoltare) headphones pl, headset

cu'gino, -a [ku'dʒino] sm/f cousin

O 'cui pron

1 (nei complementi indiretti: persona) whom; (: oggetto, animale) which; **la persona/le persone a cui accennavi** the person/people you were referring

to o to whom you were referring; **i libri di cui parlavo** the books I was talking about o about which I was talking; **il quartiere in cui abito** the district where I live; **la ragione per cui** the reason why

2 (inserito tra articolo e sostantivo) whose; **la donna i cui figli sono scomparsi** the woman whose children have disappeared; **il signore, dal cui figlio ho avuto il libro** the man from whose son I got the book

culi'naria sf cookery

'culla sf cradle

cul'lare vt to rock

'culmine sm top, summit

'culo (fam!) sm arse (BRIT!), ass (US!); (fig: fortuna) luck: **aver ~** to have the luck of the devil

'culto sm (religione) religion; (adorazione) worship, adoration; (venerazione: anche fig) cult

cul'tura sf culture, education, learning; **cultu'rale** ag cultural

cultu'rismo sm body-building

cumula'tivo, -a ag cumulative; (prezzo) inclusive; (biglietto) group cpd

'cumulo sm (mucchio) pile, heap; (Meteor) cumulus

cu'netta sf (avvallamento) dip; (di scolo) gutter

cu'ocere ['kwɔtʃere] vt (alimenti) to cook; (mattoni ecc) to fire ▸ vi to cook; **~ al forno** (pane) to bake; (arrosto) to roast; **cu'oco, -a, -chi, -che** sm/f cook; (di ristorante) chef

cu'oio sm leather; **cuoio capelluto** scalp

cu'ore sm heart; **cuori** smpl (Carte) hearts; **avere buon ~** to be kind-hearted; **stare a ~ a qn** to be important to sb

'cupo, -a ag dark; (suono) dull; (fig) gloomy, dismal

'cupola sf dome; cupola

'cura sf care; (Med: trattamento) (course of) treatment; **aver ~ di** (occuparsi di) to look after; **a ~ di** (libro) edited by; **cura dimagrante** diet

cu'rare vt (malato, malattia) to treat; (: guarire) to cure; (aver cura di) to take care of; (testo) to edit; **curarsi** vpr to take care of o.s.; (Med) to follow a course of treatment; **curarsi di** to pay attention to

curio'sare vi to look round, wander round; (tra libri) to browse; **~ nei negozi** to look o wander round the shops

curiosità sf inv curiosity; (cosa rara) curio, curiosity

curi'oso, -a ag curious; **essere ~ di** to be curious about

cur'sore sm (Inform) cursor

'curva sf curve; (stradale) bend, curve

cur'vare vt to bend ▶ vi (veicolo) to take a bend; (strada) to bend, curve; **curvarsi** vpr to bend; (legno) to warp

'curvo, -a ag curved; (piegato) bent

cusci'netto [kuʃʃi'netto] sm pad; (Tecn) bearing ▶ ag inv **stato ~** buffer state; **cuscinetto a sfere** ball bearing

cu'scino [kuʃʃino] sm cushion; (guanciale) pillow

cus'tode sm/f keeper, custodian

cus'todia sf care; (Dir) custody; (astuccio) case, holder

custo'dire vt (conservare) to keep; (assistere) to look after, take care of; (fare la guardia) to guard

CV abbr (= cavallo vapore) h.p.

cyber'caffè [tʃiberka'fɛ] sm inv cybercafé

cyber'nauta, -i, -e sm/f Internet surfer

cyber'spazio sm cyberspace

d

da

(da+il = **dal**, da+lo = **dallo**, da+l' = **dall'**, da+la = **dalla**, da+i = **dai**, da+gli = **dagli**, da+le = **dalle**) prep

1 (agente) by: **dipinto da un grande artista** painted by a great artist

2 (causa) from; **tremare dalla paura** to tremble with fear

3 (stato in luogo) at; **abito da lui** I'm living at his house o with him; **sono dal giornalaio/da Francesco** I'm at the newsagent's/Francesco's; (moto a luogo) to; (moto per luogo) through; **vado da Pietro/dal giornalaio** I'm going to Pietro's (house)/to the newsagent's; **sono passati dalla finestra** they came in through the window

5 (provenienza, allontanamento) from; **arrivare/partire da Milano** to arrive/depart from Milan; **scendere dal treno/dalla macchina** to get off the train/out of the car; **si trova a 5 km da qui** it's 5 km from here

6 (tempo: durata) for; (: a partire da: nel passato) since; (: nel futuro) from; **vivo qui da un anno** I've been living here for a year; **è dalle 3 che ti aspetto** I've been waiting for you since 3 (o'clock); **da oggi in poi** from today onwards; **da bambino** as a child, when I (o he ecc) was a child

7 (modo, maniera) like; **comportarsi da uomo** to behave like a man; **l'ho fatto**

da me I did it (by) myself

B (*descrittivo*): **una macchina da corsa** a racing car; **una ragazza dai capelli biondi** a girl with blonde hair; **un vestito da 60 euro** a 60 euros dress

dà *vb vedi* **dare**

dac'capo *av* (*di nuovo*) (once) again; (*dal principio*) all over again, from the beginning

'dado *sm* (*da gioco*) dice o die; (*Cuc*) stock (BRIT) o bouillon (US) cube; (*Tecn*) (screw)nut; **dadi** *smpl* (*game of*) dice; **giocare a dadi** to play dice

'daino *sm* (*fallow*) deer *inv*; (*pelle*) buckskin

dal'tonico, -a, -ci, -che *ag* colour-blind

'dama *sf* lady; (*nei balli*) partner; (*gioco*) draughts *sg* (BRIT), checkers *sg* (US)

damigi'ana [dami'dʒana] *sf* demijohn

da'nese *ag* Danish ▶ *sm/f* Dane ▶ *sm* (*Ling*) Danish

Dani'marca *sf* la ~ Denmark

dannazi'one *sf* damnation

danneggi'are [danned'dʒare] *vt* to damage; (*rovinare*) to spoil; (*nuocere*) to harm

'danno *sm* damage; (*a persona*) harm, injury; **danni** *smpl* (*Dir*) damages; **dan'noso, -a** *ag* dannoso, (*a, per*) harmful (to), bad (for)

Da'nubio *sm* il ~ the Danube

'danza ['dantsa] *sf* la ~ dancing; **una ~ danza** a dance

dan'zare [dan'tsare] *vt, vi* to dance

dapper'tutto *av* everywhere

dap'prima *av* at first

'dare (*Comm*) debit ▶ *vt* to give; (*produrre*: frutti, suono) to produce ▶ *vi* (*guardare*): ~ **su** to look (out) onto; **darsi** *vpr* **darsi a** to dedicate o.s. to; **darsi al commercio** to go into business; **darsi al bere** to take to drink; ~ **da mangiare a qn** to give sb

sth to eat; ~ **per certo qc** to consider sth certain; ~ **per morto qn** to give sb up for dead; **darsi per vinto** to give in

'data *sf* date; ~ **limite d'utilizzo** *or* **di consumo** best-before date; **data di nascita** date of birth; **data di scadenza** expiry date

'dato, -a *ag* (*stabilito*) given ▶ *sm* datum; **dati** *smpl* data *pl*; ~ **che** given that; un ~ **di fatto** a fact; **dati sensibili** personal information

da'tore, -'trice *sm/f*; **datore di lavoro** employer

'dattero *sm* date

dattilogra'fia *sf* typing

datti'lografo, -a *sm/f* typist

da'vanti *av* in front; (*dirimpetto*) opposite ▶ *ag* in front ▶ *sm* front; ~ **a** in front of; facing, opposite; (*in presenza di*) before, in front of

davan'zale [davan'tsale] *sm* windowsill

dav'vero *av* really, indeed

d.C. *adv abbr* (= *dopo Cristo*) A.D.

'dea *sf* goddess

'debbo *ecc vb vedi* **dovere**

'debito, -a *ag* due, proper ▶ *sm* debt; (*Comm*: dare) debit; **a tempo** ~ at the right time

'debole *ag* weak, feeble; (*suono*) faint; (*luce*) dim ▶ *sm* weakness; **debo'lezza** *sf* weakness

debut'tare *vi* to make one's debut

deca'denza [deka'dentsa] *sf* decline; (*Dir*) loss, forfeiture

decaffei'nato, -a *ag* decaffeinated

decapi'tare *vt* to decapitate, behead

decappot'tabile *ag, sf* convertible

de'cennio [de'tʃɛnnjo] *sm* decade

de'cente [de'tʃɛnte] *ag* decent, respectable, proper; (*accettabile*) satisfactory, decent

de'cesso [de'tʃɛsso] *sm* death

de'cidere [de'tʃidere] *vt* ~ **qc** to decide

on sth; (questione, lite) to settle sth; ~ di fare/che to decide to do/that; ~ di qc (cosa) to determine sth; decidersi (a fare) to decide (to do), make up one's mind (to do)

deci'frare [detʃi'frare] vt to decode; (fig) to decipher, make out

deci'male [detʃi'male] ag decimal

'decimo, -a ['dɛtʃimo] num tenth

de'cina [de'tʃina] sf ten; (circa dieci): una ~ (di) about ten

de'cisi ecc [de'tʃizi] vb vedi decidere

decisi'one [detʃi'zjone] sf decision; prendere una ~ to make a decision

deci'sivo, -a [detʃi'zivo] ag (gen) decisive; (fattore) deciding

de'ciso, -a [de'tʃizo] pp di decidere

decli'nare vi (pendio) to slope down; (fig: diminuire) to decline ▶ vt to decline

declinazi'one sf (Ling) declension

de'clino sm decline

decodifica'tore sm (Tel) decoder

decol'lare vi (Aer) to take off; de'collo sm take-off

deco'rare vt to decorate; decorazi'one sf decoration

de'creto sm decree; decreto legge decree with the force of law

'dedica, -che sf dedication

dedi'care vt to dedicate; dedicarsi vpr dedicarsi a to devote o.s. to

dedicherò ecc [dedike'rɔ] vb vedi dedicare

'dedito, -a ag ~ a (studio ecc) dedicated o devoted to; (vizio) addicted to

de'duco ecc vb vedi dedurre

de'durre vt (concludere) to deduce; (defalcare) to deduct

de'dussi ecc vb vedi dedurre

defici'ente [defi'tʃɛnte] ag (mancante): ~ di deficient in; (insufficiente) insufficient ▶ sm/f mental defective; (peg: cretino) idiot

'deficit ['dɛfitʃit] sm inv (Econ) deficit

defi'nire vt to define; (risolvere) to settle; defini'tiva sf in ~ (dopotutto) in the end; (dunque) hence; defini'tivo, -a ag definitive, final; definizi'one sf definition; settlement

defor'mare vt (alterare) to put out of shape; (corpo) to deform; (pensiero, fatto) to distort; deformarsi vpr to lose its shape

de'forme ag deformed; disfigured

de'funto, -a ag late cpd ▶ sm/f deceased

degene'rare [dedʒene'rare] vi to degenerate

de'gente [de'dʒɛnte] sm/f (in ospedale) in-patient

deglu'tire vt to swallow

de'gnare [deɲ'ɲare] vt ~ qn della propria presenza to honour sb with one's presence; degnarsi vpr degnarsi di fare qc to deign o condescend to do sth

'degno, -a [deɲɲo] ag dignified; ~ di worthy of; ~ di lode praiseworthy

de'grado sm; degrado urbano urban decline

'delega, -ghe sf (procura) proxy

dele'terio, -a ag damaging; (per salute ecc) harmful

del'fino sm (Zool) dolphin; (Storia) dauphin; (fig) probable successor

deli'cato, -a ag delicate; (salute) delicate, frail; (fig: gentile) thoughtful, considerate; (: che dimostra tatto) tactful

delin'quente sm/f criminal, delinquent; delinquente abituale regular offender, habitual offender; delin'quenza sf criminality, delinquency; delinquenza minorile juvenile delinquency

deli'rare vi to be delirious, rave; (fig) to rave

de'lirio sm delirium; (ragionamento insensato) raving; (fig): andare/

mandare in ~ to go/send into a frenzy

de'litto sm crime

delizi'oso, -a ag delightful; (*cibi*) delicious

delta'plano sm hang-glider; **volo col ~** hang-gliding

delu'dente ag disappointing

de'ludere vt to disappoint; **delusi'one** sf disappointment; **de'luso, -a** pp di **deludere**

'demmo vb vedi **dare**

demo'cratico, -a, -ci, -che ag democratic

democra'zia [demokrat'tsia] sf democracy

demo'lire vt to demolish

de'monio sm demon, devil; **il D~** the Devil

de'naro sm money

densità sf inv density

'denso, -a ag thick, dense

den'tale ag dental

'dente sm tooth; (*di forchetta*) prong; **al ~** (*Cuc*: *pasta*) al dente; **denti del giudizio** wisdom teeth; **denti da latte** milk teeth; **denti'era** sf (set of) false teeth pl

denti'fricio [denti'fritʃo] sm toothpaste

den'tista, -i, -e sm/f dentist

'dentro av inside; (*in casa*) indoors; (*fig*: *nell'intimo*) inwardly ▶ prep ~(**a**) in; **piegato in ~** folded over; **qui/là ~** in here/there; **~ di sé** (*pensare, brontolare*) to oneself

de'nuncia, -ce o **cie** [de'nuntʃa] sf denunciation; declaration; **denuncia dei redditi** (*income*) tax return

denunci'are [denun'tʃare] vt to denounce; (*dichiarare*) to declare; (*persona, nascita ecc*) to report; **vorrei ~ un furto** I'd like to report a theft

denu'trito, -a ag undernourished

denutrizi'one [denutrit'tsjone] sf malnutrition

deodo'rante sm deodorant

depe'rire vi to waste away

depi'larsi vpr ~ (**le gambe**) (*con rasoio*) to shave (one's legs); (*con ceretta*) to wax (one's legs)

depila'tivo, -a ag hair-removing cpd, depilatory

dépli'ant [depli'ɑ̃] sm inv leaflet; (*opuscolo*) brochure

deplo'revole ag deplorable

de'pone, de'pongo ecc vb vedi **deporre**

de'porre vt (*depositare*) to put down; (*rimuovere: da una carica*) to remove; (: *re*) to depose; (*Dir*) to testify

depor'tare vt to deport

de'posi ecc vb vedi **deporre**

deposi'tare vt (*gen, Geo, Econ*) to deposit; (*lasciare*) to leave; (*merci*) to store; **depositarsi** vpr (*sabbia, polvere*) to settle

de'posito sm deposit; (*luogo*) warehouse; depot; (: *Mil*) depot; **deposito bagagli** left-luggage office

deposizi'one [depozit'tsjone] sf deposition; (*da una carica*) removal

depra'vato, -a ag depraved ▶ sm/f degenerate

depre'dare vt to rob, plunder

depressi'one sf depression

de'presso, -a pp di **deprimere** ▶ ag depressed

deprez'zare [depret'tsare] vt (*Econ*) to depreciate

depri'mente ag depressing

de'primere vt to depress

depu'rare vt to purify

depu'tato sm (*Pol*) deputy, ≈ Member of Parliament (*BRIT*), ≈ Member of Congress (*US*)

deragli'are [deraʎ'ʎare] vi to be derailed; **far ~** to derail

de'ridere vt to mock, deride

de'risi *ecc vb vedi* **deridere**

de'riva *sf* (*Naut, Aer*) drift; **andare alla ~** (*anche fig*) to drift

deri'vare *vi ~ da* to derive from ▶ *vt* to derive; (*corso d'acqua*) to divert

derma'tologo, -a, -gi, -ghe *sm/f* dermatologist

deru'bare *vt* to rob

des'crivere *vt* to describe; **descrizi'one** *sf* description

de'serto, -a *ag* deserted ▶ *sm* (*Geo*) desert; **isola deserta** desert island

deside'rare *vt* to want, wish for; (*sessualmente*) to desire; **~ fare/che qn faccia** to want o wish to do/sb to do; **desidera fare una passeggiata?** would you like to go for a walk?

desi'derio *sm* wish; (*più intenso, carnale*) desire

deside'roso, -a *ag ~ di* longing o eager for

desi'nenza [dezi'nɛntsa] *sf* (*Ling*) ending, inflexion

de'sistere *vi ~ da* to give up, desist from

deso'lato, -a *ag* (*paesaggio*) desolate; (*persona: spiacente*) sorry

'dessi *ecc vb vedi* **dare**

'deste *ecc vb vedi* **dare**

desti'nare *vt* to destine; (*assegnare*) to appoint, assign; (*indirizzare*) to address; **~ qc a qn** to intend to give sth to sb, intend sb to have sth; **destina'tario, -a** *sm/f* (*di lettera*) addressee

destinazi'one [destinat'tsjone] *sf* destination; (*uso*) purpose

des'tino *sm* destiny, fate

destitu'ire *vt* to dismiss, remove

'destra *sf* (*mano*) right hand; (*parte*) right (side); (*Pol*): **la ~** the Right; **a ~** (*essere*) on the right; (*andare*) to the right

destreggi'arsi [destred'dʒarsi] *vpr* to manoeuvre (*BRIT*), maneuver (*US*)

des'trezza [des'trettsa] *sf* skill, dexterity

'destro, -a *ag* right, right-hand

dete'nuto, -a *sm/f* prisoner

deter'gente [deter'dʒɛnte] *ag* (*crema, latte*) cleansing ▶ *sm* cleanser

⚠ Attenzione! In inglese esiste la parola **detergent** che però significa **detersivo**.

determi'nare *vt* to determine

determina'tivo, -a *ag* determining; **articolo ~** (*Ling*) definite article

determi'nato, -a *ag* (*particolare*) specific; (*risoluto*) determined, resolute

deter'sivo *sm* detergent

detes'tare *vt* to detest, hate

de'trae, de'traggo *ecc vb vedi* **detrarre**

de'trarre *vt ~* (*da*) to deduct (from), take away (from)

de'trassi *ecc vb vedi* **detrarre**

'detta *sf a ~ di* according to

det'taglio [det'taʎʎo] *sm* detail; (*Comm*): **il ~** retail; **al ~** (*Comm*) retail; separately

det'tare *vt* to dictate; **~ legge** (*fig*) to lay down the law; **det'tato** *sm* dictation

'detto, -a *pp di* **dire** ▶ *ag* (*soprannominato*) called, known as; (*già nominato*) above-mentioned ▶ *sm* saying; **~ fatto** no sooner said than done

devas'tare *vt* to devastate; (*fig*) to ravage

devi'are *vi ~* (*da*) to turn off (from) ▶ *vt* to divert; **deviazi'one** *sf* (*anche Aut*) diversion

'devo *ecc vb vedi* **dovere**

de'volvere *vt* (*Dir*) to transfer, devolve

de'voto, -a *ag* (*Rel*) devout, pious; (*affezionato*) devoted

devozi'one [devot'tsjone] *sf* devoutness; (*anche Rel*) devotion

di
(di+il = **del**, di+lo = **dello**, di+l' = **dell'**,
di+la = **della**, di+i = **dei**, di+gli = **degli**, di+le
= **delle**) prep

1 (possesso, specificazione) of; (composto
da, scritto da) by: **la macchina di Paolo/
mio fratello** Paolo's/my brother's car;
un amico di mio fratello a friend of my
brother's, one of my brother's friends;
un quadro di Botticelli a painting by
Botticelli

2 (caratterizzazione, misura) of: **una
casa di mattoni** a brick house, a house
made of bricks; **un orologio d'oro** a
gold watch; **un bimbo di 3 anni** a child
of 3, a 3-year-old child

3 (causa, mezzo, modo) with; **tremare
di paura** to tremble with fear; **morire
di cancro** to die of cancer; **spalmare di
burro** to spread with butter

4 (argomento) about, of: **discutere di
sport** to talk about sport

5 (luogo: provenienza) from; out of:
essere di Roma to be from Rome;
uscire di casa to come out o leave
the house

6 (tempo) in; **d'estate/d'inverno** in
(the) summer/winter; **di notte** by
night, at night; **di mattina/sera** in
the morning/evening; **di lunedì** on
Mondays

▶ det (una certa quantità di) some;
(: negativo) any; (interrogativo) any;
some; **del pane** (some) bread; **delle
caramelle** (some) sweets; **degli amici
miei** some friends of mine; **vuoi del
vino?** do you want o any wine?

dia'bete sm diabetes sg
dia'betico, -a, ci, che ag, sm/f
diabetic
dia'framma, -i sm (divisione) screen;
(Anat, Fot, contraccettivo) diaphragm
d'agnosi [di'annozi] sf diagnosis sg
diago'nale ag, sf diagonal
dia'gramma, -i sm diagram

dia'letto sm dialect
di'alisi sf dialysis sg
di'alogo, -ghi sm dialogue
dia'mante sm diamond
di'ametro sm diameter
diaposi'tiva sf transparency, slide
di'ario sm diary
diar'rea sf diarrhoea
di'avolo sm devil
di'battito sm debate, discussion
'dice ['ditʃe] vb vedi **dire**
di'cembre [di'tʃembre] sm December
dice'ria [ditʃe'ria] sf rumour, piece
of gossip
dichia'rare [dikja'rare] vt to declare;
dichiararsi vpr to declare o.s.;
(innamorato) to declare one's love;
dichiararsi vinto to acknowledge
defeat; **dichiarazi'one** sf declaration;
dichiarazione dei redditi statement
of income; (modulo) tax return
dician'nove [ditʃan'nove] num
nineteen
dicias'sette [ditʃas'sette] num
seventeen
dici'otto [di'tʃɔtto] num eighteen
dici'tura [ditʃi'tura] sf words pl,
wording
'dico ecc vb vedi **dire**
didasca'lia sf (di illustrazione)
caption; (Cine) subtitle; (Teatro) stage
directions pl
di'eci [dj'ɛtʃi] num ten
'dieci ecc vb vedi **dare**
'diesel ['dizəl] sm inv diesel engine
dies'sino, -a sm/f member of the DS
political party
di'eta sf diet; **essere a ~** to be on a diet
di'etro av behind; (in fondo) at the back
▶ prep behind; (tempo: dopo) after ▶ sm
back, rear ▶ ag inv back cpd; **le zampe
di ~** the hind legs; **~ richiesta** on
demand; (scritta) on application
di'fendere vt to defend; **difendersi**
vpr (cavarsela) to get by; **difendersi**

da/contro to defend o.s. from/
against; **difendersi dal freddo** to
protect o.s. from the cold; **difen'sore,
-a** sm/f defender; **avvocato difensore**
counsel for the defence; **di'fesa** sf
defence

di'fesi ecc vb vedi **difendere**

di'fetto sm (mancanza): **~ di** lack of;
shortage of; (di fabbricazione) fault,
flaw, defect; (morale) fault, failing,
defect; (fisico) defect; **far ~** to be
lacking; **in ~** at fault; in the wrong;
difet'toso, -a ag defective, faulty

diffe'rente [diffe'rɛnte] ag different

diffe'renza [diffe'rɛntsa] sf
difference; **a ~ di** unlike

diffe'rire vt to postpone, defer ▸ vi to
be different

diffe'rita sf **in ~** (trasmettere)
prerecorded

dif'ficile [dif'fitʃile] ag difficult;
(persona) hard to please, difficult
(to please); (poco probabile): **è ~ che
sia libero** it is unlikely that he'll be
free ▸ sm difficult part; difficulty;
difficoltà sf inv difficulty

diffi'dente ag suspicious, distrustful

diffi'denza sf suspicion, distrust

dif'fondere vt (luce, calore) to
diffuse; (notizie) to spread, circulate;
diffondersi vpr to spread

dif'fusi ecc vb vedi **diffondere**

dif'fuso, -a pp di **diffondere** ▸ ag
(malattia, fenomeno) widespread

'diga, -ghe sf dam; (portuale)
breakwater

dige'rente [didʒe'rɛnte] ag (apparato)
digestive

dige'rire [didʒe'rire] vt to digest;
digesti'one sf digestion; **diges'tivo,
-a** ag digestive ▸ sm (after-dinner)
liqueur

digi'tale [didʒi'tale] ag digital; (delle
dita) finger cpd, digital ▸ sf (Bot)
foxglove

digi'tare [didʒi'tare] vt, vi (Inform)
to key (in)

digiu'nare [didʒu'nare] vi to starve
o.s.; (Rel) to fast; **digi'uno, -a** ag
essere digiuno not to have eaten ▸ sm
fast; **a digiuno** on an empty stomach

dignità [dinni'ta] sf inv dignity

'DIGOS ['digos] sigla f (= Divisione
Investigazioni Generali e Operazioni
Speciali) police department dealing with
political security

digri'gnare [digrin'nare] vt **~ i denti**
to grind one's teeth

dilapi'dare vt to squander, waste

dila'tare vt to dilate; (gas) to cause
to expand; (passaggio, cavità) to open
(up); **dilatarsi** vpr to dilate; (Fisica)
to expand

dilazio'nare [dilattsjo'nare] vt to
delay, defer

di'lemma, -i sm dilemma

dilet'tante sm/f dilettante; (anche
Sport) amateur

dili'gente [dili'dʒɛnte] ag (scrupoloso)
diligent; (accurato) careful, accurate

dilu'ire vt to dilute

dilun'garsi vpr (fig): **~ su** to talk at
length on a subject

diluvi'are vb impers to pour (down)

di'luvio sm downpour; (inondazione,
fig) flood

dima'grante ag slimming cpd

dima'grire vi to get thinner, lose
weight

dime'nare vt to wave, shake;
dimenarsi vpr to toss and turn; (fig)
to struggle; **~ la coda** (cane) to wag
its tail

dimensi'one sf dimension;
(grandezza) size

dimenti'canza [dimenti'kantsa] sf
forgetfulness; (errore) oversight, slip;
per ~ inadvertently

dimenti'care vt to forget; **ho
dimenticato la chiave/il passaporto**

I forgot the key/my passport;
dimenticarsi vpr **dimenticarsi di qc**
to forget sth

dimesti'chezza [dimesti'kettsa] sf
familiarity

di'mettere vt ~ **qn da** to dismiss sb
from; (dall'ospedale) to discharge sb
from; **dimettersi** vpr **dimettersi (da)**
to resign (from)

dimez'zare [dimed'dzare] vt to halve

diminu'ire vt to reduce, diminish;
(prezzi) to bring down, reduce ▶ vi
to decrease, diminish; (rumore) to
die down, die away; (prezzi) to fall,
go down

diminu'tivo, -a ag, sm diminutive

diminuzi'one sf decreasing,
diminishing

di'misi ecc vb vedi **dimettere**

dimissi'oni sfpl resignation sg; **dare**
o **presentare le ~** to resign, hand in
one's resignation

dimos'trare vt to demonstrate,
show; (provare) to prove,
demonstrate; **dimostrarsi** vpr
dimostrarsi molto abile to show o.s.
o prove to be very clever; **dimostra
30 anni** he looks about 30 (years old);
dimostrazi'one sf demonstration,
proof

di'namica sf dynamics sg

di'namico, -a, -ci, -che ag dynamic

dina'mite sf dynamite

'dinamo sf inv dynamo

dino'sauro sm dinosaur

din'torni smpl outskirts; **nei ~ di** in the
vicinity o neighbourhood of

'dio (pl **'dei**) sm god; **D~** God; **gli dei** the
gods; **D~ mio!** my goodness!, my God!

diparti'mento sm department

dipen'dente ag dependent ▶ sm/f
employee; **dipendente statale** state
employee

di'pendere vi ~ **da** to depend on;
(finanziariamente) to be dependent on;

(derivare) to come from, be due to

di'pesi ecc vb vedi **dipendere**

di'pingere [di'pindʒere] vt to paint

di'pinsi ecc vb vedi **dipingere**

di'pinto, -a pp di **dipingere** ▶ sm
painting

di'ploma, -i sm diploma

diplo'matico, -a, -ci, -che ag
diplomatic ▶ sm diplomat

diploma'zia [diplomat'tsia] sf
diplomacy

di'porto: **imbarcazione da ~** sf
pleasure craft

dira'dare vt to thin (out); (visite) to
reduce, make less frequent; **diradarsi**
vpr to disperse; (nebbia) to clear (up)

'dire vt to say; (segreto, fatto) to tell; ~
qc a qn to tell sb sth; ~ **a qn di fare qc**
to tell sb to do sth; ~ **di sì/no** to say
yes/no; **si dice che ...** they say that
...; **si ~bbe che ...** it looks (o sounds)
as though ...; **dica, signora?** (in un
negozio) yes, Madam, can I help you?;
come si dice in inglese ...? what's the
English (word) for ...?

di'ressi ecc vb vedi **dirigere**

di'retta sf vedi **diretto**

di'retto, -a pp di **dirigere** ▶ ag direct
▶ sm (Ferr) through train

diret'tore, -'trice sm/f (di azienda)
director: manager/ess; (di scuola
elementare) head (teacher) (BRIT),
principal (US); **direttore d'orchestra**
conductor; **direttore vendite** sales
director o manager

direzi'one [diret'tsjone] sf board of
directors; management; (senso di
movimento) direction; **in ~ di** in the
direction of, towards

diri'gente sm/f
executive; (Pol) leader ▶ ag **classe ~**
ruling class

di'rigere [diri'dʒere] vt to direct;
(impresa) to run, manage; (Mus) to
conduct; **dirigersi** vpr **dirigersi verso**

o a to make *o* head for

dirim'petto *av* opposite; **~ a** opposite, facing

di'ritto, -a *ag* straight; *(onesto)* straight, upright ▶ *av* straight, directly; **andare ~** to go straight on ▶ *sm* right side; *(Tennis)* forehand; *(Maglia)* plain stitch; *(prerogativa)* right; *(legi, scienza)*: **il ~** law; **diritti** *smpl (tasse)* duty sg: **stare ~** to stand up straight; **aver ~ a qc** to be entitled to sth; **diritti d'autore** royalties

dirotta'mento *sm*; **dirottamento (aereo)** hijack

dirot'tare *vt (nave, aereo)* to change the course of; *(aereo sotto minaccia)* to hijack; *(traffico)* to divert ▶ *vi (nave, aereo)* to change course; **dirotta'tore, -'trice** *sm/f* hijacker

di'rotto, -a *ag (pioggia)* torrential; *(pianto)* unrestrained; **piovere a ~** to pour; **piangere a ~** to cry one's heart out

di'rupo *sm* crag, precipice

di'sabile *sm/f* disabled person ▶ *ag* disabled; **i disabili** the disabled

disabi'tato, -a *ag* uninhabited

disabitu'arsi *vpr* **~ a** to get out of the habit of

disac'cordo *sm* disagreement

disadat'tato, -a *ag (Psic)* maladjusted

disa'dorno, -a *ag* plain, unadorned

disagi'ato, -a [diza'dʒato] *ag* poor, needy; *(vita)* hard

di'sagio [di'zadʒo] *sm* discomfort; *(disturbo)* inconvenience; *(fig: imbarazzo)* embarrassment; **essere a ~** to be ill at ease

disappro'vare *vt* to disapprove of; **disapprovazi'one** *sf* disapproval

disap'punto *sm* disappointment

disar'mare *vt, vi* to disarm; **di'sarmo** *sm (Mil)* disarmament

di'sastro *sm* disaster

disas'troso, -a *ag* disastrous

disat'tento, -a *ag* inattentive; **disattenzi'one** *sf* carelessness, lack of attention

disavven'tura *sf* misadventure, mishap

dis'capito *sm* **a ~ di** to the detriment of

dis'carica, -che *sf (di rifiuti)* rubbish tip *o* dump

di'scendere [diʃ'ʃɛndere] *vt* to go *(o* come) down ▶ *vi* to go *(o* come) down; *(strada)* to go down; *(smontare)* to get off; **~ da** *(famiglia)* to be descended from; **~ dalla macchina/dal treno** to get out of the car/out of *o* off the train; **~ da cavallo** to dismount, get off one's horse

di'scesa [diʃ'ʃesa] *sf* descent; *(pendio)* slope; **in ~** *(strada)* downhill *cpd*, sloping; **discesa libera** *(Sci)* downhill *(race)*

disci'plina [diʃʃi'plina] *sf* discipline

'disco, -schi *sm* disc; *(Sport)* discus; *(fonografico)* record; *(Inform)* disk; **disco orario** *(Aut)* parking disc; **disco rigido** *(Inform)* hard disk; **disco volante** flying saucer

disco'grafico, -a, ci, che *ag* record *cpd*, recording *cpd* ▶ *sm* record producer; **casa discografica** record(ing) company

dis'correre *vi* **~ (di)** to talk (about)

dis'corso, -a *pp di* **discorrere** ▶ *sm* speech; *(conversazione)* conversation, talk

disco'teca, -che *sf (raccolta)* record library; *(locale)* disco

discre'panza [diskre'pantsa] *sf* disagreement

dis'creto, -a *ag* discreet; *(abbastanza buono)* reasonable, fair

discriminazi'one [diskriminat'tsjone] *sf* discrimination

dis'cussi *ecc vb vedi* **discutere**

discussi'one *sf* discussion; (*litigio*) argument; **fuori ~** out of the question

dis'cutere *vt* to discuss, debate; (*contestare*) to question ▶ *vi* (*conversare*): **~ (di)** to discuss; (*litigare*) to argue

dis'detta *sf* (*di prenotazione ecc*) cancellation; (*sfortuna*) bad luck

dis'dire *vt* (*prenotazione*) to cancel; (*Dir*): **~ un contratto d'affitto** to give notice (to quit); **vorrei ~ la mia prenotazione** I want to cancel my booking

dise'gnare [diseɲˈɲare] *vt* to draw; (*progettare*) to design; (*fig*) to outline

disegna'tore, -'trice *sm/f* designer

di'segno [diˈseɲɲo] *sm* drawing; design; outline; **disegno di legge** (*Dir*) bill

diser'bante *sm* weed-killer

diser'tare *vt, vi* to desert

dis'fare *vt* to undo; (*valigie*) to unpack; (*meccanismo*) to take to pieces; (*neve*) to melt; **disfarsi** *vpr* to come undone; (*neve*) to melt; **~ il letto** to strip the bed; **disfarsi di qn** (*liberarsi*) to get rid of sb; **dis'fatto, -a** *pp di* **disfare**

dis'gelo [dizˈdʒɛlo] *sm* thaw

dis'grazia [dizˈɡrattsja] *sf* (*sventura*) misfortune; (*incidente*) accident, mishap

disgu'ido *sm* hitch; **disguido postale** error in postal delivery

disgus'tare *vt* to disgust

dis'gusto *sm* disgust; **disgus'toso, -a** *ag* disgusting

disidra'tare *vt* to dehydrate

disimpa'rare *vt* to forget

disinfet'tante *ag, sm* disinfectant

disinfet'tare *vt* to disinfect

disini'bito, -a *ag* uninhibited

disinstal'lare *vt* (*software*) to uninstall

disinte'grare *vt, vi* to disintegrate;

disintegrarsi *vpr* to disintegrate

disinteres'sarsi *vpr* **~ di** to take no interest in

disinte'resse *sm* indifference; (*generosità*) unselfishness

disintossi'carsi *vpr* to clear out one's system; (*alcolizzato, drogato*) to be treated for alcoholism (*o drug addiction*)

disin'volto, -a *ag* casual, free and easy

dismi'sura *sf* excess; **a ~** to excess, excessively

disoccu'pato, -a *ag* unemployed ▶ *sm/f* unemployed person; **disoccupazi'one** *sf* unemployment

diso'nesto, -a *ag* dishonest

disordi'nato, -a *ag* untidy; (*privo di misura*) irregular, wild

di'sordine *sm* (*confusione*) disorder, confusion; (*sregolatezza*) debauchery; **disordini** *smpl* (*Pol ecc*) disorder *sg*; (*tumulti*) riots

disorien'tare *vt* to disorientate

disorien'tato, -a *ag* disorientated

dispari *ag inv* odd, uneven

dis'parte: **in ~** *av* (*da lato*) aside, apart; **tenersi o starsene in ~** to keep to o.s., hold o.s. aloof

dispendi'oso, -a *ag* expensive

dis'pensa *sf* pantry, larder; (*mobile*) sideboard; (*Dir*) dispensation; (*Rel*) dispensation; (*fascicolo*) number, issue

dispe'rare *vi, vt* to disorientate *[...]*

dis'perato, -a *ag* (*persona*) in despair; (*caso, tentativo*) desperate

disperazi'one *sf* despair

dis'perdere *vt* (*disseminare*) to disperse; (*Mil*) to scatter, rout; (*fig*: *consumare*) to waste, squander; **disperdersi** *vpr* to disperse; to scatter; **dis'perso, -a** *pp di* **disperdere** ▶ *sm/f* missing person

dis'petto *sm spite no pl*, spitefulness *no pl*; **fare un ~ a qn** to play a (nasty) trick on sb; **a ~ di** in spite of;

dispet'toso, -a *ag* spiteful

dispia'cere [dispja'tʃere] *sm* (*rammarico*) regret, sorrow; (*dolore*) grief; **dispiaceri** *smpl* (*preoccupazioni*) troubles, worries *vi* **~ a** to displease ♦ *vb impers* **mi dispiace (che)** I am sorry (that); **le dispiace se...?** do you mind if ...?

dis'pone, dis'pongo *ecc vb vedi* **disporre**

dispo'nibile *ag* available

dis'porre *vt* (*sistemare*) to arrange; (*preparare*) to prepare; (*Dir*) to order; (*persuadere*): **~ qn a** to incline o dispose sb towards ♦ *vi* (*decidere*) to decide; (*usufruire*): **~ di** to use, have at one's disposal; (*essere dotato*): **~ di** to have

dis'posi *ecc vb vedi* **disporre**

dispo'sitivo *sm* (*meccanismo*) device

disposizi'one [dispozit'tsjone] *sf* arrangement, layout; (*stato d'animo*) mood; (*tendenza*) bent, inclination; (*comando*) order; (*Dir*) provision, regulation; **a ~ di qn** at sb's disposal

dis'posto, -a *pp di* **disporre**

disprez'zare [dispret'tsare] *vt* to despise

dis'prezzo [dis'prettso] *sm* contempt

'disputa *sf* dispute, quarrel

dispu'tare *vt* (*contendere*) to dispute, contest; (*gara*) to take part in ♦ *vi* to quarrel; **~ di** to discuss; **disputarsi qc** to fight for sth

'disse *vb vedi* **dire**

dissente'ria *sf* dysentery

dissen'tire *vi* **~ (da)** to disagree (with)

disse'tante *ag* refreshing

'dissi *vb vedi* **dire**

dissimu'lare *vt* (*fingere*) to dissemble; (*nascondere*) to conceal

dissi'pare *vt* to dissipate; (*scialacquare*) to squander, waste

dissu'adere *vt* **~ qn da** to dissuade sb from

distac'care *vt* to detach, separate; (*Sport*) to leave behind; **distaccarsi** *vpr* to be detached; (*fig*) to stand out; **distaccarsi da** (*fig: allontanarsi*) to grow away from

dis'tacco, -chi *sm* (*separazione*) separation; (*indifferenza*) detachment; (*Sport*): **vincere con un ~ di ...** to win by a distance of ...

dis'tante *av* far away ♦ *ag* **~ (da)** distant (from), far away (from)

dis'tanza [dis'tantsa] *sf* distance

distanzi'are [distan'tsjare] *vt* to space out, place at intervals; (*Sport*) to outdistance; (*fig: superare*) to outstrip, surpass

dis'tare *vi* **distiamo pochi chilometri da Roma** we are only a few kilometres (away) from Rome; **quanto dista il centro da qui?** how far is the town centre?

dis'tendere *vt* (*coperta*) to spread out; (*gambe*) to stretch (out); (*mettere a giacere*) to lay; (*rilassare: muscoli, nervi*) to relax; **distendersi** *vpr* (*rilassarsi*) to relax; (*sdraiarsi*) to lie down

dis'tesa *sf* expanse, stretch

dis'teso, -a *pp di* **distendere**

distil'lare *vt* to distil

distille'ria *sf* distillery

distin'guere *vt* to distinguish; **distinguersi** *vpr* (*essere riconoscibile*) to be distinguished; (*emergere*) to stand out, be conspicuous, distinguish o.s.

dis'tinta *sf* (*nota*) note; (*elenco*) list; **distinta di versamento** pay-in slip

distin'tivo, -a *ag* distinctive; distinguishing ♦ *sm* badge

dis'tinto, -a *pp di* **distinguere** ♦ *ag* (*dignitoso ed elegante*) distinguished; **"distinti saluti"** (*in lettera*) yours faithfully

distinzi'one [distin'tsjone] *sf* distinction

dis'togliere [dis'tɔʎʎere] *vt* **~ da** to

take away from; (fig) to dissuade from

distorsi'one sf (Med) sprain; (Fisica, Ottica) distortion

dis'trarre vt to distract; (divertire) to entertain, amuse; **distrarsi** vpr (non fare attenzione) to be distracted, let one's mind wander; (svagarsi) to amuse o enjoy o.s.; **dis'tratto, -a** pp di **distrarre** ▶ ag absent-minded; (disattento) inattentive; **distrazi'one** sf absent-mindedness; inattention; (svago) distraction, entertainment

dis'tretto sm district

distribu'ire vt to distribute; (Carte) to deal (out); (posta) to deliver; (lavoro) to allocate, assign; (ripartire) to share out; **distribu'tore** sm (di benzina) petrol (BRIT) o gas (US) pump; (Aut, Elettr) distributor; **distributore automatico** vending machine

distri'care vt to disentangle, unravel; **districarsi** vpr (tirarsi fuori): **districarsi da** to get out of, disentangle o.s. from

dis'truggere [dis'trudʒere] vt to destroy; **distruzi'one** sf destruction

distur'bare vt to disturb, trouble; (sonno, lezioni) to disturb, interrupt; **disturbarsi** vpr to put o.s. out

dis'turbo sm trouble, bother, inconvenience; (indisposizione) (slight) disorder, ailment; **scusi il ~** I'm sorry to trouble you

disubbidi'ente ag disobedient

disubbi'dire vi ~ (a qn) to disobey (sb)

disu'mano, -a ag inhuman

di'tale sm thimble

'dito sm (pl(f) 'dita) sm finger; (misura) finger, finger's breadth; **dito (del piede)** toe

'ditta sf firm, business

ditta'tore sm dictator

ditta'tura sf dictatorship

dit'tongo, -ghi sm diphthong

d'urno, -a ag day cpd, daytime cpd

'diva sf vedi divo

di'vano sm sofa; divan; **divano letto** bed settee, sofa bed

divari'care vt to open wide

di'vario sm difference

diven'tare vi to become; ~ **famoso/professore** to become famous/a teacher

diversifi'care vt to diversify, vary; to differentiate; **diversificarsi** vpr **diversificarsi (per)** to differ (in)

diversità sf inv difference, diversity; (varietà) variety

diver'sivo sm diversion

di'verso, -a ag (differente) ~ **(da)** different (from); **diversi, -e** det pl several, various; (Comm) sundry pron pl several (people), many (people)

diver'tente ag amusing

diverti'mento sm amusement, pleasure; (passatempo) pastime, recreation

diver'tire vt to amuse, entertain; **divertirsi** vpr to amuse o enjoy o.s.

di'videre vt (anche Mat) to divide; (distribuire, ripartire) to divide (up), split (up); **dividersi** vpr (separarsi) to separate; (strade) to fork

divi'eto sm prohibition; "~ **di sosta**" (Aut) "no parking"

divinco'larsi vpr to wriggle, writhe

di'vino, -a ag divine

di'visa sf (Mil ecc) uniform; (Comm) foreign currency

di'visi ecc vb vedi **dividere**

divisi'one sf division

'divo, -a sm/f star

divo'rare vt to devour

divorzi'are [divor'tsjare] vi ~ **(da qn)** to divorce (sb)

di'vorzio [di'vortsjo] sm divorce

divul'gare vt to divulge, disclose; (rendere comprensibile) to popularize

dizio'nario [ditsjo'narjo] sm dictionary

DJ [di'dʒei] sigla m/f (= Disk Jockey) DJ

do sm (Mus) C; (: solfeggiando) do(h)

dobbi'amo vb vedi **dovere**

D.O.C. [dɔk] abbr (= denominazione di origine controllata) label guaranteeing the quality of wine

'doccia, -ce ['dɔttʃa] sf (bagno) shower; **fare la ~** to have a shower

do'cente [do'tʃente] ag teaching ▶ sm/f teacher; (di università) lecturer

'docile ['dɔtʃile] ag docile

documen'tario sm documentary

documen'tarsi vpr **~ (su)** to gather information o material (about)

docu'mento sm document; **documenti** smpl (d'identità ecc) papers

dodi'cesimo, -a [dodi'tʃezimo] num twelfth

'dodici ['doditʃi] num twelve

do'gana sf (ufficio) customs pl; (tassa) (customs) duty; **passare la ~** to go through customs; **dogani'ere** sm customs officer

'doglie ['dɔʎʎe] sfpl (Med) labour sg, labour pains

'dolce ['doltʃe] ag sweet; (carattere, persona) gentle, mild; (fig: mite: clima) mild; (non ripido: pendio) gentle ▶ sm (sapore dolce) sweetness, sweet taste; (Cuc: portata) sweet, dessert; (: torta) cake; **dolci'ficante** sm sweetener

'dollaro sm dollar

Dolo'miti sfpl **le ~** the Dolomites

do'lore sm (fisico) pain; (morale) sorrow, grief; **dolo'roso, -a** ag painful; sorrowful, sad

do'manda sf (interrogazione) question; (richiesta) demand; (: cortese) request; (Dir: richiesta scritta) application; (Econ): **la ~** demand; **fare una ~ a qn** to ask sb a question; **fare ~ (per un lavoro)** to apply (for a job)

doman'dare vt (per avere) to ask for; (per sapere) to ask; (esigere) to demand; **domandarsi** vpr to wonder; to ask o.s.; **~ qc a qn** to ask sb for sth; to

ask sb sth

do'mani av tomorrow ▶ sm **il ~** (il futuro) the future; (il giorno successivo) the next day; **~ l'altro** the day after tomorrow

do'mare vt to tame

doma'tore, -'trice sm/f (gen) tamer; **domatore di cavalli** horsebreaker; **domatore di leoni** lion tamer

domat'tina av tomorrow morning

do'menica, -che [do'menika] sf Sunday; **di** o **la ~** on Sundays

do'mestico, -a, -ci, -che ag domestic ▶ sm/f servant, domestic

domi'cilio [domi'tʃiljo] sm (Dir) domicile, place of residence

domi'nare vt to dominate; (fig: sentimenti) to control, master ▶ vi to be in the dominant position

do'nare vt to give, present; (per beneficenza ecc) to donate ▶ vi (fig): **~ a** to suit, become; **~ sangue** to give blood; **dona'tore, -'trice** sm/f donor; **donatore di sangue/di organi** blood/organ donor

dondo'lare vt (cullare) to rock; **dondolarsi** vpr to swing, sway; **'dondolo** sm **sedia/cavallo a dondolo** rocking chair/horse

'donna sf woman; **donna di casa** housewife; home-loving woman; **donna di servizio** maid

donnai'olo sm ladykiller

'donnola sf weasel

'dono sm gift

doping ['dɔpiŋ] sm doping

'dopo av (tempo) afterwards; (più tardi) later; (luogo) after, next ▶ prep after ▶ cong (temporale): **~ aver studiato** after having studied; **~ mangiato** va **a dormire** after having eaten o after a meal he goes for a sleep ▶ ag inv **il giorno ~** the following day; **un anno ~** a year later; **~ di me/lui** after me/him; **~, a ~!** see you later!

dopo'barba sm inv after-shave

dopodo'mani av the day after tomorrow

doposci [dopoʃˈʃi] sm inv après-ski outfit

dopo'sole sm inv aftersun (lotion)

dopo'tutto av (tutto considerato) after all

doppi'aggio [dopˈpjaddʒo] sm (Cinema) dubbing

doppi'are vt (Naut) to round; (Sport) to lap; (Cinema) to dub

doppio, -a ag double; (fig: falso) double-dealing, deceitful ▸ sm (quantità): **il ~ (di)** twice as much (o many), double the amount (o number) of; (Sport) doubles pl ▸ av double

doppi'one sm duplicate (copy)

doppio'petto sm double-breasted jacket

dormicchi'are [dormikˈkjare] vi to doze

dormigli'one, -a [dormiʎˈʎone] sm/f sleepyhead

dor'mire vt, vi to sleep; **andare a ~** to go to bed; **dor'mita** sf **farsi una dormita** to have a good sleep

dormi'torio sm dormitory

dormi'veglia [dormiˈveʎʎa] sm drowsiness

'dorso sm back; (di montagna) ridge, crest; (di libro) spine; **a ~ di cavallo** on horseback

do'sare vt to measure out; (Med) to dose

'dose sf quantity, amount; (Med) dose

do'tato, -a ag **~ di** (attrezzature) equipped with; (bellezza, intelligenza) endowed with; **un uomo ~** a gifted man

'dote sf (di sposa) dowry; (assegnata a un ente) endowment; (fig) gift, talent

Dott. abbr (= dottore) Dr.

dotto'rato sm degree; **dottorato di**

ricerca doctorate, doctor's degree

dot'tore, -essa sm/f doctor; **chiamate un ~** call a doctor

● **dottore**

● In Italy, anyone who has a degree
● in any subject can use the title
● **dottore**. Thus a person who
● is addressed as **dottore** is not
● necessarily a doctor of medicine.

dot'trina sf doctrine

Dott.ssa abbr (= dottoressa) Dr.

'dove av (gen) where; (in cui) where, in which; (dovunque) wherever ▸ cong (mentre, laddove) whereas; **~ sei?/vai?** where are you?/are you going?; **dimmi dov'è** tell me where it is; **di ~ sei?** where are you from?; **per ~ si passa?** which way should we go?; **la città ~ abito** the town where o in which I live; **siediti ~ vuoi** sit wherever you like

do'vere sm (obbligo) duty ▸ vt (essere debitore): **~ qc (a qn)** to owe (sb) sth ▸ vi (seguito dall'infinito: obbligo) to have to; **rivolgersi a chi di ~** to apply to the appropriate authority o person; **lui deve farlo** he has to do it, he must do it; **quanto le devo?** how much do I owe you?; **è dovuto partire** he had to leave; **ha dovuto pagare** he had to pay; (: intenzione): **devo partire domani** I'm (due) to leave tomorrow; (: probabilità): **dev'essere tardi** it must be late; **come si deve** (lavorare, comportarsi) properly; **una persona come si deve** a respectable person

dove'roso, -a ag (right and) proper

dovrò ecc vb vedi **dovere**

do'vunque av (in qualunque luogo) wherever; (dappertutto) everywhere; **~ io vada** wherever I go

do'vuto, -a ag (causato): **~ a** due to

doz'zina [dodˈdzina] sf dozen; **una ~ di uova** a dozen eggs

dozzi'nale [doddziˈnale] ag cheap,

second-rate

'drago, -ghi sm dragon

'dramma, -i sm drama; **dram'matico, -a, -ci, -che** ag dramatic

'drastico, -a, -ci, -che ag drastic

'dritto, -a ag, av = **diritto**

'droga, -ghe sf (sostanza aromatica) spice; (stupefacente) drug; **droghe leggere/pesanti** soft/hard drugs

drogarsi vpr to take drugs

dro'gato, -a sm/f drug addict

droghe'ria [droge'ria] sf grocer's shop (BRIT), grocery (store) (US)

drome'dario sm dromedary

DS [di'esse] sigla mpl (= Democratici di Sinistra) Italian left-wing party

'dubbio, -a ag (incerto) doubtful, dubious; (ambiguo) dubious ▶ sm (incertezza) doubt; **avere il ~ che** to be afraid that, suspect that; **mettere in ~ qc** to question sth

dubi'tare vi ~ **di** to doubt; (risultato) to be doubtful of

Dub'lino sm Dublin

'duca, -chi sm duke

du'chessa [du'kessa] sf duchess

'due num two

due'cento [due'tʃento] num two hundred ▶ sm **il D~** the thirteenth century

due'pezzi [due'pettsi] sm (costume da bagno) two-piece swimsuit; (abito femminile) two-piece suit

'dunque (perciò) so, therefore; (riprendendo il discorso) well (then) ▶ sm inv **venire al ~** to come to the point

du'omo sm cathedral

> Attenzione! In inglese esiste la parola **dome**, che però significa **cupola**.

dupli'cato sm duplicate

'duplice ['duplitʃe] ag double, twofold; **in ~ copia** in duplicate

du'rante prep during

du'rare vi to last; ~ **fatica a** to have difficulty in

du'rezza [du'rettsa] sf hardness; stubbornness; harshness; toughness

'duro, -a ag (pietra, lavoro, materasso, problema) hard; (persona: ostinato) stubborn, obstinate; (severo) harsh, hard; (voce) harsh; (carne) tough ▶ sm hardness; (difficoltà) hard part; (persona) tough guy; **tener ~** to stand firm, hold out; **~ d'orecchi** hard of hearing

DVD [divu'di] sigla m (= digital versatile (or) video disc) DVD; (lettore) DVD player

e

e (dav V spesso **ed**) cong and; **e lui?** what about him?; **e comprало!** well buy it then!

E abbr (= est) E

è vb vedi **essere**

'ebbi ecc vb vedi **avere**

e'braico, -a, -ci, -che ag Hebrew, Hebraic ▶ sm (Ling) Hebrew

e'breo, -a ag Jewish ▶ sm/f Jew/ess

EC abbr (= Eurocity) fast train connecting Western European cities

ecc. av abbr (= eccetera) etc

eccel'lente [ettʃel'lɛnte] ag excellent

ec'centrico, -a, -ci, -che [et'tʃɛntriko] ag eccentric

ecces'sivo, -a [ettʃes'sivo] ag excessive

ec'cesso [et'tʃɛsso] sm excess; **all'~** (gentile, generoso) excessively; **eccesso di velocità** (Aut) speeding

ec'cetera [et'tʃɛtera] av et cetera, and so on

ec'cetto [et'tʃɛtto] prep except, with the exception of; **~ che** except, other than; **~ che (non)** unless

eccezio'nale [ettʃetsjo'nale] ag exceptional

eccezi'one [ettʃet'tsjone] sf exception; (Dir) objection; **a ~ di** with the exception of, except for; **d'~** exceptional

ecci'tare [ettʃi'tare] vt (curiosità, interesse) to excite, arouse; (folla) to incite; **eccitarsi** vpr to get excited; (sessualmente) to become aroused

'ecco av (per dimostrare): **~ il treno!** here's o here comes the train!; (dav pron): **~mi!** here I am!; **~ne uno!** here's one (of them)!; (dav pp): **~ fatto!** there, that's it done!

ec'come av rather; **ti piace? —~!** do you like it? — I'll say! o and how! o rather! (BRIT)

e'clisse sf eclipse

'eco (pl(m) **'echi**) sm o f echo

ecogra'fia sf (Med) scan

ecolo'gia [ekolo'dʒia] sf ecology

eco'logico, -a, ci, che [eko'lɔdʒiko] ag ecological

econo'mia sf economy; (scienza) economics sg; (risparmio: azione) saving; **fare ~** to economize, make economies; **eco'nomico, -a, -ci, -che** ag economic; (poco costoso) economical

ecstasy ['ɛkstazi] sf Ecstasy

'edera sf ivy

e'dicola sf newspaper kiosk o stand (US)

edi'ficio [edi'fitʃo] sm building

e'dile ag building cpd

Edim'burgo sf Edinburgh

edi'tore, -'trice ag publishing cpd
▶ sm/f publisher

⚠ Attenzione! In inglese esiste la parola editor, che però significa redattore.

edizi'one [edit'tsjone] sf edition; (tiratura) printing; **edizione straordinaria** special edition

edu'care vt to educate; (gusto, mente) to train; **~ qn a fare** to train sb to do; **edu'cato, -a** ag polite, well-mannered; **educazi'one** sf education; (familiare) upbringing; (comportamento) (good) manners pl; **educazione fisica** (Ins) physical training o education

⚠ Attenzione! In inglese esiste la parola educated, che però significa istruito.

educherò ecc [eduke'rɔ] vb vedi educare

effemi'nato, -a ag effeminate

efferve'scente [efferveʃ'ʃɛnte] ag effervescent

effet'tivo, -a ag (reale) real, actual; (impiegato, professore) permanent; (Mil) regular ▶ sm (Mil) strength; (di patrimonio ecc) sum total

ef'fetto sm effect; (Comm: cambiale) bill; (fig: impressione) impression; **in effetti** in fact, actually; **effetto serra** greenhouse effect; **effetti personali** personal effects, personal belongings

effi'cace [effi'katʃe] ag effective

effici'ente [effi'tʃɛnte] ag efficient

E'geo [e'dʒɛo] sm **l'~, il mare ~** the Aegean (Sea)

E'gitto [e'dʒitto] sm **l'~** Egypt

egizi'ano, -a [edʒit'tsjano] ag, sm/f Egyptian

'egli ['eʎʎi] pron he; **~ stesso** he himself

ego'ismo sm selfishness, egoism;

ego'ista, -i, -e ag selfish, egoistic ▸ sm/f egoist

Egr. abbr = **egregio**

e'gregio, -a, -gi, -gie [e'grɛdʒo] ag (nelle lettere): **E~ Signore** Dear Sir

E.I. abbr = **Esercito Italiano**

elabo'rare vt (progetto) to work out, elaborate; (dati) to process

elasticiz'zato, -a [elastitʃid'dzato] ag stretch cpd

e'lastico, -a, -ci, -che ag elastic; (fig: andatura) springy; (: decisione, vedute) flexible ▸ sm (di gomma) rubber band; (per il cucito) elastic no pl

ele'fante sm elephant

ele'gante ag elegant

e'leggere [e'lɛddʒere] vt to elect

elemen'tare ag elementary; **le (scuole) elementari** sfpl primary (BRIT) o grade (US) school

ele'mento sm element; (parte componente) element, component, part; **elementi** smpl (della scienza ecc) elements, rudiments

ele'mosina sf charity, alms pl; **chiedere l'~** to beg

elen'care vt to list

elencherò ecc [elenke'rɔ] vb vedi **elencare**

e'lenco, -chi sm list; **elenco telefonico** telephone directory

e'lessi ecc vb vedi **eleggere**

eletto'rale ag electoral, election cpd

elet'tore, -'trice sm/f voter, elector

elet'trauto sm inv workshop for car electrical repairs; (tecnico) car electrician

elettri'cista, -i [elettri'tʃista] sm electrician

elettricità [elettritʃi'ta] sf electricity

e'lettrico, -a, -ci, -che ag electric(al)

elettriz'zante [elettrid'dzante] ag (fig) electrifying, thrilling

elettriz'zare [elettrid'dzare] vt to electrify; **elettrizzarsi** vpr to become

charged with electricity

e'lettro... prefisso:

elettrodo'mestico, -a, -ci, -che ag apparecchi elettrodomestici domestic (electrical) appliances;

elet'tronico, -a, -ci, -che ag electronic

elezi'one [elet'tsjone] sf election; **elezioni** sfpl (Pol) election(s)

'elica, -che sf propeller

eli'cottero sm helicopter

elimi'nare vt to eliminate

elisoc'corso sm helicopter ambulance

el'metto sm helmet

elogi'are [elo'dʒare] vt to praise

elo'quente ag eloquent

e'ludere vt to evade

e'lusi ecc vb vedi **eludere**

e-mail [i'meil] sf inv (messaggio, sistema) e-mail ▸ ag inv (indirizzo) e-mail

emargi'nato, -a [emardʒi'nato] sm/f outcast; **emarginazione** [emardʒinat'tsjone] sf marginalization

embri'one sm embryo

emenda'mento sm amendment

emer'genza [emer'dʒɛntsa] sf emergency; **in caso di ~** in an emergency

e'mergere [e'mɛrdʒere] vi to emerge; (sommergibile) to surface; (fig: distinguersi) to stand out

e'mersi ecc vb vedi **emergere**

e'mettere vt (suono, luce) to give out, emit; (onde radio) to send out; (assegno, francobollo, ordine) to issue

emi'crania sf migraine

emi'grare vi to emigrate

emis'fero sm hemisphere; **emisfero australe** southern hemisphere; **emisfero boreale** northern hemisphere

e'misi ecc vb vedi **emettere**

emit'tente ag (banca) issuing; (Radio)

broadcasting, transmitting ▶ *sf* (*Radio*) transmitter

emorra'gia, -'gie [emorra'dʒia] *sf* haemorrhage

emor'roidi *sfpl* haemorrhoids *pl* (*BRIT*), hemorrhoids *pl* (*US*)

emo'tivo, -a *ag* emotional

emozio'nante [emottsjo'nante] *ag* exciting, thrilling

emozionare [emottsjo'nare] *vt* (*commuovere*) to move; (*agitare*) to make nervous; (*elettrizzare*) to excite; **emozionarsi** *vpr* to be moved: to be nervous; to be excited: **emozionato, -a** [emottsjo'nato] *ag* (*commosso*) moved; (*agitato*) nervous; (*elettrizzato*) excited

emozi'one [emot'tsjone] *sf* emotion; (*agitazione*) excitement

enciclope'dia [entʃiklope'dia] *sf* encyclopaedia

endove'noso, -a *ag* (*Med*) intravenous

'E.N.E.L. ['enel] *sigla m* (= *Ente Nazionale per l'Energia Elettrica*) *national electricity company*

ener'getico, -a, ci, che [ener'dʒetiko] *ag* (*risorse, crisi*) energy *cpd*; (*sostanza, alimento*) energy-giving

ener'gia, -'gie [ener'dʒia] *sf* (*Fisica*) energy; (*fig*) energy, strength, vigour; **energia eolica** wind power; **energia solare** solar power; **e'nergico, -a, -ci, -che** *ag* energetic, vigorous

'enfasi *sf* emphasis; (*peg*) bombast, pomposity

en'nesimo, -a *ag* (*Mat, fig*) nth; **per l'ennesima volta** for the umpteenth time

e'norme *ag* enormous, huge

'ente *sm* (*istituzione*) body, board, corporation; (*Filosofia*) being; **enti pubblici** public bodies; **ente di ricerca** research organization

en'trambi, -e *pron pl* both (of them) ▶ *ag pl* ~ **i ragazzi** both boys, both of the boys

en'trare *vi* to go (o come) in; ~ **in** (*luogo*) to enter, go (o come) into; (*trovar posto, poter stare*) to fit into; (*essere ammesso a: club ecc*) to join, become a member of; ~ **in automobile** to get into the car; **far ~ qn** (*visitatore ecc*) to show sb in; **questo non c'entra** (*fig*) that's got nothing to do with it; **en'trata** *sf* entrance, entry; **dov'è l'entrata?** where's the entrance?; **entrate** *sfpl* (*Comm*) receipts, takings; (*Econ*) income *sg*

'entro *prep* (*temporale*) within

entusias'mare *vt* to excite, fill with enthusiasm; **entusiasmarsi** *vpr* **entusiasmarsi (per qc/qn)** to become enthusiastic (about sth/sb); **entusi'asmo** *sm* enthusiasm; **entusi'asta, -i, -e** *ag* enthusiastic ▶ *sm/f* enthusiast

epa'tite *sf* hepatitis

epide'mia *sf* epidemic

epiles'sia *sf* epilepsy

epi'lettico, -a, ci, che *ag, sm/f* epileptic

epi'sodio *sm* episode

'epoca, -che *sf* (*periodo storico*) age, era; (*tempo*) time; (*Geo*) age

ep'pure *cong* and yet, nevertheless

EPT *sigla m* (= *Ente Provinciale per il Turismo*) *district tourist bureau*

equa'tore *sm* equator

equazi'one [ekwat'tsjone] *sf* (*Mat*) equation

e'questre *ag* equestrian

equi'librio *sm* balance, equilibrium; **perdere l'equilibrare** to lose one's balance

e'quino, -a *ag* horse *cpd*, equine

equipaggia'mento [ekwipaddʒa'mento] *sm* (*operazione*)

di nave) equipping, fitting out; (: *di spedizione, esercito*) equipping, kitting out; (*attrezzatura*) equipment

equipaggi'are [ekwipad'dʒare] vt (*di persone*) to man; (*di mezzi*) to equip; **equipaggiarsi** vpr to equip o.s.; **equi'paggio** sm crew

equitazi'one [ekwitat'tsjone] sf (*horse-)riding

equiva'lente ag, sm equivalent

e'quivoco, -a, -ci, -che ag equivocal, ambiguous; (*sospetto*) dubious ▶ sm misunderstanding; **a scanso di equivoci** to avoid any misunderstanding; **giocare sull'~** to equivocate

'equo, -a ag fair, just

'era sf era

'era ecc vb vedi **essere**

'erba sf grass; **in ~** (*fig*) budding; **erbe aromatiche** herbs; **erba medica** lucerne; **er'baccia, -ce** sf weed

erboriste'ria sf (*scienza*) study of medicinal herbs; (*negozio*) herbalist's (shop)

e'rede sm/f heir; **eredità** sf (*Dir*) inheritance; (*Biol*) heredity; **lasciare** qc **in eredità a** qn to leave o bequeath sth to sb; **eredi'tare** vt to inherit; **eredi'tario, -a** ag hereditary

ere'mita, -i sm hermit

er'gastolo sm (*Dir: pena*) life imprisonment

'erica sf heather

er'metico, -a, -ci, -che ag hermetic

'ernia sf (*Med*) hernia

'ero vb vedi **essere**

e'roe sm hero

ero'gare vt (*somme*) to distribute; (*gas, servizi*) to supply

e'roico, -a, -ci, -che ag heroic

ero'ina sf heroine; (*droga*) heroin

erosi'one sf erosion

e'rotico, -a, -ci, -che ag erotic

er'rato, -a ag wrong

er'rore sm error, mistake; (*morale*) error; **per ~** by mistake; **ci dev'essere un ~** there must be some mistake; **errore giudiziario** miscarriage of justice

eruzi'one [erut'tsjone] sf eruption

esacer'bare [ezatʃer'bare] vt to exacerbate

esage'rare [ezadʒe'rare] vt to exaggerate ▶ vi to exaggerate; (*eccedere*) to go too far

esal'tare vt to exalt; (*entusiasmare*) to excite, stir

e'same sm examination; (*Ins*) exam, examination; **fare** o **dare un ~** to sit o take an exam; **esame di guida** driving test; **esame del sangue** blood test

esami'nare vt to examine

esaspe'rare vt to exasperate; to exacerbate

esatta'mente av exactly; accurately, precisely

esat'tezza [ezat'tettsa] sf exactitude, accuracy, precision

e'satto, -a pp di **esigere** ▶ ag (*calcolo, ora*) correct, right, exact; (*preciso*) accurate, precise; (*puntuale*) punctual

esau'dire vt to grant, fulfil

esau'riente ag exhaustive

esauri'mento sm exhaustion; **esaurimento nervoso** nervous breakdown

esau'rire vt (*stancare*) to exhaust, wear out; (*provviste, miniera*) to exhaust; **esaurirsi** vpr to exhaust o.s., wear o.s. out; (*provviste*) to run out; **esau'rito, -a** ag exhausted; (*merci*) sold out; **registrare il tutto esaurito** (*Teatro*) to have a full house; **e'sausto, -a** ag exhausted

'esca (*pl* **'esche**) sf bait

'esce [ˈɛʃʃe] vb vedi **uscire**

eschi'mese [eski'mese] ag, sm/f

Eskimo

'esci ['ɛʃʃi] vb vedi **uscire**

escla'mare vi to exclaim, cry out

esclama'tivo, -a ag **punto ~** exclamation mark

esclamazi'one sf exclamation

es'cludere vt to exclude

es'clusi ecc vb vedi **escludere**

esclusi'one sf exclusion; **a ~ di, fatta ~ per** except (for), apart from; **senza ~ (alcuna)** without exception; **procedere per ~** to follow a process of elimination; **senza ~ di colpi** (fig) with no holds barred; **esclusione sociale** social exclusion

esclu'siva sf (Dir, Comm) exclusive o sole rights pl

esclusiva'mente av exclusively, solely

esclu'sivo, -a ag exclusive

es'cluso, -a pp di **escludere**

'esco vb vedi **uscire**

escogi'tare [eskodʒi'tare] vt to devise, think up

'escono vb vedi **uscire**

escursi'one sf (gita) excursion, trip; (: a piedi) hike, walk; (Meteor) range; **escursione termica** temperature range

esecuzi'one [ezekut'tsjone] sf execution, carrying out; (Mus) performance; **esecuzione capitale** execution

esegu'ire vt to carry out, execute; (Mus) to perform, execute

e'sempio sm example; **per ~ for** example, for instance; **fare un ~** to give an example; **esem'plare** ag exemplary ▶ sm example; (copia) copy

eserci'tare [ezertʃi'tare] vt (professione) to practise (BRIT), practice (US); (allenare: corpo, mente) to exercise, train; (diritto) to exercise; (influenza, pressione) to exert; **esercitarsi** vpr to practise;

esercitarsi alla lotta to practise fighting

e'sercito [e'zɛrtʃito] sm army

eser'cizio [ezer'tʃittsjo] sm practice; exercising; (fisico: di matematica) exercise; (Econ) financial year; (azienda) business, concern; **in ~** (medico ecc) practising; **esercizio pubblico** (Comm) commercial concern

esi'bire vt to exhibit, display; (documenti) to produce, present; **esibirsi** vpr (attore) to perform; (fig) to show off; **esibizi'one** sf exhibition; (di documento) presentation; (spettacolo) show, performance

esi'gente [ezi'dʒente] ag demanding

e'sigere [e'zidʒere] vt (pretendere) to demand; (richiedere) to demand, require; (imposte) to collect

'esile ag (persona) slender, slim; (stelo) thin; (voce) faint

esili'are vt to exile; **e'silio** sm exile

esis'tenza [ezis'tɛntsa] sf existence

e'sistere vi to exist

esi'tare vi to hesitate

'esito sm result, outcome

'esodo sm exodus

esone'rare vt to exempt

e'sordio sm debut

esor'tare vt ~ qn a fare to urge sb to do

e'sotico, -a, -ci, -che ag exotic

es'pandere vt to expand; (confini) to extend; (influenza) to extend, spread; **espandersi** vpr to expand; **espansi'one** sf expansion; **espansione di memoria** (Inform) memory upgrade; **espan'sivo, -a** ag expansive, communicative

espatri'are vi to leave one's country

espedi'ente sm expedient

es'pellere vt to expel

esperi'enza [espe'rjɛntsa] sf experience

esperi'mento sm experiment

es'perto, -a ag, sm expert

espi'rare vt, vi to breathe out

es'plicito, -a [es'plitʃito] ag explicit
► vt to fire

es'plodere vi (anche fig) to explode

esplo'rare vt to explore

esplosi'one sf explosion

es'pone ecc vb vedi **esporre**

es'pongo, es'poni ecc vb vedi **esporre**

es'porre vt (merci) to display; (quadro) to exhibit, show; (fatti, idee) to explain, set out; (porre in pericolo, Fot) to expose; **esporsi** vpr **esporsi a** (sole, pericolo) to expose o.s. to; (critiche) to lay o.s. open to

espor'tare vt to export

es'pose ecc vb vedi **esporre**

esposizi'one [espozit'tsjone] sf displaying; exhibiting; setting out; (anche Fot) exposure; (mostra) exhibition; (narrazione) explanation, exposition

es'posto, -a pp di **esporre** ► ag ~ **a nord** facing north ► sm (Amm) statement, account; (: petizione) petition

espressi'one sf expression

espres'sivo, -a ag expressive

es'presso, -a pp di **esprimere** ► ag express ► sm (lettera) express letter; (anche: treno ~) express train; (anche: caffè ~) espresso

es'primere vt to express; **esprimersi** vpr to express o.s.

es'pulsi ecc vb vedi **espellere**

espulsi'one sf expulsion

es'senza [es'sentsa] sf essence;
essenzi'ale ag essential; **l'essenziale** the main o most important thing

essere sm being; **essere umano** human being
► vb copulativo

1 (con attributo, sostantivo) to be; **sei giovane/simpatico** you are o you're young/nice; **è medico** he is o he's a doctor

2 (+ di: appartenere) to be; **di chi è la penna?** whose pen is it?; **è di Carla** it is o it's Carla's, it belongs to Carla

3 (+ di: provenire) to be; **è di Venezia** he is o he's from Venice

4 (data, ora): **è il 15 agosto/lunedì** it is o it's the 15th of August/Monday; **che ora è, che ore sono?** what time is it?; **è l'una** it is o it's one o'clock; **sono le due** it is o it's two o'clock

5 (costare): **quant'è?** how much is it?; **sono 10 euro** it's o it's 10 euros
► vb aus

1 (attivo): **essere arrivato/venuto** to have arrived/come; **è già partita** she has already left

2 (passivo) to be; **essere fatto da** to be made by; **è stata uccisa** she has been killed

3 (riflessivo): **si sono lavati** they washed, they got washed

4 (+ da + infinito): **è da farsi subito** it must be o is to be done immediately
► vi

1 (esistere, trovarsi) to be; **sono a casa** I'm at home; **essere in piedi/seduto** to be standing/sitting

2 **esserci: c'è** there is; **ci sono** there are; **che c'è?** what's the matter?, what is it?; **ci sono!** (fig: ho capito) I get it!;
vedi anche **ci**
► vb impers **è tardi/Pasqua** it's late/ Easter; **è possibile che venga** he may come; **è così** that's the way it is.

'essi pron mpl vedi **esso**

'esso, -a pron (riferito a persona: soggetto) he/she; (: complemento) him/her

est sm east

es'tate sf summer

esteri'ore ag outward, external

es'terno, -a ag (porta, muro) outer, outside; (scala) outside; (alunno, impressione) external ▸ sm outside, exterior ▸ sm/f (allievo) day pupil; all'~ outside; per uso ~ for external use only; esterni smpl (Cinema) location shots

'estero, -a ag foreign ▸ sm all'~ abroad

es'teso, -a pp di estendere ▸ ag extensive, large; scrivere per ~ to write in full

es'tetico, -a, -ci, -che ag aesthetic ▸ sf (disciplina) aesthetics sg; (bellezza) attractiveness; este'tista, -i, -e sm/f beautician

es'tinguere vt to extinguish, put out; (debito) to pay off; estinguersi vpr to go out; (specie) to become extinct

es'tinsi ecc vb vedi estinguere

estin'tore sm (fire) extinguisher

estinzi'one sf putting out; (di specie) extinction

estir'pare vt (pianta) to uproot, pull up; (fig: vizio) to eradicate

es'tivo, -a ag summer cpd

es'torcere [es'tɔrtʃere] vt ~ qc (a qn) to extort sth (from sb)

estradizi'one [estradit'tsjone] sf extradition

es'trae, es'traggo ecc vb vedi estrarre

es'traneo, -a ag foreign ▸ sm/f stranger; rimanere ~ a qc to take no part in sth

es'trarre vt to extract; (minerali) to mine; (sorteggiare) to draw

es'trassi ecc vb vedi estrarre

estrema'mente av extremely

estre'mista, -i, e sm/f extremist

estremità sf inv extremity, end ▸ sfpl (Anat) extremities

es'tremo, -a ag extreme; (ultimo: ora, tentativo) final, last ▸ sm extreme; (di pazienza, forze) limit, end; estremi smpl (Amm: dati essenziali) details,

particulars; l'~ Oriente the Far East

estro'verso, -a ag, sm extrovert

età sf inv age; all'~ di 8 anni at the age of 8, at 8 years of age; ha la mia ~ he (o she) is the same age as me o as I am; raggiungere la maggiore ~ to come of age; essere in ~ minore to be under age

etere sm ether

eternità sf eternity

e'terno, -a ag eternal

etero'geneo, -a [etero'dʒɛneo] ag heterogeneous

eterosessu'ale ag, sm/f heterosexual

'etica sf ethics sg; vedi anche etico

eti'chetta [eti'ketta] sf label; (cerimoniale): l'~ etiquette

'etico, -a, -ci, -che ag ethical

eti'lometro sm Breathalyzer®

etimolo'gia, -'gie [etimolo'dʒia] sf etymology

Eti'opia sf l'~ Ethiopia

'etnico, -a, -ci, -che ag ethnic

e'trusco, -a, -schi, -sche ag, sm/f Etruscan

'ettaro sm hectare (= 10,000 m²)

'etto sm abbr (= ettogrammo) 100 grams

'euro sm inv (divisa) euro

Eu'ropa sf l'~ Europe

europarlamen'tare sm/f Member of the European Parliament, MEP

euro'peo, -a ag, sm/f European

eutana'sia sf euthanasia

evacu'are vt to evacuate

e'vadere vi (fuggire): ~ da to escape from ▸ vt (sbrigare) to deal with, dispatch; (tasse) to evade

evapo'rare vi to evaporate

e'vasi ecc vb vedi evadere

evasi'one sf (vedi evadere) escape; dispatch; evasione fiscale tax evasion

eva'sivo, -a ag evasive

e'vaso, -a pp di evadere ▸ sm escapee

e'vento sm event

eventu'ale ag possible
Attenzione! In inglese esiste la parola eventual, che però significa finale.

eventual'mente av if necessary
Attenzione! In inglese esiste la parola eventually, che però significa alla fine.

evi'dente ag evident, obvious

evidente'mente av evidently; (palesemente) obviously, evidently

evi'tare vt to avoid; ~ di fare to avoid doing; ~ qc a qn to spare sb sth

evoluzi'one [evolut'tsjone] sf evolution

e'volversi vpr to evolve

ev'viva escl hurrah!; ~ il re! long live the king!, hurrah for the king!

ex prefisso ex, former

'extra ag inv first-rate; top-quality ▶ sm inv extra; **extracomuni'tario, -a** ag from outside the EC ▶ sm/f non-EC citizen

extrater'restre ag, sm/f extraterrestrial

f

fa vb vedi **fare** ▶ sm inv (Mus) F; (: solfeggiando la scala) fa ▶ av **10 anni fa** 10 years ago

'fabbrica sf factory; **fabbri'care** vt to build; (produrre) to manufacture, make; (fig) to fabricate, invent
Attenzione! In inglese esiste la parola fabric, che però significa stoffa.

fac'cenda [fat'tʃɛnda] sf matter, affair; (cosa da fare) task, chore

fac'chino [fak'kino] sm porter

'faccia, -ce ['fattʃa] sf face; (di moneta, medaglia) side; **faccia a faccia** face to face

facci'ata [fat'tʃata] sf façade; (di pagina) side

'faccio [fattʃo] vb vedi **fare**

fa'cessi ecc [fa'tʃɛssi] vb vedi **fare**

fa'cevo ecc [fa'tʃevo] vb vedi **fare**

'facile ['fatʃile] ag easy; (disposto): ~ a inclined to, prone to; (probabile): è ~ che piova it's likely to rain

facoltà sf inv faculty; (autorità) power

facolta'tivo, -a ag optional; (fermata d'autobus) request cpd

'faggio ['faddʒo] sm beech

fagi'ano [fa'dʒano] sm pheasant

fagio'lino [fadʒo'lino] sm French (BRIT) o string bean

fagi'olo [fa'dʒɔlo] sm bean

'fai vb vedi **fare**

'fai-da-'te sm inv DIY, do-it-yourself

'falce ['faltʃe] sf scythe; **falci'are** vt to cut; (fig) to mow down

falcia'trice [faltʃa'tritʃe] sf (per fieno) reaping machine; (per erba) mowing machine

'falco, -chi sm hawk

'falda sf layer, stratum; (di cappello) brim; (di cappotto) tails pl; (di monte) lower slope; (di tetto) pitch

fale'gname [faleɲ'ɲame] sm joiner

falli'mento sm failure; bankruptcy

fal'lire vi (non riuscire): ~ (in) to fail (in); (Dir) to go bankrupt ▶ vt (colpo, bersaglio) to miss

'fallo sm error, mistake; (imperfezione) defect, flaw; (Sport) foul; fault; **senza ~** without fail

falò sm inv bonfire

falsifi'care vt to forge; (*monete*) to forge, counterfeit

'falso, -a ag false; (*errato*) wrong; (*falsificato*) forged; fake; (*: oro, gioielli*) imitation cpd ▶ sm forgery; **giurare il ~** to commit perjury

'fama sf fame; (*reputazione*) reputation, name

'fame sf hunger; **aver ~** to be hungry

fa'miglia [fa'miʎʎa] sf family

famili'are ag (*della famiglia*) family cpd; (*ben noto*) familiar; (*rapporti, atmosfera*) friendly; (*Ling*) informal, colloquial ▶ sm/f relative, relation

fa'moso, -a ag famous, well-known

fa'nale sm (*Aut*) light, lamp (BRIT); (*luce stradale, Naut*) light; (*di faro*) beacon

fa'natico, -a, -ci, -che ag fanatical; (*del teatro, calcio ecc*): **~ di o per** mad o crazy about ▶ sm/f fanatic; (*tifoso*) fan

'fango, -ghi sm mud

'fanno vb vedi **fare**

fannul'lone, -a sm/f idler, loafer

fantasci'enza [fantaʃ'ʃɛntsa] sf science fiction

fanta'sia sf fantasy, imagination; (*capriccio*) whim, caprice ▶ ag inv **vestito ~** patterned dress

fan'tasma, -i sm ghost, phantom

fan'tastico, -a, -ci, -che ag fantastic; (*potenza, ingegno*) imaginative

fan'tino sm jockey

fara'butto sm crook

fard sm inv blusher

'fare
sm

1 (*modo di fare*): **con fare distratto** absent-mindedly; **ha un fare simpatico** he has a pleasant manner

2: **sul far del giorno/della notte** at daybreak/nightfall
▶ vt

1 (*fabbricare, creare*) to make; (*: casa*) to build; (*: assegno*) to make out; **fare un pasto/una promessa/un film** to make a meal/a promise/a film; **fare rumore** to make a noise

2 (*effettuare: lavoro, attività, studi*) to do; (*: sport*) to play; **cosa fa?** (*adesso*) what are you doing?; (*di professione*) what do you do?; (*di professione*) what do you do?; **fare psicologia/italiano** (*Ins*) to do psychology/Italian; **fare un viaggio** to go on a trip o journey; **fare una passeggiata** to go for a walk; **fare la spesa** to do the shopping

3 (*funzione*) to be; (*Teatro*) to play, be; **fare il medico** to be a doctor; **fare il malato** (*fingere*) to act the invalid

4 (*suscitare: sentimenti*): **fare paura a qn** to frighten sb; **(non) fa niente** (*non importa*) it doesn't matter

5 (*ammontare*): **3 più 3 fa 6** 3 and 3 are o make 6; **fanno 3 euro** that's 3 euros; **Roma fa 2.000.000 di abitanti** Rome has 2,000,000 inhabitants; **che ora fai?** what time do you make it?

6 (*+ infinito*): **far fare qc a qn** (*obbligare*) to make sb do sth; (*permettere*) to let sb do sth; **fammi vedere** let me see; **far partire il motore** to start (up) the engine; **far riparare la macchina/costruire una casa** to get o have the car repaired/a house built

7: **farsi: farsi una gonna** to make o.s. a skirt; **farsi un nome** to make a name for o.s.; **farsi la permanente** to get a perm; **farsi tagliare i capelli** to get one's hair cut; **farsi operare** to have an operation

8 (*fraseologia*): **farcela** to succeed, manage; **non ce la faccio più** I can't go on; **ce la faremo** we'll make it; **me l'hanno fatta!** (*imbrogliare*) I've been done!; **lo facevo più giovane** I thought he was younger; **fare sì/no con la testa** to nod/shake one's head
▶ vi

1 (agire) to act, do; **fate come volete** do as you like; **fare presto** to be quick; **fare da** to act as; **non c'è niente da fare** it's no use; **saperci fare con qn/qc** to know how to deal with sb/sth; **faccia pure!** go ahead!

2 (dire) to say; **"davvero?" fece** "really?" he said

3: **fare per** (essere adatto) to be suitable for; **fare per fare qc** to be about to do sth; **fece per andarsene** he made as if to leave

4: **farsi: si fa così** you do it like this, this is the way it's done; **non si fa così!** (rimprovero) that's no way to behave!; **la festa non si fa** the party is off

5: **fare a gara con qn** to compete o vie with sb; **fare a pugni** to come to blows; **fare in tempo a fare** to be in time to do
▶ vb impers **fa bel tempo** the weather is fine; **fa caldo/freddo** it's hot/cold; **fa notte** it's getting dark
▶ vpr **farsi**

1 (diventare) to become; **farsi prete** to become a priest; **farsi grande/vecchio** to grow tall/old

2 (spostarsi): **farsi avanti/indietro** to move forward/back

3 (fam: drogarsi) to be a junkie

far'falla sf butterfly

fa'rina sf flour

farma'cia, -'cie [farma'tʃia] sf pharmacy; (negozio) chemist's (shop) (BRIT), pharmacy; **farma'cista, -i, -e** sm/f chemist (BRIT), pharmacist

'farmaco, -ci o **chi** sm drug, medicine

'faro sm (Naut) lighthouse; (Aer) beacon; (Aut) headlight

'fascia, -sce ['faʃʃa] sf band, strip; (Med) bandage; (di sindaco, ufficiale) sash; (parte di territorio) strip, belt; (di contribuenti ecc) group, band; **essere in fasce** (anche fig) to be in one's infancy; **fascia oraria** time band

fasci'are [faʃʃare] vt to bind; (Med)

to bandage

fa'scicolo [faʃʃikolo] sm (di documenti) file, dossier; (di rivista) issue, number; (opuscolo) booklet, pamphlet

fa'scino ['faʃʃino] sm charm, fascination

fa'scismo [faʃʃizmo] sm fascism

'fase sf phase; (Tecn) stroke; **fuori ~** (motore) rough

fas'tidio sm bother, trouble; **dare ~ a qn** to bother o annoy sb; **sento ~ allo stomaco** my stomach's upset; **avere fastidi con la polizia** to have trouble o bother with the police; **fastidi'oso, -a** ag annoying, tiresome

> Attenzione! In inglese esiste la parola fastidious, che però significa pignolo.

'fata sf fairy

fa'tale ag fatal; (inevitabile) inevitable; (irresistibile) irresistible

fa'tica, -che sf hard work, toil; (sforzo) effort; (di metalli) fatigue; **a ~** with difficulty; **fare ~ a fare qc** to have a job doing sth; **fati'coso, -a** ag tiring, exhausting; (lavoro) laborious

'fatto, -a pp di **fare** ▶ ag **un uomo ~** a grown man; **~ a mano/in casa** hand-/home-made ▶ sm fact; (azione) deed; (avvenimento) event, occurrence; (di romanzo, film) action, story; **cogliere qn sul ~** to catch sb red-handed; **il ~ sta o è che** the fact remains o is that; **in ~ di** as for, as far as … is concerned

fat'tore sm (Agr) farm manager; (Mat, elemento costitutivo) factor; **fattore di protezione** (di lozione solare) factor; **vorrei una crema solare con ~ di protezione 15** I'd like a factor 15 suntan cream

fatto'ria sf farm; farmhouse

> Attenzione! In inglese esiste la parola factory, che però significa fabbrica.

fatto'rino sm errand-boy; (di ufficio)

office-boy; (d'albergo) porter
fat'tura sf (Comm) invoice; (di abito) tailoring; (malìa) spell
fattu'rato sm (Comm) turnover
'fauna sf fauna
'fava sf broad bean
'favola sf (fiaba) fairy tale; (d'intento morale) fable; (fandonia) yarn;
favo'loso, -a ag fabulous; (incredibile) incredible
fa'vore sm favour; **per ~** please; **fare un ~ a qn** to do sb a favour
favo'rire vt to favour; (il commercio, l'industria, le arti) to promote, encourage; **vuole ~?** won't you help yourself?; **favorisca in salotto** please come into the sitting room
fax sm inv fax; **mandare qc via ~** to fax sth
fazzo'letto [fattso'letto] sm (head)scarf; (per la testa) handkerchief; **fazzoletto di carta** tissue
feb'braio sm February
'febbre sf fever; **aver la ~** to have a high temperature; **febbre da fieno** hay fever
'feci ecc ['fetʃi] vb vedi **fare**
fecondazi'one [fekondat'tsjone] sf fertilization; **fecondazione artificiale** artificial insemination
fe'condo, -a ag fertile
'fede sf (credenza) belief, faith; (Rel) faith; (fiducia) faith, trust; (fedeltà) loyalty; (anello) wedding ring; (attestato) certificate; **aver ~ in qn** to have faith in sb; **in buona/mala ~** in good/bad faith; **"in ~"** (Dir) "in witness whereof"; **fe'dele** ag faithful (to) ▶ sm/f follower; **i fedeli** (Rel) the faithful
'federa sf pillowslip, pillowcase
fede'rale ag federal
'fegato sm liver; (fig) guts pl, nerve
'felce ['feltʃe] sf fern

fe'lice [fe'litʃe] ag happy; (fortunato) lucky; **felicità** sf happiness
felici'tarsi [felitʃi'tarsi] vpr (congratularsi) **~ con qn per qc** to congratulate sb on sth
fe'lino, -a ag, sm feline
'felpa sf sweatshirt
'femmina sf (Zool, Tecn) female; (figlia) girl, daughter; (spesso peg) woman; **femmi'nile** ag feminine; (sesso) female; (lavoro, giornale, moda) woman's ▶ sm (Ling) feminine
'femore sm thighbone, femur
fe'nomeno sm phenomenon
feri'ale ag **giorno ~** weekday
'ferie sfpl holidays (BRIT), vacation sg (US); **andare in ~** to go on holiday o vacation
fe'rire vt to injure; (deliberatamente: Mil ecc) to wound; (colpire) to hurt; **ferirsi** vpr to hurt o.s., injure o.s; **fe'rita** sf injury, wound; **fe'rito, -a** sm/f wounded o injured man/woman
fer'maglio [fer'maʎʎo] sm clasp; (per documenti) clip
fer'mare vt to stop, halt; (Polizia) to detain, hold ▶ vi to stop; **fermarsi** vpr to stop, halt; **fermarsi a fare qc** to stop to do sth; **può fermarsi qui/all'angolo?** could you stop here/at the corner?
fer'mata sf stop; **fermata dell'autobus** bus stop
fer'menti smpl **~ lattici** probiotic bacteria
fer'mezza [fer'mettsa] sf (fig) firmness, steadfastness
'fermo, -a ag still, motionless; (veicolo, macchina; orologio) not working; (saldo: anche fig) firm; (voce, mano) steady ▶ escl stop!; keep still! ▶ sm (chiusura) catch, lock; (Dir); **fermo di polizia** police detention
fe'roce [fe'rotʃe] ag (animale) fierce, ferocious; (persona) cruel, fierce;

(*fame, dolore*) raging; **le bestie feroci** wild animals

ferra'gosto *sm* (*festa*) feast of the Assumption; (*periodo*) August holidays *pl*

● **Ferragosto**
● **Ferragosto**, August 15th, is a
● national holiday. Marking the Feast
● of the Assumption, its origins are
● religious but in recent years it has
● simply become the most important
● public holiday of the summer
● season. Most people take some
● extra time off work and head out of
● town to the holiday resorts.

ferra'menta *sfpl negozio di* ~ ironmonger's (*BRIT*), hardware shop *o* store (*US*)

'ferro *sm* iron; **una bistecca ai ferri** a grilled steak; **ferro battuto** wrought iron; **ferro da calza** knitting needle; **ferro di cavallo** horseshoe; **ferro da stiro** iron

ferro'via *sf* railway (*BRIT*), railroad (*US*); **ferrovi'ario, -a** *ag* railway (*BRIT*), railroad *cpd* (*US*); **ferrovi'ere** *sm* railwayman (*BRIT*), railroad man (*US*)

fertile *ag* fertile

'fesso, -a *pp di* **fendere ▶** *ag* (*fam: sciocco*) crazy, cracked

fes'sura *sf* crack, split; (*per gettone, moneta*) slot

'festa *sf* (*religiosa*) feast; (*pubblica*) holiday; (*compleanno*) birthday; (*onomastico*) name day; (*ricevimento*) celebration, party; **far** ~ to have a holiday; **to live it up; far ~ a qn** to give sb a warm welcome

festeggi'are [fested'dʒare] *vt* to celebrate; (*persona*) to have a celebration for

fes'tivo, -a *ag* (*atmosfera*) festive; **giorno** ~ holiday

'feto *sm* foetus (*BRIT*), fetus (*US*)

'fetta *sf* slice

fettuc'cine [fettut'tʃine] *sfpl* (*Cuc*) ribbon-shaped pasta

FF.SS. *abbr* = **Ferrovie dello Stato**

FI *sigla* = **Firenze ▶** *abbr* (= *Forza Italia*) Italian centre-right political party

fi'aba *sf* fairy tale

fi'acca *sf* weariness; (*svogliatezza*) listlessness

fi'acco, -a, -chi, -che *ag* (*stanco*) tired, weary; (*svogliato*) listless; (*debole*) weak; (*mercato*) slack

fi'accola *sf* torch

fi'ala *sf* phial

fi'amma *sf* flame

fiam'mante *ag* (*colore*) flaming; **nuovo** ~ brand new

fiam'mifero *sm* match

fia'mmingo, -a, -ghi, -ghe *ag* Flemish **▶** *sm/f* Fleming **▶** *sm* (*Ling*) Flemish; **i Fiamminghi** the Flemish

fi'anco, -chi *sm* side; (*Mil*) flank; **di** ~ sideways, from the side; **a ~ a ~** side by side

fi'asco, -schi *sm* flask; (*fig*) fiasco; **fare** ~ to fail

fia'tare *vi* (*fig: parlare*): **senza** ~ without saying a word

fi'ato *sm* breath; (*resistenza*) stamina; **avere il ~ grosso** to be out of breath; **prendere** ~ to catch one's breath

'fibbia *sf* buckle

'fibra *sf* fibre; (*fig*) constitution

fic'care *vt* to push, thrust, drive; **ficcarsi** *vpr* (*andare a finire*) to get to

ficcherò *ecc* [fikke'rɔ] *vb vedi* **ficcare**

'fico, -chi *sm* (*pianta*) fig tree; (*frutto*) fig; **fico d'India** prickly pear; **fico secco** dried fig

fidanza'mento [fidantsa'mento] *sm* engagement

fidan'zarsi [fidan'tsarsi] *vpr* to get engaged; **fidan'zato, -a** *sm/f* fiancé/fiancée

fi'darsi vpr ~ **di** to trust; **fi'dato, -a** ag reliable, trustworthy

fi'ducia [fi'dutʃa] sf confidence, trust; **incarico di ~** position of trust, responsible position; **persona di ~** reliable person

fie'nile sm barn; hayloft

fi'eno sm hay

fi'era sf fair

fi'ero, -a ag proud; (audace) bold

'fifa (fam) sf **aver ~** to have the jitters

fig. abbr (= figura) fig

'figlia ['fiλλa] sf daughter

figli'astro, -a [fiλ'λastro] sm/f stepson/daughter

'figlio ['fiλλo] sm son; (senza distinzione di sesso) child; **figlio di papà** spoilt, wealthy young man; **figlio unico** only child

fi'gura sf figure; (forma, aspetto esterno) form, shape; (illustrazione) picture, illustration; **far ~** to look smart; **fare una brutta ~** to make a bad impression

figu'rina sf figurine; (cartoncino) picture card

'fila sf row, line; (coda) queue; (serie) series, string; **di ~** in succession; **fare la ~** to queue; **in ~ indiana** in single file

fi'lare vt to spin ▶ vi (baco, ragno) to spin; (formaggio fuso) to go stringy; (discorso) to hang together; (fam: amoreggiare) to go steady; (muoversi a forte velocità) to go at full speed; ~ **diritto** (fig) to toe the line; ~ **via** to dash off

filas'trocca, -che sf nursery rhyme

filate'lia sf philately, stamp collecting

fi'letto sm (di vite) thread; (di carne) fillet

fili'ale ag (di figlio) filial ▶ sf (di impresa) branch

film sm inv film

'filo sm (anche fig) thread; (filato) yarn; (metallico) wire; (di lama, rasoio) edge;

per ~ **e per segno** in detail; **con un ~ di voce** in a whisper; **filo d'erba** blade of grass; **filo interdentale** dental floss; **filo di perle** string of pearls; **filo spinato** barbed wire

fi'lone sm (di minerali) seam, vein; (pane) ≈ Vienna loaf; (fig) trend

filoso'fia sf philosophy; **fi'losofo, -a** sm/f philosopher

fil'trare vt, vi to filter

'filtro sm filter; **filtro dell'olio** (Aut) oil filter

fi'nale ag final ▶ sm (di opera) end, ending; (: Mus) finale ▶ sf (Sport) final; **final'mente** av finally, at last

fi'nanza [fi'nantsa] sf finance; **finanze** sfpl (di individuo, Stato) finances

finché [fin'ke] cong (per tutto il tempo che) as long as; (fino al momento in cui) until; **aspetta ~ io (non) sia ritornato** wait until I get back

'fine ag (lamina, carta) thin; (capelli, polvere) fine; (vista, udito) keen, sharp; (persona: raffinata) refined, distinguished; (osservazione) subtle ▶ sf end ▶ sm aim, purpose; (esito) result, outcome; **secondo ~** ulterior motive; **in o alla ~** in the end, finally

fi'nestra sf window; **fines'trino** sm window; **vorrei un posto vicino al finestrino** I'd like a window seat

'fingere ['findʒere] vt to feign; (supporre) to imagine, suppose; **fingersi** vpr **fingersi ubriaco/pazzo** to pretend to be drunk/mad; **~ di fare** to pretend to do

fi'nire vt to finish ▶ vi to finish, end; **quando finisce lo spettacolo?** when does the show finish?; **~ di fare** (compiere) to finish doing; (smettere) to stop doing; **~ in galera** to end up o finish up in prison

finlan'dese ag, sm (Ling) Finnish ▶ sm/f Finn

Fin'landia sf la ~ Finland

'fino, -a ag (capelli, seta) fine; (oro) pure; (fig: acuto) shrewd ▶ av (spesso troncato in fin: pure, anche) even ▶ prep (spesso troncato in fin: tempo): **fin quando?** till when?; (: luogo): **fin qui** as far as here; **~ a** (tempo) until, till; (luogo) as far as, (up) to; **fin da domani** from tomorrow onwards; **fin da ieri** since yesterday; **fin dalla nascita** from o since birth

fi'nocchio [fi'nɔkkjo] sm fennel; (fam: peg: omosessuale) queer

fi'nora av up till now

'finsi ecc vb vedi **fingere**

'finta sf pretence, sham; (Sport) feint; **far ~ (di fare)** to pretend (to do)

'finto, -a pp di **fingere** ▶ ag false; artificial

finzi'one [fin'tsjone] sf pretence, sham

fi'occo, -chi sm (di nastro) bow; (di stoffa, lana) flock; (di neve) flake; (Naut) jib; **coi fiocchi** (fig) first-rate; **fiocchi di avena** oatflakes; **fiocchi di granturco** cornflakes

fi'ocina ['fjɔtʃina] sf harpoon

fi'oco, -a, -chi, -che ag faint, dim

fi'onda sf catapult

fio'raio, -a sm/f florist

fi'ore sm flower; **fiori** smpl (Carte) clubs; **a fior d'acqua** on the surface of the water; **avere i nervi a fior di pelle** to be on edge; **fior di latte** cream; **fiori di campo** wild flowers

fioren'tino, -a ag Florentine

fio'retto sm (Scherma) foil

fio'rire vi (rosa) to flower; (albero) to blossom; (fig) to flourish

Fi'renze [fi'rɛntse] sf Florence

'firma sf signature

> Attenzione! In inglese esiste la parola **firm**, che però significa **ditta**.

fir'mare vt to sign; **un abito firmato** a designer suit; **dove devo ~?** where do I sign?

fisar'monica, -che sf accordion

fis'cale ag fiscal, tax cpd; **medico ~** doctor employed by Social Security to verify cases of sick leave

fischi'are [fis'kjare] vi to whistle ▶ vt to whistle; (attore) to boo, hiss

fischi'etto [fis'kjetto] sm (strumento) whistle

'fischio ['fiskjo] sm whistle

'fisco sm tax authorities pl, ≈ Inland Revenue (BRIT), ≈ Internal Revenue Service (US)

'fisica sf physics sg

'fisico, -a, -ci, -che ag physical ▶ sm/f physicist ▶ sm physique

fisiotera'pia sf physiotherapy

fisiotera'pista sm/f physiotherapist

fis'sare vt to fix, fasten; (guardare intensamente) to stare at; (data, condizioni) to fix, establish, set; (prenotare) to book; **fissarsi** vpr **fissarsi su** (sguardo, attenzione) to focus on; (fig: idea) to become obsessed with

'fisso, -a ag fixed; (stipendio, impiego) regular ▶ av **guardare ~ qc/qn** to stare at sth/sb

'fitta sf sharp pain; vedi anche **fitto**

fit'tizio, -a ag fictitious, imaginary

'fitto, -a ag thick, dense; (pioggia) heavy ▶ sm depths pl, middle; (affitto, pigione) rent

fi'ume sm river

fiu'tare vt to smell, sniff; (animale) to scent; (fig: inganno) to get wind of, smell; **~ tabacco/cocaina** to take snuff/cocaine

fla'grante ag **cogliere qn in ~** to catch sb red-handed

fla'nella sf flannel

flash [flaʃ] sm inv (Fot) flash; (giornalistico) newsflash

'flauto sm flute

fles'sibile ag pliable; (fig: che si adatta)

flexible

flessibili'tà sf (anche fig) flexibility

flessi'one sf (gen) bending; (Ginnastica: a terra) sit-up; (: in piedi) forward bend; (: sulle gambe) knee-bend; (diminuzione) slight drop, slight fall; (Ling) inflection; **fare una ~** to bend; **una ~ economica** a downward trend in the economy

flettere vt to bend

'flipper sm inv pinball machine

F.lli abbr (= fratelli) Bros.

'flora sf flora

'florido, -a ag flourishing; (fig) glowing with health

'floscio, -a, -sci, -sce ['flɔʃʃo] ag (cappello) floppy, soft; (muscoli) flabby

'flotta sf fleet

'fluido, -a ag, sm fluid

flu'oro sm fluorine

'flusso sm flow; (Fisica, Med) flux; **~ e ri~** ebb and flow

fluvi'ale ag river cpd, fluvial

FMI sigla m (= Fondo Monetario Internazionale) IMF

'foca, -che (Zool) seal

fo'caccia, -ce [fo'kattʃa] sf kind of pizza; (dolce) bun

'foce ['fotʃe] sf (Geo) mouth

foco'laio sm (Med) centre of infection; (fig) hotbed

foco'lare sm hearth, fireside; (Tecn) furnace

'fodera sf (di vestito) lining; (di libro, poltrona) cover

'fodero sm (di spada) scabbard; (di pugnale) sheath; (di pistola) holster

'foga sf enthusiasm, ardour

'foglia ['fɔʎʎa] sf leaf; **foglia d'argento/d'oro** silver/gold leaf

'foglio ['fɔʎʎo] sm (di carta) sheet (of paper); (di metallo) sheet; **foglio di calcolo** (Inform) spreadsheet; **foglio rosa** (Aut) provisional licence; **foglio di via** (Dir) expulsion order; **foglio**

volante pamphlet

'fogna ['foɲɲa] sf drain, sewer

föhn [fø:n] sm inv hair dryer

'folla sf crowd, throng

'folle ag mad, insane; (Tecn) idle; **in ~** (Aut) in neutral

fol'lia sf folly, foolishness; foolish act; (pazzia) madness, lunacy

'folto, -a ag thick

fon sm inv hair dryer

fondamen'tale ag fundamental, basic

fonda'mento sm foundation; **fondamenta** sfpl (Edil) foundations

fon'dare vt to found; (fig: dar base): **~ qc su** to base sth on

fon'dente ag cioccolato ~ plain o dark chocolate

'fondere vt (neve) to melt; (metallo) to fuse, melt; (fig: colori) to merge, blend; (: imprese, gruppi) to merge ▶ vi to melt; **fondersi** vpr to melt; (fig: partiti, correnti) to unite, merge

'fondo, -a ag deep ▶ sm (di recipiente, pozzo) bottom; (di stanza) back; (quantità di liquido che resta, deposito) dregs pl; (sfondo) background; (unità immobiliare) property, estate; (somma di denaro) fund; (Sport) long-distance race; **fondi** smpl (denaro) funds; **a notte fonda** at dead of night; **in ~ a** at the bottom of; at the back of; (strada) at the end of; **andare a ~** (nave) to sink; **conoscere a ~** to know inside out; **dar ~ a** (fig: provviste, soldi) to use up; **in ~** (fig) after all, all things considered; **andare fino in ~ a** (fig) to examine thoroughly; **a ~ perduto** (Comm) without security; **fondi di magazzino** old o unsold stock sg; **fondi di caffè** coffee grounds; **fondo comune di investimento** investment trust

fondo'tinta sm inv (cosmetico) foundation

fo'netica sf phonetics sg

fon'tana sf fountain

'fonte sf spring, source; (fig) source ▶ sm; **fonte battesimale** (Rel) font; **fonte energetica** source of energy

fo'raggio [fo'raddʒo] sm fodder, forage

fo'rare vt to pierce, make a hole in; (pallone) to burst; (biglietto) to punch; **~ una gomma** to burst a tyre (BRIT) o tire (US)

'forbici ['fɔrbitʃi] sfpl scissors

'forca, -che sf (Agr) fork, pitchfork; (patibolo) gallows sg

for'chetta [for'ketta] sf fork

for'cina [for'tʃina] sf hairpin

fo'resta sf forest

foresti'ero, -a ag foreign ▶ sm/f foreigner

'forfora sf dandruff

'forma sf form; (aspetto esteriore) form, shape; (Dir: procedura) procedure; (per calzature) last; (stampo di cucina) mould

formag'gino [formad'dʒino] sm processed cheese

for'maggio [for'maddʒo] sm cheese

for'male ag formal

for'mare vt to form, shape, make; (numero di telefono) to dial; (fig: carattere) to form, mould; **formarsi** vpr to form, take shape; **for'mato** sm format, size; **formazi'one** sf formation; (fig: educazione) training; **formazione professionale** vocational training

for'mica®, -che sf ant

formica® ['fɔrmika] sf (materiale) Formica®

formi'dabile ag powerful, formidable; (straordinario) remarkable

'formula sf formula; **formula di cortesia** courtesy form

formu'lare vt to formulate; to express

for'naio sm baker

for'nello sm (elettrico, a gas) ring; (di pipa) bowl

for'nire vt **~ qn di qc, ~ qc a qn** to provide o supply sb with sth, supply sth to sb

'forno sm (di cucina) oven; (panetteria) bakery; (Tecn: per calce ecc) kiln; (: per metalli) furnace; **forno a microonde** microwave oven

'foro sm (buco) hole; (Storia) forum; (tribunale) (law) court

'forse av perhaps, maybe; (circa) about; **essere in ~** to be in doubt

'forte ag strong; (suono) loud; (spesa) considerable, great; (passione, dolore) great, deep ▶ av strongly; (velocemente) fast; (a voce alta) loud(ly); (violentemente) hard ▶ sm (edificio) fort; (specialità) forte, strong point; **essere ~ in qc** to be good at sth

for'tezza [for'tettsa] sf (morale) strength; (luogo fortificato) fortress

for'tuito, -a ag fortuitous, chance

for'tuna sf (destino) fortune, luck; (buona sorte) success, fortune; (eredità, averi) fortune; **per ~** luckily, fortunately; **di ~** makeshift, improvised; **atterraggio di ~** emergency landing; **fortu'nato, -a** ag lucky, fortunate; (coronato da successo) successful

'forza ['fɔrtsa] sf strength; (potere) power; (Fisica) force; **forze** sfpl (fisiche) strength sg; (Mil) forces; **forza!** escl come on!; **per ~** against one's will; (naturalmente) of course; **a viva ~** by force; **a ~ di** by dint of; **~ maggiore** circumstances beyond one's control; **la ~ pubblica** the police pl; **forze armate** armed forces; **forze dell'ordine** the forces of law and order; **Forza Italia** Italian centre-right political party; **forza di pace** peacekeeping force

for'zare [for'tsare] vt to force; **~ qn a fare** to force sb to do

for'zista, -i, e [for'tsista] *ag* of Forza Italia ▸ *sm/f* member (o supporter) of Forza Italia

fos'chia [fos'kia] *sf* mist, haze

fosco, -a, -schi, -sche *ag* dark, gloomy

'fosforo *sm* phosphorous

fossa *sf* pit; (*di cimitero*): grave; **fossa biologica** septic tank

fos'sato *sm* ditch; (*di fortezza*) moat

fos'setta *sf* dimple

'fossi *ecc vb vedi* **essere**

'fossile *ag, sm* fossil

'fosso *sm* ditch; (*Mil*) trench

'foste *ecc vb vedi* **essere**

'foto *sf* photo; **può farci una ~, per favore?** would you take a picture of us, please? ▸ *prefisso*: **foto ricordo** souvenir photo; **foto tessera** passport(-type) photo; **foto'camera** *sf* **fotocamera digitale** digital camera; **foto'copia** *sf* photocopy; **fotocopi'are** *vt* to photocopy; **fotocopia'trice** [fotokopja'tritʃe] *sf* photocopier; **fotogra'fare** *vt* to photograph; **fotogra'fia** (*immagine*) photograph; (*procedimento*) photography; **una fotografia a colori/in bianco e nero** a colour/black and white photograph; **fare una fotografia** to take a photograph; **foto'grafico, -a, ci, che** *ag* photographic; **macchina fotografica** camera; **fo'tografo, -a** *sm/f* photographer; **fotoro'manzo** *sm* romantic picture story

fou'lard [fu'lar] *sm inv* scarf

fra *prep* = **tra**

'fradicio, -a, -ci, -ce ['fraditʃo] *ag* (*molto bagnato*) soaking (wet); **ubriaco ~** blind drunk

'fragile ['fradʒile] *ag* fragile; (*fig: salute*) delicate

'fragola *sf* strawberry

fra'grante *ag* fragrant

frain'tendere *vt* to misunderstand

fram'mento *sm* fragment

'frana *sf* landslide; (*fig: persona*): **essere una ~** to be useless

fran'cese [fran'tʃeze] *ag* French ▸ *sm/f* Frenchman/woman ▸ *sm* (*Ling*) French; **i Francesi** the French

'Francia ['frantʃa] *sf* la ~ France

'franco, -a, -chi, -che *ag* (*Comm*) free; (*sincero*) frank, open, sincere ▸ *sm* (*moneta*) franc; **farla franca** (*fig*) to get off scot-free; **prezzo ~ fabbrica** ex-works price; **franco di dogana** duty-free

franco'bollo *sm* (*postage*) stamp

'frangia, -ge ['frandʒa] *sf* fringe

frap'pé *sm* milk shake

'frase *sf* (*Ling*) sentence; (*locuzione, espressione, Mus*) phrase; **frase fatta** set phrase

'frassino *sm* ash (tree)

frastagli'ato, -a [frasta'ʎʎato] *ag* (*costa*) indented, jagged

frastor'nare *vt* to daze; to befuddle

frastu'ono *sm* hubbub, din

'frate *sm* friar, monk

fratel'lastro *sm* stepbrother; (*con genitore in comune*) half-brother

fra'tello *sm* brother; **fratelli** *smpl* brothers; (*nel senso di fratelli e sorelle*) brothers and sisters

fra'terno, -a *ag* fraternal, brotherly

frat'tempo *sm* **nel ~ in** the meantime, meanwhile

frat'tura *sf* fracture; (*fig*) split, break

frazi'one [frat'tsjone] *sf* fraction; (*di comune*) small town

'freccia, -ce ['frettʃa] *sf* arrow; **freccia di direzione** (*Aut*) indicator

fred'dezza [fred'dettsa] *sf* coldness

'freddo, -a *sm* cold; **fa ~** it's cold; **aver ~** to be cold; **a ~** (*fig*) deliberately; **freddo'loso, -a** *ag* sensitive to the cold

fre'gare *vt* to rub; (*fam: truffare*) to

take in, cheat; (: *rubare*) to swipe, pinch; **fregarsene** (*faml*): **chi se ne frega?** who gives a damn (about it)?

fregherò *ecc* [frege'rɔ] *vb vedi* **fregare**

fre'nare *vt* (*veicolo*) to slow down; (*cavallo*) to rein in; (*lacrime*) to restrain, hold back ▸ *vi* to brake; **frenarsi** *vpr* (*fig*) to restrain o.s., control o.s.

'freno *sm* brake; (*morso*) bit; **tenere a ~** to restrain; **freno a disco** disc brake; **freno a mano** handbrake

frequen'tare *vt* (*scuola, corso*) to attend; (*locale, bar*) to go to, frequent; (*persone*) to see (often)

frequen'tato, -a *ag* (*locale*) busy

fre'quente *ag* frequent; **di ~** frequently

fres'chezza [fres'kettsa] *sf* freshness

'fresco, -a, -schi, -sche *ag* fresh; (*temperatura*) cool; (*notizia*) recent, fresh ▸ *sm* **godere il ~** to enjoy the cool air; **stare ~** (*fig*) to be in for it; **mettere al ~** to put in a cool place

'fretta *sf* hurry, haste; **in ~** in a hurry; **in ~ e furia** in a mad rush; **aver ~** to be in a hurry

'friggere ['friddʒere] *vt* to fry ▸ *vi* (*olio ecc*) to sizzle

'frigido, -a ['fridʒido] *ag* (*Med*) frigid

'frigo *sm* fridge

frigo'bar *sm inv* minibar

frigo'rifero, -a *ag* refrigerating ▸ *sm* refrigerator

fringu'ello *sm* chaffinch

'frissi *ecc vb vedi* **friggere**

frit'tata *sf* omelette; **fare una ~** (*fig*) to make a mess of things

frit'tella *sf* (*Cuc*) fritter

'fritto, -a *pp di* **friggere** ▸ *ag* fried ▸ *sm* fried food; **fritto misto** mixed fry

frit'tura *sf* (*Cuc*): **frittura di pesce** mixed fried fish

'frivolo, -a *ag* frivolous

frizi'one [frit'tsjone] *sf* friction; (*sulla pelle*) rub, rub-down; (*Aut*) clutch

friz'zante [frid'dzante] *ag* (*anche fig*) sparkling

fro'dare *vt* to defraud, cheat

'frode *sf* fraud; **frode fiscale** tax evasion

'fronda *sf* (*leafy*) branch; (*di partito politico*) internal opposition; **fronde** *sfpl* (*di albero*) foliage *sg*

fron'tale *ag* frontal; (*scontro*) head-on

'fronte *sf* (*Anat*) forehead; (*di edificio*) front, façade ▸ *sm* (*Mil, Pol, Meteor*) front; **a ~, di ~** facing, opposite; **di ~ a** (*posizione*) opposite, facing, in front of; (*a paragone di*) compared with

fronti'era *sf* border, frontier

'frottola *sf* fib

fru'gare *vi* to rummage ▸ *vt* to search

frugherò *ecc* [fruge'rɔ] *vb vedi* **frugare**

frul'lare *vt* (*Cuc*) to whisk ▸ *vi* (*uccelli*) to flutter; **frul'lato** *sm* milk shake; fruit drink; **frulla'tore** *sm* electric mixer

fru'mento *sm* wheat

fru'scio [fruʃ'ʃio] *sm* rustle; rustling; (*di acque*) murmur

'frusta *sf* whip; (*Cuc*) whisk

frus'tare *vt* to whip

frus'trato, -a *ag* frustrated

'frutta *sf* fruit; (*portata*) dessert; **frutta candita** candied fruit; **frutta secca** dried fruit

frut'tare *vi* to bear dividends, give a return

frut'teto *sm* orchard

frutti'vendolo, -a *sm/f* greengrocer (BRIT), produce dealer (US)

'frutto *sm* fruit; (*fig: risultato*) result(s); (*Econ: interesse*) interest; (: *reddito*) income; **frutti di bosco** berries; **frutti di mare** seafood *sg*

FS *abbr* = **Ferrovie dello Stato**

fu *vb vedi* **essere** ▸ *ag inv* **il fu Paolo Bianchi** the late Paolo Bianchi

fuci'lare [futʃi'lare] *vt* to shoot

fu'cile [fu'tʃile] sm rifle, gun; (da caccia) shotgun, gun

'fucsia sf fuchsia

'fuga sf escape, flight; (di gas, liquidi) leak; (Mus) fugue; **fuga di cervelli** brain drain

fug'gire [fud'dʒire] vi to flee, run away; (fig: passar veloce) to fly ▶ vt to avoid

'fui vb vedi **essere**

fu'liggine [fu'liddʒine] sf soot

'fulmine sm thunderbolt; lightning no pl

fu'mare vi to smoke; (emettere vapore) to steam ▶ vt to smoke; **le dà fastidio se fumo?** do you mind if I smoke?; **fuma'tore, -'trice** sm/f smoker

fu'metto sm comic strip; **giornale** sm, **a fumetti** comic

'fummo vb vedi **essere**

'fumo sm smoke; (vapore) steam; (il fumare tabacco) smoking; **fumi** smpl (industriali ecc) fumes; **i fumi dell'alcool** the after-effects of drink; **vendere ~** to deceive, cheat; **fumo passivo** passive smoking

'fune sf rope, cord; (più grossa) cable

'funebre sm funeral; (rito) funeral; (aspetto) gloomy, funereal

fune'rale sm funeral

'fungere ['fundʒere] vi ~ **da** to act as

'fungo, -ghi sm fungus; (commestibile) mushroom; **fungo velenoso** toadstool

funico'lare sf funicular railway

funi'via sf cable railway

'funsi ecc vb vedi **fungere**

funzio'nare [funtsjo'nare] vi to work, function; (fungere): ~ **da** to act as; **come funziona?** how does this work?; **la TV non funziona** the TV isn't working

funzio'nario [funtsjo'narjo] sm official; **funzionario statale** civil servant

funzi'one [fun'tsjone] sf function; (carica) post, position; (Rel) service; **in ~** (meccanismo) in operation; **in ~ di** (come) as; **fare le ~ di qn** (farne le veci) to take sb's place

fu'oco, -chi sm fire; (fornello) ring; (Fot, Fisica) focus; **dare ~ a qc** to set fire to sth; **far ~** (sparare) to fire; **al ~!** fire!; **fuoco d'artificio** firework

fuorché [fwor'ke] cong, prep except

fu'ori av outside; (all'aperto) outdoors, outside; (fuori di casa, Sport) out; (esclamativo) get out! ▶ prep ~ **(di)** out of, outside ▶ sm outside; **lasciar ~ qc/qn** to leave sth/sb out; **far ~ qn** (fam) to kill sb, do sb in; **essere ~ di sé** to be beside o.s.; ~ **luogo** (inopportuno) out of place, uncalled for; ~ **mano** out of the way, remote; ~ **pericolo** out of danger; ~ **uso** old-fashioned, obsolete; **fuorigi'oco** sm offside; **fuori'strada** sm (Aut) cross-country vehicle

'furbo, -a ag clever, smart; (peg) cunning

fu'rente ag ~ **(contro)** furious (with)

fur'fante sm rascal, scoundrel

fur'gone sm van

'furia sf (ira) fury, rage; (fig: impeto) fury, violence; (fretta) rush; **a ~ di** by dint of; **andare su tutte le furie** to get into a towering rage; **furi'bondo, -a** ag furious

furi'oso, -a ag furious

'furono vb vedi **essere**

fur'tivo, -a ag furtive

'furto sm theft; **vorrei denunciare un ~** I'd like to report a theft; **furto con scasso** burglary

'fusa sfpl **fare le ~** to purr

fu'seaux smpl inv leggings

'fusi ecc vb vedi **fondere**

fu'sibile sm (Elettr) fuse

fusi'one sf (di metalli) fusion, melting; (colata) casting; (Comm) merger; (fig)

merging
'fuso, -a pp di **fondere ▶** sm (Filatura)
spindle; **fuso orario** time zone
fus'tino sm (di detersivo) tub
'fusto sm stem; (Anat, di albero) trunk;
(recipiente) drum, can
fu'turo, -a ag, sm future

g

'gabbia sf cage; (da imballaggio) crate;
gabbia dell'ascensore lift (BRIT) o
elevator (US) shaft; **gabbia toracica**
(Anat) rib cage
gabbi'ano sm (sea)gull
gabi'netto sm (Med ecc) consulting
room; (Pol) ministry; (WC) toilet,
lavatory; (Ins: di fisica ecc) laboratory
'gaffe [gaf] sf inv blunder
ga'lante ag gallant, courteous;
(avventura) amorous
ga'lassia sf galaxy
ga'lera sf (Naut) galley; (prigione)
prison
'galla sf a ~ afloat; **venire a ~** to
surface, come to the surface; (fig:
verità) to come out
galleggi'are [galled'dʒare] vi to float
galle'ria sf (traforo) tunnel; (Archit,
d'arte) gallery; (Teatro) circle; (strada
coperta con negozi) arcade
'Galles sm **il ~** Wales
gal'lina sf hen

'gallo sm cock
galop'pare vi to gallop
ga'loppo sm gallop; **al o di ~** at a gallop
'gamba sf leg; (asta: di lettera) stem; **in
~** (in buona salute) well; (bravo, sveglio)
bright, smart; **prendere qc sotto ~**
(fig) to treat sth too lightly
gambe'retto sm shrimp
'gambero sm (di acqua dolce) crayfish;
(di mare) prawn
'gambo sm stem; (di frutta) stalk
'gamma sf (Mus) scale; (di colori, fig)
range
'gancio ['gantʃo] sm hook
'gara sf competition; (Sport)
competition; contest; match; (: corsa)
race; **fare a ~** to compete, vie
ga'rage [ga'raʒ] sm inv garage
garan'tire vt to guarantee; (debito)
to stand surety for; (dare per certo)
to assure
garan'zia [garan'tsia] sf guarantee;
(pegno) security
gar'bato, -a ag courteous, polite
gareggi'are [gared'dʒare] vi to
compete
garga'rismo sm gargle; **fare i
gargarismi** to gargle
ga'rofano sm carnation; **chiodo di
~** clove
'garza ['gardza] sf (per bende) gauze
gar'zone [gar'dzone] sm (di negozio)
boy
gas sm inv gas; **sento odore di ~** I can
smell gas; **a tutto ~** at full speed; **dare
~** (Aut) to accelerate
ga'solio sm diesel (oil)
gas'sato, -a ag fizzy
gast'rite sf gastritis
gastrono'mia sf gastronomy
gat'tino sm kitten
'gatto, -a sm/f cat, tomcat/she-cat;
gatto delle nevi (Aut, Sci) snowcat;
gatto selvatico wildcat
'gazza ['gaddza] sf magpie

gel [dʒɛl] *sm inv* gel

ge'lare [dʒe'lare] *vt, vi, vb impers* to freeze

gelate'ria [dʒelate'ria] *sf* ice-cream shop

gela'tina [dʒela'tina] *sf* gelatine; **gelatina esplosiva** gelignite; **gelatina di frutta** fruit jelly

ge'lato, -a [dʒe'lato] *ag* frozen ▶ *sm* ice cream

'gelido, -a ['dʒɛlido] *ag* icy, ice-cold

'gelo ['dʒɛlo] *sm* (*temperatura*) intense cold; (*brina*) frost; (*fig*) chill

gelo'sia [dʒelo'sia] *sf* jealousy

ge'loso, -a [dʒe'loso] *ag* jealous

'gelso ['dʒɛlso] *sm* mulberry (tree)

gelso'mino [dʒelso'mino] *sm* jasmine

ge'mello, -a [dʒe'mɛllo] *ag, sm/f* twin; **gemelli** *smpl* (*di camicia*) cufflinks; (*dello zodiaco*): **Gemelli** Gemini *sg*

ge'mere ['dʒɛmere] *vi* to moan, groan; (*cigolare*) to creak

'gemma ['dʒɛmma] *sf* (*Bot*) bud; (*pietra preziosa*) gem

gene'rale [dʒene'rale] *ag, sm* general; **in ~** (*per sommi capi*) in general terms; (*di solito*) usually, in general

gene'rare [dʒene'rare] *vt* (*dar vita*) to give birth to; (*produrre*) to produce; (*causare*) to arouse; (*Tecn*) to produce, generate; **generazi'one** *sf* generation

'genere ['dʒɛnere] *sm* kind, type, sort; (*Biol*) genus; (*merce*) article, product; (*Ling*) gender; (*Arte, Letteratura*) genre; **in ~** generally, as a rule; **genere umano** mankind; **generi alimentari** foodstuffs

ge'nerico, -a, -ci, -che [dʒe'nɛriko] *ag* generic; (*vago*) vague, imprecise

'genero ['dʒɛnero] *sm* son-in-law

gene'roso, -a [dʒene'roso] *ag* generous

ge'netica [dʒe'nɛtika] *sf* genetics *sg*

ge'netico, -a, -ci, -che [dʒe'nɛtiko]

ag genetic

gen'giva [dʒen'dʒiva] *sf* (*Anat*) gum

geni'ale [dʒen'jale] *ag* (*persona*) of genius; (*idea*) ingenious, brilliant

'genio ['dʒɛnjo] *sm* genius; **andare a ~ a qn** to be to sb's liking, appeal to sb

geni'tore [dʒeni'tore] *sm* parent, father *o* mother; **i miei genitori** my parents, my father and mother

gen'naio [dʒen'najo] *sm* January

'Genova ['dʒɛnova] *sf* Genoa

'gente ['dʒɛnte] *sf* people *pl*

gen'tile [dʒen'tile] *ag* (*persona, atto*) kind; (*: garbato*) courteous, polite; (*nelle lettere*): **G~ Signore** Dear Sir; (*: sulla busta*): **G~ Signor Fernando Villa** Mr Fernando Villa

genu'ino, -a [dʒenu'ino] *ag* (*prodotto*) natural; (*persona, sentimento*) genuine, sincere

geogra'fia [dʒeogra'fia] *sf* geography

geolo'gia [dʒeolo'dʒia] *sf* geology

ge'ometra, -i, -e [dʒe'ɔmetra] *sm/f* (*professionista*) surveyor

geome'tria [dʒeome'tria] *sf* geometry

ge'ranio [dʒe'ranjo] *sm* geranium

gerar'chia [dʒerar'kia] *sf* hierarchy

'gergo, -ghi ['dʒɛrgo] *sm* jargon; slang

geria'tria [dʒerja'tria] *sf* geriatrics *sg*

Ger'mania [dʒer'manja] *sf* **la ~ occidentale/orientale** West/East Germany

'germe ['dʒɛrme] *sm* germ; (*fig*) seed

germogli'are [dʒermoʎ'ʎare] *vi* to sprout; to germinate

gero'glifico, -ci [dʒero'glifiko] *sm* hieroglyphic

ge'rundio [dʒe'rundjo] *sm* gerund

'gesso ['dʒɛsso] *sm* chalk; (*Scultura, Med, Edil*) plaster; (*statua*) plaster figure; (*minerale*) gypsum

gesti'one [dʒes'tjone] *sf* management

ges'tire [dʒes'tire] *vt* to run, manage

'gesto ['dʒɛsto] *sm* gesture

Gesù [dʒe'zu] sm Jesus

gesu'ita, -i [dʒezu'ita] sm Jesuit

get'tare [dʒet'tare] vt to throw; (anche: ~ **via**) to throw away or out; (Scultura) to cast; (Edil) to lay; (acqua) to spout; (grido) to utter; **gettarsi** vpr **gettarsi in** (fiume) to flow into; ~ **uno sguardo su** to take a quick look at

'getto ['dʒetto] sm (di gas, liquido, Aer) jet; **a ~ continuo** uninterruptedly; **di ~** (fig) straight off, in one go

get'tone [dʒet'tone] sm token; (per giochi) counter; (: roulette ecc) chip; **gettone telefonico** telephone token

ghiacci'aio [gjat'tʃajo] sm glacier

ghiacci'ato, -a ag frozen; (bevanda) ice-cold

ghi'accio [ɡjattʃo] sm ice

ghiacci'olo [gjat'tʃolo] sm icicle; (tipo di gelato) ice lolly (BRIT), Popsicle® (US)

ghi'aia ['gjaja] sf gravel

ghi'anda ['gjanda] sf(Bot) acorn

ghi'andola [gjandola] sf gland

ghi'otto, -a ['gjotto] ag greedy; (cibo) delicious, appetizing

ghir'landa [gir'landa] sf garland, wreath

'ghiro ['giro] sm dormouse

'ghisa ['giza] sf cast iron

già [dʒa] av already; (ex, in precedenza) formerly > escl of course; **sì, già** indeed!

gi'acca, -che ['dʒakka] sf jacket; **giacca a vento** windcheater (BRIT), windbreaker (US)

giacché [dʒak'ke] cong since, as

giac'cone [dʒak'kone] sm heavy jacket

gi'ada ['dʒada] sf jade

giagu'aro [dʒa'gwaro] sm jaguar

gi'allo ['dʒallo] ag yellow; (carnagione) sallow > sm yellow; (anche: romanzo ~) detective novel; (anche: film ~) detective film; **giallo dell'uovo** yolk

Giama'ica [dʒa'maika] sf la ~ Jamaica

Giap'pone [dʒap'pone] sm Japan; **giappo'nese** ag, sm/f, sm Japanese inv

giardi'naggio [dʒardi'naddʒo] sm gardening

giardini'ere, -a [dʒardi'njere] sm/f gardener

giar'dino [dʒar'dino] sm garden; **giardino d'infanzia** nursery school; **giardino pubblico** public gardens pl, (public) park; **giardino zoologico** zoo

giavel'lotto [dʒavel'lotto] sm javelin

gigabyte [dʒiga'bait] sm inv gigabyte

gi'gante, -'essa [dʒi'gante] sm/f giant > ag giant, gigantic; (Comm) giant-size

'giglio ['dʒiʎʎo] sm lily

gilè [dʒi'le] sm inv waistcoat

gin [dʒin] sm inv gin

gine'cologo, -a, -gi, -ghe [dʒine'kɔlogo] sm/f gynaecologist

gi'nepro [dʒi'nepro] sm juniper

gi'nestra [dʒi'nestra] sf(Bot) broom

Gi'nevra [dʒi'nevra] sf Geneva

gin'nastica [dʒin'nastika] sf gymnastics sg; (esercizio fisico) keep-fit exercises; (Ins) physical education

gi'nocchio [dʒi'nɔkkjo] (pl(m) **gi'nocchi**, o pl(f) **gi'nocchia**) sm knee; **stare in ~** to kneel, be on one's knees; **mettersi in ~** to kneel (down)

gio'care [dʒo'kare] vt to play; (scommettere) to stake, wager, bet; (ingannare) to take in > vi to play; (a roulette ecc) to gamble; (fig) to play a part, be important; ~ **a** (gioco, sport) to play; (cavalli) to bet on; **giocarsi la carriera** to put one's career at risk; **gioca'tore, -'trice** sm/f player; gambler

gio'cattolo [dʒo'kattolo] sm toy

giocherò [dʒoke'ro] vb vedi **giocare**

gi'oco, -chi [dʒɔko] sm game; (divertimento, Tecn) play; (al casinò) gambling; (Carte) hand; (insieme di *pezzi ecc necessari per un gioco*) set; **per ~** for fun; **fare il doppio ~ con qn** to double-cross sb; **i Giochi Olimpici** the Olympic Games; **gioco d'azzardo** game of chance; **gioco degli scacchi** chess set

giocoli'ere [dʒokoˈljɛre] *sm* juggler

gi'oia [ˈdʒɔja] *sf* joy, delight; (*pietra preziosa*) jewel, precious stone

gioielle'ria [dʒojelleˈria] *sf* jeweller's craft; jeweller's (shop)

gioielli'ere, -a [dʒojelˈljɛre] *sm/f* jeweller

gioi'ello [dʒoˈjɛllo] *sm* jewel, piece of jewellery; **i miei gioielli** my jewels or jewellery; **gioielli** *smpl* (*anelli, collane ecc*) jewellery; **i gioielli della Corona** the crown jewels

Gior'dania [dʒorˈdanja] *sf* la ~ Jordan

giorna'laio, -a [dʒornaˈlajo] *sm/f* newsagent (*BRIT*), newsdealer (*US*)

gior'nale [dʒorˈnale] *sm* (*news*) paper; (*diario*) journal, diary; (*Comm*) journal; **giornale di bordo** log; **giornale radio** news *sg*

giornali'ero, -a [dʒornaˈljɛro] *ag* daily; (*che varia: umore*) changeable ▸ *sm* day labourer

giorna'lismo [dʒornaˈlizmo] *sm* journalism

giorna'lista, -i, -e [dʒornaˈlista] *sm/f* journalist

gior'nata [dʒorˈnata] *sf* day; **giornata lavorativa** working day

gi'orno [ˈdʒorno] *sm* day; (*opposto alla notte*) day, daytime; (*anche:* **luce del ~**) daylight; **al ~** per day; **di ~** by day; **al d'oggi** nowadays

gi'ostra [ˈdʒɔstra] *sf* (*per bimbi*) merry-go-round; (*torneo storico*) joust

gio'vane [dʒoˈvane] *ag* young; (*aspetto*) youthful ▸ *sm/f* youth/girl, young man/woman; **i giovani** young people

gio'vare [dʒoˈvare] *vi* a ~ (*essere utile*) to be useful to; (*far bene*) to be good for ▸ *vb impers* (*essere bene, utile*) to be useful; **giovarsi di qc** to make use of sth

giovedì [dʒoveˈdi] *sm inv* Thursday; **di ~ il ~** on Thursdays

gioventù [dʒovenˈtu] *sf* (*periodo*) youth; (*i giovani*) young people *pl*, youth

G.I.P. [dʒip] *sigla m inv* (= *Giudice per le Indagini Preliminari*) judge for preliminary enquiries

gira'dischi [dʒiraˈdiski] *sm inv* record player

gi'raffa [dʒiˈraffa] *sf* giraffe

gi'rare [dʒiˈrare] *vt* (*far ruotare*) to turn; (*percorrere, visitare*) to go round; (*Cinema*) to shoot; to make; (*Comm*) to endorse ▸ *vi* to turn; (*più veloce*) to spin; (*andare in giro*) to wander, go around; **girarsi** *vr* to turn; **~ attorno a** to go round; to revolve round; **al prossimo incrocio giri a destra/sinistra** turn right/left at the next junction; **far ~ la testa a qn** to make sb dizzy; (*fig*) to turn sb's head

girar'rosto [dʒirarˈrɔsto] *sm* (*Cuc*) spit

gira'sole [dʒiraˈsole] *sm* sunflower

gi'revole [dʒiˈrevole] *ag* revolving, turning

gi'rino [dʒiˈrino] *sm* tadpole

'giro [ˈdʒiro] *sm* (*circuito, cerchio*) circle; (*di chiave, manovella*) turn; (*viaggio*) tour, excursion; (*passeggiata*) stroll, walk; (*in macchina*) ride; (*in bicicletta*) ride; (*Sport: della pista*) lap; (*di denaro*) circulation; (*Carte*) hand; (*fig*) revolution; **prendere in ~ qn** (*fig*) to pull sb's leg; **fare un ~** to go for a walk (*o a drive o a ride*); **andare in ~** to go about, walk around; **a stretto ~ di posta** by return of post; **nel ~ di un mese** in a month's time; **essere nel ~** (*fig*) to belong to a circle (of friends); **giro d'affari** (*Comm*) turnover; **giro**

di parole circumlocution; **giro di prova** (Aut) test drive; **giro turistico** sightseeing tour; **giro'collo** sm a girocollo crew-neck cpd

gironzo'lare [dʒirondzo'lare] vi to stroll about

'gita ['dʒita] sf excursion, trip; **fare una ~** to go for a trip, go on an outing

gi'tano, -a [dʒi'tano] sm/f gipsy

giù [dʒu] av down; (dabbasso) downstairs; **in ~** downwards, down; **~ di lì** (pressappoco) thereabouts; **bambini dai 6 anni in ~** children aged 6 and under; **~ per, cadere ~ per le scale** to fall down the stairs; **essere ~** (fig: di salute) to be run down; (: di spirito) to be depressed

giub'botto [dʒub'bɔtto] sm jerkin; **giubbotto antiproiettile** bulletproof vest; **giubbotto salvagente** life jacket

giudi'care [dʒudi'kare] vt to judge; (accusato) to try; (lite) to arbitrate in; **~ qn/qc bello** to consider sb/sth (to be) beautiful

gi'udice ['dʒuditʃe] sm judge; **giudice conciliatore** justice of the peace; **giudice istruttore** examining (BRIT) o committing (US) magistrate; **giudice popolare** member of a jury

giu'dizio [dʒu'dittsjo] sm judgment; (opinione) opinion; (Dir) judgment, sentence; (: processo) trial; (: verdetto) verdict; **aver ~** to be wise o prudent; **citare in ~** to summons

gi'ugno ['dʒuɲɲo] sm June

gi'ungere ['dʒundʒere] vi to arrive ▶ vt (mani ecc) to join; **~ a** to arrive at, reach

gi'ungla ['dʒungla] sf jungle

gi'unsi ecc ['dʒunsi] vb vedi **giungere**

giura'mento [dʒura'mento] sm oath; **giuramento falso** perjury

giu'rare [dʒu'rare] vt to swear ▶ vi to swear, take an oath

giu'ria [dʒu'ria] sf jury

giu'ridico, -a, -ci, -che [dʒu'ridiko] ag legal

giustifi'care [dʒustifi'kare] vt to justify; **giustificazi'one** sf justification; (Ins) (note of) excuse

gius'tizia [dʒus'tittsja] sf justice; **giustizi'are** vt to execute, put to death

gi'usto, -a ['dʒusto] ag (equo) fair, just; (vero) true, correct; (adatto) right, suitable; (preciso) exact, correct ▶ av (esattamente) exactly, precisely; (per l'appunto, appena) just; **arrivare ~** to arrive just in time; **ho ~ bisogno di te** you're just the person I need

glaci'ale [gla'tʃale] ag glacial

gli [ʎi] (davV, s impura, gn, pn, ps, x, z) det mpl the ▶ pron (a lui) to him; (a essa) to it; (in coppia con la, la, li, le, ne: a lui, a lei, a loro ecc): **~ele do** I'm giving them to him (o her o them); vedi anche **il**

glo'bale ag overall

'globo sm globe

'globulo sm (Anat): **globulo rosso/bianco** red/white corpuscle

'gloria sf glory

'gnocchi ['ɲɔkki] smpl (Cuc) small dumplings made of semolina pasta o potato

'gobba sf (Anat) hump; (protuberanza) bump

'gobbo, -a ag hunchbacked; (ricurvo) round-shouldered ▶ sm/f hunchback

'goccia, -ce ['gottʃa] sf drop; **goccio'lare** vi, vt to drip

go'dere vi (compiacersi): **~ (di)** to be delighted (at), rejoice (at); (trarre vantaggio): **~ di** benefit from ▶ vt to enjoy; **godersi la vita** to enjoy life; **godersela** to have a good time, enjoy o.s.

godrò ecc vb vedi **godere**

'goffo, -a ag clumsy, awkward

'gola sf (Anat) throat; (golosità)

gluttony, greed; (di camino) flue; (di monte) gorge; **fare ~** (anche fig) to tempt

golf sm inv (Sport) golf; (maglia) cardigan

'golfo sm gulf

go'loso, -a ag greedy

gomi'tata sf **dare una ~ a qn** to elbow sb; **farsi avanti a (forza o furia di) gomitate** to elbow one's way through; **fare a gomitate per qc** to fight to get sth

go'mito sm elbow; (di strada ecc) sharp bend

go'mitolo sm ball

'gomma sf rubber; (per cancellare) rubber, eraser; (di veicolo) tyre (BRIT), tire (US); **gomma americana o da masticare** chewing gum; **gomma a terra** flat tyre (BRIT) o tire (US); **ho una ~ a terra** I've got a flat tyre; **gom'mone** sm rubber dinghy

gonfi'are vt (pallone) to blow up, inflate; (dilatare, ingrossare) to swell; (fig: notizia) to exaggerate; **gonfiarsi** vpr to swell; (fiume) to rise; **'gonfio, -a** ag swollen; (stomaco) bloated; (vela) full; **gonfi'ore** sm swelling

'gonna sf skirt; **gonna pantalone** culottes pl

'gorgo, -ghi sm whirlpool

gorgogli'are [gorgoʎ'ʎare] vi to gurgle

go'rilla sm inv gorilla; (guardia del corpo) bodyguard

'gotico, -a, ci, che ag, sm Gothic

'gotta sf gout

gover'nare vt (stato) to govern, rule; (pilotare, guidare) to steer; (bestiame) to tend, look after

go'verno sm government

GPL sigla m (= Gas di Petrolio Liquefatto) LPG

GPS sigla m (= Global Positioning System) GPS

graci'dare [gratʃi'dare] vi to croak

'gracile ['gratʃile] ag frail, delicate

gradazi'one [gradat'tsjone] sf (sfumatura) gradation; **gradazione alcolica** alcoholic content, strength

gra'devole ag pleasant, agreeable

gradi'nata sf flight of steps; (in teatro, stadio) tiers pl

gra'dino sm step; (Alpinismo) foothold

gra'dire vt (accettare con piacere) to accept; (desiderare) to wish, like; **gradisce una tazza di tè?** would you like a cup of tea?

'grado sm (Mat, Fisica ecc) degree; (stadio) degree, level; (Mil, sociale) rank; **essere in ~ di fare** to be in a position to do

gradu'ale ag gradual

graf'fetta sf paper clip

graffi'are vt to scratch; **graffiarsi** vpr to get scratched; (con unghie) to scratch o.s.

'graffio sm scratch

gra'fia sf spelling; (scrittura) handwriting

'grafico, -a, -ci, -che ag graphic ▶ sm graph; (persona) graphic designer

gram'matica, -che sf grammar

'grammo sm gram(me)

'grana sf (granello, di minerali, corpi spezzati) grain; (fam: seccatura) trouble; (: soldi) cash ▶ sm inv Parmesan (cheese)

gra'naio sm granary, barn

gra'nata sf (proiettile) grenade

Gran Bre'tagna [-bre'taɲɲa] sf **la ~** Great Britain

'granchio ['grankjo] sm crab; (fig) blunder; **prendere un ~** (fig) to blunder

'grande (qualche volta gran + C, grand' + V) ag (grosso, largo, vasto) big, large; (alto) tall; (lungo) long; (in sensi astratti) great ▶ sm/f (persona adulta) adult, grown-up; (chi ha ingegno e potenza) great man/woman; **fare le cose in ~** to do things in style; **una gran bella donna** a very beautiful woman; **non è una gran cosa** o **un gran che** it's nothing special; **non ne so gran che** I don't know very much about it

gran'dezza [gran'dettsa] *sf* (*dimensione*) size; magnitude; (*fig*) greatness; **in ~ naturale** life-size(d)

grandi'nare *vb impers* to hail

'grandine *sf* hail

gra'nello *sm* (*di cereali, uva*) seed; (*di frutta*) pip; (*di sabbia, sale ecc*) grain

gra'nito *sm* granite

'grano *sm* (*in quasi tutti i sensi*) grain; (*frumento*) wheat; (*di rosario, collana*) bead; **grano di pepe** peppercorn

gran'turco *sm* maize

'grappa *sf* rough, strong brandy

'grappolo *sm* bunch, cluster

gras'setto (*Tip*) bold (type)

'grasso, -a *ag* fat; (*cibo*) fatty; (*pelle*) greasy; (*terreno*) rich; (*fig: guadagno, annata*) plentiful ▶ *sm* (*di persona, animale*) fat; (*sostanza che unge*) grease

'grata *sf* grating

gra'ticola *sf* grill

'gratis *av* free, for nothing

grati'tudine *sf* gratitude

'grato, -a *ag* grateful; (*gradito*) pleasant, agreeable

gratta'capo *sm* worry, headache

grattaci'elo [gratta'tʃɛlo] *sm* skyscraper

gratta e vinci ['gratta e 'vintʃi] *sm inv* (*biglietto*) scratchcard; (*lotteria*) scratchcard lottery

grat'tare *vt* (*pelle*) to scratch; (*raschiare*) to scrape; (*pane, formaggio, carote*) to grate; (*fam: rubare*) to pinch ▶ *vi* (*stridere*) to grate; (*Aut*) to grind;

grattarsi *vpr* to scratch o.s.; **grattarsi la pancia** (*fig*) to twiddle one's thumbs

grat'tugia, -gie [grat'tudʒa] *sf* grater; **grattugi'are** *vt* to grate; **pane grattugiato** breadcrumbs *pl*

gra'tuito, -a *ag* free; (*fig*) gratuitous

'grave *ag* (*danno, pericolo, peccato ecc*) grave, serious; (*responsabilità*) heavy, grave; (*contegno*) grave, solemn; (*voce, suono*) deep, low-pitched; (*Ling*): **accento ~** grave accent; **un malato ~** a person who is seriously ill

grave'mente *av* (*ammalato, ferito*) seriously

gravi'danza [gravi'dantsa] *sf* pregnancy

gravità *sf* seriousness; (*anche Fisica*) gravity

gra'voso, -a *ag* heavy, onerous

'grazia ['grattsja] *sf* grace; (*favore*) favour; (*Dir*) pardon

'grazie ['grattsje] *escl* thank you!; **~ mille!** o **tante!** o **infinite!** thank you very much!; **~ a** thanks to

grazi'oso, -a [grat'tsjoso] *ag* charming, delightful; (*gentile*) gracious

'Grecia ['grɛtʃa] *sf* **la ~** Greece; **'greco, -a, -ci, -che** *ag, sm/f, sm* Greek

'gregge ['greddʒe] (*pl(f)* **-i**) *sm* flock

grembi'ule *sm* apron; (*sopravveste*) overall

'grembo *sm* lap; (*ventre della madre*) womb

'grezzo, -a ['greddzo] *ag* raw, unrefined; (*diamante*) rough, uncut; (*tessuto*) unbleached

gri'dare *vi* (*per chiamare*) to shout, cry (out); (*strillare*) to scream, yell ▶ *vt* to shout (out), yell (out); **~ aiuto** to cry o shout for help

'grido (*pl(m)* **-i**, o *pl(f)* **-a**) *sm* shout, cry; scream, yell; (*di animale*) cry; **di ~** famous

'grigio, -a, -gi, -gie ['gridʒo] *ag, sm* grey

'griglia ['griʎʎa] *sf* (*per arrostire*) grill; (*Elettr*) grid; (*inferriata*) grating; **alla ~** (*Cuc*) grilled

gril'letto sm trigger

grillo sm (Zool) cricket; (fig) whim

'grinta sf grim expression; (Sport) fighting spirit

gris'sino sm bread-stick

Groen'landia sf la ~ Greenland

gron'daia sf gutter

gron'dare vi to pour; (essere bagnato): ~ **di** to be dripping with ▶ vt to drip with

'groppa sf (di animale) back, rump; (fam: dell'uomo) back, shoulders pl

gros'sezza [gros'settsa] sf size; thickness

gros'sista, -i, -e sm/f (Comm) wholesaler

'grosso, -a ag big, large; (di spessore) thick; (grossolano: anche fig) coarse; (grave, insopportabile) serious, great; (tempo, mare) rough ▶ sm **il ~ di** the bulk of; **un pezzo ~** (fig) a VIP, a bigwig; **farla grossa** to do something very stupid; **dirle grosse** to tell tall stories; **sbagliarsi di ~** to be completely wrong

'grotta sf cave; grotto

grot'tesco, -a, -schi, -sche ag grotesque

gro'viglio [gro'viλλo] sm tangle; (fig) muddle

gru sf inv crane

'gruccia, -ce ['gruttʃa] sf (per camminare) crutch; (per abiti) coat-hanger

'grumo sm (di sangue) clot; (di farina ecc) lump

'gruppo sm group; **gruppo sanguigno** blood group

GSM sigla m (= Global System for Mobile Communication) GSM

guada'gnare [gwadaɲ'ɲare] vt (ottenere) to gain; (soldi, stipendio) to earn; (vincere) to win; (raggiungere) to reach

gua'dagno [gwa'daɲɲo] sm earnings

pl; (Comm) profit; (vantaggio, giovamento) advantage, gain; **guadagno lordo/netto** gross/net earnings pl

gu'ado sm ford; **passare a ~** to ford

gu'ai escl ~ **a te** (o lui ecc)! woe betide you (o him ecc)!

gu'aio sm trouble, mishap; (inconveniente) trouble, snag

gua'ire vi to whine, yelp

gu'ancia, -ce ['gwantʃa] sf cheek

guanci'ale [gwan'tʃale] sm pillow

gu'anto sm glove

guarda'linee sm inv (Sport) linesman

guar'dare vt (con lo sguardo: osservare) to look at; (film, televisione) to watch; (custodire) to look after, take care of ▶ vi to look; (badare): ~ **a** to pay attention to; (luoghi: essere orientato): ~ **a** to face; **guardarsi** vpr to look at o.s.; **guardarsi da** (astenersi) to refrain from; (stare in guardia) to beware of; **guardarsi dal fare** to take care not to do; **guardarsi di non sbagliare** try not to make a mistake; ~ **a vista qn** to keep a close watch on sb

guarda'roba sm inv wardrobe; (locale) cloakroom

gu'ardia sf (individuo, corpo) guard; (sorveglianza) watch; **fare la ~ a qc/qn** to guard sth/sb; **stare in ~** (fig) to be on one's guard; **di ~** (medico) on call; **guardia carceraria** (prison) warder; **guardia del corpo** bodyguard; **Guardia di finanza** (corpo) customs pl; (persona) customs officer; **guardia medica** emergency doctor service

● **Guardia di finanza**
● The Guardia di Finanza is a
● military body which deals with
● infringements of the laws governing
● income tax and monopolies. It
● reports to the Ministers of Finance,
● Justice or Agriculture, depending on
● the function it is performing.

guardi'ano, -a sm/f (di carcere)

warder; (di villa ecc) caretaker; (di museo) custodian; (di zoo) keeper; **guardiano notturno** night watchman

guarigi'one [gwari'dʒone] sf recovery

gua'rire vt (persona, malattia) to cure; (ferita) to heal ▶ vi to recover, be cured; to heal (up)

guar'nire vt (ornare: abiti) to trim; (Cuc) to garnish

guasta'feste sm/f inv spoilsport

guastarsi vpr (cibo) to go bad; (meccanismo) to break down; (tempo) to change for the worse

gu'asto, -a ag (non funzionante) broken; (: telefono ecc) out of order; (andato a male) bad, rotten; (: dente) decayed, bad; (fig: corrotto) depraved ▶ sm breakdown; (avaria) failure; **guasto al motore** engine failure

gu'erra sf war; (tecnica: atomica, chimica ecc) warfare; **fare la ~ (a)** to wage war (against); **guerra mondiale** world war; **guerra preventiva** preventive war

'gufo sm owl

gu'ida sf (libro) guidebook; (persona) guide; (comando, direzione) guidance, direction; (Aut) driving; (tappeto: di tenda, cassetto) runner; **avete una ~ in italiano?** do you have a guidebook in Italian?; **c'è una ~ che parla italiano?** is there an Italian-speaking guide?; **guida a destra/a sinistra** (Aut) right-/left-hand drive; **guida telefonica** telephone directory; **guida turistica** tourist guide

gui'dare vt to guide; (squadra, rivolta) to lead; (auto) to drive; (aereo, nave) to pilot; **sai ~?** can you drive?; **guida'tore, -trice** sm/f (conducente) driver

guin'zaglio [gwin'tsaʎʎo] sm leash, lead

'guscio ['guʃʃo] sm shell

gu'stare vt (cibi) to taste; (: assaporare con piacere) to enjoy, savour; (fig) to enjoy, appreciate ▶ vi **~ a** to please; **non mi gusta affatto** I don't like it at all

'gusto sm taste; (sapore) flavour; (godimento) enjoyment; **che gusti avete?** which flavours do you have?; **al ~ di fragola** strawberry-flavoured; **mangiare di ~** to eat heartily; **prenderci ~:** **ci ha preso ~** he's acquired a taste for it, he's got to like it; **gus'toso, -a** ag tasty; (fig) agreeable

h

H, h ['akka] sf o m inv (lettera) H, h ▶ abbr (= ora) hr; (= etto, altezza) h; **H come hotel** ≈ H for Harry (BRIT), H for How (US)

ha'cker [hæ'kə⁽ʳ⁾] sm inv hacker

ha, 'hai [a, ai] vb vedi **avere**

hall [hɔl] sf inv hall, foyer

hamburger [am'burger] sm inv (carne) hamburger; (panino) burger

'handicap ['handikap] sm inv handicap; **handicap'pato, -a** ag handicapped ▶ sm/f handicapped person, disabled person

'hanno ['anno] vb vedi **avere**

hard discount [ardi'kaunt] sm inv discount supermarket

hard disk [ar'disk] *sm inv* hard disk

hardware ['ardwer] *sm inv* hardware

hascisch [aʃ'ʃiʃ] *sm* hashish

Hawaii [a'vai] *sfpl* le ~ Hawaii *sg*

help [ɛlp] *sm inv (Inform)* help

herpes ['ɛrpes] *sm (Med)* herpes *sg*;
herpes zoster shingles *sg*

'hi-fi ['haifai] *sm inv*, *ag inv* hi-fi

ho [ɔ] *vb vedi* **avere**

hobby ['hɔbi] *sm inv* hobby

hockey ['hɔki] *sm* hockey; **hockey su
ghiaccio** ice hockey

home page ['houm'peidʒ] *sf inv*
home page

Hong Kong ['hɔ̃g] *sf* Hong Kong

hostess ['hɔustis] *sf inv* air hostess
(BRIT) o stewardess

hot dog ['hɔtdɔg] *sm inv* hot dog

ho'tel *sm inv* hotel

humour ['hju:mə] *sm inv (sense of)*
humour

humus *sm* humus

husky ['aski] *sm inv (cane)* husky *m inv*

i *det mpl* the

IC *abbr* (= Intercity) Intercity

ICI ['itʃi] *sigla f* (= Imposta Comunale sugli
Immobili) ≈ Council Tax

i'cona *sf* (Rel, Inform, fig) icon

i'dea *sf* idea; (opinione) opinion, view;
(ideale) ideal; **dare l'~ di** to seem,

look like; **neanche** o **neppure per ~!**
certainly not!; **idea fissa** obsession

ide'ale *ag*, *sm* ideal

ide'are *vt* (immaginare) to think up,
conceive; (progettare) to plan

i'dentico, -a, -ci, -che *ag* identical

identifi'care *vt* to identify;
identificarsi *vpr* **identificarsi (con)**
to identify o.s. (with)

identità *sf inv* identity

ideolo'gia, -'gie [ideolo'dʒia] *sf*
ideology

idio'matico, -a, -ci, -che *ag*
idiomatic; **frase idiomatica** idiom

idi'ota, -i, -e *ag* idiotic ► *sm/f* idiot

'idolo *sm* idol

idoneità *sf* suitability

i'doneo, -a *ag* ~ **a** suitable for, fit for;
(Mil) fit for; (qualificato) qualified for

i'drante *sm* hydrant

idra'tante *ag* moisturizing ► *sm*
moisturizer

i'draulico, -a, -ci, -che *ag* hydraulic
► *sm* plumber

idroe'lettrico, -a, -ci, -che *ag*
hydroelectric

i'drofilo, -a *ag vedi* **cotone**

i'drogeno [i'drɔdʒeno] *sm* hydrogen

idrovo'lante *sm* seaplane

i'ena *sf* hyena

i'eri *av*, *sm* yesterday; **il giornale di ~**
yesterday's paper; **~ l'altro** the day
before yesterday; **~ sera** yesterday
evening

igi'ene [i'dʒɛne] *sf* hygiene; **igiene
pubblica** public health; **igi'enico, -a,
-ci, -he** *ag* hygienic; (salubre) healthy

i'gnaro, -a [iɲ'naro] *ag* ~ **di** unaware
of, ignorant of

i'gnobile [iɲ'nɔbile] *ag* despicable,
vile

igno'rante [iɲɲo'rante] *ag* ignorant

igno'rare [iɲɲo'rare] *vt* (non sapere,
conoscere) to be ignorant o unaware
of, not to know; (fingere di non vedere,

sentire) to ignore

i'gnoto, -a [iɲˈɲɔto] *ag* unknown

il

(pl(m)**i**; diventa **lo** (pl **gli**) *davanti a s impura, gn, pn, ps, x, z,* **l**a (pl **le**)) *det m*

1 the; **il libro/lo studente/l'acqua** the book/the student/the water; **gli scolari** the pupils

2 (*astrazione*): an; **2 euro il chilo/la giovinezza** courage/love/youth

3 (*tempo*): **il mattino/la sera** in the morning/evening; **il venerdì** ecc (*abitualmente*) on Fridays ecc; (*quel giorno*) the Friday ecc; **la settimana prossima** next week

4 (*distributivo*): a, an; **2 euro il chilo/paio** 2 euros per kilo/pair

5 (*partitivo*): some, any; **hai messo lo zucchero?** have you added sugar?; **hai comprato il latte?** did you buy (some o any) milk?

6 (*possesso*): **aprire gli occhi** to open one's eyes; **rompersi la gamba** to break one's leg; **avere i capelli neri/il naso rosso** to have dark hair/a red nose

7 (*con nomi propri*): **il Petrarca** Petrarch; **il Presidente Bush** President Bush; **dov'è la Francesca?** where's Francesca?

8 (*con nomi geografici*): **il Tevere** the Tiber; **l'Italia** Italy; **il Regno Unito** the United Kingdom; **l'Everest** Everest

ille'gale *ag* illegal

illeg'gibile [illedˈdʒibile] *ag* illegible

ille'gittimo, -a [illeˈdʒittimo] *ag* illegitimate

il'leso, -a *ag* unhurt, unharmed

illimi'tato, -a *ag* boundless; unlimited

ill.mo *abbr* = **illustrissimo**

il'ludere *vt* to deceive, delude; **illudersi** *vpr* to deceive o.s., delude o.s.

illumi'nare *vt* to light up, illuminate; (*fig*) to enlighten; **illuminarsi** *vpr*

to light up; **~ a giorno** to floodlight; **illuminazi'one** *sf* lighting; illumination; floodlighting; (*fig*) flash of inspiration

il'lusi ecc *vb vedi* **illudere**

illusi'one *sf* illusion; **farsi delle illusioni** to delude o.s.; **illusione ottica** optical illusion

il'luso, -a *pp di* **illudere**

illus'trare *vt* to illustrate; **illustrazi'one** *sf* illustration

il'lustre *ag* eminent, renowned; **illus'trissimo, -a** *ag* (*negli indirizzi*) very revered

imbal'laggio [imbalˈladdʒo] *sm* packing *no pl*

imbal'lare *vt* to pack; (*Aut*) to race

imbalsa'mare *vt* to embalm

imbambo'lato, -a *ag* (*sguardo*) vacant, blank

imbaraz'zante [imbaratˈtsante] *ag* embarrassing, awkward

imbaraz'zare [imbaratˈtsare] *vt* (*mettere a disagio*) to embarrass; (*ostacolare movimenti*) to hamper

imbaraz'zato, -a [imbaratˈtsato] *ag* embarrassed; **avere lo stomaco ~** to have an upset stomach

imba'razzo [imbaˈrattso] *sm* (*disagio*) embarrassment; (*perplessità*) puzzlement, bewilderment; **imbarazzo di stomaco** indigestion

imbar'care *vt* (*passeggeri*) to embark; (*merci*) to load; **imbarcarsi** *vpr* imbarcarsi su to board; **imbarcarsi per l'America** to sail for America; **imbarcarsi in** (*fig: affare ecc*) to embark on

imbarcazi'one [imbarkatˈtsjone] *sf* (*small*) boat, (*small*) craft *inv*; **imbarcazione di salvataggio** lifeboat

im'barco, -chi *sm* embarkation; loading; boarding; (*banchina*) landing stage

imbas'tire vt (cucire) to tack; (fig: abbozzare) to sketch, outline

im'battersi vpr ~ in (incontrare) to bump o run into

imbat'tibile ag unbeatable, invincible

imbavagli'are [imbavaʎˈʎare] vt to gag

imbe'cille [imbeˈtʃille] ag idiotic ▶ sm/f idiot; (Med) imbecile

imbian'care vt to whiten; (muro) to whitewash ▶ vi to become o turn white

imbian'chino [imbjanˈkino] sm (house) painter, painter and decorator

imboc'care vt (bambino) to feed; (entrare: strada) to enter, turn into

imbocca'tura sf mouth; (di strada, porto) entrance; (Mus, del morso) mouthpiece

imbos'cata sf ambush

imbottigli'are [imbottiʎˈʎare] vt to bottle; (Naut) to blockade; (Mil) to hem in; **imbottigliarsi** vpr to be stuck in a traffic jam

imbot'tire vt to stuff; (giacca) to pad; **imbottirsi** vpr imbottirsi di (rimpinzarsi) to stuff o.s. with; **imbot'tito, -a** ag stuffed; (giacca) padded; **panino imbottito** filled roll

imbra'nato, -a ag clumsy, awkward ▶ sm/f clumsy person

imbrogli'are [imbroʎˈʎare] vt to mix up; (fig: raggirare) to deceive, cheat; (: confondere) to confuse, mix up; **imbrogli'one, -a** sm/f cheat, swindler

imbronci'ato, -a ag sulky

imbu'care vt to post; **dove posso ~ queste cartoline?** where can I post these cards?

imbur'rare vt to butter

im'buto sm funnel

imi'tare vt to imitate; (riprodurre) to copy; (assomigliare) to look like

immagazzi'nare [immagaddziˈnare] vt to store

immagi'nare [immadʒiˈnare] vt to imagine; (supporre) to suppose; (inventare) to invent; **s'immagini!** don't mention it!, not at all!; **immaginazi'one** sf imagination; (cosa immaginata) fancy

im'magine [imˈmadʒine] sf image; (rappresentazione grafica, mentale) picture

imman'cabile ag certain; unfailing

im'mane ag (smisurato) enormous; (spaventoso) terrible

immangi'abile [imman'dʒabile] ag inedible

immatrico'lare vt to register; **immatricolarsi** vpr (Ins) to matriculate, enrol

imma'turo, -a ag (frutto) unripe; (persona) immature; (prematuro) premature

immedesi'marsi vpr ~ in to identify with

immediata'mente av immediately, at once

immedi'ato, -a ag immediate

im'menso, -a ag immense

im'mergere [imˈmɛrdʒere] vt to immerse, plunge; **immergersi** vpr to plunge; (sommergibile) to dive, submerge; (dedicarsi a): **immergersi in** to immerse o.s. in

immeri'tato, -a ag undeserved

immersi'one sf immersion; (di sommergibile) submersion, dive; (di palombaro) dive

im'mettere vt ~ (in) to introduce (into); ~ **dati in un computer** to enter data on a computer

immi'grato, -a sm/f immigrant

immi'nente ag imminent

immischiarsi vpr ~ in to interfere o meddle in

im'mobile ag motionless, still;

immobili'are ag (Dir) property cpd
immon'dizia [immon'dittsja] sf dirt,
filth; (spesso al pl: spazzatura, rifiuti)
rubbish no pl, refuse no pl
immo'rale ag immoral
immor'tale ag immortal
im'mune ag (esente) exempt; (Med,
Dir) immune
immu'tabile ag immutable;
unchanging
impacchet'tare [impakket'tare] vt
to pack up
impacci'ato, -a ag awkward, clumsy;
(imbarazzato) embarrassed
im'pacco, -chi sm (Med) compress
impadro'nirsi vpr ~ **di** to seize, take
possession of; (fig: apprendere a fondo)
to master
impa'gabile ag priceless
impa'lato, -a ag (fig) stiff as a board
impalca'tura sf scaffolding
impalli'dire vi to turn pale; (fig)
to fade
impa'nato, -a ag (Cuc) coated in
breadcrumbs
impan'tanarsi vpr to sink (in the
mud); (fig) to get bogged down
impappi'narsi vpr to stammer, falter
impa'rare vt to learn
impar'tire vt to bestow, give
imparzi'ale [impar'tsjale] ag
impartial, unbiased
impas'sibile ag impassive
impas'tare vt (pasta) to knead
impas'ticcarsi vpr to pop pills
im'pasto sm (l'impastare: di pane)
kneading; (: di cemento) mixing;
(pasta) dough; (anche fig) mixture
im'patto sm impact
impau'rire vt to scare, frighten ▸ vi
(anche: **impaurirsi**) to become scared
o frightened
impazi'ente [impat'tsjɛnte] ag
impatient
impaz'zata [impat'tsata] sf **all'~**

(precipitosamente) at breakneck
speed
impaz'zire [impat'tsire] vi to go mad;
~ **per qn/qc** to be crazy about sb/sth
impec'cabile ag impeccable
impedi'mento sm obstacle,
hindrance
impe'dire vt (vietare): ~ **a qn di fare**
to prevent sb from doing; (ostruire)
to obstruct; (impacciare) to hamper,
hinder
impegnarsi vpr (vincolarsi): ~ **a
fare** to undertake to do; (mettersi
risolutamente): ~ **in qc** to devote o.s. to
sth; ~ **con qn** (accordarsi) to come to
an agreement with sb
impegna'tivo, -a ag binding; (lavoro)
demanding, exacting
impe'gnato, -a ag (occupato) busy;
(fig: romanzo, autore) committed,
engagé
im'pegno [im'peɲɲo] sm (obbligo)
obligation; (promessa) promise,
pledge; (zelo) diligence, zeal; (compito,
d'autore) commitment
impel'lente ag pressing, urgent
impen'narsi vpr (cavallo) to rear up;
(Aer) to nose up; (fig) to bridle
impensie'rire vt to worry;
impensierirsi vpr to worry
impera'tivo, -a ag, sm imperative
impera'tore, -'trice sm/f emperor/
empress
imperdo'nabile ag unforgivable,
unpardonable
imper'fetto, -a ag imperfect ▸ sm
(Ling) imperfect (tense)
imperi'ale ag imperial
imperi'oso, -a ag (persona) imperious;
(motivo, esigenza) urgent, pressing
imperme'abile ag waterproof ▸ sm
raincoat
im'pero sm empire; (forza, autorità)
rule, control
imperso'nale ag impersonal
imperso'nare vt to personify; (Teatro)

to play, act (the part of)

imperter'rito, -a *ag* fearless, undaunted; impassive

imperti'nente *ag* impertinent

'impeto *sm (moto, forza)* force, impetus; *(assalto)* onslaught; *(fig: impulso)* impulse; *(: slancio)* transport; **con ~** energetically; vehemently

impet'tito, -a *ag* stiff, erect

impetu'oso, -a *ag (vento)* strong, raging; *(persona)* impetuous

impi'anto *sm (installazione)* installation; *(apparecchiature)* plant; *(sistema)* system; **impianto elettrico** wiring; **impianto di risalita** *(Sci)* ski lift; **impianto di riscaldamento** heating system; **impianto sportivo** sports complex

impic'care *vt* to hang; **impiccarsi** *vpr* to hang o.s.

impicciarsi [impit'tʃarsi] *vpr (immischiarsi)*: **~ (in)** to meddle (in); **impicciati degli affari tuoi!** mind your own business!

impicci'one, -a [impit'tʃone] *sm/f* busybody

impie'gare *vt (usare)* to use, employ; *(spendere: denaro, tempo)* to spend; *(investire)* to invest; **impie'gato, -a** *sm/f* employee

impi'ego, -ghi *sm (uso)* use; *(occupazione)* employment; *(posto di lavoro)* (regular) job, post; *(Econ)* investment

impieto'sire *vt* to move to pity; **impietosirsi** *vpr* to be moved to pity

impigli'arsi *vpr* to get caught up o entangled

impi'grirsi *vpr* to grow lazy

impli'care *vt* to imply; *(coinvolgere)* to involve

im'plicito, -a [im'plitʃito] *ag* implicit

implo'rare *vt* to implore; *(pietà ecc)* to beg for

impolve'rarsi *vpr* to get dusty

im'pone *ecc vb vedi* **imporre**

impo'nente *ag* imposing, impressive

im'pongo *ecc vb vedi* **imporre**

impo'nibile *ag* taxable ▶ *sm* taxable income

impopo'lare *ag* unpopular

im'porre *vt* to impose; *(costringere)* to force, make; *(far valere)* to impose, enforce; **imporsi** *vpr (persona)* to assert o.s.; *(cosa: rendersi necessario)* to become necessary; *(aver successo: moda, attore)* to become popular; **~ a qn di fare** to force sb to do, make sb do

impor'tante *ag* important

impor'tanza *sf* importance; **dare importanza a qc** to attach importance to sth; **darsi importanza** to give o.s. airs

impor'tare *vt (introdurre dall'estero)* to import ▶ *vi* to matter, be important ▶ *vb impers (essere necessario)* to be necessary; *(interessare)* to matter; **non importa!** it doesn't matter!; **non me ne importa!** I don't care!

im'porto *sm (total)* amount

importu'nare *vt* to bother

im'posi *ecc vb vedi* **imporre**

imposizi'one [impozit'tsjone] *sf* imposition; order, command; *(onere, imposta)* tax

imposses'sarsi *vpr* **~ di** to seize, take possession of

impos'sibile *ag* impossible; **fare l'~** to do one's utmost, do all one can

im'posta *sf (di finestra)* shutter; *(tassa)* tax; **imposta sul reddito** income tax; **imposta sul valore aggiunto** value added tax *(BRIT)*, sales tax *(US)*

impos'tare *vt (imbucare)* to post; *(preparare)* to plan, set out; *(avviare)* to begin, start off; *(voce)* to pitch

impostazi'one [impostat'tsjone] *sf (di lettera)* posting *(BRIT)*, mailing *(US)*; *(di problema, questione)*

formulation, statement; (di lavoro)
organization, planning; (di attività)
setting up; (Mus: di voce) pitch;
impostazioni sfpl (di computer)
settings

impo'tente ag weak, powerless;
(anche Med) impotent

impratʹicabile ag (strada)
impassable; (campo di gioco)
unplayable

impreʹcare vi to curse, swear; ~
contro to hurl abuse at

imprecaziʹone [imprekatʹtsjone] sf
abuse, curse

impreʹgnare [imprepʹpare] vt ~
(di) (imbevere) to soak o impregnate
(with); (riempire) to fill (with)

imprendiʹtore sm (industriale)
entrepreneur; (appaltatore)
contractor; **piccolo ~** small
businessman

imʹpresa sf (iniziativa) enterprise;
(azione) exploit; (azienda) firm,
concern

impressioʹnante ag impressive,
upsetting

impressioʹnare vt to impress;
(turbare) to upset; (Fot) to expose;
impressionarsi vpr to be easily upset

impressiʹone sf impression; (fig:
sensazione) sensation, feeling;
(stampa) printing; **fare ~ (colpire)** to
impress; (turbare) to frighten, upset;
fare buona/cattiva ~ a to make a
good/bad impression on

impreveʹdibile ag unforeseeable;
(persona) unpredictable

impreʹvisto, -a ag unexpected,
unforeseen ▸ sm unforeseen event;
salvo imprevisti unless anything
unexpected happens

imprigioʹnare [impridʒoʹnare] vt to
imprison

improʹbabile ag improbable, unlikely

imʹpronta sf imprint, impression;

sign; (di piede, mano) print; (fig)
mark, stamp; **impronta digitale**
fingerprint

improvvisaʹmente av suddenly;
unexpectedly

improvviʹsare vt to improvise

improvviʹviso, -a ag (imprevisto)
unexpected; (subitaneo) sudden; **all'~**
unexpectedly; suddenly

impruʹdente ag unwise, rash

impuʹgnare [impupʹpare] vt to grasp,
grip; (Dir) to contest

impulʹsivo, -a ag impulsive

imʹpulso sm impulse

impunʹtarsi vpr to stop dead, refuse
to budge; (fig) to be obstinate

impuʹtato, -a sm/f (Dir) accused,
defendant

in
(in + il = **nel**, in + lo = **nello**, in + l' =
nell', in + la = **nella**, in + i = **nei**, in + gli =
negli, in + le = **nelle**) prep

1 (stato in luogo); in; **vivere in Italia/**
città to live in Italy/town; **essere in**
casa/ufficio to be at home/the office;
se fossi in te if I were you

2 (moto a luogo) to; (: dentro) into;
andare in Germania/città to go to
Germany/town; **andare in ufficio** to
go to the office; **entrare in macchina/**
casa to get into the car/go into the
house

3 (tempo): in; **nel 1989** in 1989; **in**
giugno/estate in June/summer

4 (modo, maniera); in; **in silenzio** in
silence; **in abito da sera** in evening
dress; **in guerra** at war; **in vacanza** on
holiday; **Maria Bianchi in Rossi** Maria
Rossi née Bianchi

5 (mezzo) by; **viaggiare in autobus/**
treno to travel by bus/train

6 (materia) made of; **in marmo** made
of marble, marble cpd; **una collana in**
oro a gold necklace

7 (misura) in; **siamo in quattro** there

are four of us; **in tutto** in all
8 (fine): **dare in dono** to give as a gift;
spende tutto in alcool he spends all
his money on drink; **in onore di** in
honour of

inabi'tabile ag uninhabitable
inacces'sibile [inattʃes'sibile]
ag (luogo) inaccessible; (persona)
unapproachable
inaccet'tabile [inattʃet'tabile] ag
unacceptable
ina'datto, -a ag ~ (a) unsuitable o
unfit (for)
inadegu'ato, -a ag inadequate
inaffi'dabile ag unreliable
inami'dato, -a ag starched
inar'care vt (schiena) to arch;
(sopracciglia) to raise
inaspet'tato, -a ag unexpected
inas'prire vt (disciplina) to tighten up,
make harsher; (carattere) to embitter;
inasprirsi vpr to become harsher; to
become bitter; to become worse
inattac'cabile ag (anche fig)
unassailable; (alibi) cast-iron
inatten'dibile ag unreliable
inat'teso, -a ag unexpected
inattu'abile ag impracticable
inau'dito, -a ag unheard of
inaugu'rare vt to inaugurate, open;
(monumento) to unveil
inaugurazi'one [inaugurat'tsjone] sf
inauguration; unveiling
incal'lito, -a ag calloused; (fig)
hardened, inveterate; (: insensibile)
hard
incande'scente [inkande'ʃʃente] ag
incandescent, white-hot
incan'tare vt to enchant, bewitch;
incantarsi vpr (rimanere intontito)
to be spellbound; to be in a daze;
(meccanismo: bloccarsi) to jam;
incan'tevole ag charming,
enchanting
in'canto sm spell, charm,

enchantment; (asta) auction; **come
per ~** as if by magic; **mettere all'~** to
put up for auction
inca'pace [inka'patʃe] ag incapable
incarce'rare [inkartʃe'rare] vt to
imprison
incari'care vt ~ qn di fare to give
sb the responsibility of doing;
incaricarsi di to take care o charge of
in'carico, -chi sm task, job
incarta'mento sm dossier, file
incar'tare vt to wrap (in paper)
incas'sare vt (merce) to pack (in
cases); (gemma: incastonare) to set;
(Econ: riscuotere) to collect; (Pugilato:
colpi) to take, stand up to; **in'casso**
sm cashing, encashment; (introito)
takings pl
incas'trare vt to fit in, insert; (fig:
intrappolare) to catch; **incastrarsi** vpr
(combaciare) to fit together; (restare
bloccato) to become stuck
incate'nare vt to chain up
in'cauto, -a ag imprudent, rash
inca'vato, -a ag hollow; (occhi)
sunken
incendi'are [intʃen'djare] vt to set fire
to; **incendiarsi** vpr to catch fire, burst
into flames
in'cendio [in'tʃendjo] sm fire
incene'ritore [intʃeneri'tore] sm
incinerator
in'censo [in'tʃenso] sm incense
incensu'rato, -a [intʃensu'rato] ag
(Dir): **essere ~** to have a clean record
incenti'vare [intʃenti'vare] vt
(produzione, vendite) to boost; (persona)
to motivate
incen'tivo [intʃen'tivo] sm incentive
inceppar'si vpr to jam
incer'tezza [intʃer'tettsa] sf
uncertainty
in'certo, -a [in'tʃerto] ag uncertain;
(irresoluto) undecided, hesitating ▶ sm
uncertainty

in'cetta [in'tʃetta] sf buying up; **fare ~ di** qc to buy up sth

inchi'esta [in'kjɛsta] sf investigation, inquiry

inchinarsi vpr to bend down; (per riverenza) to bow; (: donna) to curtsy

inchio'dare [inkjo'dare] vt to nail (down); **~ la macchina** (Aut) to jam on the brakes

inchi'ostro [in'kjɔstro] sm ink; **inchiostro simpatico** invisible ink

inciam'pare [intʃam'pare] vi to trip, stumble

inci'dente [intʃi'dɛnte] sm accident; **ho avuto un ~** I've had an accident; **incidente automobilistico** o **d'auto** car accident; **incidente diplomatico** diplomatic incident

in'cidere [in'tʃidere] vi **~ su** to bear upon, affect ▶ vt (tagliare incavando) to cut into; (Arte) to engrave; to etch; (canzone) to record

in'cinta [in'tʃinta] ag f pregnant

incipri'are [intʃi'prjare] vt to powder

incipriarsi ▶ vpr to powder one's face

in'circa [in'tʃirka] av **all'~** more or less, very nearly

in'cisi ecc [in'tʃizi] vb vedi **incidere**

incisi'one [intʃi'zjone] sf cut; (disegno) engraving; etching; (registrazione) recording; (Med) incision

in'ciso, -a [in'tʃizo] pp di **incidere** ▶ sm **per ~** incidentally, by the way

inci'tare [intʃi'tare] vt to incite

inci'vile [intʃi'vile] ag uncivilized; (villano) impolite

incl. abbr (= incluso) encl.

incli'nare vt to tilt; **inclinarsi** vpr (barca) to list; (aereo) to bank

in'cludere vt to include; (accludere) to enclose; **in'cluso, -a** pp di **includere** ▶ ag included; enclosed

incoe'rente ag incoherent; (contraddittorio) inconsistent

in'cognita [in'kɔɲɲita] sf (Mat, fig) unknown quantity

in'cognito, -a [in'kɔɲɲito] ag unknown ▶ sm **in ~** incognito

incol'lare vt to glue, gum; (unire con colla) to stick together

inco'lore ag colourless

incol'pare vt **~ qn di** to charge sb with

in'colto, -a ag (terreno) uncultivated; (trascurato: capelli) neglected; (persona) uneducated

in'colume ag safe and sound, unhurt

incom'benza [inkom'bɛntsa] sf duty, task

in'combere vi (sovrastare minacciando): **~ su** to threaten, hang over

incominci'are [inkomin'tʃare] vi, vt to begin, start

incompe'tente ag incompetent

incompi'uto, -a ag unfinished, incomplete

incom'pleto, -a ag incomplete

incompren'sibile ag incomprehensible

inconce'pibile [inkontʃe'pibile] ag inconceivable

inconcili'abile [inkontʃi'ljabile] ag irreconcilable

inconclu'dente ag inconclusive; (persona) ineffectual

incondizio'nato, -a [inkondittsjo'nato] ag unconditional

inconfon'dibile ag unmistakable

inconsa'pevole ag **~ di** unaware of, ignorant of

in'conscio, -a, -sci, -sce [in'kɔnʃo] ag unconscious ▶ sm (Psic): **l'~** the unconscious

inconsis'tente ag insubstantial; unfounded

inconsu'eto, -a ag unusual

incon'trare vt to meet; (difficoltà) to meet with; **incontrarsi** vpr to meet

in'contro av **~ a** (verso) towards ▶ sm meeting; (Sport) match; meeting; **incontro di calcio** football match

inconveni'ente sm drawback, snag
incoraggia'mento [inkoraddʒa'mento] sm encouragement
incoraggi'are [inkorad'dʒare] vt to encourage
incornici'are [inkorni'tʃare] vt to frame
incoro'nare vt to crown
in'correre vi ~ **in** to meet with, run into
incosci'ente [inkoʃ'ʃente] ag (inconscio) unconscious; (irresponsabile) reckless, thoughtless
incre'dibile ag incredible, unbelievable
in'credulo, -a ag incredulous, disbelieving
incremen'tare vt to increase; (dar sviluppo a) to promote
incre'mento sm (sviluppo) development; (aumento numerico) increase, growth
incresci'oso, -a [inkreʃ'ʃoso] ag (incidente ecc) regrettable
incrimi'nare vt (Dir) to charge
incri'nare vt to crack; (fig: rapporti, amicizia) to cause to deteriorate; **incrinarsi** vpr to crack; to deteriorate
incroci'are [inkro'tʃare] vt to cross; (incontrare) to meet ▶ vi (Naut, Aer) to cruise; **incrociarsi** vpr (strade) to cross, intersect; (persone, veicoli) to pass each other; **~ le braccia/le gambe** to fold one's arms/cross one's legs
in'crocio [in'krotʃo] sm (anche Ferr) crossing; (di strade) crossroads
incuba'trice [inkuba'tritʃe] sf incubator
'incubo sm nightmare
incu'rabile ag incurable
incu'rante ag ~ **(di)** heedless (of), careless (of)
incurio'sire vt to make curious;

incuriosirsi vpr to become curious
incursi'one sf raid
incur'vare vt to bend, curve; **incurvarsi** vpr to bend, curve
incus'todito, -a ag unguarded, unattended
in'cutere vt ~ **timore/rispetto a qn** to strike fear into sb/command sb's respect
'indaco sm indigo
indaffa'rato, -a ag busy
inda'gare vt to investigate
in'dagine [in'dadʒine] sf investigation, inquiry; (ricerca) research, study; **indagine di mercato** market survey
indebi'tarsi vpr to run o get into debt
indebo'lire vt, vi (anche: **indebolirsi**) to weaken
inde'cente [inde'tʃente] ag indecent
inde'ciso, -a [inde'tʃizo] ag indecisive; (irresoluto) undecided
indefi'nito, -a ag (anche Ling) indefinite; (impreciso, non determinato) undefined
in'degno, -a [in'deɲɲo] ag (atto) shameful; (persona) unworthy
indemoni'ato, -a ag possessed (by the devil)
in'denne ag unhurt, uninjured
indenniz'zare [indennid'dzare] vt to compensate
indetermina'tivo, -a ag (Ling) indefinite
'India sf l'~ India; **indi'ano, -a** ag Indian ▶ sm/f(d'India) Indian; (d'America) NativeAmerican, (American) Indian
indi'care vt (mostrare) to show, indicate; (: col dito) to point to, point out; (consigliare) to suggest, recommend; **indica'tivo, -a** ag indicative ▶ sm (Ling) indicative (mood); **indicazi'one** sf indication; (informazione) piece of information

'**indice** ['inditʃe] *sm* index; (*fig*) sign; (*dito*) index finger, forefinger; **indice di gradimento** (*Radio*, *TV*) popularity rating

indicherò *ecc* [indike'rɔ] *vb vedi* **indicare**

indi'cibile [indi'tʃibile] *ag* inexpressible

indietreggi'are [indjetred'dʒare] *vi* to draw back, retreat

indi'etro *av back*; (*guardare*) behind, back; (*andare, cadere: anche:* **all'~**) backwards; **rimanere ~** to be left behind; **essere ~** (*col lavoro*) to be behind; (*orologio*) to be slow; **rimandare qc ~** to send sth back

indi'feso, -a *ag* (*città ecc*) undefended; (*persona*) defenceless

indiffe'rente *ag* indifferent

in'digeno, -a [in'didʒeno] *ag* indigenous, native ▸ *sm/f* native

indigesti'one [indidʒes'tjone] *sf* indigestion

indi'gesto, -a [indi'dʒesto] *ag* indigestible

indi'gnare [indiɲ'ɲare] *vt* to fill with indignation; **indignarsi** *vpr* to get indignant

indimenti'cabile *ag* unforgettable

indipen'dente *ag* independent

in'dire *vt* (*concorso*) to announce; (*elezioni*) to call

indi'retto, -a *ag* indirect

indiriz'zare [indirit'tsare] *vt* (*dirigere*) to direct; (*mandare*) to send; (*lettera*) to address

indi'rizzo [indi'rittso] *sm* address; (*direzione*) direction; (*avvio*) trend, course; **il mio ~ è...** my address is ...

indis'creto, -a *ag* indiscreet

indis'cusso, -a *ag* unquestioned

indispen'sabile *ag* indispensable, essential

indispet'tire *vt* to irritate, annoy ▸ *vi* (*anche:* **indispettirsi**) to get irritated

o annoyed

individu'ale *ag* individual

individu'are *vt* (*dar forma distinta a*) to characterize; (*determinare*) to locate; (*riconoscere*) to single out

indi'viduo *sm* individual

indizi'ato, -a *ag* suspected ▸ *sm/f* suspect

in'dizio [in'dittsjo] *sm* (*segno*) sign, indication; (*Polizia*) clue; (*Dir*) piece of evidence

'indole *sf* nature, character

indolen'zito, -a [indolen'tsito] *ag* stiff, aching; (*intorpidito*) numb

indo'lore *ag* painless

indo'mani *sm* **l'~** the next day, the following day

Indo'nesia *sf* **l'~** Indonesia

indos'sare *vt* (*mettere indosso*) to put on; (*avere indosso*) to have on; **indossa'tore, -'trice** *sm/f* model

indottri'nare *vt* to indoctrinate

indovi'nare *vt* (*scoprire*) to guess; (*immaginare*) to imagine, guess; (*il futuro*) to foretell; **indovi'nello** *sm* riddle

indubbia'mente *av* undoubtedly

in'dubbio, -a *ag* certain, undoubted

in'duco *ecc vb vedi* **indurre**

indugi'are [indu'dʒare] *vi* to take one's time, delay

in'dugio [in'dudʒo] *sm* (*ritardo*) delay; **senza ~** without delay

indul'gente [indul'dʒɛnte] *ag* indulgent; (*giudice*) lenient

indu'mento *sm* article of clothing, garment

indu'rire *vt* to harden ▸ *vi* (*anche:* **indurirsi**) to harden, become hard

in'durre *vt* **~ qn a fare qc** to induce o persuade sb to do sth; **~ qn in errore** to mislead sb

in'dussi *ecc vb vedi* **indurre**

in'dustria *sf* industry; **industri'ale** *ag* industrial ▸ *sm* industrialist

inecce'pibile [inettʃe'pibile] *ag* unexceptionable

i'nedito, -a *ag* unpublished

ine'rente *ag* ~ **a** concerning, regarding

i'nerme *ag* unarmed; defenceless

inerpi'carsi *vpr* ~ **(su)** to clamber (up)

i'nerte *ag* inert; (*inattivo*) indolent, sluggish

ine'satto, -a *ag* (*impreciso*) inexact; (*erroneo*) incorrect; (*Amm: non riscosso*) uncollected

inesis'tente *ag* non-existent

inesperi'enza [inespe'rjentsa] *sf* inexperience

ines'perto, -a *ag* inexperienced

inevi'tabile *ag* inevitable

i'nezia [i'nettsja] *sf* trifle, thing of no importance

infagot'tare *vt* to bundle up, wrap up; **infagottarsi** *vpr* to wrap up

infal'libile *ag* infallible

infa'mante *ag* defamatory

in'fame *ag* infamous; (*fig: cosa, compito*) awful, dreadful

infan'gare *vt* to cover with mud; (*fig: reputazione*) to sully; **infangarsi** *vpr* to get covered in mud; to be sullied

infan'tile *ag* child *cpd*; childlike; (*adulto, azione*) childish; **letteratura ~** children's books *pl*

in'fanzia [in'fantsja] *sf* childhood; (*bambini*) children *pl*; **prima ~** babyhood, infancy

infari'nare *vt* to cover with (*o sprinkle* with *o* dip in) flour; **infarina'tura** *sf* (*fig*) smattering

in'farto *sm* (*Med*) heart attack

infasti'dire *vt* to annoy, irritate; **infastidirsi** *vpr* to get annoyed *o* irritated

infati'cabile *ag* tireless, untiring

in'fatti *cong* actually, as a matter of fact

Attenzione! In inglese esiste

l'espressione *in fact* che però vuol dire *in effetti*.

infatu'arsi *vpr* ~ **di** to become infatuated with, fall for

infe'dele *ag* unfaithful

infe'lice [infe'litʃe] *ag* unhappy; (*sfortunato*) unlucky, unfortunate; (*inopportuno*) inopportune, ill-timed; (*mal riuscito: lavoro*) bad, poor

inferi'ore *ag* lower; (*per intelligenza, qualità*) inferior ▶ *sm/f* inferior; ~ **a** (*numero, quantità*) less *o* smaller than; (*meno buono*) inferior to; ~ **alla media** below average; **inferiorità** *sf* inferiority

infer'meria *sf* infirmary; (*di scuola, nave*) sick bay

infermi'ere, -a *sm/f* nurse

infermità *sf inv* illness; infirmity; **infermità mentale** mental illness; (*Dir*) insanity

in'fermo, -a *ag* (*ammalato*) ill; (*debole*) infirm

infer'nale *ag* infernal; (*proposito, complotto*) diabolical

in'ferno *sm* hell

inferri'ata *sf* grating

infes'tare *vt* to infest

infet'tare *vt* to infect; **infettarsi** *vpr* to become infected; **infezi'one** *sf* infection

infiam'mabile *ag* inflammable

infiam'mare *vt* to set alight; (*fig, Med*) to inflame; **infiammarsi** *vpr* to catch fire; (*Med*) to become inflamed; **infiammazi'one** *sf* (*Med*) inflammation

infie'rire *vi* ~ **su** (*fisicamente*) to attack furiously; (*verbalmente*) to rage at

infi'lare *vt* (*ago*) to thread; (*mettere: chiave*) to insert; (: *anello, vestito*) to slip *o* put on; (*strada*) to turn into, take; **infilarsi** *vpr* infilarsi in to slip into; (*indossare*) to slip on; ~ **l'uscio** to slip in; to slip out

infil'trarsi vpr to penetrate, seep through; (Mil) to infiltrate

infil'zare [infil'tsare] vt (infilare) to string together; (trafiggere) to pierce

'infimo, -a ag lowest

in'fine av finally; (insomma) in short

infinità sf infinity; (in quantità): **un'~ di** an infinite number of

infi'nito, -a ag infinite; (Ling) infinitive ▸ sm infinity; (Ling) infinitive; **all'~** (senza fine) endlessly

infinocchi'are [infinok'kjare] (fam) vt to hoodwink

infischi'arsi [infis'kjarsi] vpr **~ di** not to care about

in'fisso, -a (pp) di **infiggere** sm fixture; (di porta, finestra) frame

inflazi'one [inflat'tsjone] sf inflation

in'fliggere [in'flidʒere] vt to inflict

in'flissi ecc vb vedi **infliggere**

influ'ente ag influential; **influ'enza** sf influence; (Med) influenza, flu

influen'zare [influen'tsare] vt to influence, have an influence on

influ'ire vi **~ su** to influence

in'flusso sm influence

infon'dato, -a ag unfounded, groundless

in'fondere vt **~ qc in qn** to instill sth in sb

infor'mare vt to inform, tell; **informarsi** vpr informarsi (di o su) to inquire (about)

infor'matica sf computer science

informa'tivo, -a ag informative

infor'mato, -a ag informed; **tenersi ~** to keep o.s. (well-)informed

informa'tore sm informer

informazi'one [informat'tsjone] sf piece of information; **prendere informazioni sul conto di qn** to get information about sb; **chiedere un'~** to ask for (some) information

in'forme ag shapeless

informico'larsi vpr to have pins and needles

infortu'nato, -a ag injured, hurt ▸ sm/f injured person

infor'tunio sm accident; **infortunio sul lavoro** industrial accident, accident at work

infra'dito sm inv (calzatura) flip flop (BRIT), thong (US)

infrazi'one [infrat'tsjone] sf **~ a** breaking of, violation of

infred'datura sf slight cold

infred'dolito, -a ag cold, chilled

infu'ori av out; **all'~ outwards**; **all'~ di** (eccetto) except, with the exception of

infuri'arsi vpr to fly into a rage

infusi'one sf infusion

in'fuso, -a pp di **infondere** ▸ sm infusion

Ing. abbr = **ingegnere**

ingaggi'are [ingad'dʒare] vt (assumere con compenso) to take on, hire; (Sport) to sign on; (Mil) to engage

ingan'nare vt to deceive; (fisco) to cheat; (eludere) to dodge, elude; (fig: tempo) to while away ▸ vi (apparenza) to be deceptive; **ingannarsi** vpr to be mistaken, be wrong

in'ganno sm deceit, deception; (azione) trick; (menzogna, frode) cheat, swindle; (illusione) illusion

inge'gnarsi [indʒen'narsi] vpr to do one's best, try hard; **~ per vivere** to live by one's wits

inge'gnere [indʒen'nɛre] sm engineer; **~ civile/navale** civil/ naval engineer; **ingegne'ria** sf engineering; **ingegneria genetica** genetic engineering

in'gegno [in'dʒenno] sm (intelligenza) intelligence, brains pl; (capacità creativa) ingenuity; (disposizione) talent; **inge'gnoso, -a** ag ingenious, clever

ingelo'sire [indʒelo'zire] vt to make jealous ▸ vi (anche: **ingelosirsi**) to become jealous

in'gente [in'dʒɛnte] *ag* huge, enormous

ingenuità [indʒenui'ta] *sf* ingenuousness

in'genuo, -a [in'dʒɛnuo] *ag* naïve
Attenzione! In inglese esiste la parola *ingenious*, che però significa *ingegnoso*.

inge'rire [indʒe'rire] *vt* to ingest

inges'sare [indʒes'sare] *vt* (*Med*) to put in plaster; **ingessa'tura** *sf* plaster

Inghil'terra [ingil'tɛrra] *sf* l'~ England

inghiot'tire [ingjot'tire] *vt* to swallow

ingial'lire [indʒal'lire] *vi* to go yellow .

inginocchi'arsi [indʒinok'kjarsi] *vpr* to kneel (down)

ingiù [in'dʒu] *av* down, downwards

ingi'uria [in'dʒurja] *sf* insult; (*fig: danno*) damage

ingiu'stizia [indʒus'tittsja] *sf* injustice

ingi'usto, -a [in'dʒusto] *ag* unjust, unfair

in'glese *ag* English ▶ *sm/f* Englishman/woman ▶ *sm* (*Ling*) English; **gli Inglesi** the English; **andarsene** o **filare all'~** to take French leave

ingoi'are *vt* to gulp (down); (*fig*) to swallow (up)

ingol'farsi *vpr* to flood

ingom'brante *ag* cumbersome

ingom'brare *vt* (*strada*) to block; (*stanza*) to clutter up

in'gordo, -a *ag ~ di* greedy for; (*fig*) greedy o avid for

in'gorgo, -ghi *sm* blockage, obstruction; (*anche:* ~ **stradale**) traffic jam

ingoz'zarsi *vpr ~* **(di)** to stuff o.s. (with)

ingra'naggio [ingra'naddʒo] *sm* (*Tecn*) gear; (*di orologio*) mechanism;

gli **ingranaggi della burocrazia** the bureaucratic machinery

ingra'nare *vi* to mesh, engage ▶ *vt* to engage; ~ **la marcia** to get into gear

ingrandi'mento *sm* enlargement; extension

ingran'dire *vt* (*anche Fot*) to enlarge; (*estendere*) to extend; (*Ottica, fig*) to magnify ▶ *vi* (*anche:* **ingrandirsi**) to become larger o bigger; (*aumentare*) to grow, increase; (*espandersi*) to expand

ingras'sare *vt* to make fat; (*animali*) to fatten; (*lubrificare*) to oil, lubricate ▶ *vi* (*anche:* **ingrassarsi**) to get fat, put on weight

in'grato, -a *ag* ungrateful; (*lavoro*) thankless, unrewarding

ingredi'ente *sm* ingredient

in'gresso *sm* (*porta*) entrance; (*atrio*) hall; (*l'entrare*) entrance, entry; (*facoltà di entrare*) admission; **ingresso libero** admission free

ingros'sare *vt* to increase; (*folla, livello*) to swell ▶ *vi* (*anche:* **ingrossarsi**) to increase; to swell

in'grosso *av* **all'~** (*Comm*) wholesale; (*all'incirca*) roughly, about

ingua'ribile *ag* incurable

'inguine *sm* (*Anat*) groin

ini'bire *vt* to forbid, prohibit; (*Psic*) to inhibit; **inibirsi** *vpr* to restrain o.s.

ini'bito, -a *ag* inhibited ▶ *sm/f* inhibited person

iniet'tare *vt* to inject; **iniezi'one** *sf* injection

ininterrotta'mente *av* non-stop, continuously

ininter'rotto, -a *ag* unbroken; uninterrupted

inizi'ale [init'tsjale] *ag, sf* initial

inizi'are [init'tsjare] *vi, vt* to begin, start; **a che ora inizia il film?** when does the film start?; ~ **qn a** to initiate sb into; (*pittura ecc*) to introduce sb to; ~ **a fare qc** to start doing sth

inizia'tiva [inittsja'tiva] *sf* initiative; **iniziativa privata** private enterprise

i'nizio [i'nittsjo] *sm* beginning; **all'~** at the beginning, at the start; **dare ~ a qc** to start sth, get sth going

innaffi'are *ecc* = **annaffiare** *ecc*

innamo'rarsi *vpr* **~ (di qn)** to fall in love (with); **innamo'rato, -a** *ag (che nutre amore)*: **innamorato (di)** in love (with); *(appassionato)*: **innamorato di** very fond of ▸ *sm/f* lover; sweetheart

innanzi'tutto *av* first of all

in'nato, -a *ag* innate

innatu'rale *ag* unnatural

inne'gabile *ag* undeniable

innervo'sire *vt* **~ qn** to get on sb's nerves; **innervosirsi** *vpr* to get irritated o upset

innes'care *vt* to prime

'inno *sm* hymn; **inno nazionale** national anthem

inno'cente [inno'tʃɛnte] *ag* innocent

in'nocuo, -a *ag* innocuous, harmless

innova'tivo, -a *ag* innovative

innume'revole *ag* innumerable

inol'trare *vt (Amm)* to pass on, forward

i'noltre *av* besides, moreover

inon'dare *vt* to flood

inoppor'tuno, -a *ag* untimely, ill-timed; *(inappropriato)*: *(momento)* inopportune

inorri'dire *vt* to horrify ▸ *vi* to be horrified

inosser'vato, -a *ag (non notato)* unobserved; *(non rispettato)* not observed, not kept

inossi'dabile *ag* stainless

INPS *sigla m (= Istituto Nazionale Previdenza Sociale)* social security service

inqua'drare *vt (foto, immagine)* to frame; *(fig)* to situate, set

inqui'eto, -a *ag* restless; *(preoccupato)* worried, anxious

inqui'lino, -a *sm/f* tenant

inquina'mento *sm* pollution

inqui'nare *vt* to pollute

insab'biare *vt (fig: pratica)* to shelve; **insabbiarsi** *vpr (arenarsi: barca)* to run aground; *(fig: pratica)* to be shelved

insac'cati *smpl (Cuc)* sausages

insa'lata *sf* salad; **insalata mista** mixed salad; **insalata russa** *(Cuc)* Russian salad *(comprised of cold diced cooked vegetables in mayonnaise)*; **insalati'era** *sf* salad bowl

insa'nabile *ag (piaga)* which cannot be healed; *(situazione)* irremediable; *(odio)* implacable

insa'puta *sf* **all'~ di qn** without sb knowing

inse'diarsi *vpr* to take up office; *(popolo, colonia)* to settle

in'segna [in'seɲɲa] *sf* sign; *(emblema)* sign, emblem; *(bandiera)* flag, banner

insegna'mento [inseɲɲa'mento] *sm* teaching

inse'gnante [inseɲ'ɲante] *ag* teaching ▸ *sm/f* teacher

inse'gnare [inseɲ'ɲare] *vt, vi* to teach; **~ a qn qc** to teach sb sth; **~ a qn a fare qc** to teach sb (how) to do sth

insegui'mento *sm* pursuit, chase

insegui're *vt* to pursue, chase

insena'tura *sf* inlet, creek

insen'sato, -a *ag* senseless, stupid

insen'sibile *ag (nervo)* insensible; *(persona)* indifferent

inse'rire *vt* to insert; *(Elettr)* to connect; *(allegare)* to enclose; *(annuncio)* to put in, place; **inserirsi** *vpr (fig)*: **inserirsi in** to become part of

inservi'ente *sm/f* attendant

inserzi'one [inser'tsjone] *sf* insertion; *(avviso)* advertisement; **fare un'~ sul giornale** to put an advertisement in the paper

insetti'cida, -i [insetti'tʃida] *sm* insecticide

in'setto sm insect

insi'curo, -a ag insecure

insi'eme av together ▶ prep – a o con together with ▶ sm whole; (Mat, servizio, assortimento) set; (Moda) ensemble, outfit; **tutti** ~ all together; **tutto** ~ all together; (in una volta) at one go; **nell'** ~ on the whole; **d'** ~ (veduta ecc) overall

in'segne [in'siɲɲe] ag (persona) famous, distinguished; (città, monumento) notable

insignifi'cante [insiɲɲifi'kante] ag insignificant

insinu'are vt (introdurre): ~ qc in to slip o slide sth into; (fig) to insinuate, imply; **insinuarsi** vpr **insinuarsi in** to seep into; (fig) to creep into; to worm one's way into

in'sipido, -a ag insipid

insis'tente ag insistent; persistent

in'sistere vi ~ **su qc** to insist on sth; ~ **in qc/a fare** (perseverare) to persist in sth/in doing

insoddis'fatto, -a ag dissatisfied

insoffe'rente ag intolerant

insolazi'one [insolat'tsjone] sf (Med) sunstroke

inso'lente ag insolent

in'solito, -a ag unusual, out of the ordinary

inso'luto, -a ag (non risolto) unsolved

in'somma av (in conclusione) in short; (dunque) well ▶ escl for heaven's sake!

in'sonne ag sleepless; **in'sonnia** sf insomnia, sleeplessness

insonno'lito, -a ag sleepy, drowsy

insoppor'tabile ag unbearable

in'sorgere [in'sordʒere] vi (ribellarsi) to rise up, rebel; (apparire) to come up, arise

in'sorsi ecc vb vedi **insorgere**

insospet'tire vt to make suspicious ▶ vi (anche: **insospettirsi**) to become suspicious

inspi'rare vt to breathe in, inhale

in'stabile ag (carico, indole) unstable; (tempo) unsettled; (equilibrio) unsteady

instal'lare vt to install

instan'cabile ag untiring, indefatigable

instau'rare vt to introduce, institute

insuc'cesso [insut'tʃesso] sm failure, flop

insuffici'ente [insuffi'tʃente] ag insufficient; (compito, allievo) inadequate; **insuffici'enza** sf insufficiency; inadequacy; (Ins) fail; **insufficienza di prove** (Dir) lack of evidence; **insufficienza renale** renal insufficiency

insu'lina sf insulin

in'sulso, -a ag (sciocco) inane, silly; (persona) dull, insipid

insul'tare vt to insult, affront

in'sulto sm insult, affront

intac'care vt (fare tacche) to cut into; (corrodere) to corrode; (fig: cominciare ad usare: risparmi) to break into; (: ledere) to damage

intagli'are [intaʎ'ʎare] vt to carve

in'tanto av (nel frattempo) meanwhile, in the meantime; (per cominciare) just to begin with; ~ **che** while

inta'sare vt to choke (up), block (up); (Aut) to obstruct, block; **intasarsi** vpr to become choked o blocked

intas'care vt to pocket

in'tatto, -a ag intact; (puro) unsullied

intavo'lare vt to start, enter into

inte'grale ag complete; (pane, farina) wholemeal (BRIT), whole-wheat (US); (Mat): **calcolo** ~ integral calculus

inte'grante ag **parte** ~ integral part

inte'grare vt to complete; (Mat) to integrate; **integrarsi** vpr (persona) to become integrated

integra'tore sm **integratori alimentari** nutritional supplements

integrità sf integrity

'integro, -a ag (intatto, intero) complete, whole; (retto) upright

intelaia'tura sf frame; (fig) structure, framework

intel'letto sm intellect;
intellettu'ale sm/f intellectual

intelli'gente [intelli'dʒɛnte] ag intelligent

intem'perie sfpl bad weather sg

in'tendere vt (avere intenzione) to: **fare qc** to intend o mean to do sth; (comprendere) to understand; (udire) to hear; (significare) to mean; **intendersi** vpr (conoscere): **intendersi di** to know a lot about, be a connoisseur of; (accordarsi) to get on (well); **intendersela con qn** (avere una relazione amorosa) to have an affair with sb; **intendi'tore, -'trice** sm/f connoisseur, expert

inten'sivo, -a ag intensive

in'tenso, -a ag intense

in'tento, -a ag (teso, assorto): **~ (a)** intent (on), absorbed (in) ▶ sm aim, purpose

intenzio'nale [intentsjo'nale] ag intentional

intenzi'one [inten'tsjone] sf intention; (Dir) intent; **avere ~ di fare qc** to intend o to do sth, have the intention of doing sth

interat'tivo, -a [interat'tivo] ag interactive

intercet'tare [intertʃet'tare] vt to intercept

intercity [intaʃi'ti] sm inv (Ferr) ≈ intercity (train)

inter'detto, -a pp di **interdire** ▶ ag forbidden, prohibited; (sconcertato) dumbfounded ▶ sm (Rel) interdict

interes'sante ag interesting; **essere in stato ~** to be expecting (a baby)

interes'sare vt to interest; (concernere) to concern, be of interest to; (far intervenire): **~ qn a** to draw

sb's attention to ▶ vi **~ a** to interest, matter to; **interessarsi** vpr (mostrare interesse): **interessarsi a** to take an interest in, be interested in; (occuparsi): **interessarsi di** to take care of

inte'resse sm (anche Comm) interest

inter'faccia, -ce [inter'fattʃa] sf (Inform) interface

interfe'renza [interfe'rentsa] sf interference

interfe'rire vi to interfere

interiezi'one [interjet'tsjone] sf exclamation, interjection

interi'ora sfpl entrails

interi'ore ag interior, inner, inside, internal; (fig) inner

inter'medio, -a ag intermediate

inter'nare vt (arrestare) to intern; (Med) to commit (to a mental institution)

inter'nauta sm/f Internet user

internazio'nale [internattsjo'nale] ag international

'Internet ['internet] sf Internet; **in ~** on the Internet

in'terno, -a ag (di dentro) internal, interior, inner; (: mare) inland; (nazionale) domestic; (allievo) boarding ▶ sm inside, interior; (di paese) interior; (fodera) lining; (di appartamento) flat (number); (Tel) extension ▶ sm/f (Ins) boarder; **interni** smpl (Cinema) interior shots; **all'~** inside; **Ministero degli Interni** Ministry of the Interior, ≈ Home Office (BRIT), Department of the Interior (US)

in'tero, -a ag (integro, intatto) whole, entire; (completo, totale) complete; (numero) whole; (non ridotto: biglietto) full; (latte) full-cream

interpel'lare vt to consult

interpre'tare vt to interpret;
in'terprete sm/f interpreter;

(Teatro) actor/actress, performer; (Mus) performer; **ci potrebbe fare da interprete?** could you act as an interpreter for us?

interregio'nale [interredʒo'nale] sm train that travels between two or more regions of Italy, stopping frequently

interro'gare vt to question; (Ins) to test; **interrogazi'one** sf questioning no pl; (Ins) oral test

inter'rompere vt to interrupt; (studi, trattative) to break off, interrupt; **interrompersi** vpr to break off, stop

interrut'tore sm switch

interruzi'one [interrut'tsjone] sf interruption; break

interur'bana sf trunk o long-distance call

inter'vallo sm interval; (spazio) space, gap

interve'nire vi (partecipare): ~ **a** to take part in; (intromettersi: anche Pol) to intervene; (Med: operare) to operate; **inter'vento** sm participation; (intromissione) intervention; (Med) operation; **fare un intervento nel corso di** (dibattito, programma) to take part in

inter'vista sf interview; **intervis'tare** vt to interview

intes'tare vt (lettera) to address; (proprietà): ~ **a** to register in the name of; **~ un assegno a qn** to make out a cheque to sb

intes'tato, -a ag (proprietà, casa, conto) in the name of; (assegno) made out to; **carta intestata** headed paper

intes'tino sm (Anat) intestine

intimidazi'one [intimidat'tsjone] sf intimidation

intimi'dire vt to intimidate ▸ vi (intimidirsi) to grow shy

intimità sf intimacy; privacy; (familiarità) familiarity

intimo, -a ag intimate; (affetti, vita)

private; (fig: profondo) inmost ▸ sm (persona) intimate o close friend; (dell'animo) bottom, depths pl; **parti intime** (Anat) private parts

in'tingolo sm sauce; (pietanza) stew

intito'lare vt to give a title to; (dedicare) to dedicate; **intitolarsi** vpr (libro, film) to be called

intolle'rabile ag intolerable

intolle'rante ag intolerant

in'tonaco, -ci o **chi** sm plaster

into'nare vt (canto) to start to sing; (armonizzare) to match; **intonarsi** vpr (colori) to go together; **intonarsi a** (carnagione) to suit; (abito) to go with, match

inton'tito, -a ag stunned, dazed; **~ dal sonno** stupid with sleep

in'toppo sm stumbling block, obstacle

in'torno av around; **~ a** (attorno a) around; (riguardo, circa) about

intossi'care vt to poison; **intossicazi'one** sf poisoning

intral'ciare [intral'tʃare] vt to hamper, hold up

intransi'tivo, -a ag, sm intransitive

intrapren'dente ag enterprising, go-ahead

intra'prendere vt to undertake

intrat'tabile ag intractable

intratte'nere vt to entertain; to engage in conversation; **intrattenersi** vpr to linger; **intrattenersi su qc** to dwell on sth

intrave'dere vt to catch a glimpse of; (fig) to foresee

intrecci'are [intret'tʃare] vt (capelli) to plait, braid; (intessere: anche fig) to weave, interweave, intertwine

intri'gante ag scheming ▸ sm/f schemer, intriguer

in'trinseco, -a, -ci, -che ag intrinsic

in'triso, -a ag **~ (di)** soaked (in)

intro'durre vt to introduce; (chiave)

ecc): **~ qc in** to insert sth into; (*persone: far entrare*) to show in; **introdursi** *vpr* (*moda, tecniche*) to be introduced; **introdursi in** (*persona: penetrare*) to enter; (: *entrare furtivamente*) to steal *o* slip into; **introduzi'one** *sf* introduction

in'troito *sm* income, revenue

intro'mettersi *vpr* to interfere, meddle; (*interporsi*) to intervene

in'truglio [in'truʎʎo] *sm* concoction

intrusi'one *sf* intrusion; interference

in'truso, -a *sm/f* intruder

intu'ire *vt* to perceive by intuition; (*rendersi conto*) to realize; **in'tuito** *sm* intuition; (*perspicacia*) perspicacity

inu'mano, -a *ag* inhuman

inumi'dire *vt* to dampen, moisten; **inumidirsi** *vpr* to become damp *o* wet

i'nutile *ag* useless; (*superfluo*) pointless, unnecessary

inutil'mente *av* unnecessarily; (*senza risultato*) in vain

inva'dente *ag* (*fig*) interfering, nosey

in'vadere *vt* to invade; (*affollare*) to swarm into, overrun; (*acque*) to flood

inva'ghirsi [inva'girsi] *vpr* **~ di** to take a fancy to

invalidità *sf* infirmity; disability; (*Dir*) invalidity

in'valido, -a *ag* (*infermo*) infirm, invalid; (*al lavoro*) disabled; (*Dir: nullo*) invalid ▶ *sm/f* invalid; disabled person

in'vano *av* in vain

invasi'one *sf* invasion

inva'sore, invadi'trice [invadi'tritʃe] *ag* invading ▶ *sm* invader

invecchi'are [invek'kjare] *vi* (*persona*) to grow old; (*vino, popolazione*) to age; (*moda*) to become dated ▶ *vt* to age; (*far apparire più vecchio*) to make look older

in'vece [in'vetʃe] *av* instead; (*al contrario*) on the contrary; **~ di**

instead of

inve'ire *vi* **~ contro** to rail against

inven'tare *vt* to invent; (*pericoli, pettegolezzi*) to make up, invent

inven'tario *sm* inventory; (*Comm*) stocktaking *no pl*

inven'tore *sm* inventor

invenzi'one [inven'tsjone] *sf* invention; (*bugia*) lie, story

inver'nale *ag* winter *cpd*; (*simile all'inverno*) wintry

in'verno *sm* winter

invero'simile *ag* unlikely

inversi'one *sf* inversion; reversal; **"divieto d'~"** (*Aut*) "no U-turns"

in'verso, -a *ag* opposite; (*Mat*) inverse ▶ *sm* contrary, opposite; **in senso ~** in the opposite direction; **in ordine ~** in reverse order

inver'tire *vt* to invert, reverse; **~ la marcia** (*Aut*) to do a U-turn

investi'gare *vt, vi* to investigate; **investiga'tore, -'trice** *sm/f* investigator, detective; **investigatore privato** private investigator

investi'mento *sm* (*Econ*) investment

inves'tire *vt* (*denaro*) to invest; (*veicolo: pedone*) to knock down; (: *altro veicolo*) to crash into; (*apostrofare*) to assail; (*incaricare*): **~ qn di** to invest sb with

invi'are *vt* to send; **invi'ato, -a** *sm/f* envoy; (*Stampa*) correspondent; **inviato speciale** (*Pol*) special envoy; (*di giornale*) special correspondent

in'vidia *sf* envy; **invidi'are** *vt*: **invidiare qn (per qc)** to envy sb for sth; **invidiare qc a qn** to envy sb sth; **invidi'oso, -a** *ag* envious

in'vio, -'vii *sm* sending; (*insieme di merci*) consignment; (*tasto*) Return (key), Enter (key)

invipe'rito, -a *ag* furious

invi'sibile *ag* invisible

invi'tare vt to invite; ~ **qn a fare** to invite sb to do; **invi'tato, -a** sm/f guest; **in'vito** sm invitation

invo'care vt (chiedere: aiuto, pace) to cry out for; (appellarsi: la legge, Dio) to appeal to, invoke

invogli'are [invoʎ'ʎare] vt ~ **qn a fare** to tempt sb to do, induce sb to do

involon'tario, -a ag (errore) unintentional; (gesto) involuntary

invol'tino sm (Cuc) roulade

in'volto sm (pacco) parcel; (fagotto) bundle

in'volucro sm cover, wrapping

inzup'pare [intsup'pare] vt to soak; **inzupparsi** vpr to get soaked

'io pron I ▶ sm inv I'~ the ego, the self; ~ **stesso(a)** I myself

i'odio sm iodine

l'onio sm Io ~, **il mar** ~ the Ionian (Sea)

ipermer'cato sm hypermarket

ipertensi'one sf high blood pressure, hypertension

iper'testo sm hypertext

ip'nosi sf hypnosis; **ipnotiz'zare** vt to hypnotize

ipocri'sia sf hypocrisy

i'pocrita, -i, -e ag hypocritical ▶ sm/f hypocrite

ipo'teca, -che sf mortgage

i'potesi sf inv hypothesis

'ippica sf horseracing

'ippico, -a, -ci, -che ag horse cpd

ippocas'tano sm horse chestnut

ip'podromo sm racecourse

ippo'potamo sm hippopotamus

'ipsilon sf o m inv (lettera) Y, y; (: del'alfabeto greco) upsilon

IR abbr (= Interregionale) long distance train which stops frequently

ira'cheno, -a [ira'kɛno] ag, sm/f Iraqi

l'ran sm I'~ Iran

irani'ano, -a ag, sm/f Iranian

l'raq sm I'~ Iraq

l'iride sf (arcobaleno) rainbow; (Anat, Bot) iris

'iris sm inv iris

Ir'landa sf I'~ Ireland; I'~ **del Nord** Northern Ireland, Ulster; **la Repubblica d'**~ Eire, the Republic of Ireland; **irlan'dese** ag Irish ▶ sm/f Irishman/woman; **gli Irlandesi** the Irish

iro'nia sf irony; **i'ronico, -a, -ci, -che** ag ironic(al)

irrago'nevole [irradʒo'nevole] ag irrational; unreasonable

irrazio'nale [irrattsjo'nale] ag irrational

irre'ale ag unreal

irrego'lare ag irregular; (terreno) uneven

irremo'vibile ag (fig) unshakeable, unyielding

irrequi'eto, -a ag restless

irresis'tibile ag irresistible

irrespon'sabile ag irresponsible

irri'gare vt (annaffiare) to irrigate; (fiume ecc) to flow through

irrigi'dire [irridʒi'dire] vt to stiffen; **irrigidirsi** vpr to stiffen

irri'sorio, -a ag derisory

irri'tare vt (mettere di malumore) to irritate, annoy; (Med) to irritate; **irritarsi** vpr (stizzirsi) to become irritated o annoyed; (Med) to become irritated

ir'rompere vi ~ **in** to burst into

irru'ente ag (fig) impetuous, violent

ir'ruppi ecc vb vedi **irrompere**

irruzi'one [irrut'tsjone] sf **fare** ~ **in** to burst into; (polizia) to raid

is'crissi ecc vb vedi **iscrivere**

is'critto, -a pp di **iscrivere** ▶ sm/f member; **per o in** ~ in writing

is'crivere vt to register, enter; (persona): ~ **(a)** to register (in), enrol (in); **iscriversi** vpr **iscriversi (a)** (club, partito) to join; (università) to register o enrol (at); (esame, concorso) to register o enter (for); **iscrizi'one** sf (epigrafe ecc) inscription; (a scuola, società) enrolment, registration; (registrazione) registration

Is'lam sm l'~ Islam

Is'landa sf l'~ Iceland

islan'dese ag Icelandic ▸ sm/f Icelander ▸ sm (Ling) Icelandic

'isola sf island; **isola pedonale** (Aut) pedestrian precinct

isola'mento sm isolation; (Tecn) insulation

iso'lante ag insulating ▸ sm insulator

iso'lare vt to isolate; (Tecn) to insulate; (: acusticamente) to soundproof; **isolarsi** vpr to isolate o.s.; **iso'lato, -a** ag isolated; insulated ▸ sm (gruppo di edifici) block

ispet'tore sm inspector

ispezio'nare [ispettsjo'nare] vt to inspect

'ispido, -a ag bristly, shaggy

ispi'rare vt to inspire

Isra'ele sm l'~ Israel; **israeli'ano, -a** ag, sm/f Israeli

is'sare vt to hoist

istan'taneo, -a ag instantaneous ▸ sf (Fot) snapshot

is'tante sm instant, moment; **all'~**, **sull'~** instantly, immediately

is'terico, -a, -ci, -che ag hysterical

isti'gare vt to incite

is'tinto sm instinct

istitu'ire vt (fondare) to institute, found; (porre: confronto) to establish; (intraprendere: inchiesta) to set up

isti'tuto sm institute; (di università) department; (ente, Dir) institution; **istituto di bellezza** beauty salon; **istituto di credito** bank, banking institution; **istituto di ricerca** research institute

istituzi'one [istitut'tsjone] sf institution

'istmo sm (Geo) isthmus

'istrice ['istritʃe] sm porcupine

istru'ito, -a ag educated

istrut'tore, -'trice sm/f instructor ▸ ag giudice – vedi giudice

istruzi'one sf education; training; (direttiva) instruction; **istruzioni** sfpl (norme) instructions; **istruzioni per l'uso** instructions for use; ~ **obbligatoria** (Scol) compulsory education

l'talia sf l'~ Italy

itali'ano, -a ag Italian ▸ sm/f Italian ▸ sm (Ling) Italian; **gli Italiani** the Italians

itine'rario sm itinerary

'ittico, -a, -ci, -che ag fish cpd; fishing cpd

Iugos'lavia = Jugoslavia

IVA ['iva] sigla f (= imposta sul valore aggiunto) VAT

◆

j

jazz [dʒaz] sm jazz

jeans [dʒinz] smpl jeans

jeep® [dʒip] sf inv jeep

'jogging ['dʒɔgin] sm jogging; **fare ~** to go jogging

'jolly ['dʒɔli] sm inv joker

joystick [dʒɔis'tik] sm inv joystick

ju'do [dʒu'dɔ] sm judo

Jugos'lavia [jugoz'lavja] sf (Storia): **la ~** Yugoslavia; **la ex~** former

Yugoslavia; **jugos'lavo, -a** *ag, sm/f*
(*Storia*) Yugoslav(ian)

K

K, k ['kappa] *sf o m inv* (*lettera*) K, k
▶ *abbr* (= *kilo-, chilo-*) k; (*Inform*) K;
come Kursaal ≈ K for King
kamikaze [kami'kaddze] *sm inv*
kamikaze
karaoke [ka'raokε] *sm inv* karaoke
karatè *sm* karate
ka'yak [ka'jak] *sm inv* kayak
Kenia ['kεnja] *sm* **il ~** Kenya
kg *abbr* (= *chilogrammo*) kg
'killer *sm inv* gunman, hired gun
kitsch [kitʃ] *sm* kitsch
'kiwi ['kiwi] *sm inv* kiwi fruit
K.O. [kappa'o] *sm inv* knockout
ko'ala [ko'ala] *sm inv* koala (bear)
koso'varo, -a [koso'varo] *ag, sm/f*
Kosovan
Ko'sovo *sm* Kosovo
'krapfen *sm inv* (*Cuc*) doughnut
Kuwait [ku'vait] *sm* **il ~** Kuwait

l' *det vedi* **la**; **lo**; **il**
la (*davV* **l'**) *det f* the ▶ *pron* (*oggetto:
persona*) her; (: *cosa*) it; (: *forma di
cortesia*) you; *vedi anche* **il**
là *av* there; **di là** (*da quel luogo*) from
there; (*in quel luogo*) in there; (*dall'altra
parte*) over there; **di là di** beyond;
per di là that way; **più in là** further
on; (*tempo*) later on; **fatti in là** move
up; **là dentro/sopra/sotto** in/up (*o
on*)/under there; *vedi anche* **quello**
'labbro (*pl*(*f*) **labbra**) (*solo nel senso
Anat*) *sm* lip
labi'rinto *sm* labyrinth, maze
labora'torio *sm* (*di ricerca*) laboratory;
(*di arti, mestieri*) workshop;
laboratorio linguistico language
laboratory
labori'oso, -a *ag* (*faticoso*) laborious;
(*attivo*) hard-working
'lacca, -che *sf* lacquer
'laccio ['lattʃo] *sm* noose; (*legaccio,
tirante*) lasso; (*di scarpa*) lace; **laccio
emostatico** tourniquet
lace'rare [latʃe'rare] *vt* to tear to
shreds, lacerate; **lacerarsi** *vpr* to tear
'lacrima *sf* tear; **in lacrime** in
tears; **lacri'mogeno, -a** *ag* **gas
lacrimogeno** tear gas
la'cuna *sf* (*fig*) gap
'ladro *sm* thief
laggiù [lad'dʒu] *av* down there; (*di là*)
over there
la'gnarsi [laɲ'narsi] *vpr* **~ (di)** to

complain (about)

'lago, -ghi *sm* lake

la'guna *sf* lagoon

'laico, -a, -ci, -che *ag* (apostolato) lay; (vita) secular; (scuola) non-denominational ▶ *sm/f* layman/woman

'lama *sm inv* (Zool) llama; (Rel) lama ▶ *sf* blade

lamentarsi *vpr* (emettere lamenti) to moan, groan; (rammaricarsi): **~ (di)** to complain (about)

lamen'tela *sf* complaining *no pl*

la'metta *sf* razor blade

'lamina *sf* (lastra sottile) thin sheet (o layer o plate); **lamina d'oro** gold leaf; gold foil

'lampada *sf* lamp; **lampada a gas** gas lamp; **lampada da tavolo** table lamp

lampa'dario *sm* chandelier

lampa'dina *sf* light bulb; **lampadina tascabile** pocket torch (BRIT) *o* flashlight (US)

lam'pante *ag* (fig: evidente) crystal clear, evident

lampeggi'are [lamped'dʒare] *vi* (luce, fari) to flash ▶ *vb impers* **lampeggia** there's lightning; **lampeggia'tore** *sm* (Aut) indicator

lampi'one *sm* street light *o* lamp (BRIT)

'lampo *sm* (Meteor) flash of lightning; (di luce: fig) flash

lam'pone *sm* raspberry

'lana *sf* wool; **pura ~ vergine** pure new wool; **lana d'acciaio** steel wool; **lana di vetro** glass wool

lan'cetta [lan'tʃetta] *sf* (indice) pointer, needle; (di orologio) hand

'lancia ['lantʃa] *sf* (arma) lance; (: picca) spear; (di pompa antincendio) nozzle; (imbarcazione) launch; **lancia di salvataggio** lifeboat

lanciafi'amme [lantʃa'fjamme] *sm*

inv flamethrower

lanci'are [lan'tʃare] *vt* to throw, hurl, fling; (Sport) to throw; (far partire: automobile) to get up to full speed; (bombe) to drop; (razzo, prodotto, moda) to launch; **lanciarsi** *vpr* **lanciarsi contro/su** to throw *o* hurl *o* fling o.s. against/on; **lanciarsi in** (fig) to embark on

lanci'nante [lantʃi'nante] *ag* (dolore) shooting, throbbing; (grido) piercing

'lancio ['lantʃo] *sm* throwing *no pl*; throw; dropping *no pl*; drop; launching *no pl*; launch; **lancio del disco** (Sport) throwing the discus; **lancio del peso** putting the shot

'languido, -a *ag* (fiacca) languid, weak; (tenero, malinconico) languishing

lan'terna *sf* lantern; (faro) lighthouse

'lapide *sf* (di sepolcro) tombstone; (commemorativa) plaque

'lapsus *sm inv* slip

'lardo *sm* bacon fat, lard

lar'ghezza [lar'gettsa] *sf* width; breadth; looseness; generosity; **larghezza di vedute** broad-mindedness

'largo, -a, -ghi, -ghe *ag* wide; broad; (maniche) wide; (abito: troppo ampio) loose; (fig) generous ▶ *sm* width; breadth; (mare aperto) open sea ▶ *sf* **stare** *o* **tenersi alla larga (da qn/qc)** to keep one's distance (from sb/sth), keep away (from sb/sth); **~ due metri** two metres wide; **~ di spalle** broad-shouldered; **di larghe vedute** broad-minded; **su larga scala** on a large scale; **di manica larga** generous, open-handed; **al ~ di Genova** off the coast of) Genoa; **farsi ~ tra la folla** to push one's way through the crowd

'larice ['laritʃe] *sm* (Bot) larch

larin'gite [larin'dʒite] *sf* laryngitis

'larva *sf* larva; (*fig*) shadow

la'sagne [la'zaɲɲe] *sfpl* lasagna *sg*

lasci'are [laʃ'ʃare] *vt* to leave; (*abbandonare*) to leave, abandon, give up; (*cessare di tenere*) to let go of ▶ *vb aus* **~ fare qn** to let sb do; **~ andare** *o* **correre** *o* **perdere** to let things go their own way; **~ stare qc/qn** to leave sth/sb alone; **lasciarsi** *vpr* (*persone*) to part; (*coppia*) to split up; **lasciarsi andare** to let o.s. go

'laser ['lazer] *ag*, *sm inv* (**raggio**) **~** laser (beam)

lassa'tivo, -a *ag*, *sm* laxative

'lasso *sm*: **lasso di tempo** interval, lapse of time

lassù *av* up there

'lastra *sf* (*di pietra*) slab; (*di metallo*, *Fot*) plate; (*di ghiaccio*, *vetro*) sheet; (*radiografica*) X-ray (plate)

lastri'cato *sm* paving

late'rale *ag* lateral, side *cpd*; (*uscita*, *ingresso ecc*) side *cpd* ▶ *sm* (*Calcio*) half-back

la'tino, -a *ag*, *sm* Latin

lati'tante *sm/f* fugitive (from justice)

lati'tudine *sf* latitude

'lato, -a *ag* (*fig*) wide, broad ▶ *sm* side; (*fig*) aspect, point of view; **in senso ~** broadly speaking

'latta *sf* tin (plate); (*recipiente*) tin, can

lat'tante *ag* unweaned

'latte *sm* milk; **latte detergente** cleansing milk *o* lotion; **latte intero** full-cream milk; **latte a lunga conservazione** UHT milk, long-life milk; **latte magro** *o* **scremato** skimmed milk; **latte in polvere** dried *o* powdered milk; **latte solare** suntan lotion; **latti'cini** *smpl* dairy products

lat'tina *sf* (*di birra ecc*) can

lat'tuga, -ghe *sf* lettuce

'laurea *sf* degree; **laurea in ingegneria** engineering degree; **laurea in lettere** = arts degree

○ **laurea**
The **laurea** is awarded to students who successfully complete their degree courses. Traditionally, this takes between four and six years; a major element of the final examinations is the presentation and discussion of a dissertation. A shorter, more vocational course of study, taking from two to three years, is also available; at the end of this time students receive a diploma called the **laurea breve**.

laure'arsi *vpr* to graduate

laure'ato, -a *ag*, *sm/f* graduate

'lauro *sm* laurel

'lauto, -a *ag* (*pranzo*, *mancia*) lavish

'lava *sf* lava

la'vabo *sm* washbasin

la'vaggio [la'vaddʒo] *sm* washing *no pl*; **lavaggio del cervello** brainwashing *no pl*; **lavaggio a secco** dry-cleaning

la'vagna [la'vaɲɲa] *sf* (*Geo*) slate; (*di scuola*) blackboard

la'vanda *sf* (*anche Med*) wash; (*Bot*) lavender; **lavande'ria** *sf* laundry; **lavanderia automatica** launderette; **lavanderia a secco** dry-cleaner's; **lavan'dino** *sm* sink

lavapi'atti *sm/f* dishwasher

la'vare *vt* to wash; **lavarsi** *vpr* to wash, have a wash; **~ a secco** to dry-clean; **lavarsi le mani/i denti** to wash one's hands/clean one's teeth

lava'secco *sm o f inv* dry cleaner's

lavasto'viglie [lavasto'viʎʎe] *sm o f inv* (*macchina*) dishwasher

lava'trice [lava'tritʃe] *sf* washing machine

lavo'rare *vi* to work; (*fig*: *bar*, *studio ecc*) to do good business ▶ *vt* to work; **lavorarsi qn** (*persuaderlo*) to work on sb; **~ a** to work on; **~ a maglia** to knit; **lavora'tivo, -a** *ag* working;

lavora'tore, -'trice *sm/f* worker ▶ *ag* working

la'voro *sm* work; (*occupazione*) job, work *no pl*; (*opera*) piece of work, job; (Econ) labour; **che ~ fa?** what do you do?; **lavori forzati** hard labour *sg*; **lavoro interinale** *o* **in affitto** temporary work

le *det fpl* **le** ▶ *pron* (*oggetto*) them; (: *a lei, a essa*) (to) her; (: *forma di cortesia*) (to) you; *vedi anche* **il**

l'ale *ag* loyal; (*sincero*) sincere; (*onesto*) fair

'lecca 'lecca *sm inv* lollipop

leccapi'edi (*peg*) *sm/f inv* toady, bootlicker

lec'care *vt* to lick; (*gatto: latte ecc*) to lick *o* lap up; (*fig*) to flatter; **leccarsi i baffi** to lick one's lips

leccherò *ecc* [lekke'rɔ] *vb vedi* **leccare**

'leccio [ˈlɛttʃo] *sm* holm oak, ilex

leccor'nia *sf* titbit, delicacy

'lecito, -a [ˈlɛtʃito] *ag* permitted, allowed

'lega, -ghe *sf* league; (*di metalli*) alloy

le'gaccio [leˈgattʃo] *sm* string, lace

le'gale *ag* legal ▶ *sm* lawyer

legaliz'zare *vt* to authenticate; (*regolarizzare*) to legalize

le'game *sm* (*corda, fig: affettivo*) tie, bond; (*nesso logico*) link, connection

le'gare *vt* (*prigioniero, capelli, cane*) to tie (up); (*libro*) to bind; (Chim) to alloy; (*fig: collegare*) to bind, join ▶ *vi* (*far lega*) to unite; (*fig*) to get on well

le'genda [leˈdʒɛnda] *sf* (*di carta geografica ecc*) = **leggenda**

'legge [ˈlɛddʒe] *sf* law

leg'genda [ledˈdʒɛnda] *sf* (*narrazione*) legend; (*di carta geografica ecc*) key, legend

'leggere [ˈlɛddʒere] *vt, vi* to read

legge'rezza [leddʒeˈrettsa] *sf* lightness; thoughtlessness; fickleness

leg'gero, -a [ledˈdʒero] *ag* light; (*agile, snello*) nimble, agile, light; (*tè, caffè*) weak; (*fig: non grave, piccolo*) slight; (: *spensierato*) thoughtless; (: *incostante*) fickle; free and easy; **alla leggera** thoughtlessly

leg'gio, -'gii [ledˈdʒio] *sm* lectern; (Mus) music stand

legherò *ecc* [legeˈrɔ] *vb vedi* **legare**

legisla'tivo, -a [ledʒislaˈtivo] *ag* legislative

legisla'tura [ledʒislaˈtura] *sf* legislature

le'gittimo, -a [leˈdʒittimo] *ag* legitimate; (*fig: giustificato, lecito*) justified, legitimate; **legittima difesa** (Dir) self-defence

'legna [ˈlenna] *sf* firewood

'legno [ˈlenno] *sm* wood; (*pezzo di legno*) piece of wood; **di ~** wooden; **legno compensato** plywood

'lei *pron* (*soggetto*) she; (*oggetto: per dare rilievo, con preposizione*) her; (*forma di cortesia: anche:* **L~**) you ▶ *sm* **dare del ~ a qn** to address sb as "lei"; **~ stessa** she herself; you yourself

■ **lei**

■ **lei** is the third person singular pronoun. It is used in Italian to address an adult whom you do not know or with whom you are on formal terms.

lenta'mente *av* slowly

'lente *sf* (Ottica) lens *sg*; **lenti a contatto** *o* **corneali** contact lenses; **lenti (a contatto) morbide/rigide** soft/hard contact lenses; **lente d'ingrandimento** magnifying glass; **lenti** *sfpl* (*occhiali*) lenses

len'tezza [lenˈtettsa] *sf* slowness

len'ticchia [lenˈtikkja] *sf* (Bot) lentil

len'tiggine [lenˈtiddʒine] *sf* freckle

'lento, -a *ag* slow; (*molle: fune*) slack; (*non stretto: vite, abito*) loose ▶ *sm* (*ballo*) slow dance

'lenza ['lentsa] *sf* fishing-line

lenzu'olo [len'tswɔlo] *sm* sheet

le'one *sm* lion; (*dello zodiaco*): **L~** Leo

lepo'rino, -a *ag* labbro ~ harelip

'lepre *sf* hare

'lercio, -a, -ci, -cie ['lɛrtʃo] *ag* filthy

lesi'one *sf* (*Med*) lesion; (*Dir*) injury, damage; (*Edil*) crack

les'sare *vt* (*Cuc*) to boil

'lessi *ecc vb vedi* **leggere**

'lessico, -ci *sm* vocabulary; lexicon

'lesso, -a *ag* boiled ▶ *sm* boiled meat

le'tale *ag* lethal; fatal

leta'maio *sm* dunghill

le'tame *sm* manure, dung

le'targo, -ghi *sm* lethargy; (*Zool*) hibernation

'lettera *sf* letter; **lettere** *sfpl* (*letteratura*) literature *sg*; (*studi umanistici*) arts (subjects); **alla ~** literally; **in lettere** in words, in full

letteral'mente *av* literally

lette'rario, -a *ag* literary

lette'rato, -a *ag* well-read, scholarly

lettera'tura *sf* literature

let'tiga, -ghe *sf* (*barella*) stretcher

let'tino *sm* cot (*BRIT*), crib (*US*); **lettino solare** sunbed

'letto, -a *pp di* **leggere** ▶ *sm* bed; **andare a ~** to go to bed; **letto a castello** bunk beds *pl*; **letto a una piazza** single; **letto a due piazze** *o* **matrimoniale** double bed

let'tore, -'trice *sm/f* reader; (*Ins*) (foreign language) assistant (*BRIT*), (foreign) teaching assistant (*US*) ▶ *sm* (*Tecn*): **~ ottico** optical character reader; **lettore CD** CD player; **lettore DVD** DVD player

let'tura *sf* reading

> Attenzione! In inglese esiste la parola **lecture**, che però significa *lezione* oppure *conferenza*.

leuce'mia [leutʃe'mia] *sf* leukaemia

'leva *sf* lever; (*Mil*) conscription; **far ~ su qn** to work on sb; **leva del cambio** (*Aut*) gear lever

le'vante *sm* east; (*vento*) East wind; **il L~** the Levant

le'vare *vt* (*occhi, braccio*) to raise; (*sollevare, togliere: tassa, divieto*) to lift; (*indumenti*) to take off, remove; (*rimuovere*) to take away; (: *dal di sopra*) to take off; (: *dal di dentro*) to take out

leva'toio, -a *ag* ponte ~ drawbridge

lezi'one [let'tsjone] *sf* lesson; (*Univ*) lecture; **fare ~** to teach; to lecture; **dare una ~ a qn** to teach sb a lesson; **lezioni private** private lessons

li *pron pl* (*oggetto*) them

lì *av* there; **di o da lì** from there; **per di lì** that way; **di lì a pochi giorni** a few days later; **lì per lì** there and then; at first; **essere lì (lì) per fare** to be on the point of doing, be about to do; **lì dentro** in there; **lì sotto** under there; **lì sopra** on there; up there; *vedi anche* **quello**

liba'nese *ag, sm/f* Lebanese *inv*

Li'bano *sm* **il ~** the Lebanon

'libbra *sf* (*peso*) pound

li'beccio [li'bettʃo] *sm* south-west wind

li'bellula *sf* dragonfly

libe'rale *ag, sm/f* liberal

liberaliz'zare [liberalid'dzare] *vt* to liberalize

libe'rare *vt* (*rendere libero: prigioniero*) to release; (: *popolo*) to free, liberate; (*sgombrare: passaggio*) to clear; (: *stanza*) to vacate; (*produrre: energia*) to release; **liberarsi** *vpr* **liberarsi di qc/ qn** to get rid of sth/sb; **liberazi'one** *sf* liberation, freeing; release; rescuing

• **Liberazione**
• The **Liberazione** is a national
• holiday which falls on April 25th.
• It commemorates the liberation
• of Italy at the end of the Second
• World War.

'libero, -a *ag* free; (*strada*) clear; (*non occupato: posto ecc*) vacant; free; not taken; empty; not engaged; **~ di fare qc** free to do sth; **~ da** free from; **è ~ questo posto?** is this seat free? **~ arbitrio** free will; **~ professionista** self-employed professional person; **~ scambio** free trade; **libertà** *sf* freedom; (*tempo disponibile*) free time ▶ *sfpl* (*licenza*) liberties; **in libertà provvisoria/vigilata** released without bail/on probation

'Libia *sf la* ~ Libya; **'libico, -a, -ci, -che** *ag, sm/f* Libyan

li'bidine *sf* lust

li'braio *sm* bookseller

li'brarsi *vpr* to hover

libre'ria *sf* (*bottega*) bookshop; (*mobile*) bookcase

> Attenzione! In inglese esiste la parola **library**, che però significa *biblioteca*.

li'bretto *sm* booklet; (*taccuino*) notebook; (*Mus*) libretto; **libretto degli assegni** cheque book; **libretto di circolazione** (*Aut*) logbook; **libretto di risparmio** (*savings*) bank-book, passbook; **libretto universitario** student's report book

'libro *sm* book; **libro di cassa** cash book; **libro mastro** ledger; **libro paga** payroll; **libro di testo** textbook

li'cenza [li'tʃɛntsa] *sf* (*permesso*) permission, leave; (*di pesca, caccia, circolazione*) permit, licence; (*Mil*) leave; (*Ins*) school leaving certificate; (*libertà*) liberty; licence; licentiousness; **andare in ~** (*Mil*) to go on leave

licenzia'mento [litʃentsja'mento] *sm* dismissal

licenzi'are [litʃen'tsjare] *vt* (*impiegato*) to dismiss; (*Comm: per eccesso di personale*) to make redundant; (*Ins*) to award a certificate to; **licenziarsi**

vpr (*impiegato*) to resign, hand in one's notice; (*Ins*) to obtain one's school-leaving certificate

li'ceo [li'tʃɛo] *sm* (*Ins*) secondary (*BRIT*) o high (*US*) school (*for 14- to 19-year-olds*)

'lido *sm* beach, shore

Liechtenstein ['liktənstain] *sm il* ~ Liechtenstein

li'eto, -a *ag* happy, glad; **"molto ~"** (*nelle presentazioni*) "pleased to meet you"

li'eve *ag* light; (*di poco conto*) slight; (*sommesso: voce*) faint, soft

lievi'tare *vi* (*anche fig*) to rise ▶ *vt* to leaven

li'evito *sm* yeast; **lievito di birra** brewer's yeast

'ligio, -a, -gi, -gie ['lidʒo] *ag* faithful, loyal

'lilla *sm inv* lilac

'lillà *sm inv* lilac

'lima *sf* file; **lima da unghie** nail file

limacci'oso, -a [limat'tʃoso] *ag* slimy; muddy

li'mare *vt* to file (down); (*fig*) to polish

limi'tare *vt* to limit, restrict; (*circoscrivere*) to bound, surround; **limitarsi** *vpr* **limitarsi nel mangiare** to limit one's eating; **limitarsi a qc/a fare qc** to limit o.s. to sth/to doing sth

'limite *sm* limit; (*confine*) border, boundary; **limite di velocità** speed limit

limo'nata *sf* lemonade (*BRIT*), (*lemon*) soda (*US*); lemon squash (*BRIT*), lemonade (*US*)

li'mone *sm* (*pianta*) lemon tree; (*frutto*) lemon

'limpido, -a *ag* clear; (*acqua*) limpid, clear

'lince ['lintʃe] *sf* lynx

linci'are *vt* to lynch

'linea *sf* line; (*di mezzi pubblici di*

trasporto: itinerario) route; (: *servizio*) service; **a grandi linee** in outline; **mantenere la ~ look** to look after one's figure; **aereo di ~** airliner; **nave di ~** liner; **volo di ~** scheduled flight; **linea aerea** airline; **linea di partenza/ d'arrivo** (*Sport*) starting/finishing line; **linea di tiro** line of fire

linea'menti *smpl* features; (*fig*) outlines

line'are *ag* linear; (*fig*) coherent, logical

line'etta *sf* (*trattino*) dash; (*d'unione*) hyphen

lin'gotto *sm* ingot, bar

'lingua *sf* (*Anat*, *Cuc*) tongue; (*idioma*) language; **mostrare la ~** to stick out one's tongue; **~ italiana** Italian-speaking; **che lingue parla?** what languages do you speak?; **una ~ di terra** a spit of land; **lingua madre** mother tongue

lingu'aggio [lin'gwaddʒo] *sm* language

lingu'etta *sf* (*di strumento*) reed; (*di scarpa*, *Tecn*) tongue; (*di busta*) flap

'lino *sm* (*pianta*) flax; (*tessuto*) linen

li'noleum *sm inv* linoleum, lino

liposuzi'one [liposut'tsjone] *sf* liposuction

lique'fatto, -a *pp di* liquefare

liqui'dare *vt* (*società, beni: persona: uccidere*) to liquidate; (*persona: sbarazzarsene*) to get rid of; (*conto, problema*) to settle; (*Comm: merce*) to sell off, clear; **liquidazi'one** *sf* liquidation; settlement; clearance sale

liquidità *sf* liquidity

'liquido, -a *ag, sm* liquid; **liquido per freni** brake fluid

liqui'rizia [likwi'rittsja] *sf* liquorice

li'quore *sm* liqueur

'lira *sf* (*Storia: unità monetaria*) lira; (*Mus*) lyre; **lira sterlina** pound

sterling

'lirico, -a, -ci, -che *ag* lyric(al); (*Mus*) lyric; **cantante/teatro ~** opera singer/house

Lis'bona *sf* Lisbon

'lisca, -sche *sf* (*di pesce*) fishbone

lisci'are [liʃʃare] *vt* to smooth; (*fig*) to flatter

'liscio, -a, -sci, -sce ['liʃʃo] *ag* smooth; (*capelli*) straight; (*mobile*) plain; (*bevanda alcolica*) neat; (*fig*) straightforward, simple ▶ *av* **andare ~** to go smoothly; **passarla liscia** to get away with it

'liso, -a *ag* worn out, threadbare

'lista *sf* (*elenco*) list; **lista elettorale** electoral roll; **lista delle spese** shopping list; **lista dei vini** wine list; **lista delle vivande** menu

lis'tino *sm* list; **listino dei cambi** (foreign) exchange rate; **listino dei prezzi** price list

'lite *sf* quarrel, argument; (*Dir*) lawsuit

liti'gare *vi* to quarrel; (*Dir*) to litigate

li'tigio [li'tidʒo] *sm* quarrel

lito'rale *ag* coastal, coast *cpd* ▶ *sm* coast

'litro *sm* litre

livel'lare *vt* to level, make level

li'vello *sm* level; (*fig*) level, standard; **ad alto ~** (*fig*) high-level; **livello del mare** sea level

'livido, -a *ag* livid; (*per percosse*) bruised, black and blue; (*cielo*) leaden ▶ *sm* bruise

Li'vorno *sf* Livorno, Leghorn

'lizza ['littsa] *sf* lists *pl*; **scendere in ~** to enter the lists

lo (*dav s impura, gn, pn, ps, x, z; dav V* **l'**) *det m* the ▶ *pron* (*oggetto: persona*) him; (: *cosa*) it; **lo sapevo** I knew it; **lo so** I know; **sii buono, anche se lui non lo è** be good, even if he isn't; *vedi anche* **il**

lo'cale *ag* local ▶ *sm* room; (*luogo pubblico*) premises *pl*; **locale**

notturno nightclub; **località** sf inv locality

lo'canda sf inn

locomo'tiva sf locomotive

locuzi'one [lokut'tsjone] sf phrase, expression

lo'dare vt to praise

'lode sf praise; (Ins): **laurearsi con 110 e ~ ≈** to graduate with a first-class honours degree (BRIT), graduate summa cum laude (US)

'loden sm inv (stoffa) loden; (cappotto) loden overcoat

lo'devole ag praiseworthy

loga'ritmo sm logarithm

'loggia, -ge ['lɔddʒa] sf (Archit) loggia; (circolo massonico) lodge; **loggi'one** sm (di teatro): **il loggione** the Gods sg

'logico, -a, -ci, -che ['lɔdʒiko] ag logical

logo'rare vt to wear out; (sciupare) to waste; **logorarsi** vpr to wear out; (fig) to wear o.s. out

'logoro, -a ag (stoffa) worn out, threadbare; (persona) worn out

Lombar'dia sf la ~ Lombardy

lom'bata sf (taglio di carne) loin

lom'brico, -chi sm earthworm

londi'nese ag London cpd ▶ sm/f Londoner

'Londra sf London

lon'gevo, -a [lon'dʒevo] ag long-lived

longi'tudine [londʒi'tudine] sf longitude

lonta'nanza [lonta'nantsa] sf distance; absence

lon'tano, -a ag (distante) distant, faraway; (assente) absent; (vago: sospetto) slight, remote; (tempo: remoto) far-off, distant; (parente) distant, remote ▶ av far; **è lontana la casa?** is it far to the house?, is the house far from here?; **è un chilometro** it's a kilometre away o a kilometre from here; **più ~** farther; **da**

o di ~ from a distance; **~ da** a long way from; **è molto ~ da qui?** is it far from here?; **alla lontana** slightly, vaguely

lo'quace [lo'kwatʃe] ag talkative, loquacious; (fig: gesto ecc) eloquent

'lordo, -a ag dirty, filthy; (peso, stipendio) gross

'loro pron pl (oggetto, con preposizione) them; (complemento di termine) to them; (soggetto) they; (forma di cortesia: anche: L~) you; to you; **il(la) ~, i(le) ~** det their; (forma di cortesia: anche: L~) your ▶ pron theirs; (forma di cortesia: anche: L~) yours; **~ stessi(e)** they themselves; you yourselves

'losco, -a, -schi, -sche ag (fig) shady, suspicious

'lotta sf struggle, fight; (Sport) wrestling; **lotta libera** all-in wrestling; **lot'tare** vi to fight, struggle; to wrestle

lotte'ria sf lottery; (di gara ippica) sweepstake

'lotto sm (gioco) (state) lottery; (parte) lot; (Edil) site

● **Lotto**
● The Lotto is an official lottery run
● by the Italian Finance Ministry.
● It consists of a weekly draw of
● numbers and is very popular.

lozi'one [lot'tsjone] sf lotion

lubrifi'cante sm lubricant

lubrifi'care vt to lubricate

luc'chetto [luk'ketto] sm padlock

lucci'care [luttʃi'kare] vi to sparkle, glitter, twinkle

'luccio ['luttʃo] sm (Zool) pike

'lucciola ['luttʃola] sf (Zool) firefly; glowworm

'luce ['lutʃe] sf light; (finestra) window; **alla ~ di** by the light of; **fare ~ su qc** (fig) to shed o throw light on sth; **~ del sole/della luna** sun/moonlight

lucer'nario [lutʃer'narjo] sm skylight

lu'certola [lu'tʃertola] sf lizard

luci'dare [lutʃi'dare] *vt* to polish

lucida'trice [lutʃida'tritʃe] *sf* floor polisher

'lucido, -a [lutʃido] *ag* shining, bright; (*lucidato*) polished; (*fig*) lucid ▶ *sm* shine, lustre; (*disegno*) tracing; **lucido per scarpe** shoe polish

'lucro *sm* profit, gain

'luglio ['luʎʎo] *sm* July

'lugubre *ag* gloomy

'lui *pron* (*soggetto*) he; (*oggetto: per dare rilievo, con preposizione*) him; **~ stesso** he himself

lu'maca, -che *sf* slug; (*chiocciola*) snail

lumi'noso, -a *ag* (*che emette luce*) luminous; (*cielo, colore, stanza*) bright; (*sorgente*) of light, light *cpd*; (*fig: sorriso*) bright, radiant

'luna *sf* moon; **luna nuova/piena** new/full moon; **luna di miele** honeymoon; **siamo in ~ di miele** we're on honeymoon

'luna park *sm inv* amusement park, funfair

lu'nare *ag* lunar, moon *cpd*

lu'nario *sm* almanac; **sbarcare il ~ to** make ends meet

lu'natico, -a, -ci, -che *ag* whimsical, temperamental

lunedì *sm inv* Monday; **di** o **il ~ on** Mondays

lun'ghezza [lun'gettsa] *sf* length; **lunghezza d'onda** (*Fisica*) wavelength

'lungo, -a, -ghi, -ghe *ag* long; (*lento: persona*) slow; (*diluito: caffè, brodo*) weak, watery, thin ▶ *sm* length ▶ *prep* along; **~ 3 metri** 3 metres long; **a ~ for** a long time; **a ~ andare** in the long run; **di gran lunga** (*molto*) by far; **andare in ~** o **per le lunghe** to drag on; **saperla lunga** to know what's what; **in ~ e in largo** far and wide, all over; **~ il corso dei secoli** throughout the centuries

lungo'mare *sm* promenade

lu'notto *sm* (*Aut*) rear o back window; **lunotto termico** heated rear window

lu'ogo, -ghi *sm* place; (*posto: di incidenze ecc*) scene, site; (*punto, passo di libro*) passage; **in ~ di** instead of; **in primo ~** in the first place; **aver ~ to** take place; **dar ~ a** to give rise to; **luogo di nascita** birthplace; (*Amm*) place of birth; **luogo di provenienza** place of origin; **luogo comune** commonplace

'lupo, -a *sm/f* wolf

'luppolo *sm* (*Bot*) hop

'lurido, -a *ag* filthy

lusin'gare *vt* to flatter

Lussem'burgo *sm* (*stato*): **il ~** Luxembourg ▶ *sf* (*città*) Luxembourg

'lusso *sm* luxury; **di ~** luxury *cpd*; **lussu'oso, -a** *ag* luxurious

lus'suria *sf* lust

lus'trino *sm* sequin

'lutto *sm* mourning; **essere in/ portare il ~** to be in/wear mourning

m. *abbr* = **mese**; **metro**; **miglia**

ma *cong* but; **ma insomma!** for goodness sake!; **ma no!** of course not!

'macabro, -a *ag* gruesome, macabre

macché [mak'ke] *escl* not at all!, certainly not!

macche'roni [makke'roni] *smpl* macaroni sg

'macchia ['makkja] *sf* stain, spot; (*chiazza di diverso colore*) spot, splash, patch; (*tipo di boscaglia*) scrub; **alla ~** (*fig*) in hiding; **macchi'are** *vt* (*sporcare*) to stain, mark; **macchiarsi** *vpr* (*persona*) to get o.s. dirty; (*stoffa*) to stain; to get stained or marked

macchi'ato, -a [mak'kjato] *ag* (*pelle, pelo*) spotted; ~ **di** stained with; **caffè ~** coffee with a dash of milk

'macchina ['makkina] *sf* machine; (*motore, locomotiva*) engine; (*automobile*) car; (*fig: meccanismo*) machinery; **andare in ~** (*Aut*) to go by car; (*Stampa*) to press; **macchina da cucire** sewing machine; **macchina fotografica** camera; **macchina da presa** cine o movie camera; **macchina da scrivere** typewriter; **macchina a vapore** steam engine

macchi'nario [makki'narjo] *sm* machinery

macchi'nista, -i [makki'nista] *sm* (*di treno*) engine-driver; (*di nave*) engineer

Macedonia [matʃe'dɔnja] *sf* **la ~** Macedonia

mace'donia [matʃe'dɔnja] *sf* fruit salad

macel'laio [matʃel'lajo] *sm* butcher

macelle'ria *sf* butcher's (shop)

ma'cerie [ma'tʃerje] *sfpl* rubble sg, debris sg

ma'cigno [ma'tʃiɲɲo] *sm* (*masso*) rock, boulder

maci'nare [matʃi'nare] *vt* to grind; (*carne*) to mince (BRIT), grind (US)

macrobi'otico, -a *ag* macrobiotic ▶ **macrobiotica** sg

Ma'donna *sf* (*Rel*) Our Lady

mador'nale *ag* enormous, huge

'madre *sf* mother; (*matrice di bolletta*) counterfoil ▶ *ag inv* mother cpd; **ragazza ~** unmarried mother; **scena ~** (*Teatro*) principal scene; (*fig*) terrible scene

madre'lingua *sf* mother tongue, native language

madre'perla *sf* mother-of-pearl

ma'drina *sf* godmother

maestà *sf inv* majesty

ma'estra *sf vedi* maestro

maes'trale *sm* north-west wind, mistral

ma'estro, -a *sm/f* (*Ins: anche:* ~ **di scuola o elementare**) primary (BRIT) o grade school (US) teacher; (*esperto*) expert ▶ *sm* (*artigiano, fig: guida*) master; (*Mus*) maestro ▶ *ag* (*principale*) main; (*di grande abilità*) masterly, skilful; **maestra d'asilo** nursery teacher; **~ di cerimonie** master of ceremonies

'mafia *sf* Mafia

'maga *sf* sorceress

ma'gari *escl* (*esprime desiderio*) **~ fosse vero!** if only it were true!; **ti piacerebbe andare in Scozia? — magari!** would you like to go to Scotland? — and how! ▶ *av* (*anche*) even; (*forse*) perhaps

magaz'zino [magad'dzino] *sm* warehouse; **grande ~** department store

> Attenzione! In inglese esiste la parola *magazine* che però significa *rivista*.

'maggio ['maddʒo] *sm* May

maggio'rana [maddʒo'rana] *sf* (*Bot*) (sweet) marjoram

maggio'ranza [maddʒo'rantsa] *sf* majority

maggior'domo [maddʒor'dɔmo] *sm* butler

maggi'ore [mad'dʒore] *ag*

(*comparativo: più grande*) bigger, larger; taller; greater; (: *più vecchio: sorella, fratello*) older, elder; (: *di grado superiore*) senior; (: *più importante: Mil, Mus*) major; (*superlativo*) biggest, largest; tallest; greatest; oldest, eldest ▶ *sm/f* (*di grado*) superior; (*di età*) elder; (*Mil*) major; (: *Aer*) squadron leader; **la maggior parte** the majority; **andare per la ~** (*cantante ecc*) to be very popular; **maggio'renne** *ag* of age ▶ *sm/f* person who has come of age

ma'gia [ma'dʒia] *sf* magic; **'magico, -a, -ci, -che** *ag* magic; (*fig*) fascinating, charming, magical

magis'trato [madʒis'trato] *sm* magistrate

'maglia ['maʎʎa] *sf* stitch; (*lavoro ai ferri*) knitting *no pl*; (*tessuto, Sport*) jersey; (*maglione*) jersey, sweater; (*di catena*) link; (*di rete*) mesh; **maglia diritta/rovescia** plain/purl; **magli'etta** *sf* (*canottiera*) vest; (*tipo camicia*) T-shirt

magli'one *sm* sweater, jumper

ma'gnetico, -a, -ci, -che *ag* magnetic

ma'gnifico, -a, -ci, -che [maɲ'ɲifiko] *ag* magnificent, splendid; (*ospite*) generous

ma'gnolia [maɲ'ɲɔlja] *sf* magnolia

'mago, -ghi *sm* (*stregone*) magician, wizard; (*illusionista*) magician

ma'grezza [ma'grettsa] *sf* thinness

'magro, -a *ag* (*very*) thin, skinny; (*carne*) lean; (*formaggio*) low-fat; (*fig: scarso, misero*) meagre, poor; (: *meschino: scusa*) poor, lame; **mangiare di ~** not to eat meat

'mai *av* (*nessuna volta*) never; (*talvolta*) ever; **non ... ~** never ... ; **~ più** never again; **non sono ~ stato in Spagna** I've never been to Spain; **come ~?** (*o how*) how?; **chi/dove/quando**

~**?** whoever/wherever/whenever?

mai'ale *sm* (*Zool*) pig; (*carne*) pork

maio'nese *sf* mayonnaise

'mais *sm inv* maize

mai'uscolo, -a *ag* (*lettera*) capital; (*fig*) enormous, huge

mala'fede *sf* bad faith

malan'dato, -a *ag* (*persona: di salute*) in poor health; (: *di condizioni finanziarie*) badly off; (*trascurato*) shabby

ma'lanno *sm* (*disgrazia*) misfortune; (*malattia*) ailment

mala'pena *sf* **a ~** hardly, scarcely

ma'laria *sf* (*Med*) malaria

ma'lato, -a *ag* ill, sick; (*gamba*) bad; (*pianta*) diseased ▶ *sm/f* sick person; (*in ospedale*) patient; **malat'tia** *sf* (*infettivo ecc*) illness, disease; (*cattiva salute*) illness, sickness; (*di pianta*) disease

mala'vita *sf* underworld

mala'voglia [mala'vɔʎʎa] *sf* **di ~** unwillingly, reluctantly

Mala'ysia *sf* Malaysia

mal'concio, -a, -ci, -ce [mal'kontʃo] *ag* in a sorry state

malcon'tento *sm* discontent

malcos'tume *sm* immorality

mal'destro, -a *ag* (*inabile*) inexpert, inexperienced; (*goffo*) awkward

'male *av* badly ▶ *sm* (*ciò che è ingiusto, disonesto*) evil; (*danno, svantaggio*) harm; (*sventura*) misfortune; (*dolore fisico, morale*) pain, ache; **di ~ in peggio** from bad to worse; **sentirsi ~ to** feel ill; **far ~** (*dolere*) to hurt; **far ~ alla salute** to be bad for one's health; **far del ~ a qn** to hurt *o* harm sb; **restare o rimanere ~** to be sorry; to be disappointed; to be hurt; **andare a ~** to go bad; **come va? — non c'è ~** how are you? — not bad; **avere mal di gola/testa** to have a sore throat/a headache; **aver ~ ai piedi** to have sore feet; **mal d'auto** carsickness; **mal di cuore** heart trouble; **male di dente** toothache; **mal di mare** seasickness

male'detto, -a pp di **maledire** ▶ ag cursed, damned; (fig: fam) damned, blasted

male'dire vt to curse; **maledizi'one** sf curse; **maledizione!** damn it!

maledu'cato, -a ag rude, ill-mannered

maleducazi'one [maledukat'tsjone] sf rudeness

ma'lefico, -a, -ci, -che ag (influsso, azione) evil

ma'lessere sm indisposition, slight illness; (fig) uneasiness

malfa'mato, -a ag notorious

malfat'tore, -'trice sm/f wrongdoer

mal'fermo, -a ag unsteady, shaky; (salute) poor, delicate

mal'grado prep in spite of, despite ▶ cong although; **mio** (o **tuo** ecc) ~ against my (o your ecc) will

ma'ligno, -a [ma'liɲɲo] ag (malvagio) malicious, malignant; (Med) malignant

malinco'nia sf melancholy, gloom; **malin'conico, -a, -ci, -che** ag melancholy

malincu'ore: a ~ av reluctantly, unwillingly

malin'teso, -a ag misunderstood; (riguardo, senso del dovere) mistaken, wrong ▶ sm misunderstanding; **c'è stato un ~** there's been a misunderstanding

ma'lizia [ma'littsja] sf (malignità) malice; (furbizia) cunning; (espediente) trick; **malizi'oso, -a** ag malicious; cunning; (vivace, birichino) mischievous

malme'nare vt to beat up

ma'locchio [ma'lɔkkjo] sm evil eye

ma'lora sf **andare in ~** to go to the dogs

ma'lore sm (sudden) illness

mal'sano, -a ag unhealthy

'malta sf (Edil) mortar

mal'tempo sm bad weather

'malto sm malt

maltrat'tare vt to ill-treat

malu'more sm bad mood; (irritabilità) bad temper; (discordia) ill feeling; **di ~** in a bad mood

'malva sf (Bot) mallow ▶ ag, sm inv mauve

mal'vagio, -a, -gi, -gie [mal'vadʒo] ag wicked, evil

malvi'vente sm criminal

malvolenti'eri av unwillingly, reluctantly

'mamma sf mummy, mum; **~ mia!** my goodness!

mam'mella sf (Anat) breast; (di vacca, capra ecc) udder

mam'mifero sm mammal

ma'nata sf (colpo) slap; (quantità) handful

man'canza [man'kantsa] sf lack; (carenza) shortage, scarcity; (fallo) fault; (imperfezione) failing, shortcoming; **per ~ di tempo** through lack of time; **in ~ di meglio** for lack of anything better

man'care vi (essere insufficiente) to be lacking; (venir meno) to fail; (sbagliare) to be wrong, make a mistake; (non esserci) to be missing, not to be there; (essere lontano): **~ (da)** to be away (from) ▶ vt to miss; **~ di** to lack; **~ a** (promessa) to fail to keep; **tu mi manchi** I miss you; **mancò poco che morisse** he very nearly died; **mancano ancora 10 sterline** we're still £10 short; **manca un quarto alle 6** it's a quarter to 6

mancherò ecc vb vedi **mancare**

'mancia [ˈmantʃa] sf tip; **quanto devo lasciare di ~?** how much should I tip?; **~ competente** reward

manci'ata [man'tʃata] sf handful

man'cino, -a [man'tʃino] ag (braccio) left; (persona) left-handed; (fig) underhand

manda'rancio [manda'rantʃo] sm clementine

man'dare vt to send; (far funzionare: macchina) to drive; (emettere) to send out; (: grido) to give, utter, let out; **~ a chiamare qn** to send for sb; **~ avanti** (fig: famiglia) to provide for; (: fabbrica) to run, look after; **~ giù** to send down; (anche fig) to swallow; **~ via** to send away; (licenziare) to fire

manda'rino sm mandarin (orange); (cinese) mandarin

man'data sf (quantità) lot, batch; (di chiave) turn; **chiudere a doppia ~** to double-lock

man'dato sm (incarico) commission; (Dir: provvedimento) warrant; (di deputato ecc) mandate; (ordine di pagamento) postal o money order; **mandato d'arresto** warrant for arrest

man'dibola sf mandible, jaw

'mandorla sf almond; **'mandorlo** sm almond tree

'mandria sf herd

maneggi'are [maned'dʒare] vt (creta, cera) to mould, work, fashion; (arnesi, utensili) to handle; (: adoperare) to use; (fig: persone, denaro) to handle, deal with; **ma'neggio** sm moulding; handling; use; (intrigo) plot, scheme; (per cavalli) riding school

ma'nesco, -a, -schi, -sche ag free with one's fists

ma'nette sfpl handcuffs

manga'nello sm club

mangi'are [man'dʒare] vt to eat; (intaccare) to eat into o away; (Carte, Scacchi ecc) to take ▸ vi to eat ▸ sm eating; (cibo) food; (cucina) cooking;

possiamo ~ qualcosa? can we have something to eat?; **mangiarsi le parole** to mumble; **mangiarsi le unghie** to bite one's nails

man'gime [man'dʒime] sm fodder

'mango, -ghi sm mango

ma'nia sf (Psic) mania; (fig) obsession, craze; **ma'niaco, -a, -ci, -che** ag suffering from a mania; **maniaco (di)** obsessed (by), crazy (about)

'manica sf sleeve; (fig: gruppo) gang, bunch; (Geo): **la M~, il Canale della M~** the (English) Channel; **essere di ~ larga/stretta** to be easy-going/ strict; **manica a vento** (Aer) wind sock

mani'chino [mani'kino] sm (di sarto, vetrina) dummy

'manico, -ci sm handle; (Mus) neck

mani'comio sm mental hospital; (fig) madhouse

mani'cure sm o f inv manicure ▸ sf inv manicurist

mani'era sf way, manner; (stile) style, manner; **maniere** sfpl (comportamento) manners; **in ~ che** so that; **in ~ da** so as to; **in tutte le maniere** at all costs

manifes'tare vt to show, display; (esprimere) to express; (rivelare) to reveal, disclose ▸ vi to demonstrate; **manifestazi'one** sf show, display; expression; (sintomo) sign, symptom; (dimostrazione pubblica) demonstration; (cerimonia) event

mani'festo, -a ag obvious, evident ▸ sm poster, bill; (scritto ideologico) manifesto

ma'niglia [ma'niʎʎa] sf handle; (sostegno: negli autobus ecc) strap

manipo'lare vt to manipulate; (alterare: vino) to adulterate

man'naro: lupo ~ sm werewolf

'mano, -i sf hand; (strato: di vernice ecc) coat; **di prima ~** (notizia) first-hand;

di seconda ~ second-hand; **man ~** little by little, gradually; **man ~ che** as; **darsi** o **stringersi la ~** to shake hands; **mettere le mani avanti** (*fig*) to safeguard o.s.; **restare a mani vuote** to be left empty-handed; **venire alle mani** to come to blows; **a ~** by hand; **mani in alto!** hands up!

mano'dopera *sf* labour

ma'nometro *sm* gauge, manometer

mano'mettere *vt* (*alterare*) to tamper with; (*aprire indebitamente*) to break open illegally

ma'nopola *sf* (*dell'armatura*) gauntlet; (*guanto*) mitt; (*di impugnatura*) hand-grip; (*pomello*) knob

manos'critto, -a *ag* handwritten ▶ *sm* manuscript

mano'vale *sm* labourer

mano'vella *sf* handle; (*Tecn*) crank

ma'novra *sf* manoeuvre (BRIT), maneuver (US); (*Ferr*) shunting

man'sarda *sf* attic

mansi'one *sf* task, duty, job

mansu'eto, -a *ag* gentle, docile

man'tello *sm* cloak; (*fig: di neve ecc*) blanket, mantle; (*Zool*) coat

mante'nere *vt* to maintain; (*adempiere: promesse*) to keep, abide by; (*provvedere a*) to support, maintain; **mantenersi** *vpr* **mantenersi calmo/giovane** to stay calm/young

'Mantova *sf* Mantua

manu'ale *ag* manual ▶ *sm* (*testo*) manual, handbook

ma'nubrio *sm* handle; (*di bicicletta ecc*) handlebars *pl*; (*Sport*) dumbbell

manutenzi'one [manuten'tsjone] *sf* maintenance, upkeep; (*d'impianti*) maintenance, servicing

'manzo ['mandzo] *sm* (*Zool*) steer; (*carne*) beef

'mappa *sf* (*Geo*) map; **mappa'mondo** *sm* map of the world; (*globo girevole*)

globe

mara'tona *sf* marathon

'marca, -che *sf* (*Comm: di prodotti*) brand; (*contrassegno, scontrino*) ticket, check; **prodotto di ~** (*di buona qualità*) high-class product; **marca da bollo** official stamp

mar'care *vt* (*munire di contrassegno*) to mark; (*a fuoco*) to brand; (*Sport: gol*) to score; (*: avversario*) to mark; (*accentuare*) to stress; **~ visita** (*Mil*) to report sick

marcherò *ecc* [marke'rɔ] *vb vedi* **marcare**

mar'chese, -a [mar'keze] *sm/f* marquis o marquess/marchioness

marchi'are [mar'kjare] *vt* to brand

'marcia, -ce ['martʃa] *sf* (*anche Mus, Mil*) march; (*funzionamento*) running; (*il camminare*) walking; (*Aut*) gear; **mettere in ~** to start; **mettersi in ~** to get moving; **far ~ indietro** (*Aut*) to reverse; (*fig*) to back-pedal

marciapi'ede [martʃa'pjede] *sm* (*di strada*) pavement (BRIT), sidewalk (US); (*Ferr*) platform

marci'are [mar'tʃare] *vi* to march; (*andare: treno, macchina*) to go; (*funzionare*) to run, work

'marcio, -a, -ci, -ce ['martʃo] *ag* (*frutta, legno*) rotten, bad; (*Med*) festering; (*fig*) corrupt, rotten

mar'cire [mar'tʃire] *vi* (*andare a male*) to go bad, rot; (*suppurare*) to fester; (*fig*) to rot, waste away

'marco, -chi (*unità monetaria*) mark

'mare *sm* sea; **in ~** at sea; **andare al ~** (*in vacanza ecc*) to go to the seaside; **il M~ del Nord** the North Sea

ma'rea *sf* tide; **alta/bassa ~** high/low tide

mareggi'ata [mared'dʒata] *sf* heavy sea

mare'moto *sm* seaquake

maresci'allo [mareʃ'ʃallo] *sm* (*Mil*)

marshal; (: *sottufficiale*) warrant officer

marga'rina sf margarine

marghe'rita [marge'rita] sf (ox-eye) daisy, marguerite; (*di stampante*) daisy wheel

'margine ['mardʒine] sm margin; (*di bosco, via*) edge, border

mariju'ana [mæri'wa:na] sf marijuana

ma'rina sf navy; (*costa*) coast; (*quadro*) seascape; **marina mercantile/ militare** navy/merchant navy (BRIT) o marine (US)

mari'naio sm sailor

mari'nare vt (Cuc) to marinate; **~ la scuola** to play truant

ma'rino, -a ag sea cpd, marine

mario'netta sf puppet

ma'rito sm husband

ma'rittimo, -a ag maritime, sea cpd

marmel'lata sf jam; (*di agrumi*) marmalade

mar'mitta sf (*recipiente*) pot; (Aut) silencer; **marmitta catalitica** catalytic converter

'marmo sm marble

mar'motta sf (Zool) marmot

maroc'chino, -a [marok'kino] ag, sm/f Moroccan

Ma'rocco sm il ~ Morocco

mar'rone ag inv brown ▶ sm (Bot) chestnut

> ⚠ Attenzione! In inglese esiste la parola *maroon*, che però indica un altro colore, il rosso bordeaux.

mar'supio sm pouch; (*per denaro*) bum bag; (*per neonato*) sling

marte'dì sm inv Tuesday; **di** o **il ~ on** Tuesdays; **martedì grasso** Shrove Tuesday

martel'lare vt to hammer ▶ vi (*pulsare*) to throb; (: *cuore*) to thump

mar'tello sm hammer; (*di uscio*) knocker; **martello pneumatico** pneumatic drill

'martire sm/f martyr

mar'xista, -i, -e ag, sm/f Marxist

marza'pane [martsa'pane] sm marzipan

'marzo ['martso] sm March

mascal'zone [maskal'tsone] sm rascal, scoundrel

mas'cara sm inv mascara

ma'scella [maʃ'ʃella] sf (Anat) jaw

'maschera ['maskera] sf mask; (*travestimento*) disguise; (: *per un ballo ecc*) fancy dress; (Teatro, Cinema) usher/usherette; (*personaggio del teatro*) stock character; **masche'rare** vt to mask; (*travestire*) to disguise; to dress up; (*fig: celare*) to hide, conceal; (Mil) to camouflage; **mascherarsi da** to disguise o.s. as; to dress up as; (*fig*) to masquerade as

mas'chile [mas'kile] ag masculine (*sesso, popolazione*) male; (*abiti*) men's; (*per ragazzi: scuola*) boys'

mas'chilista, -i, -e ag, sm/f (*uomo*) (male) chauvinist, sexist; (*donna*) sexist

'maschio, -a ['maskjo] ag (Biol) male; (*virile*) manly ▶ sm (*anche Zool, Tecn*) male; (*uomo*) man; (*ragazzo*) boy; (*figlio*) son

masco'lino, -a ag masculine

'massa sf mass; (*di errori ecc*): **una ~ di** heaps of, masses of; (*di gente*) mass, multitude; (Elettr) earth; **in ~** (Comm) in bulk; (*tutti insieme*) en masse; **adunata in ~** mass meeting; **di ~** (*cultura, manifestazione*) mass cpd

mas'sacro sm massacre, slaughter; (*fig*) mess, disaster

massaggi'are [massad'dʒare] vt to massage

mas'saggio [mas'saddʒo] sm massage; **massaggio cardiaco** cardiac massage

mas'saia sf housewife

masse'rizie [masse'rittsje] *sfpl* (household) furnishings

mas'siccio, -a, -ci, -ce [mas'sittʃo] *ag* (oro, legno) solid; (palazzo) massive; (corporatura) stout ▸ *sm* (Geo) massif

'massima *sf* (sentenza, regola) maxim; (Meteor) maximum temperature; **in linea di ~** generally speaking; *vedi* **massimo**

massi'male *sm* maximum

'massimo, -a *ag, sm* maximum; **al ~** at (the) most

'masso *sm* rock, boulder

masteriz'zare [masterid'dzare] *vt* (CD, DVD) to burn

masterizza'tore [masteriddza'tore] *sm* CD burner o writer

masti'care *vt* to chew

'mastice ['mastitʃe] *sm* mastic; (per vetri) putty

mas'tino *sm* mastiff

ma'tassa *sf* skein

mate'matica *sf* mathematics *sg*

mate'matico, -a, -ci, -che *ag* mathematical ▸ *sm/f* mathematician

materas'sino *sm* mat; **materassino gonfiabile** air bed

mate'rasso *sm* mattress; **materasso a molle** spring o interior-sprung mattress

ma'teria *sf* (Fisica) matter; (Tecn, Comm) material, matter *no pl*; (disciplina) subject; (argomento) subject matter, material; **in ~ di** (per quanto concerne) on the subject of; **materie prime** raw materials

materi'ale *ag* material; (fig: grossolano) rough, rude ▸ *sm* material; (insieme di strumenti ecc) equipment *no pl*, materials *pl*

mater'nità *sf* motherhood, maternity; (reparto) maternity ward

ma'terno, -a *ag* (amore, cura ecc) maternal, motherly; (nonno) maternal; (lingua, terra) mother *cpd*

ma'tita *sf* pencil; **matite colorate** coloured pencils; **matita per gli occhi** eyeliner (pencil)

ma'tricola *sf* (registro) register; (numero) registration number; (nell'università) freshman, fresher

ma'trigna [ma'triɲɲa] *sf* stepmother

matrimoni'ale *ag* matrimonial, marriage *cpd*

matri'monio *sm* marriage, matrimony; (durata) marriage, married life; (cerimonia) wedding

mat'tina *sf* morning

'matto, -a *ag* mad, crazy; (fig: falso) false, imitation ▸ *sm/f* madman/woman; **avere una voglia matta di qc** to be dying for sth

mat'tone *sm* brick; (fig): **questo libro/film è un ~** this book/film is heavy going

matto'nella *sf* tile

matu'rare *vi* (anche: maturarsi: frutta, grano) to ripen; (ascesso) to come to a head; (fig: persona, idea, Econ) to mature ▸ *vt* to ripen, to (make) mature

maturità *sf* maturity; (di frutta) ripeness, maturity; (Ins) school-leaving examination, ≈ GCE A-levels (BRIT)

ma'turo, -a *ag* mature; (frutto) ripe, mature

max. *abbr* (= massimo) max

maxischermo [maxis'kermo] *sm* giant screen

'mazza ['mattsa] *sf* (bastone) club; (martello) sledge-hammer; (Sport: da golf) club; (: da baseball, cricket) bat

maz'zata [mat'tsata] *sf* (anche fig) heavy blow

'mazzo ['mattso] *sm* (di fiori, chiavi ecc) bunch; (di carte da gioco) pack

me *pron* me; **me stesso(a)** myself; **sei bravo quanto me** you are as clever as I (am) o as me

mec'canico, -a, -ci, -che *ag*
mechanical ▶ *sm* mechanic; **può
mandare un ~?** can you send a
mechanic?

mecca'nismo *sm* mechanism

me'daglia [me'daʎʎa] *sf* medal

me'desimo, -a *ag* same; (in *persona*):
io ~ I myself

'media *sf* average; (Mat) mean; (Ins:
voto) end-of-term average; **le medie**
sfpl = **scuola media**; **in ~** on average;
vedi anche **medio**

medi'ante *prep* by means of

media'tore, -'trice *sm/f* mediator;
(Comm) middle man, agent

medi'care *vt* to treat; (*ferita*) to dress

medi'cina [medi'tʃina] *sf* medicine;
medicina legale forensic medicine

'medico, -a, -ci, -che *ag* medical
▶ *sm* doctor; **chiamate un ~** call a
doctor; **medico generico** general
practitioner, GP

medie'vale *ag* medieval

'medio, -a *ag* average; (*punto, ceto*)
middle; (*altezza, statura*) medium ▶ *sm*
(*dito*) middle finger; **licenza media**
*leaving certificate awarded at the end of
3 years of secondary education*; **scuola
media** *first 3 years of secondary school*

medi'ocre *ag* mediocre, poor

medi'tare *vt* to ponder over, meditate
on; (*progettare*) to plan, think out ▶ *vi*
to meditate

mediter'raneo, -a *ag*
Mediterranean; **il (mare) M~** the
Mediterranean (Sea)

me'dusa *sf* (Zool) jellyfish

'mega'byte *sm inv* (Comput) megabyte

mega'fono *sm* megaphone

'meglio ['mɛʎʎo] *av, ag inv* better; (con
senso superlativo) best ▶ *sm* (*la cosa
migliore*) il ~ the best (thing); **faresti
~ ad andartene** you had better leave;
alla ~ as best one can; **andar di bene
in ~** to get better and better; **fare del**

proprio ~ to do one's best; **per il ~** for
the best; **aver la ~ su qn** to get the
better of sb

'mela *sf* apple; **mela cotogna** quince

mela'grana *sf* pomegranate

melan'zana [melan'dzana] *sf*
aubergine (BRIT), eggplant (US)

melato'nina *sf* melatonin

'melma *sf* mud, mire

'melo *sm* apple tree

melo'dia *sf* melody

me'lone *sm* (musk)melon

'membro *sm* member (pl(f) **membra**)
(*arto*) limb

memo'randum *sm inv* memorandum

me'moria *sf* memory; **memorie** *sfpl*
(*opera autobiografica*) memoirs; **a ~**
(*imparare, sapere*) by heart; **a ~ d'uomo**
within living memory

mendi'cante *sm/f* beggar

○ **'meno**
　 av

1 (in *minore misura*) less; **dovresti
mangiare meno** you should eat less,
you shouldn't eat so much

2 (*comparativo*): **meno ... di** not as ...
as, less ... than; **sono meno alto di te**
I'm not as tall as you (are), I'm less tall
than you (are); **meno ... che** not as ...
as, less ... than; **meno che mai** less
than ever; **è meno intelligente che
ricco** he's more rich than intelligent;
meno fumo più mangio the less I
smoke the more I eat

3 (*superlativo*) least; **il meno dotato
degli studenti** the least gifted of the
students; **è quello che compro meno
spesso** it's the one I buy least often

4 (*Mat*) minus; **8 meno 5** 8 minus 5, 8
take away 5; **sono le 8 meno un quarto**
it's a quarter to 8; **meno 5 gradi** 5
degrees below zero, minus 5 degrees; **1
euro in meno** 1 euro less

5 (*fraseologia*): **quanto meno poteva
telefonare** he could at least have

phoned; **non so se accettare o meno** I don't know whether to accept or not; **fare a meno di qc/qn** to do without sth/sb; **non potevo fare a meno di ridere** I couldn't help laughing; **meno male!** thank goodness!; **meno male che sei arrivato** it's a good job that you've come

▶ *ag inv (tempo, denaro)* less; *(errori, persone)* fewer; **ha fatto meno errori di tutti** he made fewer mistakes than anyone, he made the fewest mistakes of all

▶ *sm inv*

1: **il meno** *(il minimo)* the least; **parlare del più e del meno** to talk about this and that

2 *(Mat)* minus

▶ *prep (eccetto)* except (for), apart from; **a meno che, a meno di** unless; **a meno che non piova** unless it rains; **non posso, a meno di prendere ferie** I can't, unless I take some leave

meno'pausa *sf* menopause

'mensa *sf (locale)* canteen; *(: Mil)* mess; *(: nelle università)* refectory

men'sile *ag* monthly ▶ *sm (periodico)* monthly *(magazine)*; *(stipendio)* monthly salary

'mensola *sf* bracket; *(ripiano)* shelf; *(Archit)* corbel

'menta *sf* mint; *(anche: ~ piperita)* peppermint; *(bibita)* peppermint cordial; *(caramella)* mint, peppermint

men'tale *ag* mental; **mentalità** *sf inv* mentality

'mente *sf* mind; **imparare/sapere qc a ~** to learn/know sth by heart; **avere in ~ qc** to have sth in mind; **passare di ~ a qn** to slip sb's mind

men'tire *vi* to lie

'mento *sm* chin

'mentre *cong (temporale)* while; *(avversativo)* whereas

menù *sm inv* menu; **ci può portare**

il ~? could we see the menu?; **menù turistico** set menu

menzio'nare [mentsjo'nare] *vt* to mention

men'zogna [men'tsɔɲɲa] *sf* lie

mera'viglia [mera'viλλa] *sf* amazement, wonder; *(persona, cosa)* marvel, wonder; **a ~** perfectly, wonderfully; **meravigli'are** *vt* to amaze, astonish; **meravigliarsi (di)** to marvel (at); *(stupirsi)* to be amazed (at), be astonished (at); **meravigli'oso, -a** *ag* wonderful, marvellous

mer'cante *sm* merchant; **mercante d'arte** art dealer

merca'tino *sm (rionale)* local street market; *(Econ)* unofficial stock market

mer'cato *sm* market; **mercato dei cambi** exchange market; **mercato nero** black market

'merce ['mɛrtʃe] *sf* goods *pl*, merchandise

mercé [mer'tʃe] *sf* mercy

merce'ria [mertʃe'ria] *sf (articoli)* haberdashery *(BRIT)*, notions *pl (US)*; *(bottega)* haberdasher's shop *(BRIT)*, notions store *(US)*

mercoledì *sm inv* Wednesday; **di o il ~** on Wednesdays; **mercoledì delle Ceneri** Ash Wednesday

mer'curio *sm* mercury

'merda *(fam!)* *sf* shit (!)

me'renda *sf* afternoon snack

meren'dina *sf* snack

meridi'ana *sf (orologio)* sundial

meridi'ano, -a *ag* meridian; midday *cpd*, noonday ▶ *sm* meridian

meridio'nale *ag* southern ▶ *sm/f* southerner

meridi'one *sm* south

me'ringa, -ghe *sf (Cuc)* meringue

meri'tare *vt* to deserve, merit ▶ *vb impers* **merita andare** it's worth going meri'tevole ag worthy

'merito sm merit; (valore) worth; in ~ a as regards, with regard to; dare ~ a qn di to give sb credit for; finire a pari ~ to finish joint first (o second ecc); to tie

mer'letto sm lace

'merlo sm (Zool) blackbird; (Archit) battlement

mer'luzzo [mer'luttso] sm (Zool) cod

mes'chino, -a [mes'kino] ag wretched; (scarso) scanty, poor; (persona: gretta) mean; (: limitata) narrow-minded, petty

mesco'lare vt to mix; (vini, colori) to blend; (mettere in disordine) to mix up, muddle up; (carte) to shuffle

'mese sm month

'messa sf (Rel) mass; (il mettere): messa in moto starting; messa in piega set; messa a punto (Tecn) adjustment; (Aut) tuning; (fig) clarification; messa in scena = messinscena

mes'saggero [messad'dʒɛro] sm messenger

messaggino [messad'dʒino] sm (di telefonino) text (message)

mes'saggio [mes'saddʒo] sm message; (messaggio telefonico): posso lasciare un ~? can I leave a message?; ci sono messaggi per me? are there any messages for me?; messaggio di posta elettronica e-mail message

messag'gistica [messad'dʒistica] sf ~ immediata (Inform) instant messaging; programma di ~ immediata instant messenger

mes'sale sm (Rel) missal

messi'cano, -a ag, sm/f Mexican

'Messico sm il ~ Mexico

messin'scena [messin'ʃɛna] sf (Teatro) production

'messo, -a pp di mettere ▶ sm messenger

mesti'ere sm (professione) job; (: manuale) trade; (: artigianale) craft; (fig: abilità nel lavoro) skill, technique; essere del ~ to know the tricks of the trade

'mestolo sm (Cuc) ladle

mestruazi'one [mestruat'tsjone] sf menstruation

'meta sf destination; (fig) aim, goal

metà sf inv half; (punto di mezzo) middle; dividere qc a o per ~ to divide sth in half, halve sth; fare a ~ (di qc con qn) to go halves (with sb in sth); a ~ prezzo at half price; a ~ strada halfway

meta'done sm methadone

me'tafora sf metaphor

me'tallico, -a, -ci, -che ag (di metallo) metal cpd; (splendore, rumore ecc) metallic

me'tallo sm metal

metalmec'canico, -a, -ci, -che ag engineering cpd ▶ sm engineering worker

me'tano sm methane

me'ticcio, -a, -ci, -ce [me'tittʃo] sm/f half-caste, half-breed

me'todico, -a, -ci, -che ag methodical

'metodo sm method

'metro sm metre; (nastro) tape measure; (asta) (metre) rule

metropoli'tana sf underground, subway

'mettere vt to put; (abito) to put on; (: portare) to wear; (installare: telefono) to put in; (fig: provocare): ~ fame/allegria a qn to make sb hungry/happy; (supporre): mettiamo che ... let's suppose o say that ...; mettersi vpr (persona) to put o.s.; (oggetto) to go; (: disporsi: faccenda) to turn out; mettersi a sedere to sit down; mettersi a letto to get into bed; (per malattia) to take to one's bed; **mettersi il cappello** to put on one's hat; **mettersi a** (*cominciare*) to begin to, start to; **mettersi al lavoro** to set to work; **mettersi con qn** (*in società*) to team up with sb; (*in coppia*) to start going out with sb; **metterci: metterci molta cura/molto tempo** to take a lot of care/a lot of time; **ci ho messo 3 ore per venire** it's taken me 3 hours to get here; **mettercela tutta** to do one's best; **~ a tacere qn/qc** to keep sb/sth quiet; **~ su casa** to set up house; **~ su un negozio** to start a shop; **~ via** to put away

mezza'notte [meddza'nɔtte] *sf* midnight

'mezzo, -a ['mɛddzo] *ag* half; **un ~ litro/panino** half a litre/roll ▶ *av* half-; **~ morto** half-dead ▶ *sm* (*metà*) half; (*parte centrale*: *di strada ecc*) middle; (*per raggiungere un fine*) means *sg*; (*veicolo*) vehicle; (*nell'indicare l'ora*): **le nove e ~** half past nine; **~ giorno e ~** half past twelve; **mezzi** *smpl* (*possibilità economiche*) means; **di mezza età** middle-aged; **un soprabito di mezza stagione** a spring (*o autumn*) coat; **di ~** middle, in the middle; **andarci di ~** (*patir danno*) to suffer; **levarsi o togliersi di ~** to get out of the way; **in ~ a** in the middle of; **per o a ~ di** by means of; **mezzi di comunicazione di massa** mass media *pl*; **mezzi pubblici** public transport *sg*; **mezzi di trasporto** means of transport

mezzogiorno [meddzo'dʒorno] *sm* midday, noon; **a ~** at 12 (o'clock) *o* midday *o* noon; **il ~ d'Italia** southern Italy

mi (*dav lo, la, li, le, ne diventa* **me**) *pron* (*oggetto*) me; (*complemento di termine*) to me; (*riflessivo*) myself ▶ *sm* (*Mus*) E; (: *solfeggiando la scala*) mi

miago'lare *vi* to miaow, mew

'mica *av* (*fam*): **non ... ~** not ... at all; **non sono ~ stanco** I'm not a bit tired; **non sarà ~ partito?** he wouldn't have left, would he?; **~ male** not bad

'miccia, -ce ['mittʃa] *sf* fuse

micidi'ale [mitʃi'djale] *ag* fatal; (*dannosissimo*) deadly

micro'fibra *sf* microfibre

mi'crofono *sm* microphone

micros'copio *sm* microscope

mi'dollo (*pl(f)* **midolla**) *sm* (*Anat*) marrow; **midollo osseo** bone marrow

mi'ele *sm* honey

'miglia ['miʎʎa] *sfpl di* **miglio**

migli'aio [miʎ'ʎajo] (*(pl)f* **migliaia**) *sm* thousand; **un ~ (di)** about a thousand; **a migliaia** by the thousand, in thousands

'miglio ['miʎʎo] *sm* (*Bot*) millet (*pl(f)* **miglia**) (*unità di misura*) mile; **~ marino** *o* **nautico** nautical mile

migliora'mento [miʎʎora'mento] *sm* improvement

miglio'rare *vt, vi* to improve

migli'ore [miʎ'ʎore] *ag* (*comparativo*) better; (*superlativo*) best ▶ *sm* **il ~** the best (thing) ▶ *sm/f* **il(la) ~** the best (person); **il miglior vino di questa regione** the best wine in this area

'mignolo ['miɲɲolo] *sm* (*Anat*) little finger, pinkie; (: *dito del piede*) little toe

Mi'lano *sf* Milan

miliar'dario, -a *sm/f* millionaire

mili'ardo *sm* thousand million, billion (*US*)

mili'one *sm* million; **mille euro** one thousand euros

mili'tante *ag*, *sm/f* militant

mili'tare *vi* (*Mil*) to be a soldier, serve; (*fig*: *in un partito*) to be a member ▶ *ag* military ▶ *sm* serviceman; **fare il ~** to do one's military service

'mille (*pl* **mila**) *num* a *o* one thousand;

dieci mila ten thousand

mil'lennio sm millennium

millepi'edi sm inv centipede

mil'lesimo, -a ag, sm thousandth

milli'grammo sm milligram(me)

mil'limetro sm millimetre

'milza ['miltsa] sf (Anat) spleen

mimetiz'zare [mimetid'dzare] vt to camouflage; **mimetizzarsi** vpr to camouflage o.s.

'mimo sm (attore, componimento) mime

mi'mosa sf mimosa

min. abbr (= minuto, minimo) min

'mina sf (esplosivo) mine; (di matita) lead

mi'naccia, -ce [mi'nattʃa] sf threat; **minacci'are** vt to threaten; **minacciare qn di morte** to threaten to kill sb; **minacciare di fare qc** to threaten to do sth

mi'nare vt (Mil) to mine; (fig) to undermine

mina'tore sm miner

mine'rale ag, sm mineral

mine'rario, -a ag (delle miniere) mining; (dei minerali) ore cpd

mi'nestra sf soup; **minestra in brodo** noodle soup; **minestra di verdure** vegetable soup

minia'tura sf miniature

'mini'bar sm inv minibar

mini'era sf mine

mini'gonna sf miniskirt

'minimo, -a ag minimum, least, slightest; (piccolissimo) very small, slight; (il più basso) lowest, minimum ▶ sm minimum; **al ~ at least; girare al ~ (Aut) to idle**

minis'tero sm (Pol, Rel) ministry; (governo) government; **M~ delle Finanze** Ministry of Finance, ≈ Treasury

mi'nistro sm (Pol, Rel) minister

mino'ranza [mino'rantsa] sf minority

mi'nore ag (comparativo) less; (più piccolo) smaller; (numero) lower; (inferiore) lower, inferior; (meno importante) minor; (più giovane) younger; (superlativo) least; smallest; lowest; youngest ▶ sm/f = **minorenne**

mino'renne ag under age ▶ sm/f minor, person under age

mi'nuscolo, -a ag (scrittura, carattere) small; (piccolissimo) tiny ▶ sf small letter

mi'nuto, -a ag tiny, minute; (pioggia) fine; (corporatura) delicate, fine ▶ sm (unità di misura) minute; **al ~ (Comm)** retail

'mio (f'mia, pl mi'ei or'mie) det **il ~, la mia** ecc my ▶ pron **il ~, la mia** ecc mine; **i miei** my family; **un ~ amico** a friend of mine

'miope ag short-sighted

'mira sf (anche fig) aim; **prendere la ~** to take aim; **prendere di ~ qn** (fig) to pick on sb

mi'racolo sm miracle

mi'raggio [mi'raddʒo] sm mirage

mi'rare vi **~ a** to aim at

mi'rino sm (Tecn) sight; (Fot) viewer, viewfinder

mir'tillo sm bilberry (BRIT), blueberry (US), whortleberry

mi'scela [miʃʃela] sf mixture; (di caffè) blend

'mischia ['miskja] sf scuffle; (Rugby) scrum, scrummage

mis'cuglio [mis'kuʎʎo] sm mixture, hotchpotch, jumble

'mise vb vedi **mettere**

mise'rabile ag (infelice) miserable, wretched; (povero) poverty-stricken; (di scarso valore) miserable

mi'seria sf extreme poverty; (infelicità) misery

miseri'cordia sf mercy, pity

'misero, -a ag miserable, wretched; (povero) poverty-stricken;

(insufficiente) miserable

'**misi** vb vedi **mettere**

mi'**sogino** [mi'zɔdʒino] sm misogynist

'**missile** sm missile

missio'**nario**, -**a** ag, sm/f missionary

missi'**one** sf mission

misteri'**oso**, -**a** ag mysterious

mis'**tero** sm mystery

'**misto**, -**a** ag mixed; (scuola) mixed, coeducational ▶ sm mixture

mis'**tura** sf mixture

mi'**sura** sf measure; (misurazione, dimensione) measurement; (taglia) size; (provvedimento) measure, step; (moderazione) moderation; (Mus) time; (: divisione) bar; (fig: limite) bounds pl, limit; **nella ~ in cui** inasmuch as, insofar as; (fatto) **su ~** made to measure

misu'**rare** vt (ambiente, stoffa) to measure; (terreno) to survey; (abito) to try on; (pesare) to weigh up; (fig: parole ecc) to weigh up; (: spese, cibo) to limit ▶ vi to measure; **misurarsi** vpr **misurarsi con qn** to have a confrontation with sb; to compete with sb

'**mite** ag mild

'**mitico**, -**a**, -**ci**, -**che** ag mythical

'**mito** sm myth; **mitolo'gia**, -'**gie** sf mythology

'**mitra** sf (Rel) mitre ▶ sm inv (arma) sub-machine gun

mit'**tente** sm/f sender

mm abbr (= millimetro) mm

'**mobile** ag mobile; (parte di macchina) moving; (Dir: bene) movable, personal ▶ sm (arredamento) piece of furniture; **mobili** smpl (mobilia) furniture sg

mocas'**sino** sm moccasin

'**moda** sf fashion; **alla ~**, **di ~** fashionable, in fashion

modalità sf inv formality

mo'**della** sf model

mo'**dello** sm model; (stampo) mould ▶ ag inv model cpd

'**modem** sm inv modem

modera'**tore**, -'**trice** sm/f moderator

mo'**derno**, -**a** ag modern

mo'**desto**, -**a** ag modest

'**modico**, -**a**, -**ci**, -**che** ag reasonable, moderate

mo'**difica**, -**che** sf modification

modifi'**care** vt to modify, alter

'**modo** sm way, manner; (mezzo) means, way; (occasione) opportunity; (Ling) mood; (Mus) mode; **modi** smpl (comportamento) manners; **a suo ~**, **a ~ suo** in his own way; **ad o in ogni ~** anyway; **di o in ~ che** so that; **in ~ da** so as to; **in tutti i modi** at all costs; (comunque) anyway; (in ogni caso) in any case; **per ~ di dire** so to speak; **modo di dire** turn of phrase

'**modulo** sm (modello) form; (Archit, lunare, di comando) module

mo'**gano** sm mahogany

'**mogio**, -**a**, -**gi**, -**gie** ['mɔdʒo] ag down in the dumps, dejected

'**moglie** ['mɔʎʎe] sf wife

mo'**ine** sfpl cajolery sg; (leziosità) affectation sg

mo'**lare** sm (dente) molar

'**mole** sf mass; (dimensioni) size; (edificio grandioso) massive structure

moles'**tare** vt to bother, annoy; mo'**lestia** sf annoyance, bother; **recar molestia a qn** to bother sb; **molestie sessuali** sexual harassment sg

'**molla** sf spring; **molle** sfpl (per camino) tongs

mol'**lare** vt to release, let go; (Naut) to ease; (fig: ceffone) to give ▶ vi (cedere) to give in

'**molle** ag soft; (muscoli) flabby

mol'**letta** sf (per capelli) hairgrip; (per

panni stesi) clothes peg
'mollica, -che sf crumb, soft part
mol'lusco, -schi sm mollusc
'molo sm mole, breakwater; jetty
moltipli'care vt to multiply;
  moltiplicarsi vpr to multiply;
  to increase in number;
  moltiplicazi'one sf multiplication

⭕ **'molto, -a**
  det (quantità) a lot of, much;
  (numero) a lot of, many; **molto pane/
  carbone** a lot of bread/coal; **molta
  gente** a lot of people, many people;
  molti libri a lot of books, many books;
  non ho molto tempo I haven't got
  much time; **per molto (tempo)** for a
  long time
  ▶ av
  1 a lot, (very) much; **viaggia molto**
  he travels a lot; **non viaggia molto** he
  doesn't travel much o a lot
  2 (intensivo: con aggettivi, avverbi)
  very; (: con participio passato) (very)
  much; **molto buono** very good; **molto
  migliore, molto meglio** much o a
  lot better
  ▶ pron much, a lot

momentanea'mente av at the
  moment, at present
momen'taneo, -a ag momentary,
  fleeting
mo'mento sm moment; **da
  un ~ all'altro** at any moment;
  (all'improvviso) suddenly; **al ~ di fare
  just as I was (o you were o he was ecc)
  doing; **per il ~** for the time being; **dal
  ~ che** ever since; (dato che) since; **a
  momenti** (da un momento all'altro) any
  time o moment now; (quasi) nearly
'monaca, -che sf nun
'Monaco sf Monaco; **Monaco (di
  Baviera)** Munich
'monaco, -ci sm monk
monar'chia sf monarchy
monas'tero sm (di monaci)

monastery; (di monache) convent
mon'dano, -a ag (anche fig) worldly;
  (anche: dell'alta società) society cpd;
  fashionable
mondi'ale ag (campionato, popolazione)
  world cpd; (influenza) world-wide
'mondo sm world; (grande quantità):
  un ~ di lots of, a host of; **il bel ~** high
  society
mo'nello, -a sm/f street urchin;
  (ragazzo vivace) scamp, imp
mo'neta sf coin; (Econ: valuta)
  currency; (denaro spicciolo) (small)
  change; **moneta estera** foreign
  currency; **moneta legale** legal
  tender
mongol'fiera sf hot-air balloon
'monitor sm inv (Tecn, TV) monitor
monolo'cale sm studio flat
mono'polio sm monopoly
mo'notono, -a ag monotonous
monovo'lume ag inv, sf inv
  (automobile) = people carrier, MPV
mon'sone sm monsoon
monta'carichi [monta'kariki] sm inv
  hoist, goods lift
mon'taggio [mon'taddʒo] sm (Tecn)
  assembly; (Cinema) editing
mon'tagna [mon'taɲɲa] sf
  mountain; (zona montuosa): **la ~** the
  mountains pl; **andare in ~** to go to the
  mountains; **montagne russe** roller
  coaster sg, big dipper sg (BRIT)
monta'naro, -a ag mountain cpd
  ▶ sm/f mountain dweller
mon'tano, -a ag mountain cpd;
  alpine
mon'tare vt to go (o come) up;
  (cavallo) to ride; (apparecchiatura) to
  set up, assemble; (Cuc) to whip; (Zool)
  to cover; (incastonare) to mount, set;
  (Cinema) to edit; (Fot) to mount ▶ vi
  to go (o come) up; (a cavallo): **~ bene/
  male** to ride well/badly; (aumentare di
  livello, volume) to rise

monta'tura sf assembling no pl; (di occhiali) frames pl; (di gioiello) mounting, setting; (fig): **montatura pubblicitaria** publicity stunt

'monte sm mountain; **a ~ upstream**; **mandare a ~ qc** to upset sth, cause sth to fail; **il M~ Bianco** Mont Blanc; **monte di pietà** pawnshop; **monte premi** prize

mon'tone sm (Zool) ram; **carne di ~** mutton

montu'oso, -a ag mountainous

monu'mento sm monument

mo'quette [mo'ket] sf inv fitted carpet

'mora sf (del rovo) blackberry; (del gelso) mulberry; (Dir) delay; (: somma) arrears pl

mo'rale ag moral ▶ sf (scienza) ethics sg, moral philosophy; (complesso di norme) moral standards pl, morality; (condotta) morals pl; (insegnamento morale) moral ▶ sm morale; **essere giù di ~** to be feeling down

'morbido, -a ag soft; (pelle) soft, smooth

> Attenzione! In inglese esiste la parola morbid, che però significa morboso.

mor'billo sm (Med) measles sg

'morbo sm disease

mor'boso, -a ag (fig) morbid

'mordere vt to bite; (addentare) to bite into

mori'bondo, -a ag dying, moribund

mo'rire vi to die; (abitudine, civiltà) to die out; **~ di fame** to die of hunger; (fig) to be starving; **~ di noia/paura** to be bored/scared to death; **fa un caldo da ~** it's terribly hot

mormo'rare vi to murmur; (brontolare) to grumble

'moro, -a ag dark(-haired), dark(-complexioned)

'morsa sf (Tecn) vice; (fig: stretta) grip

morsi'care vt to nibble (at), gnaw (at); (insetto) to bite

'morso, -a pp di **mordere** ▶ sm bite; (di insetto) sting; (parte della briglia) bit; **morsi della fame** pangs of hunger

morta'della sf (Cuc) mortadella (type of salted pork meat)

mor'taio sm mortar

mor'tale, ag, sm mortal

'morte sf death

'morto, -a pp di **morire** ▶ ag dead ▶ sm/f dead man/woman; **i morti** the dead; **fare il ~** (nell'acqua) to float on one's back; **il Mar M~** the Dead Sea

mo'saico, -ci sm mosaic

'Mosca sf Moscow

'mosca, -sche sf fly; **mosca cieca** blind-man's-buff

mosce'rino [moʃʃe'rino] sm midge, gnat

mos'chea [mos'kea] sf mosque

'moscio, -a, -sci, -sce ['moʃʃo] ag (fig) lifeless

mos'cone sm (Zool) bluebottle; (barca) pedalo; (: a remi) kind of pedalo with oars

'mossa sf movement; (nel gioco) move

'mossi ecc vb vedi **muovere**

'mosso, -a pp di **muovere** ▶ ag (mare) rough; (capelli) wavy; (Fot) blurred

mos'tarda sf mustard; **mostarda di Cremona** pickled fruit with mustard

'mostra sf exhibition, show; (ostentazione) show; **in ~** on show; **far ~ di** (fingere) to pretend; **far ~ di sé** to show off

mos'trare vt to show; **può mostrarmi dov'è, per favore?** can you show me where it is, please?

'mostro sm monster; **mostru'oso, -a** ag monstrous

mo'tel sm inv motel

moti'vare vt (causare) to cause; (giustificare) to justify, account for

mo'tivo sm (causa) reason, cause; (movente) motive; (letterario) (central) theme; (*disegno*) motif, design, pattern; (*Mus*) motif; **per quale ~?** why?, for what reason?

'moto sm (*anche Fisica*) motion; (*movimento, gesto*) movement; (*esercizio fisico*) exercise; (*sommossa*) rising, revolt; (*commozione*) feeling, impulse ▶ sf inv (*motocicletta*) motorbike; **mettere in ~** to set in motion; (*Aut*) to start up

motoci'clista, -i, -e sm/f motorcyclist

mo'tore, -'trice ag motor; (*Tecn*) driving ▶ sm engine, motor; **a ~** motor cpd, power-driven; **~ a combustione interna/a reazione** internal combustion/jet engine; **motore di ricerca** (*Inform*) search engine; **moto'rino** sm moped; **motorino di avviamento** (*Aut*) starter

motos'cafo sm motorboat

'motto sm (*battuta scherzosa*) witty remark; (*frase emblematica*) motto, maxim

'mouse ['maus] sm inv (*Inform*) mouse

mo'vente sm motive

movi'mento sm movement; (*fig*) activity, hustle and bustle; (*Mus*) tempo, movement

mozi'one [mot'tsjone] sf (*Pol*) motion

mozza'rella [mottsa'rella] sf mozzarella, *a moist Neapolitan curd cheese*

mozzi'cone [mottsi'kone] sm stub, butt, end; (*anche:* **~ di sigaretta**) cigarette end

'mucca, -che sf cow; **mucca pazza** mad cow disease

mucchio ['mukkjo] sm pile, heap; (*fig*): **un ~ di** lots of, heaps of

'muco, -chi sm mucus

'muffa sf mould, mildew

mug'gire [mud'dʒire] vi (*vacca*) to low, moo; (*toro*) to bellow; (*fig*) to roar

mu'ghetto [mu'getto] sm lily of the valley

mu'lino sm mill; **mulino a vento** windmill

'mulo sm mule

'multa sf fine

multi'etnico, -a, -ci, -che ag multiethnic

multirazziale [multirat'tsjale] ag multiracial

multi'sala ag inv multiscreen

multivitami'nico, -a, -ci, -che ag complesso ~ multivitamin

'mummia sf mummy

'mungere ['mundʒere] vt (*anche fig*) to milk

munici'pale [munitʃi'pale] ag municipal; town cpd

muni'cipio [muni'tʃipjo] sm town council, corporation; (*edificio*) town hall

munizi'oni [munit'tsjoni] sfpl (*Mil*) ammunition sg

'munsi ecc vb vedi **mungere**

mu'oio ecc vb vedi **morire**

mu'overe vt to move; (*ruota, macchina*) to drive; (*sollevare: questione, obiezione*) to raise, bring up; (: *accusa*) to make, bring forward; **muoversi** vpr to move; **muoviti!** hurry up!, get a move on!

'mura sfpl vedi **muro**

mu'rale ag wall cpd; mural

mura'tore sm mason; bricklayer

'muro sm wall

'muschio ['muskjo] sm (*Zool*) musk; (*Bot*) moss

musco'lare ag muscular, muscle cpd

'muscolo sm (*Anat*) muscle

mu'seo sm museum

museru'ola sf muzzle

'musica sf music; **musica da ballo/ camera** dance/chamber music; **musi'cale** ag musical; **musi'cista, -i, -e** sm/f musician

'müsli ['mysli] sm muesli

'**muso** *sm* muzzle; (*di auto, aereo*) nose; **tenere il ~** to sulk

mussul'mano, -a *ag, sm/f* Muslim, Moslem

'**muta** *sf* (*di animali*) moulting; (*di serpenti*) sloughing; (*per immersioni subacquee*) diving suit; (*gruppo di cani*) pack

mu'tande *sfpl* (*da uomo*) (under)pants

'**muto, -a** *ag* (*Med*) dumb; (*emozione, dolore, Cinema*) silent; (*Ling*) silent, mute; (*carta geografica*) blank; **~ per lo stupore** *ecc* speechless with amazement *ecc*

'**mutuo, -a** *ag* (*reciproco*) mutual ▸ *sm* (*Econ*) (long-term) loan

n

N *abbr* (= *nord*) N

n. *abbr* (= *numero*) no

'**nafta** *sf* naphtha; (*per motori diesel*) diesel oil

nafta'lina *sf* (*Chim*) naphthalene; (*tarmicida*) mothballs *pl*

'**naia** *sf* (*Mil*) slang term for national service

na'ïf [na'if] *ag inv* naïve

'**nanna** *sf* (*linguaggio infantile*): **andare a ~** to go to beddy-byes

'**nano, -a** *ag, sm/f* dwarf

napole'tano, -a *ag, sm/f* Neapolitan

'**Napoli** *sf* Naples

nar'ciso [nar'tʃizo] *sm* narcissus

nar'cotico, -ci *sm* narcotic

na'rice [na'ritʃe] *sf* nostril

nar'rare *vt* to tell the story of, recount; **narra'tiva** *sf* (*branca letteraria*) fiction

na'sale *ag* nasal

'**nascere** ['naʃʃere] *vi* (*bambino*) to be born; (*pianta*) to come o spring up; (*fiume*) to rise, have its source; (*sole*) to rise; (*dente*) to come through; (*fig: derivare, conseguire*): **~ da** to arise from, be born out of; **è nata nel 1952** she was born in 1952; '**nascita** *sf* birth

nas'condere *vt* to hide, conceal; **nascondersi** *vpr* to hide; **nascon'diglio** *sm* hiding place; **nascon'dino** *sm* (*gioco*) hide-and-seek; **nas'cosi** *ecc vb vedi* **nascondere**; **nas'costo, -a** *pp di* **nascondere** ▸ *ag* hidden; **di nascosto** secretly

na'sello *sm* (*Zool*) hake

'**naso** *sm* nose

'**nastro** *sm* ribbon; (*magnetico, isolante, Sport*) tape; **nastro adesivo** adhesive tape; **nastro trasportatore** conveyor belt

nas'turzio [nas'turtsjo] *sm* nasturtium

na'tale *ag* of one's birth ▸ *sm* (*Rel*): **N~** Christmas; (*giorno della nascita*) birthday; **nata'lizio, -a** *ag* (*del Natale*) Christmas *cpd*

na'tica, -che *sf* (*Anat*) buttock

'**nato, -a** *pp di* **nascere** ▸ *ag* **un attore ~** a born actor; **nata Pieri** née Pieri

na'tura *sf* nature; **pagare in ~** to pay in kind; **natura morta** still life

natu'rale *ag* natural

natural'mente *av* naturally; (*certamente, sì*) of course

natu'rista, -i, e *ag, sm/f* naturist, nudist

naufra'gare *vi* (*nave*) to be wrecked; (*persona*) to be shipwrecked; (*fig*)

to fall through; **'naufrago, -ghi** sm
castaway, shipwreck victim

'nausea sf nausea; **nause'ante**
ag (odore) nauseating; (sapore)
disgusting; (fig) sickening

'nautico, -a, -ci, -che ag nautical

na'vale ag naval

na'vata sf (anche: ~ centrale) nave;
(anche: ~ laterale) aisle

'nave sf ship, vessel; **nave cisterna**
tanker; **nave da guerra** warship;
nave passeggeri passenger ship

na'vetta sf shuttle; (servizio di
collegamento) shuttle (service)

navi'cella [navi't∫ɛlla] sf (di aerostato)
gondola; **navicella spaziale**
spaceship

navi'gare vi to sail; ~ **in Internet**
to surf the Net; **navigazi'one** sf
navigation

nazio'nale [nattsjo'nale] ag
national ▸ sf (Sport) national team;
nazionalità sf inv nationality

nazi'one [nat'tsjone] sf nation

naziskin ['nɑːtsiskin] sm inv Nazi
skinhead

NB abbr (= nota bene) NB

ne pron

1 (di lui, lei, loro) of him/her/them;
about him/her/them; **ne riconosco la
voce** I recognize his/her voice

2 (di questa, quella cosa) of it; about it;
ne voglio ancora I want some more (of
it o them); **non parliamone più!** let's
not talk about it any more!

3 (con valore partitivo): **hai dei libri?
— sì, ne ho** have you any books? — yes,
I have (some); **hai del pane? — no,
non ne ho** have you any bread? — no, I
haven't any; **quanti anni hai? — ne ho
17** how old are you? — I'm 17

▸ av (moto a luogo: da lì) from there; **ne
vengo ora** I've just come from there

né cong né ... né neither ... nor; né

l'uno né l'altro lo vuole neither of
them wants it; **non parla né l'italiano
né il tedesco** he speaks neither
Italian nor German, he doesn't speak
either Italian or German; **non piove
né nevica** it isn't raining or snowing

ne'anche [ne'anke] av, cong not
even; ~ **per idea o sogno!** not on your life!

'nebbia sf fog; (foschia) mist

necessaria'mente
[net∫essarjamente] av necessarily

neces'sario, -a [net∫es'sarjo] ag
necessary

necessità [net∫essi'ta] sf inv necessity;
(povertà) need, poverty

necro'logio [nekro'lɔdʒo] sm obituary
notice

ne'gare vt to deny; (rifiutare) to deny,
refuse; ~ **di aver fatto/che** to deny
having done/that; **nega'tivo, -a** ag,
sf, sm negative

negherò ecc [nege'rɔ] vb vedi **negare**

negli'gente [negli'dʒente] ag
negligent, careless

negozi'ante [negot'tsjante] sm/f
trader, dealer; (bottegaio) shopkeeper
(BRIT), storekeeper (US)

negozi'are [negot'tsjare] vt to
negotiate ▸ vi ~ **in** to trade o deal in;
negozi'ato sm negotiation

ne'gozio [ne'gɔttsjo] sm (locale) shop
(BRIT), store (US)

'negro, -a sm/f Negro

ne'mico, -a, -ci, -che ag hostile; (Mil)
enemy cpd ▸ sm/f enemy; **essere ~ di**
to be strongly averse o opposed to

nem'meno av, cong = **neanche**

'neo sm mole; (fig) (slight) flaw

'neon sm (Chim) neon

neo'nato, -a ag newborn ▸ sm/f

newborn baby

neozelan'dese [neoddzelan'dese]
ag New Zealand *cpd* ▶ *sm/f* New
Zealander

'**Nepal** *sm* il ~ Nepal

nep'pure *av, cong* = **neanche**

'**nero, -a** *ag* black; (*scuro*) dark ▶ *sm*
black; **il Mar N~** the Black Sea

'**nervo** *sm* (*Anat*) nerve; (*Bot*) vein;
avere i nervi to be on edge; **dare
sui nervi a qn** to get on sb's nerves;
ner'voso, -a *ag* nervous; (*irritabile*)
irritable ▶ *sm* (*fam*): **far venire il
nervoso a qn** to get on sb's nerves

'**nespola** *sf* (*Bot*) medlar; (*fig*) blow,
punch

'**nesso** *sm* connection, link

ⓞ **nes'suno, -a**

(*det: dav sm* **nessun** +*C, V,*
nessuno +*s impura, gn, pn, ps, x, z; dav sf*
nessuna +*C,* **nessun'** +*V*) *det*

1 (*non uno*) no; (*, espressione negativa
+*) any; **non c'è nessun libro** there
isn't any book, there is no book;
nessun altro no one else, nobody else;
nessun'altra cosa nothing else; **in
nessun luogo** nowhere

2 (*qualche*) any; **hai nessuna
obiezione?** do you have any
objections?

▶ *pron*

1 (*non uno*) no one, nobody; (*, espressione negativa +*) any(one); (*: cosa*) none; (*, espressione negativa +*)
any; **nessuno è venuto, non è venuto
nessuno** nobody came

2 (*qualcuno*) anyone, anybody; **ha
telefonato nessuno?** did anyone
phone?

net'tare *vt* to clean

net'tezza [net'tettsa] *sf* cleanness,
cleanliness; **nettezza urbana**
cleansing department

'**netto, -a** *ag* (*pulito*) clean; (*chiaro*)
clear, clear-cut; (*deciso*) definite;

(*Econ*) net

nettur'bino *sm* dustman (*BRIT*),
garbage collector (*US*)

neu'trale *ag* neutral

'**neutro, -a** *ag* neutral; (*Ling*) neuter
▶ *sm* (*Ling*) neuter

'**neve** *sf* snow; **nevi'care** *vb impers* to
snow; **nevi'cata** *sf* snowfall

ne'vischio [ne'viskjo] *sm* sleet

ne'voso, -a *ag* snowy; snow-covered

neval'gia [nevral'dʒia] *sf* neuralgia

nevras'tenico, -a, -ci, -che *ag* (*Med*)
neurasthenic; (*fig*) hot-tempered

ne'vrosi *sf* neurosis

ne'vrotico, -a, ci, che *ag, sm/f* (*anche
fig*) neurotic

'**nicchia** ['nikkja] *sf* niche; (*naturale*)
cavity, hollow; **nicchia di mercato**
(*Comm*) niche market

nicchi'are [nik'kjare] *vi* to shilly-
shally, hesitate

'**nichel** ['nikel] *sm* nickel

nico'tina *sf* nicotine

'**nido** *sm* nest; **a ~ d'ape** (*tessuto ecc*)
honeycomb *cpd*

ⓞ **ni'ente**
pron

1 (*nessuna cosa*) nothing; **niente
può fermarlo** nothing can stop him;
niente di niente absolutely nothing;
nient'altro nothing else; **nient'altro
che** nothing but, just, only; **niente
affatto** not at all, not in the least;
come se niente fosse as if nothing
had happened; **cose da niente** trivial
matters; **per niente** (*gratis, invano*)
for nothing

2 (*qualcosa*): **hai bisogno di niente?** do
you need anything?

3 : **non ... niente** nothing; (*espressione
negativa +*) anything; **non ho visto
niente** I saw nothing, I didn't see
anything; **non ho niente da dire** I have
nothing o haven't anything to say
▶ *sm* nothing; **un bel niente** absolutely

nothing; **basta un niente per farla piangere** the slightest thing is enough to make her cry
▶ *av* (*in nessuna misura*): **non… niente** not … at all; **non è (per) niente buono** it isn't good at all

Ni'geria [ni'dʒɛrja] *sf* la ~ Nigeria

'ninfa *sf* nymph

nin'fea *sf* water lily

ninna-'nanna *sf* lullaby

'ninnolo *sm* (*gingillo*) knick-knack

ni'pote *sm/f* (*di zii*) nephew/niece; (*di nonni*) grandson/daughter, grandchild

'nitido, -a *ag* clear; (*specchio*) bright

ni'trire *vi* to neigh

ni'trito *sm* (*di cavallo*) neighing *no pl*; neigh; (*Chim*) nitrite

nitroglice'rina [nitroɡlitʃe'rina] *sf* nitroglycerine

no (*risposta*) no; **vieni o no?** are you coming or not?; **perché no?** why not?; **lo conosciamo? — tu no ma io sì** do we know him? — you don't but I do; **verrai, no?** you'll come, won't you?

'nobile *ag* noble ▶ *sm/f* noble, nobleman/woman

'nocca, -che [f] (*Anat*) knuckle

'noccio *ecc* [f 'nɔttʃo] *vb vedi* **nuocere**

nocci'ola [not'tʃɔla] *ag inv* (*colore*) hazel, light brown ▶ *sf* hazelnut

noccio'lina [nottʃo'lina] *sf*: **nocciolina americana** peanut

noccio'lo ['nɔttʃolo] *sm* (*di frutto*) stone; (*fig*) heart, core

'noce ['noʃe] *sm* (*albero*) walnut tree ▶ *sf* (*frutto*) walnut; **noce di cocco** coconut; **noce moscata** nutmeg

no'cevo *ecc* [no'tʃevo] *vb vedi* **nuocere**

no'civo, -a [no'tʃivo] *ag* harmful, noxious

'nocqui *ecc vb vedi* **nuocere**

'nodo *sm* (*di cravatta, legname, Naut*) knot; (*Aut, Ferr*) junction; (*Med, Astr, Bot*) node; (*fig: legame*) bond, tie;

(: *punto centrale*) heart, crux; **avere un ~ alla gola** to have a lump in one's throat

no-'global *sm/f* anti-globalization protester ▶ *ag* (*movimento, manifestante*) anti-globalization

'noi *pron* (*soggetto*) we; (*oggetto: per dare rilievo, con preposizione*) us; **~ stessi(e)** we ourselves; (*oggetto*) ourselves

'noia *sf* boredom; (*disturbo, impaccio*) bother *no pl*, trouble *no pl*; **avere qn/qc a ~** not to like sb/sth; **mi è venuta a ~** I'm tired of it; **dare ~ a** to annoy; **avere delle noie con qn** to have trouble with sb

noi'oso, -a *ag* boring; (*fastidioso*) annoying, troublesome

▌ Attenzione! In inglese esiste la parola *noisy*, che però significa *rumoroso*.

noleggi'are [noled'dʒare] *vt* (*prendere a noleggio*) to hire (BRIT), rent; (*dare a noleggio*) to hire out (BRIT), rent (out); (*aereo, nave*) to charter; **vorrei ~ una macchina** I'd like to hire a car; **no'leggio** *sm* hire (BRIT), rental; charter

'nomade *ag* nomadic ▶ *sm/f* nomad

'nome *sm* name; (*Ling*) noun; **in/a ~ di** in the name of; **di o per ~** (*chiamato*) called, named; **conoscere qn di ~** to know sb by name; **nome d'arte** stage name; **nome di battesimo** Christian name; **nome di famiglia** surname

no'mignolo [no'miɲɲolo] *sm* nickname

'nomina *sf* appointment

nomi'nale *ag* nominal; (*Ling*) noun *cpd*

nomi'nare *vt* to name; (*eleggere*) to appoint; (*citare*) to mention

nomina'tivo, -a *ag* (*Ling*) nominative; (*Econ*) registered ▶ *sm* (*Ling: anche:* **caso ~**) nominative (case); (*Amm*) name

non av not ▶ prefisso non-; vedi **affatto**; **appena** ecc

nonché [non'ke] cong (tanto più, tanto meno) let alone; (e inoltre) as well as

noncu'rante ag ~ (di) careless (of), indifferent (to)

'nonno, -a sm/f grandfather/ mother; (in senso più familiare) grandma/grandpa; **i nonni** smpl the grandparents

non'nulla sm inv un ~ nothing, a trifle

'nono, -a ag, sm ninth

nonos'tante prep in spite of, notwithstanding ▶ cong although, even though

nontiscordardimé sm inv (Bot) forget-me-not

nord sm North ▶ ag inv north; northern; **il Mare del N~** the North Sea; **nor'dest** sm north-east; **nor'dovest** sm north-west

'norma sf (principio) norm; (regola) regulation, rule; (consuetudine) custom, rule; **a ~ di legge** according to law, as laid down by law; **norme per l'uso** instructions for use; **norme di sicurezza** safety regulations

nor'male ag normal; standard cpd

normal'mente av normally

norve'gese [norve'dʒese] ag, sm/f, sm Norwegian

Nor'vegia [nor'vedʒa] sf la ~ Norway

nostal'gia [nostal'dʒia] sf (di casa, paese) homesickness; (del passato) nostalgia

nos'trano, -a ag local; national; home-produced

'nostro, -a det il (la) ~ (-a) ecc our ▶ pron il (la) ~ (-a) ecc ours ▶ sm il ~ our money; our belongings; **i nostri** our family; our own people; **è dei nostri** he's one of us

'nota sf (segno) mark; (comunicazione scritta, Mus) note; (fattura) bill; (elenco) list; **degno di ~** noteworthy, worthy of note

no'taio sm notary

no'tare vt (segnare: errori) to mark; (registrare) to note (down), write down; (rilevare, osservare) to note, notice; **farsi ~** to get o.s. noticed

no'tevole ag (talento) notable, remarkable; (peso) considerable

no'tifica, -che sf notification

no'tizia [no'tittsja] sf (piece of) news sg; (informazione) piece of information; **notizi'ario** sm (Radio, TV, Stampa) news sg

'noto, -a ag (well-)known

notorietà sf fame; notoriety

no'torio, -a ag well-known; (peg) notorious

not'tambulo, -a sm/f night-bird; (fig)

not'tata sf night

'notte sf night; **di ~** at night; (durante la notte) in the night, during the night; **notte bianca** sleepless night

not'turno, -a ag nocturnal; (servizio, guardiano) night cpd

no'vanta num ninety; **novan'tesimo, -a** num ninetieth

'nove num nine

nove'cento [nove'tʃento] num nine hundred ▶ sm **il N~** the twentieth century

no'vella sf (Letteratura) short story

no'vello, -a ag (piante, patate) new; (insalata, verdura) early; (sposo) newly-married

no'vembre sm November

novità sf inv novelty; (innovazione) innovation; (cosa originale, insolita) something new; (notizia) piece of news sg; **le ~ della moda** the latest fashions

nozi'one [not'tsjone] sf notion, idea

'nozze ['nɔttse] sfpl wedding sg, marriage sg; **nozze d'argento/d'oro** silver/golden wedding sg

'nubile ag (donna) unmarried, single

'nuca sf nape of the neck
nucle'are ag nuclear
'nucleo sm nucleus; (gruppo) team, unit, group; (Mil, Polizia) squad; **nucleo familiare** family unit
nu'dista, -i, -e sm/f nudist
'nudo, -a ag (persona) bare, naked, nude; (membra) bare, naked; (montagna) bare ▶ sm (Arte) nude
'nulla pron, av = **niente** ▶ sm = **il nulla** nothing
nullità sf inv nullity; (persona) nonentity
'nullo, -a ag useless, worthless; (Dir) null (and void); (Sport): **incontro ~** draw
nume'rale ag, sm numeral
nume'rare vt to number
nu'merico, -a, -ci, -che ag numerical
'numero sm number; (romano, arabo) numeral; (di spettacolo) act, turn; **numero civico** house number; **numero di scarpe** shoe size; **numero di telefono** telephone number; **nume'roso, -a** ag numerous, many; (con sostantivo sg) large
nu'occio ecc ['nwɔttʃo] vb vedi **nuocere**
nu'ocere ['nwɔtʃere] vi **~ a** to harm, damage
nu'ora sf daughter-in-law
nuo'tare vi to swim; (galleggiare: oggetti) to float; **nuota'tore, -'trice** sm/f swimmer; **nu'oto** sm swimming
nu'ova sf (notizia) (piece of) news sg; vedi anche **nuovo**
nuova'mente av again
Nu'ova Ze'landa [-dze'landa] sf **la ~** New Zealand
nu'ovo, -a ag new; **di ~** again; **~ fiammante** o **di zecca** brand-new
nutri'ente ag nutritious, nourishing
nutri'mento sm food, nourishment
nu'trire vt to feed; (fig: sentimenti) to

harbour, nurse; **nutrirsi** vpr **nutrirsi di** to feed on, to eat
'nuvola sf cloud; **nuvo'loso, -a** ag cloudy
nuzi'ale [nut'tsjale] ag nuptial; wedding cpd
'nylon ['nailən] sm nylon

O

o (dav V spesso **od**) cong or; **o ... o** either ... or; **o l'uno o l'altro** either (of them)
O abbr (= ovest) W
'oasi sf inv oasis
obbedi'ente ecc = **ubbidiente** ecc
obbli'gare vt (costringere): **~ qn a fare** to force o oblige sb to do; (Dir) to bind; **obbliga'torio, -a** ag compulsory, obligatory; **'obbligo, -ghi** sm obligation; (dovere) duty; **avere l'obbligo di fare** to be obliged to do; **essere d'obbligo** (discorso, applauso) to be called for
o'beso, -a ag obese
obiet'tare vt **~ che** to object that; **~ su qc** to object to sth, raise objections concerning sth
obiet'tivo, -a ag objective ▶ sm (Ottica, Fot) lens sg, objective; (Mil, fig) objective
obiet'tore sm objector; **obiettore di coscienza** conscientious objector
obiezi'one [objet'tsjone] sf objection

obi'torio sm morgue, mortuary

o'bliquo, -a ag oblique; (inclinato) slanting; (fig) devious, underhand

oblite'rare vt (biglietto) to stamp; (francobollo) to cancel

oblò sm inv porthole

'oboe sm (Mus) oboe

'oca (pl 'oche) sf goose

occasi'one sf (caso favorevole) opportunity; (causa, motivo, circostanza) occasion; (Comm) bargain; **d'~** (a buon prezzo) bargain cpd; (usato) secondhand

occhi'aia [ok'kjaja] sf avere le **occhiaie** to have shadows under one's eyes

occhi'ali [ok'kjali] smpl glasses, spectacles; **occhiali da sole/da vista** sunglasses/(prescription) glasses

occhi'ata [ok'kjata] sf look, glance; **dare un'~ a** to have a look at

occhi'ello [ok'kjɛllo] sm buttonhole; (asola) eyelet

'occhio ['ɔkkjo] sm eye; **~!** carefully, watch out!; **a ~ nudo** with the naked eye; **a quattr'occhi** privately, tête-à-tête; **dare all'~ o nell'~ a qn** to catch sb's eye; **fare l'~ a qc** to get used to sth; **tenere d'~ qn** to keep an eye on sb; **vedere di buon/mal ~ qc** to look favourably/unfavourably on sth

occhio'lino [okkjo'lino] sm fare l'~ a **qn** to wink at sb

occiden'tale [ottʃiden'tale] ag western ▶ sm/f Westerner

occi'dente [ottʃi'dente] sm west; (Pol): **l'O~** the West; **a ~** in the west

occor'rente ag necessary ▶ sm all that is necessary

occor'renza [okkor'rɛntsa] sf necessity, need; **all'~** in case of need

oc'correre vt to be needed, be required ▶ vb impers **occorre farlo** it must be done; **occorre che tu parta** you must leave, you'll have to leave;

mi occorrono i soldi I need the money

| Attenzione! In inglese esiste il verbo to occur, che però significa succedere.

oc'culto, -a ag hidden, concealed; (scienze, forze) occult

occu'pare vt to occupy; (manodopera) to employ; (ingombrare) to occupy, take up; **occuparsi** vpr to occupy o.s., keep o.s. busy; (impiegarsi) to get a job; **occuparsi di** (interessarsi) to take an interest in; (prendersi cura di) to look after, take care of;

occu'pato, -a ag (Mil, Pol) occupied; (persona: affaccendato) busy; (posto, sedia) taken; (toilette, Tel) engaged; **la linea è occupata** the line's engaged; **è occupato questo posto?** is this seat taken?; **occupazi'one** sf occupation; (impiego, lavoro) job; (Econ) employment

o'ceano [o'tʃeano] sm ocean

'ocra sf ochre

'OCSE sigla f (= Organizzazione per la Cooperazione e lo Sviluppo Economico) OECD (Organization for Economic Cooperation and Development)

ocu'lare ag ocular, eye cpd; **testimone ~** eye witness

ocu'lato, -a ag (attento) cautious, prudent; (accorto) shrewd

ocu'lista, -i, -e sm/f eye specialist, oculist

odi'are vt to hate, detest

odi'erno, -a ag today's, of today; (attuale) present

'odio sm hatred; **avere in ~ qc/qn** to hate o detest sth/sb; **odi'oso, -a** ag hateful, odious

odo'rare vt (annusare) to smell; (profumare) to perfume, scent ▶ vi **~ (di)** to smell (of)

o'dore sm smell; **odori** smpl (Cuc) (aromatic) herbs

of'fendere vt to offend; (violare) to

break, violate; (*insultare*) to insult; (*ferire*) to hurt; **offendersi** *vpr* (*con senso reciproco*) to insult one another; (*risentirsi*): **offendersi (di)** to take offence (at), be offended (by)

offe'rente *sm* (*in aste*): **al maggior ~** to the highest bidder

of'ferta *sf* offer; (*donazione, anche Rel*) offering; (*in gara d'appalto*) tender; (*in aste*) bid; (*Econ*) supply: **fare un'~** to make an offer; to tender; to bid; **"offerte d'impiego"** "situations vacant"; **offerta speciale** special offer

of'fesa *sf* insult, affront; (*Mil*) attack; (*Dir*) offence; *vedi anche* **offeso**

of'feso, -a *pp di* **offendere** ▶ *ag* offended; (*fisicamente*) hurt, injured ▶ *sm/f* offended party; **essere ~ con qn** to be annoyed with sb; **parte offesa** (*Dir*) plaintiff

offi'cina [offi'tʃina] *sf* workshop

of'frire *vt* to offer; (*proporsi*) (*proporsi*) to offer (o.s.), volunteer; (*occasione*) to present itself; (*esporsi*): **offrirsi a** to expose o.s. to; **ti offro da bere** I'll buy you a drink

offus'care *vt* to obscure, darken; (*fig: intelletto*) to dim, cloud; (: *fama*) to obscure, overshadow; **offuscarsi** *vpr* (*cielo*) to grow dark; to cloud, grow dim; to be obscured

ogget'tivo, -a [oddʒet'tivo] *ag* objective

og'getto [od'dʒetto] *sm* object; (*materia, argomento*) subject (matter); **oggetti smarriti** lost property *sg*

'oggi ['ɔddʒi] *av, sm* today; **~ a otto** a week today; **oggigi'orno** *av* nowadays

OGM *sigla m* (= *organismo geneticamente modificato*) GMO

'ogni ['oɲɲi] *det* every, each; (*tutti*) all; (*con valore distributivo*) every; **~ uomo è mortale** all men are mortal; **viene**

~ due giorni he comes every two days; **~ cosa** everything; **ad ~ costo** at all costs, at any price; **in ~ luogo** everywhere; **~ tanto** every so often; **~ volta che** every time that

Ognis'santi [oɲɲis'santi] *sm* All Saints' Day

o'gnuno [oɲ'ɲuno] *pron* everyone, everybody

O'landa *sf* l'**~** Holland; **olan'dese** *ag* Dutch ▶ *sm* (*Ling*) Dutch ▶ *sm/f* Dutchman/woman; **gli Olandesi** the Dutch

ole'andro *sm* oleander

oleo'dotto *sm* oil pipeline

ole'oso, -a *ag* oily; (*che contiene olio*) oil-yielding

ol'fatto *sm* sense of smell

oli'are *vt* to oil

oli'era *sf* oil cruet

Olim'piadi *sfpl* Olympic games; **o'limpico, -a, -ci, -che** *ag* Olympic

'olio *sm* oil; **sott'~** (*Cuc*) in oil; **~ di fegato di merluzzo** cod liver oil; **olio d'oliva** olive oil; **olio di semi** vegetable oil

o'liva *sf* olive; **o'livo** *sm* olive tree

'olmo *sm* elm

OLP *sigla f* (= *Organizzazione per la Liberazione della Palestina*) PLO

ol'traggio [ol'traddʒo] *sm* outrage, offence, insult; **~ a pubblico ufficiale** (*Dir*) insulting a public official; **oltraggio al pudore** (*Dir*) indecent behaviour

ol'tranza [ol'trantsa] *sf* a **~** to the last, to the bitter end

'oltre *av* (*più in là*) further; (*di più: aspettare*) longer, more ▶ *prep* (*di là da*) beyond, over, on the other side of; (*più di*) more than, over; (*in aggiunta a*) besides; (*eccetto*): **~ a** except, apart from; **oltrepas'sare** *vt* to go beyond, exceed

o'maggio [o'maddʒo] *sm* (*dono*)

gift; (segno di rispetto) homage, tribute; **omaggi** smpl (complimenti) respects; **rendere ~ a** to pay homage o tribute to; **in ~** (copia, biglietto) complimentary

ombe'lico, -chi sm navel

'ombra sf (zona non assolata, fantasma) shade; (sagoma scura) shadow; **sedere all'~** to sit in the shade; **restare nell'~** (fig) to remain in obscurity

om'brello sm umbrella; **ombrel'lone** sm beach umbrella

om'bretto sm eye shadow

O.M.C. sigla f (= Organizzazione Mondiale del Commercio) WTO

ome'lette [ɔmɛˈlɛt] sf inv omelet(te)

ome'lia sf (Rel) homily, sermon

omeopa'tia sf homoeopathy

omertà sf conspiracy of silence

o'mettere vt to omit, leave out; **~ di fare** to omit o fail to do

omi'cida, -i, -e [omiˈtʃida] ag homicidal, murderous ▶ sm/f murderer/eress

omi'cidio [omiˈtʃidjo] sm murder; **omicidio colposo** culpable homicide

o'misi ecc vb vedi **omettere**

omissi'one sf omission; **omissione di soccorso** (Dir) failure to stop and give assistance

omogeneiz'zato [omodʒeneidˈdzato] sm baby food

omo'geneo, -a [omoˈdʒɛneo] ag homogeneous

o'monimo, -a sm/f namesake ▶ sm (Ling) homonym

omosessu'ale ag, sm/f homosexual

O.M.S. sigla f (= Organizzazione Mondiale della Sanità) WHO

On. abbr (Pol) = **onorevole**

'onda sf wave; **mettere** o **mandare in ~** (Radio, TV) to broadcast; **andare in ~** (Radio, TV) to go on the air; **onde corte/lunghe/medie** short/long/ medium wave

'onere sm burden; **oneri fiscali** taxes

onestà sf honesty

o'nesto, -a ag (probo, retto) honest; (giusto) fair; (casto) chaste, virtuous

ONG sigla f inv **Organizzazione Non Governativa** NGO

onnipo'tente ag omnipotent

ono'mastico, -ci sm name-day

ono'rare vt to honour; (far onore a) to do credit to

ono'rario, -a ag honorary ▶ sm fee

o'nore sm honour; **in ~ di** in honour of; **fare gli onori di casa** to play host (o hostess); **fare ~ a** to honour; (pranzo) to do justice to; (famiglia) to be a credit to; **farsi ~** to distinguish o.s.; **ono'revole** ag honourable ▶ sm/f (Pol) = Member of Parliament (BRIT), ≈ Congressman/woman (US)

on'tano sm (Bot) alder

'O.N.U. ['ɔnu] sigla f (= Organizzazione delle Nazioni Unite) UN, UNO

o'paco, -a, -chi, -che ag (vetro) opaque; (metallo) dull, matt

o'pale sm o f opal

'opera sf work; (azione rilevante) action, deed, work; (Mus) work; opus; (: melodramma) opera; (: teatro) opera house; (ente) institution, organization; **opere pubbliche** public works; **opera d'arte** work of art; **opera lirica** (grand) opera

ope'raio, -a ag working-class; workers' ▶ sm/f worker; **classe operaia** working class

ope'rare vt to carry out, make; (Med) to operate on ▶ vi to operate, work; (rimedio) to act, work; (Med) to operate; **operarsi** vpr (Med) to have an operation; **operarsi d'appendicite** to have one's appendix out; **operazi'one** sf operation

ope'retta sf (Mus) operetta, light opera

opini'one sf opinion; **opinione**

pubblica public opinion

'oppio sm opium

op'pongo ecc vb vedi **opporre**

op'porre vt to oppose; **opporsi** vpr **opporsi (a qc)** to oppose (sth); to object (to sth); **~ resistenza/un rifiuto** to offer resistance/refuse

opportu'nista, -i, -e sm/f opportunist

opportunità sf inv opportunity; (convenienza) opportuneness, timeliness

oppor'tuno, -a ag timely, opportune

op'posi ecc vb vedi **opporre**

opposizi'one sf (opposit'tsjone) opposition; (Dir) objection

op'posto, -a pp di **opporre** ▶ ag opposite; (opinioni) conflicting ▶ sm opposite, contrary; **all'~** on the contrary

oppressi'one sf oppression

oppri'mente vt (premere, gravare) to weigh down; (estenuare: caldo) to suffocate, oppress; (tiranneggiare: popolo) to oppress

op'pure cong or (else)

op'tare vi **~ per** to opt for

o'puscolo sm booklet, pamphlet

opzi'one sf (op'tsjone) option

'ora sf (60 minuti) hour; (momento) time; **che ~ è?, che ore sono?** what time is it? **a che ~ apre il museo/negozio?** what time does the museum/shop open? **non vedo l'~ di fare** to long to do, look forward to doing; **di buon'~** early; **alla buon'~!** at last!; **~ legale** o **estiva** summer time (BRIT), daylight saving time (US); **ora di cena** dinner time; **ora locale** local time; **ora di pranzo** lunchtime; **ora di punta** (Aut) rush hour

o'racolo sm oracle

o'rale ag, sm oral

o'rario, -a ag hourly; (fuso, segnale) time cpd; (velocità) per hour ▶ sm timetable, schedule; (di ufficio, visite ecc) hours pl, time(s pl); **in ~** on time

o'rata sf (Zool) sea bream

ora'tore, -'trice sm/f speaker; orator

'orbita sf (Astr, Fisica) orbit; (Anat) (eye-)socket

or'chestra sf (or'kestra) sf orchestra

orchi'dea (orki'dεa) sf orchid

or'digno (or'diɲɲo) sm (esplosivo) explosive device

ordi'nale ag, sm ordinal

ordi'nare vt (mettere in ordine) to arrange, organize; (Comm) to order; (prescrivere: medicina) to prescribe; (comandare): **posso ~ per favore?** can I order now please?; **~ a qn di fare qc** to order o command sb to do sth; (Rel) to ordain

ordi'nario, -a ag (comune) ordinary; everyday; standard; (grossolano) coarse, common ▶ sm ordinary; (Ins: di università) full professor

ordi'nato, -a ag tidy, orderly

ordinazi'one sf (ordinat'tsjone) sf (Comm) order; (Rel) ordination; **eseguire qc su ~** to make sth to order

'ordine sm order; (carattere): **d'~ pratico** of a practical nature; **all'~** (Comm: assegno) to order; **di prim'~** first-class; **fino a nuovo ~** until further notice; **essere in ~** (documenti) to be in order; (stanza, persona) to be tidy; **mettere in ~** to put in order, tidy (up); **l'~ pubblico** law and order; **ordini (sacri)** (Rel) holy orders; **ordine del giorno** (di seduta) agenda; (Mil) order of the day; **ordine di pagamento** (Comm) order for payment

orec'chino (orek'kino) sm earring

o'recchio (o'rekkjo) (pl(f) o'recchie) sm (Anat) ear

orecchi'oni [orek'kjoni] smpl (Med) mumps sg

o'refice [o'refitʃe] sm goldsmith; jeweller; **orefice'ria** sf (arte) goldsmith's art; (negozio) jeweller's (shop)

'orfano, -a ag orphan(ed) ▶ sm/f orphan; **~ di padre/madre** fatherless/ motherless

orga'netto sm barrel organ; (fam: armonica a bocca) mouth organ; (: fisarmonica) accordion

or'ganico, -a, -ci, -che ag organic ▶ sm personnel, staff

organi'gramma, -i sm organization chart

orga'nismo sm (Biol) organism; (corpo umano) body; (Amm) body, organism

organiz'zare [organid'dzare] vt to organize; **organizzarsi** vpr to get organized; **organizzazi'one** sf organization

'organo sm organ; (di congegno) part; (portavoce) spokesman, mouthpiece

'orgia, -ge ['ɔrdʒa] sf orgy

or'goglio [or'gɔʎʎo] sm pride; **orgogli'oso, -a** ag proud

orien'tale ag oriental; eastern; east

orienta'mento sm positioning; orientation; direction; **senso d ~** sense of direction; **perdere l'~** to lose one's bearings; **orientamento professionale** careers guidance

orien'tare vpr to find one's bearings; (fig: tendere) to tend, lean; (: indirizzarsi) to take up, go in for

ori'ente sm east; **l'O~** the East, the Orient; **a ~** in the east

o'rigano sm oregano

origi'nale [oridʒi'nale] ag original; (bizzarro) eccentric ▶ sm original

origi'nario, -a [oridʒi'narjo] ag original; **essere ~ di** to be a native of; (provenire da) to originate from; to be

native to

o'rigine [o'ridʒine] sf origin; **all'~** originally; **d'~ inglese** of English origin; **dare ~ a** to give rise to

origli'are [oriʎ'ʎare] vi **~ (a)** to eavesdrop (on)

o'rina sf urine

ori'nare vi to urinate ▶ vt to pass

orizzon'tale [oriddzon'tale] ag horizontal

oriz'zonte [orid'dzonte] sm horizon

'orlo sm edge, border; (di recipiente) rim, brim; (di vestito ecc) hem

'orma sf (di persona) footprint; (di animale) track; (impronta, traccia) mark, trace

or'mai av by now, by this time; (adesso) now; (quasi) almost, nearly

ormeggi'are [ormed'dʒare] vt (Naut) to moor

or'mone sm hormone

ornamen'tale ag ornamental, decorative

or'nare vt to adorn, decorate; **ornarsi** vpr **ornarsi (di)** to deck o.s. (out) (with)

ornitolo'gia [ornitolo'dʒia] sf ornithology

'oro sm gold; **d'~, in ~** gold cpd; **d'~** (colore, occasione) golden; (persona) marvellous

oro'logio [oro'lɔdʒo] sm clock; (da tasca, da polso) watch; **orologio al quarzo** quartz watch; **orologio da polso** wristwatch

o'roscopo sm horoscope

or'rendo, -a ag (spaventoso) horrible, awful; (bruttissimo) hideous

or'ribile ag horrible

or'rore sm horror; **avere in ~ qn/qc** to loathe o detest sb/sth; **mi fanno ~** I loathe o detest them

orsacchi'otto [orsak'kjɔtto] sm teddy bear

'orso sm bear; **orso bruno/bianco**

brown/polar bear

or'taggio [or'taddʒo] *sm* vegetable

or'tensia *sf* hydrangea

or'tica, -che *sf* (stinging) nettle

orti'caria *sf* nettle rash

'orto *sm* vegetable garden, kitchen garden; (*Agr*) market garden (*BRIT*), truck farm (*US*); **orto botanico** botanical garden(s) (*pl*)

orto'dosso, -a *ag* orthodox

ortogra'fia *sf* spelling

orto'pedico, -a, -ci, -che *ag* orthopaedic ▸ *sm* orthopaedic specialist

orzai'olo [ordza'jɔlo] *sm* (*Med*) stye

'orzo ['ɔrdzo] *sm* barley

o'sare *vt, vi* to dare; ~ **fare** to dare (to) do

oscenità [oʃʃeni'ta] *sf inv* obscenity

o'sceno, -a [oʃʃeno] *ag* obscene; (*ripugnante*) ghastly

oscil'lare [oʃʃil'lare] *vi* (*pendolo*) to swing; (*dondolare: al vento ecc*) to rock; (*variare*) to fluctuate; (*Tecn*) to oscillate; (*fig*): ~ **fra** to waver o hesitate between

oscu'rare *vt* to darken, obscure; (*fig*) to obscure; **oscurarsi** *vpr* (*cielo*) to darken, cloud over; (*persona*): **si oscurò in volto** his face clouded over

oscurità *sf* (*vedi ag*) darkness, obscurity

os'curo, -a *ag* dark; (*fig*) obscure; humble, lowly ▸ *sm* **all'~** in the dark; **tenere qn all'~ di qc** to keep sb in the dark about sth

ospe'dale *sm* hospital; **dov'è l'~ più vicino?** where's the nearest hospital?

ospi'tale *ag* hospitable

ospi'tare *vt* to give hospitality to; (*albergo*) to accommodate

'ospite *sm/f* (*persona che ospita*) host/ hostess; (*persona ospitata*) guest

os'pizio [os'pittsjo] *sm* (*per vecchi ecc*) home

osser'vare *vt* to observe, watch; (*esaminare*) to examine; (*notare, rilevare*) to notice, observe; (*Dir: la legge*) to observe, respect; (*mantenere: silenzio*) to keep, observe; **far ~ qc a qn** to point sth out to sb; **osservazi'one** *sf* observation; (*di legge ecc*) observance; (*considerazione critica*) observation, remark; (*rimprovero*) reproof; **in osservazione** under observation

ossessio'nare *vt* to obsess, haunt; (*tormentare*) to torment, harass

ossessi'one *sf* obsession

os'sia *cong* that is, to be precise

os'sido *sm* oxide; **ossido di carbonio** carbon monoxide

ossige'nare [ossidʒe'nare] *vt* to oxygenate; (*decolorare*) to bleach; **acqua ossigenata** hydrogen peroxide

os'sigeno *sm* oxygen

'osso (*pl(f) ***ossa**) (*nel senso Anat*) *sm* bone; **d'~** (*bottone ecc*) of bone, bone *cpd*; **osso di seppia** cuttlebone

ostaco'lare *vt* to block, obstruct

os'tacolo *sm* obstacle; (*Equitazione*) hurdle, jump

os'taggio [os'taddʒo] *sm* hostage

os'tello *sm*; **ostello della gioventù** youth hostel

osten'tare *vt* to make a show of, flaunt

oste'ria *sf inn*

os'tetrico, -a, -ci, -che *ag* obstetric ▸ *sm* obstetrician

'ostia *sf* (*Rel*) host; (*per medicinali*) wafer

'ostico, -a, -ci, -che *ag* (*fig*) harsh; hard, difficult; unpleasant

os'tile *ag* hostile

osti'narsi *vpr* to insist, dig one's heels in; ~ **a fare** to persist (obstinately) in doing; **osti'nato, -a** *ag* (*caparbio*) obstinate; (*tenace*) persistent, determined

'ostrica, -che sf oyster
  Attenzione! In inglese esiste la parola ostrich, che però significa struzzo.

ostru'ire vt to obstruct, block

o'tite sf ear infection

ot'tanta num eighty

ot'tavo, -a num eighth

otte'nere vt to obtain, get; (risultato) to achieve, obtain

'ottica sf (scienza) optics sg; (Fot: lenti, prismi ecc) optics pl

'ottico, -a, -ci, -che ag (della vista: nervo) optic; (dell'ottica) optical ▶ sm optician

ottima'mente av excellently, very well

otti'mismo sm optimism

otti'mista, -i, -e sm/f optimist

'ottimo, -a ag excellent, very good

'otto num eight

ot'tobre sm October

otto'cento [otto'tʃɛnto] num eight hundred ▶ sm l'O~ the nineteenth century

ot'tone sm brass; **gli ottoni** (Mus) the brass

ottu'rare vt to close (up); (dente) to fill; **il lavandino è otturato** the sink is blocked; **otturarsi** vpr to become o get blocked up; **otturazi'one** sf closing (up); (dentaria) filling

ot'tuso, -a ag (Mat, fig) obtuse; (suono) dull

o'vaia sf (Anat) ovary

o'vale ag, sm oval

o'vatta sf cotton wool; (per imbottire) padding, wadding

'ovest sm west

o'vile sm pen, enclosure

ovulazi'one [ovulat'tsjone] sf ovulation

'ovulo sm (Fisiol) ovum

o'vunque av = dovunque

ovvi'are vi ~ a to obviate

'ovvio, -a ag obvious

ozi'are [ot'tsjare] vi to laze, idle

'ozio ['ɔttsjo] sm idleness; (tempo libero) leisure; **ore d'~** leisure time; **stare in ~** to be idle

o'zono [o'dzono] sm ozone

p

P abbr (= parcheggio) P; (Aut: = principiante) L

p. abbr (= pagina) p

pac'chetto [pak'ketto] sm packet; **pacchetto azionario** (Comm) shareholding

'pacco, -chi sm parcel; (involto) bundle; **pacco postale** parcel

'pace ['patʃe] sf peace; **darsi ~** to resign o.s.; **fare la ~ con** to make it up with

pa'cifico, -a, -ci, -che [pa'tʃiːfiko] ag (persona) peaceable; (vita) peaceful; (fig: indiscusso) indisputable; (: ovvio) obvious, clear ▶ sm il P~, l'Oceano P~ the Pacific (Ocean)

paci'fista, -i, -e [patʃi'fista] sm/f pacifist

pa'della sf frying pan; (per infermi) bedpan

padigli'one [padiʎ'ʎone] sm pavilion

'Padova sf Padua

'padre sm father

pa'drino sm godfather

padro'nanza [padro'nantsa] sf

command, mastery

pa'drone, -a sm/f master/mistress; (proprietario) owner; (datore di lavoro) employer; **essere ~ di sé** to be in control of o.s.; **padrone(a) di casa** master/mistress of the house; (per gli inquilini) landlord/lady

pae'saggio [pae'zaddʒo] sm landscape

pa'ese sm (nazione) country, nation; (terra) country, land; (villaggio) village, (small) town; **i Paesi Bassi** the Netherlands; **paese di provenienza** country of origin

'paga, -ghe sf pay, wages pl

paga'mento sm payment

pa'gare vt to pay; (acquisto, fig: colpa) to pay for; (contraccambiare) to repay, pay back ▸ vi to pay; **quanto l'hai pagato?** how much did you pay for it?; **posso ~ con la carta di credito?** can I pay by credit card?; **~ in contanti** to pay cash

pa'gella [pa'dʒɛlla] sf (Ins) report card

paghe'rò [page'rɔ] sm inv acknowledgement of a debt, IOU

'pagina ['padʒina] sf page; **pagine bianche** phone book, telephone directory; **pagine gialle** Yellow Pages

'paglia ['paʎʎa] sf straw

pagli'accio [paʎ'ʎattʃo] sm clown

pagli'etta [paʎ'ʎetta] sf (cappello per uomo) (straw) boater; (per tegami ecc) steel wool

pa'gnotta [paɲ'ɲɔtta] sf round loaf

'paio (pl(f)**'paia**) sm pair; **un ~ di** (alcuni) a couple of

'Pakistan sm **il ~** Pakistan

'pala sf shovel; (di remo, ventilatore, elica) blade; (di ruota) paddle

pa'lato sm palate

pa'lazzo [pa'lattso] sm (reggia) palace; (edificio) building; **palazzo di giustizia** courthouse; **palazzo dello sport** sports stadium

'palco, -chi sm (Teatro) box; (tavolato) platform, stand; (ripiano) layer

palco'scenico, -ci [palko'ʃɛniko] sm (Teatro) stage

pa'lese ag clear, evident

Pales'tina sf **la ~** Palestine

palesti'nese ag, sm/f Palestinian

pa'lestra sf gymnasium; (esercizio atletico) exercise, training; (fig) training ground, school

pa'letta sf spade; (per il focolare) shovel; (del capostazione) signalling disc

pa'letto sm stake, peg; (spranga) bolt

'palio sm (gara): **il P~** horse race run at Siena; **mettere qc in ~** to offer sth as a prize

● **palio**

● The **palio** is a horse race which takes
● place in a number of Italian towns,
● the most famous being the one in
● Siena. This is usually held twice a
● year on July and August 16th
● in the Piazza del Campo in Siena.
● 10 of the 17 **contrade** or districts
● take part, each represented by a
● horse and rider. The winner is the
● first horse to complete the course,
● whether it has a rider or not.

'palla sf ball; (pallottola) bullet; **palla di neve** snowball; **palla ovale** rugby ball; **palla'canestro** sf basketball; **palla'mano** sf handball; **pallanu'oto** sf water polo; **palla'volo** sf volleyball

palleggi'are [palled'dʒare] vi (Calcio) to practise with the ball; (Tennis) to knock up

pallia'tivo sm palliative; (fig) stopgap measure

'pallido, -a ag pale

pal'lina sf (bilia) marble

pallon'cino [pallon'tʃino] sm balloon; (lampioncino) Chinese lantern

pal'lone sm (palla) ball; (Calcio) football; (aerostato) balloon; **gioco**

del ~ football

pal'lottola sf pellet; (proiettile) bullet

'palma sf (Anat) = **palmo**; (Bot, simbolo) palm; **palma da datteri** date palm

'palmo sm (Anat) palm; **restare con un ~ di naso** to be badly disappointed

'palo sm (legno appuntito) stake; (sostegno) pole; **fare da o il ~** (fig) to act as look-out

palom'baro sm diver

pal'pare vt to feel, finger

'palpebra sf eyelid

pa'lude sf marsh, swamp

pan'cetta [pan'tʃetta] sf (Cuc) bacon

pan'china [pan'kina] sf garden seat; (di giardino pubblico) (park) bench

'pancia, -ce ['pantʃa] sf belly, stomach; **mettere o fare ~** to be getting a paunch; **avere mal di ~** to have stomachache o a sore stomach

panci'otto [pan'tʃotto] sm waistcoat

'pancreas sm inv pancreas

'panda sm inv panda

'pane sm bread; (pagnotta) loaf (of bread); (forma) **un ~ di burro** a pat of butter; **guadagnarsi il ~** to earn one's living; **pane a cassetta** sliced bread; **pane di Spagna** sponge cake; **pane integrale** wholemeal bread; **pane tostato** toast

panet'teria sf (forno) bakery; (negozio) baker's (shop), bakery

panet'tiere, -a sm/f baker

panet'tone sm a kind of spiced brioche with sultanas, eaten at Christmas

pangrat'tato sm breadcrumbs pl

'panico, -a, -ci, -che ag, sm panic

pani'ere sm basket

pani'ficio [pani'fitʃo] sm (forno) bakery; (negozio) baker's (shop), bakery

pa'nino sm roll; **panino caldo** toasted sandwich; **panino imbottito** filled roll; sandwich

'panna sf (Cuc) cream; (Tecn) = **panne**;

panna da cucina cooking cream; **panna montata** whipped cream

'panne sf inv **essere in ~** (Aut) to have broken down

pan'nello sm panel; **pannello solare** solar panel

'panno sm cloth; **panni** smpl (abiti) clothes; **mettiti nei miei panni** (fig) put yourself in my shoes

pan'nocchia [pan'nɔkkja] sf (di mais ecc) ear

panno'lino sm (per bambini) nappy (BRIT), diaper (US)

pano'rama, -i sm panorama

panta'loni smpl trousers (BRIT), pants (US), pair sg. of trousers o pants

pan'tano sm bog

pan'tera sf panther

pan'tofola sf slipper

'Papa, -i sm pope

papà sm inv dad(dy)

pa'pavero sm poppy

'pappa sf baby cereal; **pappa reale** royal jelly

pappa'gallo sm parrot; (fig: uomo) Romeo, wolf

pa'rabola sf (Mat) parabola; (Rel) parable

para'bolico, -a, ci, che ag (Mat) parabolic; vedi anche **antenna**

para'brezza [para'breddza] sm inv (Aut) windscreen (BRIT), windshield (US)

paraca'dute sm inv parachute

para'diso sm paradise

parados'sale ag paradoxical

para'fulmine sm lightning conductor

pa'raggi [pa'raddʒi] smpl **nei ~** in the vicinity, in the neighbourhood

parago'nare vt ~ **con/a** to compare with/to

para'gone sm comparison; (esempio analogo) analogy, parallel; **reggere al ~** to stand comparison

pa'ragrafo sm paragraph
pa'ralisi sf paralysis
paral'lelo, -a ag parallel ▶ sm (Geo) parallel; (comparazione): **fare un ~ tra** to draw a parallel between
para'lume sm lampshade
pa'rametro sm parameter
para'noia sf paranoia; **para'noico, -a, -ci, -che** ag, sm/f paranoid
para'occhi [para'okki] smpl blinkers
para'petto sm balustrade
pa'rare vt (addobbare) to adorn, deck; (proteggere) to shield, protect; (scansare: colpo) to parry; (Calcio) to save ▶ vi **dove vuole andare a ~?** what are you driving at?
pa'rata sf (Sport) save; (Mil) review, parade
para'urti sm inv (Aut) bumper
para'vento sm folding screen; **fare da ~ a qn** (fig) to shield sb
par'cella [par'tʃɛlla] sf account, fee (of lawyer etc)
parcheg'giare [parked'dʒare] vt to park; **posso ~ qui?** can I park here?; **parcheggiatore, -trice** [parkeddʒa'tore] sm/f (Aut) parking attendant
par'cheggio sm parking no pl; (luogo) car park; (singolo posto) parking space
par'chimetro [par'kimetro] sm parking meter
'parco, -chi sm park; (spazio per deposito) depot; (complesso di veicoli) fleet
par'cometro sm (pay-and-display) ticket machine
pa'recchio, -a [pa'rekkjo] det quite a lot of; (tempo) quite a lot of, a long
pareggi'are [pared'dʒare] vt to make equal; (terreno) to level, make level; (bilancio, conti) to balance ▶ vi (Sport) to draw; **pa'reggio** sm (Econ) balance; (Sport) draw
pa'rente sm/f relative, relation

▌ Attenzione! In inglese esiste la parola **parent**, che però significa **genitore**.

paren'tela sf (vincolo di sangue, fig) relationship
pa'rentesi sf (segno grafico) bracket, parenthesis; (frase incisa) parenthesis; (digressione) parenthesis, digression
pa'rere sm (opinione) opinion; (consiglio) advice, opinion; **a mio ~** in my opinion ▶ vi to seem, appear ▶ vb impers **pare che** it seems o appears that, they say that; **mi pare che** it seems to me that; **mi pare di sì** I think so; **fai come ti pare** do as you like; **che ti pare del mio libro?** what do you think of my book?
pa'rete sf wall
'pari ag inv (uguale) equal, same; (in giochi) equal; drawn, tied; (Mat) even ▶ sm inv (Pol: di Gran Bretagna) peer ▶ sm/f inv peer; **copiato ~ ~** copied word for word; **alla ~** on the same level; **ragazza alla ~** au pair girl; **mettersi alla ~ con** to place o.s. on the same level as; **mettersi in ~ con** to catch up with; **andare di ~ passo con** qn to keep pace with sb
Pa'rigi [pa'ridʒi] sf Paris
pari'gino, -a [pari'dʒino] ag, sm/f Parisian
pa'rità sf parity, equality; (Sport) draw, tie
parlamen'tare ag parliamentary ▶ sm/f = Member of Parliament (BRIT), ≈ Congressman/woman (US) ▶ vi to negotiate, parley
parla'mento sm parliament

- **parlamento**
- The Italian **Parlamento** is made
- up of two chambers, the **Camera**
- **dei deputati** and the **Senato**.
- Parliamentary elections are held
- every 5 years.

parlan'tina (fam) sf talkativeness;

avere ~ to have the gift of the gab
par'lare vi to speak, talk; (confidare cose segrete) to talk ▶ vt to speak; **~ (a qn) di** to speak o talk (to sb) about; **posso ~ con...?** can I speak to ...?; **parla italiano?** do you speak Italian?; **non parlo inglese** I don't speak English

parmigi'ano [parmi'dʒano] sm (grana) Parmesan (cheese)

pa'rola sf word; (facoltà) speech; **parole** sfpl (chiacchiere) talk sg; **chiedere la ~** to ask permission to speak; **prendere la ~** to take the floor; **parola d'onore** word of honour; **parola d'ordine** (Mil) password; **parole incrociate** crossword (puzzle) sg; **paro'laccia, -ce** sf bad word, swearword

parrò ecc vb vedi **parere**

par'rocchia [par'rɔkkja] sf parish; parish church

par'rucca, -che sf wig

parrucchi'ere, -a [parruk'kjɛre] sm/f hairdresser ▶ sm barber

'parte sf part; (lato) side; (quota spettante a ciascuno) share; (direzione) direction; (Pol) party; faction; (Dir) party; **a ~** ag separate ▶ av separately; **scherzi a ~** joking aside; **a ~ ciò** apart from that; **da ~** (in disparte) on one side, aside; **d'altra ~** on the other hand; **da ~ di** (per conto di) on behalf of; **da ~ mia** as far as I'm concerned, as for me; **da ~ a ~** right through; **da ogni ~** on all sides, everywhere; (moto da luogo) from all sides; **da nessuna ~** nowhere; **da questa ~** (in questa direzione) this way; **prendere ~ a qc** to take part in sth; **mettere da ~** to put aside; **mettere qn a ~ di** to inform sb of

parteci'pare [partetʃi'pare] vi: **~ a** to take part in, participate in; (utili ecc) to share in; (spese ecc) to contribute

to; (dolore, successo di qn) to share (in)

parteggi'are [parted'dʒare] vi: **~ per** to side with, be on the side of

par'tenza [par'tɛntsa] sf departure; (Sport) start; **essere in ~** to be about to leave, be leaving

parti'cipio [parti'tʃipjo] sm participle

partico'lare ag (specifico) particular; (proprio) personal, private; (speciale) special, particular; (caratteristico) distinctive, characteristic; (fuori dal comune) peculiar ▶ sm detail, particular; **in ~** in particular, particularly

par'tire vi to go, leave; (allontanarsi) to go (o drive ecc) away o off; (petardo, colpo) to go off; (fig: avere inizio, Sport) to start; **sono partita da Roma alle 7** I left Rome at 7; **a che ora parte il treno/l'autobus?** what time does the train/bus leave?; **il volo parte da Ciampino** the flight leaves from Ciampino; **a ~ da** from

par'tita sf (Comm) lot, consignment; (Econ: registrazione) entry, item; (Carte, Sport: gioco) game; (: competizione) match, game; **partita di caccia** hunting party; **partita IVA** VAT registration number

par'tito sm (Pol) party; (decisione) decision, resolution; (persona da maritare) match

'parto sm (Med) delivery, (child) birth; labour

parvi ecc vb vedi **parere**

parzi'ale [par'tsjale] ag (limitato) partial; (non obiettivo) biased, partial

pasco'lare vt, vi to graze

'pascolo sm pasture

'Pasqua sf Easter; **Pas'quetta** sf Easter Monday

pas'sabile ag fairly good, passable

pas'saggio [pas'saddʒo] sm passing no pl, passage; (traversata) crossing no pl, passage; (luogo, prezzo della *traversata, brano di libro ecc)* passage; *(su veicolo altrui)* lift *(BRIT)*, ride; *(Sport)* pass; **di ~** *(persona)* passing through; **può darmi un ~ fino alla stazione?** can you give me a lift to the station?; **passaggio a livello** level *(BRIT)* o grade *(US)* crossing; **passaggio pedonale** pedestrian crossing

passamon'tagna [passamon'taɲɲa] *sm inv* balaclava

pas'sante *sm/f* passer-by ▶ *sm* loop

passa'porto *sm* passport

pas'sare *vi (andare)* to go; *(veicolo, pedone)* to pass (by), go by; *(fare una breve sosta: postino ecc)* to come, call; *(: amico: per fare una visita)* to call o drop in; *(sole, aria, luce)* to get through; *(trascorrere: giorni, tempo)* to pass, go by; *(fig: proposta di legge)* to be passed; *(: dolore)* to pass, go away; *(Carte)* to pass ▶ *vt (attraversare)* to cross; *(trasmettere: messaggio)*: **~ qc a qn** to pass sth on to sb; *(dare)*: **~ qc a qn** to pass sth to sb, give sb sth; *(trascorrere: tempo)* to spend; *(superare: esame)* to pass; *(triturare: verdura)* to strain; *(approvare)* to pass, approve; *(oltrepassare, sorpassare: anche fig)* to go beyond; *(fig: subire)* to go through; **mi passa il sale/l'olio per favore?** could you pass the salt/oil please?; **~ da ... a** to pass from ... to; **~ padre in figlio** to be handed down o to pass from father to son; **~ per** *(anche fig)* to go through; **~ per stupido/un genio** to be taken for a fool/a genius; **~ sopra** *(anche fig)* to pass over; **~ attraverso** *(anche fig)* to go through; **~ alla storia** to pass into history; **~ a un esame** to go up (to the next class) after an exam; **~ inosservato** to go unnoticed; **~ di moda** to go out of fashion; **le passo il Signor X** *(al telefono)* here is Mr X; I'm putting you through to Mr X; **lasciar**

~ qn/qc to let sb/sth through; **come te la passi?** how are you getting on o along?

passa'tempo *sm* pastime, hobby

pas'sato, -a *ag* past; *(sfiorito)* faded ▶ *sm* past; *(Ling)* past (tense); **passato prossimo** *(Ling)* present perfect/past historic; **passato di verdura** *(Cuc)* vegetable purée

passeg'gero, -a [passed'dʒero] *ag* passing ▶ *sm/f* passenger

passeggi'are [passed'dʒare] *vi* to go for a walk; *(in veicolo)* to go for a drive; **passeggi'ata** *sf* walk; drive; *(luogo)* promenade; **fare una passeggiata** to go for a walk (o drive); **passeg'gino** *sm* pushchair *(BRIT)*, stroller *(US)*

passe'rella *sf* footbridge; *(di nave, aereo)* gangway; *(pedana)* catwalk

'passero *sm* sparrow

passi'one *sf* passion

pas'sivo, -a *ag* passive ▶ *sm (Ling)* passive; *(Econ)* debit; *(: complesso dei debiti)* liabilities *pl*

'passo *sm* step; *(andatura)* pace; *(rumore)* (foot)step; *(orma)* footprint; *(passaggio, fig: brano)* passage; *(valico)* pass; **a ~ d'uomo** at walking pace; **~ (a)** step by step; **fare due** o **quattro passi** to go for a walk o stroll; **di questo ~** at this rate; **"passo carraio"** "vehicle entrance — keep clear"

'pasta *sf (Cuc)* dough; *(: impasto per dolce)* pastry; *(: anche: ~ alimentare)* pasta; *(massa molle di materia)* paste; *(fig: indole)* nature; **paste** *sfpl (pasticcini)* pastries; **pasta in brodo** noodle soup; **pasta sfoglia** puff pastry o paste *(US)*

pastasci'utta [pastaʃ'ʃutta] *sf* pasta

pas'tella *sf* batter

pas'tello *sm* pastel

pastic'ceria [pastittʃe'ria] *sf (pasticcini)* pastries *pl*, cakes *pl*; *(negozio)* cake shop; *(arte)* confectionery

pasticci'ere, -a [pastit'tʃɛre] sm/f pastrycook; confectioner

pastic'cino [pastit'tʃino] sm petit four

pas'ticcio [pas'tittʃo] sm (Cuc) pie; (lavoro disordinato, imbroglio) mess; **trovarsi nei pasticci** to get into trouble

pas'tiglia [pas'tiʎʎa] sf pastille, lozenge

pas'tina sf small pasta shapes used in soup

'pasto sm meal

pas'tore sm shepherd; (Rel) pastor, minister; (anche: **cane** ~) sheepdog; **pastore tedesco** (Zool) Alsatian, German shepherd

pa'tata sf potato; **patate fritte** chips (BRIT), French fries; **pata'tine** sfpl (potato) crisps; **patatine fritte** chips (BRIT), French fries

pa'tente sf licence; **patente di guida** driving licence (BRIT), driver's license (US); **patente a punti** driving licence with penalty points

> Attenzione! In inglese esiste la parola patent, che però significa brevetto.

pater'nità sf paternity, fatherhood

pa'tetico, -a, -ci, -che ag pathetic; (commovente) moving, touching

pa'tibolo sm gallows sg, scaffold

'patina sf (su rame ecc) patina; (sulla lingua) fur, coating

pa'tire vt, vi to suffer

pa'tito, -a sm/f enthusiast, fan, lover

patolo'gia [patolo'dʒia] sf pathology

'patria sf homeland

pa'trigno [pa'trinno] sm stepfather

patri'monio sm estate, property; (fig) heritage

pa'trono sm (Rel) patron saint; (socio di patronato) patron; (Dir) counsel

patteggi'are [patted'dʒare] vt, vi to negotiate; (Dir) to plea-bargain

patti'naggio [patti'naddʒo] sm

skating; **pattinaggio a rotelle/sul ghiaccio** roller-/ice-skating

patti'nare vi to skate; ~ **sul ghiaccio** to ice-skate; **pattina'tore, -'trice** sm/f skater; **'pattino** sm skate; (di slitta) runner; (Aer) skid; (Tecn) sliding block; **pattini in linea** Rollerblades®; **pattini da ghiaccio/a rotelle** ice/roller skates

'patto sm (accordo) pact, agreement; (condizione) term, condition; **a ~ che** on condition that

pat'tuglia [pat'tuʎʎa] sf (Mil) patrol

pattu'ire vt to reach an agreement on

pattumi'era sf (dust)bin (BRIT), ashcan (US)

pa'ura sf fear; **aver ~ di/di fare/che** to be frightened o afraid of/of doing/that; **far ~ a** to frighten; **per ~ di/che** for fear of/that; **pau'roso, -a** ag (che fa paura) frightening; (che ha paura) fearful, timorous

'pausa sf (sosta) break; (nel parlare, Mus) pause

pavi'mento sm floor

> Attenzione! In inglese esiste la parola pavement, che però significa marciapiede.

pa'vone sm peacock

pazien'tare [pattsjen'tare] vi to be patient

pazi'ente [pat'tsjɛnte] ag, sm/f patient; **pazi'enza** sf patience

paz'zesco, -a, -schi, -sche [pat'tsesko] ag mad, crazy

paz'zia [pat'tsia] sf (Med) madness, insanity; (azione) folly; (di azione, decisione) madness, folly

'pazzo, -a ['pattso] ag (Med) mad, insane; (strano) wild, mad ▸ sm/f madman/woman; **~ di** (gioia, amore ecc) mad o crazy with; **~ per qc/qn** mad o crazy about sth/sb

PC [pit'tʃi] sigla m inv (= personal computer) PC; **PC portatile** laptop

pec'care vi to sin; (fig) to err

pec'cato sm sin; **è un ~ che** it's a pity that; **che ~!** what a shame o pity!

peccherò ecc [pekke'rɔ] vb vedi **peccare**

pece ['petʃe] sf pitch

Pe'chino [pe'kino] sf Beijing

pecora sf sheep; **peco'rino** sm sheep's milk cheese

pe'daggio [pe'daddʒo] sm toll

pedago'gia [pedago'dʒia] sf pedagogy, educational methods pl

peda'lare vi to pedal; (andare in bicicletta) to cycle

pe'dale sm pedal

pe'dana sf footboard; (Sport: nel salto) springboard; (: nella scherma) piste

pe'dante ag pedantic ▶ smf pedant

pe'data sf (impronta) footprint; (colpo) kick; **prendere a pedate qn/qc** to kick sb/sth

pedi'atra, -i, -e smf paediatrician

pedi'cure smf/inv chiropodist

pe'dina sf (della dama) draughtsman (BRIT), draftsman (US); (fig) pawn

pedi'nare vt to shadow, tail

pe'dofilo, -a ag, sm/f paedophile

pedo'nale ag pedestrian

pe'done, -a sm/f pedestrian ▶ sm (Scacchi) pawn

'peggio ['peddʒo] av, ag inv worse ▶ sm o f **il o la ~** the worst; **alla ~** at worst, if the worst comes to the worst; **peggio'rare** vt to make worse, worsen ▶ vi to grow worse, worsen; **peggi'ore** ag (comparativo) worse; (superlativo) worst ▶ sm/f **il(la più) peggiore** the worst (person)

'pegno ['peɲɲo] sm (Dir) security, pledge; (nei giochi di società) forfeit; (fig) pledge, token; **dare in ~ qc** to pawn sth

pe'lare vt (spennare) to pluck; (spellare) to skin; (sbucciare) to peel; (fig) to make pay through the nose

pe'lato, -a ag pomodori pelati tinned tomatoes

'pelle sf skin; (di animale) skin, hide; (cuoio) leather; **avere la ~ d'oca** to have goose pimples o goose flesh

pellegri'naggio [pellegri'naddʒo] sm pilgrimage

pelle'rossa (pl **pelli'rosse**) sm/f Red Indian

pelli'cano sm pelican

pel'liccia, -ce [pel'littʃa] sf (mantello di animale) coat, fur; (indumento) fur coat; **pelliccia ecologica** fake fur

pel'licola sf (membrana sottile) film, layer; (Fot, Cinema) film

'pelo sm hair; (pelame) coat, hair; (pelliccia) fur; (di tappeto) pile; (di liquido) surface; **per un ~: per un ~ non ho perduto il treno** I very nearly missed the train; **c'è mancato un ~ che affogasse** he escaped drowning by the skin of his teeth; **pe'loso, -a** ag hairy

'peltro sm pewter

pe'luche [pə'lyʃ] sm plush; **giocattoli di ~** soft toys

pe'luria sf down

'pena sf (Dir) sentence; (punizione) punishment; (sofferenza) sadness no pl, sorrow; (fatica) trouble no pl, effort; (difficoltà) difficulty; **far ~** to be pitiful; **mi fai ~** I feel sorry for you; **prendersi o darsi la ~ di fare** to go to the trouble of doing; **pena di morte** death sentence; **pena pecuniaria** fine; **pe'nale** ag penal

pen'dente ag hanging; leaning ▶ sm (ciondolo) pendant; (orecchino) drop earring

'pendere vi (essere appeso): **~ da** to hang from; (essere inclinato) to lean; (fig: incombere): **~ su** to hang over

pen'dio, -'dii sm slope, slant; (luogo in pendenza) slope

'pendola sf pendulum clock

pendo'lare sm/f commuter

pendo'lino sm high-speed train

pene'trante ag piercing, penetrating

pene'trare vi to come o get in ▶ vt to penetrate; **~ in** to enter; (proiettile) to penetrate; (: acqua, aria) to go o come into

penicil'lina [penitʃil'lina] sf penicillin

pe'nisola sf peninsula

penitenzi'ario [peniten'tsjarjo] sm prison

'penna sf (di uccello) feather; (per scrivere) pen; **penne** sfpl (Cuc) quills (type of pasta); **penna a sfera** ballpoint pen; **penna stilografica** fountain pen

penna'rello sm felt-(tip) pen

pen'nello sm brush; (per dipingere) (paint)brush; **a ~** (perfettamente) to perfection, perfectly; **pennello per la barba** shaving brush

pe'nombra sf half-light, dim light

pen'sare vi to think ▶ vt to think; (inventare, escogitare) to think out; **~ a** to think of; (amico, vacanze) to think of o about; (problema) to think about; **~ di fare qc** to think of doing sth; **ci penso io** I'll see to o take care of it

pensi'ero sm thought; (modo di pensare, dottrina) thinking no pl; (preoccupazione) worry, care, trouble; **stare in ~ per qn** to be worried about sb; **pensie'roso, -a** ag thoughtful

'pensile ag hanging

pensio'nato, -a sm/f pensioner

pensi'one sf (al prestatore di lavoro) pension; (vitto e alloggio) board and lodging; (albergo) boarding house; **andare in ~** to retire; **mezza ~** half board; **pensione completa** full board

pen'tirsi vpr **~ di** to repent of; (rammaricarsi) to regret, be sorry for

'pentola sf pot; **pentola a pressione** pressure cooker

pe'nultimo, -a ag last but one (BRIT),

next to last, penultimate

penzo'lare [pendzo'lare] vi to dangle, hang loosely

'pepe sm pepper; **pepe in grani/ macinato** whole/ground pepper

pepe'rone [pepe'rone] sm chilli pepper

pepe'rone sm pepper, capsicum; (piccante) chilli

pe'pita sf nugget

 per prep

1 (moto attraverso luogo) through; **i ladri sono passati per la finestra** the thieves got in (o out) through the window; **l'ho cercato per tutta la casa** I've searched the whole house o all over the house for it

2 (moto a luogo) for, to; **partire per la Germania/il mare** to leave for Germany/the sea; **il treno per Roma** the Rome train, the train for o to Rome

3 (stato in luogo): **seduto/sdraiato per terra** sitting/lying on the ground

4 (tempo) for; **per anni/lungo tempo** for years/a long time; **per tutta l'estate** throughout the summer, all summer long; **lo rividi per Natale** I saw him again at Christmas; **lo faccio per lunedì** I'll do it for Monday

5 (mezzo, maniera) by; **per lettera/via aerea/ferrovia** by letter/airmail/rail; **prendere qn per un braccio** to take sb by the arm

6 (causa, scopo) for; **assente per malattia** absent because of o through o owing to illness; **ottimo per il mal di gola** excellent for sore throats

7 (limitazione) for; **è troppo difficile per lui** it's too difficult for him; **per quel che mi riguarda** as far as I'm concerned; **per poco che sia** however little it may be; **per questa volta ti perdono** I'll forgive you this time

8 (prezzo, misura) for; (distributivo) a,

per; **venduto per 3 milioni** sold for 3 million; **1 euro per persona** 1 euro a o per person; **uno per volta** one at a time; **uno per uno** one by one; **5 per cento** 5 per cent; **3 per 4 fa 12** 3 times 4 equals 12; **dividere/moltiplicare 12 per 4** to divide/multiply 12 by 4

9 (in qualità di) as; (al posto di) for; **avere qn per professore** to have sb as a teacher; **ti ho preso per Mario** I mistook you for Mario, I thought you were Mario; **dare per morto qn** to give sb up for dead

10 (seguito da vb: finale): **per fare qc** so as to do sth, in order to do sth; (: causale): **per aver fatto qc** for having done sth; (: consecutivo): **è abbastanza grande per andarci da solo** he's big enough to go on his own

'pera sf pear

per'bene ag inv respectable, decent ▸ av (con cura) properly, well

percentu'ale [pertʃentu'ale] sf percentage

perce'pire [pertʃe'pire] vt (sentire) to perceive; (ricevere) to receive

perché
 [per'ke] av why; **perché no?** why not?; **perché non vuoi andarci?** why don't you want to go?; **spiegami perché l'hai fatto** tell me why you did it
▸ cong

1 (causale) because; **non posso uscire perché ho da fare** I can't go out because o as I've a lot to do

2 (finale) in order that, so that; **te lo do perché tu lo legga** I'm giving it to you so (that) you can read it

3 (consecutivo): **è troppo forte perché si possa batterlo** he's too strong to be beaten
▸ sm inv reason; **il perché di** the reason for

perciò [per'tʃɔ] cong so, for this (o

that) reason

per'correre vt (luogo) to go all over; (: paese) to travel up and down, go all over; (distanza) to cover

per'corso, -a pp di percorrere ▸ sm (tragitto) journey; (tratto) route

percu'otere vt to hit, strike

percussi'one sf percussion; **strumenti a ~** (Mus) percussion instruments

'perdere vt to lose; (lasciarsi sfuggire) to miss; (sprecare: tempo, denaro) to waste ▸ vi to lose; (serbatoio ecc) to leak; **perdersi** vpr (smarrirsi) to get lost; (svanire) to disappear, vanish; **mi sono perso** I'm lost; **ho perso il portafoglio/passaporto** I've lost my wallet/passport; **abbiamo perso il treno** we missed our train; **saper ~** to be a good loser; **lascia ~!** forget it!, never mind!

perdigi'orno [perdi'dʒorno] sm/f inv idler, waster

'perdita sf loss; (spreco) waste; (fuoriuscita) leak; **siamo in ~** (Comm) we are running at a loss; **a ~ d'occhio** as far as the eye can see

perdo'nare vt to pardon, forgive; (scusare) to excuse, pardon

per'dono sm forgiveness; (Dir) pardon

perduta'mente av desperately, passionately

pe'renne ag eternal, perpetual, perennial; (Bot) perennial

perfetta'mente av perfectly; **sai ~ che ...** you know perfectly well that ...

per'fetto, -a ag perfect ▸ sm (Ling) perfect (tense)

perfeziona'mento [perfettsjona'mento] sm ~ **(di)** improvement (in), perfection (of); **corso di ~** proficiency course

perfezio'nare [perfettsjo'nare] vt to improve, perfect; **perfezionarsi** vpr to improve

perfezi'one [perfet'tsjone] sf
perfection

per'fino av even

perfo'rare vt to perforate, to punch
a hole (o holes) in; (banda, schede) to
punch; (trivellare) to drill

perga'mena sf parchment

perico'lante ag precarious

pe'ricolo sm danger; **mettere in ~** to
endanger, to put in danger; **perico'loso,
-a** ag dangerous

perife'ria sf (di città) outskirts pl

pe'rifrasi sf circumlocution

pe'rimetro sm perimeter

peri'odico, -a, -ci, -che ag
periodic(al); (Mat) recurring ▶ sm
periodical

pe'riodo sm period

peripe'zie [peripet'tsie] sfpl ups and
downs, vicissitudes

pe'rito, -a ag expert, skilled ▶ sm/f
expert; (agronomo, navale) surveyor;
perito chimico qualified chemist

peri'zoma, -i [peri'dzɔma] sm
G-string

'perla sf pearl; **per'lina** sf bead

perlus'trare vt to patrol

perma'loso, -a ag touchy

perma'nente ag permanent
▶ sf permanent wave, perm;
perma'nenza sf permanence; (di
soggiorno) stay

perme'are vt to permeate

per'messo, -a pp di **permettere**
▶ sm (autorizzazione) permission,
leave; (dato a militare, impiegato) leave;
(licenza) licence, permit; (Mil: foglio)
pass; **~?, è ~?** (posso entrare?) may I
come in?; (posso passare?) excuse
me; **permesso di lavoro/pesca**
work/fishing permit; **permesso di
soggiorno** residence permit

per'mettere vt to allow, permit; **~ a
qn qc/di fare qc** to allow sb sth/to
do sth; **permettersi qc/di fare qc**

to allow o.s. sth/to do sth; (avere la
possibilità) to afford sth/to do sth

per'misi ecc vb vedi **permettere**

per'nacchia [per'nakkja] (fam) sf **fare
una ~** to blow a raspberry

per'nice [per'nitʃe] sf partridge

'perno sm pivot

pernot'tare vi to spend the night,
stay overnight

'pero sm pear tree

però cong (ma) but; (tuttavia) however,
nevertheless

perpendico'lare ag, sf perpendicular

per'plesso, -a ag perplexed;
uncertain, undecided

perqui'sire vt to search;
perquisizi'one sf (police) search

'perse ecc vb vedi **perdere**

persecuzi'one [persekut'tsjone] sf
persecution

persegui'tare vt to persecute

perseve'rante ag persevering

'persi ecc vb vedi **perdere**

persi'ana sf shutter; **persiana
avvolgibile** roller shutter

per'sino av = **perfino**

persis'tente ag persistent

'perso, -a pp di **perdere**

per'sona sf person; (qualcuno): **una
~ someone, somebody;** (espressione
interrogativa) anyone o anybody

perso'naggio [perso'naddʒo] sm
(persona ragguardevole) personality,
figure; (tipo) character, individual;
(Letteratura) character

perso'nale ag personal ▶ sm staff;
personnel; (figura fisica) build

personalità sf inv personality

perspi'cace [perspi'katʃe] ag shrewd,
discerning

persu'adere vt **~ qn (di qc/a fare)** to
persuade sb (of sth/to do)

per'tanto cong (quindi) so, therefore

'pertica, -che sf pole

perti'nente ag **~ (a)** relevant (to),

pertinent (to)

per'tosse sf whooping cough

perturbazi'one [perturbat'tsjone] sf disruption; perturbation; **perturbazione atmosferica** atmospheric disturbance

per'vadere vt to pervade

per'verso, -a ag depraved; perverse

perver'tito, -a sm/f pervert

p.es. abbr (= per esempio) e.g.

pe'sante ag heavy; **è troppo ~** it's too heavy

pe'sare vt to weigh ▸ vi (avere un peso) to weigh; (essere pesante) to be heavy; (fig) to carry weight; **~ su** (fig) to lie heavy on; to influence; to hang over; **pesarsi** vpr to weigh o.s.; **~ le parole** to weigh one's words; **~ sulla coscienza** to weigh on sb's conscience; **mi pesa ammetterlo** I don't like admitting it; **tutta la responsabilità pesa su di lui** all the responsibility rests on him; **è una situazione che mi pesa** I find the situation difficult; **il suo parere pesa molto** his opinion counts for a lot

'pesca (pl pesche) (: frutto) sf peach; (il pescare) fishing; **andare a ~** to go fishing; **~ con la lenza** angling; **pesca di beneficenza** (lotteria) lucky dip

pes'care vt (pesce) to fish for; to catch; (qc nell'acqua) to fish out; (fig: trovare) to get hold of, find; **andare a ~** to go fishing

pesca'tore sm fisherman; angler

'pesce ['peʃʃe] sm fish gen inv; **Pesci** (dello zodiaco) Pisces; **pesce d'aprile!** April Fool!; **pesce rosso** goldfish; **pesce spada** swordfish; **pesce'cane** sm shark

peschere'ccio [peske'rettʃo] sm fishing boat

pesche'ria [peske'ria] sf fishmonger's (shop) (BRIT), fish store (US)

pescherò ecc [peske'rɔ] vb vedi

pescare

'peso sm weight; (Sport) shot; **rubare sul ~** to give short weight; **essere di ~ a qn** (fig) to be a burden to sb; **peso lordo/netto** gross/net weight; **peso massimo/medio** (Pugilato) heavy/middleweight

pessi'mismo sm pessimism; **pessi'mista, -i, -e** ag pessimistic ▸ sm/f pessimist

'pessimo, -a ag very bad, awful

pes'tare vt to tread on, trample on; (sale, pepe) to grind; (uva, aglio) to crush; (fig: picchiare): **~ qn** to beat sb up

'peste sf plague; (persona) nuisance, pest

pes'tello sm pestle

'petalo sm (Bot) petal

pe'tardo sm firecracker, banger (BRIT)

petizi'one [petit'tsjone] sf petition

petroli'era sf (nave) oil tanker

pe'trolio sm oil, petroleum; (per lampada, fornello) paraffin

▍ Attenzione! In inglese esiste la parola petrol che però significa benzina.

pettego'lare vi to gossip

pettego'lezzo [pettego'leddzo] sm gossip no pl; **fare pettegolezzi** to gossip

pet'tegolo, -a ag gossipy ▸ sm/f gossip

petti'nare vt to comb (the hair of); **pettinarsi** vpr to comb one's hair; **pettina'tura** sf (acconciatura) hairstyle

'pettine sm comb; (Zool) scallop

petti'rosso sm robin

'petto sm chest; (seno) breast, bust; (Cuc: di carne bovina) brisket; (: di pollo ecc) breast; **a doppio ~** (abito) double-breasted

petu'lante ag insolent

'pezza ['pettsa] sf piece of cloth;

(toppa) patch; (cencio) rag, cloth

pez'zente [pet'tsɛnte] sm/f beggar

'pezzo ['pɛttso] sm (gen) piece; (brandello, frammento) piece, bit; (di macchina, arnese ecc) part; (Stampa) article; (di tempo): **aspettare un ~** to wait quite a while o some time; **in o a pezzi** in pieces; **andare in pezzi** to break into pieces; **un bel ~ d'uomo** a fine figure of a man; **abito a due pezzi** two-piece suit; **pezzo di cronaca** (Stampa) report; **pezzo grosso** (fig) bigwig; **pezzo di ricambio** spare part

pi'accio ecc ['pjattʃo] vb vedi **piacere**

pia'cente [pja'tʃɛnte] ag attractive

pia'cere [pja'tʃere] vi to please; **una ragazza che piace** a likeable girl; an attractive girl; **~ a: mi piace** I like it; **quei ragazzi non mi piacciono** I don't like those boys; **gli ~bbe andare al cinema** he would like to go to the cinema ▶ sm pleasure; (favore) favour; **"-!"** (nelle presentazioni) "pleased to meet you"; **~** (di conoscerla) nice to meet you; **con ~** certainly, with pleasure; **per ~!** please; **fare un ~ a qn** to do sb a favour; **pia'cevole** ag pleasant, agreeable

pi'acqui ecc vedi **piacere**

pi'aga, -ghe ['pjaga] sf (lesione) sore; (ferita: anche fig) wound; (fig: flagello) scourge, curse; (: persona) pest, nuisance

piagnuco'lare [pjaɲɲuko'lare] vi to whimper

pianeggi'ante [pjaned'dʒante] ag flat, level

piane'rottolo sm landing

pia'neta sm (Astr) planet

pi'angere ['pjandʒere] vi to cry, weep; (occhi) to water ▶ vt to cry, weep; (lamentare) to bewail, lament; **~ la morte di qn** to mourn sb's death

pianifi'care vt to plan

pia'nista, -i, -e sm/f pianist

pi'ano, -a ag (piatto) flat, level;

(Mat) plane; (chiaro) clear, plain ▶ av (adagio) slowly; (a bassa voce) softly; (con cautela) slowly, carefully ▶ sm (Mat) plane; (Geo) plain; (livello) level, plane; (di edificio) floor; (programma) plan; (Mus) piano; **a che ~ si trova?** what floor is it on?; **pian ~** very slowly; (poco a poco) little by little; **in primo/secondo ~** in the foreground/background; **di primo ~** (fig) prominent, high-ranking

piano'forte sm piano, pianoforte

piano'terra sm inv ground floor

pi'ansi ecc vb vedi **piangere**

pi'anta sf (Bot) plant; (Anat: anche: ~ del piede) sole (of the foot); (grafico) plan; (topografica) map; **in ~ stabile** on the permanent staff; **pian'tare** vt to plant; (conficcare) to drive o hammer in; (tenda) to put up, pitch; (fig: lasciare) to leave, desert; **piantarsi** vpr **piantarsi davanti a qn** to plant o.s. in front of sb; **piantala!** (fam) cut it out!

pianter'reno sm = **pianoterra**

pia'nura sf plain

pi'astra sf plate; (di pietra) slab; (di fornello) hotplate; **panino alla ~** toasted sandwich; **piastra di registrazione** tape deck

pias'trella sf tile

pias'trina sf (Mil) identity disc

piatta'forma sf (anche fig) platform

piat'tino sm saucer

pi'atto, -a ag (Tav; fig: scialbo) dull ▶ sm (recipiente, vivanda) dish; (grafico) course; (parte piana) flat (part); **piatti** smpl (Mus) cymbals; **piatto fondo** soup dish; **piatto forte** main course; **piatto del giorno** dish of the day, plat du jour; **piatto del giradischi** turntable; **piatto piano** dinner plate

pi'azza ['pjattsa] sf square; (Comm) market; **far ~ pulita** to make a clean sweep; **piazza d'armi** (Mil) parade ground; **piaz'zale** sm (large) square

piaz'zola [pjat'tsɔla] *sf* (Aut) lay-by; (*di tenda*) pitch

pic'cante *ag* hot, pungent; (*fig*) racy; biting

pic'chetto [pik'ketto] *sm* (Mil, *di scioperanti*) picket; (*di tenda*) peg

picchi'are [pik'kjare] *vt* (*persona: colpire*) to hit, strike; (: *prendere a botte*) to beat (up); (*battere*) to beat; (*sbattere*) to bang ▶ *vi* (*bussare*) to knock; (: *con forza*) to bang; (*colpire*) to hit, strike; (*sole*) to beat down; **picchi'ata** *sf* (Aer) dive

'picchio [pikkjo] *sm* woodpecker

pic'cino, -a [pit'tʃino] *ag* tiny, very small

picci'one [pit'tʃone] *sm* pigeon

'picco, -chi *sm* peak; **a ~** vertically

'piccolo, -a *ag* small; (*oggetto, mano, di età: bambino*) small, little; (*dav sostantivo: di breve durata: viaggio*) short; (*fig*) mean, petty ▶ *sm/f* child, little one

pic'cone *sm* pick(-axe)

pic'cozza [pik'kɔttsa] *sf* ice-axe

pic'nic *sm inv* picnic

pi'docchio [pi'dɔkkjo] *sm* louse

pi'ede *sm* foot; (*di mobile*) leg; **in piedi** standing; **a piedi** on foot; **a piedi nudi** barefoot; **su due piedi** (*fig*) at once; **prendere ~** (*fig*) to gain ground, catch on; **sul ~ di guerra** (Mil) ready for action; **piede di porco** crowbar

pi'ega, -ghe *sf* (*piegatura, Geo*) fold; (*di gonna*) pleat; (*di pantaloni*) crease; (*grinza*) wrinkle, crease; **prendere una brutta ~** (*fig*) to take a turn for the worse

pie'gare *vt* to fold; (*braccia, gambe, testa*) to bend ▶ *vi* to bend; **piegarsi** *vpr* to bend; (*fig*): **piegarsi (a)** to yield (to), submit (to)

piegherò *ecc* [pjege'rɔ] *vb vedi* **piegare**

pie'ghevole *ag* pliable, flexible; (*porta*) folding

Pie'monte *sm* il ~ Piedmont

pi'ena *sf* (*di fiume*) flood, spate

pi'eno, -a *ag* full; (*muro, mattone*) solid ▶ *sm* (*colmo*) height, peak; (*carico*) full load; **~ di** full of; **in ~ giorno** in broad daylight; **il ~, per favore** (Aut) fill it up, please

piercing ['pirsing] *sm* piercing; **farsi il ~ all'ombelico** to have one's navel pierced

pietà *sf* pity; (Rel) piety; **senza ~** pitiless, merciless; **avere ~ di** (*compassione*) to pity, feel sorry for; (*misericordia*) to have pity o mercy on

pie'tanza [pje'tantsa] *sf* dish, course

pie'toso, -a *ag* (*compassionevole*) pitying, compassionate; (*che desta pietà*) pitiful

pi'etra *sf* stone; **pietra preziosa** precious stone, gem

'piffero *sm* (Mus) pipe

pigi'ama, -i [pi'dʒama] *sm* pyjamas *pl*

pigli'are [piʎ'ʎare] *vt* to take, grab; (*afferrare*) to catch

'pigna [pinna] *sf* pine cone

pi'gnolo, -a [pin'nɔlo] *ag* pernickety

pi'grizia [pi'grittsja] *sf* laziness

'pigro, -a *ag* lazy

PIL *sigla m* (= *prodotto interno lordo*) GDP

'pila *sf* (*catasta, di ponte*) pile; (Elettr) battery; (*torcia*) torch (BRIT), flashlight

pi'lastro *sm* pillar

'pile ['pail] *sm inv* fleece

'pillola *sf* pill; **prendere la ~** to be on the pill

pi'lone *sm* (*di ponte*) pier; (*di linea elettrica*) pylon

pi'lota, -i, -e *sm/f* pilot; (Aut) driver ▶ *ag inv* pilot *cpd*; **pilota automatico** automatic pilot

pinaco'teca, -che *sf* art gallery

pi'neta *sf* pinewood

ping-'pong [piŋ'pɔŋ] *sm* table tennis

pingu'ino *sm* (Zool) penguin

'**pinna** sf (di pesce) fin; (di cetaceo, per nuotare) flipper

'**pino** sm pine (tree); **pi'nolo** sm pine kernel

'**pinza** ['pintsa] sf pliers pl; (Med) forceps pl; (Zool) pincer

pinzette [pin'tsette] sfpl tweezers

pi'oggia, -ge ['pjɔddʒa] sf rain; **pioggia acida** acid rain

pi'olo sm peg; (di scala) rung

piom'bare vi to fall heavily; (gettarsi con impeto): **~ su** to fall upon, assail ▶ vt (dente) to fill; **piomba'tura** sf (di dente) filling

piom'bino sm (sigillo) (lead) seal; (del filo a piombo) plummet; (Pesca) sinker

pi'ombo sm (Chim) lead; **a ~** (cadere) straight down; **senza ~** (benzina) unleaded

pioni'ere, -a sm/f pioneer

pi'oppo sm poplar

pi'overe vb impers to rain ▶ vi (fig: scendere dall'alto) to rain down; (lettere, regali) to pour into; **pioviggi'nare** vb impers to drizzle; **pio'voso, -a** ag rainy

pi'ovra sf octopus

pi'ovve ecc vb vedi **piovere**

'**pipa** sf pipe

pipì (fam) sf **fare ~** to have a wee (wee)

pipis'trello sm (Zool) bat

pi'ramide sf pyramid

pi'rata, -i sm pirate; **pirata della strada** hit-and-run driver; **pirata informatica** hacker

Pire'nei smpl i ~ the Pyrenees

pi'romane sm/f pyromaniac; arsonist

pi'roscafo sm steamer, steamship

pisci'are [piʃʃare] (fam!) vi to piss (!), pee (!)

pi'scina [piʃʃina] sf (swimming) pool; (stabilimento) (swimming) baths pl

pi'sello sm pea

piso'lino sm nap

'**pista** sf (traccia) track, trail; (di stadio) track; (di pattinaggio) rink; (da sci) run;

(Aer) runway; (di circo) ring; **pista da ballo** dance floor

pis'tacchio [pis'takkjo] sm pistachio (tree); pistachio (nut)

pis'tola sf pistol, gun

pis'tone sm piston

pi'tone sm python

pit'tore, -'trice sm/f painter; **pitto'resco, -a, -schi, -sche** ag picturesque

pit'tura sf painting; **pittu'rare** vt to paint

più

av

1 (in maggiore quantità) more; **più del solito** more than usual; **in più, di più** more; **ne voglio di più** I want some more; **ci sono 3 persone in o di più** there are 3 more o extra people; **più o meno** more or less; **per di più** (inoltre) what's more, moreover

2 (comparativo) more; (aggettivo corto +) ...er; **più ... di/che** more ... than; **lavoro più di te/Paola** I work harder than you/Paola; **è più intelligente che ricco** he's more intelligent than rich

3 (superlativo) most; (aggettivo corto +) ...est; **il più grande/intelligente** the biggest/most intelligent; **è quello che compro più spesso** that's the one I buy most often; **al più presto** as soon as possible; **al più tardi** at the latest

4 (negazione): **non ... più** no more, no longer; **non ho più soldi** I've got no more money, I don't have any more money; **non lavoro più** I'm no longer working, I don't work any more; **a più non posso** (gridare) at the top of one's voice; (correre) as fast as one can

5 (Mat) plus; **4 più 5 fa 9** 4 plus 5 equals 9; **più 5 gradi** 5 degrees above freezing, plus 5

▶ prep plus

▶ ag inv

1: **più ... (di)** more ... (than); **più**

denaro/tempo more money/time; **più persone di quante ci aspettassimo** more people than we expected **2** (numerosi, diversi) several; **l'aspettai per più giorni** I waited for it for several days

▶ sm

1 (la maggior parte): **il più è fatto** most of it is done

2 (Mat) plus (sign)

3 **i più** the majority

pi'uma sf feather; **piu'mino** sm (eider)down; (per letto) eiderdown; (: tipo danese) duvet, continental quilt; (giacca) quilted jacket (with goose-feather padding); (per cipria) powder puff; (per spolverare) feather duster

piut'tosto av rather; **~ che** (anziché) rather than

'**pizza** ['pittsa] sf pizza; **pizze'ria** sf place where pizzas are made, sold or eaten

pizzi'care [pittsi'kare] vt (stringere) to nip, pinch; (pungere) to sting; to bite; (Mus) to pluck ▶ vi (prudere) to itch, be itchy; (cibo) to be hot o spicy

'**pizzico, -chi** ['pittsiko] sm (pizzicotto) pinch, nip; (piccola quantità) pinch, dash; (d'insetto) sting; bite

pizzi'cotto [pittsi'kɔtto] sm pinch, nip

'**pizzo** ['pittso] sm (merletto) lace; (barbetta) goatee beard

plagi'are [pla'dʒare] vt (copiare) to plagiarize

plaid [plɛd] sm inv (travelling) rug (BRIT), lap robe (US)

pla'nare vi (Aer) to glide

'**plasma** sm plasma

plas'mare vt to mould, shape

'**plastica, -che** sf (arte) plastic arts pl; (Med) plastic surgery; (sostanza) plastic; **plastica facciale** face lift

'**platano** sm plane tree

pla'tea sf (Teatro) stalls pl

'**platino** sm platinum

plau'sibile ag plausible

pleni'lunio sm full moon

'**plettro** sm plectrum

pleu'rite sf pleurisy

'**plico, -chi** sm (pacco) parcel; **in ~ a parte** (Comm) under separate cover

plo'tone sm (Mil) platoon; **plotone d'esecuzione** firing squad

plu'rale ag, sm plural

PM abbr (Pol) = **Pubblico Ministero**; (= Polizia Militare) MP (Military Police)

pneu'matico, -a, -ci, -che ag inflatable; pneumatic ▶ sm (Aut) tyre (BRIT), tire (US)

po' av, sm vedi **poco**

○ '**poco, -a, -chi, -che** ag (quantità) little, not much; (numero) few, not many; **poco pane/denaro/spazio** little o not much bread/money/space; **poche persone/ idee** few o not many people/ideas; **ci vediamo tra poco** (sottinteso: tempo) see you soon

▶ av

1 (in piccola quantità) little, not much; (numero limitato) few, not many; **guadagna poco** he doesn't earn much, he earns little

2 (con ag, av) (a) little; not very; **sta poco bene** he isn't very well; **è poco più vecchia di lui** she's a little o slightly older than him

3 (tempo): **poco dopo/prima** shortly afterwards/before; **il film dura poco** the film doesn't last very long; **ci vediamo molto poco** we don't see each other very often, we hardly ever see each other

4: **un po'** a little, a bit; **è un po' corto** it's a little o a bit short; **arriverà fra un po'** he'll arrive shortly o in a little while

5: **a dir poco** to say the least; **a poco a poco** little by little; **per poco non cadevo** I nearly fell; **è una cosa da poco** it's nothing, it's of no importance; **una persona da poco** a worthless person

▶ *pron* (a) little

po'dere *sm* (Agr) farm

'podio *sm* dais, platform; (Mus) podium

poe'sia *sf* (arte) poetry; (componimento) poem

po'eta, -'essa *sm/f* poet/poetess

poggi'are [pod'dʒare] *vt* to lean, rest; (posare) to lay, place; **poggia'testa** *sm inv* (Aut) headrest

'poggio ['pɔddʒo] *sm* hillock, knoll

poi *av* then; (alla fine) finally, at last; **e ~** (inoltre) and besides; **questa ~ (è bella)!** (ironico) that's a good one!

poiché [poi'ke] *cong* since, as

'poker *sm* poker

po'lacco, -a, -chi, -che *ag* Polish ▶ *sm/f* Pole

po'lare *ag* polar

po'lemica, -che *sf* controversy

po'lemico, -a, -ci, -che *ag* polemic(al), controversial

po'lenta *sf* (Cuc) sort of thick porridge made with maize flour

'polio(mie'lite) *sf* polio(myelitis)

po'lipo *sm* polyp

polisti'rolo *sm* polystyrene

po'litica, -che *sf* politics *sg*; (linea di condotta) policy; (anche: politico); **politica'mente** *av* politically; **politicamente corretto** politically correct

po'litico, -a, -ci, -che *ag* political ▶ *sm/f* politician

poli'zia [polit'tsia] *sf* police; **polizia giudiziaria** ≈ Criminal Investigation Department (BRIT), ≈ Federal Bureau of Investigation (US); **polizia stradale** traffic police; **polizi'esco, -a, -schi, -sche** *ag* police *cpd*; (film, romanzo) detective *cpd*; **polizi'otto** *sm* policeman; **cane poliziotto** police dog; **donna poliziotto** policewoman; **poliziotto di quartiere** local police officer

● **polizia di stato**
● The function of the **polizia di stato**
● is to maintain public order, to
● uphold the law and prevent and
● investigate crime. They are a civil
● body, reporting to the Minister of
● the Interior.

po'lizza ['polittsa] *sf* (Comm) bill; **~ di assicurazione** insurance policy; **polizza di carico** bill of lading

pol'laio *sm* henhouse

'pollice ['pollitʃe] *sm* thumb

'polline *sm* pollen

'pollo *sm* chicken

pol'mone *sm* lung; **polmone d'acciaio** (Med) iron lung; **polmo'nite** *sf* pneumonia; **polmonite atipica** SARS

'polo *sm* (Geo, Fisica) pole; (gioco) polo; **polo nord/sud** North/South Pole

Po'lonia *sf* la ~ Poland

'polpa *sf* flesh, pulp; (carne) lean meat

pol'paccio [pol'pattʃo] *sm* (Anat) calf

polpas'trello *sm* fingertip

pol'petta *sf* (Cuc) meatball

'polpo *sm* octopus

pol'sino *sm* cuff

'polso *sm* (Anat) wrist; (pulsazione) pulse; (fig: forza) drive, vigour

pol'trire *vi* to laze about

pol'trona *sf* armchair; (Teatro: posto) seat in the front stalls (BRIT) o orchestra (US)

'polvere *sf* dust; (sostanza ridotta minutissima) powder, dust; **latte in ~** powdered milk; **caffè in ~** instant coffee; **sapone in ~** soap powder; **polvere da sparo/pirica** gunpowder

po'mata *sf* ointment, cream

po'mello *sm* knob

pome'riggio [pome'riddʒo] *sm* afternoon

'pomice ['pomitʃe] *sf* pumice

'pomo sm (mela) apple; (ornamentale) knob; (di sella) pommel; **pomo d'Adamo** (Anat) Adam's apple

pomo'doro sm tomato; **pomodori pelati** skinned tomatoes

'pompa sf pump; (sfarzo) pomp (and ceremony); **pompe funebri** funeral parlour sg (BRIT), undertaker's sg; **pompa di benzina** petrol (BRIT) o gas (US) pump; (distributore) filling o gas (US) station; **pom'pare** vt to pump; (trarre) to pump out; (gonfiare d'aria) to pump up

pom'pelmo sm grapefruit

pompi'ere sm fireman

po'nente sm west

pongo, poni ecc vb vedi **porre**

'ponte sm bridge; (di nave) deck; (: anche: **~ di comando**) bridge; (impalcatura) scaffold; **fare il ~** (fig) to take the extra day off (between 2 public holidays); **governo ~** interim government; **ponte aereo** airlift; **ponte levatoio** drawbridge; **ponte sospeso** suspension bridge

pon'tefice [pon'tefitʃe] sm (Rel) pontiff

'popcorn ['pɔpkɔːn] sm inv popcorn

popo'lare ag popular; (quartiere, clientela) working-class ▸ vt (rendere abitato) to populate; **popolarsi** vpr to fill with people, get crowded; **popolazi'one** sf population

'popolo sm people

'poppa sf (di nave) stern; (seno) breast

porcel'lana [portʃel'lana] sf porcelain, china; piece of china

porcel'lino, -a [portʃel'lino] sm/f piglet; **porcellino d'India** guinea pig

por'cheria [porke'ria] sf filth, muck; (fig: oscenità) obscenity; (: azione disonesta) dirty trick; (: cosa mal fatta) rubbish

por'cile [por'tʃile] sm pigsty

por'cino, -a [por'tʃino] ag of pigs,

pork cpd ▸ sm (fungo) type of edible mushroom

'porco, -ci sm pig; (carne) pork

porcos'pino sm porcupine

'porgere ['pɔrdʒere] vt to hand, give; (tendere) to hold out

porno'fia sf pornography; **porno'grafico, -a, -ci, -che** ag pornographic

'poro sm pore

'porpora sf purple

'porre vt (mettere) to put; (collocare) to place; (posare) to lay (down), put (down); (fig: supporre): **poniamo (il caso) che ...** let's suppose that ...

'porro sm (Bot) leek; (Med) wart

'porsi ecc vb vedi **porgere**

'porta sf door; (Sport) goal; **porta'bagagli** sm inv (facchino) porter; (Aut, Ferr) luggage rack; **porta-CD** [portati'di] sm inv (mobile) CD rack; (astuccio) CD holder; **porta'cenere** sm inv ashtray; **portachi'avi** sm inv keyring; **porta'erei** sf inv (nave) aircraft carrier; **portafi'nestra** (pl **portefi'nestre**) sf French window; **porta'foglio** sm wallet; (Pol, Borsa) portfolio; **non trovo il portafoglio** I can't find my wallet; **portafor'tuna** sm inv lucky charm; mascot

por'tale sm (di chiesa, Inform) portal

porta'mento sm carriage, bearing

portamo'nete sm inv purse

por'tante ag (muro ecc) supporting, load-bearing

portan'tina sf sedan chair; (per ammalati) stretcher

portaom'brelli sm inv umbrella stand

porta'pacchi [porta'pakki] sm inv (di moto, bicicletta) luggage rack

por'tare vt (sostenere, sorreggere: peso, bambino, pacco) to carry; (indossare: abito, occhiali) to wear; (: capelli lunghi) to have; (avere: nome, titolo) to have, bear; (*recare*): **~ qc a qn** to take (o bring) sth to sb; (*fig: sentimenti*) to bear

portasiga'rette *sm inv* cigarette case

por'tata *sf* (*vivanda*) course; (*Aut*) carrying (o loading) capacity; (*di arma*) range; (*volume d'acqua*) rate of flow; (*fig: limite*) scope, capability; (: *importanza*) impact, import; **alla ~ di tutti** (*conoscenza*) within everybody's capabilities; (*prezzo*) within everybody's means; **a/fuori ~ (di)** within/out of reach (of); **a ~ di mano** within (arm's) reach

por'tatile *ag* portable

por'tato, -a *ag* (*incline*): **~ a** inclined o apt to

portau'ovo *sm inv* eggcup

porta'voce [porta'vot∫e] *sm/f inv* spokesman/woman

por'tento *sm* wonder, marvel

porti'era *sf* (*Aut*) door

porti'ere *sm* (*portinaio*) concierge, caretaker; (*di hotel*) porter; (*nel calcio*) goalkeeper

porti'naio, -a *sm/f* concierge, caretaker

portine'ria *sf* caretaker's lodge

'porto, -a *pp di* **porgere** ▶ *sm* (*Naut*) harbour, port ▶ *sm inv* port (wine); **porto d'armi** (*documento*) gun licence

Porto'gallo *sm* **il ~** Portugal; **porto'ghese** *ag, sm/f, sm* Portuguese *inv*

por'tone *sm* main entrance, main door

portu'ale *ag* harbour *cpd*, port *cpd* ▶ *sm* dock worker

porzi'one [por'tsjone] *sf* portion, share; (*di cibo*) portion, helping

'posa *sf* (*Fot*) exposure; (*atteggiamento, di modello*) pose

po'sare *vt* to put (down), lay (down) ▶ *vi* (*ponte, edificio, teoria*): **~ su** to rest on; (*Fot: atteggiarsi*) to pose; **posarsi**

vpr (*aereo*) to land; (*uccello*) to alight; (*sguardo*) to settle

po'sata *sf* piece of cutlery

pos'critto *sm* postscript

'posi *ecc vb vedi* **porre**

posi'tivo, -a *ag* positive

posizi'one [pozit'tsjone] *sf* position; **prendere ~** (*fig*) to take a stand; **luci di ~** (*Aut*) sidelights

pos'porre *vt* to place after; (*differire*) to postpone, defer

posse'dere *vt* to own, possess; (*qualità, virtù*) to have, possess

posses'sivo, -a *ag* possessive

pos'sesso *sm* ownership *no pl*; possession

posses'sore *sm* owner

pos'sibile *ag* possible ▶ *sm* **fare tutto il ~** to do everything possible; **nei limiti del ~** as far as possible; **al più tardi ~** as late as possible; **possibilità** *sf inv* possibility ▶ *sfpl* (*mezzi*) means; **aver la possibilità di fare** to be in a position to do; **to have the opportunity to do**

possi'dente *sm/f* landowner

possi'edo *ecc vb vedi* **possedere**

'posso *ecc vb vedi* **potere**

'posta *sf* (*servizio*) post, postal service; (*corrispondenza*) post, mail; (*ufficio postale*) post office; (*nei giochi d'azzardo*) stake; **Poste** *sfpl* (*amministrazione*) post offices; **c'è ~ per me?** are there any letters for me?; **ministro delle Poste e Telecomunicazioni** Postmaster General; **posta aerea** airmail; **posta elettronica** E-mail, e-mail, electronic mail; **posta ordinaria** ≈ second-class mail; **posta prioritaria** ≈ first-class post; **pos'tale** *ag* postal, post office *cpd*

posteggi'are [posted'dʒare] *vt, vi* to park; **pos'teggio** *sm* car park (*BRIT*), parking lot (*US*); (*di taxi*) rank (*BRIT*), stand (US)

'poster sm inv poster

posteri'ore ag (dietro) back; (dopo) later ▶ sm (fam: sedere) behind

postici'pare [postitʃi'pare] vt to defer, postpone

pos'tino sm postman (BRIT), mailman (US)

'posto, -a pp di **porre** ▶ sm (sito, posizione) place; (impiego) job; (spazio libero) room, space; (di parcheggio) space; (sedile: al teatro, in treno ecc) seat; (Mil) post; **a ~** (in ordine) in place, tidy; (fig) settled; (: persona) reliable; **vorrei prenotare due posti** I'd like to book two seats; **al ~ di** in place of; **sul ~** on the spot; **mettere a ~** to tidy (up), put in order; (faccende) to straighten out; **posto di blocco** roadblock; **posto di lavoro** job; **posti in piedi** (in teatro, in autobus) standing room; **posto di polizia** police station

po'tabile ag drinkable; **acqua ~** drinking water

po'tare vt to prune

po'tassio sm potassium

po'tente ag (nazione) strong, powerful; (veleno, farmaco) strong, potent; **po'tenza** sf power; (forza) strength

potenzi'ale [poten'tsjale] ag, sm potential

○ **po'tere**

sm power; **al potere** (partito ecc) in power; **potere d'acquisto** purchasing power

▶ vb aus

1 (essere in grado di) can, be able to; **non ha potuto ripararlo** he couldn't o he wasn't able to repair it; **non è potuto venire** he couldn't o he wasn't able to come; **spiacente di non poter aiutare** sorry not to be able to help

2 (avere il permesso) can, may, be allowed to; **posso entrare?** can o may I

come in?; **si può sapere dove sei stato?** where on earth have you been?

3 (eventualità) may, might, could; **potrebbe essere vero** it might o could be true; **può aver avuto un incidente** he may o might o could have had an accident; **può darsi** perhaps; **può darsi o essere che non venga** he may o might not come

4 (augurio): **potessi almeno parlargli!** if only I could speak to him!

5 (suggerimento): **potresti almeno scusarti!** you could at least apologize!

▶ vt can, be able to; **può molto per noi** he can do a lot for us; **non ne posso più** (per stanchezza) I'm exhausted; (per rabbia) I can't take any more

potrò ecc vb vedi **potere**

'povero, -a ag poor; (disadorno) plain, bare ▶ sm/f poor man/woman; **i poveri** the poor; **~ di** lacking in, having little; **po'vertà** sf poverty

poz'zanghera [pot'tsangera] sf puddle

'pozzo ['pottso] sm well; (cava: di carbone) pit; (di miniera) shaft; **pozzo petrolifero** oil well

P.R.A. [pra] sigla m (= Pubblico Registro Automobilistico) ≈ DVLA

pran'zare [pran'dzare] vi to dine, have dinner; to lunch, have lunch

'pranzo ['prandzo] sm dinner; (a mezzogiorno) lunch

'prassi sf usual procedure

'pratica, -che sf practice; (esperienza) experience; (conoscenza) knowledge, familiarity; (tirocinio) training, practice; (Amm: affare) matter, case; (: incartamento) file, dossier; **in ~** (praticamente) in practice; **mettere in ~** to put into practice

prati'cabile ag (progetto) practicable, feasible; (luogo) passable, practicable

pratica'mente av (in modo pratico) in a practical way, practically; (quasi) practically, almost

prati'care vt to practise; (Sport: tennis ecc) to play; (: nuoto, scherma ecc) to go in for; (eseguire: apertura, buco) to make; **~ uno sconto** to give a discount

'pratico, -a, -ci, -che ag practical; **~ di** (esperto) experienced o skilled in; (familiare) familiar with

'prato sm meadow; (di giardino) lawn

preav'viso sm notice; **telefonata con ~ personal** o person to person call

pre'cario, -a ag precarious; (Ins) temporary

precauzi'one [prekaut'tsjone] sf caution, care; (misura) precaution

prece'dente [pretʃe'dɛnte] ag previous ▶ sm precedent; **il discorso/film ~** the previous o preceding speech/film; **senza precedenti** unprecedented; **precedenti penali** criminal record sg; **prece'denza** sf priority, precedence; (Aut) right of way

pre'cedere [pre'tʃɛdere] vt to precede, go (o come) before

precipi'tare [pretʃipi'tare] vi (cadere) to fall headlong; (fig: situazione) to get out of control ▶ vt (gettare dall'alto in basso) to hurl, fling; (fig: affrettare) to rush; **precipitarsi** vpr (gettarsi) to hurl o fling o.s.; (affrettarsi) to rush; **precipi'toso, -a** ag (caduta, fuga) headlong; (fig: avventato) rash, reckless; (: affrettato) hasty, rushed

preci'pizio [pretʃi'pittsjo] sm precipice; **a ~** (fig: correre) headlong

precisa'mente [pretʃiza'mente] av (gen) precisely; (con esattezza) exactly

preci'sare [pretʃi'zare] vt to state, specify; (spiegare) to explain (in detail)

precisi'one [pretʃi'zjone] sf precision; accuracy

pre'ciso, -a [pre'tʃizo] ag (esatto) precise; (accurato) accurate; precise;

(deciso: idee) precise, definite; (uguale): **2 vestiti precisi** 2 dresses exactly the same; **sono le 9 precise** it's exactly 9 o'clock

pre'cludere vt to block, obstruct

pre'coce [pre'kɔtʃe] ag early; (bambino) precocious; (vecchiaia) premature

precon'cetto [prekon'tʃɛtto] sm preconceived idea, prejudice

precur'sore sm forerunner, precursor

'preda sf (bottino) booty; (animale, fig) prey; **essere ~ di** to fall prey to; **essere in ~ a** to be prey to

'predica, -che sf sermon; (fig) lecture, talking-to

predi'care vt, vi to preach

predi'cato sm (Ling) predicate

predi'letto, -a pp di **prediligere** ▶ ag, sm/f favourite

predi'ligere [predi'lidʒere] vt to prefer, have a preference for

pre'dire vt to foretell, predict

predis'porre vt to get ready, prepare; **~ qn a qc** to predispose sb to sth

predizi'one [predit'tsjone] sf prediction

prefazi'one [prefat'tsjone] sf preface, foreword

prefe'renza [prefe'rɛntsa] sf preference

prefe'rire vt to prefer, like better; **~ il caffè al tè** to prefer coffee to tea, like coffee better than tea

pre'figgersi [pre'fiddʒersi] vpr **~ uno scopo** to set o.s. a goal

pre'fisso, -a pp di **prefiggere** ▶ sm (Ling) prefix; (Tel) dialling (BRIT) o dial (US) code; **qual è il ~ telefonico di Londra?** what is the dialling code for London?

pre'gare vi to pray ▶ vt (Rel) to pray to; (implorare) to beg; (chiedere): **~ qn di fare** to ask sb to do; **farsi ~** to need coaxing o persuading

pre'gevole [pre'dʒevole] ag valuable

pregherò ecc [pregeˈrɔ] vb vedi
pregare

preghi'era [preˈgjɛra] sf (Rel) prayer;
(domanda) request

pregi'ato, -a [preˈdʒato] ag (di valore)
valuable; **vino ~** vintage wine

'pregio [ˈprɛdʒo] sm (stima) esteem,
regard; (qualità) (good) quality, merit;
(valore) value, worth

pregiudi'care [predʒudiˈkare] vt to
prejudice, harm, be detrimental to

pregiu'dizio [predʒuˈdittsjo] sm (idea
errata) prejudice; (danno) harm no pl

'prego escl (a chi ringrazia) don't
mention it!; (invitando qn ad
accomodarsi) please sit down!;
(invitando qn ad andare prima) after you!

pregus'tare vt to look forward to

prele'vare vt (denaro) to withdraw;
(campione) to take; (polizia) to take,
capture

preli'evo sm (di denaro) withdrawal;
(Med) **fare un ~ (di)** to take a sample
(of); **prelievo di sangue: fare un ~ di
sangue** to take a blood sample

prelimi'nare ag preliminary

'premere vt to press ▶ vi **~ su** to press
down on; (fig) to put pressure on; **~ a**
(fig: importare) to matter to

pre'mettere vt to put before; (dire
prima) to start by saying, state first

premi'are vt to give a prize to; (fig:
merito, onestà) to reward

premiazi'one [premjatˈtsjone] sf
prize giving

'premio sm prize; (ricompensa) reward;
(Comm) premium; (Amm: indennità)
bonus

pre'misi ecc vb vedi **premettere**

premu'nirsi vpr **~ di** to provide o.s.
with; **~ contro** to protect o.s. from,
guard o.s. against

pre'mura sf (fretta) haste, hurry;
(riguardo) attention, care; **premure**
sfpl (attenzioni, cure) care sg; **aver ~ to**

be in a hurry; **far ~ a qn** to hurry sb;
usare ogni ~ nei riguardi di qn to be
very attentive to sb; **premu'roso, -a**
ag thoughtful, considerate

'prendere vt to take; (andare a
prendere) to get, fetch; (ottenere)
to get; (guadagnare) to get, earn;
(catturare: ladro, pesce) to catch;
(collaboratore, dipendente) to take
on; (passeggero) to pick up; (chiedere:
somma, prezzo) to charge, ask;
(trattare: persona) to handle ▶ vi (colla,
cemento) to set; (pianta) to take;
(fuoco: nel camino) to catch; (voltare):
~ a destra to turn (to the) right;
prendersi vr (azzuffarsi): **prendersi
a pugni** to come to blows; **dove si
prende il traghetto per...** where
do we get the ferry to ...; **prendi
qualcosa?** (da bere, da mangiare) would
you like something to eat (o drink)?;
prendo un caffè I'll have a coffee; **~
qn/qc per** (scambiare) to take sb/sth
for; **~ fuoco** to catch fire; **~ parte a**
to take part in; **prendersi cura di qn/qc**
to look after sb/sth; **prendersela**
(adirarsi) to get annoyed; (preoccuparsi)
to get upset, worry

preno'tare vt to book, reserve; **vorrei
~ una camera doppia** I'd like to book
a double room; **ho prenotato un
tavolo al nome di ...** I booked a table
in the name of ...; **prenotazi'one** sf
booking, reservation; **ho confermato
la prenotazione per fax/e-mail** I
confirmed my booking by fax/e-mail

preoccu'pare vt to worry; to
preoccupy; **preoccuparsi** vpr
preoccuparsi di qn/qc to worry
about sb/sth; **preoccuparsi per qn** to
be anxious for sb; **preoccupazi'one** sf
worry, anxiety

prepa'rare vt to prepare; (esame,
concorso) to prepare for; **prepararsi**
vpr (vestirsi) to get ready; **prepararsi**

a qc/a fare to get ready o **prepare** (o.s.) for sth/to do; **~ da mangiare** to prepare a meal; **prepara'tivi** smpl preparations

preposizi'one [prepozit'tsjone] sf (Ling) preposition

prepo'tente ag (persona) domineering, arrogant; (bisogno, desiderio) overwhelming, pressing ▶ sm/f bully

'presa sf taking no pl; (di persona) catching no pl; (di città) capture; (indurimento: di cemento) setting; (appiglio, Sport) hold; (di acqua, gas) (supply) point; (piccola quantità: di sale ecc) pinch; (Carte) trick; **far ~ (colla)** to set; **far ~ sul pubblico** to catch the public's imagination; **essere alle prese con** (fig) to be struggling with; **presa d'aria** air inlet; **presa (di corrente)** (Elettr) socket; (: al muro) point

pre'sagio [pre'zadʒo] sm omen

'presbite ag long-sighted

pres'crivere vt to prescribe

'prese ecc vb vedi **prendere**

presen'tare vt ~ (qca qn) (far conoscere): **~ qn (a)** to introduce sb (to); (Amm: inoltrare) to submit; **presentarsi** vpr (recarsi, farsi vedere) to present o.s., appear; (farsi conoscere) to introduce o.s.; (occasione) to arise; **presentarsi come candidato** (Pol) to stand as a candidate; **presentarsi bene/male** to have a good/poor appearance

pre'sente ag present; (questo) this ▶ sm present; **i presenti** those present; **aver ~ qc/qn** to remember sth/sb; **presenti** (persone) people present; **aver ~ qc/qn** to remember sth/sb; **tenere ~ qn/qc** to keep sth/sb in mind

presenti'mento sm premonition

pre'senza [pre'zɛntsa] sf presence; (aspetto esteriore) appearance;

presenza di spirito presence of mind

pre'sepio, pre'sepe sm crib

preser'vare vt to protect; to save; **preserva'tivo** sm sheath, condom

'presi ecc vb vedi **prendere**

'preside sm/f (Ins) head (teacher) (BRIT), principal (US); (di facoltà universitaria) dean; **preside di facoltà** (Univ) dean of faculty

presi'dente sm (Pol) president; (di assemblea, Comm) chairman; **presidente del consiglio** prime minister

presi'edere vt to preside over ▶ vi **~ a** to direct, be in charge of

pressap'poco av about, roughly

pres'sare vt to press

pressi'one sf pressure; **far ~ su qn** to put pressure on sb; **pressione sanguigna** blood pressure; **pressione atmosferica** atmospheric pressure

'presso av (vicino) nearby, close at hand ▶ prep (vicino a) near; (accanto a) beside, next to; (in casa di) **~ qn** at sb's home; (nelle lettere) care of, c/o; (alle dipendenze di): **lavora ~ di noi** he works for o with us ▶ smpl **nei pressi di** near, in the vicinity of

pres'tante ag good-looking

pres'tare vt **~ (qca qn)** to lend (sth to sb o sth to sb); **prestarsi** vpr (offrirsi) to offer to; (essere adatto): **prestarsi a** to lend itself to, be suitable for; **mi può ~ dei soldi?** can you lend me some money?; **~ aiuto** to lend a hand; **~ attenzione** to pay attention; **~ fede a qc/qn** to give credence to sth/sb; **~ orecchio** to listen; **prestazi'one** sf (Tecn, Sport) performance

prestigia'tore, -'trice [prestidʒa'tore] sm/f conjurer

pres'tigio [pres'tidʒo] sm (fama) prestige; (illusione): **gioco di ~**

conjuring trick

'prestito sm lending no pl; loan; **dar in ~ to** lend; **prendere in ~ to** borrow

'presto av (tra poco) soon; (in fretta) quickly; (di buon'ora) early; **a ~** see you soon; **fare ~** to hurry up and do sth; (non costare fatica) to have no trouble doing sth; **si fa ~ a criticare** it's easy to criticize

pre'sumere vt to presume, assume

pre'sunsi ecc vb vedi **presumere**

presuntu'oso, -a ag presumptuous

presunzi'one [prezun'tsjone] sf presumption

'prete sm priest

preten'dente sm/f pretender ▶ sm (corteggiatore) suitor

pre'tendere vt (esigere) to demand, require; (sostenere): **~ che** to claim that; **pretende di aver sempre ragione** he thinks he's always right
Attenzione! In inglese esiste il verbo **to pretend**, che però significa **far finta**.

pre'tesa sf (esigenza) claim, demand; (presunzione, sfarzo) pretentiousness; **senza pretese** unpretentious

pre'teso, -a pp di **pretendere**

pre'testo sm pretext, excuse

preva'lere vi to prevail

preve'dere vt (indovinare) to foresee; (presagire) to foretell; (considerare) to make provision for

preve'nire vt (anticipare) to forestall; to anticipate; (evitare) to avoid, prevent

preven'tivo, -a ag preventive ▶ sm (Comm) estimate

prevenzi'one [preven'tsjone] sf prevention; (preconcetto) prejudice

previ'dente ag showing foresight, prudent; **previ'denza** sf foresight; **istituto di previdenza** provident institution; **previdenza sociale** social security (BRIT); welfare (US)

pre'vidi ecc vb vedi **prevedere**

previsi'one sf forecast, prediction; **previsioni meteorologiche** weather forecast sg; **previsioni del tempo** weather forecast sg

pre'visto, -a pp di **prevedere** ▶ sm **più/meno del ~** more/less than expected

prezi'oso, -a [pret'tsjoso] ag precious; invaluable ▶ sm jewel; valuable

prez'zemolo [pret'tsemolo] sm parsley

'prezzo ['prettso] sm price; **prezzo d'acquisto/di vendita** buying/selling price

prigi'one [pri'dʒone] sf prison; **prigioni'ero, -a** ag captive ▶ sm/f prisoner

'prima sf (Teatro) first night; (Cinema) première; (Aut) first gear; vedi anche **primo** ▶ av before; (in anticipo) in advance, beforehand; (per l'addietro) at one time, formerly; (più presto) sooner, earlier; (in primo luogo) first ▶ cong ~ **di fare/che parta** before doing/he leaves; ~ **di** before; ~ **o poi** sooner or later

pri'mario, -a ag primary; (principale) chief, leading, primary ▶ sm (Med) chief physician

prima'tista, -i, e sm/f (Sport) record holder

pri'mato sm supremacy; (Sport) record

prima'vera sf spring

primi'tivo, -a ag primitive; original

pri'mizie [pri'mittsje] sfpl early produce sg

'primo, -a ag first; (fig) initial; basic; prime ▶ sm/f first (one) ▶ sm (Cuc) first course; (in date): **il ~ luglio** the first of July; **le prime ore del mattino** the early hours of the morning; **ai primi di maggio** at the beginning of May; **viaggiare in prima** to travel first-class; **in ~ luogo** first of all, in the first place; **di prim'ordine** o **prima qualità**

first-class, first-rate; **in un ~ tempo** at first; **prima donna** leading lady; (di opera lirica) prima donna

primordi'ale ag primordial

'primula sf primrose

princi'pale [printʃi'pale] ag main, principal ▶ sm manager, boss

principal'mente [printʃipal'mente] av mainly, principally

'principe ['printʃipe] sm prince; **principe ereditario** crown prince; **princi'pessa** sf princess

principi'ante [printʃi'pjante] sm/f beginner

prin'cipio [prin'tʃipjo] sm (inizio) beginning, start; (origine) origin, cause; (concetto, norma) principle; **al di ~** at first; **per ~** on principle; **principi** smpl (concetti fondamentali) principles; **una questione di ~** a matter of principle

priorità sf priority

priori'tario, -a ag having priority, of utmost importance

pri'vare vt ~ **qn di** to deprive sb of; **privarsi di** to go o do without

pri'vato, -a ag private ▶ sm/f private citizen; **in ~** in private

privilegi'are [privile'dʒare] vt to grant a privilege to

privilegi'ato, -a [privile'dʒato] ag (individuo, classe) privileged; (trattamento, Comm: credito) preferential; **azioni ~e** preference shares (BRIT), preferred stock (US)

privi'legio [privi'ledʒo] sm privilege

'privo, -a ag ~ **di** without, lacking

pro prep for, on behalf of ▶ sm inv (utilità) advantage, benefit; **a che ~?** what's the use?; **il ~ e il contro** the pros and cons

pro'babile ag probable, likely; **probabilità** sf inv probability

probabil'mente av probably

pro'blema, -i sm problem

pro'boscide [pro'bɔʃʃide] sf (di elefante) trunk

pro'cedere [pro'tʃɛdere] vi to proceed; (comportarsi) to behave; (iniziare): **~ a** to start; **~ contro** (Dir) to start legal proceedings against; **proce'dura** sf (Dir) procedure

proces'sare [protʃes'sare] vt (Dir) to try

processi'one [protʃes'sjone] sf procession

pro'cesso [pro'tʃɛsso] sm (Dir) trial; proceedings pl; (metodo) process

pro'cinto [pro'tʃinto] sm **in ~ di fare** about to do, on the point of doing

procla'mare vt to proclaim

procre'are vt to procreate

procu'rare vt ~ **qc a qn** (fornire) to get o obtain sth for sb; (causare: noie ecc) to bring o give sb sth

pro'digio [pro'didʒo] sm marvel, wonder; (persona) prodigy

pro'dotto, -a pp di **produrre** ▶ sm product; **prodotti agricoli** farm produce sg

pro'duco ecc vb vedi **produrre**

pro'durre vt to produce

pro'dussi ecc vb vedi **produrre**

produzi'one sf production; (rendimento) output

Prof. abbr (= professore) Prof

profa'nare vt to desecrate

profes'sare vt to profess; (medicina ecc) to practise

professio'nale ag professional

professi'one sf profession; **professio'nista, -i, -e** sm/f professional

profes'sore, -'essa sm/f (Ins) teacher; (: di università) lecturer; (: titolare di cattedra) professor

pro'filo sm profile; (breve descrizione) sketch, outline; **di ~** in profile

pro'fitto sm advantage, profit, benefit; (fig: progresso) progress;

(*Comm*) profit

profondità sf inv depth

pro'fondo, -a ag deep; (*rancore, meditazione*) profound ▸ sm depth(s pl), bottom; **quanto è profonda l'acqua?** how deep is the water?; **~ 8 metri** 8 metres deep

'profugo, -a, -ghi, -ghe sm/f refugee

profu'mare vt to perfume ▸ vi to be fragrant; **profumarsi** vpr to put on perfume o scent

profu'mato, -a ag (*fiore, aria*) fragrant; (*fazzoletto, saponetta*) scented; (*pelle*) sweet-smelling; (*persona*) with perfume on

profume'ria sf perfumery; (*negozio*) perfume shop

pro'fumo sm (*prodotto*) perfume, scent; (*fragranza*) scent, fragrance

proget'tare [prodʒet'tare] vt to plan; (*edificio*) to plan, design; **pro'getto** sm plan, project; (*idea*) plan, project; **progetto di legge** bill

pro'gramma, -i sm programme; (*TV, Radio*) programmes pl; (*Ins*) syllabus, curriculum; (*Inform*) program; **program'mare** vt (*TV, Radio*) to put on; (*Inform*) to program; (*Econ*) to plan; **programma'tore, -'trice** sm/f (*Inform*) computer programmer

progre'dire vi to progress, make progress

pro'gresso sm progress no pl; **fare progressi** to make progress

proi'bire vt to forbid, prohibit

proiet'tare vt (*gen, Geom, Cinema*) to project; (: *presentare*) to show, screen; (*luce, ombra*) to throw, cast, project; **proi'ettile** sm projectile, bullet (*o shell ecc*); **proiet'tore** sm (*Cinema*) projector; (*Aut*) headlamp; (*Mil*) searchlight; **proiezi'one** sf (*Cinema*) projection; showing

prolife'rare vi (*fig*) to proliferate

pro'lunga, -ghe sf (*di cavo ecc*)

extension

prolun'gare vt (*discorso, attesa*) to prolong; (*linea, termine*) to extend

prome'moria sm inv memorandum

pro'messa sf promise

pro'mettere vt to promise ▸ vi to look promising ▸ a qn di fare to promise sb that one will do

promi'nente ag prominent

pro'misi ecc vb vedi **promettere**

promon'torio sm promontory, headland

promozi'one [promot'tsjone] sf promotion

promu'overe vt to promote

proni'pote sm/f (*di nonni*) great-grandchild, great-grandson/granddaughter; (*di zii*) great-nephew/niece

pro'nome sm (*Ling*) pronoun

pron'tezza [pron'tettsa] sf readiness; quickness, promptness

'pronto, -a ag ready; (*rapido*) fast, quick, prompt; **quando saranno pronte le mie foto?** when will my photos be ready?; **~!** (*Tel*) hello!; **~ all'ira** quick-tempered; **pronto soccorso** (*cure*) first aid; (*reparto*) A&E (*BRIT*), ER (*US*)

prontu'ario sm manual, handbook

pro'nuncia [pro'nuntʃa] sf pronunciation

pronunci'are [pronun'tʃare] vt (*parola, sentenza*) to pronounce; (*dire*) to utter; (*discorso*) to deliver; **come si pronuncia?** how do you pronounce it?

propa'ganda sf propaganda

pro'pendere vi ~ per to favour, lean towards

propi'nare vt to administer

pro'porre vt (*suggerire*): ~ qc (a qn) to suggest sth (to sb); (*candidato*) to put forward; (*legge, brindisi*) to propose; ~ di fare to suggest o propose doing;

propor'si di fare to propose o intend to do; **proporsi una meta** to set o.s. a goal

proporzio'nale [proportsjo'nale] ag proportional

proporzi'one [propor'tsjone] sf proportion; **in ~ a** in proportion to; **proporzioni** sfpl (dimensioni) proportions; **di vaste proporzioni** huge

pro'posito sm (intenzione) intention, aim; (argomento) subject, matter; **a ~ di** regarding, with regard to; **di ~** (apposta) deliberately, on purpose; **a ~** by the way; **capitare a ~** (cosa, persona) to turn up at the right time

proposizi'one [propozit'tsjone] sf (Ling) clause; (: periodo) sentence

pro'posta sf proposal; (suggerimento) suggestion; **proposta di legge** bill

propri'età sf inv (ciò che si possiede) property gen no pl, estate; (caratteristica) property; (correttezza) correctness; **proprietà privata** private property; **proprie'tario, -a** sm/f owner; (di albergo ecc) proprietor, owner; (per l'inquilino) landlord/lady

'proprio, -a ag (possessivo) own; (: impersonale) one's; (esatto) exact, correct, proper; (senso, significato) literal; (Ling: nome) proper; (particolare) ~ **di** characteristic of, peculiar to ▶ av (precisamente) just, exactly; (davvero) really; (affatto) **non ... ~** not ... at all; **l'ha visto con i (suoi) propri occhi** he saw it with his own eyes

proro'gare vt to extend; (differire) to postpone, defer

'prosa sf prose

pro'sciogliere [proʃ'ʃɔʎʎere] vt to release; (Dir) to acquit

prosciu'gare [proʃʃu'gare] vt (terreni) to drain, reclaim; **prosciugarsi** vpr to dry up

prosci'utto [proʃ'ʃutto] sm ham; **prosciutto cotto/crudo** cooked/cured ham

prosegu'imento sm continuation; **buon ~!** all the best!; (a chi viaggia) enjoy the rest of your journey!

prosegu'ire vt to carry on with, continue ▶ vi to carry on, go on

prospe'rare vi to thrive

prospet'tare vt (esporre) to point out, show; **prospettarsi** vpr to look, appear

prospet'tiva sf (Arte) perspective; (veduta) view; (fig: previsione, possibilità) prospect

pros'petto sm (Disegno) elevation; (veduta) view, prospect; (facciata) façade, front; (tabella) table; (sommario) summary; **prospetto informativo** prospectus

prossi'mità sf nearness, proximity; **in ~ di** near (to), close to

'prossimo, -a ag (vicino): **~ a** near (to), close to; (che viene subito dopo) next; (parente) close ▶ sm neighbour, fellow man

prostitu'irsi vpr to prostitute o.s.

prosti'tuta sf prostitute

protago'nista, -i, -e sm/f protagonist

pro'teggere [pro'teddʒere] vt to protect

prote'ina sf protein

pro'tendere vt to stretch out

pro'testa sf protest

protes'tante ag, sm/f Protestant

protes'tare vt, vi to protest

pro'tetto, -a pp di **proteggere**

protezi'one [protet'tsjone] sf protection; (patrocinio) patronage

pro'totipo sm prototype

pro'trarre vt (prolungare) to prolong; **protrarsi** vpr to go on, continue

protube'ranza [protube'rantsa] sf protuberance, bulge

'**prova** sf (esperimento, cimento) test, trial; (tentativo) attempt, try; (Mat, testimonianza, documento ecc) proof; (Dir) evidence no pl, proof; (Ins) exam, test; (Teatro) rehearsal; (di abito) fitting; **a ~ di** (in testimonianza) as proof of; **a ~ di fuoco** fireproof; **fino a ~ contraria** until it is proved otherwise; **mettere alla ~** to put to the test; **giro di ~** test o trial run; **prova generale** (Teatro) dress rehearsal

pro'**vare** vt (sperimentare) to test; (tentare) to try, attempt; (assaggiare) to try, taste; (sperimentare in sé) to experience; (sentire) to feel; (cimentare) to put to the test; (dimostrare) to prove; (abito) to try on; **~ a fare** to try o attempt to do

proveni'**enza** [prove'njɛntsa] sf origin, source

prove'**nire** vi **~ da** to come from

pro'**venti** smpl revenue sg

pro'**verbio** sm proverb

pro'**vetta** sf test tube; **bambino in ~** test-tube baby

pro'**vider** [pro'vaider] sm inv (Inform) service provider

pro'**vincia**, **-ce** o **cie** [pro'vintʃa] sf province

pro'**vino** sm (Cinema) screen test; (campione) specimen

provo'**cante** ag (attraente) provocative

provo'**care** vt (causare) to cause, bring about; (eccitare: riso, pietà) to arouse; (irritare, sfidare) to provoke; **provocazi'one** sf provocation

prov've'**dere** vi (disporre) **~ (a)** to provide (for); (prendere un provvedimento) to take steps, act; **provvedi'mento** sm measure; (di previdenza) precaution

provvi'**denza** [provvi'dɛntsa] sf **la ~** providence

provvigi'**one** [provvi'dʒone] sf (Comm) commission

provvi'**sorio**, **-a** ag temporary

prov'**viste** sfpl supplies

'**prua** sf (Naut) bow(s) (pl), prow

pru'**dente** ag cautious, prudent; (assennato) sensible, wise; **pru'denza** sf prudence, caution; wisdom

'**prudere** vi to itch, be itchy

'**prugna** ['pruɲɲa] sf plum; **prugna secca** prune

pru'**rito** sm itchiness no pl; itch

P.S. abbr (= postscriptum) P.S.; (Polizia) = **Pubblica Sicurezza**

pseu'**donimo** sm pseudonym

psica'**nalisi** sf psychoanalysis

psicana'**lista**, **-i**, **-e** sm/f psychoanalyst

'**psiche** ['psike] sf (Psic) psyche

psichi'**atra**, **-i**, **-e** [psi'kjatra] sm/f psychiatrist; **psichi'atrico**, **-a**, **-ci**, **-che** ag psychiatric

psicolo'**gia** [psikolo'dʒia] sf psychology; **psico'logico**, **-a**, **-ci**, **-che** ag psychological; **psi'cologo**, **-a**, **-gi**, **-ghe** sm/f psychologist

psico'**patico**, **-a**, **-ci**, **-che** ag psychopathic ▶ sm/f psychopath

pubbli'**care** vt to publish

pubblicazi'**one** [pubblikat'tsjone] sf publication

pubblici'**tà** [pubbliʧi'ta] sf (diffusione) publicity; (attività) advertising; (annunci nei giornali) advertisements pl

'**pubblico**, **-a**, **-ci**, **-che** ag public; (statale: scuola ecc) state cpd ▶ sm public; (spettatori) audience; **in ~** in public; **P~ Ministero** Public Prosecutor's Office; **la Pubblica Sicurezza** the police; **pubblico funzionario** civil servant

'**pube** sm (Anat) pubis

puber'**tà** sf puberty

'**pudico**, **-a**, **-ci**, **-che** ag modest

pu'**dore** sm modesty

pue'**rile** ag childish

pugi'lato [pudʒi'lato] *sm* boxing

'**pugile** ['pudʒile] *sm* boxer

pugna'lare [puɲɲa'lare] *vt* to stab

pu'gnale [puɲ'ɲale] *sm* dagger

'**pugno** [puɲɲo] *sm* fist; (*colpo*) punch; (*quantità*) fistful

'**pulce** ['pultʃe] *sf* flea

pul'cino [pul'tʃino] *sm* chick

pu'lire *vt* to clean; (*lucidare*) to polish; **pu'lito, -a** *ag* (*anche fig*) clean; (*ordinato*) neat, tidy; **puli'tura** *sf* cleaning; **pulitura a secco** dry cleaning; **puli'zia** *sf* cleaning; cleanness; **fare le pulizie** to do the cleaning *o* the housework; **pulizia etnica** ethnic cleansing

'**pullman** *sm inv* coach

pul'lover *sm inv* pullover, jumper

pullu'lare *vi* to swarm, teem

pul'mino *sm* minibus

'**pulpito** *sm* pulpit

pul'sante *sm* (push-)button

pul'sare *vi* to pulsate, beat

pul'viscolo *sm* fine dust; **pulviscolo atmosferico** specks *pl* of dust

'**puma** *sm inv* puma

pun'gente [pun'dʒente] *ag* prickly; stinging; (*anche fig*) biting

'**pungere** ['pundʒere] *vt* to prick; (*insetto, ortica*) to sting; (: *freddo*) to bite

pungigli'one [pundʒiʎ'ʎone] *sm* sting

pu'nire *vt* to punish; **punizi'one** *sf* punishment; (*Sport*) penalty

'**punsi** *ecc vb vedi* **pungere**

'**punta** *sf* point; (*parte terminale*) tip, end; (*di monte*) peak; (*di costa*) promontory; (*minima parte*) touch, trace; **in ~ di piedi** on tip-toe; **ore di ~** peak hours; **uomo di ~** front-rank *o* leading man

pun'tare *vt* (*piedi a terra, gomiti sul tavolo*) to plant; (*dirigere: pistola*) to point; (*scommettere*) to bet ▶ *vi* (*mirare*): **~ a** to aim at; **~ su** (*dirigersi*)

to head *o* make for; (*fig: contare*) to count *o* rely on

pun'tata *sf* (*gita*) short trip; (*scommessa*) bet; (*parte di opera*) instalment; **romanzo a puntate** serial

punteggia'tura [punteddʒa'tura] *sf* (*Ling*) punctuation

pun'teggio [pun'teddʒo] *sm* score

puntel'lare *vt* to support

pun'tello *sm* prop, support

pun'tina *sf*; **puntina da disegno** drawing pin

pun'tino *sm* dot; **fare qc a ~** to do sth properly

'**punto, -a** *pp di* **pungere** ▶ *sm* (*segno, macchiolina*) dot; (*Ling*) full stop; (*di indirizzo e-mail*) dot; (*Mat, momento, di punteggio: fig: argomento*) point; (*posto*) spot; (*a scuola*) mark; (*nel cucire, nella maglia, Med*) stitch ▶ *av* **non ... ~** not at all; **punto cardinale** point of the compass, cardinal point; **punto debole** weak point; **punto esclamativo** exclamation mark; **punto interrogativo** question mark; **punto nero** (*comedone*) blackhead; **punto di partenza** (*anche fig*) starting point; **punto di riferimento** landmark; (*fig*) point of reference; **punto (di) vendita** retail outlet; **punto e virgola** semicolon; **punto di vista** (*fig*) point of view

puntu'ale *ag* punctual

pun'tura *sf* (*di ago*) prick; (*Med*) puncture; (*: iniezione*) injection; (*dolore*) sharp pain; **puntura d'insetto** sting, bite

▌ Attenzione! In inglese esiste la parola *puncture*, che si usa per indicare la foratura di una gomma.

punzecchi'are [puntsek'kjare] *vt* to prick; (*fig*) to tease

può *ecc*, **-puo'i** *vb vedi* **potere**

pu'pazzo [pu'pattso] *sm* puppet

pu'pilla *sf* (Anat) pupil

purché [pur'ke] *cong* provided that, on condition that

'pure *cong* (tuttavia) and yet, nevertheless; (anche se) even if ▸ *av* (anche) too, also; **pur di** ~ (al fine di) just to; **faccia ~!** go ahead!, please do!

purè *sm* (Cuc) purée; (: di patate) mashed potatoes

pu'rezza [pu'rettsa] *sf* purity

pur'gante *sm* (Med) purgative, purge

purga'torio *sm* purgatory

purifi'care *vt* to purify; (metallo) to refine

'puro, -a *ag* pure; (acqua) clear, limpid; (vino) undiluted; **puro'sangue** *sm/f inv* thoroughbred

pur'troppo *av* unfortunately

pus *sm* pus

'pustola *sf* pimple

puti'ferio *sm* rumpus, row

putre'fatto, -a *pp di* **putrefare**

put'tana (fam!) *sf* whore (!)

puz'zare [put'tsare] *vi* to stink

'puzzo ['puttso] *sm* stink, foul smell

'puzzola ['puttsola] *sf* polecat

puzzo'lente [puttso'lente] *ag* stinking

pvc [pivi'tʃi] *sigla m* (= polyvinyl chloride) PVC

q *abbr* (= quintale) q

qua *av* here; **in ~** (verso questa parte) this way; **da un anno in ~** for a year now; **da ~ndo in ~?** since when?; **per di ~** (passare) this way; **al di ~ di** (fiume, strada) on this side of; **~ dentro/fuori** ecc in/out here ecc; *vedi anche* ecc; *vedi anche* **questo**

qua'derno *sm* notebook; (per scuola) exercise book

qua'drante *sm* quadrant; (di orologio) face

qua'drare *vi* (bilancio) to balance, tally; (descrizione) to correspond ▸ *vt* (Mat) to square; **non mi quadra** I don't like it; **qua'drato, -a** *ag* square; (fig: equilibrato) level-headed, sensible; (: peg) square ▸ *sm* (Mat) square; (Pugilato) ring; **5 al quadrato** 5 squared

quadri'foglio [kwadri'fɔʎʎo] *sm* four-leaf clover

quadri'mestre *sm* (periodo) four-month period; (Ins) term

'quadro *sm* (pittura) painting, picture; (quadrato) square; (tabella) table, chart; (Tecn) board, panel; (Teatro) scene; (fig: scena, spettacolo) sight; (: descrizione) outline, description; **quadri** *smpl* (Pol) party organizers; (Mil) cadres; (Comm) managerial staff; (Carte) diamonds

qua'druplo, -a *ag, sm* quadruple

quaggiù [kwad'dʒu] *av* down here

'quaglia ['kwaʎʎa] *sf* quail

'qualche
['kwalke] det

1 some, a few; (*in interrogative*) any; **ho comprato qualche libro** I've bought some *o* a few books; **qualche volta** sometimes; **hai qualche sigaretta?** have you any cigarettes?

2 (*uno*): **c'è qualche medico?** is there a doctor?; **in qualche modo** somehow

3 (*un certo, parecchio*) some; **un personaggio di qualche rilievo** a figure of some importance

4: **qualche cosa = qualcosa**

qual'cosa *pron* something; (*in espressioni interrogative*) anything; **qualcos'altro** something else; anything else; **~ di nuovo** something new; anything new; **~ da mangiare** something to eat; anything to eat; **c'è ~ che non va?** is there something *o* anything wrong?

qual'cuno *pron* (*persona*) someone, somebody; (: *in espressioni interrogative*) anyone, anybody; (*alcuni*) some; **~ è favorevole a noi** some are on our side; **qualcun altro** someone *o* somebody else; anyone *o* anybody else

'quale
(*spesso troncato in* **qual**) det

1 (*interrogativo*) what; (: *scegliendo tra due o più cose o persone*) which; **quale uomo/denaro?** what man/money?, which man/money?; **quali sono i tuoi programmi?** what are your plans?; **quale stanza preferisci?** which room do you prefer?

2 (*relativo: come*): **il risultato fu quale ci si aspettava** the result was as expected

3 (*esclamativo*) what; **quale disgrazia!** what bad luck!

▶ *pron*

1 (*interrogativo*) which; **quale dei due scegli?** which of the two do you want?

2 (*relativo*): **il (la) quale** (*persona: soggetto*) who; (: *oggetto, con preposizione*) whom; (*cosa*) which; (*possessivo*) whose; **suo padre, il quale è avvocato, ...** his father, who is a lawyer, ...; **il signore con il quale parlavo** the gentleman to whom I was speaking; **l'albergo al quale ci siamo fermati** the hotel where we stayed *o* which we stayed at; **la signora della quale ammiriamo la bellezza** the lady whose beauty we admire

3 (*relativo: in elenchi*) such as, like; **piante quali l'edera** plants like *o* such as ivy; **quale sindaco di questa città** as mayor of this town

qua'lifica, -che *sf* qualification; (*titolo*) title

qualifi'cato, -a *ag* (*dotato di qualifica*) qualified; (*esperto, abile*) skilled; **non mi ritengo ~ per questo lavoro** I don't think I'm qualified for this job; **è un medico molto ~** he is a very distinguished doctor

qualificazi'one *sf* **gara di ~** (*Sport*) qualifying event

qualità *sf inv* quality; **in ~ di** in one's capacity as

qua'lora *cong* in case, if

qual'siasi *det inv* = **qualunque**

qua'lunque *det inv* any; (*quale che sia*) whatever; (*discriminativo*) whichever; (*posposto: mediocre*) poor, indifferent; ordinary; **mettiti un vestito ~** put on any old dress; **~ cosa** anything; **~ cosa accada** whatever happens; **a ~ costo** at any cost, whatever the cost; **l'uomo ~** the man in the street; **~ persona** anyone, anybody

'quando *cong, av* when; **~ sarò ricco** when I'm rich; **da ~** (*dacché*) since; (*interrogativo*) **da ~ sei qui?** how long have you been here?; **quand'anche** even if

quantità *sf inv* quantity; (*gran*

numero): **una ~ di** a great deal of; a lot of; **in grande ~** in large quantities

○ **'quanto, -a**
  det

1 (*interrogativo: quantità*) how much; (: *numero*) how many; **quanto pane/denaro?** how much bread/money?; **quanti libri/ragazzi?** how many books/boys?; **quanto tempo?** how long?; **quanti anni hai?** how old are you?

2 (*esclamativo*): **quante storie!** what a lot of nonsense!; **quanto tempo sprecato!** what a waste of time!

3 (*relativo: quantità*) as much ... as; (: *numero*) as many ... as; **ho quanto denaro mi occorre** I have as much money as I need; **prendi quanti libri vuoi** take as many books as you like
  ▶ *pron*

1 (*interrogativo: quantità*) how much; (: *numero*) how many; (: *tempo*) how long; **quanto mi dai?** how much will you give me?; **quanti me ne hai portati?** how many did you bring me?; **da quanto sei qui?** how long have you been here?; **quanti ne abbiamo oggi?** what's the date today?

2 (*relativo: quantità*) as much as; (: *numero*) as many as; **farò quanto posso** I'll do as much as I can; **possono venire quanti sono stati invitati** all those who have been invited can come
  ▶ *av*

1 (*interrogativo: con ag, av*) how; (: *con vb*) how much; **quanto stanco ti sembrava?** how tired did he seem to you?; **quanto corre la tua moto?** how fast can your motorbike go?; **quanto costa?** how much does it cost?; **quant'è?** how much is it?

2 (*esclamativo: con ag, av*) how; (: *con vb*) how much; **quanto sono felice!** how happy I am!; **sapessi quanto abbiamo camminato!** if you knew how far we've

walked!; **studierò quanto posso** I'll study as much as I can; **quanto prima** as soon as possible

3 : **in quanto** (*in qualità di*) as; (*perché, per il fatto che*) as, since; **(in) quanto a** (*per ciò che riguarda*) as for, as regards

4 : **per quanto** (*nonostante, anche se*) however; **per quanto si sforzi, non ce la farà** try as he may, he won't manage it; **per quanto sia brava, fa degli errori** however good she may be, she makes mistakes; **per quanto io sappia** as far as I know

qua'ranta *num* forty
quaran'tena *sf* quarantine
quaran'tesimo, -a *num* fortieth
quaran'tina *sf* **una ~ (di)** about forty
'quarta *sf* (*Aut*) fourth (gear); *vedi anche* **quarto**
quar'tetto *sm* quartet(te)
quarti'ere *sm* district, area; (*Mil*) quarters *pl*; **quartier generale** headquarters *pl*
'quarto, -a *ag* fourth ▶ *sm* fourth; (*quarta parte*) quarter; **le 6 e un ~** a quarter past six; **quarti di finale** quarter final; **quarto d'ora** quarter of an hour
'quarzo ['kwartso] *sm* quartz
'quasi *av* almost, nearly ▶ *cong* (*anche: ~ che*) as if; **(non) ... ~ mai** hardly ever; **~ ~ me ne andrei** I've half a mind to leave
quas'sù *av* up here
quat'tordici [kwat'tordit∫i] *num* fourteen
quat'trini *smpl* money *sg*, cash *sg*
'quattro *num* four; **in ~ e quatt'otto** in less than no time; **quattro'cento** *num* four hundred ▶ *sm* il Quattrocento the fifteenth century
○ **'quello, -a**
  (*dav sm* quel + C, quell' + V, quello + *s impura, gn, pn, ps, x, z, pl* quei + C, quegli + V o *s impura, gn, pn, ps, x, z; dav*

sf quella + C, quell' +V; *pl* quelle) *det*
that; those *pl*: **quella casa** that house;
quegli uomini those men; **voglio
quella camicia (lì o là)** I want that shirt
▶ *pron*

1 (*dimostrativo*) that (one), those
(ones) *pl*: (*ciò*) that; **conosci quella?**
do you know that woman?; **prendo
quello bianco** I'll take the white one;
chi è quello? who's that?; **prendi
quello (lì o là)** take that one (there)

2 (*relativo*) **quello(a) che** (*persona*)
the one (who); (*cosa*) the one (which),
the one (that); **quelli(e) che** (*persone*)
those who; (*cose*) those which; **è lui
quello che non voleva venire** he's the
one who didn't want to come; **ho fatto
quello che potevo** I did what I could

quercia, -ce ['kwɛrtʃa] *sf* oak (tree);
(*legno*) oak

que'rela *sf* (*Dir*) (legal) action

que'sito *sm* question, query; problem

questio'nario *sm* questionnaire

questi'one *sf* problem, question;
(*controversia*) issue; (*litigio*) quarrel;
in ~ in question; **è ~ di tempo** it's a
matter o question of time

○ 'questo, -a
det

1 (*dimostrativo*) this; these *pl*: **questo
libro (qui o qua)** this book; **io prendo
questo cappotto, tu quello** I'll
take this coat, you take that one;
quest'oggi today; **questa sera** this
evening

2 (*enfatico*): **non fatemi più prendere
di queste paure** don't frighten me like
that again
▶ *pron* (*dimostrativo*) this (one); these
(ones) *pl*: (*ciò*) this; **prendo questo
(qui o qua)** I'll take this one; **preferisci
questi o quelli?** do you prefer these
(ones) or those (ones)?; **questo
intendevo** this is what I meant;
**vengono Paolo e Luca: questo da

Roma, quello da Palermo** Paolo and
Luca are coming: the former from
Palermo, the latter from Rome

ques'tura *sf* police headquarters *pl*

qui *av* here; **da o di ~ from** here; **di ~ in
avanti** from now on; **di ~ a poco/una
settimana** in a little while/a week's
time; **~ dentro/sopra/vicino** in/up/
near here; *vedi anche* **questo**

quie'tanza [kwje'tantsa] *sf* receipt

qui'ete *sf* quiet, quietness; calmness;
stillness; peace

qui'eto, -a *ag* quiet; (*notte*) calm, still;
(*mare*) calm

'quindi *av* then ▶ *cong* therefore, so

'quindici ['kwindit∫i] *num* fifteen; **~
giorni** a fortnight (BRIT), two weeks

quindi'cina [kwindi't∫ina] *sf* (*serie*):
una ~ (di) about fifteen; **fra una ~ di
giorni** in a fortnight

quinta *sf vedi* **quinto**

quin'tale *sm* quintal (100 kg)

'quinto, -a *num* fifth

quiz [kwidz] *sm inv* (*domanda*)
question; (*anche*): **gioco a ~** quiz game

'quota *sf* (*parte*) quota, share; (*Aer*)
height, altitude; (*Ippica*) odds
pl: **prendere/perdere ~** (*Aer*) to
gain/lose height o altitude; **quota
d'iscrizione** enrolment fee; (*a club*)
membership fee

quotidi'ano, -a *ag* daily; (*banale*)
everyday ▶ *sm* (*giornale*) daily (paper)

quozi'ente [kwot'tsjɛnte] *sm* (*Mat*)
quotient; **quoziente d'intelligenza**
intelligence quotient, IQ

r

R, r ['ɛrre] *sf o m (lettera)* R, r; **R come Roma** ≈ R for Robert (BRIT), R for Roger (US)

'**rabbia** *sf (ira)* anger, rage; *(accanimento, furia)* fury; *(Med: idrofobia)* rabies *sg*

rab'bino *sm* rabbi

rabbi'oso, -a *ag* angry, furious; *(facile all'ira)* quick-tempered; *(forze, acqua ecc)* furious, raging; *(Med)* rabid, mad

rabbo'nire *vt* to calm down

rabbrivi'dire *vi* to shudder, shiver

raccapez'zarsi [rakkapet'tsarsi] *vpr* **non ~** to be at a loss

raccapricci'ante [rakkaprit'ʃante] *ag* horrifying

raccatta'palle *sm inv (Sport)* ballboy

raccat'tare *vt* to pick up

rac'chetta [rak'ketta] *sf (per tennis)* racket; *(per ping-pong)* bat; **racchetta da neve** snowshoe; **racchetta da sci** ski stick

racchi'udere [rak'kjudere] *vt* to contain

rac'cogliere [rak'kɔʎʎere] *vt* to collect; *(raccattare)* to pick up; *(frutti, fiori)* to pick, pluck; *(Agr)* to harvest; *(approvazione, voti)* to win

rac'colta *sf* collecting *no pl*; collection *no pl*; *(Agr)* harvesting *no pl*, gathering *no pl*; harvest, crop; **raccolta differenziata** *(dei rifiuti) separate collection of different kinds of household waste*

rac'colto, -a *pp di* **raccogliere** ▸ *ag (persona: pensoso)* thoughtful; *(luogo: appartato)* secluded, quiet ▸ *sm (Agr)* crop, harvest

raccoman'dabile *ag (highly)* commendable; **è un tipo poco ~** he is not to be trusted

raccoman'dare *vt* to recommend; *(affidare)* to entrust; *(esortare)*: **~ a qn di non fare** to tell o warn sb not to do; **raccoman'darsi** *vt (anche: lettera raccomandata)* recorded-delivery letter

raccon'tare *vt*: **~ (a qn)** *(dire)* to tell (sb); *(narrare)* to relate (to sb), tell (sb) about; **rac'conto** *sm* telling *no pl*, relating *no pl*; *(fatto raccontato)* story, tale; **racconti per bambini** children's stories

rac'cordo *sm (Tecn: giunto)* connection, joint; *(Aut)*: **raccordo anulare** *(Aut)* ring road (BRIT), beltway (US); **raccordo autostradale** slip road (BRIT), entrance *(o exit)* ramp (US); **raccordo ferroviario** siding; **raccordo stradale** link road

racimo'lare [ratʃimo'lare] *vt (fig)* to scrape together, glean

'**rada** *sf (natural)* harbour

'**radar** *sm* radar

raddoppi'are *vt, vi* to double

raddriz'zare [raddrit'tsare] *vt* to straighten; *(fig: correggere)* to put straight, correct

'**radere** *vt (barba)* to shave off; *(mento)* to shave; *(fig: rasentare)* to graze; to skim; **radersi** *vpr* to shave (o.s.); **~ al suolo** to raze to the ground

radi'are *vt* to strike off

radia'tore *sm* radiator

radiazi'one [radjat'tsjone] *sf (Fisica)* radiation; *(cancellazione)* striking off

radi'cale *ag* radical ▸ *sm (Ling)* root

ra'dicchio [ra'dikkjo] *sm* chicory

ra'dice [ra'ditʃe] sf root

'radio sf inv radio ▸ sm (Chim) radium;
radioat'tivo, -a ag radioactive;
radio'cronaca, -che sf radio
commentary; **radiogra'fia** sf
radiography; (foto) X-ray photograph

radi'oso, -a ag radiant

radios'veglia [radjoz'veʎʎa] sf radio
alarm

'rado, -a ag (capelli) sparse, thin;
(visite) infrequent; di ~ rarely

radu'nare vt to gather, assemble;
radunarsi vpr to gather, assemble

ra'dura sf clearing

raf'fermo, -a ag stale

'raffica, -che sf (Meteor) gust (of
wind); (di colpi: scarica) burst of gunfire

raffigu'rare vt to represent

raffi'nato, -a ag refined

raffor'zare [raffor'tsare] vt to
reinforce

raffredda'mento sm cooling

raffred'dare vt to cool; (fig) to
dampen, have a cooling effect on;
raffreddarsi vpr to grow cool o cold;
(prendere un raffreddore) to catch a cold;
(fig) to cool (off)

raffred'dato, -a ag (Med): essere ~ to
have a cold

raffred'dore sm (Med) cold

raf'fronto sm comparison

'rafia sf (fibra) raffia

rafting ['rafting] sm white-water
rafting

ra'gazza [ra'gattsa] sf girl; (fam:
fidanzato) girlfriend; **nome da ~**
maiden name; **ragazza madre**
unmarried mother

ra'gazzo [ra'gattso] sm boy; (fam:
fidanzato) boyfriend; **ragazzi** smpl
(figli) kids; **ciao ragazzi!** (gruppo)
hi guys!

raggi'ante [rad'dʒante] ag radiant,
shining

'raggio ['raddʒo] sm (di sole ecc) ray;

(Mat, distanza) radius; (di ruota ecc)
spoke; **raggio d'azione** range; **raggi
X** X-rays

raggi'rare [raddʒi'rare] vt to take
in, trick

raggi'ungere [rad'dʒundʒere] vt to
reach; (persona: riprendere) to catch
up (with); (bersaglio) to hit; (fig: meta)
to achieve

raggomito'larsi vpr to curl up

raggranel'lare vt to scrape together

raggrup'pare vt to group (together)

ragiona'mento [radʒona'mento]
sm reasoning no pl; arguing no pl;
argument

ragio'nare [radʒo'nare] vi to reason; ~
di (discorrere) to talk about

ragi'one [ra'dʒone] sf reason;
(dimostrazione, prova) argument,
reason; (diritto) right; aver ~ to be
right; aver ~ di qn to get the better
of sb; dare ~ a qn to agree with sb;
to prove sb right; perdere la ~ to
become insane; (fig) to take leave of
one's senses; in ~ di at the rate of; to
the amount of; according to; a o con
~ rightly, justly; a ragion veduta after
due consideration; **ragione sociale**
(Comm) corporate name

ragione'ria [radʒone'ria] sf
accountancy; accounts department

ragio'nevole [radʒo'nevole] ag
reasonable

ragioni'ere, -a [radʒo'njɛre] sm/f
accountant

ragli'are [raʎ'ʎare] vi to bray

ragna'tela [raɲɲa'tela] sf cobweb,
spider's web

'ragno ['raɲɲo] sm spider

ragù sm inv (Cuc) meat sauce; stew

RAI-TV [raiti'vu] sigla f = Radio
televisione italiana

ralle'grare vt to cheer up; **rallegrarsi**
vpr to cheer up; (provare allegrezza)
to rejoice; **rallegrarsi con qn** to

congratulate sb

rallen'tare vt to slow down; (fig) to lessen, slacken ▶ vi to slow down

rallenta'tore sm (Cinema) slow-motion camera; **al ~** (anche fig) in slow motion

raman'zina [raman'dzina] sf lecture, telling-off

'rame sm (Chim) copper

rammari'carsi vpr **~ (di)** (rincrescersi) to be sorry (about), regret; (lamentarsi) to complain (about)

rammen'dare vt to mend; (calza) to darn

'ramo sm branch

ramo'scello [ramoʃ'ʃello] sm twig

'rampa sf flight (of stairs); **rampa di lancio** launching pad

rampi'cante ag (Bot) climbing

'rana sf frog

'rancido, -a ['rantʃido] ag rancid

ran'core sm rancour, resentment

ran'dagio, -a, -gi, -gie o ge [ran'dadʒo] ag (gatto, cane) stray

ran'dello sm club, cudgel

'rango, -ghi sm (condizione sociale, Mil, riga) rank

rannicchi'arsi [rannik'kjarsi] vpr to crouch, huddle

rannuvo'larsi vpr to cloud over, become overcast

'rapa sf (Bot) turnip

ra'pace [ra'patʃe] ag (animale) predatory; (fig) rapacious, grasping ▶ sm bird of prey

ra'pare vt (capelli) to crop, cut very short

rapida'mente av quickly, rapidly

rapidità sf speed

'rapido, -a ag fast; (esame, occhiata) quick, rapid ▶ sm (Ferr) express (train)

rapi'mento sm kidnapping; (fig) rapture

ra'pina sf robbery; **rapina in banca** bank robbery; **rapina a mano**

armata armed robbery; **rapi'nare** vt to rob; **rapina'tore, -'trice** sm/f robber

ra'pire vt (cose) to steal; (persone) to kidnap; (fig) to enrapture, delight; **rapi'tore, -'trice** sm/f kidnapper

rap'porto sm (resoconto) report; (legame) relationship; (Mat, Tecn) ratio; **rapporti sessuali** sexual intercourse sg

rappre'saglia [rappre'saʎʎa] sf reprisal, retaliation

rappresen'tante sm/f representative

rappresen'tare vt to represent; (Teatro) to perform; **rappresentazi'one** sf representation; performing no pl; (spettacolo) performance

rara'mente av seldom, rarely

rare'fatto, -a ag rarefied

'raro, -a ag rare

ra'sare vt (barba ecc) to shave off; (siepi, erba) to trim, cut; **rasarsi** vpr to shave (o.s.)

raschi'are [ras'kjare] vt (vernice) to scrape off; (macchia, fango) to scrape off ▶ vi to clear one's throat

ra'sente prep **~ (a)** close to, very near

'raso, -a pp di **radere** ▶ ag (barba) shaved; (capelli) cropped; (con misure di capacità) level; (pieno: bicchiere) full to the brim ▶ sm (tessuto) satin; **un cucchiaio ~** a level spoonful; **raso terra** close to the ground

ra'soio sm razor; **rasoio elettrico** electric shaver o razor

ras'segna [ras'seɲɲa] sf (Mil) inspection, review; (esame) inspection; (resoconto) review, survey; (pubblicazione letteraria ecc) review; (mostra) exhibition, show; **passare in ~** (Mil, fig) to review

rassegnarsi vpr (accettare): **~ (a qc/a fare)** to resign o.s. (to sth/to doing)

rassicu'rare vt to reassure

rasso'dare vt to harden, stiffen; **rassodarsi** vpr to harden, to strengthen

rassomigli'anza [rassomiʎ'ʎantsa] sf resemblance

rassomigli'are [rassomiʎ'ʎare] vi ~ a to resemble, look like

rastrel'lare vt to rake; (fig: perlustrare) to comb

ras'trello sm rake

'rata sf (quota) instalment; **pagare a rate** to pay by instalments o on hire purchase (BRIT)

ratifi'care vt (Dir) to ratify

'ratto sm (Dir) abduction; (Zool) rat

rattop'pare vt to patch

rattris'tare vt to sadden; **rattristarsi** vpr to become sad

'rauco, -a, -chi, -che ag hoarse

rava'nello sm radish

ravi'oli smpl ravioli sg

ravvi'vare vt to revive; (fig) to brighten up, enliven

razio'nale [rattsjo'nale] ag rational

razio'nare [rattsjo'nare] vt to ration

razi'one [rat'tsjone] sf ration; (porzione) portion, share

'razza ['rattsa] sf race; (Zool) breed; (discendenza, stirpe) stock, race; (sorta) sort, kind

razzi'ale [rat'tsjale] ag racial

raz'zismo [rat'tsizmo] sm racism, racialism

raz'zista, -i, -e [rat'tsista] ag, sm/f racist, racialist

'razzo ['raddzo] sm rocket

R.C. sigla m (= partito della Rifondazione Comunista) left-wing Italian political party

re sm inv king; (Mus) D; (: solfeggiando) re

rea'gire [rea'dʒire] vi to react

re'ale ag real; (di, da re) royal ▸ sm il ~ reality

realiz'zare [realid'dzare] vt (progetto ecc) to realize, carry out; (sogno, desiderio) to realize, fulfil; (scopo) to achieve; (Comm: titoli ecc) to realize; (Calcio ecc) to score; **realizzarsi** vpr to be realized

real'mente av really, actually

realtà sf inv reality

re'ato sm offence

reat'tore sm (Fisica) reactor; (Aer: aereo) jet; (: motore) jet engine

reazio'nario, -a [reattsjo'narjo] ag (Pol) reactionary

reazi'one [reat'tsjone] sf reaction

'rebus sm inv rebus; (fig) puzzle; enigma

recapi'tare vt to deliver

re'capito sm (indirizzo) address; (consegna) delivery; **recapito a domicilio** home delivery (service); **recapito telefonico** phone number

re'cedere [re'tʃɛdere] vi to withdraw

recensi'one [retʃen'sjone] sf review

re'cente [re'tʃɛnte] ag recent; **di ~** recently; **recente'mente** av recently

re'cidere [re'tʃidere] vt to cut off, chop off

recin'tare [retʃin'tare] vt to enclose, fence off

re'cinto [re'tʃinto] sm enclosure; (ciò che recinge) fence; surrounding wall

recipi'ente [retʃi'pjɛnte] sm container

re'ciproco, -a, -ci, -che [re'tʃiproko] ag reciprocal

'recita ['rɛtʃita] sf performance

reci'tare [retʃi'tare] vt (poesia, lezione) to recite; (dramma) to perform; (ruolo) to play o act (the part of)

recla'mare vi to complain ▸ vt (richiedere) to demand

re'clamo sm complaint

recli'nabile ag (sedile) reclining

reclusi'one sf (Dir) imprisonment

re'cluta sf recruit

re'condito, -a ag secluded; (fig) secret, hidden

'record ag inv record cpd ▸ sm inv record; **in tempo ~, a tempo di ~** in record time; **detenere il ~ di** to hold the record for; **record mondiale** world record

recriminazi'one [rekriminat'tsjone] sf recrimination

recupe'rare vt (rientrare in possesso di) to recover, get back; (tempo perduto) to make up for; (Naut) to salvage; (: naufraghi) to rescue; (delinquente) to rehabilitate; **~ lo svantaggio** (Sport) to close the gap

redargu'ire vt to rebuke

re'dassi ecc vb vedi **redigere**

reddi'tizio, -a [reddi'tittsjo] ag profitable

'reddito sm income; (dello Stato) revenue; (di un capitale) yield

re'digere [re'didʒere] vt to write; (contratto) to draw up

redini sfpl reins

'reduce ['rɛdutʃe] ag ~ **da** returning from, back from ▸ sm/f survivor

refe'rendum sm inv referendum

refe'renze [refe'rɛntse] sfpl references

re'ferto sm medical report

rega'lare vt to give (as a present), make a present of

re'galo sm gift, present

re'gata sf regatta

'reggere ['rɛddʒere] vt (tenere) to hold; (sostenere) to support, bear, hold up; (portare) to carry, bear; (resistere) to withstand; (dirigere: impresa) to manage, run; (governare) to rule, govern; (Ling) to take, be followed by ▸ vi (resistere): **~ a** to stand up to, hold out against; (sopportare): **~ a** to stand; (durare) to last; (fig: teoria ecc) to hold water; **reggersi** vpr (stare ritto) to stand

'reggia, -ge ['rɛddʒa] sf royal palace

reggi'calze [reddʒi'kaltse] sm inv suspender belt

reggi'mento [reddʒi'mento] sm (Mil) regiment

reggi'seno [reddʒi'seno] sm bra

re'gia, -'gie [re'dʒia] sf (TV, Cinema ecc) direction

re'gime [re'dʒime] sm (Pol) regime; (Dir: aureo, patrimoniale ecc) system; (Med) diet; (Tecn) (engine) speed

re'gina [re'dʒina] sf queen

regio'nale [redʒo'nale] ag regional ▸ sm local train (stopping frequently)

regi'one [re'dʒone] sf region; (territorio) region, district, area

re'gista, -i, -e [re'dʒista] sm/f (TV, Cinema ecc) director

regis'trare [redʒis'trare] vt (Amm) to register; (Comm) to enter; (notare) to note, take note of; (canzone, conversazione: strumento di misura) to record; (mettere a punto) to adjust, regulate; (bagagli) to check in; **registra'tore** sm (strumento) recorder, register; (magnetofono) tape recorder; **registratore di cassa** cash register; **registratore a cassette** cassette recorder

re'gistro [re'dʒistro] sm (libro, Mus, Tech) register; ledger; logbook; (Dir) registry

re'gnare [reɲ'nare] vi to reign, rule

'regno [reɲɲo] sm kingdom; (periodo) reign; (fig) realm; **il R~ Unito** the United Kingdom; **regno animale/ vegetale** animal/vegetable kingdom

'regola sf rule; **a ~ d'arte** duly; perfectly; **in ~** in order

rego'labile ag adjustable

regola'mento sm (complesso di norme) regulations pl; (di debito) settlement; **regolamento di conti** (fig) settling of scores

rego'lare ag regular; (in regola: domanda) in order, lawful ▸ vt to regulate, control; (apparecchio) to adjust, regulate; (questione, conto, *debito*) to settle; **regolarsi** *vpr* (*moderarsi*): **regolarsi nel bere/nello spendere** to control one's drinking/ spending; (*comportarsi*) to behave, act

rela'tivo, -a *ag* relative

relazi'one [relat'tsjone] *sf* (*fra cose, persone*) relation(ship); (*resoconto*) report, account

rele'gare *vt* to banish; (*fig*) to relegate

religi'one [reli'dʒone] *sf* religion

re'liquia *sf* relic

re'litto *sm* wreck; (*fig*) down-and-out

re'mare *vi* to row

remini'scenze [reminif'fentse] *sfpl* reminiscences

remis'sivo, -a *ag* submissive, compliant

'remo *sm* oar

re'moto, -a *ag* remote

'rendere *vt* (*ridare*) to return, give back; (: *saluto ecc*) to return; (*produrre*) to yield, bring in; (*esprimere, tradurre*) to render; **~ qc possibile** to make sth possible; **rendersi** *vpr* **rendersi utile** to make o.s. useful; **rendersi conto di qc** to realize sth; **~ qc possibile** to make sth possible; **~ grazie a qn** give thanks to sb; **~ omaggio a qn** to pay homage to sb; **~ un servizio a qn** to do sb a service; **~ una testimonianza** to give evidence; **non so se mi rendo l'idea** I don't know if I'm making myself clear

rendi'mento *sm* (*reddito*) yield; (*di manodopera, Tecn*) efficiency; (*capacità di produrre*) output; (*di studenti*) performance

'rendita *sf* (*di individuo*) private *o* unearned income; (*Comm*) revenue; **rendita annua** annuity

'rene *sm* kidney

'renna *sf* reindeer *inv*

re'parto *sm* department, section; (*Mil*) detachment

repel'lente *ag* repulsive

repen'taglio [repen'taʎʎo] *sm* **mettere a ~** to jeopardize, risk

repen'tino, -a *ag* sudden, unexpected

reper'torio *sm* (*Teatro*) repertory; (*elenco*) index, (alphabetical) list

'replica, -che *sf* repetition; reply, answer; (*obiezione*) objection; (*Teatro, Cinema*) repeat performance; (*copia*) replica

repli'care *vt* (*ripetere*) to repeat; (*rispondere*) to answer, reply

repressi'one *sf* repression

re'presso, -a *pp di* **reprimere**

re'primere *vt* to suppress, repress

re'pubblica, -che *sf* republic

reputazi'one [reputat'tsjone] *sf* reputation

requi'sire *vt* to requisition

requi'sito *sm* requirement

'resa *sf* (*l'arrendersi*) surrender; (*restituzione, rendimento*) return; **resa dei conti** rendering of accounts; (*fig*) day of reckoning

'resi *ecc vb vedi* **rendere**

resi'dente *ag* resident; **residenzi'ale** *ag* residential

re'siduo, -a *ag* residual, remaining ▶ *sm* remainder; (*Chim*) residue

'resina *sf* resin

resis'tente *ag* (*che resiste*): **~ a** resistant to; (*forte*) strong; (*duraturo*) long-lasting, durable; **~ al caldo** heat-resistant; **resis'tenza** *sf* resistance; (*di persona: fisica*) stamina, endurance; (: *mentale*) endurance, resistance

Resistenza

The **Resistenza** in Italy fought against the Nazis and the Fascists during the Second World War. Members of the **Resistenza** spanned a wide political spectrum and played a vital role in the Liberation and in the formation of the new democratic government at the end of the war.

re'sistere vi to resist; ~ **a** (assalto, tentazioni) to resist; (dolore: pianta) to withstand; (non patir danno) to be resistant to

reso'conto sm report, account

res'pingere [res'pindʒere] vt to drive back, repel; (rifiutare) to reject; (Ins: bocciare) to fail

respi'rare vi to breathe; (fig) to get one's breath; to breathe again ▶ vt to breathe (in), inhale; **respirazi'one** sf breathing; **respirazione artificiale** artificial respiration; **res'piro** sm breathing no pl; (singolo atto) breath; (fig) respite, rest; **mandare un respiro di sollievo** to give a sigh of relief

respon'sabile ag responsible ▶ sm/f person responsible; (capo) person in charge; ~ **di** responsible for; (Dir) liable for; **responsabilità** sf inv responsibility; (legale) liability

res'ponso sm answer

'ressa sf crowd, throng

'ressi ecc vb vedi **reggere**

res'tare vi (rimanere) to remain, stay; (avanzare) to be left; (diventare): ~ **orfano/cieco** to become o be left an orphan/become blind; ~ **d'accordo** to agree; **non resta più niente** there's nothing left; **restano pochi giorni** there are only a few days left

restau'rare vt to restore

res'tio, -a, -'tii, -'tie ag ~ **a** reluctant to

restitu'ire vt to return, give back; (energie, forze) to restore

'resto sm remainder, rest; (denaro) change; (Mat) remainder; **resti** smpl (di cibo) leftovers; (di città) remains; **del** ~ moreover, besides; **tenga pure il** ~ keep the change; **resti mortali** (mortal) remains

res'tringere [res'trindʒere] vt to reduce; (vestito) to take in; (stoffa) to shrink; (fig) to restrict, limit;

restringersi vpr (strada) to narrow; (stoffa) to shrink

'rete sf net; (fig) trap, snare; (di recinzione) netting; (Aut, Ferr, di spionaggio ecc) network; **segnare una ~** (Calcio) to score a goal; **la R~** the Web; **rete ferroviaria** railway network; **rete del letto** (sprung) bed base; **rete stradale** road network; **rete (televisiva)** (sistema) network; (canale) channel

reti'cente [reti'tʃɛnte] ag reticent

retico'lato sm grid; (rete) wire netting; (di filo spinato) barbed wire (fence)

'retina sf (Anat) retina

re'torico, -a, -ci, -che ag rhetorical ▶ sf rhetoric

retribu'ire vt to pay

'retro sm inv back ▶ av (dietro): **vedi ~** see over(leaf)

retro'cedere [retro'tʃɛdere] vi to withdraw ▶ vt (Calcio) to relegate; (Mil) to degrade

re'trogrado, -a ag (fig) reactionary, backward-looking

retro'marcia [retro'martʃa] sf (Aut) reverse; (: dispositivo) reverse gear

retro'scena [retro'ʃɛna] sm inv (Teatro) backstage; **i ~** (fig) the behind-the-scenes activities

retrovi'sore sm (Aut) (rear-view) mirror

'retta sf (Mat) straight line; (di convitto) charge for bed and board; (fig: ascolto): **dar ~ a** to listen to, pay attention to

rettango'lare ag rectangular

ret'tangolo, -a ag right-angled ▶ sm rectangle

ret'tifica, -che sf rectification, correction

'rettile sm reptile

retti'lineo, -a ag rectilinear

'retto, -a pp di **reggere** ▶ ag straight; (Mat): **angolo ~** right angle; (onesto) honest, upright; (giusto, esatto) correct, proper, right

ret'tore sm (Rel) rector; (di università) ≈ chancellor

reuma'tismo sm rheumatism

revisi'one sf auditing no pl; audit; servicing no pl; overhaul; review; revision; **revisione di bozze** proofreading

revi'sore sm; **revisore di bozze** proofreader; **revisore di conti** auditor

revival [ri'vaivel] sm inv revival

'revoca sf revocation

revo'care vt to revoke

re'volver sm inv revolver

ri'abbia ecc vb vedi **riavere**

riabili'tare vt to rehabilitate

rianimazi'one [rianimat'tsjone] sf (Med) resuscitation; **centro di ~** intensive care unit

ria'prire vt to reopen, open again; **riaprirsi** vpr to reopen, open again

ri'armo sm (Mil) rearmament

rias'sumere vt (riprendere) to resume; (impiegare di nuovo) to re-employ; (sintetizzare) to summarize; **rias'sunto, -a** pp di **riassumere** ▶ sm summary

riattac'care vt (attaccare di nuovo): ~ (a) (manifesto, francobollo) to stick back (on); (bottone) to sew back (on); (quadro, chiavi) to hang back up (on); ~ (il telefono o il ricevitore) to hang up (the receiver)

ria'vere vt to have again; (avere indietro) to get back; (riacquistare) to recover; **riaversi** vpr to recover

riba'dire vt (fig) to confirm

ri'balta sf flap; (Teatro: proscenio) front of the stage; (fig) limelight; **luci della ~** footlights pl

ribal'tabile ag (sedile) tip-up

ribal'tare vt, vi (anche: **ribaltarsi**) to turn over, tip over

ribas'sare vt to lower, bring down ▶ vi

to come down, fall

ri'battere vt to return, hit back; (confutare) to refute; ~ **che** to retort that

ribel'larsi vpr ~ (a) to rebel (against); **ri'belle** ag (soldati) rebel; (ragazzo) rebellious ▶ sm/f rebel

'ribes sm inv currant; **ribes nero** blackcurrant; **ribes rosso** redcurrant

ri'brezzo [ri'breddzo] sm disgust, loathing; **far ~ a** to disgust

ribut'tante ag disgusting, revolting

rica'dere vi to fall again; (scendere a terra: fig: nel peccato ecc) to fall back; (vestiti, capelli ecc) to hang (down); (riversarsi: fatiche, colpe): ~ **su** to fall on; **rica'duta** sf (Med) relapse

rica'mare vt to embroider

ricambi'are vt to change again; (contraccambiare) to repay, return; **ri'cambio** sm exchange, return; (Fisiol) metabolism

ri'camo sm embroidery

ricapito'lare vt to recapitulate, sum up

ricari'care vt (arma, macchina fotografica) to reload; (pipa) to refill; (orologio) to rewind; (batteria) to recharge

ricat'tare vt to blackmail; **ri'catto** sm blackmail

rica'vare vt (estrarre) to draw out, extract; (ottenere) to obtain, gain

ric'chezza [rik'kettsa] sf wealth; (fig) richness

'riccio, -a [ˈrittʃo] ag curly ▶ sm (Zool) hedgehog; **riccio di mare** sea urchin; **'ricciolo** sm curl

'ricco, -a, -chi, -che ag rich; (persona, paese) rich, wealthy ▶ sm/f rich man/woman; **i ricchi** the rich; ~ **di** full of; rich in

ri'cerca, -che [ri'tʃerka] sf search; (indagine) investigation, inquiry; (studio): **la ~** research; **una ~** piece of research; **ricerca di mercato** market research

ricer'care [ritʃer'kare] vt (motivi, cause) to look for, try to determine; (successo, piacere) to pursue; (onore, gloria) to seek; **ricer'cato, -a** ag (apprezzato) much sought-after; (affettato) studied, affected ▶ sm/f (Polizia) wanted man/woman

ricerca'tore, -'trice [ritʃerka'tore] sm/f (Ins) researcher

ri'cetta [ri'tʃetta] sf (Med) prescription; (Cuc) recipe; **mi può fare una ~ medica?** could you write me a prescription?

ricettazi'one [ritʃettat'tsjone] sf (Dir) receiving (stolen goods)

ri'cevere [ri'tʃevere] vt to receive; (stipendio, lettera) to get, receive; (accogliere: ospite) to welcome; (vedere: cliente, rappresentante ecc) to see; **ricevi'mento** sm receiving no pl; (festa) reception; **ricevi'tore** sm (Tecn) receiver; **rice'vuta** sf receipt; **posso avere una ricevuta, per favore?** can I have a receipt, please?; **ricevuta fiscale** receipt for tax purposes; **ricevuta di ritorno** (Posta) advice of receipt

richia'mare [rikja'mare] vt (chiamare indietro, ritelefonare) to call back; (ambasciatore, truppe) to recall; (rimproverare) to reprimand; (attirare) to attract, draw; **può ~ più tardi?** can you call back later?; **richiamarsi a** (riferirsi a) to refer to

richi'edere [ri'kjɛdere] vt to ask again for; (chiedere indietro): **~ qc** to ask for sth back; (chiedere: per sapere) to ask; (: per avere) to ask for; (Amm: documenti) to apply for; (esigere) to need, require; **richi'esta** sf (domanda) request; (Amm) application, request; (esigenza) demand, request; **a richiesta** on request

rici'clare [ritʃi'klare] vt to recycle

'ricino ['ritʃino] sm **olio di ~** castor oil

ricognizi'one [rikoɲɲit'tsjone] sf (Mil) reconnaissance; (Dir) recognition, acknowledgement

ricomin'ciare [rikomin'tʃare] vt, vi to start again, begin again

ricom'pensa sf reward **ricompen'sare** vt to reward **riconciliarsi** vpr to be reconciled **ricono'scente** ag grateful

rico'noscere [riko'noʃʃere] vt to recognize; (Dir: figlio, debito) to acknowledge; (ammettere: errore) to admit, acknowledge

rico'perto, -a pp di **ricoprire**

ricopi'are vt to copy

rico'prire vt (coprire) to cover; (occupare: carica) to hold

ricor'dare vt to remember, recall; (richiamare alla memoria): **~ qc a qn** to remind sb of sth; **ricordarsi** vpr ricordarsi (di) to remember; ricordarsi di qc/di aver fatto to remember sth/having done

ri'cordo sm memory; (regalo) keepsake, souvenir; (di viaggio) souvenir

ricor'rente ag recurrent, recurring; **ricor'renza** sf recurrence; (festività) anniversary

ri'correre vi (ripetersi) to recur; **~ a** (rivolgersi) to turn to; (: Dir) to appeal to; (servirsi di) to have recourse to

ricostitu'ente ag (Med): **cura ~** tonic

ricostru'ire vt (casa) to rebuild; (fatti) to reconstruct

ri'cotta sf soft white unsalted cheese made from sheep's milk

ricove'rare vt to give shelter to; **~ qn in ospedale** to admit sb to hospital

ri'covero sm shelter, refuge; (Mil) shelter; (Med) admission (to hospital)

ricreazi'one [rikreat'tsjone] sf

recreation, entertainment; (*Ins*) break

ri'credersi *vpr* to change one's mind

ridacchi'are [ridak'kjare] *vi* to snigger

ri'dare *vt* to return, give back

'ridere *vi* to laugh; (*deridere, beffare*): ~ **di** to laugh at, make fun of

ri'dicolo, -a *ag* ridiculous, absurd

ridimensio'nare *vt* to reorganize; (*fig*) to see in the right perspective

ri'dire *vt* to repeat; (*criticare*) to find fault with; to object to; **trova sempre qualcosa da ~** he always manages to find fault

ridon'dante *ag* redundant

ri'dotto, -a *pp di* **ridurre** ▶ *ag* (*biglietto*) reduced; (*formato*) small

ri'duco *ecc vb vedi* **ridurre**

ri'durre *vt* (*anche Chim, Mat*) to reduce; (*prezzo, spese*) to cut, reduce; (*accorciare: opera letteraria*) to abridge; (*Radio, TV*) to adapt; **ridursi** *vpr* (*diminuirsi*) to be reduced, shrink; **ridursi a** to be reduced to; **ridursi pelle e ossa** to be reduced to skin and bone; **ri'dussi** *ecc vb vedi* **ridurre**; **ridut'tore** *sm* (*Elec*) adaptor; **riduzi'one** *sf* reduction; abridgement; adaptation; **ci sono riduzioni per i bambini/gli studenti?** is there a reduction for children/students?

ri'ebbi *ecc vb vedi* **riavere**

riem'pire *vt* to fill (up); (*modulo*) to fill in o out; **riempirsi** *vpr* to fill (up); ~ **qc di** to fill sth (up) with

rien'tranza [rien'trantsa] *sf* recess; indentation

rien'trare *vi* (*entrare di nuovo*) to go (o come) back in; (*tornare*) to return; (*fare una rientranza*) to go in, curve inwards; to be indented; (*riguardare*): ~ **in** to be included among, form part of ▶

riepilo'gare *vt* to summarize ▶ *vi* to recapitulate

ri'esco *ecc vb vedi* **riuscire**

ri'fare *vt* to do again; (*ricostruire*) to make again; (*nodo*) to tie again, do up again; (*imitare*) to imitate, copy; **rifarsi** *vpr* (*risarcirsi*): **rifarsi di** to make up for; (*vendicarsi*): **rifarsi di qc su qn** to get one's own back on sb for sth; (*riferirsi*): **rifarsi a** to go back to; to follow; ~ **il letto** to make the bed; **rifarsi una vita** to make a new life for o.s.

riferi'mento *sm* reference; **in** *o* **con** ~ **a** with reference to

rife'rire *vt* (*riportare*) to report ▶ *vi* to do a report; **riferirsi** *vpr* **riferirsi a** to refer to

rifi'nire *vt* to finish off, put the finishing touches to

rifiu'tare *vt* to refuse; ~ **di fare** to refuse to do; **rifi'uto** *sm* refusal; **rifiuti** *smpl* (*spazzatura*) rubbish *sg*, refuse *sg*

rifles'sione *sf* (*Fisica, meditazione*) reflection; (*il pensare*) thought, reflection; (*osservazione*) remark

rifles'sivo, -a *ag* thoughtful, reflective; (*Ling*) reflexive

ri'flesso, -a *pp di* **riflettere** ▶ *sm* (*di luce, allo specchio*) reflection; (*Fisiol*) reflex; **di** *o* **per** ~ indirectly

riflessolo'gia [riflessolo'dʒia] *sf* reflexology

ri'flettere *vt* to reflect ▶ *vi* to think; **riflettersi** *vpr* to be reflected; ~ **su** to think over

riflet'tore *sm* reflector; (*proiettore*) floodlight; searchlight

ri'flusso *sm* flowing back; (*della marea*) ebb; **un'epoca di** ~ an era of nostalgia

ri'forma *sf* reform; **la R~** (*Rel*) the Reformation

riforma'torio *sm* (*Dir*) community home (*BRIT*), reformatory (*US*)

riforni'mento *sm* supplying, providing; restocking; **rifornimenti**

smpl (provviste) supplies, provisions

rifor'nire *vt (provvedere)*: **~ di** to supply o provide with; *(fornire di nuovo: casa ecc)* to restock; **rifornirsi** *vpr* **rifornirsi di qc** to stock up on sth

rifu'giarsi [rifu'dʒarsi] *vpr* to take refuge; **rifugi'ato, -a** *sm/f* refugee; **ri'fugio** [ri'fudʒo] *sm* refuge, shelter; *(in montagna)* shelter; **rifugio antiaereo** air-raid shelter

'riga, -ghe *sf* line; *(striscia)* stripe; *(di persone, cose)* line, row; *(regolo)* ruler; *(scriminatura)* parting; **mettersi in ~** to line up; **a riga** *(foglio)* lined; *(vestito)* striped

ri'gare *vt (foglio)* to rule ▸ *vi* **~ diritto** *(fig)* to toe the line

rigatti'ere *sm* junk dealer

righerò *ecc* [rige'rɔ] *vb vedi* **rigare**

'rigido, -a ['ridʒido] *ag* rigid, stiff; *(membra ecc: indurite)* stiff; *(Meteor)* harsh, severe; *(fig)* strict

rigogli'oso, -a [rigoʎ'ʎoso] *ag (pianta)* luxuriant; *(fig: commercio, sviluppo)* thriving

ri'gore *sm (Meteor)* harshness, rigours *pl; (fig)* severity, strictness; *(anche:* **calcio di ~**) penalty; **di ~** compulsory; **a rigor di termini** strictly speaking

riguar'dare *vt* to look at again; *(considerare)* to regard, consider; *(concernere)* to regard, concern; **riguardarsi** *vpr (aver cura di sé)* to look after o.s.

rigu'ardo *sm (attenzione)* care; *(considerazione)* regard, respect; **~ a** concerning, with regard to; **non aver riguardi nell'agire/nel parlare** to act/speak freely

rilasci'are [rilaʃ'ʃare] *vt (rimettere in libertà)* to release; *(Amm: documenti)* to issue

rilassarsi *vpr* to relax; *(fig: disciplina)* to become slack

rile'gare *vt (libro)* to bind

ri'leggere [ri'lɛddʒere] *vt* to reread, read again; *(rivedere)* to read over

ri'lento: a ~ *av* slowly

rile'vante *ag* considerable, important

rile'vare *vt (ricavare)* to find; *(notare)* to notice; *(mettere in evidenza)* to point out; *(venire a conoscere: notizia)* to learn; *(raccogliere: dati)* to gather, collect; *(Topografia)* to survey; *(Mil)* to relieve; *(Comm)* to take over

ri'lievo *sm (Arte, Geo)* relief; *(fig: rilevanza)* importance; *(Topografia)* survey; **dar ~ a** o **mettere in ~ qc** *(fig)* to bring sth out, highlight sth

rilut'tante *ag* reluctant

'rima *sf* rhyme; *(verso)* verse

riman'dare *vt* to send again; *(restituire, rinviare)* to send back, return; *(differire)*: **~ qc (a)** to postpone o put sth off (till); *(far riferimento)*: **~ qn a** to refer sb to; **essere rimandato** *(Ins)* to have to repeat one's exams

ri'mando *sm (rinvio)* return; *(dilazione)* postponement; *(riferimento)* cross-reference

rima'nente *ag* remaining ▸ *sm* rest, remainder; **i rimanenti** *(persone)* the rest of them, the others

rima'nere *vi (restare)* to remain, stay; *(avanzare)* to be left, remain; *(restare stupito)* to be amazed; *(restare, mancare)*: **rimangono poche settimane a Pasqua** there are only a few weeks left till Easter; **rimane da vedere se** it remains to be seen whether; *(diventare)*: **~ vedovo** to be left a widower; *(trovarsi)*: **~ sorpreso** to be surprised

rimangi'are [riman'dʒare] *vt* to eat again; **~si la parola, ~si una promessa** *(fig)* to go back on one's word/one's promise

ri'mango *ecc vb vedi* **rimanere**

rimargi'narsi vpr to heal

rimbal'zare [rimbal'tsare] vi to bounce back, rebound; (proiettile) to ricochet

rimbam'bito, -a ag senile, in one's dotage

rimboc'care vt (coperta) to tuck in; (maniche, pantaloni) to turn o roll up

rimbom'bare vi to resound

rimbor'sare vt to pay back, repay

rimedi'are vi ~ a to remedy ▶ vt (fam: procurarsi) to get o scrape together

ri'medio sm (medicina) medicine; (cura, fig) remedy, cure

ri'mettere vt (mettere di nuovo) to put back; (indossare di nuovo): ~ qc to put sth back on, put sth on again; (affidare) to entrust; (: decisione) to refer; (condonare) to remit; (Comm: merci) to deliver; (: denaro) to remit; (vomitare) to bring up; (perdere: anche: rimetterci) to lose; **rimettersi al bello** (tempo) to clear up; **rimettersi in salute** to get better, recover one's health

ri'misi ecc vb vedi **rimettere**

'rimmel® sm inv mascara

rimoder'nare vt to modernize

rimorchi'are [rimor'kjare] vt to tow; (fig: ragazza) to pick up

ri'morchio [ri'mɔrkjo] sm tow; (veicolo) trailer

ri'morso sm remorse

rimozi'one [rimot'tsjone] sf removal; (da un impiego) dismissal; (Psic) repression

rimpatri'are vi to return home ▶ vt to repatriate

rimpi'angere [rim'pjandʒere] vt to regret; (persona) to miss; **rimpi'anto, -a** pp di **rimpiangere** ▶ sm regret

rimpiaz'zare [rimpjat'tsare] vt to replace

rimpiccio'lire [rimpittʃo'lire] vt to make smaller ▶ vi (anche:

rimpicciolirsi) to become smaller

rimpinzarsi [rimpin'tsarsi] vpr ~ (di qc) to stuff o.s. (with sth)

rimprove'rare vt to rebuke, reprimand

rimu'overe vt to remove; (destituire) to dismiss

Rinasci'mento [rinaʃʃi'mento] sm il ~ the Renaissance

ri'nascita [ri'naʃʃita] sf rebirth, revival

rinca'rare vt to increase the price of ▶ vi to go up, become more expensive

rinca'sare vi to go home

rinchi'udere [rin'kjudere] vt to shut (o lock) up; **rinchiudersi** vpr **rinchiudersi in** to shut o.s. up in; **rinchiudersi in se stesso** to withdraw into o.s.

rin'correre vt to chase, run after; **rin'corsa** sf short run

rin'crescere [rin'kreʃʃere] vb impers **mi rincresce che/di non poter fare** I'm sorry that/I can't do, I regret that/being unable to do

rinfacci'are [rinfat'tʃare] vt (fig): ~ qc a qn to throw sth in sb's face

rinfor'zare [rinfor'tsare] vt to reinforce, strengthen ▶ vi (anche: **rinforzarsi**) to grow stronger

rinfres'care (atmosfera, temperatura) to cool (down); (abito, pareti) to freshen up ▶ vi (tempo) to grow cooler; **rinfrescarsi** vpr (ristorarsi) to refresh o.s.; (lavarsi) to freshen up; **rin'fresco, -schi** sm (festa) party; **rinfreschi** smpl refreshments

rin'fusa sf alla ~ in confusion, higgledy-piggledy

ringhi'are [rin'gjare] vi to growl, snarl

ringhi'era [rin'gjera] sf railing; (delle scale) banister(s) (pl)

ringiova'nire [rindʒova'nire] vt (vestito, acconciatura ecc): ~ qn to make sb look younger; (: vacanze ecc) to rejuvenate ▶ vi (anche: **ringiovanirsi**) to become (o look) younger

ringrazia'mento
[ringrattsja'mento] *sm* thanks *pl*

ringrazi'are [ringrat'tsjare] *vt* to
thank; **~ qn di qc** to thank sb for sth

rinne'gare *vt (fede)* to renounce;
(figlio) to disown, repudiate

rinnova'mento *sm* renewal;
(economico) revival

rinno'vare *vt* to renew; *(ripetere)* to
repeat, renew

rinoce'ronte [rinotʃe'ronte] *sm*
rhinoceros

rino'mato, -a *ag* renowned,
celebrated

rintracci'are [rintrat'tʃare] *vt* to
track down

rintro'nare *vi* to boom, boom ▶ *vt*
(assordare) to deafen; *(stordire)* to stun

rinunci'are [rinun'tʃare] *vi* **~ a** to give
up, renounce; **~ a fare qc** to give up
doing sth

rinvi'are *vt (rimandare indietro)* to
send back, return; *(differire)*: **~ qc (a)**
to postpone sth *o* put sth off *(till; to
adjourn sth (till); (fare un rimando)*: **~
qn a** to refer sb to

rin'vio, -'vii *sm (rimando)* return;
(differimento) postponement; *(: di
seduta)* adjournment; *(in un testo)*
cross-reference; **rinvio a giudizio**
(Dir) indictment

riò *ecc vb vedi* **riavere**

ri'one *sm* district, quarter

riordi'nare *vt (rimettere in ordine)* to
tidy; *(riorganizzare)* to reorganize

riorganiz'zare [riorganid'dzare] *vt*
to reorganize

ripa'gare *vt* to repay

ripa'rare *vt (proteggere)* to protect,
defend; *(correggere: male, torto)* to
make up for; *(: errore)* to put right;
(aggiustare) to repair ▶ *vi (mettere
rimedio)*: **~ a** to make up for; **ripararsi**
vpr (rifugiarsi) to take refuge *o* shelter,

dove lo posso far **~?** where can I get
this repaired?; **riparazi'one** *sf (di un
torto)* reparation; *(di guasto, scarpe)*
repairing *no pl*; repair; *(risarcimento)*
compensation

ri'paro *sm (protezione)* shelter,
protection; *(rimedio)* remedy

ripar'tire *vt (dividere)* to divide up;
(distribuire) to share out ▶ *vi* to set off
again; to leave again

ripas'sare *vi* to come (o go) back ▶ *vt
(scritto, lezione)* to go over (again)

ripen'sare *vi* to think; *(cambiare
pensiero)* to change one's mind;
(tornare col pensiero): **~ a** to recall

ripercu'otersi *vpr*: **~ su** *(fig)* to have
repercussions on

ripercussi'one *sf (fig)*: avere una
~ o delle ripercussioni su to have
repercussions on

ripes'care *vt (pesce)* to catch again;
(persona, cosa) to fish out; *(fig:
ritrovare)* to dig out

ri'petere *vt* to repeat; *(ripassare)* to
go over; **può ~ per favore?** can you
repeat that please?; **ripetizi'one**
sf repetition; *(di lezione)* revision;
ripetizioni *sfpl (Ins)* private tutoring
o coaching *sg*

ripi'ano *sm (di mobile)* shelf

ri'picca *sf* per **~** out of spite

'ripido, -a *ag* steep

ripie'gare *vt* to refold; *(piegare più
volte)* to fold up) ▶ *vi (Mil)* to retreat,
fall back; *(fig: accontentarsi)*: **~ su** to
make do with

ripi'eno, -a *ag* full; *(Cuc)* stuffed;
(: panino) filled ▶ *sm (Cuc)* stuffing

ri'pone, ri'pongo *ecc vb vedi* **riporre**

ri'porre *vt (porre al suo posto)* to put
back, replace; *(mettere via)* to put
away; *(fiducia, speranza)*: **~ qc in qn** to
place *o* put sth in sb

ripor'tare *vt (portare indietro)* to bring
(o take) back; *(riferire)* to report;

(citare) to quote; *(vittoria)* to gain; *(successo)* to have; *(Mat)* to carry; **riportarsi a** *(anche fig)* to go back to; *(riferirsi a)* to refer to; **~ danni** to suffer damage

ripo'sare vt, vi to rest; **riposarsi** vpr to rest

ri'posi ecc vb vedi **riporre**

ri'poso sm rest; *(Mil)*: **~!** at ease!; **a ~** *(in pensione)* retired; **giorno di ~** day off

ripos'tiglio [ripos'tiʎʎo] sm lumber-room

ri'prendere vt *(prigioniero, fortezza)* to recapture; *(prendere indietro)* to take back; *(ricominciare: lavoro)* to resume; *(andare a prendere)* to fetch, come back for; *(riassumere: impiegati)* to take on again, re-employ; *(rimproverare)* to tell off; *(restringere: abito)* to take in; *(Cinema)* to shoot; **riprendersi** vpr to recover; *(correggersi)* to correct o.s.; **ri'presa** sf recapture; resumption; *(economica, da malattia, emozione)* recovery; *(Aut)* acceleration no pl; *(Teatro, Cinema)* rerun; *(Cinema: presa)* shooting no pl; shot; *(Sport)* second half; *(: Pugilato)* round; **a più riprese** on several occasions, several times; **ripresa cinematografica** shot

ripristi'nare vt to restore

ripro'durre vt to reproduce; **riprodursi** vpr *(Biol)* to reproduce; *(riformarsi)* to form again

ripro'vare vt *(provare di nuovo: gen)* to try again; *(vestito)* to try on again; *(: sensazione)* to experience again ▶ vi *(tentare)*: **~ (a fare qc)** to try (to do sth); **riproverò più tardi** I'll try again later

ripudi'are vt to repudiate, disown

ripu'gnante [ripuɲ'ɲante] ag disgusting, repulsive

ri'quadro sm square; *(Archit)* panel

ri'saia sf paddy field

risa'lire vi *(ritornare in su)* to go back up; **~ a** *(ritornare con la mente)* to go back to; *(datare da)* to date back to, go back to

risal'tare vi *(fig: distinguersi)* to stand out; *(Archit)* to project, jut out

risa'puto, -a ag **è ~ che ...** everyone knows that ..., it is common knowledge that ...

risarci'mento [risartʃi'mento] sm **~ (di)** compensation (for); **risarcimento danni** damages

risar'cire [risar'tʃire] vt *(cose)* to pay compensation for; *(persona)*: **~ qn di qc** to compensate sb for sth

ri'sata sf laugh

riscalda'mento sm heating; **riscaldamento centrale** central heating

riscal'dare vt *(scaldare)* to heat; *(: mani, persona)* to warm; *(minestra)* to reheat; **riscaldarsi** vpr to warm up

ris'catto sm ransom; redemption

rischia'rare [riskja'rare] vt *(illuminare)* to light up; *(colore)* to make lighter; **rischiararsi** vpr *(tempo)* to clear up; *(cielo)* to clear; *(fig: volto)* to brighten up; **rischiararsi la voce** to clear one's throat

rischi'are [ris'kjare] vt to risk ▶ vi **~ di fare qc** to risk o run the risk of doing sth

'rischio ['riskjo] sm risk; **rischi'oso, -a** ag risky, dangerous

risci'acquare [riʃʃa'kware] vt to rinse

riscon'trare vt *(rilevare)* to find

ris'cuotere vt *(ritirare: somma)* to collect; *(: stipendio)* to draw, collect; *(assegno)* to cash; *(fig: successo ecc)* to win, earn

'rise ecc vb vedi **ridere**

risenti'mento sm resentment

risen'tire vt to hear again; *(provare)* to feel ▶ vi **~ di** to feel o (show) the effects of; **risentirsi** vpr **risentirsi di o per** to

take offence at, resent; **risen'tito, -a**
ag resentful

ri'serbo sm reserve

ri'serva sf reserve; (di caccia, pesca)
preserve; (restrizione, di indigeni)
reservation; **di ~** (provviste ecc) in
reserve

riser'vare vt (tenere in serbo) to
keep, put aside; (prenotare) to book,
reserve; **ho riservato un tavolo a
nome...** I booked a table in the name
of ...; **riser'vato, -a** ag (prenotato:
fig: persona) reserved; (confidenziale)
confidential

'risi ecc vb vedi **ridere**

risi'edere vi ~ **a o in** to reside in

'risma sf (di carta) ream; (fig) kind, sort

'riso (pl(f) **risa**) (: il ridere) sm **il ~**
laughter; (pianta) rice ▶ pp di **ridere**

riso'lino sm snigger

ri'solsi ecc vb vedi **risolvere**

ri'solto, -a pp di **risolvere**

riso'luto, -a ag determined, resolute

risoluzi'one [risolut'tsjone] sf solving
no pl; (Mat) solution; (decisione, di
schermo, immagine) resolution

ri'solvere vt (difficoltà, controversia) to
resolve; (problema) to solve; (decidere):
~ **di fare** to resolve to do; **risolversi**
vpr (decidersi): **risolversi a fare** to
make up one's mind to do; (andare a
finire): **risolversi in** to end up, turn
out; **risolversi in nulla** to come to
nothing

riso'nanza [riso'nantsa] sf
resonance; **aver vasta ~** (fig: fatto ecc)
to be known far and wide

ri'sorgere [ri'sordʒere] vi to rise
again; **risorgi'mento** sm revival;
il Risorgimento (Storia) the
Risorgimento

● **Risorgimento**
● The Risorgimento was the
● political movement which led to
● the proclamation of the Kingdom

● of Italy in 1861, and eventually to
● unification in 1871.

ri'sorsa sf expedient, resort; **risorse
umane** human resources

ri'sorsi ecc vb vedi **risorgere**

ri'sotto sm (Cuc) risotto

risparmi'are vt to save; (non uccidere)
to spare ▶ vi to save; ~ **qc a qn** to
spare sb sth

ris'parmio sm saving no pl; (denaro)
savings pl; **risparmi** smpl (denaro)
savings

rispec'chiare [rispek'kjare] vt to
reflect

rispet'tabile ag respectable

rispet'tare vt to respect; **farsi ~** to
command respect

rispet'tivo, -a ag respective

ris'petto sm respect; **rispetti** smpl
(saluti) respects, regards; ~ **a** (in
paragone a) compared to; (in relazione
a) as regards, as for

ris'pondere vi to answer, reply;
(freni) to respond; ~ **a** (domanda) to
answer, reply to; (persona) to answer;
(invito) to respond to; (provocazione:
veicolo, apparecchio) to respond to;
(corrispondere a) to correspond to;
(: speranze, bisogno) to answer; ~ **di** to
answer for; **ris'posta** sf answer, reply;
in risposta a in reply to

'rissa sf brawl

ris'tampa sf reprinting no pl; reprint

risto'rante sm restaurant; **mi può
consigliare un buon ~?** can you
recommend a good restaurant?

ris'tretto, -a pp di **restringere** ▶ ag
(racchiuso) enclosed, hemmed in;
(angusto) narrow; (limitato): ~ **(a)**
restricted o limited (to); (Cuc: brodo)
thick; (: caffè) extra strong

ristruttu'rare vt (azienda) to
reorganize; (edificio) to restore;
(appartamento) to alter; (crema,
balsamo) to repair

risucchi'are [risuk'kjare] vt to suck in

risul'tare vi (dimostrarsi) to prove (to be), turn out (to be); (riuscire): **~ vincitore** to emerge as the winner; **~ da** (provenire) to result from, be the result of; **mi risulta che ...** I understand that ...; **non mi risulta** not as far as I know; **risul'tato** sm result

risuo'nare vi (rimbombare) to resound

risurrezi'one [risurret'tsjone] sf (Rel) resurrection

risusci'tare [risuʃʃi'tare] vt to resuscitate, restore to life; (fig) to revive, bring back ▶ vi to rise (from the dead)

ris'veglio [riz'veʎʎo] sm waking up; (fig) revival

ris'volto sm (di giacca) lapel; (di pantaloni) turn-up; (di manica) cuff; (di tasca) flap; (di libro) inside flap; (fig) implication

ritagli'are [ritaʎ'ʎare] vt (tagliar via) to cut out

ritar'dare vi (persona, treno) to be late; (orologio) to be slow ▶ vt (rallentare) to slow down; (impedire) to hold up; (differire) to postpone, delay

ri'tardo sm delay; (di persona aspettata) lateness no pl; (fig: mentale) backwardness; **in ~** late; **il volo ha due ore di ~** the flight is two hours late; **scusi il ~** sorry I'm late

ri'tegno [ri'teɲɲo] sm restraint

rite'nere vt (trattenere) to hold back; (: somma) to deduct; (giudicare) to consider, believe

ri'tengo, ri'tenni ecc vb vedi **ritenere**

riterrò, ritiene ecc vb vedi **ritenere**

riti'rare vt to withdraw; (Pol: richiamare) to recall; (andare a prendere: pacco ecc) to collect, pick up; **ritirarsi** vpr to withdraw; (da un'attività) to retire; (stoffa) to shrink; (marea) to recede

'ritmo sm rhythm; (fig) rate; (: della vita) pace, tempo

'rito sm rite; **di ~** usual, customary

ritoc'care vt (disegno, fotografia) to touch up; (testo) to alter

ritor'nare vi to return, go (o come) back, to get back; (ripresentarsi) to recur; (ridiventare): **~ ricco** to become rich again ▶ vt (restituire) to return, give back; **quando ritorniamo?** when do we get back?

ritor'nello sm refrain

ri'torno sm return; **essere di ~** to be back; **avere un ~ di fiamma** (Aut) to backfire; (fig: persona) to be back in love again

ri'trarre vt (trarre indietro, via) to withdraw; (distogliere: sguardo) to turn away; (rappresentare) to portray, depict; (ricavare) to get, obtain

ritrat'tare vt (disdire) to retract, take back; (trattare nuovamente) to deal with again

ri'tratto, -a pp di **ritrarre** ▶ sm portrait

ritro'vare vt to find; (salute) to regain; (persona) to find; to meet again; **ritrovarsi** vpr (essere, capitare) to find o.s.; (raccapezzarsi) to find one's way; (con senso reciproco) to meet (again)

'ritto, -a ag (in piedi) standing, on one's feet; (levato in alto) erect, raised; (: capelli) standing on end; (posto verticalmente) upright

ritu'ale ag, sm ritual

riuni'one sf (adunanza) meeting; (riconciliazione) reunion

riu'nire vt (ricongiungere) to join (together); (riconciliare) to reunite, bring together ▶ **riunirsi** vpr (adunarsi) to meet; (tornare insieme) to be reunited

riu'scire [riuʃ'ʃire] vi (uscire di nuovo) to go out again, go back out; (aver esito: fatti, azioni) to go, turn out; (*aver successo*) to succeed, be successful; (*essere, apparire*) to be, prove; (*raggiungere il fine*) to manage, succeed; ~ **a fare qc** to manage to do o succeed in doing o be able to do sth

'riva *sf* (*di fiume*) bank; (*di lago, mare*) shore

ri'vale *sm/f* rival; **rivalità** *sf* rivalry

rivalu'tare *vt* (*Econ*) to revalue

rive'dere *vt* to see again; (*ripassare*) to revise; (*verificare*) to check

rivedrò *ecc vb vedi* **rivedere**

rive'lare *vt* to reveal; (*divulgare*) to reveal, disclose; (*dare indizio*) to reveal, show; **rivelarsi** *vpr* (*manifestarsi*) to be revealed; **rivelarsi onesto** *ecc* to prove to be honest *ecc*; **rivelazi'one** *sf* revelation

rivendi'care *vt* to claim, demand

rivendi'tore, -'trice *sm/f* retailer; **rivenditore autorizzato** (*Comm*) authorized dealer

ri'verbero *sm* (*di luce, calore*) reflection; (*di suono*) reverberation

rivesti'mento *sm* covering; coating

rives'tire *vt* to dress again; (*ricoprire*) to cover; to coat; (*fig: carica*) to hold

ri'vidi *ecc vb vedi* **rivedere**

ri'vincita [ri'vintʃita] *sf* (*Sport*) return match; (*fig*) revenge

ri'vista *sf* review; (*periodico*) magazine, review; (*Teatro*) revue; variety show

ri'volgere [ri'vɔldʒere] *vt* (*attenzione, sguardo*) to turn, direct; (*parole*) to address; **rivolgersi** *vpr* to turn round; (*fig: dirigersi per informazioni*): **rivolgersi a** to go and see, go and speak to; (: *ufficio*) to enquire at

ri'volsi *ecc vb vedi* **rivolgere**

ri'volta *sf* revolt, rebellion

rivol'tella *sf* revolver

rivoluzio'nare [rivoluttsjo'nare] *vt* to revolutionize

rivoluzio'nario, -a [rivoluttsjo'narjo] *ag*, *sm/f* revolutionary

rivoluzi'one [rivolut'tsjone] *sf* revolution

riz'zare [rit'tsare] *vt* to raise, erect; **rizzarsi** *vpr* to stand up; (*capelli*) to stand on end

'roba *sf* stuff, things *pl*; (*possessi, beni*) belongings *pl*, things *pl*, possessions *pl*; ~ **da mangiare** things *pl* to eat, food; ~ **da matti** sheer madness o lunacy

'robot *sm inv* robot

ro'busto, -a *ag* robust, sturdy; (*solido: catena*) strong

roc'chetto [rok'ketto] *sm* reel, spool

'roccia, -ce [r'ɔttʃa] *sf* rock; **fare** ~ (*Sport*) to go rock climbing

'roco, -a, chi, che *ag* hoarse

ro'daggio [ro'daddʒo] *sm* running (BRIT) o breaking (US) in; **in** ~ running (BRIT) o breaking (US) in

rodi'tore *sm* (*Zool*) rodent

rodo'dendro *sm* rhododendron

ro'gnone [roɲ'none] *sm* (*Cuc*) kidney

'rogo, -ghi *sm* (*per cadaveri*) (funeral) pyre; (*supplizio*): **il** ~ the stake

rol'lio *sm* roll(ing)

'Roma *sf* Rome

Roma'nia *sf* la ~ Romania

ro'manico, -a, -ci, -che *ag* Romanesque

ro'mano, -a *ag*, *sm/f* Roman

ro'mantico, -a, -ci, -che *ag* romantic

romanzi'ere [roman'dzjɛre] *sm* novelist

ro'manzo, -a [ro'mandzo] *ag* (*Ling*) romance *cpd* ▶ *sm* novel; **romanzo d'appendice** serial (story); **romanzo giallo/poliziesco** detective story; **romanzo rosa** romantic novel

'rombo *sm* rumble, thunder, roar; (*Mat*) rhombus; (*Zool*) turbot; brill

'rompere *vt* to break; (*fidanzamento*)

to break off ▶ vi to break; **rompersi** vpr to break; **mi rompe le scatole** (fam) he (o she) is a pain in the neck; **rompersi un braccio** to break an arm; **mi si è rotta la macchina** my car has broken down; **rompis'catole** (fam) sm/f inv pest, pain in the neck

'rondine sf (Zool) swallow

ron'zare [ron'dzare] vi to buzz, hum

ron'zio [ron'dzio] sm buzzing

'rosa sf rose ▶ ag inv, sm pink; **ro'sato, -a** ag pink, rosy ▶ sm (vino) rosé (wine)

rosicchi'are [rosik'kjare] vt to gnaw (at); (mangiucchiare) to nibble (at)

rosma'rino sm rosemary

roso'lare vt (Cuc) to brown

roso'lia sf (Med) German measles sg, rubella

ro'sone sm rosette; (vetrata) rose window

'rospo sm (Zool) toad

ros'setto sm (per labbra) lipstick

'rosso, -a ag, sm, sm/f red; **il mar R∼** the Red Sea; **rosso d'uovo** egg yolk

rosticce'ria [rostitʃeˈria] sf shop selling roast meat and other cooked food

ro'taia sf rut, track; (Ferr) rail

ro'tella sf small wheel; (di mobile) castor

roto'lare vt, vi to roll; **rotolarsi** vpr to roll (about)

'rotolo sm roll; **andare a rotoli** (fig) to go to rack and ruin

ro'tondo, -a ag round

'rotta sf (Aer, Naut) course, route; (Mil) rout; **a ∼ di collo** at breakneck speed; **essere in ∼ con qn** to be on bad terms with sb

rotta'mare vt to scrap

rottamazione [rottama'tsjone] sf (come incentivo) the scrapping of old vehicles in return for incentives

rot'tame sm fragment, scrap, broken bit; **rottami** smpl (di nave, aereo ecc) wreckage sg

'rotto, -a pp di **rompere** ▶ ag broken; (calzoni) torn, split; **per il ∼ della cuffia** by the skin of one's teeth

rot'tura sf breaking no pl; break; breaking off; (Med) fracture, break

rou'lotte [ru'lɔt] sf caravan

ro'vente ag red-hot

'rovere sm oak

ro'vescia [ro'veʃʃa] sf alla ∼ upside-down; inside-out; **oggi mi va tutto alla ∼** everything is going wrong (for me) today

rovesci'are [roveʃ'ʃare] vt (versare in giù) to pour; (: accidentalmente) to spill; (capovolgere) to turn upside down; (gettare a terra) to knock down; (: fig: governo) to overthrow; (piegare all'indietro: testa) to throw back; **rovesciarsi** vpr (sedia, macchina) to overturn; (barca) to capsize; (liquido) to spill; (fig: situazione) to be reversed

ro'vescio, -sci [ro'veʃʃo] sm other side, wrong side; (della mano) back; (di moneta) reverse; (pioggia) sudden downpour; (fig) setback; (Maglia: anche: **punto ∼**) purl (stitch); (Tennis) backhand (stroke); **a ∼** upside-down; inside-out; **capire qc a ∼** to misunderstand sth

ro'vina sf ruin; **andare in ∼** (andare a pezzi) to collapse; (fig) to go to rack and ruin; **rovine** sfpl (ruderi) ruins; **mandare in ∼** to ruin

rovi'nare vi to collapse, fall down ▶ vt (danneggiare: fig) to ruin; **rovinarsi** vpr (persona) to ruin o.s.; (oggetto, vestito) to be ruined

rovis'tare vt (casa) to ransack; (tasche) to rummage in (o through)

'rovo sm (Bot) blackberry bush, bramble bush

'rozzo, -a ['roddzo] ag rough, coarse

ru'bare vt to steal; ∼ **qc a qn** to steal sth from sb; **mi hanno rubato il portafoglio** my wallet has been stolen

rubi'netto sm tap, faucet (US)

ru'bino sm ruby

ru'brica, -ghe sf (Stampa) column; (quadernetto) index book; address book; **rubrica d'indirizzi** address book; **rubrica telefonica** list of telephone numbers

'rudere sm (rovina) ruins pl

rudimen'tale ag rudimentary, basic

rudi'menti smpl rudiments; basic principles; basic knowledge sg

ruffi'ano sm pimp

'ruga, -ghe sf wrinkle

'ruggine ['ruddʒine] sf rust

rug'gire [rud'dʒire] vi to roar

rugi'ada [ru'dʒada] sf dew

ru'goso, -a ag wrinkled

rul'lino sm (Fot) film; **vorrei un ~ da 36 pose** I'd like a 36-exposure film

'rullo sm (di tamburi) roll; (arnese cilindrico, Tip) roller; **rullo compressore** steam roller; **rullo di pellicola** roll of film

rum sm rum

ru'meno, -a ag, sm/f, sm Romanian

rumi'nare vt (Zool) to ruminate

ru'more sm un ~ a noise, a sound; **il ~** noise; **non riesco a dormire a causa del ~** I can't sleep for the noise; **rumo'roso, -a** ag noisy

Attenzione! In inglese esiste la parola *rumour*, che però significa *voce* nel senso *diceria*.

ru'olo sm (Teatro: fig) role, part; (elenco) roll, register, list; **di ~** permanent, on the permanent staff

ru'ota sf wheel; **ruota anteriore/posteriore** front/back wheel; **ruota di scorta** spare wheel

ruo'tare vt, vi to rotate

'rupe sf cliff

'ruppi ecc vb vedi **rompere**

ru'rale ag rural, country cpd

ru'scello [ruʃʃello] sm stream

'ruspa sf excavator

rus'sare vi to snore

'Russia sf la ~ Russia; **'russo, -a** ag, sm/f, sm Russian

'rustico, -a, -ci, -che ag rustic; (fig) rough, unrefined

rut'tare vi to belch; **'rutto** sm belch

'ruvido, -a ag rough, coarse

S

S. abbr (= sud) S; (= santo) St

sa vb vedi **sapere**

'sabato sm Saturday; **di ~**, **il ~** on Saturdays

'sabbia sf sand; **sabbie mobili** quicksand(s); **sabbi'oso, -a** ag sandy

'sacca, -che sf bag; (bisaccia) haversack; **sacca da viaggio** travelling bag

sacca'rina sf saccharin(e)

saccheggi'are [sakked'dʒare] vt to sack, plunder

sac'chetto [sak'ketto] sm (small) bag, (small) sack; **sacchetto di carta/di plastica** paper/plastic bag

'sacco, -chi sm bag; (per carbone ecc) sack; (Anat, Biol) sac; (tela) sacking; (saccheggio) sack(ing); (fig: grande quantità): **un ~ di** lots of, heaps of, a lot of; **sacco a pelo** sleeping bag; **sacco per i rifiuti** bin bag

sacer'dote [satʃer'dɔte] sm priest

sacrifi'care vt to sacrifice;
sacrificarsi vpr to sacrifice o.s.;
(privarsi di qc) to make sacrifices

sacri'ficio [sakri'fitʃo] sm sacrifice

'sacro, -a ag sacred

'sadico, -a, -ci, -che ag sadistic
▶ sm/f sadist

sa'etta sf arrow; (fulmine)
thunderbolt; flash of lightning

sa'fari sm inv safari

sag'gezza [sad'dʒettsa] sf wisdom

'saggio, -a, -gi, -ge ['saddʒo] ag wise
▶ sm (persona) sage; (esperimento) test;
(fig: prova) proof; (campione) sample;
(scritto) essay

Sagit'tario [sadʒit'tarjo] sm
Sagittarius

'sagoma sf (profilo) outline, profile;
(forma) form, shape; (Tecn) template;
(bersaglio) target; (fig: persona)
character

'sagra sf festival

sagres'tano sm sacristan; sexton

sagres'tia sf sacristy

Sa'hara [sa'ara] sm **il (deserto del) ~**
the Sahara (Desert)

'sai vb vedi **sapere**

'sala sf hall; (stanza) room; (Cinema:
Yyy: di proiezione) cinema; **sala
d'aspetto** waiting room; **sala
da ballo** ballroom; **sala giochi**
amusement arcade; **sala operatoria**
operating theatre; **sala da pranzo**
dining room; **sala per concerti**
concert hall

sa'lame sm salami no pl, salami
sausage

sala'moia sf (Cuc) brine

sa'lato, -a ag (sapore) salty; (Cuc)
salted, salt cpd; (fig: prezzo) steep, stiff

sal'dare vt (congiungere) to join,
bind; (parti metalliche) to solder; (: con
saldatura autogena) to weld; (conto) to
settle, pay

'saldo, -a ag (resistente, forte) strong,
firm; (fermo) firm, steady, stable; (fig)
firm, steadfast ▶ sm (svendita) sale;
(di conto) settlement; (Econ) balance;
saldi smpl (Comm) sales; **essere ~
nella propria fede** (fig) to stick to
one's guns

'sale sm salt; (fig): **ha poco ~ in zucca**
he doesn't have much sense; **sale fino**
table salt; **sale grosso** cooking salt

'salgo ecc vb vedi **salire**

'salice ['salitʃe] sm willow; **salice
piangente** weeping willow

sali'ente ag (fig) salient, main

sali'era sf salt cellar

sa'lire vi to go (o come) up; (aereo ecc)
to climb, go up; (passeggero) to get
on; (sentiero, prezzi, livello) to go up,
rise ▶ vt (scale, gradini) to go (o come)
up; **~ su** to climb (up); **~ sul treno/
sull'autobus** to board the train/on the
bus; **~ in macchina** to get into the
car; **sa'lita** sf climb, ascent; (erta) hill,
slope; **in salita** ag, av uphill

sa'liva sf saliva

'salma sf corpse

'salmo sm psalm

sal'mone sm salmon

sa'lone sm (stanza) sitting room,
lounge; (in albergo) lounge; (su nave)
lounge, saloon; (mostra) show,
exhibition; **salone di bellezza**
beauty salon

sa'lotto sm lounge, sitting room;
(mobilio) lounge suite

sal'pare vi (Naut) to set sail; (anche: ~
l'ancora) to weigh anchor

'salsa sf (Cuc) sauce; **salsa di
pomodoro** tomato sauce

sal'siccia, -ce [sal'sittʃa] sf pork
sausage

sal'tare vi to jump, leap; (esplodere) to
blow up, explode; (: valvola) to blow;
(venir via) to pop off; (non aver luogo:
corso ecc) to be cancelled ▶ vt to jump

(over), leap (over); (fig: pranzo, capitolo) to skip, miss (out); (Cuc) to sauté; **far ~** to blow up; to burst open; **~ fuori** (fig: apparire all'improvviso) to turn up

saltel'lare vi to skip; to hop

'salto sm jump; (Sport) jumping; **fare un ~** to jump, leap; **fare ~ da qn** to pop over to sb's (place); **salto in alto/ lungo** high/long jump; **salto con l'asta** pole vaulting; **salto mortale** somersault

saltu'ario, -a ag occasional, irregular

sa'lubre ag healthy, salubrious

salume'ria sf delicatessen

sa'lumi smpl salted cured meats

salu'tare ag healthy; (fig) salutary, beneficial ▸ vt (incontrandosi) to greet; (congedandosi) to say goodbye to; (Mil) to salute

sa'lute sf health; **~!** (a chi starnutisce) bless you!; (nei brindisi) cheers!; **bere alla ~ di qn** to drink (to) sb's health

sa'luto sm (gesto) wave; (parola) greeting; (Mil) salute

salva'danaio sm money box, piggy bank

salva'gente [salva'dʒɛnte] sm (Naut) lifebuoy; (cintura) life belt; (giubbotto) life jacket; (stradale) traffic island

salvaguar'dare vt to safeguard

sal'vare vt to save; (trarre da un pericolo) to rescue; (proteggere) to protect; **salvarsi** vpr to save o.s.; to escape; **salvaschermo** [salvas'kermo] sm (Inform) screen saver; **salvaslip** [salva'zlip] sm inv panty liner; **salva'taggio** sm rescue

'salve (fam) escl hi!

'salvia sf (Bot) sage

salvi'etta sf napkin; **salvietta umidificata** baby wipe

'salvo, -a ag safe, unhurt, unharmed; (fuori pericolo) safe, out of danger ▸ sm in **~** safe ▸ prep (eccetto)

except; **mettere qc in ~** to put sth in a safe place; **~ che** (a meno che) unless; (eccetto che) except (that); **~ imprevisti** barring accidents

sam'buco sm elder (tree)

'sandalo sm (Bot) sandalwood; (calzatura) sandal

'sangue sm blood; **farsi cattivo ~** to fret, get in a state; **sangue freddo** (fig) sang-froid, calm; **a ~ freddo** in cold blood; **sangui'nare** vi to bleed

sani'tà sf health; (salubrità) healthiness; **Ministero della S~** Department of Health; **sanità mentale** sanity

sani'tario, -a ag health cpd; (condizioni) sanitary ▸ sm (Amm) doctor; **sanitari** smpl (impianti) bathroom o sanitary fittings

'sanno vb vedi **sapere**

'sano, -a ag healthy; (denti, costituzione) healthy, sound; (integro) whole, unbroken; (fig: politica, consigli) sound; **~ di mente** sane; **di sana pianta** completely, entirely; **~ e salvo** safe and sound

'santo, -a ag holy; (fig) saintly; (seguito da nome proprio) saint ▸ sm/f saint; **la Santa Sede** the Holy See

santu'ario sm sanctuary

sanzi'one [san'tsjone] sf sanction; (penale, civile) sanction, penalty

sa'pere vt to know; (essere capace di): **so nuotare** I know how to swim, I can swim ▸ vi **~ di** (aver sapore) to taste of; (aver odore) to smell of ▸ sm knowledge; **far ~ qc a qn** to inform sb about sth, let sb know sth; **mi sa che non sia vero** I don't think that's true; **non lo so** I don't know; **non so l'inglese** I don't speak English; **sa dove posso...?** do you know where I can ...?

sa'pone sm soap; **sapone da bucato** washing soap

sa'pore sm taste, flavour; **sapo'rito, -a** ag tasty

sappi'amo vb vedi **sapere**

saprò ecc vb vedi **sapere**

sarà ecc vb vedi **essere**

saraci'nesca [sarat∫i'neska] sf (serranda) rolling shutter

sar'castico, -a, ci, che ag sarcastic

Sar'degna [sar'deɲɲa] sf **la** ~ Sardinia

sar'dina sf sardine

sa'rei ecc vb vedi **essere**

SARS sigla f (Med: = severe acute respiratory syndrome) SARS

'sarta sf vedi **sarto**

'sarto, -a sm/f tailor/dressmaker

'sasso sm stone; (ciottolo) pebble; (masso) rock

sas'sofono sm saxophone

sas'soso, -a ag stony; pebbly

'Satana sm Satan

sa'tellite sm, ag satellite

satira sf satire

'sauna sf sauna

sazi'are [sat'tsjare] vt to satisfy, satiate; **saziarsi** vpr **saziarsi (di)** to eat one's fill (of); (fig) **saziarsi di** to grow tired o weary of

'sazio, -a ['sattsjo] ag ~ **(di)** sated (with), full (of); (fig: stufo) fed up (with), sick (of); **sono** ~ I'm full (up)

sba'dato, -a ag careless, inattentive

sbadigli'are [zbadiʎ'ʎare] vi to yawn; **sba'diglio** sm yawn

sbagli'are [zbaʎ'ʎare] vt to make a mistake in, get wrong ▶ vi to make a mistake, be mistaken, be wrong; (operare in modo non giusto) to err; **sbagliarsi** vpr to make a mistake, be mistaken, be wrong; ~ **strada/la mira** to take the wrong road/miss one's aim

sbagli'ato, -a [zbaʎ'ʎato] ag (gen) wrong; (compito) full of mistakes; (conclusione) erroneous

'sbaglio sm mistake, error; (morale)

error; **fare uno** ~ to make a mistake

sbalor'dire vt to stun, amaze ▶ vi to be stunned, be amazed

sbal'zare [zbal'tsare] vt to throw, hurl ▶ vi (balzare) to bounce; (saltare) to leap, bound

sban'dare vi (Naut) to list; (Aer) to bank; (Aut) to skid

sba'raglio [zba'raʎʎo] sm rout; defeat; **gettarsi allo** ~ to risk everything

sbaraz'zarsi [zbarat'tsarsi] vpr ~ **di** to get rid of, rid o.s. of

sbar'care vt (passeggeri) to disembark; (merci) to unload ▶ vi to disembark

'sbarra sf bar; (di passaggio a livello) barrier; (Dir): **presentarsi alla** ~ to appear before the court

sbar'rare vt (strada ecc) to block, bar; (assegno) to cross; ~ **il passo** to bar the way; ~ **gli occhi** to open one's eyes wide

'sbattere vt (porta) to slam, bang; (tappeti, ali, Cuc) to beat; (urtare) to knock, hit ▶ vi (porta, finestra) to bang; (agitarsi: ali, vele ecc) to flap; **me ne sbatto!** (fam) I don't give a damn!

sba'vare vi to dribble; (colore) to smear, smudge

'sberla sf slap

sbia'dire vi, vt to fade; **sbia'dito, -a** ag faded; (fig) colourless, dull

sbian'care vt to whiten; (tessuto) to bleach ▶ vi (impallidire) to grow pale o white

sbirci'ata [zbir't∫ata] sf **dare una** ~ a **qc** to glance at sth, have a look at sth

sblocc'are vt to unblock, free; (freno) to release; (prezzi, affitti) to decontrol; **sbloccarsi** vpr (gen) to become unblocked; (passaggio, strada) to clear, become unblocked

sboc'care vi ~ **in** (fiume) to flow into; (strada) to lead into; (persona) to come (out) into; (fig: concludersi) to end (up) in

sboc'cato, -a ag (persona) foul-mouthed; (linguaggio) foul

sbocci'are [zbot'tʃare] vi (fiore) to bloom, open (out)

sbol'lire vi (fig) to cool down, calm down

'sbornia (fam) sf **prendersi una ~** to get plastered

sbor'sare vt (denaro) to pay out

sbot'tare vi **~ in una risata/per la collera** to burst out laughing/explode with anger

sbotto'nare vt to unbutton, undo

sbrai'tare vt to yell, bawl

sbra'nare vt to tear to pieces

sbricio'lare [zbritʃo'lare] vt to crumble; **sbriciolarsi** vpr to crumble

sbri'gare vt to deal with; **sbrigarsi** vpr to hurry (up)

'sbronza ['zbrontsa] (fam) sf (ubriaco): **prendersi una ~** to get plastered

sbron'zarsi [zbron'tsarsi] vpr (fam) to get sozzled

'sbronzo, -a ['zbrontso] (fam) ag plastered

sbruf'fone, -a sm/f boaster

sbu'care vi to come out, emerge; (improvvisamente) to pop out (o up)

sbucci'are [zbut'tʃare] vt (arancia, patata) to peel; (piselli) to shell; **sbucciarsi un ginocchio** to graze one's knee

sbucherò ecc [zbuke'rɔ] vb vedi **sbucare**

sbuf'fare vi (persona, cavallo) to snort; (animare) to puff, pant; (treno) to puff

sca'broso, -a ag (fig: difficile) difficult, thorny; (: imbarazzante) embarrassing; (: sconcio) indecent

scacchi smpl (gioco) chess sg; **a ~** (tessuto) check(ed)

scacchi'era [skak'kjera] sf chessboard

scacci'are [skat'tʃare] vt to chase away o out, drive away o out

'scaddi ecc vb vedi **scadere**

sca'dente ag shoddy, of poor quality

sca'denza [ska'dentsa] sf (di cambiale, contratto) maturity; (di passaporto) expiry date; **a breve/lunga ~** short-/long-term; **data di ~** expiry date

sca'dere vi (contratto ecc) to expire; (debito) to fall due; (valore, forze, peso) to decline, go down

sca'fandro sm (di palombaro) diving suit; (di astronauta) space-suit

scaf'fale sm shelf; (mobile) set of shelves

'scafo sm (Naut, Aer) hull

scagio'nare [skadʒo'nare] vt to exonerate, free from blame

'scaglia ['skaʎʎa] sf (Zool) scale; (scheggia) chip, flake

scagli'are [skaʎ'ʎare] vt (lanciare: anche fig) to hurl, fling; **scagliarsi** (anche: vr): **scagliarsi su o contro** to hurl o fling o.s. at; (fig) to rail at

'scala sf (a gradini ecc) staircase, stairs pl; (a pioli, di corda) ladder; (Mus, Geo, di colori, valori, fig) scale; **scale** sfpl (scalinata) stairs; **su vasta ~/ ridotta** on a large/small scale; **~ mobile (dei salari)** index-linked pay scale; **scala a libretto** stepladder; **scala mobile** escalator; (Econ) sliding scale

- **Scala**

  Milan's world-famous **la Scala** theatre first opened its doors in 1778 with a performance of Salieri's opera, "L'Europa riconosciuta". It suffered serious damage in the bombing of Milan in 1943 and reopened in 1946 with a concert conducted byToscanini. It also has a famous classical dance school.

sca'lare vt (Alpinismo, muro) to climb, scale; (debito) to scale down, reduce

scalda'bagno [skalda'baɲɲo] sm water-heater

scal'dare vt to heat; **scaldarsi** vpr to

warm up, heat up; (*al fuoco, al sole*) to warm o.s.; (*fig*) to get excited

scal'fire *vt* to scratch

scali'nata *sf* staircase

sca'lino *sm* (*anche fig*) step; (*di scala a pioli*) rung

'scalo *sm* (*Naut*) slipway; (: *porto d'approdo*) port of call; (*Aer*) stopover; **fare ~ (a)** (*Naut*) to call (at), put in (at); (*Aer*) to land (at), make a stop (at); **scalo merci** (*Ferr*) goods (*BRIT*) o freight yard

scalop'pina *sf* (*Cuc*) escalope

scal'pello *sm* chisel

scal'pore *sm* noise, row; **far ~** (*notizia*) to cause a sensation o a stir

scaltro, -a *ag* cunning, shrewd

'scalzo, -a ['skaltso] *ag* barefoot

scambi'are *vt* to exchange; (*confondere*): **~ qn/qc per** to take o mistake sb/sth for; **mi hanno scambiato il cappello** they've given me the wrong hat; **scambiarsi** *vpr* (*auguri, confidenze, visite*) to exchange; **~ qn/qc per** (*confondere*) to mistake sth/sb for

'scambio *sm* exchange; (*Ferr*) points *pl*; **fare (uno) ~** to make a swap

scampa'gnata [skampaɲ'ɲata] *sf* trip to the country

scam'pare *vt* (*salvare*) to rescue, save; (*evitare: morte, prigione*) to escape ▶ *vi* **~ a** (*pericolo*) to survive (sth), escape (sth); **scamparla bella** to have a narrow escape

'scampo *sm* (*salvezza*) escape; (*Zool*) prawn; **cercare ~ nella fuga** to seek safety in flight

'scampolo *sm* remnant

scanala'tura *sf* (*incavo*) channel, groove

scandagli'are [skandaʎ'ʎare] *vt* (*Naut*) to sound; (*fig*) to sound out; to probe

scandaliz'zare [skandalid'dzare] *vt*

to shock, scandalize; **scandalizzarsi** *vpr* to be shocked

'scandalo *sm* scandal

Scandi'navia *sf* la ~ Scandinavia; **scandi'navo, -a** *ag*, *sm/f* Scandinavian

scanner ['skanner] *sm inv* (*Inform*) scanner

scansafa'tiche [skansafa'tike] *sm/f inv* idler, loafer

scan'sare *vt* (*rimuovere*) to move (aside), shift; (*schivare: schiaffo*) to dodge; (*sfuggire*) to avoid; **scansarsi** *vpr* to move aside

scan'sia *sf* shelves *pl*; (*per libri*) bookcase

'scanso *sm* **a ~ di** in order to avoid, as a precaution against

scanti'nato *sm* basement

scapacci'one [skapat'tʃone] *sm* clout

scapes'trato, -a *ag* dissolute

'scapola *sf* shoulder blade

'scapolo *sm* bachelor

scappa'mento *sm* (*Aut*) exhaust

scap'pare *vi* (*fuggire*) to escape; (*andare via in fretta*) to rush off; **lasciarsi ~ un'occasione** to let an opportunity go by; **~ di prigione** to escape from prison; **~ di mano** (*oggetto*) to slip out of one's hands; **~ di mente a qn** to slip sb's mind; **mi scappò detto** I let it slip; **scappa'toia** *sf* way out

scara'beo *sm* beetle

scarabocchi'are [skarabok'kjare] *vt* to scribble, scrawl; **scara'bocchio** *sm* scribble, scrawl

scara'faggio [skara'faddʒo] *sm* cockroach

scaraman'zia [skaraman'tsia] *sf* **per ~** for luck

scaraven'tare *vt* to fling, hurl; **scaraventarsi** *vpr* to fling o.s.

scarce'rare [skartʃe'rare] *vt* to release (from prison)

scardi'nare vt ~ **una porta** to take a door off its hinges

scari'care vt (merci, camion ecc) to unload; (passeggeri) to set down, put off; (arma) to unload; (: sparare, Elettr) to discharge; (corso d'acqua) to empty, pour; (fig: liberare da un peso) to unburden, relieve; (da Internet) to download; **scaricarsi** vpr (orologio) to run down; (batteria, accumulatore) to go flat o dead; (fig: rilassarsi) to unwind; (: sfogarsi) to let off steam

'scarico, -a, -chi, -che ag unloaded; (orologio) run down; (accumulatore) dead, flat ▶ sm (di merci, materiali) unloading; (di immondizie) dumping, tipping (BRIT); (Tecn: deflusso) draining; (: dispositivo) drain; (Aut) exhaust

scarlat'tina sf scarlet fever

scar'latto, -a ag scarlet

'scarpa sf shoe; **scarpe da ginnastica/tennis** gym/tennis shoes

scar'pata sf escarpment

scarpi'era sf shoe rack

scar'pone sm boot; **scarponi da montagna** climbing boots; **scarponi da sci** ski-boots

scarseggi'are [skarsed'dʒare] vi to be scarce; ~ **di** to be short of, lack

'scarso, -a ag (insufficiente) insufficient, meagre; (povero: annata) poor, lean; (Ins: voto) poor; ~ **di** lacking in; **3 chili scarsi** just under 3 kilos, barely 3 kilos

scar'tare vt (pacco) to unwrap; (idea) to reject; (Mil) to declare unfit for military service; (carte da gioco) to discard; (Calcio) to dodge (past) ▶ vi to swerve

'scarto sm (cosa scartata: anche Comm) reject; (di veicolo) swerve; (differenza) gap, difference

scassi'nare vt to break, force

scate'nare vt (fig) to incite, stir up; **scatenarsi** vpr (temporale) to break; (rivolta) to break out; (persona: infuriarsi) to rage

'scatola sf box; (di latta) tin (BRIT), can; **cibi in ~** tinned (BRIT) o canned foods; **scatola cranica** cranium; **scato'lone** sm (big) box

scat'tare vt (fotografia) to take ▶ vi (congegno, molla ecc) to be released; (balzare) to spring up; (Sport) to put on a spurt; (fig: per l'ira) to fly into a rage; ~ **in piedi** to spring to one's feet

'scatto sm (dispositivo) release; (: di arma da fuoco) trigger mechanism; (rumore) click; (balzo) jump, start; (Sport) spurt; (fig: di ira ecc) fit; (: di stipendio) increment; **di ~** suddenly

scaval'care vt (ostacolo) to pass (o climb) over; (fig) to get ahead of, overtake

sca'vare vt (terreno) to dig; (legno) to hollow out; (pozzo, galleria) to bore; (città sepolta ecc) to excavate

'scavo sm excavating no pl; excavation

'scegliere ['ʃeʎʎere] vt to choose, select

sce'icco, -chi [ʃe'ikko] sm sheik

'scelgo ecc ['ʃelgo] vb vedi **scegliere**

scel'lino [ʃel'lino] sm shilling

'scelta ['ʃelta] sf choice; selection; **di prima** ~ top grade o quality; **frutta o formaggi a** ~ choice of fruit or cheese

'scelto, -a ['ʃelto] pp di **scegliere** ▶ ag (gruppo) carefully selected; (frutta, verdura) choice, top quality; (Mil: specializzato) crack cpd, highly skilled

'scemo, -a ['ʃemo] ag stupid, silly

'scena ['ʃena] sf (gen) scene; (palcoscenico) stage; **le scene** (fig: teatro) the stage; **fare una** ~ to make a scene; **andare in** ~ to be staged o put on o performed; **mettere in** ~ to stage

sce'nario [ʃe'narjo] sm scenery; (di film) scenario

sce'nata [ʃeˈnata] sf row, scene

'scendere [ˈʃendere] vi to go o come) down; (strada, sole) to go down; (notte) to fall; (passeggero: fermarsi) to get out, alight; (fig: temperatura, prezzi) to go o come down, fall, drop ▶ vt (scale, pendio) to go o come) down; ~ **dalle scale** to go o come) down the stairs; ~ **dal treno** to get off o out of the train; **dove devo** ~? where do I get off?; ~ **dalla macchina** to get out of the car; ~ **da cavallo** to dismount, get off one's horse

sceneggi'ato [ʃenedˈdʒato] sm television drama

'scettico, -a, -ci, -che [ˈʃɛttiko] ag sceptical

'scettro [ˈʃɛttro] sm sceptre

'scheda [ˈskɛda] sf (index) card; **scheda elettorale** ballot paper; **scheda ricaricabile** (Tel) top-up card; **scheda telefonica** phone card; **sche'dario** sm file; (mobile) filing cabinet

sche'dina [skeˈdina] sf ≈ pools coupon (BRIT)

'scheggia, -ge [ˈskeddʒa] sf splinter, sliver

'scheletro [ˈskɛletro] sm skeleton

'schema, -i [ˈskɛma] sm (diagramma) diagram, sketch; (progetto, abbozzo) outline, plan

'scherma [ˈskɛrma] sf fencing

scher'maglia [skerˈmaʎʎa] sf (fig) skirmish

'schermo [ˈskɛrmo] sm shield, screen; (Cinema, TV) screen

scher'nire [skerˈnire] vt to mock, sneer at

scher'zare [skerˈtsare] vi to joke

'scherzo [ˈskɛrtso] sm joke; (tiro) trick; (Mus) scherzo; **è uno** ~ (una cosa facile) it's child's play!, it's easy!; **per** ~ in jest; for a joke o a laugh; **fare un brutto** ~ **a qn** to play a nasty trick on sb

schiaccia'noci [skjattʃaˈnotʃi] sm inv nutcracker

schiacci'are [skjatˈtʃare] vt (dito) to crush; (noci) to crack; ~ **un pisolino** to have a nap; **schiacciarsi** vpr (appiattirsi) to get squashed; (frantumarsi) to get crushed

schiaffeggi'are [skjaffedˈdʒare] vt to slap

schi'affo [ˈskjaffo] sm slap

schian'tarsi vpr to break (up), shatter

schia'rire [skjaˈrire] vt to lighten, make lighter; **schiarirsi** vpr to grow lighter; (tornar sereno) to clear, brighten up; **schiarirsi la voce** to clear one's throat

schiavitù [skjaviˈtu] sf slavery

schi'avo, -a [ˈskjavo] sm/f slave

schi'ena [ˈskjɛna] sf (Anat) back; **schie'nale** sm (di sedia) back

schi'era [ˈskjɛra] sf (Mil) rank; (gruppo) group, band

schiera'mento [skjeraˈmento] sm (Mil, Sport) formation; (fig) alliance

schie'rare [skjeˈrare] vt (esercito) to line up, draw up, marshal; **schierarsi** vpr to line up; (fig): **schierarsi con o dalla parte di/contro qn** to side with/oppose sb

schifo [ˈskifo] sm disgust; **fare** ~ (essere fatto male, dare pessimi risultati) to be awful; **mi fa** ~ it makes me sick, it's disgusting; **quel libro è uno** ~ that book's rotten; **schi'foso, -a** ag disgusting, revolting; (molto scadente) rotten, lousy

schioc'care [skjokˈkare] vt (frusta) to crack; (dita) to snap; (lingua) to click; ~ **le labbra** to smack one's lips

schiudersi vpr to open

schi'uma [ˈskjuma] sf foam; (di sapone) lather; (di latte) froth; (fig: feccia) scum

schi'vare [skiˈvare] vt to dodge, avoid

'schivo, -a [ˈskivo] ag (ritroso) standoffish, reserved; (timido) shy

schiz'zare [skit'tsare] vt (spruzzare) to spurt, squirt; (sporcare) to splash, spatter; (fig: abbozzare) to sketch ▸ vi to spurt, squirt; (saltar fuori) to dart up (o off ecc)

schizzi'noso, -a [skittsi'noso] ag fussy, finicky

'schizzo ['skittso] sm (di liquido) spurt; splash, spatter; (abbozzo) sketch

sci [ʃi] sm (attrezzo) ski; (attività) skiing; **sci d'acqua** water-skiing; **sci di fondo** cross-country skiing, ski touring (US); **sci nautico** water-skiing

'scia ['ʃia] (pl scie) sf (di imbarcazione) wake; (di profumo) trail

scià [ʃa] sm inv shah

sci'abola ['ʃabola] sf sabre

scia'callo [ʃa'kallo] sm jackal

sciac'quare [ʃak'kware] vt to rinse

scia'gura [ʃa'gura] sf disaster, calamity; misfortune

scialac'quare [ʃalak'kware] vt to squander

sci'albo, -a ['ʃalbo] ag pale, dull; (fig) dull, colourless

sci'alle ['ʃalle] sm shawl

scia'luppa [ʃa'luppa] sf: **scialuppa di salvataggio** lifeboat

sci'ame ['ʃame] sm swarm

sci'are [ʃi'are] vi to ski

sci'arpa [ʃi'arpa] sf scarf; (fascia) sash

scia'tore, -'trice [ʃia'tore] sm/f skier

sci'atto, -a ['ʃatto] ag (persona) slovenly, unkempt

scien'tifico, -a, -ci, -che [ʃen'tifiko] ag scientific

sci'enza ['ʃentsa] sf science; (sapere) knowledge; **scienze** sfpl (Ins) science sg; **scienze naturali** natural sciences; **scienzi'ato, -a** sm/f scientist

'scimmia ['ʃimmja] sf monkey

scimpanzé [ʃimpan'tse] sm inv chimpanzee

scin'tilla [ʃin'tilla] sf spark; **scintil'lare** vi to spark; (acqua, occhi) to sparkle

scioc'chezza [ʃok'kettsa] sf stupidity no pl; stupid o foolish thing; **dire sciocchezze** to talk nonsense

sci'occo, -a, -chi, -che [ʃokko] ag stupid, foolish

sci'ogliere ['ʃɔʎʎere] vt (nodo) to untie; (capelli) to loosen; (persona, animale) to untie, release; (fig: persona): ~ **da** to release from; (neve) to melt; (nell'acqua: zucchero ecc) to dissolve; (fig: mistero) to solve; (porre fine a: contratto) to cancel; (: società, matrimonio) to dissolve; (: riunione) to bring to an end; **sciogliersi** vpr to loosen, come untied; (: neve) to melt; to dissolve; (assemblea ecc) to break up; ~ **i muscoli** to limber up; **scioglilingua** [ʃoʎʎi'lingwa] sm inv tongue-twister

sci'olgo ecc ['ʃɔlgo] vb vedi **sciogliere**

sci'olto, -a ['ʃɔlto] pp di **sciogliere** ▸ ag loose; (agile) agile, nimble; supple; (disinvolto) free and easy; **versi sciolti** (Poesia) blank verse

sciope'rare [ʃope'rare] vi to strike, go on strike

sci'opero ['ʃopero] sm strike; **fare ~** to strike; **sciopero bianco** work-to-rule (BRIT), slowdown (US); **sciopero selvaggio** wildcat strike; **sciopero a singhiozzo** on-off strike

scio'via [ʃio'via] sf ski lift

scip'pare [ʃip'pare] vt ~ **qn** to snatch sb's bag; **mi hanno scippato** they snatched my bag

sci'rocco [ʃi'rɔkko] sm sirocco

sci'roppo [ʃi'rɔppo] sm syrup

'scisma, -i ['ʃizma] sm (Rel) schism

scissi'one [ʃis'sjone] sf (anche fig) split, division; (Fisica) fission

sciu'pare [ʃu'pare] vt (abito, libro, appetito) to spoil, ruin; (tempo, denaro) to waste

scivo'lare [ʃivoʼlare] *vi* to slide o glide along; (*involontariamente*) to slip, slide; **'scivolo** *sm* slide; (*Tecn*) chute; **scivo'loso, -a** *ag* slippery

scle'rosi *sf* sclerosis

scoc'care *vt* (*freccia*) to shoot ▸ *vi* (*guizzare*) to shoot up; (*battere: ora*) to strike

scoccherò *ecc* [skokke'rɔ] *vb vedi* **scoccare**

scocci'are [skot'tʃare] (*fam*) *vt* to bother, annoy; **scocciarsi** *vpr* to be bothered o annoyed

sco'della *sf* bowl

scodinzo'lare [skodintso'lare] *vi* to wag its tail

scogli'era [skoʎ'ʎɛra] *sf* reef; cliff

'scoglio ['skɔʎʎo] *sm* (*al mare*) rock

scoi'attolo *sm* squirrel

scola'pasta *sm inv* colander

scolapi'atti *sm inv* drainer (*for plates*)

sco'lare *ag* età scolare = school age ▸ *vt* to drain ▸ *vi* to drip

scola'resca *sf* schoolchildren *pl*, pupils *pl*

sco'laro, -a *sm/f* pupil, schoolboy/girl

Attenzione! In inglese esiste la parola *scholar*, che però significa *studioso*.

sco'lastico, -a, -ci, -che *ag* school *cpd*; scholastic

scol'lato, -a *ag* (*vestito*) low-cut, low-necked; (*donna*) wearing a low-cut dress (*o blouse ecc*)

scolla'tura *sf* neckline

scolle'gare *vt* (*fili, apparecchi*) to disconnect

'scolo *sm* drainage

scolo'rire *vt* to fade; to discolour; **scolorirsi** *vpr* to fade; to become discoloured; (*impallidire*) to turn pale

scol'pire *vt* to carve, sculpt

scombus'solare *vt* to upset

scom'messa *sf* bet, wager

scom'mettere *vt, vi* to bet

scomo'dare *vt* to trouble, bother; to disturb; **scomodarsi** *vpr* to put o.s. out; **scomodarsi a fare** to go to the bother o trouble of doing

'scomodo, -a *ag* uncomfortable; (*sistemazione, posto*) awkward, inconvenient

scompa'rire *vi* (*sparire*) to disappear, vanish; (*fig*) to be insignificant

scomparti'mento *sm* compartment; **uno ~ per non-fumatori** a non-smoking compartment

scompigli'are [skompiʎ'ʎare] *vt* (*cassetto, capelli*) to mess up, disarrange; (*fig: piani*) to upset

scomuni'care *vt* to excommunicate

'sconcio, -a, -ci, -ce ['skontʃo] *ag* (*osceno*) indecent, obscene ▸ *sm* disgrace

scon'figgere [skon'fiddʒere] *vt* to defeat, overcome

sconfi'nare *vi* to cross the border; (*in proprietà privata*) to trespass; (*fig*): **~ da** to stray o digress from

scon'fitta *sf* defeat

scon'forto *sm* despondency

sconge'lare [skondʒe'lare] *vt* to defrost

scongiu'rare [skondʒu'rare] *vt* (*implorare*) to entreat, beseech, implore; (*eludere: pericolo*) to ward off, avert; **scongi'uro** *sm* entreaty; (*esorcismo*) exorcism; **fare gli scongiuri** to touch wood (*BRIT*), knock on wood (*US*)

scon'nesso, -a *ag* incoherent

sconosci'uto, -a [skonoʃ'ʃuto] *ag* unknown; new, strange ▸ *sm/f* stranger; unknown person

sconsigli'are [skonsiʎ'ʎare] *vt* ~ qc a qn to advise sb against sth; ~ qn dal fare qc to advise sb not to do o against doing sth

sconso'lato, -a *ag* inconsolable; desolate

scon'tare vt (Comm: detrarre) to deduct; (: debito) to pay off; (: cambiale) to discount; (pena) to serve; (colpa, errori) to pay for, suffer for

scon'tato, -a ag (previsto) foreseen, taken for granted; **dare per ~ che** to take it for granted that

scon'tento, -a ag ~ (di) dissatisfied (with) ▶ sm dissatisfaction

'sconto sm discount; **fare uno ~** to give a discount; **ci sono sconti per studenti?** are there discounts for students?

scon'trarsi vpr (treni ecc) to crash, collide; (venire ad uno scontro, fig) to clash; **~ con** to crash into, collide with

scon'trino sm ticket; (di cassa) receipt; **potrei avere lo ~ per favore?** can I have a receipt, please?

'scontro sm clash, encounter; crash, collision

scon'troso, -a ag sullen, surly; (permaloso) touchy

sconveni'ente ag unseemly, improper

scon'volgere [skon'voldʒere] vt to throw into confusion, upset; (turbare) to shake, disturb, upset; **scon'volto, -a** pp di **sconvolgere**

scooter ['skuter] sm inv scooter

'scopa sf broom; (Carte) Italian card game; **sco'pare** vt to sweep

sco'perta sf discovery

sco'perto, -a pp di **scoprire** ▶ ag uncovered; (capo) uncovered, bare; (macchina) open; (Mil) exposed, without cover; (conto) overdrawn

'scopo sm aim, purpose; **a che ~?** what for?

scoppi'are vi (spaccarsi) to burst; (esplodere) to explode; (fig) to break out; **~ in pianto o a piangere** to burst out crying; **~ dalle risa o dal ridere** to split one's sides laughing

scoppiet'tare vi to crackle

'scoppio sm explosion; (di tuono, arma ecc) crash, bang; (fig: di risa, ira) fit, outburst; (: di guerra) outbreak; **a ~ ritardato** delayed-action

sco'prire vt to discover; (liberare da ciò che copre) to uncover; (: monumento) to unveil; **scoprirsi** vpr to put on lighter clothes; (fig) to give o.s. away

scoraggi'are [skoradʒare] vt to discourage; **scoraggiarsi** vpr to become discouraged, lose heart

scorcia'toia [skortʃa'toja] sf short cut

'scorcio [skortʃo] sm (Arte) foreshortening; (di secolo, periodo) end, close; **scorcio panoramico** vista

scor'dare vt to forget; **scordarsi** vpr **scordarsi di qc/di fare** to forget sth/to do

'scorgere ['skordʒere] vt to make out, distinguish, see

scorpacci'ata [skorpatʃ'tʃata] sf **fare una ~ (di)** to stuff o.s. (with), eat one's fill (of)

scorpi'one sm scorpion; (dello zodiaco); **S~** Scorpio

'scorrere vt (giornale, lettera) to run o skim through ▶ vi (liquido, fiume) to run, flow; (fune) to run; (cassetto, porta) to slide easily; (tempo) to pass (by)

scor'retto, -a ag incorrect; (sgarbato) impolite; (sconveniente) improper

scor'revole ag (porta) sliding; (fig: stile) fluent, flowing

'scorsi ecc vb vedi **scorgere**

'scorso, -a pp di **scorrere** ▶ ag last

scor'soio, -a ag **nodo ~** noose

'scorta sf (di personalità, convoglio) escort; (provvista) supply, stock

scor'tese ag discourteous, rude

'scorza ['skordza] sf (di albero) bark; (di agrumi) peel, skin

sco'sceso, -a ag [skoʃ'feso] steep

'scossa sf jerk, jolt, shake; (Elettr, fig) shock; **scossa di terremoto** earth tremor

'scosso, -a pp di **scuotere** ▸ ag (turbato) shaken, upset

scos'tante ag (fig) off-putting (BRIT), unpleasant

scotch [skɔtʃ] sm inv (whisky) Scotch; (nastro adesivo) Scotch tape®, Sellotape®

scot'tare vt (ustionare) to burn; (: con liquido bollente) to scald ▸ vi to burn; (caffè) to be too hot; **scottarsi** vpr to burn/scald o.s.; (fig) to have one's fingers burnt; **scotta'tura** sf burn; scald

'scotto, -a ag overcooked ▸ sm (fig): **pagare lo ~ (di)** to pay the penalty (for)

sco'vare vt to drive out, flush out; (fig) to discover

'Scozia ['skɔttsia] sf la ~ Scotland; **scoz'zese** ag Scottish ▸ sm/f Scot

scredi'tare vt to discredit

screen saver ['skriːn'seivər] sm inv (Inform) screen saver

scre'mato, -a ag skimmed; **parzialmente ~** semi-skimmed

screpo'lato, -a ag (labbra) chapped; (muro) cracked

'screzio ['skrettsjo] sm disagreement

scricchio'lare [skrikkjo'lare] vi to creak, squeak

'scrigno ['skriɲɲo] sm casket

scrimina'tura sf parting

'scrissi ecc vb vedi **scrivere**

'scritta sf inscription

'scritto, -a pp di **scrivere** ▸ ag written ▸ sm writing; (lettera) letter, note

scrit'toio sm writing desk

scrit'tore, -'trice sm/f writer

scrit'tura sf writing; (Comm) entry; (contratto) contract; (Rel): **la Sacra S~** the Scriptures pl

scrittu'rare vt (Teatro, Cinema) to sign up, engage; (Comm) to enter

scriva'nia sf desk

'scrivere vt to write; **come si scrive?** how is it spelt?, how do you write it?

scroc'cone, -a sm/f scrounger

'scrofa sf (Zool) sow

scrol'lare vt to shake; **scrollarsi** vpr (anche fig) to give o.s. a shake; (anche: **~ le spalle/il capo**) to shrug one's shoulders/shake one's head

'scrupolo sm scruple; (meticolosità) care, conscientiousness

scrupo'loso, -a ag scrupulous; conscientious

scru'tare vt to scrutinize; (intenzioni, causa) to examine, scrutinize

scu'cire [sku'tʃire] vt (orlo ecc) to unpick, undo; **scucirsi** vpr to come unstitched

scude'ria sf stable

scu'detto sm (Sport) (championship) shield; (distintivo) badge

'scudo sm shield

sculacci'are [skulat'tʃare] vt to spank

scul'tore, -'trice sm/f sculptor

scul'tura sf sculpture

scu'ola sf school; **scuola elementare/materna** primary (BRIT) o grade (US) /nursery school; **scuola guida** driving school; **scuola media** secondary (BRIT) o high (US) school; **scuola dell'obbligo** compulsory education; **scuola tecnica** technical college; **scuole serali** evening classes, night school sg

scu'otere vt to shake

'scure sf axe

'scuro, -a ag dark; (fig: espressione) grim ▸ sm darkness; dark colour; (imposta) (window) shutter; **verde/rosso ecc ~** dark green/red ecc

'scusa sf apology; (pretesto) excuse; **chiedere ~ a qn (per)** to apologize to sb (for); **chiedo ~** I'm sorry; (disturbando ecc) excuse me

scu'sare vt to excuse; **scusarsi** vpr

scusarsi (di) to apologize (for); **(mi) scusi** I'm sorry; (*per richiamare l'attenzione*) excuse me

sde'gnato, -a [zdeɲ'ɲato] *ag* indignant, angry

'sdegno ['zdeɲɲo] *sm* scorn, disdain

sdolci'nato, -a [zdoltʃi'nato] *ag* mawkish, oversentimental

sdrai'arsi *vpr* to stretch out, lie down

'sdraio *sm* **sedia a ~** deck chair

sdruccio'levole [zdruttʃo'levole] *ag* slippery

se
  pron vedi **si**
  ▷ *cong*

1 (*condizionale, ipotetica*) if; **se nevica non vengo** I won't come if it snows; **sarei rimasto se me l'avessero chiesto** I would have stayed if they'd asked me; **non puoi fare altro se non telefonare** all you can do is phone; **se mai** if, if ever; **siamo noi se mai che lo siamo grati** it is we who should be grateful to you; **se no** (*altrimenti*) or (else), otherwise

2 (*in frasi dubitative, interrogative indirette*) if, whether; **non so se scrivere o telefonare** I don't know whether or if I should write or phone

sé *pron* (*gen*) oneself; (*esso, essa, lui, lei, loro*) itself; himself; herself; themselves; **sé stesso(a)** *pron* oneself; itself; himself; herself

seb'bene *cong* although, though

sec. *abbr* (= *secolo*) c

'secca *sf* (*del mare*) shallows *pl*; *vedi anche* **secco**

sec'care *vt* to dry up; (*prosciugare*) to dry up; (*fig: importunare*) to annoy, bother ▷ *vi* to dry; to dry up; **seccarsi** *vpr* to dry; to dry up; (*fig*) to grow annoyed

sec'cato, -a *ag* (*fig: infastidito*) bothered, annoyed; (*: stufo*) fed up

secca'tura *sf* (*fig*) bother *no pl*, trouble *no pl*

seccherò *ecc* [sekke'rɔ] *vb vedi* **seccare**

secchi'ello [sek'kjɛllo] *sm* bucket; **secchiello del ghiaccio** ice bucket

'secchio ['sekkjo] *sm* bucket, pail

'secco, -a, -chi, -che *ag* dry; (*fichi, pesce*) dried; (*foglie, ramo*) withered; (*magro: persona*) thin, skinny; (*fig: risposta, modo di fare*) curt, abrupt; (*: colpo*) clean, sharp ▷ *sm* (*siccità*) drought; **restarci ~** (*fig: morire sul colpo*) to drop dead; **mettere in ~** (*barca*) to beach; **rimanere a ~** (*fig*) to be left in the lurch

seco'lare *ag* age-old, centuries-old; (*laico, mondano*) secular

'secolo *sm* century; (*epoca*) age

secon'dario, -a *ag* secondary

secon'dino *sm* prison guard

se'condo, -a *ag* second ▷ *sm* second; (*di pranzo*) main course ▷ *prep* according to; (*nel modo prescritto*) in accordance with; **~ me** in my opinion, to my mind; **di seconda mano** second-hand; **a seconda di** according to; in accordance with; **seconda classe** second-class

'sedano *sm* celery

seda'tivo, -a *ag, sm* sedative

'sede *sf* seat; (*di ditta*) head office; (*di organizzazione*) headquarters *pl*; **sede centrale** head office; **sede sociale** registered office

seden'tario, -a *ag* sedentary

se'dere *vi* to sit, be seated

'sedia *sf* chair; **sedia elettrica** electric chair; **sedia a rotelle** wheelchair

'sedici ['sedit ʃi] *num* sixteen

se'dile *sm* seat; (*panchina*) bench

sedu'cente [sedu'tʃɛnte] *ag* seductive; (*proposta*) very attractive

se'durre *vt* to seduce

se'duta *sf* session, sitting; (*riunione*)

meeting; **seduta spiritica** séance;
seduta stante (fig) immediately
seduzi'one [sedut'tsjone] sf
seduction; (fascino) charm, appeal
SEeO abbr (= salvo errori e omissioni)
E and OE
'sega, -ghe sf saw
'segale sf rye
se'gare vt to saw; (recidere) to saw off
'seggio ['sɛddʒo] sm seat; **seggio elettorale** polling station
'seggiola ['sɛddʒola] sf chair;
seggio'lone sm (per bambini)
highchair
seggio'via [seddʒo'via] sf chairlift
segherò [sege'rɔ] vb vedi **segare**
segna'lare [seɲɲa'lare] vt (manovra ecc) to signal; to indicate; (annunciare) to announce; to report; (fig: far conoscere) to point out; (: persona) to single out
se'gnale [seɲ'ɲale] sm signal;
(cartello) sign; **segnale acustico** acoustic o sound signal; **segnale d'allarme** alarm; (Ferr) communication cord;
segnale orario (Radio) time signal;
segnale stradale road sign
segna'libro [seɲɲa'libro] sm (anche Inform) bookmark
se'gnare [seɲ'ɲare] vt to mark;
(prendere nota) to note; (indicare) to indicate, mark; (Sport: goal) to score
'segno ['seɲɲo] sm sign; (impronta, contrassegno) mark; (limite) limit, bounds pl; (bersaglio) target; **fare ~ di sì/no** to nod (one's head)/shake one's head; **fare ~ a qn di fermarsi** to motion (to) sb to stop; **cogliere o colpire nel ~** (fig) to hit the mark;
segno zodiacale star sign
segre'taria, -a sf secretary;
segretario comunale town clerk;
Segretario di Stato Secretary of State
segrete'ria sf (di ditta, scuola)

(secretary's) office; (d'organizzazione internazionale) secretariat; (Pol ecc: carica) office of Secretary; **segreteria telefonica** answering service
se'greto, -a ag secret ▶ sm secret;
secrecy no pl; **in ~** in secret, secretly
segu'ace [se'gwatʃe] sm/f follower, disciple
segu'ente ag following, next
segu'ire vt to follow; (frequentare: corso) to attend ▶ vi to follow;
(continuare: testo) to continue
segui'tare vt to continue, carry on with ▶ vi to continue, carry on
'seguito sm (scorta) suite, retinue; (discepoli) followers pl;
(favore) following; (continuazione) continuation; (conseguenza) result; **di ~** at a stretch, on end; **in ~** later on; **in ~ a, a ~ di** following; (a causa di) as a result of, owing to
'sei vb vedi **essere** ▶ num six
sei'cento [sei'tʃɛnto] num six hundred ▶ sm **il S~** the seventeenth century
selci'ato [sel'tʃato] sm cobbled surface
selezio'nare [selettsjo'nare] vt to select
selezi'one [selet'tsjone] sf selection
'sella sf saddle
sel'lino sm saddle
selvag'gina [selvad'dʒina] sf (animali) game
sel'vaggio, -a, -gi, -ge [sel'vaddʒo] ag wild; (tribù) savage, uncivilized;
(fig) savage, brutal ▶ sm/f savage
sel'vatico, -a, -ci, -che ag wild
se'maforo sm (Aut) traffic lights pl
sem'brare vi to seem ▶ vb impers
sembra che it seems that; **mi sembra che** it seems to me that, I think (that);
~ di essere to seem to be
'seme sm seed; (sperma) semen;
(Carte) suit
se'mestre sm half-year, six-month period

semifi'nale sf semifinal

semi'freddo sm ice-cream cake

semi'nare vt to sow

semi'nario sm seminar; (Rel) seminary

seminter'rato sm basement; (appartamento) basement flat

'semola sf; **semola di grano duro** durum wheat

semo'lino sm semolina

'semplice ['semplitʃe] ag simple; (di un solo elemento) single

'sempre av always; (ancora) still; **posso ~ tentare** I can always o still try; **da ~** always; **per ~** forever; **una volta per ~** once and for all; **~ che** provided (that); **~ più** more and more; **~ meno** less and less

sempre'verde ag, sm o f (Bot) evergreen

'senape sf (Cuc) mustard

se'nato sm senate; **sena'tore, -'trice** sm/f senator

'senno sm judgment, (common) sense; **col ~ di poi** with hindsight

'seno sm (Anat: petto, mammella) breast; (: grembo, fig) womb; (: cavità) sinus

sen'sato, -a ag sensible

sensazio'nale [sensattsjo'nale] ag sensational

sensazi'one [sensat'tsjone] sf feeling, sensation; **avere la ~ che** to have a feeling that; **fare ~** to cause a sensation, create a stir

sen'sibile ag sensitive; (ai sensi) perceptible; (rilevante, notevole) appreciable, noticeable; **~ a** sensitive to

> Attenzione! In inglese esiste la parola sensible, che però significa ragionevole.

'senso sm (Fisiol, istinto) sense; (impressione, sensazione) feeling, sensation; (significato) meaning,

sense; (direzione) direction; **sensi** smpl (coscienza) consciousness sg; (sensualità) senses; **ciò non ha ~** that doesn't make sense; **fare ~ a** (ripugnare) to disgust, repel; **in ~ orario/antiorario** clockwise/anticlockwise; **senso di colpa** sense of guilt; **senso comune** common sense; **senso unico** (strada) one-way; **senso vietato** (Aut) no entry

sensu'ale ag sensual; sensuous

sen'tenza [sen'tɛntsa] sf (Dir) sentence; (massima) maxim

senti'ero sm path

sentimen'tale ag sentimental; (vita, avventura) love cpd

senti'mento sm feeling

senti'nella sf sentry

sen'tire vt (percepire al tatto, fig) to feel; (udire) to hear; (ascoltare) to listen to; (odore) to smell; (aroma, sapore) to taste ▷ vi: **~ di** (avere sapore) to taste of; (avere odore) to smell of; **sentirsi** vpr (uso reciproco) to be in touch; **sentirsi bene/male** to feel well/unwell o ill; **non mi sento bene** I don't feel well; **sentirsi di fare qc** (essere disposto) to feel like doing sth

sen'tito, -a ag (sincero) sincere, warm; **per ~ dire** by hearsay

'senza ['sɛntsa] prep, cong without; **~ nulla** without saying a word; **fare ~ qc** to do without sth; **~ di me** without me o my; **~ che io lo sapessi** without me o my knowing; **senz'altro** of course, certainly; **~ dubbio** no doubt; **~ scrupoli** unscrupulous; **~ amici** friendless

sepa'rare vt to separate; (dividere) to divide; (tenere distinto) to distinguish; **separarsi** vpr (coniugi) to separate, part; (amici) to part, leave each other; **separarsi da** (coniuge) to separate o part from; (amico, socio) to part company with; (oggetto) to part with; **sepa'rato, -a** ag (letti, conto ecc) separate; (coniugi) separated

seppel'lire vt to bury

'**seppi** ecc vb vedi **sapere**

'**seppia** sf cuttlefish ▶ ag inv sepia

se'**quenza** [se'kwɛntsa] sf sequence

seques'**trare** vt (Dir) to impound; (rapire) to kidnap; **se'questro** sm (Dir) impoundment; **sequestro di persona** kidnapping

'**sera** sf evening; **di ~** in the evening; **domani ~** tomorrow evening, tomorrow night; **se'rale** ag evening cpd; **se'rata** sf evening; (ricevimento) party

ser'**bare** vt to keep; (mettere da parte) to put aside; **~ rancore/odio verso qn** to bear sb a grudge/hate sb

serba'**toio** sm tank; (cisterna) cistern

'**Serbia** sf la ~ Serbia

'**serbo** ag Serbian ▶ sm/f Serbian, Serb ▶ sm (Ling) Serbian; (il serbare): **mettere/tenere o avere in ~ qc** to put/keep sth aside

se'**reno, -a** ag (tempo, cielo) clear; (fig) serene, calm

ser'**gente** [ser'dʒɛnte] sm (Mil) sergeant

'**serie** sf inv (successione) series inv; (gruppo, collezione) set; (Sport) division; league; (Comm): **modello di ~/fuori ~** standard/custom-built model; **in ~** in quick succession; (Comm) mass cpd

seri'**età** sf seriousness; reliability

'**serio, -a** ag serious; (impiegato) responsible, reliable; (ditta, cliente) reliable, dependable; **sul ~** (davvero) really, truly; (seriamente) seriously, in earnest

ser'**pente** sm snake; **serpente a sonagli** rattlesnake

'**serra** sf greenhouse; hothouse

ser'**randa** sf roller shutter

serra'**tura** sf lock

'**server** ['sɛrver] sm inv (Inform) server

ser'**vire** vt to serve; (clienti: al ristorante) to wait on; (: al negozio) to serve, attend to; (fig: giovare) to aid, help; (Carte) to deal ▶ vi (Tennis) to serve; (essere utile): **~ a qn** to be of use to sb; (fig: giovare): **~ a qc/a fare** (utensile ecc) to be used for sth/for doing; (~ a qn) da to serve as (for sb); **servirsi** vpr (usare): **servirsi di** to use; (prendere: cibo): **servirsi (di)** to help o.s. (to); **serviti pure!** help yourself!; (essere cliente abituale): **servirsi da** to be a regular customer at, go to

servi'**zievole** [servit'tsjevole] ag obliging, willing to help

ser'**vizio** [ser'vittsjo] sm service; (al ristorante: sul conto) service (charge); (Stampa, TV, Radio) report; (da tè, caffè ecc) set, service; **servizi** smpl (di casa) kitchen and bathroom; (Econ) services; **essere di ~** to be on duty; **fuori ~** (telefono ecc) out of order; **~ compreso** service included; **servizio militare** military service; **servizio di posate** set of cutlery; **servizi segreti** secret service sg; **servizio da tè** tea set

ses'**santa** num sixty; **sessan'tesimo, -a** num sixtieth

sessi'**one** sf session

'**sesso** sm sex; **sessu'ale** ag sexual, sex cpd

ses'**tante** sm sextant

'**sesto, -a** ag, sm sixth

'**seta** sf silk

'**sete** sf thirst; **avere ~** to be thirsty

'**setola** sf bristle

'**setta** sf sect

set'**tanta** num seventy; **settan'tesimo, -a** num seventieth

set'**tare** vt (Inform) to set up

'**sette** num seven

sette'**cento** [sette'tʃɛnto] num seven hundred ▶ sm il S~ the eighteenth century

set'tembre sm September

settentrio'nale ag northern

settentri'one sm north

setti'mana sf week; **settima'nale** ag, sm weekly

● **settimana bianca**
● Settimana bianca is the name
● given to a week-long winter-sports
● holiday taken by many Italians some
● time in the skiing season.

'settimo, -a ag, sm seventh

set'tore sm sector

severità sf severity

se'vero, -a ag severe

sevizi'are [sevit'tsjare] vt to torture

sezio'nare [settsjo'nare] vt to divide into sections; (Med) to dissect

sezi'one [set'tsjone] sf section

sfacchi'nata [sfakki'nata] sf (fam) chore, drudgery no pl

sfacci'ato, -a [sfat'tʃato] ag (maleducato) cheeky, impudent; (vistoso) gaudy

sfa'mare vt to feed; (cibo) to fill; **sfamarsi** vpr to satisfy one's hunger, fill o.s. up

sfasci'are [sfaʃ'ʃare] vt (ferita) to unbandage; (distruggere) to smash, shatter; **sfasciarsi** vpr (rompersi) to smash, shatter

sfavo'revole ag unfavourable

'sfera sf sphere

sfer'rare vt (fig: colpo) to land, deal; (: attacco) to launch

'sfida sf challenge

sfi'dare vt to challenge; (fig) to defy, brave

sfi'ducia [sfi'dutʃa] sf distrust, mistrust

sfi'gato, -a (fam) ag (sfortunato) unlucky

sfigu'rare vt (persona) to disfigure; (quadro, statua) to deface ▶ vi (far cattiva figura) to make a bad

impression

sfi'lare vt (ago) to unthread; (abito, scarpe) to slip off ▶ vi (truppe) to march past; (atleti) to parade; **sfilarsi** vpr (perle ecc) to come unstrung; (orlo, tessuto) to fray; (calza) to run, ladder; **sfi'lata** sf march past; parade; **sfilata di moda** fashion show

'sfinge ['sfindʒe] sf sphinx

sfi'nito, -a ag exhausted

sfio'rare vt to brush (against); (argomento) to touch upon

sfio'rire vi to wither, fade

sfo'cato, -a ag (Fot) out of focus

sfoci'are [sfo'tʃare] vi: ~ **in** to flow into; (fig: malcontento) to develop into

sfode'rato, -a ag (vestito) unlined

sfogarsi vpr (sfogare la propria rabbia) to give vent to one's anger; (confidarsi): ~ **(con)** to pour out one's feelings (to); **non sfogarti su di me!** don't take your bad temper out on me!

sfoggi'are [sfod'dʒare] vt, vi to show off

'sfoglia ['sfoʎʎa] sf sheet of pasta dough; **pasta ~** (Cuc) puff pastry

sfogli'are [sfoʎ'ʎare] vt (libro) to leaf through

'sfogo, -ghi sm (eruzione cutanea) rash; (fig) outburst; **dare ~ a** (fig) to give vent to

sfon'dare vt (porta) to break down; (scarpe) to wear a hole in; (cesto, scatola) to burst, knock the bottom out of; (Mil) to break through ▶ vi (riuscire) to make a name for o.s.

'sfondo sm background

sfor'mato sm (Cuc) type of soufflé

sfor'tuna sf misfortune, ill luck no pl; **avere ~** to be unlucky; **sfortu'nato, -a** ag unlucky; (impresa, film) unsuccessful

sforzarsi vpr ~ **di** o **a** o **per fare** to try hard to do

'sforzo ['sfɔrtso] sm effort; (tensione

eccessiva, Tecn) strain; **fare uno ~ to make an effort**

sfrat'tare vt to evict; **'sfratto** sm eviction

sfrecci'are [sfret'tʃare] vi to shoot o flash past

sfre'gare [sfre'dʒare] vt (strofinare) to rub; (graffiare) to scratch; **sfregarsi le mani** to rub one's hands; **~ un fiammifero** to strike a match

sfregi'are [sfre'dʒare] vt to slash, gash; (persona) to disfigure; (quadro) to deface

sfre'nato, -a ag (fig) unrestrained, unbridled

sfron'tato, -a ag shameless

sfrutta'mento sm exploitation

sfrut'tare vt (terreno) to overwork, exhaust; (miniera) to exploit, work; (fig: operai, occasione, potere) to exploit

sfug'gire [sfud'dʒire] vi to escape; **~ a** (custode) to escape (from); (morte) to escape; **~ a qn** (dettaglio, nome) to escape sb; **~ di mano a qn** to slip out of sb's hand (o hands)

sfu'mare vt (colori, contorni) to soften, shade off ▶ vi to shade (off), fade; (fig: svanire) to vanish, disappear; (: speranze) to come to nothing

sfuma'tura sf shading off no pl; (tonalità) shade, tone; (fig) touch, hint

sfuri'ata sf (scatto di collera) fit of anger; (rimprovero) sharp rebuke

sga'bello sm stool

sgabuz'zino [zgabud'dzino] sm lumber room

sgambet'tare vi to kick one's legs about

sgam'betto sm far lo **~ a qn** to trip sb up; (fig) to oust sb

sganci'are [zgan'tʃare] vt to unhook; (Ferr) to uncouple; (bombe: da aereo) to release, drop; (fig: fam: soldi) to fork out; **sganciarsi** vpr (fig): **sganciarsi (da)** to get away (from)

sganghe'rato, -a ag [zganghe'rato] (off its hinges; (auto) ramshackle; (risata) wild, boisterous

sgar'bato, -a ag rude, impolite

'sgarbo sm fare uno **~ a qn** to be rude to sb

sgargi'ante [zgar'dʒante] ag gaudy, showy

sgattaio'lare vi to sneak away o off

sge'lare [zdʒe'lare] vi, vt to thaw

sghignaz'zare [zgiɲɲat'tsare] vi to laugh scornfully

sgob'bare (fam) vi (scolaro) to swot; (operaio) to slog

sgombe'rare vt (tavolo, stanza) to clear; (piazza, città) to evacuate ▶ vi to move

'sgombro, -a ag **~ (di)** clear (of), free (from) ▶ sm (Zool) mackerel; (anche: **sgombero**) clearing; vacating; evacuation; (: trasloco) removal

sgonfi'are vt to let down, deflate; **sgonfiarsi** vpr to go down

'sgonfio, -a ag (pneumatico, pallone) flat

'sgorbio sm blot; scribble

sgra'devole ag unpleasant, disagreeable

sgra'dito, -a ag unpleasant, unwelcome

sgra'nare vt (piselli) to shell; **~ gli occhi** to open one's eyes wide

sgranchire [zgran'kire] vt (anche: **sgranchirsi**) to stretch; **~ le gambe** to stretch one's legs

sgranocchi'are [zgranok'kjare] vt to munch

'sgravio sm **~ fiscale** tax relief

sgrazi'ato, -a ag [zgrat'tsjato] ag clumsy, ungainly

sgri'dare vt to scold

sgual'cire [zgwal'tʃire] vt to crumple (up), crease

sgual'drina (peg) sf slut

sgu'ardo sm (occhiata) look, glance;

(espressione) look (in one's eye)

sguaz'zare [zgwat'tsare] *vi* *(nell'acqua)* to splash about; *(nella melma)* to wallow; **~ nell'oro** to be rolling in money

sguinzagli'are [zgwintsaʎ'ʎare] *vt* to let off the leash; *(fig: persona):* **~ qn dietro a qn** to set sb on sb

sgusci'are [zguʃ'ʃare] *vt* to shell ▶ *vi* *(sfuggire di mano)* to slip; **~ via** to slip o slink away

'shampoo ['ʃampo] *sm inv* shampoo

shiatzu [ʃi'atstsu] *sm inv* shiatsu

shock [ʃɔk] *sm inv* shock

si

⊙ *(dav lo, la, li, le, ne diventa* **se**) *pron*

1 *(riflessivo: maschile)* himself; *(: femminile)* herself; *(: neutro)* itself; *(: impersonale)* oneself; *(: pl)* themselves; **lavarsi** to wash (oneself); **si è tagliato** he has cut himself; **si credono importanti** they think a lot of themselves

2 *(riflessivo: con complemento oggetto):* **lavarsi le mani** to wash one's hands; **si sta lavando i capelli** he (o she) is washing his (o her) hair

3 *(reciproco)* one another, each other; **si amano** they love one another o each other

4 *(passivo):* **si ripara facilmente** it is easily repaired

5 *(impersonale):* **si dice che ...** they o people say that ...; **si vede che è vecchio** one o you can see that it's old

6 *(noi)* we; **tra poco si parte** we're leaving soon

sì *av* yes; **un giorno sì e uno no** every other day

'sia *cong* **~ ... ~** *(o ... o):* **~ che lavori, ~ che non lavori** whether he works or not; *(tanto ... quanto):* **verranno ~ Luigi ~ suo fratello** both Luigi and his brother will be coming

si'amo *vb vedi* **essere**

si'cario *sm* hired killer

sicché [sik'ke] *cong* *(perciò)* so (that), therefore; *(e quindi)* (and) so

sic'cità [sittʃi'ta] *sf* drought

sic'come *cong* since, as

Si'cilia [si'tʃilja] *sf* **la ~** Sicily

si'cura *sf* safety catch; *(Aut)* safety lock

sicu'rezza [siku'rettsa] *sf* safety; security; *(fiducia)* confidence; *(certezza)* certainty; **di ~** safety *cpd*; **la ~ stradale** road safety

si'curo, -a *ag* safe; *(ben difeso)* secure; *(fiducioso)* confident; *(certo)* sure, certain; *(notizia, amico)* reliable; *(esperto)* skilled ▶ *av (anche: di ~)* certainly; **essere/mettere al ~** to be safe/put in a safe place; **~ di sé** self-confident, sure of o.s.; **sentirsi ~** to feel safe o secure

si'edo *ecc vb vedi* **sedere**

si'epe *sf* hedge

si'ero *sm (Med)* serum; **sieronega'tivo, -a** *ag* HIV-negative; **sieroposi'tivo, -a** *ag* HIV-positive

si'ete *vb vedi* **essere**

si'filide *sf* syphilis

Sig. *abbr* (= *signore*) Mr

siga'retta *sf* cigarette

'sigaro *sm* cigar

Sigg. *abbr* (= *signori*) Messrs

sigil'lare [sidʒil'lare] *vt* to seal

si'gillo [si'dʒillo] *sm* seal

'sigla *sf* initials *pl*; acronym, abbreviation; **sigla automobilistica** *abbreviation of province on vehicle number plate*; **sigla musicale** signature tune

Sig.na *abbr* (= *signorina*) Miss

si'gnora [siɲ'ɲora] *sf* lady; **la ~ X** Mrs X; **buon giorno S~/Signore/Signorina** good morning; *(deferente)* good morning Madam/Sir/Madam; *(quando si conosce il nome)* good morning Mrs/Mr/Miss X; **Gentile S~/Signore/Signorina** (in una lettera) Dear Madam/Sir/Madam; **il signor Rossi e~** Mr Rossi and his wife; **signore e signori** ladies and gentlemen

si'gnore [siɲˈɲore] sm gentleman; (padrone) lord, master; (Rel): **il S~** the Lord; **il signor e~** Mr X; **i signori Bianchi** (coniugi) Mr and Mrs Bianchi; vedi anche **signora**

signo'rile [siɲɲoˈrile] ag refined

signo'rina [siɲɲoˈrina] sf young lady; **la~X** Miss X; vedi anche **signora**

Sig.ra abbr (= signora) Mrs

silenzia'tore [silentsjaˈtore] sm silencer

si'lenzio [siˈlentsjo] sm silence; **fare~** to be quiet, stop talking; **silenzi'oso, -a** ag silent, quiet

si'licio [siˈlitʃo] sm silicon

sili'cone sm silicone

'sillaba sf syllable

si'luro sm torpedo

simboleggi'are [simboledˈdʒare] vt to symbolize

'simbolo sm symbol

'simile (analogo) similar; (di questo tipo): **un uomo~** such a man, a man like this; **libri simili** such books; **~a** similar to; **i suoi simili** one's fellow men; one's peers

simme'tria sf symmetry

simpa'tia sf (qualità) pleasantness; (inclinazione) liking; **avere~per qn** to like sb, have a liking for sb

sim'patico, -a, -ci, -che ag (persona) nice, pleasant, likeable; (casa, albergo ecc) nice, pleasant

> Attenzione! In inglese esiste la parola sympathetic, che però significa comprensivo.

simpatiz'zare [simpatidˈdzare] vi **~con** to take a liking to

simu'lare vt to sham, simulate; (Tecn)

to simulate

simul'taneo, -a ag simultaneous

sina'goga, -ghe sf synagogue

since'rità [sintʃeriˈta] sf sincerity

sin'cero, -a [sinˈtʃero] ag sincere; genuine; heartfelt

sinda'cale ag (trade-)union cpd

sinda'cato sm (di lavoratori) (trade) union; (Amm, Econ, Dir) syndicate, trust, pool

'sindaco, -ci sm mayor

sinfo'nia sf (Mus) symphony

singhioz'zare [singjotˈtsare] vi to sob; to hiccup

singhi'ozzo [sinˈgjottso] sm sob; (Med) hiccup; **avere il~** to have the hiccups; **a~** (fig) by fits and starts

single [ˈsingol] ag inv, sm/f inv single

singo'lare ag (insolito) remarkable, singular; (Ling) singular ▶ sm (Ling) singular; (Tennis): **~maschile/femminile** men's/women's singles

'singolo, -a ag single, individual ▶ sm (persona) individual; (Tennis) = **singolare**

si'nistra sf (Pol) left (wing); **a~** on the left; (direzione) to the left

si'nistro, -a ag left, left-hand; (fig) sinister ▶ sm (incidente) accident

si'nonimo sm synonym; **~di** synonymous with

sin'tassi sf syntax

'sintesi sf synthesis; (riassunto) summary, résumé

sin'tetico, -a, -ci, -che ag synthetic

sintetiz'zare [sintetidˈdzare] vt to synthesize; (riassumere) to summarize

sinto'matico, -a, -ci, -che ag symptomatic

'sintomo sm symptom

sintonizzarsi vpr **~su** to tune in to

si'pario sm (Teatro) curtain

si'rena sf (apparecchio) siren; (nella mitologia, fig) siren, mermaid

'Siria sf **la~** Syria

si'ringa, -ghe sf syringe

'sismico, -a, -ci, -che ag seismic

sis'tema, -i sm system; method; way; **sistema nervoso** nervous system; **sistema operativo** (Inform) operating system; **sistema solare** solar system

siste'mare vt (mettere a posto) to tidy, put in order; (risolvere: questione) to sort out, settle; (procurare un lavoro a) to find a job for; (dare un alloggio a) to settle, find accommodation for; **sistemarsi** vpr (problema) to be settled; (persona: trovare alloggio) to find accommodation (BRIT) o accommodations (US); (: trovarsi un lavoro) to get fixed up with a job; **ti sistemo io!** I'll soon sort you out!

siste'matico, -a, -ci, -che ag systematic

sistemazi'one [sistemat'tsjone] sf arrangement, order; settlement; employment; accommodation (BRIT), accommodations (US)

'sito sm ~ Internet website

situazi'one [situat'tsjone] sf situation

ski-lift ['ski:lift] sm inv ski tow

slacci'are [zlat'tʃare] vt to undo, unfasten

slanci'ato, -a [zlan'tʃato] ag slender

'slancio sm dash, leap; (fig) surge; **di ~** impetuously

'slavo, -a ag Slav(onic), Slavic

sle'ale ag disloyal; (concorrenza ecc) unfair

sle'gare vt to untie

slip [zlip] sm inv briefs pl

'slitta sf sledge; (trainata) sleigh

slit'tare vi to slip, slide; (Aut) to skid

s.l.m. abbr (= sul livello del mare) a.s.l.

slo'gare vt (Med) to dislocate

sloggi'are [zlod'dʒare] vt (inquilino) to turn out ▶ vi to move out

Slo'vacchia [zlo'vakkja] sf Slovakia

slo'vacco, -a, -chi, -che ag, sm/f Slovák

Slovenia [zlo'vɛnja] sf Slovenia

slo'veno, -a ag, sm/f Slovene, Slovenian ▶ sm (Ling) Slovene

smacchi'are [zmak'kjare] vt to remove stains from; **smacchia'tore** sm stain remover

'smacco, -chi sm humiliating defeat

smagli'ante [zmaʎ'ʎante] ag brilliant, dazzling

smaglia'tura [zmaʎʎa'tura] sf (su maglia, calza) ladder; (della pelle) stretch mark

smalizi'ato, -a [zmalit'tsjato] ag shrewd, cunning

smalti'mento sm (di rifiuti) disposal

smal'tire vt (merce) to sell off; (rifiuti) to dispose of; (cibo) to digest; (peso) to lose; (rabbia) to get over; **~ la sbornia** to sober up

'smalto sm (anche: di denti) enamel; (per ceramica) glaze; **smalto per unghie** nail varnish

smantel'lare vt to dismantle

smarri'mento sm loss; (fig) bewilderment; dismay

smar'rire vt to lose; (non riuscire a trovare) to mislay; **smarrirsi** vpr (perdersi) to lose one's way, get lost; (: oggetto) to go astray

smasche'rare [zmaske'rare] vt to unmask

SME sigla m (= Sistema Monetario Europeo) EMS (European Monetary System)

smen'tire vt (negare) to deny; (testimonianza) to refute; **smentirsi** vpr to be inconsistent

sme'raldo sm emerald

'smesso, -a pp di smettere

'smettere vt to stop; (vestiti) to stop wearing ▶ vi to stop, cease; **~ di fare** to stop doing

'smilzo, -a ['zmiltso] ag thin, lean

sminu'ire vt to diminish, lessen; (fig) to belittle

sminuz'zare [zminut'tsare] vt to break into small pieces; to crumble

'smisi ecc vb vedi **smettere**

smis'tare vt (pacchi ecc) to sort; (Ferr) to shunt

smisu'rato, -a ag boundless, immeasurable; (grandissimo) immense, enormous

smoking ['sməʊkiŋ] sm inv dinner jacket

smon'tare vt (mobile, macchina ecc) to take to pieces, dismantle; (fig: scoraggiare) to dishearten ▶ vi (scendere: da cavallo) to dismount; (: da treno) to get off; (terminare il lavoro) to stop (work); **smontarsi** vpr to lose heart; to lose one's enthusiasm

'smorfia sf grimace; (atteggiamento lezioso) simpering; **fare smorfie** to make faces; to simper

'smorto, -a ag (viso) pale, wan; (colore) dull

smor'zare [zmor'tsare] vt (suoni) to deaden; (colori) to tone down; (luce) to dim; (sete) to quench; (entusiasmo) to dampen; **smorzarsi** vpr (suono, luce) to fade; (entusiasmo) to dampen

SMS sigla m inv (= short message service) text (message)

smu'overe vt to move, shift; (fig: commuovere) to move; (: dall'inerzia) to rouse, stir

snatu'rato, -a ag inhuman, heartless

'snello, -a ag (agile) agile; (svelto) slender, slim

sner'vante ag (attesa, lavoro) exasperating

snob'bare vt to snub

sno'dare vt (rendere agile, mobile) to loosen; **snodarsi** vpr to come loose; (articolarsi) to bend; (strada, fiume) to wind

sno'dato, -a ag (articolazione, persona) flexible; (fune ecc) undone

so vb vedi **sapere**

sobbar'carsi vpr ~ **a** to take on, undertake

'sobrio, -a ag sober

socchi'udere [sok'kjudere] vt (porta) to leave ajar; (occhi) to half-close; **socchi'uso, -a** pp di **socchiudere**

soc'correre vt to help, assist

soccorri'tore, -'trice sm/f rescuer

soc'corso, -a pp di **soccorrere** ▶ sm help, aid, assistance; **soccorso stradale** breakdown service

soci'ale [so'tʃale] ag social; (di associazione) club cpd, association cpd

socia'lismo [sotʃa'lizmo] sm socialism; **socia'lista, -i, -e** ag, sm/f socialist

società [sotʃe'ta] sf inv society; (sportiva) club; (Comm) company; ~ **a responsabilità limitata** type of limited liability company; **società per azioni** limited (BRIT) o incorporated (US) company

soci'evole [so'tʃevole] ag sociable

'socio ['sɔtʃo] sm (Dir, Comm) partner; (membro di associazione) member

'soda sf (Chim) soda; (bibita) soda (water)

soddisfa'cente [soddisfa'tʃɛnte] ag satisfactory

soddis'fare vt, vi ~ **a** to satisfy; (impegno) to fulfil; (debito) to pay off; (richiesta) to meet, comply with; **soddis'fatto, -a** pp di **soddisfare** ▶ ag satisfied; **soddisfatto di** happy o satisfied with; pleased with; **soddisfazi'one** sf satisfaction

'sodo, -a ag firm, hard; (uovo) hard-boiled ▶ av (picchiare, lavorare) hard; (dormire) soundly

sofà sm inv sofa

soffe'renza [soffe'rɛntsa] sf suffering

sof'ferto, -a pp di **soffrire**

soffi'are vt to blow; (notizia, segreto)

to whisper ▶ vi to blow; (sbuffare) to puff (and blow); **soffiarsi il naso** to blow one's nose; **~ qc/qn a qn** (fig) to pinch o steal sth/sb from sb; **~ via qc** to blow sth away

soffi'ata sf (fam) tip-off; **fare una ~ alla polizia** to tip off the police

'soffice ['sɔffitʃe] ag soft

'soffio sm (di vento) breath; **soffio al cuore** heart murmur

sof'fitta sf attic

sof'fitto sm ceiling

soffo'cante ag suffocating, stifling

soffo'care vi (anche: **soffocarsi**) to suffocate, choke ▶ vt to suffocate, choke; (fig) to stifle, suppress

sof'frire vt to suffer, endure; (sopportare) to bear, stand ▶ vi to suffer; to be in pain; **~ (di) qc** (Med) to suffer from sth

sof'fritto, -a pp di **soffriggere** ▶ sm (Cuc) fried mixture of herbs, bacon and onions

sofisti'cato, -a ag sophisticated; (vino) adulterated

'software ['sɔftwɛə] sm **~ applicativo** applications package

sogget'tivo, -a [soddʒet'tivo] ag subjective

sog'getto, -a [sod'dʒɛtto] ag **~ a** (sottomesso) subject to; (esposto: a variazioni, danni ecc) subject o liable to ▶ sm subject

soggezi'one [soddʒet'tsjone] sf subjection; (timidezza) awe; **avere ~ di qn** to stand in awe of sb; to be ill at ease in sb's presence

soggi'orno sm (invernale, marino) stay; (stanza) living room

'soglia ['sɔʎʎa] sf doorstep; (anche fig) threshold

sogliola ['sɔʎʎola] sf (Zool) sole

so'gnare [soɲ'ɲare] vt, vi to dream; **~ a occhi aperti** to daydream

'sogno ['soɲɲo] sm dream

'soia sf (Bot) soya

sol sm (Mus) G; (: solfeggiando) so(h)

so'laio sm (soffitta) attic

sola'mente av only, just

so'lare ag solar, sun cpd

'solco, -chi sm (scavo, fig: ruga) furrow; (incavo) rut, track; (di disco) groove

sol'dato sm soldier; **soldato semplice** private

soldi smpl (denaro) money sg; **non ho ~** I haven't got any money

'sole sm sun; (luce) sun(light); (tempo assolato) sun(shine); **prendere il ~** to sunbathe

soleggi'ato, -a [soled'dʒato] ag sunny

so'lenne ag solemn

soli'dale ag **essere ~ (con)** to be in agreement (with)

solidarietà sf solidarity

'solido, -a ag solid; (forte, robusto) sturdy, solid; (fig: ditta) sound, solid ▶ sm (Mat) solid

so'lista, -i, -e ag solo ▶ sm/f soloist

solita'mente av usually, as a rule

soli'tario, -a ag (senza compagnia) solitary, lonely; (solo, isolato) solitary, lone; (deserto) lonely ▶ sm (gioiello, gioco) solitaire

'solito, -a ag usual; **essere ~ fare** to be in the habit of doing; **di ~** usually; **più tardi del ~** later than usual; **come al ~** as usual

soli'tudine sf solitude

sol'letico sm tickling; **soffrire il ~** to be ticklish

solleva'mento sm raising; lifting; revolt; **sollevamento pesi** (Sport) weight-lifting

solle'vare vt to lift, raise; (fig: persona: alleggerire): **~ (da)** to relieve (of); (: dar conforto) to comfort, relieve; (: questione) to raise; (: far insorgere) to stir (to revolt); **sollevarsi** vpr to rise; (fig: riprendersi) to recover; (: ribellarsi) to rise up

solli'evo sm relief; (conforto) comfort

'solo, -a ag alone; (in senso spirituale: isolato) lonely; (unico): **un ~ libro** only one book, a single book; (con ag numerale): **veniamo noi tre soli** just o only the three of us are coming ▶ av (soltanto) only, just; **non ~ ... ma anche** not only ... but also; **fare qc da ~** to do sth (all) by oneself

sol'tanto av only

so'lubile ag (sostanza) soluble

soluzi'one [solut'tsjone] sf solution

sol'vente ag, sm solvent

so'maro sm ass, donkey

somigli'anza [somiλ'λantsa] sf resemblance

somigli'are [somiλ'λare] vi **~ a** to be like, resemble; (nell'aspetto fisico) to look like; **somigliarsi** vpr to be o look) alike

'somma sf (Mat) sum; (di denaro) sum (of money)

som'mare vt to add up; (aggiungere) to add; **tutto sommato** all things considered

som'mario, -a ag (racconto, indagine) brief; (giustizia) summary ▶ sm summary

sommer'gibile [sommer'dʒibile] sm submarine

som'merso, -a pp di **sommergere**

sommità sf inv summit, top; (fig) height

som'mossa sf uprising

'sonda sf (Med, Meteor, Aer) probe; (Mineralogia) drill ▶ ag inv **pallone** m ~ weather balloon

son'daggio [son'daddʒo] sm sounding; probe; boring, drilling; (indagine) survey; **sondaggio d'opinioni** opinion poll

son'dare vt (Naut) to sound; (atmosfera, piaga) to probe; (Mineralogia) to bore, drill; (fig: opinione ecc) to survey, poll

so'netto sm sonnet

son'nambulo, -a sm/f sleepwalker

sonnel'lino sm nap

son'nifero sm sleeping drug (o pill)

'sonno sm sleep; **prendere ~** to fall asleep; **aver ~** to be sleepy

'sono vb vedi **essere**

so'noro, -a ag (ambiente) resonant; (voce) sonorous, ringing; (onde, film) sound cpd

sontu'oso, -a ag sumptuous; lavish

sop'palco, -chi sm mezzanine

soppor'tare vt (subire: perdita, spese) to bear, sustain; (soffrire: dolore) to bear, endure; (cosa: freddo) to withstand; (persona: freddo, vino) to take; (tollerare) to put up with, tolerate

> Attenzione! In inglese esiste il verbo to support, che però non significa sopportare.

sop'primere vt (carica, privilegi, testimone) to do away with; (pubblicazione) to suppress; (parola, frase) to delete

'sopra prep (gen) on; (al di sopra di, più in alto di) above; over; (riguardo a) on, about ▶ av on top; (attaccato, scritto) on it; (al di sopra) above; (al piano superiore) upstairs; **donne ~ i 30 anni** women over 30 (years of age); **abito di ~** I live upstairs; **dormirci ~** (fig) to sleep on it

so'prabito sm overcoat

soprac'ciglio [soprat'tʃiλλo] (pl(f) **soprac'ciglia**) sm eyebrow

sopraf'fare vt to overcome, overwhelm

sopral'luogo, -ghi sm (di esperti) inspection; (di polizia) on-the-spot investigation

sopram'mobile sm ornament

soprannatu'rale ag supernatural

sopran'nome sm nickname

so'prano, -a sm/f (persona) soprano

▶ *sm* (*voce*) soprano

soprappensi'ero *av* lost in thought

sopras'salto *sm* **di ~** with a start; suddenly

soprasse'dere *vi* **~ a** to delay, put off

soprat'tutto *av* (*anzitutto*) above all; (*specialmente*) especially

sopravvalu'tare *vt* to overestimate

soprav'vento *sm* **avere/prendere il ~ su** to have/get the upper hand over

sopravvis'suto, -a *pp di* **sopravvivere**

soprav'vivere *vi* to survive; (*continuare a vivere*): **~ (in)** to live on (in); **~ a** (*incidente ecc*) to survive; (*persona*) to outlive

so'pruso *sm* abuse of power; **subire un ~** to be abused

soq'quadro *sm* **mettere a ~** to turn upside-down

sor'betto *sm* sorbet, water ice

sor'dina *sf* **in ~** softly; (*fig*) on the sly

'sordo, -a *ag* deaf; (*rumore*) muffled; (*dolore*) dull; (*odio, rancore*) veiled ▶ *sm/f* deaf person; **sordo'muto, -a** *ag* deaf-and-dumb ▶ *sm/f* deaf-mute

so'rella *sf* sister; **sorel'lastra** *sf* stepsister; (*con genitore in comune*) half-sister

sor'gente [sor'dʒɛnte] *sf* (*d'acqua*) spring; (*di fiume, Fisica, fig*) source

'sorgere ['sordʒere] *vi* to rise; (*scaturire*) to spring; rise; (*fig: difficoltà*) to arise

sorni'one, -a *ag* sly

sorpas'sare *vt* (*Aut*) to overtake; (*fig*) to surpass; (: *eccedere*) to exceed, go beyond; **~ in altezza** to be higher than; (*persona*) to be taller than

sorpren'dente *ag* surprising

sor'prendere *vt* (*cogliere: in flagrante ecc*) to catch; (*stupire*) to surprise; **sorprendersi** *vpr* **sorprendersi (di)** to be surprised (at); **sor'presa** *sf* surprise; **fare una sorpresa a qn** to

give sb a surprise; **sor'preso, -a** *pp di* **sorprendere**

sor'reggere [sor'rɛddʒere] *vt* to support, hold up; (*fig*) to sustain; **sorreggersi** *vpr* (*tenersi ritto*) to stay upright

sor'ridere *vi* to smile; **sor'riso, -a** *di* **sorridere** ▶ *sm* smile

'sorsi *ecc vb vedi* **sorgere**

'sorso *sm* sip

'sorta *sf* sort, kind; **di ~** whatever, of any kind, at all

'sorte *sf* (*fato*) fate, destiny; (*evento fortuito*) chance; **tirare a ~** to draw lots

sor'teggio [sor'tɛddʒo] *sm* draw

sorvegli'ante [sorveʎ'ʎante] *sm/f* (*di carcere*) guard, warder (BRIT); (*di fabbrica ecc*) supervisor

sorvegli'anza [sorveʎ'ʎantsa] *sf* watch; supervision; (*Polizia, Mil*) surveillance

sorvegli'are [sorveʎ'ʎare] *vt* (*bambino, bagagli, prigioniero*) to watch, keep an eye on; (*malato*) to watch over; (*territorio, casa*) to watch o keep watch over; (*lavori*) to supervise

sorvo'lare *vt* (*territorio*) to fly over ▶ *vi*: **~ su** (*fig*) to skim over

S.O.S. *sigla m* mayday, SOS

'sosia *sm inv* double

sos'pendere *vt* (*appendere*) to hang (up); (*interrompere, privare di una carica*) to suspend; (*rimandare*) to defer; (*appendere*) to hang

sospet'tare *vt* to suspect ▶ *vi*: **~ di** to suspect; (*diffidare*) to be suspicious of

sos'petto, -a *ag* suspicious ▶ *sm* suspicion; **sospet'toso, -a** *ag* suspicious

sospi'rare *vi* to sigh ▶ *vt* to long for, yearn for; **sos'piro** *sm* sigh

'sosta *sf* (*fermata*) stop, halt; (*pausa*) pause, break; **senza ~** non-stop, without a break

sostan'tivo *sm* noun, substantive

sos'tanza [sos'tantsa] *sf* substance;
sostanze *sfpl* (*ricchezze*) wealth *sg*,
possessions; **in ~** in short, to sum up

sos'tare *vi* (*fermarsi*) to stop (for a
while), stay; (*fare una pausa*) to take
a break

sos'tegno [sos'teɲɲo] *sm* support

soste'nere *vt* to support; (*prendere
su di sé*) to take on, bear; (*resistere*) to
withstand, stand up to; (*affermare*):
~ che to maintain that; **sostenersi**
vpr to hold o.s. up, support o.s.; (*fig*)
to keep up one's strength; **~ gli esami**
to sit exams

sostenta'mento *sm* maintenance,
support

sostitu'ire *vt* (*mettere al posto di*): **~ qn/
qc a** to substitute sb/sth for; (*prendere
il posto di: persona*) to substitute for;
(*: cosa*) to take the place of

sosti'tuto, -a *sm/f* substitute

sostituzi'one [sostitut'tsjone] *sf*
substitution; **in ~ di** as a substitute
for, in place of

sotta'ceti [sotta'tʃeti] *smpl* pickles

sot'tana *sf* (*sottoveste*) underskirt;
(*gonna*) skirt; (*Rel*) soutane, cassock

sotter'fugio [sotter'fudʒo] *sm*
subterfuge

sotter'raneo, -a *ag* underground
▶ *sm* cellar

sotter'rare *vt* to bury

sot'tile *ag* thin; (*figura, caviglia*) thin,
slim, slender; (*fine: polvere, capelli*)
fine; (*fig: leggero*) light; (*: vista*) sharp,
keen; (*: olfatto*) fine, discriminating;
(*: mente*) subtle; shrewd ▶ *sm* **non
andare per il ~** not to mince matters

sottin'teso, -a *pp di* **sottintendere**
▶ *sm* allusion; **parlare senza
sottintesi** to speak plainly

'sotto *prep* (*gen*) under; (*più in basso
di*) below ▶ *av* underneath, beneath;
below; (*al piano*) **di ~** downstairs; **~
forma di** in the form of; **~ il monte**

at the foot of the mountain; **siamo
~ Natale** it's nearly Christmas;
~ la pioggia/il sole in the rain/
sun(shine); **~ terra** underground;
chiuso ~ vuoto vacuum-packed

sotto'fondo *sm* background;
sottofondo musicale background
music

sottoline'are *vt* to underline; (*fig*) to
emphasize, stress

sottoma'rino, -a *ag* (*flora*)
submarine; (*cavo, navigazione*)
underwater ▶ *sm* (*Naut*) submarine

sottopas'saggio [sottopas'saddʒo]
sm (*Aut*) underpass; (*pedonale*)
subway, underpass

sotto'porre *vt* (*costringere*) to subject;
(*fig: presentare*) to submit; **sottoporsi**
vpr to submit; **sottoporsi a** (*subire*)
to undergo

sottos'critto, -a *pp di* **sottoscrivere**

sotto'sopra *av* upside-down

sotto'terra *av* underground

sotto'titolo *sm* subtitle

sottovalu'tare *vt* to underestimate

sotto'veste *sf* underskirt

sotto'voce [sotto'votʃe] *av* in a low
voice

sottovu'oto *av* **confezionare ~** to
vacuum-pack ▶ *ag* **confezione f ~**
vacuum packed

souve'nir [suv(a)'nir] *sm inv* souvenir

sovi'etico, -a, -ci, -che *ag* Soviet
▶ *sm/f* Soviet citizen

sovrac'carico, -a, chi, che *ag* **~ (di)**
overloaded (with) ▶ *sm* excess load; **~
di lavoro** extra work

sovraffol'lato, -a *ag* overcrowded

sovrannatu'rale *ag*
= **soprannatu'rale**

so'vrano, -a *ag* sovereign; (*fig:
sommo*) supreme ▶ *sm/f* sovereign,
monarch

sovrap'porre *vt* to place on top of,
put on top of

sovvenzi'one [sovven'tsjone] *sf*
subsidy, grant

'sozzo, -a ['sottso] *ag* filthy, dirty

S.P.A. *abbr* = **società per azioni**

spac'care *vt* to split, break; (*legna*) to
chop; **spaccarsi** *vpr* to split, break;
spacca'tura *sf* split

spaccherò *ecc* [spakke'rɔ] *vb vedi*
spaccare

spacci'are [spat'tʃare] *vt* (*vendere*) to
sell (off); (*mettere in circolazione*) to
circulate; (*droga*) to peddle, push;
spacciarsi *vpr* **spacciarsi per** (*farsi
credere*) to pass o.s. off as, pretend
to be; **spaccia'tore, -'trice** *sm/f* (*di
droga*) pusher; (*di denaro falso*) dealer;
'spaccio *sm* (*di merce rubata, droga*):
spaccio (di) trafficking (in); **spaccio
(di)** passing (of); (*vendita*) sale;
(*bottega*) shop

'spacco, -chi *sm* (*fenditura*) split,
crack; (*strappo*) tear; (*di gonna*) slit

spac'cone *sm/f* boaster, braggart

spada *sf* sword

spae'sato, -a *ag* disorientated, lost

spa'ghetti [spa'getti] *smpl* (*Cuc*)
spaghetti *sg*

'Spagna ['spaɲɲa] *sf* la ~ Spain;
spa'gnolo, -a *ag* Spanish ▶ *sm/f*
Spaniard ▶ *sm* (*Ling*) Spanish; **gli
Spagnoli** the Spanish

'spago, -ghi *sm* string, twine

spai'ato, -a *ag* (*calza, guanto*) odd

spalan'care *vt* to open wide;
spalancarsi *vpr* to open wide

spa'lare *vt* to shovel

'spalla *sf* shoulder; (*fig: Teatro*) stooge;
spalle *sfpl* (*dorso*) back

spalli'era *sf* (*di sedia ecc*) back; (*di
letto: da capo*) head(board); (: *da piedi*)
foot(board); (*Ginnastica*) wall bars *pl*

spal'lina *sf* (*bretella*) strap;
(*imbottitura*) shoulder pad

spal'mare *vt* to spread

'spalti *smpl* (*di stadio*) terracing

'spandere *vt* to spread; (*versare*) to
pour (out)

spa'rare *vt* to fire ▶ *vi* (*far fuoco*) to
fire; (*tirare*) to shoot; **spara'toria** *sf*
exchange of shots

sparecchi'are [sparek'kjare] *vt* ~ (**la
tavola**) to clear the table

spa'reggio [spa'reddʒo] *sm* (*Sport*)
play-off

'spargere ['spardʒere] *vt* (*sparpagliare*)
to scatter; (*versare: vino*) to spill; (:
lacrime, sangue) to shed; (*diffondere*) to
spread; (*emanare*) to give off (*o* out);
spargersi *vpr* to spread

spa'rire *vi* to disappear, vanish

spar'lare *vi* ~ **di** to run down, speak
ill of

'sparo *sm* shot

spar'tire *vt* (*eredità, bottino*) to share
out; (*avversari*) to separate

spar'tito *sm* (*Mus*) score

sparti'traffico *sm inv* (*Aut*) central
reservation (*BRIT*), median (strip) (*US*)

sparvi'ero *sm* (*Zool*) sparrowhawk

spasi'mante *sm* suitor

spassio'nato, -a *ag* dispassionate,
impartial

'spasso *sm* (*divertimento*) amusement,
enjoyment; **andare a ~** to go out for
a walk; **essere a ~** (*fig*) to be out of
work; **mandare qn a ~** (*fig*) to give
sb the sack

'spatola *sf* spatula; (*di muratore*)
trowel

spa'valdo, -a *ag* arrogant, bold

spaventa'passeri *sm inv* scarecrow

spaven'tare *vt* to frighten, scare;
spaventarsi *vpr* to be frightened,

be scared; to get a fright; **spa'vento**
sm fear, fright; **far spavento a qn**
to give sb a fright; **spaven'toso,
-a** ag frightening, terrible; (fig: fam)
tremendous, fantastic

spazientirsi [spattsjen'tirsi] vpr to
lose one's patience

'spazio ['spattsjo] sm space; **spazio
aereo** airspace; **spazi'oso, -a** ag
spacious

spazzaca'mino [spattsaka'mino] sm
chimney sweep

spazza'neve [spattsa'neve] sm inv
snowplough

spaz'zare [spat'tsare] vt to sweep;
(foglie ecc) to sweep up; (cacciare)
to sweep away; **spazza'tura** sf
sweepings pl; (immondizia) rubbish;
spaz'zino sm street sweeper

'spazzola ['spattsola] sf brush;
spazzola da capelli hairbrush;
spazzola per abiti clothesbrush;
spazzo'lare vt to brush; **spazzo'lino**
sm (small) brush; **spazzolino da
denti** toothbrush

specchi'arsi [spek'kjarsi] vpr to look
at o.s. in a mirror; (riflettersi) to be
mirrored, be reflected

specchi'etto [spek'kjetto] sm
(tabella) table, chart; **specchietto da
borsetta** pocket mirror; **specchietto
retrovisore** (Aut) rear-view mirror

'specchio ['spekkjo] sm mirror

speci'ale [spe'tʃale] ag special;
specia'lista, -i, -e sm/f specialist;
specialità sf inv speciality; (branca
di studio) special field, speciality;
**vorrei assaggiare una specialità del
posto** I'd like to try a local speciality;
special'mente av especially,
particularly

'specie ['spetʃe] sf inv (Biol, Bot, Zool)
species inv; (tipo) kind, sort ▶ av
especially, particularly; **una ~ di** a
kind of; **fare ~ a qn** to surprise sb; **la ~**

umana mankind

specifi'care [spetʃifi'kare] vt to
specify, state

spe'cifico, -a, -ci, -che [spe'tʃifiko]
ag specific

specu'lare vi ~ **su** (Comm) to speculate
in; (sfruttare) to exploit; (meditare)
to speculate on; **speculazi'one** sf
speculation

spe'dire vt to send

'spegnere ['spɛɲɲere] vt (fuoco,
sigaretta) to put out, extinguish;
(apparecchio elettrico) to turn o
switch off; (gas) to turn off; (fig:
suoni, passioni) to stifle; (debito) to
extinguish; **spegnersi** vpr to go out;
(morire) to pass away; **puoi
~ la luce?** could you switch off the
light?; **non riesco a ~ il riscaldamento**
I can't turn the heating off

spellarsi vpr to peel

'spendere vt to spend

'spengo ecc vb vedi **spegnere**

spensi ecc vb vedi **spegnere**

spensie'rato, -a ag carefree

'spento, -a pp di **spegnere** ▶ ag
(suono) muffled; (colore) dull;
(sigaretta) out; (civiltà, vulcano) extinct

spe'ranza [spe'rantsa] sf hope

spe'rare vt to hope for ▶ vi ~ **in** to trust
in; ~ **che/di fare** to hope that/to do;
lo spero, spero di sì I hope so

sper'duto, -a ag (isolato) out-of-the-
way; (persona: smarrita, a disagio) lost

sperimen'tale ag experimental

sperimen'tare vt to experiment
with, test; (fig) to test, put to the test

'sperma, -i sm sperm

spe'rone sm spur

sperpe'rare vt to squander

'spesa sf (somma di denaro) expense;
(costo) cost; (acquisto) purchase; (fam:
acquisto del cibo quotidiano) shopping;
spese postali postage sg; **spese di
viaggio** travelling expenses

'spesso, -a ag (fitto) thick; (frequente) frequent ▸ av often; **spesse volte** frequently, often

spes'sore sm thickness

Spett. abbr vedi **spettabile**

spet'tabile (abbr: Spett.: in lettere) ag ~ **Ditta X** Messrs X and X

spet'tacolo sm (rappresentazione) performance, show; (vista, scena) sight; **dare ▸ di sé** to make an exhibition o a spectacle of o.s.

spet'tare vi ~ **a** (decisione) to be up to; (stipendio) to be due to; **spetta a te decidere** it's up to you to decide

spetta'tore, -'trice sm/f (Cinema, Teatro) member of the audience; (di avvenimento) onlooker, witness

spettego'lare vi to gossip

spetti'nato, -a ag dishevelled

'spettro sm (fantasma) spectre; (Fisica) spectrum

'spezie ['spettsje] sfpl (Cuc) spices

spez'zare [spet'tsare] vt (rompere) to break; (fig: interrompere) to break up; **spezzarsi** vpr to break

spezza'tino [spettsa'tino] sm (Cuc) stew

spezzet'tare [spettset'tare] vt to break up (o chop) into small pieces

'spia sf spy; (della polizia) informer; (Elettr) indicating light; warning light; (fessura) peep-hole; (fig: sintomo) sign, indication

spia'cente [spja'tʃɛnte] ag sorry; **essere ~ di qc/di fare qc** to be sorry about sth/for doing sth

spia'cevole [spja'tʃevole] ag unpleasant

spi'aggia, -ge ['spjaddʒa] sf beach; **spiaggia libera** public beach

spia'nare vt (terreno) to level, make level; (edificio) to raze to the ground; (pasta) to roll out; (rendere liscio) to smooth (out)

spi'are vt to spy on

spi'azzo ['spjattso] sm open space; (radura) clearing

'spicchio ['spikkjo] sm (di agrumi) segment; (di aglio) clove; (parte) piece, slice

spicci'arsi vpr to hurry up

spiccioli smpl (small) change; **mi dispiace, non ho ~** sorry, I don't have any change

'spicco, -chi sm **di ~** outstanding; (tema) main, principal; **fare ~** to stand out

spie'dino sm (utensile) skewer; (pietanza) kebab

spi'edo sm (Cuc) spit

spie'gare vt (far capire) to explain; (tovaglia) to unfold; (vele) to unfurl; **spiegarsi** vpr to explain o.s., make o.s. clear; ~ **qc a qn** to explain sth to sb; **spiegazi'one** sf explanation

spiegherò ecc [spjege'rɔ] vb vedi **spiegare**

spie'tato, -a ag ruthless, pitiless

spiffe'rare (fam) vt to blurt out, blab

'spiffero sm draught (BRIT), draft (US)

'spiga, -ghe sf (Bot) ear

spigli'ato, -a [spiʎ'ʎato] ag self-possessed, self-confident

'spigolo sm corner; (Mat) edge

'spilla sf brooch; (da cravatta, cappello) pin; ~ **di sicurezza** o **da balia** safety pin

'spillo sm pin; **spillo da balia** o **di sicurezza** safety pin

spi'lorcio, -a, -ci, -ce [spi'lortʃo] ag mean, stingy

'spina sf (Zool) thorn, prickle; (di pesce) bone; (Elettr) plug; (di botte) bunghole; **birra alla ~** draught beer; **spina dorsale** (Anat) backbone

spinaci [spi'natʃi] smpl spinach sg

spi'nello sm (Droga: gergo) joint

'spingere ['spindʒere] vt to push; (condurre: anche fig) to drive; (stimolare): ~ **qn a fare** to urge o press sb to do

spi'noso, -a ag thorny, prickly

'spinsi ecc vb vedi **spingere**

'spinta sf (urto) push; (Fisica) thrust; (fig: stimolo) incentive, spur; (: appoggio) string-pulling no pl; **dare una ~ a qn** (fig) to pull strings for sb

'spinto, -a pp di **spingere**

spio'naggio [spjo'nadd3o] sm espionage, spying

spion'cino [spjon'tʃino] sm peephole

spi'raglio [spi'raʎʎo] sm (fessura) chink, narrow opening; (raggio di luce, fig) glimmer, gleam

spi'rale sf spiral; (contraccettivo) coil; **a ~ spiral(-shaped)**

spiri'tato, -a ag possessed; (fig: persona, espressione) wild

spiri'tismo sm spiritualism

'spirito sm (Rel, Chim, disposizione d'animo, di legge ecc, fantasma) spirit; (pensieri, intelletto) mind; (arguzia) wit; (umorismo) humour, wit; **lo S~ Santo** the Holy Spirit o Ghost

spirito'saggine [spirito'sadd3ine] sf witticism; (peg) wisecrack

spiri'toso, -a ag witty

spiritu'ale ag spiritual

'splendere vi to shine

'splendido, -a ag splendid; (splendente) shining; (sfarzoso) magnificent, splendid

splen'dore sm splendour; (luce intensa) brilliance, brightness

spogli'are [spoʎ'ʎare] vt (svestire) to undress; (privare, fig: depredare): **~ qn di qc** to deprive sb of sth; (togliere ornamenti: anche fig): **~ qn/qc di** to strip sb/sth of; **spogliarsi** vpr to undress, strip; **spogliarsi di** (ricchezze ecc) to deprive o.s. of, give up; (pregiudizi) to rid o.s. of; **spoglia'rello** [spoʎʎa'rello] sm striptease; **spoglia'toio** sm dressing room; (di scuola ecc) cloakroom; (Sport)

changing room

'spola sf (bobina di filo) cop; **fare la ~ (fra)** to go to and fro o shuttle (between)

spolve'rare vt (anche Cuc) to dust; (con spazzola) to brush; (con battipanni) to beat; (fig) to polish off ▶ vi to dust

spon'taneo, -a ag spontaneous; (persona) unaffected, natural

spor'care vt to dirty, make dirty; (fig) to sully, soil; **sporcarsi** vpr to get dirty

spor'cizia [spor'tʃittsja] sf (stato) dirtiness; (sudiciume) dirt, filth; (cosa sporca) dirt no pl, something dirty

'sporco, -a, -chi, -che ag dirty, filthy

spor'genza [spor'd3ɛntsa] sf projection

'sporgere [spord3ere] vt to put out, stretch out ▶ vi (venire in fuori) to stick out; **sporgersi** vpr to lean out; **~ querela contro qn** (Dir) to take legal action against sb

'sporsi ecc vb vedi **sporgere**

sport sm inv sport

spor'tello sm (di treno, auto ecc) door; (di banca, ufficio) window, counter; **sportello automatico** (Banca) cash dispenser, automated telling machine

spor'tivo, -a ag (gara, giornale, centro) sports cpd; (persona) sporty; (abito) casual; (spirito, atteggiamento) sporting

'sposa sf bride; (moglie) wife

sposa'lizio [spoza'littsjo] sm wedding

spo'sare vt to marry; (fig: idea, fede) to espouse; **sposarsi** vpr to get married, marry; **sposarsi con qn** to marry sb, get married to sb; **spo'sato, -a** ag married

'sposo sm (bride)groom; (marito) husband

spos'sato, -a ag exhausted, weary

spos'tare vt to move, shift; (cambiare: orario) to change; **spostarsi** vpr to move; **può ~ la macchina, per favore?** can you move your car please?

'spranga, -ghe sf (sbarra) bar

spre'care vt to waste

spre'gevole [spre'dʒevole] ag contemptible, despicable

'spremere vt to squeeze

spremia'grumi sm inv lemon squeezer

spre'muta sf fresh juice; **spremuta d'arancia** fresh orange juice

sprez'zante [spret'tsante] ag scornful, contemptuous

sprofon'dare vi to sink; (casa) to collapse; (suolo) to give way, subside

spro'nare vt to spur (on)

sproporzio'nato, -a [sproportsjo'nato] ag disproportionate, out of all proportion

sproporzi'one [spropor'tsjone] sf disproportion

spro'posito sm blunder; **a ~** at the wrong time; (rispondere, parlare) irrelevantly

sprovve'duto, -a ag inexperienced, naïve

sprov'visto, -a ag (mancante): **~ di** lacking in, without; **alla sprovvista** unawares

spruz'zare [sprut'tsare] vt (a nebulizzazione) to spray; (aspergere) to sprinkle; (inzaccherare) to splash

'spugna ['spuɲɲa] sf (Zool) sponge; (tessuto) towelling

'spuma sf (schiuma) foam; (bibita) fizzy drink

spu'mante sm sparkling wine

spun'tare vt (coltello) to break the point of; (capelli) to trim ▶ vi (uscire: germogli) to sprout; (: capelli) to begin to grow; (: denti) to come through; (apparire) to appear (suddenly)

spun'tino sm snack

'spunto sm (Teatro, Mus) cue; (fig)

starting point; **dare lo ~ a** (fig) to give rise to

spu'tare vt to spit out; (fig) to belch (out) ▶ vi to spit

'squadra sf (strumento) (set) square; (gruppo) team, squad; (di operai) gang, squad; (Mil) squad; (: Aer, Naut) squadron; (Sport) team; **lavoro a squadre** teamwork

squagli'arsi [skwaʎ'ʎarsi] vpr to melt; (fig) to sneak off

squa'lifica sf disqualification

squalifi'care vt to disqualify

squ'allido, -a ag wretched, bleak

'squalo sm shark

'squama sf scale

squarcia'gola [skwartʃa'gola]: **a ~** av at the top of one's voice

squattri'nato, -a ag penniless

squili'brato, -a ag (Psic) unbalanced

squil'lante ag shrill, sharp

squil'lare vi (campanello, telefono) to ring (out); (tromba) to blare; **'squillo** sm ring, ringing no pl; blare; **ragazza f squillo** inv call girl

squi'sito, -a ag exquisite; (cibo) delicious; (persona) delightful

squit'tire vi (uccello) to squawk; (topo) to squeak

sradi'care vt to uproot; (fig) to eradicate

srego'lato, -a ag (senza ordine: vita) disorderly; (smodato) immoderate; (dissoluto) dissolute

S.r.l. abbr = **società a responsabilità limitata**

sroto'lare vt, **sroto'larsi** ▶ vpr to unroll

SS sigla = **strada statale**

S.S.N. abbr (= Servizio Sanitario Nazionale) ≈ NHS

sta ecc vb vedi **stare**

'stabile ag stable, steady; (tempo: non variabile) settled; (Teatro: compagnia) resident ▶ sm (edificio) building

stabili'mento sm (edificio) establishment; (fabbrica) plant, factory

stabi'lire vt to establish; (fissare: prezzi, data) to fix; (decidere) to decide; **stabilirsi** vpr (prendere dimora) to settle

stac'care vt (levare) to detach, remove; (separare: anche fig) to separate, divide; (strappare) to tear off (o out); (scandire: parole) to pronounce clearly; (Sport) to leave behind; **staccarsi** vpr (bottone ecc) to come off; (scostarsi) **staccarsi (da)** to come away (from); (fig: separarsi): **staccarsi da** to leave; **non ~ gli occhi da qn** not to take one's eyes off sb

'stadio sm (Sport) stadium; (periodo, fase) phase, stage

'staffa sf (di sella, Tecn) stirrup; **perdere le staffe** (fig) to fly off the handle

staf'fetta sf (messo) dispatch rider; (Sport) relay race

stagio'nale [stadʒo'nale] ag seasonal

stagio'nato, -a [stadʒo'nato] ag (vedi vb) seasoned; matured; (scherzoso: attempato) getting on in years

stagi'one [sta'dʒone] sf season; **alta/bassa ~** high/low season

stagista, -i, -e [sta'dʒista] sm/f trainee, intern (US)

'stagno, -a ['staɲɲo] ag watertight; (a tenuta d'aria) airtight ▶ sm (acquitrino) pond; (Chim) tin

sta'gnola [stan'ɲɔla] sf tinfoil

'stalla sf (per bovini) cowshed; (per cavalli) stable

stal'lone sm stallion

stamat'tina av this morning

stam'becco, -chi sm ibex

'stampa sf (Tip, Fot: tecnica) printing; (impressione, copia fotografica) print; (insieme di quotidiani, giornali ecc) press

stam'pante sf (Inform) printer

stam'pare vt to print; (pubblicare) to publish; (coniare) to strike, coin; (imprimere: anche fig) to impress

stampa'tello sm block letters pl

stam'pella sf crutch

'stampo sm mould; (fig: indole) type, kind, sort

sta'nare vt to drive out

stan'care vt to tire, make tired; (annoiare) to bore; (infastidire) to annoy; **stancarsi** vpr to get tired, tire o.s. out; **stancarsi (di)** to grow weary (of), grow tired (of)

stan'chezza [stan'kettsa] sf tiredness, fatigue

'stanco, -a, -chi, -che ag tired; **~ di** tired of, fed up with

stan'ghetta [stan'getta] sf (di occhiali) leg; (Mus, di scrittura) bar

'stanno vb vedi **stare**

sta'notte av tonight; (notte passata) last night

'stante prep a sé ~ (appartamento, casa) independent, separate

stan'tio, -a, -'tii, -'tie ag stale; (burro) rancid; (fig) old

stan'tuffo sm piston

'stanza ['stantsa] sf room; (Poesia) stanza; **stanza da bagno** bathroom; **stanza da letto** bedroom

stap'pare vt to uncork; to uncap

'stare vi (restare in un luogo) to stay, remain; (abitare) to stay, live; (essere situato) to be, be situated; (anche: **~ in piedi**) to be, stand; (essere, trovarsi) to be; (dipendere): **se stesse in me** if it were up to me, if it depended on me; (seguito da gerundio): **sta studiando** he's studying; **starci** (esserci spazio): **nel baule non ci sta più niente** there's no more room in the boot; (accettare) to accept; (essere, trovarsi) **ci stai?** is that okay with you?; **~ a** (attenersi a) to follow, stick to; (seguito dall'infinito): **stiamo a discutere** we're talking; (toccare *a*): **sta te giocare** it's your turn to play; **~ per fare qc** to be about to do sth; **come sta?** how are you?; **io sto bene/male** I'm very well/not very well; **~ a qn** (*abiti ecc*) to fit sb; **queste scarpe mi stanno strette** these shoes are tight for me; **il rosso ti sta bene** red suits you

starnu'tire *vi* to sneeze; **star'nuto** *sm* sneeze

sta'sera *av* this evening, tonight

sta'tale *ag* state *cpd*; **government** *cpd* ▶ *sm/f* state employee, local authority employee; (*nell'amministrazione*) ≈ civil servant; **strada statale** ≈ trunk (*Brit*) *o* main road

sta'tista, -i *sm* statesman

sta'tistica *sf* statistics *sg*

'stato, -a *pp di* **essere; stare** ▶ *sm* (*condizione*) state, condition; (*Pol*) state; (*Dir*) status; **essere in ~ d'accusa** (*Dir*) to be committed for trial; **~ d'assedio/d'emergenza** state of siege/emergency; **~ civile** (*Amm*) marital status; **gli Stati Uniti (d'America)** the United States (of America); **stato d'animo** mood; **stato maggiore** (*Mil*) staff

'statua *sf* statue

statuni'tense *ag* United States *cpd*, of the United States

sta'tura *sf* (*Anat*) height, stature; (*fig*) stature

sta'tuto *sm* (*Dir*) statute; constitution

sta'volta *av* this time

stazio'nario, -a [stattsjo'narjo] *ag* stationary; (*fig*) unchanged

stazi'one [stat'tsjone] *sf* station; (*balneare, termale*) resort; **stazione degli autobus** bus station; **stazione balneare** seaside resort; **stazione ferroviaria** railway (*Brit*) *o* railroad (*US*) station; **stazione invernale** winter sports resort; **stazione di polizia** police station (*in small town*);

stazione di servizio service *o* petrol (*Brit*) *o* filling station

'stecca, -che *sf* stick; (*di ombrello*) rib; (*di sigarette*) carton; (*Med*) splint; (*stonatura*) **fare una ~** to sing (*o* play) a wrong note

stec'cato *sm* fence

'stella *sf* star; **stella alpina** (*Bot*) edelweiss; **stella cadente** shooting star; **stella di mare** (*Zool*) starfish

'stelo *sm* stem; (*asta*) rod; **lampada a ~** standard lamp

'stemma, -i *sm* coat of arms

'stemmo *vb vedi* **stare**

stempi'ato, -a *ag* with a receding hairline

'stendere *vt* (*braccia, gambe*) to stretch (out); (*tovaglia*) to spread (out); (*bucato*) to hang out; (*mettere a giacere*) to lay (down); (*spalmare: colore*) to spread; (*mettere per iscritto*) to draw up; **stendersi** *vpr* (*coricarsi*) to stretch out, lie down; (*estendersi*) to extend, stretch

stenogra'fia *sf* shorthand

sten'tare *vi* **~ a fare** to find it hard to do, have difficulty doing

'stento *sm* (*fatica*) difficulty; **stenti** *smpl* (*privazioni*) hardship *sg*, privation *sg*; **a ~** with difficulty, barely

'sterco *sm* dung

stereo ['stereo] *ag inv* stereo ▶ *sm inv* (*impianto*) stereo

'sterile *ag* sterile; (*terra*) barren; (*fig*) futile, fruitless

steriliz'zare [sterilid'dzare] *vt* to sterilize

ster'lina *sf* pound (sterling)

stermi'nare *vt* to exterminate, wipe out

stermi'nato, -a *ag* immense; endless

ster'minio *sm* extermination, destruction

'sterno *sm* (*Anat*) breastbone

ste'roide *sm* steroid

ster'zare [ster'tsare] vt, vi (Aut) to steer; **'terzo** sm steering; (volante) steering wheel

'stessi ecc vb vedi **stare**

'stesso, -a ag same; (rafforzativo: in persona, proprio): **il re ~** the king himself o in person ▶ pron **lo(la) ~(a)** the same (one); **i suoi stessi avversari lo ammirano** even his enemies admire him; **fa lo ~** it doesn't matter; **per me è lo ~** it's all the same to me, it doesn't matter to me; vedi **io**; **tu** ecc

ste'sura sf drafting no pl, drawing up no pl; draft

'stetti ecc vb vedi **stare**

'stia ecc vb vedi **stare**

sti'lare vt to draw up, draft

'stile sm style; **stile libero** freestyle; **sti'lista, -i** sm designer

stilo'grafica, -che sf (anche: **penna ~**) fountain pen

'stima sf esteem; valuation; assessment, estimate

sti'mare vt (persona) to esteem, hold in high regard; (terreno, casa ecc) to value; (stabilire in misura approssimativa) to estimate, assess; (ritenere): **~ che** to consider that; **stimarsi fortunato** to consider o.s. (to be) lucky

stimo'lare vt to stimulate; (incitare): **~ qn (a fare)** to spur sb on (to do)

'stimolo sm (anche fig) stimulus

'stingere ['stindʒere] vt, vi (anche: **stingersi**) to fade; **'stinto, -a** pp di **stingere**

sti'pare vt to cram, pack; **stiparsi** vpr (accalcarsi) to crowd, throng

sti'pendio sm salary

'stipite sm (di porta, finestra) jamb

stipu'lare vt (redigere) to draw up

sti'rare vt (abito) to iron; (distendere) to stretch; (strappare: muscolo) to strain; **stirarsi** vpr to stretch (o.s.)

stiti'chezza [stiti'kettsa] sf

constipation

'stitico, -a, -ci, -che ag constipated

'stiva sf (di nave) hold

sti'vale sm boot

'stizza ['stittsa] sf anger, vexation

'stoffa sf material, fabric; (fig): **aver la ~ di** to have the makings of

'stomaco, -chi sm stomach; **dare di ~** to vomit, be sick

sto'nato, -a ag (persona) off-key; (strumento) off-key, out of tune

stop sm inv (Tel) stop; (Aut: cartello) stop sign; (: fanalino d'arresto) brake-light

'storcere ['stɔrtʃere] vt to twist; **storcersi** vpr to writhe, twist; **~ il naso** (fig) to turn up one's nose; **storcersi la caviglia** to twist one's ankle

stor'dire vt (intontire) to stun, daze; **stor'dito, -a** ag stunned

'storia sf (scienza, avvenimenti) history; (racconto, bugia) story; (faccenda, questione) business no pl; (pretesto) excuse, pretext; **storie** sfpl (smancerie) fuss sg; **'storico, -a, -ci, -che** ag historic(al) ▶ sm historian

stori'one sm (Zool) sturgeon

'stormo sm (di uccelli) flock

'storpio, -a ag crippled, maimed

'storsi ecc vb vedi **storcere**

'storta sf (distorsione) sprain, twist

'storto, -a pp di **storcere** ▶ ag (chiodo) twisted, bent; (gamba, quadro) crooked

sto'viglie [sto'viʎʎe] sfpl dishes pl, crockery

'strabico, -a, -ci, -che ag squint-eyed; (occhi) squint

strac'chino [strak'kino] sm type of soft cheese

stracci'are [strat'tʃare] vt to tear; **stracciarsi** vpr to tear

'straccio, -a, -ci, -ce [strat'tʃo] ag **carta straccia** waste paper ▶ sm rag;

(*per pulire*) cloth, duster; **stracci** *smpl* (*peg: indumenti*) rags; **si è ridotto a uno** ~ he's worn himself out; **non ha uno ~ di lavoro** he's not got a job of any sort

'**strada** *sf* road; (*di città*) street; (*cammino, via, fig*) way; **che ~ devo prendere per andare a ...?** which road do I take for ...?; **farsi ~** (*fig*) to do well for o.s.; **essere fuori ~** (*fig*) to be on the wrong track; **~ facendo** on the way; **strada senza uscita** dead end; **stra'dale** *ag* road *cpd*

strafalci'one [strafal'tʃone] *sm* blunder, howler

stra'fare *vi* to overdo it

strafot'tente *ag* **è ~** he doesn't give a damn, he couldn't care less

'**strage** ['stradʒe] *sf* massacre, slaughter

stralu'nato, -a *ag* (*occhi*) rolling; (*persona*) beside o.s., very upset

stram'bo, -a *ag* strange, queer

strampa'lato, -a *ag* odd, eccentric

stra'nezza [stra'nettsa] *sf* strangeness

strango'lare *vt* to strangle

strani'ero, -a *ag* foreign ▶ *sm/f* foreigner

Attenzione! In inglese esiste la parola *stranger*, che però significa *sconosciuto* oppure *estraneo*.

'**strano, -a** *ag* strange, odd

straordi'nario, -a *ag* extraordinary; (*treno ecc*) special ▶ *sm* (*lavoro*) overtime

strapi'ombo *sm* overhanging rock; **a ~** overhanging

strap'pare *vt* (*gen*) to tear, rip; (*pagina ecc*) to tear out; (*sradicare*) to pull up; (*togliere*): **~ qc a qn** to snatch sth from sb; (*fig*) to wrest sth from sb; **strapparsi** *vpr* (*lacerarsi*) to rip, tear; (*rompersi*) to break; **strapparsi un muscolo** to tear a muscle

'**strappo** *sm* pull, tug; tear, rip; **fare uno strappo alla regola** to make an exception to the rule; **strappo muscolare** torn muscle

strari'pare *vi* to overflow

stras'cico, -chi ['straʃʃiko] *sm* (*di abito*) train; (*conseguenza*) after-effect

strata'gemma, -i [strata'dʒemma] *sm* stratagem

strate'gia, -'gie [strate'dʒia] *sf* strategy; **stra'tegico, -a, -ci, -che** *ag* strategic

'**strato** *sm* layer; (*rivestimento*) coat, coating; (*Geo, fig*) stratum; (*Meteor*) stratus; **strato d'ozono** ozone layer

strat'tone *sm* tug, jerk; **dare uno ~ a qc** to tug o **~ a** jerk sth, give sth a tug o **~**

strava'gante *ag* odd, eccentric

stra'volto, -a *pp di* **stravolgere**

stra'zio ['stratsjo] *sm* torture; (*fig: cosa fatta male*): **essere uno ~** to be appalling

'**strega, -ghe** *sf* witch

stre'gare *vt* to bewitch

stre'gone *sm* (*mago*) wizard; (*di tribù*) witch doctor

strepi'toso, -a *ag* clamorous, deafening; (*fig: successo*) resounding

stres'sante *ag* stressful

stres'sato, -a *ag* under stress

stretch [stretʃ] *ag inv* stretch

'**stretta** *sf* (*di mano*) grasp; (*finanziaria*) squeeze; (*fig: dolore, turbamento*) pang; **una ~ di mano** a handshake; **essere alle strette** to have one's back to the wall; *vedi anche* **stretto**

stretta'mente (*rigorosamente*) strictly

'**stretto, -a** *pp di* **stringere** ▶ *ag* (*corridoio, limiti*) narrow; (*gonna, scarpe, nodo, curva*) tight; (*intimo: parente, amico*) close; (*rigoroso: osservanza*) strict; (*preciso: significato*) precise, exact ▶ *sm* (*braccio di mare*) strait; **a denti stretti** with clenched teeth;

lo ~ necessario the bare minimum; **stret'toia** sf bottleneck; (fig) tricky situation

stri'ato, -a ag streaked

'stridulo, -a ag shrill

stril'lare vt, vi to scream, shriek; **'strillo** sm scream, shriek

strimin'zito, -a [strimin'tsito] ag (misero) shabby; (magro) skinny

strimpel'lare vt (Mus) to strum

'stringa, -ghe sf lace

strin'gato, -a ag (fig) concise

'stringere ['strindʒere] vt (avvicinare due cose) to press (together), squeeze (together); (tenere stretto) to hold tight, clasp, clutch; (pugno, mascella, denti) to clench; (labbra) to compress; (avvitare) to tighten; (abito) to take in; (scarpe) to pinch, be tight for; (fig: concludere: patto) to make; (: accelerare: passo, tempo) to quicken ▶ vi (essere stretto) to be tight; (tempo: incalzare) to be pressing

'strinsi ecc vb vedi **stringere**

'striscia, -sce ['striʃʃa] sf (di carta, tessuto ecc) strip; (riga) stripe; **strisce (pedonali)** zebra crossing sg

strisci'are [striʃʃare] vt (piedi) to drag; (muro, macchina ecc) to graze ▶ vi to crawl, creep

'striscio ['striʃʃo] sm graze; (Med) smear; **colpire di ~** to graze

strisci'one [striʃʃone] sm banner

strito'lare vt to grind

striz'zare [strit'tsare] vt (panni) to wring (out); **~ l'occhio** to wink

'strofa sf strophe

strofi'naccio [strofi'nattʃo] sm duster, cloth; (per piatti) dishcloth; (per pavimenti) floorcloth

strofi'nare vt to rub

stron'care vt to break off; (fig: ribellione) to suppress, put down; (: film, libro) to tear to pieces

'stronzo ['strontso] sm (sterco) turd; (fig fam!: persona) shit (!)

stroz'zare [strot'tsare] vt (soffocare) to choke, strangle

struccarsi vpr to remove one's make-up

strumen'tale ag (Mus) instrumental

strumentaliz'zare [strumentalid'dzare] vt to exploit, use to one's own ends

stru'mento sm (arnese, fig) instrument, tool; (Mus) instrument; **~ a corda o ad arco/a fiato** stringed/ wind instrument

'strutto sm lard

strut'tura sf structure

'struzzo ['struttso] sm ostrich

stuc'care vt (muro) to plaster; (vetro) to putty; (decorare con stucchi) to stucco

'stucco, -chi sm plaster; (da vetri) putty; (ornamentale) stucco; **rimanere di ~** (fig) to be dumbfounded

stu'dente, -essa sm/f student; (scolaro) pupil, schoolboy/girl

studi'are vt to study

'studio sm studying; (ricerca, saggio, stanza) study; (di professionista) office; (di artista, Cinema, TV, Radio) studio; **studi** smpl (Ins) studies; **studio medico** doctor's surgery (BRIT) o office (US)

studi'oso, -a ag studious, hard-working ▶ sm/f scholar

'stufa sf stove; **stufa elettrica** electric fire o heater

stu'fare vt (Cuc) to stew; (fig: fam) to bore; **stufarsi** vpr (fam): **stufarsi (di)** (fig) to get fed up (with); **'stufo, -a** (fam) ag **essere stufo di** to be fed up with, be sick and tired of

stu'oia sf mat

stupefa'cente [stupefa'tʃente] ag stunning, astounding ▶ sm drug, narcotic

stupe'fatto, -a pp di **stupefare**

stu'pendo, -a *ag* marvellous, wonderful

stupi'daggine [stupi'daddʒine] *sf* stupid thing (to do o say)

stupidità *sf* stupidity

'stupido, -a *ag* stupid

stu'pire *vt* to amaze, stun ▶ *vi* **stupirsi**; ~ **(di)** to be amazed (at), be stunned (by)

stu'pore *sm* amazement, astonishment

stu'prare *vt* to rape

'stupro *sm* rape

stu'rare *vt* (*lavandino*) to clear

stuzzica'denti [stuttsika'dɛnti] *sm* toothpick

stuzzi'care [stuttsi'kare] *vt* (*ferita ecc*) to poke (at), prod (at); (*fig*) to tease; (: *appetito*) to whet; (: *curiosità*) to stimulate; ~ **i denti** to pick one's teeth

su

(*su +il* = **sul**, *su +lo* = **sullo**, *su +l'* = **sull'**, *su +la* = **sulla**, *su +i* = **sui**, *su +gli* = **sugli**, *su +le* = **sulle**) *prep*

1 (*gen*) on; (*moto*) on(to); (*in cima a*) on (top of); **mettilo sul tavolo** put it on the table; **un paesino sul mare** a village by the sea

2 (*argomento*) about, on; **un libro su Cesare** a book on *o* about Caesar

3 (*circa*) about; **costerà sui 3 milioni** it will cost about 3 million; **una ragazza sui 17 anni** a girl of about 17 (years of age)

4: **su misura** made to measure; **su richiesta** on request; **3 casi su dieci** 3 cases out of 10

▶ *av*

1 (*in alto, verso l'alto*) up; **vieni su** come on up; **guarda su** look up; **su le mani!** hands up!; **in su** (*verso l'alto*) up(wards); (*in poi*) onwards; **dai 20 anni in su** from the age of 20 onwards

2 (*addosso*) on; **cos'hai su?** what have you got on?

▶ *escl* come on!; **su coraggio!** come on, cheer up!

sub'acqueo, -a *ag* underwater ▶ *sm* skin-diver

sub'buglio [sub'buʎʎo] *sm* confusion, turmoil

'subdolo, -a *ag* underhand, sneaky

suben'trare *vi* ~ **a qn in qc** to take over sth from sb

su'bire *vt* to suffer, endure

'subito *av* immediately, at once, straight away

subodo'rare *vt* (*insidia ecc*) to smell, suspect

subordi'nato, -a *ag* subordinate; (*dipendente*): ~ **a** dependent on, subject to

suc'cedere [sut'tʃedere] *vi* (*prendere il posto di qn*): ~ **a** to succeed; (*venire dopo*): ~ **a** to follow; (*accadere*) to happen; **cos'è successo?** what happened?; **succes'sivo, -a** *ag* successive; **suc'cesso, -a** *pp di* **succedere** ▶ *sm* (*esito*) outcome; (*buona riuscita*) success; **di successo** (*libro, personaggio*) successful

succhi'are [suk'kjare] *vt* to suck (up); **succhi'otto** *sm* (*per bambino*) dummy

succhi'otto [suk'kjɔtto] *sm* dummy (BRIT), pacifier (US), comforter (US)

suc'cinto, -a [sut'tʃinto] *ag* (*discorso*) succinct; (*abito*) brief

'succo, -chi *sm* juice; (*fig*) essence, gist; **succo di frutta/pomodoro** fruit/tomato juice

succur'sale *sf* branch (office)

sud *sm* south ▶ *ag inv* south; (*lato*) south, southern

Su'dafrica *sm* **il** ~ South Africa; **sudafri'cano, -a** *ag, sm/f* South African

Suda'merica *sm* **il** ~ South America

su'dare *vi* to perspire, sweat; ~ **freddo** to come out in a cold sweat

su'dato, -a *ag* (*persona, mani*) sweaty;

(fig: denaro) hard-earned ▶ sf (anche fig) sweat; **una vittoria sudata** a hard-won victory; **ho fatto una bella sudata per finirlo in tempo** it was a real sweat to get it finished in time

suddi'videre vt to subdivide

su'dest sm south-east

'sudicio, -a, -ci, -ce ['suditʃo] ag dirty, filthy

su'dore sm perspiration, sweat

su'dovest sm south-west

suffici'ente [suffi'tʃɛnte] ag enough, sufficient; (borioso) self-important; (Ins) satisfactory; **suffici'enza** sf self-importance; pass mark; **a sufficienza** enough; **ne ho avuto a sufficienza!** I've had enough of this!

suf'fisso sm (Ling) suffix

sugge'rimento [suddʒeri'mento] sm suggestion; (consiglio) piece of advice, advice no pl

sugge'rire [suddʒe'rire] vt (risposta) to tell; (consigliare) to advise; (proporre) to suggest; (Teatro) to prompt

suggestio'nare [suddʒestjo'nare] vt to influence

sugges'tivo, -a [suddʒes'tivo] ag (paesaggio) evocative; (teoria) interesting, attractive

'sughero ['sugero] sm cork

'sugo, -ghi (succo) juice; (di carne) gravy; (condimento) sauce; (fig) gist, essence

sui'cida, -i, -e [sui'tʃida] ag suicidal ▶ sm/f suicide

suici'darsi [suitʃi'darsi] vpr to commit suicide

sui'cidio [sui'tʃidjo] sm suicide

su'ino, -a ag **carne suina** pork ▶ sm pig

sul'tano, -a sm/f sultan/sultana

'suo (f'sua, pl'suoi, pl'sue) det **il ~, la sua** ecc (di lui) his; (di lei) her; (di esso) its; (con valore indefinito) one's, his/her; (anche: **S~**: forma di cortesia) your ▶ pron

il ~, la sua ecc his; hers; yours; **i~i** his (o her o one's o your) family

su'ocero, -a ['swotʃero] sm/f father/mother-in-law

su'ola sf (di scarpa) sole

su'olo sm (terreno) ground; (terra) soil

suo'nare vt (Mus) to play; (campana) to ring; (ore) to strike; (clacson, allarme) to sound ▶ vi to play; (telefono, campana) to ring; (ore) to strike; (clacson, fig: parole) to sound

suone'ria sf alarm

su'ono sm sound

su'ora sf (Rel) sister

'super sf (anche: **benzina ~**) = four-star (petrol) (BRIT), premium (US)

supe'rare vt (oltrepassare: limite) to exceed, surpass; (percorrere) to cover; (attraversare: fiume) to cross; (sorpassare: veicolo) to overtake; (fig: essere più bravo di) to surpass, outdo; (: difficoltà) to overcome; (: esame) to get through; **~ qn in altezza/peso** to be taller/heavier than sb; **ha superato la cinquantina** he's over fifty (years of age)

su'perbia sf pride; **su'perbo, -a** ag proud; (fig) magnificent, superb

superfici'ale [superfi'tʃale] ag superficial

super'ficie, -ci [super'fitʃe] sf surface

su'perfluo, -a ag superfluous

superi'ore ag (piano, arto, classi) upper; (più elevato: temperatura, livello): **~ (a)** higher (than); (migliore): **~ (a)** superior (to)

superla'tivo, -a ag, sm superlative

supermer'cato sm supermarket

su'perstite ag surviving ▶ sm/f survivor

superstizi'one [superstit'tsjone] sf superstition; **superstizi'oso, -a** ag superstitious

super'strada sf ≈ (toll-free) motorway

su'pino, -a ag supine

supplemen'tare ag extra; (treno) relief cpd; (entrate) additional

supple'mento sm supplement

sup'plente sm/f temporary member of staff, supply (o substitute) teacher

'supplica, -che sf (preghiera) plea; (domanda scritta) petition, request

suppli'care vt to implore, beseech

sup'plizio [sup'plittsjo] sm torture

sup'pongo, sup'poni ecc vb vedi **supporre**

sup'porre vt to suppose

sup'porto sm (sostegno) support

sup'posta sf (Med) suppository

su'premo, -a ag supreme

surge'lare [surdʒe'lare] vt to (deep-)freeze

surge'lato, -a [surdʒe'lato] ag (deep-)frozen ▶ smpl i **surgelati** frozen food sg

'surplus sm inv (Econ) surplus

surriscal'dare vt to overheat

suscet'tibile [suʃʃet'tibile] ag (sensibile) touchy, sensitive

susci'tare [suʃʃi'tare] vt to provoke, arouse

su'sina sf plum

susseguirsi vpr to follow one another

sus'sidio sm subsidy; **sussidi didattici** teaching aids

sussul'tare vi to start

sussur'rare vt, vi to whisper, murmur; **sus'surro** sm whisper, murmur

svagarsi vpr to amuse o.s.; to enjoy o.s.

'svago, -ghi sm (riposo) relaxation; (ricreazione) amusement; (passatempo) pastime

svaligi'are [zvali'dʒare] vt to rob, burgle (BRIT), burglarize (US)

svalutarsi vpr (Econ) to be devalued

svalutazi'one sf devaluation

sva'nire vi to disappear, vanish

svantaggi'ato, -a [zvantad'dʒato] ag at a disadvantage

svan'taggio [zvan'taddʒo] sm disadvantage; (inconveniente) drawback, disadvantage

svari'ato, -a ag varied; various

'svastica sf swastika

sve'dese ag Swedish ▶ sm/f Swede ▶ sm (Ling) Swedish

'sveglia ['zveʎʎa] sf waking up; (orologio) alarm (clock); **sveglia telefonica** alarm call

svegli'are [zveʎ'ʎare] vt to wake up; (fig) to awaken, arouse; **svegliarsi** vpr to wake up; (fig) to be revived, reawaken; **vorrei essere svegliato alle 7, per favore** could I have an alarm call at 7 am, please?

'sveglio, -a ['zveʎʎo] ag awake; (fig) quick-witted

sve'lare vt to reveal

'svelto, -a ag (passo) quick; (mente) quick, alert; **alla svelta** quickly

'svendere vt to sell off, clear

'svendita sf (Comm) (clearance) sale

'svengo ecc vb vedi **svenire**

sveni'mento sm fainting fit, faint

sve'nire vi to faint

sven'tare vt to foil, thwart

sven'tato, -a ag (distratto) scatterbrained; (imprudente) rash

sven'tola sf: **orecchie a sventola** sticking-out ears

svento'lare vt, vi to wave, flutter

sven'tura sf misfortune

sver'rò ecc vb vedi **svenire**

sves'tire vt to undress; **svestirsi** vpr to get undressed

'Svezia ['zvettsja] sf la ~ Sweden

svi'are vt to divert; (fig) to lead astray

svi'gnarsela [zviɲ'ɲarsela] vpr to slip away, sneak off

svilup'pare vt to develop; **svilupparsi** vpr to develop; **può ~ questo rullino?** can you develop this film?

svi'luppo sm development

'svincolo sm (stradale) motorway (BRIT) o expressway (US) intersection

'svista sf oversight

svi'tare vt to unscrew

Svizzera ['zvittsera] sf la ~ Switzerland

svizzero, -a ['zvittsero] ag, sm/f Swiss

svogli'ato, -a [zvoʎ'ʎato] ag listless; (pigro) lazy

'svolgere ['zvɔldʒere] vt to unwind; (srotolare) to unroll; (fig: argomento) to develop; (: piano, programma) to carry out; **svolgersi** vpr to unwind; to unroll; (fig: aver luogo) to take place; (: procedere) to go on

'svolsi ecc vb vedi **svolgere**

'svolta sf (atto) turning no pl; (curva) turn, bend; (fig) turning-point

svol'tare vi to turn

svuo'tare vt to empty (out)

t

T, t [ti] sf o m inv (lettera) T, t; **T come Taranto** ≈ T for Tommy

t abbr = **tonnellata**

tabacche'ria [tabakke'ria] sf tobacconist's (shop)

● **tabaccheria**
● Tabaccherie sell cigarettes and
● tobacco and can easily be identified
● by their sign, a large white "T" on

● a black background. You can buy
● postage stamps and bus tickets at
● a tabaccheria and some also sell
● newspapers.

ta'bacco, -chi sm tobacco

ta'bella sf (tavola) table; (elenco) list

tabel'lone sm (pubblicitario) billboard; (con orario) timetable board

TAC sigla f (Med: = Tomografia Assiale Computerizzata) CAT

tac'chino [tak'kino] sm turkey

'tacco, -chi sm heel; **tacchi a spillo** stiletto heels

taccu'ino sm notebook

ta'cere [ta'tʃere] vi to be silent o quiet; (smettere di parlare) to fall silent ▶ vt to keep to oneself, say nothing about; **far ~ qn** to make sb be quiet; (fig) to silence sb

ta'chimetro [ta'kimetro] sm speedometer

'tacqui ecc vb vedi **tacere**

ta'fano sm horsefly

'taglia ['taʎʎa] sf (statura) height; (misura) size; (riscatto) ransom; (ricompensa) reward; **taglia forte** (di abito) large size

taglia'carte [taʎʎa'karte] sm inv paperknife

tagli'ando [taʎ'ʎando] sm coupon

tagli'are [taʎ'ʎare] vt to cut; (recidere, interrompere) to cut off; (intersecare) to cut across, intersect; (carne) to carve; (vini) to blend ▶ vi to cut; (prendere una scorciatoia) to take a short-cut; **tagliarsi** vpr to cut o.s.; **mi sono tagliato** I've cut myself; ~ **corto** (fig) to cut short; ~ **la corda** (fig) to sneak off; ~ **i ponti (con)** (fig) to break off relations (with); ~ **la strada a qn** to cut across sb; **mi sono tagliato** I've cut myself

taglia'telle [taʎʎa'telle] sfpl tagliatelle pl

taglia'unghie [taʎʎa'ungje] sm inv

nail clippers pl
tagli'ente [taʎˈʎɛnte] *ag* sharp
'taglio [ˈtaʎʎo] *sm* cutting *no pl*; cut; (*parte tagliente*) cutting edge; (*di abito*) cut, style; (*di stoffa: lunghezza*) length; (*di vini*) blending; **di ~** on edge, edgeways; **banconote di piccolo/grosso ~** notes of small/large denomination; **taglio cesareo** Caesarean section
tailan'dese *ag, sm/f, sm* Thai
Tai'landia *sf* la ~ Thailand
'talco *sm* talcum powder

O tale *det*

1 (*simile, così grande*) such; **un(a) tale ... such (a) ...; non accetto tali discorsi** I won't allow such talk; **è di una tale arroganza** he is so arrogant; **fa una tale confusione!** he makes such a mess!

2 (*persona o cosa indeterminata*) such-and-such; **il giorno tale all'ora tale** on such-and-such a day at such-and-such a time; **la tal persona** that person; **ha telefonato una tale Giovanna** somebody called Giovanna phoned

3 (*nelle similitudini*): **tale ... tale** like ...; like; **tale padre tale figlio** like father, like son; **hai il vestito tale quale il mio** your dress is just *o* exactly like mine

▶ *pron* (*indefinito: persona*): **un(a) tale** someone; **quel (o quella) tale** that person, that man (*o* woman); **il tal dei tali** what's-his-name

tale'bano *sm* Taliban
ta'lento *sm* talent
talis'mano *sm* talisman
tallon'cino [tallonˈtʃino] *sm* counterfoil
tal'lone *sm* heel
tal'mente *av* so
'talpa *sf* (*Zool*) mole
tal'volta *av* sometimes, at times
tambu'rello *sm* tambourine

tam'buro *sm* drum
Ta'migi [taˈmidʒi] *sm* il ~ the Thames
tampo'nare *vt* (*otturare*) to plug; (*urtare: macchina*) to crash *o* ram into
tam'pone *sm* (*Med*) wad, pad; (*per timbri*) ink-pad; (*respingente*) buffer; **tampone assorbente** tampon
'tana *sf* lair, den
'tanga *sm inv* G-string
tan'gente [tanˈdʒɛnte] *ag* (*Mat*): ~ **a** tangential to ▶ *sf* tangent; (*quota*) share
tangenzi'ale [tandʒenˈtsjale] *sf* (*Aut*) bypass
'tanica *sf* (*contenitore*) jerry can

O 'tanto, -a *det*

1 (*molto: quantità*) a lot of, much; (: *numero*) a lot of, many; (*così tanto: quantità*) so much, such a lot of; (: *numero*) so many, such a lot of; **tante volte** so many times, so often; **tanti auguri** all the best!; **tante grazie** many thanks; **tanto tempo** so long, such a long time; **ogni tanti chilometri** every so many kilometres

2: **tanto ... quanto** (*quantità*) as much ... as; (*numero*) as many ... as; **ho tanta pazienza quanta ne hai tu** I have as much patience as you have *o* as you; **ha tanti amici quanti nemici** he has as many friends as he has enemies

3 (*rafforzativo*) such; **ho aspettato per tanto tempo** I waited so long *o* for such a long time

▶ *pron*

1 (*molto*) much, a lot; (*così tanto*) so much, such a lot; **tanti, e** many, a lot; so many, such a lot; **credevo ce ne fosse tanto** I thought there was (such) a lot, I thought there was plenty

2: **tanto quanto** (*denaro*) as much; (*cioccolatini*) as many as; **ne ho tanto quanto basta** I have as much as I need; **due volte tanto** twice as much

3 (indeterminato) so much; **tanto per l'affitto, tanto per il gas** so much for the rent, so much for the gas; **costa un tanto al metro** it costs so much per metre; **di tanto in tanto, ogni tanto** every so often; **tanto vale che ...** I (o we ecc) may as well ...; **tanto meglio!** so much the better!; **tanto peggio per lui!** so much the worse for him!

▶ av

1 (molto) very; **vengo tanto volentieri** I'd be very glad to come; **non ci vuole tanto a capirlo** it doesn't take much to understand it

2 (così tanto: con ag, av) so; (: con vb) so much, such a lot; **è tanto bella!** she's so beautiful!; **non urlare tanto** don't shout so much; **sto tanto meglio adesso** I'm so much better now; **tanto ... che** so ... (that); **tanto ... da** so ... as

3 : **tanto ... quanto** as ... as; **conosco tanto Carlo quanto suo padre** I know both Carlo and his father; **non è poi tanto complicato quanto sembri** it's not as difficult as it seems; **tanto più insisti, tanto più non mollerà** la the more you insist, the more stubborn he'll be; **quanto più ... tanto meno** the more ... the less

4 (solamente) just; **tanto per cambiare/scherzare** just for a change/a joke; **una volta tanto** for once

5 (a lungo) (for) long

▶ cong after all

'tappa sf (luogo di sosta, fermata) stop, halt; (parte di un percorso) stage, leg; (Sport) lap; **a tappe** in stages

tap'pare vt to plug, stop up; (bottiglia) to cork; **tapparsi** vpr **tapparsi in casa** to shut o.s. up at home; **tapparsi la bocca** to shut up; **tapparsi le orecchie** to turn a deaf ear

tappa'rella sf rolling shutter

tappe'tino sm (per auto) car mat;

tappetino antiscivolo (da bagno) non-slip mat

tap'peto sm carpet; (anche: tappetino) rug; (Sport) **andare al ~** to go down for the count; **mettere sul ~** (fig) to bring up for discussion

tappez'zare [tappet'tsare] vt (con carta) to paper; (rivestire): **~ qc (di)** to cover sth (with); **tappezze'ria** sf (tessuto) tapestry; (carta da parati) wallpaper; (arte) upholstery; **far da tappezzeria** (fig) to be a wallflower

'tappo sm stopper; (in sughero) cork

tar'dare vi to be late ▶ vt to delay; **~ a fare** to delay doing

'tardi av late; (più ~ later (on); **al più ~** at the latest; **sul ~** (verso sera) late in the day; **far ~** to be late; (restare alzato) to stay up late; **è troppo ~** it's too late

'targa, -ghe sf plate; (Aut) number (BRIT) o license (US) plate; **tar'ghetta** sf (su bagaglio) name tag; (su porta) nameplate

ta'riffa sf (gen) rate, tariff; (di trasporti) fare; (elenco) price list; tariff

'tarlo sm woodworm

'tarma sf moth

tarocchi smpl (gioco) tarot sg

tarta'ruga, -ghe sf tortoise; (di mare) turtle; (materiale) tortoiseshell

tar'tina sf canapé

tar'tufo sm (Bot) truffle

'tasca, -sche sf pocket; **tas'cabile** ag (libro) pocket cpd

'tassa sf (imposta) tax; (doganale) duty; (per iscrizione: a scuola ecc) fee; **tassa di circolazione** road tax; **tassa di soggiorno** tourist tax

tas'sare vt to levy a duty on

tas'sello sm plug; wedge

tassì sm inv = **taxi**; **tas'sista, -i, -e** sm/f taxi driver

'tasso sm (di natalità, d'interesse ecc) rate; (Bot) yew; (Zool) badger; **tasso di cambio/d'interesse** rate of exchange/interest

tas'tare vt to feel; **~ il terreno** (fig) to see how the land lies

tasti'era sf keyboard

'tasto sm key; (tatto) touch, feel

tas'toni avv **procedere (a) ~** to grope one's way forward

'tatto sm (senso) touch; (fig) tact; **duro al ~** hard to the touch; **aver ~** to be tactful, have tact

tatu'aggio [tatu'addʒo] sm tattooing; (disegno) tattoo

tatu'are vt to tattoo

'tavola sf table; (asse) plank, board; (lastra) tablet; (quadro) panel (painting); (illustrazione) plate; **tavola calda** snack bar; **tavola rotonda** (fig) round table; **tavola a vela** windsurfer

tavo'letta sf tablet, bar; **a ~** (Aut) flat out

tavo'lino sm small table; (scrivania) desk

'tavolo sm table; **un ~ per 4 per favore** a table for 4, please

'taxi sm inv taxi; **può chiamarmi un ~ per favore?** can you call me a taxi, please?

'tazza ['tattsa] sf cup; **una ~ di caffè/tè** a cup of coffee/tea; **tazza da tè/caffè** tea/coffee cup

TBC abbr f (= tubercolosi) TB

te pron (soggetto: in forme comparative, oggetto) you

tè sm inv tea; (trattenimento) tea party

tea'trale ag theatrical

te'atro sm theatre

techno ['tεkno] ag inv (musica) techno

tecnica, -che sf technique; (tecnologia) technology

'tecnico, -a, -ci, -che ag technical ▶ sm/f technician

tecnolo'gia [teknolo'dʒia] sf technology

te'desco, -a, -schi, -sche ag, sm/f,

sm German

te'game sm (Cuc) pan

'tegola sf tile

tei'era sf teapot

tel. abbr (= telefono) tel

'tela sf (tessuto) cloth; (per vele, quadri) canvas; (dipinto) canvas, painting; **di ~** (calzoni) (heavy) cotton cpd; (scarpe, borsa) canvas cpd; **tela cerata** oilcloth

te'laio sm (apparecchio) loom; (struttura) frame

tele'camera sf television camera

teleco'mando sm remote control

tele'cronaca sf television report

telefo'nare vi to telephone, ring; to make a phone call ▶ vt to telephone; **~ a** to phone up, ring up, call up

telefo'nata sf (telephone) call; **~ a carico del destinatario** reverse charge (BRIT) o collect (US) call

tele'fonico, -a, -ci, -che ag (tele)phone cpd

telefo'nino sm mobile phone

te'lefono sm telephone; **telefono a gettoni** pay phone

telegior'nale [teledʒor'nale] sm television news (programme)

tele'gramma, -i sm telegram

telela'voro sm teleworking

Tele'pass® sm inv automatic payment card for use on Italian motorways

telepa'tia sf telepathy

teles'copio sm telescope

teleselezi'one [teleselet'tsjone] sf direct dialling

telespetta'tore, -'trice sm/f (television) viewer

tele'vendita sf teleshopping

televisi'one sf television

televi'sore sm television set

'tema, -i sm theme; (Ins) essay, composition

te'mere vt to fear, be afraid of; (essere sensibile a: freddo, calore) to be sensitive to ▶ vi to be afraid; (essere *preoccupato*; **~ per** to worry about, fear for; **~ di/che** to be afraid of/that

temperama'tite *sm inv* pencil sharpener

tempera'mento *sm* temperament

tempera'tura *sf* temperature

tempe'rino *sm* penknife

tem'pesta *sf* storm; **tempesta di sabbia/neve** sand/snowstorm

'tempia *sf* (Anat) temple

'tempio *sm* (edificio) temple

'tempo *sm* (Meteor) weather; (cronologico) time; (epoca) time, times *pl*; (di film, gioco: parte) part; (Mus) time; (: battuta) beat; (Ling) tense; **che ~ fa?** what's the weather like?; **un ~** once; **~ fa** some time ago; **al ~ stesso o a un ~** at the same time; **per ~** early; **ha fatto il suo ~** it has had its day; **primo/secondo ~** (Teatro) first/second part; (Sport) first/second half; **in ~ utile** in due time *o* course; **a ~ pieno** full-time; **tempo libero** free time

tempo'rale *ag* temporal ▶ *sm* (Meteor) (thunder)storm

tempo'raneo, -a *ag* temporary

te'nace [te'natʃe] *ag* strong, tough; (fig) tenacious

te'naglie [te'naʎʎe] *sfpl* pincers *pl*

'tenda *sf* (riparo) awning; (di finestra) curtain; (per campeggio ecc) tent

ten'denza [ten'dɛntsa] *sf* tendency; (orientamento) trend; **avere ~ a o per qc** to have a bent for sth

'tendere *vt* (allungare al massimo) to stretch, draw tight; (porgere: mano) to hold out; (fig: trappola) to lay, set ▶ *vi* **~ a qc/a fare** to tend towards sth/to do; **~ l'orecchio** to prick up one's ears; **il tempo tende al caldo** the weather is getting hot; **un blu che tende al verde** a greenish blue

'tendine *sm* tendon, sinew

ten'done *sm* (da circo) tent

'tenebre *sfpl* darkness *sg*

'tenente *sm* lieutenant

te'nere *vt* to hold; (conservare, mantenere) to keep; (ritenere, considerare) to consider; (spazio: occupare) to take up, occupy; (seguire: strada) to keep to ▶ *vi* to hold; (colori) to be fast; (dare importanza): **~ a** to care about; **~ a fare** to want to do, be keen to do; **tenersi** *vpr* (stare in una determinata posizione) to stand; (stimarsi) to consider o.s.; (aggrapparsi): **tenersi a** to hold on to; (attenersi): **tenersi a** to stick to; **~ una conferenza** to give a lecture; **~ conto di qc** to take sth into consideration; **~ presente qc** to bear sth in mind

'tenero, -a *ag* tender; (pietra, cera, colore) soft; (fig) tender, loving

'tengo *ecc vb vedi* **tenere**

'tenni *ecc vb vedi* **tenere**

'tennis *sm* tennis

ten'nista, -i, e *sm/f* tennis player

te'nore *sm* (tono) tone; (Mus) tenor; **tenore di vita** (livello) standard of living

tensi'one *sf* tension

ten'tare *vt* (indurre) to tempt; (provare): **~ qc/di fare** to attempt *o* try sth/to do; **tenta'tivo** *sm* attempt; **tentazi'one** *sf* temptation

tenten'nare *vi* to shake, be unsteady; (fig) to hesitate, waver

ten'toni *av* **andare a ~** (anche fig) to grope one's way

'tenue *ag* (sottile) fine; (colore) soft; (fig) slender, slight

te'nuta *sf* (capacità) capacity; (divisa) uniform; (abito) dress; (Agr) estate; **a ~ d'aria** airtight; **tenuta di strada** roadholding power

teolo'gia [teolo'dʒia] *sf* theology

teo'ria *sf* theory

te'pore *sm* warmth

tep'pista, -i *sm* hooligan

tera'pia sf therapy; **terapia intensiva** intensive care

tergicris'tallo [terdʒikris'tallo] sm windscreen (BRIT) o windshield (US) wiper

tergiver'sare [terdʒiver'sare] vi to shilly-shally

ter'male ag thermal; **stazione** sf ~ spa

'terme sfpl thermal baths

termi'nale ag, sm terminal

termi'nare vt to end; (lavoro) to finish ▶ vi to end

'termine sm term; (fine, estremità) end; (di territorio) boundary, limit; **contratto a ~** (Comm) forward contract; **a breve/lungo ~** short-/long-term; **parlare senza mezzi termini** to talk frankly, not to mince one's words

ter'mometro sm thermometer

'termos sm inv = **thermos®**

termosi'fone sm radiator

ter'mostato sm thermostat

'terra sf (gen, Elettr) earth; (sostanza) soil, earth; (opposto al mare) land no pl; (regione, paese) land; (argilla) clay; **terre** sfpl (possedimento) lands, land sg; **a o per ~** (stato) on the ground (o floor); (moto) to the ground, down; **mettere a ~** (Elettr) to earth

terra'cotta sf terracotta; **vasellame** sm di ~ earthenware

terra'ferma sf dry land, terra firma; (continente) mainland

ter'razza [ter'rattsa] sf terrace

ter'razzo [ter'rattso] sm = **terrazza**

terre'moto sm earthquake

ter'reno, -a ag (vita, beni) earthly ▶ sm (suolo, fig) ground; (Comm) land no pl, plot (of land); site; (Sport, Mil) field

ter'restre ag (superficie) of the earth, earth's; (di terra: battaglia, animale) land cpd; (Rel) earthly, worldly

ter'ribile ag terrible, dreadful

terrifi'cante ag terrifying

ter'rina sf tureen

territori'ale ag territorial

terri'torio sm territory

ter'rore sm terror; **terro'rismo** sm terrorism; **terro'rista, -i, -e** sm/f terrorist

terroriz'zare [terrorid'dzare] vt to terrorize

terza ['tertsa] sf (Scol: elementare) ≈ third year at primary school; (: medie) ≈ second year at secondary school; (: superiore) ≈ fifth year at secondary school; (Aut) third gear

ter'zino [ter'tsino] sm (Calcio) fullback, back

'terzo, -a ['tertso] ag third ▶ sm (frazione) third; (Dir) third party; **terza pagina** (Stampa) Arts page; **terzi** smpl (altri) others, other people

teschio ['teskjo] sm skull

'tesi sf thesis; **tesi di laurea** degree thesis

'tesi ecc² vb vedi **tendere**

'teso, -a pp di **tendere** ▶ ag (tirato) taut, tight; (fig) tense

te'soro sm treasure; **il Ministero del T~** the Treasury

'tessera sf (documento) card

tes'suto sm fabric, material; (Biol) tissue

test ['test] sm inv test

'testa sf head; (di cose: estremità, parte anteriore) head, front; **di ~** (vettura ecc) front; **tenere ~ a qn** (nemico ecc) to stand up to sb; **fare di ~ propria** to go one's own way; **in ~** (Sport) in the lead; **~ o croce?** heads or tails?; **avere la ~ dura** to be stubborn; **testa d'aglio** bulb of garlic; **testa di serie** (Tennis) seed, seeded player

testa'mento sm (atto) will; **l'Antico/il Nuovo T~** (Rel) the Old/New Testament

tes'tardo, -a ag stubborn, pig-headed

tes'tata *sf* (*parte anteriore*) head; (*intestazione*) heading

tes'ticolo *sm* testicle

testi'mone *sm/f* (*Dir*) witness; **testimone oculare** eye witness

testimoni'are *vt* to testify; (*fig*) to bear witness to, testify to ▶ *vi* to give evidence, testify

'testo *sm* text; **fare ~** (*opera, autore*) to be authoritative; **questo libro non fa ~** this book is not essential reading

tes'tuggine [tes'tuddʒine] *sf* tortoise; (*di mare*) turtle

'tetano *sm* (*Med*) tetanus

'tetto *sm* roof; **tet'toia** *sf* roofing; canopy

tettuccio [tet'tuttʃo] *sm* **~ apribile** (*Aut*) sunroof

'Tevere *sm* **il ~** the Tiber

TG, Tg *abbr* = **telegiornale**

'thermos® ['tɛrmos] *sm inv* vacuum o Thermos® flask

ti *pron* (*dav lo, la, li, le, ne diventa* **te** ▶ *pron* (*oggetto*) you; (*complemento di termine*) (to) you; (*riflessivo*) yourself

'Tibet *sm* **il ~** Tibet

'tibia *sf* tibia, shinbone

tic *sm inv* tic, (nervous) twitch; (*fig*) mannerism

ticchet'tio [tikket'tio] *sm* (*di macchina da scrivere*) clatter; (*di orologio*) ticking; (*della pioggia*) patter

'ticket *sm inv* (*su farmaci*) prescription charge

ti'ene *ecc vb vedi* **tenere**

ti'epido, -a *ag* lukewarm, tepid

'tifo *sm* (*Med*) typhus; (*fig*): **fare il ~ per** to be a fan of

ti'fone *sm* typhoon

ti'foso, -a *sm/f* (*Sport ecc*) fan

tigì [ti'dʒi] *sm inv* TV news

'tiglio ['tiʎʎo] *sm* lime (tree), linden (tree)

'tigre *sf* tiger

tim'brare *vt* to stamp; (*annullare:*

francobolli) to postmark; **~ il cartellino** to clock in

'timbro *sm* stamp; (*Mus*) timbre, tone

'timido, -a *ag* shy; timid

'timo *sm* thyme

ti'mone *sm* (*Naut*) rudder

ti'more *sm* (*paura*) fear; (*rispetto*) awe

'timpano *sm* (*Anat*) eardrum; (*Mus*)

'tingere ['tindʒere] *vt* to dye

'tinsi *ecc vb vedi* **tingere**

'tinta *sf* (*materia colorante*) dye; (*colore*) colour, shade

tintin'nare *vi* to tinkle

tinto'ria *sf* (*lavasecco*) dry cleaner's (shop)

tin'tura *sf* (*operazione*) dyeing; (*colorante*) dye; **tintura di iodio** tincture of iodine

'tipico, -a, -ci, -che *ag* typical

'tipo *sm* type; (*genere*) kind, type; (*fam*) chap, fellow; **che ~ di...?** what kind of...?

tipogra'fia *sf* typography; (*procedimento*) letterpress (printing); (*officina*) printing house

TIR *sigla m* (= *Transports Internationaux Routiers*) International Heavy Goods Vehicle

ti'rare *vt* (*gen*) to pull; (*estrarre*): **~ qc da** to take o pull sth out of; to get sth out of; to extract sth from; (*chiudere:* **tenda** *ecc*) to draw, pull; (*tracciare, disegnare*) to draw, trace; (*lanciare: sasso, palla*) to throw; (*stampare*) to print; (*pistola, freccia*) to fire ▶ *vi* (*pipa, camino*) to draw; (*vento*) to blow; (*abito*) to be tight; (*fare fuoco*) to fire; (*fare del tiro, Calcio*) to shoot; **~ avanti** *vi* to struggle on ▶ *vt* to keep going; **~ fuori** (*estrarre*) to take out, pull out; **~ giù** (*abbassare*) to bring down, to lower; (*da scaffale ecc.*) to take down; **~ su** to pull up; (*capelli*) to put up; (*fig: bambino*) to bring up; **tirarsi** *vpr*

tirarsi indietro to draw back; (*fig*)

to back out; **~ a indovinare** to take a guess; **~ sul prezzo** to bargain; **tirar dritto** to keep right on going; **tirati su!** (fig) cheer up!; **~ via** (togliere) to take off

tira'tura sf(azione) printing; (di libro) (print) run; (di giornale) circulation

'tirchio, -a ['tirkjo] ag mean, stingy

'tiro sm shooting no pl, firing no pl; (colpo, sparo) shot; (di palla: lancio) throwing no pl; throw; (fig) trick; **cavallo da ~** draught (BRIT) o draft (US) horse; **tiro a segno** target shooting; (luogo) shooting range; **tiro con l'arco** archery

tiro'cinio [tiro'tʃinjo] sm apprenticeship; (professionale) training

ti'roide sf thyroid (gland)

Tir'reno sm **il (mar) ~** the Tyrrhenian Sea

ti'sana sf herb tea

tito'lare ag/sm incumbent; (proprietario) owner; (Calcio) regular player

'titolo sm title; (di giornale) headline; (diploma) qualification; (Comm) security; (: azione) share; **a che ~?** for what reason?; **a ~ di amicizia** out of friendship; **a ~ di premio** as a prize; **titolo di credito** share; **titoli di stato** government securities; **titoli di testa** (Cinema) credits

titu'bante ag hesitant, irresolute

toast [toust] sm inv toasted sandwich (generally with ham and cheese)

toc'cante ag touching

toc'care vt to touch; (tastare) to feel; (fig: riguardare) to concern; (: commuovere) to touch, move; (: pungere) to hurt, wound; (: far cenno a: argomento) to touch on, mention ▸ vi **~ a** (accadere) to happen to; (spettare) to be up to; **~ (il fondo)** (in acqua) to touch the bottom; **tocca a**

te difenderci it's up to you to defend us; **a chi tocca?** whose turn is it?; **mi toccò pagare** I had to pay

toccherò ecc [tokke'rɔ] vb vedi **toccare**

'togliere ['tɔʎʎere] vt (rimuovere) to take away (o off), remove; (riprendere, non concedere più) to take away, remove; (Mat) to take away, subtract; **~ qc a qn** to take sth (away) from sb; **ciò non toglie che** nevertheless, be that as it may; **togliersi il cappello** to take off one's hat

toi'lette [twa'lɛt] sf inv toilet; (mobile) dressing table; **dov'è la ~?** where's the toilet?

'Tokyo sf Tokyo

'tolgo ecc vb vedi **togliere**

tolle'rare vt to tolerate

'tolsi ecc vb vedi **togliere**

'tomba sf tomb

tom'bino sm manhole cover

'tombola sf(gioco) tombola; (ruzzolone) tumble

'tondo, -a ag round

'tonfo sm splash; (rumore sordo) thud; (caduta): **fare un ~** to take a tumble

tonifi'care vt (muscoli, pelle) to tone up; (irrobustire) to invigorate, brace

tonnel'lata sf ton

'tonno sm tuna (fish)

'tono sm (gen) tone; (Mus: di pezzo) key; (di colore) shade, tone

ton'silla sf tonsil

'tonto, -a ag dull, stupid

to'pazio [to'pattsjo] sm topaz

'topo sm mouse

'toppa sf(serratura) keyhole; (pezza) patch

to'race [to'ratʃe] sm chest

'torba sf peat

'torcere ['tɔrtʃere] vt to twist; **torcersi** vpr to twist, writhe

'torcia, -ce ['tɔrtʃa] sf torch; **torcia elettrica** torch (BRIT), flashlight (US)

torci'collo [tortʃi'kɔllo] sm stiff neck

'tordo sm thrush

To'rino sf Turin

tor'menta sf snowstorm

tormen'tare vt to torment; **tormentarsi** vpr to fret, worry o.s.

tor'nado sm tornado

tor'nante sm hairpin bend

tor'nare vi to return, go (o come) back; (ridiventare: anche fig) to become (again); (riuscire giusto, esatto: conto) to work out; (risultare) to turn out (to be), prove (to be); **~ utile** to prove o turn out (to be) useful; **~ a casa** to go (o come) home; **torno a casa martedì** I'm going home on Tuesday

tor'neo sm tournament

'tornio sm lathe

'toro sm bull; (dello zodiaco) **T~** Taurus

'torre sf tower; (Scacchi) rook, castle; **torre di controllo** (Aer) control tower

tor'rente sm torrent

torri'one sm keep

tor'rone sm nougat

'torsi ecc vb vedi **torcere**

torsi'one sf twisting; torsion

'torso sm torso, trunk; (Arte) torso

'torsolo sm (di cavolo ecc) stump; (di frutta) core

'torta sf cake

tortel'lini smpl (Cuc) tortellini

'torto, -a pp di **torcere** ▶ ag (ritorto) twisted; (storto) twisted, crooked ▶ sm (ingiustizia) wrong; (colpa) fault; **a ~** wrongly; **aver ~** to be wrong

'tortora sf turtle dove

tor'tura sf torture; **tortu'rare** vt to torture

to'sare vt (pecora) to shear; (siepe) to clip

Tos'cana sf **la ~** Tuscany

'tosse sf cough; **ho la ~** I've got a cough

'tossico, -a, -ci, -che ag toxic

tossicodipen'dente sm/f drug addict

tos'sire vi to cough

tosta'pane sm inv toaster

to'tale ag, sm total

toto'calcio [toto'kaltʃo] sm gambling pool betting on football results, ≈ (football) pools pl (BRIT)

to'vaglia [to'vaʎʎa] sf tablecloth; **tovagli'olo** sm napkin

tra prep (di due persone, cose) between; (di più persone, cose) among(st); (tempo: entro) within, in; **~ 5 giorni** in 5 days' time; **sia detto ~ noi ...** between you and me ...; **litigano ~ (di) loro** they're fighting amongst themselves; **~ breve** soon; **~ sé e sé** (parlare ecc) to oneself

traboc'care vi to overflow

traboc'chetto [trabok'ketto] sm (fig) trap

'traccia, -ce ['trattʃa] sf (segno, striscia) trail, track; (orma) tracks pl; (residuo, testimonianza) trace, sign; (abbozzo) outline

tracci'are [trat'tʃare] vt to trace, mark (out); (disegnare) to draw; (fig: abbozzare) to outline

tra'chea [tra'kɛa] sf windpipe, trachea

tra'colla sf shoulder strap; **borsa a ~** shoulder bag

tradi'mento sm betrayal; (Dir, Mil) treason

tra'dire vt to betray; (coniuge) to be unfaithful to; (doveri: mancare) to fail in; (rivelare) to give away, reveal; **tradirsi** vpr to give o.s. away

tradizio'nale [traditsjo'nale] ag traditional

tradizi'one [tradit'tsjone] sf tradition

tra'durre vt to translate; (spiegare) to render, convey; **me lo può ~?** can you translate this for me?; **traduzi'one** sf translation

'trae vb vedi **trarre**

traffi'cante sm/f dealer; (peg)

trafficker

traffi'care vi (commerciare): **~ (in)** to trade (in), deal (in); (affaccendarsi) to busy o.s. ▶ vt (peg) to traffic in

'traffico, -ci sm traffic; (commercio) trade, traffic; **traffico di armi/droga** arms/drug trafficking

tra'gedia [tra'dʒɛdja] sf tragedy

'traggo ecc vb vedi **trarre**

tra'ghetto [tra'getto] sm ferry(boat)

'tragico, -a, -ci, -che ['tradʒiko] ag tragic

tra'gitto [tra'dʒitto] sm (passaggio) crossing; (viaggio) journey

tragu'ardo sm (Sport) finishing line; (fig) goal, aim

'trai ecc vb vedi **trarre**

traiet'toria sf trajectory

trai'nare vt to drag, haul; (rimorchiare) to tow

tralasci'are [tralaʃ'ʃare] vt (studi) to neglect; (dettagli) to leave out, omit

tra'liccio [tra'littʃo] sm (Elettr) pylon

tram sm inv tram

'trama sf (filo) weft, woof; (fig: argomento, maneggio) plot

traman'dare vt to pass on, hand down

tram'busto sm turmoil

tramez'zino [tramed'dzino] sm sandwich

'tramite prep through

tramon'tare vi to set, go down; (del sole) sunset

tra'monto sm setting; (del sole) sunset

trampo'lino sm (per tuffi) springboard, diving board; (per lo sci) ski-jump

tra'nello sm trap

'tranne prep except (for), but (for); **~ che** unless

tranquil'lante sm (Med) tranquillizer

tranquillità sf calm, stillness; quietness; peace of mind

tranquilliz'zare [trankwillid'dzare]

vt to reassure

> Attenzione! In inglese esiste il verbo to tranquillize, che però significa "calmare con un tranquillante".

tran'quillo, -a ag calm, quiet; (bambino, scolaro) quiet; (sereno) with one's mind at rest; **sta' ~** don't worry

transazi'one [transat'tsjone] sf compromise; (Dir) settlement; (Comm) transaction, deal

tran'senna sf barrier

transgenico, -a, -ci, -che [trans'dʒɛniko] ag genetically modified

tran'sigere [tran'sidʒere] vi (venire a patti) to compromise, come to an agreement

transi'tabile ag passable

transi'tare vi to pass

transi'tivo, -a ag transitive

'transito sm transit; **di ~** (merci) in transit; (stazione) transit cpd; **"divieto di ~"** "no entry"

'trapano sm (utensile) drill; (Med) trepan

trape'lare vi to leak, drip; (fig) to leak out

tra'pezio [tra'pɛttsjo] sm (Mat) trapezium; (attrezzo ginnico) trapeze

trapian'tare vt to transplant; **trapi'anto** sm transplanting; (Med) transplant; **trapianto cardiaco** heart transplant

'trappola sf trap

tra'punta sf quilt

'trarre vt to draw, pull; (portare) to take; (prendere, tirare fuori) to take (out), draw; (derivare) to obtain; **~ origine da qc** to have its origins o originate in sth

trasa'lire vi to start, jump

trasan'dato, -a ag shabby

trasci'nare [traʃʃi'nare] vt to drag; **trascinarsi** vpr to drag o.s. along; (fig)

to drag on
tras'correre vt (tempo) to spend, pass ▶ vi to pass

tras'crivere vt to transcribe

trascu'rare vt to neglect; (non considerare) to disregard

trasferi'mento sm transfer; (trasloco) removal, move; **trasferimento di chiamata** (Tel) call forwarding

trasfe'rire vt to transfer; **trasferirsi** vpr to move; **tras'ferta** sf transfer; (indennità) travelling expenses pl; (Sport) away game

trasfor'mare vt to transform, change; **trasformarsi** vpr to be transformed; **trasformarsi in qc** to turn into sth; **trasforma'tore** sm (Elec) transformer

trasfusi'one sf (Med) transfusion

trasgre'dire vt to disobey, contravene

traslo'care vt to move, transfer; **tras'loco, -chi** sm removal

tras'mettere vt (passare) ~ **qc a qn** to pass sth on to sb; (mandare) to send; (Tecn, Tel, Med) to transmit; (TV, Radio) to broadcast; **trasmissi'one** sf (gen, Fisica, Tecn) transmission; (passaggio) transmission, passing on; (TV, Radio) broadcast

traspa'rente ag transparent

traspor'tare vt to carry, move; (merce) to transport, convey; **lasciarsi ~ (da qc)** (fig) to let o.s. be carried away (by sth); **tras'porto** sm transport

'trassi ecc vb vedi **trarre**

trasver'sale ag transverse, cross(-); running at right angles

'tratta sf (Econ) draft; (di persone): **la ~ delle bianche** the white slave trade

tratta'mento sm treatment; (servizio) service

trat'tare vt (gen) to treat; (commerciare) to deal in; (svolgere: argomento) to discuss, deal with; (negoziare) to negotiate ▶ vi ~ **di** to deal with; ~ **con** (persona) to deal with; **si tratta di ...** it's about ...

tratte'nere vt (far rimanere: persona) to detain; (intrattenere: ospiti) to entertain; (tenere, frenare, reprimere) to hold back, keep back; (astenersi dal consegnare) to hold, keep; (detrarre: somma) to deduct; **trattenersi** vpr (astenersi) to restrain o.s., stop o.s.; (soffermarsi) to stay, remain

trat'tino sm dash; (in parole composte) hyphen

'tratto, -a pp di **trarre** ▶ sm (di penna, matita) stroke; (parte) part, piece; (di strada) stretch; (di mare, cielo) expanse; (di tempo) period (of time)

trat'tore sm tractor

tratto'ria sf restaurant

'trauma, -i sm trauma

tra'vaglio [tra'vaʎʎo] sm (angoscia) pain, suffering; (Med) pains pl

trava'sare vt to decant

tra'versa sf (trave) crosspiece; (via) side street; (Ferr) sleeper (BRIT), (railroad) tie (US); (Calcio) crossbar

traver'sata sf crossing; (Aer) flight, trip; **quanto dura la ~?** how long does the crossing take?

traver'sie sfpl mishaps, misfortunes

tra'verso, -a ag oblique; **di ~** ag askew ▶ av sideways; **andare di ~** (cibo) to go down the wrong way; **guardare di ~** to look askance at

travesti'mento sm disguise

travestirsi vpr to disguise o.s.

tra'volgere [tra'vɔldʒere] vt to sweep away, carry away; (fig) to overwhelm

tre num three

'treccia, -ce ['trettʃa] sf plait, braid

tre'cento [tre'tʃento] num three hundred ▶ sm il **T~** the fourteenth century

'tredici ['treditʃi] num thirteen

'tregua sf truce; (fig) respite

tre'mare vi ~ **di** (freddo ecc) to shiver o tremble with; (paura, rabbia) to shake o tremble with

tre'mendo, -a ag terrible, awful

> Attenzione! In inglese esiste la parola tremendous, che però significa enorme oppure fantastico, strepitoso.

'tremito sm trembling no pl; shaking no pl; shivering no pl

'treno sm train; **è questo il ~ per...?** is this the train for ...?; **treno di gomme** set of tyres (BRIT) o tires (US); **treno merci** goods (BRIT) o freight train; **treno viaggiatori** passenger train

* There are various types of train in
* Italy. For short journeys there are
* the "Regionali" (R), which generally
* operate within a particular region,
* and the "Interregionali" (IR),
* which operate beyond regional
* boundaries. Medium- and long-
* distance passenger journeys are
* carried out by "Intercity" (I) and
* "Eurocity" (EC) trains. The "Eurostar"
* service (ES) offers fast connections
* between the major Italian cities.
* Night services are operated by
* "Intercity Notte" (ICN), "Euronight"
* (EN) and by "Espressi" (EXP).

'trenta num thirty; **tren'tesimo, -a** num thirtieth; **tren'tina** sf una trentina (di) thirty or so, about thirty

'trepidante ag anxious

tri'angolo sm triangle

tribù sf inv tribe

tri'buna sf (podio) platform; (in aule ecc) gallery; (di stadio) stand

tribu'nale sm court

tri'ciclo [tri'tʃiklo] sm tricycle

tri'foglio [tri'fɔʎʎo] sm clover

'triglia ['triʎʎa] sf red mullet

tri'mestre sm period of three months;

(Ins) term, quarter (US); (Comm) quarter

trin'cea [trin'tʃea] sf trench

trion'fare vi to triumph, win; **~ su** to triumph over, overcome; **tri'onfo** sm triumph

tripli'care vt to triple

'triplo, -a ag triple; treble ▶ sm **il ~ (di)** three times as much (as); **la spesa è tripla** it costs three times as much

'trippa sf (Cuc) tripe

'triste ag sad; (luogo) dreary, gloomy

tri'tare vt to mince, grind (US)

trivi'ale ag vulgar, low

tro'feo sm trophy

'tromba sf (Mus) trumpet; (Aut) horn; **tromba d'aria** whirlwind; **tromba delle scale** stairwell

trom'bone sm trombone

trom'bosi sf thrombosis

tron'care vt to cut off; (spezzare) to break off

'tronco, -a, -chi, -che ag cut off; broken off; (Ling) truncated; (fig) cut short ▶ sm (Bot, Anat) trunk; (fig: tratto) section; **licenziare qn in ~** to fire sb on the spot

'trono sm throne

tropi'cale ag tropical

🅞 **'troppo, -a**
det (in eccesso: quantità) too much; (: numero) too many; **c'era troppa gente** there were too many people; **fa troppo caldo** it's too hot
▶ pron (in eccesso: quantità) too much; (: numero) too many; **ne hai messo troppo** you've put in too much; **meglio troppi che pochi** better too many than too few
▶ av (eccessivamente: con ag, av) too; (: con vb) too much; **troppo amaro/tardi** too bitter/late; **lavora troppo** he works too much; **costa troppo** it costs too much; **di troppo** too much; too many; **qualche tazza di troppo** a

few cups too many; **2 euro di troppo** 2 euros too much; **essere di troppo** to be in the way

'trota sf trout

'trottola sf spinning top

tro'vare vt to find; (giudicare): **trovo che** I find o think that; **trovarsi** vpr (reciproco: incontrarsi) to meet; (essere, stare) to be; (arrivare, capitare) to find o.s.; **non trovo più il portafoglio** I can't find my wallet; **andare a ~ qn** to go and see sb; **~ qn colpevole** to find sb guilty; **trovarsi bene** (in un luogo, con qn) to get on well

truc'care vt (falsare) to fake; (attore ecc) to make up; (travestire) to disguise; (Sport) to fix; (Aut) to soup up; **truccarsi** vpr to make up (one's face)

'trucco, -chi sm trick; (cosmesi) make-up

'truffa sf fraud, swindle; **truf'fare** vt to swindle, cheat

truffa'tore, -'trice sm/f swindler, cheat

'truppa sf troop

tu pron you; **tu stesso(a)** you yourself; **dare del tu a qn** to address sb as "tu"

'tubo sm tube; pipe; **tubo digerente** (Anat) alimentary canal, digestive tract; **tubo di scappamento** (Aut) exhaust pipe

tuffarsi vpr to plunge, dive

'tuffo sm dive; (breve bagno) dip

tuli'pano sm tulip

tu'more sm (Med) tumour

Tuni'sia sf la ~ Tunisia

'tuo (f'tua, pl tu'oi, 'tue) det il ~, la tua ecc your ▶ pron il ~, la tua ecc yours

tuo'nare vi to thunder; **tuona** it is thundering, there's some thunder

tu'ono sm thunder

tu'orlo sm yolk

tur'bante sm turban

tur'bare vt to disturb, disturb

tur'bato, -a ag upset; (preoccupato, ansioso) anxious

turbo'lenza [turbo'lɛntsa] sf turbulence

tur'chese [tur'kese] sf turquoise

Tur'chia [tur'kia] sf la ~ Turkey

'turco, -a, -chi, -che ag Turkish ▶ sm/f Turk/Turkish woman ▶ sm (Ling) Turkish; **parlare ~** (fig) to talk double-dutch

tu'rismo sm tourism; tourist industry; **tu'rista, -i, -e** sm/f tourist; **turismo sessuale** sex tourism; **tu'ristico, -a, -ci, -che** ag tourist cpd

'turno sm turn; (di lavoro) shift; **di ~** (soldato, medico, custode) on duty; **a ~** (rispondere) in turn; (lavorare) in shifts; **fare a ~ a fare qc** to take turns to do sth; **è il suo ~** it's your (o his ecc turn)

'turpe ag filthy, vile

'tuta sf overalls pl; (Sport) tracksuit

tu'tela sf (Dir: di minore) guardianship; (: protezione) protection; (difesa) defence

tutta'via cong nevertheless, yet

'tutto, -a

○ det

1 (intero) all; **tutto il latte** all the milk; **tutta la notte** all night, the whole night; **tutto il libro** the whole book; **tutta una bottiglia** a whole bottle

2 (pl, collettivo) all; every; **tutti i libri** all the books; **tutte le notti** every night; **tutti i venerdì** every Friday; **tutti gli uomini** all the men; (collettivo) all men; **tutto l'anno** all year long; **tutti e due** both o each of us (o them o you); **tutti e cinque** all five of us (o them o you)

3 (completamente): **era tutta sporca** she was all dirty; **tremava tutto** he was trembling all over; **è tutta sua madre** she's just o exactly like her mother

4: **a tutt'oggi** so far, up till now; **a tutta velocità** at full o top speed

▶ *pron*

1 (*ogni cosa*) everything, all; (*qualsiasi cosa*) anything; **ha mangiato tutto** he's eaten everything; **tutto considerato** all things considered; **in tutto: 5 euro in tutto** 5 euros in all; **in tutto eravamo 50** there were 50 of us in all

2: **tutti, e** (*ognuno*) all, everybody; **vengono tutti** they are all coming, everybody's coming; **tutti quanti** all and sundry

▶ *av* (*completamente*) entirely, quite; **è tutto il contrario** it's quite o exactly the opposite; **tutt'al più: saranno stati tutt'al più una cinquantina** there were about fifty of them at (the very) most; **tutt'al più possiamo prendere un treno** if the worst comes to the worst we can take a train; **tutt'altro** on the contrary; **è tutt'altro che felice** he's anything but happy; **tutt'a un tratto** suddenly

▶ *sm* **il tutto** the whole lot, all of it

tut'tora *av* still

TV [ti'vu] *sf inv* (= *televisione*) TV ▶ *sigla* = Treviso

u

ubbidi'ente *ag* obedient

ubbi'dire *vi* to obey; **~ a** to obey; (*veicolo, macchina*) to respond to

ubria'care *vt* **~ qn** to get sb drunk;

(*alcool*) to make sb drunk; (*fig*) to make sb's head spin o reel; **ubriacarsi** *vpr* to get drunk; **ubriacarsi di** (*fig*) to become intoxicated with

ubri'aco, -a, -chi, -che *ag, sm/f* drunk

uc'cello [ut'tʃɛllo] *sm* bird

uc'cidere [ut'tʃidere] *vt* to kill; **uccidersi** *vpr* (*suicidarsi*) to kill o.s.; (*perdere la vita*) to be killed

u'dito (*sense of*) hearing

UE *sigla f* (= *Unione Europea*) EU

UEM *sigla f* (= *Unione economica e monetaria*) EMU

'uffa *escl* tut!

uffici'ale [uffi'tʃale] *ag* official ▶ *sm* (*Amm*) official, officer; (*Mil*) officer; **~ di stato civile** registrar

uf'ficio [uf'fitʃo] *sm* (*gen*) office; (*dovere*) duty; (*mansione*) task, function, job; (*agenzia*) agency, bureau; (*Rel*) service; **d'~** *ag* official *cpd*; ▶ *av* officially; **ufficio di collocamento** employment office; **ufficio informazioni** information bureau; **ufficio oggetti smarriti** lost property office (*BRIT*), lost and found (*US*); **ufficio (del) personale** personnel department; **ufficio postale** post office

uffici'oso, -a [uffi'tʃoso] *ag* unofficial

uguagli'anza [ugwaʎ'ʎantsa] *sf* equality

uguagli'are [ugwaʎ'ʎare] *vt* to make equal; (*essere uguale*) to equal, be equal to; (*livellare*) to level; **uguagliarsi a o con qn** (*paragonarsi*) to compare o.s. to sb

ugu'ale *ag* equal; (*identico*) identical, the same; (*uniforme*) level, even ▶ *av* **costano ~** they cost the same; **sono bravi ~** they're equally good

UIL *sigla f* (= *Unione Italiana del Lavoro*) trade union federation

'ulcera ['ultʃera] *sf* ulcer

U'livo sm l'~ centre-left Italian political grouping

u'livo = olivo

ulteri'ore ag further

ultima'mente av lately, of late

ulti'mare vt to finish, complete

'ultimo, -a ag (finale) last; (estremo) farthest, utmost; (recente: notizia, moda) latest; (fig: sommo, fondamentale) ultimate ▶ sm/f last (one); **fino all'~** to the last, until the end; **da ~, in ~** in the end; **abitare all'~ piano** to live on the top floor; **per ~** (entrare, arrivare) last

ulu'lare vi to howl

umanità sf humanity

u'mano, -a ag human; (comprensivo) humane

umidità sf dampness; humidity

'umido, -a ag damp; (mano, occhi) moist; (clima) humid ▶ sm dampness, damp; **carne in ~** stew

'umile ag humble

umili'are vt to humiliate; **umiliarsi** vpr to humble o.s.

u'more sm (disposizione d'animo) mood; (carattere) temper; **di buon/cattivo ~** in a good/bad mood

umo'rismo sm humour; **avere il senso dell'~** to have a sense of humour; **umo'ristico, -a, -ci, -che** ag humorous, funny

u'nanime ag unanimous

unci'netto [untʃi'netto] sm crochet hook

un'cino [un'tʃino] sm hook

undi'cenne [undi'tʃenne] ag, sm/f eleven-year-old

undi'cesimo, -a [undi'tʃezimo] ag eleventh

'undici ['unditʃi] num eleven

'ungere ['undʒere] vt to grease, oil; (Rel) to anoint; (fig) to flatter, butter up

unghe'rese [unge'rese] ag, sm/f, sm Hungarian

Unghe'ria [unge'ria] sf l'~ Hungary

'unghia ['ungja] sf (Anat) nail; (di animale) claw; (di rapace) talon; (di cavallo) hoof

ungu'ento sm ointment

'unico, -a, -ci, -che ag (solo) only; (ineguagliabile) unique; (singolo: binario) single; **figlio(a) ~(a)** only son/daughter, only child

unifi'care vt to unite, unify; (sistemi) to standardize; **unificazi'one** sf uniting; unification; standardization

uni'forme ag uniform; (superficie) even ▶ sf (divisa) uniform

uni'one sf union; (fig: concordia) unity, harmony; **Unione europea** European Union; **ex Unione Sovietica** former Soviet Union

u'nire vt to unite; (congiungere) to join, connect; (: ingredienti, colori) to combine; (in matrimonio) to unite, join together; **unirsi** vpr to unite; (in matrimonio) to be joined together; **~ qc** to unite sth with; to join o connect sth with; to combine sth with; **unirsi a** (gruppo, società) to join

unità sf inv (unione, concordia) unity; (Mat, Mil, Comm, di misura) unit; **unità di misura** unit of measurement

u'nito, -a ag (paese) united; (amici, famiglia) close; **in tinta unita** plain, self-coloured

univer'sale ag universal; general

università sf inv university

uni'verso sm universe

'uno, -a (dav sm +C, V, uno +s impura, gn, pn, ps, x, z; dav sf un' +V, una +C) art indef

1 a; (dav vocale) an; **un bambino** a child; **una strada** a street; **uno zingaro** a gypsy

2 (intensivo): **ho avuto una paura!** I got such a fright!

▶ pron

1 one; **prendine uno** take one (of them); **l'uno o l'altro** either (of them); **l'uno e l'altro** both (of them); **aiutarsi l'un l'altro** to help one another o each other; **sono entrati l'uno dopo l'altro** they came in one after the other **2** (un tale) someone, somebody **3** (con valore impersonale) one, you; **se uno vuole** if one wants, if you want ▶ num one; **una mela e due pere** one apple and two pears; **uno più uno fa due** one plus one equals two, one and one are two

▶ sf **è l'una** it's one (o'clock)

'unsi ecc vb vedi **ungere**

'unto, -a pp di **ungere** ▶ ag greasy, oily ▶ sm grease

u'omo (pl u'omini) sm man; **da ~** (abito, scarpe) men's, for men; **uomo d'affari** businessman; **uomo di paglia** stooge; **uomo politico** politician; **uomo rana** frogman

u'ovo (pl(f) u'ova) sm egg; **uovo affogato/alla coque** poached/ boiled egg; **uovo bazzotto/sodo** soft-/hard-boiled egg; **uovo di Pasqua** Easter egg; **uovo in camicia** poached egg; **uova strapazzate/al tegame** scrambled/fried eggs

ura'gano sm hurricane

urba'nistica sf town planning

ur'bano, -a ag urban, city cpd, town cpd; (Tel: chiamata) local; (fig) urbane

ur'gente [ur'dʒɛnte] ag urgent; **ur'genza** sf urgency; **in caso d'urgenza** (in case of) an emergency; **d'urgenza** as emergency ▶ av urgently, as a matter of urgency

ur'lare vi (persona) to scream, yell; (animale, vento) to howl ▶ vt to scream, yell

'urlo (pl(m) 'urli, pl(f) 'urla) sm scream, yell; howl

urrà escl hurrah!

U.R.S.S. abbr f **l'U.R.S.S.** the USSR

ur'tare vt to bump into, knock against; (fig: irritare) to annoy ▶ vi **~ contro o in** to bump into, knock against, crash into; (fig: imbattersi) to come up against; **urtarsi** vpr (reciproco: scontrarsi) to collide; (: fig) to clash; (irritarsi) to get annoyed

'U.S.A. ['uza] smpl **gli U.S.A.** the USA

u'sanza [u'zantsa] sf custom; (moda) fashion

u'sare vt to use, employ ▶ vi (servirsi): **~ di** to use; (: diritto) to exercise; (essere di moda) to be fashionable; (essere solito): **~ fare** to be in the habit of doing, be accustomed to doing ▶ vb impers **qui usa così** it's the custom round here; **u'sato, -a** ag used; (consumato) worn; (di seconda mano) used, second-hand ▶ sm second-hand goods pl

u'scire [uʃʃire] vi (gen) to come out; (partire, andare a passeggio, a uno spettacolo ecc) to go out; (essere sorteggiato: numero) to come up; **~ da** (gen) to come o (posto) to go o (come) out of, leave; (solco, vasca ecc) to come out of; (muro) to stick out of; (competenza ecc) to be outside; (infanzia, adolescenza) to leave behind; (famiglia nobile ecc) to come from; **~ da o di casa** to go out; (fig) to leave home; **~ in automobile** to go out in the car, go for a drive; **~ di strada** (Aut) to go off o leave the road

u'scita [uʃʃita] sf (passaggio, varco) exit, way out; (per divertimento) outing; (Econ: somma) expenditure; (Teatro) entrance; (fig: battuta) witty remark; **dov'è l'~?** where's the exit?; **uscita di sicurezza** emergency exit

usi'gnolo [uziɲ'ɲɔlo] sm nightingale

'uso sm (utilizzazione) use; (esercizio) practice; (abitudine) custom; **a ~ di** for (the use of); **d'~** (corrente) in use; **fuori ~** out of use; **uso esterno** per-

esterno for external use only
usti'one sf burn
usu'ale ag common, everyday
u'sura sf usury; (logoramento) wear (and tear)
uten'sile sm tool, implement; **utensili da cucina** kitchen utensils
u'tente sm/f user
utero sm uterus
'utile ag useful ▶ sm (vantaggio) advantage, benefit; (Econ: profitto) profit
utiliz'zare [utilid'dzare] vt to use, make use of, utilize
'uva sf grapes pl; **uva passa** raisins pl; **uva spina** gooseberry
UVA abbr (= ultravioletto prossimo) UVA
UVB abbr (= ultravioletto remoto) UVB

V

v. abbr (= vedi) v
va, va' vb vedi **andare**
va'cante ag vacant
va'canza [va'kantsa] sf (riposo, ferie) holiday(s) pl (BRIT), vacation (US); (giorno di permesso) day off, holiday; **vacanze** sfpl (periodo di ferie) holidays (BRIT), vacation sg (US); **essere/andare in ~** to be/go on holiday o vacation; **sono qui in ~** I'm on holiday here; **vacanze estive** summer holiday(s) o vacation; **vacanze**

natalizie Christmas holidays o vacation

Attenzione! In inglese esiste la parola vacancy che però indica un posto vacante o una camera disponibile.

'vacca, -che sf cow
vacci'nare [vattʃi'nare] vt to vaccinate
vac'cino [vat'tʃino] sm (Med) vaccine
vacil'lare [vatʃil'lare] vi to sway, wobble; (luce) to flicker; (fig: memoria, coraggio) to be failing, falter
'vacuo, -a ag (fig) empty, vacuous
'vado ecc vb vedi **andare**
vaga'bondo, -a sm/f tramp, vagrant
va'gare vi to wander
vagherò ecc [vage'rɔ] vb vedi **vagare**
va'gina [va'dʒina] sf vagina
'vaglia ['vaʎʎa] sm inv money order; **vaglia postale** postal order
vagli'are [vaʎ'ʎare] vt to sift; (fig) to weigh up
'vago, -a, -ghi, -ghe ag vague
va'gone sm (Ferr: per passeggeri) coach; (: per merci) truck, wagon; **vagone letto** sleeper, sleeping car; **vagone ristorante** dining o restaurant car
'vai vb vedi **andare**
vai'olo sm smallpox
va'langa, -ghe sf avalanche
va'lere vi (avere forza, potenza) to have influence; (essere valido) to be valid; (avere vigore, autorità) to hold, apply; (essere capace: poeta, studente) to be good, be able ▶ vt (prezzo, sforzo) to be worth; (corrispondere) to correspond to; (procurare): **~ qc a qn** to earn sb sth; **valersi di** to make use of, take advantage of; **far ~** (autorità ecc) to assert; **vale a dire** that is to say; **~ la pena** to be worth the effort o worth it
'valgo ecc vb vedi **valere**
vali'care vt to cross

'valico, -chi sm (passo) pass

'valido, -a ag valid; (rimedio) effective; (aiuto) real; (persona) worthwhile

vali'getta [vali'dʒetta] sf briefcase; **valigetta ventiquattrore** overnight bag o case

va'ligia, -gie o **ge** [va'lidʒa] sf (suit)case; **fare le valigie** to pack (up)

'valle sf valley; **a ~** (di fiume) downstream; **scendere a ~** to go downhill

va'lore sm (gen) value; (merito) merit, worth; (coraggio) valour, courage; (Comm: titolo) security; **valori** smpl (oggetti preziosi) valuables

valoriz'zare [valorid'dzare] vt (terreno) to develop; (fig) to make the most of

va'luta sf currency, money; (Banca): **~ 15 gennaio** interest to run from January 15th

valu'tare vt (casa, gioiello, fig) to value; (stabilire: peso, entrate, fig) to estimate

'valvola sf (Tecn, Anat) valve; (Elettr) fuse

'valzer ['valtser] sm inv waltz

vam'pata sf (di fiamma) blaze; (di calore) blast; (: al viso) flush

vam'piro sm vampire

vanda'lismo sm vandalism

'vandalo sm vandal

vaneggi'are [vaned'dʒare] vi to rave

'vanga, -ghe sf spade

van'gelo [van'dʒɛlo] sm gospel

va'niglia [va'niʎʎa] sf vanilla

vanità sf vanity; (di promessa) emptiness; (di sforzo) futility; **vani'toso, -a** ag vain, conceited

'vanno vb vedi **andare**

'vano, -a ag vain ▶ sm (spazio) space; (apertura) opening; (stanza) room

van'taggio [van'taddʒo] sm advantage; **essere/portarsi in ~** (Sport) to be in/take the lead; **vantaggi'oso, -a** ag advantageous;

favourable

vantarsi vpr **~ (di/di aver fatto)** to boast o brag (about/about having done)

'vanvera sf **a ~** haphazardly; **parlare a ~** to talk nonsense

va'pore sm vapour; (anche: **~ acqueo**) steam; (nave) steamer; **a ~** (turbina ecc) steam cpd; **al ~** (Cuc) steamed

va'rare vt (Naut, fig) to launch; (Dir) to pass

var'care vt to cross

'varco, -chi sm passage; **aprirsi un ~ tra la folla** to push one's way through the crowd

vare'china [vare'kina] sf bleach

vari'abile ag variable; (tempo, umore) changeable, variable ▶ sf (Mat) variable

vari'cella [vari'tʃɛlla] sf chickenpox

vari'coso, -a ag varicose

varietà sf inv variety ▶ sm inv variety show

'vario, -a ag varied; (parecchi: col sostantivo al pl) various; (mutevole: umore) changeable

'varo sm (Naut: fig) launch; (di leggi) passing

varrò ecc vb vedi **valere**

Var'savia sf Warsaw

va'saio sm potter

'vasca, -sche sf basin; **vasca da bagno** bathtub, bath

vas'chetta [vas'ketta] sf (per gelato) tub; (per sviluppare fotografie) dish

vase'lina sf Vaseline®

'vaso sm (recipiente) pot; (: barattolo) jar; (: decorativo) vase; (Anat) vessel; **vaso da fiori** vase; (per piante) flowerpot

vas'soio sm tray

'vasto, -a ag vast, immense

Vati'cano sm **il ~** the Vatican

ve pron, av vedi **vi**

vecchi'aia [vek'kjaja] sf old age

'vecchio, -a [ˈvɛkkjo] *ag* old ▶ *sm/f* old man/woman; **i vecchi** the old

ve'dere *vt, vi* to see; **vedersi** *vpr* to meet, see one another; **avere a che ~ con** to have something to do with; **far ~ qc a qn** to show sb sth; **farsi ~** to show o.s.; *(farsi vivo)* to show one's face; **vedi di non farlo** make sure o see you don't do it; **non (ci) si vede** *(è buio ecc)* you can't see a thing; **non lo posso ~** *(fig)* I can't stand him

ve'detta *sf (sentinella, posto)* look-out; *(Naut)* patrol boat

'vedovo, -a *sm/f* widower/widow

vedrò *ecc vb vedi* **vedere**

ve'duta *sf view;* **vedute** *sfpl (fig: opinioni)* views; **di larghe** *o* **ampie vedute** broad-minded; **di vedute limitate** narrow-minded

vege'tale [vedʒeˈtale] *ag, sm* vegetable

vegetari'ano, -a [vedʒetaˈrjano] *ag, sm/f* vegetarian; **avete piatti vegetariani?** do you have any vegetarian dishes?

vegetazi'one [vedʒetatˈtsjone] *sf* vegetation

'vegeto, -a [ˈvɛdʒeto] *ag (pianta)* thriving; *(persona)* strong, vigorous

'veglia [ˈveʎʎa] *sf* wakefulness; *(sorveglianza)* watch; *(trattenimento)* evening gathering; **fare la ~ a un malato** to watch over a sick person

vegli'one [veʎˈʎone] *sm* ball, dance; **veglione di Capodanno** New Year's Eve party

ve'icolo *sm* vehicle

'vela *sf (Naut: tela)* sail; *(Sport)* sailing

ve'leno *sm* poison; **vele'noso, -a** *ag* poisonous

veli'ero *sm* sailing ship

vel'luto *sm* velvet; **velluto a coste** cord

'velo *sm* veil; *(tessuto)* voile

ve'loce [veˈlotʃe] *ag* fast, quick ▶ *av*

fast, quickly; **velocità** *sf* speed; **a forte velocità** at high speed; **velocità di crociera** cruising speed

'vena *sf (gen)* vein; *(filone)* vein, seam; *(fig: ispirazione)* inspiration; *(: umore)* mood; **essere in ~ di qc** to be in the mood for sth

ve'nale *ag (prezzo, valore)* market *cpd*; *(fig)* venal; mercenary

ven'demmia *sf (raccolta)* grape harvest; *(quantità d'uva)* grape crop, grapes *pl*; *(vino ottenuto)* vintage

'vendere *vt* to sell; **"vendesi"** "for sale"

ven'detta *sf* revenge

vendicarsi *vpr* **~ (di)** to avenge o.s. (for); *(per rancore)* to take one's revenge (for); **~ su qn** to revenge o.s. on sb

'vendita *sf* sale; **la ~** *(attività)* selling; *(smercio)* sales *pl*; **in ~** on sale; **vendita all'asta** sale by auction; **vendita per telefono** telesales *sg*

vene'rare *vt* to venerate

venerdì *sm inv* Friday; **di** *o* **il ~** on Fridays; **V~ Santo** Good Friday

ve'nereo, -a *ag* venereal

Ve'nezia [veˈnɛttsja] *sf* Venice

'vengo *ecc vb vedi* **venire**

veni'ale *ag* venial

ve'nire *vi* to come; *(riuscire: dolce, fotografia)* to turn out; *(come ausiliare: essere)*: **viene ammirato da tutti** he is admired by everyone; **~ da** to come from; **quanto viene?** how much does it cost?; **far ~** *(mandare a chiamare)* to send for; **~ giù** to come down; **~ meno** *(svenire)* to faint; **~ meno a qc** not to fulfil sth; **~ su** to come up; **~ a trovare qn** to come and see sb; **~ via** to come away

'venni *ecc vb vedi* **venire**

ven'taglio [venˈtaʎʎo] *sm* fan

ven'tata *sf* gust *(of wind)*

ven'tenne *ag* **una ragazza ~** a twenty-year-old girl, a girl of twenty

ven'tesimo, -a *num* twentieth

'venti *num* twenty

venti'lare *vt (stanza)* to air, ventilate; *(fig: idea, proposta)* to air; **ventila'tore** *sm* ventilator, fan

ven'tina *sf* **una ~ (di)** around twenty, twenty or so

'vento *sm* wind

'ventola *sf (Aut, Tecn)* fan

ven'tosa *sf (Zool)* sucker; *(di gomma)* suction pad

ven'toso, -a *ag* windy

'ventre *sm* stomach

'vera *sf* wedding ring

vera'mente *av* really

ve'randa *sf* veranda(h)

ver'bale *ag* verbal ▶ *sm (di riunione)* minutes *pl*

'verbo *sm (Ling)* verb; *(parola)* word; *(Rel):* **il V~** the Word

'verde *ag, sm* green; **essere al ~** to be broke; **verde bottiglia/oliva** bottle/olive green

ver'detto *sm* verdict

ver'dura *sf* vegetables *pl*

'vergine ['vɛrdʒine] *sf* virgin; *(dello zodiaco):* **V~** Virgo ▶ *ag* virgin; *(ragazza):* **essere ~** to be a virgin

ver'gogna [ver'ɡoɲɲa] *sf* shame; *(timidezza)* shyness, embarrassment; **vergo'gnarsi** *vpr* **vergognarsi (di)** to be o feel ashamed (of); to be shy (about), be embarrassed (about); **vergo'gnoso, -a** *ag* ashamed; *(timido)* shy, embarrassed (about); *(causa di vergogna: azione)* shameful

ve'rifica, -che *sf* checking *no pl*, check

verifi'care *vt (controllare)* to check; *(confermare)* to confirm, bear out

verità *sf inv* truth

'verme *sm* worm

ver'miglio [ver'miʎʎo] *sm* vermilion, scarlet

ver'nice [ver'nitʃe] *sf (coloritura)* paint; *(trasparente)* varnish; *(pelle)* patent leather; **"~ fresca"** "wet paint"; **vernici'are** *vt* to paint; to varnish

'vero, -a *ag (veridico: fatti, testimonianza)* true; *(autentico)* real ▶ *sm (verità)* truth; *(realtà)* (real) life; **un ~ e proprio delinquente** a real criminal, an out-and-out criminal

vero'simile *ag* likely, probable

verrò *ecc vb vedi* **venire**

ver'ruca, -che *sf* wart

versa'mento *sm (pagamento)* payment; *(deposito di denaro)* deposit

ver'sante *sm* slopes *pl*, side

ver'sare *vt (fare uscire: vino, farina)* to pour (out); *(spargere: lacrime, sangue)* to shed; *(rovesciare)* to spill; *(Econ)* to pay; *(: depositare)* to deposit, pay in

versa'tile *ag* versatile

versi'one *sf* version; *(traduzione)* translation

'verso *sm (di poesia)* verse, line; *(di animale, uccello)* cry; *(direzione)* direction; *(modo)* way; *(di foglio di carta)* verso; *(di moneta)* reverse; **versi** *smpl (poesia)* verse *sg*; **non c'è ~ di persuaderlo** there's no way of persuading him, he can't be persuaded ▶ *prep (in direzione di)* toward(s); *(nei pressi di)* near, around (about); *(in senso temporale)* around, around; *(nei confronti di)* for; **~ di me** towards me; **~ sera** towards evening

'vertebra *sf* vertebra

verte'brale *ag* vertebral; **colonna ~** spinal column, spine

verti'cale *ag, sf* vertical

'vertice *sm* summit, top; *(Mat)* vertex; **conferenza al ~** *(Pol)* summit conference

ver'tigine [ver'tidʒine] *sf* dizziness *no pl*; dizzy spell; *(Med)* vertigo; **avere le vertigini** to feel dizzy

ve'scica, -che [veʃʃika] *sf (Anat)* bladder; *(Med)* blister

'vescovo *sm* bishop

'**vespa** *sf* wasp

ves'taglia [ves'taʎʎa] *sf* dressing gown

ves'tire *vt* (*bambino, malato*) to dress; (*avere indosso*) to have on, wear; **vestirsi** *vpr* to dress, get dressed; **ves'tito, -a** *ag* dressed ▶ *sm* garment; (*da donna*) dress; (*da uomo*) suit; **vestiti** *smpl* (*indumenti*) clothes; **vestito di bianco** dressed in white

veteri'nario, -a *ag* veterinary ▶ *sm* veterinary surgeon (*BRIT*), veterinarian (*US*), vet

'**veto** *sm inv* veto

ve'traio *sm* glassmaker; glazier

ve'trata *sf* glass door (*o* window); (*di chiesa*) stained glass window

ve'trato, -a *ag* (*porta, finestra*) glazed; (*che contiene vetro*) glass *cpd* ▶ *sf* glass door (*o* window); (*di chiesa*) stained glass window; **carta vetrata** sandpaper

ve'trina *sf* (*di negozio*) (shop) window; (*armadio*) display cabinet; **vetri'nista, -i, -e** *sm/f* window dresser

'**vetro** *sm* glass; (*per finestra, porta*) pane (of glass)

'**vetta** *sf* peak, summit, top

vet'tura *sf* (*carrozza*) carriage; (*Ferr*) carriage (*BRIT*), car (*US*); (*auto*) car (*BRIT*), automobile (*US*)

vezzeggia'tivo [vettseddʒa'tivo] *sm* (*Ling*) term of endearment

vi (*dav lo, la, li, le, ne diventa* **ve**) *pron* (*oggetto*) you; (*complemento di termine*) (to) you; (*riflessivo*) yourselves; (*reciproco*) each other ▶ *av* (*lì*) there; (*qui*) here; (*per questo/quel luogo*) through here/there; **vi è/sono** there is/are

'**via** *sf* (*gen*) way; (*strada*) street; (*sentiero, pista*) path, track; (*Amm: procedimento*) channels *pl* ▶ *prep* (*passando per*) via, by way of ▶ *av* away ▶ *escl* go away!; (*suvvia*) come on!;

(*Sport*) go! ▶ *sm* (*Sport*) starting signal; **in ~ di guarigione** on the road to recovery; **per ~ di** (*a causa di*) because of, on account of; **in o per ~** on the way; **per ~ aerea** by air; (*lettere*) by airmail; **andare/essere ~** to go/be away; **~ ~ che** (*a mano a mano*) as; **dare il ~** (*Sport*) to give the starting signal; **dare il ~ a** (*fig*) to start; **in ~ provvisoria** provisionally; **Via lattea** (*Astr*) Milky Way; **via di mezzo** middle course; **via d'uscita** (*fig*) way out

via'dotto *sm* viaduct

viaggi'are [viad'dʒare] *vi* to travel; **viaggia'tore, -'trice** *ag* travelling ▶ *sm* traveller; (*passeggero*) passenger

vi'aggio ['vjaddʒo] *sm* travel(ling); (*tragitto*) journey, trip; **buon ~!** have a good trip!; **com'è andato il ~?** how was your journey?; **il ~ dura due ore** the journey takes two hours; **viaggio di nozze** honeymoon; **siamo in ~ di nozze** we're on honeymoon

vi'ale *sm* avenue

via'vai *sm* coming and going, bustle

vi'brare *vi* to vibrate

'**vice** ['vitʃe] *sm/f* deputy ▶ *prefisso*

vi'cenda [vi'tʃɛnda] *sf* event; **a ~** in turn

vice'versa [vitʃe'vɛrsa] *av* vice versa; **da Roma a Pisa e ~** from Rome to Pisa and back

vici'nanza [vitʃi'nantsa] *sf* nearness, closeness

vi'cino, -a [vi'tʃino] *ag* (*gen*) near; (*nello spazio*) near, nearby; (*accanto*) next; (*nel tempo*) near, close at hand ▶ *sm/f* neighbour ▶ *av* near, close; **da ~** (*guardare*) close up; (*esaminare, seguire*) closely; (*conoscere*) well, intimately; **~ a** near (to), close to; (*accanto a*) beside; **c'è una banca qui ~?** is there a bank nearby?; **~ di casa** neighbour

'**vicolo** *sm* alley; **vicolo cieco** blind alley

'video sm inv (TV: schermo) screen;
video'camera sf camcorder;
videocas'setta sf videocassette;
videoclip [video'klip] sm inv
videoclip; **videogi'oco, -chi**
[video'dʒɔko] sm video game;
videoregistra'tore sm video
(recorder); **videote'lefono** sm
videophone
'vidi ecc vb vedi **vedere**
vie'tare vt to forbid; (Amm) to
prohibit; ~ a qn di fare to forbid sb
to do; to prohibit sb from doing;
"vietato fumare/l'ingresso" "no
smoking/admittance"
vie'tato, -a ag (vedi vb) forbidden;
prohibited; banned; "~ fumare/
l'ingresso" "no smoking/
admittance"; ~ ai minori di 14/18 anni
prohibited to children under 14/18;
"senso ~" (Aut) "no entry"; "sosta
vietata" (Aut) "no parking"
Viet'nam sm il ~ Vietnam;
vietna'mita, -i, -e ag, sm/f, sm
Vietnamese inv
vi'gente [vi'dʒɛnte] ag in force
'vigile ['vidʒile] ag watchful ▶ sm
(anche: ~ urbano) policeman (in
towns); **vigile del fuoco** fireman
vi'gilia [vi'dʒilja] sf (giorno antecedente)
eve; **la ~ di Natale** Christmas Eve
vigli'acco, -a, -chi, -che [viʎ'ʎakko]
ag cowardly ▶ sm/f coward
vi'gneto [vin'neto] sm vineyard
vi'gnetta [vin'netta] sf cartoon
vi'gore sm vigour; (Dir): **essere/
entrare in ~** to be in/come into force
'vile ag (spregevole) low, mean, base;
(codardo) cowardly
'villa sf villa
vil'laggio [vil'laddʒo] sm village;
villaggio turistico holiday village
vil'lano, -a ag rude, ill-mannered
villeggia'tura [villeddʒa'tura] sf
holiday(s) pl (BRIT), vacation (US)

vil'letta sf, **vil'lino** ▶ sm small house
(with a garden), cottage
'vimini smpl di ~ wicker
'vincere ['vintʃere] vt (in guerra, al
gioco, a una gara) to defeat, beat;
(premio, guerra, partita) to win; (fig) to
overcome, conquer ▶ vi to win; ~ qn in
bellezza to be better-looking than sb;
vinci'tore sm winner; (Mil) victor
vi'nicolo, -a ag wine cpd
'vino sm wine; **vino bianco/rosato/
rosso** white/rosé/red wine; **vino da
pasto** table wine
'vinsi ecc vb vedi **vincere**
vi'ola sf (Bot) violet; (Mus) viola ▶ ag,
sm inv (colore) purple
vio'lare vt (chiesa) to desecrate,
violate; (giuramento, legge) to violate
violen'tare vt to use violence on;
(donna) to rape
vio'lento, -a ag violent; **vio'lenza** sf
violence; **violenza carnale** rape
vio'letta sf (Bot) violet
vio'letto, -a ag, sm (colore) violet
violi'nista, -i, -e sm/f violinist
vio'lino sm violin
violon'cello [violon'tʃɛllo] sm cello
vi'ottolo sm path, track
vip [vip] sigla m (= very important
person) VIP
'vipera sf viper, adder
vi'rare vi (Naut, Aer) to turn; (Fot) to
tone; ~ **di bordo** (Naut) to tack
'virgola sf (Ling) comma; (Mat) point;
virgo'lette sfpl inverted commas,
quotation marks
vi'rile ag (proprio dell'uomo) masculine;
(non puerile, da uomo) manly, virile
virtù sf inv virtue; in o per ~ di by
virtue of, by
virtu'ale ag virtual
'virus sm inv (anche Inform) virus
'viscere ['viʃʃere] sfpl (di animale)
entrails pl; (fig) bowels pl
'vischio ['viskjo] sm (Bot) mistletoe;

(pania) birdlime

'**viscido, -a** ['viʃʃido] ag slimy

vi'**sibile** ag visible

visibilità sf visibility

visi'era sf (di elmo) visor; (di berretto) peak

visi'one sf vision; **prendere ~ di qc** to examine sth, look over; **prima/seconda** (Cinema) first/second showing

'**visita** sf visit; (Med) visit, call; (: esame) examination; **visita guidata** guided tour; **a che ora comincia la ~ guidata?** what time does the guided tour start?; **visita medica** medical examination; visi'**tare** vt to visit; (Med) to visit, call on; (: esaminare) to examine; visita'**tore, -'trice** sm/f visitor

vi'**sivo, -a** ag visual

'**viso** sm face

vi'**sone** sm mink

'**vispo, -a** ag quick, lively

'**vissi** ecc vb vedi **vivere**

'**vista** sf (facoltà) (eye)sight; (fatto di vedere): **la ~ di** the sight of; (veduta) view; **sparare a ~** to shoot on sight; **in ~** in sight; **perdere qn di ~** to lose sight of sb; (fig) to lose touch with sb; **a ~ d'occhio** as far as the eye can see; (fig) before one's very eyes; **far ~ di fare** to pretend to do

'**visto, -a** pp di **vedere** ▶ sm visa; **~ che** seeing (that)

vis'**toso, -a** ag gaudy, garish; (ingente) considerable

visu'ale ag visual

'**vita** sf life; (Anat) waist; **a ~** for life

vi'**tale** ag vital

vita'**mina** sf vitamin

'**vite** sf (Bot) vine; (Tecn) screw

vi'**tello** sm (Zool) calf; (carne) veal; (pelle) calfskin

'**vittima** sf victim

'**vitto** sm food; (in un albergo ecc) board;

vitto e alloggio board and lodging

vit'**toria** sf victory

'**viva** escl ~ **il re!** long live the king!

vi'**vace** [vi'vatʃe] ag (vivo, animato) lively; (: mente) lively, sharp; (colore) bright

vi'**vaio** sm (di pesci) hatchery; (Agr) nursery

vivavoce [viva'votʃe] sm inv (dispositivo) loudspeaker; **mettere il ~** to switch on the loudspeaker

vi'**vente** ag living, alive; **i viventi** the living

'**vivere** vi to live ▶ vt to live; (passare: brutto momento) to live through, go through; (sentire: gioie, pene di qn) to share ▶ sm life; (anche: modo di ~) way of life; **viveri** smpl (cibo) food sg, provisions; **~ di** to live on

'**vivido, -a** ag (colore) vivid, bright

vivisezi'one [viviset'tsjone] sf vivisection

'**vivo, -a** ag (vivente) alive, living; (: animale) live; (fig) lively; (: colore) bright, brilliant; **i vivi** the living; **~ e vegeto** hale and hearty; **farsi ~** to show one's face; to be heard from; **ritrarre dal ~** to paint from life; **pungere qn nel ~** (fig) to cut sb to the quick

vivrò ecc vb vedi **vivere**

vizi'**are** [vit'tsjare] vt (bambino) to spoil; (corrompere moralmente) to corrupt; **vizi'ato, -a** ag spoilt; (aria, acqua) polluted

'**vizio** sm (morale) vice; (cattiva abitudine) bad habit; (imperfezione) flaw, defect; (errore) fault, mistake

V.le abbr = **viale**

vocabo'**lario** sm (dizionario) dictionary; (lessico) vocabulary

vo'**cabolo** sm word

vo'**cale** ag vocal ▶ sf vowel

vocazi'one [vokat'tsjone] sf vocation; (fig) natural bent

voce ['votʃe] sf voice; (diceria) rumour; (di un elenco, in elenco) item; **aver ~ in capitolo** (fig) to have a say in the matter

voga sf (Naut) rowing; (usanza): **essere in ~** to be in fashion o in vogue

vo'gare vi to row

vogherò ecc [voge'rɔ] vb vedi **vogare**

voglia ['vɔʎʎa] sf desire, wish; (macchia) birthmark; **aver ~ di qc/di fare** to feel like sth/like doing; (più forte) to want sth/to do

voglio ecc ['vɔʎʎo] vb vedi **volere**

voi pron you; **voi'altri** pron you

vo'lante ag flying ▶ sm (steering) wheel

volan'tino sm leaflet

vo'lare vi (uccello, aereo, fig) to fly; (cappello) to blow away o off, fly away o off; **~ via** to fly away o off

vo'latile ag (Chim) volatile ▶ sm (Zool) bird

volente'roso, -a ag willing

volenti'eri av willingly; **"~"** "with pleasure", "I'd be glad to"

vo'lere

O   sm will, wish(es); **contro il volere di** against the wishes of; **per volere di qn** in obedience to sb's will o wishes ▶ vt

1 (esigere, desiderare) to want; **voler fare/che qn faccia** to want to do/sb to do; **volete del caffè?** would you like o do you want some coffee?; **vorrei questo/fare** I would o I'd like this/to do; **come vuoi** as you like; **senza volere** (inavvertitamente) without meaning to, unintentionally

2 (consentire): **vogliate attendere, per piacere** please wait; **vogliamo andare?** shall we go?; **vuole essere così gentile da …?** would you be so kind as to …?; **non ha voluto ricevermi** he wouldn't see me

3: **volerci** (essere necessario: materiale,

attenzione) to need; (: tempo) to take; **quanta farina ci vuole per questa torta?** how much flour do you need for this cake?; **ci vuole un'ora per arrivare a Venezia** it takes an hour to get to Venice

4: **voler bene a qn** (amore) to love sb; (affetto) to be fond of sb, like sb very much; **voler male a qn** to dislike sb; **volerne a qn** to bear sb a grudge; **voler dire** to mean

vol'gare ag vulgar

voli'era sf aviary

voli'tivo, -a ag strong-willed

'volli ecc vb vedi **volere**

'volo sm flight; **al ~: colpire qc al ~** to hit sth as it flies past; **capire al ~** to understand straight away; **volo charter** charter flight; **volo di linea** scheduled flight

volontà sf will; **a ~** (mangiare, bere) as much as one likes; **buona/cattiva ~** goodwill/lack of goodwill

volon'tario, -a ag voluntary ▶ sm (Mil) volunteer

'volpe sf fox

'volta sf (momento, circostanza) time; (turno, giro) turn; (curva) turn, bend; (Archit) vault; (direzione): **partire alla ~ di** to set off for; **a mia (o tua ecc) ~** in turn; **una ~** once; **una ~ sola** only once; **due volte** twice; **una cosa per ~** one thing at a time; **una ~ per tutte** once and for all; **a volte** at times, sometimes; **una ~ che** (temporale) once; (causale) since; **3 volte 4** 3 times 4

volta'faccia [volta'fattʃa] sm inv (fig) volte-face

vol'taggio [vol'taddʒo] sm (Elettr) voltage

vol'tare vt to turn; (girare: moneta) to turn over; (rigirare) to turn round ▶ vi to turn; **voltarsi** vpr to turn; to turn over; to turn round

voltas'tomaco sm nausea; (fig) disgust

'volto, -a pp di **volgere** ▶ sm face

vo'lubile ag changeable, fickle

vo'lume sm volume

vomi'tare vt, vi to vomit; **'vomito** sm vomiting no pl; vomit

'vongola sf clam

vo'race [vo'ratʃe] ag voracious, greedy

vo'ragine [vo'radʒine] sf abyss, chasm

vorrò ecc vb vedi **volere**

'vortice ['vɔrtitʃe] sm whirlwind; whirlpool; (fig) whirl

'vostro, -a det il(la) ~(a) ecc your ▶ pron il(la) ~(a) ecc yours

vo'tante sm/f voter

vo'tare vi to vote ▶ vt (sottoporre a votazione) to take a vote on; (approvare) to vote for; (Rel): **~ qc a** to dedicate sth to

'voto sm (Pol) vote; (Ins) mark; (Rel) vow; (: offerta) votive offering; **aver voti belli/brutti** (Ins) to get good/bad marks

vs. abbr (Comm) = **vostro**

vul'cano sm volcano

vulne'rabile ag vulnerable

vu'oi, vu'ole vb vedi **volere**

vuo'tare vt to empty; **vuotarsi** vpr to empty

vu'oto, -a ag empty; (fig: privo): **~ di** (senso ecc) devoid of ▶ sm empty space, gap; (spazio in bianco) blank; (Fisica) vacuum; (fig: mancanza) gap, void; **a mani vuote** empty-handed; **vuoto d'aria** air pocket; **vuoto a rendere** returnable bottle

W

'wafer ['vafer] sm inv (Cuc, Elettr) wafer

'water ['wɔːtəʳ] sm inv toilet

watt [vat] sm inv watt

W.C. sm inv WC

web [ueb] sm il ~ the Web; **cercare nel ~** to search the Web ▶ ag inv **pagina ~** web page

'weekend ['wiːkend] sm inv weekend

'western ['wɛstern] ag (Cinema) cowboy cpd ▶ sm inv western, cowboy film; **western all'italiana** spaghetti western

'whisky ['wiski] sm inv whisky

'windsurf ['windsəːf] sm inv (tavola) windsurfer; (sport) windsurfing

'würstel ['vyrstəl] sm inv frankfurter

X

xe'nofobo, -a [kse'nɔfobo] ag xenophobic ▶ sm/f xenophobe

xi'lofono [ksi'lɔfono] sm xylophone

y

yacht [jɔt] *sm inv* yacht
'yoga ['jɔga] *ag inv, sm* yoga (*cpd*)
yogurt ['jɔgurt] *sm inv* yog(h)urt

z

zabai'one [dzaba'jone] *sm* dessert made of egg yolks, sugar and marsala
zaf'fata [tsaf'fata] *sf* (*tanfo*) stench
zaffe'rano [dzaffe'rano] *sm* saffron
zaf'firo [dzaf'firo] *sm* sapphire
'zaino ['dzaino] *sm* rucksack
'zampa ['tsampa] *sf* (*di animale: gamba*) leg; (*: piede*) paw; **a quattro zampe** on all fours
zampil'lare [tsampil'lare] *vi* to gush, spurt
zan'zara [dzan'dzara] *sf* mosquito; **zanzari'era** *sf* mosquito net
'zappa ['tsappa] *sf* hoe
'zapping ['tsapiŋ] *sm* (*TV*) channel-hopping

zar, za'rina [tsar, tsa'rina] *sm/f* tsar/tsarina
'zattera ['dzattera] *sf* raft
'zebra ['dzɛbra] *sf* zebra; **zebre** *sfpl* (*Aut*) zebra crossing *sg* (BRIT), crosswalk *sg* (US)
'zecca, -che ['tsekka] *sf* (*Zool*) tick; (*officina di monete*) mint
'zelo ['dzɛlo] *sm* zeal
zen'zero ['dzendzero] *sm* ginger
'zeppa ['tseppa] *sf* wedge
'zeppo, -a ['tseppo] *ag* **~ di** crammed *o* packed with
zer'bino [dzer'bino] *sm* doormat
'zero ['dzɛro] *sm* zero, nought; **vincere per tre a ~** (*Sport*) to win three-nil
'zia ['tsia] *sf* aunt
zibel'lino [dzibel'lino] *sm* sable
'zigomo ['dzigomo] *sm* cheekbone
zig'zag [dzig'dzag] *sm inv* zigzag; **andare a ~** to zigzag
Zimbabwe [tsim'babwe] *sm* **lo ~** Zimbabwe
'zinco ['dzinko] *sm* zinc
'zingaro, -a ['dzingaro] *sm/f* gipsy
'zio ['tsio] (*pl* **'zii**) *sm* uncle
zip'pare *vt* (*Inform: file*) to zip
zi'tella [dzi'tella] *sf* spinster; (*peg*) old maid
'zitto, -a ['tsitto] *ag* quiet, silent; **sta' ~!** be quiet!
'zoccolo ['tsɔkkolo] *sm* (*calzatura*) clog; (*di cavallo ecc*) hoof; (*basamento*) base; plinth
zodia'cale [dzodia'kale] *ag* zodiac *cpd*; **segno ~** sign of the zodiac
zo'diaco [dzo'diako] *sm* zodiac
'zolfo ['tsolfo] *sm* sulphur
'zolla ['dzɔlla] *sf* clod (of earth)
zol'letta [dzol'letta] *sf* sugar lump
'zona ['dzɔna] *sf* zone, area; **zona di depressione** (*Meteor*) trough of low pressure; **zona disco** (*Aut*) ≈ meter zone; **zona industriale** industrial estate; **zona pedonale** pedestrian

precinct; **zona verde** (*di abitato*) green area

'zonzo ['dzondzo]: **a ~** *av*, **andare a ~** to wander about, stroll about

zoo ['dzɔɔ] *sm inv* zoo

zoolo'gia [dzoolo'dʒia] *sf* zoology

zoppi'care [tsoppi'kare] *vi* to limp; to be shaky, rickety

'zoppo, -a ['tsɔppo] *ag* lame; (*fig: mobile*) shaky, rickety

Z.T.L. *sigla f* (= *Zona a Traffico Limitato*) controlled traffic zone

'zucca, -che ['tsukka] *sf* (*Bot*) marrow; pumpkin

zucche'rare [tsukke'rare] *vt* to put sugar in; **zucche'rato, -a** *ag* sweet, sweetened

zuccheri'era [tsukke'rjɛra] *sf* sugar bowl

'zucchero ['tsukkero] *sm* sugar; **zucchero di canna** cane sugar; **zucchero filato** candy floss, cotton candy (*US*)

zuc'china [tsuk'kina] *sf* courgette (*BRIT*), zucchini (*US*)

'zuffa ['tsuffa] *sf* brawl

'zuppa ['tsuppa] *sf* soup; (*fig*) mixture, muddle; **zuppa inglese** (*Cuc*) dessert made with sponge cake, custard and chocolate, ≈ trifle (*BRIT*)

'zuppo, -a ['tsuppo] *ag* **~ (di)** drenched (with), soaked (with)

ENGLISH - ITALIAN
INGLESE - ITALIANO

a

A [eɪ] n (Mus) la m; (letter) A, a for m inv

a
[ə] (before vowel or silent h **an**) indef art
1 (un (uno + s impure, gn, pn, ps, x, z), una f (un' + vowel); **a book** un libro; **a mirror** uno specchio; **an apple** una mela; **she's a doctor** è medico
2 (instead of the number "one") un(o), f una; **a year ago** un anno fa; **a hundred/thousand** etc pounds cento/mille etc sterline
3 (in expressing ratios, prices etc) a, per; **3 a day/week** 3 al giorno/alla settimana; **10 km an hour** 10 km all'ora; **£5 a person** 5 sterline a persona or per persona

A.A. n abbr (= Alcoholics Anonymous) AA; (BRIT: = Automobile Association) ≈ A.C.I. m

A.A.A. (US) n abbr (= American Automobile Association) ≈ A.C.I. m

aback [ə'bæk] adv **to be taken ~** essere sbalordito(-a)

abandon [ə'bændən] vt abbandonare ▶ n **with ~** sfrenatamente, spensieratamente

abattoir [ˈæbətwɑːʳ] (BRIT) n mattatoio

abbey [ˈæbɪ] n abbazia, badia

abbreviation [əbriːvɪˈeɪʃən] n abbreviazione f

abdomen [ˈæbdəmən] n addome m

abduct [æbˈdʌkt] vt rapire

abide [əˈbaɪd] vt **I can't ~ it/him** non lo posso soffrire or sopportare ▶ **abide by** vt fus conformarsi a

ability [əˈbɪlɪtɪ] n abilità f inv

able [ˈeɪbl] adj capace; **to be ~ to do sth** essere capace di fare qc, poter fare qc

abnormal [æbˈnɔːməl] adj anormale

aboard [əˈbɔːd] adv a bordo ▶ prep a bordo di

abolish [əˈbɒlɪʃ] vt abolire

abolition [æbəʊˈlɪʃən] n abolizione f

abort [əˈbɔːt] vt abortire; **abortion** [əˈbɔːʃən] n aborto; **to have an abortion** abortire

about
[əˈbaʊt] adv
1 (approximately) circa, quasi; **about a hundred/thousand** etc un centinaio/migliaio etc, circa cento/mille etc; **it takes about 10 hours** ci vogliono circa 10 ore; **at about 2 o'clock** verso le 2; **I've just about finished** ho quasi finito
2 (referring to place) qua e là, in giro; **to leave things lying about** lasciare delle cose in giro; **to run about** correre qua e là; **to walk about** camminare
3: **to be about to do sth** stare per fare qc
▶ prep
1 (relating to) su, di; **a book about London** un libro su Londra; **what is it about?** di che si tratta?; (book, film etc) di cosa tratta?; **we talked about it** ne abbiamo parlato; **what or how about doing this?** che ne dici di fare questo?
2 (referring to place): **to walk about the town** camminare per la città; **her clothes were scattered about the room** i suoi vestiti erano sparsi or in giro per tutta la stanza

above [əˈbʌv] adv, prep sopra; **mentioned ~** suddetto; **~ all** soprattutto

abroad [əˈbrɔːd] adv all'estero

abrupt [əˈbrʌpt] adj (sudden)

improvviso); (gruff, blunt) brusco(-a)

abscess ['æbsɪs] n ascesso

absence ['æbsəns] n assenza

absent ['æbsənt] adj assente; **absent-minded** adj distratto(-a)

absolute ['æbsəlu:t] adj assoluto(-a); **absolutely** [-'lu:tlɪ] adv assolutamente

absorb [əb'zɔ:b] vt assorbire; **to be ~ed in a book** essere immerso in un libro; **absorbent cotton** [əb'zɔ:bənt-] (US) n cotone m idrofilo; **absorbing** adj avvincente, molto interessante

abstain [əb'steɪn] vi to ~ (from) astenersi (da)

abstract ['æbstrækt] adj astratto(-a)

absurd [əb'sə:d] adj assurdo(-a)

abundance [ə'bʌndəns] n abbondanza

abundant [ə'bʌndənt] adj abbondante

abuse [n ə'bju:s, vb ə'bju:z] n abuso; (insults) ingiurie fpl ▶ vt abusare di; **abusive** adj ingiurioso(-a)

abysmal [ə'bɪzməl] adj spaventoso(-a)

academic [ækə'dɛmɪk] adj accademico(-a); (pej: issue) puramente formale ▶ n universitario(-a); **academic year** n anno accademico

academy [ə'kædəmɪ] n (learned body) accademia; (school) scuola privata; **academy of music** n conservatorio

accelerate [æk'sɛləreɪt] vt, vi accelerare; **acceleration** n accelerazione f; **accelerator** n acceleratore m

accent ['æksɛnt] n accento

accept [ək'sɛpt] vt accettare; **acceptable** adj accettabile; **acceptance** n accettazione f

access ['æksɛs] n accesso; **accessible** [æk'sɛsəbl] adj accessibile

accessory [æk'sɛsərɪ] n accessorio;

(Law): **~ to** complice m/f di

accident ['æksɪdənt] n incidente m; (chance) caso; **I've had an ~** ho avuto un incidente; **by ~** per caso; **accidental** [-'dɛntl] adj accidentale; **accidentally** [-'dɛntəlɪ] adv per caso; **Accident and Emergency Department** n (BRIT) pronto soccorso; **accident insurance** n assicurazione f contro gli infortuni

acclaim [ə'kleɪm] n acclamazione f

accommodate [ə'kɒmədeɪt] vt alloggiare; (oblige, help) favorire

accommodation [əkɒmə'deɪʃən] (US **accommodations**) n alloggio

accompaniment [ə'kʌmpənɪmənt] n accompagnamento

accompany [ə'kʌmpənɪ] vt accompagnare

accomplice [ə'kʌmplɪs] n complice m/f

accomplish [ə'kʌmplɪʃ] vt compiere; (goal) raggiungere; **accomplishment** n compimento; realizzazione f

accord [ə'kɔ:d] n accordo ▶ vt accordare; **of his own ~** di propria iniziativa; **accordance** n in **accordance with** in conformità con; **according: according to** prep secondo; **accordingly** adv in conformità

account [ə'kaunt] n (Comm) conto; (report) descrizione f; **~s** npl (Comm) conti mpl; **of no ~** di nessuna importanza; **on ~** in acconto; **on no ~** per nessun motivo; **on ~ of** a causa di; **to take into ~, take ~ of** tener conto di ▶ **account for** vt fus spiegare; giustificare; **accountable** adj accountable **(to)** responsabile (verso); **accountant** [ə'kauntənt] n ragioniere(-a); **account number** n numero di conto

accumulate [ə'kju:mjuleɪt] vt

accumulare ▸ vi accumularsi

accuracy [ˈækjʊrəsɪ] n precisione f

accurate [ˈækjʊrɪt] adj preciso(-a);
accurately adv precisamente

accusation [ækjʊˈzeɪʃən] n accusa

accuse [əˈkjuːz] vt accusare; **accused**
n accusato(-a)

accustomed [əˈkʌstəmd] adj ~ **to**
abituato(-a) a

ace [eɪs] n asso

ache [eɪk] n male m, dolore m ▸ vi (be
sore) far male, dolere; **my head ~s** mi
fa male la testa

achieve [əˈtʃiːv] vt (aim) raggiungere;
(victory, success) ottenere;
achievement n compimento;
successo

acid [ˈæsɪd] adj acido(-a) ▸ n acido

acknowledge [əkˈnɔlɪdʒ] vt (letter:
also: ~ **receipt of**) confermare la
ricevuta di; (fact) riconoscere;
acknowledgement n conferma;
riconoscimento

acne [ˈæknɪ] n acne f

acorn [ˈeɪkɔːn] n ghianda

acoustic [əˈkuːstɪk] adj acustico(-a)

acquaintance [əˈkweɪntəns] n
conoscenza; (person) conoscente m/f

acquire [əˈkwaɪəˈ] vt acquistare;
acquisition [ækwɪˈzɪʃən] n acquisto

acquit [əˈkwɪt] vt assolvere; **to ~ o.s.
well** comportarsi bene

acre [ˈeɪkəˈ] n acro; = 4047 m²

acronym [ˈækrənɪm] n acronimo

across [əˈkrɔs] prep (on the other
side) dall'altra parte di; (crosswise)
attraverso ▸ adv dall'altra parte;
in larghezza; **to run/swim ~**
attraversare di corsa/a nuoto; **~ from**
di fronte a

acrylic [əˈkrɪlɪk] adj acrilico(-a)

act [ækt] n atto; (in music-hall etc)
numero; (Law) decreto ▸ vi agire;
(Theatre) recitare; (pretend) fingere ▸ vt
(part) recitare; **to ~ as** agire da ▸ **act**

up (inf) vi (person) comportarsi male;
(knee, back, injury) fare male; (machine)
non funzionare; **acting** adj che fa le
funzioni di ▸ n (of actor) recitazione f;
(activity): **to do some acting** fare del
teatro (or del cinema)

action [ˈækʃən] n azione f; (Mil)
combattimento; (Law) processo;
out of ~ fuori combattimento; fuori
servizio; **to take ~** agire; **action
replay** n (TV) replay m inv

activate [ˈæktɪveɪt] vt (mechanism)
attivare

active [ˈæktɪv] adj attivo(-a); **actively**
adv (participate) attivamente;
(discourage, dislike) vivamente

activist [ˈæktɪvɪst] n attivista m/f

activity [ækˈtɪvɪtɪ] n attività f inv;
activity holiday n vacanza organizzata
con attività ricreative per ragazzi

actor [ˈæktəˈ] n attore m

actress [ˈæktrɪs] n attrice f

actual [ˈæktjʊəl] adj reale,
effettivo(-a).
Be careful not to translate **actual**
by the Italian word *attuale*.

actually [ˈæktjʊəlɪ] adv veramente;
(even) addirittura
Be careful not to translate **actually**
by the Italian word *attualmente*.

acupuncture [ˈækjʊpʌŋktʃəˈ] n
agopuntura

acute [əˈkjuːt] adj acuto(-a); (mind,
person) perspicace

ad [æd] n abbr = **advertisement**

A.D. adv abbr (= Anno Domini) d.C.

adamant [ˈædəmənt] adj irremovibile

adapt [əˈdæpt] vt adattare ▸ vi to ~ (to)
adattarsi (a); **adapter, adaptor** n
(Elec) adattatore m

add [æd] vt aggiungere ▸ vi to ~ **to**
(increase) aumentare ▸ **add up** vt
(figures) addizionare ▸ vi (fig): **it
doesn't ~ up** non ha senso ▸ **add up
to** vt fus (Math) ammontare a; (fig:

mean) significare; **it doesn't ~ up to much** non è un granché

addict ['ædɪkt] *n* tossicomane *m/f*; (*fig*) fanatico(-a); **addicted** [ə'dɪktɪd] *adj* **to be addicted to** (*drink etc*) essere dedito(-a) a; (*fig*: *football etc*) essere tifoso(-a) di; (*Med*) tossicodipendenza; **addictive** [ə'dɪktɪv] *adj* che dà assuefazione

addition [ə'dɪʃən] *n* addizione *f*; (*thing added*) aggiunta; **in ~** inoltre; **in ~ to** oltre; **additional** *adj* supplementare

additive ['ædɪtɪv] *n* additivo

address [ə'dres] *n* indirizzo; (*talk*) discorso ▶ *vt* indirizzare; (*speak to*) fare un discorso a; (*issue*) affrontare; **my ~ is ...** il mio indirizzo è ...; **address book** *n* rubrica

adequate ['ædɪkwɪt] *adj* adeguato(-a), sufficiente

adhere [əd'hɪə'] *vi* **to ~ to** aderire a; (*fig: rule, decision*) seguire

adhesive [əd'hi:zɪv] *n* adesivo; **adhesive tape** *n* (BRIT: *for parcels etc*) nastro adesivo; (US *Med*) cerotto adesivo

adjacent [ə'dʒeɪsənt] *adj* adiacente; **~ to** accanto a

adjective ['ædʒɛktɪv] *n* aggettivo

adjoining [ə'dʒɔɪnɪŋ] *adj* accanto *inv*, adiacente

adjourn [ə'dʒə:n] *vt* rimandare ▶ *vi* essere aggiornato(-a)

adjust [ə'dʒʌst] *vt* aggiustare; (*change*) rettificare ▶ *vi* **to ~ (to)** adattarsi (a); **adjustable** *adj* regolabile; **adjustment** *n* (*Psych*) adattamento; (*of machine*) regolazione *f*; (*of prices, wages*) modifica

administer [əd'mɪnɪstə'] *vt* amministrare; (*justice, drug*) somministrare; **administration** [ədmɪnɪs'treɪʃən] *n* amministrazione *f*; **administrative** [əd'mɪnɪstrətɪv] *adj* amministrativo(-a)

administrator [əd'mɪnɪstreɪtə'] *n* amministratore(-trice)

admiral ['ædmərəl] *n* ammiraglio

admiration [ædmə'reɪʃən] *n* ammirazione *f*

admire [əd'maɪə'] *vt* ammirare; **admirer** *n* ammiratore(-trice)

admission [əd'mɪʃən] *n* ammissione *f*; (*to exhibition, nightclub etc*) ingresso; (*confession*) confessione *f*

admit [əd'mɪt] *vt* ammettere; far entrare; (*agree*) riconoscere ▶ **admit to** *vt fus* riconoscere; **admittance** *n* ingresso; **admittedly** *adv* bisogna pur riconoscere (che)

adolescent [ædəu'lɛsnt] *adj*, *n* adolescente *m/f*

adopt [ə'dɔpt] *vt* adottare; **adopted** *adj* adottivo(-a); **adoption** [ə'dɔpʃən] *n* adozione *f*

adore [ə'dɔ:'] *vt* adorare

adorn [ə'dɔ:n] *vt* ornare

Adriatic [eɪdrɪ'ætɪk] *n* **the ~ (Sea)** il mareAdriatico, l'Adriatico

adrift [ə'drɪft] *adv* alla deriva

adult ['ædʌlt] *adj* adulto(-a); (*work, education*) per adulti ▶ *n* adulto(-a); **adult education** *n* scuola per adulti

adultery [ə'dʌltərɪ] *n* adulterio

advance [əd'vɑ:ns] *n* avanzamento; (*money*) anticipo ▶ *adj* (*booking etc*) in anticipo ▶ *vt* (*money*) anticipare ▶ *vi* avanzare; **in ~** in anticipo; **do I need to book in ~?** occorre che prenoti in anticipo?; **advanced** *adj* avanzato(-a); (*Scol: studies*) superiore

advantage [əd'vɑ:ntɪdʒ] *n* (*also Tennis*) vantaggio; **to take ~ of** approfittarsi di

advent ['ædvənt] *n* avvento; (*Rel*): **A~** Avvento

adventure [əd'ventʃə'] *n* avventura; **adventurous** [əd'ventʃərəs] *adj* avventuroso(-a)

adverb ['ædvə:b] *n* avverbio

adversary ['ædvəsərɪ] n
avversario(-a)

adverse ['ædvɜːs] adj avverso(-a)

advert ['ædvɜːt] (BRIT) n abbr
= **advertisement**

advertise ['ædvətaɪz] vi, vt fare
pubblicità or réclame (a); fare
un'inserzione (per vendere); **to ~
for** (staff) mettere un annuncio sul
giornale per trovare; **advertisement**
[əd'vɜːtɪsmənt] n (Comm) réclame
f inv, pubblicità f inv; (in classified
ads) inserzione f; **advertiser** n
azienda che reclamizza un prodotto;
(in newspaper) inserzionista
m/f; **advertising** ['ædvətaɪzɪŋ] n
pubblicità

advice [əd'vaɪs] n consigli mpl;
piece of ~ consiglio; **to take legal ~**
consultare un avvocato

advisable [əd'vaɪzəbl] adj
consigliabile

advise [əd'vaɪz] vt consigliare; **to ~
sb of sth** informare qn di qc; **to ~ sb
against sth/doing sth** sconsigliare
qc a qn/a qn di fare qc; **adviser**
n consigliere(-a); (in business)
consulente m/f, consigliere(-a);
advisory [-ərɪ] adj consultivo(-a)

advocate [n 'ædvəkeɪt, vb 'ædvəkeɪt]
n (upholder) sostenitore(-trice); (Law)
avvocato (difensore) ▶ vt propugnare

Aegean [ɪ'dʒiːən] n **the ~ (Sea)** il mar
Egeo, l'Egeo

aerial ['ɛərɪəl] n antenna ▶ adj
aereo(-a)

aerobics [ɛə'rəubɪks] n aerobica

aeroplane ['ɛərəpleɪn] (BRIT) n
aeroplano

aerosol ['ɛərəsɒl] (BRIT) n aerosol m inv

affair [ə'fɛəʳ] n affare m; (also: **love
~**) relazione f amorosa; **~s** (business)
affari

affect [ə'fɛkt] vt toccare; (influence)
influire su, incidere su; (feign) fingere

affected adj affettato(-a); **affection**
[ə'fɛkʃən] n affezione f; **affectionate**
adj affettuoso(-a)

afflict [ə'flɪkt] vt affliggere

affluent ['æfluənt] adj ricco(-a); **the ~
society** la società del benessere

afford [ə'fɔːd] vt permettersi; (provide)
fornire; **affordable** adj (che ha un
prezzo) abbordabile

Afghanistan [æf'gænɪstaːn] n
Afganistan m

afraid [ə'freɪd] adj impaurito(-a); **to be
~ of** or **to/that** aver paura di/che; **I am
~ so/not** ho paura di sì/no

Africa ['æfrɪkə] n Africa; **African** adj, n
africano(-a); **African-American** adj, n
afroamericano(-a)

after ['aːftəʳ] prep, adv dopo ▶ conj
dopo che; **what/who are you ~?**
che/chi cerca?; **~ he left/having
done** dopo che se ne fu andato/dopo
aver fatto; **to name sb ~ sb** dare a
qn il nome di qn; **it's twenty ~ eight**
(US) sono le otto e venti; **to ask ~ sb**
chiedere di qn; **~ all** dopo tutto; **~
you!** dopo di lei!; **after-effects** npl
consequenze fpl; (of illness) postumi
mpl; **aftermath** n consequenze fpl;
in the aftermath of nel periodo
dopo; **afternoon** n pomeriggio;
after-shave (lotion) ['aːftəʃeɪv-] n
dopobarba m inv; **aftersun (lotion/
cream)** n doposole m inv; **afterwards**
(US **afterward**) adv dopo

again [ə'gɛn] adv di nuovo; **to begin/
see ~** ricominciare/rivedere; **not ...~**
non ... più; **~ and ~** ripetutamente

against [ə'gɛnst] prep contro

age [eɪdʒ] n età f inv ▶ vt, vi invecchiare;
it's been ~s since sono secoli che; **he
is 20 years of ~** ha 20 anni; **to come of
~** diventare maggiorenne; **~d 10** di 10
anni; **the ~d** ['eɪdʒɪd] gli anziani; **age
group** n generazione f; **age limit** n
limite m d'età

agency ['eɪdʒənsɪ] n agenzia

agenda [ə'dʒɛndə] n ordine m del giorno

agent ['eɪdʒənt] n agente m

aggravate ['ægrəveɪt] vt aggravare; (person) irritare

aggression [ə'grɛʃən] n aggressione f

aggressive [ə'grɛsɪv] adj aggressivo(-a)

agile ['ædʒaɪl] adj agile

agitated ['ædʒɪteɪtɪd] adj agitato(-a), turbato(-a)

AGM n abbr = **annual general meeting**

ago [ə'gəʊ] adv **2 days ~** 2 giorni fa; **not long ~** poco tempo fa; **how long ~?** quanto tempo fa?

agony ['ægənɪ] n dolore m atroce; **to be in ~** avere dolori atroci

agree [ə'griː] vt (price) pattuire ▶ vi **to ~ (with)** essere d'accordo (con); (Ling) concordare (con); **to ~ to sth/to do sth** accettare qc/di fare qc; **to ~ that** (admit) ammettere che; **to ~ on sth** accordarsi su qc; **garlic doesn't ~ with me** l'aglio non mi va; **agreeable** adj gradevole; (willing) disposto(-a); **agreed** adj (time, place) stabilito(-a); **agreement** n accordo; **in agreement** d'accordo

agricultural [ægrɪ'kʌltʃərəl] adj agricolo(-a)

agriculture ['ægrɪkʌltʃə'] n agricoltura

ahead [ə'hɛd] adv avanti; davanti; **~ of** davanti a; (fig: schedule etc) in anticipo su; **~ of time** in anticipo; **go right** or **straight ~** tiri diritto

aid [eɪd] n aiuto ▶ vt aiutare; **in ~ of** a favore di

aide [eɪd] n (person) aiutante m/f

AIDS [eɪdz] n abbr (= acquired immune deficiency syndrome) AIDS f

ailing ['eɪlɪŋ] adj sofferente; (fig: economy, industry etc) in difficoltà

ailment ['eɪlmənt] n indisposizione f

aim [eɪm] vt **to ~ sth at** (such as gun) mirare qc a, puntare qc a; (camera) rivolgere qc a; (missile) lanciare qc contro ▶ vi (also: **to ~ at**) prendere la mira ▶ n mira; **to ~ at** mirare; **to ~ to do** aver l'intenzione di fare

ain't [eɪnt] (inf) = **am not**; **aren't**; **isn't**

air [ɛə'] n aria ▶ vt (room) arieggiare; (clothes) far prendere aria a; (grievances, ideas) esprimere pubblicamente ▶ cpd (currents) d'aria; (attack) aereo(-a); **to throw sth into the ~** lanciare qc in aria; **by ~** (travel) in aereo; **on the ~** (Radio, TV) in onda; **airbag** n airbag m; **airbed** (BRIT) n materassino; **airborne** ['ɛəbɔːn] adj (plane) in volo; (troops) aerotrasportato(-a); **as soon as the plane was airborne** appena l'aereo ebbe decollato; **air-conditioned** adj con or ad aria condizionata; **air conditioning** n condizionamento d'aria; **aircraft** n inv apparecchio; **airfield** n campo d'aviazione; **Air Force** n aviazione f militare; **air hostess** (BRIT) n hostess f inv; **airing cupboard** ['ɛərɪŋ-] n armadio riscaldato per asciugare panni.; **airlift** n ponte m aereo; **airline** n linea aerea; **airliner** n aereo di linea; **airmail** n **by airmail** per via aerea; **airplane** (US) n aeroplano; **airport** n aeroporto; **air raid** n incursione f aerea; **airsick** adj **to be airsick** soffrire di mal d'aria; **airspace** n spazio aereo; **airstrip** n pista d'atterraggio; **air terminal** n air-terminal m inv; **airtight** adj ermetico(-a); **air-traffic controller** n controllore m del traffico aereo; **airy** adj arioso(-a); (manners) noncurante

aisle [aɪl] n (of church) navata laterale; navata centrale; (of plane) corridoio; **aisle seat** n (on plane) posto sul corridoio

allow | 291

ajar [əˈdʒɑːʳ] adj socchiuso(-a)

à la carte [ɑːlɑːˈkɑːt] adv alla carta

alarm [əˈlɑːm] n allarme m ▸ vt allarmare; **alarm call** n (in hotel etc) sveglia; **could I have an alarm call at 7 am, please?** vorrei essere svegliato alle 7, per favore; **alarm clock** n sveglia; **alarmed** adj (person) allarmato(-a); (house, car etc) dotato(-a) di allarme; **alarming** adj allarmante, preoccupante

Albania [ælˈbeɪnɪə] n Albania

albeit [ɔːlˈbiːɪt] conj sebbene + sub, benché + sub

album [ˈælbəm] n album m inv

alcohol [ˈælkəhɒl] n alcool m; **alcohol-free** adj analcolico(-a); **alcoholic** [-ˈhɒlɪk] adj alcolico(-a) ▸ n alcolizzato(-a)

alcove [ˈælkəʊv] n alcova

ale [eɪl] n birra

alert [əˈlɜːt] adj vigile ▸ n allarme m ▸ vt avvertire; mettere in guardia; **on the ~** all'erta

algebra [ˈældʒɪbrə] n algebra

Algeria [ælˈdʒɪərɪə] n Algeria

alias [ˈeɪlɪæs] adv alias ▸ n pseudonimo, falso nome m

alibi [ˈælɪbaɪ] n alibi m inv

alien [ˈeɪlɪən] n straniero(-a); (extraterrestrial) alieno(-a) (a) ▸ adj ~ (to) estraneo(-a) (a); **alienate** vt alienare

alight [əˈlaɪt] adj acceso(-a) ▸ vi scendere; (bird) posarsi

align [əˈlaɪn] vt allineare

alike [əˈlaɪk] adj simile ▸ adv sia ... sia; **to look ~** assomigliarsi

alive [əˈlaɪv] adj vivo(-a); (lively) vivace

all [ɔːl] adj tutto(-a); **all day** tutto il giorno; **all night** tutta la notte; **all men** tutti gli uomini; **all five came** sono venuti tutti e cinque; **all the books** tutti i libri; **all the food** tutto il cibo; **all the time** sempre; tutto il tempo; **all his**

life tutta la vita
▸ pron

1 tutto(-a); **I ate it all, I ate all of it** l'ho mangiato tutto; **all of us went** noi siamo andati; **all of the boys went** tutti i ragazzi sono andati

2 (in phrases): **above all** soprattutto; **after all** dopotutto; **at all: not at all** (in answer to question) niente affatto; (in answer to thanks) prego!, di niente!, s'immagini!; **I'm not at all tired** non sono affatto stanco(-a); **anything at all will do** andrà bene qualsiasi cosa; **all in all** tutto sommato
▸ adv tutto alone tutto(-a) solo(-a); **it's not as hard as all that** non è poi così difficile; **all the more/the better** tanto più/meglio; **all but** quasi; **the score is two all** il punteggio è di due a due

Allah [ˈælə] n Allah m

allegation [ælɪˈgeɪʃən] n asserzione f

alleged [əˈledʒd] adj presunto(-a); **allegedly** [əˈledʒɪdlɪ] adv secondo quanto si asserisce

allegiance [əˈliːdʒəns] n fedeltà

allergic [əˈlɜːdʒɪk] adj ~ **to** allergico(-a) a; **I'm ~ to penicillin** sono allergico alla penicillina

allergy [ˈælədʒɪ] n allergia

alleviate [əˈliːvɪeɪt] vt sollevare

alley [ˈælɪ] n vicolo

alliance [əˈlaɪəns] n alleanza

allied [ˈælaɪd] adj alleato(-a)

alligator [ˈælɪgeɪtəʳ] n alligatore m

all-in [ˈɔːlɪn] adj (BRIT: also adv: charge) tutto compreso

allocate [ˈæləkeɪt] vt assegnare

allot [əˈlɒt] vt assegnare

all-out [ˈɔːlaʊt] adj (effort etc) totale ▸ adv **to go all out for** mettercela tutta per

allow [əˈlaʊ] vt (practice, behaviour) permettere; (sum to spend etc) accordare; (sum, time estimated) dare; (concede): **to ~ that** ammettere che; **to**

~ **sb to do** permettere a qn di fare; **he is ~ed to** lo può fare ▶ **allow for** vt fa tener conto di **allowance** n (money received) assegno; indennità f inv; (Tax) detrazione f di imposta; **to make allowances for** tener conto di

all right adv (feel, work) bene; (as answer) va bene

ally ['ælaɪ] n alleato

almighty [ɔːl'maɪtɪ] adj onnipotente; (row etc) colossale

almond ['ɑːmənd] n mandorla

almost ['ɔːlməust] adv quasi

alone [ə'ləun] adj, adv solo(-a); **to leave sb ~** lasciare qn in pace; **to leave sth ~** lasciare stare qc; **let ~ ...** figuriamoci poi ..., tanto meno ...

along [ə'lɒŋ] prep lungo ▶ adv **is he coming ~?** viene con noi? **he was limping ~** veniva zoppicando; **~ with** insieme con; **all ~** (all the time) sempre, fin dall'inizio; **alongside** prep accanto a; lungo ▶ adv accanto

aloof [ə'luːf] adj distaccato(-a) ▶ adv **to stand ~** tenersi a distanza or in disparte

aloud [ə'laud] adv ad alta voce

alphabet ['ælfəbet] n alfabeto

Alps [ælps] npl **the ~** le Alpi

already [ɔːl'redɪ] adv già

alright [ɔːl'raɪt] (BRIT) adv = **all right**

also ['ɔːlsəu] adv anche

altar ['ɔːltə'] n altare m

alter ['ɔːltə'] vt, vi alterare; **alteration** [ɔːltə'reɪʃən] n modificazione f, alterazione f; **alterations** (Sewing, Archit) modifiche fpl; **timetable subject to alteration** orario soggetto a variazioni

alternate [adj ɔːl'tɜːnɪt, vb 'ɔːltəːneɪt] adj alterno(-a); (US: plan etc) alternativo(-a) ▶ vi **to ~ (with)** alternarsi (a); **on ~ days** ogni due giorni

alternative [ɔːl'tɜːnətɪv] adj

alternativo(-a) ▶ n (choice) alternativa; **alternatively** adv **alternatively one could ...** come alternativa si potrebbe ...

although [ɔːl'ðəu] conj benché + sub, sebbene + sub

altitude ['æltɪtjuːd] n altitudine f

altogether [ɔːltə'geðə'] adv del tutto, completamente; (on the whole) tutto considerato; (in all) in tutto

aluminium [æljuː'mɪnɪəm] (BRIT), **aluminum** [ə'luːmɪnəm] (US) n alluminio

always ['ɔːlweɪz] adv sempre

Alzheimer's (disease) ['æltshaɪməz-] n (malattia di) Alzheimer

am [æm] vb see **be**

amalgamate [ə'mælgəmeɪt] vt amalgamare ▶ vi amalgamarsi

amass [ə'mæs] vt ammassare

amateur ['æmətə'] n dilettante m/f ▶ adj (Sport) dilettante

amaze [ə'meɪz] vt stupire; **amazed** adj sbalordito(-a); **to be amazed (at)** essere sbalordito (da); **amazement** n stupore m; **amazing** adj sorprendente, sbalorditivo(-a)

Amazon ['æməzən] n (Mythology) Amazzone f; (river): **the ~** il Rio delle Amazzoni ▶ cpd (basin, jungle) amazzonico(-a)

ambassador [æm'bæsədə'] n ambasciatore(-trice)

amber ['æmbə'] n ambra; **at ~** (BRIT Aut) giallo

ambiguous [æm'bɪgjuəs] adj ambiguo(-a)

ambition [æm'bɪʃən] n ambizione f; **ambitious** [æm'bɪʃəs] adj ambizioso(-a)

ambulance ['æmbjuləns] n ambulanza; **call an ~!** chiamate un'ambulanza!

ambush ['æmbuʃ] n imboscata

amen ['ɑː'mɛn] *excl* così sia, amen

amend [ə'mɛnd] *vt (law)* emendare; *(text)* correggere; **to make ~s** fare ammenda; **amendment** *n* emendamento; correzione *f*

amenities [ə'miːnɪtɪz] *npl* attrezzature *fpl* ricreative e culturali

America [ə'mɛrɪkə] *n* America; **American** *adj*, *n* americano(-a); **American football** *n* (BRIT) football *m* americano

amicable ['æmɪkəbl] *adj* amichevole

amid(st) [ə'mɪd(st)] *prep* in mezzo a

ammunition [æmju'nɪʃən] *n* munizioni *fpl*

amnesty ['æmnɪstɪ] *n* amnistia; **to grant an ~ to** concedere l'amnistia a, amnistiare

among(st) [ə'mʌŋ(st)] *prep* fra, tra, in mezzo a

amount [ə'maunt] *n* somma; ammontare *m*; quantità *f inv* ▶ *vi* **to ~ to** *(total)* ammontare a; *(be same as)* essere come

amp(ère) ['æmp(ɛə')] *n* ampère *m inv*

ample ['æmpl] *adj* ampio(-a); spazioso(-a); *(enough)*: **this is ~** questo è più che sufficiente

amplifier ['æmplɪfaɪə'] *n* amplificatore *m*

amputate ['æmpjuteɪt] *vt* amputare

Amtrak ['æmtræk] (US) *n* società ferroviaria americana

amuse [ə'mjuːz] *vt* divertire; **amusement** *n* divertimento; **amusement arcade** *n* sala giochi; **amusement park** *n* luna park *m inv*

amusing [ə'mjuːzɪŋ] *adj* divertente

an [æn] *indef art* see **a**

anaemia [ə'niːmɪə] (US **anemia**) *n* anemia

anaemic [ə'niːmɪk] (US **anemic**) *adj* anemico(-a)

anaesthetic [ænɪs'θɛtɪk] (US **anesthetic**) *adj* anestetico(-a) ▶ *n*

anestetico

analog(ue) ['ænəlɔg] *adj (watch, computer)* analogico(-a)

analogy [ə'nælədʒɪ] *n* analogia; **to draw an ~ between** fare un'analogia tra

analyse ['ænəlaɪz] (US **analyze**) *vt* analizzare; **analysis** [ə'næləsɪs] (*pl* **analyses**) *n* analisi *f inv*; **analyst** ['ænəlɪst] *n (Pol etc)* analista *m/f*; (US) *(psic)*analista *m/f*

analyze ['ænəlaɪz] (US) *vt* = **analyse**

anarchy ['ænəkɪ] *n* anarchia

anatomy [ə'nætəmɪ] *n* anatomia

ancestor ['ænsɪstə'] *n* antenato(-a)

anchor ['æŋkə'] *n* ancora ▶ *vi (also:* **to drop ~)** gettare l'ancora ▶ *vt* ancorare; **to weigh ~** salpare *or* levare l'ancora

anchovy ['æntʃəvɪ] *n* acciuga

ancient ['eɪnʃənt] *adj* antico(-a); *(person, car)* vecchissimo(-a)

and [ænd] *conj* e; *(often before vowel)*: **~ so on** e così via; **try ~ come** cerca di venire; **he talked ~ talked** non la finiva di parlare; **better ~ better** sempre meglio

Andes ['ændiːz] *npl* **the ~** le Ande

anemia *etc* [ə'niːmɪə] (US) = **anaemia** *etc*

anesthetic [ænɪs'θɛtɪk] (US) *adj*, *n* = **anaesthetic**

angel ['eɪndʒəl] *n* angelo

anger ['æŋgə'] *n* rabbia

angina [æn'dʒaɪnə] *n* angina pectoris

angle ['æŋgl] *n* angolo; **from their ~** dal loro punto di vista

angler ['æŋglə'] *n* pescatore *m* con la lenza

Anglican ['æŋglɪkən] *adj*, *n* anglicano(-a)

angling ['æŋglɪŋ] *n* pesca con la lenza

angrily ['æŋgrɪlɪ] *adv* con rabbia

angry ['æŋgrɪ] *adj* arrabbiato(-a), furioso(-a); *(wound)* infiammato(-a); **to be ~ with sb/at sth** essere in collera con qn/per qc; **to get ~** arrabbiarsi; **to make sb ~** fare arrabbiare qn

anguish ['æŋgwɪʃ] n angoscia

animal ['ænɪməl] adj animale ▶ n animale m

animated ['ænɪmeɪtɪd] adj animato(-a)

animation [ænɪ'meɪʃən] n animazione f

aniseed ['ænɪsiːd] n semi mpl di anice

ankle ['æŋkl] n caviglia

annex [n 'æneks, vb ə'neks] n (BRIT: also: **~e**) (edificio) annesso ▶ vt annettere

anniversary [ænɪ'vɜːsərɪ] n anniversario

announce [ə'naʊns] vt annunciare; **announcement** n annuncio; (letter, card) partecipazione f; **announcer** n (Radio, TV: between programmes) annunciatore(-trice); (: in a programme) presentatore(-trice)

annoy [ə'nɔɪ] vt dare fastidio a; **don't get ~ed!** non irritarti!; **annoying** adj noioso(-a)

annual ['ænjʊəl] adj annuale ▶ n (Bot) pianta annua; (book) annuario; **annually** adv annualmente

annum ['ænəm] n see **per**

anonymous [ə'nɒnɪməs] adj anonimo(-a)

anorak ['ænəræk] n giacca a vento

anorexia [ænə'reksɪə] n (Med: also: ~ **nervosa**) anoressia

anorexic [ænə'reksɪk] adj, n anoressico(-a)

another [ə'nʌðə'] adj ~ **book** (one more) un altro libro, ancora un libro; (a different one) un altro libro ▶ pron un altro(un'altra), ancora uno(-a); see also **one**

answer ['ɑːnsə'] n risposta; soluzione f ▶ vi rispondere ▶ vt (reply to) rispondere a; (problem) risolvere;

(prayer) esaudire; **in ~ to your letter** in risposta alla sua lettera; **to ~ the phone** rispondere (al telefono); **to ~ the bell** rispondere al campanello; **to ~ the door** aprire la porta ▶ **answer back** vi ribattere; **answerphone** n (esp BRIT) segreteria telefonica

ant [ænt] n formica

Antarctic [ænt'ɑːktɪk] n **the ~** l'Antartide f

antelope ['æntɪləʊp] n antilope f

antenatal [æntɪ'neɪtl] adj prenatale

antenna [æn'tɛnə, -niː] (pl **antennae**) n antenna

anthem ['ænθəm] n **national ~** inno nazionale

anthology [æn'θɒlədʒɪ] n antologia

anthrax ['ænθræks] n antrace m

anthropology [ænθrə'pɒlədʒɪ] n antropologia

anti [ænti] prefix anti; **antibiotic** ['æntɪbaɪ'ɒtɪk] n antibiotico; **antibody** ['æntɪbɒdɪ] n anticorpo

anticipate [æn'tɪsɪpeɪt] vt prevedere; pregustare; (wishes, request) prevenire; **anticipation** [æntɪsɪ'peɪʃən] n anticipazione f; (expectation) aspettativa fpl

anticlimax ['æntɪ'klaɪmæks] n **it was an ~** fu una completa delusione

anticlockwise ['æntɪ'klɒkwaɪz] adj, adv in senso antiorario

antics ['æntɪks] npl buffonerie fpl

anti: antidote ['æntɪdəʊt] n antidoto; **antifreeze** ['æntɪfriːz] n anticongelante m; **antiglobalization** [æntɪgləʊbəlaɪ'zeɪʃən] n antiglobalizzazione f; **antihistamine** [æntɪ'hɪstəmɪn] n antistaminico; **antiperspirant** ['æntɪ'pəːspərənt] adj antitraspirante

antique [æn'tiːk] n antichità f inv ▶ adj antico(-a); **antique shop** n negozio d'antichità

antiseptic [æntɪ'sɛptɪk] n antisettico

antisocial [ˈæntɪˈsəʊʃəl] *adj* asociale

antlers [ˈæntləz] *npl* palchi *mpl*

anxiety [æŋˈzaɪətɪ] *n* ansia; *(keenness):*
~ **to do** smania di fare

anxious [ˈæŋkʃəs] *adj* ansioso(-a),
inquieto(-a); *(worrying)* angoscioso(-a);
(keen): ~ **to do/that** impaziente di
fare/che + *sub*

○ any
['ɛnɪ] *adj*

1 *(in questions etc):* **have you any
butter?** hai del burro?, hai un po' di
burro?; **have you any children?** hai
bambini?; **if there are any tickets left**
se ci sono ancora (dei) biglietti, se c'è
ancora qualche biglietto

2 *(with negative):* **I haven't any money/
books** non ho soldi/libri

3 *(no matter which)* qualsiasi,
qualunque; **choose any book you like**
scegli un libro qualsiasi

4 *(in phrases):* **in any case** in ogni caso;
any day now da un giorno all'altro; **at
any moment** in qualsiasi momento,
da un momento all'altro; **at any rate**
ad ogni modo

▶ *pron*

1 *(in questions, with negative):* **have you
got any?** ne hai?; **can any of you sing?**
qualcuno di voi sa cantare?; **I haven't
any (of them)** non ne ho

2 *(no matter which one(s)):* **take any
of those books (you like)** prendi uno
qualsiasi di quei libri

▶ *adv*

1 *(in questions etc):* **do you want any
more soup/sandwiches?** vuoi ancora
un po' di minestra/degli altri panini?;
are you feeling any better? ti senti
meglio?

2 *(with negative):* **I can't hear him any
more** non lo sento più; **don't wait any
longer** non aspettare più

any: anybody [ˈɛnɪbɒdɪ] *pron* *(in
questions etc)* qualcuno, nessuno; *(with*

negative) nessuno; *(no matter who)*
chiunque; **can you see anybody?**
vedi qualcuno *or* nessuno?; **if
anybody should phone ...** se telefona
qualcuno ...; **I can't see anybody** non
vedo nessuno; **anybody could do it**
chiunque potrebbe farlo; **anyhow**
[ˈɛnɪhaʊ] *adv* *(at any rate)* ad ogni
modo, comunque; *(haphazard):* **do it
anyhow you like** fallo come ti pare;
I shall go anyhow ci andrò lo stesso
or comunque; **she leaves things just
anyhow** lascia tutto come capita;
anyone [ˈɛnɪwʌn] *pron* = **anybody**;
anything [ˈɛnɪθɪŋ] *pron* *(in question
etc)* qualcosa, niente; *(with negative)*
niente; *(no matter what):* **you can say
anything you like** puoi dire quello
che ti pare; **can you see anything?**
vedi niente *or* qualcosa?; **if anything
happens to me ...** se mi dovesse
succedere qualcosa ...; **I can't see
anything** non vedo niente; **anything
will do** va bene qualsiasi cosa *or*
tutto; **anytime** *adv* in qualunque
momento; quando vuole; **anyway**
[ˈɛnɪweɪ] *adv* *(at any rate)* ad ogni
modo, comunque; *(besides)* ad ogni
modo; **anywhere** [ˈɛnɪwɛə] *adv* *(in
questions etc)* da qualche parte; *(with
negative)* da nessuna parte; *(no matter
where)* da qualsiasi *or* qualunque
parte, dovunque; **can you see him
anywhere?** lo vedi da qualche parte?;
I can't see him anywhere non lo vedo
da nessuna parte; **anywhere in the
world** dovunque nel mondo

apart [əˈpɑːt] *adv* *(to one side)* a parte;
(separately) separatamente; **with
one's legs ~** con le gambe divaricate;
10 miles ~ a 10 miglia di distanza
(l'uno dall'altro); **to take ~** smontare;
~ from a parte, eccetto

apartment [əˈpɑːtmənt] *(US)* *n*
appartamento; *(room)* locale *m*;

apartment building (US) n stabile m, caseggiato

apathy ['æpəθɪ] n apatia

ape [eɪp] n scimmia ▶ vt scimmiottare

aperitif [ə'perɪtɪːf] n aperitivo

aperture ['æpətʃuə'] n apertura

APEX n abbr (= advance purchase excursion) APEX m inv

apologize [ə'pɔlədʒaɪz] vi to ~ (for sth to sb) scusarsi (di qc a qn), chiedere scusa (a qn per qc)

apology [ə'pɔlədʒɪ] n scuse fpl

apostrophe [ə'pɔstrəfɪ] n (sign) apostrofo

appal [ə'pɔːl] (US **appall**) vt scioccare; **appalling** adj spaventoso(-a)

apparatus [æpə'reɪtəs] n apparato; (in gymnasium) attrezzatura

apparent [ə'pærənt] adj evidente; **apparently** adv evidentemente

appeal [ə'piːl] vi (Law) appellarsi alla legge ▶ n (Law) appello; (request) richiesta; (charm) attrattiva; **to ~ to** (person) appellarsi a; (thing) piacere a; **it doesn't ~ to me** mi dice poco; **appealing** adj (nice) attraente

appear [ə'pɪə'] vi apparire; (Law) comparire; (publication) essere pubblicato(-a); (seem) sembrare; **it would ~ that** sembra che; **appearance** n apparizione f; apparenza; (look, aspect) aspetto

appendicitis [əpendɪ'saɪtɪs] n appendicite f

appendix [ə'pendɪks] (pl **appendices**) n appendice f

appetite ['æpɪtaɪt] n appetito

appetizer ['æpɪtaɪzə'] n stuzzichino

applaud [ə'plɔːd] vt, vi applaudire

applause [ə'plɔːz] n applauso

apple ['æpl] n mela; **apple pie** n torta di mele

appliance [ə'plaɪəns] n apparecchio

applicable [ə'plɪkəbl] adj applicabile;

to be ~ to essere valido per; **the law is ~ from January** la legge entrerà in vigore in gennaio

applicant ['æplɪkənt] n candidato(-a)

application [æplɪ'keɪʃən] n applicazione f; (for a job, a grant etc) domanda; **application form** n modulo per la domanda

apply [ə'plaɪ] vt to ~ (to) (paint, ointment) dare (a); (theory, technique) applicare (a) ▶ vi **to ~ to** (ask) rivolgersi a; (be suitable for, relevant to) riguardare, riferirsi a; **to ~ (for)** (permit, grant, job) fare domanda (per); **to ~ o.s. to** dedicarsi a

appoint [ə'pɔɪnt] vt nominare; **appointment** n nomina; (arrangement to meet) appuntamento; **I have an appointment (with)** ... ho un appuntamento (con) ...; **I'd like to make an appointment (with)** vorrei prendere un appuntamento (con)

appraisal [ə'preɪzl] n valutazione f

appreciate [ə'priːʃieɪt] vt (like) apprezzare; (be grateful for) essere riconoscente di; (be aware of) rendersi conto di ▶ vi (Finance) aumentare; **I'd ~ your help** ti sono grato per l'aiuto; **appreciation** [əpriːʃi'eɪʃən] n apprezzamento; (Finance) aumento del valore

apprehension [æprɪ'henʃən] n (fear) inquietudine f

apprehensive [æprɪ'hensɪv] adj apprensivo(-a)

apprentice [ə'prentɪs] n apprendista m/f

approach [ə'prəutʃ] vi avvicinarsi ▶ vt (come near) avvicinarsi a; (ask, apply to) rivolgersi a; (subject, passer-by) avvicinare ▶ n approccio; accesso; (to problem) modo di affrontare

appropriate [adj ə'prəuprɪɪt, vb ə'prəuprɪeɪt] adj appropriato(-a), adatto(-a) ▶ vt (take) appropriarsi

approval [ə'pru:vəl] n approvazione f; **on ~** (Comm) in prova, in esame

approve [ə'pru:v] vt, vi approvare
▷ **approve of** vt fus approvare

approximate [ə'prɒksɪmɪt] adj approssimativo(-a); **approximately** adv circa

Apr. abbr (= April) apr.

apricot ['eɪprɪkɒt] n albicocca

April ['eɪprəl] n aprile m; **~ fool!** pesce d'aprile!; **April Fools' Day** n vedi nota nel riquadro

● **April Fools' Day**
● April Fool's Day è il primo aprile, il
● giorno degli scherzi e delle burle. Il
● nome deriva dal fatto che, se una
● persona cade nella trappola che gli è
● stata tesa, fa la figura del "fool", cioè
● dello sciocco. Tradizionalmente,
● gli scherzi vengono fatti entro
● mezzogiorno.

apron ['eɪprən] n grembiule m

apt [æpt] adj (suitable) adatto(-a); (able) capace; (likely): **to be ~ to do** avere tendenza a fare

aquarium [ə'kweərɪəm] n acquario

Aquarius [ə'kweərɪəs] n Acquario

Arab ['ærəb] adj, n arabo(-a)

Arabia [ə'reɪbɪə] n Arabia; **Arabian** [ə'reɪbɪən] adj arabo(-a); **Arabic** ['ærəbɪk] adj arabico(-a), arabo(-a) ▶ n arabo; **Arabic numerals** n numeri mpl arabi, numerazione f araba

arbitrary ['ɑ:bɪtrərɪ] adj arbitrario(-a)

arbitration [ɑ:bɪ'treɪʃən] n (Law) arbitrato; (Industry) arbitraggio

arc [ɑ:k] n arco

arcade [ɑ:'keɪd] n portico; (passage with shops) galleria

arch [ɑ:tʃ] n arco; (of foot) arco plantare ▶ vt inarcare

archaeology [ɑ:kɪ'ɒlədʒɪ] (US **archeology**) n archeologia

archbishop [ɑ:tʃ'bɪʃəp] n arcivescovo

archeology etc [ɑ:kɪ'ɒlədʒɪ] (US)

= **archaeology** etc

architect ['ɑ:kɪtekt] n architetto; **architectural** [ɑ:kɪ'tektʃərəl] adj architettonico(-a); **architecture** ['ɑ: kɪtektʃə*] n architettura

archive ['ɑ:kaɪv] n (often pl: also Comput) archivio

Arctic ['ɑ:ktɪk] adj artico(-a) ▶ n **the ~ l'Artico**

are [ɑ:*] vb see **be**

area ['eərɪə] n (Geom) area; (zone) zona; (: smaller) settore m; **area code** (US) (Tel) prefisso

arena [ə'ri:nə] n arena

aren't [ɑ:nt] = **are not**

Argentina [ɑ:dʒən'ti:nə] n Argentina; **Argentinian** ['-tɪnɪən] adj, n argentino(-a)

arguably ['ɑ:gjuəblɪ] adv **it is ~ ...** si può sostenere che sia ...

argue [ɑ:gju:] vi (quarrel) litigare; (reason) ragionare; **to ~ that** sostenere che

argument ['ɑ:gjumənt] n (reasons) argomento; (quarrel) lite f

Aries ['eərɪz] n Ariete m

arise [ə'raɪz] (pt arose, pp arisen) vi (opportunity, problem) presentarsi

arithmetic [ə'rɪθmətɪk] n aritmetica

arm [ɑ:m] n braccio ▶ vt armare; **~s** npl (weapons) armi fpl; **~ in ~** a braccetto; **armchair** n poltrona

armed [ɑ:md] adj armato(-a); **armed robbery** n rapina a mano armata

armour ['ɑ:mə*] (US **armor**) n armatura; (Mil: tanks) mezzi mpl blindati

armpit ['ɑ:mpɪt] n ascella

armrest ['ɑ:mrest] n bracciolo

army ['ɑ:mɪ] n esercito

A road n strada statale

aroma [ə'rəumə] n aroma; **aromatherapy** n aromaterapia

arose [ə'rəuz] pt of **arise**

around [ə'raund] adv attorno, intorno

▶ *prep* intorno a; *(fig: about)*: ~£5/3 o'clock circa 5 sterline/le 3; **is he ~?** è in giro?

arouse [əˈraʊz] *vt (sleeper)* svegliare; *(curiosity, passions)* suscitare

arrange [əˈreɪndʒ] *vt* sistemare; *(programme)* preparare; **to ~ to do sth** mettersi d'accordo per fare qc; **arrangement** *n* sistemazione *f*; *(agreement)* accordo; **arrangements** *npl (plans)* progetti *mpl*, piani *mpl*

array [əˈreɪ] *n* ~ of fila di

arrears [əˈrɪəz] *npl* arretrati *mpl*; **to be in ~ with one's rent** essere in arretrato con l'affitto

arrest [əˈrest] *vt* arrestare; *(sb's attention)* attirare ▶ *n* arresto; **under ~** in arresto

arrival [əˈraɪvl] *n* arrivo; *(person)* arrivato(-a); **a new ~** un nuovo venuto; *(baby)* un neonato

arrive [əˈraɪv] *vi* arrivare; **what time does the train from Rome ~?** a che ora arriva il treno da Roma? ▷ **arrive at** *vt fus* arrivare a

arrogance [ˈærəgəns] *n* arroganza

arrogant [ˈærəgənt] *adj* arrogante

arrow [ˈærəʊ] *n* freccia

arse [ɑːs] *(infl)* *n* culo (!)

arson [ˈɑːsn] *n* incendio doloso

art [ɑːt] *n* arte *f*; *(craft)* mestiere *m*; **art college** *n* scuola di belle arti

artery [ˈɑːtəri] *n* arteria

art gallery *n* galleria d'arte

arthritis [ɑːˈθraɪtɪs] *n* artrite *f*

artichoke [ˈɑːtɪtʃəʊk] *n* carciofo; **Jerusalem ~** topinambur *m inv*

article [ˈɑːtɪkl] *n* articolo

articulate [*adj* ɑːˈtɪkjʊlɪt, *vb* ɑːˈtɪkjʊleɪt] *adj (person)* che si esprime forbitamente; *(speech)* articolato(-a) ▶ *vi* articolare

artificial [ɑːtɪˈfɪʃl] *adj* artificiale

artist [ˈɑːtɪst] *n* artista *m/f*; **artistic** [ɑːˈtɪstɪk] *adj* artistico(-a)

art school *n* scuola d'arte

as
[æz] *conj*

1 *(referring to time)* mentre; **as the years went by** col passare degli anni; **he came in as I was leaving** arrivò mentre stavo uscendo; **as from tomorrow** da domani

2 *(in comparisons)*: **as big as** grande come; **twice as big as** due volte più grande di; **as much/many as** tanto quanto/tanti quanti; **as soon as possible** prima possibile

3 *(since, because)* dal momento che, siccome

4 *(referring to manner, way)* come; **do as you wish** fa' come vuoi; **as she said** come ha detto lei

5 *(concerning)*: **as for o to that** per quanto riguarda o quanto a quello

6: **as if o as though** come se; **he looked as if he was ill** sembrava stare male; *see also* **long**; **such**; **well**

▶ *prep* he works as a driver fa l'autista; **as chairman of the company he ...** come presidente della compagnia lui ...; **he gave me it as a present** me lo ha regalato

a.s.a.p. *abbr* = **as soon as possible**

asbestos [æzˈbestəs] *n* asbesto, amianto

ascent [əˈsent] *n* salita

ash [æʃ] *n (dust)* cenere *f*; *(wood, tree)* frassino

ashamed [əˈʃeɪmd] *adj* vergognoso(-a); **to be ~ of** vergognarsi di

ashore [əˈʃɔː] *adv* a terra

ashtray [ˈæʃtreɪ] *n* portacenere *m*

Ash Wednesday *n* mercoledì *m inv* delle Ceneri

Asia [ˈeɪʒə] *n* Asia; **Asian** *adj*, *n* asiatico(-a)

aside [əˈsaɪd] *adv* da parte ▶ *n* a parte *m*

ask [ɑːsk] *vt (question)* domandare;

(invite) invitare; **to ~ sb sth/sth to do sth** chiedere qc a qn/a qn di fare qc; **to ~ sb about sth** chiedere a qn di qc; **to ~ (sb) a question** fare una domanda (a qn); **to ~ sb out to dinner** invitare qn a mangiare fuori ▷ **ask for** *vt fus* chiedere; *(trouble etc)* cercare

asleep [əˈsliːp] *adj* addormentato(-a); **to be ~** dormire; **to fall ~** addormentarsi

asparagus [əsˈpærəgəs] *n* asparagi *mpl*

aspect [ˈæspɛkt] *n* aspetto

aspirations [æspəˈreɪʃənz] *npl* aspirazioni *fpl*

aspire [əsˈpaɪəʳ] *vi* **to ~** aspirare a

aspirin [ˈæsprɪn] *n* aspirina

ass [æs] *n* asino; *(inf)* scemo(-a); *(US: inf!)* culo (!)

assassin [əˈsæsɪn] *n* assassino; **assassinate** [əˈsæsɪneɪt] *vt* assassinare

assault [əˈsɔːlt] *n (Mil)* assalto; *(gen: attack)* aggressione *f* ▷ *vt* assaltare; aggredire; *(sexually)* violentare

assemble [əˈsɛmbl] *vt* riunire; *(Tech)* montare ▷ *vi* riunirsi

assembly [əˈsɛmblɪ] *n (meeting)* assemblea; *(construction)* montaggio

assert [əˈsəːt] *vt* asserire; *(insist on)* far valere; **assertion** [əˈsəːʃən] *n* asserzione *f*

assess [əˈsɛs] *vt* valutare; **assessment** *n* valutazione *f*

asset [ˈæsɛt] *n* vantaggio; **~s** *npl (Finance: of individual)* beni *mpl*; *(: of company)* attivo

assign [əˈsaɪn] *vt* **to ~ (to)** *(task)* assegnare (a); *(resources)* riservare (a); *(cause, meaning)* attribuire (a); **to ~ a date to sth** fissare la data di qc; **assignment** *n* compito

assist [əˈsɪst] *vt* assistere, aiutare; **assistance** *n* assistenza, aiuto; **assistant** *n* assistente *m/f*; *(BRIT:*

also: **shop assistant)** commesso(-a)

associate *[adj, n* əˈsəʊʃɪɪt, *vb* əˈsəʊʃɪeɪt] *adj* associato(-a); *(member)* aggiunto(-a) ▷ *n* collega *m/f* ▷ *vt* associare ▷ *vi* **to ~ with sb** frequentare

association [əsəʊsɪˈeɪʃən] *n* associazione *f*

assorted [əˈsɔːtɪd] *adj* assortito(-a)

assortment [əˈsɔːtmənt] *n* assortimento

assume [əˈsjuːm] *vt* supporre; *(responsibilities etc)* assumere; *(attitude, name)* prendere

assumption [əˈsʌmpʃən] *n* supposizione *f*, ipotesi *f inv*; *(of power)* assunzione *f*

assurance [əˈʃʊərəns] *n* assicurazione *f*; *(self-confidence)* fiducia in se stesso

assure [əˈʃʊəʳ] *vt* assicurare

asterisk [ˈæstərɪsk] *n* asterisco

asthma [ˈæsmə] *n* asma

astonish [əˈstɔnɪʃ] *vt* stupire; **astonished** *adj* stupito(-a), sorpreso(-a); **to be astonished (at)** essere stupito(-a) (da); **astonishing** *adj* sorprendente, stupefacente; **I find it astonishing that ...** mi stupisce che ...; **astonishment** *n* stupore *m*

astound [əˈstaund] *vt* sbalordire

astray [əˈstreɪ] *adv* **to go ~** smarrirsi; **to lead ~** portare sulla cattiva strada

astrology [əsˈtrɔlədʒɪ] *n* astrologia

astronaut [ˈæstrənɔːt] *n* astronauta *m/f*

astronomer [əsˈtrɔnəməʳ] *n* astronomo(-a)

astronomical [æstrəˈnɔmɪkl] *adj* astronomico(-a)

astronomy [əsˈtrɔnəmɪ] *n* astronomia

astute [əsˈtjuːt] *adj* astuto(-a)

asylum [əˈsaɪləm] *n (politico)* asilo; *(per malati)* manicomio

○ **at**
[æt] prep

1 (referring to position, direction) a; **at the top** in cima; **at the desk** al banco, alla scrivania; **at home/school** a casa/scuola; **at the baker's** dal panettiere; **to look at sth** guardare qc; **to throw sth at sb** lanciare qc a qn

2 (referring to time) a; **at 4 o'clock** alle 4; **at night** di notte; **at Christmas** a Natale; **at times** a volte

3 (referring to rates, speed etc) a; **at £1 a kilo** a sterlina al chilo; **two at a time** due alla volta, due per volta; **at 50 km/h** a 50 km/h

4 (referring to manner) **at a stroke** d'un solo colpo; **at peace** in pace

5 (referring to activity): **to be at work** essere al lavoro; **to play at cowboys** giocare ai cowboy; **to be good at sth/doing sth** essere bravo in qc/fare qc

6 (referring to cause): **shocked/surprised/annoyed at sth** colpito da/sorpreso da/arrabbiato per qc; **I went at his suggestion** ci sono andato dietro suo consiglio

ate [eɪt] pt of **eat**

atheist ['eɪθɪɪst] n ateo(-a)

Athens ['æθɪnz] n Atene f

athlete ['æθliːt] n atleta m/f

athletic [æθ'lɛtɪk] adj atletico(-a); **athletics** n atletica

Atlantic [ət'læntɪk] adj atlantico(-a) ▸ n **the ~ (Ocean)** l'Atlantico, l'Oceano Atlantico

atlas ['ætləs] n atlante m

A.T.M. n abbr (= automated telling machine) cassa automatica prelievi, sportello automatico

atmosphere ['ætməsfɪər] n atmosfera

atom ['ætəm] n atomo; **atomic** [ə'tɒmɪk] adj atomico(-a); **atom(ic) bomb** n bomba atomica

A to Z® n (map) stradario

atrocity [ə'trɒsɪti] n atrocità f inv

attach [ə'tætʃ] vt attaccare; (document, letter) allegare; (importance etc) attribuire; **to be ~ed to sb/sth** (to like) essere affezionato(-a) a qn/qc;

attachment [ə'tætʃmənt] n (tool) accessorio; (love): **attachment (to)** affetto (per)

attack [ə'tæk] vt attaccare; (person) aggredire; (task etc) iniziare; (problem) affrontare ▸ n attacco; **heart ~** infarto; **attacker** n aggressore m

attain [ə'teɪn] vt (also: **~ to**) arrivare a, raggiungere

attempt [ə'tɛmpt] n tentativo ▸ vt tentare; **to make an ~ on sb's life** attentare alla vita di qn

attend [ə'tɛnd] vt frequentare; (meeting, talk) andare a; (patient) assistere ▸ **attend to** vt fus (needs, affairs etc) prendersi cura di; (customer) occuparsi di; **attendance** n (being present) presenza; (people present) gente f presente; **attendant** n custode m/f; persona di servizio ▸ adj concomitante

▌ Be careful not to translate **attend** by the Italian word **attendere**.

attention [ə'tɛnʃən] n attenzione f ▸ excl (Mil) attenti!; **for the ~ of** (Admin) per l'attenzione di

attic ['ætɪk] n soffitta

attitude ['ætɪtjuːd] n atteggiamento; posa

attorney [ə'tɜːnɪ] n (lawyer) avvocato; (having proxy) mandatario; **Attorney General** n (BRIT) Procuratore m Generale; (US) Ministro della Giustizia

attract [ə'trækt] vt attirare; **attraction** [ə'trækʃən] n (gen pl: pleasant things) attrattiva; (Physics, fig: towards sth) attrazione f; **attractive** adj attraente

attribute [n 'ætrɪbjuːt, vb ə'trɪbjuːt]

n attributo ▶ *vt* **to ~ sth to** attribuire qc a

aubergine ['əubəʒiːn] *n* melanzana

auburn ['ɔːbən] *adj* tizianesco(-a)

auction ['ɔːkʃən] *n* (*also:* **sale by ~**) asta ▶ *vt* (*also:* **to sell by ~**) vendere all'asta; (*also:* **to put up for ~**) mettere all'asta

audible ['ɔːdɪbl] *adj* udibile

audience ['ɔːdɪəns] *n* (*people*) pubblico; spettatori *mpl*; ascoltatori *mpl*; (*interview*) udienza

audit ['ɔːdɪt] *vt* rivedere, verificare

audition [ɔːˈdɪʃən] *n* audizione *f*

auditor ['ɔːdɪtə*] *n* revisore *m*

auditorium [ɔːdɪˈtɔːrɪəm] *n* sala, auditorio

Aug. *abbr* (= *August*) ago., ag.

August ['ɔːɡəst] *n* agosto

aunt [ɑːnt] *n* zia; **auntie**, **aunty** *n* zietta

au pair ['əuˈpɛə*] *n* (*also:* **~ girl**) (ragazza *f*) alla pari *inv*

aura ['ɔːrə] *n* aura

austerity [ɔsˈtɛrɪtɪ] *n* austerità *f inv*

Australia [ɔsˈtreɪlɪə] *n* Australia; **Australian** *adj, n* australiano(-a)

Austria ['ɔstrɪə] *n* Austria; **Austrian** *adj, n* austriaco(-a)

authentic [ɔːˈθɛntɪk] *adj* autentico(-a)

author ['ɔːθə*] *n* autore(-trice)

authority [ɔːˈθɔrɪtɪ] *n* autorità *f inv*; (*permission*) autorizzazione *f*; **the authorities** *npl* (*government etc*) le autorità

authorize ['ɔːθəraɪz] *vt* autorizzare

auto ['ɔːtəu] (*US*) *n* auto *f inv*; **autobiography** [ɔːtəbaɪˈɔɡrəfɪ] *n* autobiografia; **autograph** ['ɔːtəɡrɑːf] *n* autografo ▶ *vt* firmare; **automatic** [ɔːtəˈmætɪk] *adj* automatico(-a) ▶ *n* (*gun*) arma automatica; (*washing machine*) lavatrice *f* automatica; (*car*) automobile *f* con cambio automatico; **automatically** *adv*

automaticamente; **automobile** ['ɔːtəməbiːl] (*US*) *n* automobile *f*; **autonomous** [ɔːˈtɔnəməs] *adj* autonomo(-a); **autonomy** [ɔːˈtɔnəmɪ] *n* autonomia

autumn ['ɔːtəm] *n* autunno

auxiliary [ɔːɡˈzɪlɪərɪ] *adj* ausiliario(-a) ▶ *n* ausiliare *m/f*

avail [əˈveɪl] *vt* **to ~ o.s. of** servirsi di; approfittarsi di ▶ *n* **to no ~** inutilmente

availability [əveɪləˈbɪlɪtɪ] *n* disponibilità

available [əˈveɪləbl] *adj* disponibile

avalanche ['ævəlɑːnʃ] *n* valanga

Ave. *abbr* = **avenue**

avenue ['ævənjuː] *n* viale *m*; (*fig*) strada, via

average ['ævərɪdʒ] *n* media ▶ *adj* medio(-a) ▶ *vt* (*a certain figure*) fare di or in media; **on ~** in media

avert [əˈvəːt] *vt* evitare, prevenire; (*one's eyes*) distogliere

avid ['ævɪd] *adj* (*supporter etc*) accanito(-a)

avocado [ævəˈkɑːdəu] *n* (BRIT: *also:* **~ pear**) avocado *m inv*

avoid [əˈvɔɪd] *vt* evitare

await [əˈweɪt] *vt* aspettare

awake [əˈweɪk] (*pt* **awoke**, *pp* **awoken, awaked**) *adj* sveglio(-a) ▶ *vt* svegliare ▶ *vi* svegliarsi

award [əˈwɔːd] *n* premio; (*Law*) risarcimento ▶ *vt* assegnare; (*Law: damages*) accordare

aware [əˈwɛə*] *adj* **~ of** (*conscious*) conscio(-a) di; (*informed*) informato(-a) di; **to become ~ of** accorgersi di; **awareness** *n* consapevolezza

away [əˈweɪ] *adj, adv* via; lontano(-a); **two kilometres ~** a due chilometri di distanza; **two hours ~ by car** a due ore di distanza in macchina; **the holiday was two weeks ~** mancavano due settimane alle vacanze; **he's ~ for a week** è andato via per una settimana; **to take ~** togliere; **he was working/pedalling** etc **~** (la particella indica la continuità e l'energia dell'azione) lavorava/pedalava etc più che poteva; **to fade/wither** etc **~** (la particella rinforza l'idea della diminuzione)

awe [ɔ:] n timore m; **awesome** adj imponente

awful ['ɔ:fəl] adj terribile; **an ~ lot of** un mucchio di; **awfully** adv (very) terribilmente

awkward ['ɔ:kwəd] adj (clumsy) goffo(-a); (inconvenient) scomodo(-a); (embarrassing) imbarazzante

awoke [ə'wəuk] pt of **awake**

awoken [ə'wəukn] pp of **awake**

axe [æks] (US **ax**) n scure f ▶ vt (project etc) abolire; (jobs) sopprimere

axle ['æksl] n (also: **~-tree**) asse m

ay(e) [aɪ] excl (yes) sì

azalea [ə'zeɪlɪə] n azalea

b

B [bi:] n (Mus) si m; (letter) B, b f or m inv

B.A. n abbr = **Bachelor of Arts**

baby ['beɪbɪ] n bambino(-a); **baby carriage** (US) n carrozzina; **baby-sit** vi fare il (o la) baby-sitter; **baby-sitter** n baby-sitter m/f inv; **baby wipe** n salvietta umidificata

bachelor ['bætʃələ*] n scapolo; **B~ of Arts/Science** ≈ laureato(-a) in lettere/scienze

back [bæk] n (of person, horse) dorso, schiena; (as opposed to front) dietro; (of hand) dorso; (of train) coda; (of chair) schienale m; (of page) rovescio; (of book) retro m; (Football) difensore m ▶ vt (candidate) appoggiare; (horse: at races) puntare su; (car) guidare a marcia indietro ▶ vi indietreggiare; (car etc) fare marcia indietro ▶ cpd posteriore, di dietro; (seat, wheels) posteriore ▶ adv (not forward) indietro; (returned): **he's ~** è tornato; **he ran ~** tornò indietro di corsa; (restitution): **throw the ball ~** ritira la palla; **can I have it ~?** posso riaverlo?; (again): **he called ~** ha richiamato ▷ **back down** vi fare marcia indietro ▷ **back out** vi (of promise) tirarsi indietro ▷ **back up** vt (support) appoggiare, sostenere; (Comput) fare una copia di riserva di; **backache** n mal m di schiena; **backbencher** (BRIT) n membro del Parlamento senza potere amministrativo; **backbone** n spina dorsale; **back door** n porta sul retro; **backfire** vi (Aut) dar ritorni di fiamma; (plans) fallire; **backgammon** n tavola reale; **background** n sfondo; (of events) background m inv; (basic knowledge) base f; (experience) esperienza; **family background** ambiente m familiare; **backing** n (fig) appoggio; **backlog** n **backlog of work** lavoro arretrato; **backpack** n zaino; **backpacker** n chi viaggia con zaino e sacco a pelo; **backslash** n backslash m inv, barra obliqua inversa; **backstage** adv nel retroscena; **backstroke** n nuoto sul dorso; **backup** adj (train, plane) supplementare; (Comput) di riserva ▶ n (support) appoggio, sostegno; (also: **backup file**) file m inv di riserva; **backward** adj (movement) indietro inv; (person) tardivo(-a); (country) arretrato(-a); **backwards** adv indietro; (fall, walk) all'indietro; **backyard** n cortile m dietro la casa

bacon ['beɪkən] n pancetta

bacteria [bæk'tɪərɪə] npl batteri mpl

bad [bæd] adj cattivo(-a); (accident, injury) brutto(-a); (meat, food) andato(-a) a male; **his ~ leg** la sua gamba malata; **to go ~** andare a male

badge [bædʒ] n insegna; (of policeman) stemma m

badger ['bædʒə'] n tasso

badly ['bædlɪ] adv (work, dress etc) male; **~ wounded** gravemente ferito; **he needs it ~** ne ha un gran bisogno

bad-mannered [bæd'mænəd] adj maleducato(-a), sgarbato(-a)

badminton ['bædmɪntən] n badminton m

bad-tempered ['bæd'tɛmpəd] adj irritabile; di malumore

bag [bæg] n sacco; (handbag etc) borsa; **~s of** (inf: lots of) un sacco di; **baggage** n bagagli mpl; **baggage allowance** n franchigia f bagaglio inv; **baggage reclaim** n ritiro m bagaglio inv; **baggy** adj largo(-a), sformato(-a); **bagpipes** npl cornamusa

bail [beɪl] n cauzione f ▶ vt (prisoner: also: **grant ~ to**) concedere la libertà provvisoria su cauzione a; (boat: also: **~ out**) aggottare; **on ~** in libertà provvisoria su cauzione

bait [beɪt] n esca ▶ vt (hook) innescare; (trap) munire di esca; (fig) tormentare

bake [beɪk] vt cuocere al forno ▶ vi cuocersi al forno; **baked beans** [-bi:nz] npl fagioli mpl in salsa di pomodoro; **baked potato** n patata cotta al forno con la buccia; **baker** n fornaio(-a), panettiere(-a); **bakery** n panetteria; **baking** n cottura (al forno); **baking powder** n lievito in polvere

balance ['bæləns] n equilibrio; (Comm: sum) bilancio; (remainder) resto; (scales) bilancia ▶ vt tenere in equilibrio; (budget) far quadrare; (account) pareggiare; (compensate) contrappesare; **~ of trade/payments** bilancia commerciale/dei pagamenti; **balanced** adj (personality, diet) equilibrato(-a); **balance sheet** n bilancio

balcony ['bælkənɪ] n balcone m; (in theatre) balconata; **do you have a room with a ~?** avete una camera con balcone?

bald [bɔ:ld] n calvo(-a); (tyre) liscio(-a)

Balearics [bælɪ'ærɪks] npl **the ~** le Baleari fpl

ball [bɔ:l] n palla; (football) pallone m; (for golf) pallina; (of wool, string) gomitolo; (dance) ballo; **to play ~** (fig) stare al gioco

ballerina [bælə'ri:nə] n ballerina

ballet ['bæleɪ] n balletto; **ballet dancer** n ballerino(-a) classico(-a)

balloon [bə'lu:n] n pallone m

ballot ['bælət] n scrutinio

ballpoint (pen) ['bɔ:lpɔɪnt(-)] n penna a sfera

ballroom ['bɔ:lrum] n sala da ballo

Baltic ['bɔ:ltɪk] adj, **n the ~ Sea** il (mar) Baltico

bamboo [bæm'bu:] n bambù m

ban [bæn] n interdizione f ▶ vt interdire

banana [bə'nɑ:nə] n banana

band [bænd] n banda; (at a dance) orchestra; (Mil) fanfara

bandage ['bændɪdʒ] n benda, fascia

Band-Aid® ['bændeɪd] (US) n cerotto

B. & B. n abbr = **bed and breakfast**

bandit ['bændɪt] n bandito

bang [bæŋ] n (of door) lo sbattere; (of gun, blow) colpo ▶ vt battere (violentemente); (door) sbattere ▶ vi scoppiare; sbattere

Bangladesh [bɑːŋgləˈdɛʃ] n Bangladesh m

bangle [ˈbæŋgl] n braccialetto

bangs [bæŋz] (US) npl (fringe) frangia, frangetta

banish [ˈbænɪʃ] vt bandire

banister(s) [ˈbænɪstə(z)] n(pl) ringhiera

banjo [ˈbændʒəu] (pl banjoes or banjos) n banjo m inv

bank [bæŋk] n banca, banco; (of river, lake) riva, sponda; (of earth) banco ▶ vi (Aviat) inclinarsi in virata ▷ **bank on** vt fus contare su; **bank account** n conto in banca; **bank balance** n saldo; **a healthy bank balance** un solido conto in banca; **bank card** n carta f assegni inv; **bank charges** npl (BRIT) spese fpl bancarie; **banker** n banchiere m; **bank holiday** (BRIT) n giorno di festa; vedi nota nel riquadro; **banking** n attività bancaria; professione f di banchiere; **bank manager** n direttore m di banca; **banknote** n banconota

- **bank holiday**
- Una **bank holiday**, in Gran
- Bretagna, è una giornata in cui
- banche e molti negozi sono chiusi.
- Generalmente le **bank holidays**
- cadono di lunedì e molti ne
- approfittano per fare una breve
- vacanza fuori città.

bankrupt [ˈbæŋkrʌpt] adj fallito(-a); **to go ~** fallire; **bankruptcy** n fallimento

bank statement n estratto conto

banner [ˈbænəʳ] n striscione m

bannister(s) [ˈbænɪstə(z)] n(pl) see **banister(s)**

banquet [ˈbæŋkwɪt] n banchetto

baptism [ˈbæptɪzəm] n battesimo

baptize [bæpˈtaɪz] vt battezzare

bar [bɑːʳ] n (place) bar m inv; (counter) banco; (rod) barra; (of window etc) sbarra; (of chocolate) tavoletta; (fig) ostacolo; restrizione f; (Mus) battuta ▶ vt (road, window) sbarrare; (person) escludere; (activity) interdire; **~ of soap** saponetta; **the B~** (Law) l'Ordine m degli avvocati; **behind ~s** (prisoner) dietro le sbarre; **~ none** senza eccezione

barbaric [bɑːˈbærɪk] adj barbarico(-a)

barbecue [ˈbɑːbɪkjuː] n barbecue m inv

barbed wire [ˈbɑːbd-] n filo spinato

barber [ˈbɑːbəʳ] n barbiere m; **barber's (shop)** (US barber (shop)) n barbiere m

bar code n (on goods) codice m a barre

bare [bɛəʳ] adj nudo(-a) ▶ vt scoprire, denudare; (teeth) mostrare; **the ~ necessities** lo stretto necessario; **barefoot** adj, adv scalzo(-a); **barely** adv appena

bargain [ˈbɑːgɪn] n (transaction) contratto; (good buy) affare m ▶ vi trattare; **into the ~** per giunta ▷ **bargain for** vt fus he got more than he ~ed for gli è andata peggio di quel che si aspettasse

barge [bɑːdʒ] n chiatta ▷ **barge in** vi (walk in) piombare dentro; (interrupt talk) intromettersi a sproposito

bark [bɑːk] n (of tree) corteccia; (of dog) abbaio ▶ vi abbaiare

barley [ˈbɑːlɪ] n orzo

barmaid [ˈbɑːmeɪd] n cameriera al banco

barman [ˈbɑːmən] (irreg) n barista m

barn [bɑːn] n granaio

barometer [bəˈrɔmɪtəʳ] n barometro

baron [ˈbærən] n barone m; **baroness** n baronessa

barracks [ˈbærəks] npl caserma f

barrage [ˈbærɑːʒ] n (Mil, dam) sbarramento; (fig) fiume m

barrel [ˈbærəl] n barile m; (of gun)

canna

barren ['bærən] *adj* sterile; *(soil)* arido(-a)

barrette [bə'rɛt] *(US) n* fermaglio per capelli

barricade [bærɪ'keɪd] *n* barricata

barrier ['bærɪə'] *n* barriera

barring ['bɑːrɪŋ] *prep* salvo

barrister ['bærɪstə'] *(BRIT) n* avvocato(-essa) *(con diritto di parlare davanti a tutte le corti)*

barrow ['bærəʊ] *n (cart)* carriola

bartender ['bɑːtɛndə'] *(US) n* barista *m*

base [beɪs] *n* base *f* ▶ *vt* to ~ **sth on** basare qc su ▶ *adj* vile

baseball ['beɪsbɔːl] *n* baseball *m*; **baseball cap** *n* berretto da baseball

basement ['beɪsmənt] *n* seminterrato; *(also: shop)* interrato

bases[1] ['beɪsiːz] *npl of* **basis**

bases[2] ['beɪsiz] *npl of* **base**

bash [bæʃ] *(inf) vt* picchiare

basic ['beɪsɪk] *adj* rudimentale; essenziale; **basically** [-lɪ] *adv* fondamentalmente; sostanzialmente; **basics** *npl* **the basics** l'essenziale *m*

basil ['bæzl] *n* basilico

basin ['beɪsn] *n (vessel: also Geo)* bacino; *(also: wash~)* lavabo

basis ['beɪsɪs] *(pl* **bases**) *n* base *f*; **on a part-time ~** part-time; **on a trial ~** in prova

basket ['bɑːskɪt] *n* cesta; *(smaller)* cestino; *(with handle)* paniere *m*; **basketball** *n* pallacanestro *f*

bass [beɪs] *n (Mus)* basso

bastard ['bɑːstəd] *n* bastardo(-a); *(infl)* stronzo (!)

bat [bæt] *n* pipistrello; *(for baseball etc)* mazza; *(BRIT: for table tennis)* racchetta ▶ *vt* **he didn't ~ an eyelid** non battè ciglio

batch [bætʃ] *n (of bread)* infornata; *(of*

papers) cumulo

bath [bɑːθ] *n* bagno; *(bathtub)* vasca da bagno ▶ *vt* far fare il bagno a; **to have a ~** fare un bagno; *see also* **baths**

bathe [beɪð] *vi* fare il bagno ▶ *vt (wound)* lavare

bathing ['beɪðɪŋ] *n* bagni *mpl*; **bathing costume** *(US* **bathing suit)** *n* costume *m* da bagno

bath: bathrobe ['bɑːθrəʊb] *n* accappatoio; **bathroom** ['bɑːθrʊm] *n* stanza da bagno; **baths** [bɑːðz] *npl* bagni *mpl* pubblici; **bath towel** *n* asciugamano da bagno; **bathtub** *n (vasca da bagno*

baton ['bætən] *n (Mus)* bacchetta; *(Athletics)* testimone *m*; *(club)* manganello

batter ['bætə'] *vt* battere ▶ *n* pastetta; **battered** *adj (hat)* sformato(-a); *(pan)* ammaccato(-a)

battery ['bætərɪ] *n* batteria; *(of torch)* pila; **battery farming** *n* allevamento in batteria

battle ['bætl] *n* battaglia ▶ *vi* battagliare, lottare; **battlefield** *n* campo di battaglia

bay [beɪ] *n (of sea)* baia; **to hold sb at ~** tenere qn a bada

bazaar [bə'zɑː'] *n* bazar *m inv*; vendita di beneficenza

BBC *n abbr* (= British Broadcasting Corporation) rete nazionale di radiotelevisione in Gran Bretagna

● **BBC**
● La BBC è l'azienda statale che
● fornisce il servizio radiofonico
● e televisivo in Gran Bretagna.
● Ha due reti televisive terrestri
● (BBC1 e BBC2), e cinque stazioni
● radiofoniche nazionali. Oggi la BBC
● ha anche diverse stazioni digitali
● radiofoniche e televisive. Da molti
● anni fornisce inoltre un servizio di
● intrattenimento e informazione

- internazionale, il "BBC World
- Service", trasmesso in tutto il
- mondo.

B.C. *adv abbr* (= *before Christ*) a.C.

be
[bi:] (*pt* was, were, *pp* been)
aux vb

1 (*with present participle: forming continuous tenses*): **what are you doing?** che fa?, che sta facendo?; **they're coming tomorrow** vengono domani; **I've been waiting for her for hours** sono ore che l'aspetto

2 (*with pp: forming passives*) essere; **to be killed** essere *or* venire ucciso(-a); **the box had been opened** la scatola era stata aperta; **the thief was nowhere to be seen** il ladro non si trovava da nessuna parte

3 (*in tag questions*): **it was fun, wasn't it?** è stato divertente, no?; **he's good-looking, isn't he?** è un bell'uomo, vero?; **she's back, is she?** così è tornata, eh?

4 (+ *to* + *infinitive*): **the house is to be sold** abbiamo *or* hanno *etc* intenzione di vendere casa; **you're to be congratulated for all your work** dovremo farvi i complimenti per tutto il vostro lavoro; **he's not to open it** non deve aprirlo

▶ *vb* + *complement*

1 (*gen*) essere; **I'm English** sono inglese; **I'm tired** sono stanco(-a); **I'm hot/cold** ho caldo/freddo; **he's a doctor** è medico; **2 and 2 are 4** 2 più 2 fa 4; **be careful!** sta attento(-a)!; **be good** sii buono(-a)

2 (*of health*) stare; **how are you?** come sta?; **he's very ill** sta molto male

3 (*of age*): **how old are you?** quanti anni hai?; **I'm sixteen (years old)** ho sedici anni

4 (*cost*) costare; **how much was the meal?** quant'era *or* quanto costava

il pranzo?; **that'll be £5, please** (fa) 5 sterline, per favore

▶ *vi*

1 (*exist, occur etc*) essere, esistere; **the best singer that ever was** il migliore cantante mai esistito *or* di tutti tempi; **be that as it may** comunque sia, sia come sia; **so be it** sia pure, e sia

2 (*referring to place*) essere, trovarsi; **I won't be here tomorrow** non ci sarò domani; **Edinburgh is in Scotland** Edimburgo si trova in Scozia

3 (*referring to movement*): **where have you been?** dov'è stato?; **I've been to China** sono stato in Cina

▶ *impers vb*

1 (*referring to time, distance*) essere; **it's 5 o'clock** sono le 5; **it's the 28th of April** è il 28 aprile; **it's 10 km to the village** di qui al paese sono 10 km

2 (*referring to the weather*) fare; **it's too hot/cold** fa troppo caldo/freddo; **it's windy** c'è vento

3 (*emphatic*): **it's me** sono io; **it was Maria who paid the bill** è stata Maria che ha pagato il conto

beach [bi:tʃ] *n* spiaggia ▶ *vt* tirare in secco

beacon ['bi:kən] *n* (*lighthouse*) faro; (*marker*) segnale *m*

bead [bi:d] *n* perlina; **~s** *npl* (*necklace*) collana

beak [bi:k] *n* becco

beam [bi:m] *n* trave *f*; (*of light*) raggio ▶ *vi* brillare

bean [bi:n] *n* fagiolo; (*of coffee*) chicco; **runner ~** fagiolino; **beansprouts** *npl* germogli *mpl* di soia

bear [bɛəʳ] (*pt* bore, *pp* borne) *n* orso ▶ *vt* portare; (*endure*) sopportare; (*produce*) generare ▶ *vi* **to ~ right/left** piegare a destra/sinistra

beard [bɪəd] *n* barba

bearer ['bɛərəʳ] *n* portatore *m*

bearing ['bɛərɪŋ] *n* portamento;

(connection) rapporto

beast [biːst] n bestia

beat [biːt] (pt beat, pp **beaten**) n colpo; (of heart) battito; (Mus) tempo; battuta; (of policeman) giro ▶ vt battere; (eggs, cream) sbattere ▶ vi battere; **off the ~en track** fuori mano; **~ it!** (inf) fila!, fuori dai piedi! ▷ **beat up** vt (person) picchiare; (eggs) sbattere; **beating** n bastonata

beautiful ['bjuːtɪful] adj bello(-a); **beautifully** adv splendidamente

beauty ['bjuːtɪ] n bellezza; **beauty parlour** [-'pɑːləʳ] (US **beauty parlor**) n salone m di bellezza; **beauty salon** n istituto di bellezza; **beauty spot** (BRIT) n (Tourism) luogo pittoresco

beaver ['biːvəʳ] n castoro

became [bɪ'keɪm] pt of **become**

because [bɪ'kɔz] conj perché; **~ of** a causa di

beckon ['bɛkən] vt (also: **~ to**) chiamare con un cenno

become [bɪ'kʌm] (irreg: like **come**) vt diventare; **to ~ fat/thin** ingrassarsi/dimagrire

bed [bɛd] n letto; (of flowers) aiuola; (of coal, clay) strato; **single/double ~** letto a una piazza/a due piazze or matrimoniale; **bed and breakfast** n (place) ≈ pensione f familiare; (terms) camera con colazione; vedi nota nel riquadro; **bedclothes** ['bɛdkləuðz] npl biancheria e coperte fpl da letto; **bedding** n coperte e lenzuola fpl; **bed linen** n biancheria da letto; **bedroom** n camera da letto; **bedside** n at sb's **bedside** al capezzale di qn; **bedside lamp** n lampada da comodino; **bedside table** n comodino; **bedsit(ter)** (BRIT) n monolocale m; **bedspread** n copriletto; **bedtime** n it's **bedtime** è ora di andare a letto

● **bed and breakfast**

● I **bed and breakfasts**, anche B & Bs,

● sono piccole pensioni a conduzione
● familiare, più economiche rispetto
● agli alberghi, dove al mattino viene
● servita la tradizionale colazione
● all'inglese.

bee [biː] n ape f

beech [biːtʃ] n faggio

beef [biːf] n manzo; **roast ~** arrosto di manzo; **beefburger** n hamburger m inv; **Beefeater** n guardia della Torre di Londra

been [biːn] pp of **be**

beer [bɪəʳ] n birra; **beer garden** n (BRIT) giardino (di pub)

beet [biːt] (US) n (also: **red ~**) barbabietola rossa

beetle ['biːtl] n scarafaggio; coleottero

beetroot ['biːtruːt] (BRIT) n barbabietola

before [bɪ'fɔːʳ] prep (in time) prima di; (in space) davanti a ▶ conj prima che + sub; prima di ▶ adv prima; **~ going** prima di andare; **~ she goes** prima che vada; **the week ~** la settimana prima; **I've seen it ~** l'ho già visto; **I've never seen it ~** è la prima volta che lo vedo; **beforehand** adv in anticipo

beg [bɛg] vi chiedere l'elemosina ▶ vt (also: **~ for**) chiedere in elemosina; (favour) chiedere; **to ~ sb to do** pregare qn di fare

began [bɪ'gæn] pt of **begin**

beggar ['bɛgəʳ] n mendicante m/f

begin [bɪ'gɪn] (pt began, pp begun) vt, vi cominciare; **to ~ doing** or **to do sth** incominciare or iniziare a fare qc; **beginner** n principiante m/f; **beginning** n inizio, principio

begun [bɪ'gʌn] pp of **begin**

behalf [bɪ'hɑːf] n **on ~ of** per conto di; a nome di

behave [bɪ'heɪv] vi comportarsi; (well: also: **~ o.s.**) comportarsi bene; **behaviour** [bɪ'heɪvjəʳ] (US **behavior**) *n* comportamento, condotta

behind [bɪˈhaɪnd] *prep* dietro; (*followed by pronoun*) dietro di; (*time*) in ritardo con ▶ *adv* dietro; (*leave, stay*) indietro ▶ *n* didietro; **to be ~ (schedule)** essere in ritardo rispetto al programma; **~ the scenes** (*fig*) dietro le quinte

beige [beɪʒ] *adj* beige inv

Beijing [ˈbeɪˈdʒɪŋ] *n* Pechino *f*

being [ˈbiːɪŋ] *n* essere *m*

belated [bɪˈleɪtɪd] *adj* tardo(-a)

belch [bɛltʃ] *vi* ruttare ▶ *vt* (*gen: belch out: smoke etc*) eruttare

Belgian [ˈbɛldʒən] *adj*, *n* belga *m/f*

Belgium [ˈbɛldʒəm] *n* Belgio

belief [bɪˈliːf] *n* (*opinion*) opinione *f*, convinzione *f*; (*trust, faith*) fede *f*

believe [bɪˈliːv] *vt, vi* credere; **to ~ in** (*God*) credere in; (*ghosts*) credere a; (*method*) avere fiducia in; **believer** *n* (*Rel*) credente *m/f*; (*in idea, activity*): **to be a believer in** credere in

bell [bɛl] *n* campana; (*small, on door, electric*) campanello

bellboy [ˈbɛlbɔɪ], (*US* **bellhop**) [ˈbɛlhɔp] *n* ragazzo d'albergo, fattorino d'albergo

bellow [ˈbɛləu] *vi* muggire

bell pepper (*esp US*) *n* peperone *m*

belly [ˈbɛlɪ] *n* pancia; **belly button** *n* ombelico

belong [bɪˈlɔŋ] *vi* **to ~ to** appartenere a; (*club etc*) essere socio di; **this book ~s here** questo libro va qui; **belongings** *npl* cose *fpl*, roba

beloved [bɪˈlʌvɪd] *adj* adorato(-a)

below [bɪˈləu] *prep* sotto, al di sotto di ▶ *adv* sotto, di sotto; giù; **see ~** vedi sotto *or* oltre

belt [bɛlt] *n* cintura; (*Tech*) cinghia ▶ *vt* (*thrash*) picchiare ▶ *vi* (*inf*) filarsela; **beltway** (*US*) *n* (*Aut: ring road*) circonvallazione *f*; (*: motorway*) autostrada

bemused [bɪˈmjuːzd] *adj*

perplesso(-a), stupito(-a)

bench [bɛntʃ] *n* panca; (*in workshop, Pol*) banco; **the B~** (*Law*) la Corte

bend [bɛnd] (*pt, pp* **bent**) *vt* curvare; (*leg, arm*) piegare ▶ *vi* curvarsi; piegarsi ▶ *n* (*BRIT: in road*) curva; (*in pipe, river*) gomito ▶ **bend down** *vi* chinarsi ▶ **bend over** *vi* piegarsi

beneath [bɪˈniːθ] *prep* sotto, al di sotto di; (*unworthy of*) indegno(-a) di ▶ *adv* sotto, di sotto

beneficial [bɛnɪˈfɪʃl] *adj* che fa bene; vantaggioso(-a)

benefit [ˈbɛnɪfɪt] *n* beneficio, vantaggio; (*allowance of money*) indennità *f inv* ▶ *vt* far bene a ▶ *vi* **he'll ~ from it** ne trarrà beneficio *or* profitto

benign [bɪˈnaɪn] *adj* (*person, smile*) benevolo(-a); (*Med*) benigno(-a)

bent [bɛnt] *pt, pp of* **bend** ▶ *n* inclinazione *f* ▶ *adj* (*inf: dishonest*) losco(-a); **to be ~ on** essere deciso(-a) a

bereaved [bɪˈriːvd] *n* **the ~** i familiari in lutto

beret [ˈbɛreɪ] *n* berretto

Berlin [bəːˈlɪn] *n* Berlino *f*

Bermuda [bəːˈmjuːdə] *n* le Bermude

berry [ˈbɛrɪ] *n* bacca

berth [bəːθ] *n* (*bed*) cuccetta; (*for ship*) ormeggio ▶ *vi* (*in harbour*) entrare in porto; (*at anchor*) gettare l'ancora

beside [bɪˈsaɪd] *prep* accanto a; **to be ~ o.s. (with anger)** essere fuori di sé (dalla rabbia); **that's ~ the point** non c'entra; **besides** [bɪˈsaɪdz] *adv* inoltre, per di più ▶ *prep* oltre a; a parte

best [bɛst] *adj* migliore ▶ *adv* meglio; **the ~ part of** (*quantity*) la maggior parte di; **at ~** tutt'al più; **to make the ~ of sth** cavare il meglio possibile da qc; **to do one's ~** fare del proprio meglio; **to the ~ of my knowledge** per quel che ne so; **to the ~ of my ability**

al massimo delle mie capacità;
best-before date n scadenza; **best man** (irreg) n testimone m dello sposo; **bestseller** n bestseller m inv

bet [bɛt] (pt, pp **bet** or **betted**) n scommessa ▶ vt, vi scommettere; **to ~ sb sth** scommettere qc con qn

betray [bɪˈtreɪ] vt tradire

better [ˈbɛtəʳ] adj migliore ▶ adv meglio ▶ vt migliorare ▶ n **to get the ~ of** avere la meglio su; **you had ~ do it** è meglio che lo faccia; **he thought ~ of it** cambiò idea; **to get ~** migliorare

betting [ˈbɛtɪŋ] n scommesse fpl; **betting shop** (BRIT) n ufficio dell'allibratore

between [bɪˈtwiːn] prep tra ▶ adv in mezzo, nel mezzo

beverage [ˈbɛvərɪdʒ] n bevanda

beware [bɪˈwɛəʳ] vt, vi **to ~ (of)** stare attento(-a) (a); **"~ of the dog"** "attenti al cane"

bewildered [bɪˈwɪldəd] adj sconcertato(-a), confuso(-a)

beyond [bɪˈjɔnd] prep oltre; (exceeding) al di sopra di ▶ adv di là: **~ doubt** senza dubbio; **~ repair** irreparabile

bias [ˈbaɪəs] n (prejudice) pregiudizio; (preference) preferenza; **bias(s)ed** adj parziale

bib [bɪb] n bavaglino

Bible [ˈbaɪbl] n Bibbia

bicarbonate of soda [baɪˈkɑːbənɪt-] n bicarbonato (di sodio)

biceps [ˈbaɪsɛps] n bicipite m

bicycle [ˈbaɪsɪkl] n bicicletta; **bicycle pump** n pompa della bicicletta

bid [bɪd] (pt **bade** or **bid**, pp **bidden** or **bid**) n offerta; (attempt) tentativo ▶ vi fare un'offerta ▶ vt fare un'offerta di; **to ~ sb good day** dire buon giorno a qn; **bidder** n **the highest bidder** il maggiore offerente

bidet [ˈbiːdeɪ] n bidè m inv

big [bɪg] adj grande; grosso(-a); **Big Apple** n vedi nota nel riquadro; **bigheaded** [ˈbɪgˈhɛdɪd] adj presuntuoso(-a); **big toe** n alluce m

Big Apple

Tutti sanno che **The Big Apple**, la Grande Mela, è New York ("apple" in gergo significa grande città), ma sicuramente i soprannomi di altre città americane non sono così conosciuti. Chicago è soprannominata "the Windy City" perché è ventosa, New Orleans si chiama "the Big Easy" per il modo di vivere tranquillo e rilassato dei suoi abitanti, e l'industria automobilistica ha fatto sì che Detroit fosse soprannominata "Motown".

bike [baɪk] n bici f inv; **bike lane** n pista ciclabile

bikini [bɪˈkiːnɪ] n bikini m inv

bilateral [baɪˈlætərl] adj bilaterale

bilingual [baɪˈlɪŋgwəl] adj bilingue

bill [bɪl] n conto; (Pol) atto; (US: banknote) banconota; (of bird) becco; (of show) locandina; **can I have the ~, please** il conto, per favore; **put it on my ~** lo metta sul mio conto; **"post no ~s"** "divieto di affissione"; **to fit** or **fill the ~** (fig) fare al caso; **billboard** n tabellone m; **billfold** [ˈbɪlfəʊld] (US) n portafoglio

billiards [ˈbɪljədz] n biliardo

billion [ˈbɪljən] num (BRIT) bilione m; (US) miliardo

bin [bɪn] n (for coal, rubbish) bidone m; (for bread) cassetta; (dustbin) pattumiera; (litter bin) cestino

bind [baɪnd] (pt, pp **bound**) vt legare; (oblige) obbligare ▶ n (inf) scocciatura

binge [bɪndʒ] (inf) n **to go on a ~** fare baldoria

bingo [ˈbɪŋgəʊ] n gioco simile alla tombola

binoculars [bɪˈnɔkjuləz] npl binocolo

bio... [baɪə'...] prefix; **biochemistry** n biochimica; **biodegradable** adj biodegradabile; **biography** [baɪˈɔgrəfɪ] n biografia; **biological** adj biologico(-a); **biology** [baɪˈɔlədʒɪ] n biologia

birch [bə:tʃ] n betulla

bird [bə:d] n uccello; (BRIT: inf: girl) bambola; **bird of prey** n (uccello) rapace m; **birdwatching** n birdwatching m

Biro® ['baɪrəu] n biro® f inv

birth [bə:θ] n nascita; **to give -** to partorire; **birth certificate** n certificato di nascita; **birth control** n controllo delle nascite; contraccezione f; **birthday** n compleanno ▶ cpd di compleanno; **birthmark** n voglia; **birthplace** n luogo di nascita

biscuit ['bɪskɪt] (BRIT) n biscotto

bishop ['bɪʃəp] n vescovo

bistro ['bi:strəu] n bistrò m inv

bit [bɪt] pt of **bite** ▶ n pezzo; (Comput) bit m inv; (of horse) morso; **a - of** un po' di; **a - mad** un po' matto; **- by -** a poco a poco

bitch [bɪtʃ] n (dog) cagna; (infl) vacca

bite [baɪt] (pt, pp **bit**, **bitten**) vt, vi mordere; (insect) pungere ▶ n morso; (insect bite) puntura; (mouthful) boccone m; **let's have a - to eat** mangiamo un boccone; **to - one's nails** mangiarsi le unghie

bitten ['bɪtn] pp of **bite**

bitter ['bɪtə'] adj amaro(-a); (wind, criticism) pungente ▶ n (BRIT: beer) birra amara

bizarre [bɪ'zɑ:'] adj bizzarro(-a)

black [blæk] adj nero(-a) ▶ n nero; (person): B~ negro(-a) ▶ vt (BRIT Industry) boicottare; **to give sb a black eye** fare un occhio nero a qn; **in the ~** (bank account) in attivo ▶ **black out**

vi (faint) svenire; **blackberry** n mora; **blackbird** n merlo; **blackboard** n lavagna; **black coffee** n caffè m inv nero; **blackcurrant** n ribes m inv; **black ice** n strato trasparente di ghiaccio; **blackmail** n ricatto ▶ vt ricattare; **black market** n mercato nero; **blackout** n oscuramento; (TV, Radio) interruzione f delle trasmissioni; (fainting) svenimento; **black pepper** n pepe m nero; **black pudding** n sanguinaccio; **Black Sea** n the Black Sea il Mar Nero

bladder ['blædə'] n vescica

blade [bleɪd] n lama; (of oar) pala; **~ of grass** filo d'erba

blame [bleɪm] n colpa ▶ vt **to ~ sb/sth for sth** dare la colpa di qc a qn/qc; **who's to ~?** chi è colpevole?

bland [blænd] adj mite; (taste) blando(-a)

blank [blæŋk] adj bianco(-a); (look) distratto(-a) ▶ n spazio vuoto; (cartridge) cartuccia a salve

blanket ['blæŋkɪt] n coperta

blast [blɑ:st] n (of wind) raffica; (of bomb etc) esplosione f ▶ vt far saltare

blatant ['bleɪtənt] adj flagrante

blaze [bleɪz] n (fire) incendio; (fig) vampata; splendore m ▶ vi (fire) ardere, fiammeggiare; (guns) sparare senza sosta; (fig: eyes) ardere ▶ vt **to ~ a trail** (fig) tracciare una via nuova; **in a ~ of publicity** circondato da grande pubblicità

blazer ['bleɪzə'] n blazer m inv

bleach [bli:tʃ] n (also: household ~) varechina ▶ vt (material) candeggiare; **bleachers** (US) npl (Sport) posti mpl di gradinata

bleak [bli:k] adj tetro(-a)

bled [bled] pt, pp of **bleed**

bleed [bli:d] (pt, pp **bled**) vi sanguinare; **my nose is ~ing** mi viene fuori sangue dal naso

blemish ['blɛmɪʃ] n macchia

blend [blɛnd] n miscela ▶ vt mescolare ▶ vi (colours etc: also: **~ in**) armonizzare; **blender** n (Culin) frullatore m

bless [blɛs] (pt, pp blessed or blest) vt benedire; **~ you!** (after sneeze) salute!; **blessing** n benedizione f; fortuna

blew [bluː] pt of **blow**

blight [blaɪt] vt (hopes etc) deludere; (life) rovinare

blind [blaɪnd] adj cieco(-a) ▶ n (for window) avvolgibile m; (Venetian blind) veneziana ▶ vt accecare; **the ~** npl i ciechi; **blind alley** n vicolo cieco; **blindfold** n benda ▶ adj, adv bendato(-a) ▶ vt bendare gli occhi a

blink [blɪŋk] vi battere gli occhi; (light) lampeggiare

bliss [blɪs] n estasi f

blister ['blɪstəʳ] n (on skin) vescica; (on paintwork) bolla ▶ vi (paint) coprirsi di bolle

blizzard ['blɪzəd] n bufera di neve

bloated ['bləʊtɪd] adj gonfio(-a)

blob [blɔb] n (drop) goccia; (stain, spot) macchia

block [blɔk] n blocco; (in pipes) ingombro; (toy) cubo; (of buildings) isolato ▶ vt bloccare; **the sink is ~ed** il lavandino è otturato ▶ **block up** vt bloccare; (pipe) ingorgare, intasare; **blockade** [-'keɪd] n blocco; **blockage** n ostacolo; **blockbuster** n (film, book) grande successo; **block capitals** npl stampatello; **block letters** npl stampatello

bloke [bləʊk] n (BRIT: inf) n tizio

blond(e) [blɔnd] adj, n biondo(-a)

blood [blʌd] n sangue m; **blood donor** n donatore(-trice) di sangue; **blood group** n gruppo sanguigno; **blood poisoning** n setticemia; **blood pressure** n pressione f sanguigna; **bloodshed** n spargimento di sangue; **bloodshot** adj **bloodshot eyes** occhi iniettati di sangue; **bloodstream** n flusso del sangue; **blood test** n analisi f inv del sangue; **blood transfusion** n trasfusione f di sangue; **blood type** n gruppo sanguigno; **blood vessel** n vaso sanguigno; **bloody** adj (fight) sanguinoso(-a); (nose) sanguinante; (BRIT: inf!): **this bloody ...** questo maledetto ...; **bloody awful/good** (inf!) veramente terribile/forte

bloom [bluːm] n fiore m ▶ vi (tree) essere in fiore; (flower) aprirsi

blossom ['blɔsəm] n fiore m; (with pl sense) fiori mpl ▶ vi essere in fiore

blot [blɔt] n macchia ▶ vt macchiare

blouse [blauz] n (feminine garment) camicetta

blow [bləʊ] (pt blew, pp blown) n colpo ▶ vi soffiare ▶ vt (fuse) far saltare; (wind) spingere; (instrument) suonare; **to ~ one's nose** soffiarsi il naso; **to ~ a whistle** fischiare ▶ **blow away** vt portare via ▶ **blow out** vi scoppiare ▶ **blow up** vi saltare in aria ▶ vt far saltare in aria; (tyre) gonfiare; (Phot) ingrandire; **blow-dry** n messa in piega a phon

blown [bləʊn] pp of **blow**

blue [bluː] adj azzurro(-a); (depressed) giù inv; **film/joke** film/barzelletta pornografico(-a); **out of the ~** (fig) all'improvviso; **bluebell** n giacinto dei boschi; **blueberry** n mirtillo; **blue cheese** n formaggio tipo gorgonzola; **blues** npl **the blues** (Mus) il blues; **to have the blues** (inf: feeling) essere a terra; **bluetit** n cinciarella

bluff [blʌf] vi bluffare ▶ n bluff m inv ▶ adj (person) brusco(-a); **to call sb's ~** mettere alla prova il bluff di qn

blunder ['blʌndəʳ] n abbaglio ▶ vi prendere un abbaglio

blunt [blʌnt] adj smussato(-a); spuntato(-a); (person) brusco(-a)

blur [bləːʳ] n forma indistinta ▶ vt

offuscare; **blurred** adj (photo)
mosso(-a); (TV) sfuocato(-a)

blush [blʌʃ] vi arrossire ▶ n rossore m;
blusher n fard m inv

board [bɔːd] n tavola; (on wall)
tabellone m; (committee) consiglio,
comitato; (in firm) consiglio
d'amministrazione; (Naut, Aviat):
on ~ a bordo ▶ vt (ship) salire a bordo
di; (train) salire su; **full ~** (BRIT)
pensione completa; **half ~** (BRIT)
mezza pensione; **~ and lodging**
vitto e alloggio; **which goes by the ~**
(fig) che viene abbandonato; **board
game** n gioco da tavolo; **boarding
card** n = **boarding pass**; **boarding
pass** n (Aviat, Naut) carta d'imbarco;
boarding school n collegio; **board
room** n sala del consiglio

boast [bəust] vi **to ~ (about** or **of)**
vantarsi (di)

boat [bəut] n nave f; (small) barca

bob [bɔb] vi (boat, cork on water: also: **~
up and down)** andare su e giù

bobby pin ['bɔbɪ-] (US) n fermaglio
per capelli

body ['bɔdɪ] n corpo; (of car)
carrozzeria; (of plane) fusoliera;
(fig: group) gruppo; (: organization)
organizzazione f; (: quantity) quantità
f inv; **body-building** n culturismo;
bodyguard n guardia del corpo;
bodywork n carrozzeria

bog [bɔg] n palude f ▶ vt **to get ~ged
down** (fig) impantanarsi

bogus ['bəugəs] adj falso(-a); finto(-a)

boil [bɔɪl] vt, vi bollire ▶ n (Med)
foruncolo; **to come to the** (BRIT) or
a (US) **~** raggiungere l'ebollizione
▷ **boil over** vi traboccare (bollendo);
boiled egg n uovo alla coque; **boiled
potatoes** npl patate fpl bollite o
lesse; **boiler** n caldaia; **boiling** adj
bollente; **I'm boiling (hot)** (inf) sto
morendo di caldo; **boiling point** n

punto di ebollizione

bold [bəuld] adj audace; (child)
impudente; (colour) deciso(-a)

Bolivia [bə'lɪvɪə] n Bolivia

Bolivian [bə'lɪvɪən] adj, n boliviano(-a)

bollard ['bɔləd] (BRIT) n (Aut)
colonnina luminosa

bolt [bəult] n chiavistello; (with nut)
bullone m ▶ adv: **~ upright** diritto(-a)
come un fuso ▶ vt serrare; (also:
~ together) imbullonare; (food)
mangiare in fretta ▶ vi scappare via

bomb [bɔm] n bomba ▶ vt
bombardare; **bombard** [bɔm'bɑːd]
vt bombardare; **bomber** n (Aviat)
bombardiere m; **bomb scare** n stato
di allarme (per sospetta presenza di
una bomba)

bond [bɔnd] n legame m; (binding
promise, Finance) obbligazione
f; (Comm): **in ~** in attesa di
sdoganamento

bone [bəun] n osso; (of fish) spina, lisca
▶ vt disossare; togliere le spine a

bonfire ['bɔnfaɪə] n falò m inv

bonnet ['bɔnɪt] n cuffia; (BRIT: of car)
cofano

bonus ['bəunəs] n premio; (fig)
sovrappiù m inv

boo [buː] excl bah! ▶ vt fischiare

book [buk] n libro; (of stamps etc)
blocchetto ▶ vt (ticket, seat, room)
prenotare; (driver) multare; (football
player) ammonire; **~s** npl (Comm) conti
mpl; **I'd like to ~ a double room** vorrei
prenotare una camera doppia; **I ~ed a
table in the name of ...** ho prenotato
un tavolo al nome di ... ▷ **book in** vi
(BRIT: at hotel) prendere una camera
▷ **book up** vt riservare, prenotare;
the hotel is ~ed up l'albergo è al
completo; **all seats are ~ed up** è
tutto esaurito; **bookcase** n scaffale
m; **booking** n (BRIT) prenotazione
f; **I confirmed my booking by**

fax/e-mail ho confermato la mia prenotazione tramite fax/e-mail; **booking office** (BRIT) n (Rail) biglietteria f; (Theatre) botteghino; **book-keeping** n contabilità; **booklet** n libricino; **bookmaker** n allibratore m; **bookmark** (also Comput) n segnalibro ▶ vt (Comput) mettere un segnalibro a; (Internet Explorer) aggiungere a "Preferiti"; **bookseller** n libraio; **bookshelf** n mensola (per libri); **bookshop**, **bookstore** n libreria

boom [bu:m] n (noise) rimbombo; (in prices etc) boom m inv ▶ vi rimbombare; andare a gonfie vele

boost [bu:st] n spinta ▶ vt spingere

boot [bu:t] n stivale m; (for hiking) scarpone m da montagna; (for football etc) scarpa; (BRIT: of car) portabagagli m inv ▶ vt (Comput) inizializzare; **to ~** (in addition) per giunta, in più

booth [bu:ð] n cabina; (at fair) baraccone m

booze [bu:z] (inf) n alcool m

border ['bɔ:dǝ'] n orlo; margine m; (of a country) frontiera; (for flowers) aiuola (laterale) ▶ vt (road) costeggiare; (another country: also: **~ on**) confinare con; **the B~s** la zona di confine tra l'Inghilterra e la Scozia; **borderline** n (fig): **on the borderline** incerto(-a)

bore [bɔ:'] pt of **bear** ▶ vt (hole etc) scavare; (person) annoiare ▶ n (person) seccatore(-trice); (of gun) calibro; **bored** adj annoiato(-a); **to be bored** annoiarsi; **he's bored to tears** or**to death** or **stiff** è annoiato a morte; **boredom** n noia

boring ['bɔ:rɪŋ] adj noioso(-a)

born [bɔ:n] adj **to be ~** nascere; **I was ~ in 1960** sono nato nel 1960

borne [bɔ:n] pp of **bear**

borough ['bʌrǝ] n comune m

borrow ['bɔrǝu] vt **to ~ sth (from sb)**

prendere in prestito qc (da qn)

Bosnia(-Herzegovina) ['bɒznɪǝ(hɜrzǝ'gǝuvi:nǝ)] n Bosnia-Erzegovina; **Bosnian** ['bɒznɪǝn] n, adj bosniaco(-a) m/f

bosom ['buzǝm] n petto; (fig) seno

boss [bɒs] n capo ▶ vt comandare; **bossy** adj prepotente

both [bǝuθ] adj entrambi(-e), tutt'e due ▶ pron **~ of them** entrambi(-e); **~ of us went, we ~ went** ci siamo andati tutt'e due ▶ adv **they sell ~ meat and poultry** vendono insieme la carne ed il pollame

bother ['bɒðǝ'] vt (worry) preoccupare; (annoy) infastidire ▶ vi (also: **~ o.s.**) preoccuparsi ▶ n **it is a ~ to have to do** è una seccatura dover fare; **it was no ~** non c'era problema; **to ~ doing sth** darsi la pena di fare qc

bottle ['bɒtl] n bottiglia; (baby's) biberon m inv ▶ vt imbottigliare; **bottle bank** n contenitore m per la raccolta del vetro; **bottle-opener** n apribottiglie m inv

bottom ['bɒtǝm] n fondo; (buttocks) sedere m ▶ adj (più basso(-a); ultimo(-a); **at the ~ of** in fondo a

bought [bɔ:t] pt, pp of **buy**

boulder ['bǝuldǝ'] n masso (tondeggiante)

bounce [bauns] vi (ball) rimbalzare; (cheque) essere restituito(-a) ▶ vt far rimbalzare ▶ n (rebound) rimbalzo; **bouncer** (inf) n buttafuori m inv

bound [baund] pt, pp of **bind** ▶ n (gen pl) limite m; (leap) salto ▶ vi saltare ▶ vt (limit) delimitare ▶ adj **~ by law** obbligato(-a) per legge; **to be ~ to do sth** (obliged) essere costretto(-a) a fare qc; **he's ~ to fail** (likely) fallirà di certo; **~ for** diretto(-a) a; **out of-s** il cui accesso è vietato

boundary ['baundrɪ] n confine m

bouquet ['bukeɪ] n bouquet m inv

bourbon ['buəbən] (US) n (also: ~ whiskey) bourbon m inv

bout [baut] n periodo; (of malaria etc) attacco; (Boxing etc) incontro

boutique [buː'tiːk] n boutique f inv

bow¹ [bəu] n nodo; (weapon) arco; (Mus) archetto

bow² [bau] n (with body) inchino; (Naut: also: ~s) prua ▶ vi inchinarsi; (yield): to ~ to or before sottomettersi a

bowels ['bauəlz] npl intestini mpl; (fig) viscere fpl

bowl [bəul] n (for eating) scodella; (for washing) bacino; (ball) boccia ▶ vi (Cricket) servire (la palla); **bowler** ['bəulə'] n (Cricket, Baseball) lanciatore m; (BRIT: also: **bowler hat**) bombetta; **bowling** ['bəulɪŋ] n (game) gioco delle bocce; **bowling alley** n pista da bowling; **bowling green** n campo di bocce; **bowls** [bəulz] n gioco delle bocce

bow tie n cravatta a farfalla

box [bɔks] n scatola; (also: **cardboard ~**) cartone m; (Theatre) palco ▶ vi inscatolare ▶ vi fare del pugilato; **boxer** n (person) pugile m; **boxer shorts** ['bɔksəʃɔːts] npl n boxer; **a pair of boxer shorts** un paio di boxer; **boxing** n (Sport) pugilato m; **Boxing Day** (BRIT) n ≈ Santo Stefano; vedi nota nel riquadro; **boxing gloves** npl guantoni mpl da pugile; **boxing ring** n ring m inv; **box office** n biglietteria

Boxing Day
Il Boxing Day è un giorno di festa e cade in genere il 26 dicembre. Prende il nome dalla tradizionale usanza di donare pacchi regalo natalizi, chiamati "Christmas boxes", a fornitori e dipendenti.

boy [bɔɪ] n ragazzo

boycott ['bɔɪkɔt] n boicottaggio ▶ vt boicottare

boyfriend ['bɔɪfrɛnd] n ragazzo

bra [brɑː] n reggipetto, reggiseno

brace [breɪs] n (on teeth) apparecchio correttore; (tool) trapano ▶ vt rinforzare, sostenere; **~s** (BRIT) npl (Dress) bretelle fpl; **to ~ o.s.** (also fig) tenersi forte

bracelet ['breɪslɪt] n braccialetto

bracket ['brækɪt] n (Tech) mensola; (group) gruppo; (Typ) parentesi f inv ▶ vt mettere fra parentesi

brag [bræg] vi vantarsi

braid [breɪd] n (trimming) passamano; (of hair) treccia

brain [breɪn] n cervello; **~s** npl (intelligence) cervella fpl; **he's got ~s** è intelligente

braise [breɪz] vt brasare

brake [breɪk] n (on vehicle) freno ▶ vi frenare; **brake light** n (fanalino dello) stop m inv

bran [bræn] n crusca

branch [brɑːntʃ] n ramo; (Comm) succursale f ▶ **branch off** vi diramarsi ▷ **branch out** vi (fig) intraprendere una nuova attività

brand [brænd] n marca; (fig) tipo ▶ vt (cattle) marcare (a ferro rovente); **brand name** n marca; **brand-new** adj nuovo(-a) di zecca

brandy ['brændɪ] n brandy m inv

brash [bræʃ] adj sfacciato(-a)

brass [brɑːs] n ottone m; **the ~** (Mus) gli ottoni; **brass band** n fanfara

brat [bræt] (pej) n marmocchio, monello(-a)

brave [breɪv] adj coraggioso(-a) ▶ vt affrontare; **bravery** n coraggio

brawl [brɔːl] n rissa

Brazil [brə'zɪl] n Brasile m; **Brazilian** adj, n brasiliano(-a)

breach [briːtʃ] vt aprire una breccia in ▶ n (gap) breccia, varco; (breaking): **~ of contract** rottura di contratto; **~ of the peace** violazione f dell'ordine pubblico

bread [brɛd] n pane m; **breadbin** n cassetta f portapane inv; **breadbox** (US) n cassetta f portapane inv; **breadcrumbs** npl briciole fpl; (Culin) pangrattato

breadth [brɛtθ] n larghezza; (fig: of knowledge etc) ampiezza

break [breɪk] (pt broke, pp broken) vt rompere; (law) violare; (record) battere ▶ vi rompersi; (storm) scoppiare; (weather) cambiare; (dawn) spuntare; (news) saltare fuori ▶ n (gap) breccia; (fracture) rottura; (rest, also Scol) intervallo; (: short) pausa; (chance) possibilità f inv; **to ~ one's leg** ecc rompersi la gamba ecc; **to ~ the news to sb** comunicare per primo la notizia a qn; **to ~ even** coprire le spese; **to ~ free o loose** spezzare i legami; **to ~ open** (door etc) sfondare ▶ **break down** vt (figures, data) analizzare ▶ vi (person) avere un esaurimento (nervoso); (Aut) guastarsi; **my car has broken down** mi si è rotta la macchina ▶ **break in** vt (horse etc) domare ▶ vi (burglar) fare irruzione; (interrupt) interrompere ▶ **break into** vt fus (house) fare irruzione in ▶ **break off** vi (speaker) interrompersi; (branch) troncarsi ▶ **break out** vi evadere; (war, fight) scoppiare; **to ~ out in spots** coprirsi di macchie ▶ **break up** vi (ship) sfondarsi; (meeting) sciogliersi; (crowd) disperdersi; (marriage) andare a pezzi; (Scol) chiudere ▶ vt fare a pezzi, spaccare; (fight etc) interrompere, far cessare; **breakdown** n (Aut) guasto; (in communications) interruzione f; (of marriage) rottura; (Med: also: **nervous breakdown**) esaurimento nervoso; (of statistics) resoconto; **breakdown truck, breakdown van** n carro m attrezzi inv

breakfast ['brɛkfəst] n colazione f;

what time is **~**? a che ora è servita la colazione?

break: **break-in** n irruzione f; **breakthrough** n (fig) passo avanti

breast [brɛst] n (of woman) seno; (chest, Culin) petto; **breast-feed** (irreg: like **feed**) vt, vi allattare (al seno); **breast-stroke** n nuoto a rana

breath [brɛθ] n respiro; **out of ~** senza fiato

Breathalyser® ['brɛθəlaɪzə'] (BRIT) n alcoltest m inv

breathe [briːð] vt, vi respirare ▶ **breathe in** vt respirare ▶ vi inspirare ▶ **breathe out** vt, vi espirare; **breathing** n respiro, respirazione f

breath: **breathless** ['brɛθlɪs] adj senza fiato; **breathtaking** ['brɛθteɪkɪŋ] adj mozzafiato inv; **breath test** n prova del palloncino

bred [brɛd] pt, pp of **breed**

breed [briːd] (pt, pp **bred**) vt allevare ▶ vi riprodursi ▶ n razza; (type, class) varietà f inv

breeze [briːz] n brezza

breezy ['briːzɪ] adj allegro(-a), ventilato(-a)

brew [bruː] vt (tea) fare un infuso di; (beer) fare ▶ vi (storm, fig: trouble etc) preparasi ▶ **brewery** n fabbrica di birra

bribe [braɪb] n bustarella ▶ vt comprare; **bribery** n corruzione f

bric-a-brac ['brɪkəbræk] n bric-a-brac m

brick [brɪk] n mattone m; **bricklayer** n muratore m

bride [braɪd] n sposa; **bridegroom** n sposo; **bridesmaid** n damigella d'onore

bridge [brɪdʒ] n ponte m; (Naut) ponte di comando; (of nose) dorso; (Cards) bridge m inv ▶ vt (fig: gap) colmare

bridle ['braɪdl] n briglia

brief [briːf] adj breve ▶ n (Law)

comparsa; (gen) istruzioni fpl ▶ vt mettere al corrente; **~s** npl (underwear) mutande fpl; **briefcase** n cartella; **briefing** n briefing m inv; **briefly** adv (glance) di sfuggita; (explain, say) brevemente

brigadier [brɪgə'dɪəʳ] n generale m di brigata

bright [braɪt] adj luminoso(-a); (clever) sveglio(-a); (lively) vivace

brilliant ['brɪljənt] adj brillante; (light, smile) radioso(-a); (inf) splendido(-a)

brim [brɪm] n orlo

brine [braɪn] n (Culin) salamoia

bring [brɪŋ] (pt, pp brought) vt portare ▷ **bring about** vt causare ▷ **bring back** vt riportare ▷ **bring down** vt portare giù; abbattere ▷ **bring in** vt (person) fare entrare; (object) portare; (Pol: bill) presentare; (: legislation) introdurre; (Law: verdict) emettere; (produce: income) rendere ▷ **bring on** vt (illness, attack) causare, provocare; (player, substitute) far scendere in campo ▷ **bring out** vt tirar fuori; (meaning) mettere in evidenza; (book, album) far uscire ▷ **bring up** vt (carry up) portare su; (child) allevare; (question) introdurre; (food: vomit) rimettere, rigurgitare

brink [brɪŋk] n orlo

brisk [brɪsk] adj (manner) spiccio(-a); (trade) vivace; (pace) svelto(-a)

bristle ['brɪsl] n setola ▶ vi rizzarsi; **bristling with** irto(-a) di

Brit [brɪt] n abbr (inf: = British person) britannico(-a)

Britain ['brɪtən] n (also: **Great ~**) Gran Bretagna

British ['brɪtɪʃ] adj britannico(-a); **British Isles** npl Isole Britanniche

Briton ['brɪtən] n britannico(-a)

brittle ['brɪtl] adj fragile

broad [brɔːd] adj largo(-a); (distinction) generale; (accent) spiccato(-a);

in ~ **daylight** in pieno giorno; **broadband** adj (Comput) a banda larga ▶ n banda larga; **broad bean** n fava; **broadcast** (pt, pp broadcast) n trasmissione f ▶ vt trasmettere per radio (or per televisione) ▶ vi fare una trasmissione; **broaden** vt allargare ▶ vi allargarsi; **broadly** adv (fig) in generale; **broad-minded** adj di mente aperta

broccoli ['brɔkəlɪ] n broccoli mpl

brochure ['brəuʃjuəʳ] n dépliant m inv

broil [brɔɪl] vt cuocere a fuoco vivo

broiler ['brɔɪləʳ] (US) n (grill) griglia

broke [brəuk] pt of **break** ▶ adj (inf) squattrinato(-a)

broken ['brəukn] pp of **break** ▶ adj rotto(-a); **a ~ leg** una gamba rotta; in ~ **English** in un inglese stentato

broker ['brəukəʳ] n agente m

bronchitis [brɔŋ'kaɪtɪs] n bronchite f

bronze [brɔnz] n bronzo

brooch [brəutʃ] n spilla

brood [bruːd] n covata ▶ vi (person) rimuginare

broom [brum] n scopa; (Bot) ginestra

Bros. abbr (= Brothers) F.lli

broth [brɔθ] n brodo

brothel ['brɔθl] n bordello

brother ['brʌðəʳ] n fratello; **brother-in-law** n cognato

brought [brɔːt] pt, pp of **bring**

brow [brau] n fronte f; (rare, gen: eyebrow) sopracciglio; (of hill) cima

brown [braun] adj bruno(-a), marrone; (tanned) abbronzato(-a) ▶ n (colour) color m bruno or marrone ▶ vt (Culin) rosolare; **brown bread** n pane m integrale, pane nero

Brownie ['braunɪ] n giovane esploratrice f

brown rice n riso greggio

brown sugar n zucchero greggio

browse [brauz] vi (among books) curiosare fra i libri; **to ~ through a**

book sfogliare un libro; **browser** n (Comput) browser m inv

bruise [bruːz] n (on person) livido ▶ vt farsi un livido a

brunette [bruːˈnɛt] n bruna

brush [brʌʃ] n spazzola; (for painting, shaving) pennello; (quarrel) schermaglia ▶ vt spazzolare; (also: ~ against) sfiorare

Brussels [ˈbrʌslz] n Bruxelles f

Brussels sprout [spraʊt] n cavolo di Bruxelles

brutal [ˈbruːtl] adj brutale

B.Sc. n abbr (Univ) = **Bachelor of Science**

BSE n abbr (= bovine spongiform encephalopathy) encefalite f bovina spongiforme

bubble [ˈbʌbl] n bolla ▶ vi ribollire; (sparkle: fig) essere effervescente; **bubble bath** n bagnoschiuma m inv; **bubble gum** n gomma americana

buck [bʌk] n maschio (di camoscio, caprone, coniglio ecc); (US: inf) dollaro ▶ vi sgroppare; **to pass the ~ to sb** scaricare (su di qn) la propria responsabilità

bucket [ˈbʌkɪt] n secchio

buckle [ˈbʌkl] n fibbia ▶ vt allacciare ▶ vi (wheel etc) piegarsi

bud [bʌd] n gemma; (of flower) bocciolo ▶ vi germogliare; (flower) sbocciare

Buddhism [ˈbudɪzəm] n buddismo

Buddhist [ˈbudɪst] adj, n buddista (m/f)

buddy [ˈbʌdɪ] (US) n compagno

budge [bʌdʒ] vt scostare; (fig) smuovere ▶ vi spostarsi; smuoversi

budgerigar [ˈbʌdʒərɪgɑːˈ] n pappagallino

budget [ˈbʌdʒɪt] n bilancio preventivo ▶ vi **to ~ for sth** fare il bilancio per qc

budgie [ˈbʌdʒɪ] n = **budgerigar**

buff [bʌf] adj color camoscio ▶ n (inf: enthusiast) appassionato(-a)

buffalo [ˈbʌfələu] n (pl **buffalo** or **buffaloes**) n bufalo; (US) bisonte m

buffer [ˈbʌfəʳ] n respingente m; (Comput) memoria tampone, buffer m inv

buffet[1] [ˈbʌfɪt] vt sferzare

buffet[2] [ˈbufeɪ] n (food, BRIT: bar) buffet m inv; **buffet car** (BRIT) n (Rail) ≈ servizio ristoro

bug [bʌg] n (esp US: insect) insetto; (Comput, fig: germ) virus m inv; (spy device) microfono spia ▶ vt mettere sotto controllo; (inf: annoy) scocciare

buggy [ˈbʌgɪ] n (baby buggy) passeggino

build [bɪld] (pt, pp **built**) n (of person) corporatura ▶ vt costruire ▷ **build up** vt accumulare; aumentare; **builder** n costruttore m; **building** n costruzione f; edificio; (industry) edilizia; **building site** n cantiere m di costruzione; **building society** (BRIT) n società f inv immobiliare

built [bɪlt] pt, pp of **build**; **built-in** adj (cupboard) a muro; (device) incorporato(-a); **built-up** adj built-up **area** abitato

bulb [bʌlb] n (Bot) bulbo; (Elec) lampadina

Bulgaria [bʌlˈgɛərɪə] n Bulgaria; **Bulgarian** adj bulgaro(-a) ▶ n bulgaro(-a); (Ling) bulgaro

bulge [bʌldʒ] n rigonfiamento ▶ vi essere protuberante o rigonfio(-a); **to be bulging with** essere pieno(-a) o zeppo(-a) di

bulimia [bəˈlɪmɪə] n bulimia

bulimic [bjuːˈlɪmɪk] adj, n bulimico(-a)

bulk [bʌlk] n massa, volume m; **in ~ pacchi o cassette etc**; (Comm) all'ingrosso; **the ~ of** il grosso di; **bulky** adj grosso(-a), voluminoso(-a)

bull [bul] n toro; (male elephant, whale) maschio

bulldozer [ˈbuldəuzəʳ] n bulldozer n

m inv

bullet ['bulɪt] *n* pallottola

bulletin ['bulɪtɪn] *n* bollettino;
bulletin board (*Comput*) bulletin
board *m inv*

bullfight ['bulfaɪt] *n* corrida;
bullfighter *n* torero; **bullfighting** *n*
tauromachia

bully ['bulɪ] *n* prepotente *m* ▶ *vt*
angariare; (*frighten*) intimidire

bum [bʌm] (*inf*) *n* (*backside*) culo;
(*tramp*) vagabondo(-a)

bumblebee ['bʌmblbi:] *n* bombo

bump [bʌmp] *n* (*in car*) piccolo
tamponamento; (*jolt*) scossa; (*on
road etc*) protuberanza; (*on head*)
bernoccolo ▶ *vt* battere ▷ **bump
into** *vt fus* scontrarsi con; (*person*)
imbattersi in; **bumper** *n* paraurti *m
inv* ▶ *adj* **bumper harvest** raccolto
eccezionale; **bumpy** ['bʌmpɪ] *adj*
(*road*) dissestato(-a)

bun [bʌn] *n* focaccia; (*of hair*) crocchia

bunch [bʌntʃ] *n* (*of flowers, keys*)
mazzo; (*of bananas*) casco; (*of people*)
gruppo; **~ of grapes** grappolo d'uva;
~es *npl* (*in hair*) codine *fpl*

bundle ['bʌndl] *n* fascio ▶ *vt* (*also:* **~ up**)
legare in un fascio; (*put*) **to ~ sth/sb
into** spingere qc/qn in

bungalow ['bʌŋɡələu] *n* bungalow
m inv

bungee jumping ['bʌndʒi:'dʒʌmpɪŋ]
n salto nel vuoto da ponti, grattacieli *etc*
con un cavo fissato alla caviglia

bunion ['bʌnjən] *n* callo (al piede)

bunk [bʌŋk] *n* cuccetta; **bunk beds** *npl*
letti *mpl* a castello

bunker ['bʌŋkəʳ] *n* (*coal store*)
ripostiglio per il carbone; (*Mil, Golf*)
bunker *m inv*

bunny ['bʌnɪ] *n* (*also:* **~ rabbit**)
coniglietto

buoy [bɔɪ] *n* boa; **buoyant** *adj*
galleggiante; (*fig*) vivace

burden ['bə:dn] *n* carico, fardello ▶ *vt*
to ~ sb with caricare qn di

bureau [bjuə'rəu] (*pl* **bureaux**) *n* (*BRIT:
writing desk*) scrivania; (*US: chest of
drawers*) cassettone *m*; (*office*) ufficio,
agenzia

bureaucracy [bjuə'rɔkrəsɪ] *n*
burocrazia

bureaucrat ['bjuərəkræt] *n* burocrate
m/f

bureau de change [-də'ʃɑ̃ʒ] (*pl*
bureaux de change) *n* cambiavalute
m inv

bureaux [bjuə'rəuz] *npl of* **bureau**

burger ['bə:gəʳ] *n* hamburger *m inv*

burglar ['bə:gləʳ] *n* scassinatore
m; **burglar alarm** *n* campanello
antifurto; **burglary** *n* furto con
scasso

burial ['bɛrɪəl] *n* sepoltura

burn [bə:n] (*pt, pp* **burned** or **burnt**) *vt,
vi* bruciare ▶ *n* bruciatura, scottatura
▷ **burn down** *vt* distruggere col fuoco
▷ **burn out** (*writer etc*): **to ~ o.s. out**
esaurirsi; **burning** *adj* in fiamme;
(*sand*) che scotta; (*ambition*) bruciante

Burns Night *n vedi nota nel riquadro*

● **Burns Night**
●
● **Burns Night** è la festa celebrata il 25
● gennaio per commemorare il poeta
● scozzese Robert Burns (1759-1796).
● Gli scozzesi festeggiano questa data
● con una cena, la "Burns supper", a
● base di "haggis", piatto tradizionale
● scozzese, e whisky.

burnt [bə:nt] *pt, pp of* **burn**

burp [bə:p] (*inf*) *n* rutto ▶ *vi* ruttare

burrow ['bʌrəu] *n* tana ▶ *vt* scavare

burst [bə:st] (*pt, pp* **burst**) *vt* far
scoppiare ▶ *vi* esplodere; (*tyre*)
scoppiare ▶ *n* scoppio; (*also:* **~ pipe**)
rottura nel tubo, perdita; **a ~ of
speed** uno scatto di velocità; **to
~ into flames/tears** scoppiare in
fiamme/lacrime; **to ~ out laughing**

scoppiare a ridere; **to be ~ing with** scoppiare di ▶ **burst into** vt fus (room etc) irrompere in

bury ['bɛrɪ] vt seppellire

bus [bʌs] (pl buses) n autobus m inv; **bus conductor** n autista m/f (dell'autobus)

bush [buʃ] n cespuglio; (scrub land) macchia; **to beat about the ~** menare il cane per l'aia

business ['bɪznɪs] n (matter) affare m; (trading) affari mpl; (firm) azienda; (job, duty) lavoro; **to be away on ~** essere andato via per affari; **it's none of my ~** questo non mi riguarda; **he means ~** non scherza; **business class** n (Aer) business class f; **businesslike** adj serio(-a), efficiente; **businessman** (irreg) n uomo d'affari; **business trip** n viaggio d'affari; **businesswoman** (irreg) n donna d'affari

busker ['bʌskə'] (BRIT) n suonatore(-trice) ambulante

bus: bus pass n tessera dell'autobus; **bus shelter** n pensilina (alla fermata dell'autobus); **bus station** n stazione f delle corriere, autostazione f; **bus-stop** n fermata di autobus

bust [bʌst] n busto; (Anat) seno ▶ adj (inf: broken) rotto(-a); **to go ~** fallire

bustling ['bʌslɪŋ] adj movimentato(-a)

busy ['bɪzɪ] adj occupato(-a); (shop, street) molto frequentato(-a) ▶ vt **to o.s.** darsi da fare; **busy signal** (US) n (Tel) segnale m di occupato

but

[bʌt] conj ma; **I'd love to come, but I'm busy** vorrei tanto venire, ma ho da fare

▶ prep (apart from, except) eccetto, tranne, meno; **he was nothing but trouble** non dava altro che guai; **no-one but him can do it** nessuno può farlo tranne lui; **but for you/your**

help se non fosse per te/il tuo aiuto; **anything but that** tutto ma non questo

▶ adv (just, only) solo, soltanto; **she's but a child** è solo una bambina; **had I but known** se solo avessi saputo; **I can but try** tentar non nuoce; **all but finished** quasi finito

butcher ['butʃə'] n macellaio ▶ vt macellare; **butcher's (shop)** n macelleria

butler ['bʌtlə'] n maggiordomo

butt [bʌt] n (cask) grossa botte f; (of gun) calcio; (of cigarette) mozzicone m; (BRIT: fig: target) oggetto ▶ vt cozzare

butter ['bʌtə'] n burro ▶ vt imburrare; **buttercup** n ranuncolo

butterfly ['bʌtəflaɪ] n farfalla; (Swimming: also: ~ stroke) (nuoto a) farfalla

buttocks ['bʌtəks] npl natiche fpl

button ['bʌtn] n bottone m; (US: badge) distintivo ▶ vt (also: ~ up) abbottonare ▶ vi abbottonarsi

buy [baɪ] (pt, pp bought) vt comprare ▶ n acquisto; **where can I ~ some postcards?** dove posso comprare delle cartoline?; **to ~ sb sth/sth from sb** comprare qc per qn/qc da qn; **to ~ sb a drink** offrire da bere a qn ▶ **buy out** vt (business) rilevare ▶ **buy up** vt accaparrare; **buyer** n compratore(-trice)

buzz [bʌz] n ronzio; (inf: phone call) colpo di telefono ▶ vi ronzare; **buzzer** ['bʌzə'] n cicalino

by

[baɪ] prep

1 (referring to cause, agent) da; **killed by lightning** ucciso da un fulmine; **surrounded by a fence** circondato da uno steccato; **a painting by Picasso** un quadro di Picasso

2 (referring to method, manner, means): **by bus/car/train** in autobus/

macchina/treno, con l'autobus/la macchina/il treno; **to pay by cheque** pagare con (un) assegno; **by moonlight** al chiaro di luna; **by saving hard, he ...** risparmiando molto, lui ...

3 (*via, through*) per; **we came by Dover** siamo venuti via Dover

4 (*close to, past*) accanto a; **the house by the river** la casa sul fiume; **a holiday by the sea** una vacanza al mare; **she sat by his bed** si sedette accanto al suo letto; **she rushed by me** mi è passata accanto correndo; **I go by the post office every day** passo davanti all'ufficio postale ogni giorno

5 (*not later than*) per, entro; **by 4 o'clock** per or entro le 4; **by this time tomorrow** domani a quest'ora; **by the time I got here it was too late** quando sono arrivato era ormai troppo tardi

6 (*during*): **by day/night** di giorno/notte

7 (*amount*) a; **by the kilo/metre** a chili/metri; **paid by the hour** pagato all'ora; **one by one** uno per uno; **little by little** a poco a poco

8 (*Math, measure*): **to divide/multiply by 3** dividere/moltiplicare per 3; **it's broader by a metre** è un metro più largo, è più largo di un metro

9 (*according to*) per; **to play by the rules** attenersi alle regole; **it's all right by me** per me va bene

10: (*all*) **by oneself** *etc* (tutto(-a)) solo(-a); **he did it (all) by himself** lo ha fatto (tutto) da solo

11: **by the way** a proposito; **this wasn't my idea by the way** tra l'altro l'idea non è stata mia
▶ *adv*

1 *see* **go**; **pass** *etc*

2: **by and by** (*in past*) poco dopo; (*in future*) fra breve; **by and large** nel complesso

bye(-bye) ['baɪ('baɪ)] *excl* ciao!,

arrivederci!

by-election ['baɪɪlɛkʃən] (*BRIT*) *n* elezione *f* straordinaria

bypass ['baɪpɑːs] *n* circonvallazione *f*; (*Med*) by-pass *m inv* ▶ *vt* fare una deviazione intorno a

byte [baɪt] *n* (*Comput*) byte *m inv*, bicarattere *m*

C

C [siː] *n* (*Mus*) do

cab [kæb] *n* taxi *m inv*; (*of train, truck*) cabina

cabaret ['kæbəreɪ] *n* cabaret *m inv*

cabbage ['kæbɪdʒ] *n* cavolo

cabin ['kæbɪn] *n* capanna; (*on ship*) cabina; **cabin crew** *n* equipaggio

cabinet ['kæbɪnɪt] *n* (*Pol*) consiglio dei ministri; (*furniture*) armadietto; (*also:* **display ~**) vetrinetta; **cabinet minister** *n* ministro (*membro del Consiglio*)

cable ['keɪbl] *n* cavo; fune *f*; (*Tel*) cablogramma *m* ▶ *vt* telegrafare; **cable car** *n* funivia; **cable television** *n* televisione *f* via cavo

cactus ['kæktəs] (*pl* **cacti**) *n* cactus *m inv*

café ['kæfeɪ] *n* caffè *m inv*

cafeteria [kæfɪ'tɪərɪə] *n* self-service *m inv*

caffein(e) ['kæfiːn] *n* caffeina

cage [keɪdʒ] n gabbia

cagoule [kə'gu:l] n K-way® m inv

cake [keɪk] n (large) torta; (small) pasticcino; **cake of soap** n saponetta

calcium ['kælsɪəm] n calcio

calculate ['kælkjuleɪt] vt calcolare; **calculation** [-'leɪʃən] n calcolo; **calculator** n calcolatrice f

calendar ['kæləndə*] n calendario

calf [kɑ:f] (pl **calves**) n (of cow) vitello; (of other animals) piccolo; (also: ~**skin**) (pelle f di) vitello; (Anat) polpaccio

calibre ['kælɪbə*] (US **caliber**) n calibro

call [kɔ:l] vt (gen: also Tel) chiamare; (meeting) indire ▶ vi chiamare; (visit: also: ~ **in**, ~ **round**) passare ▶ n (shout) grido, urlo; (Tel) telefonata; **to be ~ed** (person, object) chiamarsi; **can you ~ back later?** può richiamare più tardi?; **can I make a ~ from here?** posso telefonare da qui?; **to be on ~** essere a disposizione ▷ **call back** vi (return) ritornare; (Tel) ritelefonare, richiamare ▷ **call for** vt fus richiedere; (fetch) passare a prendere ▷ **call in** vt (doctor, expert, police) chiamare, far venire ▷ **call off** vt disdire ▷ **call on** vt fus (visit) passare da; (appeal to) chiedere a ▷ **call out** vi (in pain) urlare; (to person) chiamare ▷ **call up** vt (Mil) richiamare; (Tel) telefonare a; **callbox** [BRIT] n cabina telefonica; **call centre** (US **call center**) n centro informazioni telefoniche; **caller** n persona che chiama, visitatore(-trice)

callous ['kæləs] adj indurito(-a), insensibile

calm [kɑ:m] adj calmo(-a) ▶ n calma ▶ vt calmare ▷ **calm down** vi calmarsi ▶ vt calmare; **calmly** adv con calma

Calor gas® ['kælə*-] n butano

calorie ['kælərɪ] n caloria

calves [kɑ:vz] npl of **calf**

camcorder ['kæmkɔ:də*] n camcorder

came [keɪm] pt of **come**

camel ['kæməl] n cammello

camera ['kæmərə] n macchina fotografica; (Cinema, TV) cinepresa; **in ~ a porte chiuse; cameraman** (irreg) n cameraman m inv

camouflage ['kæməflɑ:ʒ] n (Mil, Zool) mimetizzazione f ▶ vt mimetizzare

camp [kæmp] n campeggio; (Mil) campo ▶ vi accamparsi ▶ adj effeminato(-a)

campaign [kæm'peɪn] n (Mil, Pol etc) campagna ▶ vi (also fig) fare una campagna; **campaigner** n **campaigner for** fautore(-trice) di; **campaigner against** oppositore(-trice) di

camp: **campbed** n (BRIT) brandina; **camper** ['kæmpə*] n campeggiatore(-trice); (vehicle) camper m inv; **campground** (US) n campeggio; **camping** ['kæmpɪŋ] n campeggio; **to go camping** andare in campeggio; **campsite** ['kæmpsaɪt] n campeggio

campus ['kæmpəs] n campus m inv

can[1] [kæn] n (of milk) scatola; (of oil) bidone m; (of water) tanica; (tin) scatola ▶ vt mettere in scatola

can[2]

[kæn] (negative **cannot**, **can't**, conditional and pt **could**) aux vb

1 (be able to) potere; **I can't go any further** non posso andare oltre; **you can do it if you try** sei in grado di farlo — basta provarci; **I'll help you all I can** ti aiuterò come potrò; **I can't see you** non ti vedo

2 (know how to) sapere, essere capace di; **I can swim** so nuotare; **can you speak French?** parla francese?

3 (may) potere; **could I have a word with you?** posso parlarle un momento?

4 (expressing disbelief, puzzlement etc):

it can't be true! non può essere vero!; **what CAN he want?** cosa può mai volere?

5 (*expressing possibility, suggestion etc*): **he could be in the library** può darsi che sia in biblioteca; **she could have been delayed** può aver avuto un contrattempo

Canada [ˈkænədə] n Canada m; **Canadian** [kəˈneɪdɪən] *adj, n* canadese m/f

canal [kəˈnæl] n canale m

canary [kəˈnɛərɪ] n canarino

Canary Islands, Canaries [kəˈnɛərɪz] npl **the ~** le (isole) Canarie

cancel [ˈkænsəl] vt annullare; (*train*) sopprimere; (*cross out*) cancellare; **I want to ~ my booking** vorrei disdire la mia prenotazione; **cancellation** [-ˈleɪʃən] n annullamento; soppressione f; cancellazione f; (*Tourism*) prenotazione f annullata

cancer [ˈkænsə*ʳ*] n cancro

Cancer [ˈkænsə*ʳ*] n (*sign*) Cancro

candidate [ˈkændɪdeɪt] n candidato(-a)

candle [ˈkændl] n candela; (*in church*) cero; **candlestick** n bugia; (*bigger, ornate*) candeliere m

candy [ˈkændɪ] n zucchero candito; (*US*) caramella; caramelle fpl; **candy bar** (*US*) n lungo biscotto, in genere ricoperto di cioccolato; **candyfloss** [ˈkændɪflɒs] n (*BRIT*) zucchero filato

cane [keɪn] n canna; (*for furniture*) bambù m; (*stick*) verga ▸ vt (*BRIT Scol*) punire a colpi di verga

canister [ˈkænɪstə*ʳ*] n scatola metallica

cannabis [ˈkænəbɪs] n canapa indiana

canned [kænd] *adj* (*food*) in scatola

cannon [ˈkænən] (*pl* **cannon** or **cannons**) n (*gun*) cannone m

cannot [ˈkænɒt] = **can not**

canoe [kəˈnuː] n canoa; **canoeing** n

canottaggio

canon [ˈkænən] n (*clergyman*) canonico; (*standard*) canone m

can-opener [ˈkænəupnə*ʳ*] n apriscatole m inv

can't [kænt] = **can not**

canteen [kænˈtiːn] n mensa; (*BRIT: of cutlery*) portaposate m inv

▌ Be careful not to translate **canteen** by the Italian word *cantina*.

canter [ˈkæntə*ʳ*] vi andare al piccolo galoppo

canvas [ˈkænvəs] n tela

canvass [ˈkænvəs] vi (*Pol*): **to ~ for** raccogliere voti per ▸ vt fare un sondaggio di

canyon [ˈkænjən] n canyon m inv

cap [kæp] n (*hat*) berretto; (*of pen*) coperchio; (*of bottle, toy gun*) tappo; (*contraceptive*) diaframma m ▸ vt (*outdo*) superare; (*limit*) fissare un tetto (a)

capability [keɪpəˈbɪlɪtɪ] n capacità f inv, abilità f inv

capable [ˈkeɪpəbl] *adj* capace

capacity [kəˈpæsɪtɪ] n capacità f inv; (*of lift etc*) capienza

cape [keɪp] n (*garment*) cappa; (*Geo*) capo

caper [ˈkeɪpə*ʳ*] n (*Culin*) cappero; (*prank*) scherzetto

capital [ˈkæpɪtl] n (*also: ~ city*) capitale f; (*money*) capitale m; (*also: ~ letter*) (lettera) maiuscola; **capitalism** n capitalismo; **capitalist** *adj, n* capitalista m/f; **capital punishment** n pena capitale

Capitol [ˈkæpɪtl] n **the ~** il Campidoglio

Capricorn [ˈkæprɪkɔːn] n Capricorno

capsize [kæpˈsaɪz] vt capovolgere ▸ vi capovolgersi

capsule [ˈkæpsjuːl] n capsula

captain [ˈkæptɪn] n capitano

caption [ˈkæpʃən] n leggenda

captivity [kæp'tɪvɪtɪ] n cattività

capture ['kæptʃə'] vt catturare; (Comput) registrare ► n cattura; (data) registrazione f per rilevazione f di dati

car [kɑː'] n (Aut) macchina, automobile f; (Rail) vagone m

carafe [kə'ræf] n caraffa

caramel ['kærəməl] n caramello

carat ['kærət] n carato; **18 ~ gold** oro a 18 carati

caravan ['kærəvæn] n (BRIT) roulotte f inv; (of camels) carovana; **caravan site** (BRIT) n campeggio per roulotte

carbohydrate [kɑː'bəu'haɪdreɪt] n carboidrato

carbon ['kɑːbən] n carbonio; **carbon dioxide** [-daɪ'ɒksaɪd] n diossido di carbonio; **carbon monoxide** [-mɔ'nɒksaɪd] n monossido di carbonio

car boot sale n vedi nota nel riquadro

- **car boot sale**
- Il **car boot sale** è un mercatino
- dell'usato molto popolare in Gran
- Bretagna. Normalmente ha luogo
- in un parcheggio o in un grande
- spiazzo, e la merce viene in genere
- esposta nei bagagliai, in inglese
- appunto "boots", aperti delle
- macchine.

carburettor [kɑːbju'rɛtə'] (US **carburetor**) n carburatore m

card [kɑːd] n carta; (visiting card etc) biglietto; (Christmas card etc) cartolina; **cardboard** n cartone m; **card game** n gioco di carte

cardigan ['kɑːdɪgən] n cardigan m inv

cardinal ['kɑːdɪnl] adj cardinale ► n cardinale m

cardphone ['kɑːdfəun] n telefono a scheda

care [kɛə'] n cura, attenzione f; (worry) preoccupazione f ► vi **to ~ about** curarsi di; (thing, idea) interessarsi di; **~ of** presso; **in sb's ~** alle cure di

qn; **to take ~ (to do)** fare attenzione (a fare); **to take ~ of** curarsi di; (bill, problem) occuparsi di; **I don't ~** non me ne importa; **I couldn't ~ less** non m'interessa affatto ▷ **care for** vt fus aver cura di; (like) volere bene a

career [kə'rɪə'] n carriera ► vi (also: **~ along**) andare di (gran) carriera

care: carefree ['kɛəfriː] adj sgombro(-a) di preoccupazioni; **careful** ['kɛəful] adj attento(-a); (cautious) cauto(-a); **(be) careful!** attenzione!; **carefully** adv con cura; cautamente; **caregiver** (US) n (professional) assistente m/f; (unpaid) persona che si prende cura di un parente malato o anziano; **careless** ['kɛəlɪs] adj negligente; (heedless) spensierato(-a); **carelessness** n negligenza; mancanza di tatto; **carer** ['kɛərə'] n assistente m/f (di persone malata o handicappata); **caretaker** ['kɛəteɪkə'] n custode m

car-ferry ['kɑːfɛrɪ] n traghetto

cargo ['kɑːgəu] (pl **cargoes**) n carico

car hire n autonoleggio

Caribbean [kærɪ'biːən] adj **the ~ Sea** il Mar dei Caraibi

caring ['kɛərɪŋ] adj (person) premuroso(-a); (society, organization) umanitario(-a)

carnation [kɑː'neɪʃən] n garofano

carnival ['kɑːnɪvəl] n (public celebration) carnevale m; (US: funfair) luna park m inv

carol ['kærəl] n **Christmas ~** canto di Natale

carousel [kærə'sɛl] (US) n giostra

car park (BRIT) n parcheggio

carpenter ['kɑːpɪntə'] n carpentiere m

carpet ['kɑːpɪt] n tappeto ► vt coprire con tappeto

car rental (US) n autonoleggio

carriage ['kærɪdʒ] n vettura; (of goods) trasporto; **carriageway** (BRIT) n (part of road) carreggiata

carrier ['kærɪə*] n (of disease) portatore(-trice); (Comm) impresa di trasporti; **carrier bag** (BRIT) n sacchetto

carrot ['kærət] n carota

carry ['kærɪ] vt (person) portare; (: vehicle) trasportare; (involve: responsibilities etc) comportare; (Med) essere portatore(-trice) di ▶ vi (sound) farsi sentire; **to be** or **get carried away** (fig) entusiasmarsi ▷ **carry on** vi **to ~ on with sth/doing** continuare qc/a fare ▶ vt mandare avanti ▷ **carry out** vt (orders) eseguire; (investigation) svolgere

cart [kɑːt] n carro ▶ vt (inf) trascinare

carton ['kɑːtən] n (box) scatola di cartone; (of yogurt) cartone m; (of cigarettes) stecca

cartoon [kɑːˈtuːn] n (Press) disegno umoristico; (comic strip) fumetto; (Cinema) disegno animato

cartridge ['kɑːtrɪdʒ] n (for gun, pen) cartuccia; (music tape) cassetta

carve [kɑːv] vt (meat) trinciare; (wood, stone) intagliare; **carving** n (in wood etc) scultura

car wash n lavaggio auto

case [keɪs] n (gen); (Law) causa, processo; (box) scatola; (BRIT: also: **suit~**) valigia; **in ~** of in caso di; **in ~ he** caso mai lui; **in any ~** in ogni caso; **just in ~** in caso di bisogno

cash [kæʃ] n denaro; (coins, notes) denaro liquido ▶ vt incassare; **I haven't got any ~** non ho contanti; **to pay (in) ~** pagare in contanti; **~ on delivery** pagamento alla consegna; **cashback** n (discount) sconto; (at supermarket etc) anticipo di contanti ottenuto presso la cassa di un negozio tramite una carta di debito; **cash card** (BRIT) n tesserino di prelievo; **cash desk** (BRIT) n cassa; **cash dispenser**

(BRIT) n sportello automatico

cashew [kæˈʃuː] n (also: ~ **nut**) anacardio

cashier [kæˈʃɪə*] n cassiere(-a)

cashmere ['kæʃmɪə*] n cachemire m

cash point n sportello bancario automatico, Bancomat® m inv

cash register n registratore m di cassa

casino [kəˈsiːnəu] n casinò m inv

casket ['kɑːskɪt] n cofanetto; (US: coffin) bara

casserole ['kæsərəul] n casseruola; (food): **chicken ~** pollo in casseruola

cassette [kæˈsɛt] n cassetta; **cassette player** n riproduttore m a cassette

cast [kɑːst] (pt, pp **cast**) vt (throw) gettare; (metal) gettare, fondere; (Theatre): **to ~ sb as Hamlet** scegliere qn per la parte di Amleto ▶ n (Theatre) cast m inv; (also: **plaster ~**) ingessatura; **to ~ one's vote** votare, dare il voto ▷ **cast off** vi (Naut) salpare; (Knitting) calare

castanets [kæstəˈnɛts] npl castagnette fpl

caster sugar ['kɑːstə*-] (BRIT) n zucchero semolato

cast-iron ['kɑːstaɪən] adj (lit) di ghisa; (fig: case) di ferro

castle ['kɑːsl] n castello

casual ['kæʒjul] adj (chance) casuale, fortuito(-a); (: work etc) avventizio(-a); (unconcerned) noncurante, indifferente; **~ wear** casual m

casualty ['kæʒjultɪ] n ferito(-a); (dead) morto(-a), vittima; (Med: department) pronto soccorso

cat [kæt] n gatto

catalogue ['kætəlɔg] (US **catalog**) n catalogo ▶ vt catalogare

catalytic converter [kætəlɪtɪk-] n marmitta catalitica, catalizzatore m

cataract ['kætərækt] n (also Med) cateratta

catarrh [kə'ta:ʳ] n catarro

catastrophe [kə'tæstrəfɪ] n catastrofe f

catch [kætʃ] (pt, pp caught) vt prendere; (ball) afferrare; (surprise: person) sorprendere; (attention) attirare; (comment, whisper) cogliere; (person) raggiungere ▶ vi (fire) prendere ▶ n (fish etc caught) retata; (of ball) presa; (trick) inganno; (Tech) gancio; (game) catch m inv; **to ~ fire** prendere fuoco; **to ~ sight of** scorgere ▷ **catch up** vi mettersi in pari ▶ vt (also: ~ up with) raggiungere; **catching** ['kætʃɪŋ] adj (Med) contagioso(-a)

category ['kætɪɡərɪ] n categoria

cater ['keɪtəʳ] vi: **~ for** (BRIT: needs) provvedere a; (: readers, consumers) incontrare i gusti di; (Comm: provide food) provvedere alla ristorazione di

caterpillar ['kætəpɪləʳ] n bruco

cathedral [kə'θi:drəl] n cattedrale f, duomo

Catholic ['kæθəlɪk] adj, n (Rel) cattolico(-a)

Catseye® ['kæts'aɪ] (BRIT) n (Aut) catarifrangente m

cattle ['kætl] npl bestiame m, bestie fpl

catwalk ['kætwɔ:k] n passerella

caught [kɔ:t] pt, pp of **catch**

cauliflower ['kɔlɪflauəʳ] n cavolfiore m

cause [kɔ:z] n causa ▶ vt causare

caution ['kɔ:ʃən] n prudenza; (warning) avvertimento ▶ vt avvertire; ammonire; **cautious** ['kɔ:ʃəs] adj cauto(-a), prudente

cave [keɪv] n caverna, grotta ▷ **cave in** vi (roof etc) crollare

caviar(e) ['kævɪa:ʳ] n caviale m

cavity ['kævɪtɪ] n cavità f inv

cc abbr = **cubic centimetres; carbon copy**

CCTV n abbr (= closed-circuit television) televisione f a circuito chiuso

CD abbr (disc) CD m inv; (player) lettore m CD inv; **CD player** n lettore m CD; **CD-ROM** [-rɔm] n abbr CD-ROM m inv

cease [si:s] vt, vi cessare; **ceasefire** n cessate il fuoco m inv

cedar ['si:dəʳ] n cedro

ceilidh ['keɪlɪ] n festa con musiche e danze popolari scozzesi o irlandesi

ceiling ['si:lɪŋ] n soffitto; (on wages etc) tetto

celebrate ['sɛlɪbreɪt] vt, vi celebrare; **celebration** [-'breɪʃən] n celebrazione f

celebrity [sɪ'lɛbrɪtɪ] n celebrità f inv

celery ['sɛlərɪ] n sedano

cell [sɛl] n cella; (of revolutionaries, Biol) cellula; (Elec) elemento (di batteria)

cellar ['sɛləʳ] n sottosuolo; cantina

cello ['tʃɛləu] n violoncello

Cellophane® ['sɛləfeɪn] n cellophane® m

cellphone ['sɛləfeɪn] n cellulare m

Celsius ['sɛlsɪəs] adj Celsius inv

Celtic ['kɛltɪk, 'sɛltɪk] adj celtico(-a)

cement [sə'mɛnt] n cemento

cemetery ['sɛmɪtrɪ] n cimitero

censor ['sɛnsəʳ] n censore m ▶ vt censurare; **censorship** n censura

census ['sɛnsəs] n censimento

cent [sɛnt] n (US: coin) centesimo (=1:100 di un dollaro); (unit of euro) centesimo; see also **per**

centenary [sɛn'ti:nərɪ] n centenario

centennial [sɛn'tɛnɪəl] (US) n centenario

center ['sɛntəʳ] (US) n, vt = **centre**

centi... [sɛntɪ] prefix: **centigrade** ['sɛntɪɡreɪd] adj centigrado(-a); **centimetre** ['sɛntɪmi:təʳ] (US **centimeter**) n centimetro; **centipede** ['sɛntɪpi:d] n centopiedi m inv

central ['sɛntrəl] adj centrale; **Central**

America n America centrale; **central heating** n riscaldamento centrale; **central reservation** n (BRITAut) banchina f spartitraffico inv

centre ['sɛntə'] (US **center**) n centro ▶ vt centrare; **centre-forward** n (Sport) centroavanti m; **centre-half** n (Sport) centromediano

century ['sɛntjʊrɪ] n secolo; **twentieth ~** ventesimo secolo

CEO n abbr = **chief executive officer**

ceramic [sɪ'ræmɪk] adj ceramico(-a)

cereal ['si:rɪəl] n cereale m

ceremony ['sɛrɪmənɪ] n cerimonia; **to stand on ~** fare complimenti

certain ['sə:tən] adj certo(-a); **to make ~ of** assicurarsi di; **for ~** per certo, di sicuro; **certainly** adv certamente, certo; **certainty** n certezza

certificate [sə'tɪfɪkɪt] n certificato; diploma m

certify ['sə:tɪfaɪ] vt certificare; (award diploma to) conferire un diploma a; (declare insane) dichiarare pazzo(-a)

cf. abbr (= compare) cfr

CFC n (= chlorofluorocarbon) CFC m inv

chain [tʃeɪn] n catena ▶ vt (also: ~ up) incatenare; **chain-smoke** vi fumare una sigaretta dopo l'altra

chair [tʃɛə'] n sedia; (armchair) poltrona; (of university) cattedra; (of meeting) presidenza ▶ vt (meeting) presiedere; **chairlift** n seggiovia; **chairman** (irreg) n presidente m; **chairperson** n presidente(-essa); **chairwoman** (irreg) n presidentessa

chalet ['ʃæleɪ] n chalet m inv

chalk [tʃɔ:k] n gesso; **chalkboard** (US) n lavagna

challenge ['tʃælɪndʒ] n sfida ▶ vt sfidare; (statement, right) mettere in dubbio; **to ~ sb to do** sfidare qn a fare; **challenging** adj (task) impegnativo(-a); (look) di sfida

chamber ['tʃeɪmbə'] n camera;

chambermaid n cameriera

champagne [ʃæm'peɪn] n champagne m inv

champion ['tʃæmpɪən] n campione(-essa); **championship** n campionato

chance [tʃɑ:ns] n caso; (opportunity) occasione f; (likelihood) possibilità f inv ▶ vt **to ~ it** rischiare, provarci ▶ adj fortuito(-a); **to take a ~** rischiare; **by ~** per caso

chancellor ['tʃɑ:nsələ'] n cancelliere m; **Chancellor of the Exchequer** [-ɪks'tʃɛkə'] (BRIT) n Cancelliere dello Scacchiere

chandelier [ʃændə'lɪə'] n lampadario

change [tʃeɪndʒ] vt cambiare; (transform): **to ~ sb into** trasformare qn in ▶ vi cambiare; (change one's clothes) cambiarsi; (be transformed): **to ~ into** trasformarsi in ▶ n cambiamento; (of clothes) cambio; (money returned) resto; (coins) spiccioli; **where can I ~ some money?** dove posso cambiare dei soldi?; **to ~ one's mind** cambiare idea; **keep the ~!** tenga pure il resto!; **sorry, I don't have any ~** mi dispiace, non ho spiccioli; **for a ~** tanto per cambiare ▶ **change over** vi (from sth to sth) passare; (players etc) scambiarsi (di posto o di campo) ▶ vi cambiare; **changeable** adj (weather) variabile; **change machine** n distributore automatico di monete; **changing room** n (BRIT: in shop) camerino; (: Sport) spogliatoio

channel ['tʃænl] n canale m; (of river, sea) alveo ▶ vt canalizzare; **Channel Tunnel** n the Channel Tunnel il tunnel sotto la Manica

chant [tʃɑ:nt] n canto; salmodia ▶ vt cantare; salmodiare

chaos ['keɪɒs] n caos m

chaotic [keɪ'ɒtɪk] adj caotico(-a)

chap [tʃæp] (BRIT: inf) n (man) tipo

chapel ['tʃæpəl] n cappella

chapped [tʃæpt] adj (skin, lips) screpolato(-a)

chapter ['tʃæptə'] n capitolo

character ['kærɪktə'] n carattere m; (in novel, film) personaggio;
characteristic [-'rɪstɪk] adj caratteristico(-a) ▶ n caratteristica;
characterize ['kærɪktəraɪz] vt caratterizzare; (describe): to characterize (as) descrivere (come)

charcoal ['tʃɑːkəul] n carbone m di legna

charge [tʃɑːdʒ] n accusa; (cost) prezzo; (responsibility) responsabilità ▶ vt (gun, battery, Mil: enemy) caricare; (customer) fare pagare a; (sum) fare pagare; (Law): to ~ sb (with) accusare qn (di) ▶ vi (gen with: up, along etc) lanciarsi; charge card n carta f clienti inv; charger n (also: battery charger) caricabatterie m inv; (old: warhorse) destriero

charismatic [kærɪz'mætɪk] adj carismatico(-a)

charity ['tʃærɪtɪ] n carità; (organization) opera pia; charity shop n (BRIT) negozi che vendono articoli di seconda mano e devolvono il ricavato in beneficenza

charm [tʃɑːm] n fascino; (on bracelet) ciondolo ▶ vt affascinare, incantare; charming adj affascinante

chart [tʃɑːt] n tabella; grafico; (map) carta nautica ▶ vt fare una carta nautica di; ~s npl (Mus) hit parade f

charter ['tʃɑːtə'] vt (plane) noleggiare ▶ n (document) carta; chartered accountant ['tʃɑːtəd-] (BRIT) n ragioniere(-a) professionista; charter flight n volo m charter inv

chase [tʃeɪs] vt inseguire; (also: ~ away) cacciare ▶ n caccia

chat [tʃæt] vi (also: have a ~) chiacchierare ▶ n chiacchierata

▷ chat up vt (BRIT inf: girl) abbordare;

chat room n (Internet) chat room f inv;
chat show (BRIT) n talk show m inv

chatter ['tʃætə'] vi (person) ciarlare; (bird) cinguettare; (teeth) battere ▶ n ciarle fpl; cinguettio

chauffeur ['ʃəufə'] n autista m

chauvinist ['ʃəuvɪnɪst] n (male chauvinist) maschilista m; (nationalist) sciovinista m/f

cheap [tʃiːp] adj economico(-a); (joke) grossolano(-a); (poor quality) di cattiva qualità ▶ adv a buon mercato; can you recommend a ~ hotel/restaurant, please? potrebbe indicarmi un albergo/ristorante non troppo caro?; cheap day return n biglietto ridotto di andata e ritorno valido in giornata; cheaply adv a buon prezzo, a buon mercato

cheat [tʃiːt] vi imbrogliare; (at school) copiare ▶ vt ingannare ▶ n imbroglione m; to ~ sb out of sth defraudare qn di qc ▷ cheat on vt fus (husband, wife) tradire

Chechnya [tʃɪtʃ'njɑː] n Cecenia

check [tʃɛk] vt verificare; (passport, ticket) controllare; (halt) fermare; (restrain) contenere ▶ n verifica; controllo; (curb) freno; (US: bill) conto; (pattern: gen pl) quadretti mpl; (US) = cheque ▶ adj (pattern, cloth) a quadretti ▷ check in vi (in hotel) registrare; (at airport) presentarsi all'accettazione ▶ vt (luggage) depositare ▷ check off vt segnare ▷ check out vi (in hotel) saldare il conto ▷ check up vi to ~ up (on sth) investigare (qc); to ~ up on sb informarsi sul conto di qn; checkbook (US) n = chequebook; checked adj a quadretti; checkers (US) n dama; check-in n (also: check-in desk: at airport) check-in m inv; check-ing n accettazione f (bagagli inv);

account (US) n conto corrente;
checklist n lista di controllo;
checkmate n scaccomatto;
checkout (in supermarket) cassa;
checkpoint n posto di blocco;
checkroom (US) n deposito m bagagli
inv; **checkup** n (Med) controllo medico

cheddar ['tʃedə'] n formaggio duro di
latte di mucca di colore bianco o arancione

cheek [tʃi:k] n guancia; (impudence)
faccia tosta; **cheekbone** n zigomo;
cheeky adj sfacciato(-a)

cheer [tʃɪə'] vt applaudire; (gladden)
rallegrare ▸ vi applaudire ▸ n grido
(di incoraggiamento); **cheer up** vi
rallegrarsi, farsi animo ▸ vt rallegrare;
cheerful adj allegro(-a)

cheerio ['tʃɪərɪ'əu] excl ciao!

cheerleader ['tʃɪəli:də'] n cheerleader
f inv

cheese [tʃi:z] n formaggio;
cheeseburger n cheeseburger m inv;
cheesecake n specie di torta di ricotta, a
volte con frutta

chef [ʃef] n capocuoco

chemical ['kemɪkəl] adj chimico(-a)
▸ n prodotto chimico

chemist ['kemɪst] n (BRIT: pharmacist)
farmacista m/f; (scientist) chimico(-a);
chemistry n chimica; **chemist's
(shop)** (BRIT) n farmacia

cheque [tʃek] (US **check**) n assegno;
chequebook n libretto degli assegni;
cheque card n carta f assegni inv

cherry ['tʃerɪ] n ciliegia; (also: ~ **tree**)
ciliegio

chess [tʃes] n scacchi mpl

chest [tʃest] n petto; (box) cassa

chestnut ['tʃesnʌt] n castagna; (also: ~
tree) castagno

chest of drawers n cassettone m

chew [tʃu:] vt masticare; **chewing
gum** n chewing gum m

chic [ʃi:k] adj elegante

chick [tʃɪk] n pulcino; (inf) pollastrella

chicken ['tʃɪkɪn] n pollo; (inf: coward)
coniglio ▸ **chicken out** (inf) vi avere
fifa; **chickenpox** n varicella

chickpea ['tʃɪkpi:] n cece m

chief [tʃi:f] n capo ▸ adj principale;
chief executive (officer) n direttore
m generale; **chiefly** adv per lo più,
soprattutto

child [tʃaɪld] (pl **children**) n
bambino(-a); **child abuse** n molestie
fpl a minori; **child benefit** n (BRIT)
= assegni mpl familiari; **childbirth**
n parto; **child-care** n il badare ai
bambini; **childhood** n infanzia;
childish adj puerile; **child minder**
[-'maɪndə'] n (BRIT) bambinaia;
children ['tʃɪldrən] npl of **child**

Chile ['tʃɪlɪ] n Cile m

Chilean ['tʃɪlɪən] adj, n cileno(-a)

chill [tʃɪl] n freddo; (Med) infreddatura
▸ vt raffreddare ▷ **chill out** (esp US) vi
(inf) darsi una calmata

chil(l)i ['tʃɪlɪ] n peperoncino

chilly ['tʃɪlɪ] adj freddo(-a), fresco(-a);
to feel ~ sentirsi infreddolito(-a)

chimney ['tʃɪmnɪ] n camino

chimpanzee [tʃɪmpæn'zi:] n
scimpanzé m inv

chin [tʃɪn] n mento

China ['tʃaɪnə] n Cina

china ['tʃaɪnə] n porcellana

Chinese [tʃaɪ'ni:z] adj cinese ▸ n inv
cinese m/f; (Ling) cinese m

chip [tʃɪp] n (gen pl: Culin) patatina
fritta; (: US: also: **potato** ~) patatina;
(of wood, glass, stone) scheggia; (also:
micro~) chip m inv ▸ vt (cup, plate)
scheggiare; **chip shop** n (BRIT) vedi
nota nel riquadro

● **chip shop**
● I **chip shops**, anche chiamati "fish
  and chip shops", sono friggitorie che
  vendono principalmente filetti di
  pesce impanati e patatine fritte.

chiropodist [kɪ'rɔpədɪst] (BRIT) n

pedicure m/f inv
chisel ['tʃɪzl] n cesello
chives [tʃaɪvz] npl erba cipollina
chlorine ['klɔ:ri:n] n cloro
choc-ice ['tʃɒkaɪs] n (BRIT) gelato ricoperto al cioccolato
chocolate ['tʃɒklɪt] ▶ n (substance) cioccolato, cioccolata; (drink) cioccolata; (a sweet) cioccolatino
choice [tʃɔɪs] n scelta ▶ adj scelto(-a)
choir ['kwaɪə'] n coro
choke [tʃəuk] vi soffocare ▶ vt soffocare; (block): to be ~d with essere intasato(-a) di ▶ n (Aut) valvola dell'aria
cholesterol [kə'lɛstərɔl] n colesterolo
choose [tʃu:z] (pt **chose**,, pp **chosen**) vt scegliere; **to ~ to do** decidere di fare; preferire fare
chop [tʃɒp] vt (wood) spaccare; (Culin: also: ~ **up**) tritare ▶ n (Culin) costoletta
  ▷ **chop down** vt (tree) abbattere
  ▷ **chop off** vt tagliare; **chopsticks** ['tʃɒpstɪks] npl bastoncini mpl cinesi
chord [kɔ:d] n (Mus) accordo
chore [tʃɔ:'] n faccenda; **household ~s** faccende fpl domestiche
chorus ['kɔ:rəs] n coro; (repeated part of song: also fig) ritornello
chose [tʃəuz] pt of **choose**
chosen ['tʃəuzn] pp of **choose**
Christ [kraɪst] n Cristo
christen ['krɪsn] vt battezzare; **christening** n battesimo
Christian ['krɪstɪən] adj, n cristiano(-a); **Christianity** [-'ænɪtɪ] n cristianesimo; **Christian name** n nome m (di battesimo)
Christmas ['krɪsməs] n Natale m; **Merry ~!** Buon Natale!; **Christmas card** n cartolina di Natale; **Christmas carol** n canto natalizio; **Christmas Day** n il giorno di Natale; **Christmas Eve** n la vigilia di Natale; **Christmas pudding** n (esp BRIT) specie di budino

con frutta secca, spezie e brandy;
Christmas tree n albero di Natale
chrome [krəum] n cromo
chronic ['krɒnɪk] adj cronico(-a)
chrysanthemum [krɪ'sænθəməm] n crisantemo
chubby ['tʃʌbɪ] adj paffuto(-a)
chuck [tʃʌk] (inf) vt buttare, gettare; (BRIT: also: ~ **up**) piantare ▶ **chuck out** vt buttar fuori
chuckle ['tʃʌkl] vi ridere sommessamente
chum [tʃʌm] n compagno(-a)
chunk [tʃʌŋk] n pezzo
church [tʃə:tʃ] n chiesa; **churchyard** n sagrato
churn [tʃə:n] n (for butter) zangola; (for milk) bidone m
chute [ʃu:t] n (also: **rubbish ~**) canale m di scarico; (BRIT: children's slide) scivolo
chutney ['tʃʌtnɪ] n salsa piccante (di frutta, zucchero e spezie)
CIA (US) n abbr (= Central Intelligence Agency) CIA f
CID (BRIT) n abbr (= Criminal Investigation Department) ≈ polizia giudiziaria
cider ['saɪdə'] n sidro
cigar [sɪ'ga:'] n sigaro
cigarette [sɪgə'rɛt] n sigaretta; **cigarette lighter** n accendino
cinema ['sɪnəmə] n cinema m inv
cinnamon ['sɪnəmən] n cannella
circle ['sə:kl] n cerchio; (of friends etc) circolo; (in cinema) galleria ▶ vi girare in circolo ▶ vt (surround) circondare; (move round) girare intorno a
circuit ['sə:kɪt] n circuito
circular ['sə:kjulə'] adj circolare ▶ n circolare f
circulate ['sə:kjuleɪt] vi circolare ▶ vt far circolare; **circulation** [-'leɪʃən] n circolazione f; (of newspaper) tiratura
circumstances ['sə:kəmstənsiz] npl

circostanze *fpl*; (*financial condition*) condizioni *fpl* finanziarie

circus ['sə:kəs] *n* circo

cite [saɪt] *vt* citare

citizen ['sɪtɪzn] *n* (*of country*) cittadino(-a); (*of town*) abitante *m/f*; **citizenship** *n* cittadinanza

citrus fruits ['sɪtrəs] *npl* agrumi *mpl*

city ['sɪtɪ] *n* città *f inv*; **the C~** la Città di Londra (*centro commerciale*); **city centre** *n* centro della città; **city technology college** *n* (BRIT) istituto tecnico superiore (*finanziato dall'industria*)

civic ['sɪvɪk] *adj* civico(-a)

civil ['sɪvɪl] *adj* civile; **civilian** [sɪ'vɪlɪən] *adj, n* borghese *m/f*

civilization [sɪvɪlaɪ'zeɪʃən] *n* civiltà *f inv*

civilized ['sɪvɪlaɪzd] *adj* civilizzato(-a); (*fig*) cortese

civil: **civil law** *n* codice *m*, civile; (*study*) diritto civile; **civil rights** *npl* diritti *mpl* civili; **civil servant** *n* impiegato(-a) statale; **Civil Service** *n* amministrazione *f* statale; **civil war** *n* guerra civile

CJD *abbr* (= Creutzfeld Jacob disease) malattia di Creutzfeldt-Jacob

claim [kleɪm] *vt* (*assert*): **to ~ (that)/to be** sostenere (che)/di essere; (*credit, rights etc*) rivendicare; (*damages*) richiedere ▸ *vi* (*for insurance*) fare una domanda d'indennizzo ▸ *n* pretesa; rivendicazione *f*; richiesta; **claim form** *n* (*gen*) modulo di richiesta; (*for expenses*) modulo di rimborso spese

clam [klæm] *n* vongola

clamp [klæmp] *n* pinza, morsa ▸ *vt* stringere con una morsa; (*Aut: wheel*) applicare i ceppi bloccaruote a

clan [klæn] *n* clan *m inv*

clap [klæp] *vi* applaudire

claret ['klærət] *n* vino di Bordeaux

clarify ['klærɪfaɪ] *vt* chiarificare,

chiarire

clarinet [klærɪ'nɛt] *n* clarinetto

clarity ['klærɪtɪ] *n* clarità *f*

clash [klæʃ] *n* frastuono; (*fig*) scontro ▸ *vi* scontrarsi; cozzare

clasp [klɑːsp] *n* (*hold*) stretta; (*of necklace, bag*) fermaglio, fibbia ▸ *vt* stringere

class [klɑːs] *n* classe *f* ▸ *vt* classificare

classic ['klæsɪk] *adj* classico(-a) ▸ *n* classico; **classical** *adj* classico(-a)

classification [klæsɪfɪ'keɪʃən] *n* classificazione *f*

classify ['klæsɪfaɪ] *vt* classificare

classmate ['klɑːsmeɪt] *n* compagno(-a) di classe

classroom ['klɑːsrum] *n* aula

classy ['klɑːsɪ] *adj* (*inf*) chic *inv*, elegante

clatter ['klætə*] *n* tintinnio; scalpitio ▸ *vi* tintinnare; scalpitare

clause [klɔːz] *n* clausola; (*Ling*) proposizione *f*

claustrophobic [klɔːstrə'fəʊbɪk] *adj* claustrofobico(-a)

claw [klɔː] *n* (*of bird of prey*) artiglio; (*of lobster*) pinza

clay [kleɪ] *n* argilla

clean [kliːn] *adj* pulito(-a); (*clear, smooth*) liscio(-a) ▸ *vt* pulire ▸ **clean up** *vt* (*also fig*) ripulire; **cleaner** *n* (*person*) donna delle pulizie; **cleaner's** *n* (*also: dry cleaner's*) tintoria; **cleaning** *n* pulizia

cleanser ['klɛnzə*] *n* detergente *m*

clear [klɪə*] *adj* chiaro(-a); (*glass etc*) trasparente; (*road, way*) libero(-a); (*conscience*) pulito(-a) ▸ *vt* sgombrare; liberare; (*table*) sparecchiare; (*cheque*) fare la compensazione di; (*Law: suspect*) discolpare; (*obstacle*) superare ▸ *vi* (*weather*) rasserenarsi; (*fog*) andarsene ▸ *adv* ~ distante da ▸ **clear away** *vt* (*things, clothes etc*) mettere a posto; **to ~ away the**

dishes sparecchiare la tavola ▷ **clear up** vt mettere in ordine; (mystery) risolvere; **clearance** n (removal) sgombro; (permission) autorizzazione f, permesso; **clear-cut** adj ben delineato(-a), distinto(-a); **clearing** n radura; **clearly** adv chiaramente; **clearway** (BRIT) n strada con divieto di sosta

clench [klɛntʃ] vt stringere

clergy ['klɜːdʒɪ] n clero

clerk [klɑːk, (US) klɜːrk] n (BRIT) impiegato(-a); (US) commesso(-a)

clever ['klɛvə²] adj (mentally) intelligente; (deft, skilful) abile; (device, arrangement) ingegnoso(-a)

cliché ['kliːʃeɪ] n cliché m inv

click [klɪk] vi scattare ▶ vt (heels etc) battere; (tongue) far schioccare

client ['klaɪənt] n cliente m/f

cliff [klɪf] n scogliera scoscesa, rupe f

climate ['klaɪmɪt] n clima m

climax ['klaɪmæks] n culmine m; (sexual) orgasmo

climb [klaɪm] vi salire; (clamber) arrampicarsi ▶ vt salire; (Climbing) scalare ▶ n salita; arrampicata; scalata ▷ **climb down** vi scendere; (BRIT fig) far marcia indietro; **climber** n rocciatore(-trice); alpinista m/f; **climbing** n alpinismo

clinch [klɪntʃ] vt (deal) concludere

cling [klɪŋ] (pt, pp clung) vi to ~ (to) aggrapparsi (a); (of clothes) aderire strettamente a

Clingfilm® ['klɪŋfɪlm] n pellicola trasparente (per alimenti)

clinic ['klɪnɪk] n clinica

clip [klɪp] n (for hair) forcina; (also: **paper** ~) graffetta; (TV, Cinema) sequenza ▶ vt attaccare insieme; (hair, nails) tagliare; (hedge) tosare; **clipping** n (from newspaper) ritaglio

cloak [kləʊk] n mantello ▶ vt avvolgere; **cloakroom** n (for coats

etc) guardaroba m inv; (BRIT: W.C.) gabinetti mpl

clock [klɒk] n orologio ▷ **clock in** or **on** vi timbrare il cartellino (all'entrata) ▷ **clock off** or **out** vi timbrare il cartellino (all'uscita); **clockwise** adv in senso orario; **clockwork** n movimento or meccanismo a orologeria ▶ adj a molla

clog [klɒg] n zoccolo ▶ vt intasare ▶ vi (also: ~ **up**) intasarsi, bloccarsi

clone [kləʊn] n clone m

close¹ [kləʊs] adj ~ **(to)** vicino(-a); (watch, link, relative) stretto(-a); (examination) attento(-a); (contest) combattuto(-a); (weather) afoso(-a) ▶ adv vicino, dappresso; ~ **to** vicino a; ~ **by, ~ at hand** a pochi passi; **a ~ friend** un amico intimo; **to have a ~ shave** (fig) scamparla bella

close² [kləʊz] vt chiudere ▶ vi (shop etc) chiudere; (lid, door etc) chiudersi; (end) finire ▶ n (end) fine f; **what time do you ~?** a che ora chiudete? ▷ **close down** vi cessare (definitivamente); **closed** adj chiuso(-a)

closely ['kləʊslɪ] adv (examine, watch) da vicino; (related) strettamente

closet ['klɒzɪt] n (cupboard) armadio

close-up ['kləʊsʌp] n primo piano

closing time n orario di chiusura

closure ['kləʊʒə²] n chiusura

clot [klɒt] n (also: **blood** ~) coagulo; (inf: idiot) scemo(-a) ▶ vi coagularsi

cloth [klɒθ] n (material) tessuto, stoffa; (rag) strofinaccio

clothes [kləʊðz] npl abiti mpl, vestiti mpl; **clothes line** n corda (per stendere il bucato); **clothes peg** (US **clothes pin**) n molletta

clothing ['kləʊðɪŋ] n = **clothes**

cloud [klaʊd] n nuvola ▷ **cloud over** vi rannuvolarsi; (fig) offuscarsi; **cloudy** adj nuvoloso(-a); (liquid) torbido(-a)

clove [kləʊv] n chiodo di garofano;

clove of garlic n spicchio d'aglio
clown [klaʊn] n pagliaccio ▶ vi (also: ~
about, ~ around) fare il pagliaccio
club [klʌb] n (society) club m inv,
circolo; (weapon, Golf) mazza
▶ vt bastonare ▶ vi to ~ together
associarsi; ~s npl (Cards) fiori mpl;
club class n (Aviat) classe f club inv
clue [kluː] n indizio; (in crosswords)
definizione f; **I haven't a** ~ non ho la
minima idea
clump [klʌmp] n (of flowers, trees)
gruppo; (of grass) ciuffo
clumsy ['klʌmzɪ] adj goffo(-a)
clung [klʌŋ] pt, pp of **cling**
cluster ['klʌstə] n gruppo ▶ vi
raggrupparsi
clutch [klʌtʃ] n (grip, grasp) presa,
stretta; (Aut) frizione f ▶ vt afferrare,
stringere forte
cm abbr (= centimetre) cm
Co. abbr = **county**; **company**
c/o abbr (= care of) presso
coach [kəʊtʃ] n (bus) pullman m
inv; (horse-drawn, of train) carrozza;
(Sport) allenatore(-trice); (tutor) chi
dà ripetizioni a ▶ vt allenare; dare
ripetizioni a; **coach station** (BRIT)
n stazione f delle corriere; **coach trip** n
viaggio in pullman
coal [kəʊl] n carbone m
coalition [kəʊə'lɪʃən] n coalizione f
coarse [kɔːs] adj (salt, sand etc)
grosso(-a); (cloth, person) rozzo(-a)
coast [kəʊst] n costa ▶ vi (with cycle etc)
scendere a ruota libera; **coastal** adj
costiero(-a); **coastguard** n guardia
costiera; **coastline** n linea costiera
coat [kəʊt] n cappotto; (of animal)
pelo; (of paint) mano f ▶ vt coprire;
coat hanger n attaccapanni m inv; **a**
coating n rivestimento
coax [kəʊks] vt indurre (con moine)
cob [kɔb] n see **corn**
cobbled ['kɔbld] adj ~ **street** strada

pavimentata a ciottoli
cobweb ['kɔbwɛb] n ragnatela
cocaine [kə'keɪn] n cocaina
cock [kɔk] n (rooster) gallo; (male bird)
maschio ▶ vt (gun) armare; **cockerel**
n galletto
cockney ['kɔknɪ] n cockney m/f inv
(abitante dei quartieri popolari dell'East
End di Londra)
cockpit ['kɔkpɪt] n abitacolo
cockroach ['kɔkrəʊtʃ] n blatta
cocktail ['kɔkteɪl] n cocktail m inv
cocoa ['kəʊkəʊ] n cacao
coconut ['kəʊkənʌt] n noce f di cocco
cod [kɔd] n merluzzo
C.O.D. abbr = **cash on delivery**
code [kəʊd] n codice m
coeducational ['kəʊɛdjuː'keɪʃənl]
adj misto(-a)
coffee ['kɔfɪ] n caffè m inv; **coffee bar**
(BRIT) n caffè m inv; **coffee bean** n
grano or chicco di caffè; **coffee break**
n pausa per il caffè; **coffee maker** n
bollitore m per il caffè; **coffeepot** n
caffettiera; **coffee shop** n = caffè m
inv; **coffee table** n tavolino
coffin ['kɔfɪn] n bara
cog [kɔg] n dente m
cognac ['kɔnjæk] n cognac m inv
coherent [kəʊ'hɪərənt] adj coerente
coil [kɔɪl] n rotolo; (Elec) bobina;
(contraceptive) spirale f ▶ vt avvolgere
coin [kɔɪn] n moneta ▶ vt (word)
coniare
coincide [kəʊɪn'saɪd] vi coincidere;
coincidence [kəʊ'ɪnsɪdəns] n
combinazione f
Coke® [kəʊk] n coca
coke [kəʊk] n coke m
colander ['kɔləndə] n colino
cold [kəʊld] adj freddo(-a) ▶ n freddo;
(Med) raffreddore m; **it's** ~ fa freddo;
to be ~ (person) aver freddo; (object)
essere freddo(-a); **to catch** ~ prendere
freddo; **to catch a** ~ prendere un

raffreddore; **in ~ blood** a sangue freddo; **cold sore** n erpete m

coleslaw ['kəʊlslɔː] n insalata di cavolo bianco

colic ['kɒlɪk] n colica

collaborate [kə'læbəreɪt] vi collaborare

collapse [kə'læps] vi crollare ► n crollo; (Med) collasso

collar ['kɒlər] n (of coat, shirt) colletto; (of dog, cat) collare m; **collarbone** n clavicola

colleague ['kɒliːɡ] n collega m/f

collect [kə'lekt] vt (gen) raccogliere; (as a hobby) fare collezione di; (BRIT: call and pick up) prendere; (money owed, pension) riscuotere; (donations, subscriptions) fare una colletta di ► vi adunarsi, riunirsi, ammucchiarsi; **to call ~** (US Tel) fare una chiamata a carico del destinatario; **collection** [kə'lekʃən] n raccolta; collezione f; (for money) colletta; **collective** adj collettivo(-a) ► n collettivo; **collector** [kə'lektər] n collezionista m/f

college ['kɒlɪdʒ] n college m inv; (of technology etc) istituto superiore

collide [kə'laɪd] vi **to ~ with** scontrarsi (con)

collision [kə'lɪʒən] n collisione f, scontro

cologne [kə'ləʊn] n (also: **eau de ~**) acqua di colonia

Colombia [kə'lɒmbɪə] n Colombia; **Colombian** adj, n colombiano(-a)

colon ['kəʊlən] n (sign) due punti mpl; (Med) colon m inv

colonel ['kɜːnl] n colonnello

colonial [kə'ləʊnɪəl] adj coloniale

colony ['kɒlənɪ] n colonia

colour etc ['kʌlər] (US **color**) n colore m ► vt colorare; (tint, dye) tingere; (fig: affect) influenzare ► vi (blush) arrossire ▷ **colour in** vt colorare; **colour-blind** adj daltonico(-a); **coloured** adj (photo)

a colori; (person) di colore; **colour film** n (for camera) pellicola a colori; **colourful** adj (US **colorful**) a colori, a vivaci colori; (personality) colorato(-a); **colouring** n (substance) colorante m; (complexion) colorito; **colour television** n televisione f a colori

column ['kɒləm] n colonna

coma ['kəʊmə] n coma m inv

comb [kəʊm] n pettine m ► vt (hair) pettinare; (area) battere a tappeto

combat ['kɒmbæt] n combattimento ► vt combattere, lottare contro

combination [kɒmbɪ'neɪʃən] n combinazione f

combine [vb kəm'baɪn, n 'kɒmbaɪn] vt **to ~ (with)** combinare (con); (one quality with another) unire (a) ► vi unirsi; (Chem) combinarsi ► n (Econ) associazione f

come [kʌm] (pt **came**, pp **come**) vi venire; arrivare; **to ~ to** (decision etc) raggiungere; **I've ~ to like him** ho cominciato a piacermi; **to ~ undone** slacciarsi; **to ~ loose** allentarsi ▷ **come across** vt fus trovare per caso ▷ **come along** vi (pupil, work) fare progressi; **~ along!** avanti!, andiamo!, forza! ▷ **come back** vi ritornare ▷ **come down** vi scendere; (prices) calare; (buildings) essere demolito(-a) ▷ **come from** vt fus venire da; provenire da ▷ **come in** vi entrare ▷ **come off** vi (button) staccarsi; (stain) andar via; (attempt) riuscire ▷ **come on** vi (pupil, work, project) fare progressi; (lights) accendersi; (electricity) entrare in funzione; **~ on!** avanti!, andiamo!, forza! ▷ **come out** vi uscire; (stain) andare via ▷ **come round** vi (after faint, operation) riprendere conoscenza, rinvenire ▷ **come to** vi rinvenire ▷ **come up** vi (sun) salire; (problem) sorgere; (event) essere in arrivo; (in conversation)

334 | comeback

saltar fuori ▷ **come up with** vt fus he came up with an idea venne fuori con un'idea

comeback ['kʌmbæk] n (Theatre etc) ritorno

comedian [kə'miːdɪən] n comico

comedy ['kɒmɪdɪ] n commedia

comet ['kɒmɪt] n cometa

comfort ['kʌmfət] n comodità f inv, benessere m; (relief) consolazione f, conforto ▶ vt consolare, confortare; **comfortable** adj comodo(-a); (financially) agiato(-a); **comfort station** (US) n gabinetti mpl

comic ['kɒmɪk] adj (also: ~al) comico(-a) ▶ n comico; (BRIT: magazine) giornaletto; **comic book** (US) n giornalino (a fumetti); **comic strip** n fumetto

comma ['kɒmə] n virgola

command [kə'mɑːnd] n ordine m, comando; (Mil: authority) comando; (mastery) padronanza ▶ vt comandare; **to ~ sb to do** ordinare a qn di fare; **commander** n capo; (Mil) comandante m

commemorate [kə'meməreɪt] vt commemorare

commence [kə'mens] vt, vi cominciare; **commencement** (US) n (Univ) cerimonia di consegna dei diplomi

commend [kə'mend] vt lodare; raccomandare

comment ['kɒment] n commento ▶ vi **to ~ (on)** fare commenti (su); **commentary** ['kɒməntərɪ] n commentario; (Sport) radiocronaca; telecronaca; **commentator** ['kɒmənteɪtə*] n commentatore(-trice); radiocronista m/f; telecronista m/f

commerce ['kɒmɜːs] n commercio

commercial [kə'mɜːʃl] adj commerciale ▶ n (TV, Radio:

advertisement) pubblicità f inv; **commercial break** n intervallo pubblicitario

commission [kə'mɪʃən] n commissione f ▶ vt (work of art) commissionare; **out of ~** (Naut) in disarmo; **commissioner** n (Police) questore m

commit [kə'mɪt] vt (act) commettere; (to sb's care) affidare; **to o.s. to do** impegnarsi (a fare); **to ~ suicide** suicidarsi; **commitment** n impegno; promessa

committee [kə'mɪtɪ] n comitato

commodity [kə'mɒdɪtɪ] n prodotto, articolo

common ['kɒmən] adj comune; (pej) volgare; (usual) normale ▶ n terreno comune; **the C~s** (BRIT) ▶ npl la Camera dei Comuni; **in ~** in comune; **commonly** adv comunemente, usualmente; **commonplace** adj banale, ordinario(-a); **Commons** npl (BRIT Pol): **the (House of) Commons** la Camera dei Comuni; **common sense** n buon senso; **Commonwealth** n **the Commonwealth** il Commonwealth

* **Commonwealth**
* Il Commonwealth è
* un'associazione di stati sovrani
* indipendenti e di alcuni territori
* annessi che facevano parte
* dell'antico Impero Britannico.
* Nel 1931 questi assunsero il nome
* di "Commonwealth of Nations",
* denominazione successivamente
* semplificata in "Commonwealth".
* Attualmente gli stati del
* "Commonwealth" riconoscono
* ancora il proprio capo di stato.

communal ['kɒmjuːnl] adj (for common use) pubblico(-a)

commune n ['kɒmjuːn, vb kə'mjuːn] n (group) comune f ▶ vi **to ~ with**

mettersi in comunione con

communicate [kə'mju:nɪkeɪt] *vt* comunicare, trasmettere ▶ *vi* **to ~ with** comunicare (con)

communication [kəmju:nɪ'keɪʃən] *n* comunicazione *f*

communion [kə'mju:nɪən] *n* (*also:* **Holy C~**) comunione *f*

communism ['kɔmjunɪzəm] *n* comunismo; **communist** *adj, n* comunista *m/f*

community [kə'mju:nɪtɪ] *n* comunità *f inv*; **community centre** (*US* **community center**) *n* circolo ricreativo; **community service** *n* (*BRIT*) ≈ lavoro sostitutivo

commute [kə'mju:t] *vi* fare il pendolare ▶ *vt* (*Law*) commutare; **commuter** *n* pendolare *m/f*

compact [*adj* kəm'pækt, *n* 'kɔmpækt] *adj* compatto(-a) ▶ *n* (*also:* **powder ~**) portacipria *m inv*; **compact disc** *n* compact disc *m inv*; **compact disc player** *n* lettore *m* CD *inv*

companion [kəm'pænɪən] *n* compagno(-a)

company ['kʌmpənɪ] *n* (*also* Comm, Mil, Theatre) compagnia; **to keep sb ~** tenere compagnia a qn; **company car** *n* macchina (di proprietà) della ditta; **company director** *n* amministratore *m*, consigliere *m* di amministrazione

comparable ['kɔmpərəbl] *adj* simile

comparative [kəm'pærətɪv] *adj* relativo(-a); (*adjective etc*) comparativo(-a); **comparatively** *adv* relativamente

compare [kəm'pεə'] *vt* **to ~ sth/sb with/to** confrontare qc/qn con/a ▶ *vi* **to ~ (with)** reggere il confronto (con); **comparison** [-'pærɪsn] *n* confronto; **in comparison (with)** in confronto (a)

compartment [kəm'pɑ:tmənt] *n* compartimento; (*Rail*)

scompartimento; **a non-smoking ~** uno scompartimento per non-fumatori

compass ['kʌmpəs] *n* bussola; **~es** *npl* (*Math*) compasso

compassion [kəm'pæʃən] *n* compassione *f*

compatible [kəm'pætɪbl] *adj* compatibile

compel [kəm'pεl] *vt* costringere, obbligare; **compelling** *adj* (*fig: argument*) irresistibile

compensate ['kɔmpənseɪt] *vt* risarcire ▶ *vi* **to ~ for** compensare; **compensation** [-'seɪʃən] *n* compensazione *f*; (*money*) risarcimento

compete [kəm'pi:t] *vi* (*take part*) concorrere; (*vie*): **to ~ with** fare concorrenza (a)

competent ['kɔmpɪtənt] *adj* competente

competition [kɔmpɪ'tɪʃən] *n* gara, concorso; (*Econ*) concorrenza

competitive [kəm'pεtɪtɪv] *adj* (*Econ*) concorrenziale; (*sport*) agonistico(-a); (*person*) che ha spirito di competizione; che ha spirito agonistico

competitor [kəm'pεtɪtə'] *n* concorrente *m/f*

complacent [kəm'pleɪsnt] *adj* compiaciuto(-a) di sé

complain [kəm'pleɪn] *vi* lagnarsi, lamentarsi; **complaint** *n* lamento; (*in shop etc*) reclamo; (*Med*) malattia

complement [*n* 'kɔmplɪmənt, *vb* 'kɔmplɪmənt] *n* complemento; (*especially of ship's crew etc*) effettivo ▶ *vt* (*enhance*) accompagnarsi bene a; **complementary** [kɔmplɪ'mεntərɪ] *adj* complementare

complete [kəm'pli:t] *adj* completo(-a) ▶ *vt* completare; (*a form*) riempire; **completely** *adv* completamente;

completion n completamento

complex ['kɒmplɛks] adj complesso(-a) ▸ n (Psych, of buildings etc) complesso

complexion [kəm'plɛkʃən] n (of face) carnagione f

compliance [kəm'plaɪəns] n acquiescenza; **in ~ with** (orders, wishes etc) in conformità con

complicate ['kɒmplɪkeɪt] vt complicare; **complicated** adj complicato(-a); **complication** [-'keɪʃən] n complicazione f

compliment [n 'kɒmplɪmənt, vb 'kɒmplɪment] n complimento ▸ vt fare un complimento a; **complimentary** [-'mɛntərɪ] adj complimentoso(-a), elogiativo(-a); (free) in omaggio

comply [kəm'plaɪ] vi **to ~ with** assentire a; conformarsi a

component [kəm'pəʊnənt] adj componente ▸ n componente m

compose [kəm'pəʊz] vt (form): **to be ~d of** essere composto di; (music, poem etc) comporre; **to o.s.** ricomporsi; **composer** n (Mus) compositore(-trice); **composition** [kɒmpə'zɪʃən] n composizione f

composure [kəm'pəʊʒəʳ] n calma

compound ['kɒmpaʊnd] n (Chem, Ling) composto; (enclosure) recinto ▸ adj composto(-a)

comprehension [kɒmprɪ'hɛnʃən] n comprensione f

comprehensive [kɒmprɪ'hɛnsɪv] adj completo(-a); **comprehensive (school)** (BRIT) n scuola secondaria aperta a tutti

Be careful not to translate **comprehensive** by the Italian word **comprensivo**.

compress [vb kəm'prɛs, n 'kɒmprɛs] vt comprimere ▸ n (Med) compressa

comprise [kəm'praɪz] vt (also: **be ~d**) comprendere

compromise ['kɒmprəmaɪz] n compromesso ▸ vt compromettere ▸ vi venire a un compromesso

compulsive [kəm'pʌlsɪv] adj (liar, gambler) che non riesce a controllarsi; (viewing, reading) cui non si può fare a meno

compulsory [kəm'pʌlsərɪ] adj obbligatorio(-a)

computer [kəm'pjuːtəʳ] n computer m inv, elaboratore m elettronico; **computer game** n gioco per computer; **computer-generated** adj realizzato(-a) al computer; **computerize** vt computerizzare; **computer programmer** n programmatore(-trice); **computer programming** n programmazione f di computer; **computer science** n informatica; **computer studies** npl informatica; **computing** n informatica

con [kɒn] (inf) vt truffare ▸ n truffa

conceal [kən'siːl] vt nascondere

concede [kən'siːd] vt ammettere

conceited [kən'siːtɪd] adj presuntuoso(-a), vanitoso(-a)

conceive [kən'siːv] vt concepire ▸ vi concepire un bambino

concentrate ['kɒnsəntreɪt] vi concentrarsi ▸ vt concentrare

concentration [kɒnsən'treɪʃən] n concentrazione f

concept ['kɒnsɛpt] n concetto

concern [kən'sɜːn] n affare m; (Comm) azienda, ditta; (anxiety) preoccupazione f ▸ vt riguardare; **to be ~ed (about)** preoccuparsi (di); **concerning** prep riguardo a, circa

concert ['kɒnsət] n concerto; **concert hall** n sala da concerti

concerto [kən'tʃɛːtəu] n concerto

concession [kən'sɛʃən] n concessione f

concise [kən'saɪs] adj conciso(-a)

conclude [kənˈkluːd] vt concludere; **conclusion** [-ˈkluːʒən] n conclusione f

concrete [ˈkɒnkriːt] n calcestruzzo ▶ adj concreto(-a), di calcestruzzo

concussion [kənˈkʌʃən] n commozione f cerebrale

condemn [kənˈdɛm] vt condannare; (building) dichiarare pericoloso(-a)

condensation [kɒndɛnˈseɪʃən] n condensazione f

condense [kənˈdɛns] vi condensarsi ▶ vt condensare

condition [kənˈdɪʃən] n condizione f; (Med) malattia ▶ vt condizionare; **on ~ that** a condizione che + sub, a condizione di; **conditional** adj condizionale; **to be conditional upon** dipendere da; **conditioner** n (for hair) balsamo; (for fabrics) ammorbidente m

condo [ˈkɒndəʊ] (US) n abbr (inf) = **condominium**

condom [ˈkɒndəm] n preservativo

condominium [kɒndəˈmɪnɪəm] (US) n condominio

condone [kənˈdəʊn] vt condonare

conduct [n ˈkɒndʌkt, vb kənˈdʌkt] n condotta ▶ vt condurre; (manage) dirigere; amministrare; (Mus) dirigere; **to ~ o.s.** comportarsi; **conducted tour** [kənˈdʌktɪd-] n gita accompagnata; **conductor** n (of orchestra) direttore m d'orchestra; (on bus) bigliettaio m; (US: on train) controllore m; (Elec) conduttore m

cone [kəʊn] n cono; (Bot) pigna; (traffic cone) birillo

confectionery [kənˈfɛkʃənrɪ] n dolciumi mpl

confer [kənˈfəː] vt **to ~ sth on** conferire qc a ▶ vi conferire

conference [ˈkɒnfərns] n congresso

confess [kənˈfɛs] vt confessare, ammettere ▶ vi confessarsi; **confession** [kənˈfɛʃən] n confessione f

confide [kənˈfaɪd] vi **to ~ in** confidarsi con

confidence [ˈkɒnfɪdns] n confidenza; (trust) fiducia; (self-assurance) sicurezza di sé; **in ~** (speak, write) in confidenza, confidenzialmente; **confident** adj sicuro(-a), sicuro(-a) di sé; **confidential** [kɒnfɪˈdɛnʃəl] adj riservato(-a), confidenziale

confine [kənˈfaɪn] vt limitare; (shut up) rinchiudere; **confined** adj (space) ristretto(-a)

confirm [kənˈfəːm] vt confermare; **confirmation** [kɒnfəˈmeɪʃən] n conferma; (Rel) cresima

confiscate [ˈkɒnfɪskeɪt] vt confiscare

conflict [n ˈkɒnflɪkt, vb kənˈflɪkt] n conflitto ▶ vi essere in conflitto

conform [kənˈfɔːm] vi **to ~** conformarsi (a)

confront [kənˈfrʌnt] vt (enemy, danger) affrontare; **confrontation** [kɒnfrənˈteɪʃən] n scontro

confuse [kənˈfjuːz] vt (one thing with another) confondere; **confused** adj confuso(-a); **confusing** adj che fa confondere; **confusion** [-ˈfjuːʒən] n confusione f

congestion [kənˈdʒɛstʃən] n congestione f

congratulate [kənˈgrætjuleɪt] vt **to ~ sb (on)** congratularsi con qn (per or di); **congratulations** [-ˈleɪʃənz] npl auguri mpl; (on success) complimenti mpl, congratulazioni fpl

congregation [kɒŋgrɪˈgeɪʃən] n congregazione f

congress [ˈkɒŋgrɛs] n congresso; **congressman** (irreg: US) n membro del Congresso; **congresswoman** (irreg: US) n (donna) membro del Congresso

conifer [ˈkɒnɪfə'] n conifero

conjugate [ˈkɒndʒugeɪt] vt coniugare

conjugation [kɔndʒə'geɪʃən] n coniugazione f

conjunction [kən'dʒʌŋkʃən] n congiunzione f

conjure ['kʌndʒə'] vi fare giochi di prestigio

connect [kə'nɛkt] vt connettere, collegare; (Elec, Tel) collegare; (fig) associare ▶ vi (train): to ~ with essere in coincidenza con; to be ~ed with (associated) aver rapporti con; **connecting flight** n volo in coincidenza; **connection** [-ʃən] ▶ n relazione f, rapporto; (Elec) connessione f; (train, plane) coincidenza; (Tel) collegamento

conquer ['kɔŋkə'] vt conquistare; (feelings) vincere

conquest ['kɔŋkwɛst] n conquista

cons [kɔnz] npl see **convenience**; **pro**

conscience ['kɔnʃəns] n coscienza

conscientious [kɔnʃɪ'ɛnʃəs] adj coscienzioso(-a)

conscious ['kɔnʃəs] adj consapevole; (Med) cosciente; **consciousness** n consapevolezza; coscienza

consecutive [kən'sɛkjutɪv] adj consecutivo(-a); on 3 ~ occasions 3 volte di fila

consensus [kən'sɛnsəs] n consenso; the ~ of opinion l'opinione f unanime or comune

consent [kən'sɛnt] n consenso ▶ vi to ~ (to) acconsentire (a)

consequence ['kɔnsɪkwəns] n conseguenza, risultato; importanza

consequently ['kɔnsɪkwəntlɪ] adv di conseguenza, dunque

conservation [kɔnsə'veɪʃən] n conservazione f

conservative [kən'sə:vətɪv] adj conservatore(-trice); (cautious) cauto(-a); **Conservative** (BRIT) adj, n (Pol) conservatore(-trice)

conservatory [kən'sə:vətrɪ] n

(greenhouse) serra; (Mus) conservatorio

consider [kən'sɪdə'] vt considerare; (take into account) tener conto di; **to ~ doing sth** considerare la possibilità di fare qc; **considerable** [kən'sɪdərəbl] adj considerevole, notevole; **considerably** adv notevolmente, decisamente; **considerate** [kən'sɪdərɪt] adj premuroso(-a); **consideration** [kənsɪdə'reɪʃən] n considerazione f; **considering** [kən'sɪdərɪŋ] prep in considerazione di

consignment [kən'saɪnmənt] n (of goods) consegna; spedizione f

consist [kən'sɪst] vi to ~ of constare di, essere composto(-a) di

consistency [kən'sɪstənsɪ] n consistenza; (fig) coerenza

consistent [kən'sɪstənt] adj coerente

consolation [kɔnsə'leɪʃən] n consolazione f

console¹ [kən'səul] vt consolare

console² ['kɔnsəul] n quadro di comando

consonant ['kɔnsənənt] n consonante f

conspicuous [kən'spɪkjuəs] adj cospicuo(-a)

conspiracy [kən'spɪrəsɪ] n congiura, cospirazione f

constable ['kʌnstəbl] (BRIT) n ≈ poliziotto, agente m di polizia; **chief ~** ≈ questore m

constant ['kɔnstənt] adj costante, continuo(-a); **constantly** adv costantemente; continuamente

constipated ['kɔnstɪpeɪtɪd] adj stitico(-a); **constipation** [kɔnstɪ'peɪʃən] n stitichezza

constituency [kən'stɪtjuənsɪ] n collegio elettorale

constitute ['kɔnstɪtju:t] vt costituire

constitution [kɔnstɪ'tju:ʃən] n costituzione f

constraint [kən'streɪnt] n
costrizione f

construct [kən'strʌkt] vt costruire;
construction [-ʃən] n costruzione f;
constructive adj costruttivo(-a)

consul ['kɔnsl] n console m;
consulate ['kɔnsjulɪt] vt consolato

consult [kən'sʌlt] vt consultare;
consultant [n (Med) consulente m
medico; (other specialist) consulente;
consultation [-'teɪʃən] n (Med)
consulto; (discussion) consultazione f;
consulting room [kən'sʌltɪŋ-] (BRIT)
n ambulatorio

consume [kən'sjuːm] vt consumare;
consumer n consumatore(-trice)

consumption [kən'sʌmpʃən] n
consumo

cont. abbr = **continued**

contact ['kɔntækt] n contatto;
(person) conoscenza ▶ vt mettersi in
contatto con; **contact lenses** npl
lenti fpl a contatto

contagious [kən'teɪdʒəs] adj (also fig)
contagioso(-a)

contain [kən'teɪn] vt contenere;
to ~ o.s. contenersi; **container**
n recipiente m; (for shipping etc)
container m inv

contaminate [kən'tæmɪneɪt] vt
contaminare

cont'd abbr = **continued**

contemplate ['kɔntəmpleɪt] vt
contemplare; (consider) pensare a
(or di)

contemporary [kən'tɛmpərərɪ] adj, n
contemporaneo(-a)

contempt [kən'tɛmpt] n disprezzo; **~
of court** (Law) oltraggio alla Corte

contend [kən'tɛnd] vt **to ~ that**
sostenere che ▶ vi **to ~ with** lottare
contro

content¹ ['kɔntɛnt] n contenuto; **~s**
npl (of box, case etc) contenuto; **(table
of) ~s** indice m

content² [kən'tɛnt] adj contento(-a),
soddisfatto(-a) ▶ vt contentare,
soddisfare; **contented** adj
contento(-a), soddisfatto(-a)

contest [n 'kɔntɛst, vb kən'tɛst] n
lotta; (competition) gara, concorso
▶ vt contestare; impugnare; (compete
for) essere in lizza per; **contestant**
[kən'tɛstənt] n concorrente m/f; (in
fight) avversario(-a)

context ['kɔntɛkst] n contesto

continent ['kɔntɪnənt] n
continente m; **the C~** (BRIT) l'Europa
continentale; **continental** [-'nɛntl]
adj continentale; **continental
breakfast** n colazione f all'europea
(senza piatti caldi); **continental quilt**
(BRIT) n piumino

continual [kən'tɪnjuəl] adj
continuo(-a); **continually** adv di
continuo

continue [kən'tɪnjuː] vi continuare
▶ vt continuare; (start again)
riprendere

continuity [kɔntɪ'njuːɪtɪ] n
continuità f; (TV, Cinema) (ordine m
della) sceneggiatura

continuous [kən'tɪnjuəs] adj
continuo(-a), ininterrotto(-a);
continuous assessment
(BRIT) valutazione f continua;
continuously adv (repeatedly)
continuamente; (uninterruptedly)
ininterrottamente

contour ['kɔntuə'] n contorno,
profilo; (also: **~ line**) curva di livello

contraception [kɔntrə'sɛpʃən] n
contraccezione f

contraceptive [kɔntrə'sɛptɪv] adj
contraccettivo(-a) ▶ n contraccettivo

contract [n 'kɔntrækt, vb kən'trækt]
n contratto ▶ vi (become smaller)
contrarsi; (Comm) **to ~ to do sth**
fare un contratto per fare qc ▶ vt
(illness) contrarre; **contractor** n

imprenditore m

contradict [kɒntrə'dɪkt] vt contraddire; **contradiction** [kɒntrə'dɪkʃən] n contraddizione f; **to be in contradiction with** discordare con

contrary[1] ['kɒntrərɪ] adj contrario(-a); (unfavourable) avverso(-a), contrario(-a) ▶ n contrario; **on the ~** al contrario; **unless you hear to the ~** salvo contrordine

contrary[2] [kən'treərɪ] adj (perverse) bisbetico(-a)

contrast [n 'kɒntrɑːst, vb kən'trɑːst] n contrasto ▶ vt mettere in contrasto; **in ~ to** contrariamente a

contribute [kən'trɪbjuːt] vi contribuire ▶ vt **to ~ to £10/an article to** dare 10 sterline/un articolo a; **to ~ to** contribuire a; (newspaper) scrivere per; **contribution** [kɒntrɪ'bjuːʃən] n contributo; **contributor** n (to newspaper) collaboratore(-trice)

control [kən'trəul] vt controllare; (firm, operation etc) dirigere ▶ n controllo; **~s** npl (of vehicle etc) comandi mpl; (governmental) controlli mpl; **under ~** sotto controllo; **to be in ~ of** avere il controllo di; **to go out of ~** (car) non rispondere ai comandi; (situation) sfuggire di mano; **control tower** n (Aviat) torre f di controllo

controversial [kɒntrə'vəːʃl] adj controverso(-a), polemico(-a)

controversy ['kɒntrəvəːsɪ] n controversia, polemica

convenience [kən'viːnɪəns] n comodità f inv; **at your ~** a suo comodo; **all modern ~s** (BRIT), **all mod cons** tutte le comodità moderne

convenient [kən'viːnɪənt] adj comodo(-a)

> Be careful not to translate **convenient** by the Italian word **conveniente**.

convent ['kɒnvənt] n convento

convention [kən'venʃən] n convenzione f; (meeting) convegno; **conventional** adj convenzionale

conversation [kɒnvə'seɪʃən] n conversazione f

conversely [kən'vəːslɪ] adv al contrario, per contro

conversion [kən'vəːʃən] n conversione f; (BRIT: of house) trasformazione f, rimodernamento

convert [vb kən'vəːt, n 'kɒnvəːt] vt (Comm, Rel) convertire; (alter) trasformare ▶ n convertito(-a); **convertible** n macchina decappottabile

convey [kən'veɪ] vt trasportare; (thanks) comunicare; (idea) dare; **conveyor belt** [kən'veɪə'-] n nastro trasportatore

convict [vb kən'vɪkt, n 'kɒnvɪkt] vt dichiarare colpevole ▶ n carcerato(-a); **conviction** [-ʃən] n condanna; (belief) convinzione f

convince [kən'vɪns] vt convincere, persuadere; **convinced** adj **convinced of/that** convinto(-a) di/ che; **convincing** adj convincente

convoy ['kɒnvɔɪ] n convoglio

cook [kuk] vt cucinare, cuocere ▶ vi cuocere; (person) cucinare ▶ n cuoco(-a); **cook book** n libro di cucina; **cooker** n fornello, cucina; **cookery** n cucina; **cookery book** (BRIT) n = **cook book**; **cookie** (US) n biscotto; **cooking** n cucina

cool [kuːl] adj fresco(-a); (not afraid, calm) calmo(-a); (unfriendly) freddo(-a) ▶ vt raffreddare; (room) rinfrescare ▶ vi (water) raffreddarsi; (air) rinfrescarsi ▷ **cool down** vi raffreddarsi; (fig: person, situation) calmarsi ▷ **cool off** vi (become calmer) calmarsi ▷ (lose enthusiasm) perdere interesse

cop [kɒp] (inf) n sbirro

cope [kəup] vi to ~ with (problems) far fronte a

copper ['kɒpəʳ] n rame m; (inf: policeman) sbirro

copy ['kɒpɪ] n copia ▶ vt copiare; **copyright** n diritto d'autore

coral ['kɒrəl] n corallo

cord [kɔːd] n corda; (Elec) filo; ~s npl (trousers) calzoni mpl (di velluto) a coste; **cordless** adj senza cavo

corduroy ['kɔːdərɔɪ] n fustagno

core [kɔːʳ] n (of fruit) torsolo m; (of organization etc) cuore m ▶ vt estrarre il torsolo da

coriander [kɒrɪ'ændəʳ] n coriandolo

cork [kɔːk] n sughero m; (of bottle) tappo; **corkscrew** n cavatappi m inv

corn [kɔːn] n (BRIT: wheat) grano; (US: maize) granturco; (on foot) callo; ~ **on the cob** (Culin) pannocchia cotta

corned beef ['kɔːnd'biːf] n carne f di manzo in scatola

corner ['kɔːnəʳ] n angolo; (Aut) curva ▶ vt intrappolare; mettere con le spalle al muro; (Comm: market) accaparrare ▶ vi prendere una curva

corner shop (BRIT) piccolo negozio di generi alimentari

cornflakes ['kɔːnfleɪks] npl fiocchi mpl di granturco

cornflour ['kɔːnflauəʳ] (BRIT) n farina finissima di granturco

cornstarch ['kɔːnstɑːtʃ] (US) n = **cornflour**

Cornwall ['kɔːnwəl] n Cornovaglia

coronary ['kɒrənərɪ] n ~ (**thrombosis**) trombosi f coronaria

coronation [kɒrə'neɪʃən] n incoronazione f

coroner ['kɒrənəʳ] n magistrato incaricato di indagare la causa di morte in circostanze sospette

corporal ['kɔːpərl] n caporalmaggiore m ▶ adj ~ **punishment** pena corporale

corporate ['kɔːpərɪt] adj costituito(-a)

(in corporazione), comune

corporation [kɔːpə'reɪʃən] n (of town) consiglio comunale; (Comm) ente m

corps [kɔːʳ, pl kɔːz] n inv corpo

corpse [kɔːps] n cadavere m

correct [kə'rɛkt] adj (accurate) corretto(-a), esatto(-a); (proper) corretto(-a) ▶ vt correggere; **correction** [-ʃən] n correzione f

correspond [kɒrɪs'pɔnd] vi corrispondere; **correspondence** n corrispondenza; **correspondent** n corrispondente m/f; **corresponding** adj corrispondente

corridor ['kɒrɪdɔːʳ] n corridoio

corrode [kə'rəud] vt corrodere ▶ vi corrodersi

corrupt [kə'rʌpt] adj corrotto(-a); (Comput) alterato(-a) ▶ vt corrompere; **corruption** n corruzione f

Corsica ['kɔːsɪkə] n Corsica

cosmetic [kɒz'mɛtɪk] n cosmetico ▶ adj (fig: measure etc) superficiale; **cosmetic surgery** n chirurgia plastica

cosmopolitan [kɒzmə'pɔlɪtn] adj cosmopolita

cost [kɒst] (pt, pp **cost**) n costo ▶ vt costare; (find out the cost of) stabilire il prezzo di; ~s npl (Comm, Law) spese fpl; **how much does it ~?** quanto costa?; **at all ~s** a ogni costo

co-star ['kəustɑːʳ] n attore/trice della stessa importanza del protagonista

Costa Rica ['kɒstə'riːkə] n Costa Rica

costly ['kɒstlɪ] adj costoso(-a), caro(-a)

cost of living adj ~ **allowance** indennità f inv di contingenza

costume ['kɒstjuːm] n costume m; (lady's suit) tailleur m inv; (BRIT: also: **swimming ~**) costume m da bagno

cosy ['kəuzɪ] (US **cozy**) adj intimo(-a); **I'm very ~ here** sto proprio bene qui

cot [kɒt] n (BRIT: child's) lettino; (US: campbed) brandina

cottage ['kɔtɪdʒ] n cottage m inv;
cottage cheese n fiocchi mpl di
latte magro

cotton ['kɔtn] n cotone m ▷ **cotton on**
vi (inf): **to ~ on** (to sth) afferrare (qc);
cotton bud (BRIT) cotton fioc® m
inv; **cotton candy** (US) n zucchero
filato; **cotton wool** (BRIT) n cotone
idrofilo

couch [kautʃ] n sofà m inv

cough [kɔf] vi tossire ▶ n tosse f; **I've
got a ~** ho la tosse; **cough mixture,
cough syrup** n sciroppo per la tosse

could [kud] pt of **can²**

couldn't = could not

council ['kaunsl] n consiglio; **city or
town ~** consiglio comunale; **council
estate** (BRIT) n quartiere m di case
popolari; **council house** (BRIT) n casa
popolare; **councillor** (US **councilor**)
n consigliere(-a); **council tax** (BRIT)
tassa comunale sulla proprietà

counsel ['kaunsl] n avvocato;
consultazione f ▶ vt consigliare;
counselling (US **counseling**) n
(Psych) assistenza psicologica;
counsellor (US **counselor**) n
consigliere(-a); (US) avvocato

count [kaunt] vt, vi contare ▶ n (of
votes etc) conteggio; (of pollen etc)
livello; (nobleman) conte m ▷ **count
in** (inf) vt includere; **~ me in** ci sto
anch'io ▷ **count on** vt fus contare su;
countdown n conto alla rovescia

counter ['kauntə'] n banco ▶ vt
opporsi a ▶ adv: **~ to** contro; in
opposizione a; **counter clockwise**
[-'klɔkwaɪz] (US) adv in senso
antiorario

counterfeit ['kauntəfɪt] n
contraffazione f, falso ▶ vt
contraffare, falsificare ▶ adj falso(-a)

counterpart ['kauntəpɑːt] n (of
document etc) copia; (of person)
corrispondente m/f

countess ['kauntɪs] n contessa

countless ['kauntlɪs] adj
innumerevole

country ['kʌntrɪ] n paese m; (native
land) patria; (as opposed to town)
campagna; (region) regione f;
country and western (music)
musica country e western, country m;
country house n villa in campagna;
countryside n campagna

county ['kauntɪ] n contea

coup [kuː] n (pl **coups**) n colpo; (also: **~
d'état**) colpo di Stato

couple ['kʌpl] n coppia; **a ~ of** un
paio di

coupon ['kuːpɔn] n buono; (detachable
form) coupon m inv

courage ['kʌrɪdʒ] n coraggio;
courageous adj coraggioso(-a)

courgette [kuə'ʒet] (BRIT) n zucchina

courier ['kurɪə'] n corriere m; (for
tourists) guida

course [kɔːs] n corso; (of ship) rotta;
(for golf) campo; (part of meal) piatto;
of ~ senz'altro, naturalmente;
~ of action modo d'agire; **a ~ of
treatment** (Med) una cura

court [kɔːt] n corte f; (Tennis) campo
▶ vt (woman) fare la corte a; **to take to
~** citare in tribunale

courtesy ['kəːtəsɪ] n cortesia; (by) **~** di
per gentile concessione di; **courtesy
bus, courtesy coach** n autobus m inv
gratuito (di hotel, aeroporto)

court: court-house (US) n palazzo di
giustizia; **courtroom** n tribunale m;
courtyard n cortile m

cousin ['kʌzn] n cugino(-a); **first ~**
cugino di primo grado

cover ['kʌvə'] vt coprire; (book, table)
rivestire; (include) comprendere;
(Press) fare un servizio su ▶ n (of pan)
coperchio; (over furniture) fodera; (of
bed) copriletto; (of book) copertina;
(shelter) riparo; (Comm, Insurance, of

spy) copertura; **~s** npl (on bed) lenzuola fpl e coperte fpl; **to take ~** (shelter) ripararsi; **under ~** al riparo; **under ~ of darkness** protetto dall'oscurità; **under separate ~** (Comm) a parte, in plico separato ▸ **cover up** vi **to ~ up for sb** coprire qn; **coverage** n (Press, Radio, TV): **to give full coverage to sth** fare un ampio servizio su qc; **cover charge** n coperto; **cover-up** n occultamento (di informazioni)

cow [kau] n vacca ▸ vt (person) intimidire

coward ['kauəd] n vigliacco(-a); **cowardly** adj vigliaccio(-a)

cowboy ['kaubɔɪ] n cow-boy m inv

cozy ['kəuzɪ] (US) adj = **cosy**

crab [kræb] n granchio

crack [kræk] n fessura, crepa, incrinatura; (noise) schiocco; (: of gun) scoppio; (drug) crack m inv ▸ vt spaccare; incrinare; (whip) schioccare; (nut) schiacciare; (problem) risolvere; (code) decifrare ▸ adj (troops) fuori classe; **to ~ a joke** fare una battuta ▸ **crack down on** vt fus porre freno a; **cracked** adj (inf) matto(-a); **cracker** n cracker m inv; petardo

crackle ['krækl] vi crepitare

cradle ['kreɪdl] n culla

craft [krɑːft] n mestiere m; (cunning) astuzia; (boat) naviglio; **craftsman** (irreg) n artigiano; **craftsmanship** n abilità

cram [kræm] vt (fill): **to ~ sth with** riempire qc di; (put): **to ~ sth into** stipare qc in ▸ vi (for exams) prepararsi (in gran fretta)

cramp [kræmp] n crampo; **I've got ~ in my leg** ho un crampo alla gamba; **cramped** adj ristretto(-a)

cranberry ['krænbərɪ] n mirtillo

crane [kreɪn] n gru f inv

crap [kræp] n (inf!) fesserie fpl; **to have a ~** cacare (!)

crash [kræʃ] n fragore m; (of car) incidente m; (of plane) caduta; (of business etc) crollo ▸ vt fracassare ▸ vi (plane) fracassarsi; (car) avere un incidente; (two cars) scontrarsi; (business etc) fallire, andare in rovina; **crash course** n corso intensivo; **crash helmet** n casco

crate [kreɪt] n cassa

crave [kreɪv] vt, vi **to ~ (for)** desiderare ardentemente

crawl [krɔːl] vi strisciare carponi; (vehicle) avanzare lentamente ▸ n (swimming) crawl m

crayfish ['kreɪfɪʃ] n inv (freshwater) gambero (d'acqua dolce); (saltwater) gambero

crayon ['kreɪən] n matita colorata

craze [kreɪz] n mania

crazy ['kreɪzɪ] adj matto(-a); (inf: keen): **~ about sb** pazzo(-a) di qn; **~ about sth** matto(-a) per qc

creak [kriːk] vi cigolare, scricchiolare

cream [kriːm] n crema; (fresh) panna ▸ adj (colour) color crema inv; **cream cheese** n formaggio fresco; **creamy** adj cremoso(-a)

crease [kriːs] n grinza; (deliberate) piega ▸ vt sgualcire ▸ vi sgualcirsi

create [kriː'eɪt] vt creare; **creation** [-ʃən] n creazione f; **creative** adj creativo(-a); **creator** n creatore(-trice)

creature ['kriːtʃə] n creatura

crèche [kreʃ] n asilo infantile

credentials [krɪ'denʃlz] npl credenziali fpl

credibility [kredɪ'bɪlɪtɪ] n credibilità

credible ['kredɪbl] adj credibile; (witness, source) attendibile

credit ['kredɪt] n credito; onore m ▸ vt (Comm) accreditare; (believe: also: **give ~ to**) credere, prestar fede a; **~s** npl (Cinema) titoli mpl; **to ~ sb with**

(fig) attribuire a qn; **to be in ~** (person) essere creditore(-trice); (bank account) essere coperto(-a); **credit card** n carta di credito; **do you take credit cards?** accettate carte di credito?

creek [kriːk] n insenatura; (US) piccolo fiume m

creep [kriːp] (pt, pp **crept**) vi avanzare furtivamente (or pian piano)

cremate [krɪ'meɪt] vt cremare

crematorium [krɛmə'tɔːrɪəm] (pl **crematoria**) n forno crematorio

crept [krɛpt] pt, pp of **creep**

crescent ['krɛsnt] n (shape) mezzaluna; (street) strada semicircolare

cress [krɛs] n crescione m

crest [krɛst] n cresta; (of coat of arms) cimiero

crew [kruː] n equipaggio; **crew-neck** n girocollo

crib [krɪb] n culla ▶ vt (inf) copiare

cricket ['krɪkɪt] n (insect) grillo; (game) cricket m; **cricketer** n giocatore m di cricket

crime [kraɪm] n crimine m; **criminal** ['krɪmɪnl] adj, n criminale m/f

crimson ['krɪmzn] adj color cremisi inv

cringe [krɪndʒ] vi acquattarsi; (in embarrassment) sentirsi sprofondare

cripple ['krɪpl] n zoppo(-a) ▶ vt azzoppare

crisis ['kraɪsɪs] (pl **crises**) n crisi f inv

crisp [krɪsp] adj croccante; (fig) frizzante; vivace; deciso(-a); **crispy** adj croccante

criterion [kraɪ'tɪərɪən] (pl **criteria**) n criterio

critic ['krɪtɪk] n critico; **critical** adj critico(-a); **criticism** ['krɪtɪsɪzm] n critica; **criticize** ['krɪtɪsaɪz] vt criticare

Croat ['krəʊæt] adj, n = **Croatian**

Croatia [krəʊ'eɪʃə] n Croazia; **Croatian** adj croato(-a) ▶ n croato(-a);

(Ling) croato

crockery ['krɔkərɪ] n vasellame m

crocodile ['krɔkədaɪl] n coccodrillo

crocus ['krəʊkəs] n croco

croissant ['krwɑːs] n brioche f inv, croissant m inv

crook [kruk] n truffatore m; (of shepherd) bastone m; **crooked** ['krukɪd] adj curvo(-a), storto(-a); (action) disonesto(-a)

crop [krɔp] n (produce) coltivazione f; (amount produced) raccolto; (riding crop) frustino ▶ vt (hair) rapare ▶ **crop up** vi presentarsi

cross [krɔs] n croce f; (Biol) incrocio ▶ vt (street etc) attraversare; (arms, legs, Biol) incrociare; (cheque) sbarrare ▶ adj di cattivo umore ▶ **cross off** vt cancellare (tirando una riga con la penna) ▶ **cross out** vt cancellare ▶ **cross over** vi attraversare; **cross-Channel ferry** ['krɔs'tʃænl-] n traghetto che attraversa la Manica; **crosscountry (race)** n cross-country m inv; **crossing** n incrocio; (sea passage) traversata; (also: **pedestrian crossing**) passaggio pedonale; **how long does the crossing take?** quanto dura la traversata?; **crossing guard** (US) n dipendente comunale che aiuta i bambini ad attraversare la strada; **crossroads** n incrocio; **crosswalk** (US) n strisce fpl pedonali, passaggio pedonale; **crossword** n cruciverba m inv

crotch [krɔtʃ] n (Anat) inforcatura; (of garment) pattina

crouch [krautʃ] vi acquattarsi; rannicchiarsi

crouton ['kruːtɔn] n crostino

crow [krəʊ] n (bird) cornacchia; (of cock) canto del gallo ▶ vi (cock) cantare

crowd [kraud] n folla ▶ vt affollare, stipare ▶ vi to **~ round/in** affollarsi intorno a/in; **crowded**

adj affollato(-a); **crowded with** stipato(-a) di

crown [kraun] *n* corona; (*of head*) calotta cranica; (*of hat*) cocuzzolo; (*of hill*) cima ▶ *vt* incoronare; (*fig: career*) coronare; **crown jewels** *npl* gioielli *mpl* della Corona

crucial ['kru:ʃl] *adj* cruciale, decisivo(-a)

crucifix ['kru:sɪfɪks] *n* crocifisso

crude [kru:d] *adj* (*materials*) greggio(-a), non raffinato(-a); (*fig: basic*) crudo(-a), primitivo(-a); (*: vulgar*) rozzo(-a), grossolano(-a); **crude (oil)** *n* (petrolio) greggio

cruel ['kruəl] *adj* crudele; **cruelty** *n* crudeltà *f inv*

cruise [kru:z] *n* crociera ▶ *vi* andare a velocità di crociera; (*taxi*) circolare

crumb [krʌm] *n* briciola

crumble ['krʌmbl] *vt* sbriciolare ▶ *vi* sbriciolarsi; (*plaster etc*) sgretolarsi; (*land, earth*) franare; (*building, fig*) crollare

crumpet ['krʌmpɪt] *n* specie di frittella

crumple ['krʌmpl] *vt* raggrinzare, spiegazzare

crunch [krʌntʃ] *vt* sgranocchiare; (*underfoot*) scricchiolare ▶ *vi* scricchiolare; *n* momento cruciale; **crunchy** *adj* croccante

crush [krʌʃ] *n* folla; (*love*): **to have a ~ on sb** avere una cotta per qn; (*drink*): **lemon ~** spremuta di limone ▶ *vt* schiacciare; (*crumple*) sgualcire

crust [krʌst] *n* crosta; **crusty** *adj* (*bread*) croccante; (*person*) brontolone(-a); (*remark*) brusco(-a)

crutch [krʌtʃ] *n* gruccia

cry [kraɪ] *vi* piangere; (*shout*) urlare ▶ *n* urlo, grido ▶ **cry out** *vi*, *vt* gridare

crystal ['krɪstl] *n* cristallo

cub [kʌb] *n* cucciolo; (*also: ~ scout*) lupetto

Cuba ['kju:bə] *n* Cuba

Cuban ['kju:bən] *adj*, *n* cubano(-a)

cube [kju:b] *n* cubo ▶ *vt* (*Math*) elevare al cubo; **cubic** *adj* cubico(-a); (*metre, foot*) cubo(-a)

cubicle ['kju:bɪkl] *n* scompartimento separato; cabina

cuckoo ['kuku:] *n* cucù *m inv*

cucumber ['kju:kʌmbə'] *n* cetriolo

cuddle ['kʌdl] *vt* abbracciare, coccolare ▶ *vi* abbracciarsi

cue [kju:] *n* (*snooker cue*) stecca; (*Theatre etc*) segnale *m*

cuff [kʌf] *n* (*BRIT: of shirt, coat etc*) polsino; (*US: of trousers*) risvolto; **off the ~** improvvisando; **cufflinks** *npl* gemelli *mpl*

cuisine [kwɪ'zi:n] *n* cucina

cul-de-sac ['kʌldəsæk] *n* vicolo cieco

cull [kʌl] *vt* (*ideas etc*) scegliere ▶ *n* (*of animals*) abbattimento selettivo

culminate ['kʌlmɪneɪt] *vi* **to ~ in** culminare con

culprit ['kʌlprɪt] *n* colpevole *m/f*

cult [kʌlt] *n* culto

cultivate ['kʌltɪveɪt] *vt* (*also fig*) coltivare

cultural ['kʌltʃərəl] *adj* culturale

culture ['kʌltʃə'] *n* (*also fig*) cultura

cumin ['kʌmɪn] *n* (*spice*) cumino

cunning ['kʌnɪŋ] *n* astuzia, furberia ▶ *adj* astuto(-a), furbo(-a)

cup [kʌp] *n* tazza; (*prize, of bra*) coppa

cupboard ['kʌbəd] *n* armadio

cup final *n* (*BRIT Football*) finale *f* di coppa

curator [kjuə'reɪtə'] *n* direttore *m* (*di museo ecc*)

curb [kə:b] *vt* tenere a freno ▶ *n* freno; (*US*) bordo del marciapiede

curdle ['kə:dl] *vi* cagliare

cure [kjuə'] *vt* guarire; (*Culin*) trattare; affumicare; essiccare ▶ *n* rimedio

curfew ['kə:fju:] *n* coprifuoco

curiosity [kjuərɪ'ɔsɪtɪ] *n* curiosità

curious ['kjuərɪəs] *adj* curioso(-a)

curl [kə:l] n riccio ▸ vt ondulare; (*tightly*) arricciare ▸ vi arricciarsi
▷ **curl up** vi rannicchiarsi; **curler** n bigodino; **curly** ['kə:lɪ] adj ricciuto(-a)
currant ['kʌrnt] n (*dried*) sultanina; (*bush, fruit*) ribes m inv
currency ['kʌrnsɪ] n moneta; **to gain ~** (*fig*) acquistare larga diffusione
current ['kʌrnt] adj corrente ▸ n corrente f; **current account** (*BRIT*) n conto corrente; **current affairs** npl attualità fpl; **currently** adv attualmente
curriculum [kə'rɪkjuləm] (*pl* **curriculums** or **curricula**) n curriculum m inv; **curriculum vitae** [-'viːtaɪ] n curriculum vitae m inv
curry ['kʌrɪ] n curry m inv ▸ vt **to ~ favour with** cercare di attirarsi i favori di; **curry powder** n curry m
curse [kə:s] vt maledire ▸ vi bestemmiare ▸ n maledizione f; bestemmia
cursor ['kə:sə'] n (*Comput*) cursore m
curt [kə:t] adj secco(-a)
curtain ['kə:tn] n tenda; (*Theatre*) sipario
curve [kə:v] n curva ▸ vi curvarsi; **curved** adj curvo(-a)
cushion ['kuʃən] n cuscino ▸ vt (*shock*) fare da cuscinetto a
custard ['kʌstəd] n (*for pouring*) crema
custody ['kʌstədɪ] n (*of child*) tutela; **to take into ~** (*suspect*) mettere in detenzione preventiva
custom ['kʌstəm] n costume m, consuetudine f; (*Comm*) clientela
customer ['kʌstəmə'] n cliente m/f
customized ['kʌstəmaɪzd] adj (*car etc*) fuoriserie inv
customs ['kʌstəmz] npl dogana; **customs officer** n doganiere m
cut [kʌt] (*pt, pp* cut) vt tagliare; (*shape, make*) intagliare; (*reduce*) ridurre ▸ vi tagliare ▸ n taglio; (*in salary etc*)

riduzione f; **I've ~ myself** mi sono tagliato; **to ~ a tooth** mettere un dente ▷ **cut back** vt (*plants*) tagliare; (*production, expenditure*) ridurre ▷ **cut down** vt (*tree etc*) abbattere ▸ vt fus (*also*: **~ down on**) ridurre ▷ **cut off** vt tagliare; (*fig*) isolare ▷ **cut out** vt tagliare fuori; eliminare; tagliare ▷ **cut up** vt tagliare a pezzi; **cutback** n riduzione f
cute [kjuːt] adj (*sweet*) carino(-a)
cutlery ['kʌtlərɪ] n posate fpl
cutlet ['kʌtlɪt] n costoletta; (*nut etc cutlet*) cotoletta vegetariana
cut: **cut-price** (*BRIT*) adj a prezzo ridotto; **cut-rate** (*US*) adj = **cut-price**; **cutting** ['kʌtɪŋ] adj tagliente ▸ n (*from newspaper*) ritaglio (di giornale); (*from plant*) talea
CV n abbr = **curriculum vitae**
cwt abbr = **hundredweight(s)**
cybercafé ['saɪbəkæfeɪ] n cybercaffè m inv
cyberspace ['saɪbəspeɪs] n ciberspazio
cycle ['saɪkl] n ciclo; (*bicycle*) bicicletta ▸ vi andare in bicicletta; **cycle hire** n noleggio m biciclette inv; **cycle lane** n pista ciclabile; **cycle path** n pista ciclabile; **cycling** ['saɪklɪŋ] n ciclismo; **cyclist** ['saɪklɪst] n ciclista m/f
cyclone ['saɪkləun] n ciclone m
cylinder ['sɪlɪndə'] n cilindro
cymbal ['sɪmbl] n piatto
cynical ['sɪnɪkl] adj cinico(-a)
Cypriot ['sɪprɪət] adj, n cipriota (m/f)
Cyprus ['saɪprəs] n Cipro
cyst [sɪst] n cisti f inv; **cystitis** [sɪs'taɪtɪs] n cistite f
czar [zɑː'] n zar m inv
Czech [tʃɛk] adj ceco(-a) ▸ n ceco(-a); (*Ling*) ceco; **Czech Republic** n the Czech Republic la Repubblica Ceca

d

D [di:] n (Mus) re m

dab [dæb] vt (eyes, wound) tamponare; (paint, cream) applicare (con leggeri colpetti)

dad, daddy [dæd, 'dædɪ] n babbo, papà m inv

daffodil ['dæfədɪl] n trombone m, giunchiglia

daft [dɑːft] adj sciocco(-a)

dagger ['dægə'] n pugnale m

daily ['deɪlɪ] adj quotidiano(-a), giornaliero(-a) ▶ n quotidiano ▶ adv tutti i giorni

dairy ['dɛərɪ] n (BRIT: shop) latteria; (on farm) caseificio ▶ adj caseario(-a); **dairy produce** npl latticini mpl

daisy ['deɪzɪ] n margherita

dam [dæm] n diga ▶ vt sbarrare; costruire dighe su

damage ['dæmɪdʒ] n danno, danni mpl; (fig) danno ▶ vt danneggiare; **~s** npl (Law) danni

damn [dæm] vt condannare; (curse) maledire ▶ n (inf): **I don't give a ~** non me ne frega niente ▶ adj (inf: also: **~ed**): **this ~ ...** questo maledetto ...; **~ it!** accidenti!

damp [dæmp] adj umido(-a), n umidità, umido ▶ vt (also: **~en**: cloth, rag) inumidire, bagnare; (: enthusiasm etc) spegnere

dance [dɑːns] n danza, ballo; (ball) ballo ▶ vi ballare; **dance floor** n pista da ballo; **dancer** n danzatore(-trice)

(professional) ballerino(-a); **dancing** ['dɑːnsɪŋ] n danza, ballo

dandelion ['dændɪlaɪən] n dente m di leone

dandruff ['dændrəf] n forfora

Dane [deɪn] n danese m/f

danger ['deɪndʒə'] n pericolo; **there is a ~ of fire** c'è pericolo di incendio; **in ~** in pericolo; **he was in ~ of falling** rischiava di cadere; **dangerous** adj pericoloso(-a)

dangle ['dæŋgl] vt dondolare; (fig) far balenare ▶ vi pendolare

Danish ['deɪnɪʃ] adj danese ▶ n (Ling) danese m

dare [dɛə'] vt **to ~ sb to do** sfidare qn a fare ▶ vi **to ~ to do sth** osare fare qc; **I ~ say** (I suppose) immagino (che); **daring** adj audace, ardito(-a) ▶ n audacia

dark [dɑːk] adj (night, room) buio(-a), scuro(-a); (colour, complexion) scuro(-a); (fig) cupo(-a), tetro(-a), nero(-a) ▶ n **in the ~** al buio; **in the ~ about** (fig) all'oscuro di; **after ~** a notte fatta; **darken** vt (colour) scurire ▶ vi (sky, mood) oscurarsi; **darkness** n oscurità, buio; **darkroom** n camera oscura

darling ['dɑːlɪŋ] adj caro(-a) ▶ n tesoro

dart [dɑːt] n freccetta; (Sewing) pince f inv ▶ vi **to ~ away/along** sfrecciare via/lungo; **dartboard** n bersaglio (per freccette); **darts** n tiro al bersaglio (con freccette)

dash [dæʃ] n (sign) lineetta; (small quantity) punta ▶ vt (missile) gettare; (hopes) infrangere ▶ vi **to ~ towards** precipitarsi verso

dashboard ['dæʃbɔːd] n (Aut) cruscotto

data ['deɪtə] npl dati mpl; **database** n base f di dati, data base m inv; **data processing** n elaborazione f

(elettronica) dei dati
date [deɪt] n data; appuntamento;
(fruit) dattero ▶ vt datare; (person)
uscire con; **what's the ~ today?**
quanti ne abbiamo oggi?; **~ of birth**
data di nascita; **to ~** (until now) fino a
oggi; **dated** adj passato(-a) di moda
daughter ['dɔːtə'] n figlia; **daughter-
in-law** n nuora
daunting ['dɔːntɪŋ] adj non
invidiabile
dawn [dɔːn] n alba ▶ vi (day) spuntare;
(fig): **it ~ed on him that ...** gli è venuto
in mente che ...
day [deɪ] n giorno; (as duration)
giornata; (period of time, age) tempo,
epoca; **the ~ before** il giorno avanti
or prima; **the ~ after, the following
~** il giorno dopo or seguente; **the ~
after tomorrow** dopodomani; **the
~ before yester~** l'altroieri; **by ~** di
giorno; **day-care centre** n scuola
materna; **daydream** vi sognare a
occhi aperti; **daylight** n luce f del
giorno; **day return** (BRIT) n biglietto
giornaliero di andata e ritorno;
daytime n giorno; **day-to-day** adj
(life, organization) quotidiano(-a); **day
trip** n gita (in un giorno)
dazed [deɪzd] adj stordito(-a)
dazzle ['dæzl] vt abbagliare; **dazzling**
adj (light) abbagliante; (colour)
violento(-a); (smile) smagliante
DC abbr (= direct current) c.c.
dead [dɛd] adj morto(-a); (numb)
intirizzito(-a); (telephone)
muto(-a); (battery) scarico(-a) ▶ adv
assolutamente, perfettamente ▶ npl
the ~ i morti; **he was shot ~** fu colpito
a morte; **~ tired** stanco(-a) morto(-a);
to stop ~ fermarsi di colpo; **dead end**
n vicolo cieco; **deadline** n scadenza;
deadly adj mortale; (weapon, poison)
micidiale; **Dead Sea** n the Dead Sea
il mar Morto

deaf [dɛf] adj sordo(-a); **deafen**
vt assordare; **deafening** adj
fragoroso(-a)
deal [diːl] n (pt, pp dealt) n accordo;
(business deal) affare m ▶ vt (blow, cards)
dare; **a great ~ (of)** molto(-a) ▶ **deal
with** vt fus (Comm) fare affari con,
trattare con; (handle) occuparsi di;
(be about: book etc) trattare di; **dealer**
n commerciante m/f; **dealings**
npl (Comm) relazioni fpl; (relations)
rapporti mpl
dealt [dɛlt] pt, pp of **deal**
dean [diːn] n (Rel) decano; (Scol)
preside m di facoltà (or di collegio)
dear [dɪə'] adj caro(-a) ▶ n **my ~** caro
mio/cara mia ▶ excl **~ me!** Dio mio!;
D~ Sir/Madam (in letter) Egregio
Signore/Egregia Signora; **D~ Mr/Mrs
X** Gentile Signor/Signora X; **dearly**
adv (love) moltissimo; (pay) a caro
prezzo
death [dɛθ] n morte f; (Admin)
decesso; **death penalty** n pena di
morte; **death sentence** n condanna
a morte
debate [dɪ'beɪt] n dibattito ▶ vt
dibattere; discutere
debit ['dɛbɪt] n debito ▶ vt **to ~ a sum
to sb** or **to sb's account** addebitare
una somma a qn; **debit card** n carta
di debito
debris ['dɛbriː] n detriti mpl
debt [dɛt] n debito; **to be in ~** essere
indebitato(-a)
debut ['deɪbjuː] n debutto
Dec. abbr (= December) dic
decade ['dɛkeɪd] n decennio
decaffeinated [dɪ'kæfɪneɪtɪd] adj
decaffeinato(-a)
decay [dɪ'keɪ] n decadimento; (also:
tooth ~) carie f ▶ vi (rot) imputridire
deceased [dɪ'siːst] n defunto(-a)
deceit [dɪ'siːt] n inganno; **deceive**
[dɪ'siːv] vt ingannare

December [dɪ'sɛmbəʳ] n dicembre m

decency ['di:sənsɪ] n decenza

decent ['di:sənt] adj decente;
(respectable) per bene; (kind) gentile

deception [dɪ'sɛpʃən] n inganno

deceptive [dɪ'sɛptɪv] adj ingannevole

decide [dɪ'saɪd] vt (person) far prendere
una decisione a; (question, argument)
risolvere, decidere ▶ vi decidere,
decidersi; **to ~ to do/that** decidere di
fare/che; **to ~ on** decidere per

decimal ['dɛsɪml] adj decimale ▶ n
decimale m

decision [dɪ'sɪʒən] n decisione f

decisive [dɪ'saɪsɪv] adj decisivo(-a);
(person) deciso(-a)

deck [dɛk] n (Naut) ponte m; (of bus):
top ~ imperiale m; (record deck) piatto;
(of cards) mazzo; **deckchair** n sedia
a sdraio

declaration [dɛklə'reɪʃən] n
dichiarazione f

declare [dɪ'klɛəʳ] vt dichiarare

decline [dɪ'klaɪn] n (decay) declino;
(lessening) ribasso ▶ vt declinare;
rifiutare ▶ vi declinare; diminuire

decorate ['dɛkəreɪt] vt (adorn, give
a medal to) decorare; (paint and
paper) tinteggiare e tappezzare;
decoration [-'reɪʃən] n (medal etc,
adornment) decorazione f; **decorator**
n decoratore m

decrease [n 'di:kri:s, vb di:'kri:s] n
diminuzione f ▶ vt, vi diminuire

decree [dɪ'kri:] n decreto

dedicate ['dɛdɪkeɪt] vt consacrare;
(book etc) dedicare; **dedicated**
adj coscienzioso(-a); (Comput)
specializzato(-a), dedicato(-a);
dedication [dɛdɪ'keɪʃən] n (devotion)
dedizione f; (in book) dedica

deduce [dɪ'dju:s] vt dedurre

deduct [dɪ'dʌkt] vt **to ~ sth from**
dedurre qc (da); **deduction**
[dɪ'dʌkʃən] n deduzione f

deed [di:d] n azione f, atto; (Law) atto

deem [di:m] vt (formal) giudicare,
ritenere; **to ~ it wise to do** ritenere
prudente fare

deep [di:p] adj profondo(-a); **4
metres ~** profondo(-a) 4 metri ▶ adv
spectators stood 20 ~ c'erano 20 file
di spettatori; **how ~ is the water?**
quanto è profonda l'acqua?; **deep-
fry** vt friggere in olio abbondante;
deeply adv profondamente

deer [dɪəʳ] n inv **the ~** i cervidi; (red) ~
cervo; (fallow) ~ daino; roe ~ capriolo

default [dɪ'fɔ:lt] n (Comput: also: ~
value) default m inv; **by ~** (Sport) per
abbandono

defeat [dɪ'fi:t] n sconfitta ▶ vt (team,
opponents) sconfiggere

defect [n 'di:fɛkt, vb di'fɛkt] n difetto
▶ vi **to ~ to the enemy** passare al
nemico; **defective** [dɪ'fɛktɪv] adj
difettoso(-a)

defence [dɪ'fɛns] (US **defense**) n
difesa

defend [dɪ'fɛnd] vt difendere;
defendant n imputato(-a); **defender**
n difensore(-a)

defense [dɪ'fɛns] (US) n = **defence**

defensive [dɪ'fɛnsɪv] adj difensivo(-a)
▶ n **on the ~** sulla difensiva

defer [dɪ'fə:ʳ] vt (postpone) differire,
rinviare

defiance [dɪ'faɪəns] n sfida; **in ~ of** a
dispetto di; **defiant** [dɪ'faɪənt] adj
(attitude) di sfida; (person) ribelle

deficiency [dɪ'fɪʃənsɪ] n deficienza,
carenza; **deficient** adj deficiente;
insufficiente; **to be deficient in**
mancare di

deficit ['dɛfɪsɪt] n deficit m inv

define [dɪ'faɪn] vt definire

definite ['dɛfɪnɪt] adj (fixed)
definito(-a), preciso(-a); (clear,
obvious) ben definito(-a), esatto(-a);
(Ling) determinativo(-a); **he was ~**

about it ne era sicuro; **definitely** adv indubbiamente

definition [dɛfɪˈnɪʃən] n definizione f

deflate [diːˈfleɪt] vt sgonfiare

deflect [dɪˈflɛkt] vt deflettere, deviare

defraud [dɪˈfrɔːd] vt defraudare

defrost [diːˈfrɒst] vt (fridge) disgelare

defuse [diːˈfjuːz] vt disinnescare; (fig) distendere

defy [dɪˈfaɪ] vt sfidare; (efforts etc) resistere a; **it defies description** supera ogni descrizione

degree [dɪˈgriː] n grado; (Scol) laurea (universitaria); **a first ~ in maths** una laurea in matematica; **by ~s** (gradually) gradualmente; **a poco a poco; to some ~** fino a un certo punto, **to some** fino a un certo punto, in certa misura

dehydrated [diːhaɪˈdreɪtɪd] adj disidratato(-a); (milk, eggs) in polvere

de-icer [diːˈaɪsə*] n sbrinatore m

delay [dɪˈleɪ] vt ritardare ▶ vi **to ~ (in doing sth)** ritardare (a fare qc) ▶ n ritardo; **to be ~ed** subire un ritardo; (person) essere trattenuto(-a)

delegate [n ˈdɛlɪgɪt, vb ˈdɛlɪgeɪt] n delegato(-a) ▶ vt delegare

delete [dɪˈliːt] vt cancellare

deli [ˈdɛlɪ] n = **delicatessen**

deliberate [adj dɪˈlɪbərɪt, vb dɪˈlɪbəreɪt] adj (intentional) intenzionale; (slow) misurato(-a) ▶ vi deliberare, riflettere; **deliberately** adv (on purpose) deliberatamente

delicacy [ˈdɛlɪkəsɪ] n delicatezza

delicate [ˈdɛlɪkɪt] adj delicato(-a)

delicatessen [dɛlɪkəˈtɛsn] n ≈ salumeria

delicious [dɪˈlɪʃəs] adj delizioso(-a), squisito(-a)

delight [dɪˈlaɪt] n delizia, gran piacere m ▶ vt dilettare; **to take (a)~ in** dilettarsi in; **delighted** adj **delighted (at or with)** contentissimo(-a) (di), felice (di); **delighted to do** felice di

fare; **delightful** adj delizioso(-a), incantevole

delinquent [dɪˈlɪŋkwənt] adj, n delinquente m/f

deliver [dɪˈlɪvə*] vt (mail) distribuire; (goods) consegnare; (speech) pronunciare; (Med) far partorire; **delivery** n distribuzione f; consegna; (of speaker) dizione f; (Med) parto

delusion [dɪˈluːʒən] n illusione f

de luxe [dəˈlʌks] adj di lusso

delve [dɛlv] vi **to ~ into** frugare in; (subject) far ricerche in

demand [dɪˈmɑːnd] vt richiedere; (rights) rivendicare ▶ n domanda; (claim) rivendicazione f; **in ~** ricercato(-a), richiesto(-a); **on ~** a richiesta; **demanding** adj (boss) esigente; (work) impegnativo(-a)

demise [dɪˈmaɪz] n decesso

demo [ˈdɛməu] (inf) n abbr (= demonstration) manifestazione f

democracy [dɪˈmɔkrəsɪ] n democrazia; **democrat** [ˈdɛməkræt] n democratico(-a); **democratic** [dɛməˈkrætɪk] adj democratico(-a)

demolish [dɪˈmɔlɪʃ] vt demolire; **demolition** [dɛməˈlɪʃən] n demolizione f

demon [ˈdiːmən] n (also fig) demonio ▶ cpd **a ~ squash player** un mago dello squash; **a ~ driver** un guidatore folle

demonstrate [ˈdɛmənstreɪt] vt dimostrare, provare ▶ vi dimostrare, manifestare; **demonstration** [ˈstreɪʃən] n dimostrazione f; (Pol) dimostrazione, manifestazione f; **demonstrator** n (Pol) dimostrante m/f; (Comm) dimostratore(-trice)

demote [dɪˈməut] vt far retrocedere

den [dɛn] n tana, covo; (room) buco

denial [dɪˈnaɪəl] n diniego; rifiuto

denim [ˈdɛnɪm] n tessuto di cotone ritorto; **~s** npl (jeans) blue jeans mpl

Denmark [ˈdɛnmɑːk] n Danimarca

denomination [dɪnɒmɪ'neɪʃən] n (money) valore m; (Rel) confessione f

denounce [dɪ'naʊns] vt denunciare

dense [dɛns] adj fitto(-a); (smoke) denso(-a); (inf: person) ottuso(-a), duro(-a)

density ['dɛnsɪtɪ] n densità f inv

dent [dɛnt] n ammaccatura ▶ vt (also: **make a ~ in**) ammaccare

dental ['dɛntl] adj dentale; **dental floss** [-flɔs] n filo interdentale; **dental surgery** n ambulatorio del dentista

dentist ['dɛntɪst] n dentista m/f

dentures ['dɛntʃəz] npl dentiera f

deny [dɪ'naɪ] vt negare; (refuse) rifiutare

deodorant [di:'əʊdərənt] n deodorante m

depart [dɪ'pɑːt] vi partire; **to ~ from** (fig) deviare da

department [dɪ'pɑːtmənt] n (Comm) reparto; (Scol) sezione f, dipartimento; (Pol) ministero; **department store** n grande magazzino

departure [dɪ'pɑːtʃə] n partenza; (fig): **~ from** deviazione f da; **a new ~** una svolta (decisiva); **departure lounge** n (at airport) sala d'attesa

depend [dɪ'pɛnd] vi **to ~ on** dipendere da; (rely on) contare su; **it ~s** dipende; **~ing on the result ...** a seconda del risultato ...; **dependant** n persona a carico; **dependent** adj **to be dependent on** dipendere da; (child, relative) essere a carico di ▶ n = **dependant**

depict [dɪ'pɪkt] vt (in picture) dipingere; (in words) descrivere

deport [dɪ'pɔːt] vt deportare; espellere

deposit [dɪ'pɔzɪt] n (Comm, Geo) deposito; (of ore, oil) giacimento; (Chem) sedimento; (part payment) acconto; (for hired goods etc) cauzione f ▶ vt depositare; dare in acconto;

mettere or lasciare in deposito; **deposit account** n conto vincolato

depot ['dɛpəʊ] n deposito; (US) stazione f ferroviaria

depreciate [dɪ'priːʃɪeɪt] vi svalutarsi

depress [dɪ'prɛs] vt deprimere; (price, wages) abbassare; (press down) premere; **depressed** adj (person) depresso(-a), abbattuto(-a); (price) in ribasso; (industry) in crisi; **depressing** adj deprimente; **depression** [dɪ'prɛʃən] n depressione f

deprive [dɪ'praɪv] vt **to ~ sb of** privare qn di; **deprived** adj disgraziato(-a)

dept. abbr = **department**

depth [dɛpθ] n profondità f inv; **in the ~s of** nel profondo di; nel cuore di; **out of one's ~** (in water) dove non si tocca; (fig) a disagio

deputy ['dɛpjutɪ] adj **~ head** (BRIT Scol) vicepreside m/f ▶ n (assistant) vice m/f inv; (US: also: **~ sheriff**) vice-sceriffo

derail [dɪ'reɪl] vt **to be ~ed** deragliare

derelict ['dɛrɪlɪkt] adj abbandonato(-a)

derive [dɪ'raɪv] vt **to ~ sth from** derivare qc da; trarre qc da ▶ vi **to ~ from** derivare da

descend [dɪ'sɛnd] vt, vi discendere, scendere; **to ~ from** discendere da; **to ~ to** (lying, begging) abbassarsi a; **descendant** n discendente m/f; **descent** [dɪ'sɛnt] n discesa; (origin) discendenza, famiglia

describe [dɪs'kraɪb] vt descrivere; **description** [-'krɪpʃən] n descrizione f; (sort) genere m, specie f

desert [n 'dɛzət, vb dɪ'zəːt] n deserto ▶ vt lasciare, abbandonare ▶ vi (Mil) disertare; **deserted** [dɪ'zəːtɪd] adj deserto(-a)

deserve [dɪ'zəːv] vt meritare

design [dɪ'zaɪn] n (art, sketch) disegno; (layout, shape) linea; (pattern) fantasia; (intention) intenzione f ▶ vt disegnare;

progettare

designate vt [vb 'dezigneit,
adj 'dezignit] designare ▶ adj
designato(-a)

designer [di'zainə*] n (Art, Tech)
disegnatore(-trice); (of fashion)
modellista m/f

desirable [di'zaiərəbl] adj
desiderabile; **it is ~ that** è opportuno
che + sub

desire [di'zaiə*] n desiderio, voglia ▶ vt
desiderare, volere

desk [desk] n (in office) scrivania; (for
pupil) banco; (BRIT: in shop, restaurant)
cassa; (in hotel) ricevimento; (at
airport) accettazione f; **desk-top
publishing** n desktop publishing m

despair [dis'peə*] n disperazione f ▶ vi
to ~ of disperare di

despatch [dis'pætʃ] n, vt = **dispatch**

desperate ['despərit] adj
disperato(-a); (fugitive) capace
di tutto; **to be ~ for sth/to do**
volere disperatamente qc/fare;
desperately adv disperatamente;
(very) terribilmente, estremamente;
desperation [despə'reiʃən] n
disperazione f

despise [dis'paiz] vt disprezzare,
sdegnare

despite [dis'pait] prep malgrado, a
dispetto di, nonostante

dessert [di'zə:t] n dolce m; frutta;
dessertspoon n cucchiaio da dolci

destination [desti'neiʃən] n
destinazione f

destined ['destind] adj **to be ~ to do/
for** essere destinato(-a) a fare/per

destiny ['destini] n destino

destroy [dis'trɔi] vt distruggere

destruction [dis'trʌkʃən] n
distruzione f

destructive [dis'trʌktiv] adj
distruttivo(-a)

detach [di'tætʃ] vt staccare,

distaccare; **detached** adj (attitude)
distante; **detached house** n villa

detail ['di:teil] n particolare
m, dettaglio ▶ vt dettagliare,
particolareggiare; **in ~** nei particolari;
detailed adj particolareggiato(-a)

detain [di'tein] vt trattenere; (in
captivity) detenere

detect [di'tekt] vt scoprire, scorgere;
(Med, Police, Radar etc) individuare;
detection [di'tekʃən] n scoperta;
individuazione f; **detective** n
investigatore(-trice); **detective
story** n giallo

detention [di'tenʃən] n detenzione f;
(Scol) permanenza forzata per punizione

deter [di'tə:*] vt dissuadere

detergent [di'tə:dʒənt] n detersivo

deteriorate [di'tiəriəreit] vi
deteriorarsi

determination [ditə:mi'neiʃən] n
determinazione f

determine [di'tə:min] vt
determinare; **determined** adj (person)
risoluto(-a), deciso(-a); **determined
to do** deciso(-a) a fare

deterrent [di'terənt] n deterrente m;
to act as a ~ fungere da deterrente

detest [di'test] vt detestare

detour ['di:tuə*] n deviazione f

detract [di'trækt] vi **to ~ from**
detrarre da

detrimental [detri'mentl] adj **~ to**
dannoso(-a) a, nocivo(-a) a

devastating ['devəsteitiŋ] adj
devastatore(-trice), sconvolgente

develop [di'veləp] vt sviluppare;
(habit) prendere (gradualmente) ▶ vi
svilupparsi; (facts, symptoms: appear)
manifestarsi, rivelarsi; **can you ~ this
film?** può sviluppare questo rullino?;
developing country n paese m in via
di sviluppo; **development** n sviluppo

device [di'vais] n (apparatus) congegno

devil ['devl] n diavolo; demonio

devious ['diːvɪəs] adj (person) subdolo(-a)

devise [dɪ'vaɪz] vt escogitare, concepire

devote [dɪ'vəut] vt **to ~ sth to** dedicare qc a q; **devoted** adj devoto(-a); **to be devoted to sb** essere molto affezionato(-a) a qn; **devotion** [dɪ'vəʊʃən] n devozione f, attaccamento; (Rel) atto di devozione, preghiera

devour [dɪ'vauə*] vt divorare

devout [dɪ'vaut] adj pio(-a), devoto(-a)

dew [djuː] n rugiada

diabetes [daɪə'biːtiːz] n diabete m

diabetic [daɪə'bɛtɪk] adj, n diabetico(-a)

diagnose [daɪəg'nəʊz] vt diagnosticare

diagnosis [daɪəg'nəʊsɪs] (pl **diagnoses**) n diagnosi f inv

diagonal [daɪ'ægənl] adj diagonale ▷ n diagonale f

diagram ['daɪəgræm] n diagramma m

dial ['daɪəl] n quadrante m; (on radio) lancetta; (on telephone) disco combinatore ▷ vt (number) fare

dialect ['daɪəlɛkt] n dialetto

dialling code, (US **area code**) n prefisso; **what's the ~ for Paris?** qual è il prefisso telefonico di Parigi?

dialling tone, (US **dial tone**) n segnale m di linea libera

dialogue, (US **dialog**) ['daɪəlɒg] n dialogo

diameter [daɪ'æmɪtə*] n diametro

diamond ['daɪəmənd] n diamante m; (shape) rombo; **~s** npl (Cards) quadri mpl

diaper ['daɪəpə*] (US) n pannolino

diarrhoea, (US **diarrhea**) [daɪə'riːə] n diarrea

diary ['daɪərɪ] n (daily account) diario; (book) agenda

dice [daɪs] n inv dado ▷ vt (Culin) tagliare a dadini

dictate [dɪk'teɪt] vt dettare; **dictation** [dɪk'teɪʃən] n dettatura; (Scol) dettato

dictator [dɪk'teɪtə*] n dittatore m

dictionary ['dɪkʃənrɪ] n dizionario

did [dɪd] pt of **do**

didn't [dɪdnt] = **did not**

die [daɪ] vi morire; **to be dying for sth/to do sth** morire dalla voglia di qc/di fare qc ▷ **die down** vi abbassarsi ▷ **die out** vi estinguersi

diesel ['diːzəl] n (vehicle) diesel m inv

diet ['daɪət] n alimentazione f; (restricted food) dieta ▷ vi (also: **be on a ~**) stare a dieta

differ ['dɪfə*] vi **to ~ from sth** differire da qc, essere diverso(-a) da qc; **to ~ from sb over sth** essere in disaccordo con qn su qc; **difference** n differenza; (disagreement) screzio; **different** adj diverso(-a); **differentiate** [-'rɛnʃɪeɪt] vi **to differentiate between** discriminare or fare differenza fra; **differently** adv diversamente

difficult ['dɪfɪkəlt] adj difficile; **difficulty** n difficoltà f inv

dig [dɪg] (pt, pp **dug**) vt (hole) scavare; (garden) vangare ▷ n (prod) gomitata; (archaeological) scavo; (fig) frecciata ▷ **dig up** vt (tree etc) sradicare; (information) scavare fuori

digest [vb daɪ'dʒɛst, n 'daɪdʒɛst] vt digerire ▷ n compendio; **digestion** [dɪ'dʒɛstʃən] n digestione f

digit ['dɪdʒɪt] n cifra; (finger) dito; **digital** adj digitale; **digital camera** n macchina fotografica digitale; **digital TV** n televisione f digitale

dignified ['dɪgnɪfaɪd] adj dignitoso(-a)

dignity ['dɪgnɪtɪ] n dignità

digs [dɪgz] (BRIT: inf) npl camera ammobiliata

dilemma [daɪˈlɛmə] n dilemma m

dill [dɪl] n aneto

dilute [daɪˈluːt] vt diluire; (with water) annacquare

dim [dɪm] adj (light) debole; (shape etc) vago(-a); (room) in penombra; (inf: person) tonto(-a) ▶ vt (light) abbassare

dime [daɪm] (US) n = 10 cents

dimension [daɪˈmɛnʃən] n dimensione f

diminish [dɪˈmɪnɪʃ] vt, vi diminuire

din [dɪn] n chiasso, fracasso

dine [daɪn] vi pranzare; **diner** n (person) cliente m/f; (US: place) tavola calda

dinghy [ˈdɪŋgɪ] n battello pneumatico; (also: **rubber ~**) gommone m

dingy [ˈdɪndʒɪ] adj grigio(-a)

dining car [ˈdaɪnɪŋ-] (BRIT) n vagone m ristorante

dining room n sala da pranzo

dining table n tavolo da pranzo

dinner [ˈdɪnə^r] n (lunch) pranzo; (evening meal) cena; (public) banchetto; **dinner jacket** n smoking m inv; **dinner party** n cena; **dinner time** n ora di pranzo (or cena)

dinosaur [ˈdaɪnəsɔː^r] n dinosauro

dip [dɪp] n discesa; (in sea) bagno; (Culin) salsetta ▶ vt immergere; bagnare; (BRITAut: lights) abbassare ▶ vi abbassarsi

diploma [dɪˈpləʊmə] n diploma m

diplomacy [dɪˈpləʊməsɪ] n diplomazia

diplomat [ˈdɪpləmæt] n diplomatico; **diplomatic** [dɪpləˈmætɪk] adj diplomatico(-a)

dipstick [ˈdɪpstɪk] n (Aut) indicatore m di livello dell'olio

dire [daɪə^r] adj terribile; estremo(-a)

direct [daɪˈrɛkt] adj diretto(-a) ▶ vt dirigere; (order): **to ~ sb to do sth** dare direttive a qn di fare qc ▶ adv direttamente; **can you ~ me to ...?** mi

può indicare la strada per ...?; **direct debit** n (Banking) addebito effettuato per ordine di un cliente di banca

direction [dɪˈrɛkʃən] n direzione f; **~s** npl (advice) chiarimenti mpl; **sense of ~** senso dell'orientamento; **~s for use** istruzioni fpl

directly [dɪˈrɛktlɪ] adv (in straight line) direttamente; (at once) subito

director [dɪˈrɛktə^r] n direttore(-trice), amministratore(-trice); (Theatre, Cinema) regista m/f

directory [dɪˈrɛktərɪ] n elenco; **directory enquiries** (US **directory assistance**) n informazioni fpl elenco abbonati inv

dirt [dəːt] n sporcizia; immondizia; (earth) terra; **dirty** adj sporco(-a) ▶ vt sporcare

disability [dɪsəˈbɪlɪtɪ] n invalidità f inv; (Law) incapacità f inv

disabled [dɪsˈeɪbld] adj invalido(-a); (mentally) ritardato(-a) ▶ npl **the ~** gli invalidi

disadvantage [dɪsədˈvɑːntɪdʒ] n svantaggio

disagree [dɪsəˈgriː] vi (differ) discordare; (be against, think otherwise): **to ~ (with)** essere in disaccordo (con), dissentire (da); **disagreeable** adj sgradevole; (person) antipatico(-a); **disagreement** n disaccordo; (argument) dissapore m

disappear [dɪsəˈpɪə^r] vi scomparire; **disappearance** n scomparsa

disappoint [dɪsəˈpɔɪnt] vt deludere; **disappointed** adj deluso(-a); **disappointing** adj deludente; **disappointment** n delusione f

disapproval [dɪsəˈpruːvəl] n disapprovazione f

disapprove [dɪsəˈpruːv] vi **to ~ of** disapprovare

disarm [dɪsˈɑːm] vt disarmare; **disarmament** n disarmo

disaster [dɪˈzɑːstəʳ] n disastro; **disastrous** [dɪˈzɑːstrəs] adj disastroso(-a)

disbelief [ˈdɪsbəˈliːf] n incredulità

disc [dɪsk] n disco; (Comput) = **disk**

discard [dɪsˈkɑːd] vt (old things) scartare; (fig) abbandonare

discharge [vb dɪsˈtʃɑːdʒ, n ˈdɪstʃɑːdʒ] vt (duties) compiere; (Elec, waste etc) scaricare; (Med) emettere; (patient) dimettere; (employee) licenziare; (soldier) congedare; (defendant) liberare ▶ n (Elec) scarica; (Med) emissione f; (dismissal) licenziamento; congedo; liberazione f

discipline [ˈdɪsɪplɪn] n disciplina ▶ vt disciplinare; (punish) punire

disc jockey n disc jockey m inv

disclose [dɪsˈkləʊz] vt rivelare, svelare

disco [ˈdɪskəʊ] n abbr discoteca

discoloured (US **discolored**) [dɪsˈkʌləd] adj scolorito(-a), ingiallito(-a)

discomfort [dɪsˈkʌmfət] n disagio; (lack of comfort) scomodità f inv

disconnect [dɪskəˈnɛkt] vt sconnettere, staccare; (Elec, Radio) staccare; (gas, water) chiudere

discontent [dɪskənˈtɛnt] n scontentezza

discontinue [dɪskənˈtɪnjuː] vt smettere, cessare; "~d" (Comm) "fuori produzione"

discount [n ˈdɪskaʊnt, vb dɪsˈkaʊnt] n sconto ▶ vt scontare; (idea) non badare a; **are there ~s for students?** ci sono sconti per studenti?

discourage [dɪsˈkʌrɪdʒ] vt scoraggiare

discover [dɪsˈkʌvəʳ] vt scoprire; **discovery** n scoperta

discredit [dɪsˈkrɛdɪt] vt screditare; mettere in dubbio

discreet [dɪsˈkriːt] adj discreto(-a)

discrepancy [dɪsˈkrɛpənsɪ] n discrepanza

discretion [dɪsˈkrɛʃən] n discrezione f; **use your own ~** giudichi lei

discriminate [dɪsˈkrɪmɪneɪt] vi **to ~ between** distinguere tra; **to ~ against** discriminare contro; **discrimination** [-ˈneɪʃən] n discriminazione f; (judgment) discernimento

discuss [dɪsˈkʌs] vt discutere; (debate) dibattere; **discussion** [dɪsˈkʌʃən] n discussione f

disease [dɪˈziːz] n malattia

disembark [dɪsɪmˈbɑːk] vt, vi sbarcare

disgrace [dɪsˈgreɪs] n vergogna; (disfavour) disgrazia ▶ vt disonorare, far cadere in disgrazia; **disgraceful** adj scandaloso(-a), vergognoso(-a)

disgruntled [dɪsˈgrʌntld] adj scontento(-a), di cattivo umore

disguise [dɪsˈgaɪz] n travestimento ▶ vt **to ~ (as)** travestire (da); **in ~** vt travestito(-a)

disgust [dɪsˈgʌst] n disgusto, nausea ▶ vt disgustare, far schifo a; **disgusted** [dɪsˈgʌstɪd] adj indignato(-a); **disgusting** [dɪsˈgʌstɪŋ] adj disgustoso(-a), ripugnante

dish [dɪʃ] n piatto; **to do** or **wash the ~es** lavare i piatti; **dishcloth** n strofinaccio

dishonest [dɪsˈɔnɪst] adj disonesto(-a)

dishtowel [ˈdɪʃtaʊəl] (US) n strofinaccio dei piatti

dishwasher [ˈdɪʃwɔʃəʳ] n lavastoviglie f inv

disillusion [dɪsɪˈluːʒən] vt disilludere, disingannare

disinfectant [dɪsɪnˈfɛktənt] n disinfettante m

disintegrate [dɪsˈɪntɪgreɪt] vi disintegrarsi

disk [dɪsk] n (Comput) disco; **single-/double-sided ~** disco a facciata singola/doppia; **disk drive** n lettore m; **diskette** (US) n = disk

dislike [dɪsˈlaɪk] n antipatia, avversione f; (gen pl) cosa che non piace ▶ vt **he ~s it** non gli piace

dislocate [ˈdɪslǝkeɪt] vt slogare

disloyal [dɪsˈlɔɪǝl] adj sleale

dismal [ˈdɪzml] adj tetro

dismantle [dɪsˈmæntl] vt (machine) smontare

dismay [dɪsˈmeɪ] n costernazione f ▶ vt sgomentare

dismiss [dɪsˈmɪs] vt congedare; (employee) licenziare; (idea) scacciare; (Law) respingere; **dismissal** n congedo; licenziamento

disobedient [dɪsǝˈbiːdɪǝnt] adj disubbidiente

disobey [dɪsǝˈbeɪ] vt disubbidire a

disorder [dɪsˈɔːdǝ] n disordine m; (rioting) tumulto; (Med) disturbo

disorganized [dɪsˈɔːgǝnaɪzd] adj (person, life) disorganizzato(-a); (system, meeting) male organizzato(-a)

disown [dɪsˈǝun] vt rinnegare

dispatch [dɪsˈpætʃ] vt spedire, inviare ▶ n spedizione f, invio; (Mil, Press) dispaccio

dispel [dɪsˈpel] vt dissipare, scacciare

dispense [dɪsˈpens] vt distribuire, amministrare ▶ **dispense with** vt fus fare a meno di; **dispenser** n (container) distributore m

disperse [dɪsˈpǝːs] vt disperdere; (knowledge) disseminare ▶ vi disperdersi

display [dɪsˈpleɪ] n esposizione f; (of feeling etc) manifestazione f; (screen) schermo ▶ vt mostrare; (goods) esporre; (pej) ostentare

displease [dɪsˈpliːz] vt dispiacere a, scontentare; **~d with** scontento di

disposable [dɪsˈpǝuzǝbl] adj (pack etc) a perdere; (income) disponibile

disposal [dɪsˈpǝuzl] n eliminazione f;

(of property) cessione f; **at one's ~** alla sua disposizione

dispose [dɪsˈpǝuz] vi **~ of** sbarazzarsi di; **disposition** [-ˈzɪʃǝn] n disposizione f; (temperament) carattere m

disproportionate [dɪsprǝˈpɔːʃǝnǝt] adj sproporzionato(-a)

dispute [dɪsˈpjuːt] n disputa; (also: **industrial ~**) controversia (sindacale) ▶ vt contestare; (matter) discutere; (victory) disputare

disqualify [dɪsˈkwɔlɪfaɪ] vt (Sport) squalificare; **to ~ sb from sth/from doing** rendere qn incapace di qc/a fare; squalificare qn da qc/da fare; **to ~ sb from driving** ritirare la patente a qn

disregard [dɪsrɪˈgɑːd] vt non far caso a, non badare a

disrupt [dɪsˈrʌpt] vt disturbare; creare scompiglio in; **disruption** [dɪsˈrʌpʃǝn] n disordine m; interruzione f

dissatisfaction [dɪssætɪsˈfækʃǝn] n scontentezza, insoddisfazione f

dissatisfied [dɪsˈsætɪsfaɪd] adj **~ (with)** scontento(a) or insoddisfatto(a) (di)

dissect [dɪˈsekt] vt sezionare

dissent [dɪˈsent] n dissenso

dissertation [dɪsǝˈteɪʃǝn] n tesi f inv, dissertazione f

dissolve [dɪˈzɔlv] vt dissolvere, sciogliere; (Pol, marriage etc) sciogliere ▶ vi dissolversi, sciogliersi

distance [ˈdɪstns] n distanza; **in the ~** in lontananza

distant [ˈdɪstnt] adj lontano(-a), distante; (manner) riservato(-a), freddo(-a)

distil [dɪsˈtɪl] (US **distill**) vt distillare; **distillery** n distilleria

distinct [dɪsˈtɪŋkt] adj distinto(-a); **as ~ from** a differenza di; **distinction**

[dɪsˈtɪŋkʃən] n distinzione f; (in exam)
lode f; **distinctive** adj distintivo(-a)
distinguish [dɪsˈtɪŋɡwɪʃ]
vt distinguere; discernere;
distinguished adj (eminent) eminente
distort [dɪsˈtɔːt] vt distorcere; (Tech)
deformare
distract [dɪsˈtrækt] vt distrarre;
distracted adj distratto(-a);
distraction [dɪsˈtrækʃən] n
distrazione f
distraught [dɪsˈtrɔːt] adj stravolto(-a)
distress [dɪsˈtres] n angoscia
▶ vt affliggere; **distressing** adj
doloroso(-a)
distribute [dɪsˈtrɪbjuːt] vt distribuire;
distribution [-ˈbjuːʃən] n
distribuzione f; **distributor** n
distributore m
district [ˈdɪstrɪkt] n (of country)
regione f; (of town) quartiere m;
(Admin) distretto; **district attorney**
(US) n = sostituto procuratore m della
Repubblica
distrust [dɪsˈtrʌst] n diffidenza,
sfiducia ▶ vt non aver fiducia in
disturb [dɪsˈtəːb] vt disturbare;
disturbance n disturbo; (political etc)
disordini mpl; **disturbed** adj (worried,
upset) turbato(-a); **emotionally**
disturbed con turbe emotive;
disturbing adj sconvolgente
ditch [dɪtʃ] n fossa ▶ vt (inf) piantare
in asso
ditto [ˈdɪtəu] adv idem
dive [daɪv] n tuffo; (of submarine)
immersione f ▶ vi tuffarsi;
immergersi; **diver** n tuffatore(-trice),
palombaro
diverse [daɪˈvəːs] adj vario(-a)
diversion [daɪˈvəːʃən] n (BRIT
Aut) deviazione f; (distraction)
divertimento
diversity [daɪˈvəːsɪtɪ] n diversità f inv,
varietà f inv

divert [daɪˈvəːt] vt deviare
divide [dɪˈvaɪd] vt dividere; (separate)
separare ▶ vt dividersi; **divided**
highway (US) n strada a doppia
carreggiata
divine [dɪˈvaɪn] adj divino(-a)
diving [ˈdaɪvɪŋ] n tuffo; **diving board**
n trampolino
division [dɪˈvɪʒən] n divisione f;
separazione f; (esp Football) serie f
divorce [dɪˈvɔːs] n divorzio ▶ vt
divorziare da; (dissociate) separare;
divorced adj divorziato(-a); **divorcee**
[-ˈsiː] n divorziato(-a)
D.I.Y. (BRIT) n abbr = **do-it-yourself**
dizzy [ˈdɪzɪ] adj **to feel** ~ avere il
capogiro
DJ n abbr = **disc jockey**
DNA n abbr (= deoxyribonucleic acid) DNA
m; **DNA test** n test m inv del DNA

do
[duː] (pt did, pp done) n (inf:
party etc) festa; **it was rather a grand**
do è stato un ricevimento piuttosto
importante
▶ vb
1 (in negative constructions: non
tradotto): **I don't understand** non
capisco
2 (to form questions: non tradotto):
didn't you know? non lo sapevi?;
why didn't you come? perché non
sei venuto?
3 (for emphasis, in polite expressions):
she does seem rather late sembra
essere piuttosto in ritardo; **do sit**
down si accomodi la prego, prego si
sieda; **do take care!** mi raccomando,
sta attento!
4 (used to avoid repeating vb): **she swims**
better than I do lei nuota meglio di
me; **do you agree? —yes, I do/no, I**
don't sei d'accordo? —sì/no; **she lives**
in Glasgow —so do I lei vive a Glasgow
— anch'io; **he asked me to help him**

and I did mi ha chiesto di aiutarlo ed io l'ho fatto

5 (in question tags): **you like him, don't you?** ti piace, vero?; **I don't know him, do I?** non lo conosco, vero?

▶ vt (gen, carry out, perform etc) fare; **what are you doing tonight?** che fa stasera?; **to do the cooking** cucinare; **to do the washing-up** fare i piatti; **to do one's teeth** lavarsi i denti; **to do one's hair/nails** farsi i capelli/le unghie; **the car was doing 100** la macchina faceva i 100 all'ora

▶ vi

1 (act, behave) fare; **do as I do** faccia come me, faccia come faccio io

2 (get on, fare) andare; **he's doing well/badly at school** va bene/male a scuola; **how do you do?** piacere!

3 (suit) andare bene; **this room will do** questa stanza va bene

4 (be sufficient) bastare; **will £10 do?** basteranno 10 sterline?; **that'll do** basta così; **that'll do!** (in annoyance) ora basta!; **to make do (with)** arrangiarsi (con)

▷ **do away with** vt fus (kill) far fuori; (abolish) abolire

▷ **do up** vt (laces) allacciare; (dress, buttons) abbottonare; (renovate: room, house) rimettere a nuovo, rifare

▷ **do with** vt fus (need) aver bisogno di; (be connected): **what has it got to do with you?** e tu che c'entri?; **I won't have anything to do with it** non voglio avere niente a che farci; **it has to do with money** si tratta di soldi

▷ **do without** vi fare senza ▶ vt fus fare a meno di

dock [dɔk] n (Naut) bacino; (Law) banco degli imputati ▶ vi entrare in bacino; (Space) agganciarsi; **~s** npl (Naut) dock m inv

doctor ['dɔktə'] n medico(-a); (Ph. D. etc) dottore(-essa) ▶ vt (drink etc)

adulterare; **call a ~!** chiamate un dottore!; **Doctor of Philosophy** n dottorato di ricerca; (person) titolare m/f di un dottorato di ricerca

document ['dɔkjumənt] n documento; **documentary** [-'mɛntərɪ] adj (evidence) documentato(-a) ▶ n documentario; **documentation** [dɔkjumən'teɪʃən] n documentazione f

dodge [dɔdʒ] n trucco; schivata ▶ vt schivare, eludere

dodgy ['dɔdʒɪ] adj (inf: uncertain) rischioso(-a); (untrustworthy) sospetto(-a)

does [dʌz] vb see **do**

doesn't ['dʌznt] = **does not**

dog [dɔg] n cane m ▶ vt (follow closely) pedinare; (fig: memory etc) perseguitare; **doggy bag** n sacchetto per gli avanzi (da portare a casa)

do-it-yourself ['du:ɪtjɔ:'sɛlf] n il far da sé

dole [dəul] (BRIT) n sussidio di disoccupazione; **to be on the ~** vivere del sussidio

doll [dɔl] n bambola

dollar ['dɔlə'] n dollaro

dolphin ['dɔlfɪn] n delfino

dome [dəum] n cupola

domestic [də'mɛstɪk] adj (duty, happiness, animal) domestico(-a); (policy, affairs, flights) nazionale; **domestic appliance** n elettrodomestico

dominant ['dɔmɪnənt] adj dominante

dominate ['dɔmɪneɪt] vt dominare

domino ['dɔmɪnəu] (pl dominoes) n domino; **dominoes** n (game) gioco del domino

donate [də'neɪt] vt donare; **donation** [də'neɪʃən] n donazione f

done [dʌn] pp of **do**

donkey ['dɔŋkɪ] n asino

donor ['dəunə'] n donatore(-trice);

donor card n tessera di donatore di organi

don't [dəʊnt] = **do not**

donut ['dəʊnət] (US) n = **doughnut**

doodle ['duːdl] vi scarabocchiare

doom [duːm] n destino; rovina ▸ vt **to be ~ed (to failure)** essere predestinato(-a) (a fallire)

door [dɔːʳ] n porta; **doorbell** n campanello; **door handle** n maniglia; **doorknob** ['dɔːnɔb] n pomello, maniglia; **doorstep** n gradino della porta; **doorway** n porta

dope [dəʊp] n (inf: drugs) roba ▸ vt (horse etc) drogare

dormitory ['dɔːmɪtrɪ] n dormitorio; (US) casa dello studente

DOS [dɔs] n abbr (= disk operating system) DOS m

dosage ['dəʊsɪdʒ] n posologia

dose [dəʊs] n dose f; (bout) attacco

dot [dɔt] n punto; macchiolina ▸ vt **~ted with** punteggiato(-a) di; **on the ~** in punto; **dotted line** ['dɔtɪd-] n linea punteggiata

double ['dʌbl] adj doppio(-a) ▸ adv (twice) **to cost ~ sth** costare il doppio (di qc) ▸ n sosia m inv ▸ vt raddoppiare; (fold) piegare doppio or in due ▸ vi raddoppiarsi; **at the ~** (BRIT), **on the ~** a passo di corsa ▸ **double back** vi (person) tornare sui propri passi; **double bass** n contrabbasso; **double bed** n letto matrimoniale; **double-check** vt, vi ricontrollare; **double-click** vi (Comput) fare doppio click; **double-cross** vt fare il doppio gioco con; **doubledecker** n autobus m inv a due piani; **double glazing** (BRIT) n doppi vetri mpl; **double room** n camera matrimoniale; **doubles** n (Tennis) doppio; **double yellow lines** npl (BRIT: Aut) linea gialla doppia continua che segnala il divieto di sosta

doubt [daʊt] n dubbio ▸ vt dubitare di;

to ~ that dubitare che + sub; **doubtful** adj dubbioso(-a), incerto(-a); (person) equivoco(-a); **doubtless** adv indubbiamente

dough [dəʊ] n pasta, impasto; **doughnut** (US **donut**) n bombolone m

dove [dʌv] n colombo(-a)

down [daʊn] n piume fpl ▸ adv giù, di sotto ▸ prep giù per ▸ vt (inf: drink) scolarsi; **~ with X!** abbasso X!; **down-and-out** n barbone m; **downfall** n caduta; rovina; **downhill** adv **to go downhill** andare in discesa; (fig) lasciarsi andare; andare a rotoli

Downing Street ['daʊnɪŋ-] n **lo ~** residenza del primo ministro inglese

○ **Downing Street**
● Al numero 10 di **Downing Street**, nel
○ quartiere di Westminster a Londra,
○ si trova la residenza del primo
○ ministro inglese, al numero 11 quella
● del **Chancellor of the Exchequer**.

down: **download** vt (Comput) scaricare; **downright** adj franco(-a); (refusal) assoluto(-a)

Down's syndrome n sindrome f di Down

down: **downstairs** adv di sotto; al piano inferiore; **down-to-earth** adj pratico(-a); **downtown** adv in città; **down under** n (Australia etc) agli antipodi; **downward** ['daʊnwəd] adj, adv in giù, in discesa; **downwards** ['daʊnwədz] adv = **downward**

doz. abbr = **dozen**

doze [dəʊz] vi sonnecchiare

dozen ['dʌzn] n dozzina; **a ~ books** una dozzina di libri; **~s of** decine fpl di

Dr. abbr (= doctor) dott.; (in street names) = **drive**

drab [dræb] adj tetro(-a), grigio(-a)

draft [drɑːft] n abbozzo; (Pol) bozza; (Comm) tratta; (US: call-up) leva ▸ vt abbozzare; see also **draught**

drag [dræg] vt trascinare; (river)
dragare ▶ vi trascinarsi ▶ n (inf)
noioso(-a); noia, fatica; (women's
clothing): **in ~** travestito (da donna)

dragon ['drægən] n drago

dragonfly ['drægənflaɪ] n libellula

drain [dreɪn] n (for sewage) fogna; (on
resources) salasso ▶ vt (land, marshes)
prosciugare; (vegetables) scolare
▶ vi (water) defluire (via); **drainage**
n prosciugamento; fognatura;
drainpipe n tubo di scarico

drama ['drɑːmə] n (art) dramma
m, teatro; (play) commedia; (event)
dramma; **dramatic** [drə'mætɪk] adj
drammatico(-a)

drank [dræŋk] pt of **drink**

drape [dreɪp] vt drappeggiare; **~s**
npl (curtains) tende fpl

drastic ['dræstɪk] adj drastico(-a)

draught [drɑːft] (US **draft**) n corrente
f d'aria; (Naut) pescaggio; on **~** (beer)
alla spina; **draught beer** n birra
alla spina; **draughts** (BRIT) n (gioco
della) dama

draw [drɔː] (pt **drew**, pp **drawn**) vt
tirare; (take out) estrarre; (attract)
attirare; (picture) disegnare; (line,
circle) tracciare; (money) ritirare ▶ vi
(Sport) pareggiare ▶ n pareggio;
(in lottery) estrazione f; **to ~ near**
avvicinarsi ▶ **draw out** vi (lengthen)
allungarsi ▶ vt (money) ritirare ▷ **draw
up** vi (stop) arrestarsi, fermarsi
▶ vt (chair) avvicinare; (document)
compilare; **drawback** n svantaggio,
inconveniente m

drawer [drɔːʳ] n cassetto

drawing ['drɔːɪŋ] n disegno; **drawing
pin** (BRIT) n puntina da disegno;
drawing room n salotto

drawn [drɔːn] pp of **draw**

dread [drɛd] n terrore m ▶ vt tremare
all'idea di; **dreadful** adj terribile

dream [driːm] n (pt, pp **dreamed** or
dreamt) n sogno ▶ vt, vi sognare;
dreamer n sognatore(-trice)

dreamt [drɛmt] pt, pp of **dream**

dreary ['drɪərɪ] adj tetro(-a);
monotono(-a)

drench [drɛntʃ] vt inzuppare

dress [drɛs] n vestito; (no pl: clothing)
abbigliamento ▶ vt vestire; (wound)
fasciare ▶ vi vestirsi; **to get ~ed**
vestirsi ▶ **dress up** vi vestirsi a festa;
(in fancy dress) vestirsi in costume;
dress circle (BRIT) n prima galleria;
dresser n (BRIT: cupboard) credenza;
(US) cassettone m; **dressing** n (Med)
benda; (Culin) condimento; **dressing
gown** (BRIT) n vestaglia; **dressing
room** n (Theatre) camerino; (Sport)
spogliatoio; **dressing table** n toilette
f inv; **dressmaker** n sarta

drew [druː] pt of **draw**

dribble ['drɪbl] vi (baby) sbavare ▶ vt
(ball) dribblare

dried [draɪd] adj (fruit, beans) secco(-a);
(eggs, milk) in polvere

drier ['draɪəʳ] n = **dryer**

drift [drɪft] n (of current etc) direzione
f; forza; (of snow) cumulo; turbine
m; (general meaning) senso ▶ vi (boat)
essere trasportato(-a) dalla corrente;
(sand, snow) ammucchiarsi

drill [drɪl] n trapano; (Mil)
esercitazione f ▶ vt trapanare;
(troops) addestrare ▶ vi (for oil) fare
trivellazioni

drink [drɪŋk] n (pt **drank**, pp **drunk**)
n bevanda, bibita; (alcoholic drink)
bicchierino; (sip) sorso ▶ vt, vi bere;
to have a ~ bere qualcosa; **would you
like a ~?** vuoi qualcosa da bere?; **a ~ of
water** un po' d'acqua; **drink-driving**
n guida in stato di ebbrezza; **drinker**
n bevitore(-trice); **drinking water** n
acqua potabile

drip [drɪp] n goccia; gocciolamento;
(Med) fleboclisi f inv ▶ vi gocciolare;

(tap) sgocciolare

drive [draɪv] *(pt* **drove,** *pp* **driven)** *n* passeggiata *or* giro in macchina; *(also:* **-way)** viale *m* d'accesso; *(energy)* energia; *(campaign)* campagna; *(also:* **disk ~)** lettore *m* ▶ *vt* guidare; *(nail)* piantare; *(push)* cacciare, spingere; *(Tech: motor)* azionare; far funzionare ▶ *vi (Aut: at controls)* guidare; *(: travel)* andare in macchina; **left-/right-hand ~** guida a sinistra/destra; **to ~ sb mad** far impazzire qn ▶ **drive out** *vt (force out)* cacciare, mandare via; **drive-in** *(esp US) adj,* n drive-in (*m inv*)

driven ['drɪvn] *pp of* **drive**

driver ['draɪvə'] *n* conducente *m/f; (of taxi)* tassista *m; (chauffeur: of bus)* autista *m/f;* **driver's license** *(US)* n patente *f* di guida

driveway ['draɪvweɪ] *n* viale *m* d'accesso

driving ['draɪvɪŋ] *n* guida; **driving instructor** *n* istruttore(-trice) di scuola guida; **driving lesson** *n* lezione *f* di guida; **driving licence** *(BRIT)* n patente *f* di guida; **driving test** *n* esame *m* di guida

drizzle ['drɪzl] *n* pioggerella

droop [druːp] *vi (flower)* appassire; *(head, shoulders)* chinarsi

drop [drɔp] *n (of water)* goccia; *(lessening)* diminuzione *f; (fall)* caduta ▶ *vt* lasciare cadere; *(voice, eyes, price)* abbassare; *(set down from car)* far scendere; *(name from list)* lasciare fuori ▶ *vi* cascare; *(wind)* abbassarsi ▶ **drop in** *vi (inf: visit):* **to ~ in (on)** far un salto (da), passare (da) ▶ **drop off** *vi (sleep)* addormentarsi ▶ *vt (passenger)* far scendere ▶ **drop out** *vi (withdraw)* ritirarsi; *(student etc)* smettere di studiare

drought [draʊt] *n* siccità *f inv*

drove [drəʊv] *pt of* **drive**

drown [draʊn] *vt* affogare *(fig: noise)*

soffocare ▶ *vi* affogare

drowsy ['draʊzɪ] *adj* sonnolento(-a), assonnato(-a)

drug [drʌg] *n* farmaco; *(narcotic)* droga ▶ *vt* drogare; **to be on ~s** drogarsi; *(Med)* prendere medicinali; **hard/soft ~s** droghe pesanti/leggere; **drug addict** *n* tossicomane *m/f;* **drug dealer** *n* trafficante *m/f* di droga; **druggist** *(US)* n persona che gestisce un *drugstore;* **drugstore** *(US)* n drugstore *m inv*

drum [drʌm] *n* tamburo; *(for oil, petrol)* fusto ▶ *vi* tamburellare; **~s** *npl (set of drums)* batteria; **drummer** *n* batterista *m/f*

drunk [drʌŋk] *pp of* **drink** ▶ *adj* ubriaco(-a); ebbro(-a) ▶ *n (also:* **~ard)** ubriacone(-a); **drunken** *adj* ubriaco(-a); da ubriaco

dry [draɪ] *adj* secco(-a); *(day, clothes)* asciutto(-a) ▶ *vt* seccare; *(clothes, hair, hands)* asciugare ▶ *vi* asciugarsi ▶ **dry off** *vi* asciugarsi ▶ *vt* asciugare ▶ **dry up** *vi* seccarsi; **dry-cleaner's** *n* lavasecco *m inv;* **dry-cleaning** *n* pulitura a secco; **dryer** *n (for hair)* föhn *m inv,* asciugacapelli *m inv; (for clothes)* asciugabiancheria; *(US: spin-dryer)* centrifuga

DSS *n abbr (= Department of Social Security)* ministero della Previdenza sociale

DTP *n abbr (= desk-top publishing)* desktop publishing *m inv*

dual ['djuəl] *adj* doppio(-a); **dual carriageway** *(BRIT)* n strada a doppia carreggiata

dubious ['djuːbɪəs] *adj* dubbio(-a)

Dublin ['dʌblɪn] *n* Dublino *f*

duck [dʌk] *n* anatra ▶ *vi* abbassare la testa

due [djuː] *adj* dovuto(-a); *(expected)* atteso(-a); *(fitting)* giusto(-a) ▶ *n* dovuto ▶ *adv* **~ north** diritto verso nord

duel ['djuəl] n duello

duet [dju:'ɛt] n duetto

dug [dʌg] pt, pp of **dig**

duke [dju:k] n duca m

dull [dʌl] adj (light) debole; (boring)
noioso(-a); (slow-witted) ottuso(-a);
(sound, pain) sordo(-a); (weather, day)
fosco(-a), scuro(-a) ▶ vt (pain, grief)
attutire; (mind, senses) intorpidire

dumb [dʌm] adj muto(-a); (pej)
stupido(-a)

dummy ['dʌmɪ] n (tailor's model)
manichino; (Tech, Comm)
riproduzione f; (BRIT: for baby)
tettarella ▶ adj falso(-a), finto(-a)

dump [dʌmp] n (also: **rubbish** ~)
discarica di rifiuti; (inf: place) buco ▶ vt
(put down) scaricare; mettere giù; (get
rid of) buttar via

dumpling ['dʌmplɪŋ] n specie di gnocco

dune [dju:n] n duna

dungarees [dʌŋgə'ri:z] npl tuta

dungeon ['dʌndʒən] n prigione f
sotterranea

duplex ['dju:plɛks] (US) n (house)
casa con muro divisorio in comune con
un'altra; (apartment) appartamento
su due piani

duplicate [n 'dju:plɪkət, vb 'dju:
plɪkeɪt] n doppio ▶ vt duplicare; **in** ~ in
doppia copia

durable ['djuərəbl] adj durevole;
(clothes, metal) resistente

duration [djuə'reɪʃən] n durata

during ['djuərɪŋ] prep durante, nel
corso di

dusk [dʌsk] n crepuscolo

dust [dʌst] n polvere f ▶ vt (furniture)
spolverare; (cake etc) to ~ **with**
cospargere con; **dustbin** (BRIT) n
pattumiera; **duster** n straccio per
la polvere; **dustman** (irreg: BRIT) n
netturbino; **dustpan** n pattumiera;
dusty adj polveroso(-a)

Dutch [dʌtʃ] adj olandese ▶ n (Ling)
olandese m; **the** ~ npl gli Olandesi;
to go ~ (inf) fare alla romana;
Dutchman, Dutchwoman (irreg) n
olandese m/f

duty ['dju:tɪ] n dovere m; (tax) dazio,
tassa; **on** ~ di servizio; **off** ~ libero(-a),
fuori servizio; **duty-free** adj esente
da dazio

duvet ['du:veɪ] (BRIT) n piumino,
piumone m

DVD n abbr (= digital versatile or video
disk) DVD m inv; **DVD player** n lettore
m DVD

dwarf [dwɔːf] n nano(-a) ▶ vt far
apparire piccolo

dwell [dwɛl] (pt, pp **dwelt**) vi dimorare
▶ **dwell on** vt fus indugiare su

dwelt [dwɛlt] pt, pp of **dwell**

dwindle ['dwɪndl] vi diminuire

dye [daɪ] n tinta ▶ vt tingere

dying ['daɪɪŋ] adj morente,
moribondo(-a)

dynamic [daɪ'næmɪk] adj
dinamico(-a)

dynamite ['daɪnəmaɪt] n dinamite f

dyslexia [dɪs'lɛksɪə] n dislessia

dyslexic [dɪs'lɛksɪk] adj, n
dislessico(-a)

e

E [iː] n (Mus) mi m

E111 n abbr (also: **form ~**) E111 (modulo CEE per rimborso spese mediche)

each [iːtʃ] adj ogni, ciascuno(-a) ▶ pron ciascuno(-a), ognuno(-a); **~ one** ognuno(-a); **~ other** si or ci etc; **they hate ~ other** si odiano (l'un l'altro); **you are jealous of ~ other** siete gelosi l'uno dell'altro; **they have 2 books ~** hanno 2 libri ciascuno

eager ['iːɡər] adj impaziente, desideroso(-a); ardente; **to be ~ for** essere desideroso di, aver gran voglia di

eagle ['iːɡl] n aquila

ear [ɪər] n orecchio; (of corn) pannocchia; **earache** n mal m d'orecchi; **eardrum** n timpano

earl [əːl] (BRIT) n conte m

earlier ['əːlɪər] adj precedente ▶ adv prima

early ['əːlɪ] adv presto, di buon'ora; (ahead of time) in anticipo ▶ adj (near the beginning) primo(-a); (sooner than expected) prematuro(-a); (quick: reply) veloce; **at an ~ hour** di buon'ora; **to have an ~ night** andare a letto presto; **in the ~** or **~ in the spring/19th century** all'inizio della primavera/dell'Ottocento; **early retirement** n ritiro anticipato

earmark ['ɪəmɑːk] vt **to ~ sth for** destinare qc a

earn [əːn] vt guadagnare; (rest, reward)

meritare

earnest ['əːnɪst] adj serio(-a); **in ~** sul serio

earnings ['əːnɪŋz] npl guadagni mpl; (salary) stipendio

ear: earphones ['ɪəfəʊnz] npl cuffia; **earplugs** npl tappi mpl per le orecchie; **earring** ['ɪərɪŋ] n orecchino

earth [əːθ] n terra ▶ vt (BRIT Elec) mettere a terra; **earthquake** n terremoto

ease [iːz] n agio, comodo ▶ vt (soothe) calmare; (loosen) allentare; **to ~ sth out/in** tirare fuori/infilare qc con delicatezza; facilitare l'uscita/l'entrata di qc; **at ~** a proprio agio; (Mil) a riposo

easily ['iːzɪlɪ] adv facilmente

east [iːst] n est m ▶ adj dell'est ▶ adv a oriente; **the E~** l'Oriente m; (Pol) l'Est; **eastbound** ['iːstbaʊnd] adj (traffic) diretto(-a) a est; (carriageway) che porta a est

Easter ['iːstər] n Pasqua; **Easter egg** n uovo di Pasqua

eastern ['iːstən] adj orientale, d'oriente; dell'est

Easter Sunday n domenica di Pasqua

easy ['iːzɪ] adj facile; (manner) disinvolto(-a) ▶ adv **to take it** or **things ~** prendersela con calma; **easy-going** adj accomodante

eat [iːt] (pt **ate**, pp **eaten**) vt, vi mangiare; **can we have something to ~?** possiamo mangiare qualcosa? ▶ **eat out** vi mangiare fuori

eavesdrop ['iːvzdrɒp] vi **to ~ (on a conversation)** origliare (una conversazione)

e-book ['iːbuk] n libro elettronico

e-business ['iːbɪznɪs] n (company) azienda che opera in Internet; (commerce) commercio elettronico

EC n abbr (= European Community) CE f

eccentric [ɪk'sentrɪk] adj, n

364 | echo

eccentrico(-a)
echo ['ekəʊ] (pl **echoes**) n eco m or f ▶ vt
ripetere; fare eco a ▶ vi echeggiare;
dare un eco
eclipse [ɪ'klɪps] n eclissi f inv
eco-friendly [i:kəʊ'frendlɪ] adj
ecologico(-a)
ecological [i:kə'lɒdʒɪkəl] adj
ecologico(-a)
ecology [ɪ'kɒlədʒɪ] n ecologia
e-commerce [i:kɒmɜːs] n commercio
elettronico
economic [i:kə'nɒmɪk] adj
economico(-a); **economical** adj
economico(-a); (person) economica;
economics n economia ▶ npl lato
finanziario
economist [ɪ'kɒnəmɪst] n
economista m/f
economize [ɪ'kɒnəmaɪz] vi
risparmiare, fare economia
economy [ɪ'kɒnəmɪ] n economia;
economy class n (Aviat) classe f
turistica; **economy class syndrome**
n sindrome f della classe economica
ecstasy ['ekstəsɪ] n estasi f inv;
ecstatic [eks'tætɪk] adj estatico(-a),
in estasi
eczema ['eksɪmə] n eczema m
edge [edʒ] n margine m; (of table,
plate, cup) orlo; (of knife etc) taglio ▶ vt
bordare; **on** ~ (fig) = **edgy**; **to edge
away from** sgattaiolare da
edgy ['edʒɪ] adj nervoso(-a)
edible ['edɪbl] adj commestibile; (meal)
mangiabile
Edinburgh ['edɪnbərə] n Edimburgo f
edit ['edɪt] vt curare; **edition** [ɪ'dɪʃən]
n edizione f; **editor** n (in newspaper)
redattore(-trice), redattore(-trice)
capo; (of sb's work) curatore(-trice);
editorial [-'tɔːrɪəl] adj redazionale,
editoriale ▶ n editoriale m
Be careful not to translate **editor**
by the Italian word **editore**.

educate ['edjʊkeɪt] vt istruire;
educare; **educated** adj istruito(-a)
education [edjʊ'keɪʃən] n educazione
f; (schooling) istruzione f; **educational**
adj pedagogico(-a); scolastico(-a);
istruttivo(-a)
eel [i:l] n anguilla
eerie ['ɪərɪ] adj che fa accapponare
la pelle
effect [ɪ'fekt] n effetto ▶ vt effettuare;
to take ~ (law) entrare in vigore; (drug)
fare effetto; **in** ~ effettivamente;
~s npl (Theat) effetti mpl scenici;
(property) effetti mpl; **effective**
adj efficace; (actual) effettivo(-a);
effectively adv efficacemente;
effettivamente
efficiency [ɪ'fɪʃənsɪ] n efficienza;
rendimento effettivo
efficient [ɪ'fɪʃənt] adj efficiente;
efficiently adv efficientemente;
efficacemente
effort ['efət] n sforzo; **effortless** adj
senza sforzo, facile
e.g. adv abbr (= exempli gratia) per
esempio, p.es.
egg [eg] n uovo; **hard-boiled/soft-
boiled** ~ uovo sodo/alla coque;
eggcup n portauovo m inv; **eggplant**
(esp US) n melanzana; **eggshell** n
guscio d'uovo; **egg white** n albume
m, bianco d'uovo; **egg yolk** n tuorlo,
rosso (d'uovo)
ego ['i:gəʊ] n ego m inv
Egypt ['i:dʒɪpt] n Egitto; **Egyptian**
[ɪ'dʒɪpʃən] adj, n egiziano(-a)
eight [eɪt] num otto; **eighteen**
num diciotto; **eighteenth** num
diciottesimo(-a); **eighth** [eɪtθ] num
ottavo(-a); **eightieth** ['eɪtɪɪθ] num
ottantesimo(-a); **eighty** num ottanta
Eire ['eərə] n Repubblica d'Irlanda
either ['aɪðə] adj l'uno(-a) o l'altro(-a);
(both, each) ciascuno(-a) ▶ pron ~ **(of
them)** (o) l'uno(-a) o l'altro(-a) ▶ adv

neanche ▸ *conj* = **good or bad** o buono o cattivo; **on ~ side** su ciascun lato; **I don't like ~** non mi piace né l'uno né l'altro; **no, I don't ~** no, neanch'io

eject [ɪˈdʒɛkt] *vt* espellere; lanciare

elaborate [*adj* ɪˈlæbərɪt, *vb* ɪˈlæbəreɪt] *adj* elaborato(-a), minuzioso(-a) ▸ *vt* elaborare ▸ *vi* fornire i particolari

elastic [ɪˈlæstɪk] *adj* elastico(-a) ▸ *n* elastico; **elastic band** (BRIT) *n* elastico

elbow [ˈɛlbəu] *n* gomito

elder [ˈɛldəʳ] *adj* maggiore, più vecchio(-a) ▸ *n* (*tree*) sambuco; **one's ~s** i più anziani; **elderly** *adj* anziano(-a) ▸ *npl* **the elderly** gli anziani

eldest [ˈɛldɪst] *adj*, *n* **the ~ (child)** il(la) maggiore (dei bambini)

elect [ɪˈlɛkt] *vt* eleggere ▸ *adj* **the president ~** il presidente designato; **to ~ to do** decidere di fare; **election** [ɪˈlɛkʃən] *n* elezione *f*; **electoral** [ɪˈlɛktərəl] *adj* elettorale; **electorate** *n* elettorato

electric [ɪˈlɛktrɪk] *adj* elettrico(-a); **electrical** *adj* elettrico(-a); **electric blanket** *n* coperta elettrica; **electric fire** *n* stufa elettrica; **electrician** [ɪlɛkˈtrɪʃən] *n* elettricista *m*; **electricity** [ɪlɛkˈtrɪsɪtɪ] *n* elettricità; **electric shock** *n* scossa (elettrica); **electrify** [ɪˈlɛktrɪfaɪ] *vt* (*Rail*) elettrificare; (*audience*) elettrizzare

electronic [ɪlɛkˈtrɔnɪk] *adj* elettronico(-a); **electronic mail** *n* posta elettronica; **electronics** *n* elettronica

elegance [ˈɛlɪgəns] *n* eleganza

elegant [ˈɛlɪgənt] *adj* elegante

element [ˈɛlɪmənt] *n* elemento; (*of heater, kettle etc*) resistenza

elementary [ɛlɪˈmɛntərɪ] *adj* elementare; **elementary school** (US) *n* scuola elementare

elephant [ˈɛlɪfənt] *n* elefante(-essa)

elevate [ˈɛlɪveɪt] *vt* elevare

elevator [ˈɛlɪveɪtəʳ] *n* elevatore *m*; (US: *lift*) ascensore *m*

eleven [ɪˈlɛvn] *num* undici; **eleventh** *adj* undicesimo(-a)

eligible [ˈɛlɪdʒəbl] *adj* eleggibile; (*for membership*) che ha i requisiti

eliminate [ɪˈlɪmɪneɪt] *vt* eliminare

elm [ɛlm] *n* olmo

eloquent [ˈɛləkwənt] *adj* eloquente

else [ɛls] *adv* altro; **something ~** qualcos'altro; **somewhere ~** altrove; **everywhere ~** in qualsiasi altro luogo; **nobody ~** nessun altro; **where ~?** in quale altro luogo?; **little ~** poco altro; **elsewhere** *adv* altrove

elusive [ɪˈluːsɪv] *adj* elusivo(-a)

e-mail *n abbr* (= *electronic mail*) posta elettronica ▸ *vt* mandare un messaggio di posta elettronica a; **e-mail address** *n* indirizzo di posta elettronica

embankment [ɪmˈbæŋkmənt] *n* (*of road, railway*) terrapieno

embargo [ɪmˈbɑːgəu] *n* (*pl* **embargoes**) (*Comm, Naut*) embargo ▸ *vt* mettere l'embargo su; **to put an ~ on sth** mettere l'embargo su qc

embark [ɪmˈbɑːk] *vi* **to ~ (on)** imbarcarsi (su) ▸ *vt* imbarcare; **to ~ on** (*fig*) imbarcarsi in

embarrass [ɪmˈbærəs] *vt* imbarazzare; **embarrassed** *adj* imbarazzato(-a); **embarrassing** *adj* imbarazzante; **embarrassment** *n* imbarazzo

embassy [ˈɛmbəsɪ] *n* ambasciata

embrace [ɪmˈbreɪs] *vt* abbracciare ▸ *vi* abbracciarsi ▸ *n* abbraccio

embroider [ɪmˈbrɔɪdəʳ] *vt* ricamare; **embroidery** *n* ricamo

embryo [ˈɛmbrɪəu] *n* embrione *m*

emerald [ˈɛmərəld] *n* smeraldo

emerge [ɪˈməːdʒ] *vi* emergere

emergency [ɪ'məːdʒənsɪ] n
emergenza; **in an ~** in caso di
emergenza; **emergency brake** (US)
n freno a mano; **emergency exit**
n uscita di sicurezza; **emergency
landing** n atterraggio forzato;
emergency room (US: Med) n pronto
soccorso; **emergency services** npl
(fire, police, ambulance) servizi mpl di
pronto intervento

emigrate ['emɪɡreɪt] vi emigrare;
emigration [emɪ'ɡreɪʃən] n
emigrazione f

eminent ['emɪnənt] adj eminente

emissions [ɪ'mɪʃənz] npl emissioni fpl

emit [ɪ'mɪt] vt emettere

emotion [ɪ'məʊʃən] n emozione f;
emotional adj (person) emotivo(-a);
(scene) commovente; (tone, speech)
carico(-a) d'emozione

emperor ['empərə'] n imperatore m

emphasis ['emfəsɪs] (pl -ases) n enfasi
f inv; importanza

emphasize ['emfəsaɪz] vt (word,
point) sottolineare; (feature) mettere
in evidenza

empire ['empaɪə'] n impero

employ [ɪm'plɔɪ] vt impiegare;
employee [-'iː] n impiegato(-a);
employer n principale m/f, datore m
di lavoro; **employment** n impiego;
employment agency n agenzia di
collocamento

empower [ɪm'paʊə'] vt **to ~ sb to do**
concedere autorità a qn di fare

empress ['emprɪs] n imperatrice f

emptiness ['emptɪnɪs] n vuoto m

empty ['emptɪ] adj vuoto(-a); (threat,
promise) vano(-a) ▶ vt svuotare ▶ vi
vuotarsi; (liquid) scaricarsi; **empty-
handed** adj a mani vuote

EMU n abbr (= economic and monetary
union) unione f economica e
monetaria

emulsion [ɪ'mʌlʃən] n emulsione f

enable [ɪ'neɪbl] vt **to ~ sb to do**
permettere a qn di fare

enamel [ɪ'næməl] n smalto; (also: ~
paint) vernice f a smalto

enchanting [ɪn'tʃɑːntɪŋ] adj
incantevole, affascinante

encl. abbr (= enclosed) all

enclose [ɪn'kləʊz] vt (land) circondare,
recingere; (letter etc) allegare; **to ~ (with)**
allegare (con); **please find ~d** trovi
qui accluso

enclosure [ɪn'kləʊʒə'] n recinto

encore [ɔŋ'kɔː'] excl bis ▶ n bis m inv

encounter [ɪn'kaʊntə'] n incontro
▶ vt incontrare

encourage [ɪn'kʌrɪdʒ] vt
incoraggiare; **encouragement** n
incoraggiamento

encouraging [ɪn'kʌrɪdʒɪŋ] adj
incoraggiante

encyclop(a)edia [ensaɪkləʊ'piːdɪə] n
enciclopedia

end [end] n fine f; (aim) fine m; (of table)
bordo estremo; (of pointed object)
punta ▶ vt finire; (also: **bring to an ~,
put an ~ to**) mettere fine a ▶ vi finire;
in the ~ alla fine; **on ~** (object) ritto(-a);
to stand on ~ (hair) rizzarsi; **for hours
on ~** per ore ed ore ▶ **end up** vi **to ~ up
in** finire in

endanger [ɪn'deɪndʒə'] vt mettere
in pericolo

endearing [ɪn'dɪərɪŋ] adj accattivante

endeavour [ɪn'dɛvə'] (US **endeavor**)
n sforzo, tentativo ▶ vi **to ~** sforzarsi,
cercare or sforzarsi di fare

ending ['endɪŋ] n fine f, conclusione f;
(Ling) desinenza

endless ['endlɪs] adj senza fine

endorse [ɪn'dɔːs] vt (cheque) girare;
(approve) approvare, appoggiare;
endorsement n approvazione f; (on
driving licence) contravvenzione registrata
sulla patente

endurance [ɪn'djʊərəns] n

resistenza; pazienza
endure [ɪn'djʊəʳ] vt sopportare, resistere a ▸ vi durare
enemy ['ɛnəmɪ] adj, n nemico(-a)
energetic [ɛnə'dʒɛtɪk] adj energico(-a), attivo(-a)
energy ['ɛnədʒɪ] n energia
enforce [ɪn'fɔːs] vt (Law) applicare, far osservare
engaged [ɪn'geɪdʒd] adj (BRIT: busy, in use) occupato(-a); (betrothed) fidanzato(-a); **the line's ~** la linea è occupata; **to get ~** fidanzarsi; **engaged tone** (BRIT) n (Tel) segnale m di occupato
engagement [ɪn'geɪdʒmənt] n impegno, obbligo; appuntamento; (to marry) fidanzamento; **engagement ring** n anello di fidanzamento
engaging [ɪn'geɪdʒɪŋ] adj attraente
engine ['ɛndʒɪn] n (Aut) motore m; (Rail) locomotiva
engineer [ɛndʒɪ'nɪəʳ] n ingegnere m; (BRIT: for repairs) tecnico; on ship: US: Rail) macchinista m; **engineering** n ingegneria
England ['ɪŋglənd] n Inghilterra
English ['ɪŋglɪʃ] adj inglese ▸ n (Ling) inglese m; **the ~** npl gli Inglesi; **English Channel** n the English Channel la Manica; **Englishman** (irreg) n inglese m; **Englishwoman** (irreg) n inglese f
engrave [ɪn'greɪv] vt incidere
engraving [ɪn'greɪvɪŋ] n incisione f
enhance [ɪn'hɑːns] vt accrescere
enjoy [ɪn'dʒɔɪ] vt godere; (have: success, fortune) avere; **to ~ o.s.** godersela, divertirsi; **enjoyable** adj piacevole; **enjoyment** n piacere m, godimento
enlarge [ɪn'lɑːdʒ] vt ingrandire ▸ vi **to ~ on** (subject) dilungarsi su; **enlargement** n (Phot) ingrandimento
enlist [ɪn'lɪst] vt arruolare; (support)

procurare ▸ vi arruolarsi
enormous [ɪ'nɔːməs] adj enorme
enough [ɪ'nʌf] adj, n ~**time/books** assai tempo/libri; **have you got ~?** ne ha abbastanza ora a sufficienza? ▸ adv **big ~** abbastanza grande; **he has not worked ~** non ha lavorato abbastanza; **~! basta!; that's ~,** **thanks** basta così, grazie; **I've had** **~ of him** ne ho abbastanza di lui; **…which, funnily or oddly ~** … che, strano a dirsi
enquire [ɪn'kwaɪəʳ] vt, vi (esp BRIT) = **inquire**
enquiry [ɪn'kwaɪərɪ] n (esp BRIT) = **inquiry**
enrage [ɪn'reɪdʒ] vt fare arrabbiare
enrich [ɪn'rɪtʃ] vt arricchire
enrol [ɪn'rəul] (US **enroll**) vt iscrivere ▸ vi iscriversi; **enrolment** (US **enrollment**) n iscrizione f
en route [ɔn'ruːt] adv ~ **for/from/to** in viaggio per/da/a
en suite [ɔn'swiːt] adj **room with ~** **bathroom** camera con bagno
ensure [ɪn'ʃʊəʳ] vt assicurare; garantire
entail [ɪn'teɪl] vt comportare
enter ['ɛntəʳ] vt entrare in; (army) arruolarsi in; (competition) partecipare a; (sb for a competition) iscrivere; (write down) registrare; (Comput) inserire ▸ vi entrare
enterprise ['ɛntəpraɪz] n (undertaking, company) impresa; (spirit) iniziativa; **free ~** liberalismo economico; **private** **~** iniziativa privata; **enterprising** ['ɛntəpraɪzɪŋ] adj intraprendente
entertain [ɛntə'teɪn] vt divertire; (invite) ricevere; (idea, plan) nutrire; **entertainer** n comico(-a); **entertaining** adj divertente; **entertainment** n (amusement) divertimento; (show) spettacolo
enthusiasm [ɪn'θuːzɪæzəm] n

entusiasmo
enthusiast [ɪn'θuːzɪæst] n entusiasta
m/f; **enthusiastic** [-'æstɪk] adj
entusiasta, entusiastico(-a); **to be
enthusiastic about sth/sb** essere
appassionato(-a) di qc/entusiasta
di qn
entire [ɪn'taɪəʳ] adj intero(-a); **entirely**
adv completamente, interamente
entitle [ɪn'taɪtl] vt (give right): **to ~
sb to sth/to do** dare diritto a qn a
qc/a fare; **entitled** adj (book) che si
intitola; **to be entitled to do** avere il
diritto di fare
entrance [n 'entrns, vb ɪn'trɑːns] n
entrata, ingresso; (of person) entrata
▶ vt incantare, rapire; **where's the
~?** dov'è l'entrata?; **to gain ~ to**
(university etc) essere ammesso a;
entrance examination n esame
m di ammissione; **entrance fee**
n tassa d'iscrizione; (to museum
etc) prezzo d'ingresso; **entrance
ramp** (US) n (Aut) rampa di accesso;
entrant [ɪn'entrnt] n partecipante m/f;
concorrente m/f
entrepreneur [ɔntrəprə'nəːʳ] n
imprenditore m
entrust [ɪn'trʌst] vt **to ~ sth to**
affidare qc a
entry [ɪn'entrɪ] n entrata; (way in)
entrata, ingresso; (item: on list)
iscrizione f; (in dictionary) voce f; **no
~ vietato l'ingresso; (Aut) divieto di
accesso; **entry phone** n citofono
envelope [ɪn'envələup] n busta
envious [ɪn'envɪəs] adj invidioso(-a)
environment [ɪn'vaɪərnmənt]
n ambiente m; **environmental**
[-'mentl] adj ecologico(-a);
ambientale; **environmentally**
[ɪnvaɪərən'mentəlɪ] adv
environmentally **sound/friendly**
che rispetta l'ambiente
envisage [ɪn'vɪzɪdʒ] vt immaginare;

prevedere
envoy [ɪn'envɔɪ] n inviato(-a)
envy [ɪn'envɪ] n invidia ▶ vt invidiare; **to
~ sb sth** invidiare qn per qc
epic [ɪn'epɪk] n poema m epico ▶ adj
epico(-a)
epidemic [ɛpɪ'dɛmɪk] n epidemia
epilepsy [ɪn'epɪlɛpsɪ] n epilessia
epileptic [ɛpɪ'lɛptɪk] adj, n
epilettico(-a); **epileptic fit** n attacco
epilettico
episode [ɪn'epɪsəud] n episodio
equal [ɪn'iːkwl] adj uguale ▶ n pari
m/f inv ▶ vt uguagliare; **~ to** (task)
all'altezza di; **equality** [iː'kwɔlɪtɪ] n
uguaglianza; **equalize** vi pareggiare;
equally adv ugualmente
equation [ɪ'kweɪʃən] n (Math)
equazione f
equator [ɪ'kweɪtəʳ] n equatore m
equip [ɪ'kwɪp] vt equipaggiare,
attrezzare; **to ~ sb/sth with** fornire
qn/qc di; **to be well ~ped** (office
etc) essere ben attrezzato(-a); **he is
well ~ped for the job** ha i requisiti
necessari per quel lavoro; **equipment**
n attrezzatura; (electrical etc)
apparecchiatura
equivalent [ɪ'kwɪvəlnt] adj
equivalente ▶ n equivalente m; **to be ~
to** equivalere a
ER abbr (BRIT) = Elizabeth Regina (US:
Med) = **emergency room**
era [ɪn'ɪərə] n era, età f inv
erase [ɪ'reɪz] vt cancellare; **eraser** n
gomma
erect [ɪ'rɛkt] adj eretto(-a) ▶ vt
costruire; (assemble) montare;
erection [ɪ'rɛkʃən] n costruzione f;
montaggio m; (Physiol) erezione f
ERM n (= Exchange Rate Mechanism)
ERM m
erode [ɪ'rəud] vt erodere; (metal)
corrodere
erosion [ɪ'rəuʒən] n erosione f

erotic [ɪˈrɒtɪk] adj erotico(-a)

errand [ˈɛrnd] n commissione f

erratic [ɪˈrætɪk] adj imprevedibile; (person, mood) incostante

error [ˈɛrə*] n errore m

erupt [ɪˈrʌpt] vi (volcano) mettersi (or essere) in eruzione; (war, crisis) scoppiare; **eruption** [ɪˈrʌpʃən] n eruzione f; scoppio

escalate [ˈɛskəleɪt] vi intensificarsi

escalator [ˈɛskəleɪtə*] n scala mobile

escape [ɪˈskeɪp] n evasione f; fuga; (of gas etc) fuga, fuoriuscita ▶ vi fuggire; (from jail) evadere, scappare; (leak) uscire ▶ vt sfuggire a; **to ~ from** (place) fuggire da; (person) sfuggire a

escort [n ˈɛskɔːt, vb ɪˈskɔːt] n scorta; (male companion) cavaliere m ▶ vt scortare; accompagnare

especially [ɪˈspɛʃlɪ] adv specialmente; soprattutto; espressamente

espionage [ˈɛspɪənɑːʒ] n spionaggio

essay [ˈɛseɪ] n (Scol) composizione f; (Literature) saggio

essence [ˈɛsns] n essenza

essential [ɪˈsɛnʃl] adj essenziale ▶ n elemento essenziale; **essentially** adv essenzialmente; **essentials** npl the essentials l'essenziale msg

establish [ɪˈstæblɪʃ] vt stabilire; (business) mettere su; (one's power etc) affermare; **establishment** n stabilimento; **the Establishment** la classe dirigente, l'establishment m

estate [ɪˈsteɪt] n proprietà f inv; beni mpl, patrimonio; (BRIT: also: housing ~) complesso edilizio; **estate agent** (BRIT) n agente m immobiliare; **estate car** (BRIT) n giardiniera

estimate [n ˈɛstɪmət, vb ˈɛstɪmeɪt] n stima; (Comm) preventivo ▶ vt stimare, valutare

etc abbr (= et cetera) etc, ecc

eternal [ɪˈtəːnl] adj eterno(-a)

eternity [ɪˈtəːnɪtɪ] n eternità

ethical [ˈɛθɪkl] adj etico(-a), morale; **ethics** [ˈɛθɪks] n etica ▶ npl morale f

Ethiopia [iːθɪˈəupɪə] n Etiopia

ethnic [ˈɛθnɪk] adj etnico(-a); **ethnic minority** n minoranza etnica

etiquette [ˈɛtɪkɛt] n etichetta

EU n abbr (= European Union) UE f

euro [ˈjuərəu] n (currency) euro m inv

Europe [ˈjuərəp] n Europa; **European** [-ˈpiːən] adj, n europeo(-a); **European Community** n Comunità Europea; **European Union** n Unione f europea

Eurostar® [ˈjuərəustɑː*] n Eurostar® m inv

evacuate [ɪˈvækjueɪt] vt evacuare

evade [ɪˈveɪd] vt (tax) evadere; (duties etc) sottrarsi a; (person) schivare

evaluate [ɪˈvæljueɪt] vt valutare

evaporate [ɪˈvæpəreɪt] vi evaporare

eve [iːv] n on the ~ of alla vigilia di

even [ˈiːvn] adj regolare; (number) pari inv ▶ adv anche, perfino; **~ if, ~ though** anche se; **~ more** ancora di più; **~ so** ciò nonostante; **not ~** nemmeno; **to get ~ with sb** dare la pari a qn

evening [ˈiːvnɪŋ] n sera; (as duration, event) serata; **in the ~** la sera; **evening class** n corso serale; **evening dress** n (woman's) abito da sera; **in evening dress** (man) in abito scuro; (woman) in abito lungo

event [ɪˈvɛnt] n avvenimento; (Sport) gara; **in the ~ of** in caso di; **eventful** adj denso(-a) di eventi

eventual [ɪˈvɛntʃuəl] adj finale

> Be careful not to translate
> eventual by the Italian word
> eventuale.

eventually [ɪˈvɛntʃuəlɪ] adv alla fine

> Be careful not to translate
> eventually by the Italian word
> eventualmente.

ever [ˈɛvə*] adv mai; (at all times) sempre; **the best~** il migliore che ci sia mai stato; **have you ~ seen it?**

l'ha mai visto?; ~ **since** adv da allora
▶ conj sin da quando; ~ **so pretty** così
bello(-a); **evergreen** n sempreverde m

every ['εvrɪ] adj ogni; ~ **day** tutti i
giorni, ogni giorno; ~ **other/third day**
ogni due/tre giorni; ~ **other** car una
macchina su due; ~ **now and then**
ogni tanto, di quando in quando;
everybody pron = **everyone**;
everyday adj quotidiano(-a); di ogni
giorno; **everyone** pron ognuno, tutti,
pl; **everything** pron tutto, ogni cosa;
everywhere adv (gen) dappertutto;
(wherever) ovunque

evict [ɪ'vɪkt] vt sfrattare

evidence ['εvɪdns] n (proof) prova;
(of witness) testimonianza; (sign):
to show ~ of dare segni di; **to give**
~ deporre

evident ['εvɪdnt] adj evidente;
evidently adv evidentemente

evil ['iːvl] adj cattivo(-a), maligno(-a)
▶ n male m

evoke [ɪ'vəʊk] vt evocare

evolution [iːvə'luːʃən] n evoluzione f

evolve [ɪ'vɒlv] vt elaborare ▶ vi
svilupparsi, evolversi

ewe [juː] n pecora

ex (inf) [εks] n **my ex** il (la) mio(-a) ex

ex- [εks] prefix ex

exact [ɪg'zækt] adj esatto(-a) ▶ vt **to ~**
sth (from) estorcere qc (da); esigere
qc (da); **exactly** adv esattamente

exaggerate [ɪg'zædʒəreɪt] vt, vi
esagerare; **exaggeration** [-'reɪʃən] n
esagerazione f

exam [ɪg'zæm] n abbr (Scol)
= **examination**

examination [ɪgzæmɪ'neɪʃən] n (Scol)
esame m; (Med) controllo

examine [ɪg'zæmɪn] vt esaminare;
examiner n esaminatore(-trice)

example [ɪg'zɑːmpl] n esempio; **for** ~
ad or per esempio

exasperated [ɪg'zɑːspəreɪtɪd] adj

esasperato(-a)

excavate ['εkskəveɪt] vt scavare

exceed [ɪk'siːd] vt superare; (one's
powers, time limit) oltrepassare;
exceedingly adv eccessivamente

excel [ɪk'sεl] vi eccellere ▶ vt
sorpassare; **to ~ o.s** (BRIT) superare
se stesso

excellence ['εksələns] n eccellenza

excellent ['εksələnt] adj eccellente

except [ɪk'sεpt] prep (also: ~ **for**,
~**ing**) salvo, all'infuori di, eccetto
▶ vt escludere; ~ **if/when** salvo
se/quando; ~ **that** salvo che;
exception [ɪk'sεpʃən] n eccezione
f; **to take exception to** trovare da
ridire su; **exceptional** [ɪk'sεpʃənl]
adj eccezionale; **exceptionally**
[ɪk'sεpʃənəlɪ] adv eccezionalmente

excerpt [εk'səːpt] n estratto

excess [ɪk'sεs] n eccesso; **excess**
baggage n bagaglio in eccedenza;
excessive adj eccessivo(-a)

exchange [ɪks'tʃeɪndʒ] n scambio;
(also: **telephone ~**) centralino m ▶ vt to
~ **(for)** scambiare (con); **could I ~ this,**
please? posso cambiarlo, per favore?;
exchange rate n tasso di cambio

excite [ɪk'saɪt] vt eccitare; **to get ~d**
eccitarsi; **excited** adj **to get excited**
essere elettrizzato(-a); **excitement**
n eccitazione f; agitazione f; **exciting**
adj avventuroso(-a); (film, book)
appassionante

exclaim [ɪk'skleɪm] vi esclamare;
exclamation [εksklə'meɪʃən] n
esclamazione f; **exclamation mark**
(US **exclamation point**) n punto
esclamativo

exclude [ɪk'skluːd] vt escludere

excluding [ɪk'skluːdɪŋ] prep ~ **VAT**
IVA esclusa

exclusion [ɪk'skluːʒən] n esclusione f;
to the ~ of escludendo

exclusive [ɪk'skluːsɪv] adj

esclusivo(-a); ~ **of** VAT I.V.A. esclusa;
exclusively adv esclusivamente

excruciating [ɪkˈskruːʃɪeɪtɪŋ] adj
straziante, atroce

excursion [ɪkˈskəːʃən] n escursione
f, gita

excuse [n ɪkˈskjuːs, vb ɪkˈskjuːz]
n scusa ▶ vt scusare; **to ~ sb from**
(activity) dispensare qn da; ~ **me!** mi
scusi!; **now, if you will ~ me ...** ora, mi
scusi ma ...

ex-directory [ˈɛksdɪˈrɛktərɪ] (BRIT)
(Tel): **to be ~** non essere sull'elenco

execute [ˈɛksɪkjuːt] vt (prisoner)
giustiziare; (plan etc) eseguire;
execution [ɛksɪˈkjuːʃən] n
esecuzione f

executive [ɪgˈzɛkjutɪv] n (Comm)
dirigente m; (Pol) esecutivo ▶ adj
esecutivo(-a)

exempt [ɪgˈzɛmpt] adj esentato(-a)
▶ vt **to ~ sb from** non essere all'altezza

exercise [ˈɛksəsaɪz] n (keep fit) moto;
(Scol, Mil etc) esercizio ▶ vt esercitare;
(patience) usare; (dog) portar fuori ▶ vi
(also: **take ~**) fare del moto; **exercise
book** n quaderno

exert [ɪgˈzəːt] vt esercitare; **to ~ o.s.**
sforzarsi; **exertion** [-ʃən] n sforzo

exhale [ɛksˈheɪl] vt, vi espirare

exhaust [ɪgˈzɔːst] n (also: ~ **fumes**)
scappamento; (also: ~ **pipe**) tubo
di scappamento ▶ vt esaurire;
exhausted adj esaurito(-a);
exhaustion [ɪgˈzɔːstʃən] n
esaurimento; **nervous exhaustion**
sovraffaticamento mentale

exhibit [ɪgˈzɪbɪt] n (Art) oggetto
esposto; (Law) documento or oggetto
esibito ▶ vt esporre; (courage, skill)
dimostrare; **exhibition** [ɛksɪˈbɪʃən] n
mostra, esposizione f

exhilarating [ɪgˈzɪləreɪtɪŋ] adj
esilarante; stimolante

exile [ˈɛksaɪl] n esilio; (person)

esiliato(-a) ▶ vt esiliare

exist [ɪgˈzɪst] vi esistere; **existence** n
esistenza; **existing** adj esistente

exit [ˈɛksɪt] n uscita ▶ vi (Theatre,
Comput) uscire; **where's the ~?** dov'è
l'uscita?; **exit ramp** (US) n (Aut) rampa
di uscita

exotic [ɪgˈzɔtɪk] adj esotico(-a)

expand [ɪkˈspænd] vt espandere;
estendere; allargare ▶ vi (business, gas)
espandersi; (metal) dilatarsi

expansion [ɪkˈspænʃən] n (gen)
espansione f; (of town, economy)
sviluppo; (of metal) dilatazione f

expect [ɪkˈspɛkt] vt (anticipate)
prevedere, aspettarsi, prevedere
or aspettarsi che + sub; (require)
richiedere, esigere; (suppose)
supporre; (await, also baby) aspettare
▶ vi **to be ~ing** essere in stato
interessante; **to ~ sb to do** aspettarsi
che qn faccia; **expectation**
[ɛkspɛkˈteɪʃən] n aspettativa;
speranza

expedition [ɛkspəˈdɪʃən] n spedizione
f

expel [ɪkˈspɛl] vt espellere

expenditure [ɪkˈspɛndɪtʃəʳ] n spesa

expense [ɪkˈspɛns] n spesa; (high
cost) costo; **~s** npl (Comm) spese fpl,
indennità fpl; **at the ~ of** a spese di;
expense account n conto m spese inv

expensive [ɪkˈspɛnsɪv] adj caro(-a),
costoso(-a); **it's too ~** è troppo caro

experience [ɪkˈspɪərɪəns] n
esperienza ▶ vt (pleasure) provare;
(hardship) soffrire; **experienced** adj
esperto(-a)

experiment [n ɪkˈspɛrɪmənt, vb
ɪkˈspɛrɪmɛnt] n esperimento,
esperienza ▶ vi **to ~ (with/on)** fare
esperimenti (con/su); **experimental**
[ɪkspɛrɪˈmɛntl] adj sperimentale;
at the experimental stage in via di
sperimentazione

expert ['ɛkspəːt] adj, n esperto(-a);
expertise [-'tiːz] n competenza

expire [ɪk'spaɪəʳ] vi (period of time,
licence) scadere; **expiry** n scadenza;
expiry date n (of medicine, food item)
data di scadenza

explain [ɪk'spleɪn] vt spiegare;
explanation [ɛksplə'neɪʃən] n
spiegazione f

explicit [ɪk'splɪsɪt] adj esplicito(-a)

explode [ɪk'spləud] vi esplodere

exploit [n 'ɛksplɔɪt, vb ɪk'splɔɪt] n
impresa ▶ vt sfruttare; **exploitation**
[-'teɪʃən] n sfruttamento

explore [ɪk'splɔːʳ] vt esplorare;
(possibilities) esaminare; **explorer** n
esploratore(-trice)

explosion [ɪk'spləuʒən] n esplosione
f; **explosive** [ɪk'spləusɪv] adj
esplosivo(-a) ▶ n esplosivo m

export [vb ɛk'spɔːt, n 'ɛkspɔːt] vt
esportare ▶ n esportazione f; articolo
di esportazione ▶ cpd d'esportazione
◆ **exporter** n esportatore m

expose [ɪk'spəuz] vt esporre; (unmask)
smascherare; **exposed** adj (position)
esposto(-a); **exposure** [ɪk'spəuʒəʳ]
n esposizione f; (Phot) posa; (Med)
assideramento

express [ɪk'sprɛs] adj (definite)
chiaro(-a), espresso(-a); (BRIT:
letter etc) espresso ▶ n (train)
espresso ▶ vt esprimere; **expression**
[ɪk'sprɛʃən] n espressione f;
expressway (US) n (urban motorway)
autostrada che attraversa la città

exquisite [ɛk'skwɪzɪt] adj squisito(-a)

extend [ɪk'stɛnd] vt (visit) protrarre;
(road, deadline) prolungare; (building)
ampliare; (offer) offrire, porgere ▶ vi
(land, period) estendersi; **extension**
[ɪk'stɛnʃən] n (of road, term)
prolungamento; (of contract, deadline)
proroga; (building) annesso; (to wire,
table) prolunga; (telephone) interno;

(: in private house) apparecchio
supplementare; **extension lead** n
prolunga

extensive [ɪk'stɛnsɪv] adj esteso(-a),
ampio(-a); (damage) su larga scala;
(coverage, discussion) esauriente; (use)
grande

extent [ɪk'stɛnt] n estensione f; **to
some ~** fino a un certo punto; **to such
an ~ that ...** a tal punto che ...; **to
what ~?** fino a che punto?; **to the ~ of
...** fino al punto di ...

exterior [ɛk'stɪərɪəʳ] adj esteriore,
esterno(-a) ▶ n esteriore m, esterno;
aspetto (esteriore)

external [ɛk'stəːnl] adj esterno(-a),
esteriore

extinct [ɪk'stɪŋkt] adj estinto(-a);
extinction [ɪk'stɪŋkʃən] n estinzione f

extinguish [ɪk'stɪŋgwɪʃ] vt estinguere

extra ['ɛkstrə] adj extra inv,
supplementare ▶ adv (in addition)
di più ▶ n extra m inv; (surcharge)
supplemento; (Cinema, Theatre)
comparsa

extract [vb ɪk'strækt, n 'ɛkstrækt] vt
estrarre; (money, promise) strappare
▶ n estratto; (passage) brano

extradite ['ɛkstrədaɪt] vt estradare

extraordinary [ɪk'strɔːdnrɪ] adj
straordinario(-a)

extravagance [ɪk'strævəgəns] n
sperpero; stravaganza

extravagant [ɪk'strævəgənt]
adj (lavish) prodigo(-a); (wasteful)
dispendioso(-a)

> Be careful not to translate
> **extravagant** by the Italian word
> **stravagante**.

extreme [ɪk'striːm] adj estremo(-a)
▶ n estremo; **extremely** adv
estremamente

extremist [ɪk'striːmɪst] adj, n
estremista (m/f)

extrovert ['ɛkstrəvəːt] n

estroverso(-a)
eye [aɪ] n occhio; (of needle) cruna ▶ vt osservare; **to keep an ~ on** tenere d'occhio; **eyeball** n globo dell'occhio; **eyebrow** n sopracciglio; **eyedrops** npl gocce fpl oculari, collirio; **eyelash** n ciglio; **eyelid** n palpebra; **eyeliner** n eye-liner m inv; **eyeshadow** n ombretto; **eyesight** n vista; **eye witness** n testimone m/f oculare

f

F [ɛf] n (Mus) fa m
fabric ['fæbrɪk] n stoffa, tessuto
fabulous ['fæbjuləs] adj favoloso(-a); (super) favoloso(-a), fantastico(-a)
face [feɪs] n faccia, viso, volto; (expression) faccia; (of clock) quadrante m; (of building) facciata ▶ vt essere di fronte a; (facts, situation) affrontare; **~ down** a faccia in giù; **to make** or **pull a ~** fare una smorfia; **in the ~ of** (difficulties etc) di fronte a; **on the ~ of it** a prima vista; **~ to ~** faccia a faccia ▶ **face up to** vt fus affrontare, far fronte a; **face cloth** (BRIT) n guanto di spugna; **face pack** n (BRIT) maschera di bellezza
facial ['feɪʃəl] adj del viso
facilitate [fə'sɪlɪteɪt] vt facilitare
facilities [fə'sɪlɪtɪz] npl attrezzature fpl; **credit ~** facilitazioni fpl di credito

fact [fækt] n fatto; **in ~** in effetti
faction ['fækʃən] n fazione f
factor ['fæktə] n fattore m; **I'd like a ~ 15 suntan lotion** vorrei una crema solare con fattore di protezione 15
factory ['fæktərɪ] n fabbrica, stabilimento

▌ Be careful not to translate **factory** by the Italian word **fattoria**.

factual ['fæktjuəl] adj che si attiene ai fatti
faculty ['fækəltɪ] n facoltà f inv; (US) corpo insegnante
fad [fæd] n mania; capriccio
fade [feɪd] vi sbiadire, sbiadirsi; (light, sound, hope) attenuarsi, affievolirsi; (flower) appassire ▶ **fade away** vi (sound) affievolirsi
fag [fæg] (BRIT: inf) n (cigarette) cicca
Fahrenheit ['fɑːrənhaɪt] n Fahrenheit m inv
fail [feɪl] vt (exam) non superare; (candidate) bocciare; (courage, memory) mancare a ▶ vi fallire; (student) essere respinto(-a); (eyesight, health, light) venire a mancare; **to ~ to do sth** (neglect) mancare di fare qc; (be unable) non riuscire a fare qc; **without ~** senza fallo; certamente; **failing** n difetto ▶ prep in mancanza di; **failure** ['feɪljə] n fallimento; (person) fallito(-a); (mechanical etc) guasto
faint [feɪnt] adj debole; (recollection) vago(-a); (mark) indistinto(-a) ▶ n (Med) svenimento ▶ vi svenire; **to feel ~** sentirsi svenire; **faintest** adj **I haven't the faintest idea** non ho la più pallida idea; **faintly** adv debolmente; vagamente
fair [fɛə] adj (person, decision) giusto(-a), equo(-a); (quite large, quite good) discreto(-a); (hair etc) biondo(-a); (skin, complexion) chiaro(-a); (weather) bello(-a), clemente ▶ adv (play) lealmente

▶ n fiera; (BRIT: funfair) luna park m inv; **fairground** n luna park m inv

fair-haired [fɛəˈhɛəd] adj (person) biondo(-a); **fairly** adv equamente; (quite) abbastanza; **fairway** n (Golf) fairway m inv

fairy [ˈfɛərɪ] n fata; **fairy tale** n fiaba

faith [feɪθ] n fede f; (trust) fiducia; (sect) religione f, fede f; **faithful** adj fedele; **faithfully** adv fedelmente; **yours faithfully** (BRIT: in letters) distinti saluti

fake [feɪk] n imitazione f; (picture) falso; (person) impostore(-a) ▶ adj falso(-a) ▶ vt (accounts) falsificare; (illness) fingere; (painting) contraffare

falcon [ˈfɔːlkən] n falco, falcone m

fall [fɔːl] (pt fell, pp fallen) n caduta; (in temperature) abbassamento; (in price) ribasso; (US: autumn) autunno ▶ vi cadere; (temperature, price, night) scendere; **~s** npl (waterfall) cascate fpl; **to ~ flat** (on one's face) cadere bocconi; (joke) fare cilecca; (plan) fallire ▶ **fall apart** vi cadere a pezzi ▶ **fall down** vi (person) cadere; (building) crollare ▶ **fall for** vt fus (person) prendere una cotta per; **to ~ for a trick** (or a story etc) cascarci ▶ **fall off** vi cadere; (diminish) diminuire, abbassarsi ▶ **fall out** vi (hair, teeth) cadere; (friends etc) litigare ▶ **fall over** vi cadere ▶ **fall through** vi (plan, project) fallire

fallen [ˈfɔːlən] pp of **fall**

fallout [ˈfɔːlaut] n fall-out m

false [fɔːls] adj falso(-a); **under ~ pretences** con l'inganno; **false alarm** n falso allarme m; **false teeth** (BRIT) npl denti mpl finti

fame [feɪm] n fama, celebrità

familiar [fəˈmɪlɪəʳ] adj familiare; (close) intimo(-a); **to be ~ with** (subject) conoscere; **familiarize** [fəˈmɪlɪəraɪz] vt **to familiarize o.s. with** familiarizzare con

family [ˈfæmɪlɪ] n famiglia; **family doctor** n medico di famiglia; **family planning** n pianificazione f familiare

famine [ˈfæmɪn] n carestia

famous [ˈfeɪməs] adj famoso(-a)

fan [fæn] n (folding) ventaglio; (Elec) ventilatore m; (person) ammiratore(-trice), tifoso(-a) ▶ vt far vento a; (fire, quarrel) alimentare

fanatic [fəˈnætɪk] n fanatico(-a)

fan belt n cinghia del ventilatore

fan club n fan club m inv

fancy [ˈfænsɪ] n immaginazione f, fantasia; (whim) capriccio ▶ adj (hat) stravagante; (hotel, food) speciale ▶ vt (feel like, want) aver voglia di; (imagine, think) immaginare; **to take a ~ to** incapricciarsi di; **he fancies her** (inf) gli piace; **fancy dress** n costume m (per maschera)

fan heater n (BRIT) stufa ad aria calda

fantasize [ˈfæntəsaɪz] vi fantasticare, sognare

fantastic [fænˈtæstɪk] adj fantastico(-a)

fantasy [ˈfæntəsɪ] n fantasia, immaginazione f; fantasticheria; chimera

fanzine [ˈfænziːn] n rivista specialistica (per appassionati)

FAQs abbr (= frequently asked questions) FAQ fpl

far [fɑːʳ] adj lontano(-a) ▶ adv lontano; (much, greatly) molto; **is it ~ from here?** è molto lontano da qui?; **how ~?** quanto lontano?; (referring to activity etc) fino a dove?; **how ~ is the town centre?** quanto dista il centro da qui?; **~ away, ~ off** lontano, distante; **~ better** assai migliore; **by ~** di gran lunga; **go as ~ as the farm** vada fino alla fattoria; **as ~ as I know** per quel che so

farce [fɑːs] n farsa

fare [fɛəʳ] n (on trains, buses) tariffa;

(*in taxi*) prezzo della corsa; (*food*) vitto, cibo; **half ~** metà tariffa; **full ~** tariffa intera

Far East *n* **the ~** l'Estremo Oriente *m*

farewell [fɛəˈwɛl] *excl*, *n* addio

farm [fɑːm] *n* fattoria, podere *m* ▶ *vt* coltivare; **farmer** *n* coltivatore(-trice), agricoltore(-trice); **farmhouse** *n* fattoria; **farming** *n* (*gen*) agricoltura; (*of crops*) coltivazione *f*; (*of animals*) allevamento; **farmyard** *n* aia

far-reaching [fɑːˈriːtʃɪŋ] *adj* di vasta portata

fart [fɑːt] (*infl*) *vi* scoreggiare (!)

farther [ˈfɑːðə*] *adv* più lontano ▶ *adj* più lontano(-a)

farthest [ˈfɑːðɪst] *superl* of **far**

fascinate [ˈfæsɪneɪt] *vt* affascinare; **fascinated** *adj* affascinato(-a); **fascinating** *adj* affascinante; **fascination** [-ˈneɪʃən] *n* fascino

fascist [ˈfæʃɪst] *adj*, *n* fascista (*m/f*)

fashion [ˈfæʃən] *n* moda; (*manner*) maniera, modo ▶ *vt* foggiare, formare; **in ~** alla moda; **out of ~** passato(-a), di moda; **fashionable** *adj* alla moda, di moda; **fashion show** *n* sfilata di moda

fast [fɑːst] *adj* rapido(-a), svelto(-a), veloce; (*clock*): **to be ~** andare avanti; (*dye*, *colour*) solido(-a) ▶ *adv* rapidamente; (*stuck*, *held*) saldamente ▶ *n* digiuno ▶ *vi* digiunare; **~ asleep** profondamente addormentato(-a)

fasten [ˈfɑːsn] *vt* chiudere, fissare; (*coat*) abbottonare, allacciare ▶ *vi* chiudersi, fissarsi; abbottonarsi, allacciarsi

fast food *n* fast food *m*

fat [fæt] *adj* grasso(-a); (*book*, *profit etc*) grosso(-a) ▶ *n* grasso

fatal [ˈfeɪtl] *adj* fatale; mortale; disastroso(-a); **fatality** [fəˈtælɪtɪ] *n* (*road death etc*) morto(-a), vittima;

fatally *adv* a morte

fate [feɪt] *n* destino; (*of person*) sorte *f*

father [ˈfɑːðə*] *n* padre *m*; **Father Christmas** *n* Babbo Natale; **father-in-law** *n* suocero

fatigue [fəˈtiːg] *n* stanchezza

fattening [ˈfætnɪŋ] *adj* (*food*) che fa ingrassare

fatty [ˈfætɪ] *adj* (*food*) grasso(-a) ▶ *n* (*inf*) ciccione(-a)

faucet [ˈfɔːsɪt] (*US*) *n* rubinetto

fault [fɔːlt] *n* colpa; (*Tennis*) fallo; (*defect*) difetto; (*Geo*) faglia ▶ *vt* criticare; **it's my ~** è colpa mia; **to find ~ with** trovare da ridire su; **at ~** in fallo; **faulty** *adj* difettoso(-a)

fauna [ˈfɔːnə] *n* fauna

favour *etc* [ˈfeɪvə*] (*US* **favor**) *n* favore *m* ▶ *vt* (*proposition*) favorire, essere favorevole a; (*pupil etc*) favorire; (*team*, *horse*) dare per vincente; **to do sb a ~** fare un favore or una cortesia a qn; **to find ~ with** (*person*) entrare nelle buone grazie di; (*suggestion*) avere l'approvazione di; **in ~ of** in favore di; **favourable** *adj* favorevole; **favourite** [-rɪt] *adj*, *n* favorito(-a)

fawn [fɔːn] *n* daino ▶ *adj* (*also*: **~-coloured**) marrone chiaro *inv* ▶ *vi* **to ~ (up)on** adulare servilmente

fax [fæks] *n* (*document*) facsimile *m inv*, telecopia; (*machine*) telecopiatrice *f* ▶ *vt* telecopiare, trasmettere in facsimile

FBI (*US*) *n abbr* (= *Federal Bureau of Investigation*) F.B.I. *f*

fear [fɪə*] *n* paura, timore *m* ▶ *vt* aver paura di, temere; **for ~ of** per paura di; **fearful** *adj* pauroso(-a); (*sight*, *noise*) terribile, spaventoso(-a); **fearless** *adj* intrepido(-a), senza paura

feasible [ˈfiːzəbl] *adj* possibile, realizzabile

feast [fiːst] *n* festa, banchetto; (*Rel*: *also*: **~ day**) festa ▶ *vi* banchettare

feat [fi:t] n impresa, fatto insigne

feather ['feðəʳ] n penna

feature ['fi:tʃəʳ] n caratteristica; (Press, TV) articolo ▸ vt (film) avere come protagonista ▸ vi figurare; **~s** npl (of face) fisionomia; **feature film** n film m inv principale

Feb. [fɛb] abbr (= February) feb

February ['fɛbruəri] n febbraio

fed [fɛd] pt, pp of **feed**

federal ['fɛdərəl] adj federale

federation [fɛdə'reiʃən] n federazione f

fed up adj to be ~ essere stufo(-a)

fee [fi:] n pagamento; (of doctor, lawyer) onorario; (for examination) tassa d'esame; **school ~s** tasse fpl scolastiche

feeble ['fi:bl] adj debole

feed [fi:d] (pt, pp fed) n (of baby) pappa; (of animal) mangime m; (on printer) meccanismo di alimentazione ▸ vt nutrire; (baby) allattare; (horse etc) dare da mangiare a; (fire, machine) alimentare; (data, information): **to ~ into** inserire in; **feedback** n feed-back m

feel [fi:l] (pt, pp felt) n consistenza; (sense of touch) tatto ▸ vt toccare; palpare; tastare; (cold, pain, anger) sentire; (think, believe): **to ~ (that)** pensare che; **to ~ hungry/cold** aver fame/freddo; **to ~ lonely/better** sentirsi solo/meglio; **I don't ~ well** non mi sento bene; **it ~s soft** è morbido al tatto; **to ~ like** (want) aver voglia di; **to ~ about** or **around for** cercare a tastoni; **feeling** n sensazione f; (emotion) sentimento

feet [fi:t] npl of **foot**

fell [fɛl] pt of **fall** ▸ vt (tree) abbattere

fellow ['fɛləu] n individuo, tipo; compagno; (of learned society) membro cpd; **fellow citizen** n concittadino(-a); **fellow countryman** (irreg) n

compatriota m; **fellow men** npl simili mpl; **fellowship** n associazione f; compagnia; specie di borsa di studio universitaria

felony ['fɛləni] n reato, crimine m

felt [fɛlt] pt, pp of **feel** ▸ n feltro

female ['fi:meil] n (Zool) femmina; (pej: woman) donna, femmina ▸ adj (Biol, Elec) femmina inv; (sex, character) femminile; (vote etc) di donne

feminine ['fɛminin] adj femminile

feminist ['fɛminist] n femminista m/f

fence [fɛns] n recinto ▸ vt (also: ~ in) recingere ▸ vi (Sport) tirare di scherma; **fencing** n (Sport) scherma

fend [fɛnd] vi **to ~ for o.s.** arrangiarsi
▷ **fend off** vt (attack, questions) respingere, difendersi da

fender ['fɛndəʳ] n parafuoco; (on boat) parabordo; (US) parafango; paraurti m inv

fennel ['fɛnl] n finocchio

ferment [vb fə'mɛnt, n 'fə:mɛnt] vi fermentare ▸ n (fig) agitazione f, eccitazione f

fern [fə:n] n felce f

ferocious [fə'rəuʃəs] adj feroce

ferret ['fɛrit] n furetto

ferry ['fɛri] n (small) traghetto; (large: also: **~boat**) nave f traghetto inv ▸ vt traghettare

fertile ['fə:tail] adj fertile; (Biol) fecondo(-a); **fertilize** ['fə:tilaiz] vt fertilizzare; fecondare; **fertilizer** ['fə:tilaizə] n fertilizzante m

festival ['fɛstivəl] n (Rel) festa; (Art, Mus) festival m inv

festive ['fɛstiv] adj di festa; **the ~ season** (BRIT: Christmas) il periodo delle feste

fetch [fɛtʃ] vt andare a prendere; (sell for) essere venduto(-a) per

fête [feit] n festa

fetus ['fi:təs] (US) n = **foetus**

feud [fju:d] n contesa, lotta

fever ['fiːvə'] n febbre f; **feverish** adj febbrile

few [fjuː] adj pochi(-e); **a ~** adj qualche inv ▶ pron alcuni(-e); **fewer** adj meno inv, meno numerosi(-e); **fewest** adj il minor numero di

fiancé [fɪ'ɑ̃ːŋseɪ] n fidanzato; **fiancée** n fidanzata

fiasco [fɪ'æskəʊ] n fiasco

fib [fɪb] n piccola bugia

fibre ['faɪbə'] (US **fiber**) n fibra; **Fibreglass®** ['faɪbəglɑːs] (US **fiberglass**) n fibra di vetro

fickle ['fɪkl] adj incostante, capriccioso(-a)

fiction ['fɪkʃən] n narrativa, romanzi mpl; (sth made up) finzione f; **fictional** adj immaginario(-a)

fiddle ['fɪdl] n (Mus) violino; (cheating) imbroglio; truffa ▶ vt (BRIT: accounts) falsificare, falsare ▷ **fiddle with** vt fus gingillarsi con

fidelity [fɪ'dɛlɪtɪ] n fedeltà f; (accuracy) esattezza

field [fiːld] n campo; **field marshal** n feldmaresciallo

fierce [fɪəs] adj (animal, person, fighting) feroce; (loyalty) assoluto(-a); (wind) furioso(-a); (heat) intenso(-a)

fifteen [fɪf'tiːn] num quindici; **fifteenth** num quindicesimo(-a)

fifth [fɪfθ] num quinto(-a)

fiftieth ['fɪftɪɪθ] num cinquantesimo(-a)

fifty ['fɪftɪ] num cinquanta; **fifty-fifty** adj **a fifty-fifty chance** una possibilità su due ▶ adv fifty-fifty, metà per ciascuno

fig [fɪg] n fico

fight [faɪt] (pt, pp **fought**) n zuffa, rissa; (Mil) battaglia, combattimento; (against cancer etc) lotta ▶ vt (person) azzuffarsi con; (enemy: also Mil) combattere; (cancer, alcoholism, emotion) lottare contro,

combattere; (election) partecipare a ▶ vi combattere ▷ **fight back** vi difendersi; (Sport, after illness) riprendersi ▶ vt (tears) ricacciare ▷ **fight off** vt (attack, attacker) respingere; (disease, sleep, urge) lottare contro; **fighting** n combattimento

figure ['fɪgə'] n figura; (number, cipher) cifra ▶ vt (think: esp US) pensare ▶ vi (appear) figurare ▷ **figure out** vt riuscire a capire; calcolare

file [faɪl] n (tool) lima; (dossier) incartamento; (folder) cartellina; (Comput) archivio; (row) fila ▶ vt (nails, wood) limare; (papers) archiviare; (Law: claim) presentare; passare agli atti; **filing cabinet** ['faɪlɪŋ-] n casellario

Filipino [fɪlɪ'piːnəʊ] n filippino(-a); (Ling) tagal m

fill [fɪl] vt riempire; (job) coprire ▶ n **to eat one's ~** mangiare a sazietà ▷ **fill in** vt (hole) riempire; (form) compilare ▷ **fill out** vt (form, receipt) riempire ▷ **fill up** vt riempire; **~ it up, please** (Aut) il pieno, per favore

fillet ['fɪlɪt] n filetto; **fillet steak** n bistecca di filetto

filling ['fɪlɪŋ] n (Culin) impasto, ripieno; (for tooth) otturazione f; **filling station** n stazione f di rifornimento

film [fɪlm] n (Cinema) film m inv; (Phot) pellicola, rullino; (of powder, liquid) sottile strato ▶ vt, vi girare; **I'd like a 36-exposure ~** vorrei un rullino da 36 pose; **film star** n divo(-a) dello schermo

filter ['fɪltə'] n filtro ▶ vt filtrare; **filter lane** (BRIT) n (Aut) corsia di svincolo

filth [fɪlθ] n sporcizia; **filthy** adj lordo(-a), sozzo(-a); (language) osceno(-a)

fin [fɪn] n (of fish) pinna

final ['faɪnl] adj finale, ultimo(-a);

definitivo(-a) ▸ n (Sport) finale f; **~s** npl
(Scol) esami mpl finali; **finale** [fɪˈnɑːlɪ]
n finale m; **finalist** [ˈfaɪnəlɪst] n (Sport)
finalista m/f; **finalize** [ˈfaɪnəlaɪz] vt
mettere a punto; **finally** [ˈfaɪnəlɪ]
adv (lastly) alla fine; (eventually)
finalmente

finance [faɪˈnæns] n finanza;
(capital) capitale m ▸ vt finanziare;
~s npl (funds) finanze fpl; **financial**
[faɪˈnænʃəl] adj finanziario; **financial
year** n anno finanziario,
esercizio finanziario

find [faɪnd] (pt, pp found) vt trovare;
(lost object) ritrovare ▸ n trovata,
scoperta; **to ~ sb guilty** (Law)
giudicare qn colpevole ▸ **find out**
vt (truth, secret) scoprire; (person)
cogliere in fallo; **to ~ out about**
informarsi su; (by chance) scoprire;
findings npl (Law) sentenza,
conclusioni fpl; (of report) conclusioni

fine [faɪn] adj bello(-a); ottimo(-a);
(thin, subtle) fine ▸ adv (well) molto
bene ▸ n (Law) multa ▸ vt (Law)
multare; **to be ~** (person) stare bene;
(weather) far bello; **fine arts** npl belle
arti fpl

finger [ˈfɪŋɡər] n dito ▸ vt toccare,
tastare; **little/index ~** mignolo/(dito)
indice m; **fingernail** n unghia;
fingerprint n impronta digitale;
fingertip n punta del dito

finish [ˈfɪnɪʃ] n fine f; (polish etc)
finitura ▸ vt, vi finire; **when does
the show ~?** quando finisce lo
spettacolo?; **to ~ doing sth** finire di
fare qc; **to ~ third** arrivare terzo(-a)
▸ **finish off** vt compiere; (kill) uccidere
▸ **finish up** vi, vt finire

Finland [ˈfɪnlənd] n Finlandia; **Finn**
[fɪn] n finlandese m/f; **Finnish** adj
finlandese ▸ n (Ling) finlandese m

fir [fəːr] n abete m

fire [faɪər] n fuoco; (destructive)

incendio; (gas fire, electric fire) stufa
▸ vt (gun) far fuoco con; (arrow)
sparare; (fig) infiammare; (inf: dismiss)
licenziare ▸ vi sparare, far fuoco; **~!**
al fuoco!; **on ~** in fiamme; **fire alarm**
n allarme m d'incendio; **firearm**
n arma da fuoco; **fire brigade**
[-brɪˈɡeɪd] (US **fire department**) n
(corpo dei) pompieri mpl; **fire engine**
n autopompa; **fire escape** n scala
di sicurezza; **fire exit** n uscita di
sicurezza; **fire extinguisher**
[-ɪkˈstɪŋɡwɪʃər] n estintore m; **fireman**
(irreg) n pompiere m; **fireplace** n
focolare m; **fire station** n caserma
dei pompieri; **firetruck** (US) n = **fire
engine**; **firewall** n (Internet) firewall m
inv; **firewood** n legna; **fireworks** npl
fuochi d'artificio

firm [fəːm] adj fermo(-a) ▸ n ditta,
azienda; **firmly** adv fermamente

first [fəːst] adj primo(-a) ▸ adv (before
others) il primo, la prima; (before
other things) per primo; (when listing
reasons etc) per prima cosa ▸ n (person:
in race) primo(-a); (BRIT Scol) laurea
con lode; (Aut) prima; **at ~** dapprima,
all'inizio; **~ of all** prima di tutto; **first
aid** n pronto soccorso; **first-aid kit** n
cassetta pronto soccorso; **first-class**
adj di prima classe; **first-hand** adj di
prima mano; **first lady** (US) n moglie
f del presidente; **firstly** adv in primo
luogo; **first name** n prenome m; **first-
rate** adj di prima qualità, ottimo(-a)

fiscal [ˈfɪskəl] adj fiscale; **fiscal year** n
anno fiscale

fish [fɪʃ] n inv pesce m ▸ vt (river,
area) pescare in ▸ vi pescare; **to go
~ing** andare a pesca; **fish and chip
shop** n see chip shop; **fisherman**
(irreg) n pescatore m; **fish fingers**
(BRIT) npl bastoncini mpl di pesce
(surgelati); **fishing** n pesca; **fishing
boat** n barca da pesca; **fishing line** n

lenza; **fishmonger** n pescivendolo;
fishmonger's (shop) n pescheria;
fish sticks (US) npl = **fish fingers**;
fishy (inf) adj (tale, story) sospetto(-a)
fist [fɪst] n pugno
fit [fɪt] adj (Med, Sport) in forma;
(proper) adatto(-a), appropriato(-a);
conveniente ▶ vt (clothes) stare bene
a; (put in, attach) mettere; installare;
(equip) fornire, equipaggiare ▶ vi
(clothes) stare bene; (parts) andare
bene, adattarsi; (in space, gap) entrare
▶ n (Med) accesso, attacco; **~ to** in
grado di; **~ for** adatto(-a) a, degno(-a)
di; **a ~ of anger** un accesso d'ira;
this dress is a good ~ questo vestito sta
bene; **~s and starts** a sbalzi ▶ **fit
in** vi accordarsi; adattarsi; **fitness** n
(Med) forma fisica; **fitted** adj fitted
cupboards armadi mpl a muro; **fitted
carpet** moquette f inv; **fitted kitchen**
(BRIT) cucina componibile; **fitting** adj
appropriato(-a) ▶ n (of dress) prova;
(of piece of equipment) montaggio,
aggiustaggio; **fitting room** n
camerino; **fittings** npl (in building)
impianti mpl
five [faɪv] num cinque; **fiver** (inf) n
(BRIT) biglietto da cinque sterline;
(US) biglietto da cinque dollari
fix [fɪks] vt fissare; (mend) riparare;
(meal, drink) preparare ▶ n **to be in a
~** essere nei guai ▶ **fix up** vt (meeting)
fissare; **to ~ sb up with sth** procurare
qc a qn; **fixed** [fɪkst] adj (prices
etc) fisso(-a); **fixture** ['fɪkstʃəʳ] n
impianto (fisso); (Sport) incontro del
calendario sportivo
fizzy ['fɪzɪ] adj frizzante; gassato(-a)
flag [flæg] n bandiera; (also: **~stone**)
pietra da lastricare ▶ vi stancarsi;
affievolirsi; **flagpole** ['flæɡpəul]
n albero
flair [flɛəʳ] n (for business etc) fiuto; (for
languages etc) facilità; (style) stile m

flak [flæk] n (Mil) fuoco d'artiglieria;
(inf: criticism) critiche fpl
flake [fleɪk] n (of rust, paint) scaglia; (of
snow, soap powder) fiocco ▶ vi (also: **~
off**) sfaldarsi
flamboyant [flæm'bɔɪənt] adj
sgargiante
flame [fleɪm] n fiamma
flamingo [flə'mɪŋɡəu] n fenicottero,
fiammingo
flammable ['flæməbl] adj
infiammabile
flan [flæn] (BRIT) n flan m inv
flank [flæŋk] n fianco ▶ vt
fiancheggiare
flannel ['flænl] n (BRIT: also: **face ~**)
guanto di spugna; (fabric) flanella
flap [flæp] n (of pocket) patta; (of
envelope) lembo ▶ vt (wings) battere
▶ vi (sail, flag) sbattere; (inf: also: **be in
a ~**) essere in agitazione
flare [flɛəʳ] n razzo; (in skirt etc)
svasatura; **~s** (trousers) pantaloni
mpl a zampa d'elefante ▶ **flare up**
vi andare in fiamme; (fig: person)
infiammarsi di rabbia; (: revolt)
scoppiare
flash [flæʃ] n vampata; (also: **news
~**) notizia flampo inv; (Phot) flash
m inv ▶ vt accendere e spegnere;
(send: message) trasmettere; (: look,
smile) lanciare ▶ vi brillare; (light on
ambulance, eyes etc) lampeggiare;
in a ~ in un lampo; **to ~ one's
headlights** lampeggiare; **he ~ed
by** or **past** ci passò davanti come
un lampo; **flashback** n flashback
m inv; **flashbulb** n cubo m flash inv;
flashlight n lampadina tascabile
flask [flɑːsk] n fiasco; (also: **vacuum ~**)
Thermos® m inv
flat [flæt] n piatto(-a); (tyre)
sgonfio(-a), a terra; (battery)
scarico(-a); (beer) svampito(-a);
(denial) netto(-a); (Mus) bemolle inv;

(: *voice*) stonato(-a); (*rate, fee*) unico(-a) ▶ n (BRIT: *rooms*) appartamento; (*Aut*) pneumatico sgonfio; (*Mus*) bemolle *m*; **to work ~ out** lavorare a più non posso; **flatten** *vt* (*also*: **flatten out**) appiattire; (*building, city*) spianare

flatter ['flætə*] *vt* lusingare; **flattering** *adj* lusinghiero(-a); (*dress*) che dona

flaunt [flɔːnt] *vt* fare mostra di

flavour *etc* ['fleɪvə*] (US **flavor**) *n* gusto *m* ▶ *vt* insaporire, aggiungere sapore a; **what ~ do you have?** che gusti avete?; **strawberry-~ed** al gusto di fragola; **flavouring** *n* essenza (artificiale)

flaw [flɔː] *n* difetto; **flawless** *adj* senza difetti

flea [fliː] *n* pulce *f*; **flea market** *n* mercato delle pulci

flee [fliː] (*pt, pp* **fled**) *vt* fuggire da ▶ *vi* fuggire, scappare

fleece [fliːs] *n* vello ▶ *vt* (*inf*) pelare

fleet [fliːt] *n* flotta; (*of lorries etc*) convoglio; parco

fleeting ['fliːtɪŋ] *adj* fugace, fuggitivo(-a); (*visit*) volante

Flemish ['flemɪʃ] *adj* fiammingo(-a)

flesh [fleʃ] *n* carne *f*; (*of fruit*) polpa

flew [fluː] *pt of* **fly**

flex [fleks] *n* filo (flessibile) ▶ *vt* flettere; (*muscles*) contrarre; **flexibility** *n* flessibilità; **flexible** *adj* flessibile; **flexitime** ['fleksɪtaɪm] *n* orario flessibile

flick [flɪk] *n* colpetto; scarto ▶ *vt* dare un colpetto a ▶ **flick through** *vt fus* sfogliare

flicker ['flɪkə*] *vi* tremolare

flies [flaɪz] *npl of* **fly**

flight [flaɪt] *n* volo; (*escape*) fuga; (*also*: **~ of steps**) scalinata; **flight attendant** (US) *n* steward *m inv*, hostess *f inv*

flimsy ['flɪmzɪ] *adj* (*shoes, clothes*) leggero(-a); (*building*) poco solido(-a); (*excuse*) che non regge

flinch [flɪntʃ] *vi* ritirarsi; **to ~ from** tirarsi indietro di fronte a

fling [flɪŋ] (*pt, pp* **flung**) *vt* lanciare, gettare

flint [flɪnt] *n* selce *f*; (*in lighter*) pietrina

flip [flɪp] *vt* (*switch*) far scattare; (*coin*) lanciare in aria

flip-flops ['flɪpflɔps] *npl* (*esp BRIT*: *sandals*) infradito *mpl*

flipper ['flɪpə*] *n* pinna

flirt [fləːt] *vi* flirtare ▶ *n* civetta

float [fləut] *n* galleggiante *m*; (*in procession*) carro; (*money*) somma ▶ *vi* galleggiare

flock [flɔk] *n* (*of sheep, Rel*) gregge *m*; (*of birds*) stormo ▶ *vi* **to ~ to** accorrere in massa a

flood [flʌd] *n* alluvione *m*; (*of letters etc*) marea ▶ *vt* allagare; (*people*) invadere ▶ *vi* (*place*) allagarsi; (*people*): **to ~ into** riversarsi in; **flooding** *n* inondazione *f*; **floodlight** *n* riflettore *m* ▶ *vt* illuminare a giorno

floor [flɔː*] *n* pavimento; (*storey*) piano; (*of sea, valley*) fondo ▶ *vt* (*blow*) atterrare; (: *question*) ridurre al silenzio; **which ~ is it on?** a che piano si trova?; **ground ~** (BRIT), **first ~** (US) pianterreno; **first ~** (BRIT), **second ~** (US) primo piano; **floorboard** *n* tavellone *m* di legno; **flooring** *n* (*floor*) pavimento; (*material*) materiale *m* per pavimentazioni; **floor show** *n* spettacolo di varietà

flop [flɔp] *n* fiasco ▶ *vi* far fiasco; (*fall*) lasciarsi cadere; **floppy** ['flɔpɪ] *adj* floscio(-a), molle

floral ['flɔːrl] *adj* floreale

Florence ['flɔrəns] *n* Firenze *f*

Florentine ['flɔrəntaɪn] *adj* fiorentino(-a)

florist ['flɔrɪst] *n* fioraio(-a); **florist's**

(shop) n fioraio(-a)

flotation [fləʊ'teɪʃən] n (Comm) lancio

flour ['flaʊəʳ] n farina

flourish ['flʌrɪʃ] vi fiorire ▸ n (bold gesture): **with a ~** con ostentazione

flow [fləʊ] n flusso; circolazione f ▸ vi fluire; (traffic, blood in veins) circolare; (hair) scendere

flower ['flaʊəʳ] n fiore m ▸ vi fiorire; **flower bed** n aiuola; **flowerpot** n vaso da fiori

flown [fləʊn] pp of **fly**

fl. oz. abbr = **fluid ounce**

flu [fluː] n influenza

fluctuate ['flʌktjueɪt] vi fluttuare, oscillare

fluent ['fluːənt] adj (speech) facile, sciolto(-a); corrente; **he speaks ~ Italian, he's ~ in Italian** parla l'italiano correntemente

fluff [flʌf] n lanugine f; **fluffy** adj lanuginoso(-a); (toy) di peluche

fluid ['fluːɪd] adj fluido(-a) ▸ n fluido; **fluid ounce** n (BRIT) = 0.028 l; 0.05 pints

fluke [fluːk] (inf) n colpo di fortuna

flung [flʌŋ] pt, pp of **fling**

fluorescent [fluə'rɛsnt] adj fluorescente

fluoride ['fluəraɪd] n fluoruro

flurry ['flʌrɪ] n (of snow) tempesta; **a ~ of activity** una scoppio di attività

flush [flʌʃ] n rossore m; (fig: of youth, beauty etc) rigoglio, pieno vigore ▸ vt ripulire con un getto d'acqua ▸ vi arrossire ▸ adj ~ **with** a livello di, pari a; **to ~ the toilet** tirare l'acqua

flute [fluːt] n flauto

flutter ['flʌtəʳ] n agitazione f; (of wings) battito ▸ vi (bird) battere le ali

fly [flaɪ] (pt **flew**, pp **flown**) n (insect) mosca; (on trousers: also: **flies**) chiusura ▸ vt pilotare; (passengers, cargo) trasportare (in aereo); (distances) percorrere ▸ vi volare;

(passengers) andare in aereo; (escape) fuggire; (flag) sventolare ▸ **fly away** vi vola via; **fly-drive** n fly-drive holiday fly and drive m inv; **flying** n (activity) aviazione f; (action) volo ▸ adj **flying visit** visita volante; **with flying colours** con risultati brillanti; **flying saucer** n disco volante; **flyover** (BRIT) n (bridge) cavalcavia m inv

FM abbr = **frequency modulation**

foal [fəʊl] n puledro

foam [fəʊm] n schiuma; (also: ~ **rubber**) gommapiuma® ▸ vi schiumare; (soapy water) fare la schiuma

focus ['fəʊkəs] (pl **focuses**) n fuoco; (of interest) centro ▸ vt (field glasses etc) mettere a fuoco ▸ vi **to ~ on** (with camera) mettere a fuoco; (person) fissare lo sguardo su; **in ~** a fuoco; **out of ~** sfocato(-a)

foetus ['fiːtəs] (US **fetus**) n feto

fog [fɔg] n nebbia; **foggy** adj **it's foggy** c'è nebbia; **fog lamp** (US **fog light**) n (Aut) faro m antinebbia inv

foil [fɔɪl] vt confondere, frustrare ▸ n lamina di metallo; (kitchen foil) foglio di alluminio; (Fencing) fioretto; **to act as a ~ to** (fig) far risaltare

fold [fəʊld] n (bend, crease) piega; (Agr) ovile m; (fig) gregge m ▸ vt piegare; (arms) incrociare ▸ **fold up** vi (map, bed, table) piegarsi; (business) crollare ▸ vt (map etc) piegare, ripiegare; **folder** n (for papers) cartella; cartellina; **folding** adj (chair, bed) pieghevole

foliage ['fəʊlɪɪdʒ] n fogliame m

folk [fəʊk] npl gente f ▸ adj popolare; **~s** npl (family) famiglia; **folklore** ['fəʊkɔ:ʳ] n folclore m; **folk music** n musica folk inv; **folk song** n canto popolare

follow ['fɔləʊ] vt seguire ▸ vi seguire; (result) conseguire, risultare; **to ~**

suit fare lo stesso ▷ **follow up** vt
(letter, offer) fare seguito a; (case)
seguire; **follower** n seguace m/f,
discepolo(-a); **following** adj seguente
▶ n seguito, discepoli mpl; **follow-up**
n seguito

fond [fɔnd] adj (memory, look)
tenero(-a), affettuoso(-a); **to be ~ of
sb** volere bene a qn; **he's ~ of walking**
gli piace fare camminate

food [fuːd] n cibo; **food mixer** n
frullatore m; **food poisoning** n
intossicazione f; **food processor**
[-'prəʊsesə] n tritatutto m inv
elettrico; **food stamp** (US) n buono
alimentare dato agli indigenti

fool [fuːl] n sciocco(-a); (Culin) frullato
▶ vt ingannare ▶ vi (gen: fool around)
fare lo sciocco ▷ **fool about** vi
(waste time) perdere tempo;
foolish adj scemo(-a), stupido(-a);
imprudente; **foolproof** adj (plan etc)
sicurissimo(-a)

foot [fut] (pl **feet**) n piede m; (measure)
piede (= 304 mm; 12 inches); (of
animal) zampa ▶ vt (bill) pagare; **on
~ a** piedi; **footage** n (Cinema: length)
= metraggio; (: material) sequenza;

foot-and-mouth (disease)
[futənd'maʊθ-] n afta epizootica;
football n pallone m; (sport: BRIT)
calcio; (: US) football m americano;
footballer n (BRIT) = **football player**;
football match n (BRIT) partita
di calcio; **football player** n (BRIT:
also: **footballer**) calciatore m; (US)
giocatore m di football americano;
footbridge n passerella; **foothills**
npl contrafforti fpl; **foothold** n punto
d'appoggio; **footing** n (fig) posizione
f; **to lose one's footing** mettere un
piede in fallo; **footnote** n nota (a piè
di pagina); **footpath** n sentiero; (in
street) marciapiede m; **footprint** n
orma, impronta; **footstep** n passo;

(footprint) orma, impronta; **footwear**
n calzatura

for
[fɔːʳ] prep
1 (indicating destination, intention,
purpose) per; **the train for London**
il treno per Londra; **he went for the
paper** è andato a prendere il giornale;
it's time for lunch è ora di pranzo;
what's it for? a che serve?; **what for?**
(why) perché?
2 (on behalf of, representing) per; **to
work for sb/sth** lavorare per qn/qc; **I'll
ask him for you** glielo chiederò a nome
tuo; **G for George** G come George
3 (because of) per, a causa di; **for this
reason** per questo motivo
4 (with regard to) per; **it's cold for July**
è freddo per luglio; **for everyone who
voted yes, 50 voted no** per ogni voto a
favore ce n'erano 50 contro
5 (in exchange for) per; **I sold it for £5**
l'ho venduto per 5 sterline
6 (in favour of) per, a favore di; **are you
for or against us?** è con noi o contro di
noi?; **I'm all for it** sono completamente
a favore
7 (referring to distance, time) per; **there
are roadworks for 5 km** ci sono lavori
in corso per 5 km; **he was away for 2
years** è stato via per 2 anni; **she will
be away for a month** starà via un
mese; **it hasn't rained for 3 weeks** non
piove da 3 settimane; **can you do it for
tomorrow?** può farlo per domani?
8 (with infinitive clauses): **it is not for
me to decide** non sta a me decidere; **it
would be best for you to leave** sarebbe
meglio che lei se ne andasse; **there
is still time for you to do it** hai ancora
tempo per farlo; **for this to be possible
... perché ciò sia possibile ...**
9 (in spite of) nonostante; **for all his
complaints, he's very fond of her**
nonostante tutte le sue lamentele, le

vuole molto bene
▶ *conj* (since, as: rather formal) dal momento che, poiché

forbid [fə'bɪd] (*pt* forbad(e), *pp* **forbidden**) *vt* vietare, interdire; to ~ sb to do sth proibire a qn di fare qc; **forbidden** *pt of* forbid ▶ *adj* (food) proibito(-a); (area, territory) vietato(-a); (word, subject) tabù *inv*

force [fɔ:s] *n* forza ▶ *vt* forzare; **forced** *adj* forzato(-a); **forceful** *adj* forte, vigoroso(-a)

ford [fɔ:d] *n* guado

fore [fɔ:] *n* to come to the ~ mettersi in evidenza; **forearm** ['fɔ:rɑ:m] *n* avambraccio; **forecast** ['fɔ:kɑ:st] (irreg: like cast) *n* previsione *f* ▶ *vt* prevedere; **forecourt** ['fɔ:kɔ:t] *n* (of garage) corte esterna; **forefinger** ['fɔ:fɪŋgə'] *n* (dito) indice *m*; **forefront** ['fɔ:frʌnt] *n* in the forefront of all'avanguardia in; **foreground** ['fɔ:graund] *n* primo piano; **forehead** ['fɔrɪd] *n* fronte *f*

foreign ['fɔrɪn] *adj* straniero(-a); (trade) estero(-a); (object, matter) estraneo(-a); **foreign currency** *n* valuta estera; **foreigner** *n* straniero(-a); **foreign exchange** (currency) valuta estera; **Foreign Office** (BRIT) *n* Ministero degli Esteri; **Foreign Secretary** (BRIT) *n* ministro degli Affari esteri

fore: **foreman** ['fɔ:mən] (irreg) *n* caposquadra *m*; **foremost** ['fɔ:məust] *adj* principale; più in vista ▶ *adv* first and foremost innanzitutto; **forename** *n* nome *m* di battesimo

forensic [fə'rensɪk] *adj* ~ medicine medicina legale

foresee [fɔ:'si:] (irreg: like see) *vt* prevedere; **foreseeable** *adj* prevedibile

forest ['fɔrɪst] *n* foresta; **forestry** ['fɔrɪstrɪ] *n* silvicoltura

forever [fə'revə'] *adv* per sempre; (endlessly) sempre, di continuo

foreword ['fɔ:wə:d] *n* prefazione *f*

forfeit ['fɔ:fɪt] *vt* perdere; (one's happiness, health) giocarsi

forgave [fə'geɪv] *pt of* forgive

forge [fɔ:dʒ] *n* fucina ▶ *vt* (signature, money) contraffare, falsificare; (wrought iron) fucinare, foggiare; **forger** *n* contraffattore *m*; **forgery** *n* falso; (activity) contraffazione *f*

forget [fə'get] (*pt* forgot, *pp* forgotten) *vt*, *vi* dimenticare; I've forgotten my key/passport ho dimenticato la chiave/il passaporto; **forgetful** *adj* di corta memoria; **forgetful of** dimentico(-a) di

forgive [fə'gɪv] (*pt* forgave, *pp* forgiven) *vt* perdonare; to ~ sb for sth perdonare qc a qn

forgot [fə'gɒt] *pt of* forget

forgotten [fə'gɒtn] *pp of* forget

fork [fɔ:k] *n* (for eating) forchetta; (for gardening) forca; (of roads, rivers, railways) biforcazione *f* ▶ *vi* (road etc) biforcarsi

forlorn [fə'lɔ:n] *adj* (person) sconsolato(-a); (place) abbandonato(-a); (attempt) disperato(-a); (hope) vano(-a)

form [fɔ:m] *n* forma; (Scol) classe *f*; (questionnaire) scheda ▶ *vt* formare; in top ~ in gran forma

formal ['fɔ:məl] *adj* formale; (gardens) simmetrico(-a), regolare; **formality** [fɔ:'mælɪtɪ] *n* formalità *f inv*

format ['fɔ:mæt] *n* formato ▶ *vt* (Comput) formattare

formation [fɔ:'meɪʃən] *n* formazione *f*

former ['fɔ:mə'] *adj* vecchio(-a); (before n) ex *inv* (before n); the ~ ... the latter quello ... questo; **formerly** *adv* in passato

formidable ['fɔ:mɪdəbl] *adj*

formidabile

formula ['fɔ:mjulə] n formula

fort [fɔ:t] n forte m

forthcoming [fɔ:θ'kʌmɪŋ] adj (event) prossimo(-a); (help) disponibile; (character) aperto(-a), comunicativo(-a)

fortieth ['fɔ:tɪɪθ] num quarantesimo(-a)

fortify ['fɔ:tɪfaɪ] vt (city) fortificare; (person) armare

fortnight ['fɔ:tnaɪt] (BRIT) n quindici giorni mpl, due settimane fpl; **fortnightly** adj bimensile ▶ adv ogni quindici giorni

fortress ['fɔ:trɪs] n fortezza, rocca

fortunate ['fɔ:tʃənɪt] adj fortunato(-a); **it is ~ that** è una fortuna che; **fortunately** adv fortunatamente

fortune ['fɔ:tʃən] n fortuna; **fortune-teller** n indovino(-a)

forty ['fɔ:tɪ] num quaranta

forum ['fɔ:rəm] n foro

forward ['fɔ:wəd] adj (ahead of schedule) in anticipo; (movement, position) in avanti; (not shy) aperto(-a), diretto(-a) ▶ n (Sport) avanti m inv ▶ vt (letter) inoltrare; (parcel, goods) spedire; (career, plans) promuovere, appoggiare; **to move ~** avanzare; **forwarding address** n nuovo recapito cui spedire la posta; **forward(s)** adv avanti; **forward slash** n barra obliqua

fossil ['fɔsl] adj fossile ▶ n fossile m

foster ['fɔstə'] vt incoraggiare, nutrire; (child) avere in affidamento; **foster child** n bambino(-a) preso(-a) in affidamento; **foster mother** n madre f affidataria

fought [fɔ:t] pt, pp of **fight**

foul [faul] adj (smell, food, temper etc) cattivo(-a); (weather) brutto(-a); (language) osceno(-a) ▶ n (Sport) fallo ▶ vt sporcare; **foul play** n (Law): **the**

police suspect foul play la polizia sospetta un atto criminale

found [faund] pt, pp of **find** ▶ vt (establish) fondare; **foundation** [-'deɪʃən] n (act) fondazione f; (base) base f; (also: **foundation cream**) fondo tinta; **foundations** npl (of building) fondamenta fpl

founder ['faundə'] n fondatore(-trice) ▶ vi affondare

fountain ['fauntɪn] n fontana; **fountain pen** n penna stilografica

four [fɔ:'] num quattro; **on all ~s** a carponi; **four-letter word** ['fɔ:letə-] n parolaccia; **four-poster** n (also: **four-poster bed**) letto a quattro colonne; **fourteen** num quattordici; **fourteenth** num quattordicesimo(-a); **fourth** num quarto(-a); **four-wheel drive** ['fɔ:wi:l-] n (Aut): **with four-wheel drive** con quattro ruote motrici

fowl [faul] n pollame m; volatile m

fox [fɔks] n volpe f ▶ vt confondere

foyer ['fɔɪeɪ] n atrio; (Theatre) ridotto

fraction ['frækʃən] n frazione f

fracture ['fræktʃə'] n frattura

fragile ['frædʒaɪl] adj fragile

fragment ['frægmənt] n frammento

fragrance ['freɪgrəns] n fragranza, profumo

frail [freɪl] adj debole, delicato(-a)

frame [freɪm] n (of building) armatura; (of human, animal) ossatura, corpo; (of picture) cornice f; (of door, window) telaio; (of spectacles: also: **~s**) montatura ▶ vt (picture) incorniciare; **framework** n struttura

France [frɑ:ns] n Francia

franchise ['fræntʃaɪz] n (Pol) diritto di voto; (Comm) concessione f

frank [fræŋk] adj franco(-a), aperto(-a) ▶ vt (letter) affrancare; **frankly** adv francamente, sinceramente

frantic ['fræntɪk] adj frenetico(-a)

fraud [frɔːd] n truffa; (Law) frode f; (person) impostore(-a)

fraught [frɔːt] adj ~ **with** pieno(-a) di, intriso(-a) da

fray [freɪ] vt logorare ▶ vi logorarsi

freak [friːk] n fenomeno, mostro

freckle ['frɛkl] n lentiggine f

free [friː] adj libero(-a); (gratis) gratuito(-a) ▶ vt (prisoner, jammed person) liberare; (jammed object) districare; **is this seat ~?** è libero questo posto?; **~ of charge, for ~** gratuitamente; **freedom** ['friːdəm] n libertà; **Freefone®** n numero verde; **free gift** n regalo, omaggio; **free kick** n calcio libero; **freelance** adj indipendente; **freely** adv liberamente; (liberally) liberamente; **Freepost®** n affrancatura a carico del destinatario; **free-range** adj (hen) ruspante; (eggs) di gallina ruspante; **freeway** (US) n superstrada; **free will** n libero arbitrio; **of one's own free will** di spontanea volontà

freeze [friːz] (pt **froze**, pp **frozen**) vi gelare ▶ vt gelare; (food) congelare; (prices, salaries) bloccare ▶ n gelo; blocco; **freezer** n congelatore m; **freezing** ['friːzɪŋ] adj (wind, weather) gelido(-a); **freezing point** n punto di congelamento; **3 degrees below freezing point** 3 gradi sotto zero

freight [freɪt] n (goods) merce f, merci fpl; (money charged) spese fpl di trasporto; **freight train** (US) n treno m merci inv

French [frɛntʃ] adj francese ▶ n (Ling) francese m; **the ~** npl i Francesi; **French bean** n fagiolino; **French bread** n baguette f inv; **French dressing** n (Culin) condimento per insalata; **French fried potatoes** (US **French fries**) npl patate fpl fritte; **Frenchman** (irreg) n francese

m; **French stick** n baguette f inv; **French window** n portafinestra; **Frenchwoman** (irreg) n francese f

frenzy ['frɛnzɪ] n frenesia

frequency ['friːkwənsɪ] n frequenza

frequent [adj 'friːkwənt, vb frɪ'kwɛnt] adj frequente ▶ vt frequentare; **frequently** adv frequentemente, spesso

fresh [frɛʃ] adj fresco(-a); (new) nuovo(-a); (cheeky) sfacciato(-a); **freshen** vi (wind, air) rinfrescare ▷ **freshen up** vi rinfrescarsi; **fresher** (BRIT: inf) n (Scol) matricola; **freshly** adv di recente, di fresco; **freshman** (irreg: US) n = **fresher**; **freshwater** adj (fish) d'acqua dolce

fret [frɛt] vi agitarsi, affliggersi

Fri abbr (= Friday) ven

friction ['frɪkʃən] n frizione f, attrito

Friday ['fraɪdɪ] n venerdì m inv

fridge [frɪdʒ] (BRIT) n frigo, frigorifero

fried [fraɪd] pt, pp of **fry** ▶ adj fritto(-a)

friend [frɛnd] n amico(-a); **friendly** adj amichevole; **friendship** n amicizia

fries [fraɪz] (esp US) npl patate fpl fritte

frigate ['frɪgɪt] n (Naut: modern) fregata

fright [fraɪt] n paura, spavento; **to take ~** spaventarsi; **frighten** vt spaventare, far paura a; **frightened** adj spaventato(-a); **frightening** adj spaventoso(-a), pauroso(-a); **frightful** adj orribile

frill [frɪl] n balza

fringe [frɪndʒ] n (decoration: BRIT: of hair) frangia; (edge: of forest etc) margine m

Frisbee® ['frɪzbɪ] n frisbee® m inv

fritter ['frɪtə*] n frittella

frivolous ['frɪvələs] adj frivolo(-a)

fro [frəu] see **to**

frock [frɔk] n vestito

frog [frɔg] n rana; **frogman** (irreg) n uomo m rana inv

from [frɒm] prep

1 (indicating starting place, origin etc) da; **where do you come from?**, **where are you from?** da dove viene?, di dove'è?; **from London to Glasgow** da Londra a Glasgow; **a letter from my sister** una lettera da mia sorella; **tell him from me that ...** gli dica da parte mia che ...

2 (indicating time) da; **from one o'clock to or until or till two** dall'una alle due; **from January (on)** da gennaio, a partire da gennaio

3 (indicating distance) da; **the hotel is 1 km from the beach** l'albergo è a 1 km dalla spiaggia

4 (indicating price, number etc) da; **prices range from £10 to £50** i prezzi vanno dalle 10 alle 50 sterline

5 (indicating difference) da; **he can't tell red from green** non sa distinguere il rosso dal verde

6 (because of, on the basis of): **from what he says** da quanto dice lui; **weak from hunger** debole per la fame

front [frʌnt] n (of house, dress) davanti m inv; (of train) testa; (of beach) copertina; (promenade: also: **sea ~**) lungomare m; (Mil, Pol, Meteor) fronte m; (fig: appearances) fronte ▶ adj primo(-a); anteriore, davanti inv; **in ~ of** davanti a; **front door** n porta d'entrata; (of car) sportello anteriore; **frontier** ['frʌntɪə*] n frontiera; **front page** n prima pagina; **front-wheel drive** ['frʌntwiːl-] n trasmissione f anteriore

frost [frɒst] n gelo m; (also: **hoar~**) brina; **frostbite** n congelamento; **frosting** (US) n (on cake) glassa; **frosty** adj (weather, look) gelido(-a)

froth ['frɒθ] n spuma; schiuma

frown [fraʊn] vi accigliarsi

froze [frəʊz] pt of **freeze**

frozen ['frəʊzn] pp of **freeze**

fruit [fruːt] n inv (also fig) frutto; (collectively) frutta; **fruit juice** n succo di frutta; **fruit machine** (BRIT) n macchina f mangiasoldi inv; **fruit salad** n macedonia

frustrate [frʌs'treɪt] vt frustrare; **frustrated** adj frustrato(-a)

fry [fraɪ] (pt, pp **fried**) vt friggere; see also **small**; **frying pan** n padella

ft. abbr = **foot**; **feet**

fudge [fʌdʒ] n (Culin) specie di caramella a base di latte, burro e zucchero

fuel [fjʊəl] n (for heating) combustibile m; (for propelling) carburante m; **fuel tank** n deposito m nafta inv; (on vehicle) serbatoio (della benzina)

fulfil [fʊl'fɪl] vt (function) compiere; (order) eseguire; (wish, desire) soddisfare, appagare

full [fʊl] adj pieno(-a); (details, skirt) ampio(-a) ▶ adv **to know ~ well that** sapere benissimo che; **I'm ~ (up)** sono sazio; **a ~ two hours** due ore intere; **at ~ speed** a tutta velocità; **in ~** per intero; **full-length** adj (film) a lungometraggio; (coat, novel) lungo(-a); (portrait) in piedi; **full moon** n luna piena; **full-scale** adj (attack, war) su larga scala; (model) in grandezza naturale; **full stop** n punto; **full-time** adj, adv (work) a tempo pieno; **fully** adv interamente, pienamente, completamente; (at least) almeno

fumble ['fʌmbl] vi **to ~ with sth** armeggiare con qc

fume [fjuːm] vi essere furioso(-a); **fumes** npl esalazioni fpl, vapori mpl

fun [fʌn] n divertimento, spasso; **to have ~** divertirsi; **for ~** per scherzo; **to make ~ of** prendersi gioco di

function ['fʌŋkʃən] n funzione f; cerimonia, ricevimento ▶ vi funzionare

fund [fʌnd] n fondo, cassa; (source)

fondo; (store) riserva; **~s** npl (money)
fondi mpl

fundamental [fʌndə'mɛntl] adj
fondamentale

funeral ['fju:nərəl] n funerale m;
funeral director n impresario di
pompe funebri; **funeral parlour**
[-'pɑ:lə'] n impresa di pompe funebri

funfair ['fʌnfɛə'] n luna park m inv

fungus ['fʌŋgəs] (pl fungi) n fungo;
(mould) muffa

funnel ['fʌnl] n imbuto; (of ship)
ciminiera

funny ['fʌnɪ] adj divertente, buffo(-a);
(strange) strano(-a), bizzarro(-a)

fur [fə:'] n pelo; pelliccia; (BRIT: in
kettle etc) deposito calcare; **fur coat**
n pelliccia

furious ['fjuərɪəs] adj furioso(-a);
(effort) accanito(-a)

furnish ['fə:nɪʃ] vt ammobiliare;
(supply) fornire; **furnishings** npl
mobili mpl, mobilia

furniture ['fə:nɪtʃə'] n mobili mpl;
piece of ~ mobile m

furry ['fə:rɪ] adj (animal) peloso(-a)

further ['fə:ðə'] adj supplementare,
altro(-a); nuovo(-a); più lontano(-a)
▶ adv più lontano; (more) di più;
(moreover) inoltre ▶ vt favorire,
promuovere; **further education** n
corsi mpl di formazione; **college
of further education** istituto statale
con corsi specializzati (di formazione
professionale, aggiornamento
professionale ecc); **furthermore**
[fə:ðə'mɔ:'] adv inoltre, per di più

furthest ['fə:ðɪst] superl of **far**

fury ['fjuərɪ] n furore m

fuse [fju:z] (US **fuze**) n fusibile m; (for
bomb etc) miccia, spoletta ▶ vt fondere
▶ vi fondersi; **to ~ the lights** (BRIT
Elec) far saltare i fusibili; **fuse box** n
cassetta dei fusibili

fusion ['fju:ʒən] n fusione f

fuss [fʌs] n agitazione f; (complaining)
storie fpl; **to make a ~** fare delle storie;
fussy adj (person) puntiglioso(-a),
esigente; che fa le storie; (dress)
carico(-a) di fronzoli; (style)
elaborato(-a)

future ['fju:tʃə'] adj futuro(-a) ▶ n
futuro, avvenire m; (Ling) futuro; **in ~**
in futuro; **~s** npl (Comm) operazioni
fpl a termine

fuze [fju:z] (US) = **fuse**

fuzzy ['fʌzɪ] adj (Phot) indistinto(-a),
sfocato(-a); (hair) crespo(-a)

g

G [dʒi:] n (Mus) sol m

g. abbr (= gram, gravity) g

gadget ['gædʒɪt] n aggeggio

Gaelic ['geɪlɪk] adj gaelico(-a) ▶ n (Ling)
gaelico

gag [gæg] n bavaglio; (joke) facezia,
scherzo ▶ vt imbavagliare

gain [geɪn] n guadagno, profitto ▶ vt
guadagnare ▶ vi (clock, watch) andare
avanti; (benefit): **to ~ (from)** trarre
beneficio (da); **to ~ 3lbs (in weight)**
aumentare di 3 libbre; **to ~ on sb** (in
race etc) guadagnare su qn

gal. abbr = **gallon**

gala ['gɑ:lə] n gala; **swimming ~**
manifestazione f di nuoto

galaxy ['gæləksɪ] n galassia

gale [geɪl] *n* vento forte; burrasca

gall bladder ['gɔːl-] *n* cistifellea

gallery ['gælərɪ] *n* galleria

gallon ['gælən] *n* gallone *m* (= 8 pints; BRIT = 4.543l; US = 3.785l)

gallop ['gæləp] *n* galoppo ▶ *vi* galoppare

gallstone ['gɔːlstəun] *n* calcolo biliare

gamble ['gæmbl] *n* azzardo, rischio calcolato ▶ *vt, vi* giocare; **to ~ on** (*fig*) giocare su; **gambler** *n* giocatore(-trice) d'azzardo; **gambling** *n* gioco d'azzardo

game [geɪm] *n* gioco; (*event*) partita; (*Tennis*) game *m* inv; (*Culin, Hunting*) selvaggina ▶ *adj* (*ready*): **to be ~ (for sth/to do)** essere pronto(-a) (a qc/a fare); **big ~** selvaggina grossa; **~s** *npl* (*Scol*) attività *fpl* sportive; **big ~** selvaggina grossa; **games console** [geɪmz-] *n* console *f* inv dei videogame; **game show** ['geɪmʃəu] *n* gioco a premi

gammon ['gæmən] *n* (*bacon*) quarto di maiale; (*ham*) prosciutto affumicato

gang [gæŋ] *n* banda, squadra ▶ *vi* **to ~ up on sb** far combutta contro qn

gangster ['gæŋstə*] *n* gangster *m* inv

gap [gæp] *n* (*space*) buco; (*in time*) intervallo; (*difference*): **~ (between)** divario (tra)

gape [geɪp] *vi* (*person*) restare a bocca aperta; (*shirt, hole*) essere spalancato(-a)

gap year *n* (*Scol*) anno di pausa durante il quale gli studenti viaggiano o lavorano

garage ['gæraːʒ] *n* garage *m* inv; **garage sale** *n* vendita di oggetti usati nel garage di un privato

garbage ['gaːbɪdʒ] (US) *n* immondizie *fpl*, rifiuti *mpl*; (*inf*) sciocchezze *fpl*; **garbage can** (US) *n* bidone *m* della spazzatura; **garbage collector** (US) *n* spazzino(-a)

garden ['gaːdn] *n* giardino; **~s** *npl* (*public park*) giardini pubblici; **garden centre** *n* giardineria; **gardener** *n* giardiniere(-a); **gardening** *n* giardinaggio

garlic ['gaːlɪk] *n* aglio

garment ['gaːmənt] *n* indumento

garnish ['gaːnɪʃ] *vt* (*food*) guarnire

garrison ['gærɪsn] *n* guarnigione *f*

gas [gæs] *n* gas *m* inv; (US: *gasoline*) benzina ▶ *vt* asfissiare con il gas; **I can smell ~** sento odore di gas; **gas cooker** (BRIT) *n* cucina a gas; **gas cylinder** *n* bombola del gas; **gas fire** (BRIT) *n* radiatore *m* a gas

gasket ['gæskɪt] *n* (*Aut*) guarnizione *f*

gasoline ['gæsəliːn] (US) *n* benzina

gasp [gaːsp] *n* respiro affannoso, ansito ▶ *vi* ansare, ansimare; (*in surprise*) restare senza fiato

gas: gas pedal (*esp US*) *n* pedale *m* dell'acceleratore; **gas station** (US) *n* distributore *m* di benzina; **gas tank** (US) *n* (*Aut*) serbatoio (di benzina)

gate [geɪt] *n* cancello; *m* (*at airport*) uscita

gateau ['gætəu, -z] (*pl* **gateaux**) *n* torta

gatecrash ['geɪtkræʃ] (BRIT) *vt* partecipare senza invito a

gateway ['geɪtweɪ] *n* porta

gather ['gæðə*] *vt* (*flowers, fruit*) cogliere; (*pick up*) raccogliere; (*assemble*) radunare; (*understand*) capire; (*Sewing*) increspare ▶ *vi* (*assemble*) radunarsi; **to ~ speed** acquistare velocità; **gathering** *n* adunanza

gauge [geɪdʒ] *n* (*instrument*) indicatore *m* ▶ *vt* misurare; (*fig*) valutare

gave [geɪv] *pt of* **give**

gay [geɪ] *adj* (*homosexual*) omosessuale; (*cheerful*) gaio(-a), allegro(-a); (*colour*) vivace, vivo(-a)

gaze [geɪz] *n* sguardo fisso ▶ *vi* **to ~ at**

guardare fisso

GB *abbr* = **Great Britain**

GCSE *(BRIT) n abbr* General Certificate of Secondary Education

gear [gɪəʳ] *n* attrezzi *mpl*, equipaggiamento; *(Tech)* ingranaggio; *(Aut)* marcia ▶ *vt (fig: adapt)*: **to ~ sth to** adattare qc a; **in top** *or (US)* **high/low ~** in quarta (*or* quinta)/seconda; **in ~** in marcia
▷ **gear up** *vi* **to ~ up (to do)** prepararsi (a fare); **gear box** *n* scatola del cambio; **gear lever** *n* leva del cambio; **gear shift** *(US)*, **gear stick** *(BRIT) n* = **gear lever**

geese [giːs] *npl of* **goose**

gel [dʒɛl] *n* gel *m inv*

gem [dʒɛm] *n* gemma

Gemini [ˈdʒɛmɪnaɪ] *n* Gemelli *mpl*

gender [ˈdʒɛndəʳ] *n* genere *m*

gene [dʒiːn] *n (Biol)* gene *m*

general [ˈdʒɛnərl] *n* generale *m*
▶ *adj* generale; **in ~** in genere;
general anaesthetic *(US* **general anesthetic**) *n* anestesia totale;
general election *n* elezioni *fpl* generali; **generalize** *vi* generalizzare;
generally *adv* generalmente;
general practitioner *n* medico generico; **general store** *n* emporio

generate [ˈdʒɛnəreɪt] *vt* generare

generation [dʒɛnəˈreɪʃən] *n* generazione *f*

generator [ˈdʒɛnəreɪtəʳ] *n* generatore *m*

generosity [dʒɛnəˈrɔsɪtɪ] *n* generosità

generous [ˈdʒɛnərəs] *adj* generoso(-a); *(copious)* abbondante

genetic [dʒɪˈnɛtɪk] *adj* genetico(-a);
~ engineering ingegneria genetica; **genetically modified** *adj* geneticamente modificato(-a), transgenico(-a); **genetics** *n* genetica

Geneva [dʒɪˈniːvə] *n* Ginevra

genitals [ˈdʒɛnɪtlz] *npl* genitali *mpl*

genius [ˈdʒiːnɪəs] *n* genio

Genoa [ˈdʒɛnəʊə] *n* Genova

gent [dʒɛnt] *n abbr* = **gentleman**

gentle [ˈdʒɛntl] *adj* delicato(-a); *(person)* dolce

  Be careful not to translate **gentle**
  by the Italian word *gentile*.

gentleman [ˈdʒɛntlmən] *(irreg) n* signore *m*; *(well-bred man)* gentiluomo

gently [ˈdʒɛntlɪ] *adv* delicatamente

gents [dʒɛnts] *n* W.C. *m* (per signori)

genuine [ˈdʒɛnjuɪn] *adj* autentico(-a); sincero(-a); **genuinely** *adv* genuinamente

geographic(al) [dʒɪəˈɡræfɪk(l)] *adj* geografico(-a)

geography [dʒɪˈɔɡrəfɪ] *n* geografia

geology [dʒɪˈɔlədʒɪ] *n* geologia

geometry [dʒɪˈɔmɪtrɪ] *n* geometria

geranium [dʒɪˈreɪnjəm] *n* geranio

geriatric [dʒɛrɪˈætrɪk] *adj* geriatrico(-a)

germ [dʒəːm] *n (Med)* microbo; *(Biol, fig)* germe *m*

German [ˈdʒəːmən] *adj* tedesco(-a) ▶ *n* tedesco(-a); *(Ling)* tedesco; **German measles** *(BRIT) n* rosolia

Germany [ˈdʒəːmənɪ] *n* Germania

gesture [ˈdʒɛstʃəʳ] *n* gesto

get
[gɛt] *(pt, pp* **got**, *(US) pp* **gotten**) *vi*
1 *(become, be)* diventare, farsi; **to get old** invecchiare; **to get tired** stancarsi; **to get drunk** ubriacarsi; **to get killed** venire *or* rimanere ucciso(-a); **how do I get paid?** quando mi pagate?; **it's getting late** si sta facendo tardi
2 *(go)*: **to get to/from** andare a/da; **to get home** arrivare *or* tornare a casa; **how did you get here?** come sei venuto?
3 *(begin)* mettersi a, cominciare a; **to get to know sb** incominciare a conoscere qn; **let's get going** *or*

started muoviamoci
4 (*modal aux vb*): **you've got to do it** devi farlo
▶ *vt*
1: **to get sth done** (*do*) fare qc; (*have done*) far fare qc; **to get one's hair cut** farsi tagliare i capelli; **to get sb to do sth** far fare qc a qn
2 (*obtain: money, permission, results*) ottenere; (*find: job, flat*) trovare; (*fetch: person, doctor*) chiamare; (*object*) prendere; **to get sth for sb** prendere or procurare qc a qn; **get me Mr Jones, please** (*Tel*) mi passi il signor Jones, per favore; **can I get you a drink?** le posso offrire da bere?
3 (*receive: present, letter, prize*) ricevere; (*acquire: reputation*) farsi; **how much did you get for the painting?** quanto le hanno dato per il quadro?
4 (*catch*) prendere; (*hit: target etc*) colpire; **to get sb by the arm/throat** afferrare qn per un braccio/alla gola; **get him!** prendetelo!
5 (*take, move*) portare; **to get sth to sb** far avere qc a qn; **do you think we'll get it through the door?** pensi che riusciremo a farlo passare per la porta?
6 (*catch, take: plane, bus etc*) prendere; **where do we get the ferry to …?** dove si prende il traghetto per …?
7 (*understand*) afferrare; (*hear*) sentire; **I've got it!** ci sono arrivato!, ci sono!; **I'm sorry, I didn't get your name** scusi, non ho capito (*or* sentito) il suo nome
8 (*have, possess*): **to have got** avere; **how many have you got?** quanti ne ha?
▷ **get along** *vi* (*agree*) andare d'accordo; (*depart*) andarsene; (*manage*) = **get by**
▷ **get at** *vt fus* (*attack*) prendersela con; (*reach*) raggiungere, arrivare a
▷ **get away** *vi* partire, andarsene; (*escape*) scappare
▷ **get away with** *vt fus* cavarsela;

farla franca
▷ **get back** *vi* (*return*) ritornare, tornare
▶ *vt* riottenere, riavere; **when do we get back?** quando ritorniamo?
▷ **get by** *vi* (*pass*) passare; (*manage*) farcela
▷ **get down** *vi*, *vt fus* scendere ▶ *vt* far scendere; (*depress*) buttare giù
▷ **get down to** *vt fus* (*work*) mettersi a (fare)
▷ **get in** *vi* entrare; (*train*) arrivare; (*arrive home*) ritornare, tornare
▷ **get into** *vt fus* entrare in; **to get into a rage** incavolarsi
▷ **get off** *vi* (*from train etc*) scendere; (*depart: person, car*) andare via; (*escape*) cavarsela ▶ *vt* (*remove: clothes, stain*) levare ▶ *vt fus* (*train, bus*) scendere da; **where do I get off?** dove devo scendere?
▷ **get on** *vi* (*at exam etc*) andare; (*agree*): **to get on (with)** andare d'accordo (con) ▶ *vt fus* montare in; (*horse*) montare su
▷ **get out** *vi* uscire; (*of vehicle*) scendere ▶ *vt* tirar fuori, far uscire
▷ **get out of** *vt fus* uscire da; (*duty etc*) evitare
▷ **get over** *vt fus* (*illness*) riaversi da
▷ **get round** *vt fus* aggirare; (*fig: person*) rigirare
▷ **get through** *vi* (*Tel*) avere la linea
▷ **get through to** *vt fus* (*Tel*) parlare a
▷ **get together** *vi* riunirsi ▶ *vt* raccogliere; (*people*) adunare
▷ **get up** *vi* (*rise*) alzarsi ▶ *vt fus* salire su per
▷ **get up to** *vt fus* (*reach*) raggiungere; (*prank etc*) fare
getaway ['gɛtəweɪ] *n* fuga
Ghana ['gɑːnə] *n* Ghana *m*
ghastly ['gɑːstlɪ] *adj* orribile, orrendo(-a); (*pale*) spettrale
ghetto ['gɛtəu] *n* ghetto
ghost [gəust] *n* fantasma *m*, spettro
giant ['dʒaɪənt] *n* gigante *m* ▶ *adj*

gigantesco(-a), enorme
gift [gɪft] n regalo; (donation, ability) dono; **gifted** adj dotato(-a); **gift shop** (US **gift store**) n negozio di souvenir
gift token, **gift voucher** n buono m omaggio inv
gig [gɪg] n (inf: of musician) serata
gigabyte [gi:gəbaɪt] n gigabyte m inv
gigantic [dʒaɪˈgæntɪk] adj gigantesco(-a)
giggle [ˈgɪgl] vi ridere scioccamente
gills [gɪlz] npl (of fish) branchie fpl
gilt [gɪlt] n doratura ▶ adj dorato(-a)
gimmick [ˈgɪmɪk] n trucco
gin [dʒɪn] n (liquor) gin m inv
ginger [ˈdʒɪndʒəˈr] n zenzero
gipsy [ˈdʒɪpsɪ] n zingaro(-a)
giraffe [dʒɪˈrɑːf] n giraffa
girl [gəːl] n ragazza; (young unmarried woman) signorina; (daughter) figlia, figliola; **girlfriend** n (of girl) amica; (of boy) ragazza; **Girl Scout** (US) n Giovane Esploratrice f
gist [dʒɪst] n succo
give [gɪv] (pt **gave**, pp **given**) vt dare ▶ vi cedere; to ~ **sb sth**, ~ **sth to sb** dare qc a qn; **I'll ~ you £5 for it** te lo pago 5 sterline; to ~ **a cry/sigh** emettere un grido/sospiro; to ~ **a speech** fare un discorso ▶ **give away** vt dare via; (disclose) rivelare; (bride) condurre all'altare ▶ **give back** vt rendere ▶ **give in** vi cedere ▶ vt consegnare ▶ **give out** vt distribuire; annunciare ▶ **give up** vi rinunciare ▶ vt rinunciare a; to ~ **up smoking** smettere di fumare; to ~ **o.s. up** arrendersi
given [ˈgɪvn] pp of **give** ▶ adj (fixed: time, amount) dato(-a), determinato(-a) ▶ conj: ~ (**that**) ... dato che ...; ~ **the circumstances** ... date le circostanze ...
glacier [ˈglæsɪəˈr] n ghiacciaio
glad [glæd] adj lieto(-a), contento(-a); **gladly** [ˈglædlɪ] adv volentieri

glamorous [ˈglæmərəs] adj affascinante, seducente
glamour [ˈglæməˈr] (US **glamor**) n fascino
glance [glɑːns] n occhiata, sguardo ▶ vi to ~ **at** dare un'occhiata a; to ~ **off** (bullet) rimbalzare su
gland [glænd] n ghiandola
glare [glɛəˈr] n (of anger) sguardo furioso; (of light) riverbero, luce f abbagliante; (of publicity) chiasso ▶ vi abbagliare; to ~ **at** guardare male; **glaring** adj (mistake) madornale
glass [glɑːs] n (substance) vetro; (tumbler) bicchiere m; ~**es** npl (spectacles) occhiali mpl
glaze [gleɪz] vt (door) fornire di vetri; (pottery) smaltare ▶ n smalto
gleam [gliːm] vi luccicare
glen [glɛn] n valletta
glide [glaɪd] vi scivolare; (Aviat, birds) planare; **glider** n (Aviat) aliante m
glimmer [ˈglɪməˈr] n barlume m
glimpse [glɪmps] n impressione f fugace ▶ vt vedere al volo
glint [glɪnt] vi luccicare
glisten [ˈglɪsn] vi luccicare
glitter [ˈglɪtəˈr] vi scintillare
global [ˈgləʊbl] adj globale; **global warming** n effetto m serra inv
globe [gləʊb] n globo, sfera
gloom [gluːm] n oscurità, buio; (sadness) tristezza, malinconia; **gloomy** adj scuro(-a), fosco(-a), triste
glorious [ˈglɔːrɪəs] adj glorioso(-a), magnifico(-a)
glory [ˈglɔːrɪ] n gloria; splendore m
gloss [glɒs] n (shine) lucentezza; (also: ~ **paint**) vernice f a olio
glossary [ˈglɒsərɪ] n glossario
glossy [ˈglɒsɪ] adj lucido(-a)
glove [glʌv] n guanto; **glove compartment** n (Aut) vano portaoggetti
glow [gləʊ] vi ardere; (face) essere

luminoso(-a)
glucose ['glu:kəus] n glucosio
glue [glu:] n colla ▷ vt incollare
GM adj abbr (= genetically modified)
geneticamente modificato(-a)
gm abbr = **gram**
GMO n abbr (= genetically modified
organism) OGM m inv
GMT abbr (= Greenwich Mean Time) T.M.G
gnaw [nɔ:] vt rodere
go [gəu] (pt **went**, pp **gone**) (pl **goes**) vi
andare; (depart) partire, andarsene;
(work) funzionare; (time) passare;
(break etc) rompersi; (be sold): **to go
for £10** essere venduto per 10 sterline;
(fit, suit): **to go with** andare bene
con; (become): **to go pale** diventare
pallido(-a); **to go mouldy** ammuffire
▷ n **to have a go (at)** provare; **to be
on the go** essere in moto; **whose
go is it?** a chi tocca?; **he's going
to do** sta per fare; **to go for a walk**
andare a fare una passeggiata; **to
go dancing/shopping** andare a
ballare/fare la spesa; **just then the
bell went** proprio allora suonò il
campanello; **how did it go?** com'è
andato?; **to go round the back/by
the shop** passare da dietro/davanti al
negozio ▷ **go ahead** vi andare avanti
▷ **go away** vi partire, andarsene ▷ **go
back** vi tornare, ritornare ▷ **go by**
(years, time) scorrere ▷ vt fus attenersi
a, seguire (alla lettera); **prest
fede a** ▷ **go down** vi scendere; (ship)
affondare; (sun) tramontare ▷ vt fus
scendere ▷ **go for** vt fus (fetch) andare
a prendere; (like) andar matto(-a) per;
(attack) attaccare; saltare addosso
a ▷ **go in** vi entrare ▷ **go into** vt fus
entrare in; (investigate) indagare,
esaminare; (embark on) lanciarsi
in ▷ **go off** vi partire, andar via;
(food) guastarsi; (explode) esplodere,
scoppiare; (event) passare ▷ vt fus

I've ~ne off chocolate la cioccolata
non mi piace più; **the gun went off** il
fucile si scaricò ▷ **go on** vi continuare;
(happen) succedere; **to ~ on doing**
continuare a fare ▷ **go out** vi uscire;
(couple): **they went out for 3 years**
sono stati insieme per 3 anni; (fire,
light) spegnersi ▷ **go over** vi (ship)
ribaltarsi ▷ vt fus (check) esaminare
▷ **go past** vi passare ▷ vt fus passare
davanti a ▷ **go round** vi (circulate:
news, rumour) circolare; (revolve):
girare; (visit): **to ~ round (to sb's)**
passare (da qn); (make a detour): **to
~ round (by)** passare (per); (suffice)
bastare (per tutti) ▷ **go through** vt fus
(town etc) attraversare; (files, papers)
passare in rassegna; (examine: list
etc) leggere da cima a fondo ▷ **go up**
vi salire ▷ **go with** vt fus (accompany)
accompagnare ▷ **go without** vt fus
fare a meno di
go-ahead ['gəuəhed] adj
intraprendente ▷ n via m
goal [gəul] n (Sport) gol m, rete f;
(: place) porta; (fig: aim) fine m, scopo;
goalkeeper n portiere m; **goal-post** n
palo (della porta)
goat [gəut] n capra
gobble ['gɔbl] vt (also: **~ down**, **~ up**)
ingoiare
god [gɔd] n dio; **G~** Dio; **godchild**
n figlioccio(-a); **goddaughter** n
figlioccia; **goddess** n dea; **godfather**
n padrino; **godmother** n madrina;
godson n figlioccio
goggles ['gɔglz] npl occhiali mpl (di
protezione)
going ['gəuɪŋ] n (conditions) andare
m, stato del terreno ▷ adj **the ~ rate** la
tariffa in vigore
gold [gəuld] n oro ▷ adj d'oro; **golden**
adj (made of gold) d'oro; (gold in colour)
dorato(-a); **goldfish** n pesce m dorato
or rosso; **goldmine** n (also fig) miniera

d'oro; **gold-plated** adj placcato(-a) oro inv

golf [gɒlf] n golf m; **golf ball** n (for game) pallina da golf; (on typewriter) pallina; **golf club** n circolo di golf; (stick) bastone m or mazza da golf; **golf course** n campo di golf; **golfer** n giocatore(-trice) di golf

gone [gɒn] pp of **go** ▸ adj partito(-a)

gong [gɒŋ] n gong m inv

good [gud] adj buono(-a); (kind) buono(-a), gentile; (child) bravo(-a) ▸ n bene m; (Comm etc) beni mpl; merci fpl; ~! bene!, ottimo!; **to be ~ at** essere bravo(-a) in; **to be ~ for** andare bene per; **it's ~ for you** fa bene; **would you be ~ enough to …?** avrebbe la gentilezza di …?; **a ~ deal (of)** molto(-a), una buona quantità (di); **a ~ many** molti(-e); **to make ~** (loss, damage) compensare; **it's no ~ complaining** brontolare non serve a niente; **for ~** per sempre, definitivamente; **~ morning!** buon giorno!; **~ afternoon/evening!** buona sera!; **~ night!** buona notte!; **goodbye** excl arrivederci!; **Good Friday** n Venerdì Santo; **good-looking** adj bello(-a); **good-natured** adj affabile; **goodness** n (of person) bontà; **for goodness sake!** per amor di Dio!; **goodness gracious!** santo cielo!, mamma mia!; **goods train** (BRIT) n treno m merci inv; **goodwill** n amicizia, benevolenza

goose [gu:s] (pl **geese**) n oca

gooseberry ['guzbərɪ] n uva spina; **to play ~** (BRIT) tenere la candela

goose bumps, goose pimples npl pelle f d'oca

gorge [gɔ:dʒ] n gola ▸ vt **to ~ o.s. (on)** ingozzarsi (di)

gorgeous ['gɔ:dʒəs] adj magnifico(-a)

gorilla [gə'rɪlə] n gorilla m inv

gosh (inf) [gɒʃ] excl perdinci!

gospel ['gɒspl] n vangelo

gossip ['gɒsɪp] n chiacchiere fpl; pettegolezzi mpl; (person) pettegolo(-a) ▸ vi chiacchierare; **gossip column** n cronaca mondana

got [gɒt] pt, pp of **get**

gotten ['gɒtn] (US) pp of **get**

gourmet ['guəmeɪ] n buongustaio(-a)

govern ['gʌvən] vt governare; **government** ['gʌvnmənt] n governo; **governor** ['gʌvənə*] n (of state, bank) governatore m; (of school, hospital) amministratore m; (BRIT: of prison) direttore(-trice)

gown [gaun] n vestito lungo; (of teacher, BRIT: of judge) toga

G.P. n abbr = **general practitioner**

grab [græb] vt afferrare, arraffare; (property, power) impadronirsi di ▸ vi **to ~ at** cercare di afferrare

grace [greɪs] n grazia ▸ vt onorare; **5 days' ~** dilazione f di 5 giorni; **graceful** adj elegante, aggraziato(-a); **gracious** ['greɪʃəs] adj grazioso(-a), misericordioso(-a)

grade [greɪd] n (Comm) qualità f inv; classe f; categoria; (in hierarchy) grado; (Scol: mark) voto; (US: school class) classe ▸ vt classificare; ordinare; **graduare**; **grade crossing** (US) n passaggio a livello; **grade school** (US) n scuola elementare

gradient ['greɪdɪənt] n pendenza, inclinazione f

gradual ['grædjuəl] adj graduale; **gradually** adv man mano, a poco a poco

graduate [n 'grædjuɪt, vb 'grædjueɪt] n (of university) laureato(-a); (US: of high school) diplomato(-a) ▸ vi laurearsi; diplomarsi; **graduation** [-'eɪʃən] n (ceremony) consegna delle lauree (or dei diplomi)

graffiti [grə'fi:tɪ] npl graffiti mpl

graft [grɑ:ft] n (Agr, Med) innesto;

(bribery) corruzione f; (BRIT: hard work): **it's hard ~** è un lavoraccio ▶ vt innestare

grain [greɪn] n grano; (of sand) granello; (of wood) venatura

gram [græm] n grammo

grammar ['græmə*] n grammatica; **grammar school** (BRIT) n = liceo

gramme [græm] n = **gram**

gran (inf) [græn] n (BRIT) nonna

grand [grænd] adj grande, magnifico(-a); grandioso(-a); **granddad** (inf) n = **granddad**; **grandchild** (pl **-children**) n nipote m; **granddad** (inf) n nonno; **granddaughter** n nipote f; **grandfather** n nonno; **grandma** (inf) n nonna; **grandmother** n nonna; **grandpa** (inf) n = **granddad**; **grandparents** npl nonni mpl; **grand piano** n pianoforte m a coda; **Grand Prix** ['grɑ̃ː'priː] n (Aut) Gran Premio, Grand Prix m inv; **grandson** n nipote m

granite ['grænɪt] n granito

granny ['grænɪ] (inf) n nonna

grant [grɑːnt] vt accordare; (a request) accogliere; (admit) ammettere, concedere ▶ n (Scol) borsa; (Admin) sussidio, sovvenzione f; **to take sth for ~ed** dare qc per scontato; **to take sb for ~ed** dare per scontata la presenza di qn

grape [greɪp] n chicco d'uva, acino

grapefruit ['greɪpfruːt] n pompelmo

graph [grɑːf] n grafico; **graphic** adj grafico(-a); (vivid) vivido(-a); **graphics** n grafica ▶ npl illustrazioni fpl

grasp [grɑːsp] vt afferrare ▶ n (grip) presa; (fig) potere m; comprensione f

grass [grɑːs] n erba; **grasshopper** n cavalletta

grate [greɪt] n graticola (del focolare) ▶ vi cigolare, stridere ▶ vt (Culin)

grattugiare

grateful ['greɪtful] adj grato(-a), riconoscente

grater ['greɪtə*] n grattugia

gratitude ['grætɪtjuːd] n gratitudine f

grave [greɪv] n tomba ▶ adj grave, serio(-a)

gravel ['grævl] n ghiaia

gravestone ['greɪvstəun] n pietra tombale

graveyard ['greɪvjɑːd] n cimitero

gravity ['grævɪtɪ] n (Physics) gravità; pesantezza; (seriousness) gravità, serietà

gravy ['greɪvɪ] n intingolo della carne; salsa

gray [greɪ] adj = **grey**

graze [greɪz] vi pascolare, pascere ▶ vt (touch lightly) sfiorare; (scrape) escoriare ▶ n (Med) escoriazione f

grease [griːs] n (fat) grasso; (lubricant) lubrificante m ▶ vt ingrassare; lubrificare; **greasy** adj grasso(-a), untuoso(-a)

great [greɪt] adj grande; (inf) magnifico(-a), meraviglioso(-a); **Great Britain** n Gran Bretagna; **great-grandfather** n bisnonno; **great-grandmother** n bisnonna; **greatly** adv molto

Greece [griːs] n Grecia

greed [griːd] n (also: **-iness**) avarizia; (for food) golosità, ghiottoneria; **greedy** adj avido(-a); goloso(-a), ghiotto(-a)

Greek [griːk] adj greco(-a) ▶ n greco(-a); (Ling) greco

green [griːn] adj verde; (inexperienced) inesperto(-a), ingenuo(-a) ▶ n verde m; (stretch of grass) prato; (on golf course) green m inv; **~s** npl (vegetables) verdura; **green card** n (BRITAut) carta verde; (USAdmin) permesso di soggiorno e di lavoro; **greengage** ['griːngeɪdʒ] n susina Regina Claudia; **greengrocer**

(BRIT) n fruttivendolo(-a), erbivendolo(-a); **greenhouse** n serra; **greenhouse effect** n effetto serra

Greenland ['gri:nlənd] n Groenlandia

green salad n insalata verde

greet [gri:t] vt salutare; **greeting** n saluto; **greeting(s) card** n cartolina d'auguri

grew [gru:] pt of **grow**

grey [greɪ] (US **gray**) adj grigio(-a); **grey-haired** adj dai capelli grigi; **greyhound** n levriere m

grid [grɪd] n grata; (Elec) rete f; **gridlock** ['grɪdlɒk] n (traffic jam) paralisi f inv del traffico; **gridlocked** adj paralizzato(-a) dal traffico; (talks etc) in fase di stallo

grief [gri:f] n dolore m

grievance ['gri:vəns] n lagnanza

grieve [gri:v] vi addolorarsi; rattristarsi ▶ vt addolorare; **to ~ for sb** (dead person) piangere qn

grill [grɪl] n (on cooker) griglia; (also: **mixed ~**) grigliata mista ▶ vt (BRIT) cuocere ai ferri; (inf: question) interrogare senza sosta

grille [grɪl] n grata; (Aut) griglia

grim [grɪm] adj sinistro(-a), brutto(-a)

grime [graɪm] n sudiciume m

grin [grɪn] n sorriso smagliante ▶ vi fare un gran sorriso

grind [graɪnd] (pt, pp **ground**) vt macinare; (make sharp) arrotare ▶ n (work) sgobbata

grip [grɪp] n impugnatura; presa; (holdall) borsa di viaggio ▶ vt (object) afferrare; (attention) catturare; **to come to ~s with** affrontare; cercare di risolvere; **gripping** ['grɪpɪŋ] adj avvincente

grit [grɪt] n minato; (courage) fegato ▶ vt (road) coprire di sabbia; **to ~ one's teeth** stringere i denti

grits [grɪts] (US) npl macinato grosso (di avena etc)

groan [grəʊn] n gemito ▶ vi gemere

grocer ['grəʊsə*] n negoziante m di generi alimentari; **groceries** npl provviste fpl; **grocer's (shop)** n negozio di (generi) alimentari

grocery ['grəʊsəri] n (shop) (negozio di) alimentari

groin [grɔɪn] n inguine m

groom [gru:m] n palafreniere m; (also: **bride~**) sposo ▶ vt (horse) strigliare; (fig): **to ~ sb for** avviare qn a; **well-~ed** (person) curato(-a)

groove [gru:v] n scanalatura, solco

grope [grəʊp] vi **to ~ for** cercare a tastoni

gross [grəʊs] adj grossolano(-a); (Comm) lordo(-a); **grossly** adv (greatly) molto

grotesque [grəʊ'tɛsk] adj grottesco(-a)

ground [graʊnd] pt, pp of **grind** ▶ n suolo, terra; (land) terreno; (Sport) campo; (reason: gen pl) ragione f; (US: also: **~ wire**) terra ▶ vt (plane) tenere a terra; (US Elec) mettere la presa a terra a; **~s** npl (of coffee etc) fondi mpl; (gardens etc) terreno, giardini mpl; **on/to the ~** per/a terra; **to gain/lose ~** guadagnare/perdere terreno; **ground floor** n pianterreno; **groundsheet** (BRIT) n telone m impermeabile; **groundwork** n preparazione f

group [gru:p] n gruppo ▶ vt (also: **~ together**) raggruppare ▶ vi (also: **~ together**) raggrupparsi

grouse [graʊs] n inv (bird) tetraone m ▶ vi (complain) brontolare

grovel ['grɔvl] vi (fig): **to ~ (before)** strisciare (di fronte a)

grow [grəʊ] (pt **grew**, pp **grown**) vi crescere; (increase) aumentare; (develop) svilupparsi; (become): **to ~ rich/weak** arricchirsi/indebolirsi ▶ vt coltivare, far crescere ▶ **grow on** vt

fus that painting is ~ing on me quel quadro più lo guardo più mi piace
▷ **grow up** *vi* farsi grande, crescere

growl [graul] *vi* ringhiare

grown [grəun] *pp of* **grow**; **grown-up** *n* adul to(-a), grande *m/f*

growth [grəuθ] *n* crescita, sviluppo; (*what has grown*) crescita; (*Med*) escrescenza, tumore *m*

grub [grʌb] *n* larva; (*inf: food*) roba (da mangiare)

grubby ['grʌbɪ] *adj* sporco(-a)

grudge [grʌdʒ] *n* rancore *m* ▶ *vt* to ~ **sb sth** dare qc a qn di malavoglia; invidiare qc a qn; **to bear sb a ~ (for)** serbar rancore a qn (per)

gruelling ['gruəlɪŋ] (*US* **grueling**) *adj* estenuante

gruesome ['gru:səm] *adj* orribile

grumble ['grʌmbl] *vi* brontolare, lagnarsi

grumpy ['grʌmpɪ] *adj* scorbutico(-a)

grunt [grʌnt] *vi* grugnire

guarantee [gærən'ti:] *n* garanzia ▶ *vt* garantire

guard [gɑːd] *n* guardia; (*one man*) guardia, sentinella; (*BRIT Rail*) capotreno; (*on machine*) schermo protettivo; (*also:* **fire~**) parafuoco ▶ *vt* fare la guardia a; (*protect*): **to ~ (against)** proteggere (da); **to be on one's ~** stare in guardia; **guardian** *n* custode *m*; (*of minor*) tutore(-trice)

guerrilla [gə'rɪlə] *n* guerrigliero

guess [ges] *vi* indovinare ▶ *vt* indovinare; (*US*) credere, pensare ▶ *n* **to take** *or* **have a ~** provare a indovinare

guest [gest] *n* ospite *m/f*; (*in hotel*) cliente *m/f*; **guest house** *n* pensione *f*; **guest room** *n* camera degli ospiti

guidance ['gaɪdəns] *n* guida, direzione *f*

guide [gaɪd] *n* (*person, book etc*) guida; (*BRIT: also:* **girl ~**) giovane esploratrice

f ▶ *vt* guidare; **is there an English-speaking ~?** c'è una guida che parla inglese?; **guidebook** *n* guida; **do you have a guidebook in English?** avete una guida in inglese?; **guide dog** *n* cane *m* guida *inv*; **guided tour** *n* visita guidata; **what time does the guided tour start?** a che ora comincia la visita guidata?; **guidelines** *npl* (*fig*) indicazioni *fpl*, linee *fpl* direttive

guild [gɪld] *n* arte *f*, corporazione *f*; associazione *f*

guilt [gɪlt] *n* colpevolezza; **guilty** *adj* colpevole

guinea pig ['gɪnɪ-] *n* cavia

guitar [gɪ'tɑː] *n* chitarra; **guitarist** *n* chitarrista *m/f*

gulf [gʌlf] *n* golfo; (*abyss*) abisso

gull [gʌl] *n* gabbiano

gulp [gʌlp] *vi* deglutire; (*from emotion*) avere il nodo in gola ▶ *vt* (*also:* ~ **down**) tracannare, inghiottire

gum [gʌm] *n* (*Anat*) gengiva; (*glue*) colla; (*also:* **~drop**) caramella gommosa; (*also:* **chewing ~**) chewing-gum *m inv* ▶ *vt* **to ~ (together)** incollare

gun [gʌn] *n* fucile *m*; (*small*) pistola, rivoltella; (*rifle*) carabina; (*shotgun*) fucile da caccia; (*cannon*) cannone *m*; **gunfire** *n* spari *mpl*; **gunman** (*irreg*) *n* bandito armato; **gunpoint** *n* at **gunpoint** sotto minaccia di fucile; **gunpowder** *n* polvere *f* da sparo; **gunshot** *n* sparo

gush [gʌʃ] *vi* sgorgare; (*fig*) abbandonarsi ad effusioni

gust [gʌst] *n* (*of wind*) raffica; (*of smoke*) buffata

gut [gʌt] *n* intestino, budello; ~**s** *npl* (*Anat*) interiora *fpl*; (*courage*) fegato

gutter ['gʌtə] *n* (*of roof*) grondaia; (*in street*) cunetta

guy [gaɪ] *n* (*inf: man*) tipo, elemento; (*also:* ~**rope**) cavo o corda di

fissaggio; *(figure)* effigie di Guy Fawkes
Guy Fawkes Night [-'fɔːks-] *n* (*BRIT*)
vedi nota nel riquadro

● **Guy Fawkes Night**
● La sera del 5 novembre, in occasione
● della **Guy Fawkes Night**, altrimenti
● chiamata **Bonfire Night**
● commemoro con falò e fuochi
● d'artificio il fallimento della
● Congiura delle Polveri contro
● Giacomo I nel 1605. La festa prende
● il nome dal principale congiurato
● della cospirazione, Guy Fawkes, la
● cui effigie viene bruciata durante i
● festeggiamenti.

gym [dʒɪm] *n* (*also:* **~nasium**)
palestra; (*also:* **~nastics**) ginnastica;
gymnasium [dʒɪm'neɪzɪəm] *n*
palestra; **gymnast** ['dʒɪmnæst] *n*
ginnasta *m/f*; **gymnastics** [-'næstɪks]
n, npl ginnastica; **gym shoes** *npl*
scarpe *fpl* da ginnastica
gynaecologist [gaɪnɪ'kɔlədʒɪst] (*US*
gynecologist) *n* ginecologo(-a)
gypsy ['dʒɪpsɪ] *n* = **gipsy**

h

haberdashery ['hæbə'dæʃərɪ] (*BRIT*)
n merceria
habit ['hæbɪt] *n* abitudine *f*; (*costume*)
abito; (*Rel*) tonaca
habitat ['hæbɪtæt] *n* habitat *m inv*

hack [hæk] *vt* tagliare, fare a pezzi
▶ *n* (*pej: writer*) scribacchino(-a);
hacker ['hækə'] *n* (*Comput*) pirata *m*
informatico
had [hæd] *pt, pp of* **have**
haddock ['hædək] (*pl* **haddock** or
haddocks) *n* eglefino
hadn't ['hædnt] = **had not**
haemorrhage ['hɛmərɪdʒ] (*US*
hemorrhage) *n* emorragia
haemorrhoids ['hɛmərɔɪdz] (*US*
hemorrhoids) *npl* emorroidi *fpl*
haggle ['hægl] *vi* mercanteggiare
Hague [heɪg] *n* The ~ L'Aia
hail [heɪl] *n* grandine *f*; (*of criticism
etc*) pioggia ▶ *vt* (*call*) chiamare; (*flag
down: taxi*) fermare; (*greet*) salutare
▶ *vi* grandinare; **hailstone** *n* chicco
di grandine
hair [hɛə'] *n* capelli *mpl*; (*single hair:
on head*) capello; (: *on body*) pelo; **to
do one's ~** pettinarsi; **hairband**
['hɛəbænd] *n* (*elastic*) fascia per i
capelli; (*rigid*) cerchietto; **hairbrush**
n spazzola per capelli; **haircut** *n*
taglio di capelli; **hairdo** ['hɛəduː]
n acconciatura, pettinatura;
hairdresser *n* parrucchiere(-a);
hairdresser's *n* parrucchiere(-a);
hair dryer *n* asciugacapelli *m inv*;
hair gel *n* gel *m inv* per capelli; **hair
spray** *n* lacca per capelli; **hairstyle** *n*
pettinatura, acconciatura; **hairy** *adj*
irsuto(-a), peloso(-a); (*inf: frightening*)
spaventoso(-a)
hake [heɪk] (*pl* **hake** or **hakes**) *n*
nasello
half [hɑːf] (*pl* **halves**) *n* mezzo, metà
f inv ▶ *adj* mezzo(-a) ▶ *adv* a mezzo, a
metà; **~ an hour** mezz'ora; **~ a dozen**
mezza dozzina; **~ a pound** mezza
libbra; **two and a ~** due e mezzo; **a
week and a ~** una settimana e mezzo;
~ (of it) la metà; **~ (of)** la metà di;
to cut sth in ~ tagliare qc in due; **~**

asleep mezzo(-a) addormentato(-a);
half board (BRIT) n mezza pensione;
half-brother n fratellastro; **half day**
n mezza giornata; **half fare** n tariffa
a metà prezzo; **half-hearted** adj
tiepido(-a); **half-hour** n mezz'ora;
half-price adj, adv a metà prezzo; **half
term** (BRIT) (Scol) vacanza a or di
metà trimestre; **half-time** n (Sport)
intervallo; **halfway** adv a metà strada
hall [hɔːl] n sala, salone m; (entrance
way) entrata
hallmark ['hɔːlmɑːk] n marchio di
garanzia; (fig) caratteristica
hallo [hə'ləu] excl = hello
hall of residence (BRIT) n casa dello
studente
Halloween [hæləu'iːn] n vigilia
d'Ognissanti

● **Halloween**
● Negli Stati Uniti e in Gran Bretagna
  il 31 ottobre si festeggia **Halloween**,
  la notte delle streghe e dei fantasmi.
  I bambini, travestiti da fantasmi,
  streghe o mostri, bussano alle porte
  e ricevono dolci e piccoli doni.

hallucination [həluːsɪ'neɪʃən] n
allucinazione f
hallway ['hɔːlweɪ] n corridoio;
(entrance) ingresso
halo ['heɪləu] n (of saint etc) aureola
halt [hɔːlt] n fermata ▷ vt fermare ▷ vi
fermarsi
halve [hɑːv] vt (apple etc) dividere a
metà; (expense) ridurre di metà
halves [hɑːvz] npl of **half**
ham [hæm] n prosciutto
hamburger ['hæmbəːgə'] n
hamburger m inv
hamlet ['hæmlɪt] n paesetto
hammer ['hæmə'] n martello ▷ vt
martellare ▷ vi to ~ on or at the door
picchiare alla porta
hammock ['hæmək] n amaca
hamper ['hæmpə'] vt impedire ▷ n

cesta
hamster ['hæmstə'] n criceto
hamstring ['hæmstrɪŋ] n (Anat)
tendine m del ginocchio
hand [hænd] n mano f; (of clock)
lancetta; (handwriting) scrittura; (at
cards) mano; (: game) partita; (worker)
operaio(-a) m/f ▷ vt dare, passare; **to
give sb a ~** dare una mano a qn; **at ~**
a portata di mano; **in ~** a disposizione;
(work) in corso; **on ~** (person)
disponibile; (services) pronto(-a) a
intervenire; **to ~** (information etc) a
portata di mano; **on the one ~ ...,**
on the other ~ da un lato ..., dall'altro
▷ **hand down** vt passare giù;
(tradition, heirloom) tramandare; (US:
sentence, verdict) emettere ▷ **hand in** vt
consegnare ▷ **hand out** vt distribuire
▷ **hand over** vt passare; cedere;
handbag n borsetta; **hand baggage**
n bagaglio a mano; **handbook** n
manuale m; **handbrake** n freno a
mano; **handcuffs** npl manette fpl;
handful n manciata, pugno
handicap ['hændɪkæp] n
handicap m inv ▷ vt handicappare;
to be physically ~ped essere
handicappato(-a); **to be mentally
~ped** essere un(a) handicappato(-a)
mentale
handkerchief ['hæŋkətʃɪf] n
fazzoletto
handle ['hændl] n (of door etc)
maniglia; (of cup etc) ansa; (of knife etc)
impugnatura; (of saucepan) manico;
(for winding) manovella ▷ vt toccare,
maneggiare; (deal with) occuparsi
di; (treat: people) trattare; "**~ with
care**" "fragile"; **to fly off the ~** (fig)
perdere le staffe, uscire dai gangheri;
handlebar(s) n(pl) manubrio
hand: hand luggage n bagagli mpl
a mano; **handmade** adj fatto(-a)
a mano; **handout** n (money, food)

elemosina; (*leaflet*) volantino; (*at lecture*) prospetto

handsome ['hænsəm] *adj* bello(-a); (*profit, fortune*) considerevole

handwriting ['hændraıtıŋ] *n* scrittura

handy ['hændı] *adj* (*person*) bravo(-a); (*close at hand*) a portata di mano; (*convenient*) comodo(-a)

hang [hæŋ] (*pt, pp* hung) *vt* appendere; (*criminal: pt, pp* hanged) impiccare ▶ *vi* (*painting*) essere appeso(-a); (*hair*) scendere; (*drapery*) cadere; **to get the ~ of sth** (*inf*) capire come qc funziona ▶ **hang about** o **hang around** *vi* bighellonare, ciondolare ▶ **hang down** *vi* ricadere ▶ **hang on** *vi* (*wait*) aspettare ▶ **hang out** *vt* (*washing*) stendere (fuori); (*inf: live*) stare ▶ *vi* penzolare, pendere ▶ **hang round** *vi* = **hang around** ▶ **hang up** *vi* (*Tel*) riattaccare ▶ *vt* appendere

hanger ['hæŋə'] *n* gruccia

hang-gliding ['-glaıdıŋ] *n* volo col deltaplano

hangover ['hæŋəuvə'] *n* (*after drinking*) postumi *mpl* di sbornia

hankie ['hæŋkı] *n abbr* = **handkerchief**

happen ['hæpən] *vi* accadere, succedere; (*chance*): **to ~ to do sth** fare qc per caso; **what ~ed?** cos'è successo?; **as it ~s** guarda caso

happily ['hæpılı] *adv* felicemente, fortunatamente

happiness ['hæpınıs] *n* felicità, contentezza

happy ['hæpı] *adj* felice, contento(-a); **~ with** (*arrangements etc*) soddisfatto(-a) di; **to be ~ to do** (*willing*) fare volentieri; **~ birthday!** buon compleanno!

harass ['hærəs] *vt* molestare; **harassment** *n* molestia

harbour ['hɑːbə'] (*US* **harbor**) *n* porto

▶ *vt* (*hope, fear*) nutrire; (*criminal*) dare rifugio a

hard [hɑːd] *adj* duro(-a) ▶ *adv* (*work*) sodo; (*think, try*) bene; **to look ~ at** guardare fissamente; esaminare attentamente; **no ~ feelings!** senza rancore!; **to be ~ of hearing** essere duro(-a) d'orecchio; **to be ~ done by** essere trattato(-a) ingiustamente; **hardback** *n* libro rilegato; **hardboard** *n* legno precompresso; **hard disk** *n* (*Comput*) disco rigido; **harden** *vt, vi* indurire

hardly ['hɑːdlı] *adv* (*scarcely*) appena; **it's ~ the case** non è proprio il caso; **~ anyone/anywhere** quasi nessuno/da nessuna parte; **~ ever** quasi mai

hard: hardship ['hɑːdʃıp] *n* avversità *f inv*; privazioni *fpl*; **hard shoulder** (*BRIT*) *n* (*Aut*) corsia d'emergenza; **hard-up** (*inf*) *adj* al verde; **hardware** ['hɑːdwɛə'] *n* ferramenta *fpl*; (*Comput*) hardware *m*; (*Mil*) armamenti *mpl*; **hardware shop** (*US* **hardware store**) *n* (negozio di) ferramenta *fpl*; **hard-working** ['-'wɜːkıŋ] *adj* lavoratore(-trice)

hardy ['hɑːdı] *adj* robusto(-a); (*plant*) resistente al gelo

hare [hɛə'] *n* lepre *f*

harm [hɑːm] *n* male *m*; (*wrong*) danno ▶ *vt* (*person*) fare male a; (*thing*) danneggiare; **out of ~'s way** al sicuro; **harmful** *adj* dannoso(-a); **harmless** *adj* innocuo(-a), inoffensivo(-a)

harmony ['hɑːmənı] *n* armonia

harness ['hɑːnıs] *n* (*for horse*) bardatura, finimenti *mpl*; (*for child*) briglie *fpl*; (*safety harness*) imbracatura ▶ *vt* (*horse*) bardare; (*resources*) sfruttare

harp [hɑːp] *n* arpa ▶ *vi* **to ~ on about** insistere tediosamente su

harsh [hɑːʃ] *adj* (*life, winter*) duro(-a); (*judge, criticism*) severo(-a); (*sound*) rauco(-a); (light) violento(-a)

harvest ['hɑːvɪst] n raccolto; (of grapes) vendemmia ▶ vt fare il raccolto di, raccogliere; vendemmiare

has [hæz] vb see **have**

hasn't ['hæznt] = **has not**

hassle ['hæsl] (inf) n sacco di problemi

haste [heɪst] n fretta; precipitazione f; **hasten** ['heɪsn] vt affrettare ▶ vi to **hasten (to)** affrettarsi (a); **hastily** adv in fretta; precipitosamente; **hasty** adj affrettato(-a), precipitoso(-a)

hat [hæt] n cappello

hatch [hætʃ] n (Naut: also: **~way**) boccaporto; (also: **service ~**) portello di servizio ▶ vi (bird) uscire dal guscio; (egg) schiudersi

hatchback ['hætʃbæk] n (Aut) tre (or cinque) porte f inv

hate [heɪt] vt odiare, detestare ▶ n odio; **hatred** ['heɪtrɪd] n odio

haul [hɔːl] vt trascinare, tirare ▶ n (of fish) pescata; (of stolen goods etc) bottino

haunt [hɔːnt] vt (fear) pervadere; (person) frequentare ▶ n rifugio; **this house is ~ed** questa casa è abitata da un fantasma; **haunted** adj (castle etc) abitato(-a) dai fantasmi or dagli spiriti; (look) ossessionato(-a), tormentato(-a)

have
[hæv] (pt, pp **had**) aux vb

1 (gen) avere; essere; **to have arrived/ gone** essere arrivato(-a)/andato(-a); **to have eaten/slept** avere mangiato/ dormito; **he has been kind/promoted** è stato gentile/promosso; **having finished** or when he had finished, he left dopo aver finito, se n'è andato

2 (in tag questions): **you've done it, haven't you?** l'hai fatto, (non è vero?); **he hasn't done it, has he?** non l'ha fatto, vero?

3 (in short answers and questions):

you've made a mistake — no I haven't/so I have ha fatto un errore — ma no, niente affatto/sì, è vero; **we haven't paid — yes we have!** non abbiamo pagato — ma sì che abbiamo pagato!; **I've been there before, have you?** ci sono già stato, e lei?

▶ modal aux vb (be obliged): **to have (got) to do sth** dover fare qc; **I haven't got** or **I don't have to wear glasses** non ho bisogno di portare gli occhiali

▶ vt

1 (possess, obtain) avere; **he has (got) blue eyes/dark hair** ha gli occhi azzurri/i capelli scuri; **do you have** or **have you got a car/phone?** ha la macchina/il telefono?; **may I have your address?** potrebbe darmi il suo indirizzo?; **you can have it for £5** te lo lascio per 5 sterline

2 (+ noun: take, hold etc): **to have breakfast/a swim/a bath** fare colazione/una nuotata/un bagno; **to have lunch** pranzare; **to have dinner** cenare; **to have a drink** bere qualcosa; **to have a cigarette** fumare una sigaretta

3: **to have sth done** far fare qc; **to have one's hair cut** farsi tagliare i capelli; **to have sb do sth** far fare qc a qn

4 (experience, suffer) avere; **to have a cold/flu** avere il raffreddore/ l'influenza; **she had her bag stolen** le hanno rubato la borsa

5 (inf: dupe): **you've been had!** ci sei cascato!

▷ **have out** vt **to have it out with sb** (settle a problem etc) mettere le cose in chiaro con qn

haven ['heɪvn] n porto; (fig) rifugio

haven't ['hævnt] = **have not**

havoc ['hævək] n caos m

Hawaii [hə'waɪiː] n le Hawaii

hawk [hɔːk] n falco

hawthorn ['hɔːθɔːn] n biancospino

hay [heɪ] n fieno; **hay fever** n febbre f
da fieno; **haystack** n pagliaio

hazard ['hæzəd] n azzardo,
ventura; pericolo, rischio ▶ vt (guess
etc) azzardare; **hazardous** adj
pericoloso(-a); **hazard warning
lights** npl (Aut) luci fpl di emergenza

haze [heɪz] n foschia

hazel ['heɪzl] n (tree) nocciolo ▶ adj
(eyes) (color) nocciola inv; **hazelnut**
['heɪzlnʌt] n nocciola

hazy ['heɪzɪ] adj fosco(-a); (idea)
vago(-a)

he [hi:] pron lui, egli; **it is he who ...**
è lui che ...

head [hɛd] n testa; (leader) capo; (of
school) preside m/f ▶ vt (list) essere
in testa a; (group) essere a capo di;
~s or tails testa (o croce), pari (o
dispari); **~ first** a capofitto, di testa;
~ over heels in love pazzamente
innamorato(-a); **to ~ the ball** colpire
una palla di testa ▶ **head for** vt
fus dirigersi verso ▶ **head off** vt
(threat, danger) sventare; **headache**
n mal m di testa; **heading** n titolo;
intestazione f; **headlamp** (BRIT)
n = **headlight**; **headlight** n fanale
m; **headline** n titolo; **head office**
n sede f (centrale); **headphones**
npl cuffia; **headquarters** npl
ufficio centrale; (Mil) quartier
m generale; **headroom** n (in car)
altezza dell'abitacolo; (under bridge)
altezza limite; **headscarf** n foulard
m inv; **headset** n = **headphones**;
headteacher n (of primary school)
direttore(-trice); (of secondary
school) preside; **head waiter** n
capocameriere m

heal [hi:l] vt, vi guarire

health [hɛlθ] n salute f; **health
care** n assistenza sanitaria; **health
centre** (BRIT) n poliambulatorio;
health food n cibo macrobiotico;

Health Service (BRIT) n the **Health
Service** ≈ il Servizio Sanitario Statale;
healthy adj sano(-a), in
buona salute; (climate) salubre;
(appetite, economy etc) sano(-a)

heap [hi:p] n mucchio ▶ vt (stones,
sand): **to ~ (up)** ammucchiare; (plate,
sink): **to ~ sth with** riempire qc di; **~s
of** (inf) un mucchio di

hear [hɪər] (pt, pp heard) vt sentire;
(news) ascoltare ▶ vi sentire; **to ~
about** sentire notizie di; sentire parlare
di; **to ~ from sb** ricevere notizie da qn

hearing ['hɪərɪŋ] n (sense) udito;
(of witnesses) audizione f; (of a case)
udienza; **hearing aid** n apparecchio
acustico

hearse [hə:s] n carro funebre

heart [hɑ:t] n cuore m; **~s** npl (Cards)
cuori mpl; **to lose ~** scoraggiarsi; **to
take ~** farsi coraggio; **at ~** in fondo;
by ~ (learn, know) a memoria; **heart
attack** n attacco di cuore; **heartbeat**
n battito del cuore; **heartbroken**
adj to be heartbroken avere il cuore
spezzato; **heartburn** n bruciore m di
stomaco; **heart disease** n malattia
di cuore

hearth [hɑ:θ] n focolare m

heartless ['hɑ:tlɪs] adj senza cuore

hearty ['hɑ:tɪ] adj caloroso(-a);
robusto(-a), sano(-a); vigoroso(-a)

heat [hi:t] n calore m; (fig) ardore
m; fuoco; (Sport: also: **qualifying**
~) prova eliminatoria ▶ vt scaldare
▶ **heat up** vi (liquids) scaldarsi; (room)
riscaldarsi ▶ vt riscaldare; **heated** adj
riscaldato(-a); (argument) acceso(-a);
heater n radiatore m; (stove) stufa

heather ['hɛðər] n erica

heating ['hi:tɪŋ] n riscaldamento

heatwave ['hi:tweɪv] n ondata di
caldo

heaven ['hɛvn] n paradiso, cielo;
heavenly adj divino(-a), celeste

heavily ['hevɪlɪ] adv pesantemente; (drink, smoke) molto

heavy ['hevɪ] adj pesante; (sea) grosso(-a); (rain, blow) forte; (weather) afoso(-a); (drinker, smoker) gran (before noun); **it's too ~** è troppo pesante

Hebrew ['hi:bru:] adj ebreo(-a) ▶ n (Ling) ebraico

hectare ['hektaːʳ] n (BRIT) ettaro

hectic ['hektɪk] adj movimentato(-a)

he'd [hi:d] = **he would; he had**

hedge [hedʒ] n siepe f ▶ vi essere elusivo(-a); **to ~ one's bets** (fig) coprirsi dai rischi

hedgehog ['hedʒhog] n riccio

heed [hi:d] vt (also: **take ~ of**) badare a, far conto di

heel [hi:l] n (Anat) calcagno; (of shoe) tacco ▶ vt (shoe) rifare i tacchi a

hefty ['heftɪ] adj (person) robusto(-a); (parcel) pesante; (profit) grosso(-a)

height [haɪt] n altezza; (high ground) altura; (fig: of glory) apice m; (: of stupidity) colmo; **heighten** vt (fig) accrescere

heir [ɛəʳ] n erede m; **heiress** n erede f

held [held] pt, pp of **hold**

helicopter ['helɪkɔptəʳ] n elicottero

hell [hel] n inferno; **~!** (inf) porca miseria!, accidenti!

he'll [hi:l] = **he will; he shall**

hello [hə'ləu] excl buon giorno!; ciao! (to sb one addresses as "tu"); (surprise) ma guarda!

helmet ['helmɪt] n casco

help [help] n aiuto; (charwoman) donna di servizio ▶ vt aiutare; **~!** aiuto!; **can you ~ me?** può aiutarmi?; **~ yourself (to bread)** si serva (del pane); **he can't ~ it** non ci può far niente; **help out** vi aiutare ▶ vt to **~ sb out** aiutare qn; **helper** n aiutante m/f, assistente m/f; **helpful** adj di grande aiuto; (useful) utile; **helping** n porzione f; **helpless** adj impotente; (weak) debole; **helpline** adj

≈ telefono amico; (Comm) servizio m informazioni inv (a pagamento)

hem [hem] n orlo ▶ vt fare l'orlo a

hemisphere ['hemɪsfɪəʳ] n emisfero

hemorrhage ['hemərɪdʒ] (US) n = **haemorrhage**

hemorrhoids ['hemərɔɪdz] (US) npl = **haemorrhoids**

hen [hen] n gallina; (female bird) femmina

hence [hens] adv (therefore) dunque; **2 years ~** di qui a 2 anni

hen night n (inf) addio al nubilato

hepatitis [hepə'taɪtɪs] n epatite f

her [həːʳ] pron (direct) la, l' + vowel; (indirect) le; (stressed, after prep) lei ▶ adj il (la) suo(-a), i (le) suoi (sue); see also **me; my**

herb [həːb] n erba; **herbal** adj di erbe; **herbal tea** n tisana

herd [həːd] n mandria

here [hɪəʳ] adv qui, qua ▶ excl ehi!; **~!** (at roll call) presente!; **~ is/are** ecco; **~ he/she is** eccolo/eccola

hereditary [hɪ'redɪtrɪ] adj ereditario(-a)

heritage ['herɪtɪdʒ] n eredità; (fig) retaggio

hernia ['həːnɪə] n ernia

hero ['hɪərəu] (pl **heroes**) n eroe m; **heroic** [hɪ'rəuɪk] adj eroico(-a)

heroin ['herəuɪn] n eroina

heroine ['herəuɪn] n eroina

heron ['herən] n airone m

herring ['herɪŋ] n aringa

hers [həːz] pron il (la) suo(-a), i (le) suoi (sue); see also **mine[1]**

herself [həː'self] pron (reflexive) si; (emphatic) lei stessa; (after prep) se stessa, sé; see also **oneself**

he's [hi:z] = **he is; he has**

hesitant ['hezɪtənt] adj esitante, indeciso(-a)

hesitate ['hezɪteɪt] vi to **~ (about/to do)** esitare (su/a fare); **hesitation**

[-'teɪʃən] n esitazione f

heterosexual ['hetərəʊ'seksjʊəl] adj, n eterosessuale m/f

hexagon ['heksəgən] n esagono

hey [heɪ] excl ehi!

heyday ['heɪdeɪ] n the ~ of i bei giorni di, l'età d'oro di

HGV n abbr = **heavy goods vehicle**

hi [haɪ] excl ciao!

hibernate ['haɪbəneɪt] vi ibernare

hiccough ['hɪkʌp] vi singhiozzare

hiccup ['hɪkʌp] = **hiccough**

hid [hɪd] pt of **hide**

hidden ['hɪdn] pp of **hide**

hide [haɪd] (pt hid, pp hidden) n (skin) pelle f ▶ vt to ~ sth (from sb) nascondere qc (a qn) ▶ vi to ~ (from sb) nascondersi (da qn)

hideous ['hɪdɪəs] adj laido(-a); orribile

hiding ['haɪdɪŋ] n (beating) bastonata; to be in ~ (concealed) tenersi nascosto(-a)

hi-fi ['haɪfaɪ] n stereo ▶ adj ad alta fedeltà, hi-fi inv

high [haɪ] adj alto(-a); (speed, respect, number) grande; (wind) forte; (voice) acuto(-a) ▶ adv alto, in alto; **zom** ~ alto(-a) **zom**; **highchair** n seggiolone m; **high-class** adj (neighbourhood) elegante; (hotel) di prim'ordine; (person) di gran classe; (food) raffinato(-a); **higher education** n studi mpl superiori; **high heels** npl (heels) tacchi mpl alti; (shoes) scarpe fpl con i tacchi alti; **high jump** n (Sport) salto in alto; **the Highlands** npl zona montuosa; **the Highlands** le Highlands scozzesi; **highlight** n (fig: of event) momento culminante; (in hair) colpo m di sole ▶ vt mettere in evidenza; **highlights** npl (in hair) colpi mpl di sole; **highlighter** n (pen) evidenziatore m; **highly** adv molto; to speak highly of parlare molto bene di; **highness** n Her/His **Highness** Sua

Altezza; **high-rise** n (also: high-rise block, high-rise building) palazzone m; **high school** n scuola secondaria; (US) istituto superiore di istruzione; **high season** (BRIT) n alta stagione; **high street** (BRIT) n strada principale; **high-tech** (inf) adj high-tech inv; **highway** ['haɪweɪ] n strada maestra; **Highway Code** (BRIT) n codice m della strada

hijack ['haɪdʒæk] vt dirottare; **hijacker** n dirottatore(-trice)

hike [haɪk] vi fare un'escursione a piedi ▶ n escursione f a piedi; **hiker** n escursionista m/f; **hiking** n escursioni fpl a piedi

hilarious [hɪ'lɛərɪəs] adj (behaviour, event) spassosissimo(-a)

hill [hɪl] n collina, colle m; (fairly high) montagna; (on road) salita; **hillside** n fianco della collina; **hill walking** n escursioni fpl in collina; **hilly** adj collinoso(-a); montagnoso(-a)

him [hɪm] pron (direct) lo, l' + vowel; (indirect) gli; (stressed, after prep) lui; see also **me**; **himself** pron (reflexive) si; (emphatic) lui stesso; (after prep) se stesso; see also **oneself**

hind [haɪnd] adj posteriore ▶ n cerva

hinder ['hɪndə*] vt ostacolare

hindsight ['haɪndsaɪt] n with ~ con il senno di poi

Hindu ['hɪnduː] n indù m/f inv; **Hinduism** n (Rel) induismo

hinge [hɪndʒ] n cardine m ▶ vi (fig): to ~ on dipendere da

hint [hɪnt] n (suggestion) allusione f; (advice) consiglio; (sign) accenno ▶ vt to ~ that lasciar capire che ▶ vi to ~ at alludere a

hip [hɪp] n anca, fianco

hippie ['hɪpɪ] n hippy m/f inv

hippo ['hɪpəʊ] (pl hippos) n ippopotamo

hippopotamus [hɪpə'pɒtəməs] (pl

hippopotamuses or **hippopotami** n
ippopotamo

hippy ['hɪpɪ] n = **hippie**

hire ['haɪə'] vt (BRIT: car, equipment)
noleggiare; (worker) assumere; dare
lavoro a ▸ n nolo, noleggio; **for ~** da
nolo; (taxi) libero(-a); **I'd like to ~ a
car** vorrei noleggiare una macchina;
hire(d) car (BRIT) n macchina a nolo;
hire purchase (BRIT) n acquisto (or
vendita) rateale

his [hɪz] adj, pron il (la) suo (sua), i (le)
suoi (sue); see also **my**; **mine**¹

Hispanic [hɪs'pænɪk] adj ispanico(-a)

hiss [hɪs] vi fischiare; (cat, snake)
sibilare

historian [hɪ'stɔːrɪən] n storico(-a)

historic(al) [hɪ'stɔrɪk(l)] adj
storico(-a)

history ['hɪstərɪ] n storia

hit [hɪt] (pt, pp **hit**) vt colpire,
picchiare; (knock against) battere;
(reach: target) raggiungere; (collide
with: car) urtare contro; (fig: affect)
colpire; (find: problem etc) incontrare
▸ n colpo; (success, song) successo; **to ~
it off with sb** andare molto d'accordo
con qn ▸ **hit back** vi to ~ back at sb
restituire il colpo a qn

hitch [hɪtʃ] vt (fasten) attaccare;
(also: ~ up) tirare su ▸ n (difficulty)
intoppo, difficoltà f inv; **to ~ a
lift** fare l'autostop; **hitch-hike**
vi fare l'autostop; **hitch-hiker** n
autostoppista m/f; **hitch-hiking** n
autostop m

hi-tech ['haɪ'tek] adj high-tech inv

hitman ['hɪtmæn] (irreg) n (inf) sicario

HIV abbr ~-**negative/-positive** adj
sieronegativo(-a)/sieropositivo(-a)

hive [haɪv] n alveare m

hoard [hɔːd] n (of food) provviste fpl; (of
money) gruzzolo ▸ vt ammassare

hoarse [hɔːs] adj rauco(-a)

hoax [həuks] n scherzo; falso allarme

hob [hɔb] n piastra (con fornelli)

hobble ['hɔbl] vi zoppicare

hobby ['hɔbɪ] n hobby m inv,
passatempo

hobo ['həubəu] (US) n vagabondo

hockey ['hɔkɪ] n hockey m; **hockey
stick** n bastone m da hockey

hog [hɔg] n maiale m ▸ vt (fig)
arraffare; **to go the whole ~** farlo fino
in fondo

Hogmanay [hɔgmə'neɪ] n (Scottish)
≈ San Silvestro

hoist [hɔɪst] n paranco ▸ vt issare

hold [həuld] (pt, pp **held**) vt tenere;
(contain) contenere; (keep back)
trattenere; (believe) mantenere;
considerare; (possess) avere,
possedere; detenere ▸ vi (withstand
pressure) tenere; (be valid) essere
valido(-a) ▸ n presa; (control): **to have
a ~ over** avere controllo su; (Naut)
stiva; **~ the line!** (Tel) resti in linea!;
to ~ one's own (fig) difendersi bene;
to catch or **get (a) ~ of** afferrare
▸ **hold back** vt trattenere; (secret)
tenere celato(-a) ▸ **hold on** vi tener
fermo; (wait) aspettare; **~ on!** (Tel)
resti in linea! ▸ **hold out** vt offrire
▸ vi (resist) resistere ▸ **hold up** vt
(raise) alzare; (support) sostenere;
(delay) ritardare; (rob) assaltare;
holdall (BRIT) n borsone m; **holder**
n (container) contenitore m; (of ticket,
title) possessore/posseditrice; (of
office etc) incaricato(-a); (of record)
detentore(-trice)

hole [həul] n buco, buca

holiday ['hɔlɪdɪ] n vacanza; (day off)
giorno di vacanza; (public) giorno
festivo; **on ~** in vacanza; **I'm on ~
here** sono qui in vacanza; **holiday
camp** (BRIT) n (also: holiday centre)
≈ villaggio (di vacanze); **holiday job**
(BRIT) ≈ lavoro estivo; **holiday-maker**
(BRIT) n villeggiante m/f; **holiday**

resort n luogo di villeggiatura
Holland ['hɔlənd] n Olanda
hollow ['hɔləu] adj cavo(-a); (container, claim) vuoto(-a); (laugh, sound) cupo(-a) ▶ n cavità f inv; (in land) valletta, depressione f ▶ vt **to ~ out** scavare
holly ['hɔlɪ] n agrifoglio
Hollywood ['hɔlɪwud] n Hollywood f
holocaust ['hɔləkɔːst] n olocausto
holy ['həulɪ] adj santo(-a); (bread, ground) benedetto(-a), consacrato(-a)
home [həum] n casa; (country) patria; (institution) casa, ricovero ▶ cpd familiare; (cooking etc) casalingo(-a); (Econ, Pol) nazionale, interno(-a); (Sport) di casa ▶ adv a casa; in patria; (right in: nail etc) fino in fondo; **at ~** a casa; (in situation) a proprio agio; **to go** or **come ~** tornare a casa (or in patria); **make yourself at ~** si metta a suo agio; **home address** n indirizzo di casa; **homeland** n patria; **homeless** adj senza tetto; **homely** adj semplice, alla buona; accogliente; **home-made** adj casalingo(-a); **home match** n partita in casa; **Home Office** (BRIT) n ministero degli Interni; **home owner** n proprietario/a; **home page** n (Comput) home page f inv; **Home Secretary** (BRIT) n ministro degli Interni; **homesick** adj **to be homesick** avere la nostalgia; **home town** n città natale; **homework** n compiti mpl (per casa)
homicide ['hɔmɪsaɪd] (US) n omicidio
homoeopathic [həumɪə'pæθɪk] (US **homeopathic**) adj omeopatico(-a)
homoeopathy [həumɪ'ɔpəθɪ] (US **homeopathy**) n omeopatia
homosexual [həmə'sɛksjuəl] adj, n omosessuale m/f
honest ['ɔnɪst] adj onesto(-a); sincero(-a); **honestly** adv

onestamente; sinceramente;
honesty n onestà
honey ['hʌnɪ] n miele m; **honeymoon** n luna di miele, viaggio di nozze; **we're on honeymoon** siamo in luna di miele; **honeysuckle** n (Bot) caprifoglio
Hong Kong ['hɔŋ'kɔŋ] n Hong Kong f
honorary ['ɔnərərɪ] adj onorario(-a); (duty, title) onorifico(-a)
honour ['ɔnə²] (US **honor**) vt onorare ▶ n onore m; **honourable** (US **honorable**) adj onorevole; **honours degree** n (Scol) laurea specializzata
hood [hud] n cappuccio; (on cooker) cappa; (BRIT Aut) capote f; (US Aut) cofano
hoof [huːf] (pl **hooves**) n zoccolo
hook [huk] n gancio; (for fishing) amo ▶ vt uncinare; (dress) agganciare
hooligan ['huːlɪɡən] n giovinastro, teppista m
hoop [huːp] n cerchio
hooray [huːˈreɪ] excl = **hurray**
hoot [huːt] vi (Aut) suonare il clacson; (siren) ululare; (owl) gufare
Hoover® ['huːvə²] (BRIT) n aspirapolvere m inv ▶ vt hoover pulire con l'aspirapolvere
hooves [huːvz] npl of **hoof**
hop [hɔp] vi saltellare, saltare; (on one foot) saltare su una gamba
hope [həup] vt **to ~ that/to do** sperare che/di fare ▶ vi sperare ▶ n speranza; **I ~ so/not** spero di sì/no; **hopeful** adj (person) pieno(-a) di speranza; (situation) promettente; **hopefully** adv con speranza; **hopefully he will recover** speriamo che si riprenda; **hopeless** adj senza speranza, disperato(-a); (useless) inutile
hops [hɔps] npl luppoli mpl
horizon [hə'raɪzn] n orizzonte m; **horizontal** [hɔrɪ'zɔntl] adj orizzontale

hormone ['hɔːməʊn] n ormone m
horn [hɔːn] n (Zool, Mus) corno; (Aut)
clacson m inv
horoscope ['hɒrəskəʊp] n oroscopo
horrendous [hə'rendəs] adj
orrendo(-a)
horrible ['hɒrɪbl] adj orribile,
tremendo(-a)
horrid ['hɒrɪd] adj orrido(-a); (person)
odioso(-a)
horrific [hɒ'rɪfɪk] adj (accident)
spaventoso(-a); (film) orripilante
horrifying ['hɒrɪfaɪɪŋ] adj terrificante
horror ['hɒrə'] n orrore m; **horror film**
n film m inv dell'orrore
hors d'œuvre [ɔː'dɜːvrə] n antipasto
horse [hɔːs] n cavallo; **horseback:
on horseback**, adv a cavallo;
horse chestnut n ippocastano;
horsepower n cavallo (vapore);
horse-racing n ippica; **horseradish**
n rafano; **horse riding** n (BRIT)
equitazione f
hose [həʊz] n (also: ~**pipe**) tubo; (also:
garden ~) tubo per annaffiare
hospital ['hɒspɪtl] n ospedale
m; **where's the nearest ~?** dov'è
l'ospedale più vicino?
hospitality [hɒspɪ'tælɪtɪ] n ospitalità
host [həʊst] n ospite m; (Rel) ostia;
(large number): **a ~ of** una schiera di
hostage ['hɒstɪdʒ] n ostaggio(-a)
hostel ['hɒstl] n ostello; (also: **youth ~**)
ostello della gioventù
hostess ['həʊstɪs] n ospite f; (BRIT: air
hostess) hostess f inv
hostile ['hɒstaɪl] adj ostile
hostility [hɒ'stɪlɪtɪ] n ostilità f inv
hot [hɒt] adj caldo(-a); (as opposed to
only warm) molto caldo(-a); (spicy)
piccante; (fig) accanito(-a); ardente,
violento(-a), focoso(-a); **to be ~**
(person) aver caldo; (object) essere
molto caldo(-a); (weather) far caldo; **hot dog**
n hot dog m inv

hotel [həʊ'tɛl] n albergo
hot-water bottle [hɒt'wɔːtə-] n
borsa dell'acqua calda
hound [haʊnd] vt perseguitare ▶ n
segugio
hour ['auə'] n ora; **hourly** adj all'ora
house [n haus, pl 'hauzɪz] [vb hauz]
n (also: firm) casa; (Pol) camera;
(Theatre): sala; pubblico; spettacolo;
(dynasty) casata ▶ vt (person) ospitare,
alloggiare; **on the ~** (fig) offerto(-a)
dalla casa; **household** n famiglia;
casa; **householder** n padrone(-a)
di casa; (head of house) capofamiglia
m/f; **housekeeper** n governante f;
housekeeping n (work) governo della
casa; (money) soldi mpl per le spese di
casa; **housewife** (irreg) n massaia,
casalinga; **house wine** n vino della
casa; **housework** n faccende fpl
domestiche
housing ['hauzɪŋ] n alloggio;
housing development (BRIT),
housing estate n zona residenziale con
case popolari e/o private
hover ['hɒvə'] vi (bird) librarsi;
hovercraft n hovercraft m inv
how [hau] adv come: **~ are you?** come
sta?; **~ do you do?** piacere!; **~ far is
it to the river?** quanto è lontano il
fiume?; **~ long have you been here?**
da quando è qui?; **~ lovely/awful!**
che bello!/orrore!; **~ many?**
quanti(-e)?; **~ much?** quanto(-a)?;
~ much milk? quanto latte?; **~ many
people?** quante persone?; **~ old are
you?** quanti anni ha?
however [hau'ɛvə'] adv in qualsiasi
modo or maniera che; (+ adjective) per
quanto + sub; (in questions) come ▶ conj
comunque, però
howl [haul] vi ululare; (baby, person)
urlare
H.P. abbr = **hire purchase;
horsepower**

h.p. n abbr = **H.P**

HQ n, abbr = **headquarters**

hr(s) abbr (= hour(s)) h

HTML abbr (= hypertext markup language) HTML m inv

hubcap ['hʌbkæp] n coprimozzo

huddle ['hʌdl] vi to ~ together rannicchiarsi l'uno contro l'altro

huff [hʌf] n in a ~ stizzito(-a)

hug [hʌg] vt abbracciare; (shore, kerb) stringere

huge [hjuːdʒ] adj enorme, immenso(-a)

hull [hʌl] n (of ship) scafo

hum [hʌm] vt (tune) canticchiare ▶ vi canticchiare; (insect, plane, tool) ronzare

human ['hjuːmən] (irreg) adj umano(-a) ▶ n essere m umano

humane [hjuːˈmeɪn] adj umanitario(-a)

humanitarian [hjuːmænɪˈtɛərɪən] adj umanitario(-a)

humanity [hjuːˈmænɪtɪ] n umanità

human rights npl diritti mpl dell'uomo

humble ['hʌmbl] adj umile, modesto(-a) ▶ vt umiliare

humid ['hjuːmɪd] adj umido(-a); **humidity** [hjuːˈmɪdɪtɪ] n umidità

humiliate [hjuːˈmɪlɪeɪt] vt umiliare; **humiliating** adj umiliante; **humiliation** [-ˈeɪʃən] n umiliazione f

hummus ['huməs] n purè di ceci

humorous ['hjuːmərəs] adj umoristico(-a); (person) buffo(-a)

humour ['hjuːmər] (US **humor**) n umore m ▶ vt accontentare

hump [hʌmp] n gobba

hunch [hʌntʃ] n (premonition) intuizione f

hundred ['hʌndrəd] num cento; ~s of centinaia fpl di; **hundredth** [-ɪdθ] num centesimo(-a)

hung [hʌŋ] pt, pp of **hang**

Hungarian [hʌŋˈgɛərɪən] adj ungherese ▶ n ungherese m/f; (Ling) ungherese m

Hungary ['hʌŋgərɪ] n Ungheria

hunger ['hʌŋgər] n fame f ▶ vi to ~ for desiderare ardentemente

hungry ['hʌŋgrɪ] adj affamato(-a); **to be ~** aver fame

hunt [hʌnt] vt (seek) cercare; (Sport) cacciare ▶ vi to ~ (for) andare a caccia (di) ▶ n caccia; **hunter** n cacciatore m; **hunting** n caccia

hurdle ['hɜːdl] n (Sport, fig) ostacolo

hurl [hɜːl] vt lanciare con violenza

hurrah [hu'rɑː] excl = **hurray**

hurray [hu'reɪ] excl urra!, evviva!

hurricane ['hʌrɪkən] n uragano

hurry ['hʌrɪ] n fretta ▶ vi (also: ~ up) affrettarsi ▶ vt (also: ~ up: person) affrettare; (work) far in fretta; **to be in a ~** aver fretta ▶ **hurry up** vi sbrigarsi

hurt [hɜːt] (pt, pp **hurt**) vt (cause pain to) far male a; (injure, fig) ferire ▶ vi far male

husband ['hʌzbənd] n marito

hush [hʌʃ] n silenzio, calma ▶ vt zittire

husky ['hʌskɪ] adj roco(-a) ▶ n cane m eschimese

hut [hʌt] n rifugio; (shed) ripostiglio

hyacinth ['haɪəsɪnθ] n giacinto

hydrangea [haɪˈdreɪndʒə] n ortensia

hydrofoil ['haɪdrəufɔɪl] n aliscafo

hydrogen ['haɪdrədʒən] n idrogeno

hygiene ['haɪdʒiːn] n igiene f; **hygienic** [haɪˈdʒiːnɪk] adj igienico(-a)

hymn [hɪm] n inno; cantica

hype [haɪp] (inf) n campagna pubblicitaria

hyphen ['haɪfn] n trattino

hypnotize ['hɪpnətaɪz] vt ipnotizzare

hypocrite ['hɪpəkrɪt] n ipocrita m/f

hypocritical [hɪpəˈkrɪtɪkl] adj ipocrita

hypothesis [haɪˈpɒθɪsɪs] (pl **hypotheses**) n ipotesi f inv

hysterical [hɪ'stɛrɪkl] *adj* isterico(-a)
hysterics [hɪ'stɛrɪks] *npl* accesso di
isteria; (*laughter*) attacco di riso

♦

I [aɪ] *pron* io
ice [aɪs] *n* ghiaccio; (*on road*) gelo; (*ice
cream*) gelato ▶ *vt* (*cake*) glassare ▶ *vi*
(*also:* ~ **over**) ghiacciare; (*also:* ~ **up**)
gelare; **iceberg** *n* iceberg *m inv*; **ice
cream** *n* gelato; **ice cube** *n* cubetto
di ghiaccio; **ice hockey** *n* hockey *m*
su ghiaccio
Iceland ['aɪslənd] *n* Islanda;
Icelander *n* islandese *m/f*; **Icelandic**
[aɪs'lændɪk] *adj* islandese ▶ *n* (*Ling*)
islandese *m*
ice: ice lolly (BRIT) *n* ghiacciolo;
ice rink *n* pista di pattinaggio; **ice
skating** *n* pattinaggio sul ghiaccio
icing ['aɪsɪŋ] *n* (*Culin*) glassa; **icing
sugar** (BRIT) *n* zucchero a velo
icon ['aɪkɔn] *n* icona
icy ['aɪsɪ] *adj* ghiacciato(-a); (*weather,
temperature*) gelido(-a)
I'd [aɪd] = **I would**; **I had**
ID card *n* = **identity card**
idea [aɪ'dɪə] *n* idea
ideal [aɪ'dɪəl] *adj* ideale ▶ *n* ideale *m*;
ideally [aɪ'dɪəlɪ] *adv* perfettamente,
assolutamente; **ideally the book
should have ...** l'ideale sarebbe che il

libro avesse ...
identical [aɪ'dɛntɪkl] *adj* identico(-a)
identification [aɪdɛntɪfɪ'keɪʃən] *n*
identificazione *f*; (**means of**) ~ carta
d'identità
identify [aɪ'dɛntɪfaɪ] *vt* identificare
identity [aɪ'dɛntɪtɪ] *n* identità *f inv*;
identity card *n* carta d'identità
ideology [aɪdɪ'ɔlədʒɪ] *n* ideologia
idiom ['ɪdɪəm] *n* idioma *m*; (*phrase*)
espressione *f* idiomatica
idiot ['ɪdɪət] *n* idiota *m/f*
idle ['aɪdl] *adj* inattivo(-a); (*lazy*)
pigro(-a), ozioso(-a); (*unemployed*)
disoccupato(-a); (*question, pleasures*)
ozioso(-a) ▶ *vi* (*engine*) girare al
minimo
idol ['aɪdl] *n* idolo
idyllic [ɪ'dɪlɪk] *adj* idillico(-a)
i.e. *adv abbr* (= *that is*) cioè
if [ɪf] *conj* se; **if I were you ...** se fossi in
te ..., io al tuo posto ...; **if so** se è così;
if not se no; **if only** se solo *or* soltanto
ignite [ɪg'naɪt] *vt* accendere ▶ *vi*
accendersi
ignition [ɪg'nɪʃən] *n* (*Aut*) accensione
f; **to switch on/off the** ~ accendere/
spegnere il motore
ignorance ['ɪgnərəns] *n* ignoranza;
to keep sb in ~ **of sth** tenere qn
all'oscuro di qc
ignorant ['ɪgnərənt] *adj* ignorante; **to
be** ~ **of** (*subject*) essere ignorante in;
(*events*) essere ignaro(-a) di
ignore [ɪg'nɔ:r] *vt* non tener conto di;
(*person, fact*) ignorare
I'll [aɪl] = **I will**; **I shall**
ill [ɪl] *adj* (*sick*) malato(-a); (*bad*)
cattivo(-a) ▶ *n* male *m* ▶ *adv* to **speak
etc** ~ **of sb** parlare *etc* male di qn; **to
take** *or* **be taken** ~ ammalarsi
illegal [ɪ'li:gl] *adj* illegale
illegible [ɪ'lɛdʒɪbl] *adj* illeggibile
illegitimate [ɪlɪ'dʒɪtɪmət] *adj*
illegittimo(-a)

ill health n problemi mpl di salute

illiterate [ɪˈlɪtərət] adj analfabeta, illetterato(-a); (letter) scorretto(-a)

illness [ˈɪlnɪs] n malattia

illuminate [ɪˈluːmɪneɪt] vt illuminare

illusion [ɪˈluːʒən] n illusione f

illustrate [ˈɪləstreɪt] vt illustrare

illustration [ɪləˈstreɪʃən] n illustrazione f

I'm [aɪm] = **I am**

image [ˈɪmɪdʒ] n immagine f; (public face) immagine (pubblica)

imaginary [ɪˈmædʒɪnərɪ] adj immaginario(-a)

imagination [ɪmædʒɪˈneɪʃən] n immaginazione f, fantasia

imaginative [ɪˈmædʒɪnətɪv] adj immaginoso(-a)

imagine [ɪˈmædʒɪn] vt immaginare

imbalance [ɪmˈbæləns] n squilibrio

imitate [ˈɪmɪteɪt] vt imitare; **imitation** [-ˈteɪʃən] n imitazione f

immaculate [ɪˈmækjulət] adj immacolato(-a); (dress, appearance) impeccabile

immature [ɪməˈtjuəʳ] adj immaturo(-a)

immediate [ɪˈmiːdɪət] adj immediato(-a); **immediately** adv (at once) subito, immediatamente; **immediately next to** proprio accanto a

immense [ɪˈmɛns] adj immenso(-a); enorme; **immensely** adv immensamente

immerse [ɪˈmɛːs] vt immergere

immigrant [ˈɪmɪɡrənt] n immigrante m/f; immigrato(-a); **immigration** [ɪmɪˈɡreɪʃən] n immigrazione f

imminent [ˈɪmɪnənt] adj imminente

immoral [ɪˈmɔrl] adj immorale

immortal [ɪˈmɔːtl] adj, n immortale m/f

immune [ɪˈmjuːn] adj ~ **(to)** immune (da); **immune system** n sistema m

immunitario

immunize [ˈɪmjunaɪz] vt immunizzare

impact [ˈɪmpækt] n impatto

impair [ɪmˈpɛəʳ] vt danneggiare

impartial [ɪmˈpɑːʃl] adj imparziale

impatience [ɪmˈpeɪʃəns] n impazienza

impatient [ɪmˈpeɪʃənt] adj impaziente; **to get** or **grow ~** perdere la pazienza

impeccable [ɪmˈpɛkəbl] adj impeccabile

impending [ɪmˈpɛndɪŋ] adj imminente

imperative [ɪmˈpɛrətɪv] adj imperativo(-a); necessario(-a), urgente; (voice) imperioso(-a)

imperfect [ɪmˈpəːfɪkt] adj imperfetto(-a); (goods etc) difettoso(-a) ▶ n (Ling: also: **~ tense**) imperfetto

imperial [ɪmˈpɪərɪəl] adj imperiale; (measure) legale

impersonal [ɪmˈpəːsənl] adj impersonale

impersonate [ɪmˈpəːsəneɪt] vt impersonare; (Theatre) fare la mimica di

impetus [ˈɪmpətəs] n impeto

implant [ɪmˈplɑːnt] vt (Med) innestare; (fig: idea, principle) inculcare

implement [n ˈɪmplɪmənt, vb ˈɪmplɪment] n attrezzo; (for cooking) utensile m ▶ vt effettuare

implicate [ˈɪmplɪkeɪt] vt implicare

implication [ɪmplɪˈkeɪʃən] n implicazione f; **by ~** implicitamente

implicit [ɪmˈplɪsɪt] adj implicito(-a); (complete) completo(-a)

imply [ɪmˈplaɪ] vt insinuare; suggerire

impolite [ɪmpəˈlaɪt] adj scortese

import [vb ɪmˈpɔːt, n ˈɪmpɔːt] vt importare ▶ n (Comm) importazione f

importance [ɪmˈpɔːtns] n

importanza
important [ɪmˈpɔːtnt] *adj*
importante; **it's not ~** non ha
importanza
importer [ɪmˈpɔːtə²] *n*
importatore(-trice)
impose [ɪmˈpəʊz] *vt* imporre ▶ *vi*
to ~ on sb sfruttare la bontà di qn;
imposing [ɪmˈpəʊzɪŋ] *adj* imponente
impossible [ɪmˈpɒsɪbl] *adj*
impossibile
impotent [ˈɪmpətnt] *adj* impotente
impoverished [ɪmˈpɒvərɪʃt] *adj*
impoverito(-a)
impractical [ɪmˈpræktɪkl] *adj* non
pratico(-a)
impress [ɪmˈprɛs] *vt* impressionare;
(*mark*) imprimere, stampare; **to ~ sth
on sb** far capire qc a qn
impression [ɪmˈprɛʃən] *n*
impressione *f*; **to be under the ~ that**
avere l'impressione che
impressive [ɪmˈprɛsɪv] *adj* notevole
imprison [ɪmˈprɪzn] *vt* imprigionare;
imprisonment *n* imprigionamento
improbable [ɪmˈprɒbəbl] *adj*
improbabile; (*excuse*) inverosimile
improper [ɪmˈprɒpə²] *adj*
scorretto(-a); (*unsuitable*)
inadatto(-a), improprio(-a);
sconveniente, indecente
improve [ɪmˈpruːv] *vt* migliorare ▶ *vi*
migliorare; (*pupil etc*) fare progressi;
improvement *n* miglioramento;
progresso
improvise [ˈɪmprəvaɪz] *vt, vi*
improvvisare
impulse [ˈɪmpʌls] *n* impulso; **on
~ impulso**, impulsivamente;
impulsive [ɪmˈpʌlsɪv] *adj*
impulsivo(-a)

in
[ɪn] *prep*
1 (*indicating place, position*) in; **in the
house/garden** in casa/giardino; **in**
the box nella scatola; **in the fridge**
nel frigorifero; **I have it in my hand** ce
l'ho in mano; **in town/the country** in
città/campagna; **in school** a scuola; **in
here/there** qui/lì dentro
2 (*with place names: of town, region,
country*): **in London** a Londra; **in
England** in Inghilterra; **in the United
States** negli Stati Uniti; **in Yorkshire**
nello Yorkshire
3 (*indicating time: during, in the
space of*): in; **in spring/summer** in
primavera/estate; **in 1988** nel 1988; **in
May** in *or* a maggio; **I'll see you in July**
ci vediamo a luglio; **in the afternoon**
nel pomeriggio; **at 4 o'clock in the
afternoon** alle 4 del pomeriggio; **I
did it in 3 hours/days** l'ho fatto in
3 ore/giorni; **I'll see you in 2 weeks**
or **in 2 weeks' time** ci vediamo tra 2
settimane
4 (*indicating manner etc*) a: **in a
loud/soft voice** a voce alta/bassa; **in
pencil** a matita; **in English/French** in
inglese/francese; **the boy in the blue
shirt** il ragazzo con la camicia blu
5 (*indicating circumstances*): **in the sun**
al sole; **in the shade** all'ombra; **in the
rain** sotto la pioggia; **a rise in prices** un
aumento dei prezzi
6 (*indicating mood, state*): **in tears**
in lacrime; **in anger** per la rabbia;
in despair disperato(-a); **in good
condition** in buono stato, in buone
condizioni; **to live in luxury** vivere
nel lusso
7 (*with ratios, numbers*): **1 in 10** 1 su
10; **20 pence in the pound** 20 pence
per sterlina; **they lined up in twos** si
misero in fila a due a due
8 (*referring to people, works*): **the
disease is common in children** la
malattia è comune nei bambini; **in
(the works of) Dickens** in Dickens
9 (*indicating profession etc*) in; **to be in**

teaching fare l'insegnante, insegnare; **to be in publishing** essere nell'editoria **10** (after superlative) di; **the best in the class** il migliore della classe **11** (with present participle): **in saying this** dicendo questo, nel dire questo
▶ adv **to be in** (person: at home, work) esserci; (train, ship, plane) essere arrivato(-a); (in fashion) essere di moda; **to ask sb in** invitare qn ad entrare; **to run/limp** etc **in** entrare di corsa/ zoppicando etc
▶ n **the ins and outs of the problem** tutti i particolari del problema

inability [ɪnəˈbɪlɪtɪ] n ~ **(to do)** incapacità (di fare).

inaccurate [ɪnˈækjʊrət] adj inesatto(-a), impreciso(-a)

inadequate [ɪnˈædɪkwət] adj insufficiente

inadvertently [ɪnədˈvəːtntlɪ] adv senza volerlo

inappropriate [ɪnəˈprəʊprɪət] adj non adatto(-a); (word, expression) improprio(-a)

inaugurate [ɪˈnɔːɡjʊreɪt] vt inaugurare; (president, official) insediare

Inc. (US) abbr (= incorporated) S.A

incapable [ɪnˈkeɪpəbl] adj incapace

incense [n ˈɪnsɛns, vb ɪnˈsɛns] n incenso ▶ vt (anger) infuriare

incentive [ɪnˈsɛntɪv] n incentivo

inch [ɪntʃ] n pollice m (25 mm, 12 in a foot); **within an ~ of** a un pelo da; **he didn't give an ~** non ha ceduto di un millimetro

incidence [ˈɪnsɪdns] n (of crime, disease) incidenza

incident [ˈɪnsɪdnt] n incidente m; (in book) episodio

incidentally [ɪnsɪˈdɛntəlɪ] adv (by the way) a proposito

inclination [ɪnklɪˈneɪʃən] n inclinazione f

incline [n ˈɪnklaɪn, vb ɪnˈklaɪn] n pendenza, pendio ▶ vt inclinare
▶ vi (surface) essere inclinato(-a); **to be ~d to do** tendere a fare; essere propenso(-a) a fare

include [ɪnˈkluːd] vt includere, comprendere; **is service ~d?** il servizio è compreso?; **including** prep compreso(-a), incluso(-a);

inclusion [ɪnˈkluːʒən] n inclusione f;

inclusive [ɪnˈkluːsɪv] adj incluso(-a), compreso(-a); **inclusive of tax** etc tasse etc comprese

income [ˈɪnkʌm] n reddito; **income support** n (BRIT) sussidio di indigenza or povertà; **income tax** n imposta sul reddito

incoming [ˈɪnkʌmɪŋ] adj (flight, mail) in arrivo; (government) subentrante; (tide) montante

incompatible [ɪnkəmˈpætɪbl] adj incompatibile

incompetence [ɪnˈkɔmpɪtns] n incompetenza, incapacità

incompetent [ɪnˈkɔmpɪtnt] adj incompetente, incapace

incomplete [ɪnkəmˈpliːt] adj incompleto(-a)

inconsistent [ɪnkənˈsɪstənt] adj incoerente; ~ **with** non coerente con

inconvenience [ɪnkənˈviːnjəns] n inconveniente m; (trouble) disturbo
▶ vt disturbare

inconvenient [ɪnkənˈviːnjənt] adj scomodo(-a)

incorporate [ɪnˈkɔːpəreɪt] vt incorporare; (contain) contenere

incorrect [ɪnkəˈrɛkt] adj scorretto(-a); (statement) inesatto(-a)

increase [n ˈɪnkriːs, vb ɪnˈkriːs] n aumento ▶ vi, vt aumentare; **increasingly** adv sempre più

incredible [ɪnˈkrɛdɪbl] adj incredibile; **incredibly** adv incredibilmente

incur [ɪnˈkəː] vt (expenses) incorrere;

(*anger, risk*) esporsi a; (*debt*) contrarre; (*loss*) subire

indecent [ɪn'di:snt] *adj* indecente

indeed [ɪn'di:d] *adv* infatti; veramente; **yes ~!** certamente!

indefinitely [ɪn'defɪnɪtlɪ] *adv* (*wait*) indefinitamente

independence [ɪndɪ'pɛndns] *n* indipendenza; **Independence Day** (*US*) *n* vedi nota nel riquadro

● **Independence Day**
● Negli Stati Uniti il 4 luglio si
● festeggia l'**Independence Day**,
● giorno in cui, nel 1776, 13 colonie
● britanniche proclamarono la propria
● indipendenza dalla Gran Bretagna
● ed entrarono ufficialmente a far
● parte degli Stati Uniti d'America.

independent [ɪndɪ'pɛndnt] *adj* indipendente; **independent school** *n* (*BRIT*) istituto scolastico indipendente che si autofinanzia

index ['ɪndɛks] (*pl* **indexes**) *n* (*in book*) indice *m*; (: *in library etc*) catalogo; (*pl* **indices**: *ratio, sign*) indice *m*

India ['ɪndɪə] *n* India; **Indian** *adj, n* indiano(-a)

indicate ['ɪndɪkeɪt] *vt* indicare; **indication** [-'keɪʃən] *n* indicazione *f*, segno; **indicative** [ɪn'dɪkətɪv] *adj* **indicative of** indicativo(-a) di; **indicator** ['ɪndɪkeɪtə'] *n* indicatore *m*; (*Aut*) freccia

indices ['ɪndɪsi:z] *npl of* **index**

indict [ɪn'daɪt] *vt* accusare; **indictment** [ɪn'daɪtmənt] *n* accusa

indifference [ɪn'dɪfrəns] *n* indifferenza

indifferent [ɪn'dɪfrənt] *adj* indifferente; (*poor*) mediocre

indigenous [ɪn'dɪdʒɪnəs] *adj* indigeno(-a)

indigestion [ɪndɪ'dʒɛstʃən] *n* indigestione *f*

indignant [ɪn'dɪgnənt] *adj* **~ (at**

sth/**with sb**) indignato(-a) (per qc/contro qn)

indirect [ɪndɪ'rɛkt] *adj* indiretto(-a)

indispensable [ɪndɪ'spɛnsəbl] *adj* indispensabile

individual [ɪndɪ'vɪdjuəl] *n* individuo ▶ *adj* individuale; (*characteristic*) particolare, originale; **individually** *adv* singolarmente, uno(-a) per uno(-a)

Indonesia [ɪndə'ni:zɪə] *n* Indonesia

indoor ['ɪndɔ:'] *adj* da interno; (*plant*) d'appartamento; (*swimming pool*) coperto(-a); (*sport, games*) fatto(-a) al coperto; **indoors** [ɪn'dɔ:z] *adv* all'interno

induce [ɪn'dju:s] *vt* persuadere; (*bring about, Med*) provocare

indulge [ɪn'dʌldʒ] *vt* (*whim*) compiacere, soddisfare; (*child*) viziare ▶ *vi* **to ~ in** sth concedersi qc; abbandonarsi a qc; **indulgent** *adj* indulgente

industrial [ɪn'dʌstrɪəl] *adj* industriale; (*injury*) sul lavoro; **industrial estate** (*BRIT*) *n* zona industriale; **industrialist** [ɪn'dʌstrɪəlɪst] *n* industriale *m*; **industrial park** (*US*) *n* = **industrial estate**

industry ['ɪndəstrɪ] *n* industria; (*diligence*) operosità

inefficient [ɪnɪ'fɪʃənt] *adj* inefficiente

inequality [ɪnɪ'kwɔlɪtɪ] *n* ineguaglianza

inevitable [ɪn'ɛvɪtəbl] *adj* inevitabile; **inevitably** *adv* inevitabilmente

inexpensive [ɪnɪk'spɛnsɪv] *adj* poco costoso(-a)

inexperienced [ɪnɪks'pɪərɪənst] *adj* inesperto(-a), senza esperienza

inexplicable [ɪnɪk'splɪkəbl] *adj* inesplicabile

infamous ['ɪnfəməs] *adj* infame

infant ['ɪnfənt] *n* bambino(-a)

infantry ['ɪnfəntrɪ] *n* fanteria

infant school n (BRIT) scuola elementare (*per bambini dall'età di 5 a 7 anni*)

infect [ɪnˈfɛkt] vt infettare; **infection** [ɪnˈfɛkʃən] n infezione f; **infectious** [ɪnˈfɛkʃəs] adj (*disease*) infettivo(-a), contagioso(-a); (*person: fig: enthusiasm*) contagioso(-a)

infer [ɪnˈfəː] vt inferire, dedurre

inferior [ɪnˈfɪərɪə] adj inferiore; (*goods*) di qualità scadente ▶ n inferiore m/f; (*in rank*) subalterno(-a)

infertile [ɪnˈfəːtaɪl] adj sterile

infertility [ɪnfəˈtɪlɪtɪ] n sterilità f

infested [ɪnˈfɛstɪd] adj ~ (**with**) infestato(-a) (di)

infinite [ˈɪnfɪnɪt] adj infinito(-a); **infinitely** adv infinitamente

infirmary [ɪnˈfəːmərɪ] n ospedale m; (*in school, factory*) infermeria

inflamed [ɪnˈfleɪmd] adj infiammato(-a)

inflammation [ɪnfləˈmeɪʃən] n infiammazione f

inflatable [ɪnˈfleɪtəbl] adj gonfiabile

inflate [ɪnˈfleɪt] vt (*tyre, balloon*) gonfiare; (*fig*) esagerare; gonfiare; **inflation** [ɪnˈfleɪʃən] n (*Econ*) inflazione f

inflexible [ɪnˈflɛksɪbl] adj inflessibile, rigido(-a)

inflict [ɪnˈflɪkt] vt to ~ **on** infliggere a

influence [ˈɪnfluəns] n influenza ▶ vt influenzare; **under the ~ of alcohol** sotto l'effetto dell'alcool; **influential** [ɪnfluˈɛnʃl] adj influente

influx [ˈɪnflʌks] n afflusso

info (*inf*) [ˈɪnfəu] n = **information**

inform [ɪnˈfɔːm] vt to ~ **sb** (**of**) informare qn (di) ▶ vi to ~ **on sb** denunciare qn

informal [ɪnˈfɔːml] adj informale; (*announcement, invitation*) non ufficiale

information [ɪnfəˈmeɪʃən] n informazioni fpl; particolari mpl;

a piece of ~ un'informazione; **information office** n ufficio m informazioni inv; **information technology (IT)** n informatica

informative [ɪnˈfɔːmətɪv] adj istruttivo(-a)

infra-red [ɪnfrəˈrɛd] adj infrarosso(-a)

infrastructure [ˈɪnfrəstrʌktʃə] n infrastruttura

infrequent [ɪnˈfriːkwənt] adj infrequente, raro(-a)

infuriate [ɪnˈfjuərɪeɪt] vt rendere furioso(-a)

infuriating [ɪnˈfjuərɪeɪtɪŋ] adj molto irritante

ingenious [ɪnˈdʒiːnjəs] adj ingegnoso(-a)

ingredient [ɪnˈgriːdɪənt] n ingrediente m; elemento

inhabit [ɪnˈhæbɪt] vt abitare; **inhabitant** [ɪnˈhæbɪtnt] n abitante m/f

inhale [ɪnˈheɪl] vt inalare ▶ vi (*in smoking*) aspirare; **inhaler** n inalatore m

inherent [ɪnˈhɪərənt] adj ~ (**in** or **to**) inerente (a)

inherit [ɪnˈhɛrɪt] vt ereditare; **inheritance** n eredità

inhibit [ɪnˈhɪbɪt] vt (*Psych*) inibire; **inhibition** [-ˈbɪʃən] n inibizione f

initial [ɪˈnɪʃl] adj iniziale ▶ n iniziale f ▶ vt siglare; ~**s** npl (*of name*) iniziali fpl; (*as signature*) sigla; **initially** adv inizialmente, all'inizio

initiate [ɪˈnɪʃɪeɪt] vt (*start*) avviare; intraprendere; iniziare; (*person*) iniziare; to ~ **sb into a secret** mettere qn a parte di un segreto; to ~ **proceedings against sb** (*Law*) intentare causa contro qn

initiative [ɪˈnɪʃətɪv] n iniziativa

inject [ɪnˈdʒɛkt] vt (*liquid*) iniettare; (*patient*): to ~ **sb with sth** fare a qn un'iniezione di qc; (*funds*) immettere;

injection [ɪn'dʒɛkʃən] n iniezione
f, puntura

injure ['ɪndʒə'] vt ferire; (damage:
reputation etc) nuocere a; **injured** adj
ferito(-a); **injury** ['ɪndʒərɪ] n ferita

injustice [ɪn'dʒʌstɪs] n ingiustizia

ink [ɪŋk] n inchiostro; **ink-jet printer**
['ɪŋkdʒɛt-] n stampante f a getto
d'inchiostro

inland [adj 'ɪnlænd, adv ɪn'lænd] adj
interno(-a) ▸ adv all'interno; **Inland
Revenue** (BRIT) n Fisco

in-laws ['ɪnlɔːz] npl suoceri mpl;
famiglia del marito (or della moglie)

inmate ['ɪnmeɪt] n (in prison)
carcerato(-a); (in asylum)
ricoverato(-a)

inn [ɪn] n locanda

inner ['ɪnə'] adj interno(-a), interiore;
inner-city n centro di una zona
urbana

inning ['ɪnɪŋ] n (US: Baseball) ripresa;
~s (Cricket) turno di battuta

innocence ['ɪnəsns] n innocenza

innocent ['ɪnəsnt] adj innocente

innovation [ɪnəu'veɪʃən] n
innovazione f

innovative ['ɪnəu'veɪtɪv] adj
innovativo(-a)

in-patient ['ɪnpeɪʃənt] n
ricoverato(-a)

input ['ɪnput] n input m

inquest ['ɪnkwɛst] n inchiesta

inquire [ɪn'kwaɪə'] vi informarsi
▸ vt domandare, informarsi su;
inquiry n domanda; (Law) indagine
f, investigazione f; **"inquiries"**
"informazioni"

ins. abbr = **inches**

insane [ɪn'seɪn] adj matto(-a),
pazzo(-a); (Med) alienato(-a)

insanity [ɪn'sænɪtɪ] n follia; (Med)
alienazione f mentale

insect ['ɪnsɛkt] n insetto; **insect
repellent** n insettifugo

insecure [ɪnsɪ'kjuə'] adj malsicuro(-a);
(person) insicuro(-a)

insecurity [ɪnsɪ'kjuərɪtɪ] n mancanza
di sicurezza

insensitive [ɪn'sɛnsɪtɪv] adj
insensibile

insert [ɪn'sə:t] vt inserire, introdurre

inside ['ɪn'saɪd] n interno, parte f
interiore ▸ adj interno(-a), interiore
▸ adv dentro, all'interno ▸ prep dentro,
all'interno di; (of time): **~ 10 minutes**
entro 10 minuti; **inside lane** n (Aut)
corsia di marcia; **inside out** adv (turn)
a rovescio; (know) a fondo

insight ['ɪnsaɪt] n acume m,
perspicacia; (glimpse, idea)
percezione f

insignificant [ɪnsɪg'nɪfɪknt] adj
insignificante

insincere [ɪnsɪn'sɪə'] adj insincero(-a)

insist [ɪn'sɪst] vi insistere; **to ~
on doing** insistere per fare; **to ~
that** insistere perché + sub; (claim)
sostenere che; **insistent** adj
insistente

insomnia [ɪn'sɔmnɪə] n insonnia

inspect [ɪn'spɛkt] vt ispezionare;
(BRIT: ticket) controllare; **inspection**
[ɪn'spɛkʃən] n ispezione f; controllo;
inspector n ispettore(-trice); (BRIT:
on buses, trains) controllore m

inspiration [ɪnspə'reɪʃən] n
ispirazione f; **inspire** [ɪn'spaɪə'] vt
ispirare; **inspiring** adj stimolante

instability [ɪnstə'bɪlɪtɪ] n instabilità

install [ɪn'stɔ:l] (US **instal**) vt
installare; **installation** [ɪnstə'leɪʃən]
n installazione f

instalment [ɪn'stɔ:lmənt] (US
installment) n rata; (of TV serial etc)
puntata; in **~s** (pay) a rate; (receive)
una parte per volta; (: publication) a
fascicoli

instance ['ɪnstəns] n esempio, caso;
for ~ per or ad esempio; **in the first ~**

in primo luogo

instant ['ɪnstənt] n istante m, attimo ▸ adj immediato(-a); urgente; (coffee, food) in polvere; **instantly** adv immediatamente, subito

instead [ɪn'stɛd] adv invece; ~ **of** invece di

instinct ['ɪnstɪŋkt] n istinto; **instinctive** adj istintivo(-a)

institute ['ɪnstɪtjuːt] n istituto ▸ vt istituire, stabilire; (inquiry) avviare; (proceedings) iniziare

institution [ɪnstɪ'tjuːʃən] n istituzione f; (educational institution, mental institution) istituto

instruct [ɪn'strʌkt] vt to ~ **sb in sth** insegnare qc a qn; **to ~ sb to do** dare ordini a qn di fare; **instruction** [ɪn'strʌkʃən] n istruzione f; **instructions (for use)** istruzioni per l'uso; **instructor** n istruttore(-trice); (for skiing) maestro(-a)

instrument ['ɪnstrəmənt] n strumento; **instrumental** [-'mɛntl] adj (Mus) strumentale; **to be instrumental in** essere d'aiuto in

insufficient [ɪnsə'fɪʃənt] adj insufficiente

insulate ['ɪnsjuleɪt] vt isolare; **insulation** [-'leɪʃən] n isolamento

insulin ['ɪnsjulɪn] n insulina

insult [n 'ɪnsʌlt, vb ɪn'sʌlt] n insulto, affronto ▸ vt insultare; **insulting** adj offensivo(-a), ingiurioso(-a)

insurance [ɪn'ʃuərəns] n assicurazione f; **fire/life ~** assicurazione contro gli incendi/ sulla vita; **insurance company** n società di assicurazioni; **insurance policy** n polizza d'assicurazione

insure [ɪn'ʃuə'] vt assicurare

intact [ɪn'tækt] adj intatto(-a)

intake ['ɪnteɪk] n (Tech) immissione f; (of food) consumo; (BRIT: of pupils etc) afflusso

integral ['ɪntɪɡrəl] adj integrale; (part) integrante

integrate ['ɪntɪɡreɪt] vt integrare ▸ vi integrarsi

integrity [ɪn'tɛɡrɪtɪ] n integrità

intellect ['ɪntəlɛkt] n intelletto; **intellectual** [-'lɛktjuəl] adj, n intellettuale m/f

intelligence [ɪn'tɛlɪdʒəns] n intelligenza; (Mil etc) informazioni fpl

intelligent [ɪn'tɛlɪdʒənt] adj intelligente

intend [ɪn'tɛnd] vt (gift etc): **to ~ sth for** destinare qc a; **to ~ to do** aver l'intenzione di fare

intense [ɪn'tɛns] adj intenso(-a); (person) di forti sentimenti

intensify [ɪn'tɛnsɪfaɪ] vt intensificare

intensity [ɪn'tɛnsɪtɪ] n intensità

intensive [ɪn'tɛnsɪv] adj intensivo(-a); **intensive care** n terapia intensiva; **intensive care unit (ICU)** n reparto terapia intensiva

intent [ɪn'tɛnt] n intenzione f ▸ adj ~ **(on)** intento(-a) (a), immerso(-a) (in); **to all ~s and purposes** a tutti gli effetti; **to be ~ on doing sth** essere deciso a fare qc

intention [ɪn'tɛnʃən] n intenzione f; **intentional** adj intenzionale, deliberato(-a)

interact [ɪntər'ækt] vi interagire; **interaction** [ɪntər'ækʃən] n azione f reciproca, interazione f; **interactive** adj (Comput) interattivo(-a)

intercept [ɪntə'sɛpt] vt intercettare; (person) fermare

interchange ['ɪntətʃeɪndʒ] n (exchange) scambio; (on motorway) incrocio pluridirezionale

intercourse ['ɪntəkɔːs] n rapporti mpl

interest ['ɪntrɪst] n interesse m; (Comm: stake, share) interessi mpl ▸ vt interessare; **interested** adj interessato(-a); **to be interested**

in interessarsi di; **interesting** adj
interessante; **interest rate** n tasso
di interesse

interface ['ɪntəfeɪs] n (Comput)
interfaccia

interfere [ɪntəˈfɪəʳ] vi **to ~ in** (quarrel,
other people's business) immischiarsi
in; **to ~ with** (object) toccare; (plans,
duty) interferire con; **interference**
[ɪntəˈfɪərəns] n interferenza f

interim ['ɪntərɪm] adj provvisorio(-a)
▶ n **in the ~** nel frattempo

interior [ɪnˈtɪərɪəʳ] n interno; (of
country) entroterra ▶ adj interno(-a);
(minister) degli Interni; **interior
design** n architettura d'interni

intermediate [ɪntəˈmiːdɪət] adj
intermedio(-a)

intermission [ɪntəˈmɪʃən] n pausa;
(Theatre, Cinema) intermissione f,
intervallo

intern [vb ɪnˈtəːn, n ˈɪntəːn] vt
internare ▶ n (US) medico interno

internal [ɪnˈtəːnl] adj interno(-a);
Internal Revenue Service
n Fisco

international [ɪntəˈnæʃənl] adj
internazionale ▶ n (BRIT Sport)
incontro internazionale

Internet ['ɪntənɛt] n **the ~** Internet
f; **Internet café** n cybercaffè m inv;
Internet Service Provider n Provider
m inv; **Internet user** n utente m/f
Internet

interpret [ɪnˈtəːprɪt] vt
interpretare ▶ vi fare da interprete;
interpretation [ɪntəːprɪˈteɪʃən] n
interpretazione f; **interpreter** n
interprete m/f; **could you act as an
interpreter for us?** ci potrebbe fare da
interprete?

interrogate [ɪnˈtɛrəugeɪt] vt
interrogare; **interrogation** [-ˈgeɪʃən]
n interrogazione f; (of suspect etc)
interrogatorio

interrogative [ɪntəˈrɔgətɪv]
adj interrogativo(-a) ▶ n (Ling)
interrogativo

interrupt [ɪntəˈrʌpt] vt, vi
interrompere; **interruption**
[-ˈrʌpʃən] n interruzione f

intersection [ɪntəˈsɛkʃən] n
intersezione f; (of roads) incrocio

interstate ['ɪntəsteɪt] (US) n fra stati

interval ['ɪntəvl] n intervallo; **at ~s**
a intervalli

intervene [ɪntəˈviːn] vi (time)
intercorrere; (event, person)
intervenire

interview ['ɪntəvjuː] n (Radio, TV etc)
intervista; (for job) colloquio ▶ vt
intervistare; avere un colloquio con;
interviewer n intervistatore(-trice)

intimate [adj 'ɪntɪmət, vb 'ɪntɪmeɪt]
adj intimo(-a); (knowledge)
profondo(-a) ▶ vt lasciar capire

intimidate [ɪnˈtɪmɪdeɪt] vt intimidire,
intimorire

intimidating [ɪnˈtɪmɪdeɪtɪŋ] adj
(sight) spaventoso(-a); (appearance,
figure) minaccioso(-a)

into ['ɪntu:] prep dentro, in; **come ~ the
house** entra in casa; **he worked late ~
the night** lavorò fino a tarda notte; **~
Italian** in italiano

intolerant [ɪnˈtɔlərnt] adj **~ of**
intollerante di

intranet ['ɪntrənɛt] n intranet f

intransitive [ɪnˈtrænsɪtɪv] adj
intransitivo(-a)

intricate ['ɪntrɪkət] adj intricato(-a),
complicato(-a)

intrigue [ɪnˈtriːg] n intrigo ▶ vt
affascinare; **intriguing** adj
affascinante

introduce [ɪntrəˈdjuːs] vt introdurre;
to ~ sb (to sb) presentare qn (a
qn); **to ~ sb to** (pastime, technique)
iniziare qn a; **introduction**
[-ˈdʌkʃən] n introduzione f; (of person)

presentazione f; (to new experience)
iniziazione f; **introductory** adj
introduttivo(-a)

intrude [ɪn'truːd] vi (person): **to ~
(on)** intromettersi (in); **intruder** n
intruso(-a)

intuition [ɪntjuː'ɪʃən] n intuizione f

inundate ['ɪnʌndeɪt] vt **to ~ with**
inondare di

invade [ɪn'veɪd] vt invadere

invalid [n 'ɪnvəlɪd, adj ɪn'vælɪd]
n malato(-a); (with disability)
invalido(-a) ▶ adj (not valid)
invalido(-a), non valido(-a)

invaluable [ɪn'væljuəbl] adj
prezioso(-a); inestimabile

invariably [ɪn'vɛərɪəblɪ] adv
invariabilmente; sempre

invasion [ɪn'veɪʒən] n invasione f

invent [ɪn'vɛnt] vt inventare;
invention [ɪn'vɛnʃən] n invenzione f;
inventor n inventore m

inventory ['ɪnvəntrɪ] n inventario

inverted commas [ɪn'vəː tɪd-] (BRIT)
npl virgolette fpl

invest [ɪn'vɛst] vt investire ▶ vi **to ~
(in)** investire (in)

investigate [ɪn'vɛstɪgeɪt] vt
investigare, indagare; (crime) fare
indagini su; **investigation** [-'geɪʃən]
n investigazione f; (of crime) indagine f

investigator [ɪn'vɛstɪgeɪtə'] n
investigatore(-trice); **a private ~** un
investigatore privato, un detective

investment [ɪn'vɛstmənt] n
investimento

investor [ɪn'vɛstə'] n
investitore(-trice); azionista m/f

invisible [ɪn'vɪzɪbl] adj invisibile

invitation [ɪnvɪ'teɪʃən] n invito

invite [ɪn'vaɪt] vt invitare; (opinions
etc) sollecitare; **inviting** adj invitante,
attraente

invoice ['ɪnvɔɪs] n fattura ▶ vt
fatturare

involve [ɪn'vɒlv] vt (entail)
richiedere, comportare; (associate):
to ~ sb (in) implicare qn (in);
coinvolgere qn (in); **involved** adj
involuto(-a), complesso(-a); **to be
involved in** essere coinvolto(-a)
in; **involvement** n implicazione f;
coinvolgimento

inward ['ɪnwəd] adj (movement) verso
l'interno; (thought, feeling) interiore,
intimo(-a); **inward(s)** adv verso
l'interno

IQ n abbr (= intelligence quotient)
quoziente m d'intelligenza

IRA n abbr (= Irish Republican Army) IRA f

Iran [ɪ'rɑːn] n Iran m; **Iranian** adj, n
iraniano(-a)

Iraq [ɪ'rɑːk] n Iraq m; **Iraqi** adj, n
iracheno(-a)

Ireland ['aɪələnd] n Irlanda

iris ['aɪrɪs] (pl **irises**) n iride f; (Bot)
giaggiolo, iride

Irish ['aɪrɪʃ] adj irlandese ▶ npl **the ~** gli
Irlandesi; **Irishman** (irreg) n irlandese
m; **Irish Sea** n Mar m d'Irlanda;
Irishwoman (irreg) n irlandese f

iron ['aɪən] n ferro; (for clothes) ferro
da stiro ▶ adj di or in ferro ▶ vt (clothes)
stirare

ironic(al) [aɪ'rɒnɪk(l)] adj ironico(-a);
ironically adv ironicamente

ironing ['aɪənɪŋ] n (act) stirare m;
(clothes) roba da stirare; **ironing
board** n asse f da stiro

irony ['aɪrənɪ] n ironia

irrational [ɪ'ræʃənl] adj irrazionale

irregular [ɪ'rɛgjulə'] adj irregolare

irrelevant [ɪ'rɛləvənt] adj non
pertinente

irresistible [ɪrɪ'zɪstɪbl] adj irresistibile

irresponsible [ɪrɪ'spɒnsɪbl] adj
irresponsabile

irrigation [ɪrɪ'geɪʃən] n irrigazione f

irritable ['ɪrɪtəbl] adj irritabile

irritate ['ɪrɪteɪt] vt irritare; **irritating**

adj (person, sound etc) irritante; **irritation** [-'teɪʃən] n irritazione f

IRS (US) n abbr = **Internal Revenue Service**

is [ɪz] vb see **be**

ISDN n abbr (= Integrated Services Digital Network) I.S.D.N. f

Islam ['ɪzlɑːm] n Islam m; **Islamic** [ɪz'læmɪk] adj islamico(-a)

island ['aɪlənd] n isola; **islander** n isolano(-a)

isle [aɪl] n isola

isn't ['ɪznt] = **is not**

isolated ['aɪsəleɪtɪd] adj isolato(-a)

isolation [aɪsə'leɪʃən] n isolamento

ISP n abbr (= Internet Service Provider) provider m inv

Israel ['ɪzreɪl] n Israele m; **Israeli** [ɪz'reɪlɪ] adj, n israeliano(-a)

issue ['ɪʃjuː] n questione f, problema m; (of banknotes etc) emissione f; (of newspaper etc) numero ▸ vt (statement) rilasciare; (rations, equipment) distribuire; (book) pubblicare; (banknotes, cheques, stamps) emettere; **at** ~ in gioco, in discussione; **to take** ~ **with sb** (over sth) prendere posizione contro qn (riguardo a qc); **to make an** ~ **of sth** fare un problema di qc

○ it
[ɪt] pron

1 (specific: subject) esso(-a), (: direct object) lo (la), l'; (: indirect object) gli (le); **where's my book? — it's on the table** dov'è il mio libro? — è sulla tavola; **I can't find it** non lo (or la) trovo; **give it to me** dammelo (or dammela); **about/from/of it** ne; **I spoke to him about it** gliene ho parlato; **what did you learn from it?** quale insegnamento ne hai tratto?; **I'm proud of it** ne sono fiero; **did you go to it?** ci sei andato?; **put the book in it** mettici il libro

2 (impers): **it's raining** piove; **it's Friday tomorrow** domani è venerdì;

it's 6 o'clock sono le 6; **who is it? — it's me** chi è? — sono io

IT n abbr see **information technology**

Italian [ɪ'tæljən] adj italiano(-a) ▸ n italiano(-a); (Ling) italiano; **the** ~s gli Italiani; **what's the** ~ **(word) for ...?** come si dice in italiano ...?

italics [ɪ'tælɪks] npl corsivo

Italy ['ɪtəlɪ] n Italia

itch [ɪtʃ] n prurito ▸ vi (person) avere il prurito; (part of body) prudere; **to** ~ **to do sth** aver una gran voglia di fare qc; **itchy** adj che prude; **to be itchy** = **itch**

it'd ['ɪtd] = **it would**; **it had**

item ['aɪtəm] n articolo; (on agenda) punto; (also: **news** ~) notizia

it'll ['ɪtl] = **it will**; **it shall**

its [ɪts] adj il (la) suo(-a), i (le) suoi (sue)

it's [ɪts] = **it is**; **it has**

itself [ɪt'sɛlf] pron (emphatic) esso(-a) stesso(-a); (reflexive) se stesso

ITV (BRIT) n abbr (= Independent Television) rete televisiva in concorrenza con la BBC

I've [aɪv] = **I have**

ivory ['aɪvərɪ] n avorio

ivy ['aɪvɪ] n edera

j

jab [dʒæb] vt dare colpetti a ▸ n (Med: inf) puntura; **to ~ sth into** affondare or piantare qc dentro

jack [dʒæk] n (Aut) cricco; (Cards) fante m

jacket ['dʒækɪt] n giacca; (of book) copertura; **jacket potato** n patata cotta al forno con la buccia

jackpot ['dʒækpɔt] n primo premio (in denaro)

Jacuzzi® [dʒə'kuːzɪ] n vasca per idromassaggio Jacuzzi®

jagged ['dʒægɪd] adj seghettato(-a); (cliffs etc) frastagliato(-a)

jail [dʒeɪl] n prigione f ▸ vt mandare in prigione; **jail sentence** n condanna al carcere

jam [dʒæm] n marmellata; (also: **traffic ~**) ingorgo, (inf) pasticcio ▸ vt (passage etc) ingombrare, ostacolare; (mechanism, drawer etc) bloccare; (Radio) disturbare con interferenze ▸ vi incepparsi; **to ~ sth into** forzare qc dentro; infilare qc a forza dentro

Jamaica [dʒə'meɪkə] n Giamaica

jammed [dʒæmd] adj (door) bloccato(-a); (rifle, printer) inceppato(-a)

Jan abbr (= January) gen., genn.

janitor ['dʒænɪtə*] n (caretaker) portiere m; (: Scol) bidello

January ['dʒænjuərɪ] n gennaio

Japan [dʒə'pæn] n Giappone m; **Japanese** [dʒæpə'niːz] adj

giapponese ▸ n inv giapponese m/f; (Ling) giapponese m

jar [dʒɑː*] n (glass) barattolo, vasetto ▸ vi (sound) stridere; (colours etc) stonare

jargon ['dʒɑːgən] n gergo

javelin ['dʒævlɪn] n giavellotto

jaw [dʒɔː] n mascella

jazz [dʒæz] n jazz m

jealous ['dʒeləs] adj geloso(-a); **jealousy** n gelosia

jeans [dʒiːnz] npl (blue-)jeans mpl

Jello® ['dʒeləu] (US) n gelatina di frutta

jelly ['dʒelɪ] n marmellata; (also: gelatina di frutta; **jellyfish** n medusa

jeopardize ['dʒepədaɪz] vt mettere in pericolo

jerk [dʒəːk] n sobbalzo, scossa; sussulto; (inf: idiot) tonto(-a) ▸ vt dare una scossa a ▸ vi (vehicles) sobbalzare

Jersey ['dʒəːzɪ] n Jersey m

jersey ['dʒəːzɪ] n maglia; (fabric) jersey m

Jesus ['dʒiːzəs] n Gesù m

jet [dʒet] n (of gas, liquid) getto; (Aviat) aviogetto; **jet lag** n (problemi mpl dovuti allo) sbalzo dei fusi orari; **jet-ski** vi acquascooter m inv

jetty ['dʒetɪ] n molo

Jew [dʒuː] n ebreo

jewel ['dʒuːəl] n gioiello; **jeweller** (US **jeweler**) n orefice m, gioielliere(-a); **jeweller's (shop)** (US **jewelry store**) n oreficeria, gioielleria; **jewellery** (US **jewelry**) n gioielli mpl

Jewish ['dʒuːɪʃ] adj ebreo(-a), ebraico(-a)

jigsaw ['dʒɪgsɔː] n (also: ~ puzzle) puzzle m inv

job [dʒɔb] n lavoro; (employment) impiego, posto; **it's not my ~** (duty) non è compito mio; **it's a good ~ that ...** meno male che ...; **just the ~!** proprio quello che ci vuole; **job centre** (BRIT) n ufficio di collocamento; **jobless** adj senza lavoro, disoccupato(-a)

jockey ['dʒɒkɪ] n fantino, jockey m inv ▶ vi to ~ **for position** manovrare per una posizione di vantaggio

jog [dʒɒg] vt urtare ▶ vi (Sport) fare footing, fare jogging; **to ~ sb's memory** rinfrescare la memoria a qn; **to ~ along** trottare; (fig) andare avanti piano piano; **jogging** n footing m, jogging m

join [dʒɔɪn] vt unire, congiungere; (become member of) iscriversi a; (meet) raggiungere; riunirsi a ▶ vi (roads, rivers) confluire ▶ n giuntura; **join in** vi partecipare a ▶ vt fus unirsi a ▶ **join up** vi incontrarsi; (Mil) arruolarsi

joiner ['dʒɔɪnə'] (BRIT) n falegname m

joint [dʒɔɪnt] n (Tech) giuntura, giunto; (Anat) articolazione f, giuntura; (BRIT Culin) arrosto; (inf: place) locale m; (: of cannabis) spinello ▶ adj comune; **joint account** n (at bank etc) conto in partecipazione, conto comune; **jointly** adv in comune, insieme

joke [dʒəʊk] n scherzo; (funny story) barzelletta; (also: **practical ~**) beffa ▶ vi scherzare; **to play a ~ on sb** fare uno scherzo a qn; **joker** n (Cards) matta, jolly m inv

jolly ['dʒɒlɪ] adj allegro(-a), gioioso(-a) ▶ adv (BRIT: inf) veramente, proprio

jolt [dʒəʊlt] n scossa, sobbalzo ▶ vt urtare

Jordan ['dʒɔːdən] n (country) Giordania; (river) Giordano

journal ['dʒɜːnl] n giornale m; rivista; diario; **journalism** n giornalismo; **journalist** n giornalista m/f

journey ['dʒɜːnɪ] n viaggio; (distance covered) tragitto; **how was your ~?** com'è andato il viaggio?; **the ~ takes two hours** il viaggio dura due ore

joy [dʒɔɪ] n gioia; **joyrider** n chi ruba un'auto per farvi un giro; **joy stick** n (Aviat) barra di comando; (Comput) joystick m inv

Jr abbr = **junior**

judge [dʒʌdʒ] n giudice m/f ▶ vt giudicare

judo ['dʒuːdəu] n judo

jug [dʒʌg] n brocca, bricco

juggle ['dʒʌgl] vi fare giochi di destrezza; **juggler** n giocoliere(-a)

juice [dʒuːs] n succo; **juicy** ['dʒuːsɪ] adj succoso(-a)

Jul abbr (= July) lug., lu.

July ['dʒuː'laɪ] n luglio

jumble ['dʒʌmbl] n miscuglio ▶ vt (also: **~ up**) mischiare; **jumble sale** (BRIT) n vendita di beneficenza

- **jumble sale**
- Una **jumble sale** è un mercatino
- di oggetti di seconda mano
- organizzato in chiese, scuole o
- in circoli ricreativi, i cui proventi
- vengono devoluti in beneficenza.

jumbo ['dʒʌmbəu] adj ~ **jet** jumbo-jet m inv; **~ size** formato gigante

jump [dʒʌmp] vi saltare, balzare; (start) sobbalzare; (increase) rincarare ▶ vt saltare ▶ n salto, balzo; sobbalzo

jumper ['dʒʌmpə'] n (BRIT: pullover) maglione m, pullover m inv; (US: dress) scamiciato

jumper cables (US) npl = **jump leads**

jump leads (BRIT) npl cavi mpl per batteria

Jun. abbr = **junior**

junction ['dʒʌŋkʃən] n (BRIT: of roads) incrocio; (of rails) nodo ferroviario

June [dʒuːn] n giugno

jungle ['dʒʌŋgl] n giungla

junior ['dʒuːnɪə'] adj, n **he's ~ to me by 2 years, he's my ~ by 2 years** è più giovane di me (di 2 anni); **he's ~ to me** (seniority) è al di sotto di me, ho più anzianità di lui; **junior high**

K

school (US) n scuola media (da 12 a 15 anni); **junior school** (BRIT) n scuola elementare (da 8 a 11 anni)

junk [dʒʌŋk] n cianfrusaglie fpl; (cheap goods) robaccia; **junk food** n porcherie fpl

junkie ['dʒʌŋkɪ] n (inf) drogato(-a)

junk mail n stampe fpl pubblicitarie

Jupiter ['dʒu:pɪtəʳ] n (planet) Giove m

jurisdiction [dʒuərɪs'dɪkʃən] n giurisdizione f; **it falls** or **comes within/outside our ~** è/non è di nostra competenza

jury ['dʒuərɪ] n giuria

just [dʒʌst] adj giusto(-a) ▶ adv he's ~ done it/left lo ha appena fatto/è appena partito; ~ right proprio giusto; ~ 2 o'clock le 2 precise; she's ~ as clever as you è in gamba proprio quanto te; it's ~ as well that ... meno male che ...; ~ as I arrived proprio mentre arrivavo; it was ~ before/enough/here era poco prima/appena assai/proprio qui; it's ~ me sono solo io; ~ missed/caught appena perso/preso; ~ listen to this! senta un po' questo!

justice ['dʒʌstɪs] n giustizia

justification [dʒʌstɪfɪ'keɪʃən] n giustificazione f; (Typ) giustezza

justify ['dʒʌstɪfaɪ] vt giustificare

jut [dʒʌt] vi (also: ~ out) sporgersi

juvenile ['dʒu:vənaɪl] adj giovane, giovanile; (court) dei minorenni; (books) per ragazzi ▶ n giovane m/f, minorenne m/f

K abbr (= one thousand) mille; (= kilobyte) K

kangaroo [kæŋgə'ru:] n canguro

karaoke [kɑ:rə'əʊkɪ] n karaoke m inv

karate [kə'rɑ:tɪ] n karatè m

kebab [kə'bæb] n spiedino

keel [ki:l] n chiglia; **on an even ~** (fig) in uno stato normale

keen [ki:n] adj (interest, desire) vivo(-a); (eye, intelligence) acuto(-a); (competition) serrato(-a); (edge) affilato(-a); (eager) entusiasta; **to be ~ to do** or **on doing sth** avere una gran voglia di fare qc; **to be ~ on sth** essere appassionato(-a) di qc; **to be ~ on sb** avere un debole per qn

keep [ki:p] (pt, pp kept) vt tenere; (hold back) trattenere; (feed: one's family etc) mantenere, sostentare; (a promise) mantenere; (chickens, bees, pigs etc) allevare ▶ vi (food) mantenersi; (remain: in a certain state or place) restare ▶ n (of castle) maschio; (food etc): **enough for his ~** abbastanza per vitto e alloggio; (inf): **for ~s** per sempre; **to ~ doing sth** continuare a fare qc; fare qc di continuo; **to ~ sb from doing** impedire a qn di fare; **to ~ sb busy/a place tidy** tenere qn occupato(-a)/un luogo in ordine; **to ~ sth to o.s.** tenere qc per sé; **to ~ sth (back) from sb** celare qc a qn; **to ~ time** (clock) andar bene ▷ **keep away** vt **to ~ sth/sb away from sb**

tenere qc/qn lontano da qn ▸ vi **to ~ away (from)** stare lontano (da)
▷ **keep back** vt (crowds, tears, money) trattenere ▸ vi tenersi indietro ▷ **keep off** vt (dog, person) tenere lontano da ▸ vi stare alla larga; **~ your hands off!** non toccare!, giù le mani!; **"~ off the grass"** "non calpestare l'erba" ▷ **keep on** vi **to ~ doing** continuare a fare; **to ~ on (about sth)** continuare a insistere (su qc) ▷ **keep out** vt tener fuori; **"~ out"** "vietato l'accesso" ▷ **keep up** vt continuare, mantenere ▸ vi **to ~ up with** tener dietro a, andare di pari passo con; (work etc) farcela a seguire; **keeper** n custode m/f, guardiano(-a); **keeping** n (care) custodia; **in keeping with** in armonia con; in accordo con

kennel ['kɛnl] n canile m; **~s** npl canile m; **to put a dog in ~s** mettere un cane al canile

Kenya ['kɛnjə] n Kenia m

kept [kɛpt] pt, pp of **keep**

kerb [kə:b] (BRIT) n orlo del marciapiede

kerosene ['kɛrəsi:n] n cherosene m

ketchup ['kɛtʃəp] n ketchup m inv

kettle ['kɛtl] n bollitore m

key [ki:] n (gen, Mus) chiave f; (of piano, typewriter) tasto ▸ adj chiave m/f ▸ vt (also: **~ in**) digitare; **can I have my ~?** posso avere la mia chiave?; **keyboard** n tastiera; **keyhole** n buco della serratura; **keyring** n portachiavi m inv

kg abbr (= kilogram) Kg

khaki ['kɑ:kɪ] adj cachi ▸ n cachi m

kick [kɪk] vt calciare, dare calci a; (inf: habit etc) liberarsi di ▸ vi (horse) tirar calci ▸ n calcio; (thrill): **he does it for ~s** lo fa giusto per il piacere di farlo ▷ **kick off** vi (Sport) dare il primo calcio; **kick-off** n (Sport) calcio d'inizio

kid [kɪd] n (inf: child) ragazzino(-a); (animal, leather) capretto ▸ vi (inf)

scherzare

kidnap ['kɪdnæp] vt rapire, sequestrare; **kidnapping** n sequestro (di persona)

kidney ['kɪdnɪ] n (Anat) rene m; (Culin) rognone m; **kidney bean** n fagiolo borlotto

kill [kɪl] vt uccidere, ammazzare ▸ n uccisione f; **killer** n uccisore m, killer m inv; assassino(-a); **killing** n assassinio; **to make a killing** (inf) fare un bel colpo

kiln [kɪln] n forno

kilo ['ki:ləu] n chilo; **kilobyte** n (Comput) kilobyte m inv; **kilogram(me)** ['kɪləugræm] n chilogrammo; **kilometre** ['kɪləmi:tə'] (US **kilometer**) n chilometro; **kilowatt** ['kɪləuwɔt] n chilowatt m inv

kilt [kɪlt] n gonnellino scozzese

kin [kɪn] n see **next**; **kith**

kind [kaɪnd] adj gentile, buono(-a) ▸ n sorta, specie f; (species) genere m; **what ~ of ...?** che tipo di ...?; **to be two of a ~** essere molto simili; **in ~** (Comm) in natura

kindergarten ['kɪndəgɑ:tn] n giardino d'infanzia

kindly ['kaɪndlɪ] adj pieno(-a) di bontà, benevolo(-a) ▸ adv con bontà, gentilmente; **will you ~ ...** vuole ... per favore

kindness ['kaɪndnɪs] n bontà, gentilezza

king [kɪŋ] n re m inv; **kingdom** n regno, reame m; **kingfisher** n martin m inv pescatore; **king-size(d) bed** n letto king-size

kiosk ['ki:ɔsk] n edicola, chiosco; (BRIT Tel) cabina (telefonica)

kipper ['kɪpə'] n aringa affumicata

kiss [kɪs] n bacio ▸ vt baciare; **to ~ (each other)** baciarsi; **kiss of life** n respirazione f bocca a bocca

kit [kɪt] n equipaggiamento, corredo;

(set of tools etc) attrezzi mpl; (for assembly) scatola di montaggio
kitchen ['kɪtʃɪn] n cucina
kite [kaɪt] n (toy) aquilone m
kitten ['kɪtn] n gattino(-a), micino(-a)
kiwi ['ki:wi:] n (also: ~ **fruit**) kiwi m inv
km abbr (= kilometre) km
km/h abbr (= kilometres per hour) km/h
knack [næk] n **to have the ~ of** avere l'abilità di
knee [ni:] n ginocchio; **kneecap** n rotula
kneel [ni:l] (pt, pp **knelt**) vi (also: ~ **down**) inginocchiarsi
knelt [nɛlt] pt, pp of **kneel**
knew [nju:] pt of **know**
knickers ['nɪkəz] (BRIT) npl mutandine fpl
knife [naɪf] (pl **knives**) n coltello ▶ vt accoltellare, dare una coltellata a
knight [naɪt] n cavaliere m; (Chess) cavallo
knit [nɪt] vt fare a maglia ▶ vi lavorare a maglia; (broken bones) saldarsi; **to ~ one's brows** aggrottare le sopracciglia; **knitting** n lavoro a maglia; **knitting needle** n ferro (da calza); **knitwear** n maglieria
knives [naɪvz] npl of **knife**
knob [nɔb] n bottone m; manopola
knock [nɔk] vt colpire; urtare; (fig: inf) criticare ▶ vi (at door etc): **to ~ at/on** bussare a ▶ n bussata; colpo, botta ▷ **knock down** vt abbattere ▷ **knock off** vi (inf: finish) smettere (di lavorare) ▶ vt (from price) far abbassare; (inf: steal) sgraffignare ▷ **knock out** vt stendere; (Boxing) mettere K.O.; (defeat) battere ▷ **knock over** vt (person) investire; (object) far cadere; **knockout** n (Boxing) knock out m inv ▶ cpd a eliminazione
knot [nɔt] n nodo ▶ vt annodare
know [nəu] (pt **knew**, pp **known**) vt sapere; (person, author, place)

conoscere; **I don't ~** non lo so; **do you ~ where I can ...?** sa dove posso ...?; **to ~ how to do** sapere fare; **to ~ about** or **of sth/sb** sapere qc/qn; **know-all** n sapientone(-a); **know-how** n tecnica; pratica; **knowing** adj (look etc) d'intesa; **knowingly** adv (purposely) consapevolmente; (smile, look) con aria d'intesa; **know-it-all** (US) n = **know-all**
knowledge ['nɔlɪdʒ] n consapevolezza; (learning) conoscenza, sapere m; **knowledgeable** adj ben informato(-a)
known [nəun] pp of **know**
knuckle ['nʌkl] n nocca
koala [kəu'ɑ:lə] n (also: ~ **bear**) koala m inv
Koran [kɔ'rɑ:n] n Corano
Korea [kə'rɪə] n Corea; **Korean** adj, n coreano(-a)
kosher ['kəuʃə'] adj kasher inv
Kosovar, Kosovan ['kɔsəvɑ', 'kɔsəvən] adj kosovaro(-a)
Kosovo ['kusəvəu] n Kosovo
Kremlin ['krɛmlɪn] n **the ~** il Cremlino
Kuwait [ku'weɪt] n Kuwait m

L

L (BRIT) abbr = **learner driver**

l. abbr (= litre) l

lab [læb] n abbr (= laboratory) laboratorio

label ['leɪbl] n etichetta, cartellino; (brand: of record) casa ▶ vt etichettare

labor etc ['leɪbər] (US) = **labour** etc

laboratory [lə'bɒrətəri] n laboratorio

Labor Day (US) n festa del lavoro

> * **Labor Day**
> * Negli Stati Uniti e nel Canada
> * il **Labor Day**, la festa del lavoro,
> * cade il primo lunedì di settembre,
> * contrariamente a quanto accade
> * nella maggior parte dei paesi
> * europei dove tale celebrazione ha
> * luogo il primo maggio.

labor union (US) n sindacato

labour ['leɪbər] (US **labor**) n (task) lavoro; (workmen) manodopera; (Med): **to be in** ~ avere le doglie ▶ vi **to ~ (at)** lavorare duro (a); **L~, the L~ party** (BRIT) il partito laburista, i laburisti; **hard** ~ lavori mpl forzati; **labourer** n manovale m; **farm labourer** lavoratore m agricolo

lace [leɪs] n merletto, pizzo; (of shoe etc) laccio ▶ vt (shoe: also: ~ **up**) allacciare

lack [læk] n mancanza ▶ vt mancare di; **through** or **for** ~ of per mancanza di; **to be ~ing** mancare; **to be ~ing in** mancare di

lacquer ['lækər] n lacca

lacy ['leɪsɪ] adj (like lace) che sembra un pizzo

lad [læd] n ragazzo, giovanotto

ladder ['lædər] n scala; (BRIT: in tights) smagliatura

ladle ['leɪdl] n mestolo

lady ['leɪdɪ] n signora; dama; **L~ Smith** lady Smith; **the ladies' (room)** i gabinetti per signore; **ladybird** (US **ladybug**) n coccinella

lag [læg] n (of time) lasso, intervallo ▶ vi (also: ~ **behind**) trascinarsi ▶ vt (pipes) rivestire di materiale isolante

lager ['lɑːgər] n lager m inv

lagoon [lə'guːn] n laguna

laid [leɪd] pt, pp of **lay**; **laid back** (inf) adj rilassato(-a), tranquillo(-a)

lain [leɪn] pp of **lie**

lake [leɪk] n lago

lamb [læm] n agnello

lame [leɪm] adj zoppo(-a); (excuse etc) zoppicante

lament [lə'mɛnt] n lamento ▶ vt lamentare, piangere

lamp [læmp] n lampada; **lamppost** ['læmppəust] (BRIT) n lampione m; **lampshade** ['læmpʃeɪd] n paralume m

land [lænd] n (as opposed to sea) terra (ferma); (country) paese m; (soil) terreno; suolo; (estate) terreni mpl, terre fpl ▶ vi (from ship) sbarcare; (Aviat) atterrare; (fig: fall) cadere ▶ vt (passengers) sbarcare; (goods) scaricare; **to ~ sb with sth** affibbiare qc a qn; **landing** n atterraggio; (of staircase) pianerottolo; **landing card** n carta di sbarco; **landlady** n padrona o proprietaria di casa; **landlord** n padrone m or proprietario di casa; (of pub etc) padrone m; **landmark** n punto di riferimento; (fig) pietra miliare; **landowner** n proprietario(-a) terriero(-a); **landscape** n paesaggio; **landslide** n (Geo) frana; (fig: Pol) valanga

lane [leɪn] n stradina; (Aut, in race) corsia; **"get in ~"** "immettersi in corsia"

language ['læŋgwɪdʒ] n lingua; (way one speaks) linguaggio; **what ~s do you speak?** che lingue parla?; **bad ~** linguaggio volgare; **language laboratory** n laboratorio linguistico

lantern ['læntn] n lanterna

lap [læp] n (of track) giro; (of body): **in** or **on one's ~** in grembo ▶ vt (also: **~ up**) papparsi, leccare ▶ vi (waves) sciabordare

lapel [lə'pɛl] n risvolto

lapse [læps] n lapsus m inv; (longer) caduta ▶ vi (law) scadere; (membership, contract) scadere; **to ~ into bad habits** pigliare cattive abitudini; **~ of time** spazio di tempo

laptop (computer) ['læptɔp-] n laptop m inv

lard [lɑːd] n lardo

larder ['lɑːdəʳ] n dispensa

large [lɑːdʒ] adj grande; (person, animal) grosso(-a); **at ~** (free) in libertà; (generally) in generale; nell'insieme; **largely** adv in gran parte; **large-scale** adj (map, drawing etc) in grande scala; (reforms, business activities) su vasta scala

lark [lɑːk] n (bird) allodola; (joke) scherzo, gioco

laryngitis [lærɪn'dʒaɪtɪs] n laringite f

lasagne [lə'zænjə] n lasagne fpl

laser ['leɪzəʳ] n laser m inv; **laser printer** n stampante f laser inv

lash [læʃ] n frustata; (also: **eye~**) ciglio ▶ vt frustare; (tie): **to ~ to/together** legare a insieme ▶ **lash out** vi to ~ **out** (at or against sb) attaccare violentemente (qn)

lass [læs] n ragazza

last [lɑːst] adj ultimo(-a); (week, month, year) scorso(-a), passato(-a) ▶ adv per ultimo ▶ vi durare; ~ **week** la

settimana scorsa; ~ **night** ieri sera, la notte scorsa; **at ~** finalmente, alla fine; ~ **but one** penultimo(-a); **lastly** adv infine, per finire; **last-minute** adj fatto(-a) (or preso(-a) etc) all'ultimo momento

latch [lætʃ] n chiavistello ▶ **latch onto** vt fus (cling to: person) attaccarsi a, appiccicarsi a; (: idea) afferrare, capire

late [leɪt] adj (not on time) in ritardo; (far on in day etc) tardi etc; (former) ex; (dead) defunto(-a) ▶ adv tardi; (behind time, schedule) in ritardo; **sorry I'm ~** scusi il ritardo; **the flight is two hours ~** il volo ha due ore di ritardo; **it's too ~** è troppo tardi; **of ~** di recente; **in the ~ afternoon** nel tardo pomeriggio; **in ~ May** verso la fine di maggio; **latecomer** n ritardatario/a; **lately** adv recentemente; **later** ['leɪtəʳ] adj (date etc) posteriore; (version etc) successivo(-a) ▶ adv più tardi; **later on** più avanti; **latest** ['leɪtɪst] adj ultimo(-a), più recente; **at the latest** al più tardi

lather ['lɑːðəʳ] n schiuma di sapone ▶ vt insaponare

Latin ['lætɪn] n latino ▶ adj latino(-a); **Latin America** n America Latina; **Latin American** adj sudamericano(-a)

latitude ['lætɪtjuːd] n latitudine f; (fig) libertà d'azione

latter ['lætəʳ] adj secondo(-a), più recente ▶ n the ~ quest'ultimo, il secondo

laugh [lɑːf] n risata ▶ vi ridere ▶ **laugh at** vt fus (misfortune etc) ridere di; **laughter** n riso; risate fpl

launch [lɔːntʃ] n (of rocket, Comm) lancio; (of new ship) varo; (also: **motor ~**) lancia ▶ vt (rocket, Comm) lanciare; (ship, plan) varare ▶ **launch into** vt fus lanciarsi in

launder ['lɔ:ndə'] vt lavare e stirare
Launderette® [lɔ:n'drɛt] (BRIT) n
lavanderia (automatica)
Laundromat® ['lɔ:ndrəmæt] (US) n
lavanderia automatica
laundry ['lɔ:ndrɪ] n lavanderia;
(clothes) biancheria; (: dirty) panni
mpl da lavare
lava ['lɑ:və] n lava
lavatory ['lævətərɪ] n gabinetto
lavender ['lævəndə'] n lavanda
lavish ['lævɪʃ] adj copioso(-a),
abbondante; (giving freely): ~ with
prodigo(-a) di, largo(-a) in ▶ vt to ~
on sb colmare qn di qc
law [lɔ:] n legge f; **civil/criminal ~**
diritto civile/penale; **lawful** adj
legale, lecito(-a); **lawless** adj che non
conosce nessuna legge
lawn [lɔ:n] n tappeto erboso;
lawnmower n tosaerba m or finv
lawsuit ['lɔ:su:t] n processo, causa
lawyer ['lɔ:jə'] n (for sales, wills
etc) ≈ notaio; (partner, in court)
≈ avvocato(-essa)
lax [læks] adj rilassato(-a), negligente
laxative ['læksətɪv] n lassativo
lay [leɪ] (pt, pp **laid**) pt of **lie** ▶ adj
laico(-a); (not expert) profano(-a) ▶ vt
posare, mettere; (eggs) fare; (trap)
tendere; (plans) fare, elaborare; **to
~ the table** apparecchiare la tavola
▷ **lay down** vt mettere giù; (rules etc)
formulare, fissare; **to ~ down the law**
dettar legge; **to ~ down one's life** dare
la propria vita ▷ **lay off** vt (workers)
licenziare ▷ **lay on** vt (provide) fornire
▷ **lay out** vt (display) presentare,
disporre; **lay-by** (BRIT) n piazzola
(di sosta)
layer ['leɪə'] n strato
layman ['leɪmən] (irreg) n laico,
profano
layout ['leɪaut] n lay-out m inv,
disposizione f; (Press)

impaginazione f
lazy ['leɪzɪ] adj pigro(-a)
lb. abbr = **pound** (weight)
lead¹ [li:d] (pt, pp **led**) n (front position)
posizione f di testa; (distance, time
ahead) vantaggio; (clue) indizio; (Elec)
filo (elettrico); (for dog) guinzaglio;
(Theatre) parte f principale ▶ vt
guidare, condurre; (induce) indurre;
(be leader of) essere a capo di ▶ vi
condurre; (Sport) essere in testa; **in
the ~** in testa; **to ~ the way** fare strada
▷ **lead up to** vt fus portare a
lead² [led] n (metal) piombo; (in pencil)
mina
leader ['li:də'] n capo; leader m inv; (in
newspaper) articolo di fondo; (Sport)
chi è in testa; **leadership** n direzione
f; capacità di comando
lead-free ['lɛdfri:] adj senza piombo
leading ['li:dɪŋ] adj primo(-a),
principale
lead singer n cantante alla testa di
un gruppo
leaf [li:f] (pl **leaves**) n foglia ▶ vi **to ~
through sth** sfogliare qc; **to turn over
a new ~** cambiar vita
leaflet ['li:flɪt] n dépliant m inv; (Pol,
Rel) volantino
league [li:g] n lega; (Football)
campionato; **to be in ~ with** essere
in lega con
leak [li:k] n (out) fuga; (in) infiltrazione
f; (security leak) fuga d'informazioni
▶ vi (roof, bucket) perdere; (liquid)
uscire; (shoes) lasciar passare l'acqua
▶ vt (information) divulgare
lean [li:n] (pt, pp **leaned** or **leant**)
adj magro(-a) ▶ vt **to ~ sth on sth**
appoggiare qc su qc ▶ vi (slope)
pendere; (rest): **to ~ against**
appoggiarsi contro; essere
appoggiato(-a); **to ~ on** appoggiarsi
a ▶ **lean forward** vi sporgersi in
avanti ▶ **lean over** vi inclinarsi;

leaning n leaning (towards)
propensione f(per)

leant [lɛnt] pt, pp of **lean**

leap [li:p] (pt, pp **leaped** or **leapt**) n
salto, balzo ▶ vi saltare, balzare

leapt [lɛpt] pt, pp of **leap**

leap year n anno bisestile

learn [lə:n] (pt, pp **learned** or **learnt**)
vt, vi imparare; **to ~ about sth**
(hear, read) apprendere qc; **to ~ to
do sth** imparare a fare qc; **learner**
n principiante m/f; apprendista
m/f; (BRIT: also: **learner driver**)
guidatore(-a) principiante; **learning**
n erudizione f, sapienza

learnt [lə:nt] pt, pp of **learn**

lease [li:s] n contratto d'affitto ▶ vt
affittare

leash [li:ʃ] n guinzaglio

least [li:st] adj the ~ (+ noun) il (la)
più piccolo(-a), il (la) minimo(-a);
(smallest amount of) il (la) meno ▶ adv
(+ verb) meno; the ~ (+ adjective): the ~
beautiful girl la ragazza meno bella;
the ~ possible effort il minimo sforzo
possibile; **I have the ~ money** io ho
meno denaro di tutti; **at ~** almeno;
not in the ~ affatto, per nulla

leather ['lɛðə'] n cuoio

leave [li:v] (pt, pp **left**) vt lasciare; (go
away from) partire da ▶ vi partire,
andarsene; (bus, train) partire ▶ n (time
off) congedo; (Mil, consent) licenza;
what time does the train/bus ~? a
che ora parte il treno/l'autobus?; **to
be left** rimanere; **there's some milk
left over** c'è rimasto del latte; **on ~** in
congedo ▷ **leave behind** vt (person,
object) lasciare; (: forget) smenticare
▷ **leave out** vt omettere, tralasciare

leaves [li:vz] npl of **leaf**

Lebanon ['lɛbənən] n Libano

lecture ['lɛktʃə'] n conferenza; (Scol)
lezione f ▶ vi fare conferenze; fare
lezioni ▶ vt (scold): **to ~ sb on** or

about sth rimproverare qn or fare
una ramanzina a qn per qc; **to give
a ~ on** tenere una conferenza su;
lecture hall n aula magna; **lecturer**
['lɛktʃərə'] (BRIT) n (at university)
professore(-essa), docente m/f;
lecture theatre n = **lecture hall**

led [lɛd] pt, pp of **lead**

ledge [lɛdʒ] n (of window) davanzale m;
(on wall etc) sporgenza; (of mountain)
cornice f, cengia

leek [li:k] n porro

left [lɛft] pt, pp of **leave** ▶ adj
sinistro(-a) ▶ adv a sinistra ▶ n
sinistra; **on the ~, to the ~** a sinistra;
the L~ (Pol) la sinistra; **left-hand** adj
the left-hand side il lato sinistro;
left-hand drive adj guida a sinistra;
left-handed adj mancino(-a);
left-luggage locker n armadietto
per deposito bagagli; **left-luggage
(office)** (BRIT) n deposito m bagagli
inv; **left-overs** npl avanzi mpl, resti
mpl; **left-wing** adj (Pol) di sinistra

leg [lɛg] n (of animal) zampa;
(of furniture) piede m; (Culin: of chicken)
coscia; (of journey) tappa; **lst/2nd ~**
(Sport) partita di andata/ritorno

legacy ['lɛgəsɪ] n eredità f inv

legal ['li:gl] adj legale; **legal holiday**
(US) n giorno festivo, festa nazionale;
legalize vt legalizzare; **legally**
adv legalmente; **legally binding**
legalmente vincolante

legend ['lɛdʒənd] n leggenda;
legendary ['lɛdʒəndəri] adj
leggendario(-a)

leggings ['lɛgɪŋz] npl ghette fpl

legible ['lɛdʒəbl] adj leggibile

legislation [lɛdʒɪs'leɪʃən] n
legislazione f

legislative ['lɛdʒɪslətɪv] adj
legislativo(-a)

legitimate [lɪ'dʒɪtɪmət] adj
legittimo(-a)

leisure ['lɛʒəʳ] n agio, tempo libero; ricreazioni fpl; **at ~** con comodo; **leisure centre** n centro di ricreazione; **leisurely** adj tranquillo(-a), fatto(-a) con comodo or senza fretta

lemon ['lɛmən] n limone m; **lemonade** [-'neɪd] n limonata; **lemon tea** n tè m inv al limone

lend [lɛnd] (pt, pp **lent**) vt to ~ sth (to sb) prestare qc (a qn); **could you ~ me some money?** mi può prestare dei soldi?

length [lɛŋθ] n lunghezza; (distance) distanza; (section: of road, pipe etc) pezzo, tratto; (of time) periodo; **at ~** (at last) finalmente, alla fine; (lengthily) a lungo; **lengthen** vt allungare, prolungare ▶ vi allungarsi; **lengthways** adv per il lungo; **lengthy** adj molto lungo(-a)

lens [lɛnz] n lente f; (of camera) obiettivo

Lent [lɛnt] n Quaresima

lent [lɛnt] pt, pp of **lend**

lentil ['lɛntl] n lenticchia

Leo ['liːəu] n Leone m

leopard ['lɛpəd] n leopardo

leotard ['liːətɑːd] n calzamaglia

leprosy ['lɛprəsɪ] n lebbra

lesbian ['lɛzbɪən] n lesbica

less [lɛs] adj, pron, adv meno ▶ prep ~ **tax/10% discount** meno tasse/il 10% di sconto; ~ **than ever** meno che mai; ~ **than half** meno della metà; ~ **and** ~ sempre meno; **the ~ he works** ... meno lavora ...; **lessen** ['lɛsn] vi diminuire, attenuarsi ▶ vt diminuire, ridurre; **lesser** ['lɛsəʳ] adj minore, più piccolo(-a); **to a lesser extent** in grado or misura minore

lesson ['lɛsn] n lezione f; **to teach sb a ~** dare una lezione a qn

let [lɛt] (pt, pp **let**) vt lasciare; (BRIT: lease) dare in affitto; **to ~ sb do sth** lasciar fare qc a qn, lasciare che qn faccia qc; **to ~ sb know sth** far sapere qc a qn; ~**'s go** andiamo; ~ **him come** lo lasci venire; **"to ~"** "affittasi" ▶ **let down** vt (lower) abbassare; (dress) allungare; (hair) sciogliere; (tyre) sgonfiare; (disappoint) deludere ▶ **let in** vt lasciare entrare; (visitor etc) far entrare ▶ **let off** vt (allow to go) lasciare andare; (firework etc) far partire ▶ **let out** vt lasciare uscire; (scream) emettere

lethal ['liːθl] adj letale, mortale

letter ['lɛtəʳ] n lettera; **letterbox** (BRIT) n buca delle lettere

lettuce ['lɛtɪs] n lattuga, insalata

leukaemia [luː'kiːmɪə] (US **leukemia**) n leucemia

level ['lɛvl] adj piatto(-a), piano(-a); orizzontale ▶ adv **to draw ~** with mettersi alla pari di ▶ n livello ▶ vt livellare, spianare; **to be ~ with** essere alla pari di; **level crossing** (BRIT) n passaggio a livello

lever ['liːvəʳ] n leva; **leverage** ['liːvərɪdʒ] n **leverage (on or with)** forza (su); (fig) ascendente m (su)

levy ['lɛvɪ] n tassa, imposta ▶ vt imporre

liability [laɪə'bɪlətɪ] n responsabilità f inv; (handicap) peso

liable ['laɪəbl] adj (subject): ~ **to** soggetto(-a) a; passibile di; (responsible): ~ **for** responsabile (di); (likely): **to do** propenso(-a) a fare

liaise [liː'eɪz] vi **to ~ (with)** mantenere i contatti (con)

liar ['laɪəʳ] n bugiardo(-a)

liberal ['lɪbərl] adj liberale; (generous): **to be ~ with** distribuire liberalmente; **Liberal Democrat** n liberaldemocratico(-a)

liberate ['lɪbəreɪt] vt liberare

liberation [lɪbə'reɪʃən] n liberazione f

liberty ['lɪbətɪ] n libertà f inv;

~ (criminal) in libertà; **at ~ to do** libero(-a) di fare

Libra ['liːbrə] n Bilancia

librarian [laɪ'brɛərɪən] n bibliotecario(-a)

library ['laɪbrərɪ] n biblioteca

Libya ['lɪbɪə] n Libia

lice [laɪs] npl of **louse**

licence ['laɪsns] (US **license**) n autorizzazione f, permesso; (Comm) licenza; (Radio, TV) canone m, abbonamento; (also: **driving ~**: US: also: **driver's license**) patente f di guida; (excessive freedom) licenza

license ['laɪsns] n (US) = **licence** ▷ vt dare una licenza a; **licensed** adj (for alcohol) che ha la licenza di vendere bibite alcoliche; **license plate** (esp US) n (Aut) targa (automobilistica); **licensing hours** (BRIT) npl orario d'apertura (di un pub)

lick [lɪk] vt leccare; (inf: defeat) stracciare; **to ~ one's lips** (fig) leccarsi i baffi

lid [lɪd] n coperchio; (eyelid) palpebra

lie [laɪ] (pt **lay**, pp **lain**) vi (rest) giacere, star disteso(-a); (of object: be situated) trovarsi, essere; (tell lies: pt, pp **lied**) mentire, dire bugie ▷ n bugia, menzogna; **to ~ low** (fig) latitare ▷ **lie about** or **around** vi (things) essere in giro; (person) bighellonare ▷ **lie down** vi stendersi, sdraiarsi

Liechtenstein ['lɪktənstaɪn] n Liechtenstein m

lie-in ['laɪɪn] (BRIT) n **to have a ~** rimanere a letto

lieutenant [lɛf'tɛnənt, (US) luː'tɛnənt] n tenente m

life [laɪf] (pl **lives**) n vita ▷ cpd di vita; della vita; a vita; **to come to ~** rianimarsi; **life assurance** (BRIT) n = **life insurance**; **lifeboat** n scialuppa di salvataggio; **lifeguard** n bagnino; **life insurance** n assicurazione f

sulla vita; **life jacket** n giubbotto di salvataggio; **lifelike** adj verosimile; rassomigliante; **life preserver** [-prɪ'zəːvər] (US) n salvagente m; giubbotto di salvataggio; **life sentence** n ergastolo; **lifestyle** n stile m di vita; **lifetime** n **in his lifetime** durante la sua vita; **once in a lifetime** una volta nella vita

lift [lɪft] vt sollevare; (ban, rule) levare ▷ vi (fog) alzarsi ▷ n (BRIT: elevator) ascensore m; **to give sb a ~** (BRIT) dare un passaggio a qn; **can you give me a ~ to the station?** può darmi un passaggio fino alla stazione? ▷ **lift up** vt sollevare, alzare; **lift-off** n decollo

light [laɪt] (pt, pp **lighted** or **lit**) n luce f, lume m; (daylight) luce f, giorno; (lamp) lampada; (Aut: rear light) luce f di posizione; (: headlamp) fanale m; (for cigarette etc): **have you got a ~?** ha da accendere?; **~s** npl (Aut: traffic lights) semaforo ▷ vt (candle, cigarette, fire) accendere; (room): **to be lit by** essere illuminato(-a) da ▷ adj (room, colour) chiaro(-a); (not heavy, also fig) leggero(-a); **to come to ~** venire alla luce, emergere ▷ **light up** vi illuminarsi ▷ vt illuminare; **light bulb** n lampadina; **lighten** vt (make less heavy) alleggerire; **lighter** n (also: **cigarette lighter**) accendino; **light-hearted** adj gioioso(-a), gaio(-a); **lighthouse** n faro; **lighting** n illuminazione f; **lightly** adv leggermente; **to get off lightly** cavarsela a buon mercato

lightning ['laɪtnɪŋ] n lampo, fulmine m

lightweight ['laɪtweɪt] adj (suit) leggero(-a) ▷ n (Boxing) peso leggero

like [laɪk] vt (person) volere bene a; (activity, object, food): **I ~ swimming/ that book/chocolate** mi piace nuotare/quel libro/il cioccolato

▶ prep come ▶ adj simile, uguale ▶ n the —uno(-a) uguale; **his ~s and dis~s** i suoi gusti; **would you ~ a coffee?** gradirebbe un caffè?; **I'd ~** mi piacerebbe, vorrei; **would you ~ a coffee?** gradirebbe un caffè?; **to be/look ~ sb/sth** somigliare a qn/qc; **what does it look/taste ~?** che aspetto/gusto ha?; **what does it sound ~?** come fa?; **that's just ~ him** è proprio di lui; **do it ~ this** fallo così; **it is nothing ~ ...** non è affatto come ...; **likeable** adj simpatico(-a)

likelihood ['laıklıhud] n probabilità

likely ['laıklı] adj probabile; plausibile; **he's ~ to leave** probabilmente partirà, è probabile che parta; **not ~!** neanche per sogno!

likewise ['laıkwaız] adv similmente, nello stesso modo

liking ['laıkıŋ] n (**-for**) debole m (per); **to be to sb's ~** piacere a qn

lilac ['laılək] n lilla m inv

Lilo® ['laıləu] n materasso gonfiabile

lily ['lılı] n giglio

limb [lım] n arto

limbo ['lımbəu] n **to be in ~** (fig) essere lasciato(-a) nel dimenticatoio

lime [laım] n (tree) tiglio; (fruit) limetta; (Geo) calce f

limelight ['laımlaıt] n **in the ~** (fig) alla ribalta, in vista

limestone ['laımstəun] n pietra calcarea; (Geo) calcare m

limit ['lımıt] n limite m ▶ vt limitare; **limited** adj limitato(-a), ristretto(-a); **to be limited to** limitarsi a

limousine ['lıməzi:n] n limousine f inv

limp [lımp] n **to have a ~** zoppicare ▶ vi zoppicare ▶ adj floscio(-a), flaccido(-a)

foderare (di); (box): **to ~ (with)** rivestire or foderare (di); (trees, crowd) fiancheggiare; **~ of business** settore m or ramo d'attività; **in ~ with** in linea con ▶ **line up** vi allinearsi, mettersi in fila ▶ vt mettere in fila; (event, celebration) preparare

linear ['lınıə'] adj lineare

linen ['lının] n biancheria, panni mpl; (cloth) tela di lino

liner ['laınə'] n nave f di linea; (for bin) sacchetto

line-up ['laınʌp] n allineamento, fila; (Sport) formazione f di gioco

linger ['lıŋɡə'] vi attardarsi; indugiare; (smell, tradition) persistere

lingerie ['lænʒəri:] n biancheria intima femminile

linguist ['lıŋɡwıst] n linguista m/f; poliglotta m/f; **linguistic** adj linguistico(-a)

lining ['laınıŋ] n fodera

link [lıŋk] n (of a chain) anello; (relationship) legame m; (connection) collegamento ▶ vt collegare, unire, congiungere; (associate): **to ~ with** or **to** collegare a; **~s** npl (Golf) pista or terreno da golf ▶ **link up** vt collegare, unire ▶ vi riunirsi; associarsi

lion ['laıən] n leone m; **lioness** n leonessa

lip [lıp] n labbro; (of cup etc) orlo; **lip-read** vi leggere sulle labbra; **lip salve** [-sælv] n burro di cacao; **lipstick** n rossetto

liqueur [lı'kjuə'] n liquore m

liquid ['lıkwıd] n liquido ▶ adj liquido(-a); **liquidizer** n frullatore m (a brocca)

liquor ['lıkə'] n alcool m; **liquor store** (US) n negozio di liquori

Lisbon ['lızbən] n Lisbona

lisp [lısp] n pronuncia blesa della "s"

list [lıst] n lista, elenco ▶ vt (write down) mettere in lista; fare una lista di;

line [laın] n linea; (rope) corda; (for fishing) lenza; (wire) filo; (of poem) verso; (row, series) fila, riga; coda; (on face) ruga ▶ vt (clothes): **to ~ (with)**

(*enumerate*) elencare
listen ['lɪsn] *vi* ascoltare; **to ~** ascoltare; **listener** *n* ascoltatore(-trice)
lit [lɪt] *pt, pp of* **light**
liter ['li:tə*r*] (*US*) *n* = **litre**
literacy ['lɪtərəsɪ] *n* il sapere leggere e scrivere
literal ['lɪtərl] *adj* letterale; **literally** *adv* alla lettera, letteralmente
literary ['lɪtərərɪ] *adj* letterario(-a)
literate ['lɪtərət] *adj* che sa leggere e scrivere
literature ['lɪtərɪtʃə*r*] *n* letteratura; (*brochures etc*) materiale *m*
litre ['li:tə*r*] (*US* **liter**) *n* litro
litter ['lɪtə*r*] *n* (*rubbish*) rifiuti *mpl*; (*young animals*) figliata; **litter bin** (*BRIT*) *n* cestino per rifiuti; **littered** *adj* **littered with** coperto(-a) di
little ['lɪtl] *adj* (*small*) piccolo(-a); (*not much*) poco(-a) ▶ *adv* poco; **a ~** un po' (di); **a ~ bit** un pochino; **by ~ by ~** a poco a poco; **little finger** *n* mignolo
live¹ [lɪv] *vi* vivere; (*reside*) vivere, abitare; **where do you ~?** dove abita? ▷ **live together** *vi* vivere insieme, convivere ▷ **live up to** *vt fus* tener fede a, non venir meno a
live² [laɪv] *adj* (*animal*) vivo(-a); (*wire*) sotto tensione; (*bullet, missile*) inesploso(-a); (*broadcast*) diretto(-a); (*performance*) dal vivo
livelihood ['laɪvlɪhud] *n* mezzi *mpl* di sostentamento
lively ['laɪvlɪ] *adj* vivace, vivo(-a)
liven up ['laɪvn'ʌp] *vt* (*discussion, evening*) animare ▶ *vi* ravvivarsi
liver ['lɪvə*r*] *n* fegato
lives [laɪvz] *npl of* **life**
livestock ['laɪvstɔk] *n* bestiame *m*
living ['lɪvɪŋ] *adj* vivo(-a), vivente ▶ *n* **to earn** *o* **make a ~** guadagnarsi la vita; **living room** *n* soggiorno
lizard ['lɪzəd] *n* lucertola

load [ləud] *n* (*weight*) peso; (*thing carried*) carico ▶ *vt* (*also:* **~ up**): **to ~** (**with**) (*lorry, ship*) caricare (di); (*gun, camera, Comput*) caricare (con); **a ~ of**, **~s of** (*fig*) un sacco di; **loaded** *adj* (*vehicle*) carico(-a) di; (*question*) capzioso(-a) (di); (*inf: rich*) carico(-a) di soldi
loaf [ləuf] (*pl* **loaves**) *n* pane *m*, pagnotta
loan [ləun] *n* prestito ▶ *vt* dare in prestito; **on ~** in prestito
loathe [ləuð] *vt* detestare, aborrire
loaves [ləuvz] *npl of* **loaf**
lobby ['lɔbɪ] *n* atrio, vestibolo; (*Pol: pressure group*) gruppo di pressione ▶ *vt* fare pressione su
lobster ['lɔbstə*r*] *n* aragosta
local ['ləukl] *adj* locale ▶ *n* (*BRIT: pub*) ≈ bar *m inv* all'angolo; **the ~s** *npl* (*local inhabitants*) la gente della zona; **local anaesthetic** *n* anestesia locale; **local authority** *n* ente *m* locale; **local government** *n* amministrazione *f* locale; **locally** ['ləukəlɪ] *adv* da queste parti; nel vicinato
locate [ləu'keɪt] *vt* (*find*) trovare; (*situate*) collocare; situare
location [ləu'keɪʃən] *n* posizione *f*; **on ~** (*Cinema*) all'esterno
loch [lɔx] *n* lago
lock [lɔk] *n* (*of door, box*) serratura; (*of canal*) chiusa; (*of hair*) ciocca, riccio ▶ *vt* (*with key*) chiudere a chiave ▶ *vi* (*door etc*) chiudersi; (*wheels*) bloccarsi, incepparsi ▷ **lock in** *vt* chiudere dentro (a chiave) ▷ **lock out** *vt* chiudere fuori ▷ **lock up** *vt* (*criminal, mental patient*) rinchiudere; (*house*) chiudere (a chiave) ▶ *vi* chiudere tutto (a chiave)
locker ['lɔkə*r*] *n* armadietto; **locker-room** (*US*) *n* (*Sport*) spogliatoio
locksmith ['lɔksmɪθ] *n* magnano
locomotive [ləukə'məutɪv] *n*

locomotiva

lodge [lɔdʒ] n casetta, portineria; (hunting lodge) casino di caccia ▸ vi (person): **to ~ (with)** essere a pensione (presso or da); (bullet etc) conficcarsi ▸ vt (appeal etc) presentare, fare; **to ~ a complaint** presentare un reclamo; **lodger** n affittuario(-a); (with room and meals) pensionante m/f

lodging ['lɔdʒɪŋ] n alloggio; see also **board**

loft [lɔft] n solaio, soffitta

log [lɔg] n (of wood) ceppo; (also: ~book; Naut, Aviat) diario di bordo; (Aut) libretto di circolazione ▸ vt registrare ▷ **log in** vi (Comput) aprire una sessione (con codice di riconoscimento) ▷ **log off** vi (Comput) terminare una sessione

logic ['lɔdʒɪk] n logica; **logical** adj logico(-a)

logo ['ləʊgəʊ] n logo m inv

lollipop ['lɔlɪpɔp] n lecca lecca m inv

lolly ['lɔlɪ] (inf) n lecca lecca m inv; (also: **ice ~**) ghiacciolo; (money) grana

London ['lʌndən] n Londra; **Londoner** n londinese m/f

lone [ləʊn] adj solitario(-a)

loneliness ['ləʊnlɪnɪs] n solitudine f, isolamento

lonely ['ləʊnlɪ] adj solo(-a); solitario(-a), isolato(-a)

long [lɔŋ] adj lungo(-a) ▸ adv a lungo, per molto tempo ▸ vi **to ~ for sth/to do** desiderare qc/di fare, non veder l'ora di aver qc/di fare; **so or as ~ as** (while) finché; (provided that) sempre che + sub; **don't be ~!** fai presto!; **how ~ is this river/course?** quanto è lungo questo fiume/corso?; **6 metres ~** lungo 6 metri; **6 months ~** che dura 6 mesi, di 6 mesi; **all night ~** tutta la notte; **he no ~er comes** non viene più; **~ before** molto tempo prima; **before ~** (+ future) presto, fra poco;

(+ past) poco tempo dopo; **at ~ last** finalmente; **long-distance** adj (race) di fondo; (call) interurbano(-a); **long-haul** ['lɔŋhɔːl] adj (flight) a lunga percorrenza inv; **longing** n desiderio, voglia, brama

longitude ['lɔŋgɪtjuːd] n longitudine f

long: long jump n salto in lungo; **long-life** adj (milk) a lunga conservazione; (batteries) di lunga durata; **long-sighted** adj presbite; **long-standing** adj di vecchia data; **long-term** adj a lungo termine

loo [luː] (BRIT: inf) n W.C. m inv, cesso

look [lʊk] vi guardare; (seem) sembrare, parere; (building etc): **to ~ south/on to the sea** dare a sud/sul mare ▸ n sguardo; (appearance) aspetto, aria; **~s** npl (good looks) bellezza ▷ **look after** vt fus occuparsi di, prendere cura di; (keep an eye on) guardare, badare a ▷ **look around** vi guardarsi intorno ▷ **look at** vt fus guardare ▷ **look back** vi **to ~ back on** (event etc) ripensare a ▷ **look down on** vt fus (fig) guardare dall'alto, disprezzare ▷ **look for** vt fus cercare; **we're ~ing for a hotel/restaurant** stiamo cercando un albergo/ ristorante ▷ **look forward to** vt fus non veder l'ora di; (in letters): **we ~ forward to hearing from you** in attesa di una vostra gentile risposta ▷ **look into** vt fus esaminare ▷ **look out** vi (beware): **to ~ out (for)** stare in guardia (per) ▷ **look out for** vt fus cercare ▷ **look round** vi (turn) girarsi, voltarsi; (in shop) dare un'occhiata ▷ **look through** vt fus (papers, book) scorrere; (telescope) guardare attraverso ▷ **look up** vi alzare gli occhi; (improve) migliorare ▸ vt (word) cercare; (friend) andare a trovare ▷ **look up to** vt fus avere rispetto per; **lookout** n posto d'osservazione

guardia; to be on the lookout (for) stare in guardia (per)

loom [luːm] n telaio ▶ vi (also: ~ up) apparire minaccioso(-a); (event) essere imminente

loony ['luːnɪ] (inf) n pazzo(-a)

loop [luːp] n cappio ▶ vt to ~ sth round sth passare qc intorno a qc; **loophole** n via d'uscita; scappatoia

loose [luːs] adj (knot) sciolto(-a); (screw) allentato(-a); (stone) cadente; (clothes) ampio(-a), largo(-a); (animal) in libertà, scappato(-a); (life, morals) dissoluto(-a) ▶ n to be on the ~ essere in libertà; **loosely** adv senza stringere; approssimativamente; **loosen** vt sciogliere; (belt etc) allentare

loot [luːt] n bottino ▶ vt saccheggiare

lop-sided ['lɔp'saɪdɪd] adj non equilibrato(-a), asimmetrico(-a)

lord [lɔːd] n signore m; L~ Smith lord Smith; the L~ il Signore; good L~! buon Dio!; the (House of) L~s (BRIT) la Camera dei Lord

lorry ['lɔrɪ] (BRIT) n camion m inv; **lorry driver** (BRIT) n camionista m

lose [luːz] (pt, pp lost) vt perdere ▶ vi perdere; **I've lost my wallet/passport** ho perso il portafoglio/passaporto; **to ~ (time)** (clock) ritardare ▶ **lose out** vi rimetterci; **loser** n perdente m/f

loss [lɔs] n perdita; **to be at a ~** essere perplesso(-a)

lost [lɔst] pt, pp of **lose** ▶ adj perduto(-a); **I'm ~** mi sono perso; **lost property** (US **lost and found**) n oggetti mpl smarriti

lot [lɔt] n (at auctions) lotto; (destiny) destino, sorte f; **the ~** tutto(-a) quanto(-a); tutti(-e) quanti(-e); **a ~** molto; **a ~ of** una gran quantità, un sacco di; **~s of** molto(-a); **to draw ~s (for sth)** tirare a sorte (per qc)

lotion ['ləʊʃən] n lozione f

lottery ['lɔtərɪ] n lotteria

loud [laud] adj forte, alto(-a); (gaudy) vistoso(-a), sgargiante ▶ adv (speak etc) forte; **out ~** (read etc) ad alta voce; **loudly** adv fortemente, ad alta voce; **loudspeaker** n altoparlante m

lounge [laundʒ] n salotto, soggiorno; (at airport, station) sala d'attesa; (BRIT: also: ~ bar) bar m inv con servizio a tavolino ▶ vi oziare

louse [laus] (pl **lice**) n pidocchio

lousy ['lauzɪ] (inf) adj orrendo(-a), schifoso(-a); **to feel ~** stare da cani

love [lʌv] n amore m ▶ vt amare; voler bene a; **to ~ to do** mi piace fare; **to be/fall in ~ with** essere innamorato(-a)/innamorarsi di; **to make ~** fare l'amore; **"15 ~"** (Tennis) "15 a zero"; **love affair** n relazione f; **love life** n vita sentimentale

lovely ['lʌvlɪ] adj bello(-a); (delicious: smell, meal) buono(-a)

lover ['lʌvə*] n amante m/f; (person in love) innamorato(-a); (amateur): **a ~ of** un(-un') amante di; un(-un') appassionato(-a) di

loving ['lʌvɪŋ] adj affettuoso(-a)

low [ləʊ] adj basso(-a) ▶ adv in basso ▶ n (Meteor) depressione f; **to be ~ on** (supplies etc) avere scarsità di; **to feel ~** sentirsi giù; **low-alcohol** adj a basso contenuto alcolico; **low-calorie** adj a basso contenuto calorico

lower ['ləʊə*] adj (bottom: of 2 things) più basso(-a); (less important) meno importante ▶ vt calare; (prices, eyes, voice) abbassare

low-fat ['ləʊ'fæt] adj magro(-a)

loyal ['lɔɪəl] adj fedele, leale; **loyalty** n fedeltà, lealtà; **loyalty card** n carta che offre sconti a clienti abituali

L.P. n abbr = **long-playing record**

L-plates ['elpleɪts] (BRIT) npl contrassegno P principiante

Lt abbr (= lieutenant) Ten.

Ltd abbr (= limited) ≈ S.r.l.

luck [lʌk] n fortuna, sorte f; **bad ~** sfortuna, mala sorte; **good ~!** buona fortuna!; **luckily** adv fortunatamente, per fortuna; **lucky** adj fortunato(-a); (number etc) che porta fortuna

lucrative ['luːkrətɪv] adj lucrativo(-a), lucroso(-a), profittevole

ludicrous ['luːdɪkrəs] adj ridicolo(-a)

luggage ['lʌɡɪdʒ] n bagagli mpl; **our ~ hasn't arrived** i nostri bagagli non sono arrivati; **luggage rack** n portabagagli m inv

lukewarm ['luːkwɔːm] adj tiepido(-a)

lull [lʌl] n intervallo di calma ▶ vt **to ~ sb to sleep** cullare qn finché si addormenta

lullaby ['lʌləbaɪ] n ninnananna

lumber ['lʌmbəʳ] n (wood) legname m; (junk) roba vecchia

luminous ['luːmɪnəs] adj luminoso(-a)

lump [lʌmp] n pezzo; (in sauce) grumo; (swelling) gonfiore m; (also: **sugar ~**) zolletta f ▶ vt (also: **~ together**) riunire, mettere insieme; **lump sum** n somma globale; **lumpy** adj (sauce) pieno(-a) di grumi; (bed) bitorzoluto(-a)

lunatic ['luːnətɪk] adj pazzo(-a), matto(-a)

lunch [lʌntʃ] n pranzo, colazione f; **lunch break** n intervallo del pranzo; **lunch time** n ora di pranzo

lung [lʌŋ] n polmone m

lure [luəʳ] n richiamo; lusinga ▶ vt attirare (con l'inganno)

lurk [ləːk] vi stare in agguato

lush [lʌʃ] adj lussureggiante

lust [lʌst] n lussuria; cupidigia; desiderio; (fig): **~ for** sete f di

Luxembourg ['lʌksəmbəːɡ] n (state) Lussemburgo m; (city) Lussemburgo f

luxurious [lʌɡ'zjuərɪəs] adj sontuoso(-a), di lusso

luxury ['lʌkʃərɪ] n lusso ▶ cpd di lusso

⬛ Be careful not to translate **luxury** by the Italian word **lussuria**.

Lycra® ['laɪkrə] n lycra® f inv

lying ['laɪɪŋ] n bugie fpl, menzogne fpl ▶ adj bugiardo(-a)

lyrics ['lɪrɪks] npl (of song) parole fpl

m. abbr = **metre**; **mile**; **million**

M.A. abbr = **Master of Arts**

ma (inf) [maː] n mamma

mac [mæk] (BRIT) n impermeabile m

macaroni [mækə'rəʊnɪ] n maccheroni mpl

Macedonia [mæsɪ'dəʊnɪə] n Macedonia; **Macedonian** [mæsɪ'dəʊnɪən] adj macedone ▶ n macedone m/f; (Ling) macedone m

machine [mə'ʃiːn] n macchina ▶ vt (Tech) lavorare a macchina; (dress etc) cucire a macchina; **machine gun** n mitragliatrice f; **machinery** n macchinario, macchine fpl; (fig) macchina; **machine washable** adj lavabile in lavatrice

macho ['mætʃəʊ] adj macho inv

mackerel ['mækrl] n inv sgombro

mackintosh ['mækɪntɒʃ] (BRIT) n impermeabile m

mad [mæd] adj matto(-a), pazzo(-a); (foolish) sciocco(-a); (angry) furioso(-a); **to be ~ about** (*keen*) andare pazzo(-a) per

Madagascar [mædəˈgæskəʳ] n Madagascar m

madam [ˈmædəm] n signora

mad cow disease n encefalite f bovina spongiforme

made [meid] pt, pp of **make**; **made-to-measure** (*BRIT*) adj fatto(-a) su misura; **made-up** [ˈmeidʌp] adj (*story*) inventato(-a)

madly [ˈmædli] adv follemente

madman [ˈmædmən] (*irreg*) n pazzo, alienato

madness [ˈmædnis] n pazzia

Madrid [məˈdrid] n Madrid f

Mafia [ˈmæfiə] n mafia f

mag [mæg] n abbr (*BRIT inf*) = **magazine**)*Press*)

magazine [mægəˈzin] n (*Press*) rivista; (*Radio, TV*) rubrica

Be careful not to translate **magazine** by the Italian word *magazzino*.

maggot [ˈmægət] n baco, verme m

magic [ˈmædʒik] n magia ▶ adj magico(-a); **magical** adj magico(-a); **magician** [məˈdʒiʃən] n mago(-a)

magistrate [ˈmædʒistreit] n magistrato; giudice m/f

magnet [ˈmægnit] n magnete m, calamita; **magnetic** [-ˈnetik] adj magnetico(-a)

magnificent [mægˈnifisnt] adj magnifico(-a)

magnify [ˈmægnifai] vt ingrandire; **magnifying glass** n lente f d'ingrandimento

magpie [ˈmægpai] n gazza

mahogany [məˈhɔgəni] n mogano

maid [meid] n domestica; (*in hotel*) cameriera

maiden name [ˈmeidn-] n nome m da nubile or da ragazza

mail [meil] n posta ▶ vt spedire (per

posta); **mailbox** (*US*) n cassetta delle lettere; **mailing list** n elenco d'indirizzi; **mailman** (*irreg: US*) n portalettere m inv, postino; **mailorder** n vendita (or acquisto) per corrispondenza

main [mein] adj principale ▶ n (*pipe*) conduttura principale; **main course** n (*Culin*) piatto principale, piatto forte; **mainland** n continente m; **mainly** adv principalmente, soprattutto; **main road** n strada principale; **mainstream** n (*fig*) corrente f principale; **main street** n strada principale

maintain [meinˈtein] vt mantenere; (*affirm*) sostenere; **maintenance** [ˈmeintənəns] n manutenzione f; (*alimony*) alimenti mpl

maisonette [meizəˈnet] n (*BRIT*) appartamento a due piani

maize [meiz] n granturco, mais m

majesty [ˈmædʒisti] n maestà f inv

major [ˈmeidʒəʳ] n (*Mil*) maggiore m ▶ adj (*greater, Mus*) maggiore; (*in importance*) principale, importante

Majorca [məˈjɔːkə] n Maiorca

majority [məˈdʒɔriti] n maggioranza

make [meik] (pt, pp made) vt fare; (*manufacture*) fare, fabbricare; (*cause to be*): **to ~ sb sad** etc rendere qn triste etc; (*force*): **to ~ sb do sth** costringere qn a fare qc, far fare qc a qn; (*equal*): **2 and 2 ~ 4** 2 più 2 fa 4 ▶ n fabbricazione f; (*brand*) marca; **to ~ a fool of sb** far fare a qn la figura dello scemo; **to ~ a profit** realizzare un profitto; **to ~ a loss** subire una perdita; **to ~ it** (*arrive*) arrivare; (*achieve sth*) farcela; **what time do you ~ it?** che ora fai?; **to ~ do with** arrangiarsi con ▶ **make off** vi svignarsela ▶ **make out** vt (*write out*) scrivere; (: *cheque*) emettere; (*understand*) capire; (*see*) distinguere; (: *numbers*) decifrare ▶ **make up**

vt (constitute) formare; (invent) inventare; (parcel) fare ▸ vi conciliarsi; (with cosmetics) truccarsi ▸ **make up for** vt fus compensare; ricuperare; **makeover** ['meɪkəʊvə'] n (change of image) cambiamento di immagine; (of room, house) trasformazione f. **maker** n (of programme etc) creatore(-trice); (manufacturer) fabbricante m; **makeshift** adj improvvisato(-a); **make-up** n trucco

making ['meɪkɪŋ] n (fig): **in the ~** in formazione; **to have the ~s of** (actor, athlete etc) avere la stoffa di

malaria [mə'lɛərɪə] n malaria

Malaysia [mə'leɪzɪə] n Malaysia

male [meɪl] n (Biol) maschio ▸ adj maschile; maschio(-a)

malicious [mə'lɪʃəs] adj malevolo(-a); (Law) doloso(-a)

malignant [mə'lɪɡnənt] adj (Med) maligno(-a)

mall [mɔːl] n (also: **shopping ~**) centro commerciale

mallet ['mælɪt] n maglio

malnutrition [mælnjuː'trɪʃən] n denutrizione f

malpractice [mæl'præktɪs] n prevaricazione f; negligenza

malt [mɔːlt] n malto

Malta ['mɔːltə] n Malta; **Maltese** [mɔːl'tiːz] adj, n (pl inv) maltese (m/f); (Ling) maltese m

mammal ['mæml] n mammifero

mammoth ['mæməθ] adj enorme, gigantesco(-a)

man [mæn] (pl **men**) n uomo ▸ vt fornire d'uomini; stare a; **an old ~** un vecchio; **~ and wife** marito e moglie

manage ['mænɪdʒ] vi farcela ▸ vt (be in charge of) occuparsi di; gestire; **to ~ to do sth** riuscire a fare qc; **manageable** adj maneggevole; fattibile; **management** n amministrazione f, direzione f; **manager** n direttore

m; (of shop, restaurant) gerente m; (of artist, Sport) manager m inv; **manageress** [-ə'rɛs] n direttrice f; gerente f; **managerial** [-ə'dʒɪərɪəl] adj dirigenziale; **managing director** n amministratore m delegato

mandarin ['mændərɪn] n (person, fruit) mandarino

mandate ['mændeɪt] n mandato

mandatory ['mændətərɪ] adj obbligatorio(-a), ingiuntivo(-a)

mane [meɪn] n criniera

mangetout ['mɒnʒ'tuː] n pisello dolce, taccola

mango ['mæŋɡəʊ] (pl **mangoes**) n mango

man: **manhole** ['mænhəʊl] n botola stradale; **manhood** ['mænhud] n età virile; virilità

mania ['meɪnɪə] n mania; **maniac** ['meɪnɪæk] n maniaco(-a)

manic ['mænɪk] adj (behaviour, activity) maniacale

manicure ['mænɪkjuə'] n manicure f inv

manifest ['mænɪfɛst] vt manifestare ▸ adj manifesto(-a), palese

manifesto [mænɪ'fɛstəʊ] n manifesto

manipulate [mə'nɪpjuleɪt] vt manipolare

man: **mankind** [mæn'kaɪnd] n umanità, genere m umano; **manly** ['mænlɪ] adj virile; coraggioso(-a); **man-made** adj sintetico(-a), artificiale

manner ['mænə'] n maniera, modo; (behaviour) modo di fare; (type, sort): **all ~ of things** ogni genere di cosa; **~s** npl (conduct) maniere fpl; **bad ~s** maleducazione f

manoeuvre [mə'nuːvə'] (US **maneuver**) vt manovrare ▸ vi far manovre ▸ n manovra

manpower ['mænpauə'] n manodopera

mansion ['mænʃən] n casa signorile

manslaughter ['mænslɔːtə*r*] n omicidio preterintenzionale

mantelpiece ['mæntlpiːs] n mensola del caminetto

manual ['mænjuəl] adj manuale ▶ n manuale m

manufacture [mænju'fæktʃə*r*] vt fabbricare ▶ n fabbricazione f, manifattura f; **manufacturer** n fabbricante m

manure [mə'njuə*r*] n concime m

manuscript ['mænjuskrɪpt] n manoscritto

many ['mɛnɪ] adj molti(-e) ▶ pron molti(-e); **a great ~** moltissimi(-e), un gran numero (di); **~ a time** molte volte

map [mæp] n carta (geografica); (of city) cartina; **can you show it to me on the ~?** può indicarmelo sulla cartina?

maple ['meɪpl] n acero

mar [mɑː*r*] vt sciupare

Mar abbr (= March) mar.

marathon ['mærəθən] n maratona

marble ['mɑːbl] n marmo; (toy) pallina, bilia

March [mɑːtʃ] n marzo

march [mɑːtʃ] vi marciare; sfilare ▶ n marcia

mare [mɛə*r*] n giumenta

margarine [mɑːdʒə'riːn] n margarina

margin ['mɑːdʒɪn] n margine m; **marginal** adj marginale; **marginal seat** (Pol) seggio elettorale ottenuto con una stretta maggioranza; **marginally** adv (bigger, better) lievemente, di poco; (different) un po'

marigold ['mærɪɡəʊld] n calendola

marijuana [mærɪ'wɑːnə] n marijuana

marina [mə'riːnə] n marina

marinade n [mærɪ'neɪd] marinata ▶ vt ['mærɪneɪd] = **marinate**

marinate ['mærɪneɪt] vt marinare

marine [mə'riːn] adj (animal, plant)

marino(-a); (forces, engineering) marittimo(-a) ▶ n (BRIT) fante m di marina; (US) marine m inv

marital ['mærɪtl] adj maritale, coniugale; **marital status** n stato civile

maritime ['mærɪtaɪm] adj marittimo(-a)

marjoram ['mɑːdʒərəm] n maggiorana

mark [mɑːk] n segno; (stain) macchia; (of skid etc) traccia; (BRIT Scol) voto; (Sport) bersaglio; (currency) marco ▶ vt segnare; (stain) macchiare; (indicate) indicare; (BRIT Scol) dare un voto a; correggere; **to ~ time** segnare il passo; **marked** adj spiccato(-a), chiaro(-a); **marker** n (sign) segno; (bookmark) segnalibro

market ['mɑːkɪt] n mercato ▶ vt (Comm) mettere in vendita; **marketing** n marketing m; **marketplace** n (piazza del) mercato; (world of trade) piazza, mercato; **market research** n indagine f or ricerca di mercato

marmalade ['mɑːməleɪd] n marmellata d'arance

maroon [mə'ruːn] vt (also fig): **to be ~ed (in** or **at)** essere abbandonato(-a) (in) ▶ adj bordeaux inv

marquee [mɑː'kiː] n padiglione m

marriage ['mærɪdʒ] n matrimonio; **marriage certificate** n certificato di matrimonio

married ['mærɪd] adj sposato(-a); (life, love) coniugale, matrimoniale

marrow ['mærəʊ] n midollo; (vegetable) zucca

marry ['mærɪ] vt sposare, sposarsi con; (vicar, priest etc) dare in matrimonio ▶ vi (also: **get married**) sposarsi

Mars [mɑːz] n (planet) Marte m

marsh [mɑːʃ] n palude f

marshal ['mɑːʃl] n maresciallo; (US: fire) capo; (: police) capitano ▶ vt (thoughts, support) ordinare; (soldiers) adunare

martyr ['mɑːtə*] n martire m/f

marvel ['mɑːvl] n meraviglia ▶ vi to ~ (at) meravigliarsi (di); **marvellous** (US **marvelous**) adj meraviglioso(-a)

Marxism ['mɑːksɪzəm] n marxismo

Marxist ['mɑːksɪst] adj, n marxista m/f

marzipan ['mɑːzɪpæn] n marzapane m

mascara [mæs'kɑːrə] n mascara m

mascot ['mæskət] n mascotte f inv

masculine ['mæskjulɪn] adj maschile; (woman) mascolino(-a)

mash [mæʃ] vt passare, schiacciare; **mashed potatoes** npl purè m di patate

mask [mɑːsk] n maschera ▶ vt mascherare

mason ['meɪsn] n (also: **stone~**) scalpellino; (also: **free~**) massone m; **masonry** n muratura

mass [mæs] n moltitudine f, massa; (Physics) massa; (Rel) messa ▶ cpd di massa ▶ vi ammassarsi; **the ~es** npl (ordinary people) le masse; **~es of** (inf) una montagna di

massacre ['mæsəkə*] n massacro

massage ['mæsɑːʒ] n massaggio

massive ['mæsɪv] adj enorme, massiccio(-a)

mass media npl mass media mpl

mass-produce ['mæsprə'djuːs] vt produrre in serie

mast [mɑːst] n albero

master ['mɑːstə*] n padrone m; (Art etc, teacher: in primary school) maestro; (: in secondary school) professore m; (title for boys): **M~ X** Signorino X ▶ vt domare; (learn) imparare a fondo; (understand) conoscere a fondo; **mastermind** n mente f superiore ▶ vt essere il cervello di; **Master**

of Arts/Science n Master m inv in lettere/scienze; **masterpiece** n capolavoro

masturbate ['mæstəbeɪt] vi masturbare

mat [mæt] n stuoia; (also: **door~**) stoino, zerbino; (also: **table ~**) sottopiatto ▶ adj = **matt**

match [mætʃ] n fiammifero; (game) partita, incontro; (fig) uguale m/f; matrimonio; partito ▶ vt intonare; (go well with) andare benissimo con; (equal) uguagliare; (correspond to) corrispondere a; (pair: also: **~ up**) accoppiare ▶ vi combaciare; **to be a good ~** andare bene; **matchbox** n scatola per fiammiferi; **matching** adj ben assortito(-a)

mate [meɪt] n compagno(-a) di lavoro; (inf: friend) amico(-a); (animal) compagno(-a); (in merchant navy) secondo ▶ vi accoppiarsi

material [mə'tɪərɪəl] n (substance) materiale m, materia; (cloth) stoffa ▶ adj materiale; **~s** npl (equipment) materiali mpl

materialize [mə'tɪərɪəlaɪz] vi materializzarsi, realizzarsi

maternal [mə'təːnl] adj materno(-a)

maternity [mə'təːnɪtɪ] n maternità; **maternity hospital** n ≈ clinica ostetrica; **maternity leave** n congedo di maternità

math [mæθ] (US) n = **maths**

mathematical [mæθə'mætɪkl] adj matematico(-a)

mathematician [mæθəmə'tɪʃən] n matematico(-a)

mathematics [mæθə'mætɪks] n matematica

maths [mæθs] (US **math**) n matematica

matinée ['mætɪneɪ] n matinée f inv

matron ['meɪtrən] n (in hospital) capoinfermiera; (in school) infermiera

matt [mæt] adj opaco(-a)

matter ['mætə'] n questione f; (Physics) materia, sostanza; (content) contenuto; (Med: pus) pus m ▶ vi importare; **it doesn't ~** non importa; (I don't mind) non fa niente; **what's the ~?** che cosa c'è?; **no ~ what** qualsiasi cosa accada; **as a ~ of course** come cosa naturale; **as a ~ of fact** in verità; **~s** npl (affairs) questioni

mattress ['mætrɪs] n materasso

mature [mə'tjuə'] adj maturo(-a); (cheese) stagionato(-a) ▶ vi maturare; stagionare; **mature student** n studente universitario che ha più di 25 anni; **maturity** n maturità

maul [mɔːl] vt lacerare

mauve [məuv] adj malva inv

max abbr = **maximum**

maximize ['mæksɪmaɪz] vt (profits etc) massimizzare; (chances) aumentare al massimo

maximum ['mæksɪməm] (pl **maxima**) adj massimo(-a) ▶ n massimo

May [meɪ] n maggio

may [meɪ] vi (conditional **might**) (indicating possibility): **he ~ come** può darsi che venga; (be allowed to): **~ I smoke?** posso fumare?; (wishes): **God bless you!** Dio la benedica!; **you ~ as well go** tanto vale che tu te ne vada

maybe ['meɪbiː] adv forse, può darsi; **~ he'll ...** può darsi che lui ... + sub, forse lui ...

May Day n il primo maggio

mayhem ['meɪhɛm] n cagnara

mayonnaise [meɪə'neɪz] n maionese f

mayor [mɛə'] n sindaco; **mayoress** n sindaco (donna); moglie f del sindaco

maze [meɪz] n labirinto, dedalo

MD n abbr (= Doctor of Medicine) titolo di studio; (Comm) see **managing director**

me [miː] pron mi, m' + vowel or silent "h"; (stressed, after prep) me; **he heard me** mi ha o m'ha sentito; **give me a book** dammi (or mi dia) un libro; **it's me** sono io; **with me** con me; **without me** senza di me

meadow ['mɛdəu] n prato

meagre, (US **meager**) adj magro(-a)

meal [miːl] n pasto; (flour) farina; **mealtime** n l'ora di mangiare

mean [miːn] (pt, pp **meant**) adj (with money) avaro(-a), gretto(-a); (unkind) meschino(-a), maligno(-a); (shabby) misero(-a); (average) medio(-a) ▶ vt (signify) significare, voler dire; (intend): **to ~ to do** aver l'intenzione di fare ▶ n mezzo; (Math) media; **~s** npl (way, money) mezzi mpl; **by ~s of** per mezzo di; **by all ~s** ma certo, prego; **to be ~ for** essere destinato(-a) a; **do you ~ it?** dice sul serio?; **what do you ~?** che cosa vuol dire?

meaning ['miːnɪŋ] n significato, senso; **meaningful** adj significativo(-a); **meaningless** adj senza senso

meant [mɛnt] pt, pp of **mean**

meantime ['miːntaɪm] adv (also: **in the ~**) nel frattempo

meanwhile ['miːnwaɪl] adv nel frattempo

measles ['miːzlz] n morbillo

measure ['mɛʒə'] vt, vi misurare ▶ n misura; (also: **tape~**) metro

measurement ['mɛʒəmənt] n (act) misurazione f; (measure) misura; **chest/hip ~** giro petto/fianchi; **to take sb's ~s** prendere le misure di qn

meat [miːt] n carne f; **I don't eat ~** non mangio carne; **cold ~** affettato; **meatball** n polpetta di carne

Mecca ['mɛkə] n (also fig) la Mecca

mechanic [mɪ'kænɪk] n meccanico; **can you send a ~?** può mandare

un meccanico?; **mechanical** adj
meccanico(-a)

mechanism ['mɛkənɪzəm] n
meccanismo

medal ['mɛdl] n medaglia; **medallist**
(US **medalist**) n (Sport): **to be a gold
medallist** essere medaglia d'oro

meddle ['mɛdl] vi **to ~ in** immischiarsi
in, mettere le mani in; **to ~ with**
toccare

media ['miːdɪə] npl media mpl

mediaeval [mɛdɪ'iːvl] adj = **medieval**

mediate ['miːdɪeɪt] vi fare da
mediatore(-trice)

medical ['mɛdɪkl] adj medico(-a) ▶ n
visita medica; **medical certificate** n
certificato medico

medicated ['mɛdɪkeɪtɪd] adj
medicato(-a)

medication [mɛdɪ'keɪʃən] n
medicinali mpl, farmaci mpl

medicine ['mɛdsɪn] n medicina

medieval [mɛdɪ'iːvl] adj medievale

mediocre [miːdɪ'əʊkə'] adj mediocre

meditate ['mɛdɪteɪt] vi **to ~ (on)**
meditare (su)

meditation [mɛdɪ'teɪʃən] n
meditazione f

Mediterranean [mɛdɪtə'reɪnɪən]
adj mediterraneo(-a); **the ~ (Sea)** il
(mare) Mediterraneo

medium ['miːdɪəm] adj (pl **media**)
adj medio(-a) ▶ n (**means**) mezzo;
(pl **mediums**: person) medium m
inv; **medium-sized** adj (tin etc) di
grandezza media; (clothes) di taglia
media; **medium wave** n onde fpl
medie

meek [miːk] adj dolce, umile

meet [miːt] (pt, pp **met**) vt incontrare;
(for the first time) fare la conoscenza di,
(go and fetch) andare a prendere; (fig)
affrontare; soddisfare; raggiungere
▶ vi incontrarsi; (in session) riunirsi;
(join: objects) unirsi; **nice to ~ you**

piacere (di conoscerla) ▶ **meet up** vi
to ~ up with sb incontrare qn ▶ **meet
with** vt fus incontrare; **meeting** n
incontro; (session: of club etc) riunione
f; (interview) intervista; **she's at
a meeting** (Comm) è in riunione;
meeting place n luogo d'incontro

megabyte ['mɛgəbaɪt] n (Comput)
megabyte m inv

megaphone ['mɛgəfəʊn] n
megafono

melancholy ['mɛlənkəlɪ] n
malinconia ▶ adj malinconico(-a)

melody ['mɛlədɪ] n melodia

melon ['mɛlən] n melone m

melt [mɛlt] vi (gen) sciogliersi,
struggersi; (metals) fondersi ▶ vt
sciogliere, struggere; fondere

member ['mɛmbə'] n membro;
Member of Congress (US)
n membro del Congresso;
Member of Parliament (BRIT)
n deputato(-a); **Member of the
European Parliament** (BRIT) n
eurodeputato(-a); **Member of
the Scottish Parliament** (BRIT)
n deputato(-a) del Parlamento
scozzese; **membership** n iscrizione
f, (numero d')iscritti mpl, membri
mpl; **membership card** n tessera (di
iscrizione)

memento [mə'mɛntəu] n ricordo,
souvenir m inv

memo ['mɛməu] n appunto; (Comm
etc) comunicazione f di servizio

memorable ['mɛmərəbl] adj
memorabile

memorandum [mɛmə'rændəm] (pl
memoranda) n appunto; (Comm etc)
comunicazione f di servizio

memorial [mɪ'mɔːrɪəl] n
monumento commemorativo ▶ adj
commemorativo(-a)

memorize ['mɛməraɪz] vt
memorizzare

memory ['mɛmərɪ] n (also Comput) memoria; (recollection) ricordo

men [mɛn] npl of **man**

menace ['mɛnəs] n minaccia ▶ vt minacciare

mend [mɛnd] vt aggiustare, riparare; (darn) rammendare ▶ n **on the ~** in via di guarigione

meningitis [mɛnɪn'dʒaɪtɪs] n meningite f

menopause ['mɛnəupɔːz] n menopausa

men's room n **the men's room** (esp US) la toilette degli uomini

menstruation [mɛnstru'eɪʃən] n mestruazione f

menswear ['mɛnzwɛər] n abbigliamento maschile

mental ['mɛntl] adj mentale; **mental hospital** n ospedale m psichiatrico; **mentality** [mɛn'tælɪtɪ] n mentalità f inv; **mentally** adv **to be mentally handicapped** essere minorato psichico

menthol ['mɛnθɔl] n mentolo

mention ['mɛnʃən] n menzione f ▶ vt menzionare, far menzione di; **don't ~ it!** non c'è di che!, prego!

menu ['mɛnjuː] n (set menu, Comput) menù m inv; (printed) carta; **could we see the ~?** ci può portare il menù?

MEP n abbr = **Member of the European Parliament**

mercenary ['məːsɪnərɪ] adj venale ▶ n mercenario

merchandise ['məːtʃəndaɪz] n merci fpl

merchant ['məːtʃənt] n mercante m, commerciante m; **merchant navy** (US **merchant marine**) n marina mercantile

merciless ['məːsɪlɪs] adj spietato(-a)

mercury ['məːkjurɪ] n mercurio

mercy ['məːsɪ] n pietà; (Rel) misericordia; **at the ~ of** alla mercè di

mere [mɪər] adj semplice; **by a ~ chance** per mero caso; **merely** adv semplicemente, non ... che

merge [məːdʒ] vt unire ▶ vi fondersi, unirsi; (Comm) fondersi; **merger** n (Comm) fusione f

meringue [mə'ræŋ] n meringa

merit ['mɛrɪt] n merito, valore m ▶ vt meritare

mermaid ['məːmeɪd] n sirena

merry ['mɛrɪ] adj gaio(-a), allegro(-a); **M~ Christmas!** Buon Natale!; **merry-go-round** n carosello

mesh [mɛʃ] n maglia; rete f

mess [mɛs] n confusione f, disordine m; (fig) pasticcio; (dirt) sporcizia; (Mil) mensa ▷ **mess about** or **around** (inf) vi trastullarsi ▷ **mess with** (inf) vt fus (challenge, confront) litigare con; (drugs, drinks) abusare di ▷ **mess up** vt sporcare; fare un pasticcio di; rovinare

message ['mɛsɪdʒ] n messaggio; **can I leave a ~?** posso lasciare un messaggio?; **are there any ~s for me?** ci sono messaggi per me?

messenger ['mɛsɪndʒər] n messaggero(-a)

Messrs ['mɛsəz] abbr (on letters) Spett

messy ['mɛsɪ] adj sporco(-a), disordinato(-a)

met [mɛt] pt, pp of **meet**

metabolism [mɛ'tæbəlɪzəm] n metabolismo

metal ['mɛtl] n metallo; **metallic** [-'tælɪk] adj metallico(-a)

metaphor ['mɛtəfər] n metafora

meteor ['miːtɪər] n meteora; **meteorite** ['miːtɪəraɪt] n meteorite m

meteorology [miːtɪə'rɔlədʒɪ] n meteorologia

meter ['miːtər] n (instrument) contatore m; (parking meter) parchimetro; (US: unit) = **metre**

method ['mɛθəd] n metodo;

methodical [mɪ'θɒdɪkl] *adj*
metodico(-a)

meths [mɛθs] (BRIT) *n* alcool *m*
denaturato

meticulous [mɛ'tɪkjuləs] *adj*
meticoloso(-a)

metre ['miːtər] (US **meter**) *n* metro

metric ['mɛtrɪk] *adj* metrico(-a)

metro ['mɛtrəu] *n* metro *m inv*

metropolitan [mɛtrə'pɒlɪtən] *adj*
metropolitano(-a)

Mexican ['mɛksɪkən] *adj, n*
messicano(-a)

Mexico ['mɛksɪkəu] *n* Messico *m*

mg *abbr* (= milligram) mg

mice [maɪs] *npl of* **mouse**

micro... ['maɪkrəu] *prefix* micro...;
microchip *n* microcircuito
integrato; **microphone** *n* microfono;
microscope *n* microscopio;
microwave *n* (also: **microwave oven**)
forno a microonde

mid [mɪd] *adj* ~ **May** metà maggio; ~
afternoon metà pomeriggio; **in** ~ **air**
a mezz'aria; **midday** *n* mezzogiorno

middle ['mɪdl] *n* mezzo; centro;
(waist) vita ▶ *adj* di mezzo; **in the**
~ **of the night** nel bel mezzo della
notte; **middle-aged** *adj* di mezza
età; **Middle Ages** the **Middle
Ages** il Medioevo; **middle-class** *adj*
≈ borghese; **Middle East** *n* Medio
Oriente *m*; **middle name** *n* secondo
nome *m*; **middle school** *n* (US) scuola
media per ragazzi dagli 11 ai 14 anni; (BRIT)
scuola media per ragazzi dagli 8 o 9 ai
12 o 13 anni

midge [mɪdʒ] *n* moscerino

midget ['mɪdʒɪt] *n* nano(-a)

midnight ['mɪdnaɪt] *n* mezzanotte *f*

midst [mɪdst] *n* **in the** ~ **of** in mezzo a

midsummer [mɪd'sʌmər] *n* mezza or
piena estate *f*

midway [mɪd'weɪ] *adj, adv* ~
(between) a mezza strada (fra); ~

(through) a metà (di)

midweek [mɪd'wiːk] *adv* a metà
settimana

midwife ['mɪdwaɪf] (*pl* **midwives**) *n*
levatrice *f*

midwinter [mɪd'wɪntər] *n* pieno
inverno

might [maɪt] *vb see* **may** ▶ *n* potere *m*,
forza; **mighty** *adj* forte, potente

migraine ['miːgreɪn] *n* emicrania

migrant ['maɪgrənt] *adj* (bird)
migratore(-trice); (worker)
emigrato(-a)

migrate [maɪ'greɪt] *vi* (bird) migrare;
(person) emigrare

migration [maɪ'greɪʃən] *n*
migrazione *f*

mike [maɪk] *n abbr* (= microphone)
microfono

Milan [mɪ'læn] *n* Milano *f*

mild [maɪld] *adj* mite; (person, voice)
dolce; (flavour) delicato(-a); (illness)
leggero(-a); (interest) blando(-a) ▶ *n*
(beer) birra leggera; **mildly** ['maɪldlɪ]
adv mitemente; dolcemente;
delicatamente; leggermente;
blandamente; **to put it mildly** a
dire poco

mile [maɪl] *n* miglio; **mileage** *n*
distanza in miglia, ≈ chilometraggio;
mileometer [maɪ'lɒmɪtər] *n*
≈ contachilometri *m inv*; **milestone**
['maɪlstəun] *n* pietra miliare

military ['mɪlɪtərɪ] *adj* militare

militia [mɪ'lɪʃə] *n* milizia

milk [mɪlk] *n* latte *m* ▶ *vt* (cow)
mungere; (fig) sfruttare; **milk
chocolate** *n* cioccolato al latte; **milk
man** (irreg) *n* lattaio; **milky** *adj*
lattiginoso(-a); (colour) latteo(-a)

mill [mɪl] *n* mulino; (small: for coffee,
pepper etc) macinino; (factory)
fabbrica; (spinning mill) filatura ▶ *vt*
macinare ▶ *vi* (also: ~ **about**) brulicare

millennium [mɪ'lɛnɪəm] *n* (*pl*

millenniums or **millennia**) n millennio

milli... ['mɪlɪ] prefix: **milligram(me)** n milligrammo; **millilitre** ['mɪlɪliːtə'] (US **milliliter**) n millilitro; **millimetre** (US **millimeter**) n millimetro

million ['mɪljən] num milione m; **millionaire** n milionario, ≈ miliardario; **millionth** num milionesimo(-a)

milometer [maɪ'lɒmɪtə'] n = **mileometer**

mime [maɪm] n mimo ▸ vt, vi mimare

mimic ['mɪmɪk] n imitatore(-trice) ▸ vt fare la mimica di

min. abbr = **minute(s)**; **minimum**

mince [mɪns] vt tritare, macinare ▸ n (BRIT Culin) carne f tritata or macinata; **mincemeat** n frutta secca tritata per uso in pasticceria; (US) carne f tritata or macinata; **mince pie** n specie di torta con frutta secca

mind [maɪnd] n mente f ▸ vt (attend to, look after) badare a, occuparsi di; (be careful) fare attenzione a, stare attento(-a) a; (object to): **I don't ~ the noise** il rumore non mi dà alcun fastidio; **I don't ~** non m'importa; **do you ~ if ...?** le dispiace se ...?; **it is on my ~** mi preoccupa; **to my ~** secondo me, a mio parere; **to be out of one's ~** essere uscito(-a) di mente; **to keep** or **bear sth in ~** non dimenticare qc; **to make up one's ~** decidersi; **~ you, ...** sì, però va detto che ...; **never ~** non importa, non fa niente; (don't worry) non preoccuparti; **"~ the step"** "attenzione allo scalino"; **mindless** adj idiota

mine¹ [maɪn] pron il (la) mio(-a); (pl) i (le) miei (mie); **that book is ~** quel libro è mio; **yours is red, ~ is green** il tuo è rosso, il mio è verde; **a friend of ~** un mio amico

mine² [maɪn] n miniera; (explosive) mina ▸ vt (coal) estrarre; (ship, beach) minare; **minefield** n (also fig) campo minato; **miner** ['maɪnə'] n minatore m

mineral ['mɪnərəl] adj minerale ▸ n minerale m; **mineral water** n acqua minerale

mingle ['mɪŋɡl] vi **to ~ with** mescolarsi a, mischiarsi con

miniature ['mɪnətʃə'] adj in miniatura ▸ n miniatura

minibar ['mɪnɪbɑ:'] n minibar m inv

minibus ['mɪnɪbʌs] n minibus m inv

minicab ['mɪnɪkæb] n (BRIT) ≈ taxi m inv

minimal ['mɪnɪml] adj minimo(-a)

minimize ['mɪnɪmaɪz] vt minimizzare

minimum ['mɪnɪməm] (pl **minima**) n minimo ▸ adj minimo(-a)

mining ['maɪnɪŋ] n industria mineraria

miniskirt ['mɪnɪskə:t] n minigonna

minister ['mɪnɪstə'] n (BRIT Pol) ministro; (Rel) pastore m

ministry ['mɪnɪstrɪ] n ministero

minor ['maɪnə'] adj minore, di poca importanza; (Mus) minore ▸ n (Law) minorenne m/f

Minorca [mɪ'nɔ:kə] n Minorca

minority [maɪ'nɒrɪtɪ] n minoranza

mint [mɪnt] n (plant) menta; (sweet) pasticca di menta ▸ vt (coins) battere; **the (Royal) M~** (BRIT), **the (US) M~** (US) la Zecca; **in ~ condition** come nuovo(-a) di zecca

minus ['maɪnəs] n (also: **~ sign**) segno meno ▸ prep meno

minute¹ [adj maɪ'njuːt, n 'mɪnɪt] adj minuscolo(-a); (detail) minuzioso(-a) ▸ n minuto; **~s** npl (of meeting) verbale m

miracle ['mɪrəkl] n miracolo

miraculous [mɪ'rækjuləs] adj miracoloso(-a)

mirage ['mɪrɑːʒ] n miraggio

mirror ['mɪrə'] n specchio; (in car) specchietto

misbehave [mɪsbɪ'heɪv] vi comportarsi male

misc. abbr = **miscellaneous**; **miscarriage** ['mɪskærɪdʒ] n (Med) aborto spontaneo; **miscarriage of justice** errore m giudiziario

miscellaneous [mɪsɪ'leɪnɪəs] adj (items) vario(-a); (selection) misto(-a)

mischief ['mɪstʃɪf] n (naughtiness) birichineria; (maliciousness) malizia; **mischievous** adj birichino(-a)

misconception ['mɪskən'sɛpʃən] n idea sbagliata

misconduct [mɪs'kɔndʌkt] n cattiva condotta; **professional ~** reato professionale

miser ['maɪzə'] n avaro

miserable ['mɪzərəbl] adj infelice; (wretched) miserabile; (weather) deprimente; (offer, failure) misero(-a)

misery ['mɪzərɪ] n (unhappiness) tristezza; (wretchedness) miseria

misfortune [mɪs'fɔːtʃən] n sfortuna

misgiving [mɪs'gɪvɪŋ] n apprensione f; **to have ~s about** avere dei dubbi per quanto riguarda

misguided [mɪs'gaɪdɪd] adj sbagliato(-a), poco giudizioso(-a)

mishap ['mɪshæp] n disgrazia

misinterpret [mɪsɪn'tɜːprɪt] vt interpretare male

misjudge [mɪs'dʒʌdʒ] vt giudicare male

mislay [mɪs'leɪ] (irreg) vt smarrire

mislead [mɪs'liːd] (irreg) vt sviare; **misleading** adj ingannevole

misplace [mɪs'pleɪs] vt smarrire

misprint ['mɪsprɪnt] n errore m di stampa

misrepresent [mɪsrɛprɪ'zɛnt] vt travisare

Miss [mɪs] n Signorina

miss [mɪs] vt (fail to get) perdere; (fail

to hit) mancare; (fail to see): **you can't ~ it** non puoi non vederlo; (regret the absence of): **I ~ him** sento la sua mancanza ▶ vi mancare ▶ n (shot) colpo mancato; **we ~ed our train** abbiamo perso il treno ▷ **miss out** (BRIT) vt omettere ▷ **miss out on** vt fus (fun, party) perdersi; (chance, bargain) lasciarsi sfuggire

missile ['mɪsaɪl] n (Mil) missile m; (object thrown) proiettile m

missing ['mɪsɪŋ] adj perso(-a), smarrito(-a); (person) scomparso(-a); (: after disaster, Mil) disperso(-a); (removed) mancante; **to be ~** mancare

mission ['mɪʃən] n missione f; **missionary** n missionario(-a)

misspell [mɪs'spɛl] vt (irreg: like **spell**) sbagliare l'ortografia di

mist [mɪst] n nebbia, foschia ▶ vi (also: **~ over**, **~ up**) annebbiarsi; (: BRIT: windows) appannarsi

mistake [mɪs'teɪk] (irreg: like **take**) n sbaglio, errore m ▶ vt sbagliarsi di; fraintendere; **to make a ~** fare uno sbaglio, sbagliare; **there must be some ~** ci dev'essere un errore; **by ~** per sbaglio; **to ~ for** prendere per; **mistaken** pp of **mistake** ▶ adj (idea etc) sbagliato(-a); **to be mistaken** sbagliarsi

mister ['mɪstə'] (inf) n signore m; see **Mr**

mistletoe ['mɪsltəu] n vischio

mistook [mɪs'tuk] pt of **mistake**

mistress ['mɪstrɪs] n padrona; (lover) amante f; (BRIT Scol) insegnante f

mistrust [mɪs'trʌst] vt diffidare di

misty ['mɪstɪ] adj nebbioso(-a), brumoso(-a)

misunderstand [mɪsʌndə'stænd] (irreg) vt, vi capire male, fraintendere; **misunderstanding** n malinteso, equivoco; **there's been a misunderstanding** c'è stato un malinteso

misunderstood [mɪsʌndə'stud] *pt,
pp of* **misunderstand**

misuse [*n* mɪs'juːs, *vb* mɪs'juːz] *n*
cattivo uso; (*of power*) abuso ▶ *vt* far
cattivo uso di; abusare di

mitt(en) ['mɪt(n)] *n* mezzo guanto;
manopola

mix [mɪks] *vt* mescolare ▶ *vi* (*people*):
to ~ with avere a che fare con ▶ *n*
mescolanza; preparato ▶ **mix up**
vt mescolare; (*confuse*) confondere;
mixed *adj* misto(-a); **mixed grill**
n (BRIT) misto alla griglia; **mixed
salad** *n* insalata mista; **mixed-up** *adj*
(*confused*) confuso(-a); **mixer** *n* (*for
food: electric*) frullatore *m*;
(*: hand*) frullino; (*person*): **he is a good
mixer** è molto socievole; **mixture**
n mescolanza; (*blend: of tobacco etc*)
miscela; (*Med*) sciroppo; **mix-up** *n*
confusione *f*

ml *abbr* (= millilitre(s)) ml

mm *abbr* (= millimetre) mm

moan [məun] *n* gemito ▶ *vi* (*inf:
complain*): **to ~ (about)** lamentarsi (di)

moat [məut] *n* fossato

mob [mɔb] *n* calca ▶ *vt* accalcarsi
intorno a

mobile ['məubaɪl] *adj* mobile ▶ *n*
(*decoration*) mobile *m*; **mobile home** *n*
grande roulotte *f inv* utilizzata come
domicilio; **mobile phone** *n* telefono
portatile, telefonino

mobility [məu'bɪlɪtɪ] *n* mobilità; (*of
applicant*) disponibilità a viaggiare

mobilize ['məubɪlaɪz] *vt* mobilitare
▶ *vi* mobilitarsi

mock [mɔk] *vt* deridere, burlarsi di
▶ *adj* falso(-a); **~s** *npl* (BRIT: Scol: inf)
simulazione *f* degli esami; **mockery**
n derisione *f*; **to make a mockery
of** burlarsi di; (*exam*) rendere una farsa

mod cons ['mɔd'kɔnz] *npl abbr
(BRIT)* = **modern conveniences**; *see*

convenience

mode [məud] *n* modo

model ['mɔdl] *n* modello; (*person:
for fashion*) indossatore(-trice); (*: for
artist*) modello(-a) ▶ *adj* (*small-scale:
railway etc*) in miniatura; (*child,
factory*) modello *inv* ▶ *vt* modellare ▶ *vi*
fare l'indossatore (or l'indossatrice);
to ~ clothes presentare degli abiti

modem ['məudem] *n* modem *m inv*

moderate [*adj* 'mɔdərət, *vb* 'mɔdəreɪt]
adj moderato(-a) ▶ *vi* moderarsi,
placarsi ▶ *vt* moderare

moderation [mɔdə'reɪʃən] *n*
moderazione *f*, misura; **in ~** in
quantità moderata, con moderazione

modern ['mɔdən] *adj* moderno(-a);
mod cons comodità *fpl* moderne;
modernize *vt* modernizzare;
modern languages *npl* lingue *fpl*
moderne

modest ['mɔdɪst] *adj* modesto(-a);
modesty *n* modestia

modification [mɔdɪfɪ'keɪʃən] *n*
modificazione *f*; **to make ~s** fare or
apportare delle modifiche

modify ['mɔdɪfaɪ] *vt* modificare

module ['mɔdjuːl] *n* modulo

mohair ['məuhɛə'] *n* mohair *m*

Mohammed [məu'hæmɪd] *n*
Maometto

moist [mɔɪst] *adj* umido(-a);
moisture ['mɔɪstʃə'] *n* umidità;
(*on glass*) goccioline *fpl* di vapore;
moisturizer ['mɔɪstʃəraɪzə'] *n*
idratante *f*

mold *etc* [məuld] (*US*) *n, vt* = **mould**

mole [məul] *n* (*animal, fig*) talpa;
(*spot*) neo

molecule ['mɔlɪkjuːl] *n* molecola

molest [məu'lest] *vt* molestare

molten ['məultən] *adj* fuso(-a)

mom [mɔm] (*US*) *n* = **mum**

moment ['məumənt] *n* momento,
istante *m*; **at that ~** in quel

momento; **at the ~** al momento, in questo momento; **momentarily** ['məuməntrɪlɪ] adv per un momento; (US: very soon) da un momento all'altro; **momentary** adj momentaneo(-a), passeggero(-a); **momentous** [-'mɛntəs] adj di grande importanza

momentum [məu'mɛntəm] n (Physics) momento; (fig) impeto; **to gather ~** aumentare di velocità

mommy ['mɒmɪ] (US) n = **mummy**

Mon abbr (= Monday) lun.

Monaco ['mɒnəkəu] n Principato di Monaco

monarch ['mɒnək] n monarca m; **monarchy** n monarchia

monastery ['mɒnəstərɪ] n monastero

Monday ['mʌndɪ] n lunedì m inv

monetary ['mʌnɪtərɪ] adj monetario(-a)

money ['mʌnɪ] n denaro, soldi mpl; **I haven't got any ~** non ho soldi; **money belt** n marsupio (per soldi); **money order** n vaglia m inv

mongrel ['mʌŋɡrəl] n (dog) cane m bastardo

monitor ['mɒnɪtə*] n (TV, Comput) monitor m inv ▶ vt controllare

monk [mʌŋk] n monaco

monkey ['mʌŋkɪ] n scimmia

monologue ['mɒnəlɔɡ] n monologo

monopoly [mə'nɒpəlɪ] n monopolio

monosodium glutamate [mɒnə'səudɪəm'ɡluː·təmeɪt] n glutammato di sodio

monotonous [mə'nɒtənəs] adj monotono(-a)

monsoon [mɒn'suːn] n monsone m

monster ['mɒnstə*] n mostro

month [mʌnθ] n mese m; **monthly** adj mensile ▶ adv al mese; ogni mese

monument ['mɒnjumənt] n monumento

mood [muːd] n umore m; **to be in a** good/bad **~** essere di buon/cattivo umore; **moody** adj (variable) capriccioso(-a), lunatico(-a); (sullen) imbronciato(-a)

moon [muːn] n luna; **moonlight** n chiaro di luna

moor [muə*] n brughiera ▶ vt (ship) ormeggiare ▶ vi ormeggiarsi

moose [muːs] n inv alce m

mop [mɒp] n lavapavimenti m inv; (also: ~ **of hair**) zazzera ▶ vt lavare con lo straccio; (face) asciugare ▷ **mop up** vt asciugare con uno straccio

mope [məup] vi fare il broncio

moped ['məupɛd] n (BRIT) ciclomotore m

moral ['mɒrl] adj morale ▶ n morale f; **~s** (principles) moralità

morale [mɒ'rɑːl] n morale m

morality [mə'rælɪtɪ] n moralità

morbid ['mɔːbɪd] adj morboso(-a)

more
[mɔː*] adj

1 (greater in number etc) più; **more people/letters than we expected** più persone/lettere di quante ne aspettavamo; **I have more wine/ money than you** ho più vino/soldi di te; **I have more wine than beer** ho più vino che birra

2 (additional) altro(-a), ancora; **do you want (some) more tea?** vuole dell'altro tè?, vuole ancora del tè?; **I have no** or **I don't have any more money** non ho più soldi

▶ pron

1 (greater amount) più; **more than 10** più di 10; **it cost more than we expected** ha costato più di quanto ci aspettavamo

2 (further or additional amount) ancora; **is there any more?** ce n'è ancora?; **there's no more** non ce n'è più; **a little more** ancora un po'; **many/much more** molti(-e)/molto(-a) di più

▶ *adv* **more dangerous/easily (than)** più pericoloso/facilmente (di); **more and more** sempre di più; **more and more difficult** sempre più difficile; **more or less** più o meno; **more than ever** più che mai

moreover [mɔːˈrəʊvər] *adv* inoltre, di più

morgue [mɔːg] *n* obitorio

morning [ˈmɔːnɪŋ] *n* mattina, mattino; *(duration)* mattinata ▶ *cpd* del mattino; **in the ~** la mattina; **7 o'clock in the ~** le 7 di or della mattina; **morning sickness** *n* nausee *fpl* mattutine

Moroccan [məˈrɔkən] *adj, n* maroccino(-a)

Morocco [məˈrɔkəʊ] *n* Marocco

moron [ˈmɔːrɔn] *(inf)* *n* deficiente *m/f*

morphine [ˈmɔːfiːn] *n* morfina

morris dancing *n* vedi nota nel riquadro

● **morris dancing**
● Il **morris dancing** è una
● danza folcloristica inglese
● tradizionale riservata agli
● uomini. Vestiti di bianco e con dei
● campanelli attaccati alle caviglie,
● i ballerini eseguono una danza
● tenendo in mano dei fazzoletti
● bianchi e lunghi bastoni. Questa
● danza è molto popolare nelle feste
● paesane.

Morse [mɔːs] *n (also:* **~ code**) alfabeto Morse

mortal [ˈmɔːtl] *adj* mortale ▶ *n* mortale *m*

mortar [ˈmɔːtər] *n (Constr)* malta; *(dish)* mortaio

mortgage [ˈmɔːgɪdʒ] *n* ipoteca; *(loan)* prestito ipotecario ▶ *vt* ipotecare

mortician [mɔːˈtɪʃən] *(US)* *n* impresario di pompe funebri

mortified [ˈmɔːtɪfaɪd] *adj* umiliato(-a)

mortuary [ˈmɔːtjʊərɪ] *n* camera

mortuaria; obitorio

mosaic [məʊˈzeɪɪk] *n* mosaico

Moscow [ˈmɔskəʊ] *n* Mosca

Moslem [ˈmɔzləm] *adj, n* = **Muslim**

mosque [mɔsk] *n* moschea

mosquito [mɔsˈkiːtəʊ] *(pl* **mosquitoes)** *n* zanzara

moss [mɔs] *n* muschio

most [məʊst] *adj (almost all)* la maggior parte di; *(largest, greatest)*: **who has (the) ~ money?** chi ha più soldi di tutti? ► la maggior parte *di* ▶ *adv* più; *(work, sleep etc)* di più; *(very)* molto, estremamente; **the ~** *(also:* **+ adjective)** il(-la) più; **~ of** la maggior parte di; **~ of them** quasi tutti; **I saw (the) ~** ho visto più io; **at the (very) ~** al massimo; **to make the ~ of** trarre il massimo vantaggio da; **a ~ interesting book** un libro estremamente interessante; **mostly** *adv* per lo più

MOT *(BRIT)* *n abbr* = **Ministry of Transport; the ~ (test)** revisione annuale obbligatoria degli autoveicoli

motel [məʊˈtel] *n* motel *m inv*

moth [mɔθ] *n* farfalla notturna; tarma

mother [ˈmʌðər] *n* madre *f* ▶ *vt (care for)* fare da madre a; **motherhood** *n* maternità; **mother-in-law** *n* suocera; **mother-of-pearl** [ˌmʌðərəvˈpəːl] *n* madreperla; **Mother's Day** *n* la festa della mamma; **mother-to-be** [ˌmʌðətəˈbiː] *n* futura mamma; **mother tongue** *n* madrelingua

motif [məʊˈtiːf] *n* motivo

motion [ˈməʊʃən] *n* movimento, moto; *(gesture)* gesto; *(at meeting)* mozione *f* ▶ *vt, vi* **to ~ (to) sb to do** fare cenno a qn di fare; **motionless** *adj* immobile; **motion picture** *n* film *m inv*

motivate [ˈməʊtɪveɪt] *vt (act, decision)* dare origine a, motivare; *(person)* spingere

motivation [məuti'veiʃən] n
motivazione f

motive ['məutiv] n motivo

motor ['məutə'] n motore m;
(BRIT: inf: vehicle) macchina ▶ cpd
automobilistico(-a); **motorbike** n
moto f inv; **motorboat** n motoscafo;
motorcar (BRIT) n automobile
f; **motorcycle** n motocicletta;
motorcyclist n motociclista
m/f; **motoring** (BRIT) n turismo
automobilistico; **motorist** n
automobilista m/f; **motor racing**
(BRIT) n corse fpl automobilistiche;
motorway (BRIT) n autostrada

motto ['mɔtəu] (pl **mottoes**) n motto

mould [məuld] (US **mold**) n forma,
stampo; (mildew) muffa ▶ vt
formare; (fig) foggiare; **mouldy** adj
ammuffito(-a); (smell) di muffa

mound [maund] n rialzo, collinetta;
(heap) mucchio

mount [maunt] n (Geo) monte m
▶ vt montare; (horse) montare a ▶ vi
(increase) aumentare ▶ **mount up** vi
(build up) accumularsi

mountain ['mauntin] n montagna
▶ cpd di montagna; **mountain
bike** n mountain bike f inv;
mountaineer [-'niə'] n alpinista
m/f; **mountaineering** [-'niərin]
n alpinismo; **mountainous** adj
montagnoso(-a); **mountain range** n
catena montuosa

mourn [mɔːn] vt piangere, lamentare
▶ vi **to ~ (for sb)** piangere (la morte
di qn); **mourner** n parente m/f or
amico(-a) del defunto; **mourning** n
lutto; **in mourning** in lutto

mouse [maus] (pl **mice**) n topo;
(Comput) mouse m inv; **mouse mat**,
mouse pad n (Comput) tappetino
del mouse

moussaka [mu'sɑːkə] n moussaka

mousse [muːs] n mousse f inv

moustache [məs'tɑːʃ] (US **mustache**)
n baffi mpl

mouth [mauθ, pl mauðz] n bocca; (of
river) bocca, foce f; (opening) orifizio;
mouthful n boccata; **mouth organ**
n armonica; **mouthpiece** n (Mus)
imboccatura, bocchino; (spokesman)
portavoce m/f inv; **mouthwash** n
collutorio

move [muːv] n (movement)
movimento; (in game) mossa; (:
turn to play) turno; (change: of house)
trasloco; (: of job) cambiamento
▶ vt muovere; (change position of)
spostare; (emotionally) commuovere;
(Pol: resolution etc) proporre ▶ vi (gen)
muoversi, spostarsi; (also: ~ **house**)
cambiare casa, traslocare; **to get a
~ on** affrettarsi, sbrigarsi; **can you
~ your car, please?** può spostare la
macchina, per favore?; **to ~ sb to do
sth** indurre or spingere qn a fare qc;
to ~ towards andare verso ▶ **move
back** vi (return) ritornare ▶ **move in**
vi (to a house) entrare (in una nuova
casa); (police etc) intervenire ▶ **move
off** vi partire ▶ **move on** vi (riprendere
la strada ▶ **move out** vi (of house)
sgombrare ▶ **move over** vi spostarsi
▶ **move up** vi avanzare; **movement**
['muːvmənt] n (gen) movimento;
(gesture) gesto; (of stars, water,
physical) moto

movie ['muːvi] n film m inv; **the ~s**
il cinema; **movie theater** (US) n
cinema m inv

moving ['muːviŋ] adj mobile; (causing
emotion) commovente

mow [məu] (pt mowed, pp mowed
or mown) vt (grass) tagliare; (corn)
mietere; **mower** n (also: **lawnmower**)
tagliaerba m inv

Mozambique [məuzəm'biːk] n
Mozambico

MP n abbr = Member of Parliament

MP3 n abbr M3; **MP3 player** n lettore m MP3

mpg n abbr = **miles per gallon** (30 mpg = 9.4 l. per 100 km)

m.p.h. n abbr = **miles per hour** (60 m.p.h = 96 km/h)

Mr ['mɪstə*] (US **Mr.**) n Mr X Signor X, Sig. X

Mrs ['mɪsɪz] (US **Mrs.**) n Mrs X Signora X, Sig.ra X

Ms [mɪz] (US **Ms.**) n = Miss or Mrs; Ms X ≈ Signora X, ≈ Sig.ra X

● **Ms**
● In inglese si usa Ms al posto di "Mrs"
● (Signora) o "Miss" (Signorina) per
● evitare la distinzione tradizionale
● tra le donne sposate e quelle nubili.

MSP n abbr = **Member of the Scottish Parliament**

Mt abbr (Geo: = mount) M

○ **much**
[mʌtʃ] adj, pron molto(-a); **he's done so much work** ha lavorato così tanto; **I have as much money as you** ho tanti soldi quanti ne hai tu; **how much is it?** quant'è?; **it costs too much** costa troppo; **as much as you want** quanto vuoi
▶ adv

1 (greatly) molto, tanto; **thank you very much** molte grazie; **he's very much the gentleman** è il vero gentiluomo; **I read as much as I can** leggo quanto posso; **as much as you** tanto quanto te

2 (by far) molto; **it's much the biggest company in Europe** è di gran lunga la più grossa società in Europa

3 (almost) grossomodo, praticamente; **they're much the same** sono praticamente uguali

muck [mʌk] n (dirt) sporcizia ▶ **muck up** (inf) vt (ruin) rovinare; **mucky** adj (dirty) sporco(-a), lordo(-a)

mucus ['mju:kəs] n muco

mud [mʌd] n fango

muddle ['mʌdl] n confusione f, disordine m; pasticcio m ▶ vt (also: ~ **up**) confondere

muddy ['mʌdɪ] adj fangoso(-a)

mudguard ['mʌdgɑ:d] n parafango

muesli ['mju:zlɪ] n muesli m

muffin ['mʌfɪn] n specie di pasticcino soffice da tè

muffled ['mʌfld] adj smorzato(-a), attutito(-a)

muffler ['mʌflə*] (US) n (Aut) marmitta f; (: on motorbike) silenziatore m

mug [mʌg] n (cup) tazzone m; (for beer) boccale m; (inf: face) muso; (: fool) scemo(-a) ▶ vt (assault) assalire; **mugger** ['mʌgə*] n aggressore m; **mugging** n assalto

muggy ['mʌgɪ] adj afoso(-a)

mule [mju:l] n mulo

multicoloured ['mʌltɪkʌləd] (US **multicolored**) adj multicolore, variopinto(-a)

multimedia ['mʌltɪ'mi:dɪə] adj multimedia inv

multinational [mʌltɪ'næʃənl] adj, n multinazionale (f)

multiple ['mʌltɪpl] adj multiplo(-a), molteplice ▶ n multiplo; **multiple choice (test)** n esercizi mpl a scelta multipla; **multiple sclerosis** [-sklɪ'rəusɪs] n sclerosi f a placche

multiplex cinema ['mʌltɪpleks-] n cinema m inv multisala inv

multiplication [mʌltɪplɪ'keɪʃən] n moltiplicazione f

multiply ['mʌltɪplaɪ] vt moltiplicare ▶ vi moltiplicarsi

multistorey ['mʌltɪ'stɔ:rɪ] (BRIT) (building, car park) a più piani

mum [mʌm] (BRIT: inf) n mamma ▶ adj **to keep ~** non aprire bocca

mumble ['mʌmbl] vt, vi borbottare

mummy ['mʌmɪ] n (BRIT: mother)

mamma; (embalmed) mummia

mumps [mʌmps] n orecchioni mpl

munch [mʌntʃ] vt, vi sgranocchiare

municipal [mjuːˈnɪsɪpl] adj municipale

mural [ˈmjuərl] n dipinto murale

murder [ˈmɜːdəʳ] n assassinio, omicidio ▸ vt assassinare; **murderer** n omicida m, assassino

murky [ˈmɜːkɪ] adj tenebroso(-a)

murmur [ˈmɜːməʳ] n mormorio ▸ vt, vi mormorare

muscle [ˈmʌsl] n muscolo; (fig) forza; **muscular** [ˈmʌskjuləʳ] adj muscolare; (person, arm) muscoloso(-a)

museum [mjuːˈzɪəm] n museo

mushroom [ˈmʌʃrum] n fungo ▸ vi crescere in fretta

music [ˈmjuːzɪk] n musica; **musical** adj musicale; (person) portato(-a) per la musica ▸ n (show) commedia musicale; **musical instrument** n strumento musicale; **musician** [-ˈzɪʃən] n musicista m/f

Muslim [ˈmʌzlɪm] adj, n musulmano(-a)

muslin [ˈmʌzlɪn] n mussola

mussel [ˈmʌsl] n cozza

must [mʌst] aux vb (obligation): **I ~ do it** devo farlo; (probability): **he ~ be there by now** dovrebbe essere arrivato ormai; **I ~ have made a mistake** devo essermi sbagliato ▸ n **it's a ~** è d'obbligo

mustache [ˈmʌstæʃ] (US) n = **moustache**

mustard [ˈmʌstəd] n senape f, mostarda

mustn't [ˈmʌsnt] = **must not**

mute [mjuːt] adj, n muto(-a)

mutilate [ˈmjuːtɪleɪt] vt mutilare

mutiny [ˈmjuːtɪnɪ] n ammutinamento

mutter [ˈmʌtəʳ] vt, vi borbottare, brontolare

mutton [ˈmʌtn] n carne f di montone

mutual [ˈmjuːtʃuəl] adj mutuo(-a), reciproco(-a)

muzzle [ˈmʌzl] n muso; (protective device) museruola; (of gun) bocca ▸ vt mettere la museruola a

my [maɪ] adj il (la) mio(-a); (pl) i (le) miei (mie); **my house** la mia casa; **my books** i miei libri; **my brother** mio fratello; **I've washed my hair/cut my finger** mi sono lavato i capelli/ tagliato il dito

myself [maɪˈsɛlf] pron (reflexive) mi; (emphatic) io stesso(-a); (after prep) me; see also **oneself**

mysterious [mɪsˈtɪərɪəs] adj misterioso(-a)

mystery [ˈmɪstərɪ] n mistero

mystical [ˈmɪstɪkəl] adj mistico(-a)

mystify [ˈmɪstɪfaɪ] vt mistificare; (puzzle) confondere

myth [mɪθ] n mito; **mythology** [mɪˈθɔlədʒɪ] n mitologia

n

n/a abbr = **not applicable**

nag [næg] vt tormentare ▸ vi brontolare in continuazione

nail [neɪl] n (human) unghia; (metal) chiodo ▸ vt inchiodare; **to ~ sb down to (doing) sth** costringere qn a (fare) qc; **nailbrush** n spazzolino da or per unghie; **nailfile** n lima da or per unghie; **nail polish** n smalto da or per unghie; **nail polish remover** n acetone m, solvente m; **nail scissors** npl forbici fpl da or per unghie; **nail varnish** (BRIT) n = **nail polish**

naïve [naɪˈiːv] adj ingenuo(-a)

naked [ˈneɪkɪd] adj nudo(-a)

name [neɪm] n nome m; (reputation) nome, reputazione f ▶ vt (baby etc) chiamare; (plant, illness) nominare; (person, object) identificare; (price, date) fissare; **what's your ~?** come si chiama?; **by ~** di nome; **she knows them all by ~** li conosce tutti per nome; **namely** adv cioè

nanny [ˈnænɪ] n bambinaia

nap [næp] n (sleep) pisolino; (of cloth) peluria; **to be caught ~ping** essere preso alla sprovvista

napkin [ˈnæpkɪn] n (also: **table ~**) tovagliolo

nappy [ˈnæpɪ] (BRIT) n pannolino

narcotics [nɑːˈkɒtɪks] npl (drugs) narcotici, stupefacenti mpl

narrative [ˈnærətɪv] n narrativa

narrator [nəˈreɪtə*] n narratore(-trice)

narrow [ˈnærəʊ] adj stretto(-a); (fig) limitato(-a), ristretto(-a) ▶ vi restringersi; **to have a ~ escape** farcela per un pelo ▶ **narrow down** vt (search, investigation, possibilities) restringere; (list) ridurre; **narrowly** adv per un pelo; (time) per poco; **narrow-minded** adj meschino(-a)

nasal [ˈneɪzl] adj nasale

nasty [ˈnɑːstɪ] adj (person, remark: unpleasant) cattivo(-a); (: rude) villano(-a); (smell, wound, situation) brutto(-a)

nation [ˈneɪʃən] n nazione f

national [ˈnæʃənl] adj nazionale ▶ n cittadino(-a); **national anthem** n inno nazionale; **national dress** n costume m nazionale; **National Health Service** (BRIT) n servizio

nazionale di assistenza sanitaria, ≈ S.S.N. m; **National Insurance** (BRIT) n ≈ Previdenza Sociale; **nationalist** adj, n nazionalista (m/f); **nationality** [-ˈnælɪtɪ] n nazionalità f inv; **nationalize** vt nazionalizzare; **national park** n parco nazionale; **National Trust** n sovrintendenza ai beni culturali e ambientali

● **National Trust**
● Fondato nel 1895, il **National Trust**
● è un'organizzazione che si occupa
● della tutela e della salvaguardia
● di luoghi di interesse storico o
● ambientale nel Regno Unito.

nationwide [ˈneɪʃənwaɪd] adj diffuso(-a) in tutto il paese ▶ adv in tutto il paese

native [ˈneɪtɪv] n abitante m/f del paese ▶ adj indigeno(-a); (country) natio(-a); (ability) innato(-a); **a ~ of Russia** un nativo della Russia; **a ~ speaker of French** una persona di madrelingua francese; **Native American** n discendente di tribù dell'America settentrionale

NATO [ˈneɪtəʊ] n abbr (= North Atlantic Treaty Organization) N.A.T.O. f

natural [ˈnætʃrəl] adj naturale; (ability) innato(-a); (manner) semplice; **natural gas** n gas m metano; **natural history** n storia naturale; **naturally** adv naturalmente; (by nature: gifted) di natura; **natural resources** npl risorse fpl naturali

nature [ˈneɪtʃə*] n natura; (character) natura, indole f; **by ~** di natura; **nature reserve** n (BRIT) parco naturale

naughty [ˈnɔːtɪ] adj (child) birichino(-a), cattivello(-a); (story, film) spinto(-a)

nausea [ˈnɔːsɪə] n (Med) nausea; (fig: disgust) schifo

naval [ˈneɪvl] adj navale

navel ['neɪvl] n ombelico

navigate ['nævɪɡeɪt] vt percorrere navigando ▶ vi navigare; (Aut) fare da navigatore; **navigation** [-'ɡeɪʃən] n navigazione f

navy ['neɪvɪ] n marina

Nazi ['nɑːtsɪ] n nazista m/f

NB abbr (= nota bene) N.B.

near [nɪə] adj vicino(-a); (relation) prossimo(-a) ▶ adv vicino ▶ prep (also: ~ to) vicino a, presso; (: time) verso ▶ vt avvicinarsi a; **nearby** [nɪə'baɪ] adj vicino(-a) ▶ adv vicino; **is there a bank nearby?** c'è una banca qui vicino?; **nearly** adv quasi; **I nearly fell** per poco non sono caduto; **near-sighted** [nɪə'saɪtɪd] adj miope

neat [niːt] adj (person, room) ordinato(-a); (work) pulito(-a); (solution, plan) ben indovinato(-a), azzeccato(-a); (spirits) liscio(-a); **neatly** adv con ordine; (skilfully) abilmente

necessarily ['nesɪsrɪlɪ] adv necessariamente

necessary ['nesɪsrɪ] adj necessario(-a)

necessity [nɪ'sesɪtɪ] n necessità f inv

neck [nek] n collo; (of garment) colletto ▶ vi (inf) pomiciare, sbaciucchiarsi; **~ and ~** testa a testa; **necklace** ['neklɪs] n collana; **necktie** ['nektaɪ] n cravatta

nectarine ['nektərɪn] n nocepesca

need [niːd] n bisogno ▶ vt aver bisogno di; **do you ~ anything?** ha bisogno di qualcosa?; **to ~ to do** dover fare; aver bisogno di fare; **you don't ~ to go** non devi andare, non c'è bisogno che tu vada

needle ['niːdl] n ago; (on record player) puntina ▶ vt punzecchiare

needless ['niːdlɪs] adj inutile

needlework ['niːdlwɜːk] n cucito

needn't ['niːdnt] = **need not**

needy ['niːdɪ] adj bisognoso(-a)

negative ['nɛɡətɪv] n (Ling) negazione

f; (Phot) negativo ▶ adj negativo(-a)

neglect [nɪ'ɡlekt] vt trascurare ▶ n (of person, duty) negligenza; (of child, house etc) scarsa cura; **state of ~** stato di abbandono

negotiate [nɪ'ɡəʊʃɪeɪt] vi **to ~ (with)** negoziare (con) ▶ vt (Comm) negoziare; (obstacle) superare; **negotiations** [nɪɡəʊʃɪ'eɪʃənz] pl n trattative fpl, negoziati mpl

negotiator [nɪ'ɡəʊʃɪeɪtə] n negoziatore(-trice)

neighbour ['neɪbə] (US **neighbor**) n vicino(-a); **neighbourhood** n vicinato; **neighbouring** adj vicino(-a)

neither ['naɪðə] adj, pron nè l'uno(-a) nè l'altro(-a), nessuno(-a) dei (delle) due ▶ conj neanche, nemmeno, neppure ▶ adv **~ good nor bad** nè buono nè cattivo; **I didn't move and ~ did Claude** io non mi mossi e nemmeno Claude; **..., ~ do I refuse ...**, ma non ho nemmeno rifiutato

neon ['niːɔn] n neon m

Nepal [nɪ'pɔːl] n Nepal m

nephew ['nevjuː] n nipote m

nerve [nɜːv] n nervo; (courage) coraggio; (impudence) faccia tosta; **~s** (nervousness) nervoso; **a fit of ~s** una crisi di nervi

nervous ['nɜːvəs] adj nervoso(-a); (anxious) agitato(-a), in apprensione; **nervous breakdown** n esaurimento nervoso

nest [nest] n nido ▶ vi fare il nido, nidificare

net [net] n rete f ▶ adj netto(-a) ▶ vt (fish etc) prendere con la rete; (profit) ricavare un utile netto di; **the N~** (Internet) Internet f; **netball** n specie di pallacanestro

Netherlands ['neðələndz] npl **the ~** i Paesi Bassi

nett [net] adj = **net**

nettle ['netl] n ortica

network ['nɛtwəːk] n rete f

neurotic [njuə'rɔtɪk] adj, n nevrotico(-a)

neuter ['njuːtə'] adj neutro(-a) ▶ vt (cat etc) castrare

neutral ['njuːtrəl] adj neutro(-a); (person, nation) neutrale ▶ n (Aut): **in ~** in folle

never ['nɛvə'] adv (non...) mai; **I've ~ been to Spain** non sono mai stato in Spagna; **~ again** mai più; **I'll ~ go there again** non ci vado più; **~ in my life** mai in vita mia; see also **mind**; **never-ending** adj interminabile; **nevertheless** [nɛvəðə'lɛs] adv tuttavia, ciò nonostante, ciò nondimeno

new [njuː] adj nuovo(-a); (brand new) nuovo(-a) di zecca; **New Age** n New Age f inv; **newborn** adj neonato(-a); **newcomer** ['njuːkʌmə'] n nuovo(-a) venuto(-a); **newly** adv di recente

news [njuːz] n notizie fpl; (Radio) giornale m radio; (TV) telegiornale m; **a piece of ~** una notizia; **news agency** n agenzia di stampa; **newsagent** (BRIT) n giornalaio; **newscaster** n (Radio, TV) annunciatore(-trice); **news dealer** (US) n = **newsagent**; **newsletter** n bollettino; **newspaper** n giornale m; **newsreader** n = **newscaster**

newt [njuːt] n tritone m

New Year n Anno Nuovo; **New Year's Day** n il Capodanno; **New Year's Eve** n la vigilia di Capodanno

New York [-'jɔːk] n New York f

New Zealand [-'ziːlənd] n Nuova Zelanda; **New Zealander** n neozelandese m/f

next [nɛkst] adj prossimo(-a) ▶ adv accanto; (in time) dopo; **the ~ day** il giorno dopo, l'indomani; **~ time** la prossima volta; **~ year** l'anno prossimo; **when do we meet ~?**

quando ci rincontriamo?; **~ to** accanto a; **~ to nothing** quasi niente; **~ please!** (avanti) il prossimo; **next door** adv, adj accanto inv; **next-of-kin** n parente m/f prossimo(-a)

NHS n abbr = **National Health Service**

nibble ['nɪbl] vt mordicchiare

nice [naɪs] adj (holiday, trip) piacevole; (flat, picture) bello(-a); (person) simpatico(-a), gentile; **nicely** adv bene

niche [niːʃ] n (Archit) nicchia

nick [nɪk] n taglietto; tacca ▶ vt (inf) rubare; **in the ~ of time** appena in tempo

nickel ['nɪkl] n nichel m; (US) moneta da cinque centesimi di dollaro

nickname ['nɪkneɪm] n soprannome m

nicotine ['nɪkətiːn] n nicotina

niece [niːs] n nipote f

Nigeria [naɪ'dʒɪərɪə] n Nigeria

night [naɪt] n notte f; (evening) sera; **at ~** la sera; **by ~** di notte; **the ~ before last** ieri l'altro notte (or sera); **night club** n locale m notturno; **nightdress** n camicia da notte; **nightfall** n = **nightdress**; **nightlife** ['naɪtlaɪf] n vita notturna; **nightly** ['naɪtlɪ] adj di ogni notte or sera; (by night) notturno(-a) ▶ adv ogni notte or sera; **nightmare** ['naɪtmɛə'] n incubo

night: **night school** n scuola serale; **night shift** n turno di notte; **nighttime** n notte f

nil [nɪl] n nulla m; (BRIT Sport) zero

nine [naɪn] num nove; **nineteen** num diciannove; **nineteenth** [naɪn'tiːnθ] num diciannovesimo(-a); **ninetieth** ['naɪntɪɪθ] num novantesimo(-a); **ninety** num novanta; **ninth** [naɪnθ] num nono(-a)

nip [nɪp] vt pizzicare; (bite) mordere

nipple ['nɪpl] n (Anat) capezzolo

nitrogen ['naɪtrədʒən] n azoto

no
[nəʊ] (pl **noes**) adv (opposite of "yes") no; **are you coming?** — **no (I'm not)** viene? — no (non vengo); **would you like some more?** — **no thank you** ne vuole ancora un po'? — no, grazie ▶ adj (not any) nessuno(-a); **I have no money/time/books** non ho soldi/tempo/libri; **no student would have done it** nessuno studente lo avrebbe fatto; **"no parking"** "divieto di sosta"; **"no smoking"** "vietato fumare" ▶ n no m inv

nobility [nəʊˈbɪlɪtɪ] n nobiltà
noble [ˈnəʊbl] adj nobile
nobody [ˈnəʊbədɪ] pron nessuno
nod [nɒd] vi accennare col capo, fare un cenno; (in agreement) annuire con un cenno del capo; (sleep) sonnecchiare ▶ vt to ~ **one's head** fare di sì col capo ▶ n cenno ▶ **nod off** vi assopirsi
noise [nɔɪz] n rumore m; (din, racket) chiasso; **I can't sleep for the ~** non riesco a dormire a causa del rumore; **noisy** adj (street, car) rumoroso(-a); (person) chiassoso(-a)
nominal [ˈnɒmɪnl] adj nominale; (rent) simbolico(-a)
nominate [ˈnɒmɪneɪt] vt (propose) proporre come candidato; (elect) nominare; **nomination** [nɒmɪˈneɪʃən] n nomina; candidatura; **nominee** [nɒmɪˈniː] n persona nominata, candidato(-a)
none [nʌn] pron (not one thing) niente; (not one person) nessuno(-a); ~ **of you** nessuno(-a) di voi; **I've ~ left** non ne ho più; **he's ~ the worse for it** non ne ha risentito
nonetheless [nʌnðəˈlɛs] adv nondimeno
non-fiction [nɒnˈfɪkʃən] n saggistica
nonsense [ˈnɒnsəns] n sciocchezze fpl
non: **non-smoker** n non

fumatore(-trice); **non-smoking** adj (person) che non fuma; (area, section) per non fumatori; **non-stick** adj antiaderente, antiadesivo(-a)
noodles [ˈnuːdlz] npl taglierini mpl
noon [nuːn] n mezzogiorno
no-one [ˈnəʊwʌn] pron = **nobody**
nor [nɔːʳ] conj = **neither** ▶ adv see **neither**
norm [nɔːm] n norma
normal [ˈnɔːml] adj normale; **normally** adv normalmente
north [nɔːθ] n nord m, settentrione m ▶ adj inv, del nord, settentrionale ▶ adv verso nord; **North America** n America del Nord; **North American** adj, n nordamericano(-a); **northbound** [ˈnɔːθbaʊnd] adj (traffic) diretto(-a) a nord; (carriageway) nord inv; **north-east** n nord-est m; **northeastern** [ˌnɔːθˈiːstən] adj nordorientale; **northern** [ˈnɔːðən] adj del nord, settentrionale; **Northern Ireland** n Irlanda del Nord; **North Korea** n Corea del Nord; **North Pole** n Polo Nord; **North Sea** n Mare m del Nord; **northwest** n nord-ovest m; **northwestern** adj nordoccidentale
Norway [ˈnɔːweɪ] n Norvegia; **Norwegian** [nɔːˈwiːdʒən] adj norvegese ▶ n norvegese m/f; (Ling) norvegese m
nose [nəʊz] n naso; (of animal) muso ▶ vi to ~ **about** aggirarsi; **nosebleed** n emorragia nasale; **nosey** (inf) adj = **nosy**
nostalgia [nɒsˈtældʒɪə] n nostalgia
nostalgic [nɒsˈtældʒɪk] adj nostalgico(-a)
nostril [ˈnɒstrɪl] n narice f; (of horse) frogia
nosy [ˈnəʊzɪ] (inf) adj curioso(-a)
not [nɒt] adv non; **he is ~ or isn't here** non è qui, non c'è; **you must ~ or mustn't do that** non devi fare

quello; **it's too late, isn't it** *or* **is it ~?**
è troppo tardi, vero?; **~ that I don't
like him** non che (lui) non mi piaccia;
~ yet/now non ancora/ora; *see also*
all; **only**

notable ['nəʊtəbl] *adj* notevole;
 notably ['nəʊtəblɪ] *adv* (markedly)
notevolmente; (particularly) in
particolare

notch [nɒtʃ] *n* tacca; (in saw) dente *m*

note [nəʊt] *n* nota; (letter, banknote)
biglietto ▶ *vt* (also: **~ down**) prendere
nota di; **to take ~s** prendere appunti;
 notebook *n* taccuino; **noted**
['nəʊtɪd] *adj* celebre; **notepad** *n*
bloc-notes *m inv*; **notepaper** *n* carta
da lettere

nothing ['nʌθɪŋ] *n* nulla *m*, niente *m*;
(zero) zero; **he does ~** non fa niente;
 ~ new/much *etc* niente di nuovo/
speciale *etc*; **for ~** per niente

notice ['nəʊtɪs] *n* avviso; (of leaving)
preavviso ▶ *vt* notare, accorgersi
di; **to take ~ of** fare attenzione a; **to
bring sth to sb's ~** far notare qc a qn;
at short ~ con un breve preavviso;
until further ~ fino a nuovo avviso;
to hand in one's ~ licenziarsi;
 noticeable *adj* evidente

notify ['nəʊtɪfaɪ] *vt* **to ~ sth to sb** far
sapere qc a qn; **to ~ sb of sth** avvisare
qn di qc

notion ['nəʊʃən] *n* idea; (concept)
nozione *f*; **~s** *npl* (US: haberdashery)
merceria

notorious [nəʊ'tɔːrɪəs] *adj*
famigerato(-a)

notwithstanding [nɒtwɪθ'stændɪŋ]
adv nondimeno ▶ *prep* nonostante,
malgrado

nought [nɔːt] *n* zero

noun [naʊn] *n* nome *m*, sostantivo

nourish ['nʌrɪʃ] *vt* nutrire;
 nourishment *n* nutrimento

Nov. *abbr* (= November) nov.

novel ['nɒvl] *n* romanzo ▶ *adj*
nuovo(-a); **novelist** *n* romanziere(-a);
 novelty *n* novità *f inv*

November [nəʊ'vɛmbə*] *n*
novembre *m*

novice ['nɒvɪs] *n* principiante *m/f*;
(Rel) novizio(-a)

now [naʊ] *adv* ora, adesso ▶ *conj* **~
(that)** adesso che, ora che; **by ~**
ormai; **just ~** proprio ora; **right ~**
subito, immediatamente; **~ and
then, ~ and again** ogni tanto;
from ~ on da ora in poi; **nowadays**
['naʊədeɪz] *adv* oggidì

nowhere ['nəʊwɛə*] *adv* in nessun
luogo, da nessuna parte

nozzle ['nɒzl] *n* (of hose etc) boccaglio;
(of fire extinguisher) lancia

nr *abbr* (BRIT) = **near**

nuclear ['njuːklɪə*] *adj* nucleare

nucleus ['njuːklɪəs] (*pl* **nuclei**) *n*
nucleo

nude [njuːd] *adj* nudo(-a) ▶ *n* (Art)
nudo; **in the ~** tutto(-a) nudo(-a)

nudge [nʌdʒ] *vt* dare una gomitata a

nudist ['njuːdɪst] *n* nudista *m/f*

nudity ['njuːdɪtɪ] *n* nudità

nuisance ['njuːsns] *n* **it's a ~** è una
seccatura; **he's a ~** è uno scocciatore

numb [nʌm] *adj* **~ (with)**
intorpidito(-a) (da); (with fear)
impietrito(-a) (da); **~ with cold**
intirizzito(-a) (dal freddo)

number ['nʌmbə*] *n* numero ▶ *vt*
numerare; (include) contare; **a ~
of** un certo numero di; **to be ~ed
among** venire annoverato(-a) tra;
they were 10 in ~ erano in tutto 10;
 number plate (BRIT) *n* (Aut) targa;
 Number Ten (BRIT: = 10 Downing
Street) residenza del Primo Ministro del
Regno Unito

numerical [njuː'mɛrɪkl] *adj*
numerico(-a)

numerous ['njuːmərəs] *adj*

numeroso(-a)
nun [nʌn] n suora, monaca
nurse [nəːs] n infermiere(-a); (also:
~maid) bambinaia ▶ vt (patient, cold)
curare; (baby: BRIT) cullare; (: US)
allattare, dare il latte a
nursery ['nəːsərɪ] n (room) camera dei
bambini; (institution) asilo; (for plants)
vivaio; **nursery rhyme** n filastrocca;
nursery school n scuola materna;
nursery slope (BRIT) n (Ski) pista per
principianti
nursing ['nəːsɪŋ] n (profession)
professione f di infermiere (or di
infermiera); (care) cura; **nursing
home** n casa di cura
nurture ['nəːtʃə] vt allevare; nutrire
nut [nʌt] n (of metal) dado; (fruit) noce f
nutmeg ['nʌtmɛg] n noce f moscata
nutrient ['njuːtrɪənt] adj nutriente ▶ n
sostanza nutritiva
nutrition [njuːtrɪʃən] n nutrizione f
nutritious [njuːtrɪʃəs] adj nutriente
nuts [nʌts] (inf) adj matto(-a)
NVQ n abbr (BRIT) = National
Vocational Qualification
nylon ['naɪlɔn] n nailon m ▶ adj di
nailon

oak [əuk] n quercia ▶ adj di quercia
O.A.P. (BRIT) n, abbr = **old age
pensioner**
oar [ɔːʳ] n remo
oasis [əuˈeɪsɪs] (pl **oases**) n oasi f inv
oath [əuθ] n giuramento; (swear word)
bestemmia
oatmeal ['əutmiːl] n farina d'avena
oats [əuts] npl avena
obedience [əˈbiːdɪəns] n ubbidienza
obedient [əˈbiːdɪənt] adj ubbidiente
obese [əuˈbiːs] adj obeso(-a)
obesity [əuˈbiːsɪtɪ] n obesità
obey [əˈbeɪ] vt ubbidire a; (instructions,
regulations) osservare
obituary [əˈbɪtjuərɪ] n necrologia
object [n ˈɔbdʒɪkt, vb abˈdʒɛkt] n
oggetto; (purpose) scopo, intento;
(Ling) complemento oggetto ▶ vi to ~
to (attitude) disapprovare; (proposal)
protestare contro, sollevare delle
obiezioni contro; **expense is no ~** non
si bada a spese; **to ~ that** obiettare
che; **objection** [abˈdʒɛkʃən] n
obiezione f; **objective** n obiettivo
obligation [ɔblɪˈgeɪʃən] n obbligo,
dovere m; **without ~** senza impegno
obligatory [əˈblɪgətərɪ] adj
obbligatorio(-a)
oblige [əˈblaɪdʒ] vt (force): **to ~ sb to do**
costringere qn a fare; (do a favour) fare
una cortesia a; **to be ~d to sb for sth**
essere grato a qn per qc
oblique [əˈbliːk] adj obliquo(-a);

(allusion) indiretto(-a)

obliterate [ə'blɪtəreɪt] *vt* cancellare

oblivious [ə'blɪviəs] *adj* **~ of** incurante di; inconscio(-a) di

oblong ['ɔbləŋ] *adj* oblungo(-a) ▶ *n* rettangolo

obnoxious [əb'nɔkʃəs] *adj* odioso(-a); *(smell)* disgustoso(-a), ripugnante

oboe ['əubəu] *n* oboe *m*

obscene [əb'siːn] *adj* osceno(-a)

obscure [əb'skjuə'] *adj* oscuro(-a) ▶ *vt* oscurare; *(hide: sun)* nascondere

observant [əb'zə:vnt] *adj* attento(-a)

> Be careful not to translate
> **observant** by the Italian word
> *osservante*.

observation [ɔbzə'veɪʃən] *n* osservazione *f*; *(by police etc)* sorveglianza

observatory [əb'zə:vətrɪ] *n* osservatorio

observe [əb'zə:v] *vt* osservare; *(remark)* fare osservare; **observer** *n* osservatore(-trice)

obsess [əb'sɛs] *vt* ossessionare; **obsession** [əb'sɛʃən] *n* ossessione *f*; **obsessive** *adj* ossessivo(-a)

obsolete ['ɔbsəliːt] *adj* obsoleto(-a)

obstacle ['ɔbstəkl] *n* ostacolo

obstinate ['ɔbstɪnɪt] *adj* ostinato(-a)

obstruct [əb'strʌkt] *vt* *(block)* ostruire, ostacolare; *(halt)* fermare; *(hinder)* impedire; **obstruction** [əb'strʌkʃən] *n* ostruzione *f*; ostacolo

obtain [əb'teɪn] *vt* ottenere

obvious ['ɔbviəs] *adj* ovvio(-a), evidente; **obviously** *adv* ovviamente; certo

occasion [ə'keɪʒən] *n* occasione *f*; *(event)* avvenimento; **occasional** *adj* occasionale; **occasionally** *adv* ogni tanto

occult [ɔ'kʌlt] *adj* occulto(-a) ▶ *n* the **~** l'occulto

occupant ['ɔkjupənt] *n* occupante

m/f; *(of boat, car etc)* persona a bordo

occupation [ɔkju'peɪʃən] *n* occupazione *f*; *(job)* mestiere *m*, professione *f*

occupy ['ɔkjupaɪ] *vt* occupare; **to ~ o.s. in doing** occuparsi a fare

occur [ə'kə:'] *vi* succedere, capitare; **to ~ to sb** venire in mente a qn; **occurrence** *n* caso, fatto; presenza

> Be careful not to translate **occur** by the Italian word *occorrere*.

ocean ['əuʃən] *n* oceano

o'clock [ə'klɔk] *adv* **it is 5 o'clock** sono le 5

Oct. *abbr* *(= October)* ott.

October [ɔk'təubə'] *n* ottobre *m*

octopus ['ɔktəpəs] *n* polpo, piovra

odd [ɔd] *adj* *(strange)* strano(-a), bizzarro(-a); *(number)* dispari *inv*; *(not of a set)* spaiato(-a); **60~** 60 e oltre; **at ~ times** di tanto in tanto; **the ~ one out** l'eccezione *f*; **oddly** *adv* stranamente; **odds** *npl* *(in betting)* quota

odometer [ɔ'dɔmɪtə'] *n* odometro

odour ['əudə'] *(US* **odor**) *n* odore *m*; *(unpleasant)* cattivo odore

of

[ɔv, əv] *prep*

1 *(gen)* di; **a boy of 10** un ragazzo di 10 anni; **a friend of ours** un nostro amico; **that was kind of you** è stato molto gentile da parte sua

2 *(expressing quantity, amount, dates etc)* di; **a kilo of flour** un chilo di farina; **how much of this do you need?** quanto gliene serve?; **there were 3 of them** *(people)* erano in 3; *(objects)* ce n'erano 3; **3 of us went** 3 di noi sono andati; **the 5th of July** il 5 luglio

3 *(from, out of)* di, in; *of* **made of wood** (fatto) di or in legno

off

[ɔf] *adv*

1 *(distance, time)*: **it's a long way off**

è lontano; **the game is 3 days off** la partita è tra 3 giorni

2 (*departure, removal*) via; **to go off to Paris** andarsene a Parigi; **I must be off** devo andare via; **to take off one's coat** togliersi il cappotto; **the button came off** il bottone è venuto via o si è staccato; **10% off** con lo sconto del 10%

3 (*not at work*): **to have a day off** avere un giorno libero; **to be off sick** essere assente per malattia

▶ *adj* (*engine*) spento(-a); (*tap*) chiuso(-a); (*cancelled*) sospeso(-a); (*BRIT: food*) andato(-a) a male; **on the off chance** nel caso; **to have an off day** non essere in forma

▶ *prep*

1 (*motion, removal etc*) da; (*distant from*) a poca distanza da; **a street off the square** una strada che parte dalla piazza

2: **to be off meat** non mangiare più la carne

offence [ə'fɛns] (*US* **offense**) *n* (*Law*) contravvenzione *f*; (*: more serious*) reato; **to take ~ at** offendersi per

offend [ə'fɛnd] *vt* (*person*) offendere; **offender** *n* delinquente *m/f*; (*against regulations*) contravventore(-trice)

offense [ə'fɛns] (*US*) *n* = **offence**

offensive [ə'fɛnsɪv] *adj* offensivo(-a); (*smell etc*) sgradevole, ripugnante ▶ *n* (*Mil*) offensiva

offer ['ɔfə'] *n* offerta, proposta ▶ *vt* offrire; **"on ~"** (*Comm*) "in offerta speciale"

offhand [ɔf'hænd] *adj* disinvolto(-a), noncurante ▶ *adv* su due piedi

office ['ɔfɪs] *n* (*place*) ufficio; (*position*) carica; **doctor's ~** (*US*) studio; **to take ~** entrare in carica; **office block** (*US* **office building**) *n* complesso di uffici; **office hours** *npl* orario d'ufficio; (*US Med*) orario di visite

officer ['ɔfɪsə'] *n* (*Mil etc*) ufficiale *m*;

(*also*: **police ~**) agente *m* di polizia; (*of organization*) funzionario

office worker *n* impiegato(-a) d'ufficio

official [ə'fɪʃl] *adj* (*authorized*) ufficiale ▶ *n* ufficiale *m*; (*civil servant*) impiegato(-a) statale; funzionario

off: off-licence (*BRIT*) *n* (*shop*) spaccio di bevande alcoliche; **off-line** *adj, adv* (*Comput*) off line *inv*, fuori linea; (*: switched off*) spento(-a); **off-peak** *adj* (*ticket, heating etc*) a tariffa ridotta; (*time*) non di punta; **off-putting** (*BRIT*) *adj* sgradevole, antipatico(-a); **off-season** *adj, adv* fuori stagione; **offset** [*irreg*] *vt* (*counteract*) controbilanciare, compensare; **offshore** [ɔf'ʃɔː'] *adj* (*breeze*) di terra; (*island*) vicino alla costa; (*fishing*) costiero(-a); **offside** ['ɔf'saɪd] *adj* (*Sport*) fuori gioco; (*Aut: in Britain*) destro(-a); (*: in Italy etc*) sinistro(-a); **offspring** ['ɔfsprɪŋ] *n inv* prole *f*, discendenza

often ['ɔfn] *adv* spesso; **how ~ do you go?** quanto spesso ci vai?

oh [əu] *excl* oh!

oil [ɔɪl] *n* olio; (*petroleum*) petrolio; (*for central heating*) nafta ▶ *vt* (*machine*) lubrificare; **oil filter** *n* (*Aut*) filtro dell'olio; **oil painting** *n* quadro a olio; **oil refinery** *n* raffineria di petrolio; **oil rig** *n* derrick *m inv*; (*at sea*) piattaforma per l'estrazione subacquea; **oil slick** *n* chiazza d'olio; **oil tanker** *n* (*ship*) petroliera; (*truck*) autocisterna per petrolio; **oil well** *n* pozzo petrolifero; **oily** *adj* unto(-a), oleoso(-a); (*food*) grasso(-a)

ointment ['ɔɪntmənt] *n* unguento

O.K. ['əu'keɪ] *excl* d'accordo! ▶ *adj* non male *inv* ▶ *vt* approvare; **is it O.K.?, are you O.K.?** tutto bene?

old [əuld] *adj* vecchio(-a); (*ancient*) antico(-a), vecchio(-a); (*person*) vecchio(-a), anziano(-a); **how ~ are you?** quanti anni ha?; **he's 10 years ~ ha 10 anni; ~er brother** fratello maggiore; **old age** n vecchiaia; **old-age pension** n ['əuldeɪdʒ-] n (BRIT) pensione f di vecchiaia; **old-age pensioner** (BRIT) n pensionato(-a); **old-fashioned** adj vecchio(-a), fuori moda; (person) all'antica; **old people's home** n ricovero per anziani

olive ['ɔlɪv] n (fruit) oliva; (tree) olivo
▶ adj (also: **~-green**) verde oliva inv;
olive oil n olio d'oliva

Olympic [əu'lɪmpɪk] adj olimpico(-a);
the ~ Games, the ~s i giochi olimpici,
le Olimpiadi

omelet(te) ['ɔmlɪt] n omelette f inv

omen ['əumən] n presagio, augurio

ominous ['ɔmɪnəs] adj
minaccioso(-a); (event) di malaugurio

omit [əu'mɪt] vt omettere

on
[ɔn] prep

1 (indicating position) su; **on the wall** sulla parete; **on the left** a or sulla sinistra

2 (indicating means, method, condition etc): **on foot** a piedi; **on the train/plane** in treno/aereo; **on the telephone** al telefono; **on the radio/television** alla radio/televisione; **to be on drugs** drogarsi; **on holiday** in vacanza

3 (of time): **on Friday** venerdì; **on Fridays** il or di venerdì; **on June 20th** il 20 giugno; **on Friday, June 20th** venerdì, 20 giugno; **a week on Friday** venerdì a otto; **on his arrival** al suo arrivo; **on seeing this** vedendo ciò

4 (about, concerning) su, di; **information on train services** informazioni sui collegamenti ferroviari; **a book on Goldoni/physics** un libro su Goldoni/di or sulla fisica

▶ adv

1 (referring to dress, covering): **to have one's coat on** avere indosso il cappotto; **to put one's coat on** mettersi il cappotto; **what's she got on?** cosa indossa?; **she put her boots/gloves/hat on** si mise gli stivali/i guanti/il cappello; **screw the lid on tightly** avvita bene il coperchio

2 (further, continuously): **to walk on, go on** etc continuare, proseguire etc; **to read on** continuare a leggere; **on and off** ogni tanto

▶ adj

1 (in operation: machine, TV, light) acceso(-a); (: tap) aperto(-a); (: brake) inserito(-a); **is the meeting still on?** (in progress) la riunione è ancora in corso?; (not cancelled) è confermato l'incontro?; **there's a good film on at the cinema** danno un buon film al cinema

2 (inf): **that's not on!** (not acceptable) non si fa così!; (not possible) non se ne parla neanche!

once [wʌns] adv una volta ▶ conj non appena, quando; **~ he had left/it was done** dopo che se n'era andato/fu fatto; **at ~** subito; (simultaneously) a un tempo; **~ a week** una volta per settimana; **~ more** ancora una volta; **~ and for all** una volta per sempre; **~ upon a time** c'era una volta

oncoming ['ɔnkʌmɪŋ] adj (traffic) che viene in senso opposto

one
[wʌn] num uno(-a); **one hundred and fifty** centocinquanta; **one day** un giorno

▶ adj

1 (sole) unico(-a); **the one book which** l'unico libro che; **the one man who** l'unico che

2 (same) stesso(-a); **they came in the one car** sono venuti nella stessa macchina

▶ *pron*

1: this one questo(-a); that one quello(-a); **I've already got one/a red one** ne ho già uno/uno rosso; **one by one** uno per uno

2: one another l'un l'altro; **to look at one another** guardarsi; **to help one another** aiutarsi l'un l'altro o a vicenda **3** (*impersonal*) si; **one never knows** non si sa mai; **one to cut one's finger** tagliarsi un dito; **one needs to eat** bisogna mangiare

one: **one-off** (BRIT: *inf*) *n* fatto eccezionale

oneself [wʌnˈsɛlf] *pron* (*reflexive*) si; (*after prep*) sé stesso(-a), sé; **to do sth (by) ~** fare qc da sé; **to hurt ~** farsi male; **to keep sth for ~** tenere qc per sé; **to talk to ~** parlare da solo

one: **one-shot** (*US*) *n* = **one-off**; **one-sided** *adj* (*argument*) unilaterale; **one-to-one** *adj* (*relationship*) univoco(-a); **one-way** *adj* (*street, traffic*) a senso unico

ongoing [ˈɔngəʊɪŋ] *adj* in corso; in attuazione

onion [ˈʌnjən] *n* cipolla

on-line [ˈɔnlaɪn] *adj, adv* (*Comput*) on-line *inv*

onlooker [ˈɔnlʊkəʳ] *n* spettatore(-trice)

only [ˈəʊnlɪ] *adv* solo, soltanto ▶ *adj* solo(-a), unico(-a) ▶ *conj* solo che, ma; **an ~ child** un figlio unico; **not ~ ... but also** non solo ... ma anche

on-screen [ˈɔnˈskriːn] *adj* sullo schermo *inv*

onset [ˈɔnsɛt] *n* inizio

onto [ˈɔntu] *prep* = **on to**

onward(s) [ˈɔnwəd(z)] *adv* (*move*) in avanti; **from that time onward(s)** da quella volta in poi

oops [ups] *excl* ops! (*esprime rincrescimento per un piccolo contrattempo*); **~-a-daisy!** oplà!

ooze [uːz] *vi* stillare

opaque [əʊˈpeɪk] *adj* opaco(-a)

open [ˈəʊpn] *adj* aperto(-a); (*road*) libero(-a); (*meeting*) pubblico(-a) ▶ *vt* aprire ▶ *vi* (*eyes, door, debate*) aprirsi; (*flower*) sbocciare; (*shop, bank, museum*) aprire; (*book etc: commence*) cominciare; **is it ~ to the public?**; è aperto al pubblico?; **in the ~ (air)** all'aperto; **what time do you ~?** a che ora aprite? ▶ **open up** *vt* aprire; (*blocked road*) sgombrare ▶ *vi* (*shop, business*) aprire; **open-air** *adj* all'aperto; **opening** *adj* (*speech*) di apertura ▶ *n* apertura; (*opportunity*) occasione *f*, opportunità *f inv*; sbocco; **opening hours** *npl* orario d'apertura; **open learning** *n* sistema educativo secondo il quale lo studente ha maggior controllo e gestione delle modalità di apprendimento; **openly** *adv* apertamente; **open-minded** *adj* che ha la mente aperta; **open-necked** *adj* col collo slacciato; **open-plan** *adj* senza pareti divisorie; **Open University** *n* (BRIT) vedi nota nel riquadro

- **Open University**
- La **Open University**, fondata in Gran Bretagna nel 1969, organizza corsi di laurea per corrispondenza o via Internet. Alcune lezioni possono venir seguite per radio o alla televisione e vengono organizzati regolari corsi estivi.

opera [ˈɔprə] *n* opera; **opera house** *n* opera; **opera singer** *n* cantante *m/f* d'opera o lirico(-a)

operate [ˈɔpəreɪt] *vt* (*machine*) azionare, far funzionare; (*system*) usare ▶ *vi* funzionare; (*drug*) essere efficace; **to ~ on sb (for)** (*Med*) operare qn (di)

operating room (*US*) *n* = **operating theatre**

operating theatre *n* (*Med*) sala

operatoria

operation [ɔpəˈreɪʃən] n operazione f; **to be in ~** (*machine*) essere in azione or funzionamento; (*system*) essere in vigore; **to have an ~** (*Med*) subire un'operazione; **operational** adj in funzione; d'esercizio

operative [ˈɔpərətɪv] adj (*measure*) operativo(-a)

operator [ˈɔpəreɪtə*] n (*of machine*) operatore(-trice); (*Tel*) centralinista m/f

opinion [əˈpɪnɪən] n opinione f, parere m; **in my ~** secondo me, a mio avviso; **opinion poll** n sondaggio di opinioni

opponent [əˈpəunənt] n avversario(-a)

opportunity [ɔpəˈtjuːnɪtɪ] n opportunità f inv, occasione f; **to take the ~ of doing** cogliere l'occasione per fare

oppose [əˈpəuz] vt opporsi a; **~d to** contrario(-a) a; **as ~d to** in contrasto con

opposite [ˈɔpəzɪt] adj opposto(-a); (*house etc*) di fronte ▶ adv di fronte, dirimpetto ▶ prep di fronte a ▶ n the ~ il contrario, l'opposto; **the ~ sex** l'altro sesso

opposition [ɔpəˈzɪʃən] n opposizione f

oppress [əˈprɛs] vt opprimere

opt [ɔpt] vi to ~ for optare per; **to ~ to do** scegliere di fare ▷ **opt out** vi to ~ out of ritirarsi da

optician [ɔpˈtɪʃən] n ottico

optimism [ˈɔptɪmɪzəm] n ottimismo

optimist [ˈɔptɪmɪst] n ottimista m/f; **optimistic** [-ˈmɪstɪk] adj ottimistico(-a)

optimum [ˈɔptɪməm] adj ottimale

option [ˈɔpʃən] n scelta; (*Scol*) materia facoltativa; (*Comm*) opzione f; **optional** adj facoltativo(-a); (*Comm*) a scelta

or [ɔː*] conj o, oppure; (*with negative*):

he hasn't seen or heard anything non ha visto né sentito niente; **or else** se no, altrimenti; oppure

oral [ˈɔːrəl] adj orale ▶ n esame m orale

orange [ˈɔrɪndʒ] n (*fruit*) arancia ▶ adj arancione; **orange juice** n succo d'arancia; **orange squash** n succo d'arancia (*da diluire con l'acqua*)

orbit [ˈɔːbɪt] n orbita ▶ vt orbitare intorno a

orchard [ˈɔːtʃəd] n frutteto

orchestra [ˈɔːkɪstrə] n orchestra; (*US: seating*) platea

orchid [ˈɔːkɪd] n orchidea

ordeal [ɔːˈdiːl] n prova, travaglio

order [ˈɔːdə*] n ordine m; (*Comm*) ordinazione f ▶ vt ordinare; **can I ~ now, please?** posso ordinare, per favore?; **in ~** in ordine; (*of document*) in regola; **in (working) ~** funzionante; **in ~ to do** per fare; **in ~ that** affinché + sub; **on ~** (*Comm*) in ordinazione; **out of ~** non in ordine; (*not working*) guasto; **to ~ sb to do** ordinare a qn di fare; **order form** n modulo d'ordinazione; **orderly** n (*Mil*) attendente m; (*Med*) inserviente m ▶ adj (*room*) in ordine; (*mind*) metodico(-a); (*person*) ordinato(-a), metodico(-a)

ordinary [ˈɔːdnrɪ] adj normale, comune; (*pej*) mediocre; **out of the ~** diverso dal solito, fuori dell'ordinario

ore [ɔː*] n minerale m grezzo

oregano [ɔrɪˈɡɑːnəu] n origano

organ [ˈɔːɡən] n organo; **organic** [ɔːˈɡænɪk] adj organico(-a); (*of food*) biologico(-a); **organism** n organismo

organization [ɔːɡənaɪˈzeɪʃən] n organizzazione f

organize [ˈɔːɡənaɪz] vt organizzare; **to get ~d** organizzarsi; **organized** [ˈɔːɡənaɪzd] adj organizzato(-a); **organizer** n organizzatore(-trice)

orgasm [ˈɔːɡæzəm] n orgasmo

orgy ['ɔːdʒɪ] n orgia

oriental [ɔːrɪ'entl] adj, n orientale m/f

orientation [ɔːrɪen'teɪʃən] n orientamento

origin ['ɒrɪdʒɪn] n origine f

original [ə'rɪdʒɪnl] adj originale; (earliest) originario(-a) ▶ n originale m; **originally** adv (at first) all'inizio

originate [ə'rɪdʒɪneɪt] vi to ~ from essere originario(-a) di; (suggestion) provenire da; to ~ in avere origine in

Orkneys ['ɔːknɪz] npl the ~ (also: the Orkney Islands) le Orcadi

ornament ['ɔːnəmənt] n ornamento; (trinket) ninnolo; **ornamental** [-'mentl] adj ornamentale

ornate [ɔː'neɪt] adj molto ornato(-a)

orphan ['ɔːfn] n orfano(-a)

orthodox ['ɔːθədɒks] adj ortodosso(-a)

orthopaedic [ɔːθə'piːdɪk] (US **orthopedic**) adj ortopedico(-a)

osteopath ['ɒstɪəpæθ] n specialista m/f di osteopatia

ostrich ['ɒstrɪtʃ] n struzzo

other ['ʌðər] adj il (la) nostro(-a); (pl) i (le) nostri(-e) ▶ pron the ~ (one) l'altro(-a); ~s (other people) altri mpl; ~ than altro che; a parte; **otherwise** adv, conj altrimenti

otter ['ɒtər] n lontra

ouch [autʃ] excl ohi!, ahi!

ought [ɔːt] (pt ought) aux vb I ~ to do it dovrei farlo; this ~ to have been corrected questo avrebbe dovuto essere corretto; he ~ to win dovrebbe vincere

ounce [auns] n oncia (= 28.35 g, 16 in a pound)

our ['auər] adj il (la) nostro(-a); (pl) i (le) nostri(-e); see also **my**; **ours** pron il (la) nostro(-a); (pl) i (le) nostri(-e); see also **mine**; **ourselves** pron pl (reflexive) ci; (after preposition) noi; (emphatic) noi stessi(-e); see also **oneself**

oust [aust] vt cacciare, espellere

out [aut] adv (gen) fuori; ~ here/there qui/là fuori; to speak ~ loud parlare forte; to have a night ~ uscire una sera; the boat was 10 km ~ la barca era a 10 km dalla costa; 3 days ~ from Plym~h a 3 giorni da Plymouth; ~ of (outside) fuori di; (because of) per; ~ of 10 su 10; ~ of petrol senza benzina; **outback** ['autbæk] n (in Australia) interno, entroterra; **outbound** adj **outbound (for** or **from)** in partenza (per o da); **outbreak** ['autbreɪk] n scoppio; epidemia; **outburst** ['autbəːst] n scoppio; **outcast** ['autkɑːst] n esule m/f; (socially) paria m inv; **outcome** ['autkʌm] n esito, risultato; **outcry** ['autkraɪ] n protesta, clamore m; **outdated** [aut'deɪtɪd] adj (custom, clothes) fuori moda; (idea) sorpassato(-a); **outdoor** [aut'dɔːr] adj all'aperto; **outdoors** adv fuori; all'aria aperta

outer ['autər] adj esteriore; **outer space** n spazio cosmico

outfit ['autfɪt] n (clothes) completo; (: for sport) tenuta

outgoing ['autɡəuɪŋ] adj (character) socievole; **outgoings** (BRIT) npl (expenses) spese fpl, uscite fpl; **outhouse** ['authaus] n costruzione f annessa

outing ['autɪŋ] n gita; escursione f

outlaw ['autlɔː] n fuorilegge m/f ▶ vt bandire; **outlay** ['autleɪ] n spese fpl; (investment) sborsa, spesa; **outlet** ['autlet] n (for liquid etc) sbocco, scarico; (US Elec) presa di corrente; (also: **retail outlet**) punto di vendita; **outline** ['autlaɪn] n contorno, profilo; (summary) abbozzo, grandi linee fpl ▶ vt (fig) descrivere a grandi linee; **outlook** ['autluk] n prospettiva, vista; **outnumber** [aut'nʌmbər] vt superare in numero; **out-of-date** adj (passport) scaduto(-a); (clothes) fuori moda *inv*; **out-of-doors** [autəv'dɔːz] *adv* all'aperto; **out-of-the-way** *adj* (*place*) fuori mano *inv*; **out-of-town** [autəv'taun] *adj* (*shopping centre etc*) fuori città; **outpatient** ['autpeɪʃənt] *n* paziente *m/f* esterno/-a; **outpost** ['autpəust] *n* avamposto; **output** ['autput] *n* produzione *f*; (*Comput*) output *m inv*

outrage ['autreɪdʒ] *n* oltraggio; scandalo ▶ *vt* oltraggiare; **outrageous** [-'reɪdʒəs] *adj* oltraggioso(-a), scandaloso(-a)

outright [*adv* aut'raɪt, *adj* 'autraɪt] *adv* completamente; schiettamente; apertamente; sul colpo ▶ *adj* completo(-a), schietto(-a) e netto(-a)

outset ['autset] *n* inizio

outside [aut'saɪd] *n* esterno, esteriore *m* ▶ *adj* esterno(-a), esteriore ▶ *adv* fuori, all'esterno ▶ *prep* fuori di, all'esterno di; **at the ~** (*fig*) al massimo; **outside lane** *n* (*Aut*) corsia di sorpasso; **outside line** *n* (*Tel*) linea esterna; **outsider** *n* (*in race etc*) outsider *m inv*; (*stranger*) estraneo(-a)

out: **outsize** ['autsaiz] *adj* (*clothes*) per taglie forti; **outskirts** ['autskəːts] *npl* sobborghi *mpl*; **outspoken** [aut'spəukən] *adj* molto franco(-a); **outstanding** [aut'stændɪŋ] *adj* eccezionale, di rilievo; (*unfinished*) non completo(-a); non evaso(-a) non regolato(-a)

outward ['autwəd] *adj* (*sign, appearances*) esteriore; (*journey*) d'andata; **outwards** ['autwədz] *adv* (*esp BRIT*) = **outward**

outweigh [aut'weɪ] *vt* avere maggior peso di

oval ['əuvl] *adj* ovale ▶ *n* ovale *m*

ovary ['əuvərɪ] *n* ovaia

oven ['ʌvn] *n* forno; **oven glove** *n* guanto da forno; **ovenproof** *adj* da forno; **oven-ready** *adj* pronto(-a) da

infornare

over ['əuvə*] *adv* di sopra ▶ *adj* (*or adv*) (*finished*) finito(-a), terminato(-a); (*too*) troppo; (*remaining*) che avanza ▶ *prep* su; sopra; (*above*) al di sopra di; (*on the other side of*) di là di; (*more than*) più di; (*during*) durante; **~ here** qui; **~ there** là; **all ~** (*everywhere*) dappertutto; (*finished*) finito(-a); **~ and ~ (again)** più e più volte; **~ and above** oltre (a); **to ask sb ~** invitare qn (a passare)

overall [*adj, n* 'əuvərɔːl, *adv* əuvər'ɔːl] *adj* totale ▶ *n* (*BRIT*) grembiule *m* ▶ *adv* nell'insieme, complessivamente; **~s** *npl* (*worker's overalls*) tuta (da lavoro)

overboard ['əuvəbɔːd] *adv* (*Naut*) fuori bordo, in mare

overcame [əuvə'keɪm] *pt of* **overcome**

overcast ['əuvəkɑːst] *adj* (*sky*) coperto(-a)

overcharge [əuvə'tʃɑːdʒ] *vt* **to ~ sb for sth** far pagare troppo caro a qn per qc

overcoat ['əuvəkəut] *n* soprabito, cappotto

overcome [əuvə'kʌm] (*irreg*) *vt* superare; sopraffare

over: **overcrowded** [əuvə'kraudɪd] *adj* sovraffollato(-a); **overdo** [əuvə'duː] (*irreg*) *vt* esagerare; (*overcook*) cuocere troppo; **overdone** [əuvə'dʌn] *adj* troppo cotto(-a); **overdose** ['əuvədəus] *n* dose *f* eccessiva; **overdraft** ['əuvədrɑːft] *n* scoperto (di conto); **overdrawn** [əuvə'drɔːn] *adj* (*account*) scoperto(-a); **overdue** [əuvə'djuː] *adj* in ritardo; **overestimate** [əuvər'estɪmeɪt] *vt* sopravvalutare

overflow [*vb* əuvə'fləu, *n* 'əuvəfləu] *vi* traboccare ▶ *n* (*also*: **~ pipe**) troppopieno

overgrown [əuvə'grəun] *adj* (*garden*)

ricoperto(-a) di vegetazione

overhaul [vb əuvə'hɔːl, n 'əuvəhɔːl] vt revisionare ▸ n revisione f

overhead [adv əuvə'hed, adj, n 'əuvəhed] adv di sopra ▸ adj aereo(-a); (lighting) verticale ▸ n (US) = **overheads**; **overhead projector** n lavagna luminosa; **overheads** npl spese fpl generali

over: overhear [əuvə'hɪəʳ] (irreg) vt sentire (per caso); **overheat** [əuvə'hiːt] vi (engine) surriscaldare; **overland** adj, adv per via di terra; **overlap** [əuvə'læp] vi sovrapporsi; **overleaf** [əuvə'liːf] adv a tergo; **overload** [əuvə'ləud] vt sovraccaricare; **overlook** [əuvə'luk] vt (have view of) dare su; (miss) trascurare; (forgive) passare sopra a

overnight [əuvə'naɪt] adv (happen) durante la notte; (fig) tutto ad un tratto ▸ adj di notte; **he stayed there** ~ ci ha passato la notte; **overnight bag** n borsa da viaggio

overpass ['əuvəpɑːs] n cavalcavia m inv

overpower [əuvə'pauəʳ] vt soffraffare; **overpowering** adj irresistibile; (heat, stench) soffocante

over: overreact [əuvəriː'ækt] vi reagire in modo esagerato; **overrule** [əuvə'ruːl] vt (decision) annullare; (claim) respingere; **overrun** [əuvə'rʌn] (irreg: like **run**) vt (country) invadere; (time limit) superare

overseas [əuvə'siːz] adv oltremare; (abroad) all'estero ▸ adj (trade) estero(-a); (visitor) straniero(-a)

oversee [əuvə'siː] vt irreg sorvegliare

overshadow [əuvə'ʃædəu] vt far ombra su; (fig) eclissare

oversight ['əuvəsaɪt] n omissione f, svista

oversleep [əuvə'sliːp] (irreg) vt dormire troppo a lungo

overspend [əuvə'spɛnd] vi irreg spendere troppo; **we have overspent by 5000 dollars** abbiamo speso 5000 dollari di troppo

overt [əu'vəːt] adj palese

overtake [əuvə'teɪk] (irreg) vt sorpassare

over: overthrow [əuvə'θrəu] (irreg) vt (government) rovesciare; **overtime** ['əuvətaɪm] n (lavoro) straordinario

overtook [əuvə'tuk] pt of **overtake**

over: overturn [əuvə'təːn] vt rovesciare ▸ vi rovesciarsi; **overweight** [əuvə'weɪt] adj (person) troppo grasso(-a); **overwhelm** [əuvə'wɛlm] vt soffraffare; sommergere; schiacciare; **overwhelming** adj (victory, defeat) schiacciante; (heat, desire) intenso(-a)

ow [au] excl ahi

owe [əu] vt **to ~ sb sth, to ~ sth to sb** dovere qc a qn; **how much do I ~ you?** quanto le devo?; **owing to** prep a causa di

owl [aul] n gufo

own [əun] vt possedere ▸ adj proprio(-a); **a room of my ~** la mia propria camera; **to get one's ~ back** vendicarsi; **on one's ~** tutto(-a) solo(-a) ▸ **own up** vi confessare; **owner** n proprietario(-a); **ownership** n possesso

ox [ɔks] (pl **oxen**) n bue m

Oxbridge ['ɔksbrɪdʒ] n le università di Oxford e/o Cambridge

oxen ['ɔksn] npl of **ox**

oxygen ['ɔksɪdʒən] n ossigeno

oyster ['ɔɪstəʳ] n ostrica

oz. abbr = **ounce(s)**

ozone ['əuzəun] n ozono; **ozone friendly** adj che non danneggia l'ozono; **ozone layer** n fascia d'ozono

p

p [piː] abbr = **penny; pence**

P.A. n abbr = **personal assistant;**
public address system

p.a. abbr = **per annum**

pace [peɪs] n passo; (speed) passo;
velocità ▶ vi **to ~ up and down**
camminare su e giù; **to keep ~ with**
camminare di pari passo a; (events)
tenersi al corrente di; **pacemaker** n
(Med) segnapasso; (Sport: also: **pace**
setter) battistrada m inv

Pacific [pəˈsɪfɪk] n **the ~ (Ocean)** il
Pacifico, l'Oceano Pacifico

pacifier [ˈpæsɪfaɪəʳ] (US) n (dummy)
succhiotto, ciuccio (col)

pack [pæk] n pacco; (US: of cigarettes)
pacchetto; (backpack) zaino; (of
hounds) muta; (of thieves etc) banda;
(of cards) mazzo ▶ vt (in suitcase etc)
mettere; (box) riempire; (cram)
stipare, pigiare; **to ~ (one's bags)** fare
la valigia; **to ~ sb off** spedire via qn;
~ it in! (inf) dacci un taglio! ▷ **pack in**
(BRIT inf) vi (watch, car) guastarsi ▶ vt
mollare, piantare; **~ it in!** piantala!
▷ **pack up** vi (BRIT inf: machine)
guastarsi; (: person) far fagotto ▶ vt
(belongings, clothes) mettere in una
valigia; (goods, presents) imballare

package [ˈpækɪdʒ] n pacco; balla;
(also: **~ deal**) pacchetto; forfait m
inv; **package holiday** n vacanza
organizzata; **package tour** n viaggio
organizzato

packaging [ˈpækɪdʒɪŋ] n confezione
f, imballo

packed [pækt] adj (crowded)
affollato(-a); **packed lunch** n pranzo
al sacco

packet [ˈpækɪt] n pacchetto

packing [ˈpækɪŋ] n imballaggio

pact [pækt] n patto, accordo; trattato

pad [pæd] n blocco; (to prevent friction)
cuscinetto; (inf: flat) appartamentino
▶ vt imbottire; **padded** adj
imbottito(-a)

paddle [ˈpædl] n (oar) pagaia; (US: for
table tennis) racchetta da ping-pong
▶ vi sguazzare ▶ vt **to ~ a canoe** etc
vogare con la pagaia; **paddling pool**
(BRIT) n piscina per bambini

paddock [ˈpædək] n prato recintato;
(at racecourse) paddock m inv

padlock [ˈpædlɔk] n lucchetto

paedophile [ˈpiːdəʊfaɪl] (US
pedophile) n, adj pedofilo(-a)

page [peɪdʒ] n pagina; (also: **~ boy**)
paggio ▶ vt (in hotel etc) (far) chiamare

pager [ˈpeɪdʒəʳ] n (Tel) cercapersone
m inv

paid [peɪd] pt, pp of **pay** ▶ adj (work,
official) rimunerato(-a); **to put ~ to**
(BRIT) mettere fine a

pain [peɪn] n dolore m; **to be in ~**
soffrire, aver male; **to take ~ to do**
mettercela tutta per fare; **painful** adj
doloroso(-a), che fa male; difficile,
penoso(-a); **painkiller** n antalgico,
antidolorifico; **painstaking**
[ˈpeɪnzteɪkɪŋ] adj (person) sollecito(-a);
(work) accurato(-a)

paint [peɪnt] n vernice f, colore m ▶ vt
dipingere; (walls, door etc) verniciare;
to ~ the door blue verniciare la porta
di azzurro; **paintbrush** n pennello;
painter n (artist) pittore m; (decorator)
imbianchino; **painting** n pittura;
verniciatura; (picture) dipinto, quadro

pair [pɛəʳ] n (of shoes, gloves etc) paio;

(of people) coppia; duo m inv; **a ~ of scissors/trousers** un paio di forbici/ pantaloni

pajamas [pɪˈdʒɑːməz] (US) npl pigiama m

Pakistan [pɑːkɪˈstɑːn] n Pakistan m; **Pakistani** adj, n pakistano(-a)

pal [pæl] (inf) n amico(-a), compagno(-a)

palace [ˈpæləs] n palazzo

pale [peɪl] adj pallido(-a) ▶ n **to be beyond the ~** aver oltrepassato ogni limite

Palestine [ˈpælɪstaɪn] n Palestina; **Palestinian** [-ˈtɪnɪən] adj, n palestinese m/f

palm [pɑːm] n (Anat) palma, palmo; (also: **~ tree**) palma ▶ vt **to ~ sth off on sb** (inf) rifilare qc a qn

pamper [ˈpæmpə'] vt viziare, coccolare

pamphlet [ˈpæmflət] n dépliant m inv

pan [pæn] n (also: **sauce~**) casseruola; (also: **frying ~**) padella

pancake [ˈpænkeɪk] n frittella

panda [ˈpændə] n panda m inv

pane [peɪn] n vetro

panel [ˈpænl] n (of wood, cloth etc) pannello; (Radio, TV) giuria

panhandler [ˈpænhændləʳ] (US) n (inf) accattone(-a)

panic [ˈpænɪk] n panico ▶ vi perdere il sangue freddo

panorama [pænəˈrɑːmə] n panorama m

pansy [ˈpænzɪ] n (Bot) viola del pensiero, pensée f inv; (inf: pej) femminuccia

pant [pænt] vi ansare

panther [ˈpænθəʳ] n pantera

panties [ˈpæntɪz] npl slip m, mutandine fpl

pantomime [ˈpæntəmaɪm] (BRIT) n pantomima

pantomime
In Gran Bretagna la **pantomime** è

una sorta di libera interpretazione delle favole più conosciute, che vengono messe in scena a teatro durante il periodo natalizio. È uno spettacolo per tutta la famiglia che prevede la partecipazione del pubblico.

pants [pænts] npl mutande fpl, slip m; (US: trousers) pantaloni mpl

paper [ˈpeɪpəʳ] n carta; (also: **wall~**) carta da parati, tappezzeria; (also: **news~**) giornale m; (study, article) saggio; (exam) prova scritta ▶ adj di carta ▶ vt tappezzare; **~s** npl (also: **identity ~s**) carte fpl, documenti mpl; **paperback** n tascabile m; edizione f economica; **paper bag** n sacchetto di carta; **paper clip** n graffetta, clip f inv; **paper shop** n (BRIT) giornalaio m; **paperwork** n lavoro amministrativo

paprika [ˈpæprɪkə] n paprica

par [pɑːʳ] n parità, pari f; (Golf) norma; **on a ~ with** alla pari con

paracetamol [pærəˈsiːtəmɔl] (BRIT) n paracetamolo

parachute [ˈpærəʃuːt] n paracadute m inv

parade [pəˈreɪd] n parata ▶ vt (fig) fare sfoggio di ▶ vi sfilare in parata

paradise [ˈpærədaɪs] n paradiso

paradox [ˈpærədɔks] n paradosso

paraffin [ˈpærəfɪn] (BRIT) n ~ **(oil)** paraffina

paragraph [ˈpærəgrɑːf] n paragrafo

parallel [ˈpærəlɛl] adj parallelo(-a); (fig) analogo(-a) ▶ n (line) parallela; (fig, Geo) parallelo

paralysed [ˈpærəlaɪzd] adj paralizzato(-a)

paralysis [pəˈrælɪsɪs] n paralisi f inv

paramedic [pærəˈmɛdɪk] n paramedico

paranoid [ˈpærənɔɪd] adj paranoico(-a)

parasite ['pærəsaɪt] n parassita m

parcel ['pɑːsl] n pacco, pacchetto ▸ vt (also: ~ **up**) impacchare

pardon ['pɑːdn] n perdono; grazia ▸ vt perdonare; (Law) graziare; ~ **me!** mi scusi!; **I beg your ~!** scusi!; **I beg your ~?** (BRIT), ~ **me?** (US) prego?

parent ['pɛərənt] n genitore m; ~**s** npl (mother and father) genitori mpl; **parental** [pə'rɛntl] adj dei genitori

▣ Be careful not to translate **parent** by the Italian word *parente*.

Paris ['pærɪs] n Parigi f

parish ['pærɪʃ] n parrocchia; (BRIT: civil) ≈ municipio

Parisian [pə'rɪzɪən] adj, n parigino(-a)

park [pɑːk] n parco ▸ vt, vi parcheggiare; **can I ~ here?** posso parcheggiare qui?

parking ['pɑːkɪŋ] n parcheggio; "**no ~**" "sosta vietata"; **parking lot** (US) n posteggio, parcheggio; **parking meter** n parchimetro; **parking ticket** n multa per sosta vietata

parkway ['pɑːkweɪ] (US) n viale m

parliament ['pɑːləmənt] n parlamento; **parliamentary** [pɑːlə'mɛntərɪ] adj parlamentare

Parmesan [pɑːmɪ'zæn] n (also: ~ **cheese**) parmigiano

parole [pə'rəʊl] n **on ~** in libertà per buona condotta

parrot ['pærət] n pappagallo

parsley ['pɑːslɪ] n prezzemolo

parsnip ['pɑːsnɪp] n pastinaca

parson ['pɑːsn] n prete m; (Church of England) parroco

part [pɑːt] n parte f; (of machine) pezzo; (US: in hair) scriminatura ▸ adj in parte ▸ adv = **partly** ▸ vt separare ▸ vi (people) separarsi; **to take ~ in** prendere parte a; **for my ~** per parte mia; **to take sth in good ~** prendere bene qc; **to take sb's ~** parteggiare per or prendere le parti di qn; **for the**

most ~ in generale; nella maggior parte dei casi ▷ **part with** vt fus separarsi da; rinunciare a

partial ['pɑːʃl] adj parziale; **to be ~ to** avere un debole per

participant [pɑː'tɪsɪpənt] n ~ (**in**) partecipante m/f(a)

participate [pɑː'tɪsɪpeɪt] vi ~ **to** ~ (**in**) prendere parte (a), partecipare (a)

particle ['pɑːtɪkl] n particella

particular [pə'tɪkjulər] adj particolare, speciale; (fussy) difficile, meticoloso(-a); **in ~** in particolare, particolarmente; **particularly** adv particolarmente; in particolare; **particulars** npl particolari mpl, dettagli mpl; (information) informazioni fpl

parting ['pɑːtɪŋ] n separazione f; (BRIT: in hair) scriminatura f ▸ adj d'addio

partition [pɑː'tɪʃən] n (Pol) partizione f; (wall) tramezzo

partly ['pɑːtlɪ] adv parzialmente; in parte

partner ['pɑːtnər] n (Comm) socio(-a); (wife, husband etc, Sport) compagno(-a); (at dance) cavaliere/ dama; **partnership** n associazione f; (Comm) società f inv

part of speech n parte f del discorso

partridge ['pɑːtrɪdʒ] n pernice f

part-time ['pɑːt'taɪm] adj, adv a orario ridotto

party ['pɑːtɪ] n (Pol) partito; (group) gruppo; (Law) parte f; (celebration) ricevimento; serata; festa ▸ cpd (Pol) del partito, di partito

pass [pɑːs] vt (gen) passare; (place) passare davanti a; (exam) passare, superare; (candidate) promuovere; (overtake, surpass) sorpassare, superare; (approve) approvare ▸ vi passare ▸ n (permit) lasciapassare m inv; permesso; (in mountains) passo, gola; (Sport) passaggio; (Scol): **to get a ~** prendere la sufficienza; **could you ~ the salt/oil, please?** mi passa il sale/l'olio, per favore?; **to ~ sth through a hole** etc far passare qc attraverso un buco etc; **to make a ~ at sb** (inf) fare delle proposte or delle avances a qn ▷ **pass away** vi morire ▷ **pass by** vi passare ▷ vt trascurare ▷ **pass on** vt passare ▷ **pass out** vi svenire ▷ **pass over** vi (die) spirare ▷ vt lasciare da parte ▷ **pass up** vt (opportunity) lasciarsi sfuggire, perdere; **passable** adj (road) praticabile; (work) accettabile

passage ['pæsɪdʒ] n (gen) passaggio; (also: **~way**) corridoio; (in book) brano, passo; (by boat) traversata

passenger ['pæsɪndʒəʳ] n passeggero(-a)

passer-by [pɑːsə'baɪ] n passante m/f

passing place n (Aut) piazzola di sosta

passion ['pæʃən] n passione f; amore m; **passionate** adj appassionato(-a); **passion fruit** n frutto della passione

passive ['pæsɪv] adj (also Ling) passivo(-a)

passport ['pɑːspɔːt] n passaporto; **passport control** n controllo m passaporti inv; **passport office** n ufficio m, passaporti inv

password ['pɑːswəːd] n parola d'ordine

past [pɑːst] prep (further than) oltre, di là da; dopo; (later than) dopo ▷ adj passato(-a); (president etc) ex inv ▷ n passato; **he's ~ forty** ha più di quarant'anni; **ten ~ eight** le otto e dieci; **for the ~ few days** da qualche giorno; in questi ultimi giorni; **to run ~** passare di corsa

pasta ['pæstə] n pasta

paste [peɪst] n (glue) colla; (Culin) pâté m inv; pasta ▷ vt collare

pastel ['pæstl] adj pastello inv

pasteurized ['pæstəraɪzd] adj pastorizzato(-a)

pastime ['pɑːstaɪm] n passatempo

pastor ['pɑːstəʳ] n pastore m

past participle [-'pɑːtɪsɪpl] n (Ling) participio passato

pastry ['peɪstrɪ] n pasta

pasture ['pɑːstʃəʳ] n pascolo

pasty¹ ['pæstɪ] n pasticcio di carne

pasty² ['peɪstɪ] adj (face etc) smorto(-a)

pat [pæt] vt accarezzare, dare un colpetto (affettuoso) a

patch [pætʃ] n (of material, on tyre) toppa; (eye patch) benda; (spot) macchia ▷ vt (clothes) rattoppare; **(to go through) a bad ~** (attraversare) un brutto periodo; **patchy** adj irregolare

pâté ['pæteɪ] n pâté m inv

patent ['peɪtnt] n brevetto ▷ vt brevettare ▷ adj patente, manifesto(-a)

paternal [pə'təːnl] adj paterno(-a)

paternity leave [pə'təːnɪtɪ-] n congedo di paternità

path [pɑːθ] n sentiero, viottolo; viale m; (fig) strada; (of planet, missile) traiettoria

pathetic [pə'θetɪk] adj (pitiful) patetico(-a); (very bad) penoso(-a)

pathway ['pɑːθweɪ] n sentiero

patience ['peɪʃns] n pazienza; (BRIT Cards) solitario

patient ['peɪʃnt] n paziente m/f, malato(-a) ▷ adj paziente

patio ['pætɪəu] n terrazza

patriotic [pætrɪ'ɔtɪk] adj patriottico(-a)

patrol [pə'trəul] n pattuglia ▷ vt pattugliare; **patrol car** n autoradio f inv (della polizia)

patron ['peɪtrən] n (in shop) cliente m/f; (of charity) benefattore(-trice); **~ of the arts** mecenate m/f

patronizing ['pætrənaɪzɪŋ] adj

condiscendente
pattern ['pætən] n modello; (design)
disegno, motivo; **patterned** adj a
disegni, a motivi; (material) fantasia
inv

pause [pɔːz] n pausa ▶ vi fare una
pausa, arrestarsi

pave [peɪv] vt pavimentare; **to ~ the
way for** aprire la via a

pavement ['peɪvmənt] (BRIT) n
marciapiede m

|Be careful not to translate
pavement by the Italian word
pavimento.

pavilion [pə'vɪlɪən] n (Sport) edificio
annesso à campo sportivo

paving ['peɪvɪŋ] n pavimentazione f

paw [pɔː] n zampa

pawn [pɔːn] n (Chess) pedone m; (fig)
pedina ▶ vt dare in pegno; **pawn
broker** n prestatore m su pegno

pay [peɪ] (pt, pp **paid**) n stipendio;
▶ vt pagare ▶ vi (be profitable) rendere;
can I ~ by credit card? posso pagare
con la carta di credito?; **to ~ attention
(to)** fare attenzione (a); **to ~ sb a visit**
far visita a qn; **to ~ one's respects
to sb** porgere i propri rispetti a qn
▷ **pay back** vt rimborsare; **pay
for** vt fus pagare ▷ **pay in** vt versare
▷ **pay off** vt (debt) saldare; (person)
pagare; (employee) pagare e licenziare
▶ vi (scheme, decision) dare dei frutti
▷ **pay out** vt (money) sborsare, tirar
fuori; (rope) far allentare ▷ **pay up**
vt saldare; **payable** adj pagabile;
pay day n giorno di paga; **pay
envelope** (US) n = **pay packet**;
payment n pagamento; versamento;
saldo; **payout** n pagamento; (in
competition) premio; **pay packet**
(BRIT) n busta f paga inv; **pay phone**
n cabina telefonica; **payroll** n ruolo
(organico); **pay slip** n foglio m paga
inv; **pay television** n televisione f a

pagamento, pay-tv f inv

PC n abbr = **personal computer** ▶ adv
abbr = **politically correct**

p.c. abbr = **per cent**

PDA n abbr (= personal digital assistant)
PDA m inv

PE n abbr (= physical education) ed. fisica

pea [piː] n pisello

peace [piːs] n pace f; **peaceful** adj
pacifico(-a), calmo(-a)

peach [piːtʃ] n pesca

peacock ['piːkɔk] n pavone m

peak [piːk] n (of mountain) cima, vetta;
(mountain itself) picco; (of cap) visiera;
(fig) apice m, culmine m; **peak hours**
npl ore fpl di punta

peanut ['piːnʌt] n arachide f,
nocciolina americana; **peanut
butter** n burro di arachidi

pear [pɛə] n pera

pearl [pəːl] n perla

peasant ['pɛznt] n contadino(-a)

peat [piːt] n torba

pebble ['pɛbl] n ciottolo

peck [pɛk] vt (also: ~ at) beccare ▶ n
colpo di becco; (kiss) bacetto; **peckish**
(BRIT: inf) adj I feel **peckish** ho un
languorino

peculiar [pɪ'kjuːlɪə] adj strano(-a),
bizzarro(-a); peculiare; **to be ~ to**
essere peculiare
di

pedal ['pɛdl] n pedale m ▶ vi pedalare

pedalo ['pɛdələu] n pedalò m inv

pedestal ['pɛdəstl] n piedestallo

pedestrian [pɪ'dɛstrɪən] n pedone m
▶ adj pedonale; (fig) prosaico(-a),
pedestre; **pedestrian crossing**
(BRIT) n passaggio pedonale;
pedestrianized adj a **pedestrianized
street** una zona pedonalizzata;
pedestrian precinct (BRIT: US
pedestrian zone) n zona pedonale

pedigree ['pɛdɪgriː] n (of animal)
pedigree m inv; (fig) background m inv
▶ cpd (animal) di razza

pedophile ['pi:dəʊfaɪl] (US) n
= **paedophile**

pee [pi:] (inf) vi pisciare

peek [pi:k] vi guardare furtivamente

peel [pi:l] n buccia; (of orange, lemon)
scorza ▶ vt sbucciare ▶ vi (paint etc)
staccarsi

peep [pi:p] n (BRIT: look) sguardo
furtivo, sbirciata; (sound) pigolio ▶ vi
(BRIT) guardare furtivamente

peer [pɪəʳ] vi to ~ at scrutare ▶ n
(noble) pari m inv; (equal) pari
m/f inv, uguale m/f; (contemporary)
contemporaneo(-a)

peg [peg] n caviglia; (for coat etc)
attaccapanni m inv; (BRIT: also:
clothes ~) molletta

pelican ['pelɪkən] n pellicano; **pelican
crossing** (BRIT) n (Aut) attraversamento
pedonale con semaforo a controllo
manuale

pelt [pelt] vt to ~ sb (with)
bombardare qn (con) ▶ vi (rain)
piovere a dirotto; (inf: run) filare
▶ n pelle f

pelvis ['pelvɪs] n pelvi f inv, bacino

pen [pen] n penna; (for sheep) recinto

penalty ['penltɪ] n penalità f inv;
sanzione f penale; (fine) ammenda;
(Sport) penalizzazione f

pence [pens] (BRIT) npl of **penny**

pencil ['pensl] n matita ▶ **pencil in**
vt scrivere a matita; **pencil case**
n astuccio per matite; **pencil
sharpener** n temperamatite m inv

pendant ['pendnt] n pendaglio

pending ['pendɪŋ] prep in attesa di
▶ adj in sospeso

penetrate ['penɪtreɪt] vt penetrare

penfriend ['penfrend] (BRIT) n
corrispondente m/f

penguin ['peŋgwɪn] n pinguino

penicillin [penɪ'sɪlɪn] n penicillina

peninsula [pə'nɪnsjʊlə] n penisola

penis ['pi:nɪs] n pene m

penitentiary [penɪ'tenʃərɪ] (US) n
carcere m

penknife ['pennaɪf] n temperino

penniless ['penɪlɪs] adj senza un soldo

penny ['penɪ] (pl **pennies** or **pence**)
(BRIT) n penny m; (US) centesimo

penpal ['penpæl] n
corrispondente m/f

pension ['penʃən] n pensione f;
pensioner (BRIT) n pensionato(-a)

pentagon ['pentəgən] n pentagono;
the P~ (US Pol) il Pentagono

penthouse ['penthaʊs] n
appartamento (di lusso) nell'attico

penultimate [pɪ'nʌltɪmət] adj
penultimo(-a)

people ['pi:pl] npl gente f; persone
fpl; (citizens) popolo ▶ n (nation,
race) popolo; **4/several ~ came**
4/parecchie persone sono venute; ~
say that ... si dice che ...

pepper ['pepəʳ] n pepe m; (vegetable)
peperone m ▶ vt (fig) to ~ with
spruzzare di; **peppermint** n (sweet)
pasticca di menta

per [pəːʳ] prep per; a; ~ **hour** all'ora; ~
kilo etc il chilo etc; ~ **day** al giorno

perceive [pə'siːv] vt percepire; (notice)
accorgersi di

per cent adv per cento

percentage [pə'sentɪdʒ] n
percentuale f

perception [pə'sepʃən] n percezione f;
sensibilità; perspicacia

perch [pəːtʃ] n (fish) pesce m persico;
(for bird) sostegno, ramo ▶ vi
appollaiarsi

percussion [pə'kʌʃən] n percussione
f; (Mus) strumenti mpl a percussione

perfect [adj, n 'pəːfɪkt, vb pə'fekt]
adj perfetto(-a) ▶ n (also: ~ **tense**)
perfetto, passato prossimo ▶ vt
perfezionare; mettere a punto;
perfection [pə'fekʃən] n perfezione
f; **perfectly** adv perfettamente, alla

perfezione

perform [pə'fɔ:m] vt (carry out)
eseguire, fare; (symphony etc) suonare;
(play, ballet) dare; (opera) fare ▶ vi
suonare; recitare; **performance**
n esecuzione f; (at theatre etc)
rappresentazione f, spettacolo
(of an artist) interpretazione f; (of
player etc) performance f; (of car,
engine) prestazione f; **performer** n
artista m/f

perfume ['pə:fju:m] n profumo

perhaps [pə'hæps] adv forse

perimeter [pə'rɪmɪtə*] n perimetro

period ['pɪərɪəd] n periodo; (History)
epoca; (Scol) lezione f; (full stop)
punto; (Med) mestruazioni fpl
▶ adj (costume, furniture) d'epoca;
periodical [-'ɔdɪkl] n periodico;
periodically adv periodicamente

perish ['perɪʃ] vi perire, morire; (decay)
deteriorarsi

perjury ['pə:dʒərɪ] n spergiuro

perk [pə:k] (inf) n vantaggio

perm [pə:m] n (for hair) permanente f

permanent ['pə:mənənt] adj
permanente; **permanently** adv
definitivamente

permission [pə'mɪʃən] n permesso

permit [n 'pə:mɪt, vb pə'mɪt] n
permesso ▶ vt permettere; **to ~ sb to
do** permettere a qn di fare

perplex [pə'plɛks] vt lasciare
perplesso(-a)

persecute ['pə:sɪkju:t] vt
perseguitare

persecution [pə:sɪ'kju:ʃən] n
persecuzione f

persevere [pə:sɪ'vɪə*] vi perseverare

Persian ['pə:ʃən] adj persiano(-a) ▶ n
(Ling) persiano; **the (~) Gulf** n il Golfo
Persico

persist [pə'sɪst] vi **to ~ (in doing)**
persistere (nel fare); ostinarsi (a
fare); **persistent** adj persistente;

ostinato(-a)

person ['pə:sn] n persona; **in ~** di or in
persona, personalmente; **personal**
adj personale; individuale; **personal
assistant** n segretaria personale;
personal computer n personal
computer m inv; **personality** [-
'nælɪtɪ] n personalità f inv; **personally**
adv personalmente; **to take sth
personally** prendere qc come
una critica personale; **personal
organizer** n (Filofax®) Fulltime®;
(electronic) agenda elettronica;
personal stereo n Walkman® m inv

personnel [pə:sə'nɛl] n personale m

perspective [pə'spɛktɪv] n
prospettiva

perspiration [pə:spɪ'reɪʃən] n
traspirazione f, sudore m

persuade [pə'sweɪd] vt **to ~ sb to do
sth** persuadere qn a fare qc

persuasion [pə'sweɪʒən] n
persuasione f; (creed) convinzione
f, credo

persuasive [pə'sweɪsɪv] adj
persuasivo(-a)

perverse [pə'və:s] adj perverso(-a)

pervert [n 'pə:və:t, vb pə'və:t] n
pervertito(-a) ▶ vt pervertire

pessimism ['pɛsɪmɪzəm] n
pessimismo

pessimist ['pɛsɪmɪst] n pessimista
m/f; **pessimistic** [-'mɪstɪk] adj
pessimistico(-a)

pest [pɛst] n animale m (or insetto)
pestifero; (fig) peste f

pester ['pɛstə*] vt tormentare,
molestare

pesticide ['pɛstɪsaɪd] n pesticida m

pet [pɛt] n animale m domestico
▶ cpd favorito(-a) ▶ vt accarezzare;
teacher's ~ favorito(-a) del maestro

petal ['pɛtl] n petalo

petite [pə'ti:t] adj piccolo(-a) e
aggraziato(-a)

petition [pəˈtɪʃən] n petizione f
petrified [ˈpetrɪfaɪd] adj (fig) morto(-a) di paura
petrol [ˈpetrəl] (BRIT) n benzina; **two/four-star ~** ≈ benzina normale/super; **I've run out of ~** sono rimasto senza benzina

▌ Be careful not to translate **petrol** by the Italian word **petrolio**.

petroleum [pəˈtrəʊlɪəm] n petrolio
petrol: petrol pump (BRIT) n (in car, at garage) pompa di benzina; **petrol station** (BRIT) n stazione f di rifornimento; **petrol tank** (BRIT) n serbatoio della benzina
petticoat [ˈpetɪkəʊt] n sottana
petty [ˈpetɪ] adj (mean) meschino(-a); (unimportant) insignificante
pew [pju:] n panca (di chiesa)
pewter [ˈpju:tə*] n peltro
phantom [ˈfæntəm] n fantasma m
pharmacist [ˈfɑ:məsɪst] n farmacista m/f
pharmacy [ˈfɑ:məsɪ] n farmacia
phase [feɪz] n fase f, periodo ▷ **phase in** vt introdurre gradualmente ▷ **phase out** vt (machinery) eliminare gradualmente; (product) ritirare gradualmente; (job, subsidy) abolire gradualmente
Ph.D. n abbr = **Doctor of Philosophy**
pheasant [ˈfeznt] n fagiano
phenomena [fəˈnɔmɪnə] npl of **phenomenon**
phenomenal [fɪˈnɔmɪnl] adj fenomenale
phenomenon [fəˈnɔmɪnən] (pl **phenomena**) n fenomeno
Philippines [ˈfɪlɪpi:nz] npl the **~** le Filippine
philosopher [fɪˈlɔsəfə*] n filosofo(-a)
philosophical [fɪlə'sɔfɪkl] adj filosofico(-a)
philosophy [fɪˈlɔsəfɪ] n filosofia
phlegm [flɛm] n flemma

phobia [ˈfəʊbjə] n fobia
phone [fəʊn] n telefono ▶ vt telefonare; **to be on the ~** avere il telefono; (be calling) essere al telefono ▷ **phone back** vt, vi richiamare ▷ **phone up** vt telefonare a ▶ vi telefonare; **phone book** n guida del telefono, elenco telefonico; **phone booth** n = **phone box**; **phone box** n cabina telefonica; **phone call** n telefonata; **phonecard** n scheda telefonica; **phone number** n numero di telefono
phonetics [fəˈnetɪks] n fonetica
phoney [ˈfəʊnɪ] adj falso(-a), fasullo(-a)
photo [ˈfəʊtəʊ] n foto f inv
photo... [ˈfəʊtəʊ] prefix: **photo album** n (new) album m inv per fotografie; (containing photos) album m inv delle fotografie; **photocopier** n fotocopiatrice f; **photocopy** n fotocopia ▶ vt fotocopiare
photograph [ˈfəʊtəɡrɑ:f] n fotografia ▶ vt fotografare; **photographer** [fəˈtɔɡrəfə*] n fotografo; **photography** [fəˈtɔɡrəfɪ] n fotografia
phrase [freɪz] n espressione f; (Ling) locuzione f; (Mus) frase f ▶ vt esprimere; **phrase book** n vocabolarietto
physical [ˈfɪzɪkl] adj fisico(-a); **physical education** n educazione f fisica; **physically** adv fisicamente
physician [fɪˈzɪʃən] n medico
physicist [ˈfɪzɪsɪst] n fisico
physics [ˈfɪzɪks] n fisica
physiotherapist [fɪzɪəʊˈθerəpɪst] n fisioterapista m/f
physiotherapy [fɪzɪəʊˈθerəpɪ] n fisioterapia
physique [fɪˈzi:k] n fisico; costituzione f
pianist [ˈpi:ənɪst] n pianista m/f
piano [pɪˈænəʊ] n pianoforte m

pick [pɪk] n (tool: also: **~-axe**) piccone m ▶ vt scegliere; (gather) cogliere; (remove) togliere; (lock) far scattare; **take your ~** scelga; **the ~ of** il fior fiore di; **to ~ one's nose** mettersi le dita nel naso; **to ~ one's teeth** pulirsi i denti con lo stuzzicadenti; **to ~ a quarrel** attaccar briga ▶ **pick on** vt fus (person) avercela con ▶ **pick out** vt scegliere; (distinguish) distinguere ▶ **pick up** vi (improve) migliorare; ▶ vt raccogliere; (Police, Radio) prendere; (collect) passare a prendere; (Aut: give lift to) far salire; (person: for sexual encounter) rimorchiare; (learn) imparare; **to ~ up speed** acquistare velocità; **to ~ o.s. up** rialzarsi

pickle ['pɪkl] n (also: **~s**: as condiment) sottaceti mpl; (fig: mess) pasticcio ▶ vt mettere sottaceto; mettere in salamoia

pickpocket ['pɪkpɔkɪt] n borsaiolo

pick-up ['pɪkʌp] n (BRIT: on record player) pick-up m inv; (small truck: also: **~ truck, ~ van**) camioncino

picnic ['pɪknɪk] n picnic m inv; **picnic area** n area per il picnic

picture ['pɪktʃə*] n quadro; (painting) pittura; (photograph) foto(grafia); (drawing) disegno; (film) film m inv ▶ vt raffigurarsi; **~s** (BRIT) npl (cinema): **the ~s** il cinema; **would you take a ~ of us, please?** può farci una foto, per favore?; **picture frame** n cornice m inv; **picture messaging** n picture messaging m, invio di messaggini con disegni

picturesque [pɪktʃə'rɛsk] adj pittoresco(-a)

pie [paɪ] n torta; (of meat) pasticcio

piece [piːs] n pezzo; (item): **a ~ of furniture/advice** un mobile/consiglio ▶ vt **to ~ together** mettere insieme; **to take to ~s** smontare

pie chart n grafico a torta

pier [pɪə*] n molo; (of bridge etc) pila

pierce [pɪəs] vt forare; (with arrow etc) trafiggere; **pierced** adj **I've got pierced ears** ho i buchi per gli orecchini

pig [pɪg] n maiale m, porco

pigeon ['pɪdʒən] n piccione m

piggy bank ['pɪgɪ-] n salvadanaio

pigsty ['pɪgstaɪ] n porcile m

pigtail ['pɪgteɪl] n treccina

pike [paɪk] n (fish) luccio

pilchard ['pɪltʃəd] n specie di sardina

pile [paɪl] n (pillar, of books) pila; (heap) mucchio; (of carpet) pelo; **to ~ into** (car) stiparsi o ammucchiarsi in ▶ **pile up** vt ammucchiare ▶ vi ammucchiarsi; **piles** [paɪlz] npl emorroidi fpl; **pile-up** ['paɪlʌp] n (Aut) tamponamento a catena

pilgrimage ['pɪlgrɪmɪdʒ] n pellegrinaggio

pill [pɪl] n pillola; **the ~** la pillola

pillar ['pɪlə*] n colonna

pillow ['pɪləu] n guanciale m; **pillowcase** n federa

pilot ['paɪlət] n pilota m/f ▶ cpd (scheme etc) pilota ▶ vt pilotare; **pilot light** n fiamma pilota

pimple ['pɪmpl] n foruncolo

pin [pɪn] n spillo; (Tech) perno ▶ vt attaccare con uno spillo; **~s and needles** formicolio; **to ~ sb down** (fig) obbligare qn a pronunciarsi; **to ~ sth on sb** (fig) addossare la colpa di qc a qn

PIN n abbr (= personal identification number) codice m segreto

pinafore ['pɪnəfɔː*] n (also: **~ dress**) grembiule m (senza maniche)

pinch [pɪntʃ] n pizzicotto; (Culin) pizzicare; (inf: steal) grattare; **at a ~** in caso di bisogno

pine [paɪn] n (also: **~ tree**) pino ▶ vi **to ~ for** struggersi dal desiderio di

pineapple ['paɪnæpl] n ananas m inv

ping [pɪŋ] n (noise) tintinnio; **ping-pong®** n ping-pong® m

pink [pɪŋk] adj rosa inv ▶ n (colour) rosa m inv; (Bot) garofano

pinpoint ['pɪnpɔɪnt] vt indicare con precisione

pint [paɪnt] n (BRIT = 0.57l; US = 0.47l); (BRIT: inf) = birra da mezzo

pioneer [paɪə'nɪə*] n pioniere(-a)

pious ['paɪəs] adj pio(-a)

pip [pɪp] n (seed) seme m; (BRIT: time signal on radio) segnale m orario

pipe [paɪp] n tubo; (for smoking) pipa ▶ vt portare per mezzo di tubazione; **pipeline** n conduttura; (for oil) oleodotto; **piper** n piffero; suonatore(-trice) di cornamusa

pirate ['paɪərət] n pirata m ▶ vt riprodurre abusivamente

Pisces ['paɪsiːz] n Pesci mpl

piss [pɪs] (inf) vi pisciare; **pissed** (inf) adj (drunk) ubriaco(-a) fradicio(-a)

pistol ['pɪstl] n pistola

piston ['pɪstən] n pistone m

pit [pɪt] n buca, fossa; (also: **coal~**) miniera; (quarry) cava ▶ vt **to ~ sb against sb** opporre qn a qn

pitch [pɪtʃ] n (BRIT Sport) campo; (Mus) tono; (tar) pece f; (fig) grado, punto ▶ vt (throw) lanciare ▶ vi (fall) cascare; **to ~ a tent** piantare una tenda; **pitch-black** adj nero(-a) come la pece

pitfall ['pɪtfɔːl] n trappola

pith [pɪθ] n (of plant) midollo; (of orange) parte f interna della scorza; (fig) essenza, succo; vigore m

pitiful ['pɪtɪful] adj (touching) pietoso(-a)

pity ['pɪtɪ] n pietà ▶ vt aver pietà di; **what a ~!** che peccato!

pizza ['piːtsə] n pizza

placard ['plækɑːd] n affisso

place [pleɪs] n posto, luogo; (proper position, rank, seat) posto; (house) casa, alloggio; (home): **at/to his ~** a casa sua ▶ vt (object) posare, mettere; (identify) riconoscere; individuare; **to take ~** aver luogo; succedere; **to change ~s with sb** scambiare il posto con qn; **out of ~** (not suitable) inopportuno(-a); **in the first ~** in primo luogo; **to ~ an order** dare un'ordinazione; (in race, exam) classificarsi; **place mat** n sottopiatto; (in linen etc) tovaglietta; **placement** n collocamento; (job) lavoro

placid ['plæsɪd] adj placido(-a), calmo(-a)

plague [pleɪg] n peste f ▶ vt tormentare

plaice [pleɪs] n inv pianuzza

plain [pleɪn] adj (clear) chiaro(-a), palese; (simple) semplice; (frank) franco(-a), aperto(-a); (not handsome) bruttino(-a); (without seasoning etc) scondito(-a); naturale; (in one colour) tinta unita inv ▶ adv francamente, chiaramente ▶ n pianura; **plain chocolate** n cioccolato fondente; **plainly** adv chiaramente, (frankly) francamente

plaintiff ['pleɪntɪf] n attore(-trice)

plait [plæt] n treccia

plan [plæn] n pianta; (scheme) progetto, piano ▶ vt (think in advance) progettare; (prepare) organizzare ▶ vi far piani or progetti; **to ~ to do** progettare di fare

plane [pleɪn] n (Aviat) aereo; (tree) platano; (tool) pialla; (Art, Math etc) piano ▶ adj piano(-a), piatto(-a) ▶ vt (with tool) piallare

planet ['plænɪt] n pianeta m

plank [plæŋk] n tavola, asse f

planning ['plænɪŋ] n progettazione f; **family ~** pianificazione f delle nascite

plant [plɑːnt] n pianta; (machinery) impianto; (factory) fabbrica ▶ vt piantare; (bomb) mettere

plantation [plæn'teɪʃən] n
piantagione f
plaque [plæk] n placca
plaster ['plɑːstə*] n intonaco; (also: ~
of Paris) gesso; (BRIT: also: **sticking**
~) cerotto ▶ vt intonacare; ingessare;
(cover): **to ~ with** coprire di; **plaster
cast** n (Med) ingessatura, gesso;
(model, statue) modello in gesso
plastic ['plæstɪk] n plastica ▶ adj (made
of plastic) di or in plastica; **plastic
bag** n sacchetto di plastica; **plastic
surgery** n chirurgia plastica
plate [pleɪt] n (dish) piatto; (in book)
tavola; (dental plate) dentiera; **gold/
silver ~** vasellame m d'oro/d'argento
plateau ['plætəʊ] (pl **plateaus** or
plateaux) n altipiano
platform ['plætfɔːm] n (stage, at
meeting) palco; (Rail) marciapiede m;
(BRIT: of bus) piattaforma; **which ~
does the train for Rome go from?** da
che binario parte il treno per Roma?
platinum ['plætɪnəm] n platino
platoon [plə'tuːn] n plotone m
platter ['plætə*] n piatto
plausible ['plɔːzɪbl] adj plausibile,
credibile; (person) convincente
play [pleɪ] n gioco; (Theatre) commedia
▶ vt (game) giocare a; (team, opponent)
giocare contro; (instrument, piece
of music) suonare; (record, tape)
ascoltare; (role, part) interpretare
▶ vi giocare; suonare; recitare; **to
~ safe** giocare sul sicuro ▶ **play
back** vt riascoltare, risentire ▶ **play
up** vi (cause trouble) fare i capricci;
player n giocatore(-trice); (Theatre)
attore(-trice); (Mus) musicista
m/f; **playful** adj giocoso(-a);
playground n (in school) cortile m per
la ricreazione; (in park) parco m giochi
inv; **playgroup** n giardino d'infanzia;
playing card n carta da gioco;
playing field n campo sportivo

playschool n = **playgroup**; **playtime**
n (Scol) ricreazione f; **playwright** n
drammaturgo(-a)
plc abbr (= public limited company) società
per azioni a responsabilità limitata
quotata in borsa
plea [pliː] n (request) preghiera,
domanda; (Law) (argomento di)
difesa
plead [pliːd] vt patrocinare; (give as
excuse) addurre a pretesto ▶ vi (Law)
perorare la causa; (beg): **to ~ with sb**
implorare qn
pleasant ['plɛznt] adj piacevole,
gradevole
please [pliːz] excl per piacere!,
per favore!; (acceptance): **yes, ~** sì,
grazie ▶ vt piacere a ▶ vi piacere;
(think fit): **do as you ~** faccia come
le pare; **~ yourself!** come ti (or le)
pare!; **pleased** adj pleased (with)
contento(-a) (di); **pleased to meet
you!** piacere!
pleasure ['plɛʒə*] n piacere m; "**it's a
~**" "prego"
pleat [pliːt] n piega
pledge [plɛdʒ] n pegno; (promise)
promessa ▶ vt impegnare; promettere
plentiful ['plɛntɪful] adj abbondante,
copioso(-a)
plenty ['plɛntɪ] n **~ of** tanto(-a),
molto(-a); (enough) un'abbondanza di
pliers ['plaɪəz] npl pinza
plight [plaɪt] n situazione f critica
plod [plɒd] vi camminare a stento;
(fig) sgobbare
plonk [plɒŋk] (inf) n (BRIT: wine) vino
da poco ▶ vt **to ~ sth down** buttare giù
qc bruscamente
plot [plɒt] n congiura, cospirazione f;
(of story, play) trama; (of land) lotto ▶ vt
(mark out) fare la pianta di; rilevare;
(: diagram etc) tracciare; (conspire)
congiurare, cospirare ▶ vi congiurare
plough [plaʊ] (US **plow**) n aratro

▶ vt (earth) arare; **to ~ money into**
(company etc) investire danaro in;
ploughman's lunch ['plaumənz-]
(BRIT) n pasto a base di pane, formaggio
e birra

plow [plau] (US) = **plough**

ploy [plɔɪ] n stratagemma m

pluck [plʌk] vt (fruit) cogliere; (bird) spennare; (musical
instrument) pizzicare; (hairs) togliere ▶ n coraggio, fegato;
to ~ up courage farsi coraggio

plug [plʌg] n tappo; (Elec) spina; (Aut:
also: **spark(ing) ~**) candela ▶ vt (hole)
tappare; (inf: advertise) spingere
▷ **plug in** vt (Elec) attaccare a una
presa; **plughole** n (BRIT) scarico

plum [plʌm] n (fruit) susina

plumber ['plʌmə'] n idraulico

plumbing ['plʌmɪŋ] n (trade) lavoro di
idraulico; (piping) tubature fpl

plummet ['plʌmɪt] vi **to ~ (down)**
cadere a piombo

plump [plʌmp] adj grassoccio(-a) ▶ vi
to ~ for (inf: choose) decidersi per

plunge [plʌndʒ] n tuffo; (fig) caduta
▶ vt immergere ▶ vi (fall) cadere,
precipitare; (dive) tuffarsi; **to take the
~** saltare il fosso

plural ['pluərl] adj plurale ▶ n plurale m

plus [plʌs] n (also: **~ sign**) segno più
▶ prep più; **ten/twenty ~** più di
dieci/venti

ply [plaɪ] vt (a trade) esercitare ▶ vi
(ship) fare il servizio ▶ n (of wool, rope)
capo; **to ~ sb with drink** dare da bere
a qn; **plywood** n
legno compensato

P.M. n abbr = **prime minister**

p.m. adv abbr (= post meridiem) del
pomeriggio

PMS n abbr (= premenstrual syndrome)
sindrome f premestruale

PMT n abbr (= premenstrual tension)
sindrome f premestruale

pneumatic drill [njuː'mætɪk-] n

martello pneumatico

pneumonia [njuː'məunɪə] n
polmonite f

poach [pəutʃ] vt (cook: egg) affogare;
(: fish) cuocere in bianco; (steal)
cacciare (or pescare) di frodo ▶ vi fare
il bracconiere; **poached** (egg)
affogato(-a)

P.O. Box n abbr = **Post Office Box**

pocket ['pɔkɪt] n tasca ▶ vt intascare;
to be out of ~ (BRIT) rimetterci;
pocketbook (US) n (wallet)
portafoglio; **pocket money** n
paghetta, settimana

pod [pɔd] n guscio

podiatrist [pɔ'diːətrɪst] (US) n callista
m/f, pedicure m/f

podium ['pəudɪəm] n podio

poem ['pəuɪm] n poesia

poet ['pəuɪt] n poeta/essa; **poetic**
[-'ɛtɪk] adj poetico(-a); **poetry** n poesia

poignant ['pɔɪnjənt] adj struggente

point [pɔɪnt] n (gen) punto; (tip: of
needle etc) punta; (in time) punto,
momento; (Scol) voto; (main idea,
important part) nocciolo; (Elec) presa
(di corrente); (also: **decimal ~**): **2
~ 3 (2.3)** 2 virgola 3 (2,3) ▶ vt (show)
indicare; (gun etc) **to ~ sth at** puntare
qc contro ▶ vi **to ~ at** mostrare a dito;
~s npl (Aut) puntine fpl; (Rail) scambio;
to be on the ~ of doing sth essere sul
punto di or stare per fare qc; **to make
a ~** fare un'osservazione; **to get/miss
the ~** capire/non capire; **to come to
the ~** venire al fatto; **there's no ~ in
doing** è inutile (fare) ▷ **point out** vt
far notare; **point-blank** adv (also: **at
point-blank range**) a bruciapelo; (fig)
categoricamente; **pointed** adj (shape)
aguzzo(-a), appuntito(-a); (remark)
specifico(-a); **pointer** n (needle)
lancetta; (fig) indicazione f, consiglio;
pointless adj inutile, vano(-a); **point
of view** n punto di vista

poison ['pɔɪzn] n veleno ▶ vt avvelenare; **poisonous** adj velenoso(-a)

poke [pəuk] vt (fire) attizzare; (jab with finger, stick etc) punzecchiare; (put): **to ~ sth in(to)** spingere qc dentro ▶ **poke about** or **around** vi frugare ▷ **poke out** vi (stick out) spuntare fuori

poker ['pəukə'] n attizzatoio; (Cards) poker m

Poland ['pəulənd] n Polonia

polar ['pəulə'] adj polare; **polar bear** n orso bianco

Pole [pəul] n polacco(-a)

pole [pəul] n (of wood) palo; (Elec, Geo) polo; **pole bean** (US) n (runner bean) fagiolino; **pole vault** n salto con l'asta

police [pə'liːs] n polizia ▶ vt mantenere l'ordine in; **police car** n macchina della polizia; **police constable** (BRIT) n agente m di polizia; **police force** n corpo di polizia, polizia; **policeman** (irreg) n poliziotto, agente m di polizia; **police officer** n = **police constable**; **police station** n posto di polizia; **policewoman** (irreg) n donna f poliziotto inv

policy ['pɔlɪsɪ] n politica; (also: **insurance ~**) polizza (d'assicurazione)

polio ['pəulɪəu] n polio f

Polish ['pəulɪʃ] adj polacco(-a) ▶ n (Ling) polacco

polish ['pɔlɪʃ] n (for shoes) lucido; (for floor) cera; (for nails) smalto; (shine) lucentezza, lustro; (fig: refinement) raffinatezza ▶ vt lucidare; (fig: improve) raffinare ▷ **polish off** vt (food) mangiarsi; **polished** adj (fig) raffinato(-a)

polite [pə'laɪt] adj cortese; **politeness** n cortesia

political [pə'lɪtɪkl] adj politico(-a); **politically** adv politicamente; **politically correct** politicamente corretto(-a)

politician [pɔlɪ'tɪʃən] n politico

politics ['pɔlɪtɪks] n politica ▶ npl (views, policies) idee fpl politiche

poll [pəul] n scrutinio; (votes cast) voti mpl; (also: **opinion ~**) sondaggio (d'opinioni) ▶ vt ottenere

pollen ['pɔlən] n polline m

polling station ['pəulɪŋ-] (BRIT) n sezione f elettorale

pollute [pə'luːt] vt inquinare

pollution [pə'luːʃən] n inquinamento

polo ['pəuləu] n polo; **polo-neck** n collo alto; (also: **polo-neck sweater**) dolcevita ▶ adj a collo alto; **polo shirt** n polo f inv

polyester [pɔlɪ'ɛstə'] n poliestere m

polystyrene [pɔlɪ'staɪriːn] n polistirolo

polythene ['pɔlɪθiːn] n politene m; **polythene bag** n sacco di plastica

pomegranate ['pɔmɪgrænɪt] n melagrana

pompous ['pɔmpəs] adj pomposo(-a)

pond [pɔnd] n pozza; stagno

ponder ['pɔndə'] vt ponderare, riflettere su

pony ['pəunɪ] n pony m inv; **ponytail** n coda di cavallo; **pony trekking** [-trɛkɪŋ] (BRIT) n escursione f a cavallo

poodle ['puːdl] n barboncino, barbone m

pool [puːl] n (puddle) pozza; (pond) stagno; (also: **swimming ~**) piscina; (fig: of light) cerchio; (billiards) specie di biliardo a buca ▶ vt mettere in comune; **~s** npl (football pools) = totocalcio; **typing ~** servizio comune di dattilografia

poor [puə'] adj povero(-a); (mediocre) mediocre, cattivo(-a) ▶ npl **the ~** i poveri; **~ in** povero(-a) di; **poorly** adv poveramente; male ▶ adj indisposto(-a), malato(-a)

pop [pɔp] n (noise) schiocco; (Mus) musica pop; (drink) bibita gasata; (US:

inf: father) babbo ▶ vt *(put)* mettere
(in fretta) ▶ vi scoppiare; *(cork)*
schioccare ▷ **pop in** vi passare ▷ **pop
out** vi fare un salto fuori; ▷ **pop
up** vi fare un salto fuori;
pop-corn m

poplar ['pɒplə^r] n pioppo
popper ['pɒpə^r] n bottone m a
pressione
poppy ['pɒpɪ] n papavero
Popsicle® ['pɒpsɪkl] (US) n *(ice lolly)*
ghiacciolo
pop star n pop star f inv
popular ['pɒpjulə^r] adj popolare;
(fashionable) in voga; **popularity**
[-'lærɪtɪ] n popolarità
population [pɒpju'leɪʃən] n
popolazione f
porcelain ['pɔːslɪn] n porcellana
porch [pɔːtʃ] n veranda
pore [pɔː^r] n poro ▶ vi **to ~ over** essere
immerso(-a) in
pork [pɔːk] n carne f di maiale;
pork chop n braciola or costoletta
di maiale; **pork pie** n *(BRIT: Culin)*
pasticcio di maiale in crosta
porn [pɔːn] (inf) n pornografia ▶ adj
porno inv; **pornographic** [pɔː-
nə'græfɪk] adj pornografico(-a);
pornography [pɔː'nɔgrəfɪ] n
pornografia
porridge ['pɒrɪdʒ] n porridge m
port [pɔːt] n *(gen, wine)* porto; *(Naut:
left side)* babordo
portable ['pɔːtəbl] adj portatile
porter ['pɔːtə^r] n *(for luggage)* facchino,
portabagagli m inv; *(doorkeeper)*
portiere m, portinaio
portfolio [pɔːt'fəulɪəu] n *(case)*
cartella; *(Pol, Finance)* portafoglio; *(of
artist)* raccolta dei propri lavori
portion ['pɔːʃən] n porzione f
port of call n *(porto di)* scalo
portrait ['pɔːtreɪt] n ritratto
portray [pɔː'treɪ] vt fare il ritratto di;
(character on stage) rappresentare; (in

writing) ritrarre
Portugal ['pɔːtjugl] n Portogallo
Portuguese [pɔːtju'giːz] adj
portoghese ▶ n inv portoghese m/f;
(Ling) portoghese m
pose [pəuz] n posa ▶ vi posare;
(pretend): **to ~ as** atteggiarsi a, posare
a ▶ vt porre
posh [pɒʃ] (inf) adj elegante; *(family)*
per bene
position [pə'zɪʃən] n posizione f; *(job)*
posto ▶ vt sistemare
positive ['pɒzɪtɪv] adj positivo(-a);
(certain) sicuro(-a), certo(-a); *(definite)*
preciso(-a), definitivo(-a); **positively**
adv *(affirmatively, enthusiastically)*
positivamente; *(decisively)*
decisamente; *(really)* assolutamente
possess [pə'zɛs] vt possedere;
possession [pə'zɛʃən] n possesso;
possessions npl *(belongings)* beni mpl;
possessive adj possessivo(-a)
possibility [pɒsɪ'bɪlɪtɪ] n possibilità
f inv
possible ['pɒsɪbl] adj possibile; **as
big as ~** il più grande possibile;
possibly ['pɒsɪblɪ] adv *(perhaps)* forse;
if you possibly can se lo è possibile;
I cannot possibly come proprio non
posso venire
post [pəust] n *(BRIT)* posta; (: *collection)*
levata; *(job, situation)* posto; *(Mil)*
postazione f; *(pole)* palo ▶ vt *(BRIT:
send by post)* imbucare; (: *appoint)*: **to
~ to** assegnare a; **where can I ~ these
cards?** dove posso imbucare queste
cartoline?; **postage** n affrancatura;
postal adj postale; **postal order** n
vaglia m inv postale; **postbox** *(BRIT)*
n cassetta postale; **postcard** n
cartolina; **postcode** n *(BRIT)* codice m
(di avviamento) postale
poster ['pəustə^r] n manifesto, affisso
postgraduate ['pəust'grædjuət] n
laureato/a che continua gli studi

postman ['pəustmən] (irreg) n postino

postmark ['pəustmɑːk] n bollo or timbro postale

post-mortem [-'mɔːtəm] n autopsia

post office n (building) ufficio postale; (organization): the **Post Office** = le Poste e Telecomunicazioni

postpone [pəs'pəun] vt rinviare

posture ['pɒstʃəʳ] n portamento; (pose) posa, atteggiamento

postwoman ['pəustwumən] (BRIT: irreg) n postina

pot [pɒt] n (for cooking) pentola; casseruola; (teapot) teiera; (coffeepot) caffettiera; (for plants, jam) vaso; (inf: marijuana) erba ▶ vt (plant) piantare in vaso; **a ~ of tea for two** tè per due; **to go to ~** (inf: work, performance) andare in malora

potato [pə'teɪtəu] (pl **potatoes**) n patata; **potato peeler** n sbucciapatate m inv

potent ['pəutnt] adj potente, forte

potential [pə'tɛnʃl] adj potenziale ▶ n possibilità f

pothole ['pɒthəul] n (in road) buca; (BRIT: underground) caverna

pot plant n pianta in vaso

potter ['pɒtəʳ] n vasaio ▶ vi **to ~ around, ~ about** (BRIT) lavoracchiare; **pottery** n ceramiche fpl; (factory) fabbrica di ceramiche

potty ['pɒtɪ] adj (inf: mad) tocco(-a) ▶ n (child's) vasino

pouch [pautʃ] n borsa; (Zool) marsupio

poultry ['pəultrɪ] n pollame m

pounce [pauns] vi **to ~ (on)** piombare (su)

pound [paund] n (weight) libbra; (money) (lira) sterlina ▶ vt (beat) battere; (crush) pestare, polverizzare ▶ vi (beat) battere, martellare; **pound sterling** n sterlina (inglese)

pour [pɔːʳ] vt versare ▶ vi riversarsi; (rain) piovere a dirotto ▶ **pour in** vi

affluire in gran quantità ▶ **pour out** vi (people) uscire a fiumi ▶ vt vuotare; versare; (fig) sfogare; **pouring** adj **pouring rain** pioggia torrenziale

pout [paut] vi sporgere le labbra; fare il broncio

poverty ['pɒvətɪ] n povertà, miseria

powder ['paudəʳ] n polvere f ▶ vt **to ~ one's face** incipriarsi il viso; **powdered milk** n latte m in polvere

power ['pauəʳ] n (strength) potenza, forza; (ability, Pol: of party, leader) potere m; (Elec) corrente f; **to be in ~** (Pol etc) essere al potere; **power cut** (BRIT) n interruzione f or mancanza di corrente; **power failure** n interruzione f della corrente elettrica; **powerful** adj potente, forte; **powerless** adj impotente; **powerless to do** impossibilitato(-a) a fare; **power point** (BRIT) n presa di corrente; **power station** n centrale f elettrica

p.p. abbr = **per procurationem**; **p.p.J. Smith** per J. Smith; (= pages) p.

PR abbr = **public relations**

practical ['præktɪkl] adj pratico(-a); **practical joke** n beffa; **practically** adv praticamente

practice ['præktɪs] n pratica; (of profession) esercizio; (at football etc) allenamento; (business) gabinetto; clientela ▶ vt, vi (US) = **practise**; **in ~ (reality)** in pratica; **out of ~** fuori esercizio

practise ['præktɪs] (US **practice**) vt (work at: piano, one's backhand etc) esercitarsi a; (train for: skiing, running etc) allenarsi a; (sport, religion) praticare; (method) usare; (profession) esercitare ▶ vi esercitarsi; (train) allenarsi; (lawyer, doctor) esercitare; **practising** adj (Christian etc) praticante; (lawyer) che esercita la professione

practitioner [præk'tɪʃənəʳ] n
professionista m/f

pragmatic [præg'mætɪk] adj
pragmatico(-a)

prairie ['prɛərɪ] n prateria

praise [preɪz] n elogio, lode f ▸ vt
elogiare, lodare

pram [præm] (BRIT) n carrozzina

prank [præŋk] n burla

prawn [prɔ:n] n gamberetto;
prawn cocktail n cocktail m inv di
gamberetti

pray [preɪ] vi pregare; **prayer** [prɛəʳ]
n preghiera

preach [pri:tʃ] vi, vt predicare;
preacher n predicatore(-trice); (US:
minister) pastore m

precarious [prɪ'kɛərɪəs] adj
precario(-a)

precaution [prɪ'kɔ:ʃən] n
precauzione f

precede [prɪ'si:d] vt precedere;
precedent ['prɛsɪdənt] n precedente
m; **preceding** [prɪ'si:dɪŋ] adj
precedente

precinct ['pri:sɪŋkt] (US) n
circoscrizione f

precious ['prɛʃəs] adj prezioso(-a)

precise [prɪ'saɪs] adj preciso(-a);
precisely adv precisamente

precision [prɪ'sɪʒən] n precisione f

predator ['prɛdətəʳ] n predatore m

predecessor ['pri:dɪsɛsəʳ] n
predecessore(-a)

predicament [prɪ'dɪkəmənt] n
situazione f difficile

predict [prɪ'dɪkt] vt predire;
predictable adj prevedibile;
prediction [prɪ'dɪkʃən] n predizione f

predominantly [prɪ'dɔmɪnəntlɪ] adv
in maggior parte; soprattutto

preface ['prɛfəs] n prefazione f

prefect ['pri:fɛkt] n (BRIT: in school)
studente(-essa) con funzioni
disciplinari; (French etc, Admin)
prefetto

prefer [prɪ'fə:ʳ] vt preferire; **to ~ doing**
or **to do** preferire fare; **preferable**
['prɛfrəbl] adj preferibile; **preferably**
['prɛfrəblɪ] adv preferibilmente;
preference ['prɛfrəns] n preferenza

prefix ['pri:fɪks] n prefisso

pregnancy ['prɛgnənsɪ] n gravidanza

pregnant ['prɛgnənt] adj incinta ag

prehistoric ['pri:hɪs'tɔrɪk] adj
preistorico(-a)

prejudice ['prɛdʒudɪs] n pregiudizio;
(harm) torto, danno; **prejudiced** adj
(person) prevenuto(-a);
prejudiced (against) prevenuto(-a)
(contro); **prejudiced (in favour of)**
ben disposto(-a) (verso)

preliminary [prɪ'lɪmɪnərɪ] adj
preliminare

prelude ['prɛlju:d] n preludio

premature ['prɛmətʃuəʳ] adj
prematuro(-a)

premier ['prɛmɪəʳ] adj primo(-a) ▸ n
(Pol) primo ministro

première ['prɛmɪɛəʳ] n prima

Premier League n = serie A

premises ['prɛmɪsɪz] npl locale m;
on the ~ sul posto; **business ~** locali
commerciali

premium ['pri:mɪəm] n premio; **to be
at a ~** essere ricercatissimo

premonition [prɛmə'nɪʃən] n
premonizione f

preoccupied [pri:'ɔkjupaɪd] adj
preoccupato(-a)

prepaid [pri:'peɪd] adj pagato(-a) in
anticipo

preparation [prɛpə'reɪʃən] n
preparazione f; **~s** npl (for trip, war)
preparativi mpl

preparatory school [prɪ'pærətərɪ-] n
scuola elementare privata

prepare [prɪ'pɛəʳ] vt preparare ▸ vi **to ~
for** prepararsi a; **~d to** pronto(-a) a

preposition [prɛpə'zɪʃən] n
preposizione f

prep school n = preparatory school

prerequisite [priː'rɛkwɪzɪt] n requisito indispensabile

preschool ['priː'skuːl] adj (age) prescolastico(-a); (child) in età prescolastica

prescribe [prɪ'skraɪb] vt (Med) prescrivere

prescription [prɪ'skrɪpʃən] n prescrizione f; (Med) ricetta; **could you write me a ~?** mi può fare una ricetta medica?

presence ['prɛzns] n presenza; **~ of mind** presenza di spirito

present [adj, n 'prɛznt, vb prɪ'zɛnt] adj presente; (wife, residence, job) attuale ▶ n (actuality): **the ~** il presente; (gift) regalo ▶ vt presentare; (give): **to ~ sb with sth** offrire qc a qn; **to give sb a ~** fare un regalo a qn; **at ~** al momento; **presentable** [prɪ'zɛntəbl] adj presentabile; **presentation** [-'teɪʃən] n presentazione f; (ceremony) consegna ufficiale; **present-day** adj attuale, d'oggigiorno; **presenter** n (Radio, TV) presentatore(-trice); **presently** adv (soon) fra poco, presto; (at present) al momento; **present participle** n participio presente

preservation [prɛzə'veɪʃən] n preservazione f, conservazione f

preservative [prɪ'zəːvətɪv] n conservante m

preserve [prɪ'zəːv] vt (keep safe) preservare, proteggere; (maintain) conservare; (food) mettere in conserva ▶ n (often pl: jam) marmellata; (: fruit) frutta sciroppata

preside [prɪ'zaɪd] vi **to ~ (over)** presiedere a

president ['prɛzɪdənt] n presidente m; **presidential** [-'dɛnʃl] adj presidenziale

press [prɛs] n (newspapers etc): **the P~** la stampa; (tool, machine) pressa;

(for wine) torchio ▶ vt (push) premere, pigiare; (squeeze) spremere; (: hand) stringere; (clothes: iron) stirare; (pursue) incalzare; (insist): **to ~ sth on sb** far accettare qc da qn ▶ vi premere; accalcare; **we are ~ed for time** ci manca il tempo; **to ~ for sth** insistere per avere qc; **press conference** n conferenza f stampa inv; **pressing** adj urgente; **press stud** (BRIT) n bottone m a pressione; **press-up** (BRIT) n flessione f sulle braccia

pressure ['prɛʃəʳ] n pressione f; **to put ~ on sb (to do)** mettere qn sotto pressione (affinché faccia); **pressure cooker** n pentola a pressione; **pressure group** n gruppo di pressione

prestige [prɛs'tiːʒ] n prestigio

prestigious [prɛs'tɪdʒəs] adj prestigioso(-a)

presumably [prɪ'zjuːməblɪ] adv presumibilmente

presume [prɪ'zjuːm] vt supporre

pretence [prɪ'tɛns] (US **pretense**) n (claim) pretesa; **to make a ~ of doing** far finta di fare; **under false ~s** con l'inganno

pretend [prɪ'tɛnd] vt (feign) fingere ▶ vi far finta; **to ~ to do** far finta di fare

pretense [prɪ'tɛns] (US) n = **pretence**

pretentious [prɪ'tɛnʃəs] adj pretenzioso(-a)

pretext ['priːtɛkst] n pretesto

pretty ['prɪtɪ] adj grazioso(-a), carino(-a) ▶ adv abbastanza, assai

prevail [prɪ'veɪl] vi (win, be usual) prevalere; (persuade): **to ~ (up)on sb to do** persuadere qn a fare; **prevailing** adj dominante

prevalent ['prɛvələnt] adj (belief) predominante; (customs) diffuso(-a); (fashion) corrente; (disease) comune

prevent [prɪ'vɛnt] vt **to ~ sb from doing** impedire a qn di fare; **to ~**

sth from happening impedire che
qc succeda; **prevention** [-'venʃən]
n prevenzione f; **preventive** adj
preventivo(-a)
preview ['pri:vju:] n (of film)
anteprima
previous ['pri:vɪəs] adj precedente;
anteriore; **previously** adv prima
prey [preɪ] n preda ▶ vi to ~ on far
preda di; **it was ~ing on his mind** lo
stava ossessionando
price [praɪs] n prezzo ▶ vt (goods)
fissare il prezzo di; valutare; **priceless**
adj inapprezzabile; **price list** n listino
(dei) prezzi
prick [prɪk] n puntura ▶ vt pungere; **~
up one's ears** drizzare gli orecchi
prickly ['prɪklɪ] adj spinoso(-a)
pride [praɪd] n orgoglio; superbia ▶ vt
to ~ o.s. on essere orgoglioso(-a) di,
vantarsi di
priest [pri:st] n prete m, sacerdote m
primarily ['praɪmərɪlɪ] adv
principalmente, essenzialmente
primary ['praɪmərɪ] adj primario(-a);
(first in importance) primo(-a) ▶ n (US:
election) primarie fpl; **primary school**
(BRIT) n scuola elementare
prime [praɪm] adj primario(-a),
fondamentale; (excellent) di prima
qualità ▶ vt (wood) preparare; (fig)
mettere al corrente ▶ **in the ~ of life**
nel fiore della vita; **Prime Minister** n
primo ministro
primitive ['prɪmɪtɪv] adj primitivo(-a)
primrose ['prɪmrəʊz] n primavera
prince [prɪns] n principe m
princess [prɪn'ses] n principessa
principal ['prɪnsɪpl] adj principale ▶ n
(headmaster) preside m; **principally**
adv principalmente
principle ['prɪnsɪpl] n principio; **in ~** in
linea di principio; **on ~** per principio
print [prɪnt] n (mark) impronta;
(letters) caratteri mpl; (fabric) tessuto

stampato; (Art, Phot) stampa ▶ vt
imprimere; (publish) stampare,
pubblicare; (write in capitals) scrivere
in stampatello; **out of ~** esaurito(-a)
▷ **print out** vt (Comput) stampare;
printer n tipografo; (machine)
stampante f; **printout** n tabulato
prior ['praɪə*] adj precedente; (claim
etc) più importante; **~ to doing** prima
di fare
priority [praɪ'ɒrɪtɪ] n priorità f inv;
precedenza
prison ['prɪzn] n prigione f ▶ cpd
(system) carcerario(-a); (conditions,
food) nelle o delle prigioni; **prisoner**
n prigioniero(-a); **prisoner-of-war** n
prigioniero(-a) di guerra
pristine ['prɪsti:n] adj immacolato(-a)
privacy ['prɪvəsɪ] n solitudine f,
intimità
private ['praɪvɪt] adj privato(-a);
personale ▶ n soldato semplice; **"~"**
(on envelope) "riservata"; (on door)
"privato"; **in ~** in privato; **privately**
adv in privato; (within oneself) dentro
di sé; **private property** n proprietà
privata; **private school** n scuola
privata
privatize ['praɪvɪtaɪz] vt privatizzare
privilege ['prɪvɪlɪdʒ] n privilegio
prize [praɪz] n premio ▶ adj (example,
idiot) perfetto(-a); (bull, novel)
premiato(-a) ▶ vt apprezzare,
pregiare; **prize-giving** n premiazione
f; **prizewinner** n premiato(-a)
pro [prəʊ] n (Sport) professionista
m/f ▶ prep pro; **the ~s and cons** il pro
e il contro
probability [prɒbə'bɪlɪtɪ] n
probabilità f inv; **in all ~** con tutta
probabilità
probable ['prɒbəbl] adj probabile
probably ['prɒbəblɪ] adv
probabilmente
probation [prə'beɪʃən] n **on ~**

(*employee*) in prova; (*Law*) in libertà vigilata

probe [prəʊb] *n* (*Med, Space*) sonda; (*enquiry*) indagine *f*, investigazione *f* ▶ *vt* sondare, esplorare; indagare

problem ['prɒbləm] *n* problema *m*

procedure [prə'si:dʒə[r]] *n* (*Admin, Law*) procedura; (*method*) metodo, procedimento

proceed [prə'si:d] *vi* (*go forward*) avanzare, andare avanti; (*go about it*) procedere; (*continue*): **to ~ (with)** continuare; **to ~ to** andare a; passare a; **to ~ to do** mettersi a fare; **proceedings** *npl* misure *fpl*; (*Law*) procedimento; (*meeting*) riunione *f*; (*records*) rendiconti *mpl*; atti *mpl*; **proceeds** ['prəʊsi:dz] *npl* profitto, incasso

process ['prəʊses] *n* processo; (*method*) metodo, sistema *m* ▶ *vt* trattare; (*information*) elaborare

procession [prə'seʃən] *n* processione *f*, corteo; **funeral ~** corteo funebre

proclaim [prə'kleɪm] *vt* proclamare, dichiarare

prod [prɒd] *vt* dare un colpetto a; pungolare ▶ *n* colpetto

produce [*n* 'prɒdju:s, *vb* prə'dju:s] *n* (*Agr*) prodotto, prodotti *mpl* ▶ *vt* produrre; (*show*) esibire, mostrare; (*cause*) cagionare, causare; **producer** *n* (*Theatre*) regista *m/f*; (*Agr, Cinema*) produttore *m*

product ['prɒdʌkt] *n* prodotto; **production** [prə'dʌkʃən] *n* produzione *f*; **productive** [prə'dʌktɪv] *adj* produttivo(-a); **productivity** [prɒdʌk'tɪvɪtɪ] *n* produttività

Prof. *abbr* (= *professor*) Prof.

profession [prə'feʃən] *n* professione *f*; **professional** *n* professionista *m/f* ▶ *adj* professionale; (*work*) da professionista

professor [prə'fesə[r]] *n* professore

m (*titolare di una cattedra*); (*US*) professore(-essa)

profile ['prəʊfaɪl] *n* profilo

profit ['prɒfɪt] *n* profitto; beneficio ▶ *vi* **to ~ (by** *o* **from)** approfittare (di); **profitable** *adj* redditizio(-a)

profound [prə'faʊnd] *adj* profondo(-a)

programme ['prəʊgræm] (*US* **program**) *n* programma *m* ▶ *vt* programmare; **programmer** (*US* **programer**) *n* programmatore(-trice); **programming** (*US* **programing**) *n* programmazione *f*

progress [*n* 'prəʊgres, *vb* prə'gres] *n* progresso ▶ *vi* avanzare, procedere; **in ~** in corso; **to make ~** fare progressi; **progressive** [-'gresɪv] *adj* progressivo(-a); (*person*) progressista

prohibit [prə'hɪbɪt] *vt* proibire, vietare

project [*n* 'prɒdʒekt, *vb* prə'dʒekt] *n* (*plan*) piano; (*venture*) progetto; (*Scol*) studio ▶ *vt* proiettare ▶ *vi* (*stick out*) sporgere; **projection** [prə'dʒekʃən] *n* proiezione *f*; sporgenza; **projector** [prə'dʒektə[r]] *n* proiettore *m*

prolific [prə'lɪfɪk] *adj* (*artist etc*) fecondo(-a)

prolong [prə'lɒŋ] *vt* prolungare

prom [prɒm] *n abbr* = **promenade**; (*US: ball*) ballo studentesco

● **Prom**
● In Gran Bretagna i **Proms**, o
● "promenade concerts", sono
● concerti di musica classica, i più
● noti dei quali sono eseguiti nella
● prestigiosa **Royal Albert Hall** a
● Londra. Si chiamano così perché
● un tempo il pubblico seguiva i
● concerti in piedi, passeggiando
● (in inglese "promenade" voleva
● dire, appunto, passeggiare). Negli
● Stati Uniti, invece, con **prom**, si
● intende l'annuale ballo studentesco

di un'università o di una scuola secondaria.

promenade [prɒmə'nɑːd] n (by sea) lungomare m

prominent ['prɒmɪnənt] adj (standing out) prominente; (important) importante

promiscuous [prə'mɪskjuəs] adj (sexually) di facili costumi

promise ['prɒmɪs] n promessa ► vt, vi promettere; to ~ sb sth, ~ sth to sb promettere qc a qn; to ~ (sb) that/to do sth promettere (a qn) che/di fare qc; **promising** adj promettente

promote [prə'məut] vt promuovere; (venture, event) organizzare; **promotion** [-'məuʃən] n promozione f

prompt [prɒmpt] adj rapido(-a), svelto(-a); puntuale; sollecito(-a) ► adv (punctually) in punto ► n (Comput) prompt m ► vt incitare; provocare; (Theatre) suggerire a; to ~ sb to do incitare qn a fare; **promptly** adv prontamente; puntualmente

prone [prəun] adj (lying) prono(-a): ~ to propenso(-a) a, incline a

prong [prɒŋ] n rebbio, punta

pronoun ['prəunaun] n pronome m

pronounce [prə'nauns] vt pronunciare; **how do you ~ it?** come si pronuncia?

pronunciation [prənʌnsɪ'eɪʃən] n pronuncia

proof [pruːf] n prova; (of book) bozza; (Phot) provino ► adj ~ against a prova di

prop [prɒp] n sostegno, appoggio ► vt (also: ~ up) sostenere, appoggiare; (lean): to ~ sth against appoggiare qc contro o a; ~s oggetti m inv di scena ▷ prop up vt sostenere, appoggiare

propaganda [prɒpə'gændə] n propaganda

propeller [prə'pelə'] n elica

proper ['prɒpə'] adj (suited, right) adatto(-a), appropriato(-a); (seemly) decente; (authentic) vero(-a); (inf: real: noun) + vero(-a) e proprio(-a); **properly** adv (eat, study) bene; (behave) come si deve; **proper noun** n nome m proprio

property ['prɒpətɪ] n (things owned) beni mpl; (land, building) proprietà f inv; (Chem etc: quality) proprietà f

prophecy ['prɒfɪsɪ] n profezia

prophet ['prɒfɪt] n profeta m

proportion [prə'pɔːʃən] n proporzione f; (share) parte f; ~s npl (size) proporzioni fpl; **proportional** adj proporzionale

proposal [prə'pəuzl] n proposta; (plan) progetto; (of marriage) proposta di matrimonio

propose [prə'pəuz] vt proporre, suggerire ► vi fare una proposta di matrimonio; to ~ to do proporsi di fare, aver l'intenzione di fare

proposition [prɒpə'zɪʃən] n proposizione f; (offer) proposta

proprietor [prə'praɪətə'] n proprietario(-a)

prose [prəuz] n prosa

prosecute ['prɒsɪkjuːt] vt processare; **prosecution** [-'kjuːʃən] n processo; (accusing side) accusa; **prosecutor** n (also: **public prosecutor**) = procuratore m della Repubblica

prospect [n 'prɒspekt, vb prə'spekt] n prospettiva; (hope) speranza ► vi to ~ for cercare; ~s npl (for work etc) prospettive fpl; **prospective** [-'spektɪv] adj possibile; futuro(-a)

prospectus [prə'spektəs] n prospetto, programma m

prosper ['prɒspə'] vi prosperare; **prosperity** [prɒ'spɛrɪtɪ] n prosperità; **prosperous** adj prospero(-a)

prostitute ['prɒstɪtjuːt] n prostituta

male ~ uomo che si prostituisce

protect [prə'tɛkt] vt proteggere,
salvaguardare; **protection** n
protezione f; **protective** adj
protettivo(-a)

protein ['prəʊtiːn] n proteina

protest [n 'prəʊtɛst, vb prə'tɛst]
protesta ▶ vt, vi protestare

Protestant ['prɒtɪstənt] adj, n
protestante m/f

protester [prə'tɛstə'] n
dimostrante m/f

protractor [prə'træktə'] n (Geom)
goniometro

proud [praud] adj fiero(-a),
orgoglioso(-a); (pej) superbo(-a)

prove [pruːv] vt provare, dimostrare
▶ vi **to ~ (to be) correct** etc risultare
vero(-a) etc; **to ~ o.s.** mostrare le
proprie capacità

proverb ['prɒvəːb] n proverbio

provide [prə'vaɪd] vt fornire,
provvedere; **to ~ sb with sth** fornire
or provvedere qn di qc ▶ **provide
for** vt fus provvedere a; (future event)
prevedere; **provided** conj **provided
(that)** purché + sub, a condizione
che + sub; **providing** [prə'vaɪdɪn] conj
purché + sub, a condizione che + sub

province ['prɒvɪns] n provincia;
provincial [prə'vɪnʃəl] adj provinciale

provision [prə'vɪʒən] n (supply)
riserva; (supplying) provvista;
rifornimento; (stipulation) condizione
f; **~s** npl (food) provviste fpl;
provisional adj provvisorio(-a)

provocative [prə'vɒkətɪv] adj
(aggressive) provocatorio(-a); (thought-
provoking) stimolante; (seductive)
provocante

provoke [prə'vəuk] vt provocare;
incitare

prowl [praul] vi (also: ~ **about**, ~
around) aggirarsi ▶ n **to be on the
~** aggirarsi

proximity [prɒk'sɪmɪtɪ] n prossimità

proxy ['prɒksɪ] n **by ~** per procura

prudent ['pruːdnt] adj prudente

prune [pruːn] n prugna secca ▶ vt
potare

pry [praɪ] vi **to ~ into** ficcare il naso in

PS abbr (= postscript) P.S.

pseudonym ['sjuːdənɪm] n
pseudonimo

psychiatric [saɪkɪ'ætrɪk] adj
psichiatrico(-a)

psychiatrist [saɪ'kaɪətrɪst] n
psichiatra m/f

psychic ['saɪkɪk] adj (also: ~**al**)
psichico(-a); (person) dotato(-a) di
qualità telepatiche

psychoanalysis [saɪkəuə'nælɪsɪs,
-siːz] (pl -ses) n psicanalisi f inv

psychological [saɪkə'lɒdʒɪkl] adj
psicologico(-a)

psychologist [saɪ'kɒlədʒɪst] n
psicologo(-a)

psychology [saɪ'kɒlədʒɪ] n psicologia

psychotherapy [saɪkəu'θɛrəpɪ] n
psicoterapia

pt abbr (= pint; point) pt

PTO abbr (= please turn over) v.r.

pub [pʌb] n abbr (= public house) pub
m inv

puberty ['pjuːbətɪ] n pubertà

public ['pʌblɪk] adj pubblico(-a) ▶ n
pubblico; **in ~** in pubblico

publication [pʌblɪ'keɪʃən] n
pubblicazione f

public: **public company** n società f inv
per azioni (costituita tramite pubblica
sottoscrizione); **public convenience**
(BRIT) n gabinetti mpl; **public holiday**
n giorno festivo, festa nazionale;
public house (BRIT) n pub m inv

publicity [pʌb'lɪsɪtɪ] n pubblicità

publicize ['pʌblɪsaɪz] vt rendere
pubblico(-a)

public: **public limited company** n
≈ società per azioni a responsabilità

limitata (*quota in Borsa*); **publicly**
['pʌblɪklɪ] *adv* pubblicamente; **public
opinion** *n* opinione *f* pubblica; **public
relations** *n* pubbliche relazioni *fpl*;
public school *n* (BRIT) scuola privata;
(US) scuola statale; **public transport**
n mezzi *mpl* pubblici

publish ['pʌblɪʃ] *vt* pubblicare;
publisher *n* editore *m*; **publishing**
n (*industry*) editoria; (*of a book*)
pubblicazione *f*

pub lunch *n* pranzo semplice ed
economico servito nei pub

pudding ['pudɪŋ] *n* budino; (BRIT:
dessert) dolce *m*; **black ~**, (US) **blood~**
sanguinaccio

puddle ['pʌdl] *n* pozza, pozzanghera

Puerto Rico ['pwə:təu'ri:kəu] *n*
Portorico

puff [pʌf] *n* sbuffo ▶ *vt* to ~ one's pipe
tirare sboccate di fumo ▶ *vi* (*pant*)
ansare; **puff pastry** *n* pasta sfoglia

pull [pul] *n* (*tug*): **to give sth a ~** tirare
su qc ▶ *vt* tirare; (*muscle*) strappare;
(*trigger*) premere ▶ *vi* tirare; **to ~
to pieces** fare a pezzi; **to ~ one's
punches** (Boxing) risparmiare
l'avversario; **to ~ one's weight** dare il
proprio contributo; **to ~ o.s. together**
ricomporsi, riprendersi; **to ~ sb's
leg** prendere in giro qn ▶ **pull apart**
vt (*break*) fare a pezzi ▶ **pull away** *vi*
(*move off: vehicle*) muoversi, partire;
(*boat*) staccarsi dal molo, salpare;
(*draw back: person*) indietreggiare
▶ **pull back** *vt* (*lever etc*) tirare
indietro; (*curtains*) aprire ▶ *vi* (*from
confrontation etc*) tirarsi indietro;
(*Mil: withdraw*) ritirarsi ▶ **pull down**
vt (*house*) demolire; (*tree*) abbattere
▶ **pull in** *vi* (Aut: *at the kerb*) accostarsi;
(*Rail*) entrare in stazione ▶ **pull off**
vt (*clothes*) togliere; (*deal etc*) portare
a compimento ▶ **pull out** *vi* partire;
(*Aut: come out of line*) spostarsi sulla

mezzeria ▶ *vt* staccare; far uscire;
(*withdraw*) ritirare ▶ **pull over** *vi* (Aut)
accostare ▶ **pull up** *vi* (*stop*) fermarsi
▶ *vt* (*raise*) sollevare; (*uproot*) sradicare

pulley ['pulɪ] *n* puleggia, carrucola

pullover ['puləuvəʳ] *n* pullover *m inv*

pulp [pʌlp] *n* (*of fruit*) polpa

pulpit ['pulpɪt] *n* pulpito

pulse [pʌls] *n* polso; (Bot) legume *m*;
~s *npl* (Culin) legumi *mpl*

puma ['pju:mə] *n* puma *m inv*

pump [pʌmp] *n* pompa; (*shoe*)
scarpetta ▶ *vt* pompare ▶ **pump up**
vt gonfiare

pumpkin ['pʌmpkɪn] *n* zucca

pun [pʌn] *n* gioco di parole

punch [pʌntʃ] *n* (*blow*) pugno; (*tool*)
punzone *m*; (*drink*) ponce *m* ▶ *vt* (*hit*):
to ~ sb/sth dare un pugno a qn/qc;
punch-up *n* (BRIT: *inf*) rissa

punctual ['pʌŋktjuəl] *adj* puntuale

punctuation [pʌŋktju'eɪʃən] *n*
interpunzione *f*, punteggiatura

puncture ['pʌŋktʃəʳ] *n* foratura ▶ *vt*
forare

> Be careful not to translate
> **puncture** by the Italian word
> **puntura**.

punish ['pʌnɪʃ] *vt* punire;
punishment *n* punizione *f*

punk [pʌŋk] *n* (*also: ~ rocker*) punk *m/f*
inv; (*also: ~ rock*) musica punk, punk
rock *m*; (US: *inf: hoodlum*) teppista *m*

pup [pʌp] *n* cucciolo(-a)

pupil ['pju:pl] *n* allievo(-a); (Anat)
pupilla

puppet ['pʌpɪt] *n* burattino

puppy ['pʌpɪ] *n* cucciolo(-a),
cagnolino(-a)

purchase ['pə:tʃɪs] *n* acquisto,
compera ▶ *vt* comprare

pure [pjuəʳ] *adj* puro(-a); **purely**
['pjuəlɪ] *adv* puramente

purify ['pjuərɪfaɪ] *vt* purificare

purity ['pjuərɪtɪ] *n* purezza

purple ['pəːpl] *adj* di porpora; viola *inv*

purpose ['pəːpəs] *n* intenzione *f*, scopo; **on ~** apposta

purr [pəː*] *vi* fare le fusa

purse [pəːs] *n* (BRIT) borsellino; (US) borsetta ▶ *vt* contrarre

pursue [pə'sjuː] *vt* inseguire; (*fig: activity etc*) continuare con; (: *aim etc*) perseguire

pursuit [pə'sjuːt] *n* inseguimento; (*fig*) ricerca; (*pastime*) passatempo

pus [pʌs] *n* pus *m*

push [puʃ] *n* spinta; (*effort*) grande sforzo; (*drive*) energia ▶ *vt* spingere; (*button*) premere; (*thrust*): **to ~ sth (into)** ficcare qc (in); (*fig*) fare pubblicità a ▶ *vi* spingere; premere; **to ~ for** (*fig*) insistere per ▶ **push in** *vi* introdursi a forza ▶ **push off** (*inf*) *vi* filare ▶ **push on** *vi* (*continue*) continuare ▶ **push over** *vt* far cadere ▶ **push through** *vi* farsi largo spingendo ▶ *vt* (*measure*) far approvare; **pushchair** (BRIT) *n* passeggino; **pusher** *n* (*drug pusher*) spacciatore(-trice); **push-up** (US) *n* (*press-up*) flessione f sulle braccia

pussy(-cat) ['pusɪ(-)] (*inf*) *n* micio

put [put] (*pt, pp* **put**) *vt* mettere, porre; (*say*) dire, esprimere; (*a question*) fare; (*estimate*) stimare ▶ **put away** *vt* (*return*) mettere a posto ▶ **put back** *vt* (*replace*) rimettere a posto; (*postpone*) rinviare; (*delay*) ritardare ▶ **put by** *vt* (*money*) mettere da parte ▶ **put down** *vt* (*parcel etc*) posare, mettere giù; (*pay*) versare; (*in writing*) mettere per iscritto; (*revolt, animal*) sopprimere; (*attribute*) attribuire ▶ **put forward** *vt* (*ideas*) avanzare, proporre ▶ **put in** *vt* (*application, complaint*) presentare; (*time, effort*) mettere ▶ **put off** *vt* (*postpone*) rimandare, rinviare; (*discourage*) dissuadere ▶ **put on** *vt* (*clothes, lipstick*

etc) mettere; (*light etc*) accendere; (*play etc*) mettere in scena; (*food, meal*) mettere su; (*brake*) mettere; **to ~ on weight** ingrassare; **to ~ on airs** darsi delle arie ▶ **put out** *vt* mettere fuori; (*one's hand*) porgere; (*light etc*) spegnere; (*person: inconvenience*) scomodare ▶ **put through** *vt* (*Tel: call*) passare; (: *person*) mettere in comunicazione; (*plan*) far approvare ▶ **put up** *vt* (*raise*) sollevare, alzare; (: *umbrella*) aprire; (: *tent*) montare; (*pin up*) affiggere; (*hang*) appendere; (*build*) costruire, erigere; (*increase*) aumentare; (*accommodate*) alloggiare ▶ **put aside** *vt* (*lay down: book etc*) mettere da una parte, posare; (*save*) mettere da parte; (*in shop*) tenere da parte ▶ **put together** *vt* mettere insieme, riunire; (*assemble: furniture*) montare; (: *meal*) improvvisare ▶ **put up with** *vt fus* sopportare

putt [pʌt] *n* colpo leggero; **putting green** *n* green *m inv*; campo di putting

puzzle ['pʌzl] *n* enigma *m*, mistero; (*jigsaw*) puzzle *m*; (*also*: **crossword ~**) parole *fpl* incrociate, cruciverba *m inv* ▶ *vt* confondere, rendere perplesso(-a) ▶ *vi* scervellarsi; **puzzled** *adj* perplesso(-a); **puzzling** *adj* (*question*) poco chiaro(-a); (*attitude, set of instructions*) incomprensibile

pyjamas [prˈdʒɑːməz] (BRIT) *npl* pigiama *m*

pylon ['paɪlən] *n* pilone *m*

pyramid ['pɪrəmɪd] *n* piramide *f*

Pyrenees [pɪrəˈniːz] *npl* **the ~** i Pirenei

q

quack [kwæk] n (of duck) qua qua m
inv; (pej: doctor) dottoruccio(-a)

quadruple [kwɔ'drupl] vt
quadruplicare ▶ vi quadruplicarsi

quail [kweɪl] n (Zool) quaglia ▶ vi
(person): **to ~ at** or **before** perdersi
d'animo davanti a

quaint [kweɪnt] adj bizzarro(-a); (old-
fashioned) antiquato(-a); grazioso(-a),
pittoresco(-a)

quake [kweɪk] vi tremare ▶ n abbr
= **earthquake**

qualification [kwɔlɪfɪ'keɪʃən] n
(degree etc) qualifica, titolo; (ability)
competenza, qualificazione f;
(limitation) riserva, restrizione f

qualified ['kwɔlɪfaɪd] adj
qualificato(-a); (able): **~ to**
competente in, qualificato(-a) a;
(limited) condizionato(-a)

qualify ['kwɔlɪfaɪ] vt abilitare; (limit:
statement) modificare, precisare ▶ vi
to ~ (as) qualificarsi (come); **to ~ (for)**
acquistare i requisiti necessari (per);
(Sport) qualificarsi (per or a)

quality ['kwɔlɪtɪ] n qualità f inv

qualm [kwɑːm] n dubbio; scrupolo

quantify ['kwɔntɪfaɪ] vt quantificare

quantity ['kwɔntɪtɪ] n quantità f inv

quarantine ['kwɔrəntiːn] n
quarantena

quarrel ['kwɔrl] n lite f, disputa ▶ vi
litigare

quarry ['kwɔrɪ] n (for stone) cava;
(animal) preda

quart [kwɔːt] n ≈ litro

quarter ['kwɔːtə*] n quarto;
(of year) trimestre m; (district) quartiere m ▶ vt dividere in
quattro; (Mil) alloggiare; **~s** npl (living
quarters) alloggio; (Mil) alloggi mpl,
quadrato; **a ~ of an hour** un quarto
d'ora; **quarter final** n quarto di
finale; **quarterly** adj trimestrale ▶ adv
trimestrale

quartet(te) [kwɔː'tet] n quartetto

quartz [kwɔːts] n quarzo

quay [kiː] n (also: **~side**) banchina

queasy ['kwiːzɪ] adj (stomach)
delicato(-a); **to feel ~** aver la nausea

queen [kwiːn] n (gen) regina; (Cards
etc) regina, donna

queer [kwɪə*] adj strano(-a),
curioso(-a) ▶ n (inf) finocchio

quench [kwentʃ] vt **to ~ one's thirst**
dissetarsi

query ['kwɪərɪ] n domanda, questione
f ▶ vt mettere in questione

quest [kwest] n cerca, ricerca

question ['kwestʃən] n domanda,
questione f ▶ vt (person) interrogare;
(plan, idea) mettere in questione or
in dubbio; **it's a ~ of doing** si tratta
di fare; **beyond ~** fuori di dubbio;
out of the ~ fuori discussione,
impossibile; **questionable** adj
discutibile; **question mark** n punto
interrogativo; **questionnaire**
[kwestʃə'neə*] n questionario

queue [kjuː] (BRIT) n coda, fila ▶ vi
fare la coda

quiche [kiːʃ] n torta salata a base di uova,
formaggio, prosciutto o altro

quick [kwɪk] adj rapido(-a),
veloce; (reply) pronto(-a); (mind)
pronto(-a), acuto(-a) ▶ n **cut to the
~** (fig) toccato(-a) sul vivo; **be ~!** fa
presto!; **quickly** adv rapidamente,
velocemente

r

quid [kwɪd] (BRIT: inf) n inv sterlina
quiet ['kwaɪət] adj tranquillo(-a),
quieto(-a); (ceremony) semplice
▶ n tranquillità, calma ▶ vt, vi (US)
= **quieten**; **keep ~!** sta zitto!; **quieten**
(also: **quieten down**) vi calmarsi,
chetarsi ▶ vt calmare, chetare;
quietly adv tranquillamente,
calmamente; sommessamente
quilt [kwɪlt] n trapunta; (continental
quilt) piumino
quirky ['kwɜːkɪ] adj stravagante
quit [kwɪt] (pt, pp **quit** or **quitted**) vt
mollare; (premises) lasciare, partire
da ▶ vi (give up) mollare; (resign)
dimettersi
quite [kwaɪt] adv (rather) assai;
(entirely) completamente, del tutto; **I
~ understand** capisco perfettamente;
that's not ~ big enough non è proprio
sufficiente; **a few of them** non pochi
di loro; **~ (so)!** esatto!
quits [kwɪts] adj ~ **(with)** pari (con);
let's call it ~ adesso siamo pari
quiver ['kwɪvə^r] vi tremare, fremere
quiz [kwɪz] n (game) quiz m inv;
indovinello ▶ vt interrogare
quota ['kwəʊtə] n quota
quotation [kwəʊ'teɪʃən] n citazione
f; (of shares etc) quotazione f; (estimate)
preventivo; **quotation marks** npl
virgolette fpl
quote [kwəʊt] n citazione f ▶ vt
(sentence) citare; (price) dare, fissare;
(shares) quotare ▶ vi **to ~ from** citare;
~s npl = **quotation marks**

rabbi ['ræbaɪ] n rabbino
rabbit ['ræbɪt] n coniglio
rabies ['reɪbiːz] n rabbia
RAC (BRIT) n abbr = **Royal Automobile
Club**
rac(c)oon [rə'kuːn] n procione m
race [reɪs] n razza; (competition, rush)
corsa ▶ vt (horse) far correre ▶ vi
correre; (engine) imballarsi; **race
car** (US) n = **racing car**; **racecourse**
n campo di corse, ippodromo;
racehorse n cavallo da corsa;
racetrack n pista
racial ['reɪʃl] adj razziale
racing ['reɪsɪŋ] n corsa; **racing
car** (BRIT) n macchina da corsa;
racing driver (BRIT) n corridore m
automobilista
racism ['reɪsɪzəm] n razzismo; **racist**
adj, n razzista m/f
rack [ræk] n (for tennis) racchetta; (also: **luggage
~**) rete f, portabagagli m inv; (also: **roof
~**) portabagagli; (dish rack) scolapiatti
m inv ▶ vt **~ed by** torturato(-a) da; **to ~
one's brains** scervellarsi
racket ['rækɪt] n (for tennis) racchetta;
(noise) fracasso; baccano; (swindle)
imbroglio, truffa; (organized crime)
racket m inv
racquet ['rækɪt] n racchetta
radar ['reɪdɑː^r] n radar m inv
radiation [reɪdɪ'eɪʃən] n
irradiamento; (radioactive)
radiazione f

radiator [ˈreɪdɪeɪtə*] n radiatore m

radical [ˈrædɪkl] adj radicale

radio [ˈreɪdɪəʊ] n radio f inv; **on the ~** alla radio; **radioactive** [reɪdɪəʊˈæktɪv] adj radioattivo(-a); **radio station** n stazione f radio inv

radish [ˈrædɪʃ] n ravanello

RAF n abbr = **Royal Air Force**

raffle [ˈræfl] n lotteria

raft [rɑːft] n zattera; (also: **life ~**) zattera di salvataggio

rag [ræg] n straccio, cencio; (pej: newspaper) giornalaccio, bandiera; (for charity) iniziativa studentesca a scopo benefico; **~s** npl (torn clothes) stracci mpl, brandelli mpl

rage [reɪdʒ] n (fury) collera, furia ▶ vi (person) andare su tutte le furie; (storm) infuriare; **it's all the ~** fa furore

ragged [ˈrægɪd] adj (edge) irregolare; (clothes) logoro(-a); (appearance) pezzente

raid [reɪd] n (Mil) incursione f; (criminal) rapina; (by police) irruzione f ▶ vt fare un'incursione in; rapinare; fare irruzione in

rail [reɪl] n (on stair) ringhiera; (on bridge, balcony) parapetto; (of ship) battagliola; **railcard** n (BRIT) tessera di riduzione ferroviaria; **railing(s)** n(pl) ringhiere fpl; **railroad** (US) n = **railway**; **railway** (BRIT: irreg) n ferrovia; **railway line** (BRIT) n linea ferroviaria; **railway station** (BRIT) n stazione f ferroviaria

rain [reɪn] n pioggia ▶ vi piovere; **in the ~** sotto la pioggia; **it's ~ing** piove; **rainbow** n arcobaleno; **raincoat** n impermeabile m; **raindrop** n goccia di pioggia; **rainfall** n pioggia; (measurement) piovosità; **rainforest** n foresta pluviale; **rainy** adj piovoso(-a)

raise [reɪz] n aumento ▶ vt (lift) alzare; sollevare; (increase) aumentare; (a protest, doubt, question) sollevare;

(cattle, family) allevare; (crop) coltivare; (army, funds) raccogliere; (loan) ottenere; **to ~ one's voice** alzare la voce

raisin [ˈreɪzn] n uva secca

rake [reɪk] n (tool) rastrello ▶ vt (garden) rastrellare

rally [ˈrælɪ] n (Pol etc) riunione f; (Aut) rally m inv; (Tennis) scambio ▶ vt riunire, radunare ▶ vi (sick person, Stock Exchange) riprendersi

RAM [ræm] n abbr (= random access memory) memoria ad accesso casuale

ram [ræm] n montone m, ariete m ▶ vt conficcare; (crash into) cozzare, sbattere contro; percuotere; speronare

Ramadan [ˌræməˈdæn] n Ramadan m inv

ramble [ˈræmbl] n escursione f ▶ vi (pej: also: **~ on**) divagare; **rambler** n escursionista m/f; (Bot) rosa rampicante; **rambling** adj (speech) sconnesso(-a); (house) tutto(-a) a nicchie e corridoi; (Bot) rampicante

ramp [ræmp] n rampa; **on/off ~** (US Aut) raccordo di entrata/uscita

rampage [ræmˈpeɪdʒ] n **to go on the ~** scatenarsi in modo violento

ran [ræn] pt of **run**

ranch [rɑːntʃ] n ranch m inv

random [ˈrændəm] adj fatto(-a) or detto(-a) per caso; (Comput, Math) casuale ▶ n **at ~** a casaccio

rang [ræŋ] pt of **ring**

range [reɪndʒ] n (of mountains) catena; (of missile, voice) portata; (of proposals, products) gamma; (Mil: also: **shooting ~**) campo di tiro; (also: **kitchen ~**) fornello, cucina economica ▶ vt disporre ▶ vi **to ~ over** coprire; **to ~ from ... to** andare da ... a

ranger [ˈreɪndʒə*] n guardia forestale

rank [ræŋk] n fila; (status, Mil) grado; (BRIT: also: **taxi ~**) posteggio di

taxi ▸ vi to ~ among essere tra ▸ adj
puzzolente; vero(-a) e proprio(-a); **the
~ and file** (fig) la gran massa

ransom ['rænsəm] n riscatto; **to hold
sb to ~** (fig) esercitare pressione su qn

rant [rænt] vi vociare

rap [ræp] vt bussare a; picchiare su ▸ n
(music) rap m inv

rape [reɪp] n violenza carnale, stupro;
(Bot) ravizzone m ▸ vt violentare

rapid ['ræpɪd] adj rapido(-a); **rapidly**
adv rapidamente; **rapids** npl (Geo)
rapida

rapist ['reɪpɪst] n violentatore m

rapport [ræ'pɔː] n rapporto

rare [rɛə] adj raro(-a); (Culin: steak) al
sangue; **rarely** ['rɛəlɪ] adv raramente

rash [ræʃ] adj imprudente,
sconsiderato(-a) ▸ n (Med) eruzione f;
(of events etc) scoppio

rasher ['ræʃə] n fetta sottile (di lardo
or prosciutto)

raspberry ['rɑːzbərɪ] n lampone m

rat [ræt] n ratto

rate [reɪt] n (proportion) tasso,
percentuale f; (speed) velocità f inv;
(price) tariffa ▸ vt giudicare; stimare;
~s npl (BRIT: property tax) imposte fpl
comunali; (fees) tariffe fpl; **to ~ sb/sth
as** valutare qn/qc come

rather ['rɑːðə] adv piuttosto; **it's ~
expensive** è piuttosto caro; (too)
è un po' caro; **there's a lot** (too)
n'è parecchio; **I would** or **I'd ~ go**
preferirei andare

rating ['reɪtɪŋ] n (assessment)
valutazione f; (score) punteggio di
merito; **~s** npl (Radio, TV) indice m
di ascolto

ratio ['reɪʃɪəu] n proporzione f,
rapporto

ration ['ræʃən] n (gen pl) razioni fpl ▸ vt
razionare; **~s** npl razioni fpl

rational ['ræʃənl] adj razionale,
ragionevole; (solution, reasoning)

logico(-a)

rattle ['rætl] n tintinnio; (louder)
strepito; (for baby) sonaglio ▸ vi
risuonare, tintinnare; fare un
rumore di ferraglia ▸ vt scuotere (con
strepito)

rave [reɪv] vi (in anger) infuriarsi; (with
enthusiasm) andare in estasi; (Med)
delirare ▸ n (BRIT: inf: party) rave m inv

raven ['reɪvən] n corvo

ravine [rə'viːn] n burrone m

raw [rɔː] adj (uncooked) crudo(-a); (not
processed) greggio(-a); (sore) vivo(-a);
(inexperienced) inesperto(-a); (weather,
day) gelido(-a)

ray [reɪ] n raggio; **a ~ of hope** un
barlume di speranza

razor ['reɪzə] n rasoio; **razor blade** n
lama di rasoio

Rd abbr = **road**

re [riː] prep con riferimento a

RE n abbr (BRIT Mil: = Royal Engineers)
= G.M. (Genio Militare); (BRIT)
= religious education

reach [riːtʃ] n portata; (of river etc)
tratto ▸ vt raggiungere; arrivare a ▸ vi
stendersi; **out of/within ~** fuori/a
portata di mano; **within ~ of the
shops/station** vicino ai negozi/alla
stazione ▸ **reach out** vt (hand)
allungare ▸ vi **to ~ out for** stendere la
mano per prendere

react [riː'ækt] vi reagire; **reaction**
[-'ækʃən] n reazione f; **reactor**
[riː'æktə] n reattore m

read [riːd, pt, pp red] (pt, pp **read**) vi
leggere ▸ vt leggere; (understand)
intendere, interpretare; (study)
studiare ▸ **read out** vt leggere ad alta
voce; **reader** n lettore(-trice); (BRIT:
at university) professore con funzioni
preminenti di ricerca

readily ['redɪlɪ] adv volentieri; (easily)
facilmente; (quickly) prontamente

reading ['riːdɪŋ] n lettura;

(understanding) interpretazione f; *(on instrument)* indicazione f

ready ['rɛdɪ] *adj* pronto(-a); *(willing)* pronto(-a), disposto(-a); *(available)* disponibile ▸ *n* **at the ~** *(Mil)* pronto a sparare; **when will my photos be ~?** quando saranno pronte le mie foto?; **to get ~** *vi* prepararsi ▸ *vt* preparare; **ready-made** *adj* prefabbricato(-a); *(clothes)* confezionato(-a)

real [rɪəl] *adj* reale; vero(-a); **in ~ terms** in realtà; **real ale** n birra ad effervescenza naturale; **real estate** n beni mpl immobili; **realistic** [-'lɪstɪk] *adj* realistico(-a); **reality** [ri:'ælɪtɪ] n realtà f inv

realization [rɪəlaɪ'zeɪʃən] n presa di coscienza; realizzazione f

realize ['rɪəlaɪz] *vt (understand)* rendersi conto di

really ['rɪəlɪ] *adv* veramente, davvero; **~!** *(indicating annoyance)* oh, insomma!

realm [rɛlm] n reame m, regno

Realtor® ['rɪəltɔː'] *(US)* n agente m immobiliare

reappear [ri:ə'pɪə'] *vi* ricomparire, riapparire

rear [rɪə'] *adj* di dietro; *(Aut: wheel etc)* posteriore ▸ *n* didietro, parte f posteriore ▸ *vt (cattle, family)* allevare ▸ *vi (also: ~ up: animal)* impennarsi

rearrange [ri:ə'reɪndʒ] *vt* riordinare

rear: **rear-view mirror** ['rɪəvju:-] n *(Aut)* specchio retrovisore; **rear-wheel drive** n trazione fpl posteriore

reason ['ri:zn] n ragione f; *(cause, motive)* ragione, motivo ▸ *vi* **to ~ with sb** far ragionare qn; **it stands to ~ that** è ovvio che; **reasonable** *adj* ragionevole; *(not bad)* accettabile; **reasonably** *adv* ragionevolmente; **reasoning** n ragionamento

reassurance [ri:ə'ʃuərəns] n rassicurazione f

reassure [ri:ə'ʃuə'] *vt* rassicurare; **to ~**

sb of rassicurare qn di or su

rebate ['ri:beɪt] n *(on tax etc)* sgravio

rebel ['rɛbl, vb rɪ'bɛl] n ribelle m/f ▸ *vi* ribellarsi; **rebellion** n ribellione f; **rebellious** *adj* ribelle

rebuild [ri:'bɪld] *vt irreg* ricostruire

recall [rɪ'kɔ:l] *vt* richiamare; *(remember)* ricordare, richiamare alla mente ▸ *n* richiamo

rec'd *abbr = received*

receipt [rɪ'si:t] n *(document)* ricevuta; *(act of receiving)* ricevimento; **~s** npl *(Comm)* introiti mpl; **can I have a ~, please?** posso avere una ricevuta, per favore?

receive [rɪ'si:v] *vt* ricevere; *(guest)* ricevere, accogliere; **receiver** [rɪ'si:və'] n *(Tel)* ricevitore m; *(Radio, TV)* apparecchio ricevente; *(of stolen goods)* ricettatore(-trice); *(Comm)* curatore m fallimentare

recent [rɪ'si:nt] *adj* recente; **recently** *adv* recentemente

reception [rɪ'sɛpʃən] n ricevimento; *(welcome)* accoglienza; *(TV etc)* ricezione f; **reception desk** n *(in hotel)* reception f inv; *(in hospital, at doctor's)* accettazione f; *(in offices etc)* portineria f; **receptionist** n receptionist m/f inv

recession [rɪ'sɛʃən] n recessione f

recharge [ri:'tʃɑ:dʒ] *vt (battery)* ricaricare

recipe ['rɛsɪpɪ] n ricetta

recipient [rɪ'sɪpɪənt] n beneficiario(-a); *(of letter)* destinatario(-a)

recital [rɪ'saɪtl] n recital m inv

recite [rɪ'saɪt] *vt (poem)* recitare

reckless ['rɛkləs] *adj (driver etc)* spericolato(-a); *(spending)* folle

reckon ['rɛkən] *vt (count)* calcolare; *(think)*: **I ~ that ...** penso che ...

reclaim [rɪ'kleɪm] *vt (demand back)* richiedere, reclamare; *(land)*

bonificare; (materials) recuperare
recline [rɪ'klaɪn] vi stare sdraiato(-a)
recognition [rekəg'nɪʃən] n
riconoscimento; **transformed
beyond ~** irriconoscibile
recognize ['rekəgnaɪz] vt **to ~ (by/as)**
riconoscere (a or da/come)
recollection [rekə'lekʃən] n ricordo
recommend [rekə'mend] vt
raccomandare; (advise) consigliare;
can you ~ a good restaurant? mi
può consigliare un buon ristorante?;
recommendation [rekəmen'deɪʃən]
n raccomandazione f; consiglio
reconcile ['rekənsaɪl] vt (two people)
riconciliare; (two facts) conciliare,
quadrare; **to ~ o.s.** to rassegnarsi a
reconsider [ri:kən'sɪdə'] vt
riconsiderare
reconstruct [ri:kən'strʌkt] vt
ricostruire
record [n 'rekɔːd, vb rɪ'kɔːd] n ricordo,
documento; (of meeting etc) nota,
verbale m; (register) registro; (file)
pratica, dossier m inv; (Comput) record
m inv; (also: **criminal ~**) fedina penale
sporca; (Mus: disc) disco; (Sport) record
m inv, primato ▶ vt (set down) prendere
nota di, registrare; (Mus: song etc)
registrare; **in ~ time** a tempo di
record; **off the ~** adj ufficioso(-a) ▶ adv
ufficiosamente; **recorded delivery**
(BRIT) n (Post): **recorded delivery
letter** etc lettera etc raccomandata;
recorder n (Mus) flauto diritto;
recording n (Mus) registrazione f;
record player n giradischi m inv
recount [rɪ'kaʊnt] vt raccontare,
narrare
recover [rɪ'kʌvə'] vt ricuperare ▶ vi to
~ (from) riprendersi (da); **recovery**
[rɪ'kʌvərɪ] n ricupero; ristabilimento;
ripresa

> Be careful not to translate **recover**
> by the Italian word *ricoverare*.

recreate [ri:krɪ'eɪt] vt ricreare
recreation [rekrɪ'eɪʃən] n ricreazione
f; svago; **recreational drug**
[rekrɪ'eɪʃənl-] n sostanza stupefacente
usata a scopo ricreativo; **recreational
vehicle** (US) n camper m inv
recruit [rɪ'kru:t] n recluta; (in company)
nuovo(-a) assunto(-a) ▶ vt reclutare;
recruitment n reclutamento
rectangle ['rektæŋgl] n rettangolo;
rectangular [-'tæŋgjulə'] adj
rettangolare
rectify ['rektɪfaɪ] vt (error) rettificare;
(omission) riparare
rector ['rektə'] n (Rel) parroco
(anglicano)
recur [rɪ'kə:'] vi riaccadere; (symptoms)
ripresentarsi; **recurring** adj (Math)
periodico(-a)
recyclable [ri:'saɪkləbl] adj riciclabile
recycle [ri:'saɪkl] vt riciclare
recycling [ri:'saɪklɪŋ] n riciclaggio
red [red] n rosso; (Pol: pej) rosso(-a)
▶ adj rosso(-a); **in the ~** (account)
scoperto; (business) in deficit; **Red
Cross** n Croce f Rossa; **redcurrant** n
ribes m inv
redeem [rɪ'di:m] vt (debt) riscattare;
(sth in pawn) ritirare; (fig, also Rel)
redimere
red: red-haired [-'heəd] adj dai capelli
rossi; **redhead** ['redhed] n rosso(-a);
red-hot adj arroventato(-a); **red
light** n **to go through a red light** (Aut)
passare col rosso; **red-light district**
['redlaɪt-] n quartiere m a luci rosse;
red meat n carne f rossa
reduce [rɪ'dju:s] vt ridurre; (lower)
ridurre, abbassare; **"~ speed now"**
(Aut) "rallentare"; **at a ~d price**
scontato(-a); **reduced** adj (decreased)
ridotto(-a); **at a reduced price** a
prezzo ribassato or ridotto; **"greatly
reduced prices"** "grandi ribassi";
reduction [rɪ'dʌkʃən] n riduzione f;

(of price) ribasso; (discount) sconto; **is there a reduction for children/ students?** ci sono riduzioni per i bambini/gli studenti?

redundancy [rɪ'dʌndənsɪ] n licenziamento

redundant [rɪ'dʌndnt] adj (worker) licenziato(-a); (detail, object) superfluo(-a); **to be made ~** essere licenziato(-a) (per eccesso di personale)

reed [riːd] n (Bot) canna; (Mus: of clarinet etc) ancia

reef [riːf] n (at sea) scogliera

reel [riːl] n bobina, rocchetto; (Fishing) mulinello; (Cinema) rotolo; (dance) danza veloce scozzese ▸ vi (sway) barcollare

ref [ref] (inf) n abbr (= referee) arbitro

refectory [rɪ'fɛktərɪ] n refettorio

refer [rɪ'fəː'] vt **to ~ sth to** (dispute, decision) deferire qc a; **to ~ sb to** (inquirer, Med: patient) indirizzare qn a; (reader: to text) rimandare qn a ▸ vi **~ to** (allude to) accennare a; (consult) rivolgersi a

referee [rɛfə'riː] n arbitro; (BRIT: for job application) referenza ▸ vt arbitrare

reference ['rɛfrəns] n riferimento; (mention) menzione f, allusione f; (for job application) referenza; **with ~ to** (Comm: in letter) in o con riferimento a; **reference number** n numero di riferimento

refill [vb riː'fɪl, n 'riːfɪl] vt riempire di nuovo; (pen, lighter etc) ricaricare ▸ n (for pen etc) ricambio

refine [rɪ'faɪn] vt raffinare; **refined** adj (person, taste) raffinato(-a); **refinery** n raffineria

reflect [rɪ'flɛkt] vt (light, image) riflettere; (fig) rispecchiare ▸ vi (think) riflettere, considerare; **it ~s badly/ well on him** si ripercuote su di lui in senso negativo/positivo; **reflection** [-'flɛkʃən] n riflessione f; (image)

riflesso; (criticism): **reflection on** giudizio su; attacco a; **on reflection** pensandoci sopra

reflex ['riːflɛks] adj riflesso(-a) ▸ n riflesso

reform [rɪ'fɔːm] n (of sinner etc) correzione f; (of law etc) riforma ▸ vt correggere; riformare

refrain [rɪ'freɪn] vi **to ~ from doing** trattenersi dal fare ▸ n ritornello

refresh [rɪ'frɛʃ] vt rinfrescare; (food, sleep) ristorare; **refreshing** adj (drink) rinfrescante; (sleep) riposante, ristoratore(-trice); **refreshments** npl rinfreschi mpl

refrigerator [rɪ'frɪdʒəreɪtə'] n frigorifero

refuel [riː'fjuəl] vi far rifornimento (di carburante)

refuge ['rɛfjuːdʒ] n rifugio; **to take ~ in** rifugiarsi in; **refugee** [rɛfju'dʒiː] n rifugiato(-a), profugo(-a)

refund [n 'riːfʌnd, vb riː'fʌnd] n rimborso ▸ vt rimborsare

refurbish [riː'fəːbɪʃ] vt rimettere a nuovo

refusal [rɪ'fjuːzəl] n rifiuto; **to have first ~ on** avere il diritto d'opzione su

refuse [n 'rɛfjuːs, vb rɪ'fjuːz] n rifiuti mpl ▸ vt, vi rifiutare; **to ~ to do** rifiutare di fare

regain [rɪ'geɪn] vt riguadagnare; riacquistare, ricuperare

regard [rɪ'gɑːd] n riguardo, stima ▸ vt considerare, stimare; **to give one's ~ to** porgere i suoi saluti a; **"with kindest ~s"** "cordiali saluti"; **regarding** prep riguardo a, per quanto riguarda; **regardless** adv lo stesso; **regardless of** a dispetto di, nonostante

regenerate [rɪ'dʒɛnəreɪt] vt rigenerare

reggae ['rɛgeɪ] n reggae m

regiment ['rɛdʒɪmənt] n reggimento

region ['riːdʒən] n regione f; **in the ~ of** (fig) all'incirca di; **regional** adj regionale

register ['redʒɪstə'] n registro; (also: **electoral ~**) lista elettorale ▶ vt registrare; (vehicle) immatricolare; (letter) assicurare; (instrument) segnare ▶ vi iscriversi; (at hotel) firmare il registro; (make impression) entrare in testa; **registered** (BRIT) adj (letter) assicurato(-a)

registrar ['redʒɪstrɑː'] n ufficiale m di stato civile; segretario

registration [redʒɪs'treɪʃən] n (act) registrazione f; iscrizione f; (Aut: also: **~ number**) numero di targa

registry office (BRIT) n anagrafe f; **to get married in a ~** = sposarsi in municipio

regret [rɪ'gret] n rimpianto, rincrescimento ▶ vt rimpiangere; **regrettable** adj deplorevole

regular ['regjʊlə'] adj regolare; (usual) abituale, normale; (soldier) dell'esercito regolare ▶ n (client etc) cliente m/f abituale; **regularly** adv regolarmente

regulate ['regjʊleɪt] vt regolare; **regulation** [-'leɪʃən] n regolazione f; (rule) regola, regolamento

rehabilitation ['riːhəbɪlɪ'teɪʃən] n (of offender) riabilitazione f; (of disabled) riadattamento

rehearsal [rɪ'həːsəl] n prova

rehearse [rɪ'həːs] vt provare

reign [reɪn] n regno ▶ vi regnare

reimburse [riːɪm'bəːs] vt rimborsare

rein [reɪn] n (for horse) briglia

reincarnation [riːɪnkɑː'neɪʃən] n reincarnazione f

reindeer ['reɪndɪə'] n inv renna

reinforce [riːɪn'fɔːs] vt rinforzare; **reinforcements** npl (Mil) rinforzi mpl

reinstate [riːɪn'steɪt] vt reintegrare

reject [n 'riːdʒekt, vb rɪ'dʒekt] n (Comm)

scarto ▶ vt rifiutare, respingere; (Comm: goods) scartare; **rejection** [rɪ'dʒekʃən] n rifiuto

rejoice [rɪ'dʒɔɪs] vi **to ~ (at or over)** provare diletto in

relate [rɪ'leɪt] vt (tell) raccontare; (connect) collegare ▶ vi **to ~ to** (connect) riferirsi a; (get on with) stabilire un rapporto con; **relating to** che riguarda, rispetto a; **related** adj **related (to)** imparentato(-a) (con); collegato(-a) or connesso(-a) (a)

relation [rɪ'leɪʃən] n (person) parente m/f; (link) rapporto, relazione f; **~s** npl (relatives) parenti mpl; **relationship** n rapporto; (personal ties) rapporti mpl, relazioni fpl; (also: **family relationship**) legami mpl di parentela

relative ['relətɪv] n parente m/f ▶ adj relativo(-a); (respective) rispettivo(-a); **relatively** adv relativamente; (fairly, rather) abbastanza

relax [rɪ'læks] vi rilasciarsi; (person: unwind) rilassarsi ▶ vt rilasciare; (mind, person) rilassare; **relaxation** [riːlæk'seɪʃən] n rilasciamento; rilassamento; (entertainment) ricreazione f, svago; **relaxed** adj rilassato(-a); **relaxing** adj rilassante

relay ['riːleɪ] n (Sport) corsa a staffetta ▶ vt (message) trasmettere

release [rɪ'liːs] n (from prison) rilascio; (from obligation) liberazione f; (of gas etc) emissione f; (of film etc) distribuzione f; (record) disco; (device) disinnesto ▶ vt (prisoner) rilasciare; (from obligation, wreckage etc) liberare; (book, film) fare uscire; (news) rendere pubblico(-a); (gas etc) emettere; (Tech: catch, spring etc) disinnestare

relegate ['relɪgeɪt] vt relegare; (BRIT Sport): **to be ~d** essere retrocesso(-a)

relent [rɪ'lent] vi cedere; **relentless** adj implacabile

relevant ['reləvənt] adj pertinente;

(chapter) in questione; **~ to** pertinente a

▮ Be careful not to translate **relevant** by the Italian word *rilevante*.

reliable [rɪˈlaɪəbl] adj (person, firm) fidato(-a), che dà affidamento; (method) sicuro(-a); (machine) affidabile

relic [ˈrɛlɪk] n (Rel) reliquia f; (of the past) resto

relief [rɪˈliːf] n (from pain, anxiety) sollievo; (help, supplies) soccorsi mpl; (Art, Geo) rilievo

relieve [rɪˈliːv] vt (pain, patient) sollevare; (bring help) soccorrere; (take over from: gen) sostituire; (: guard) rilevare; **to ~ sb of sth** (load) alleggerire qn di qc; **to ~ o.s.** fare i propri bisogni; **relieved** adj sollevato(-a); **to be relieved that ...** essere sollevato(-a) (dal fatto) che ...; **I'm relieved to hear it** mi hai tolto un peso con questa notizia

religion [rɪˈlɪdʒən] n religione f

religious [rɪˈlɪdʒəs] adj religioso(-a); **religious education** n religione f

relish [ˈrɛlɪʃ] n (Culin) condimento; (enjoyment) gran piacere m ▶ vt (food etc) godere; **to ~ doing** adorare fare

relocate [ˌriːləʊˈkeɪt] vt trasferire ▶ vi trasferirsi

reluctance [rɪˈlʌktəns] n riluttanza

reluctant [rɪˈlʌktənt] adj riluttante, mal disposto(-a); **reluctantly** adv di mala voglia, a malincuore

rely [rɪˈlaɪ]: **to ~ on** vt fus contare su; (be dependent) dipendere da

remain [rɪˈmeɪn] vi restare, rimanere; **remainder** n resto; (Comm) rimanenza; **remaining** adj che rimane; **remains** npl resti mpl

remand [rɪˈmɑːnd] n **on ~** in detenzione preventiva ▶ vt **to ~ in custody** rinviare in carcere; trattenere a disposizione della legge

remark [rɪˈmɑːk] n osservazione f ▶ vt osservare, dire; **remarkable** adj notevole; eccezionale

remarry [ˈriːˈmærɪ] vi risposarsi

remedy [ˈrɛmədɪ] n **~ (for)** rimedio (per) ▶ vt rimediare a

remember [rɪˈmɛmbər] vt ricordare, ricordarsi di; **~ me to him** salutalo da parte mia; **Remembrance Day** [rɪˈmɛmbrəns-] n 11 novembre, giorno della commemorazione dei caduti in guerra

● **Remembrance Day**
● In Gran Bretagna, il
● **Remembrance Day** è un giorno
● di commemorazione dei caduti
● in guerra. Si celebra ogni anno
● la domenica più vicina all'11
● novembre, anniversario della firma
● dell'armistizio con la Germania
● nel 1918.

remind [rɪˈmaɪnd] vt **to ~ sb of sth** ricordare qc a qn; **to ~ sb to do** ricordare a qn di fare; **reminder** n richiamo; (note etc) promemoria m inv

reminiscent [ˌrɛmɪˈnɪsnt] adj **~ of** che fa pensare a, che richiama

remnant [ˈrɛmnənt] n resto, avanzo

remorse [rɪˈmɔːs] n rimorso

remote [rɪˈməʊt] adj remoto(-a), lontano(-a); (person) distaccato(-a); **remote control** n telecomando; **remotely** adv remotamente; (slightly) vagamente

removal [rɪˈmuːvəl] n (taking away) rimozione f; soppressione f; (BRIT: from house) trasloco; (from office: dismissal) destituzione f; (Med) ablazione f; **removal man** (irreg) n (BRIT) addetto ai traslochi; **removal van** (BRIT) n furgone m per traslochi

remove [rɪˈmuːv] vt togliere, rimuovere; (employee) destituire; (stain) far sparire; (doubt, abuse) sopprimere, eliminare

Renaissance [rɪˈneɪsɑːns] *n* the ~ il
Rinascimento

rename [riːˈneɪm] *vt* ribattezzare

render [ˈrɛndə*r*] *vt* rendere

rendezvous [ˈrɔndɪvuː] *n*
appuntamento; *(place)* luogo
d'incontro; *(meeting)* incontro

renew [rɪˈnjuː] *vt* rinnovare;
(negotiations) riprendere

renovate [ˈrɛnəveɪt] *vt* rinnovare; *(art work)* restaurare

renowned [rɪˈnaund] *adj*
rinomato(-a)

rent [rɛnt] *n* affitto ▸ *vt* *(take for rent)*
prendere in affitto; *(also:* ~ **out)** dare
in affitto; **rental** *n* *(for television,
car)* fitto

reorganize [riːˈɔːɡənaɪz] *vt*
riorganizzare

rep [rɛp] *n abbr (Comm:* = *representative)*
rappresentante *m/f; (Theatre:*
= *repertory)* teatro di repertorio

repair [rɪˈpɛə*r*] *n* riparazione ▸ *vt*
riparare; **in good/bad** ~ in buone/
cattive condizioni; **where can I get
this** ~**ed?** dove lo posso far riparare?;
repair kit *n* corredo per riparazioni

repay [riːˈpeɪ] *(irreg)* *vt (money, creditor)*
rimborsare, ripagare; *(sb's efforts)*
ricompensare; *(favour)* ricambiare;
repayment *n* pagamento; rimborso

repeat [rɪˈpiːt] *n (Radio, TV)* replica ▸ *vt*
ripetere; *(pattern)* riprodurre; *(promise,
attack, also Comm: order)* rinnovare
▸ *vi* ripetere; **can you** ~ **that, please?**
può ripetere, per favore?; **repeatedly**
adv ripetutamente, spesso; **repeat
prescription** *n (BRIT)* ricetta
ripetibile

repellent [rɪˈpɛlənt] *adj* repellente ▸ *n*
insect ~ prodotto *m* anti-insetti *inv*

repercussions [riːpəˈkʌʃənz] *npl*
ripercussioni *fpl*

repetition [rɛpɪˈtɪʃən] *n* ripetizione *f*

repetitive [rɪˈpɛtɪtɪv] *adj (movement)*

che si ripete; *(work)* monotono(-a); *(speech)* pieno(-a) di ripetizioni

replace [rɪˈpleɪs] *vt (put back)*
rimettere a posto; *(take the place of)*
sostituire; **replacement** *n* rimessa;
sostituzione *f; (person)* sostituto(-a)

replay [ˈriːpleɪ] *n (of match)* partita
ripetuta; *(of tape, film)* replay *m inv*

replica [ˈrɛplɪkə] *n* replica, copia

reply [rɪˈplaɪ] *n* risposta ▸ *vi* rispondere

report [rɪˈpɔːt] *n* rapporto; *(Press etc)*
cronaca; *(BRIT: also:* **school** ~) pagella;
(of gun) sparo ▸ *vt* riportare; *(Press
etc)* fare una cronaca su; *(bring to
notice: occurrence)* segnalare; *(: person)*
denunciare ▸ *vi (make a report)* fare un
rapporto *(or* una cronaca); *(present
o.s.)* **to** ~ **(to sb)** presentarsi (a qn);
I'd like to ~ **a theft** vorrei denunciare
un furto; **report card** *n (US, SCOTTISH)*
n pagella; **reportedly** *adv* stando a
quanto si dice; **he reportedly told
them to ...** avrebbe detto loro di ...;
reporter *n* reporter *m inv*

represent [rɛprɪˈzɛnt] *vt*
rappresentare; **representation**
[-ˈteɪʃən] *n* rappresentazione
f; (petition) rappresentanza;
representative *n* rappresentante
m/f; (US Pol) deputato(-a) ▸ *adj*
rappresentativo(-a)

repress [rɪˈprɛs] *vt* reprimere;
repression [-ˈprɛʃən] *n* repressione *f*

reprimand [ˈrɛprɪmɑːnd] *n*
rimprovero ▸ *vt* rimproverare

reproduce [riːprəˈdjuːs] *vt* riprodurre
▸ *vi* riprodursi; **reproduction**
[-ˈdʌkʃən] *n* riproduzione *f*

reptile [ˈrɛptaɪl] *n* rettile *m*

republic [rɪˈpʌblɪk] *n* repubblica;
republican *adj, n* repubblicano(-a)

reputable [ˈrɛpjutəbl] *adj* di buona
reputazione; *(occupation)* rispettabile

reputation [rɛpjuˈteɪʃən] *n*
reputazione *f*

request [rɪ'kwɛst] n domanda; (formal) richiesta ▶ vt to ~ (of or from sb) chiedere (a qn); **request stop** (BRIT) n (for bus) fermata facoltativa or a richiesta

require [rɪ'kwaɪəᵊ] vt (need: person) aver bisogno di; (: thing, situation) richiedere; (want) volere; esigere; (order): **to ~ sb to do sth** esigere da qn di fare qc; **requirement** n esigenza; bisogno; requisito

resat [ri:'sæt] pt, pp of **resit**

rescue ['rɛskju:] n salvataggio; (help) soccorso ▶ vt salvare

research [rɪ'sə:tʃ] n ricerca, ricerche fpl ▶ vt fare ricerche su

resemblance [rɪ'zɛmbləns] n somiglianza

resemble [rɪ'zɛmbl] vt assomigliare a

resent [rɪ'zɛnt] vt risentirsi di; **resentful** adj pieno(-a) di risentimento; **resentment** n risentimento

reservation [rɛzə'veɪʃən] n (booking) prenotazione f; (doubt) dubbio; (protected area) riserva; (BRIT: on road: also: **central** ~) spartitraffico m inv; **reservation desk** (US) n (in hotel) reception f inv

reserve [rɪ'zə:v] n riserva ▶ vt (seats etc) prenotare; **reserved** adj (shy) riservato(-a)

reservoir ['rɛzəvwɑ:ᵊ] n serbatoio

residence ['rɛzɪdəns] n residenza; **residence permit** (BRIT) n permesso di soggiorno

resident ['rɛzɪdənt] n residente m/f; (in hotel) cliente m/f fisso(-a) ▶ adj residente; (doctor) fisso(-a); (course, college) a tempo pieno con pernottamento; **residential** [-'dɛnʃəl] adj di residenza; (area) residenziale

residue ['rɛzɪdju:] n resto; (Chem, Physics) residuo

resign [rɪ'zaɪn] vt (one's post) dimettersi da ▶ vi dimettersi; **to ~ o.s. to** rassegnarsi a; **resignation** [rɛzɪg'neɪʃən] n dimissioni fpl; rassegnazione f

resin ['rɛzɪn] n resina

resist [rɪ'zɪst] vt resistere a; **resistance** n resistenza

resit ['ri:sɪt] (BRIT) (pt, pp **resat**) vt (exam) ripresentarsi a; (subject) ridare l'esame di ▶ n **he's got his French ~ on Friday** deve ridare l'esame di francese venerdì

resolution [rɛzə'lu:ʃən] n risoluzione f

resolve [rɪ'zɔlv] n risoluzione f ▶ vi (decide): **to ~ to do** decidere di fare ▶ vt (problem) risolvere

resort [rɪ'zɔ:t] n (town) stazione f; (recourse) ricorso ▶ vi **to ~ to** aver ricorso a; **in the last ~** come ultima risorsa

resource [rɪ'sɔ:s] n risorsa; **resourceful** adj pieno(-a) di risorse, intraprendente

respect [rɪs'pɛkt] n rispetto ▶ vt rispettare; **respectable** adj rispettabile; (quite good) discreto(-a); **respectful** adj rispettoso(-a); **respective** [rɪs'pɛktɪv] adj rispettivo(-a); **respectively** adv rispettivamente

respite ['rɛspaɪt] n respiro, tregua

respond [rɪs'pɔnd] vi rispondere; **response** [rɪs'pɔns] n risposta

responsibility [rɪspɔnsə'bɪlɪtɪ] n responsabilità f inv

responsible [rɪs'pɔnsɪbl] adj (trustworthy) fidato(-a); (job) di (grande) responsabilità; **~ (for)** responsabile (di); **responsibly** adv responsabilmente

responsive [rɪs'pɔnsɪv] adj che reagisce

rest [rɛst] n riposo; (stop) sosta, pausa; (Mus) pausa; (object: to support sth) appoggio, sostegno; (remainder) resto, avanzi mpl ▶ vi riposarsi;

(remain) rimanere, restare; *(be supported)*: **to ~ on** appoggiarsi su ▸ *(far)* riposare; *(lean)*: **to ~ sth on/against** appoggiare qc su/contro; **the ~ of them** gli altri; **it ~s with him to decide** sta a lui decidere

restaurant ['rɛstərɒn] *n* ristorante *m*; **restaurant car** *(BRIT)* *n* vagone *m* ristorante

restless ['rɛstlɪs] *adj* agitato(-a), irrequieto(-a)

restoration [rɛstə'reɪʃən] *n* restauro; restituzione *f*

restore [rɪ'stɔːʳ] *vt (building, to power)* restaurare; *(sth stolen)* restituire; *(peace, health)* ristorare

restrain [rɪs'treɪn] *vt (feeling, growth)* contenere, frenare; *(person)*: **to ~ (from doing)** trattenere (dal fare); **restraint** *n (restriction)* limitazione *f*; *(moderation)* ritegno; *(of style)* contenutezza

restrict [rɪs'trɪkt] *vt* restringere, limitare; **restriction** [-kʃən] *n* restrizione *f*; **restriction (on)** restrizione *f*(di), limitazione *f*

rest room *(US)* *n* toletta

restructure [riː'strʌktʃəʳ] *vt* ristrutturare

result [rɪ'zʌlt] *n* risultato ▸ *vi* **to ~ in** avere per risultato; **as a ~ of** in ordi conseguenza a, in seguito a

resume [rɪ'zjuːm] *vt, vi (work, journey)* riprendere

résumé ['reɪzjuːmeɪ] *n* riassunto; *(US)* curriculum *m* invivitae

resuscitate [rɪ'sʌsɪteɪt] *vt (Med)* risuscitare

retail ['riːteɪl] *adj, adv* al minuto ▸ *vt* vendere al minuto ▸ **retailer** *n* commerciante *m/f*al minuto, dettagliante *m/f*

retain [rɪ'teɪn] *vt (keep)* tenere, serbare

retaliation [rɪtælɪ'eɪʃən] *n* rappresaglia *fpl*

retarded [rɪ'tɑːdɪd] *adj* ritardato(-a)

retire [rɪ'taɪəʳ] *vi (give up work)* andare in pensione; *(withdraw)* ritirarsi, andarsene; *(go to bed)* andare a letto, ritirarsi; **retired** *adj (person)* pensionato(-a); **retirement** *n* pensione *f*; *(act)* pensionamento

retort [rɪ'tɔːt] *vi* rimbeccare

retreat [rɪ'triːt] *n* ritirata; *(place)* rifugio ▸ *vi* battere in ritirata

retrieve [rɪ'triːv] *vt (sth lost)* ricuperare, ritrovare; *(situation, honour)* salvare; *(error, loss)* rimediare a

retrospect ['rɛtrəspɛkt] *n* **in ~** guardando indietro; **retrospective** [-'spɛktɪv] *adj* retrospettivo(-a); *(law)* retroattivo(-a)

return [rɪ'tɜːn] *n (going or coming back)* ritorno; *(of sth stolen etc)* restituzione *f*; *(Finance: from land, shares)* profitto, reddito ▸ *cpd (journey, match)* di ritorno; *(BRIT: ticket)* di andata e ritorno ▸ *vi* tornare, ritornare ▸ *vt* rendere, restituire; *(bring back)* riportare; *(send back)* mandare indietro; *(put back)* rimettere; *(Pol: candidate)* eleggere; **~s** *npl (Comm)* incassi *mpl*; profitti *mpl*; **in ~ (for)** in cambio (di); **by ~ of post** a stretto giro di posta; **many happy ~s (of the day)!** cento di questi giorni!; **return ticket** *n (esp BRIT)* biglietto di andata e ritorno

reunion [riː'juːnɪən] *n* riunione *f*

reunite [riːjuː'naɪt] *vt* riunire

revamp [riː'væmp] *vt (firm)* riorganizzare

reveal [rɪ'viːl] *vt (make known)* rivelare, svelare; *(display)* rivelare, mostrare; **revealing** *adj* rivelatore(-trice); *(dress)* scollato(-a)

revel ['rɛvl] *vi* **to ~ in sth/in doing** dilettarsi di qc/a fare

revelation [rɛvə'leɪʃən] *n* rivelazione *f*

revenge [rɪ'vɛndʒ] *n* vendetta ▸ *vt*

vendicare; **to take ~ on** vendicarsi di

revenue ['rɛvənju:] n reddito

Reverend ['rɛvərənd] adj (in titles) reverendo(-a)

reversal [rɪ'və:sl] n capovolgimento

reverse [rɪ'və:s] n contrario, opposto; (back, defeat) rovescio; (Aut: also: ~ **gear**) marcia indietro ▶ adj (order, direction) contrario(-a), opposto(-a) ▶ vt (turn) invertire, rivoltare; (change) capovolgere, rovesciare; (Law: judgment) cassare; (car) fare marcia indietro con ▶ vi (BRIT Aut, person etc) fare marcia indietro; **reverse-charge call** [rɪ'və:stʃɑ:dʒ] (BRIT) n (Tel) telefonata con addebito al ricevente; **reversing lights** (BRIT) npl (Aut) luci fpl per la retromarcia

revert [rɪ'və:t] vi **to ~ to** tornare a

review [rɪ'vju:] n rivista; (of book, film) recensione f; (of situation) esame m ▶ vt passare in rivista; (book) fare la recensione di; fare il punto di

revise [rɪ'vaɪz] vt (manuscript) rivedere, correggere; (opinion) emendare, modificare; (study: subject, notes) ripassare; **revision** [rɪ'vɪʒən] n revisione f; ripasso

revival [rɪ'vaɪvl] n ripresa; ristabilimento; (of faith) risveglio

revive [rɪ'vaɪv] vt (person) rianimare; (custom) far rivivere; (hope, courage, economy) ravvivare; (play, fashion) riesumare ▶ vi (person) rianimarsi; (hope) ravvivarsi; (activity) riprendersi

revolt [rɪ'vəult] n rivolta, ribellione f ▶ vi rivoltarsi, ribellarsi ▶ vt (far) rivoltare; **revolting** adj ripugnante

revolution [rɛvə'lu:ʃən] n rivoluzione f; (of wheel etc) giro; **revolutionary** adj, n rivoluzionario(-a)

revolve [rɪ'vɔlv] vi girare

revolver [rɪ'vɔlvə*] n rivoltella

reward [rɪ'wɔ:d] n ricompensa,

premio ▶ vt **to ~ (for)** ricompensare (per); **rewarding** adj (fig) gratificante

rewind [ri:'waɪnd] (irreg) vt (watch) ricaricare; (ribbon etc) riavvolgere

rewrite [ri:'raɪt] vt irreg riscrivere

rheumatism ['ru:mətɪzəm] n reumatismo

rhinoceros [raɪ'nɔsərəs] n rinoceronte m

rhubarb ['ru:bɑ:b] n rabarbaro

rhyme [raɪm] n rima; (verse) poesia

rhythm ['rɪðm] n ritmo

rib [rɪb] n (Anat) costola ▶ vt (tease) punzecchiare

ribbon ['rɪbən] n nastro; **in ~s** (torn) a brandelli

rice [raɪs] n riso; **rice pudding** n budino di riso

rich [rɪtʃ] adj ricco(-a); (clothes) sontuoso(-a); (abundant): ~ **in** ricco(-a) di

rid [rɪd] (pt, pp rid) vt **to ~ sb of** sbarazzare o liberare qn di; **to get ~ of** sbarazzarsi di

riddle ['rɪdl] n (puzzle) indovinello ▶ vt **to be ~d with** (holes) essere crivellato(-a) di; (doubts) essere pieno(-a) di

ride [raɪd] (pt rode, pp ridden) n (on horse) cavalcata; (outing) passeggiata; (distance covered) cavalcata; corsa ▶ vi (as sport) cavalcare; (go somewhere: on horse, bicycle) andare (a cavallo or in bicicletta etc); (journey: on bicycle, motorcycle, bus) andare, viaggiare ▶ vt (a horse) montare, cavalcare; **to take sb for a ~** (fig) prendere in giro qn; fregare qn; **to ~ a horse/ bicycle/camel** montare a cavallo/in bicicletta/in groppa a un cammello; **rider** n cavalcatore(-trice); (in race) fantino; (on bicycle) ciclista m/f; (on motorcycle) motociclista m/f

ridge [rɪdʒ] n (on hill) cresta; (of roof) colmo; (on object) riga (in rilievo)

rise | 501

ridicule ['rɪdɪkjuːl] n ridicolo; scherno ▶ vt mettere in ridicolo; **ridiculous** [rɪ'dɪkjuləs] adj ridicolo(-a)

riding ['raɪdɪŋ] n equitazione f; **riding school** n scuola d'equitazione

rife [raɪf] adj diffuso(-a); **to be ~ with** abbondare di

rifle ['raɪfl] n carabina ▶ vt vuotare

rift [rɪft] n fessura, crepatura; (fig: disagreement) incrinatura, disaccordo

rig [rɪg] n (also: **oil ~:** on land) derrick m inv; (: at sea) piattaforma di trivellazione f ▶ vt (election etc) truccare

right [raɪt] adj giusto(-a); (suitable) appropriato(-a); (not left) destro(-a) ▶ n giusto; (title, claim) diritto; (not left) destra ▶ adv (answer) correttamente; (not on the left) a destra ▶ vt raddrizzare; (fig) riparare ▶ excl bene!; **to be ~** (person) aver ragione; (answer) essere giusto(-a) o corretto(-a); **by ~s** di diritto; **on the ~** a destra; **to be in the ~** aver ragione, essere nel giusto; **~ now** proprio adesso; subito; **~ away** subito; **right angle** n angolo retto; **rightful** adj (heir) legittimo(-a); **right-hand** adj: **right-hand drive** guida a destra; **the right-hand side** il lato destro; **right-handed** adj (person) che adopera la mano destra; **rightly** adv bene, correttamente; (with reason) a ragione; **right of way** n diritto di passaggio; (Aut) precedenza; **right-wing** adj (Pol) di destra

rigid ['rɪdʒɪd] adj rigido(-a); (principle) rigoroso(-a)

rigorous ['rɪgərəs] adj rigoroso(-a)

rim [rɪm] n orlo; (of spectacles) montatura; (of wheel) cerchione m

rind [raɪnd] n (of bacon) cotenna; (of lemon etc) scorza

ring [rɪŋ] (pt rang, pp rung) n anello; (of people, objects) cerchio; (of spies) giro; (of smoke etc) spirale m; (arena) pista, arena; (for boxing) ring m inv;

(sound of bell) scampanio ▶ vi (person, bell, telephone) suonare; (also: **~ out:** voice, words) risuonare; (Tel) telefonare; (ears) fischiare ▶ vt (BRIT Tel) telefonare a; (: bell, doorbell) suonare; **to give sb a ~** (BRIT Tel) dare un colpo di telefono a qn ▶ **ring back** vt, vi (Tel) richiamare ▶ **ring up** vt (Tel) telefonare a; **ringing** n (of bell) scampanio; (of telephone) squillo; (in ears) fischio; **ringing tone** n (Tel) segnale m di libero; **ringleader** n (of gang) capobanda m; **ring road** (BRIT) n raccordo anulare

rink [rɪŋk] n (also: **ice ~**) pista di pattinaggio

rinse [rɪns] n risciacquatura; (hair tint) cachet m inv ▶ vt sciacquare

riot ['raɪət] n sommossa, tumulto; (of colours) orgia ▶ vi tumultuare; **to run ~** creare disordine

rip [rɪp] n strappo ▶ vt strappare ▶ vi strapparsi ▶ **rip off** vt (inf: cheat) fregare ▶ **rip up** vt stracciare

ripe [raɪp] adj (fruit, grain) maturo(-a); (cheese) stagionato(-a)

rip-off ['rɪpɔf] n (inf): **it's a ~!** è un furto!

ripple ['rɪpl] n increspamento, ondulazione f; mormorio ▶ vi incresparsi

rise [raɪz] (pt rose, pp risen) n (slope) salita, pendio; (hill) altura; (increase: in wages: BRIT) aumento; (: in prices, temperature) rialzo, aumento; (fig: to power etc) ascesa ▶ vi alzarsi, levarsi; (prices) aumentare; (waters, river) crescere; (sun, wind, person: from chair, bed) levarsi; (also: **~ up:** building) ergersi; (: rebel) insorgere; ribellarsi; (in rank) salire; **to give ~ to** provocare, dare origine a; **to ~ to the occasion** essere all'altezza; **risen** ['rɪzn] pp of **rise**; **rising** adj (increasing: number) sempre crescente; (: prices) in aumento; (tide) montante, (sun, moon) nascente, che sorge

risk [rɪsk] n rischio; pericolo ▸ vt rischiare; **to take** or **run the ~ of doing** correre il rischio di fare; **at ~** in pericolo; **at one's own ~** a proprio rischio e pericolo; **risky** adj rischioso(-a)

rite [raɪt] n rito; **last ~s** l'estrema unzione

ritual ['rɪtjuəl] adj rituale ▸ n rituale m

rival ['raɪvl] n rivale m/f; (in business) concorrente m/f ▸ adj rivale; che fa concorrenza ▸ vt essere in concorrenza con; **to ~ sb/sth in** competere con qn/qc in; **rivalry** n rivalità; concorrenza

river ['rɪvə*] n fiume m ▸ cpd (port, traffic) fluviale; **up/down ~** a monte/valle; **riverbank** n argine m

rivet ['rɪvɪt] n ribattino, rivetto ▸ vt (fig) concentrare, fissare

Riviera [rɪvɪ'ɛərə] n **the (French) ~** la Costa Azzurra; **the Italian ~** la Riviera

road [rəud] n strada; (small) cammino; (in town) via ▸ cpd stradale; **major/minor ~** strada con/senza diritto di precedenza; **which ~ do I take for ...?** che strada devo prendere per andare a...?; **roadblock** n blocco stradale; **road map** n carta stradale; **road rage** n comportamento aggressivo al volante; **road safety** n sicurezza sulle strade; **roadside** n margine m della strada; **roadsign** n cartello stradale; **road tax** n (BRIT) tassa di circolazione; **roadworks** npl lavori mpl stradali

roam [rəum] vi errare, vagabondare

roar [rɔ:*] n ruggito; (of crowd) tumulto; (of thunder, storm) muggito; (of laughter) scoppio ▸ vi ruggire; muggire; tumultuare; **to ~ with laughter** scoppiare dalle risa; **to do a ~ing trade** fare affari d'oro

roast [rəust] n arrosto ▸ vt arrostire;

(coffee) tostare, torrefare; **roast beef** n arrosto di manzo

rob [rɔb] vt (person) rubare; (bank) svaligiare; **to ~ sb of sth** derubare qn di qc; (fig: deprive) privare qn di qc; **robber** n ladro; (armed) rapinatore m; **robbery** n furto; rapina

robe [rəub] n (for ceremony etc) abito; (also: bath ~) accappatoio; (US: also: lap ~) coperta

robin ['rɔbɪn] n pettirosso

robot ['rəubɔt] n robot m inv

robust [rəu'bʌst] adj robusto(-a); (economy) solido(-a)

rock [rɔk] n roccia; (boulder) masso; roccia; (in sea) scoglio; (US: pebble) ciottolo; (BRIT: sweet) zucchero candito ▸ vt (swing gently: cradle) dondolare; (: child) cullare; (shake) scrollare, far tremare ▸ vi dondolarsi; scrollarsi, tremare; **on the ~s** (drink) col ghiaccio; (marriage etc) in crisi; **rock and roll** n rock and roll m; **rock climbing** n roccia

rocket ['rɔkɪt] n razzo

rocking chair n sedia a dondolo

rocky ['rɔkɪ] adj (hill) roccioso(-a); (path) sassoso(-a); (fig) instabile

rod [rɔd] n (metallic, Tech) asta; (wooden) bacchetta; (also: fishing ~) canna da pesca

rode [rəud] pt of **ride**

rodent ['rəudnt] n roditore m

rogue [rəug] n mascalzone m

role [rəul] n ruolo; **role-model** n modello (di comportamento)

roll [rəul] n rotolo; (of banknotes) mazzo; (also: bread ~) panino; (register) lista; (sound: of drums etc) rullo ▸ vt rotolare; (also: ~ up: string) aggomitolare; (: sleeves) rimboccare; (cigarettes) arrotolare; (eyes) roteare; (also: ~ out: pastry) stendere; (lawn, road etc) spianare ▸ vi rotolare; (wheel) girare; (drum) rullare; (vehicle: also: ~ along) avanzare; (ship) rollare ▷ **roll over** vi rivoltarsi ▷ **roll up** (inf) vi (arrive) arrivare ▷ vt (carpet) arrotolare; **roller** n rullo; (wheel) rotella; (for hair) bigodino; **Rollerblades®** npl pattini mpl in linea; **roller coaster** ['-'kəustə'] n montagne fpl russe; **roller skates** npl pattini mpl a rotelle; **roller-skating** n pattinaggio a rotelle; **to go roller-skating** andare a pattinare (con i pattini a rotelle); **rolling pin** n matterello

ROM [rɔm] n abbr (= read only memory) memoria di sola lettura

Roman ['rəumən] adj, n romano(-a); **Roman Catholic** adj, n cattolico(-a)

romance [rə'mæns] n storia (or avventura or film m inv) romantico(-a); (charm) poesia; (love affair) idillio

Romania [rəu'meınıə] n Romania

Romanian [rəu'meınıən] adj romeno(-a) ▷ n romeno(-a); (Ling) romeno

Roman numeral n numero romano

romantic [rə'mæntık] adj romantico(-a); sentimentale

Rome [rəum] n Roma

roof [ru:f] n tetto; (of tunnel, cave) volta ▷ vt coprire (con un tetto); **~ of the mouth** palato; **roof rack** n (Aut) portabagagli m inv

rook [ruk] n (bird) corvo nero; (Chess) torre f

room [ru:m] n (in house) stanza; (bedroom, in hotel) camera; (in school etc) sala; (space) posto, spazio; **roommate** n compagno(-a) di stanza; **room service** n servizio da camera; **roomy** adj spazioso(-a); (garment) ampio(-a)

rooster ['ru:stə'] n gallo

root [ru:t] n radice f ▷ vi (plant, belief) attecchire

rope [rəup] n corda, fune f; (Naut) cavo ▷ vt (box) legare; (climbers) legare in cordata; (area: also: ~ **off**) isolare cingendo con cordoni; **to know the ~s** (fig) conoscere i trucchi del mestiere

rose [rəuz] pt of **rise** ▷ n rosa; (also: ~ **bush**) rosaio; (on watering can) rosetta

rosé ['rəuzeı] n vino rosato

rosemary ['rəuzmərı] n rosmarino

rosy ['rəuzı] adj roseo(-a)

rot [rɔt] n (decay) putrefazione f; (inf: nonsense) stupidaggini fpl ▷ vt, vi imputridire, marcire

rota ['rəutə] n tabella dei turni

rotate [rəu'teıt] vt far girare; (change round: jobs) fare a turno ▷ vi (revolve) girare

rotten ['rɔtn] adj (decayed) putrido(-a), marcio(-a); (dishonest) corrotto(-a); (inf: bad) brutto(-a); (: action) vigliacco(-a); **to feel ~** (ill) sentirsi da cani

rough [rʌf] adj (skin, surface) ruvido(-a); (terrain, road) accidentato(-a); (voice) rauco(-a); (person, manner: coarse) rozzo(-a), aspro(-a); (: violent) brutale; (district) malfamato(-a); (weather) cattivo(-a); (sea) mosso(-a); (plan) abbozzato(-a); (guess) approssimativo(-a) ▷ n (Golf) macchia; **to ~ it** far vita dura; **to sleep ~** (BRIT) dormire all'addiaccio; **roughly** adv (handle) rudemente, brutalmente; (make) grossolanamente; (speak) bruscamente; (approximately) approssimativamente

roulette [ru:'let] n roulette f

round [raund] adj rotondo(-a); (figures) tondo(-a) ▷ n (BRIT: of toast) fetta; (duty: of policeman, milkman etc) giro; (: of doctor) visite fpl; (game: of cards, golf, in competition) partita; (of ammunition) cartuccia; (Boxing) round m inv; (of talks) serie f inv ▷ vt (corner) girare; (bend) prendere ▶ prep intorno a ▶ adv all ~ tutt'attorno; **to go the long way** ~ fare il giro più lungo; **all the year** ~ tutto l'anno; **it's just ~ the corner** (also fig) è dietro l'angolo; ~ **the clock** ininterrottamente; **to go ~ to sb's house** andare da qn; **go ~ the back** passi dietro; **enough to go** ~ abbastanza per tutti; ~ **of applause** applausi mpl; ~ **of drinks** giro di bibite; ~ **of sandwiches** sandwich m inv ▶ **round off** vt (speech etc) finire ▶ **round up** vt radunare; (criminals) fare una retata di; (prices) arrotondare; **roundabout** n (BRIT Aut) rotatoria f; (at fair) giostra ▶ adj (route, means) indiretto(-a); **round trip** n (viaggio di) andata e ritorno; **roundup** n raduno; (of criminals) retata

rouse [rauz] vt (wake up) svegliare; (stir up) destare; provocare; risvegliare

route [ruːt] n itinerario m; (of bus) percorso

routine [ruːˈtiːn] adj (work) corrente, abituale; (procedure) solito(-a) ▶ n (pej) routine f, tran tran m; (Theatre) numero

row¹ [rəu] n (line) riga, fila; (Knitting) ferro; (behind one another: of cars, people) fila; (in boat) remata ▶ vi (in boat) remare; (as sport) vogare ▶ vt (boat) manovrare a remi; **in a ~** (fig) di fila

row² [rau] n (racket) baccano, chiasso; (dispute) lite f; (scolding) sgridata ▶ vi (argue) litigare

rowboat ['rəubəut] (US) n barca a remi

rowing ['rəuɪŋ] n canottaggio; **rowing boat** n (BRIT) barca a remi

royal ['rɔɪəl] adj reale; **royalty** ['rɔɪəltɪ] n (royal persons) (membri mpl della) famiglia reale; (payment: to author) diritti mpl d'autore

rpm abbr (= revolutions per minute) giri/min

R.S.V.P. abbr (= répondez s'il vous plaît) R.S.V.P.

Rt. Hon. (BRIT) abbr (= Right Honourable) ≈ Onorevole

rub [rʌb] n **to give sth a ~** strofinare qc; (sore place) massaggiare qc ▶ vt strofinare; massaggiare; (hands: also: ~ **together**) sfregarsi; **to ~ sb up** (BRIT) or ~ **sb the wrong way** (US) lisciare qn contro pelo ▶ **rub in** vt (ointment) far penetrare (massaggiando e frizionando) ▶ **rub off** vi andare via ▶ **rub out** vt cancellare

rubber ['rʌbər] n gomma; **rubber band** n elastico; **rubber gloves** npl guanti mpl di gomma

rubbish ['rʌbɪʃ] n (from household) immondizie fpl, rifiuti mpl; (fig, pej) cose fpl senza valore; robaccia; (sciocchezze fpl; **rubbish bin** (BRIT) n pattumiera; **rubbish dump** n (in town) immondezzaio

rubble ['rʌbl] n macerie fpl; (smaller) pietrisco

ruby ['ruːbɪ] n rubino

rucksack ['rʌksæk] n zaino

rudder ['rʌdər] n timone m

rude [ruːd] adj (impolite: person) scortese, rozzo(-a); (: word, manners) grossolano(-a), rozzo(-a); (shocking) indecente

ruffle ['rʌfl] vt (hair) scompigliare; (clothes, water) increspare; (fig: person) turbare

rug [rʌg] n tappeto; (BRIT: for knees) coperta

rugby ['rʌgbɪ] n (also: ~ **football**) rugby m

rugged ['rʌgɪd] adj (landscape) aspro(-a); (features, determination) duro(-a); (character) brusco(-a)

ruin ['ruːɪn] n rovina ▶ vt rovinare; ~**s** npl (of building, castle etc) rovine fpl,

ruderi *mpl*
rule [ruːl] *n* regola; *(regulation)* regolamento, regola; *(government)* governo; *(ruler)* riga ▶ *vt (country)* governare; *(person)* dominare ▶ *vi* regnare; *(decide)* decidere; *(Law)* dichiarare; **as a ~** normalmente ▷ **rule out** *vt* escludere; **ruler** *n (sovereign)* sovrano(-a); *(for measuring)* regolo, riga; **ruling** *adj (party)* al potere; *(class)* dirigente ▶ *n (Law)* decisione *f*
rum [rʌm] *n* rum *m*
Rumania etc [ruːˈmeɪnɪə] *n* = **Romania** etc
rumble [ˈrʌmbl] *n* rimbombo; brontolio ▶ *vi* rimbombare; *(stomach, pipe)* brontolare
rumour [ˈruːmə*] *(US* **rumor)** *n* voce *f* ▶ *vt* **it is ~ed that** corre voce che
⏐ Be careful not to translate **rumour** by the Italian word **rumore**.
rump steak [rʌmp-] *n* bistecca *f* girello
run [rʌn] *(pt* ran, *pp* run*)* *n* corsa; *(outing)* gita *f* in macchina*)*; *(distance travelled)* percorso, tragitto; *(Ski)* pista; *(Cricket, Baseball)* meta; *(series)* serie *f*; *(Theatre)* periodo *f* rappresentazione; *(in tights, stockings)* smagliatura ▶ *vt (distance)* correre; *(operate: business)* gestire, dirigere; *(: competition, course)* organizzare; *(: hotel)* gestire; *(: house)* governare; *(Comput)* eseguire; *(water, bath)* far scorrere; *(force through: rope, pipe)*: **to ~ sth through** far passare qc attraverso; *(pass: hand, finger)*: **to ~ sth over** passare qc su; *(Press: feature)* presentare ▶ *vi* correre; *(flee)* scappare; *(pass: road etc)* passare; *(work: machine, factory)* funzionare, andare; *(bus, train: operate)* far servizio; *(: travel)* circolare; *(continue: play, contract)* durare; *(slide: drawer; flow: river, bath)* scorrere; *(colours, washing)* stemperarsi; *(in*

election) presentarsi candidato; *(nose)* colare; **there was a ~ on ...** c'era una corsa a ...; **in the long ~** a lungo andare; **on the ~** in fuga; **to ~ a race** partecipare ad una gara; **I'll ~ you to the station** la porto alla stazione; **to ~ a risk** correre un rischio ▷ **run after** *vt fus (to catch up)* inseguire; *(chase)* correre dietro a ▷ **run away** *vi* fuggire ▷ **run down** *vt (production)* ridurre gradualmente; *(factory)* rallentare l'attività di; *(Aut)* investire; *(criticize)* criticare; **to be ~ down** *(person: tired)* essere esausto(-a) ▷ **run into** *vt fus (meet: person)* incontrare per caso; *(: trouble)* incontrare, trovare; *(collide with)* andare a sbattere contro ▷ **run off** *vi* fuggire ▶ *vt (water)* far scolare; *(copies)* fare ▷ **run out** *vi (person)* uscire di corsa; *(liquid)* colare; *(lease)* scadere; *(money)* esaurirsi ▷ **run out of** *vt fus* rimanere a corto di ▷ **run over** *vt (Aut)* investire, mettere sotto ▶ *vt fus (revise)* rivedere ▷ **run through** *vt fus (instructions)* dare una scorsa a; *(rehearse: play)* riprovare, ripetere ▷ **run up** *vt (debt)* lasciar accumulare; **to ~ up against** *(difficulties)* incontrare; **runaway** *adj (person)* fuggiasco(-a); *(horse)* in libertà; *(truck)* fuori controllo
rung [rʌŋ] *pp of* **ring** ▶ *n (of ladder)* piolo
runner [ˈrʌnə*] *n (in race)* corridore *m*; *(: horse)* partente *m/f*; *(on sledge)* pattino; *(for drawer etc)* guida; **runner bean** *(BRIT)* *n* fagiolo rampicante; **runner-up** *n* secondo(-a) arrivato(-a)
running [ˈrʌnɪŋ] *n* corsa; direzione *f*, organizzazione *f*; funzionamento ▶ *adj (water)* corrente; *(commentary)* simultaneo(-a); **in the/out of the ~ for sth** essere/non essere più in lizza per qc; **6 days ~** 6 giorni di seguito
runny [ˈrʌnɪ] *adj* che cola
run-up [ˈrʌnʌp] *n* **~ to** *(election etc)*

periodo che precede

runway ['rʌnweɪ] n (Aviat) pista (di decollo)

rupture ['rʌptʃə'] n (Med) ernia

rural ['rʊərəl] adj rurale

rush [rʌʃ] n corsa precipitosa; (hurry) furia, fretta; (sudden demand): ~ **for** corsa a; (current) flusso; (of emotion) impeto; (Bot) giunco ▶ vt mandare or spedire velocemente; (attack: town etc) precipitarsi; **rush hour** n ora di punta

Russia ['rʌʃə] n Russia; **Russian** adj russo(-a) ▶ n russo(-a); (Ling) russo

rust [rʌst] n ruggine f ▶ vi arrugginirsi

rusty ['rʌstɪ] adj arrugginito(-a)

ruthless ['ruːθlɪs] adj spietato(-a)

RV abbr (= revised version) versione riveduta della Bibbia ▶ n abbr (US) see **recreational vehicle**

rye [raɪ] n segale f

S

Sabbath ['sæbəθ] n (Jewish) sabato; (Christian) domenica

sabotage ['sæbətɑːʒ] n sabotaggio ▶ vt sabotare

saccharin(e) ['sækərɪn] n saccarina

sachet ['sæʃeɪ] n bustina

sack [sæk] n (bag) sacco ▶ vt (dismiss) licenziare, mandare a spasso; (plunder) saccheggiare; **to get the ~**

essere mandato a spasso

sacred ['seɪkrɪd] adj sacro(-a)

sacrifice ['sækrɪfaɪs] n sacrificio ▶ vt sacrificare

sad [sæd] adj triste

saddle ['sædl] n sella ▶ vt (horse) sellare; **to be ~d with sth** (inf) avere qc sulle spalle

sadistic [sə'dɪstɪk] adj sadico(-a)

sadly ['sædlɪ] adv tristemente; (regrettably) sfortunatamente; ~ **lacking in** penosamente privo di

sadness ['sædnɪs] n tristezza

s.a.e. n abbr (= stamped addressed envelope) busta affrancata e con indirizzo

safari [sə'fɑːrɪ] n safari m inv

safe [seɪf] adj sicuro(-a); (out of danger) salvo(-a), al sicuro; (cautious) prudente ▶ n cassaforte f; ~ **from** al sicuro da; ~ **and sound** sano(-a) e salvo(-a); (just) **to be on the ~ side** per non correre rischi; **could you put this in the ~, please?** lo potrebbe mettere nella cassaforte, per favore?; **safely** adv sicuramente; sano(-a) e salvo(-a); prudentemente; **safe sex** n sesso sicuro

safety ['seɪftɪ] n sicurezza; **safety belt** n cintura di sicurezza; **safety pin** n spilla di sicurezza

saffron ['sæfrən] n zafferano

sag [sæg] vi incurvarsi; afflosciarsi

sage [seɪdʒ] n (herb) salvia; (man) saggio

Sagittarius [sædʒɪ'tɛərɪəs] n Sagittario

Sahara [sə'hɑːrə] n the ~ (Desert) il (deserto del) Sahara

said [sɛd] pt, pp of **say**

sail [seɪl] n (on boat) vela; (trip): **to go for a ~** fare un giro in barca a vela ▶ vt (boat) condurre, governare ▶ vi (travel: ship) navigare; (: passenger) viaggiare per mare; (set off) salpare; (sport) fare della vela; **they ~ed into Genoa**

entrarono nel porto di Genova;
sailboat (US) n barca a vela; **sailing**
n (sport) vela; **to go sailing** fare della
vela; **sailing boat** n barca a vela;
sailor n marinaio

saint [seɪnt] n santo(-a)

sake [seɪk] n **for the ~ of** per, per
amore di

salad ['sæləd] n insalata; **salad cream**
(BRIT) n (tipo di) maionese f; **salad
dressing** n condimento per insalata

salami [sə'lɑːmɪ] n salame m

salary ['sælərɪ] n stipendio

sale [seɪl] n vendita; (at reduced
prices) svendita, liquidazione f;
(auction) vendita all'asta; **"for ~"** "in
vendita"; **on ~** in vendita; **on ~ or
return** da vendere o rimandare; **~s**
npl (total amount sold) vendite fpl;
sales assistant (US **sales clerk**) n
commesso(-a); **salesman/woman**
(irreg) n commesso(-a); (representative)
rappresentante m/f; **salesperson**
(irreg) n (in shop) commesso;
(representative) rappresentante
m/f di commercio; **sales rep** n
rappresentante m/f di commercio

saline ['seɪlaɪn] adj salino(-a)

saliva [sə'laɪvə] n saliva

salmon ['sæmən] n inv salmone m

salon ['sælɔn] n (hairdressing salon)
parrucchiere(-a); (beauty salon) salone
m di bellezza

saloon [sə'luːn] n (US) saloon m inv,
bar m inv; (BRIT: Aut) berlina; (ship's
lounge) salone m

salt [sɔlt] n sale m ▶ vt salare;
saltwater adj di mare; **salty** adj
salato(-a)

salute [sə'luːt] n saluto ▶ vt salutare

salvage ['sælvɪdʒ] n (saving)
salvataggio; (things saved) beni mpl
salvati or recuperati ▶ vt salvare,
mettere in salvo

Salvation Army [sæl'veɪʃən-] n

Esercito della Salvezza

same [seɪm] adj stesso(-a),
medesimo(-a) ▶ pron **the ~** lo (la)
stesso(-a), gli (le) stessi(-e); **the ~
book as** lo stesso libro di (o che);
at the ~ time allo stesso tempo;
all or **just the ~** tuttavia; **to do the
~ as sb** fare come qn; **the ~ to you!**
altrettanto a te!

sample ['sɑːmpl] n campione m ▶ vt
(food) assaggiare; (wine) degustare

sanction ['sæŋkʃən] n sanzione f
▶ vt sancire, sanzionare; **~s** npl (Pol)
sanzioni fpl

sanctuary ['sæŋktjuərɪ] n (holy place)
santuario; (refuge) rifugio; (for wildlife)
riserva

sand [sænd] n sabbia ▶ vt (also: ~
down) cartavetrare

sandal ['sændl] n sandalo

sand: **sandbox** ['sændbɒks] (US) n
= **sandpit**; **sandcastle** ['sændkɑːsl] n
castello di sabbia; **sand dune** n duna
di sabbia; **sandpaper** ['sændpeɪpər]
n carta vetrata; **sandpit** ['sændpɪt] n
(for children) buca di sabbia; **sands** npl
spiaggia; **sandstone** ['sændstəun]
n arenaria

sandwich ['sændwɪtʃ] n tramezzino,
panino, sandwich m inv ▶ vt **~ed
between** incastrato(-a) fra; **cheese/
ham ~** sandwich al formaggio/
prosciutto

sandy ['sændɪ] adj sabbioso(-a);
(colour) color sabbia inv, biondo(-a)
rossiccio(-a)

sane [seɪn] adj (person) sano(-a) di
mente; (outlook) sensato(-a)

sang [sæŋ] pt of **sing**

sanitary towel ['sænɪtərɪ-] (US
sanitary napkin) n assorbente m
(igienico)

sanity ['sænɪtɪ] n sanità mentale;
(common sense) buon senso

sank [sæŋk] pt of **sink**

Santa Claus [sænta'klɔːz] n Babbo Natale

sap [sæp] n (of plants) linfa ▶ vt (strength) fiaccare

sapphire ['sæfaɪəʳ] n zaffiro

sarcasm ['sɑːkæzm] n sarcasmo

sarcastic [sɑːˈkæstɪk] adj sarcastico(-a); **to be ~** fare del sarcasmo

sardine [sɑːˈdiːn] n sardina

Sardinia [sɑːˈdɪnɪə] n Sardegna

SASE (US) n abbr (= self-addressed stamped envelope) busta affrancata e con indirizzo

sat [sæt] pt, pp of **sit**

Sat. abbr (= Saturday) sab

satchel ['sætʃl] n cartella

satellite ['sætəlaɪt] n satellite ▶ adj satellite ▶ **satellite dish** n antenna parabolica; **satellite television** n televisione f via satellite

satin ['sætɪn] n raso ▶ adj di raso

satire ['sætaɪəʳ] n satira

satisfaction [sætɪsˈfækʃən] n soddisfazione f

satisfactory [sætɪsˈfæktərɪ] adj soddisfacente

satisfied ['sætɪsfaɪd] adj (customer) soddisfatto(-a); **to be ~ (with sth)** essere soddisfatto(-a) (di qc)

satisfy ['sætɪsfaɪ] vt soddisfare; (convince) convincere

Saturday ['sætədɪ] n sabato

sauce [sɔːs] n salsa; (containing meat, fish) sugo; **saucepan** n casseruola

saucer ['sɔːsəʳ] n sottocoppa m, piattino

Saudi Arabia ['saudɪ-] n Arabia Saudita

sauna ['sɔːnə] n sauna

sausage ['sɔsɪdʒ] n salsiccia; **sausage roll** n rotolo di pasta sfoglia ripieno di salsiccia

sautéed ['səuteɪd] adj saltato(-a)

savage ['sævɪdʒ] adj (cruel, fierce)

selvaggio(-a), feroce; (primitive) primitivo(-a) ▶ n selvaggio(-a) ▶ vt attaccare selvaggiamente

save [seɪv] vt (person, belongings, Comput) salvare; (money) risparmiare, mettere da parte; (time) risparmiare; (food) conservare; (avoid: trouble) evitare; (Sport) parare ▶ vi (also: **~ up**) economizzare ▶ n (Sport) parata ▶ prep salvo, a eccezione di

savings ['seɪvɪŋz] npl (money) risparmi mpl; **savings account** n libretto di risparmio; **savings and loan association** (US) n ≈ società di credito immobiliare

savoury ['seɪvərɪ] (US **savory**) adj (dish: not sweet) salato(-a)

saw [sɔː] (pt **sawed**, pp **sawed** or **sawn**) pt of **see** ▶ n (tool) sega ▶ vt segare; **sawdust** n segatura

sawn [sɔːn] pp of **saw**

saxophone ['sæksəfəun] n sassofono

say [seɪ] (pt, pp **said**) vt to have one's ~ fare sentire il proprio parere; **to have a** or **some ~** avere voce in capitolo ▶ vt dire; **could you ~ that again?** potrebbe ripeterlo?; **that goes without ~ing** va da sé; **saying** n proverbio, detto

scab [skæb] n crosta; (pej) crumiro(-a)

scaffolding ['skæfəldɪŋ] n impalcatura

scald [skɔːld] n scottatura ▶ vt scottare

scale [skeɪl] n scala; (of fish) squama ▶ vt (mountain) scalare; **~s** npl (for weighing) bilancia; **on a large ~** su vasta scala; **~ of charges** tariffa

scallion ['skæljən] n cipolla; (US: shallot) scalogna; (: leek) porro

scallop ['skɔləp] n (Zool) pettine m; (Sewing) smerlo

scalp [skælp] n cuoio capelluto ▶ vt scotennare

scalpel ['skælpl] n bisturi m inv

scam [skæm] n (inf) truffa

scampi ['skæmpi] npl scampi mpl

scan [skæn] vt scrutare; (glance at quickly) scorrere, dare un'occhiata a; (TV) analizzare; (Radar) esplorare ▶ n (Med) ecografia

scandal ['skændl] n scandalo; (gossip) pettegolezzi mpl

Scandinavia [skændɪ'neɪvɪə] n Scandinavia; **Scandinavian** adj, n scandinavo(-a)

scanner ['skænəʳ] n (Radar, Med) scanner m inv

scapegoat ['skeɪpgəʊt] n capro espiatorio

scar [skɑː] n cicatrice f ▶ vt sfregiare

scarce [skɛəs] adj scarso(-a); (copy, edition) raro(-a); **to make o.s. ~** (inf) squagliarsela; **scarcely** adv appena

scare [skɛəʳ] n spavento; panico ▶ vt spaventare, atterrire; **there was a bomb ~ at the bank** hanno evacuato la banca per paura di un attentato dinamitardo; **to ~ sb stiff** spaventare a morte qn; **scarecrow** n spaventapasseri m inv; **scared** adj **to be scared** aver paura

scarf [skɑːf] (pl **scarves** or **scarfs**) n (long) sciarpa; (square) fazzoletto da testa, foulard m inv

scarlet ['skɑːlɪt] adj scarlatto(-a)

scarves [skɑːvz] npl of **scarf**

scary ['skɛərɪ] adj che spaventa

scatter ['skætəʳ] vt spargere; (crowd) disperdere ▶ vi disperdersi

scenario [sɪ'nɑːrɪəʊ] n (Theatre, Cinema) copione m; (fig) situazione f

scene [siːn] n (Theatre, fig etc) scena; (of crime, accident) luogo, scena; (sight, view) vista, veduta; **scenery** n (Theatre) scenario; (landscape) panorama m; **scenic** adj scenico(-a), panoramico(-a)

scent [sɛnt] n profumo; (sense of smell) olfatto, odorato; (fig: track) pista

sceptical ['skɛptɪkəl] (US **skeptical**) adj scettico(-a)

schedule ['ʃɛdjuːl, (US) 'skɛdjuːl] n programma m, piano; (of trains) orario; (of prices etc) lista, tabella ▶ vt fissare; **on ~** in orario; **to be ahead of/behind ~** essere in anticipo/ritardo sul previsto; **scheduled flight** n volo di linea

scheme [skiːm] n piano, progetto; (method) sistema m; (dishonest plan, plot) intrigo, trama; (arrangement) disposizione f, sistemazione f; (pension scheme etc) programma m ▶ vi fare progetti; (intrigue) complottare

schizophrenic [skɪtsə'frɛnɪk] adj, n schizofrenico(-a)

scholar ['skɔləʳ] n (expert) studioso(-a); **scholarship** n erudizione f; (grant) borsa di studio

school [skuːl] n (primary, secondary) scuola; (university: US) università f inv ▶ cpd scolare, scolastico(-a) ▶ vt (animal) addestrare; **schoolbook** n libro scolastico; **schoolboy** n scolaro; **school children** npl scolari mpl; **schoolgirl** n scolara; **schooling** n istruzione f; **schoolteacher** n insegnante m/f, docente m/f; (primary) maestro(-a)

science ['saɪəns] n scienza; **science fiction** n fantascienza; **scientific** [-'tɪfɪk] adj scientifico(-a); **scientist** n scienziato(-a)

sci-fi ['saɪfaɪ] n abbr (inf) = **science fiction**

scissors ['sɪzəz] npl forbici fpl

scold [skəʊld] vt rimproverare

scone [skɒn] n focaccia da tè

scoop [skuːp] n mestolo; (for ice cream) cucchiaio dosatore; (Press) colpo giornalistico, notizia (in) esclusiva

scooter ['skuːtəʳ] n (motor cycle) motoretta, scooter m inv; (toy) monopattino

scope [skəʊp] n (capacity: of plan, undertaking) portata; (: of person) capacità fpl; (opportunity) possibilità fpl

scorching ['skɔ:tʃɪŋ] adj cocente, scottante

score [skɔ:ʳ] n punti mpl, punteggio; (Mus) partitura, spartito; (twenty) venti ▶ vt (goal, point) segnare, fare; (success) ottenere ▶ vi segnare; (Football) fare un goal; (keep score) segnare i punti; **~s of** (very many) un sacco di; **on that ~** a questo riguardo; **to ~ 6 out of 10** prendere 6 su 10 ▶ **score out** vt cancellare con un segno; **scoreboard** n tabellone m segnapunti; **scorer** n marcatore(-trice); (keeping score) segnapunti m inv

scorn [skɔ:n] n disprezzo ▶ vt disprezzare

Scorpio ['skɔ:pɪəʊ] n Scorpione m

scorpion ['skɔ:pɪən] n scorpione m

Scot [skɒt] n scozzese m/f

Scotch tape® n scotch® m

Scotland ['skɒtlənd] n Scozia

Scots [skɒts] adj scozzese; **Scotsman** (irreg) n scozzese m; **Scotswoman** (irreg) n scozzese f; **Scottish** ['skɒtɪʃ] adj scozzese; **Scottish Parliament** n Parlamento scozzese

scout [skaʊt] n (Mil) esploratore m; (also: **boy ~**) giovane esploratore, scout m inv

scowl [skaʊl] vi acciglarsi, aggrottare le sopracciglia; **to ~ at** guardare torvo

scramble ['skræmbl] n arrampicata ▶ vi inerpicarsi; **to ~ out** etc uscire etc in fretta; **to ~ for** azzuffarsi per; **scrambled eggs** npl uova fpl strapazzate

scrap [skræp] n pezzo, pezzetto; (fight) zuffa; (also: **~ iron**) rottami mpl di ferro, ferraglia ▶ vt demolire; (fig) scartare ▶ vi **to ~ (with sb)** fare a botte

(con qn); **~s** npl (waste) scarti mpl; **scrapbook** n album m inv di ritagli

scrape [skreɪp] vt, vi raschiare, grattare ▶ n **to get into a ~** cacciarsi in un guaio

scrap paper n cartaccia

scratch [skrætʃ] n graffio ▶ cpd **~ team** squadra raccogliticcia ▶ vt graffiare, rigare ▶ vi grattare; (paint, car) graffiare; **to start from ~** cominciare or partire da zero; **to be up to ~** essere all'altezza; **scratch card** n (BRIT) cartolina f gratta e vinci

scream [skri:m] n grido, urlo ▶ vi urlare, gridare

screen [skri:n] n schermo; (fig) muro, cortina, velo ▶ vt schermare, fare schermo a; (from the wind etc) riparare; (film) proiettare; (book) adattare per lo schermo; (candidates etc) selezionare; **screening** n (Med) dépistage m inv; **screenplay** n sceneggiatura; **screen saver** n (Comput) screen saver m inv

screw [skru:] n vite ▶ vt avvitare ▶ **screw up** vt (paper etc) spiegazzare; (inf: ruin) rovinare; **to ~ up one's eyes** strizzare gli occhi; **screwdriver** n cacciavite m

scribble ['skrɪbl] n scarabocchio ▶ vt scribacchiare in fretta ▶ vi scarabocchiare

script [skrɪpt] n (Cinema etc) copione m; (in exam) elaborato or compito d'esame

scroll [skrəʊl] n rotolo di carta

scrub [skrʌb] n (land) boscaglia ▶ vt pulire strofinando; (inf) annullare

scruffy ['skrʌfɪ] adj sciatto(-a)

scrum(mage) ['skrʌm(ɪdʒ)] n mischia

scrutiny ['skru:tɪnɪ] n esame m accurato

scuba diving ['sku:bə-] n immersioni fpl subacquee

sculptor ['skʌlptəʳ] n scultore m

sculpture ['skʌlptʃə'] n scultura
scum [skʌm] n schiuma; (pej: people) feccia
scurry ['skʌrɪ] vi sgambare, affrettarsi
sea [si:] n mare m ▶ cpd marino(-a), del mare; (bird, fish) di mare; (route, transport) marittimo(-a); **by ~** (travel) per mare; **on the ~** (boat) in mare; (town) di mare; **to be all at ~** (fig) non sapere che pesci pigliare; **out to ~** al largo; **(out) at ~** in mare; **seafood** n frutti mpl di mare; **sea front** n lungomare m; **seagull** n gabbiano
seal [si:l] n (animal) foca; (stamp) sigillo; (impression) impronta del sigillo ▶ vt sigillare **seal off** vt (close) sigillare; (forbid entry to) bloccare l'accesso a
sea level n livello del mare
seam [si:m] n cucitura; (of coal) filone m
search [sə:tʃ] n ricerca; (Law: at sb's home) perquisizione f ▶ vt frugare ▶ vi **to ~ for** ricercare; **in ~ of** alla ricerca di; **search engine** n (Comput) motore m di ricerca; **search party** n squadra di soccorso
sea: **seashore** n ['si:ʃɔ:'] n spiaggia; **seasick** ['si:sɪk] adj che soffre il mal di mare; **seaside** ['si:saɪd] n spiaggia; **seaside resort** n stazione f balneare
season ['si:zn] n stagione f ▶ vt condire, insaporire; **seasonal** adj stagionale; **seasoning** n condimento; **season ticket** n abbonamento
seat [si:t] n sedile m; (in bus, train: place) posto; (Parliament) seggio; (buttocks) didietro; (of trousers) fondo ▶ vt far sedere; (have room for) avere o essere fornito di posti a sedere per; **I'd like to book two ~s** vorrei prenotare due posti; **to be ~ed** essere seduto(-a); **seat belt** n cintura di sicurezza; **seating** n posti mpl a sedere

sea: **sea water** n acqua di mare; **seaweed** ['si:wi:d] n alghe fpl
sec. abbr = **second(s)**
secluded [sɪ'klu:dɪd] adj isolato(-a), appartato(-a)
second ['sɛkənd] num secondo(-a) ▶ adv (in race etc) al secondo posto ▶ n (unit of time) secondo; (Aut: also: **~ gear**) seconda; (Comm: imperfect) scarto; (BRIT: Scol: degree) laurea con punteggio discreto ▶ vt (motion) appoggiare; **secondary** adj secondario(-a); **secondary school** n scuola secondaria; **second-class** adj di seconda classe ▶ adv di seconda classe; **secondhand** adj di seconda mano, usato(-a); **secondly** adv in secondo luogo; **second-rate** adj scadente; **second thoughts** npl ripensamenti mpl; **on second thoughts** (BRIT) or **thought** (US) ripensandoci bene
secrecy ['si:krəsɪ] n segretezza
secret ['si:krɪt] adj segreto(-a) ▶ n segreto; **in ~** in segreto
secretary ['sɛkrətrɪ] n segretario(-a); **S~ of State (for)** (BRIT: Pol) ministro (di)
secretive ['si:krətɪv] adj riservato(-a)
secret service n servizi mpl segreti
sect [sɛkt] n setta
section ['sɛkʃən] n sezione f
sector ['sɛktə'] n settore m
secular ['sɛkjulə'] adj secolare
secure [sɪ'kjuə'] adj sicuro(-a); (firmly fixed) assicurato(-a), ben fermato(-a); (in safe place) al sicuro ▶ vt (fix) fissare, assicurare; (get) ottenere, assicurarsi; **securities** npl (Stock Exchange) titoli mpl
security [sɪ'kjuərɪtɪ] n sicurezza; (for loan) garanzia; **security guard** n guardia giurata
sedan [sə'dæn] (US) n (Aut) berlina

sedate [sɪˈdeɪt] *adj* posato(-a),
calmo(-a) ▶ *vt* calmare
sedative [ˈsedɪtɪv] *n* sedativo,
calmante *m*
seduce [sɪˈdjuːs] *vt* sedurre;
seductive [-ˈdʌktɪv] *adj* seducente
see [siː] (*pt* **saw**, *pp* **seen**) *vt* vedere;
(*accompany*) accompagnare; **to ~ sb to the door**
accompagnare qn alla porta ▶ *vi*
vedere; (*understand*) capire ▶ *n* sede
f vescovile; **to ~ that** (*ensure*) badare
che + *sub*, fare in modo che + *sub*; **~ you
soon!** a presto! ▶ **see off** *vt* salutare
alla partenza ▶ **see out** *vt* (*take to the
door*) accompagnare alla porta ▶ **see
through** *vt* portare a termine ▶ *vt fus*
non lasciarsi ingannare da ▶ **see to** *vt
fus* occuparsi di
seed [siːd] *n* seme *m*; (*fig*) germe *m*;
(*Tennis etc*) testa di serie; **to go to ~**
fare seme; (*fig*) scadere
seeing [ˈsiːɪŋ] *conj* **~ (that)** visto che
seek [siːk] (*pt*, *pp* **sought**) *vt* cercare
seem [siːm] *vi* sembrare, parere;
there ~s to be ... sembra che ci sia ...;
seemingly *adv* apparentemente
seen [siːn] *pp of* **see**
seesaw [ˈsiːsɔː] *n* altalena a bilico
segment [ˈsegmənt] *n* segmento
segregate [ˈsegrɪgeɪt] *vt* segregare,
isolare
seize [siːz] *vt* (*grasp*) afferrare; (*take
possession of*) impadronirsi di; (*Law*)
sequestrare
seizure [ˈsiːʒə] *n* (*Med*) attacco; (*Law*)
confisca, sequestro
seldom [ˈseldəm] *adv* raramente
select [sɪˈlekt] *adj* scelto(-a) ▶ *vt*
scegliere, selezionare; **selection**
[-ˈlekʃən] *n* selezione *f*, scelta;
selective *adj* selettivo(-a)
self [self] *n* the **~ l'io** *m* ▶ *prefix* auto...;
self-assured *adj* sicuro(-a) di sé;
self-catering (*BRIT*) *adj* in cui ci
si cucina da sé; **self-centred** (*US*

self-centered) *adj* egocentrico(-a);
self-confidence *n* sicurezza di sé;
self-confident *adj* sicuro(-a) di
sé; **self-conscious** *adj* timido(-a);
self-contained (*BRIT*) *adj* (*flat*)
indipendente; **self-control** *n*
autocontrollo; **self-defence** (*US*
self-defense) *n* autodifesa; (*Law*)
legittima difesa; **self-drive** *adj*
(*BRIT*: *rented car*) senza autista; **self-
employed** *adj* che lavora in proprio;
self-esteem *n* amor proprio *m*; **self-
indulgent** *adj* indulgente verso se
stesso(-a); **self-interest** *n* interesse
m personale; **selfish** *adj* egoista;
self-pity *n* autocommiserazione
f; **self-raising** (*US* **self-rising**) *adj*
self-raising flour miscela di farina
e lievito; **self-respect** *n* rispetto
di sé, amor proprio; **self-service**
adj autoservizio, self-service *m*
sell [sel] (*pt*, *pp* **sold**) *vt* vendere ▶ *vi*
vendersi; **to ~ at** *or* **for 1000 euros**
essere in vendita a 1000 euro ▶ **sell
off** *vt* svendere, liquidare ▶ **sell out**
vi **to ~ out (of sth)** esaurire (qc); **the
tickets are all sold out** i biglietti sono
esauriti; **sell-by date** [ˈselbaɪ-] *n* data
di scadenza; **seller** *n* venditore(-trice)
Sellotape® [ˈseləuteɪp] (*BRIT*) *n*
nastro adesivo, scotch® *m*
selves [selvz] *npl of* **self**
semester [sɪˈmestə] (*US*) *n* semestre
m
semi... [ˈsemɪ] *prefix* semi...;
semicircle *n* semicerchio;
semidetached (house)
[semɪdɪˈtætʃt-] (*BRIT*) *n* casa gemella;
semi-final *n* semifinale *f*
seminar [ˈsemɪnɑː] *n* seminario
semi-skimmed [ˈsemɪˈskɪmd] *adj*
(*milk*) parzialmente scremato(-a)
senate [ˈsenɪt] *n* senato; **senator**
n senatore(-trice)
send [send] (*pt*, *pp* **sent**) *vt* mandare

▷ **send back** vt rimandare ▷ **send for** vt fus mandare a chiamare, far venire ▷ **send in** vt (report, application, resignation) presentare ▷ **send off** vt (goods) spedire; (BRIT: Sport: player) espellere ▷ **send on** vt (BRIT: letter) inoltrire; (luggage etc: in advance) spedire in anticipo ▷ **send out** vt (invitation) diramare ▷ **send up** vt (person, price) far salire; (BRIT: parody) mettere in ridicolo; **sender** n mittente m/f; **send-off** n to give sb a good send-off festeggiare la partenza di qn

senile ['siːnaɪl] adj senile

senior ['siːnɪə'] adj (older) più vecchio(-a); (of higher rank) di grado più elevato; **senior citizen** n persona anziana; **senior high school** (US) n ≈ liceo

sensation [sɛnˈseɪʃən] n sensazione f; **sensational** adj sensazionale; (marvellous) eccezionale

sense [sɛns] n senso; (feeling) sensazione f, senso; (meaning) senso, significato; (wisdom) buonsenso ▶ vt sentire, percepire; **it makes ~** ha senso; **senseless** adj sciocco(-a); (unconscious) privo(-a) di sensi; **sense of humour** (BRIT) n senso dell'umorismo

sensible ['sɛnsɪbl] adj sensato(-a), ragionevole

▌ Be careful not to translate **sensible** by the Italian word **sensibile**.

sensitive ['sɛnsɪtɪv] adj sensibile; (skin, question) delicato(-a)

sensual ['sɛnsjuəl] adj sensuale

sensuous ['sɛnsjuəs] adj sensuale

sent [sɛnt] pt, pp of **send**

sentence ['sɛntns] n (Ling) frase f; (Law: judgment) sentenza; (: punishment) condanna ▶ vt to **~ sb to death/to 5 years** condannare qn a morte/a 5 anni

sentiment ['sɛntɪmənt] n sentimento; (opinion) opinione f; **sentimental** [-'mɛntl] adj sentimentale

Sep. abbr (= September) Sett.

separate [adj 'sɛprɪt, vb 'sɛpəreɪt] adj separato(-a) ▶ vt separare ▶ vi separarsi; **separately** adv separatamente; **separates** npl (clothes) coordinati mpl; **separation** [-'reɪʃən] n separazione f

September [sɛp'tɛmbə'] n settembre m

septic ['sɛptɪk] adj settico(-a); (wound) infettato(-a); **septic tank** n fossa settica

sequel ['siːkwl] n conseguenza; (of story) seguito; (of film) sequenza

sequence ['siːkwəns] n (series) serie f; (order) ordine m

sequin ['siːkwɪn] n lustrino, paillette f inv

Serb [səːb] adj, n = **Serbian**

Serbia ['səːbɪə] n Serbia

Serbian ['səːbɪən] adj serbo(-a) ▶ n serbo(-a); (Ling) serbo

sergeant ['sɑːdʒənt] n sergente m; (Police) brigadiere m

serial ['sɪərɪəl] n (Press) romanzo a puntate; (Radio, TV) trasmissione f a puntate, serial m inv; **serial killer** n serial-killer m/f inv; **serial number** n numero di serie

series ['sɪəriːz] n inv serie f inv; (Publishing) collana

serious ['sɪərɪəs] adj serio(-a), grave; **seriously** adv seriamente

sermon ['səːmən] n sermone m

servant ['səːvənt] n domestico(-a)

serve [səːv] vt (employer etc) servire, essere a servizio di; (purpose) servire a; (customer, food, meal) servire; (apprenticeship) fare; (prison term) scontare ▶ vi (also Tennis) servire; (be useful): to **~ as/for/to do** servire da/

per/per fare ▶ n (Tennis) servizio; **it ~s him right** ben gli sta, se l'è meritata; **server** n (Comput) server m inv

service ['sɜːvɪs] n servizio; (Aut: maintenance) assistenza, revisione f ▶ vt (car, washing machine) revisionare; **to be of ~ to sb** essere d'aiuto a qn; **~ included/not included** servizio compreso/escluso; **~s** (BRIT: on motorway) stazione f di servizio; (Mil): **the S~s** le Forze Armate; **service area** n (on motorway) area di servizio; **service charge** (BRIT) n servizio; **serviceman** (irreg) n militare m; **service station** n stazione f di servizio

serviette [sɜːvɪ'et] (BRIT) n tovagliolo

session ['sɛʃən] n (sitting) seduta, sessione f; (Scol) anno scolastico (or accademico)

set [sɛt] (pt, pp set) n serie f inv; (of cutlery etc) servizio; (Radio, TV) apparecchio; (Tennis) set m inv; (group of people) mondo, ambiente m; (Cinema) scenario; (Theatre: stage) scene fpl; (: scenery) scenario; (Math) insieme m; (Hairdressing) messa in piega ▶ adj (fixed) stabilito(-a), determinato(-a); (ready) pronto(-a) ▶ vt (place) posare, mettere; sistemare; (fix) fissare; (adjust) regolare; (decide: rules etc) stabilire, fissare ▶ vi (sun) tramontare; (jam, jelly) rapprendersi; (concrete) fare presa; **to be ~ on doing** essere deciso a fare; **to ~ to music** mettere in musica; **to ~ on fire** dare fuoco a; **to ~ free** liberare; **to ~ sth going** mettere in moto qc; **to ~ sail** prendere il mare ▶ **set aside** vt mettere da parte ▶ **set down** vt (bus, train) lasciare ▶ **set in** vi (infection) svilupparsi; (complications) intervenire; **the rain has ~ in for the day** ormai pioverà tutto il giorno ▶ **set off** vi partire ▶ vt (bomb) far

scoppiare; (cause to start) mettere in moto; (show up well) dare risalto a ▶ **set out** vi partire ▶ vt (arrange) disporre; (state) esporre, presentare; **to ~ out to do** proporsi di fare ▶ **set up** vt (organization) fondare, costituire; **setback** n (hitch) contrattempo, inconveniente m; **set menu** n menù m inv fisso

settee [sɛ'tiː] n divano, sofà m inv

setting ['sɛtɪŋ] n (background) ambiente m; (of controls) posizione f; (of sun) tramonto; (of jewel) montatura

settle ['sɛtl] vt (argument, matter) appianare; (accounts) regolare; (Med: calm) calmare ▶ vi (bird, dust etc) posarsi; (sediment) depositarsi; **to ~ for sth** accontentarsi di qc; **to ~ on sth** decidersi per qc ▶ **settle down** vi (get comfortable) sistemarsi; (calm down) calmarsi; (get back to normal: situation) tornare alla normalità ▶ **settle in** vi sistemarsi ▶ **settle up** vi **to ~ up with sb** regolare i conti con qn; **settlement** n (payment) pagamento, saldo; (agreement) accordo; (colony) colonia; (village etc) villaggio, comunità f inv

setup ['sɛtʌp] n (arrangement) sistemazione f; (situation) situazione f

seven ['sɛvn] num sette; **seventeen** num diciassette; **seventeenth** [sɛvn'tiːnθ] num diciassettesimo(-a); **seventh** num settimo(-a); **seventieth** ['sɛvntɪɪθ] num settantesimo(-a); **seventy** num settanta

sever ['sɛvəʳ] vt recidere, tagliare; (relations) troncare

several ['sɛvrəl] adj, pron alcuni(-e), diversi(-e); **~ of us** alcuni di noi

severe [sɪ'vɪəʳ] adj severo(-a); (serious) serio(-a), grave; (hard) duro(-a); (plain) semplice, sobrio(-a)

sew [səʊ] (pt **sewed**, pp **sewn**) vt, vi cucire

sewage ['su:ɪdʒ] n acque fpl di scolo

sewer ['su:ə'] n fogna

sewing ['səʊɪŋ] n cucitura; cucito; **sewing machine** n macchina da cucire

sewn [səʊn] pp of **sew**

sex [sɛks] n sesso; **to have ~ with** avere rapporti sessuali con; **sexism** ['sɛksɪzəm] n sessismo; **sexist** adj, n sessista m/f; **sexual** ['sɛksjuəl] adj sessuale; **sexual intercourse** n rapporti mpl sessuali; **sexuality** [sɛksjʊ'ælɪtɪ] n sessualità; **sexy** ['sɛksɪ] adj provocante, sexy inv

shabby ['ʃæbɪ] adj malandato(-a); (behaviour) vergognoso(-a)

shack [ʃæk] n baracca, capanna

shade [ʃeɪd] n ombra; (for lamp) paralume m; (of colour) tonalità f inv; (small quantity): **a ~ (more/too large)** un po' (di più/troppo grande) ▶ vt ombreggiare, fare ombra a; **in the ~** all'ombra; **~s** (US) npl (sunglasses) occhiali mpl da sole

shadow ['ʃædəʊ] n ombra ▶ vt (follow) pedinare; **shadow cabinet** (BRIT) n (Pol) governo m ombra inv

shady ['ʃeɪdɪ] adj ombroso(-a); (fig: dishonest) losco(-a), equivoco(-a)

shaft [ʃɑ:ft] n (of arrow, spear) asta; (Aut, Tech) albero; (of mine) pozzo; (of lift) tromba; (of light) raggio

shake [ʃeɪk] (pt **shook**, pp **shaken**) vt scuotere; (bottle, cocktail) agitare ▶ vi tremare; **to ~ one's head** (in refusal, dismay) scuotere la testa; **to ~ hands with sb** stringere or dare la mano a qn ▶ **shake off** vt scrollare (via); (fig) sbarazzarsi di ▶ **shake up** vt scuotere; **shaky** adj (hand, voice) tremante; (building) traballante

shall [ʃæl] aux vb **I ~ go** andrò; **~ I open the door?** apro io la porta?; **I'll get**

some, ~ I? ne prendo un po', va bene?

shallow ['ʃæləʊ] adj poco profondo(-a); (fig) superficiale

sham [ʃæm] n finzione f, messinscena; (jewellery, furniture) imitazione f

shambles ['ʃæmblz] n confusione f, baraonda, scompiglio

shame [ʃeɪm] n vergogna ▶ vt far vergognare; **it is a ~ (that/to do)** è un peccato (che ~ sub/fare); **what a ~!** che peccato!; **shameful** adj vergognoso(-a); **shameless** adj sfrontato(-a); (immodest) spudorato(-a)

shampoo [ʃæm'pu:] n shampoo m inv ▶ vt fare lo shampoo a

shandy ['ʃændɪ] n birra con gassosa

shan't [ʃɑ:nt] = **shall not**

shape [ʃeɪp] n forma ▶ vt formare; (statement) formulare; (sb's ideas) condizionare; **to take ~** prendere forma

share [ʃɛə'] n (thing received, contribution) parte f; (Comm) azione f ▶ vt dividere; (have in common) condividere, avere in comune; **shareholder** n azionista m/f

shark [ʃɑ:k] n squalo, pescecane m

sharp [ʃɑ:p] adj (razor, knife) affilato(-a); (point) acuto(-a); acuminato(-a); (nose, chin) aguzzo(-a); (outline, contrast) netto(-a); (cold, pain) pungente; (voice) stridulo(-a); (person: quick-witted) sveglio(-a); (: unscrupulous) disonesto(-a); (Mus): **C ~** do diesis ▶ n (Mus) diesis m inv ▶ adv **at 2 o'clock ~** alle due in punto; **sharpen** vt affilare; (pencil) fare la punta a; (fig) acuire; **sharpener** n (also: **pencil sharpener**) temperamatite m inv; **sharply** adv (turn, stop) bruscamente; (stand out, contrast) nettamente; (criticize, retort) duramente, aspramente

shatter ['ʃætə'] vt mandare in

frantumi, frantumare; (fig: upset)
distruggere; (: ruin) rovinare ▶ vi
frantumarsi, andare in pezzi;
shattered adj (grief-stricken)
sconvolto(-a); (exhausted) a pezzi,
distrutto(-a)

shave [ʃeɪv] vt radere, rasare ▶ vi
radersi, farsi la barba ▶ to have a ~
farsi la barba; **shaver** n (also: **electric
shaver**) rasoio elettrico

shaving cream n crema da barba

shaving foam n = **shaving cream**

shavings ['ʃeɪvɪŋz] npl (of wood etc)
trucioli mpl

shawl [ʃɔːl] n scialle m

she [ʃiː] pron ella, lei; ~-**cat** gatta;
~-**elephant** elefantessa

sheath [ʃiːθ] n fodero, guaina;
(contraceptive) preservativo

shed [ʃed] (pt, pp **shed**) n capannone
m ▶ vt (leaves, fur etc) perdere; (tears,
blood) versare; (workers) liberarsi di

she'd [ʃiːd] = **she had**; **she would**

sheep [ʃiːp] n inv pecora; **sheepdog** n
cane m da pastore; **sheepskin** n pelle
f di pecora

sheer [ʃɪəʳ] adj (utter) vero(-a)
(e proprio(-a)); (steep) a picco,
perpendicolare; (almost transparent)
sottile ▶ adv a picco

sheet [ʃiːt] n (on bed) lenzuolo; (of
paper) foglio; (of glass, ice) lastra; (of
metal) foglio, lamina

sheik(h) [ʃeɪk] n sceicco

shelf [ʃelf] (pl **shelves**) n scaffale m,
mensola

she'll [ʃiːl] = **she will**; **she shall**

shellfish ['ʃelfɪʃ] n inv (crab etc)
crostaceo; (scallop etc) mollusco; (as
food) crostacei; molluschi

shelter ['ʃeltəʳ] n riparo, rifugio ▶ vt

riparare, proteggere; (give lodging to)
dare rifugio or asilo a ▶ vi ripararsi,
mettersi al riparo; **sheltered** adj
riparato(-a)

shelves ['ʃelvz] npl of **shelf**

shelving ['ʃelvɪŋ] n scaffalature fpl

shepherd ['ʃepəd] n pastore m ▶ vt
(guide) guidare; **shepherd's pie**
(BRIT) n timballo di carne macinata e
purè di patate

sheriff [ʃerɪf] (US) n sceriffo

sherry ['ʃerɪ] n sherry m inv

she's [ʃiːz] = **she is**; **she has**

Shetland ['ʃetlənd] n (also: the ~**s**, the
~ **Isles**) le isole Shetland, le Shetland

shield [ʃiːld] n scudo; (trophy)
scudetto; (protection) schermo ▶ vt
to ~ (from) riparare (da), proteggere
(da o contro)

shift [ʃɪft] n (change) cambiamento; (of
workers) turno ▶ vt spostare, muovere;
(remove) rimuovere ▶ vi spostarsi,
muoversi

shin [ʃɪn] n tibia

shine [ʃaɪn] (pt, pp **shone**) n splendore
m, lucentezza ▶ vi (ri)splendere,
brillare ▶ vt far brillare, far
risplendere; (torch): **to ~ sth on**
puntare qc verso

shingles ['ʃɪŋglz] n (Med) herpes
zoster m

shiny ['ʃaɪnɪ] adj lucente, lucido(-a)

ship [ʃɪp] n nave f ▶ vt trasportare
(via mare); (send) spedire (via mare);
shipment n carico; **shipping** n (ships)
naviglio; (traffic) navigazione f;
shipwreck n relitto; (event) naufragio
▶ vt **to be shipwrecked** naufragare,
fare naufragio; **shipyard** n cantiere
m navale

shirt [ʃəːt] n camicia; **in ~ sleeves** in
maniche di camicia

shit [ʃɪt] (infl) excl merda (!)

shiver ['ʃɪvəʳ] n brivido ▶ vi
rabbrividire, tremare

shock [ʃɔk] n (impact) urto, colpo; (Elec) scossa; (emotional) colpo, shock m inv; (Med) shock ▶ vt colpire, scioccare; scandalizzare; **shocking** adj scioccante, traumatizzante; scandaloso(-a)

shoe [ʃuː] n (pt, pp shod) n scarpa; (also: horse~) ferro di cavallo ▶ vt (horse) ferrare; **shoelace** n stringa; **shoe polish** n lucido per scarpe; **shoeshop** n calzoleria

shone [ʃɔn] pt, pp of **shine**

shook [ʃuk] pt of **shake**

shoot [ʃuːt] (pt, pp shot) n (on branch, seedling) germoglio ▶ vt (game) cacciare, andare a caccia di; (person) sparare a; (execute) fucilare; (film) girare ▶ vi (with gun): **to ~ (at)** sparare (a), fare fuoco (su); (with bow): **to ~ (at)** tirare (su); (Football) sparare, tirare (forte) ▷ **shoot down** vt (plane) abbattere ▷ **shoot up** vi (fig) salire alle stelle; **shooting** n (shots) sparatoria; (Hunting) caccia

shop [ʃɔp] n negozio; (workshop) officina ▶ vi (also: **go ~ping**) fare spese; **shop assistant** n commesso(-a); **shopkeeper** n negoziante m/f, bottegaio(-a); **shoplifting** n taccheggio; **shopping** n (goods) spesa, acquisti mpl; **shopping bag** n borsa per la spesa; **shopping centre** (US **shopping center**) n centro commerciale; **shopping mall** n centro commerciale; **shopping trolley** n (BRIT) carrello del supermercato; **shop window** n vetrina

shore [ʃɔːʳ] n (of sea) riva, spiaggia; (of lake) riva ▶ vt **to ~ (up)** puntellare; **on ~** a terra

short [ʃɔːt] adj (not long) corto(-a); (soon finished) breve; (person) basso(-a); (curt) brusco(-a), secco(-a); (insufficient) insufficiente ▶ n (also: ~

film) cortometraggio; **to be ~ of sth** essere a corto di or mancare di qc; **in ~** in breve; **~ of doing** a meno che non si faccia; **everything ~ of** tutto fuorché; **it is ~ for** l'abbreviazione or il diminutivo di; **to cut ~** (speech, visit) accorciare, abbreviare; **to fall ~ of** venir meno a; non soddisfare; **to run ~ of** rimanere senza; **to stop ~** fermarsi di colpo; **to stop ~ of** non arrivare fino a; **shortage** n scarsezza, carenza; **shortbread** n biscotto di pasta frolla; **shortcoming** n difetto; **short(crust) pastry** (BRIT) n pasta frolla; **shortcut** n scorciatoia; **shorten** vt accorciare, ridurre; **shortfall** n deficit m; **shorthand** (BRIT) n stenografia; **short-lived** adj di breve durata; **shortly** adv fra poco; **shorts** npl (also: **a pair of shorts**) i calzoncini; **short-sighted** (BRIT) adj miope; **short-sleeved** [ˈʃɔːtsliːvd] adj a maniche corte; **short story** n racconto, novella; **short-tempered** adj irascibile; **short-term** adj (effect) di or a breve durata; (borrowing) a breve scadenza

shot [ʃɔt] pt, pp of **shoot** ▶ n sparo, colpo; (try) prova; (Football) tiro; (injection) iniezione f; (Phot) foto f inv; **like a ~** come un razzo; (very readily) immediatamente; **shotgun** n fucile m da caccia

should [ʃud] aux vb **I ~ go now** dovrei andare ora; **he ~ be there now** dovrebbe essere arrivato ora; **I ~ go if I were you** se fossi in te andrei; **I ~ like to** mi piacerebbe

shoulder [ˈʃəʊldəʳ] n spalla; (BRIT: of road) ~ banchina ▶ vt (fig) addossarsi, prendere sulle proprie spalle; **shoulder blade** n scapola

shouldn't [ˈʃudnt] = **should not**

shout [ʃaut] n urlo, grido ▶ vt gridare ▶ vi (also: **~ out**) urlare, gridare

shove [ʃʌv] vt spingere; (inf: put): **to ~ sth in** ficcare qc in

shovel [ʃʌvl] n pala ▸ vt spalare

show [ʃəu] (pt **showed**, pp **shown**) n (of emotion) dimostrazione f, manifestazione f; (semblance) apparenza; (exhibition) mostra, esposizione f; (Theatre, Cinema) spettacolo ▸ vt far vedere, mostrare; (courage etc) dimostrare, dar prova di; (exhibit) esporre ▸ vi vedersi, essere visibile; **for ~** per fare scena; **on ~** (exhibits etc) esposto(-a); **can you ~ me where it is, please?** può mostrarmi dov'è, per favore? ▸ **show in** vt (person) far entrare ▸ **show off** vi (pej) esibirsi, mettersi in mostra ▸ vt (display) mettere in risalto; (pej) mettere in mostra ▸ **show out** vt (person) accompagnare alla porta ▸ **show up** vi (stand out) essere ben visibile; (inf: turn up) farsi vedere ▸ vt mettere in risalto; **show business** n industria dello spettacolo

shower [ʃauə*] n (rain) acquazzone m; (of stones etc) pioggia; (also: ~bath) doccia ▸ vi fare la doccia ▸ vt: **to ~ sb with** (gifts, abuse etc) coprire qn di; (missiles) lanciare contro qn una pioggia di; **to have a ~** fare la doccia; **shower cap** n cuffia da doccia; **shower gel** n gel m doccia inv

showing [ʃəuɪŋ] n (of film) proiezione f

show jumping n concorso ippico (di salto ad ostacoli)

shown [ʃəun] pp of **show**

show-off [ʃəu] (inf) n (person) esibizionista m/f; **showroom** n sala d'esposizione

shrank [ʃræŋk] pt of **shrink**

shred [ʃred] n (gen pl) brandello ▸ vt fare a brandelli; (Culin) sminuzzare, tagliuzzare

shrewd [ʃru:d] adj astuto(-a), scaltro(-a)

shriek [ʃri:k] n strillo ▸ vi strillare

shrimp [ʃrɪmp] n gamberetto

shrine [ʃraɪn] n reliquario; (place) santuario

shrink [ʃrɪŋk] (pt **shrank**, pp **shrunk**) vi restringersi; (fig) ridursi; (also: ~away) ritrarsi ▸ vt (wool) far restringere ▸ n (inf: pej) psicanalista m/f; **to ~ from doing sth** rifuggire dal fare qc

shrivel [ʃrɪvl] (also: ~ up) vt raggrinzare, avvizzire ▸ vi raggrinzirsi, avvizzire

shroud [ʃraud] n lenzuolo funebre ▸ vt: **~ed in mystery** avvolto(-a) nel mistero

Shrove Tuesday [ʃrəuv-] n martedì m grasso

shrub [ʃrʌb] n arbusto

shrug [ʃrʌg] n scrollata di spalle ▸ vt, vi: **to ~ (one's shoulders)** alzare le spalle, fare spallucce ▸ **shrug off** vt passare sopra a

shrunk [ʃrʌŋk] pp of **shrink**

shudder [ʃʌdə*] n brivido ▸ vi rabbrividire

shuffle [ʃʌfl] vt (cards) mescolare; **to ~ (one's feet)** strascicare i piedi

shun [ʃʌn] vt sfuggire, evitare

shut [ʃʌt] (pt, pp **shut**) vt chiudere ▸ vi chiudersi, chiudere ▸ **shut down** vt, vi chiudere definitivamente ▸ **shut up** vi (inf: keep quiet) stare zitto(-a), fare silenzio ▸ vt (close) chiudere; (silence) far tacere; **shutter** n imposta; (Phot) otturatore m

shuttle [ʃʌtl] n spola, navetta; (space shuttle) navetta (spaziale); (also: ~ service) servizio m navetta inv; **shuttlecock** [ʃʌtlkɔk] n volano

shy [ʃaɪ] adj timido(-a)

sibling [sɪblɪŋ] n (formal) fratello/sorella

Sicily [sɪsɪlɪ] n Sicilia

sick [sɪk] adj (ill) malato(-a);

(*vomiting*): **to be ~** vomitare; (*humour*)
macabro(-a); **to feel ~** avere la nausea;
to be ~ of (*fig*) averne abbastanza di;
sickening adj (*fig*) disgustoso(-a),
rivoltante; **sick leave** n congedo per
malattia; **sickly** adj malaticcio(-a);
(*causing nausea*) nauseante; **sickness**
n malattia; (*vomiting*) vomito

side [saɪd] n lato; (*of lake*) riva; (*team*)
squadra ▶ cpd (*door, entrance*) laterale
▶ vi **to ~ with sb** parteggiare per
qn, prendere le parti di qn; **by the
~ of** di fianco di; (*road*) sul ciglio di;
~ by ~ fianco a fianco; **from ~ to ~**
da una parte all'altra; **to take ~s
(with)** schierarsi (con); **sideboard**
n credenza; **sideboards** (*BRIT*),
sideburns ['saɪdbə:nz] npl (*whiskers*)
basette fpl; **sidelight** n (*Aut*) luce f
di posizione; **sideline** n (*Sport*) linea
laterale; (*fig*) attività secondaria; **side
order** n contorno (*pietanza*); **side road**
n strada secondaria; **side street** n
traversa; **sidetrack** vt (*fig*) distrarre;
sidewalk (*US*) n marciapiede m;
sideways adv (*move*) di lato, di fianco

siege [si:dʒ] n assedio

sieve [sɪv] n setaccio ▶ vt setacciare

sift [sɪft] vt passare al crivello; (*fig*)
vagliare

sigh [saɪ] n sospiro ▶ vi sospirare

sight [saɪt] n (*faculty*) vista; (*spectacle*)
spettacolo; (*on gun*) mira ▶ vt
avvistare; **in ~** in vista; **on ~** a vista;
out of ~ non visibile; **sightseeing**
n giro turistico; **to go sightseeing**
visitare una località

sign [saɪn] n segno; (*with hand etc*)
segno, gesto; (*notice*) insegna,
cartello ▶ vt firmare; (*player*)
ingaggiare; **where do I ~?** dove devo
firmare? ▶ **sign for** vt fus (*item*) firmare
per l'accettazione di ▶ **sign in** vi
firmare il registro (all'arrivo) ▶ **sign
on** vi (*Mil*) arruolarsi; (*as unemployed*)

iscriversi sulla lista (dell'ufficio di
collocamento) ▶ vt (*Mil*) arruolare;
(*employee*) assumere ▶ **sign up** vi (*Mil*)
arruolarsi; (*for course*) iscriversi ▶ vt
(*player*) ingaggiare; (*recruits*) reclutare

signal ['sɪɡnl] n segnale m ▶ vi (*Aut*)
segnalare, mettere la freccia ▶ vt
(*person*) fare segno a; (*message*)
comunicare per mezzo di segnali

signature ['sɪɡnətʃə'] n firma

significance [sɪɡ'nɪfɪkəns] n
significato; importanza

significant [sɪɡ'nɪfɪkənt] adj
significativo(-a)

signify ['sɪɡnɪfaɪ] vt significare

sign language n linguaggio dei muti

signpost ['saɪnpəust] n cartello
indicatore

Sikh [si:k] adj, n sikh (m/f) inv

silence ['saɪləns] n silenzio ▶ vt far
tacere, ridurre al silenzio

silent ['saɪlnt] adj silenzioso(-a);
(*film*) muto(-a); **to remain ~** tacere,
stare zitto

silhouette [sɪluː'et] n silhouette f inv

silicon chip ['sɪlɪkən-] n piastrina
di silicio

silk [sɪlk] n seta ▶ adj di seta

silly ['sɪlɪ] adj stupido(-a), sciocco(-a)

silver ['sɪlvə'] n argento; (*money*)
monete da 5, 10, 20 or 50 pence; (*also:
~ware*) argenteria ▶ adj d'argento;
silver-plated adj argentato(-a)

similar ['sɪmɪlə'] adj **~ (to)** simile
(a); **similarity** [sɪmɪ'lærɪtɪ] n
somiglianza, rassomiglianza;
similarly adv allo stesso modo;
così pure

simmer ['sɪmə'] vi cuocere a fuoco
lento

simple ['sɪmpl] adj semplice;
simplicity [-'plɪsɪtɪ] n semplicità;
simplify vt semplificare; **simply** adv
semplicemente

simulate ['sɪmjuleɪt] vt fingere,

simulare
simultaneous [sɪməl'teɪnɪəs] adj simultaneo(-a); **simultaneously** adv simultaneamente, contemporaneamente
sin [sɪn] n peccato m ▶ vi peccare
since [sɪns] adv da allora ▶ prep da ◆ conj (time) da quando; (because) poiché, dato che; ~ **then, ever~** da allora
sincere [sɪn'sɪə'] adj sincero(-a); **sincerely** adv **yours sincerely** (in letters) distinti saluti
sing [sɪŋ] (pt **sang**, pp **sung**) vt, vi cantare
Singapore [sɪŋɡə'pɔ:'] n Singapore f
singer ['sɪŋə'] n cantante m/f
singing ['sɪŋɪŋ] n canto
single ['sɪŋɡl] adj solo(-a), unico(-a); (unmarried: man) celibe; (: woman) nubile; (not double) semplice ▶ n (BRIT: also: ~ **ticket**) biglietto di (sola) andata; (record) 45 giri m; ~**s** n (Tennis) singolo ▶ **single out** vt scegliere; (distinguish) distinguere; **single bed** n letto singolo; **single file** n in single file in fila indiana; **single-handed** adv senza aiuto, da solo(-a); **single-minded** adj tenace, risoluto(-a); **single parent** n (mother) ragazza f madre inv; (father) ragazzo m padre inv; **single-parent family** famiglia monoparentale; **single room** n camera singola
singular ['sɪŋɡjulə'] adj (exceptional, Ling) singolare ▶ n (Ling) singolare m
sinister ['sɪnɪstə'] adj sinistro(-a)
sink [sɪŋk] (pt **sank**, pp **sunk**) n lavandino, acquaio ▶ vt (ship) (fare) affondare, colare a picco; (foundations) scavare; (piles etc): to **~ sth into** conficcare qc in ▶ vi affondare, andare a fondo; (ground etc) cedere, avvallarsi; **my heart sank** mi sentii venir meno ▶ **sink in** vi penetrare

sinus ['saɪnəs] n (Anat) seno
sip [sɪp] n sorso ▶ vt sorseggiare
sir [sə'] n signore m; S~ **John Smith** Sir John Smith; **yes ~** sì, signore
siren ['saɪərn] n sirena
sirloin ['sə:lɔɪn] n controfiletto
sister ['sɪstə'] n sorella; (nun) suora; (BRIT: nurse) infermiera f caposala inv; **sister-in-law** n cognata
sit [sɪt] (pt, pp **sat**) vi sedere, sedersi; (assembly) essere in seduta; (for painter) posare ▶ vt (exam) sostenere, dare ▶ **sit back** vi (in seat) appoggiarsi allo schienale ▶ **sit down** vi sedersi ▶ **sit on** vt fus (jury, committee) far parte di ▶ **sit up** vi tirarsi su a sedere; (not go to bed) stare alzato(-a) fino a tardi
sitcom ['sɪtkɔm] n abbr (= situation comedy) commedia di situazione; (TV) telefilm m inv comico d'interni
site [saɪt] n posto; (also: **building ~**) cantiere m ▶ vt situare
sitting ['sɪtɪŋ] n (of assembly etc) seduta; (in canteen) turno; **sitting room** n soggiorno
situated ['sɪtjueɪtɪd] adj situato(-a)
situation [sɪtju'eɪʃən] n situazione f; (job) lavoro; (location) posizione f; "**~s vacant**" (BRIT) "offerte fpl di impiego"
six [sɪks] num sei; **sixteen** num sedici; **sixteenth** [sɪks'ti:nθ] num sedicesimo(-a); **sixth** sesto(-a); **sixth form** n (BRIT) ultimo biennio delle scuole superiori; **sixth-form college** n istituto che offre corsi di preparazione all'esame di maturità per ragazzi dai 16 ai 18 anni; **sixtieth** ['sɪkstɪɪθ] num sessantesimo(-a) ▶ pron (in series) sessantesimo(-a); (fraction) sessantesimo; **sixty** num sessanta
size [saɪz] n dimensioni fpl; (of clothing) taglia, misura; (of shoes) numero; (glue) colla; **sizeable** adj considerevole

sizzle ['sɪzl] vi sfrigolare

skate [skeɪt] n pattino; (fish: pl inv) razza ▶ vi pattinare; **skateboard** n skateboard m inv; **skateboarding** n skateboard m inv; **skater** n pattinatore(-trice); **skating** n pattinaggio; **skating rink** n pista di pattinaggio

skeleton ['skɛlɪtn] n scheletro

skeptical ['skɛptɪkl] (US) adj = **sceptical**

sketch [skɛtʃ] n (drawing) schizzo, abbozzo; (Theatre) scenetta comica, sketch m inv ▶ vt abbozzare, schizzare

skewer ['skjuːə'] n spiedino

ski [skiː] n sci m inv ▶ vi sciare; **ski boot** n scarpone m da sci

skid [skɪd] n slittamento ▶ vi slittare

ski: skier ['skiːə'] n sciatore(-trice); **skiing** ['skiːɪŋ] n sci m

skilful ['skɪlful] (US **skillful**) adj abile

ski lift n sciovia

skill [skɪl] n abilità f inv, capacità f inv; **skilled** adj esperto(-a); (worker) qualificato(-a), specializzato(-a)

skim [skɪm] vt (milk) scremare; (glide over) sfiorare ▶ vi: **to ~ through** (fig) scorrere, dare una scorsa a; **skimmed milk** (US **skim milk**) n latte m scremato

skin [skɪn] n pelle f; (fruit etc) buccia ▶ vt (fruit etc) sbucciare; (animal) scuoiare, spellare; **skinhead** n skinhead m/f inv; **skinny** adj molto magro(-a), pelle e ossa inv

skip [skɪp] n saltello, balzo; (BRIT: container) benna ▶ vi saltellare; (with rope) saltare la corda ▶ vt saltare

ski: ski pass n ski pass m; **ski pole** n racchetta (da sci)

skipper ['skɪpə'] n (Naut, Sport) capitano

skipping rope ['skɪpɪŋ-] (US **skip rope**) n corda per saltare

skirt [skəːt] n gonna, sottana ▶ vt fiancheggiare, costeggiare

skirting board (BRIT) n zoccolo

ski slope n pista da sci

ski suit n tuta da sci

skull [skʌl] n cranio, teschio

skunk [skʌŋk] n moffetta

sky [skaɪ] n cielo; **skyscraper** n grattacielo

slab [slæb] n lastra; (of cake, cheese) fetta

slack [slæk] adj (loose) allentato(-a); (slow) lento(-a); (careless) negligente; **slacks** npl (trousers) pantaloni mpl

slain [sleɪn] pp of **slay**

slam [slæm] vt (door) sbattere; (throw) scaraventare; (criticize) stroncare ▶ vi sbattere

slander ['slɑːndə'] n calunnia, diffamazione f

slang [slæŋ] n gergo, slang m

slant [slɑːnt] n pendenza, inclinazione f; (fig) angolazione f, punto di vista

slap [slæp] n manata, pacca; (on face) schiaffo ▶ vt (one a manata a; schiaffeggiare ▶ adv (directly) in pieno; **~ a coat of paint on it** dagli una mano di vernice

slash [slæʃ] vt tagliare; (face) sfregiare; (fig: prices) ridurre drasticamente, tagliare

slate [sleɪt] n ardesia; (piece) lastra di ardesia ▶ vt (fig: criticize) stroncare, distruggere

Slav [slɑːv] adj, n slavo(-a)

slave [sleɪv] n schiavo(-a) ▶ vi (also: ~ away) lavorare come uno schiavo; **slavery** n schiavitù f

slay [sleɪ] (pt **slew**, pp **slain**) vt (formal) uccidere

sleazy ['sliːzɪ] adj trasandato(-a)

sled [sled] (US) = **sledge**

sledge [slɛdʒ] n slitta

sleek [sliːk] adj (hair, fur) lucido(-a), lucente; (car, boat) slanciato(-a), affusolato(-a)

sleep [sliːp] (pt, pp **slept**) n sonno ▶ vi dormire; **to go to ~** addormentarsi ▷ **sleep in** vi (oversleep) dormire fino a tardi ▷ **sleep together** vi (have sex) andare a letto insieme; **sleeper** (BRIT) n (Rail: on track) traversina; (: train) treno di vagoni letto; **sleeping bag** n sacco a pelo; **sleeping car** n vagone m letto inv, carrozza f letto inv; **sleeping pill** n sonnifero; **sleepover** n notte f che un ragazzino passa da amici; **sleepwalk** vi camminare nel sonno; (as a habit) essere sonnambulo(-a); **sleepy** adj assonnato(-a), sonnolento(-a); (fig) addormentato(-a)

sleet [sliːt] n nevischio

sleeve [sliːv] n manica; (of record) copertina; **sleeveless** adj (garment) senza maniche

sleigh [sleɪ] n slitta

slender [ˈslɛndəʳ] adj snello(-a), sottile; (not enough) scarso(-a), esiguo(-a)

slept [slɛpt] pt, pp of **sleep**

slew [sluː] pt of **slay** ▶ vi (BRIT) girare

slice [slaɪs] n fetta ▶ vt affettare, tagliare a fette

slick [slɪk] adj (skilful) brillante; (clever) furbo(-a) ▶ n (also: **oil ~**) chiazza di petrolio

slide [slaɪd] (pt, pp **slid**) n scivolone m; (in playground) scivolo; (Phot) diapositiva; (BRIT: also: **hair ~**) fermaglio (per capelli) ▶ vt scivolare ▶ vi scivolare; **sliding** adj (door) scorrevole

slight [slaɪt] adj (slim) snello(-a), sottile; (frail) delicato(-a), fragile; (trivial) insignificante; (small)

piccolo(-a) ▶ n offesa, affronto; **not in the ~est** affatto, neppure per sogno; **slightly** adv leggermente, un po'

slim [slɪm] adj magro(-a), snello(-a) ▶ vi dimagrire; fare (or seguire) una dieta dimagrante; **slimming** [ˈslɪmɪŋ] adj (diet) dimagrante; (food) ipocalorico(-a)

slimy [ˈslaɪmɪ] adj (also fig: person) viscido(-a); (covered with mud) melmoso(-a)

sling [slɪŋ] (pt, pp **slung**) n (Med) fascia al collo; (for baby) marsupio ▶ vt lanciare, tirare

slip [slɪp] n scivolata, scivolone m; (mistake) errore m, sbaglio; (underskirt) sottoveste f; (of paper) striscia di carta; tagliando, scontrino ▶ vt (slide) far scivolare ▶ vi (slide) scivolare; (move smoothly): **to ~ into/out of** scivolare in/fuori da; (decline) declinare; **to ~ sth on/off** infilarsi/togliersi qc; **to give sb the ~** sfuggire qn; **a ~ of the tongue** un lapsus linguae ▷ **slip up** vi sbagliarsi

slipper [ˈslɪpəʳ] n pantofola

slippery [ˈslɪpərɪ] adj scivoloso(-a)

slip road (BRIT) n (to motorway) rampa di accesso

slit [slɪt] (pt, pp **slit**) n fessura, fenditura; (cut) taglio ▶ vt fendere; tagliare

slog [slɒg] (BRIT) n faticata ▶ vi lavorare con accanimento, sgobbare

slogan [ˈsləʊgən] n motto, slogan m inv

slope [sləʊp] n pendio; (side of mountain) versante m; (ski slope) pista; (of roof) pendenza; (of floor) inclinazione f ▶ vi **to ~ down** declinare; **to ~ up** essere in salita; **sloping** adj inclinato(-a)

sloppy [ˈslɒpɪ] adj (work) tirato(-a) via; (appearance) sciatto(-a)

slot [slɒt] n fessura ▶ vt **to ~ sth**

into infilare qc in; **slot machine** n (BRIT: vending machine) distributore m automatico; (for gambling) slot-machine f inv

Slovakia [sləʊˈvækɪə] n Slovacchia

Slovene [ˈsləʊviːn] adj sloveno(-a) ▶ n sloveno(-a); (Ling) sloveno

Slovenia [sləʊˈviːnɪə] n Slovenia; **Slovenian** adj, n = **Slovene**

slow [sləʊ] adj lento(-a); (watch): **to be ~** essere indietro ▶ adv lentamente ▶ vt, vi (also: **~ down**, **~ up**) rallentare; **"~"** (road sign) "rallentare" ▶ **slow down** vi rallentare; **slowly** adv lentamente; **slow motion** n **in slow motion** al rallentatore

slug [slʌɡ] n lumaca; (bullet) pallottola; **sluggish** adj lento(-a); (trading) stagnante

slum [slʌm] n catapecchia

slump [slʌmp] n crollo, caduta; (economic) depressione f, crisi f inv ▶ vi crollare

slung [slʌŋ] pt, pp of **sling**

slur [sləː*] n (fig): **~ (on)** calunnia (su) ▶ vt pronunciare in modo indistinto

sly [slaɪ] adj (smile, remark) sornione(-a); (person) furbo(-a)

smack [smæk] n (slap) pacca; (on face) schiaffo ▶ vt schiaffeggiare; (child) picchiare ▶ vi **to ~ of** puzzare di

small [smɔːl] adj piccolo(-a); **small ads** (BRIT) npl piccola pubblicità; **small change** n moneta, spiccioli mpl

smart [smɑːt] adj elegante; (fashionable) alla moda; (clever) intelligente; (quick) sveglio(-a) ▶ vi bruciare; **smartcard** n [ˈsmɑːtkɑːd] n smartcard f inv, carta intelligente

smash [smæʃ] n (also: **~up**) scontro, collisione f; (smash hit) successone m ▶ vt frantumare, fracassare; (Sport: record) battere ▶ vi frantumarsi, andare in pezzi; **smashing** (inf) adj favoloso(-a), formidabile

smear [smɪə*] n macchia; (Med) striscio ▶ vt spalmare; (make dirty) sporcare; **smear test** n (BRIT Med) Pap-test m inv

smell [smel] (pt smelt or smelled) n odore m; (sense) olfatto, odorato ▶ vt sentire (l')odore di ▶ vi (food etc): **to ~ (of)** avere odore (di); (pej) puzzare, avere un cattivo odore; **smelly** adj puzzolente

smelt [smelt] pt, pp of **smell** ▶ vt (ore) fondere

smile [smaɪl] n sorriso ▶ vi sorridere

smirk [sməːk] n sorriso furbo; sorriso compiaciuto

smog [smɒɡ] n smog m

smoke [sməʊk] n fumo ▶ vt, vi fumare; **do you mind if I ~?** le dà fastidio se fumo?; **smoke alarm** n rivelatore f di fumo; **smoked** adj (bacon, glass) affumicato(-a); **smoker** n (person) fumatore(-trice); (Rail) carrozza per fumatori; **smoking** n fumo; **"no smoking"** (sign) "vietato fumare"; **smoky** adj fumoso(-a); (taste) affumicato(-a)

smooth [smuːð] adj liscio(-a); (sauce) omogeneo(-a); (flavour, whisky) amabile; (movement) regolare; (person: pej) mellifluo(-a) ▶ vt (also: **~ out**) lisciare, spianare; (: difficulties) appianare

smother [ˈsmʌðə*] vt soffocare

SMS abbr (= short message service) SMS; **SMS message** n SMS m inv, messaggino

smudge [smʌdʒ] n macchia; sbavatura ▶ vt imbrattare, sporcare

smug [smʌɡ] adj soddisfatto(-a), compiaciuto(-a)

smuggle [ˈsmʌɡl] vt contrabbandare; **smuggling** n contrabbando

snack [snæk] n spuntino; **snack bar** n tavola calda, snack bar m inv

snag [snæɡ] n intoppo, ostacolo imprevisto

snail [sneɪl] n chiocciola

snake [sneɪk] n serpente m

snap [snæp] n (sound) schianto, colpo secco; (photograph) istantanea ▶ adj improvviso(-a) ▶ vt (far) schioccare; (break) spezzare di netto ▶ vi spezzarsi con un rumore secco; (fig: person) parlare con tono secco; **to ~ shut** chiudersi di scatto ▷ **snap at** vt fus (dog) cercare di mordere ▷ **snap up** vt afferrare; **snapshot** n istantanea

snarl [snɑːl] vi ringhiare

snatch [snætʃ] n (small amount) frammento ▶ vt strappare (con violenza); **to ~** rubare

sneak [sniːk] (pt (US) **snuck**) vi **to ~ in/out** entrare/uscire di nascosto ▶ n spione(-a); **to ~ up on sb** avvicinarsi quatto quatto a qn; **sneakers** npl scarpe fpl da ginnastica

sneer [snɪəʳ] vi sogghignare; **to ~ at** farsi beffe di

sneeze [sniːz] n starnuto ▶ vi starnutire

sniff [snɪf] n fiutata, annusata ▶ vi tirare su col naso ▶ vt fiutare, annusare

snigger ['snɪgəʳ] vi ridacchiare, ridere sotto i baffi

snip [snɪp] n pezzetto; (bargain) (buon) affare m, occasione f ▶ vt tagliare

sniper ['snaɪpəʳ] n (marksman) franco tiratore m, cecchino

snob [snɒb] n snob m/f inv

snooker ['snuːkəʳ] n tipo di gioco del biliardo

snoop ['snuːp] vi **to ~ about** curiosare

snooze [snuːz] n sonnellino, pisolino ▶ vi fare un sonnellino

snore [snɔːʳ] vi russare

snorkel ['snɔːkl] n (of swimmer) respiratore m a tubo

snort [snɔːt] n sbuffo ▶ vi sbuffare

snow [snəʊ] n neve f ▶ vi nevicare; **snowball** n palla di neve (fig)

crescere a vista d'occhio; **snowstorm** n tormenta

snub [snʌb] vt snobbare ▶ n offesa, affronto

snug [snʌg] adj comodo(-a); (room, house) accogliente, comodo(-a)

so

[səʊ] adv

1 (thus, likewise) così; **if so** se è così, quand'è così; **I didn't do it — you did so!** non l'ho fatto io — sì che l'hai fatto!; **so do I, so am I** etc anch'io; **it's 5 o'clock — so it is!** sono le 5 — davvero!; **I hope so** lo spero; **I think so** penso di sì; **so far** finora, fin qui; (in past) fino ad allora

2 (in comparisons etc: to such a degree) così; **so big (that)** così grande (che); **she's not so clever as her brother** lei non è (così) intelligente come suo fratello

3: **so much** adj tanto(-a) ▶ adv tanto; **I've got so much work/money** ho tanto lavoro/tanti soldi; **I love you so much** ti amo tanto; **so many** tanti(-e)

4 (phrases): **10 or so** circa 10; **so long!** (inf: goodbye) ciao!, ci vediamo!

▶ conj

1 (expressing purpose): **so as to do** in modo or così da fare; **we hurried so as not to be late** ci affrettammo per non fare tardi; **so (that)** affinché + sub, perché + sub

2 (expressing result): **he didn't arrive so I left** non è venuto così me ne sono andata; **so you see, I could have gone** vedi, sarei potuto andare

soak [səʊk] vt inzuppare; (clothes) mettere a mollo ▶ vi (clothes etc) essere a mollo ▷ **soak up** vt assorbire; **soaking** adj (also: **soaking wet**) fradicio(-a)

so-and-so ['səʊənsəʊ] n (somebody) un tale; **Mr/Mrs ~** signor/signora tal dei tali

soap [səʊp] n sapone m; **soap opera** n soap opera f inv; **soap powder** n detersivo

soar [sɔːʳ] vi volare in alto; (price etc) salire alle stelle; (building) ergersi

sob [sɒb] n singhiozzo ▶ vi singhiozzare

sober ['səʊbəʳ] adj sobrio(-a); (not drunk) non ubriaco(-a); (moderate) moderato(-a) ▶ **sober up** vt far passare la sbornia a ▶ vi farsi passare la sbornia

so-called ['səʊ'kɔːld] adj cosiddetto(-a)

soccer ['sɒkəʳ] n calcio

sociable ['səʊʃəbl] adj socievole

social ['səʊʃl] adj sociale ▶ n festa, serata; **socialism** n socialismo; **socialist** adj, n socialista m/f; **socialize** vi **socialize (with)** socializzare (con); **social life** n vita sociale; **socially** adv socialmente, in società; **social security** (BRIT) n previdenza sociale; **social services** npl servizi mpl sociali; **social work** n servizio sociale; **social worker** n assistente m/f sociale

society [sə'saɪətɪ] n società f inv; (club) società, associazione f; (also: **high ~**) alta società

sociology [səʊsɪ'ɒlədʒɪ] n sociologia

sock [sɒk] n calzino

socket ['sɒkɪt] n cavità f inv; (of eye) orbita; (BRIT: Elec: also: **wall ~**) presa di corrente

soda ['səʊdə] n (Chem) soda; (also: **~ water**) acqua di seltz; (US: **~ pop**) gassosa

sodium ['səʊdɪəm] n sodio

sofa ['səʊfə] n sofà m inv; **sofa bed** n divano m letto inv

soft [sɒft] adj (not rough) morbido(-a); (not hard) soffice; (not loud) sommesso(-a); (not bright) tenue; (kind) gentile; **soft**

drink n analcolico; **soft drugs** npl droghe fpl leggere; **soften** ['sɒfn] vt ammorbidire; addolcire; attenuare ▶ vi ammorbidirsi; addolcirsi; attenuarsi; **softly** adv dolcemente, morbidamente; **software** ['sɒftwɛəʳ] n (Comput) software m

soggy ['sɒgɪ] adj inzuppato(-a)

soil [sɔɪl] n terreno ▶ vt sporcare

solar ['səʊləʳ] adj solare; **solar power** n energie solare; **solar system** n sistema m solare

sold [səʊld] pt, pp of **sell**

soldier ['səʊldʒəʳ] n soldato, militare m

sold out adj (Comm) esaurito(-a)

sole [səʊl] n (of foot) pianta (del piede); (of shoe) suola; (fish: pl inv) sogliola ▶ adj solo(-a), unico(-a); **solely** adv solamente, unicamente; **I will hold you solely responsible** la considererò il solo responsabile

solemn ['sɒləm] adj solenne

solicitor [sə'lɪsɪtəʳ] (BRIT) n (for wills etc) = notaio; (in court) = avvocato

solid ['sɒlɪd] adj solido(-a); (not hollow) pieno(-a); (meal) sostanzioso(-a) ▶ n solido

solitary ['sɒlɪtərɪ] adj solitario(-a)

solitude ['sɒlɪtjuːd] n solitudine f

solo ['səʊləʊ] n assolo; **soloist** n solista m/f

soluble ['sɒljʊbl] adj solubile

solution [sə'luːʃən] n soluzione f

solve [sɒlv] vt risolvere

solvent ['sɒlvənt] adj (Comm) solvibile ▶ n (Chem) solvente m

sombre ['sɒmbəʳ] (US **somber**) adj scuro(-a); (mood, person) triste

some

[sʌm] adj

1 (a certain amount or number of): **some tea/water/cream** del tè/dell'acqua/della panna; **some children/apples** dei bambini/delle mele

2 (*certain: in contrasts*) certo(-a); **some people say that ...** alcuni dicono che ..., certa gente dice che ...
3 (*unspecified*) un(a) certo(-a), qualche; **some woman was asking for you** una tale chiedeva di lei; **some day** un giorno; **some day next week** un giorno della prossima settimana
▶ *pron*
1 (*a certain number*) alcuni(-e), certi(-e); **I've got some** (*books etc*) ne ho alcuni; **some** (*of them*) **have been sold** alcuni sono stati venduti
2 (*a certain amount*) un po'; **I've got some** (*money, milk*) ne ho un po'; **I've read some of the book** ho letto parte del libro
▶ *adv* **some 10 people** circa 10 persone

some: **somebody** ['sʌmbədɪ] *pron* = **someone**; **somehow** ['sʌmhaʊ] *adv* in un modo o nell'altro, in qualche modo; (*for some reason*) per qualche ragione; **someone** ['sʌmwʌn] *pron* qualcuno; **someplace** ['sʌmpleɪs] (*US*) *adv* = **somewhere**; **something** ['sʌmθɪŋ] *pron* qualcosa, qualche cosa; **something nice** qualcosa di bello; **something to do** qualcosa da fare; **sometime** ['sʌmtaɪm] *adv* (*in future*) una volta o l'altra; (*in past*): **sometime last month** durante il mese scorso; **sometimes** ['sʌmtaɪmz] *adv* qualche volta; **somewhat** ['sʌmwɔt] *adv* piuttosto; **somewhere** ['sʌmwɛəʳ] *adv* in or da qualche parte
son [sʌn] *n* figlio
song [sɒŋ] *n* canzone *f*
son-in-law ['sʌnɪnlɔː] *n* genero
soon [suːn] *adv* presto, fra poco; (*early, a short time after*) presto; **~ afterwards** poco dopo; *see also* **as**; **sooner** *adv* (*time*) prima; (*preference*): **I would sooner do** preferirei fare; **sooner or later** prima o poi

soothe [suːð] *vt* calmare
sophisticated [səˈfɪstɪkeɪtɪd] *adj* sofisticato(-a); raffinato(-a); complesso(-a)
sophomore ['sɒfəmɔːʳ] (*US*) *n* studente(-essa) del secondo anno
soprano [səˈprɑːnəʊ] *n* (*voice*) soprano *m*; (*singer*) soprano *m/f*
sorbet ['sɔːbeɪ] *n* sorbetto
sordid ['sɔːdɪd] *adj* sordido(-a)
sore [sɔːʳ] *adj* (*painful*) dolorante ▶ *n* piaga
sorrow ['sɒrəʊ] *n* dolore *m*
sorry ['sɒrɪ] *adj* spiacente; (*condition, excuse*) misero(-a); **~! scusa!** (or scusi! or scusate!); **to feel ~ for sb** rincrescersi per qn
sort [sɔːt] *n* specie *f*, genere *m* ▶ **sort out** *vt* (*papers*) classificare; ordinare; (*: letters etc*) smistare; (*: problems*) risolvere; (*Comput*) ordinare
SOS *n abbr* (= *save our souls*) S.O.S. *m inv*
so-so ['səʊsəʊ] *adv* così così
sought [sɔːt] *pt*, *pp of* **seek**
soul [səʊl] *n* anima
sound [saʊnd] *adj* (*healthy*) sano(-a); (*safe, not damaged*) solido(-a), in buono stato; (*reliable, not superficial*) solido(-a); (*sensible*) giudizioso(-a), di buon senso ▶ **~ asleep** profondamente addormentato ▶ *n* suono; (*noise*) rumore *m*; (*Geo*) stretto ▶ *vt* (*alarm*) suonare ▶ *vi* suonare; (*fig: seem*) sembrare; **to ~ like** rassomigliare a; **soundtrack** *n* (*of film*) colonna sonora
soup [suːp] *n* minestra; brodo; zuppa
sour ['saʊəʳ] *adj* aspro(-a); (*fruit*) acerbo(-a); (*milk*) acido(-a); (*fig*) arcigno(-a); acido(-a); **it's ~ grapes** è soltanto invidia
source [sɔːs] *n* fonte *f*, sorgente *f*; (*fig*) fonte
south [saʊθ] *n* sud *m*, meridione *m*, mezzogiorno ▶ *adj* del sud, sud

inv; meridionale ▸ *adv* verso sud;
South Africa *n* Sudafrica *m*; **South
African** *adj*, *n* sudafricano(-a); **South
America** *n* Sudamerica *m*, America
del sud *f*; **South American** *adj*, *n*
sudamericano(-a); **southbound**
['sauθbaund] *adj* (*gen*) diretto(-a)
a sud; (*carriageway*) sud inv;
southeastern [sauθ'i:stən] *adj*
sudorientale; **southern** ['sʌðən] *adj*
del sud, meridionale; esposto(-a)
a sud; **South Korea** *n* Corea *f*
del Sud; **South Pole** *n* Polo Sud;
southward(s) *adv* verso sud; **south-
west** *n* sud-ovest *m*; **southwestern**
[sauθ'westən] *adj* sudoccidentale
souvenir [su:vəˈniəʳ] *n* ricordo,
souvenir *m inv*
sovereign ['sɔvrɪn] *adj*, *n* sovrano(-a)
sow[1] [sau] (*pt* **sowed**, *pp* **sown**) *vt*
seminare
sow[2] [sau] *n* scrofa
soya ['sɔɪə] (*US* **soy**) *n* ~ **bean** *n* seme *m*
di soia; **soya sauce** *n* salsa di soia
spa [spa:] *n* (*resort*) stazione *f* termale;
(*US: also*: **health ~**) centro di cure
estetiche
space [speɪs] *n* spazio; (*room*) posto;
spazio; (*length of time*) intervallo ▸ *cpd*
spaziale ▸ *vt* (*also*: **~ out**) distanziare;
spacecraft *n inv* veicolo spaziale;
spaceship *n* = **spacecraft**
spacious ['speɪʃəs] *adj* spazioso(-a), .
ampio(-a)
spade [speɪd] *n* (*tool*) vanga; pala;
(*child's toy*) paletta; **~s** *npl* (*Cards*)
picche *fpl*
spaghetti [spə'gɛtɪ] *n* spaghetti *mpl*
Spain [speɪn] *n* Spagna
spam [spæm] *n* (*Comput*) spamming
▸ *vt* **to ~ sb** inviare a qn messaggi
pubblicitari non richiesti via email
span [spæn] *n* (*of bird, plane*) apertura
alare; (*of arch*) campata; (*in time*)
periodo; durata ▸ *vt* attraversare; (*fig*)
abbracciare
Spaniard ['spænjəd] *n* spagnolo(-a)
Spanish ['spænɪʃ] *adj* spagnolo(-a) ▸ *n*
(*Ling*) spagnolo; **the ~** *npl* gli Spagnoli
spank [spæŋk] *vt* sculacciare
spanner ['spænəʳ] *n* (*BRIT*) chiave
f inglese
spare [spɛəʳ] *adj* di riserva, di scorta;
(*surplus*) in più, d'avanzo ▸ *n* (*part*)
pezzo di ricambio ▸ *vt* (*do without*)
fare a meno di; (*afford to give*)
concedere; (*refrain from hurting, using*)
risparmiare; **to ~** (*surplus*) d'avanzo;
spare part *n* pezzo di ricambio;
spare room *n* stanza degli ospiti;
spare time *n* tempo libero; **spare
tyre** (*US* **spare tire**) *n* (*Aut*) gomma
di scorta; **spare wheel** *n* (*Aut*) ruota
di scorta
spark [spa:k] *n* scintilla; **spark(ing)
plug** *n* candela
sparkle ['spa:kl] *n* scintillio, sfavillio
▸ *vi* scintillare, sfavillare
sparrow ['spærəu] *n* passero
sparse [spa:s] *adj* sparso(-a), rado(-a)
spasm ['spæzəm] *n* (*Med*) spasmo; (*fig*)
accesso, attacco
spat [spæt] *pt*, *pp* of **spit**
spate [speɪt] *n* (*fig*): **~ of** diluvio o
fiume *m* di
spatula ['spætjulə] *n* spatola
speak [spi:k] (*pt* **spoke**, *pp* **spoken**)
vt (*language*) parlare; (*truth*) dire ▸ *vi*
parlare; **I don't ~ Italian** non parlo
italiano; **do you ~ English?** parla
inglese?; **to ~ to sb/of/about sth**
parlare a qn/di qc; **can I ~ to ...?** posso
parlare con...?; **~ up!** parla più forte!;
speaker *n* (*in public*) oratore(-trice);
(*also*: **loudspeaker**) altoparlante
m; (*Pol*): **the Speaker** *il presidente
della Camera dei Comuni* (*BRIT*) *or dei
Rappresentanti*
spear [spɪəʳ] *n* lancia ▸ *vt* infilzare
special ['spɛʃl] *adj* speciale; **special**

delivery n (Post): **by special delivery** per espresso; **special effects** npl (Cine) effetti mpl speciali; **specialist** n specialista m/f; **speciality** [spefɪˈælɪtɪ] n specialità f inv; **I'd like to try a local speciality** vorrei assaggiare una specialità del posto; **specialize** vi **to specialize (in)** specializzarsi (in); **specially** adv specialmente, particolarmente; **special needs children** bambini mpl con difficoltà di apprendimento; **special offer** n (Comm) offerta speciale; **special school** n (BRIT) scuola speciale (per portatori di handicap); **specialty** (US) n = **speciality**

species [ˈspiːʃiːz] n inv specie f inv

specific [spəˈsɪfɪk] adj specifico(-a); preciso(-a); **specifically** adv esplicitamente; (especially) appositamente

specify [ˈspesɪfaɪ] vt specificare, precisare; **unless otherwise specified** salvo indicazioni contrarie

specimen [ˈspesɪmən] n esemplare m, modello; (Med) campione m

speck [spek] n granello, macchiolina; (particle) granello

spectacle [ˈspektəkl] n spettacolo; ~s npl (glasses) occhiali mpl; **spectacular** [-ˈtækjuləʳ] adj spettacolare

spectator [spekˈteɪtəʳ] n spettatore m

spectrum [ˈspektrəm] n (pl **spectra**) n spettro

speculate [ˈspekjuleɪt] vi speculare; (try to guess): **to ~ about** fare ipotesi su

sped [sped] pt, pp of **speed**

speech [spiːtʃ] n (faculty) parola; (talk, Theatre) discorso; (manner of speaking) parlata; **speechless** adj ammutolito(-a), muto(-a)

speed [spiːd] n velocità f inv; (promptness) prontezza; **at full** or **top ~** a tutta velocità ▷ **speed up** vi, vt

accelerare; **speedboat** n motoscafo; **speeding** n (Aut) eccesso di velocità; **speed limit** n limite m di velocità; **speedometer** [spɪˈdɔmɪtəʳ] n tachimetro; **speedy** adj veloce, rapido(-a); pronto(-a)

spell [spel] (pt, pp **spelt** (BRIT) or **spelled**) n (also: **magic ~**) incantesimo; (period of time) (breve) periodo ▶ vt (in writing) scrivere (lettera per lettera); (aloud) dire lettera per lettera; (fig) significare; **to cast a ~ on sb** fare un incantesimo a qn; **he can't ~** fa errori di ortografia ▷ **spell out** vt (letter by letter) dettare lettera per lettera; (explain): **to ~ sth out for sb** spiegare qc a qn per filo e per segno; **spellchecker** [ˈspeltʃekəʳ] n correttore m ortografico; **spelling** n ortografia

spelt [spelt] (BRIT) pt, pp of **spell**

spend [spend] (pt, pp **spent**) vt (money) spendere; (time, life) passare; **spending** n **government spending** spesa pubblica

spent [spent] pt, pp of **spend**

sperm [spəːm] n sperma m

sphere [sfɪəʳ] n sfera

spice [spaɪs] n spezia ▶ vt aromatizzare

spicy [ˈspaɪsɪ] adj piccante

spider [ˈspaɪdəʳ] n ragno

spike [spaɪk] n punta

spill [spɪl] (pt, pp **spilt** or **spilled**) vt versare, rovesciare ▶ vi versarsi, rovesciarsi

spin [spɪn] (pt, pp **spun**) n (revolution of wheel) rotazione f; (Aviat) avvitamento; (trip in car) giretto ▶ vt (wool etc) filare; (wheel) far girare ▶ vi girare

spinach [ˈspɪnɪtʃ] n spinacio; (as food) spinaci mpl

spinal [ˈspaɪnl] adj spinale

spin doctor (inf) n esperto di

comunicazioni responsabile dell'immagine di un partito politico

spin-dryer [spɪn'draɪər] (BRIT) n centrifuga

spine [spaɪn] n spina dorsale; (thorn) spina

spiral ['spaɪərl] n spirale f ▶ vi (fig) salire a spirale

spire ['spaɪər] n guglia

spirit ['spɪrɪt] n spirito; (ghost) spirito, fantasma m; (mood) stato d'animo, umore m; (courage) coraggio; **~s** npl (drink) alcolici mpl; **in good ~s** di buon umore

spiritual ['spɪrɪtjuəl] adj spirituale

spit [spɪt] (pt, pp **spat**) n (for roasting) spiedo; (saliva) sputo; saliva ▶ vi sputare; (fire, fat) scoppiettare

spite [spaɪt] n dispetto ▶ vt contrariare, far dispetto a; **in ~ of** nonostante, malgrado; **spiteful** adj dispettoso(-a)

splash [splæʃ] n spruzzo; (sound) splash m inv; (of colour) schizzo ▶ vt spruzzare ▶ vi (also: **~ about**) sguazzare ▷ **splash out** (inf) vi (BRIT) fare spese folli

splendid ['splendɪd] adj splendido(-a), magnifico(-a)

splinter ['splɪntər] n scheggia ▶ vi scheggiarsi

split [splɪt] (pt, pp **split**) n spaccatura; (fig: division, quarrel) scissione f ▶ vt spaccare; (party) dividere; (work, profits) spartire, ripartire ▶ vi (divide) dividersi ▷ **split up** vi (couple) separarsi, rompere; (meeting) sciogliersi

spoil [spɔɪl] (pt, pp **spoilt** or **spoiled**) vt (damage) rovinare, guastare; (mar) sciupare; (child) viziare

spoilt [spɔɪlt] pt, pp of **spoil**

spoke [spəuk] pt of **speak** ▶ n raggio

spoken ['spəukn] pp of **speak**

spokesman ['spəuksmən] (irreg) n

portavoce m inv

spokesperson ['spəukspə:sn] n portavoce m/f

spokeswoman ['spəukswumən] (irreg) n portavoce f inv

sponge [spʌndʒ] n spugna; (also: **~ cake**) pan m di spugna ▶ vt spugnare, pulire con una spugna ▶ vi to **~ off** or **on** scroccare a; **sponge bag** (BRIT) n nécessaire m inv

sponsor ['sponsər] n (Radio, TV, Sport etc) sponsor m inv; (Pol: of bill) promotore(-trice) ▶ vt sponsorizzare; (bill) presentare; **sponsorship** n sponsorizzazione f

spontaneous [spon'teɪnɪəs] adj spontaneo(-a)

spooky ['spu:kɪ] (inf) adj che fa accapponare la pelle

spoon [spu:n] n cucchiaio; **spoonful** n cucchiaiata

sport [spɔ:t] n sport m inv; (person) persona di spirito ▶ vt sfoggiare; **sport jacket** (US) n = **sports jacket**; **sports car** n automobile f sportiva; **sports centre** (BRIT) n centro sportivo; **sports jacket** (BRIT) n giacca sportiva; **sportsman** (irreg) n sportivo; **sportswear** n abiti mpl sportivi; **sportswoman** (irreg) n sportiva; **sporty** adj sportivo(-a)

spot [spot] n punto; (mark) macchia; (dot: on pattern) pallino; (pimple) foruncolo; (place) posto; (Radio, TV) spot m inv; (small amount): **a ~ of** un po' di ▶ vt (notice) individuare, distinguere; **on the ~** sul posto; (immediately) su due piedi; (in difficulty) nei guai; **spotless** adj immacolato(-a); **spotlight** n proiettore m; (Aut) faro ausiliario

spouse [spauz] n sposo(-a)

sprain [spreɪn] n storta, distorsione f ▶ vt to **~ one's ankle** storcersi una caviglia

sprang [spræŋ] *pt of* **spring**

sprawl [sprɔːl] *vi* sdraiarsi (in modo scomposto); (*place*) estendersi (disordinatamente)

spray [spreɪ] *n* spruzzo; (*container*) nebulizzatore *m*, spray *m inv*; (*of flowers*) mazzetto ▶ *vt* spruzzare; (*crops*) irrorare

spread [sprɛd] (*pt, pp* **spread**) *n* diffusione *f*; (*distribution*) distribuzione *f*; (*Culin*) pasta (da spalmare); (*inf: food*) banchetto ▶ *vt* (*cloth*) stendere, distendere; (*butter etc*) spalmare; (*disease, knowledge*) propagare, diffondere ▶ *vi* stendersi, distendersi; spalmarsi; propagarsi, diffondersi ▷ **spread out** *vi* (*move apart*) separarsi; **spreadsheet** *n* foglio elettronico ad espansione

spree [spriː] *n* **to go on a ~** fare baldoria

spring [sprɪŋ] (*pt* **sprang**, *pp* **sprung**) *n* (*leap*) salto, balzo; (*coiled metal*) molla; (*season*) primavera; (*of water*) sorgente *f* ▶ *vi* saltare, balzare ▷ **spring up** *vi* (*problem*) presentarsi; **spring onion** *n* (*BRIT*) cipollina

sprinkle ['sprɪŋkl] *vt* spruzzare; spargere; **to ~ water** etc **on, ~ with water** etc spruzzare dell'acqua etc su

sprint [sprɪnt] *n* scatto ▶ *vi* scattare

sprung [sprʌŋ] *pp of* **spring**

spun [spʌn] *pt, pp of* **spin**

spur [spəː] *n* sperone *m*; (*fig*) sprone *m*, incentivo *m* (*also:* **~ on**) spronare; **on the ~ of the moment** lì per lì

spurt [spəːt] *n* (*of water*) getto; (*of energy*) scatto ▶ *vi* sgorgare

spy [spaɪ] *n* spia ▶ *vi* **to ~ on** spiare ▶ *vt* (*see*) scorgere

sq. *abbr* = **square**

squabble ['skwɔbl] *vi* bisticciarsi

squad [skwɔd] *n* (*Mil*) plotone *m*; (*Police*) squadra

squadron ['skwɔdrən] *n* (*Mil*)

squadrone *m*; (*Aviat, Naut*) squadriglia

squander ['skwɔndə'] *vt* dissipare

square [skweə'] *n* quadrato; (*in town*) piazza ▶ *adj* quadrato(-a); (*inf: ideas, person*) di vecchio stampo ▶ *vt* (*arrange*) regolare; (*Math*) elevare al quadrato; (*reconcile*) conciliare; **all ~** pari; **a ~ meal** un pasto abbondante; **2 metres ~** di 2 metri per 2; **1 ~ metre** 1 metro quadrato; **square root** *n* radice *f* quadrata

squash [skwɔʃ] *n* (*Sport*) squash *m*; (*BRIT: drink*): **lemon/orange ~** sciroppo di limone/arancia; (*US*) zucca; (*Sport*) squash *m* ▶ *vt* schiacciare

squat [skwɔt] *adj* tarchiato(-a), tozzo(-a) ▶ *vi* (*also:* **~ down**) accovacciarsi; **squatter** *n* occupante *m/f* abusivo(-a)

squeak [skwiːk] *vi* squittire

squeal [skwiːl] *vi* strillare

squeeze [skwiːz] *n* pressione *f*; (*also Econ*) stretta ▶ *vt* premere; (*hand, arm*) stringere

squid [skwɪd] *n* calamaro

squint [skwɪnt] *vi* essere strabico(-a) ▶ *n* **he has a ~** è strabico

squirm [skwəːm] *vi* contorcersi

squirrel ['skwɪrəl] *n* scoiattolo

squirt [skwəːt] *vi* schizzare; zampillare ▶ *vt* spruzzare

Sr *abbr* = **senior**

Sri Lanka [srɪˈlæŋkə] *n* Sri Lanka *m*

St *abbr* = **saint**; **street**

stab [stæb] *n* (*with knife etc*) pugnalata; (*of pain*) fitta; (*inf: try*): **to have a ~ at (doing) sth** provare a (fare) qc ▶ *vt* pugnalare

stability [stəˈbɪlɪtɪ] *n* stabilità

stable ['steɪbl] *n* (*for horses*) scuderia; (*for cattle*) stalla ▶ *adj* stabile

stack [stæk] *n* catasta, pila ▶ *vt* accatastare, ammucchiare

stadium ['steɪdɪəm] *n* stadio

staff [stɑːf] n (work force: gen) personale m; (: BRIT: Scol) personale insegnante ▶ vt fornire di personale

stag [stæg] n cervo

stage [steɪdʒ] n palcoscenico; (profession): **the ~** il teatro, la scena; (point) punto; (platform) palco ▶ vt (play) allestire, mettere in scena; (demonstration) organizzare; **in ~s** per gradi; a tappe

stagger ['stægə'] vi barcollare ▶ vt (person) sbalordire; (hours, holidays) scaglionare; **staggering** adj (amazing) sbalorditivo(-a)

stagnant ['stægnənt] adj stagnante

stag night, stag party n festa di addio al celibato

stain [steɪn] n macchia; (colouring) colorante m ▶ vt macchiare; (wood) tingere; **stained glass** [steɪnd'glɑː s] n vetro colorato; **stainless steel** n acciaio inossidabile

staircase ['steəkeɪs] n scale fpl, scala

stairs [steəz] npl (flight of stairs) scale fpl, scala

stairway ['steəweɪ] n = **staircase**

stake [steɪk] n palo, piolo; (Comm) interesse m; (Betting) puntata, scommessa ▶ vt (bet) scommettere; (risk) rischiare; **to be at ~** essere in gioco

stale [steɪl] adj (bread) raffermo(-a); (food) stantio(-a); (air) viziato(-a); (beer) svaporato(-a); (smell) di chiuso

stalk [stɔːk] n gambo, stelo ▶ vt inseguire

stall [stɔːl] n bancarella; (in stable) box m inv di stalla ▶ vt (Aut) far spegnere; (fig) bloccare ▶ vi (Aut) spegnersi, fermarsi; (fig) temporeggiare

stamina ['stæmɪnə] n vigore m, resistenza

stammer ['stæmə'] n balbuzie f ▶ vi balbettare

stamp [stæmp] n (postage stamp)

francobollo; (implement) timbro; (mark, also fig) marchio, impronta; (on document) bollo; timbro ▶ vi (also: **~ one's foot**) battere il piede ▶ vt battere; (letter) affrancare; (mark with a stamp) timbrare ▶ **stamp out** vt (fire) estinguere; (crime) eliminare; (opposition) soffocare; **stamped addressed envelope** n (BRIT) busta affrancata e indirizzata

▌ Be careful not to translate **stamp** the Italian word by **stampa**.

stampede [stæm'piːd] n fuggi fuggi m inv

stance [stæns] n posizione f

stand [stænd] (pt, pp **stood**) n (position) posizione f; (for taxis) posteggio; (structure) supporto, sostegno; (at exhibition) stand m inv; (in shop) banco; (at market) bancarella; (booth) chiosco; (Sport) tribuna ▶ vi stare in piedi; (rise) alzarsi in piedi; (be placed) trovarsi ▶ vt (place) mettere, porre; (tolerate, withstand) resistere, sopportare; (treat) offrire; **to make a ~** prendere posizione; **to ~ for parliament** (BRIT) presentarsi come candidato (per il parlamento) ▶ **stand back** vi (be ready) tenersi pronto(-a) ▶ vt fus (opinion) sostenere ▶ **stand down** vi (withdraw) ritirarsi ▶ **stand for** vt fus (signify) rappresentare, significare; (tolerate) sopportare, tollerare ▶ **stand in for** vt fus sostituire ▶ **stand out** vi (be prominent) spiccare ▶ **stand up** vi (rise) alzarsi in piedi ▶ **stand up for** vt fus difendere ▶ **stand up to** vt fus tener testa a, resistere a

standard ['stændəd] n modello, standard m inv; (level) livello; (flag) stendardo ▶ adj (size etc) normale, standard inv; **~s** npl (morals) principi mpl, valori mpl; **standard of living** n livello di vita

stand-by ['stændbaɪ] n riserva, sostituto; **to be on ~** (gen) tenersi pronto(-a); (doctor) essere di guardia; **stand-by ticket** n (Aviat) biglietto senza garanzia

standing ['stændɪŋ] adj diritto(-a), in piedi; (permanent) permanente ▶ n rango, condizione f, posizione f; **of many years' ~** che esiste da molti anni; **standing order** (BRIT) n (at bank) ordine m di pagamento (permanente)

stand: **standpoint** ['stændpɔɪnt] n punto di vista; **standstill** ['stændstɪl] n **at a standstill** fermo(-a); (fig) a un punto morto; **to come to a standstill** fermarsi; giungere a un punto morto

stank [stæŋk] pt of **stink**

staple ['steɪpl] n (for paper) graffetta ▶ adj (food etc) di base ▶ vt cucire

star [stɑːʳ] n stella; (celebrity) divo(-a) ▶ vi **to ~ (in)** essere la (or la) protagonista (di) ▶ vt (Cinema) essere interpretato(-a) da; **the ~s** npl (Astrology) le stelle

starboard ['stɑːbəd] n dritta

starch [stɑːtʃ] n amido

stardom ['stɑːdəm] n celebrità

stare [stɛəʳ] n sguardo fisso ▶ vi **to ~ at** fissare

stark [stɑːk] adj (bleak) desolato(-a) ▶ adv **~ naked** completamente nudo(-a)

start [stɑːt] n inizio; (of race) partenza; (sudden movement) sobbalzo; (advantage) vantaggio ▶ vt cominciare, iniziare; (car) mettere in moto ▶ vi cominciare; (on journey) partire, mettersi in viaggio; (jump) sobbalzare; **when does the film ~?** a che ora comincia il film?; **to ~ doing** or **to do sth** (in)cominciare a fare qc ▷ **start off** vi (begin) cominciare; (leave) partire ▷ **start out** vi (begin)

cominciare; (set out) partire ▷ **start up** vi cominciare; (car) avviarsi ▶ vt iniziare; (car) avviare; **starter** n (Aut) motorino d'avviamento; (Sport: official) starter m inv; (BRIT: Culin) primo piatto; **starting point** n punto di partenza

startle ['stɑːtl] vt far trasalire; **startling** adj sorprendente

starvation [stɑːˈveɪʃən] n fame f, inedia

starve [stɑːv] vi morire di fame; soffrire la fame ▶ vt far morire di fame, affamare

state [steɪt] n stato ▶ vt dichiarare, affermare; annunciare; **the S~s** (USA) gli Stati Uniti; **to be in a ~** essere agitato(-a); **statement** n dichiarazione f; **state school** n scuola statale; **statesman** (irreg) n statista m

static ['stætɪk] n (Radio) scariche fpl ▶ adj statico(-a)

station ['steɪʃən] n stazione f ▶ vt collocare, disporre

stationary ['steɪʃənəri] adj fermo(-a), immobile

stationer's (shop) n cartoleria

stationery ['steɪʃənəri] n articoli mpl di cancelleria

station wagon (US) n giardinetta

statistic [stəˈtɪstɪk] n statistica; **statistics** n (science) statistica

statue ['stætjuː] n statua

stature ['stætʃəʳ] n statura

status ['steɪtəs] n posizione f, condizione f sociale; prestigio; stato; **status quo** [-ˈkwəu] n **the status quo** lo statu quo

statutory ['stætjutrɪ] adj stabilito(-a) dalla legge, statutario(-a)

staunch [stɔːntʃ] adj fidato(-a), leale

stay [steɪ] n (period of time) soggiorno, permanenza ▶ vi rimanere; (reside) alloggiare, stare; (spend some time) trattenersi, soggiornare; **to ~ put** non muoversi; **to ~ the night** fermarsi per la notte ▷ **stay away** vi *(from person, building)* stare lontano *(from event)* non andare ▷ **stay behind** vi restare indietro ▷ **stay in** vi *(at home)* stare in casa ▷ **stay on** vi restare, rimanere ▷ **stay out** vi *(of house)* rimanere fuori *(of cable)* ▷ **stay up** vi *(at night)* rimanere alzato(-a)

steadily ['stɛdɪlɪ] adv *(firmly)* saldamente; *(constantly)* continuamente; *(fixedly)* fisso; *(walk)* con passo sicuro

steady ['stɛdɪ] adj *(not wobbling)* fermo(-a); *(regular)* costante; *(person, character)* serio(-a); *(: calm)* calmo(-a), tranquillo(-a) ▶ vt stabilizzare; calmare

steak [steɪk] n *(meat)* bistecca; *(fish)* trancia

steal [sti:l] *(pt stole, pp stolen)* vt rubare ▶ vi rubare; *(move)* muoversi furtivamente; **my wallet has been stolen** mi hanno rubato il portafoglio

steam [sti:m] n vapore m ▶ vt *(Culin)* cuocere a vapore ▶ vi fumare ▷ **steam up** vi *(window)* appannarsi; **to get ~ed up about sth** *(fig)* andare in bestia per qc; **steamy** adj *(room)* pieno(-a) di vapore; *(window)* appannato(-a)

steel [sti:l] n acciaio ▶ adj di acciaio

steep [sti:p] adj ripido(-a), scosceso(-a); *(price)* eccessivo(-a) ▶ vt inzuppare; *(washing)* mettere a mollo

steeple ['sti:pl] n campanile m

steer [stɪə'] vt guidare ▶ vi *(Naut: person)* governare; *(car)* guidarsi; **steering** n *(Aut)* sterzo; **steering wheel** n volante m

stem [stɛm] n *(of flower, plant)* stelo; *(of tree)* fusto; *(of glass)* gambo; *(of fruit, leaf)* picciolo ▶ vt contenere, arginare

step [stɛp] n passo; *(stair)* gradino, scalino; *(action)* mossa, azione f ▶ vi to ~ **forward/back** fare un passo avanti/

indietro; **~s** npl *(BRIT)* = **stepladder**; **to be in/out of ~ (with)** stare/non stare al passo *(con)* ▶ *(fig)* ritirarsi ▷ **step in** vi fare il proprio ingresso ▶ **step up** vt aumentare; intensificare; **stepbrother** n fratellastro; **stepchild** n figliastro(-a); **stepdaughter** n figliastra; **stepfather** n patrigno; **stepladder** n scala a libretto; **stepmother** n matrigna; **stepsister** n sorellastra; **stepson** n figliastro

stereo ['stɛrɪəu] n *(system)* sistema m stereofonico; *(record player)* stereo m inv ▶ adj *(also: ~phonic)* stereofonico(-a)

stereotype ['stɪərɪətaɪp] n stereotipo

sterile ['stɛraɪl] adj sterile; **sterilize** ['stɛrɪlaɪz] vt sterilizzare

sterling ['stə:lɪŋ] adj *(gold, silver)* di buona lega ▶ n *(Econ)* (lira) sterlina; **a pound ~** una lira sterlina

stern [stə:n] adj severo(-a) ▶ n *(Naut)* poppa

steroid ['stɛrɔɪd] n steroide m

stew [stju:] n stufato ▶ vt cuocere in umido

steward ['stju:əd] n *(Aviat, Naut, Rail)* steward m inv; *(in club etc)* dispensiere m; **stewardess** n assistente f di volo, hostess f inv

stick [stɪk] *(pt, pp stuck)* n bastone m; *(of rhubarb, celery)* gambo; *(of dynamite)* candelotto ▶ vt *(glue)* attaccare; *(thrust)*: **to ~ sth into** conficcare or piantare or infiggere qc in; *(inf: put)* ficcare; *(inf: tolerate)* sopportare ▶ vi attaccarsi; *(remain)* restare, rimanere ▷ **stick out** vi sporgere, spuntare ▷ **stick up** vi sporgere, spuntare ▷ **stick up for** vt fus difendere; **sticker** n cartellino adesivo; **sticking plaster** n cerotto adesivo; **stick shift** *(US)* n *(Aut)* cambio manuale

sticky ['stɪkɪ] adj attaccaticcio(-a),

vischioso(-a); (label) adesivo(-a); (fig: situation) difficile

stiff [stɪf] adj rigido(-a), duro(-a); (muscle) legato(-a), indolenzito(-a); (difficult) difficile, arduo(-a); (cold) freddo(-a), formale; (strong) forte; (high: price) molto alto(-a) ▶ adv **bored ~** annoiato(-a) a morte

stifling ['staɪflɪŋ] adj (heat) soffocante

stigma ['stɪgmə] n (fig) stigma m

stiletto [stɪ'lɛtəu] n (BRIT) (also: **~ heel**) tacco a spillo

still [stɪl] adj fermo(-a); silenzioso(-a) ▶ adv (up to this time, even) ancora; (nonetheless) tuttavia, ciò nonostante

stimulate ['stɪmjuleɪt] vt stimolare

stimulus ['stɪmjuləs] (pl **stimuli**) n stimolo

sting [stɪŋ] (pt, pp **stung**) n puntura; (organ) pungiglione m ▶ vt, vi pungere

stink [stɪŋk] (pt **stank**, pp **stunk**) n fetore m, puzzo ▶ vi puzzare

stir [stə:ʳ] n agitazione f, clamore m ▶ vt mescolare; (fig) risvegliare ▶ vi muoversi ▶ **stir up** vt provocare, suscitare; **stir-fry** vt saltare in padella ▶ n pietanza al salto

stitch [stɪtʃ] n (Sewing) punto; (Knitting) maglia; (Med) punto (di sutura); (pain) fitta ▶ vt cucire, attaccare; suturare

stock [stɔk] n riserva, provvista; (Comm) giacenza, stock m inv; (Agr) bestiame m; (Culin) brodo; (descent) stirpe f; (Finance) titoli mpl; azioni fpl ▶ adj (fig: reply etc) consueto(-a), classico(-a) ▶ vt (have in stock) avere, vendere; **~s and shares** valori mpl di borsa; **in ~** in magazzino; **out of ~** esaurito(-a); **stockbroker** ['stɔkbrəukəʳ] n agente m di cambio; **stock cube** (BRIT) n dado; **stock exchange** n Borsa (valori); **stockholder** ['stɔkhəuldəʳ] n (Finance) azionista m/f

stocking ['stɔkɪŋ] n calza

stock market n Borsa, mercato finanziario

stole [stəul] pt of **steal** ▶ n stola

stolen ['stəuln] pp of **steal**

stomach ['stʌmək] n stomaco; (belly) pancia ▶ vt sopportare, digerire; **stomachache** n mal m di stomaco

stone [stəun] n pietra; (pebble) sasso, ciottolo; (in fruit) nocciolo; (Med) calcolo; (BRIT: weight) = 6.348 kg; 14 libbre ▶ adj di pietra ▶ vt lapidare; (fruit) togliere il nocciolo a

stood [stud] pt, pp of **stand**

stool [stu:l] n sgabello

stoop [stu:p] vi (also: **have a ~**) avere una curvatura; (also: **~ down**) chinarsi, curvarsi

stop [stɔp] n arresto; (stopping place) fermata; (in punctuation) punto ▶ vt arrestare, fermare; (break off) interrompere; (also: **put a ~ to**) porre fine a ▶ vi fermarsi; (rain, noise etc) cessare, finire; **to ~ doing sth** cessare o finire di fare qc; **could you ~ here/at the corner?** può fermarsi qui/all'angolo?; **to ~ dead** fermarsi di colpo ▶ **stop by** vi passare, fare un salto ▶ **stop off** vi sostare brevemente; **stopover** n breve sosta; (Aviat) scalo; **stoppage** ['stɔpɪdʒ] n arresto, fermata; (of pay) trattenuta; (strike) interruzione f del lavoro

storage ['stɔ:rɪdʒ] n immagazzinamento

store [stɔ:ʳ] n provvista, riserva; (depot) deposito; (BRIT: department store) grande magazzino; (US: shop) negozio ▶ vt immagazzinare; **~s** npl (provisions) rifornimenti mpl, scorte fpl; **in ~** di riserva; in serbo; **storekeeper** (US) n negoziante m/f

storey ['stɔ:rɪ] (US **story**) n piano

storm [stɔ:m] n tempesta, temporale m, burrasca; uragano ▶ vi (fig)

infuriarsi ▶ vt prendere d'assalto;
stormy adj tempestoso(-a),
burrascoso(-a)

story ['stɔːrɪ] n storia; favola;
racconto; (US) = **storey**

stout [staʊt] adj solido(-a),
robusto(-a); (friend, supporter) tenace;
(fat) corpulento(-a), grasso(-a) ▶ n
birra scura

stove [stəʊv] n (for cooking) fornello;
(: small) fornelletto; (for heating) stufa

straight [streɪt] adj dritto(-a); (frank)
onesto(-a), franco(-a); (simple)
semplice ▶ adv diritto; (drink) liscio;
to put or **get ~** mettere in ordine,
mettere ordine in; **~ away, ~ off** (at
once) immediatamente; **straighten**
vt (also: **straighten out**) raddrizzare;
straightforward adj semplice;
onesto(-a), franco(-a)

strain [streɪn] n (Tech) sollecitazione
f; (physical) sforzo; (mental) tensione
f; (Med) strappo; distorsione f;
(streak, trace) tendenza; elemento
▶ vt tendere; (muscle) sforzare; (ankle)
storcere; (resources) pesare su; (food)
colare; passare; **strained** adj (muscle)
stirato(-a); (laugh etc) forzato(-a);
(relations) teso(-a); **strainer** n
passino, colino

strait [streɪt] n (Geo) stretto; **~s** npl to
be in dire **~s** (fig) essere nei guai

strand [strænd] n (of thread) filo;
stranded adj nei guai; senza mezzi
di trasporto

strange [streɪndʒ] adj (not
known) sconosciuto(-a); (odd)
strano(-a), bizzarro(-a); **strangely**
adv stranamente; **stranger** n
sconosciuto(-a); estraneo(-a)

strangle ['stræŋgl] vt strangolare

strap [stræp] n cinghia; (of slip, dress)
spallina; bretella

strategic [strə'tiːdʒɪk] adj
strategico(-a)

strategy ['strætɪdʒɪ] n strategia

straw [strɔː] n paglia; (drinking straw)
cannuccia; **that's the last ~!** è la
goccia che fa traboccare il vaso!

strawberry ['strɔːbərɪ] n fragola

stray [streɪ] adj (animal) randagio(-a);
(bullet) vagante; (scattered) sparso(-a)
▶ vi perdersi

streak [striːk] n striscia; (of hair)
mèche f inv ▶ vt striare, screziare ▶ vi
to ~ past passare come un fulmine

stream [striːm] n ruscello; corrente f;
(of people, smoke etc) fiume m ▶ vt (Scol)
dividere in livelli di rendimento ▶ vi
scorrere; **to ~ in/out** entrare/uscire
a fiotti

street [striːt] n strada, via; **streetcar**
(US) n tram m inv; **street light** n
lampione m; **street map** n pianta (di
una città)

street plan n pianta di una città

strength [streŋθ] n forza;
strengthen vt rinforzare; fortificare;
consolidare

strenuous ['strenjʊəs] adj
vigoroso(-a), energico(-a); (tiring)
duro(-a), pesante

stress [stres] n (force, pressure)
pressione f; (mental strain) tensione
f; (accent) accento ▶ vt insistere su,
sottolineare; accentare; **stressed**
adj (tense: person) stressato(-a);
(Ling, Poetry: syllable) accentato(-a);
stressful adj (job) difficile, stressante

stretch [stretʃ] n (of sand etc) distesa
▶ vi allungarsi; (extend): **to ~** or **as far
as** estendersi fino a ▶ vt tendere,
allungare; (spread) distendere; (fig)
spingere (al massimo) ▷ **stretch out**
vi allungarsi, estendersi ▶ vt (arm
etc) allungare, tendere; (to spread)
distendere

stretcher ['stretʃəʳ] n barella, lettiga

strict [strɪkt] adj (severe) rigido(-a),
severo(-a); (precise) preciso(-a),

stretto(-a); **strictly** adv severamente; rigorosamente; strettamente

stride [straɪd] (pt **strode**, pp **stridden**) n passo lungo ▶ vi camminare a grandi passi

strike [straɪk] (pt, pp **struck**) n sciopero; (of oil etc) scoperta; (attack) attacco ▶ vt colpire; (oil etc) scoprire, trovare; (bargain) fare; (fig): **the thought** or **it ~s me that ...** mi viene in mente che ... ▶ vi scioperare; (attack) attaccare; (clock) suonare; **to ~ a match** accendere un fiammifero; **striker** n scioperante m/f; (Sport) attaccante m; **striking** adj che colpisce

string [strɪŋ] (pt, pp **strung**) n spago; (row) fila; sequenza; catena; (Mus) corda ▶ vt: **to ~ out** disporre di fianco; **to ~ together** (words, ideas) mettere insieme; **the ~s** npl (Mus) gli archi; **to pull ~s for sb** (fig) raccomandare qn

strip [strɪp] n striscia ▶ vt spogliare; (paint) togliere; (also: ~ **down**: machine) smontare ▶ vi spogliarsi ▷ **strip off** vt (paint etc) staccare ▶ vi (person) spogliarsi

stripe [straɪp] n striscia, riga; (Mil, Police) gallone m; **striped** adj a strisce or righe

stripper ['strɪpəʳ] n spogliarellista m/f

strip-search ['strɪpsəːtʃ] vt: **to ~ sb** perquisire qn facendolo(-a) spogliare ▶ n perquisizione (facendo spogliare il perquisito)

strive [straɪv] (pt **strove**, pp **striven**) vi: **to ~ to do** sforzarsi di fare

strode [strəud] pt of **stride**

stroke [strəuk] n colpo; (Swimming) bracciata; (: style) stile m; (Med) colpo apoplettico ▶ vt accarezzare; **at a ~** in un attimo

stroll [strəul] n giretto, passeggiata ▶ vi andare a spasso; **stroller** (US) n passeggino

strong [strɔŋ] adj (gen) forte; (sturdy: table, fabric etc) robusto(-a); **they are 50 ~** sono in 50; **stronghold** n (also fig) roccaforte f; **strongly** adv fortemente, con forza; energicamente, vivamente

strove [strəuv] pt of **strive**

struck [strʌk] pt, pp of **strike**

structure ['strʌktʃəʳ] n struttura; (building) costruzione f, fabbricato

struggle ['strʌɡl] n lotta ▶ vi lottare

strung [strʌŋ] pt, pp of **string**

stub [stʌb] n mozzicone m; (of ticket etc) matrice f, tallonncino ▶ vt: **to ~ one's toe** urtare or sbattere il dito del piede ▷ **stub out** vt schiacciare

stubble ['stʌbl] n stoppia; (on chin) barba ispida

stubborn ['stʌbən] adj testardo(-a), ostinato(-a)

stuck [stʌk] pt, pp of **stick** ▶ adj (jammed) bloccato(-a)

stud [stʌd] n bottoncino; borchia; (also: ~ **earring**) orecchino a pressione; (also: ~ **farm**) scuderia, allevamento di cavalli; (also: ~ **horse**) stallone m ▶ vt (fig): ~**ded with** tempestato(-a) di

student ['stjuːdənt] n studente(-essa) ▶ cpd studentesco(-a); universitario(-a); degli studenti; **student driver** (US) n conducente m/f principiante; **students' union** (BRIT: association) circolo universitario; (: building) sede f del circolo universitario

studio ['stjuːdɪəu] n studio; **studio flat** (US **studio apartment**) n monolocale m

study ['stʌdɪ] n studio ▶ vt studiare; esaminare ▶ vi studiare

stuff [stʌf] n roba; (substance) sostanza, materiale m ▶ vt imbottire; (Culin) farcire; (dead animal) impagliare; (inf: push) ficcare; **stuffing** n imbottitura; (Culin) ripieno; **stuffy** adj (room) mal ventilato(-a), senz'aria; (ideas) antiquato(-a)

stumble ['stʌmbl] vi inciampare; **to ~ across** (fig) imbattersi in

stump [stʌmp] n ceppo; (of limb) moncone m ▶ vt to ~ed essere sconcertato(-a)

stun [stʌn] vt stordire; (amaze) sbalordire

stung [stʌŋ] pt, pp of **sting**

stunk [stʌŋk] pp of **stink**

stunned [stʌnd] adj (from blow) stordito(-a); (amazed, shocked) sbalordito(-a)

stunning ['stʌnɪŋ] adj sbalorditivo(-a); (girl etc) fantastico(-a)

stunt [stʌnt] n bravata; trucco pubblicitario

stupid ['stjuːpɪd] adj stupido(-a); **stupidity** [-'pɪdɪtɪ] n stupidità f inv, stupidaggine f

sturdy ['stɜːdɪ] adj robusto(-a), vigoroso(-a); solido(-a)

stutter ['stʌtər] n balbuzie f ▶ vi balbettare

style [staɪl] n stile m; (distinction) eleganza, classe f; **stylish** adj elegante; **stylist** n hair stylist parrucchiere f

sub... [sʌb] prefix sub..., sotto...; **subconscious** adj subcosciente ▶ n subcosciente m

subdued [səb'djuːd] adj pacato(-a); (light) attenuato(-a)

subject [n 'sʌbdʒɪkt, vb səb'dʒɛkt] n soggetto; (citizen etc) cittadino(-a); (Scol) materia ▶ vt **to ~ to** sottomettere a; esporre a; **to be ~ to** (law) essere sottomesso(-a) a; (disease) essere soggetto(-a) a; **subjective** [-'dʒɛktɪv] adj soggettivo(-a); **subject matter** n

argomento; contenuto

subjunctive [səb'dʒʌŋktɪv] adj congiuntivo(-a) ▶ n congiuntivo

submarine [sʌbmə'riːn] n sommergibile m

submission [səb'mɪʃən] n sottomissione f; (claim) richiesta

submit [səb'mɪt] vt sottomettere ▶ vi sottomettersi

subordinate [sə'bɔːdɪnət] adj, n subordinato(-a)

subscribe [səb'skraɪb] vi contribuire; **to ~ to** (opinion) approvare, condividere; (fund) sottoscrivere a; (newspaper) abbonarsi a; essere abbonato(-a) a

subscription [səb'skrɪpʃən] n sottoscrizione f; abbonamento

subsequent ['sʌbsɪkwənt] adj successivo(-a), seguente; conseguente; **subsequently** adv in seguito, successivamente

subside [səb'saɪd] vi cedere, abbassarsi; (flood) decrescere; (wind) calmarsi

subsidiary [səb'sɪdɪərɪ] adj sussidiario(-a); accessorio(-a) ▶ n filiale f

subsidize ['sʌbsɪdaɪz] vt sovvenzionare

subsidy ['sʌbsɪdɪ] n sovvenzione f

substance ['sʌbstəns] n sostanza

substantial [səb'stænʃl] adj solido(-a); (amount, progress etc) notevole; (meal) sostanzioso(-a)

substitute ['sʌbstɪtjuːt] n (person) sostituto(-a); (thing) succedaneo, surrogato ▶ vt **to ~ sth/sb for** sostituire qc/qn a; **substitution** [sʌbstɪ'tjuːʃən] n sostituzione f

subtle ['sʌtl] adj sottile

subtract [səb'trækt] vt sottrarre

suburb ['sʌbəːb] n sobborgo; **the ~s** la periferia; **suburban** [sə'bəːbən] adj suburbano(-a)

subway ['sʌbweɪ] n (US: underground) metropolitana; (BRIT: underpass) sottopassaggio

succeed [sək'siːd] vi riuscire; avere successo ▶ vt succedere a; **to ~ in doing** riuscire a fare

success [sək'ses] n successo; **successful** adj (venture) coronato(-a) da successo, riuscito(-a); **to be successful (in doing)** riuscire (a fare); **successfully** adv con successo

succession [sək'seʃən] n successione f

successive [sək'sesɪv] adj successivo(-a); consecutivo(-a)

successor [sək'sesə'] n successore m

succumb [sə'kʌm] vi soccombere

such [sʌtʃ] adj (of that kind): **~ a book** un tale libro, un libro del genere; **~ books** tali libri, libri del genere; (so much): **~ courage** tanto coraggio ▶ adv talmente, così; **~ a long trip** un viaggio così lungo; **~ a lot of** talmente or così tanto(-a); **~ as** (like) come; **as ~** come or in quanto tale; **such-and-such** adj tale (after noun)

suck [sʌk] vt succhiare; (breast, bottle) poppare

Sudan [suː'dɑːn] n Sudan m

sudden ['sʌdn] adj improvviso(-a); **all of a ~** improvvisamente, all'improvviso; **suddenly** adv bruscamente, improvvisamente, di colpo

sue [suː] vt citare in giudizio

suede [sweɪd] n pelle f scamosciata

suffer ['sʌfə'] vt soffrire, patire; (bear) sopportare, tollerare ▶ vi soffrire; **to ~ from** soffrire di; **suffering** n sofferenza

suffice [sə'faɪs] vi essere sufficiente, bastare

sufficient [sə'fɪʃənt] adj sufficiente; **~ money** abbastanza soldi

suffocate ['sʌfəkeɪt] vi (have difficulty breathing) soffocare; (die through lack of air) asfissiare

sugar ['ʃugə'] n zucchero ▶ vt zuccherare

suggest [sə'dʒest] vt proporre, suggerire; insinuare; **suggestion** [-'dʒestʃən] n suggerimento, proposta; indicazione f

suicide ['suɪsaɪd] n (person) suicida m/f; (act) suicidio; see also **commit**; **suicide bombing** n attentato suicida

suit [suːt] n (man's) vestito; (woman's) completo, tailleur m inv; (Law) causa; (Cards) seme m, colore m ▶ vt andar bene a or per; essere adatto(-a) a or per; (adapt): **~ to sth** adattare qc a; **well ~ed** ben assortito(-a); **suitable** adj adatto(-a); appropriato(-a); **suitcase** ['suːtkeɪs] n valigia

suite [swiːt] n (of rooms) appartamento; (Mus) suite f inv; (furniture): **bedroom/dining room ~** arredo or mobilia per la camera da letto/sala da pranzo

sulfur ['sʌlfə'] (US) n = **sulphur**

sulk [sʌlk] vi fare il broncio

sulphur ['sʌlfə'] (US sulfur) n zolfo

sultana [sʌl'tɑːnə] n (fruit) uva (secca) sultanina

sum [sʌm] n somma; (Scol etc) addizione f ▶ **sum up** vt, vi riassumere

summarize ['sʌməraɪz] vt riassumere, riepilogare

summary ['sʌmərɪ] n riassunto

summer ['sʌmə'] n estate f ▶ cpd d'estate, estivo(-a); **summer holidays** npl vacanze fpl estive; **summertime** n (season) estate f

summit ['sʌmɪt] n cima, sommità, (Pol) vertice m

summon ['sʌmən] vt chiamare, convocare

Sun. abbr (= Sunday) dom.

sun [sʌn] n sole m; **sunbathe** vi prendere un bagno di sole; **sunbed** n lettino solare; **sunblock** n protezione *f* solare totale; **sunburn** *n* (*painful*) scottatura; **sunburned, sunburnt** *adj* abbronzato(-a); (*painfully*) scottato(-a)

Sunday ['sʌndɪ] *n* domenica

Sunday paper *n* giornale *m* della domenica

● **Sunday paper**
● I Sunday papers sono i giornali
● che escono di domenica. Sono
● generalmente corredati da
● supplementi e riviste di argomento
● culturale, sportivo e di attualità.

sunflower ['sʌnflauə*] *n* girasole *m*

sung [sʌŋ] *pp of* **sing**

sunglasses ['sʌnglɑːsɪz] *npl* occhiali *mpl* da sole

sunk [sʌŋk] *pp of* **sink**

sun: sunlight *n* (luce *f* del) sole *m*; **sun lounger** *n* sedia a sdraio; **sunny** *adj* assolato(-a), soleggiato(-a); (*fig*) allegro(-a), felice; **sunrise** *n* levata del sole, alba; **sun roof** *n* (*Aut*) tetto apribile; **sunscreen** *n* (*cream*) crema solare protettiva; **sunset** *n* tramonto; **sunshade** *n* parasole *m*; **sunshine** *n* luce *f* (del) sole *m*; **sunstroke** *n* insolazione *f*, colpo di sole; **suntan** *n* abbronzatura; **suntan lotion** *n* lozione *f* solare; **suntan oil** *n* olio solare

super ['suːpə*] (*inf*) *adj* fantastico(-a)

superb [suː'pəːb] *adj* magnifico(-a)

superficial [suːpə'fɪʃəl] *adj* superficiale

superintendent [suːpərɪn'tɛndənt] *n* direttore(-trice); (*Police*) ≈ commissario (capo)

superior [su'pɪərɪə*] *adj*, *n* superiore *m/f*

superlative [su'pəːlətɪv] *adj* superlativo(-a), supremo(-a) ▸ *n* (*Ling*) superlativo

supermarket ['suːpəmɑːkɪt] *n* supermercato

supernatural [suːpə'nætʃərəl] *adj* soprannaturale ▸ *n* soprannaturale *m*

superpower ['suːpəpauə*] *n* (*Pol*) superpotenza

superstition [suːpə'stɪʃən] *n* superstizione *f*

superstitious [suːpə'stɪʃəs] *adj* superstizioso(-a)

superstore ['suːpəstɔː*] *n* (*BRIT*) grande supermercato

supervise ['suːpəvaɪz] *vt* (*person etc*) sorvegliare; (*organization*) soprintendere a; **supervision** [-'vɪʒn] *n* sorveglianza; supervisione *f*; **supervisor** *n* sorvegliante *m/f*; soprintendente *m/f*; (*in shop*) capocommesso(-a)

supper ['sʌpə*] *n* cena

supple ['sʌpl] *adj* flessibile; agile

supplement [*n* 'sʌplɪmənt, *vb* sʌplɪ'mɛnt] *n* supplemento ▸ *vt* completare, integrare

supplier [sə'plaɪə*] *n* fornitore *m*

supply [sə'plaɪ] *vt* (*provide*) fornire; (*equip*): **to ~ (with)** approvvigionare (di), attrezzare (con) ▸ *n* riserva, provvista; (*supplying*) approvvigionamento; (*Tech*) alimentazione *f*; **supplies** *npl* (*food*) viveri *mpl*; (*Mil*) sussistenza

support [sə'pɔːt] *n* (*moral, financial etc*) sostegno, appoggio; (*Tech*) supporto ▸ *vt* sostenere; (*financially*) mantenere; (*uphold*) sostenere, difendere; **supporter** *n* (*Pol etc*) sostenitore(-trice), fautore(-trice); (*Sport*) tifoso(-a)

▌ Be careful not to translate **support** by the Italian word **sopportare**.

suppose [sə'pəuz] *vt* supporre; immaginare; **to be ~d to do** essere tenuto(-a) a fare; **supposedly** [sə'pəuzɪdlɪ] *adv* presumibilmente; **supposing** *conj* se, ammesso che + *sub*

suppress [sə'prɛs] *vt* reprimere;

sopprimere; occultare
supreme [su'pri:m] adj supremo(-a)
surcharge ['sə:tʃɑ:dʒ] n supplemento
sure [ʃuə] adj sicuro(-a); (definite,
convinced) sicuro(-a), certo(-a); ~!(of
course) senz'altro!, certo!; ~ **enough**
infatti; **to make** ~ **of** sth/that
assicurarsi di qc/che; **surely** adv
sicuramente; certamente
surf [sə:f] n (waves) cavalloni mpl; ~
(foam) spuma
surface ['sə:fis] n superficie ▶ vt
(road) asfaltare ▶ vi risalire alla
superficie; (fig: news, feeling) venire
a galla
surfboard ['sə:fbɔ:d] n tavola per
surfing
surfing ['sə:fɪŋ] n surfing m
surge [sə:dʒ] n (strong movement)
-ondata; (of feeling) impeto ▶ vi
gonfiarsi; (people) riversarsi
surgeon ['sə:dʒən] n chirurgo
surgery ['sə:dʒərɪ] n chirurgia; (BRIT:
room) studio o gabinetto medico,
ambulatorio; (: also: ~ **hours**) orario
delle visite or di consultazione; **to
undergo** ~ subire un intervento
chirurgico
surname ['sə:neɪm] n cognome m
surpass [sə:'pɑ:s] vt superare
surplus ['sə:pləs] n eccedenza;
(Econ) surplus m inv ▶ adj eccedente,
d'avanzo
surprise [sə'praɪz] n sorpresa;
(astonishment) stupore m ▶ vt
sorprendere; stupire; **surprised**
[sə'praɪzd] adj (look, smile)
sorpreso(-a); **to be surprised** essere
sorpreso, sorprendersi; **surprising**
adj sorprendente, stupefacente;
surprisingly adv (easy, helpful)
sorprendentemente
surrender [sə'rɛndə] n resa,
capitolazione f ▶ vi arrendersi
surround [sə'raund] vt circondare;

(Mil etc) accerchiare; **surrounding**
adj circostante; **surroundings** npl
dintorni mpl; (fig) ambiente m
surveillance [sə:'veɪləns] n
sorveglianza, controllo
survey [n 'sə:veɪ, vb sə:'veɪ] n quadro
generale; (study) esame m; (in
housebuying etc) perizia; (of land)
rilevamento, rilievo topografico
▶ vt osservare; esaminare; valutare;
rilevare; **surveyor** n perito; geometra
m; (of land) agrimensore m
survival [sə'vaɪvl] n sopravvivenza;
(relic) reliquia, vestigio
survive [sə'vaɪv] vi sopravvivere ▶ vt
sopravvivere a; **survivor** n superstite
m/f, sopravvissuto(-a)
suspect [adj, n 'sʌspɛkt, vb səs'pɛkt]
adj sospetto(-a) ▶ n persona sospetta
▶ vt sospettare; (think likely) supporre;
(doubt) dubitare
suspend [səs'pɛnd] vt sospendere;
suspended sentence n condanna
con la condizionale; **suspenders** npl
(BRIT) giarrettiere fpl; (US) bretelle fpl
suspense [səs'pɛns] n apprensione f;
(in film etc) suspense m; **to keep sb in** ~
tenere qn in sospeso
suspension [səs'pɛnʃən] n (gen Aut)
sospensione f; (of driving licence) ritiro
temporaneo; **suspension bridge** n
ponte m sospeso
suspicion [səs'pɪʃən] n sospetto;
suspicious [səs'pɪʃəs] adj (suspecting)
sospettoso(-a); (causing suspicion)
sospetto(-a)
sustain [səs'teɪn] vt sostenere;
sopportare; (Law: charge) confermare;
(suffer) subire
swallow ['swɔləu] n (bird) rondine f
▶ vt inghiottire; (fig: story) bere
swam [swæm] pt of **swim**
swamp [swɔmp] n palude f ▶ vt
sommergere
swan [swɔn] n cigno

swap [swɔp] *vt* **to ~ (for)** scambiare (con)

swarm [swɔ:m] *n* sciame *m* ▶ *vi* (*bees*) sciamare; (*people*) brulicare; (*place*): **to be ~ing with** brulicare di

sway [sweɪ] *vi* (*tree*) ondeggiare; (*person*) barcollare ▶ *vt* (*influence*) influenzare, dominare

swear [sweəʳ] (*pt* **swore**, *pp* **sworn**) *vi* (*curse*) bestemmiare, imprecare ▶ *vt* (*promise*) giurare ▷ **swear in** *vt* prestare giuramento a; **swearword** *n* parolaccia

sweat [swet] *n* sudore *m*, traspirazione *f* ▶ *vi* sudare

sweater ['swetəʳ] *n* maglione *m*

sweatshirt ['swetʃəːt] *n* felpa

sweaty ['swetɪ] *adj* sudato(-a), bagnato(-a) di sudore

Swede [swi:d] *n* svedese *m/f*

swede [swi:d] (*BRIT*) *n* rapa svedese

Sweden ['swi:dn] *n* Svezia; **Swedish** ['swi:dɪʃ] *adj* svedese ▶ *n* (*Ling*) svedese *m*

sweep [swi:p] (*pt*, *pp* **swept**) *n* spazzata; (*also*: **chimney ~**) spazzacamino ▶ *vt* spazzare, scopare; (*current*) spazzare ▶ *vi* (*hand*) muoversi con gesto ampio; (*wind*) infuriare

sweet [swi:t] *n* (*BRIT*: *pudding*) dolce *m*; (*candy*) caramella ▶ *adj* dolce; (*fresh*) fresco(-a); (*fig*) piacevole; delicato(-a), grazioso(-a); gentile; **sweetcorn** *n* granturco dolce; **sweetener** ['swi:tnəʳ] *n* (*Culin*) dolcificante *m*; **sweetheart** *n* innamorato(-a); **sweetshop** (*BRIT*) *n* pasticceria

swell [swel] (*pt* **swelled**, *pp* **swollen**, **swelled**) *n* (*of sea*) mare *m* lungo ▶ *adj* (*US*: *inf*: *excellent*) favoloso(-a) ▶ *vt* gonfiare, ingrossare; aumentare ▶ *vi* gonfiarsi, ingrossarsi; (*sound*) crescere; (*also*: **~ up**) gonfiarsi; **swelling** *n* (*Med*) tumefazione *f*, gonfiore *m*

swept [swept] *pt*, *pp of* **sweep**

swerve [swə:v] *vi* deviare; (*driver*) sterzare; (*boxer*) scartare

swift [swɪft] *n* (*bird*) rondone *m* ▶ *adj* rapido(-a), veloce

swim [swɪm] (*pt* **swam**, *pp* **swum**) *n* **to go for a ~** andare a fare una nuotata ▶ *vi* nuotare; (*Sport*) fare del nuoto; (*head*, *room*) girare ▶ *vt* (*river*, *channel*) attraversare a or percorrere a nuoto; (*length*) nuotare; **swimmer** *n* nuotatore(-trice); **swimming** *n* nuoto; **swimming costume** (*BRIT*) *n* costume *m* da bagno; **swimming pool** *n* piscina; **swimming trunks** *npl* costume *m* da bagno (da uomo); **swimsuit** *n* costume *m* da bagno

swing [swɪŋ] (*pt*, *pp* **swung**) *n* altalena; (*movement*) oscillazione *f*; (*Mus*) ritmo; swing *m* ▶ *vt* dondolare, far oscillare; (*also*: **~ round**) far girare ▶ *vi* oscillare, dondolare; (*also*: **~ round**: *object*) roteare; (: *person*) girarsi, voltarsi; **to be in full ~** (*activity*) essere in piena attività; (*party etc*) essere nel pieno

swipe card *n* tessera magnetica

swirl [swə:l] *vi* turbinare, far mulinello

Swiss [swɪs] *adj*, *n inv* svizzero(-a)

switch [swɪtʃ] *n* (*for light*, *radio etc*) interruttore *m*; (*change*) cambiamento ▶ *vt* (*change*) cambiare; scambiare ▷ **switch off** *vt* spegnere; **could you ~ off the light?** puoi spegnere la luce? ▷ **switch on** *vt* accendere; (*engine*, *machine*) mettere in moto, avviare; **switchboard** *n* (*Tel*) centralino

Switzerland ['swɪtsələnd] *n* Svizzera

swivel ['swɪvl] *vi* (*also*: **~ round**) girare

swollen ['swəulən] *pp of* **swell**

swoop [swu:p] *n* incursione *f* ▶ *vi* (*also*: **~ down**) scendere in picchiata, piombare

swop [swɔp] *n*, *vt* = **swap**

sword [sɔːd] n spada; **swordfish** n
pesce m spada inv

swore [swɔːʳ] pt of **swear**

sworn [swɔːn] pp of **swear** ▸ adj
giurato(-a)

swum [swʌm] pp of **swim**

swung [swʌŋ] pt, pp of **swing**

syllable ['sɪləbl] n sillaba

syllabus ['sɪləbəs] n programma m

symbol ['sɪmbl] n simbolo;
symbolic(al) [sɪm'bɔlɪk(l)] adj
simbolico(-a); **to be symbolic(al) of**
sth simboleggiare qc

symmetrical [sɪ'mɛtrɪkl] adj
simmetrico(-a)

symmetry ['sɪmɪtrɪ] n simmetria

sympathetic [sɪmpə'θɛtɪk] adj
(showing pity) compassionevole; (kind)
comprensivo(-a); **~ towards** ben
disposto(-a) verso

> Be careful not to translate
> **sympathetic** by the Italian word
> **simpatico**.

sympathize ['sɪmpəθaɪz] vi **to ~ with**
(person) compatire; partecipare al
dolore di; (cause) simpatizzare per

sympathy ['sɪmpəθɪ] n compassione f

symphony ['sɪmfənɪ] n sinfonia

symptom ['sɪmptəm] n sintomo;
indizio

synagogue ['sɪnəgɔg] n sinagoga

syndicate ['sɪndɪkɪt] n sindacato

syndrome ['sɪndrəum] n sindrome f

synonym ['sɪnənɪm] n sinonimo

synthetic [sɪn'θɛtɪk] adj sintetico(-a)

Syria ['sɪrɪə] n Siria

syringe [sɪ'rɪndʒ] n siringa

syrup ['sɪrəp] n sciroppo; (also: **golden**
~) melassa raffinata

system ['sɪstəm] n sistema m;
(order) metodo; (Anat) organismo;
systematic [-'mætɪk] adj
sistematico(-a); metodico(-a);
systems analyst n analista m di
sistemi

t

ta [tɑː] (BRIT: inf) excl grazie!

tab [tæb] n (loop on coat etc) laccetto;
(label) etichetta; **to keep ~ s on** (fig)
tenere d'occhio

table ['teɪbl] n tavolo, tavola; (Math,
Chem etc) tavola ▸ vt (BRIT: motion
etc) presentare; **a ~ for 4, please** un
tavolo per 4, per favore; **to lay** or **set**
the ~ apparecchiare or preparare
la tavola; **tablecloth** n tovaglia;
table d'hôte [tɑːbl'dəut] adj (meal) a
prezzo fisso; **table lamp** n lampada
da tavolo; **tablemat** n sottopiatto;
tablespoon n cucchiaio da tavola;
(also: **tablespoonful**: as measurement)
cucchiaiata

tablet ['tæblɪt] n (Med) compressa; (of
stone) targa

table tennis n tennis m da tavolo,
ping-pong® m

tabloid ['tæblɔɪd] n (newspaper)
tabloid m inv (giornale illustrato di
formato ridotto); **the ~s, the ~ press** i
giornali popolari

taboo [tə'buː] adj, n tabù m inv

tack [tæk] n (nail) bulletta; (fig)
approccio ▸ vt imbullettare;
imbastire ▸ vi bordeggiare

tackle ['tækl] n attrezzatura,
equipaggiamento; (for lifting)
paranco; (Football) contrasto; (Rugby)
placcaggio ▸ vt (difficulty) affrontare;
(Football) contrastare; (Rugby)
placcare

tacky ['tækɪ] adj appiccicaticcio(-a); (pej) scadente

tact [tækt] n tatto: **tactful** adj delicato(-a), discreto(-a)

tactics ['tæktɪks] n, npl tattica

tactless ['tæktlɪs] adj che manca di tatto

tadpole ['tædpəʊl] n girino

taffy ['tæfɪ] (US) n caramella f mou inv

tag [tæg] n etichetta

tail [teɪl] n coda; (of shirt) falda ▶ vt (follow) seguire, pedinare; **~s** npl (formal suit) frac m inv

tailor ['teɪlə*] n sarto

Taiwan [taɪ'wɑːn] n Taiwan m; **Taiwanese** [taɪwə'niːz] adj, n taiwanese

take [teɪk] (pt took, pp taken) vt prendere; (gain: prize) ottenere, vincere; (require: effort, courage) occorrere, volerci; (tolerate) accettare, sopportare; (hold: passengers etc) contenere; (accompany) accompagnare; (bring, carry) portare; (exam) sostenere, presentarsi a; **to ~ a photo/a shower** fare una fotografia/ una doccia; **~ it that** suppongo che ▶ **take after** vt fus assomigliare a ▶ **take apart** vt smontare ▶ **take away** vt portare via; togliere ▶ **take back** vt (return) restituire; riportare; (one's words) ritirare ▶ **take down** vt (building) demolire; (letter etc) scrivere ▶ **take in** vt (deceive) imbrogliare, abbindolare; (understand) capire; (include) comprendere, includere; (lodger) prendere, ospitare ▶ **take off** vi (Aviat) decollare; (go away) andarsene ▶ vt (remove) togliere ▶ **take on** vt (work) accettare, intraprendere; (employee) assumere; (opponent) sfidare, affrontare ▶ **take out** vt portare fuori; (remove) togliere; (licence) prendere, ottenere; **to ~ sth out of sth** (drawer, pocket etc)

tirare qc fuori da qc; estrarre qc da qc ▶ **take over** vt (business) rilevare ▶ vi **to ~ over from sb** prendere le consegne or il controllo da qn ▶ **take up** vt (dress) accorciare; (occupy: time, space) occupare; (engage in: hobby etc) mettersi a; **to ~ sb up on sth** accettare qc da qn; **takeaway** (BRIT) n (shop etc) ≈ rosticceria; (food) pasto per asporto; **taken** pp of **take**; **takeoff** n (Aviat) decollo; **takeout** (US) n = **takeaway**; **takeover** n (Comm) assorbimento; **takings** ['teɪkɪŋz] npl (Comm) incasso

talc [tælk] n (also: **~um powder**) talco

tale [teɪl] n racconto, storia; **to tell ~s** (fig: to teacher, parent etc) fare la spia

talent ['tælənt] n talento; **talented** adj di talento

talk [tɔːk] n discorso; (gossip) chiacchiere fpl; (conversation) conversazione f; (interview) discussione f ▶ vi parlare; **~s** npl (Pol etc) colloqui mpl; **to ~ about** parlare di; **to ~ sb out of/into doing** dissuadere qn da/convincere qn a fare; **to ~ shop** parlare di lavoro or di affari ▶ **talk over** vt discutere; **talk show** n conversazione f televisiva, talk show m inv

tall [tɔːl] adj alto(-a); **to be 6 feet ~** ≈ essere alto 1 metro e 80

tambourine [tæmbə'riːn] n tamburello

tame [teɪm] adj addomesticato(-a); (fig: story, style) insipido(-a), scialbo(-a)

tamper ['tæmpə*] vi **to ~ with** manomettere

tampon ['tæmpɔn] n tampone m

tan [tæn] n (also: **sun~**) abbronzatura ▶ vi abbronzarsi ▶ adj (colour) marrone rossiccio inv

tandem ['tændəm] n tandem m inv

tangerine [tændʒə'riːn] n mandarino

tangle [ˈtæŋgl] *n* groviglio; **to get into a ~** aggrovigliarsi; (*fig*) combinare un pasticcio

tank [tæŋk] *n* serbatoio; (*for fish*) acquario; (*Mil*) carro armato

tanker [ˈtæŋkə*] *n* (*ship*) nave *f* cisterna *inv*; (*truck*) autobotte *f*, autocisterna

tanned [tænd] *adj* abbronzato(-a)

tantrum [ˈtæntrəm] *n* accesso di collera

Tanzania [tænzəˈniːə] *n* Tanzania

tap [tæp] *n* (*on sink etc*) rubinetto; (*gentle blow*) colpetto ▶ *vt* dare un colpetto a; (*resources*) sfruttare, utilizzare; (*telephone*) mettere sotto controllo; **on ~** (*fig: resources*) a disposizione; **tap dancing** *n* tip tap *m*

tape [teip] *n* nastro; (*also:* **magnetic ~**) nastro (magnetico); (*sticky tape*) nastro adesivo ▶ *vt* (*record*) registrare (su nastro); (*stick*) attaccare con nastro adesivo; **tape measure** *n* metro a nastro; **tape recorder** *n* registratore *m* (a nastro)

tapestry [ˈtæpistri] *n* arazzo; tappezzeria

tar [tɑː*] *n* catrame *m*

target [ˈtɑːgit] *n* bersaglio; (*fig: objective*) obiettivo

tariff [ˈtærif] *n* tariffa

tarmac [ˈtɑːmæk] *n* (*BRIT: on road*) macadam *m* al catrame; (*Aviat*) pista di decollo

tarpaulin [tɑːˈpɔːlin] *n* tela incatramata

tarragon [ˈtærəgən] *n* dragoncello

tart [tɑːt] *n* (*Culin*) crostata; (*BRIT: inf: pej: woman*) sgualdrina ▶ *adj* (*flavour*) aspro(-a), agro(-a)

tartan [ˈtɑːtn] *n* tartan *m inv*

tartar(e) sauce *n* salsa tartara

task [tɑːsk] *n* compito; **to take to ~** rimproverare

taste [teist] *n* gusto; (*flavour*) sapore *m*, gusto; (*sample*) assaggio; (*fig: glimpse, idea*) idea ▶ *vt* gustare; (*sample*) assaggiare ▶ *vi* **to ~ of** *or* **like** (*fish etc*) sapere *or* avere sapore di; **in good/bad ~** di buon/cattivo gusto; **can I have a ~?** posso assaggiarlo?; **you can ~ the garlic (in it)** (ci) si sente il sapore dell'aglio; **tasteful** *adj* di buon gusto; **tasteless** *adj* (*food*) insipido(-a); (*remark*) di cattivo gusto; **tasty** *adj* saporito(-a), gustoso(-a)

tatters [ˈtætəz] *npl* **in ~ a** brandelli

tattoo [təˈtuː] *n* tatuaggio; (*spectacle*) parata militare ▶ *vt* tatuare

taught [tɔːt] *pt, pp of* **teach**

taunt [tɔːnt] *n* scherno ▶ *vt* schernire

Taurus [ˈtɔːrəs] *n* Toro

taut [tɔːt] *adj* teso(-a)

tax [tæks] *n* (*on goods*) imposta; (*on services*) tassa; (*on income*) imposte *fpl*, tasse *fpl* ▶ *vt* tassare; (*fig: strain: patience etc*) mettere alla prova; **tax-free** *adj* esente da imposte

taxi [ˈtæksi] *n* taxi *m inv* ▶ *vi* (*Aviat*) rullare; **can you call me a ~, please?** può chiamarmi un taxi, per favore?; **taxi driver** *n* tassista *m/f*; **taxi rank** (*BRIT*) *n* = **taxi stand**; **taxi stand** *n* posteggio dei taxi

tax payer *n* contribuente *m/f*

TB *n abbr* = **tuberculosis**

tea [tiː] *n* tè *m inv*; (*BRIT: snack: for children*) merenda; **high ~** (*BRIT*) cena leggera (presa nel tardo pomeriggio); **tea bag** *n* bustina di tè; **tea break** (*BRIT*) *n* intervallo per il tè

teach [tiːtʃ] (*pt, pp* **taught**) *vt* **to ~ sb sth**, **~ sth to sb** insegnare qc a qn ▶ *vi* insegnare; **teacher** *n* insegnante *m/f*; (*in secondary school*) professore(-essa); (*in primary school*) maestro(-a); **teaching** *n* insegnamento

tea: tea cloth *n* (*for dishes*) strofinaccio; (*for trolley*) tovaglietta da tè; **teacup** [ˈtiːkʌp] *n*

tazza da tè
tea leaves npl foglie fpl di tè
team [tiːm] n squadra; (of animals) tiro
▷ **team up** vi to ~ up (with) mettersi
insieme (a)
teapot ['tiːpɔt] n teiera
tear¹ [tɛəʳ] (pt **tore**, pp **torn**) n strappo
▶ vt strappare ▶ vi strapparsi ▷ **tear
apart** vt (also fig) distruggere
▷ **tear down** vt +adv (building,
statue) demolire; (poster, flag) tirare
giù ▷ **tear off** vt (sheet of paper etc)
strappare; (one's clothes) togliersi di
dosso ▷ **tear up** vt (sheet of paper etc)
strappare
tear² [tɪəʳ] n lacrima; **in ~s** in lacrime;
tearful ['tɪəful] adj piangente,
lacrimoso(-a); **tear gas** n gas m
lacrimogeno
tearoom ['tiːruːm] n sala da tè
tease [tiːz] vt canzonare; (unkindly)
tormentare
tea: teaspoon n cucchiaino da tè;
(also: **teaspoonful**: as measurement)
cucchiaino; **teatime** n ora del tè;
tea towel (BRIT) n strofinaccio (per
i piatti)
technical ['tɛknɪkl] adj tecnico(-a)
technician [tɛk'nɪʃən] n tecnico(-a)
technique [tɛk'niːk] n tecnica
technology [tɛk'nɔlədʒɪ] n
tecnologia
teddy (bear) ['tɛdɪ-] n orsacchiotto
tedious ['tiːdɪəs] adj noioso(-a),
tedioso(-a)
tee [tiː] n (Golf) tee m inv
teen [tiːn] adj = **teenage** ▶ n (US)
= **teenager**
teenage ['tiːneɪdʒ] adj (fashions
etc) per giovani, per adolescenti;
teenager n adolescente m/f
teens [tiːnz] npl to be in one's ~ essere
adolescente
teeth [tiːθ] npl of **tooth**
teetotal ['tiː'təutl] adj astemio(-a)

telecommunications ['tɛlɪkəmjuː
nɪ'keɪʃənz] n telecomunicazioni fpl
telegram ['tɛlɪɡræm] n telegramma
m
telegraph pole n palo del telegrafo
telephone ['tɛlɪfəun] n telefono
▶ vt (person) telefonare a; (message)
comunicare per telefono; **telephone
book** n elenco telefonico; **telephone
booth** (BRIT), **telephone box** n
cabina telefonica; **telephone call**
n telefonata; **telephone directory**
n elenco telefonico; **telephone
number** n numero di telefono
telesales ['tɛlɪseɪlz] n vendita per
telefono
telescope ['tɛlɪskəup] n telescopio
televise ['tɛlɪvaɪz] vt teletrasmettere
television ['tɛlɪvɪʒən] n televisione
f; **on ~** alla televisione; **television
programme** n programma m
televisivo
tell [tɛl] (pt, pp **told**) vt dire; (relate:
story) raccontare; (distinguish): to ~
sth from distinguere qc da a ▶ vi (talk):
to ~ (of) parlare (di); (have effect)
farsi sentire, avere effetto; **to ~ sb
to do** dire a qn di fare ▷ **tell off** vt
rimproverare, sgridare; **teller** n (in
bank) cassiere(-a)
telly ['tɛlɪ] (BRIT: inf) n abbr (= television)
tivù f inv
temp [tɛmp] n abbr (= temporary)
segretaria temporanea
temper ['tɛmpəʳ] n (nature) carattere
m; (mood) umore m; (fit of anger) collera
▶ vt (moderate) moderare; **to be in
a ~** essere in collera; **to lose one's ~**
andare in collera
temperament ['tɛmprəmənt]
n (nature) temperamento;
temperamental [-'mɛntl] adj
capriccioso(-a)
temperature ['tɛmprətʃəʳ] n
temperatura; **to have or run a ~** avere

la febbre

temple ['templ] n (building) tempio; (Anat) tempia

temporary ['tempərəri] adj temporaneo(-a); (job, worker) avventizio(-a), temporaneo(-a)

tempt [tempt] vt tentare; **to ~ sb into doing** indurre qn a fare; **temptation** [-'teɪʃən] n tentazione f; **tempting** adj allettante

ten [ten] num dieci

tenant ['tenənt] n inquilino(-a)

tend [tend] vt badare a, occuparsi di ▶ vi **to ~ to do** tendere a fare; **tendency** ['tendənsɪ] n tendenza f

tender ['tendə'] adj tenero(-a); (sore) dolorante ▶ n (Comm: offer) offerta; (money): **legal ~** moneta in corso legale ▶ vt offrire

tendon ['tendən] n tendine m

tenner ['tenə'] n (BRIT inf) (banconota da) dieci sterline fpl

tennis ['tenɪs] n tennis m; **tennis ball** n palla da tennis; **tennis court** n campo da tennis; **tennis match** n partita di tennis; **tennis player** n tennista m/f; **tennis racket** n racchetta da tennis

tenor ['tenə'] n (Mus) tenore m

tenpin bowling ['tenpɪn-] n bowling m

tense [tens] adj teso(-a) ▶ n (Ling) tempo

tension ['tenʃən] n tensione f

tent [tent] n tenda

tentative ['tentətɪv] adj esitante, incerto(-a); (conclusion) provvisorio(-a)

tenth [tenθ] num decimo(-a)

tent: tent peg n picchetto da tenda; **tent pole** n palo da tenda, montante m

tepid ['tepɪd] adj tiepido(-a)

term [tə:m] n termine m; (Scol) trimestre m; (Law) sessione f ▶ vt

chiamare, definire; **~s** npl (conditions) condizioni fpl; (Comm) prezzi mpl, tariffe fpl; **in the short/long ~** a breve/lunga scadenza; **to be on good ~s with sb** essere in buoni rapporti con qn; **to come to ~s with** (problem) affrontare

terminal ['tə:mɪnl] adj finale, terminale; (disease) terminale ▶ n (Elec) morsetto; (Comput) terminale m; (Aviat, for oil, ore etc) terminal m inv; (BRIT: also: **coach ~**) capolinea m

terminate ['tə:mɪneɪt] vt mettere fine a

termini ['tə:mɪnaɪ] npl of **terminus**

terminology [tə:mɪ'nɔlədʒɪ] n terminologia

terminus ['tə:mɪnəs] (pl **termini**) n (for buses) capolinea m; (for trains) stazione f terminale

terrace ['terəs] n terrazza; (BRIT: row of houses) fila di case a schiera; **terraced** adj (garden) a terrazze

terrain [te'reɪn] n terreno

terrestrial [tɪ'restrɪəl] adj (life) terrestre; (BRIT: channel) terrestre

terrible ['terɪbl] adj terribile; **terribly** adv terribilmente; (very badly) malissimo

terrier ['terɪə'] n terrier m inv

terrific [tə'rɪfɪk] adj incredibile, fantastico(-a); (wonderful) formidabile, eccezionale

terrified ['terɪfaɪd] adj atterrito(-a)

terrify ['terɪfaɪ] vt terrorizzare; **terrifying** adj terrificante

territorial [terɪ'tɔ:rɪəl] adj territoriale

territory ['terɪtərɪ] n territorio

terror ['terə'] n terrore m; **terrorism** n terrorismo; **terrorist** n terrorista m/f

test [test] n (trial, check: of courage etc) prova; (Med) esame m; (Chem) analisi f inv; (exam: of intelligence etc) test m inv; (: in school) compito in classe; (also: **driving ~**) esame m di guida

▶ vt provare; esaminare; analizzare; sottoporre ad esame; **to ~ sb in history** esaminare qn in storia

testicle ['tɛstɪkl] n testicolo

testify ['tɛstɪfaɪ] vi (Law) testimoniare, deporre; **to ~ to sth** (Law) testimoniare qc; (gen) comprovare o dimostrare qc

testimony ['tɛstɪmənɪ] n (Law) testimonianza, deposizione f

test: test match n (Cricket, Rugby) partita internazionale; **test tube** n provetta

tetanus ['tɛtənəs] n tetano

text [tɛkst] n testo; (on mobile phone) SMS m inv, messaggino ▶ vt **to ~ sb** (inf) mandare un SMS a qn; **textbook** n libro di testo

textile ['tɛkstaɪl] n tessile m

text message n (Tel) SMS m inv, messaggino

text messaging [-'mɛsɪdʒɪŋ] n il mandarsi SMS

texture ['tɛkstʃə'] n tessitura; (of skin, paper etc) struttura

Thai [taɪ] adj tailandese ▶ n tailandese m/f; (Ling) tailandese m

Thailand ['taɪlænd] n Tailandia

Thames [tɛmz] n the ~ il Tamigi

than [ðæn, ðən] conj (in comparisons) che; (with numerals, pronouns, proper names) di; **more ~ 10/once** più di 10/una volta; **I have more/less ~ you** ne ho più/meno di te; **I have more pens ~ pencils** ho più penne che matite; **she is older ~ you think** è più vecchia di quanto tu (non) pensi

thank [θæŋk] vt ringraziare; **~ you (very much)** grazie (tante); **~ you** npl ringraziamenti mpl, grazie fpl excl grazie!; **~s to** grazie a; **thankfully** adv con riconoscenza; con sollievo; **thankfully there were few victims** grazie al cielo ci sono state poche vittime; **Thanksgiving (Day)** n giorno del ringraziamento

Thanksgiving (Day)
Negli Stati Uniti il quarto giovedì di novembre ricorre il **Thanksgiving (Day)**, festa che rievoca la celebrazione con cui i Padri Pellegrini, fondatori della colonia di Plymouth in Massachusetts, ringraziarono Dio del buon raccolto del 1621.

that [ðæt] (pl **those**) adj (demonstrative) quel (quell', quello) m; quella (quell') f; **that man/woman/book** quell'uomo/quella donna/quel libro; (not "this") quell'uomo/quella donna/quel libro là; **that one** quello(-a) là

▶ pron

1 (demonstrative) ciò; (not "this one") quello(-a); **who's that?** chi è?; **what's that?** cos'è quello?; **is that you?** sei tu?; **I prefer this to that** preferisco questo a quello; **that's what he said** questo è ciò che ha detto; **what happened after that?** che è successo dopo?; **that is** (to say) cioè

2 (relative: direct) che; (: indirect) cui; **the book (that) I read** il libro che ho letto; **the box (that) I put it in** la scatola in cui l'ho messo; **the people (that) I spoke to** le persone con cui or con le quali ho parlato

3 (relative: of time) in cui; **the day (that) he came** il giorno in cui è venuto

▶ conj che; **he thought that I was ill** pensava che io fossi malato

▶ adv (demonstrative) così; **I can't work that much** non posso lavorare (così) tanto; **that high** così alto; **the wall's about that high and that thick** il muro è alto circa così e spesso circa così

thatched [θætʃt] adj (roof) di paglia

thaw [θɔː] n disgelo ▶ vi (ice)

sciogliersi; (food) scongelarsi ▶ vt
(food: also: ~ **out**) (fare) scongelare

the
[ðiː, ðə] def art

1 (gen) il (lo, l'); la (l') f; i (gli) mpl;
le fpl; **the boy/girl/ink** il ragazzo/la
ragazza/l'inchiostro; **the books/
pencils** i libri/le matite; **the history
of the world** la storia del mondo; **give
it to the postman** dallo al postino;
I haven't the time/money non ho
tempo/soldi; **the rich and the poor** i
ricchi e i poveri

2 (in titles): **Elizabeth the First**
Elisabetta prima; **Peter the Great**
Pietro il grande

3 (in comparisons): **the more he works,
the more he earns** più lavora più
guadagna

theatre ['θɪətə'] (US **theater**) n teatro;
(also: **lecture** ~) aula magna; (also:
operating ~) sala operatoria

theft [θɛft] n furto

their [ðɛə'] adj il (la) loro; (pl) i (le) loro;
theirs pron il (la) loro; (pl) i (le) loro; see
also **my; mine**

them [ðɛm, ðəm] pron (direct) li (le);
(indirect) gli (loro after vb); (stressed,
after prep: people) loro; (: people, things)
essi(-e); see also **me**

theme [θiːm] n tema m; **theme park**
n parco di divertimenti (intorno a un
tema centrale)

themselves [ðəm'sɛlvz] pl pron
(reflexive) si; (emphatic) loro stessi(-e);
(after prep) se stessi(-e)

then [ðɛn] adv (at that time) allora;
(next) poi, dopo; (and also) e poi ▶ conj
(therefore) perciò, dunque, quindi ▶ adj
the ~ president il presidente di allora;
by ~ allora; **from ~ on** da allora in poi

theology [θɪ'ɔlədʒɪ] n teologia

theory ['θɪərɪ] n teoria

therapist ['θɛrəpɪst] n terapista m/f

therapy ['θɛrəpɪ] n terapia

there
[ðɛə'] adv

1 : **there is, there are** c'è, ci sono; **there
are 3 of them** (people) sono in 3; (things)
ce ne sono 3; **there is no-one here** non
c'è nessuno qui; **there has been an
accident** c'è stato un incidente

2 (referring to place) là, lì; **up/in/down
there** lassù/là dentro/laggiù; **he went
there on Friday** ci è andato venerdì; **I
want that book there** voglio quel libro
là or lì; **there he is!** eccolo!

3 : **there, there** (esp to child) su, su

there: thereabouts [ðɛərə'bauts]
adv (place) nei pressi, da quelle
parti; (amount) giù di lì, all'incirca;
thereafter [ðɛər'ɑːftə'] adv da allora
in poi; **thereby** [ðɛə'baɪ] adv con ciò;
therefore ['ðɛəfɔː'] adv perciò, quindi;
there's [ðɛəz] = **there is; there has**

thermal ['θəːml] adj termico(-a)

thermometer [θə'mɔmɪtə'] n
termometro

thermostat ['θəːməstæt] n
termostato

these [ðiːz] pl pron, adj questi(-e)

thesis ['θiːsɪs] (pl **theses**) n tesi f inv

they [ðeɪ] pl pron essi (esse); (people
only) loro; ~ **say that ...** (it is said
that) si dice che ...; **they'd = they
had; they would; they'll = they
shall; they will; they're = they are;
they've = they have**

thick [θɪk] adj spesso(-a); (crowd)
compatto(-a); (stupid) ottuso(-a),
lento(-a) ▶ n **in the ~ of** nel folto di;
it's 20 cm ~ ha uno spessore di 20
cm; **thicken** vi ispessire ▶ vt (sauce
etc) ispessire, rendere più denso(-a);
thickness n spessore m

thief [θiːf] (pl **thieves**) n ladro(-a)

thigh [θaɪ] n coscia

thin [θɪn] adj sottile; (person)
magro(-a); (soup) poco denso(-a) ▶ vt
to ~ (down) (sauce, paint) diluire

thing [θɪŋ] n cosa; (object) oggetto; (mania): **to have a ~ about** essere fissato(-a) con; **~s** npl (belongings) cose fpl; **poor ~** poverino(-a); **the best ~ would be to** la cosa migliore sarebbe di; **how are ~s?** come va?

think [θɪŋk] (pt, pp **thought**) vi pensare, riflettere ▶ vt pensare, credere; (imagine) immaginare; **to ~ of** pensare a; **what did you ~ of them?** cosa ne ha pensato?; **to ~ about sth/sb** pensare a qc/qn; **I'll ~ about it** ci penserò; **to ~ of doing** pensare di fare; **I ~ so/no** penso di sì/no; **to ~ well of** avere una buona opinione di ▷ **think over** vt riflettere su ▷ **think up** vt ideare

third [θəːd] num terzo(-a) ▶ n terzo(-a); (fraction) terzo, terza parte f; (Aut) terza; (BRIT: Scol: degree) laurea col minimo dei voti; **thirdly** adv in terzo luogo; **third party insurance** (BRIT) n assicurazione f contro terzi; **Third World** n the Third World il Terzo Mondo

thirst [θəːst] n sete f; **thirsty** adj (person) assetato(-a), che ha sete

thirteen [θəːˈtiːn] num tredici; **thirteenth** [-ˈtiːnθ] num tredicesimo(-a)

thirtieth [ˈθəːtɪɪθ] num trentesimo(-a)

thirty [ˈθəːtɪ] num trenta

O **this**

[ðɪs] (pl **these**) adj (demonstrative) questo(-a); **this man/woman/book** quest'uomo/questa donna/questo libro; (not "that") quest'uomo/questa donna/questo libro qui; **this one** questo(-a) qui

▶ pron (demonstrative) questo(-a); (not "that one") questo(-a) qui; **who/what is this?** chi è/che cos'è questo?; **I prefer this to that** preferisco questo a quello; **this is where I live** io abito qui; **this is what he said** questo è ciò che ha detto;

this is Mr Brown (in introductions, photo) questo è il signor Brown; (on telephone) sono il signor Brown

▶ adv (demonstrative): **this high/long** etc alto/lungo etc così; **I didn't know things were this bad** non sapevo andasse così male

thistle [ˈθɪsl] n cardo

thorn [θɔːn] n spina

thorough [ˈθʌrə] adj (search) minuzioso(-a); (knowledge, research) approfondito(-a), profondo(-a); (person) coscienzioso(-a); (cleaning) a fondo; **thoroughly** adv (search) minuziosamente; (wash, study) a fondo; (very) assolutamente

those [ðəuz] pron quelli(-e) ▶ pl adj quei (quegli) mpl; quelle fpl

though [ðəu] conj benché, sebbene ▶ adv comunque

thought [θɔːt] pt, pp of **think** ▶ n pensiero; (opinion) opinione f; **thoughtful** adj pensieroso(-a), pensoso(-a); (considerate) premuroso(-a); **thoughtless** adj sconsiderato(-a); (behaviour) scortese

thousand [ˈθauzənd] num mille; **one ~** mille; **~s of** migliaia di; **thousandth** num millesimo(-a)

thrash [θræʃ] vt picchiare; bastonare; (defeat) battere

thread [θrɛd] n filo; (of screw) filetto ▶ vt (needle) infilare

threat [θrɛt] n minaccia; **threaten** vi (storm) minacciare ▶ vt **to threaten sb with/to do** minacciare qn con/di fare; **threatening** adj minaccioso(-a)

three [θriː] num tre; **three-dimensional** adj tridimensionale; (film) stereoscopico(-a); **three-piece suite** [ˈθriːpiːs-] n salotto comprendente un divano e due poltrone; **three-quarters** npl tre quarti mpl; **three-quarters full** pieno per tre quarti

threshold ['θrɛʃhəʊld] n soglia

threw [θruː] pt of **throw**

thrill [θrɪl] n brivido ▶ vt (audience) elettrizzare; **to be ~ed** (with gift etc) essere elettrizzato(-a); **thrilled** adj **I was thrilled to get your letter** la tua lettera mi ha fatto veramente piacere; **thriller** n thriller m inv; **thrilling** adj (book) pieno(-a) di suspense; (news, discovery) elettrizzante

thriving ['θraɪvɪŋ] adj fiorente

throat [θrəʊt] n gola; **to have a sore~** avere (un or il) mal di gola

throb [θrɔb] vi palpitare; pulsare; vibrare

throne [θrəʊn] n trono

through [θruː] prep attraverso; (time) per, durante; (by means of) per mezzo di; (owing to) a causa di ▶ adj (ticket, train, passage) diretto(-a) ▶ adv attraverso; **to put sb ~ to sb** (Tel) passare qn a qn; **to be ~** (Tel) ottenere la comunicazione; (have finished) essere finito(-a); **"no-road"** (BRIT) "strada senza sbocco"; **throughout** prep (place) dappertutto in; (time) per o durante tutto(-a) ▶ adv dappertutto; sempre

throw [θrəʊ] (pt **threw**, pp **thrown**) n (Sport) lancio, tiro ▶ vt tirare, gettare; (Sport) lanciare, tirare; (rider) disarcionare; (fig) confondere; **to~a party** dare una festa ▶ **throw away** vt gettare o buttare via ▶ **throw in** vt (Sport: ball) rimettere in gioco; (include) aggiungere ▶ **throw off** vt sbarazzarsi di ▶ **throw out** vt buttare fuori; (reject) respingere ▶ **throw up** vi vomitare

thru [θruː] (US) prep, adj, adv = **through**

thrush [θrʌʃ] n tordo

thrust [θrʌst] (pt, pp **thrust**) vt spingere con forza; (push in) conficcare

thud [θʌd] n tonfo

thug [θʌg] n delinquente m

thumb [θʌm] n (Anat) pollice m; **to~a lift** fare l'autostop; **thumbtack** (US) n puntina da disegno

thump [θʌmp] n colpo forte; (sound) tonfo ▶ vt (person) picchiare; (object) battere su ▶ vi picchiare; battere

thunder ['θʌndə*] n tuono ▶ vi tuonare; (train etc): **to~past** passare con un rombo; **thunderstorm** n temporale m

Thur(s). abbr (= Thursday) gio

Thursday ['θəːzdɪ] n giovedì m inv

thus [ðʌs] adv così

thwart [θwɔːt] vt contrastare

thyme [taɪm] n timo

Tiber ['taɪbə*] n: **il Tevere**

Tibet [tɪ'bɛt] n Tibet m

tick [tɪk] n (sound: of clock) tic tac m inv; (mark) segno; spunta; (Zool) zecca; (BRIT: inf): **in a~** in un attimo ▶ vi fare tic tac ▶ vt spuntare ▶ **tick off** vt spuntare; (person) sgridare

ticket ['tɪkɪt] n (in shop: on goods) etichetta; (parking ticket) multa; (for library) scheda; **a single/return ~to...** un biglietto di sola andata/di andata e ritorno per...; **ticket barrier** n (BRIT: Rail) cancelletto d'ingresso; **ticket collector** n bigliettaio; **ticket inspector** n controllore m; **ticket machine** n distributore m di biglietti; **ticket office** n biglietteria

tickle ['tɪkl] vt fare il solletico a; (fig) solleticare ▶ vi **it~s mi** (or gli etc) fa il solletico; **ticklish** [-lɪʃ] adj che soffre il solletico; (problem) delicato(-a)

tide [taɪd] n marea; (fig: of events) corso; **high/low~** alta/bassa marea

tidy ['taɪdɪ] adj (room) ordinato(-a), lindo(-a); (dress, work) curato(-a), in ordine; (person) ordinato(-a) ▶ vt (also: **~up**) riordinare, mettere in ordine

tie [taɪ] n (string type) legaccio; (BRIT:

also: **neck~**) cravatta; (fig: link) legame m; (Sport: draw) pareggio ▶ vt (parcel) legare; (ribbon) annodare ▶ vi (Sport) pareggiare; **to ~ sth in a bow** annodare qc; **to ~ a knot in sth** fare un nodo a qc ▷ **tie down** vt legare; (to price etc) costringere ad accettare ▷ **tie up** vt (parcel, dog) legare; (boat) ormeggiare; (arrangements) concludere; **to be ~d up** (busy) essere occupato(-a) or preso(-a)

tier [tɪə*] n fila; (of cake) piano, strato

tiger ['taɪgə*] n tigre f

tight [taɪt] adj (rope) teso(-a), tirato(-a); (clothes, budget, bend etc) stretto(-a); (control) severo(-a), fermo(-a); (inf: drunk) sbronzo(-a) ▶ adv (squeeze) fortemente; (shut) ermeticamente; **tighten** vt (rope) tendere; (screw) stringere; (control) rinforzare ▶ vi tendersi; stringersi; **tightly** adv (grasp) bene, saldamente; **tights** (BRIT) npl collant m inv

tile [taɪl] n (on roof) tegola; (on wall or floor) piastrella, mattonella

till [tɪl] n registratore di cassa ▶ vt (land) coltivare ▶ prep, conj = **until**

tilt [tɪlt] vt inclinare, far pendere ▶ vi inclinarsi, pendere

timber ['tɪmbə*] n (material) legname m

time [taɪm] n tempo m; (epoch: often pl) epoca, tempo; (by clock) ora; (moment) momento; (occasion) volta; (Mus) tempo ▶ vt (race) cronometrare; (programme) calcolare la durata di; (fix moment for) programmare; (remark etc) dire (or fare) al momento giusto; **a long ~** molto tempo; **what ~ does the museum/shop open?** a che ora apre il museo/negozio?; **for the ~ being** per il momento; **4 at a ~** 4 per or alla volta; **from ~ to ~** ogni tanto; **at ~s** a volte; **in ~** (soon enough) in tempo; (after some time) col tempo;

(Mus) a tempo; **in a week's ~** fra una settimana; **in no ~** in un attimo; **any ~** in qualsiasi momento; **on ~** puntualmente; **5 ~s 5** 5 volte 5, 5 per 5; **what ~ is it?** che ora è?, che ore sono?; **to have a good ~** divertirsi; **time limit** n limite m di tempo; **timely** adj opportuno(-a); **timer** n (time switch) temporizzatore m; (in kitchen) contaminuti m inv; **time-share** adj time-share apartment/villa appartamento/villa in multiproprietà; **timetable** n orario; **time zone** n fuso orario

timid ['tɪmɪd] adj timido(-a); (easily scared) pauroso(-a)

timing ['taɪmɪŋ] n (Sport) cronometraggio; (fig) scelta del momento opportuno

tin [tɪn] n stagno; also: **~ plate** latta; (container) scatola; (BRIT: can) barattolo (di latta), lattina; **tinfoil** n stagnola

tingle ['tɪŋgl] vi pizzicare

tinker ['tɪŋkə*] n; **~ with** vt fus armeggiare intorno a; cercare di riparare

tinned [tɪnd] (BRIT) adj (food) in scatola

tin opener ['-əʊpnə*] (BRIT) n apriscatole m inv

tint [tɪnt] n tinta; **tinted** adj (hair) tinto(-a); (spectacles, glass) colorato(-a)

tiny ['taɪnɪ] adj minuscolo(-a)

tip [tɪp] n (end) punta; (gratuity) mancia; (BRIT: for rubbish) immondezzaio; (advice) suggerimento ▶ vt (waiter) dare la mancia a; (tilt) inclinare; (overturn: also: **~ over**) capovolgere; (empty: also: **~ out**) scaricare; **how much should I ~?** quanto devo lasciare di mancia? ▷ **tip off** vt fare una soffiata a

tiptoe ['tɪptəʊ] n **on ~** in punta di piedi

tire ['taɪə'] n (US) = **tyre** ▶ vt stancare ▶ vi stancarsi; **tired** adj stanco(-a); **to be tired of** essere stanco o stufo di; **tire pressure** (US) n = **tyre pressure**; **tiring** adj faticoso(-a)

tissue ['tɪʃuː] n tessuto; (paper handkerchief) fazzoletto di carta; **tissue paper** n carta velina

tit [tɪt] n (bird) cinciallegra; **to give ~ for tat** rendere pan per focaccia

title ['taɪtl] n titolo

T-junction ['tiː'dʒʌŋkʃən] n incrocio a T

TM abbr = **trademark**

to
[tuː, tə] prep

1 (direction) a; **to go to France/London/school** andare in Francia/a Londra/a scuola; **to go to Paul's/the doctor's** andare da Paul/dal dottore; **the road to Edinburgh** la strada per Edimburgo; **to the left/right** a sinistra/destra

2 (as far as) (fino) a; **from here to London** da qui a Londra; **to count to 10** contare fino a 10; **from 40 to 50 people** da 40 a 50 persone

3 (with expressions of time): **a quarter to 5** le 5 meno un quarto; **it's twenty to 3** sono le 3 meno venti

4 (for, of): **the key to the front door** la chiave della porta d'ingresso; **a letter to his wife** una lettera per la moglie

5 (expressing indirect object) a; **to give sth to sb** dare qc a qn; **to talk to sb** parlare a qn; **to be a danger to sb/sth** rappresentare un pericolo per qn/qc

6 (in relation to) a; **3 goals to 2** 3 goal a 2; **30 miles to the gallon** = 11 chilometri con un litro

7 (purpose, result): **to come to sb's aid** venire in aiuto a qn; **to sentence sb to death** condannare a morte qn; **to my surprise** con mia sorpresa

▶ with vb

1 (simple infinitive): **to go/eat** etc andare/mangiare etc

2 (following another vb): **to want/try/start to do** volere/cercare di/cominciare a fare

3 (with vb omitted): **I don't want to** non voglio (farlo); **you ought to** devi (farlo)

4 (purpose, result): **I did it to help you** l'ho fatto per aiutarti

5 (equivalent to relative clause): **I have things to do** ho da fare; **the main thing is to try** la cosa più importante è provare

6 (after adjective etc): **ready to go** pronto a partire; **too old/young to ...** troppo vecchio/giovane per ...

▶ adv **to push the door to** accostare la porta

toad [təud] n rospo; **toadstool** n fungo (velenoso)

toast [təust] n (Culin) pane m tostato; (drink, speech) brindisi m inv ▶ vt (Culin) tostare; (drink to) brindare a; **a piece** or **slice of ~** una fetta di pane tostato; **toaster** n tostapane m inv

tobacco [tə'bækəu] n tabacco

toboggan [tə'bɔgən] n toboga m inv

today [tə'deɪ] adv oggi ▶ n (also fig) oggi m

toddler ['tɔdlə'] n bambino(-a) che impara a camminare

toe [təu] n dito del piede; (of shoe) punta; **to ~ the line** (fig) stare in riga, conformarsi; **toenail** n unghia del piede

toffee ['tɔfɪ] n caramella

together [tə'gɛðə'] adv insieme; (at same time) allo stesso tempo; **~ with** insieme a

toilet ['tɔɪlət] n (BRIT: lavatory) gabinetto ▶ cpd (bag, soap etc) da toletta; **where's the ~?** dov'è il bagno?; **toilet bag** n (BRIT) nécessaire m inv da toilette; **toilet paper** n carta igienica; **toiletries** npl articoli mpl da toletta; **toilet roll** n rotolo di carta igienica

token ['təʊkən] n (sign) segno; (substitute coin) gettone m; **book/ record/gift ~** (BRIT) buono-libro/ disco/regalo

Tokyo ['təʊkjəʊ] n Tokyo f

told [təʊld] pt, pp of **tell**

tolerant ['tɔlərnt] adj **~ (of)** tollerante (nei confronti di)

tolerate ['tɔləreɪt] vt sopportare; (Med, Tech) tollerare

toll [təʊl] n (tax, charge) pedaggio ▸ vi (bell) suonare; **the accident ~ on the roads** il numero delle vittime della strada; **toll call** (US) n (Tel) (telefonata) interurbana; **toll-free** (US) adj senza addebito, gratuito(-a) ▸ adv gratuitamente; **toll-free number** n numero verde

tomato [tə'mɑːtəʊ] (pl **tomatoes**) n pomodoro; **tomato sauce** n salsa di pomodoro

tomb [tuːm] n tomba; **tombstone** ['tuːmstəʊn] n pietra tombale

tomorrow [tə'mɔrəʊ] adv domani ▸ n (also fig) domani m inv; **the day after ~** dopodomani; **~ morning** domani mattina

ton [tʌn] n tonnellata; (BRIT: 1016 kg; US: 907 kg: metric 1000 kg): **~s of** (inf) un mucchio or sacco di

tone [təʊn] n tono ▸ vi (also: **~ in**) intonarsi ▸ **tone down** vt (colour, criticism, sound) attenuare

tongs [tɔŋz] npl tenaglie fpl; (for coal) molle fpl; (for hair) arricciacapelli m inv

tongue [tʌŋ] n lingua; **~ in cheek** (say, speak) ironicamente

tonic ['tɔnɪk] n (Med) tonico; (also: **~ water**) acqua tonica

tonight [tə'naɪt] adv stanotte; (this evening) stasera ▸ n questa notte; questa sera

tonne [tʌn] n (BRIT: metric ton)

tonnellata

tonsil ['tɔnsl] n tonsilla; **tonsillitis** [-'laɪtɪs] n tonsillite f

too [tuː] adv (excessively) troppo; (also) anche; (also: **~ much**) ▸ adv troppo ▸ adj troppo(-a); **~ many** troppi(-e)

took [tʊk] pt of **take**

tool [tuːl] n utensile m, attrezzo; **tool box** n cassetta f portautensili; **tool kit** n cassetta di attrezzi

tooth [tuːθ] (pl **teeth**) n (Anat, Tech) dente m; **toothache** n mal m di denti; **toothbrush** n spazzolino da denti; **toothpaste** n dentifricio; **toothpick** n stuzzicadenti m inv

top [tɔp] n (of mountain, page, ladder) cima; (of box, cupboard, table) sopra m inv, parte f superiore; (lid: of box, jar) coperchio; (: of bottle) tappo; (blouse etc) sopra m inv; (toy) trottola ▸ adj più alto(-a); (in rank) primo(-a); (best) migliore ▸ vt (exceed) superare; (be first in) essere in testa a; **on ~ of** sopra, in cima a; (in addition to) oltre a; **from ~ to bottom** da cima a fondo ▸ **top up** (US **top off**) vt riempire; (salary) integrare; **top floor** n ultimo piano; **top hat** n cilindro

topic ['tɔpɪk] n argomento; **topical** adj d'attualità

topless ['tɔplɪs] adj (bather etc) col seno scoperto

topping ['tɔpɪŋ] n (Culin) guarnizione f

topple ['tɔpl] vt rovesciare, far cadere ▸ vi cadere; traballare

torch [tɔːtʃ] n torcia; (BRIT: electric) lampadina tascabile

tore [tɔː²] pt of **tear²**

torment [n 'tɔːment, vb tɔː'ment] n tormento ▸ vt tormentare

torn [tɔːn] pp of **tear²**

tornado [tɔː'neɪdəʊ] (pl **tornadoes**) n tornado

torpedo [tɔː'piːdəʊ] (pl **torpedoes**) n siluro

torrent ['tɔrnt] n torrente m;
torrential [tɔ'rɛnʃl] adj torrenziale
tortoise ['tɔːtəs] n tartaruga
torture ['tɔːtʃə'] n tortura ▸ vt
torturare
Tory ['tɔːrɪ] (BRIT: Pol) adj dei tories,
conservatore(-trice) ▸ n tory m/f inv,
conservatore(-trice)
toss [tɔs] vt gettare, lanciare; (one's
head) scuotere; **to ~ a coin** fare a testa
o croce; **to ~ up for sth** fare a testa
o croce per qc; **to ~ and turn** (in bed)
girarsi e rigirarsi
total ['təutl] adj totale ▸ n totale m
▸ vt (add up) sommare; (amount to)
ammontare a
totalitarian [təutælɪ'tɛərɪən] adj
totalitario(-a)
totally ['təutəlɪ] adv completamente
touch [tʌtʃ] n tocco; (sense) tatto;
(contact) contatto ▸ vt toccare; **a ~
of** (fig) un tocco di; un pizzico di; **to
get in ~ with** mettersi in contatto
con; **to lose ~** (friends) perdersi di
vista ▷ **touch down** vi (on land)
atterrare; **touchdown** n atterraggio;
(on sea) ammaraggio; (US: Football)
meta; **touched** adj commosso(-a);
touching adj commovente;
touchline n (Sport) linea laterale;
touch-sensitive adj sensibile al tatto
tough [tʌf] adj duro(-a); (resistant)
resistente
tour ['tuə'] n viaggio; (also: **package
~**) viaggio organizzato o tutto
compreso; (of town, museum) visita;
(by artist) tournée f inv ▸ vt visitare;
tour guide n guida turistica
tourism ['tuərɪzəm] n turismo
tourist ['tuərɪst] n turista m/f ▸ adv
(travel) in classe turistica ▸ cpd
turistico(-a); **tourist office** n pro
loco f inv
tournament ['tuənəmənt] n torneo
tour operator n (BRIT) operatore m

turistico
tow [təu] vt rimorchiare; **"on ~"** (BRIT),
"in ~" (US) "veicolo rimorchiato"
▷ **tow away** vt rimorchiare
toward(s) [tə'wɔːd(z)] prep verso;
(of attitude) nei confronti di; (of
purpose) per
towel ['tauəl] n asciugamano; (also:
tea ~) strofinaccio; **towelling** n
(fabric) spugna
tower ['tauə'] n torre f; **tower block**
(BRIT) n palazzone m
town [taun] n città f inv; **to go to ~**
andare in città; (fig) mettercela tutta;
town centre n centro (città); **town
hall** n ~ municipio
tow truck (US) n carro m, attrezzi inv
toxic ['tɔksɪk] adj tossico(-a)
toy [tɔɪ] n giocattolo ▸ **toy with** vt
fus giocare con; (idea) accarezzare,
trastullarsi con; **toyshop** n negozio
di giocattoli
trace [treɪs] n traccia ▸ vt (draw)
tracciare; (follow) seguire; (locate)
rintracciare
track [træk] n (of person, animal)
traccia; (on tape, Sport, path: gen) pista;
(: of bullet etc) traiettoria;
(: of suspect, animal) pista, tracce fpl;
(Rail) binario, rotaie fpl ▸ vt seguire le
tracce di; **to keep ~ of** seguire ▷ **track
down** vt (prey) scovare; snidare; (sth
lost) rintracciare; **tracksuit** n tuta
sportiva
tractor ['træktə'] n trattore m
trade [treɪd] n commercio; (skill, job)
mestiere m ▸ vi commerciare ▸ vt **to
~ sth** (for sth) barattare qc (con qc);
to ~ with/in commerciare con/in
▷ **trade in** vt (old car etc) dare come
pagamento parziale; **trademark** n
marchio di fabbrica; **trader** n
commerciante m/f; **tradesman** (irreg)
n fornitore m; (shopkeeper) negoziante
m; **trade union** n sindacato

trading ['treɪdɪŋ] n commercio
tradition [trə'dɪʃən] n tradizione f;
traditional adj tradizionale
traffic ['træfɪk] n traffico ▶ vi to ~
in (pej: liquor, drugs) trafficare in;
traffic circle n (US) isola rotatoria;
traffic island n salvagente m, isola
f, spartitraffico inv; **traffic jam** n
ingorgo (del traffico); **traffic lights**
npl semaforo; **traffic warden** n
addetto(-a) al controllo del traffico e
del parcheggio
tragedy ['trædʒədɪ] n tragedia
tragic ['trædʒɪk] adj tragico(-a)
trail [treɪl] n (tracks) tracce fpl,
pista; (path) sentiero; (of smoke etc)
scia ▶ vt trascinare, strascicare;
(follow) seguire ▶ vi essere al
traino; (dress etc) strusciare; (plant)
arrampicarsi; strisciare; (in game)
essere in svantaggio; **trailer** n (Aut)
rimorchio; (US) roulotte f inv; (Cinema)
prossimamente m inv
train [treɪn] n treno; (of dress) coda,
strascico ▶ vt (apprentice, doctor etc)
formare; (sportsman) allenare; (dog)
addestrare; (memory) esercitare;
(point: gun etc): **to ~ sth on** puntare
qc contro ▶ vi formarsi; allenarsi;
**what time does the ~ from Rome
get in?** a che ora arriva il treno da
Roma?; **is this the ~ for ...?** è questo
il treno per...?; **one's ~ of thought**
il filo dei propri pensieri; **trainee**
[treɪ'niː] n (in trade) apprendista m/f;
trainer n (Sport) allenatore(-trice);
(: shoe) scarpa da ginnastica; (of
dogs etc) addestratore(-trice);
trainers npl (shoes) scarpe fpl da
ginnastica; **training** n formazione
f; allenamento; addestramento;
in training (Sport) in allenamento;
training course n corso di
formazione professionale; **training
shoes** npl scarpe fpl da ginnastica

trait [treɪt] n tratto
traitor ['treɪtə*] n traditore m
tram [træm] (BRIT) n (also: ~ car)
tram m inv
tramp [træmp] n (person)
vagabondo(-a); (inf: pej: woman)
squaldrina
trample ['træmpl] vt **to ~ (underfoot)**
calpestare
trampoline ['træmpəlɪn] n
trampolino
tranquil ['træŋkwɪl] adj
tranquillo(-a); **tranquillizer** (US
tranquilizer) n (Med) tranquillante m
transaction [træn'zækʃən] n
transazione f
transatlantic ['trænzət'læntɪk] adj
transatlantico(-a)
transcript ['trænskrɪpt] n
trascrizione f
transfer [n 'trænsfə*, vb træns'fə*]
n (gen: also Sport) trasferimento; (of
Pol: of power) passaggio; (picture,
design) decalcomania; (: stick-on)
autoadesivo ▶ vt trasferire; passare;
to ~ the charges (BRIT: Tel) fare una
chiamata a carico del destinatario
transform [træns'fɔːm] vt
trasformare; **transformation** n
trasformazione f
transfusion [træns'fjuːʒən] n
trasfusione f
transit ['trænzɪt] n **in ~** in transito
transition [træn'zɪʃən] n passaggio,
transizione f
transitive ['trænzɪtɪv] adj (Ling)
transitivo(-a)
translate [trænz'leɪt] vt tradurre;
can you ~ this for me? me lo può
tradurre?; **translation** [-'leɪʃən]
n traduzione f; **translator** n
traduttore(-trice)
transmission [trænz'mɪʃən] n
trasmissione f
transmit [trænz'mɪt] vt trasmettere;

transmitter n trasmettitore m
transparent [træns'pærnt] adj
trasparente
transplant [vb træns'plɑːnt, n
'trænsplɑːnt] vt trapiantare ▶ n (Med)
trapianto
transport [n 'trænspɔːt, vb træns'pɔː
t] n trasporto ▶ vt trasportare;
transportation [-'teɪʃən] n (mezzo
di) trasporto
transvestite [trænz'vɛstaɪt] n
travestito(-a)
trap [træp] n (snare, trick) trappola;
(carriage) calesse m ▶ vt prendere in
trappola, intrappolare
trash [træʃ] (pej) n (goods) ciarpame m;
(nonsense) sciocchezze fpl; **trash can**
(US) n secchio della spazzatura
trauma ['trɔːmə] n trauma
m; **traumatic** [-'mætɪk] adj
traumatico(-a)
travel ['trævl] n viaggio; viaggi mpl ▶ vi
viaggiare ▶ vt (distance) percorrere;
travel agency n agenzia (di) viaggi;
travel agent n agente m di viaggio;
travel insurance n assicurazione f
di viaggio; **traveller** (US **traveler**)
n viaggiatore(-trice); **traveller's
cheque** (US **traveler's check**) n
assegno turistico; **travelling** (US
traveling) n viaggi mpl; **travel-sick**
adj to get **travel-sick** (in vehicle)
soffrire di mal d'auto; (in aeroplane)
soffrire di mal d'aria; (in boat) soffrire
di mal di mare; **travel sickness** n mal
m d'auto (or di mare or d'aria)
tray [treɪ] n (for carrying) vassoio; (on
desk) vaschetta
treacherous ['trɛtʃərəs] adj infido(-a)
treacle ['triːkl] n melassa
tread [trɛd] (pt **trod**, pp **trodden**) n
passo; (sound) rumore m di passi; (of
stairs) pedata; (of tyre) battistrada m
inv ▶ vi camminare ▷ **tread on** vt fus
calpestare

treasure ['trɛʒə'] n tesoro ▶ vt (value)
tenere in gran conto, apprezzare
molto; (store) custodire gelosamente;
treasurer ['trɛʒərə'] n tesoriere(-a)
treasury ['trɛʒərɪ] n **the T~** (BRIT),
the T~ Department (US) il ministero
del Tesoro
treat [triːt] n regalo ▶ vt trattare;
(Med) curare; **to ~ sb to sth** offrire
qc a qn; **treatment** ['triːtmənt] n
trattamento
treaty ['triːtɪ] n patto, trattato
treble ['trɛbl] adj triplo(-a), triplice ▶ vt
triplicare ▶ vi triplicarsi
tree [triː] n albero
trek [trɛk] n escursione f a piedi;
escursione f in macchina; (tiring walk)
camminata sfiancante ▶ vi (as holiday)
fare dell'escursionismo
tremble ['trɛmbl] vi tremare
tremendous [trɪ'mɛndəs] adj
(enormous) enorme; (excellent)
fantastico(-a), strepitoso(-a)

> Be careful not to translate
> **tremendous** by the Italian word
> *tremendo*.

trench [trɛntʃ] n trincea
trend [trɛnd] n (tendency) tendenza; (of
events) corso; (fashion) moda; **trendy**
adj (idea) di moda; (clothes) all'ultima
moda
trespass ['trɛspəs] vi **to ~ on**
entrare abusivamente in; **"no ~ing"**
"proprietà privata", "vietato l'accesso"
trial ['traɪəl] n (Law) processo; (test:
of machine etc) collaudo; **on ~** (Law)
sotto processo; **trial period** n periodo
di prova
triangle ['traɪæŋgl] n (Math, Mus)
triangolo
triangular [traɪ'æŋgjulə'] adj
triangolare
tribe [traɪb] n tribù f inv
tribunal [traɪ'bjuːnl] n tribunale m
tribute ['trɪbjuːt] n tributo, omaggio;

to pay - **to** rendere omaggio a

trick [trɪk] n trucco; (joke) tiro; (Cards) presa ▸ vt imbrogliare, ingannare; **to play a ~ on sb** giocare un tiro a qn; **that should do the ~** vedrai che funziona

trickle ['trɪkl] n (of water etc) rivolo; gocciolio ▸ vi gocciolare

tricky ['trɪkɪ] adj difficile, delicato(-a)

tricycle ['traɪsɪkl] n triciclo

trifle ['traɪfl] n sciocchezza; (BRIT: Culin) ≈ zuppa inglese ▸ adv a ~ **long** un po' lungo

trigger ['trɪgə*] n (of gun) grilletto

trim [trɪm] adj (house, garden) ben tenuto(-a); (figure) snello(-a) ▸ n (haircut etc) spuntata, regolata; (embellishment) finiture fpl; (on car) guarnizioni fpl ▸ vt spuntare; (decorate): **to ~ (with)** decorare (con); (Naut: a sail) orientare

trio ['triːəu] n trio

trip [trɪp] n viaggio; (excursion) gita, escursione f; (stumble) passo falso ▸ vi inciampare; (go lightly) camminare con passo leggero; **on a ~** in viaggio ▸ **trip up** vi inciampare ▸ vt fare lo sgambetto a

triple ['trɪpl] adj triplo(-a)

triplets ['trɪplɪts] npl bambini(-e) trigemini(-e)

tripod ['traɪpɔd] n treppiede m

triumph ['traɪʌmf] n trionfo ▸ vi **to ~ (over)** trionfare (su); **triumphant** [traɪ'ʌmfənt] adj trionfante

trivial ['trɪvɪəl] adj insignificante; (commonplace) banale

> Be careful not to translate **trivial** by the Italian word **triviale**.

trod [trɔd] pt of **tread**

trodden ['trɔdn] pp of **tread**

trolley ['trɔlɪ] n carrello

trombone [trɔm'bəun] n trombone m

troop [truːp] n gruppo; (Mil) squadrone m; ~s npl (Mil) truppe fpl

trophy ['trəufɪ] n trofeo

tropical ['trɔpɪkl] adj tropicale

trot [trɔt] n trotto ▸ vi trottare; **on the ~** (BRIT: fig) di fila, uno(-a) dopo l'altro(-a)

trouble ['trʌbl] n difficoltà f inv, problema m; difficoltà fpl; problemi; (worry) preoccupazione f; (bother, effort) sforzo; (Pol) conflitti mpl, disordine m; (Med): **stomach** etc ~ disturbi mpl gastrici etc ▸ vt disturbare; (worry) preoccupare ▸ vi **to ~ to do** disturbarsi a; ~s npl (Pol etc) disordini mpl; **to be in ~** avere dei problemi; **it's no ~!** di niente!; **what's the ~?** cosa c'è che non va?; **I'm sorry to ~ you** scusi il disturbo; **troubled** adj (person) preoccupato(-a), inquieto(-a); (epoch, life) agitato(-a), difficile; **troublemaker** n elemento disturbatore, agitatore(-trice); (child) discolo(-a); **troublesome** adj fastidioso(-a), seccante

trough [trɔf] n (drinking trough) abbeveratoio; (also: **feeding ~**) trogolo, mangiatoia; (channel) canale m

trousers ['trauzəz] npl pantaloni mpl, calzoni mpl; **short ~** calzoncini mpl

trout [traut] n inv trota

trowel ['trauəl] n cazzuola

truant ['truənt] (BRIT) n **to play ~** marinare la scuola

truce [truːs] n tregua

truck [trʌk] n autocarro, camion m inv; (Rail) carro merci aperto; (for luggage) carrello m portabagagli inv; **truck driver** n camionista m/f

true [truː] adj vero(-a); (accurate) accurato(-a), esatto(-a); (genuine) reale; (faithful) fedele; **to come ~** avverarsi

truly ['truːlɪ] adv veramente; (truthfully) sinceramente; (faithfully): **yours ~** (in letter) distinti saluti

trumpet ['trʌmpɪt] n tromba

trunk [trʌŋk] n (of tree, person) tronco; (of elephant) proboscide f; (case) baule m; (US: Aut) bagagliaio; **~s** (also: **swimming ~s**) calzoncini mpl da bagno

trust [trʌst] n fiducia; (Law) amministrazione f fiduciaria; (Comm) trust m inv ▶ vt (rely on) contare su; (hope) sperare; (entrust): **to ~ sth to sb** affidare qc a qn; **trusted** adj fidato(-a), **trustworthy** adj fidato(-a), degno(-a) di fiducia

truth [tru:θ, pl tru:ðz] n verità f inv; **truthful** adj (person) sincero(-a); (description) veritiero(-a), esatto(-a)

try [traɪ] n prova, tentativo; (Rugby) meta ▶ vt (Law) giudicare; (test: also: **~ out**) provare; (strain) mettere alla prova ▶ vi provare; (attempt): **to ~ to do** (seek) cercare di fare ▷ **try on** vt (clothes) provare; **trying** adj (day, experience) logorante, pesante; (child) difficile, insopportabile

T-shirt ['ti:ʃə:t] n maglietta

tub [tʌb] n tinozza; mastello; (bath) bagno

tube [tju:b] n tubo; (BRIT: underground) metropolitana, metrò m inv; (for tyre) camera d'aria

tuberculosis [tjubə:kju'ləʊsɪs] n tubercolosi f inv

tube station (BRIT) n stazione f della metropolitana

tuck [tʌk] vt (put) mettere ▷ **tuck away** vt riporre; (building): **to be ~ed away** essere in un luogo isolato ▷ **tuck in** vt mettere dentro; (child) rimboccare ▶ vi (eat) mangiare di buon appetito; abbuffarsi; **tuck shop** n negozio di pasticceria (in una scuola)

Tue(s). abbr (= Tuesday) mar

Tuesday ['tju:zdɪ] n martedì m inv

tuft [tʌft] n ciuffo

tug [tʌg] n (ship) rimorchiatore m ▶ vt

tirare con forza

tuition [tju:'ɪʃən] n (BRIT) lezioni fpl; (: private tuition) lezioni fpl private; (US: school fees) tasse fpl scolastiche

tulip ['tju:lɪp] n tulipano

tumble ['tʌmbl] n (fall) capitombolo ▶ vi capitombolare, ruzzolare; **to ~ to sth** (inf) realizzare qc; **tumble dryer** (BRIT) n asciugatrice f

tumbler ['tʌmblə'] n bicchiere m (senza stelo)

tummy ['tʌmɪ] (inf) n pancia

tumour ['tju:mə'] (US **tumor**) n tumore m

tuna ['tju:nə] n (pl inv also: **~ fish**) tonno

tune [tju:n] n (melody) melodia, aria ▶ vt (Mus) accordare; (Radio, TV, Aut) regolare, mettere a punto; **to be in/out of ~** (instrument) essere accordato(-a)/scordato(-a); (singer) essere intonato(-a)/stonato(-a) ▷ **tune in** vi (Radio, TV) sintonizzarsi (su) ▷ **tune up** vi (musician) accordare lo strumento

tunic ['tju:nɪk] n tunica

Tunisia [tju:'nɪzɪə] n Tunisia

tunnel ['tʌnl] n galleria ▶ vi scavare una galleria

turbulence ['tə:bjʊləns] n (Aviat) turbolenza

turf [tə:f] n terreno erboso; (clod) zolla ▶ vt coprire di zolle erbose

Turin [tjʊə'rɪn] n Torino f

Turk [tə:k] n turco(-a)

Turkey ['tə:kɪ] n Turchia

turkey ['tə:kɪ] n tacchino

Turkish ['tə:kɪʃ] adj turco(-a) ▶ n (Ling) turco

turmoil ['tə:mɔɪl] n confusione f, tumulto

turn [tə:n] n giro; (change) cambiamento; (in road) curva; (tendency: of mind, events) tendenza; (performance) numero; (chance) turno; (Med) crisi f inv, attacco ▶ vt girare, voltare; (change): **to ~ sth into** trasformare qc in ▶ vi girare; (person: look back) girarsi, voltarsi; (reverse direction) girare; (change) cambiare; (milk) andare a male; (become) diventare; **a good ~** un buon servizio; **it gave me quite a ~** mi ha fatto prendere un bello spavento; **"no left ~"** (Aut) "divieto di svolta a sinistra"; **it's your ~** tocca a lei; **in ~** a sua volta; a turno; **to take ~s (at sth)** fare (qc) a turno; **~ left/right at the next junction** al prossimo incrocio, giri a sinistra/destra ▶ **turn around** vi (person) girarsi; (rotate) girare ▶ vt (object) girare ▶ **turn away** vi girarsi (dall'altra parte) ▶ vt mandare via ▶ **turn back** vi ritornare, tornare indietro ▶ vt far tornare indietro; (clock) spostare indietro ▶ **turn down** vt (refuse) rifiutare; (reduce) abbassare; (fold) ripiegare ▶ **turn in** vi (inf: go to bed) andare a letto ▶ vt (fold) voltare in dentro ▶ **turn off** vi (from road) girare, voltare ▶ vt (light, radio, engine etc) spegnere; **I can't ~ the heating off** non riesco a spegnere il riscaldamento ▶ **turn on** vt (light, radio etc) accendere; **I can't ~ the heating on** non riesco ad accendere il riscaldamento ▶ **turn out** vt (light, gas) chiudere; spegnere ▶ vi (voters) presentarsi; **to ~ out to be ...** rivelarsi ..., risultare ... ▶ **turn over** vi (person) girarsi ▶ vt girare ▶ **turn round** vi girarsi; (person) girare ▶ vt (wheel) far rus **to ~** girarsi verso qn; **to ~ to sb for help** rivolgersi a qn per aiuto ▶ **turn up** vi (person) arrivare, presentarsi; (lost object) saltar fuori ▶ vt (collar, sound) alzare; **turning** n (in road) curva; **turning point** n (fig) svolta decisiva

turnip ['tə:nɪp] n rapa

turn: **turnout** ['tə:naut] n presenza,

affluenza; **turnover** ['tə:nəuvə'] n (Comm) turnover m inv; (Culin): **apple etc turnover** sfogliatella alle melle ecc; **turnstile** ['tə:nstaɪl] n tornella; **turn-up** (BRIT) n (on trousers) risvolto

turquoise ['tə:kwɔːz] n turchese m ▶ adj turchese

turtle ['tə:tl] n testuggine f; **turtleneck (sweater)** ['tə:tlnɛk-] n maglione m con il collo alto

Tuscany ['tʌskənɪ] n Toscana

tusk [tʌsk] n zanna

tutor ['tju:tə'] n (in college) docente m/f (responsabile di un gruppo di studenti); (private teacher) precettore m; **tutorial** [-'tɔ:rɪəl] n (Scol) lezione f con discussione (a un gruppo limitato)

tuxedo [tʌk'si:dəu] (US) n smoking m inv

TV [ti:'vi:] n abbr (= television) tivù f inv

tweed [twi:d] n tweed m inv

tweezers ['twi:zəz] npl pinzette fpl

twelfth [twɛlfθ] num dodicesimo(-a)

twelve [twɛlv] num dodici; **at ~ o'clock** alle dodici, a mezzogiorno; (midnight) a mezzanotte

twentieth ['twɛntɪɪθ] num ventesimo(-a)

twenty ['twɛntɪ] num venti

twice [twaɪs] adv due volte; **~ as much** due volte tanto; **~ a week** due volte alla settimana

twig [twɪg] n ramoscello ▶ vt, vi (inf) capire

twilight ['twaɪlaɪt] n crepuscolo

twin [twɪn] adj, n gemello(-a) ▶ vt **to ~ one town with another** fare il gemellaggio di una città con un'altra; **twin(-bedded) room** n stanza con letti gemelli; **twin beds** npl letti m mpl gemelli

twinkle ['twɪŋkl] vi scintillare; (eyes) brillare

twist [twɪst] n torsione f; (in wire, flex) piega; (in road) curva; (in story) colpo di scena ▶ vt attorcigliare; (ankle) slogare; (weave) intrecciare; (roll around) arrotolare; (fig) distorcere ▶ vi (road) serpeggiare

twit [twɪt] (inf) n cretino(-a)

twitch [twɪtʃ] n tiratina; (nervous) tic m inv ▶ vi contrarsi

two [tu:] num due; **to put ~ and ~ together** (fig) fare uno più uno

type [taɪp] n (category) genere m; (model) modello; (example) tipo; (Typ) tipo, carattere m ▶ vt (letter etc) battere (a macchina), dattilografare; **typewriter** n macchina da scrivere

typhoid ['taɪfɔɪd] n tifoidea

typhoon [taɪ'fu:n] n tifone m

typical ['tɪpɪkl] adj tipico(-a); **typically** adv tipicamente; **typically, he arrived late** come al solito è arrivato tardi

typing ['taɪpɪŋ] n dattilografia

typist ['taɪpɪst] n dattilografo(-a)

tyre ['taɪə'] (US **tire**) n pneumatico, gomma; **I've got a flat ~** ho una gomma a terra; **tyre pressure** n pressione f (delle gomme)

u

UFO ['ju:fəʊ] n abbr (= unidentified flying object) UFO m inv

Uganda [ju:'gændə] n Uganda

ugly ['ʌglɪ] adj brutto(-a)

UHT abbr (= ultra heat treated) UHT inv, a lunga conservazione

UK n abbr = **United Kingdom**

ulcer ['ʌlsə'] n ulcera; (also: **mouth ~**) afta

ultimate ['ʌltɪmət] adj ultimo(-a), finale; (authority) massimo(-a), supremo(-a); **ultimately** adv alla fine; in definitiva, in fin dei conti

ultimatum [ʌltɪ'meɪtəm, -tə] (pl **ultimatums** or **ultimata**) n ultimatum m inv

ultrasound ['ʌltrəsaʊnd] n (Med) ultrasuono

ultraviolet ['ʌltrə'vaɪəlɪt] adj ultravioletto(-a)

umbrella [ʌm'brelə] n ombrello

umpire ['ʌmpaɪə'] n arbitro

UN n abbr (= United Nations) ONU f

unable [ʌn'eɪbl] adj **to be ~ to** non potere, essere nell'impossibilità di; essere incapace di

unacceptable [ʌnək'sɛptəbl] adj (proposal, behaviour) inaccettabile; (price) impossibile

unanimous [ju:'nænɪməs] adj unanime

unarmed [ʌn'ɑ:md] adj (without a weapon) disarmato(-a); (combat) senz'armi

unattended [ʌnə'tɛndɪd] adj (car, child, luggage) incustodito(-a)

unattractive [ʌnə'træktɪv] adj poco attraente

unavailable [ʌnə'veɪləbl] adj (article, room, book) non disponibile; (person) impegnato(-a)

unavoidable [ʌnə'vɔɪdəbl] adj inevitabile

unaware [ʌnə'wɛə'] adj **to be ~ of** non sapere, ignorare; **unawares** adv di sorpresa, alla sprovvista

unbearable [ʌn'bɛərəbl] adj insopportabile

unbeatable [ʌn'bi:təbl] adj

imbattibile

unbelievable [ʌnbɪ'liːvəbl] *adj* incredibile

unborn [ʌn'bɔːn] *adj* non ancora nato(-a)

unbutton [ʌn'bʌtn] *vt* sbottonare

uncalled-for [ʌn'kɔːldfɔːʳ] *adj* (remark) fuori luogo *inv*; (action) ingiustificato(-a)

uncanny [ʌn'kænɪ] *adj* misterioso(-a), strano(-a)

uncertain [ʌn'sɜːtn] *adj* incerto(-a), dubbio(-a); **uncertainty** *n* incertezza

unchanged [ʌn'tʃeɪndʒd] *adj* invariato(-a)

uncle ['ʌŋkl] *n* zio

unclear [ʌn'klɪəʳ] *adj* non chiaro(-a); **I'm still ~ about what I'm supposed to do** non ho ancora ben capito cosa dovrei fare

uncomfortable [ʌn'kʌmfətəbl] *adj* scomodo(-a); (uneasy) a disagio, agitato(-a); (unpleasant) fastidioso(-a)

uncommon [ʌn'kɔmən] *adj* raro(-a), insolito(-a), non comune

unconditional [ʌnkən'dɪʃənl] *adj* incondizionato(-a), senza condizioni

unconscious [ʌn'kɔnʃəs] *adj* privo(-a) di sensi, svenuto(-a); (unaware) inconsapevole, inconscio(-a) ▸ **n** the **~** l'inconscio

uncontrollable [ʌnkən'trəuləbl] *adj* incontrollabile; indisciplinato(-a)

unconventional [ʌnkən'venʃənl] *adj* poco convenzionale

uncover [ʌn'kʌvəʳ] *vt* scoprire

undecided [ʌndɪ'saɪdɪd] *adj* indeciso(-a)

undeniable [ʌndɪ'naɪəbl] *adj* innegabile, indiscutibile

under ['ʌndəʳ] *prep* sotto; (less than) meno di; al disotto di; (according to) secondo, in conformità a ▸ *adv* (al) disotto; **~ there** là sotto; **~ repair** in riparazione; **undercover**

adj segreto(-a), clandestino(-a);

underdone *adj* (Culin) al sangue; (pej) poco cotto(-a); **underestimate** *vt* sottovalutare; **undergo** *vt* (irreg) subire; (treatment) sottoporsi a;

undergraduate *n* studente(-essa) universitario(-a); **underground** *n* (BRIT: railway) metropolitana; (Pol) movimento clandestino ▸ *adj* sotterraneo(-a); (fig) clandestino(-a) ▸ *adv* sottoterra; **to go underground** (fig) darsi alla macchia;

undergrowth *n* sottobosco;

underline *vt* sottolineare;

undermine *vt* minare; **underneath** [ʌndə'niːθ] *adv* sotto, disotto ▸ *prep* sotto, al di sotto di; **underpants** *npl* mutande *fpl*, slip *m inv*;

underpass (BRIT) *n* sottopassaggio;

underprivileged *adj* non abbiente, meno favorito(-a); **underscore** *vt* sottolineare; **undershirt** (US) *n* maglietta; **underskirt** (BRIT) *n* sottoveste f

understand [ʌndə'stænd] (irreg: like **stand**) *vt, vi* capire, comprendere; **I don't ~** non capisco; **I ~ that ...** sento che ...; credo di capire che ...; **understandable** *adj* comprensibile; **understanding** *adj* comprensivo(-a) ▸ *n* comprensione f; (agreement) accordo

understatement [ʌndə'steɪtmənt] *n* that's an **~**! a dire poco!

understood [ʌndə'stud] *pt, pp of* **understand** ▸ *adj* inteso(-a); (implied) sottinteso(-a)

undertake [ʌndə'teɪk] (irreg: like **take**) *vt* intraprendere; **to ~ to do sth** impegnarsi a fare qc

undertaker [ʌndə'teɪkəʳ] *n* impresario di pompe funebri

undertaking [ʌndə'teɪkɪŋ] *n* impresa; (promise) promessa

under: **underwater** [ʌndə'wɔːtəʳ]

adv sott'acqua ▸ adj subacqueo(-a);
underway [ʌndə'weɪ] adj to
be **underway** essere in corso;
underwear ['ʌndəweəʳ] n biancheria
(intima); **underwent** [ʌndə'wɛnt] vb
see **undergo**; **underworld**
['ʌndəwə:ld] n (of crime) malavita
undesirable [ʌndɪ'zaɪərəbl] adj
sgradevole
undisputed [ʌndɪs'pju:tɪd] adj
indiscusso(-a)
undo [ʌn'du:] vt (irreg) disfare
undone [ʌn'dʌn] pp of **undo**; to come
~ slacciarsi
undoubtedly [ʌn'dautɪdlɪ] adv senza
alcun dubbio
undress [ʌn'drɛs] vi spogliarsi
unearth [ʌn'ə:θ] vt dissotterrare;
(fig) scoprire
uneasy [ʌn'i:zɪ] adj a disagio; (worried)
preoccupato(-a); (peace) precario(-a)
unemployed [ʌnɪm'plɔɪd] adj
disoccupato(-a) ▸ npl the ~ i
disoccupati
unemployment [ʌnɪm'plɔɪmənt] n
disoccupazione f; **unemployment
benefit** (US **unemployment
compensation**) n sussidio di
disoccupazione
unequal [ʌn'i:kwəl] adj (length, objects)
disuguale; (amounts) diverso(-a);
(division of labour) ineguale
uneven [ʌn'i:vn] adj ineguale;
irregolare
unexpected [ʌnɪk'spɛktɪd] adj
inatteso(-a), imprevisto(-a);
unexpectedly adv inaspettatamente
unfair [ʌn'fɛəʳ] adj ~ (to) ingiusto(-a)
(nei confronti di)
unfaithful [ʌn'feɪθful] adj infedele
unfamiliar [ʌnfə'mɪlɪəʳ] adj
sconosciuto(-a), strano(-a); to be ~
with non avere familiarità con
unfashionable [ʌn'fæʃnəbl] adj
(clothes) fuori moda; (district) non

alla moda
unfasten [ʌn'fɑ:sn] vt slacciare;
sciogliere
unfavourable [ʌn'feɪvərəbl] (US
unfavorable) adj sfavorevole
unfinished [ʌn'fɪnɪʃt] adj
incompleto(-a)
unfit [ʌn'fɪt] adj (ill) malato(-a), in
cattiva salute; (incompetent): ~ (for)
incompetente (in); (: work, Mil)
inabile a
unfold [ʌn'fəuld] vt spiegare ▸ vi
(story, plot) svelarsi
unforgettable [ʌnfə'gɛtəbl] adj
indimenticabile
unfortunate [ʌn'fɔ:tʃnət] adj
sfortunato(-a); (event, remark) infelice;
unfortunately adv sfortunatamente,
purtroppo
unfriendly [ʌn'frɛndlɪ] adj poco
amichevole, freddo(-a)
unfurnished [ʌn'fə:nɪʃt] adj non
ammobiliato(-a)
unhappiness [ʌn'hæpɪnɪs] n
infelicità
unhappy [ʌn'hæpɪ] adj infelice;
~ about/with (arrangements etc)
insoddisfatto(-a) di
unhealthy [ʌn'hɛlθɪ] adj (gen)
malsano(-a); (person) malaticcio(-a)
unheard-of [ʌn'hə:dɔv] adj
inaudito(-a), senza precedenti
unhelpful [ʌn'hɛlpful] adj poco
disponibile
unhurt [ʌn'hə:t] adj illeso(-a)
unidentified [ʌnaɪ'dɛntɪfaɪd] adj non
identificato(-a)
uniform ['ju:nɪfɔ:m] n uniforme f,
divisa ▸ adj uniforme
unify ['ju:nɪfaɪ] vt unificare
unimportant [ʌnɪm'pɔ:tənt]
adj senza importanza, di scarsa
importanza
uninhabited [ʌnɪn'hæbɪtɪd] adj
disabitato(-a)

unintentional [ʌnɪn'tɛnʃənəl] adj involontario(-a)

union ['ju:njən] n unione f; (also: **trade ~**) sindacato ▸ cpd sindacale, dei sindacati; **Union Jack** n bandiera nazionale britannica

unique [ju:'ni:k] adj unico(-a)

unisex ['ju:nɪsɛks] adj unisex inv

unit ['ju:nɪt] n unità f inv; (section: of furniture etc) elemento; (team, squad) reparto, squadra

unite [ju:'naɪt] vt unire ▸ vi unirsi; **united** adj unito(-a); unificato(-a); (efforts) congiunto(-a); **United Kingdom** n Regno Unito; **United Nations (Organization)** n (Organizzazione f delle) Nazioni Unite; **United States (of America)** n Stati mpl Uniti (d'America)

unity ['ju:nɪti] n unità f

universal [ju:nɪ'vɜ:sl] adj universale

universe ['ju:nɪvɜ:s] n universo

university [ju:nɪ'vɜ:sɪti] n università f inv

unjust [ʌn'dʒʌst] adj ingiusto(-a)

unkind [ʌn'kaɪnd] adj scortese; crudele

unknown [ʌn'nəʊn] adj sconosciuto(-a)

unlawful [ʌn'lɔ:ful] adj illecito(-a), illegale

unleaded [ʌn'lɛdɪd] adj (petrol, fuel) verde, senza piombo

unleash [ʌn'li:ʃ] vt (fig) scatenare

unless [ʌn'lɛs] conj a meno che (non) + sub

unlike [ʌn'laɪk] adj diverso(-a) ▸ prep a differenza di, contrariamente a

unlikely [ʌn'laɪklɪ] adj improbabile

unlimited [ʌn'lɪmɪtɪd] adj illimitato(-a)

unlisted [ʌn'lɪstɪd] (US) adj (Tel): **to be ~** non essere sull'elenco

unload [ʌn'ləʊd] vt scaricare

unlock [ʌn'lɔk] vt aprire

unlucky [ʌn'lʌkɪ] adj sfortunato(-a); (object, number) che porta sfortuna

unmarried [ʌn'mærɪd] adj non sposato(-a); (man only) scapolo, celibe; (woman only) nubile

unmistak(e)able [ʌnmɪs'teɪkəbl] adj inconfondibile

unnatural [ʌn'nætʃrəl] adj innaturale; contro natura

unnecessary [ʌn'nɛsəsərɪ] adj inutile, superfluo(-a)

UNO ['ju:nəʊ] n abbr (= United Nations Organization) ONU f

unofficial [ʌnə'fɪʃl] adj non ufficiale; (strike) non dichiarato(-a) dal sindacato

unpack [ʌn'pæk] vi disfare la valigia (or le valigie) ▸ vt disfare

unpaid [ʌn'peɪd] adj (holiday) non pagato(-a); (work) non retribuito(-a); (bill, debt) da pagare

unpleasant [ʌn'plɛznt] adj spiacevole

unplug [ʌn'plʌg] vt staccare

unpopular [ʌn'pɔpjʊlə] adj impopolare

unprecedented [ʌn'prɛsɪdəntɪd] adj senza precedenti

unpredictable [ʌnprɪ'dɪktəbl] adj imprevedibile

unprotected ['ʌnprə'tɛktɪd] adj (sex) non protetto(-a)

unqualified [ʌn'kwɔlɪfaɪd] adj (teacher) non abilitato(-a); (success) assoluto(-a), senza riserve

unravel [ʌn'rævl] vt dipanare, districare

unreal [ʌn'rɪəl] adj irreale

unrealistic [ʌnrɪə'lɪstɪk] adj non realistico(-a)

unreasonable [ʌn'ri:znəbl] adj irragionevole

unrelated [ʌnrɪ'leɪtɪd] adj **~ (to)** senza rapporto (con); non imparentato(-a) (con)

unreliable [ʌnrɪ'laɪəbl] adj (person,

machine) che non dà affidamento; (*news, source of information*) inattendibile

unrest [ʌnˈrɛst] n agitazione f
unroll [ʌnˈrəʊl] vt srotolare
unruly [ʌnˈruːlɪ] adj indisciplinato(-a)
unsafe [ʌnˈseɪf] adj pericoloso(-a), rischioso(-a)
unsatisfactory [ˈʌnsætɪsˈfæktərɪ] adj che lascia a desiderare, insufficiente
unscrew [ʌnˈskruː] vt svitare
unsettled [ʌnˈsɛtld] adj (*person*) turbato(-a); indeciso(-a); (*weather*) instabile
unsettling [ʌnˈsɛtlɪŋ] adj inquietante
unsightly [ʌnˈsaɪtlɪ] adj brutto(-a), sgradevole a vedersi
unskilled [ʌnˈskɪld] adj non specializzato(-a)
unspoiled [ʌnˈspɔɪld], **unspoilt** [ˈʌnˈspɔɪlt] adj (*place*) non deturpato(-a)
unstable [ʌnˈsteɪbl] adj (*gen*) instabile; (*mentally*) squilibrato(-a)
unsteady [ʌnˈstɛdɪ] adj instabile, malsicuro(-a)
unsuccessful [ˈʌnsəkˈsɛsful] adj (*writer, proposal*) che non ha successo; (*marriage, attempt*) mal riuscito(-a), fallito(-a); **to be ~** (*in attempting sth*) non avere successo
unsuitable [ʌnˈsuːtəbl] adj inadatto(-a); inopportuno(-a), sconveniente
unsure [ʌnˈʃuə] adj incerto(-a); **to be ~ of o.s** essere insicuro(-a)
untidy [ʌnˈtaɪdɪ] adj (*room*) in disordine; (*appearance*) trascurato(-a); (*person*) disordinato(-a)
untie [ʌnˈtaɪ] vt (*knot, parcel*) disfare; (*prisoner, dog*) slegare
until [ʌnˈtɪl] prep fino a ▸ (*after negative*) prima di ▸ conj finché, fino a quando, (*in past, after negative*) prima che +sub, prima di +*infinitive*; **~ he comes** finché

or fino a quando non arriva; **~ now** finora; **~ then** fino ad allora
untrue [ʌnˈtruː] adj (*statement*) falso(-a), non vero(-a)
unused [ʌnˈjuːzd] adj nuovo(-a)
unusual [ʌnˈjuːʒuəl] adj insolito(-a), eccezionale, raro(-a); **unusually** adv insolitamente
unveil [ʌnˈveɪl] vt scoprire; svelare
unwanted [ʌnˈwɒntɪd] adj (*clothing*) smesso(-a); (*child*) non desiderato(-a)
unwell [ʌnˈwɛl] adj indisposto(-a); **to feel ~** non sentirsi bene
unwilling [ʌnˈwɪlɪŋ] adj **to be ~ to do** non voler fare
unwind [ʌnˈwaɪnd] (*irreg: like* **wind**[1]) vt svolgere, srotolare ▸ vi (*relax*) rilassarsi
unwise [ʌnˈwaɪz] adj poco saggio(-a)
unwittingly [ʌnˈwɪtɪŋlɪ] adv senza volerlo
unwrap [ʌnˈræp] vt disfare; aprire
unzip [ʌnˈzɪp] vt aprire (la chiusura lampo di); (*Comput*) dezippare

up [ʌp] prep **he went up the stairs/the hill** è salito su per le scale/sulla collina; **the cat was up a tree** il gatto era su un albero; **they live further up the street** vivono un po' più su nella stessa strada
▸ adv

1 (*upwards, higher*) su, in alto; **up in the sky/the mountains** su nel cielo/in montagna; **up there** lassù; **up above** su in alto

2 : **to be up** (*out of bed*) essere alzato(-a); (*prices, level*) essere salito(-a)

3 : **up to** (*as far as*) fino a; **up to now** finora

4 : **to be up** (*depending on*): **it's up to you** sta a lei, dipende da lei; (*equal to*): **he's not up to it** (*job, task etc*) non ne è all'altezza; (*inf: be doing*): **what is he up to?** cosa sta combinando?

▶ *n* **ups and downs** alti e bassi *mpl*
up-and-coming [ˈʌpəndˈkʌmɪŋ] *adj*
pieno(-a) di promesse, promettente
upbringing [ˈʌpbrɪŋɪŋ] *n* educazione *f*
update [ʌpˈdeɪt] *vt* aggiornare
upfront [ʌpˈfrʌnt] *adj* (*inf*) franco(-a),
aperto(-a) ▶ *adv* (*pay*) subito
upgrade [ʌpˈgreɪd] *vt* (*house, job*)
migliorare; (*employee*) avanzare di
grado
upheaval [ʌpˈhiːvl] *n*
sconvolgimento; tumulto
uphill [ʌpˈhɪl] *adj* in salita; (*fig: task*)
difficile ▶ *adv* **to go ~** andare in salita,
salire
upholstery [ʌpˈhəʊlstərɪ] *n*
tappezzeria
upmarket [ʌpˈmɑːkɪt] *adj* (*product*)
che si rivolge ad una fascia di mercato
superiore
upon [əˈpɒn] *prep* su
upper [ˈʌpəʳ] *adj* superiore ▶ *n* (*of shoe*)
tomaia; **upper-class** *adj* dell'alta
borghesia
upright [ˈʌpraɪt] *adj* diritto(-a);
verticale; (*fig*) diritto(-a), onesto(-a)
uprising [ˈʌpraɪzɪŋ] *n* insurrezione
f, rivolta
uproar [ˈʌprɔːʳ] *n* tumulto, clamore *m*
upset [*n* ˈʌpset, *vb, adj* ʌpˈset] (*irreg:
like* **set**) *n* (*to plan etc*) contrattempo;
(*stomach upset*) disturbo ▶ *vt* (*glass
etc*) rovesciare; (*plan, stomach*)
scombussolare; (*person: offend*)
contrariare; (*: grieve*) addolorare;
sconvolgere ▶ *adj* contrariato(-a),
addolorato(-a); (*stomach*)
scombussolato(-a)
upside-down [ʌpsaɪdˈdaʊn] *adv*
sottosopra
upstairs [ʌpˈsteəz] *adv, adj* di sopra, al
piano superiore ▶ *n* piano di sopra
up-to-date [ˈʌptəˈdeɪt] *adj*
moderno(-a); aggiornato(-a)
uptown [ˈʌptaʊn] (*US*) *adv* verso

i quartieri residenziali ▶ *adj* dei
quartieri residenziali
upward [ˈʌpwəd] *adj* ascendente;
verso l'alto; **upward(s)** *adv* in su,
verso l'alto
uranium [juəˈreɪnɪəm] *n* uranio
Uranus [juəˈreɪnəs] *n* (*planet*) Urano
urban [ˈəːbən] *adj* urbano(-a)
urge [əːdʒ] *n* impulso; stimolo;
forte desiderio ▶ *vt* **to ~ sb to do**
esortare qn a fare, spingere qn a fare;
raccomandare a qn di fare
urgency [ˈəːdʒənsɪ] *n* urgenza; (*of
tone*) insistenza
urgent [ˈəːdʒənt] *adj* urgente; (*voice*)
insistente
urinal [ˈjuərɪnl] *n* (*BRIT: building*)
vespasiano; (*: vessel*) orinale *m*,
pappagallo
urinate [ˈjuərɪneɪt] *vi* orinare
urine [ˈjuərɪn] *n* orina
us [ʌs] *pron* ci; (*stressed, after prep*) noi;
see also **me**
US(A) *n abbr* (= *United States (of
America)*) USA *mpl*
use [*n* juːs, *vb* juːz] *n* uso; impiego,
utilizzazione *f* ▶ *vt* usare, utilizzare,
servirsi di; **in ~** in uso; **out of ~** fuori
uso; **to be of ~** essere utile, servire;
it's no ~ non serve, è inutile; **she ~d to
do it** lo faceva (una volta), era solita
farlo; **to be ~d to** essere abituato(-a)
di ▶ **use up** *vt* consumare; esaurire;
used [*adj* (*object, car*) usato(-a);
useful *adj* utile; **useless** *adj* inutile; (*person*)
inetto(-a); **user** *n* utente *m/f*; **user-
friendly** *adj* (*computer*) di facile uso
usual [ˈjuːʒuəl] *adj* solito(-a); **as ~**
come al solito, come d'abitudine;
usually *adv* di solito
utensil [juːˈtensl] *n* utensile *m*;
kitchen ~s utensili da cucina
utility [juːˈtɪlɪtɪ] *n* utilità; (*also*: **public
~**) servizio pubblico
utilize [ˈjuːtɪlaɪz] *vt* utilizzare;

sfruttare
utmost ['ʌtməʊst] adj estremo(-a)
▶ **to do one's ~** fare il possibile or
di tutto

utter ['ʌtə'] adj assoluto(-a), totale
▶ vt pronunciare, proferire; emettere;
utterly adv completamente, del tutto

U-turn ['juːˈtəːn] n inversione f a U

V

v. abbr = **verse**; **versus**; **volt**; (= vide)
vedi, vedere

vacancy ['veɪkənsɪ] n (BRIT: job)
posto libero; (room) stanza libera; "**no
vacancies**" "completo"

⚠ Be careful not to translate **vacancy**
by the Italian word **vacanza**.

vacant ['veɪkənt] adj (job, seat etc)
libero(-a); (expression) assente

vacate [vəˈkeɪt] vt lasciare libero(-a)

vacation [vəˈkeɪʃən] (esp US)
n vacanze fpl; **vacationer** (US
vacationist) n vacanziere(-a)

vaccination [væksɪˈneɪʃən] n
vaccinazione f

vaccine ['væksiːn] n vaccino

vacuum ['vækjum] n vuoto; **vacuum
cleaner** n aspirapolvere m inv

vagina [vəˈdʒaɪnə] n vagina

vague [veɪg] adj vago(-a); (blurred:
photo, memory) sfocato(-a)

vain [veɪn] adj (useless) inutile,

vano(-a); (conceited) vanitoso(-a); **in ~**
inutilmente, invano

Valentine's Day ['væləntaɪnzdeɪ] n
San Valentino m

valid ['vælɪd] adj valido(-a), valevole;
(excuse) valido(-a)

valley ['vælɪ] n valle f

valuable ['væljuəbl] adj (jewel)
di (grande) valore; (time, help)
prezioso(-a); **valuables** npl oggetti
mpl di valore

value ['væljuː] n valore m ▶ vt (fix price)
valutare, dare un prezzo a; (cherish)
apprezzare, tenere a; **~s** npl (principles)
valori mpl

valve [vælv] n valvola

vampire ['væmpaɪə'] n vampiro

van [væn] n (Aut) furgone m; (BRIT:
Rail) vagone m

vandal ['vændl] n vandalo(-a);
vandalism n vandalismo; **vandalize**
vt vandalizzare

vanilla [vəˈnɪlə] n vaniglia ▶ cpd (ice
cream) alla vaniglia

vanish ['vænɪʃ] vi svanire, scomparire

vanity ['vænɪtɪ] n vanità

vapour ['veɪpə'] (US **vapor**) n vapore m

variable ['vɛərɪəbl] adj variabile;
(mood) mutevole

variant ['vɛərɪənt] n variante f

variation [vɛərɪˈeɪʃən] n variazione f;
(in opinion) cambiamento

varied ['vɛərɪd] adj vario(-a),
diverso(-a)

variety [vəˈraɪətɪ] n varietà f inv;
(quantity) quantità, numero

various ['vɛərɪəs] adj vario(-a),
diverso(-a); (several) parecchi(-e),
molti(-e)

varnish ['vɑːnɪʃ] n vernice f, (nail
varnish) smalto ▶ vt verniciare;
mettere lo smalto su

vary ['vɛərɪ] vt, vi variare, mutare

vase [vɑːz] n vaso

Vaseline® ['væsɪliːn] n vaselina

vast [vɑːst] adj vasto(-a); (amount, success) enorme

VAT [væt] n abbr (= value added tax) I.V.A. f

Vatican ['vætɪkən] n the ~ il Vaticano

vault [vɔːlt] n (of roof) volta; (tomb) tomba; (in bank) camera blindata ▸ vt (also: ~ over) saltare (d'un balzo)

VCR n abbr = **video cassette recorder**

VDU n abbr = **visual display unit**

veal [viːl] n vitello

veer [vɪəʳ] vi girare; virare

vegan ['viːɡən] n vegetaliano(-a)

vegetable ['vedʒtəbl] n verdura, ortaggio ▸ adj vegetale

vegetarian [vedʒɪ'teərɪən] adj, n vegetariano(-a): **do you have any ~ dishes?** avete piatti vegetariani?

vegetation [vedʒɪ'teɪʃən] n vegetazione f

vehicle ['viːɪkl] n veicolo

veil [veɪl] n velo

vein [veɪn] n vena; (on leaf) nervatura

Velcro® ['vɛlkrəu] n velcro® m inv

velvet ['vɛlvɪt] n velluto ▸ adj di velluto

vending machine ['vendɪŋ-] n distributore m automatico

vendor ['vendəʳ] n venditore(-trice)

vengeance ['vendʒəns] n vendetta; **with a ~** (fig) davvero; furiosamente

Venice ['venɪs] n Venezia

venison ['venɪsn] n carne f di cervo

venom ['venəm] n veleno

vent [vent] n foro, apertura; (in dress, jacket) spacco ▸ vt (fig: one's feelings) sfogare, dare sfogo a

ventilation [ventɪ'leɪʃən] n ventilazione f

venture ['ventʃəʳ] n impresa (rischiosa) ▸ vt rischiare, azzardare ▸ vi avventurarsi; **business ~** iniziativa commerciale

venue ['venjuː] n luogo (designato) per l'incontro

Venus ['viːnəs] n (planet) Venere m

verb [vəːb] n verbo; **verbal** adj verbale; (translation) orale

verdict ['vəːdɪkt] n verdetto

verge [vəːdʒ] n (BRIT) bordo, orlo; **"soft ~s"** (BRIT: Aut) banchine fpl cedevoli; **on the ~ of doing** sul punto di fare

verify ['verɪfaɪ] vt verificare; (prove the truth of) confermare

versatile ['vəːsətaɪl] adj (person) versatile; (machine, tool etc) (che si presta) a molti usi

verse [vəːs] n versi mpl; (stanza) strofa; (in bible) versetto

version ['vəːʃən] n versione f

versus ['vəːsəs] prep contro

vertical ['vəːtɪkl] adj verticale ▸ n verticale m

very ['verɪ] adv molto ▸ adj the ~ book which proprio il libro che; **the ~ last** proprio l'ultimo; **at the ~ least** almeno; **~ much** moltissimo

vessel ['vesl] n (Anat) vaso; (Naut) nave f; (container) recipiente m

vest [vest] n (BRIT) maglia; (: sleeveless) canottiera; (US: waistcoat) gilè m inv

vet [vet] n abbr (BRIT: = veterinary surgeon) veterinario ▸ vt esaminare minuziosamente

veteran ['vetərn] n (also: war ~) veterano

veterinary surgeon ['vetrɪnərɪ-] (US **veterinarian**) n veterinario

veto ['viːtəu] (pl **vetoes**) n veto ▸ vt opporre il veto a

via ['vaɪə] prep (by way of) via; (by means of) tramite

viable ['vaɪəbl] adj attuabile; vitale

vibrate [vaɪ'breɪt] vi to ~ (with) vibrare (di); (resound) risonare (di)

vibration [vaɪ'breɪʃən] n vibrazione f

vicar ['vɪkəʳ] n pastore m

vice [vaɪs] n (evil) vizio; (Tech) morsa; **vice-chairman** (irreg) n vicepresidente m

vice versa ['vaɪsɪ'vəːsə] adv viceversa

vicinity [vɪˈsɪnɪtɪ] n vicinanze fpl
vicious [ˈvɪʃəs] adj (remark, dog) cattivo(-a); (blow) violento(-a)
victim [ˈvɪktɪm] n vittima
victor [ˈvɪktə] n vincitore m
Victorian [vɪkˈtɔːrɪən] adj vittoriano(-a)
victorious [vɪkˈtɔːrɪəs] adj vittorioso(-a)
victory [ˈvɪktərɪ] n vittoria
video [ˈvɪdɪəʊ] cpd video... ▶ n (video film) video m inv; (also: ~ cassette) videocassetta; (also: ~ cassette recorder) videoregistratore m; **video camera** n videocamera; **video (cassette) recorder** n videoregistratore m; **video game** n videogioco; **video shop** n videonoleggio; **video tape** n videotape m inv; **video wall** n schermo m multivideo inv
vie [vaɪ] vi to ~ with competere con, rivaleggiare con
Vienna [vɪˈɛnə] n Vienna
Vietnam [vjɛtˈnæm] n Vietnam m; **Vietnamese** [vjɛtnəˈmiːz] adj, n inv vietnamita m/f
view [vjuː] n vista, veduta; (opinion) opinione f ▶ vt (look at: also fig) considerare; (house) visitare; **on ~** (in museum etc) esposto(-a); **in full ~ of** sotto gli occhi di; **in ~ of the weather/the fact that** considerato il tempo/che; **in my ~** a mio parere; **viewer** n spettatore(-trice); **viewpoint** n punto di vista; (place) posizione f
vigilant [ˈvɪdʒɪlənt] adj vigile
vigorous [ˈvɪgərəs] adj vigoroso(-a)
vile [vaɪl] adj (action) vile; (smell) disgustoso(-a), nauseante; (temper) pessimo(-a)
villa [ˈvɪlə] n villa
village [ˈvɪlɪdʒ] n villaggio; **villager** n abitante m/f di villaggio
villain [ˈvɪlən] n (scoundrel) canaglia; (BRIT: criminal) criminale m; (in novel

etc) cattivo
vinaigrette [vɪneɪˈgrɛt] n vinaigrette f inv
vine [vaɪn] n vite f; (climbing plant) rampicante m
vinegar [ˈvɪnɪgə] n aceto
vineyard [ˈvɪnjɑːd] n vigna, vigneto
vintage [ˈvɪntɪdʒ] n (year) annata, produzione f ▶ cpd d'annata
vinyl [ˈvaɪnl] n vinile m
viola [vɪˈəʊlə] n viola
violate [ˈvaɪəleɪt] vt violare
violation [vaɪəˈleɪʃən] n violazione f; **in ~ of sth** violando qc
violence [ˈvaɪələns] n violenza
violent [ˈvaɪələnt] adj violento(-a)
violet [ˈvaɪələt] adj (colour) viola inv, violetto(-a) ▶ n (plant) violetta; (colour) violetto
violin [vaɪəˈlɪn] n violino
VIP n abbr (= very important person) V.I.P. m/f inv
virgin [ˈvɜːdʒɪn] n vergine f ▶ adj vergine inv
Virgo [ˈvɜːgəʊ] n (sign) Vergine f
virtual [ˈvɜːtjʊəl] adj effettivo(-a), vero(-a); (Comput, Physics) virtuale; (in effect): **it's a ~ impossibility** è praticamente impossibile; **the ~ leader** il capo all'atto pratico; **virtually** [ˈvɜːtjʊəlɪ] adv (almost) praticamente; **virtual reality** n (Comput) realtà virtuale
virtue [ˈvɜːtjuː] n virtù f inv; (advantage) pregio, vantaggio; **by ~ of** grazie a
virus [ˈvaɪərəs] n (also Comput) virus m inv
visa [ˈviːzə] n visto
vise [vaɪs] (US) n (Tech) = **vice**
visibility [vɪzɪˈbɪlɪtɪ] n visibilità
visible [ˈvɪzəbl] adj visibile
vision [ˈvɪʒən] n (sight) vista; (foresight, in dream) visione f
visit [ˈvɪzɪt] n visita; (stay) soggiorno

▶ vt (person: US: also: ~ with) andare a trovare; (place) visitare; **visiting hours** npl (in hospital etc) orario delle visite; **visitor** n visitatore(-trice); (guest) ospite m/f; **visitor center** (US **visitor centre** n centro informazioni per visitatori di museo, zoo, parco ecc

visual ['vɪzjuəl] adj visivo(-a); visuale; ottico(-a); **visualize** ['vɪzjuəlaɪz] vt immaginare, figurarsi; (foresee) prevedere

vital ['vaɪtl] adj vitale

vitality [vaɪˈtælɪtɪ] n vitalità

vitamin ['vɪtəmɪn] n vitamina

vivid ['vɪvɪd] adj vivido(-a)

V-neck ['viːnɛk] n maglione m con lo scollo a V

vocabulary [vəuˈkæbjulərɪ] n vocabolario

vocal ['vəukl] adj (Mus) vocale; (communication) verbale

vocational [vəuˈkeɪʃənl] adj professionale

vodka ['vɔdkə] n vodka f inv

vogue [vəug] n moda; (popularity) popolarità, voga

voice [vɔɪs] n voce f ▶ vt (opinion) esprimere; **voice mail** n servizio di segreteria telefonica

void [vɔɪd] n vuoto ▶ adj (invalid) nullo(-a); (empty): ~ of privo(-a) di

volatile ['vɔlətaɪl] adj volatile; (fig) volubile

volcano [vɔlˈkeɪnəu] (pl **volcanoes**) n vulcano

volleyball ['vɔlɪbɔːl] n pallavolo f

volt [vəult] n volt m inv; **voltage** n tensione f, voltaggio

volume ['vɔljuːm] n volume m

voluntarily ['vɔləntrɪlɪ] adv volontariamente; gratuitamente

voluntary ['vɔləntərɪ] adj volontario(-a); (unpaid) gratuito(-a), non retribuito(-a)

volunteer [vɔlənˈtɪəʳ] n volontario(-a)

▶ vt offrire volontariamente ▶ vi (Mil) arruolarsi volontario; **to ~ to do** offrire (volontariamente) di fare

vomit ['vɔmɪt] n vomito ▶ vt, vi vomitare

vote [vəut] n voto, suffragio; (cast) voto; (franchise) diritto di voto ▶ vt venire eletto presidente etc; (propose): **to ~ that** approvare la proposta che ▶ vi votare; **~ of thanks** discorso di ringraziamento; **voter** n elettore(-trice); **voting** n scrutinio

voucher ['vautʃəʳ] n (for meal, petrol etc) buono

vow [vau] n voto, promessa solenne ▶ vt **to ~ to do/that** giurare di fare/che

vowel ['vauəl] n vocale f

voyage ['vɔɪdʒ] n viaggio per mare, traversata

vulgar ['vʌlgəʳ] adj volgare

vulnerable ['vʌlnərəbl] adj vulnerabile

vulture ['vʌltʃəʳ] n avvoltoio

W

waddle ['wɔdl] vi camminare come una papera

wade [weɪd] vi **to ~ through** camminare a stento in; (fig: book) leggere con fatica

wafer ['weɪfə'] n (Culin) cialda

waffle ['wɒfl] n (Culin) cialda; (inf) ciance fpl ▶ vi cianciare

wag [wæg] vt agitare, muovere ▶ vi agitarsi

wage [weɪdʒ] n (also: ~**s**) salario, paga ▶ vt **to ~ war** fare la guerra

wag(g)on ['wægən] n (horse-drawn) carro; (BRIT: Rail) vagone m (merci)

wail [weɪl] n gemito; (of siren) urlo ▶ vi gemere; urlare

waist [weɪst] n vita, cintola;
waistcoat (BRIT) n panciotto, gilè m inv

wait [weɪt] n attesa ▶ vi aspettare, attendere; **to lie in ~ for** stare in agguato a; **to ~ for** aspettare; ~ **for me, please** aspettami, per favore; **I can't ~ to ~ to** (fig) non vedo l'ora di ▶ **wait on** vt fus servire; **waiter** n cameriere m; **waiting list** n lista di attesa; **waiting room** n sala d'aspetto or d'attesa; **waitress** n cameriera

waive [weɪv] vt rinunciare a, abbandonare

wake [weɪk] (pt **woke, waked**, pp **woken, waked**) vt (also: ~ **up**) svegliare ▶ vi (also: ~ **up**) svegliarsi ▶ n (for dead person) veglia funebre; (Naut) scia

Wales [weɪlz] n Galles m

walk [wɔːk] n passeggiata; (short) giretto; (gait) passo, andatura; (path) sentiero; (in park etc) sentiero, vialetto ▶ vi camminare; (for pleasure, exercise) passeggiare ▶ vt (distance) fare o percorrere a piedi; (dog) accompagnare, portare a passeggiare; **10 minutes' ~ from** 10 minuti di cammino or a piedi da; **from all ~s of life** di tutte le condizioni sociali ▶ **walk out** vi (audience) andarsene; (workers) scendere in sciopero; **walker** n (person) camminatore(-trice); **walkie-talkie**
['wɔːkɪ'tɔːkɪ] n walkie-talkie m inv; **walking** n camminare m; **walking shoes** npl pedule fpl; **walking stick** n bastone m da passeggio; **Walkman®** ['wɔːkmən] n Walkman® m inv; **walkway** n passaggio pedonale

wall [wɔːl] n muro; (internal, of tunnel, cave) parete f

wallet ['wɒlɪt] n portafoglio; **I can't find my ~** non trovo il portafoglio

wallpaper ['wɔːlpeɪpə'] n carta da parati ▶ vt (room) mettere la carta da parati in

walnut ['wɔːlnʌt] n noce f; (tree, wood) noce m

walrus ['wɔːlrəs] (pl **walrus** or **walruses**) n tricheco

waltz [wɔːls] n valzer m inv ▶ vi ballare il valzer

wand [wɒnd] n (also: **magic ~**) bacchetta (magica)

wander ['wɒndə'] vi (person) girare senza meta, girovagare; (thoughts) vagare ▶ vt girovagare per

want [wɒnt] vt volere; (need) aver bisogno di ▶ n **for ~ of** per mancanza di; **wanted** adj (criminal) ricercato(-a); **"wanted"** (in adverts) "cercasi"

war [wɔː'] n guerra; **to make ~ (on)** far guerra (a)

ward [wɔːd] n (in hospital: room) corsia; (: section) reparto; (Pol) circoscrizione f; (Law: child: also: ~ **of court**) pupillo(-a)

warden ['wɔːdn] n (of park, game reserve, youth hostel) guardiano(-a); (BRIT: of institution) direttore(-trice); (BRIT: also: **traffic ~**) addetto(-a) al controllo del traffico e del parcheggio

wardrobe ['wɔːdrəʊb] n (cupboard) guardaroba m inv, armadio; (clothes) guardaroba m inv; (Cinema, Theatre) costumi mpl

warehouse ['wɛəhaʊs] n magazzino

warfare ['wɔːfɛə'] n guerra

warhead ['wɔːhɛd] n (Mil) testata

warm [wɔːm] adj caldo(-a); (thanks, welcome, applause) caloroso(-a); (person) cordiale; **it's ~** fa caldo; **I'm ~** ho caldo ▷ **warm up** vi scaldarsi, riscaldarsi ▷ vt scaldare, riscaldare; (engine) far scaldare; **warmly** adv (applaud, welcome) calorosamente; (dress) con abiti pesanti; **warmth** n calore m

warn [wɔːn] vt **to ~ sb that/(not) to do/of** avvertire or avvisare qn che/di (non) fare/di; **warning** n avvertimento; (notice) avviso; (signal) segnalazione f; **warning light** n spia luminosa

warrant ['wɔrnt] n (voucher) buono; (Law: to arrest) mandato di cattura; (: to search) mandato di perquisizione

warranty ['wɔrənti] n garanzia

warrior ['wɔriə'] n guerriero(-a)

Warsaw ['wɔːsɔː] n Varsavia

warship ['wɔːʃip] n nave f da guerra

wart [wɔːt] n verruca

wartime ['wɔːtaim] n **in ~** tempo di guerra

wary ['wɛəri] adj prudente

was [wɔz] pt of **be**

wash [wɔʃ] vt lavare ▷ vi lavarsi; (sea) **to ~ over/against sth** infrangersi su/contro qc ▷ n lavaggio; (of ship) scia; **to give sth a ~** lavare qc, dare una lavata a qc; **to have a ~** lavarsi ▷ **wash up** vi (BRIT) lavare i piatti; (US) darsi una lavata; **washbasin** (US **washbowl**) n lavabo; **wash cloth** (US) n pezzuola (per lavarsi); **washer** n (Tech) rondella; **washing** n (linen etc) bucato; **washing line** n (BRIT) corda del bucato; **washing machine** n lavatrice f; **washing powder** (BRIT) n detersivo (in polvere)

Washington ['wɔʃintən] n Washington f

wash: **washing-up** n rigovernatura,

lavatura dei piatti; **washing-up liquid** n detersivo liquido (per stoviglie); **washroom** n gabinetto

wasn't ['wɔznt] = **was not**

wasp [wɔsp] n vespa

waste [weist] n spreco; (of time) perdita; (rubbish) rifiuti mpl; (also: **household ~**) immondizie fpl ▷ adj (material) di scarto; (food) avanzato(-a); (land) incolto(-a) ▷ vt sprecare; **waste ground** (BRIT) n terreno incolto or abbandonato; **wastepaper basket** ['weistpeipə-] n cestino per la carta straccia

watch [wɔtʃ] n (also **wrist ~**) orologio (da polso); (act of watching, vigilance) sorveglianza; (guard: Mil, Naut) guardia; (Naut: spell of duty) quarto ▷ vt (look at) osservare; (: match, programme) guardare; (spy on, guard) sorvegliare, tenere d'occhio; (be careful of) fare attenzione a ▷ vi osservare, guardare; (keep guard) fare or montare la guardia ▷ **watch out** vi fare attenzione; **watchdog** n (also fig) cane m da guardia; **watch strap** n cinturino da orologio

water ['wɔːtə'] n acqua ▷ vt (plant) annaffiare ▷ vi (eyes) lacrimare; (mouth): **to make sb's mouth ~** far venire l'acquolina in bocca a qn; **in British ~s** nelle acque territoriali britanniche ▷ **water down** vt (milk) diluire; (fig: story) edulcorare; **watercolour** (US **watercolor**) n acquerello; **watercress** n crescione m; **waterfall** n cascata; **watering can** n annaffiatoio; **watermelon** n anguria, cocomero; **waterproof** adj impermeabile; **water-skiing** n sci m acquatico

watt [wɔt] n watt m inv

wave [weiv] n onda; (of hand) gesto, segno; (in hair) ondulazione f; (fig: surge) ondata ▷ vi fare un cenno con la mano; (*branches, grass*) ondeggiare; (*flag*) sventolare ▶ vt (*hand*) fare un gesto con; (*handkerchief*) sventolare; (*stick*) brandire; **wavelength** n lunghezza d'onda

waver ['weɪvəʳ] vi esitare; (*voice*) tremolare

wavy ['weɪvɪ] adj ondulato(-a); ondeggiante

wax [wæks] n cera ▶ vt dare la cera a; (*car*) lucidare ▶ vi (*moon*) crescere

way [weɪ] n via, strada; (*path, access*) passaggio m; (*distance*) distanza; (*direction*) parte f, direzione f; (*manner*) modo, stile m; (*habit*) abitudine f; **which ~?** — **this ~** da che parte o in quale direzione? — da questa parte or per di qua; **on the ~** (*en route*) per strada; **to be on one's ~** essere in cammino or sulla strada; **to be in the ~** bloccare il passaggio; (*fig*) essere tra i piedi or d'impiccio; **to go out of one's ~ to do** (*fig*) mettercela tutta or fare di tutto per fare; **under ~** (*project*) in corso; **to lose one's ~** perdere la strada; **in a ~** in un certo senso; **in some ~s** sotto certi aspetti; **no ~!** (*inf*) neanche per idea!; **by the ~ ...** a proposito ...; **"~ in"** (*BRIT*) "entrata", "ingresso"; **"~ out"** (*BRIT*) "uscita"; **the ~ back** la strada del ritorno; **"give ~"** (*BRIT: Aut*) "dare la precedenza"

W.C. ['dʌblju'siː] (*BRIT*) n W.C. m inv, gabinetto

we [wiː] pl pron noi

weak [wiːk] adj debole; (*health*) precario(-a); (*beam etc*) fragile; (*tea*) leggero(-a); **weaken** vi indebolirsi ▶ vt indebolire; **weakness** n debolezza f; (*fault*) punto debole, difetto; **to have a weakness for** avere un debole per

wealth [wɛlθ] n (*money, resources*) ricchezza, ricchezze fpl; (*of details*) abbondanza, profusione f; **wealthy** adj ricco(-a)

weapon ['wɛpən] n arma; **~s of mass destruction** armi mpl di distruzione di massa

wear [wɛəʳ] (*pt* **wore**, *pp* **worn**) n (*use*) uso; (*damage through use*) logorio, usura; (*clothing*): **sports/baby ~** abbigliamento sportivo/per neonati ▶ vt (*clothes*) portare; (*put on*) mettersi; (*damage: through use*) consumare ▶ vi (*last*) durare; (*rub etc through*) consumarsi; **evening ~** abiti mpl or tenuta da sera ▶ **wear off** vi sparire lentamente ▶ **wear out** vt consumare; (*person, strength*) esaurire

weary ['wɪərɪ] adj stanco(-a) ▶ vi **to ~ of** stancarsi di

weasel ['wiːzl] n (*Zool*) donnola

weather ['wɛðəʳ] n tempo ▶ vt (*storm, crisis*) superare; **What's the ~ like?** che tempo fa?; **under the ~** (*fig: ill*) poco bene; **weather forecast** n previsioni fpl del tempo, bollettino meteorologico

weave [wiːv] (*pt* **wove**, *pp* **woven**) vt (*cloth*) tessere; (*basket*) intrecciare

web [wɛb] n (*of spider*) ragnatela; (*on foot*) palma; (*fabric, also fig*) tessuto; **the (World Wide) W~** la Rete; **web page** n (*Comput*) pagina f web inv; **website** n (*Comput*) sito (Internet)

wed [wɛd] (*pt, pp* **wedded**) vt sposare ▶ vi sposarsi

we'd [wiːd] = **we had**; **we would**

Wed. abbr (= *Wednesday*) mer.

wedding ['wɛdɪŋ] n matrimonio; **wedding anniversary** n anniversario di matrimonio; **wedding day** n giorno delle nozze or del matrimonio; **wedding dress** n abito nuziale; **wedding ring** n fede f

wedge [wɛdʒ] n (*of wood etc*) zeppa; (*of cake*) fetta ▶ vt (*fix*) fissare con zeppe; (*pack tightly*) incastrare

Wednesday ['wɛdnzdɪ] n mercoledì m inv

wee [wiː] (SCOTTISH) adj piccolo(-a)
weed [wiːd] n erbaccia ▶ vt diserbare;
weedkiller n diserbante m
week [wiːk] n settimana; **a ~ today/on Friday** oggi/venerdì a otto; **weekday** n giorno feriale; (Comm) giornata lavorativa; **weekend** n fine settimana m or f inv; weekend m inv; **weekly** adv ogni settimana, settimanalmente ▶ adj settimanale ▶ n settimanale m
weep [wiːp] (pt, pp **wept**) vi (person) piangere
weigh [wei] vt, vi pesare; **to ~ anchor** salpare l'ancora ▶ **weigh up** vt valutare
weight [weit] n peso; **to lose/put on ~** dimagrire/ingrassare; **weightlifting** n sollevamento pesi
weir [wɪəʳ] n diga
weird [wɪəd] adj strano(-a), bizzarro(-a); (eerie) soprannaturale
welcome ['wɛlkəm] adj benvenuto(-a) ▶ n accoglienza, benvenuto ▶ vt dare il benvenuto a; (be glad of) rallegrarsi di; **thank you—you're ~** grazie — prego!
weld [wɛld] n saldatura ▶ vt saldare
welfare ['wɛlfɛəʳ] n benessere m; **welfare state** n stato assistenziale
well [wɛl] n pozzo ▶ adv bene ▶ adj to be ~ (person) stare bene ▶ excl allora!; ma!; ebbene!; **as ~** anche; **as ~ as** così come; oltre a; **~ done!** bravo(-a)!; **get ~ soon!** guarisci presto!; **to do ~** andare bene
we'll [wiːl] = **we will**; **we shall**
well: **well-behaved** adj ubbidiente; **well-built** adj (person) ben fatto(-a); **well-dressed** adj ben vestito(-a), vestito(-a) bene
wellies (inf) ['wɛlɪz] npl (BRIT) stivali mpl di gomma
well: **well-known** adj noto(-a), famoso(-a); **well-off** adj benestante, danaroso(-a); **well-paid** [wɛl'peɪd] adj ben pagato(-a)

Welsh [wɛlʃ] adj gallese ▶ n (Ling) gallese m; **Welshman** (irreg) n gallese m; **Welshwoman** (irreg) n gallese f
went [wɛnt] pt of **go**
wept [wɛpt] pt, pp of **weep**
were [wəːʳ] pt of **be**
we're [wɪəʳ] = **we are**
weren't [wəːnt] = **were not**
west [wɛst] n ovest m, occidente m, ponente m ▶ adj (a) ovest inv, occidentale ▶ adv verso ovest; **the W~** l'Occidente m; **westbound** ['wɛstbaund] adj (traffic) diretto(-a) a ovest; (carriageway) ovest inv; **western** adj occidentale, dell'ovest ▶ n (Cinema) western m inv; **West Indian** delle Indie Occidentali ▶ n abitante m/f delle Indie Occidentali; **West Indies** [-'ɪndɪz] npl Indie fpl Occidentali
wet [wɛt] adj umido(-a), bagnato(-a); (soaked) fradicio(-a); (rainy) piovoso(-a) ▶ n (BRIT: Pol) politico moderato; **to get ~** bagnarsi; **"~ paint"** "vernice fresca"; **wetsuit** n tuta da sub
we've [wiːv] = **we have**
whack [wæk] vt picchiare, battere
whale [weɪl] n (Zool) balena
wharf [wɔːf] (pl **wharves**) n banchina

⊙ **what**
[wɔt] adj
1 (in direct/indirect questions) che; quale; **what size is it?** che taglia è?; **what colour is it?** di che colore è?; **what books do you want?** quali or che libri vuoi?
2 (in exclamations) che; **what a mess!** che disordine!
▶ pron
1 (interrogative) che cosa, cosa, che; **what are you doing?** che or (che) cosa fai?; **what are you talking about?** di che cosa parli?; **what is it called?**

come si chiama?; **what about me?** e io?, **what about doing ...?** e se facessimo ...?

2 (relative) ciò che, quello che; **I saw what you did/was on the table** ho visto quello che hai fatto/quello che era sul tavolo

3 (indirect use) (che) cosa; **he asked me what she had said** mi ha chiesto che cosa avesse detto; **tell me what you're thinking about** dimmi a cosa stai pensando

▶ excl (disbelieving) cosa!, come!

whatever [wɒtˈɛvəᵊ] adj ~ **book** qualunque or qualsiasi libro + sub
▶ pron **do ~ is necessary/you want** faccia qualunque or qualsiasi cosa sia necessaria/lei voglia; **~ happens** qualunque cosa accada; **no reason ~ or whatsoever** nessuna ragione affatto or al mondo; **nothing ~** proprio niente

whatsoever [wɒtsəʊˈɛvəᵊ] adj = **whatever**

wheat [wiːt] n grano, frumento

wheel [wiːl] n ruota; (Aut: also: **steering ~**) volante m; (Naut) (ruota del) timone m ▶ vt spingere ▶ vi (birds) roteare; (also: **~ round**) girare; **wheelbarrow** n carriola; **wheelchair** n sedia a rotelle; **wheel clamp** n (Aut) morsa che blocca la ruota di una vettura in sosta vietata

wheeze [wiːz] vi ansimare

when [wɛn] adv quando; **when did it happen?** quando è successo?
▶ conj

1 (at, during, after the time that) quando; **she was reading when I came in** quando sono entrata lei leggeva; **that was when I needed you** era allora che avevo bisogno di te

2 (on, at which) **on the day when I met him** il giorno in cui l'ho incontrato;

one day when it was raining un giorno che pioveva

3 (whereas) quando, mentre; **you said I was wrong when in fact I was right** mi hai detto che avevo torto, quando in realtà avevo ragione

whenever [wɛnˈɛvəᵊ] adv quando mai
▶ conj quando; (every time that) ogni volta che

where [wɛəᵊ] adv, conj dove; **this is ~** è qui che; **whereabouts** adv dove
▶ n sb's **whereabouts** luogo dove qn si trova; **whereas** conj mentre; **whereby** pron per cui; **wherever** [-ˈɛvəᵊ] conj ovunque + sub; (interrogative) dove mai

whether [ˈwɛðəᵊ] conj se; **I don't know ~ to accept or not** non so se accettare o no; **it's doubtful ~** è poco probabile che; **~ you go or not** che lei vada o no

which
[wɪtʃ] adj

1 (interrogative: direct, indirect) quale; **which picture do you want?** quale quadro vuole?; **which one?** quale?; **which one of you did it?** chi di voi lo ha fatto?

2 **in which case** nel qual caso
▶ pron

1 (interrogative) quale; **which (of these) are yours?** quali di questi sono suoi?; **which of you are coming?** chi di voi viene?

2 (relative) (subject) che; (: indirect) cui, il (la) quale; **the apple which you ate/which is on the table** la mela che hai mangiato/che è sul tavolo; **the chair on which you are sitting** la sedia sulla quale or su cui sei seduto; **he said he knew, which is true** ha detto che lo sapeva, il che è vero; **after which** dopo di che

whichever [wɪtʃˈɛvəᵊ] adj take ~ **book you prefer** prenda qualsiasi libro che preferisce; **~ book you take** qualsiasi

libro prenda
while [waɪl] n momento ▸ conj
mentre; (as long as) finché; (although)
sebbene + sub; per quanto + sub; **for a
~** per un po'

whilst [waɪlst] conj = **while**

whim [wɪm] n capriccio

whine [waɪn] n gemito ▸ vi gemere;
uggiolare; piagnucolare

whip [wɪp] n frusta; (for riding)
frustino; (Pol: person) capogruppo (che
sovrintende alla disciplina dei colleghi
di partito) ▸ vt frustare; (cream, eggs)
sbattere; **whipped cream** n panna
montata

whirl [wə:l] vt (far) girare
rapidamente, (far) turbinare ▸ vi
(dancers) volteggiare; (leaves, water)
sollevarsi in vortice

whisk [wɪsk] n (Culin) frusta; frullino
▸ vt sbattere, frullare; **to ~ sb away or
off** portar via qn a tutta velocità

whiskers ['wɪskəz] npl (of animal) baffi
mpl; (of man) favoriti mpl

whisky ['wɪskɪ] (US, Ireland **whiskey**)
n whisky m inv

whisper ['wɪspə'] n sussurro ▸ vt, vi
sussurrare

whistle ['wɪsl] n (sound) fischio;
(object) fischietto ▸ vi fischiare

white [waɪt] adj bianco(-a); (with
fear) pallido(-a) ▸ n bianco; (person)
bianco(-a); **White House** n Casa
Bianca; **whitewash** n (paint) bianco
di calce ▸ vt imbiancare; (fig) coprire

whiting ['waɪtɪŋ] n inv (fish) merlango

Whitsun ['wɪtsn] n Pentecoste f

whittle ['wɪtl] vt **to ~ away, ~ down**
ridurre, tagliare

whizz [wɪz] vi **to ~ past** or **by** passare
sfrecciando

O who
[hu:] pron

1 (interrogative) chi; **who is it?, who's
there?** chi è?

2 (relative) che; **the man who spoke
to me** l'uomo che ha parlato con me;
those who can swim quelli che sanno
nuotare

whoever [hu:'ɛvə'] pron ~ **finds it**
chiunque lo trovi; **ask ~ you like**
lo chieda a chiunque vuole; ~ **she
marries** chiunque sposerà, non
importa chi sposerà; ~ **told you that?**
chi mai gliel'ha detto?

whole [həul] adj (complete) tutto(-a),
completo(-a); (not broken) intero(-a),
intatto(-a) ▸ n (all): **the ~ of** tutto(-a)
il (la); (entire unit) tutto; (not broken)
tutto; **the ~ of the town** tutta la
città, la città intera; **on the ~, as
a ~** nel complesso, nell'insieme;
wholefood(s) n(pl) cibo integrale;
wholeheartedly [həul'ha:tɪdlɪ]
adv sentitamente, di tutto cuore;
wholemeal adj (bread, flour) integrale;
wholesale n commercio or vendita
all'ingrosso ▸ adj all'ingrosso;
(destruction) totale; **wholewheat**
adj = **wholemeal**; **wholly** adv
completamente, del tutto

O whom
[hu:m] pron

1 (interrogative) chi; **whom did you
see?** chi hai visto?; **to whom did you
give it?** a chi lo hai dato?

2 (relative) che, prep + il (la) quale (check
syntax of Italian verb used); **the man
whom I saw/to whom I spoke** l'uomo
che ho visto/al quale ho parlato

whore [hɔ:] (inf: pej) n puttana

O whose
[hu:z] adj

1 (possessive: interrogative) di chi;
**whose book is this?, whose is this
book?** di chi è questo libro?; **whose
daughter are you?** di chi sei figlia?

2 (possessive: relative): **the man whose
son you rescued** l'uomo il cui figlio
hai salvato; **the girl whose sister you**

were speaking to la ragazza alla cui sorella stavi parlando

▶ *pron* di chi; **whose is this?** di chi è questo?; **I know whose it is** so di chi è

why

[waɪ] *adv* perché; **why not?** perché no?; **why not do it now?** perché non farlo adesso?

▶ *conj* **I wonder why he said that** mi chiedo perché l'abbia detto; **that's not why I'm here** non è questo il motivo per cui sono qui; **the reason why** il motivo per cui

▶ *excl* (*surprise*) ma guarda un po'!; (*remonstrating*) ma (via)!; (*explaining*) ebbene!

wicked ['wɪkɪd] *adj* cattivo(-a), malvagio(-a); maligno(-a); perfido(-a)

wicket ['wɪkɪt] *n* (*Cricket*) porta; area tra le due porte

wide [waɪd] *adj* largo(-a); (*area, knowledge*) vasto(-a); (*choice*) ampio(-a) ▶ *adv* **to open** ~ spalancare; **to shoot** ~ tirare a vuoto or fuori bersaglio; **widely** *adv* (*differing*) molto, completamente; (*travelled, spaced*) molto; (*believed*) generalmente; **widen** *vt* allargare, ampliare; **wide open** spalancato(-a); **widespread** *adj* (*belief etc*) molto or assai diffuso(-a)

widow ['wɪdəu] *n* vedova; **widower** *n* vedovo

width [wɪdθ] *n* larghezza

wield [wiːld] *vt* (*sword*) maneggiare; (*power*) esercitare

wife [waɪf] (*pl* **wives**) *n* moglie *f*

wig [wɪg] *n* parrucca

wild [waɪld] *adj* selvatico(-a); selvaggio(-a); (*sea, weather*) tempestoso(-a); (*idea, life*) folle; stravagante; (*applause*) frenetico(-a); **wilderness** ['wɪldənɪs] *n* deserto; **wildlife** *n* natura; **wildly** *adv* selvaggiamente; (*applaud*) freneticamente; (*hit, guess*) a

casaccio; (*happy*) follemente

will

[wɪl] (*pt, pp* **willed**) *aux vb*

1 (*forming future tense*): **I will finish it tomorrow** lo finirò domani; **I will have finished it by tomorrow** lo finirò entro domani; **will you do it?** — **yes I will/no I won't** lo farai? — sì (lo farò)/no (non lo farò)

2 (*in conjectures, predictions*): **he will or he'll be there by now** dovrebbe essere arrivato ora; **that will be the postman** sarà il postino

3 (*in commands, requests, offers*): **will you be quiet!** vuoi stare zitto?; **will you come?** vieni anche tu?; **will you help me?** mi puoi aiutare?; **will you have a cup of tea?** vorrebbe una tazza di tè?; **I won't put up with it!** non lo accetterò!

▶ *vt* **to will sb to do** volere che qn faccia; **he willed himself to go on** continuò grazie a un grande sforzo di volontà

▶ *n* volontà; testamento

willing ['wɪlɪŋ] *adj* volonteroso(-a); ~ **to do** disposto(-a) a fare; **willingly** *adv* volentieri

willow ['wɪləu] *n* salice *m*

willpower ['wɪlpauə'] *n* forza di volontà

wilt [wɪlt] *vi* appassire

win [wɪn] (*pt, pp* **won**) *n* (*in sports etc*) vittoria ▶ *vt* (*battle, prize, money*) vincere; (*popularity*) conquistare ▶ *vi* vincere ▶ **win over** *vt* convincere

wince [wɪns] *vi* trasalire

wind[1] [waɪnd] (*pt, pp* **wound**) *vt* attorcigliare; (*wrap*) avvolgere; (*clock, toy*) caricare ▶ *vi* (*road, river*) serpeggiare ▶ **wind down** *vt* (*car window*) abbassare; (*fig: production, business*) diminuire ▶ **wind up** *vt* (*clock*) caricare; (*debate*) concludere

wind[2] [wɪnd] *n* vento; (*Med*) flatulenza; (*breath*) respiro, fiato ▶ *vt*

(*take breath away*) far restare senza fiato; **~ power** energia eolica
windfall ['wɪndfɔːl] *n* (*money*) guadagno insperato
winding ['waɪndɪŋ] *adj* (*road*) serpeggiante; (*staircase*) a chiocciola
windmill ['wɪndmɪl] *n* mulino a vento
window ['wɪndəʊ] *n* finestra; (*in car, train, plane*) finestrino; (*in shop etc*) vetrina; (*also*: **~ pane**) vetro; **I'd like a ~ seat** vorrei un posto vicino al finestrino; **window box** *n* cassetta da fiori; **window cleaner** *n* (*person*) pulitore *m* di finestre; **window pane** *n* vetro; **window seat** *n* posto finestrino; **windowsill** *n* davanzale *m*
windscreen ['wɪndskriːn] (US **windshield**) *n* parabrezza *m inv*; **windscreen wiper** (US **windshield wiper**) *n* tergicristallo
windsurfing ['wɪndsəːfɪŋ] *n* windsurf *m inv*
windy ['wɪndɪ] *adj* ventoso(-a); **it's ~** c'è vento
wine [waɪn] *n* vino; **wine bar** *n* enoteca (*per degustazione*); **wine glass** *n* bicchiere *m* da vino; **wine list** *n* lista dei vini; **wine tasting** *n* degustazione *f* dei vini
wing [wɪŋ] *n* ala; (*Aut*) fiancata; **wing mirror** *n* (BRIT) specchietto retrovisore esterno
wink [wɪŋk] *n* ammiccamento ▸ *vi* ammiccare, fare l'occhiolino; (*light*) baluginare
winner ['wɪnər] *n* vincitore(-trice)
winning ['wɪnɪŋ] *adj* (*team, goal*) vincente; (*smile*) affascinante
winter ['wɪntər] *n* inverno; **winter sports** *npl* sport *mpl* invernali; **wintertime** *n* inverno, stagione *f* invernale
wipe [waɪp] *n* pulita, passata ▸ *vt* pulire (*strofinando*); (*erase: tape*) cancellare ▷ **wipe out** *vt*

(*debt*) pagare, liquidare; (*memory*) cancellare; (*destroy*) annientare
▷ **wipe up** *vt* asciugare
wire ['waɪər] *n* filo; (*Elec*) filo elettrico; (*Tel*) telegramma *m* ▸ *vt* (*house*) fare l'impianto elettrico di; (*also*: **~ up**) collegare, allacciare; (*person*) telegrafare a
wiring ['waɪərɪŋ] *n* impianto elettrico
wisdom ['wɪzdəm] *n* saggezza; (*of action*) prudenza; **wisdom tooth** *n* dente *m* del giudizio
wise [waɪz] *adj* saggio(-a); prudente; giudizioso(-a)
wish [wɪʃ] *n* (*desire*) desiderio; (*specific desire*) richiesta ▸ *vt* desiderare, volere; **best ~es** (*on birthday etc*) i migliori auguri; **with best ~es** (*in letter*) cordiali saluti, con i migliori saluti; **to ~ sb goodbye** dire arrivederci a qn; **he ~ed me well** mi augurò di riuscire; **to ~ to do/sb to do** desiderare o volere fare/che qn faccia; **to ~ for** desiderare
wistful ['wɪstful] *adj* malinconico(-a)
wit [wɪt] *n* (*also*: **~s**) intelligenza; presenza di spirito; (*wittiness*) spirito, arguzia; (*person*) bello spirito
witch [wɪtʃ] *n* strega

with
[wɪð, wɪθ] *prep*

1 (*in the company of*) con; **I was with him** ero con lui; **we stayed with friends** siamo stati da amici; **I'll be with you in a minute** vengo subito
2 (*descriptive*) con; **a room with a view** una stanza con vista sul mare (*or sulle montagne etc*); **the man with the grey hat/blue eyes** l'uomo con il cappello grigio/gli occhi blu
3 (*indicating manner, means, cause*): **with tears in her eyes** con le lacrime agli occhi; **red with anger** rosso dalla rabbia; **to shake with fear** tremare di paura

4: I'm with you (I understand) la seguo;
to be with it (inf: up-to-date) essere alla
moda; (: alert) essere sveglio(-a)

withdraw [wɪθ'drɔː] (irreg: like **draw**)
vt ritirare; (money from bank) ritirare;
prelevare ▶ vi ritirarsi; **withdrawal**
n ritiro; prelievo; (of army) ritirata;
withdrawal symptoms n (Med) crisi
f di astinenza; **withdrawn** adj (person)
distaccato(-a)

withdrew [wɪθ'druː] pt of **withdraw**

wither ['wɪðə*] vi appassire

withhold [wɪθ'həʊld] (irreg: like **hold**)
vt (money) trattenere; (permission): to ~
(from) rifiutare (a); (information): to ~
(from) nascondere (a)

within [wɪð'ɪn] prep all'interno, (in
time, distances) entro ▶ adv all'interno,
dentro; ~ reach (of) alla portata (di);
~ sight (of) in vista (di); ~ a mile of
entro un miglio da; ~ the week prima
della fine della settimana

without [wɪð'aʊt] prep senza; to go ~
sth fare a meno di qc

withstand [wɪθ'stænd] (irreg: like
stand) vt resistere a

witness ['wɪtnɪs] n (person, also Law)
testimone m/f ▶ vt (event) essere
testimone di; (document) attestare
l'autenticità di

witty ['wɪtɪ] adj spiritoso(-a)

wives [waɪvz] npl of **wife**

wizard ['wɪzəd] n mago

wk abbr = **week**

wobble ['wɒbl] vi tremare; (chair)
traballare

woe [wəʊ] n dolore m; disgrazia

woke [wəʊk] pt of **wake**

woken ['wəʊkn] pp of **wake**

wolf [wʊlf] (pl **wolves**) n lupo

woman ['wʊmən] (pl **women**) n
donna

womb [wuːm] n (Anat) utero

women ['wɪmɪn] npl of **woman**

won [wʌn] pt, pp of **win**

wonder ['wʌndə*] n meraviglia ▶ vi
to ~ whether/why domandarsi
se/perché; to ~ at essere sorpreso(-a)
di; meravigliarsi di; to ~ about
domandarsi di; pensare a; it's
no ~ that c'è poco or non c'è da
meravigliarsi che + sub; **wonderful**
adj meraviglioso(-a)

won't [wəʊnt] = **will not**

wood [wʊd] n (many; timber) legname
m; (forest) bosco; **wooden** adj di legno;
(fig) rigido(-a); inespressivo(-a);
woodwind npl (Mus): the **woodwind**
i legni; **woodwork** n (craft, subject)
falegnameria

wool [wʊl] n lana; to pull the ~
over sb's eyes (fig) imbrogliare
qn; **woollen** (US **woolen**) adj di
lana; (industry) laniero(-a); **woolly**
(US **wooly**) adj di lana; (fig: ideas)
confuso(-a)

word [wəːd] n parola; (news) notizie
fpl ▶ vt esprimere, formulare; in other
~s in altre parole; to break/keep
one's ~ non mantenere/mantenere
la propria parola; to have ~s with sb
avere un diverbio con qn; **wording**
n formulazione f; **word processing**
n elaborazione f di testi, word
processing m; **word processor** n
word processor m inv

wore [wɔː*] pt of **wear**

work [wəːk] n lavoro; (Art, Literature)
opera ▶ vi lavorare; (mechanism, plan
etc) funzionare; (medicine) essere
efficace ▶ vt (clay, wood etc) lavorare;
(mine etc) sfruttare; (machine) far
funzionare; (cause: effect, miracle) fare;
to be out of ~ essere disoccupato(-a);
~s n (BRIT: factory) fabbrica npl (of
clock, machine) meccanismo; **how
does this ~?** come funziona?; **the
TV isn't ~ing** la TV non funziona;
to ~ loose allentarsi ▷ **work out** vi
(plans etc) riuscire, andare bene ▶

(*problem*) risolvere; (*plan*) elaborare; **it ~s out at €100** fa 100 sterline; **worker** n lavoratore(-trice), operaio(-a); **work experience** n (*previous jobs*) esperienze fpl lavorative; (*student training placement*) tirocinio; **workforce** n forza lavoro; **working class** n classe f operaia; **working week** n settimana lavorativa; **workman** (*irreg*) n operaio m; **work of art** n opera d'arte; **workout** n (*Sport*) allenamento; **work permit** n permesso di lavoro; **workplace** n posto di lavoro; **workshop** n officina; (*practical session*) gruppo di lavoro; **work station** n stazione f di lavoro; **work surface** n piano di lavoro; **worktop** n piano di lavoro

world [wəːld] n mondo ▸ cpd (*champion*) del mondo; (*power, war*) mondiale; **to think the ~ of sb** (*fig*) pensare un gran bene di qn; **World Cup** n (*Football*) Coppa del Mondo; **world-wide** adj universale; **World-Wide Web** n World Wide Web m

worm [wəːm] n (*also: earth~*) verme m

worn [wɔːn] pp of **wear** ▸ adj usato(-a); **worn-out** adj (*object*) consumato(-a), logoro(-a); (*person*) sfinito(-a)

worried [ˈwʌrɪd] adj preoccupato(-a)

worry [ˈwʌrɪ] n preoccupazione f ▸ vt preoccupare ▸ vi preoccuparsi; **worrying** adj preoccupante

worse [wəːs] adj peggiore ▸ adv, n peggio; **a change for the ~** un peggioramento; **worsen** vt, vi peggiorare; **worse off** adj in condizioni (economiche) peggiori

worship [ˈwəːʃɪp] n culto m ▸ vt (*God*) adorare, venerare; (*person*) adorare; **Your W~** (*BRIT: to mayor*) signor sindaco; (*: to judge*) signor giudice

worst [wəːst] adj il (la) peggiore ▸ adv, n peggio; **at ~** al peggio, per male che vada

worth [wəːθ] n valore m ▸ adj to be ~ valere; **it's ~ it** ne vale la pena; **it is ~ one's while (to do)** vale la pena (fare); **worthless** adj di nessun valore; **worthwhile** adj (*activity*) utile; (*cause*) lodevole

worthy [ˈwəːðɪ] adj (*person*) degno(-a); (*motive*) lodevole; **~ of** degno di

would
[wʊd] aux vb
1 (*conditional tense*): **if you asked him he would do it** se glielo chiedesse lo farebbe; **if you had asked him he would have done it** se glielo avesse chiesto lo avrebbe fatto
2 (*in offers, invitations, requests*): **would you like a biscuit?** vorrebbe or vuole un biscotto?; **would you ask him to come in?** lo faccia entrare, per cortesia; **would you open the window please?** apra la finestra, per favore
3 (*in indirect speech*): **I said I would do it** ho detto che l'avrei fatto
4 (*emphatic*): **it would have to snow today!** doveva proprio nevicare oggi!
5 (*insistence*): **she wouldn't do it** non ha voluto farlo
6 (*conjecture*): **it would have been midnight** sarà stato mezzanotte; **it would seem so** sembrerebbe proprio di sì
7 (*indicating habit*): **he would go there on Mondays** andava lì ogni lunedì

wouldn't [ˈwʊdnt] = **would not**

wound¹ [waʊnd] pt, pp of **wind³**

wound² [wuːnd] n ferita ▸ vt ferire

wove [wəʊv] pt of **weave**

woven [ˈwəʊvn] pp of **weave**

wrap [ræp] vt avvolgere; (*pack: also: ~ up*) incartare; **wrapper** n (*on chocolate*) carta f; (*BRIT: of book*) copertina; **wrapping** [ˈræpɪŋ] n carta; **wrapping paper** n carta da pacchi; (*for gift*) carta da regali

wreath [riːθ, pl riːðz] n corona

wreck [rɛk] n (sea disaster) naufragio; (ship) relitto; (pej: person) rottame m ▶ vt demolire; (ship) far naufragare; (fig) rovinare; **wreckage** n rottami mpl; (of building) macerie fpl; (of ship) relitti mpl

wren [rɛn] n (Zool) scricciolo

wrench [rɛntʃ] n (Tech) chiave f; (tug) torsione f brusca; (fig) strazio ▶ vt strappare; storcere; **to ~ sth from** strappare qc a or da

wrestle [ˈrɛsl] vi **to ~ (with sb)** lottare (con qn); **wrestler** n lottatore(-trice); **wrestling** n lotta

wretched [ˈrɛtʃɪd] adj disgraziato(-a); (inf: weather, holiday) orrendo(-a), orribile; (: child, dog) pestifero(-a)

wriggle [ˈrɪɡl] vi (also: ~ **about**) dimenarsi; (: snake, worm) serpeggiare, muoversi serpeggiando

wring [rɪŋ] (pt, pp **wrung**) vt torcere; (wet clothes) strizzare; (fig): **to ~ sth out of** strappare qc a

wrinkle [ˈrɪŋkl] n (on skin) ruga; (on paper etc) grinza ▶ vt (nose) torcere; (forehead) corrugare ▶ vi (skin, paint) raggrinzirsi

wrist [rɪst] n polso

write [raɪt] (pt **wrote**, pp **written**) vt, vi scrivere ▶ **write down** vt annotare; (put in writing) mettere per iscritto ▷ **write off** vt (debt, plan) cancellare ▷ **write out** vt mettere per iscritto; (cheque, receipt) scrivere; **write-off** n perdita completa; **writer** n autore(-trice), scrittore(-trice)

writing [ˈraɪtɪŋ] n scrittura; (of author) scritto, opera; **in ~** per iscritto; **writing paper** n carta da lettere

written [ˈrɪtn] pp of **write**

wrong [rɔŋ] adj sbagliato(-a); (not suitable) inadatto(-a); (wicked) cattivo(-a); (unfair) ingiusto(-a) ▶ adv in modo sbagliato, erroneamente ▶ n (injustice) torto ▶ vt fare torto a; I

took a ~ turning ho sbagliato strada; **you are ~ to do it** ha torto a farlo; **you are ~ about that, you've got it ~** si sbaglia; **to be in the ~** avere torto; **what's ~?** cosa c'è che non va?; **to go ~** (person) sbagliarsi; (plan) fallire, non riuscire; (machine) guastarsi; **wrongly** adv (incorrectly, by mistake) in modo sbagliato; **wrong number** n (Tel): **you've got the wrong number** ha sbagliato numero

wrote [raut] pt of **write**

wrung [rʌŋ] pt, pp of **wring**

WWW n abbr = World Wide Web; **the ~** la Rete

X

XL abbr = **extra large**

Xmas [ˈɛksməs] n abbr = **Christmas**

X-ray [ˈɛksreɪ] n raggio X; (photograph) radiografia ▶ vt radiografare

xylophone [ˈzaɪləfəun] n xilofono

y

yacht [jɔt] *n* panfilo, yacht *m inv*; **yachting** *n* yachting *m*, sport *m* della vela

yard [jɑːd] *n* (*of house etc*) cortile *m*; (*measure*) iarda (= 914 *mm*; 3 *feet*); **yard sale** (*US*) *n* vendita di oggetti usati nel cortile di una casa privata

yarn [jɑːn] *n* filato; (*tale*) lunga storia

yawn [jɔːn] *n* sbadiglio ▶ *vi* sbadigliare

yd. *abbr* = **yard(s)**

yeah [jɛə] (*inf*) *adv* sì

year [jɪəʳ] *n* anno; (*referring to harvest, wine etc*) annata; **he is 8 ~ old** ha 8 anni; **an eight-~-old child** un(a) bambino/a di otto anni; **yearly** *adj* annuale ▶ *adv* annualmente

yearn [jəːn] *vi* **to ~ for sth/to do** desiderare ardentemente qc/di fare

yeast [jiːst] *n* lievito

yell [jɛl] *n* urlo ▶ *vi* urlare

yellow [ˈjɛləu] *adj* giallo(-a); **Yellow Pages®** *npl* pagine *fpl* gialle

yes [jɛs] *adv* sì ▶ *n* sì *m inv*; **to say/answer ~** dire/rispondere di sì

yesterday [ˈjɛstədɪ] *adv ieri* ▶ *n* ieri *m inv*; **~ morning/evening** ieri mattina/sera; **all day ~** ieri per tutta la giornata

yet [jɛt] *adv* ancora; già ▶ *conj* ma, tuttavia; **it is not finished ~** non è ancora finito; **the best ~** finora il migliore; **as ~** finora

yew [juː] *n* tasso (*albero*)

Yiddish [ˈjɪdɪʃ] *n* yiddish *m*

yield [jiːld] *n* produzione *f*, resa; reddito ▶ *vt* produrre, rendere; (*surrender*) cedere ▶ *vi* cedere; (*US: Aut*) dare la precedenza

yob(bo) [ˈjɔb(əu)] *n* (*BRIT inf*) bullo

yoga [ˈjəugə] *n* yoga *m*

yog(h)urt [ˈjəugət] *n* iogurt *m inv*

yolk [jəuk] *n* tuorlo, rosso d'uovo

you
[juː] *pron*

1 (*subject*) tu; (: *polite form*) lei; (: *pl*) voi; (: *very formal*) loro; **you Italians enjoy your food** a voi Italiani piace mangiare bene; **you and I will go** tu ed io or lei ed io andiamo

2 (*object: direct*) ti; la; vi; loro (*after vb*); (: *indirect*) ti; le; vi; loro (*after vb*); **I know you** ti or la or vi conosco; **I gave it to you** te l'ho dato; gliel'ho dato; ve l'ho dato; l'ho dato loro

3 (*stressed, after prep, in comparisons*) te; lei; voi; loro; **I told you to do it** l'ho detto a TE (*or a* LEI *etc*) di farlo; **she's younger than you** è più giovane di te (or lei *etc*)

4 (*impers: one*) si; **fresh air does you good** l'aria fresca fa bene; **you never know** non si sa mai

you'd [juːd] = **you had**; **you would**

you'll [juːl] = **you will**; **you shall**

young [jʌŋ] *adj* giovane ▶ *npl* (*of animal*) piccoli *mpl*; (*people*): **the ~** i giovani, la gioventù; **youngster** *n* giovanotto, ragazzo; (*child*) bambino/-a

your [jɔːʳ] *adj* il (la) tuo(-a) *pl*, i (le) tuoi (tue); il (la) suo(-a); (*pl*) i (le) suoi (sue); il (la) vostro(-a); (*pl*) i (le) vostri(-e); il (la) loro; (*pl*) i (le) loro; *see also* **my**

you're [juəʳ] = **you are**

yours [jɔːz] *pron* il (la) tuo(-a); (*pl*) i (le) tuoi (tue); (*polite form*) il (la) suo(-a); (*pl*) i (le) suoi (sue); il (la) vostro(-a); (*pl*) i (le) vostri(-e); (: *very formal*) il (la) loro; (*pl*) i (le) loro; *see also* mine; faithfully; sincerely

yourself [jɔːˈsɛlf] pron (reflexive) ti; si; (after prep) te; sé; (emphatic) tu stesso(-a); lei stesso(-a); **yourselves** pl pron (reflexive) vi; si; (after prep) voi; loro; (emphatic) voi stessi(-e); loro stessi(-e); see also **oneself**

youth [juːθ, pl juːðz] n gioventù f; (young man) giovane m, ragazzo; **youth club** n centro giovanile; **youthful** adj giovane; da giovane; giovanile; **youth hostel** n ostello della gioventù

you've [juːv] = **you have**

Yugoslavia [ˈjuːɡəʊˈslaːvɪə] n (Hist) Jugoslavia

Z

zeal [ziːl] n zelo; entusiasmo

zebra [ˈziːbrə] n zebra; **zebra crossing** (BRIT) n (passaggio pedonale a) strisce fpl, zebre fpl

zero [ˈzɪərəʊ] n zero

zest [zɛst] n gusto; (Culin) buccia

zigzag [ˈzɪɡzæɡ] n zigzag m inv ▸ vi zigzagare

Zimbabwe [zɪmˈbɑːbwɪ] n Zimbabwe m

zinc [zɪŋk] n zinco

zip [zɪp] n (also: ~ fastener, (US) **zipper**) chiusura f or cerniera f lampo inv ▸ vt (also: ~ up) chiudere con una cerniera lampo; **zip code** (US) n codice m di avviamento postale; **zipper** (US) n cerniera f lampo inv

zit [zɪt] n brufolo

zodiac [ˈzəʊdɪæk] n zodiaco

zone [zəʊn] n (also Mil) zona

zoo [zuː] n zoo m inv

zoology [zuːˈɒlədʒɪ] n zoologia

zoom [zuːm] vi to ~ past sfrecciare; **zoom lens** n zoom m inv, obiettivo a focale variabile

zucchini [zuːˈkiːnɪ] (US) npl (courgettes) zucchine fpl

Phrasefinder

Frasi utili
per chi viaggia

TOPICS | ARGOMENTI

TOPICS | ARGOMENTI

Hello!	Ciao!
Good evening!	Buona sera!
Good night!	Buona notte!
Goodbye!	Arrivederci!
What's your name?	Come si chiama/Come ti chiami?
My name is ...	Mi chiamo...
This is ...	Le presento/Ti presento...
my wife.	*mia moglie.*
my husband.	*mio marito.*
my partner.	*la mia compagna/il mio compagno.*
Where are you from?	Di dov'è?/Di dove sei?
I come from ...	Sono di...
How are you?	Come sta?/Come stai?
Fine, thanks.	Bene, grazie.
And you?	E lei?/E tu?
Do you speak English?	Parla/Parli l'inglese?
I don't understand Italian.	Non capisco l'italiano.
Thanks very much!	Grazie mille!

Asking the Way | Chiedere indicazioni

Where is the nearest ...?	C'è un/una... qui vicino?
How do I get to ...?	Come si va a... ?
Is it far?	È lontano?
How far is it from here?	Quanto dista da qui?
Is this the right way to ...?	È questa la strada per...?
I'm lost.	Mi sono perso/persa.
Can you show me on the map?	Me lo può/puoi far vedere sulla cartina?
You have to turn round.	Deve/Devi tornare indietro.
Go straight on.	Vada/Vai sempre dritto.
Turn left/right.	Giri/Gira a sinistra/a destra.
Take the second street on the left/right.	Prenda/Prendi la seconda a sinistra/destra.

Car Hire | Noleggiare una macchina

I want to hire ...	Vorrei noleggiare...
a car.	una macchina.
a moped.	un motorino.
a motorbike.	una motocicletta.
How much is it for ...?	Quanto costa...?
one day	al giorno
a week	alla settimana
Is there a kilometre charge?	C'è un supplemento chilometrico?
What is included in the price?	Cos'è incluso nel prezzo?
I'd like a child seat for a 2-year-old child.	Vorrei un seggiolino per un bambino di due anni.
What do I do if I have an accident/if I break down?	Cosa devo fare in caso di incidente/guasto?

Breakdowns	In caso di guasto
My car has broken down.	Mi si è fermata l'auto.
Where is the next garage?	Dov'è l'officina più vicina?
... is broken.	Si è rotto/rotta...
The exhaust	lo scappamento.
The gearbox	la scatola del cambio.
The windscreen	il parabrezza.
... are not working.	...non funziona/non funzionano.
The brakes	I freni
The headlights	Gli abbaglianti
The windscreen wipers	I tergicristalli
The battery is flat.	Ho la batteria scarica.
The car won't start.	L'auto non parte.
The engine is overheating.	Il motore si surriscalda.
The oil warning light won't go off.	La spia dell'olio resta accesa.
I have a flat tyre.	Ho una gomma a terra.
Can you repair it?	Può ripararlo?
When will the car be ready?	Quando sarà pronta la macchina?

Parking	Parcheggiare
Can I park here?	Si può parcheggiare qui?
How long can I park here?	Per quanto tempo si può parcheggiare?
Do I need to buy a (car-parking) ticket?	Bisogna prendere un biglietto per il parcheggio?
Where is the ticket machine?	Dov'è il parchimetro?
The ticket machine isn't working.	Il parchimetro non funziona.
Where do I pay the fine?	Dove si pagano le multe?

Petrol Station	Al distributore di benzina
Where is the nearest petrol station?	Dov'è il distributore (di benzina) più vicino?
Fill it up, please.	Il pieno, per favore.
30 euros' worth of ..., please.	30 euro di..., per favore.
diesel	*gasolio*
unleaded economy petrol	*benzina (super) senza piombo (95 ottani)*
premium unleaded	*benzina super senza piombo a 98 ottani*
Pump number ... please.	La pompa numero..., per favore.
Please check ...	Mi può controllare...?
the tyre pressure.	*le gomme*
the oil.	*l'olio*
the water.	*l'acqua*
A token for the car wash, please.	Mi dà un gettone per l'autolavaggio per favore?

Accident	In caso d'incidente
Please call ...	Per favore, chiami...
the police.	*la polizia.*
an ambulance.	*un'ambulanza.*
Here are my insurance details.	Ecco gli estremi della mia assicurazione.
Give me your insurance details, please.	Mi dà gli estremi della sua assicurazione per favore?
Can you be a witness for me?	Mi può fare da testimone?
You were driving too fast.	Stava andando troppo veloce.
It wasn't your right of way.	Non aveva la precedenza.

Travelling by Car	Viaggiare in auto
What's the best route to …?	Qual è la strada migliore per…?
Where can I pay the toll?	Dove si paga il pedaggio?
Do you have a road map of this area?	Ha una cartina stradale della zona?

Cycling	Viaggiare in bicicletta
Where is the cycle path to …?	Dov'è la pista ciclabile per…?
Can I keep my bike here?	Posso tenere qui la bicicletta?
My bike has been stolen.	Mi hanno rubato la bicicletta.
Where is the nearest bike repair shop?	Dov'è il negozio di biciclette più vicino che faccia riparazioni?
The brakes	*I freni*
The gears	*Il cambio*
… aren't working.	*…non funzionano/non funziona.*
The chain is broken.	Si è rotta la catena.
I've got a flat tyre.	Ho una gomma a terra.
I need a puncture repair kit.	Vorrei di un kit di riparazione per le gomme.

Train	Viaggiare in treno
How much is …?	Quanto costa…?
a single	*un biglietto di sola andata*
a return	*un biglietto di andata e ritorno*
A single to …, please.	Un biglietto di sola andata per…, per favore.

I would like to travel first/second class.	Vorrei viaggiare in prima/seconda classe.
Two returns to ..., please.	Due biglietti di andata e ritorno per..., per favore.
Is there a reduction ...?	Ci sono riduzioni...?
for students	per gli studenti
for pensioners	per i pensionati
for children	per i bambini
with this pass	con questa tessera
I'd like to reserve a seat on the train to ... please.	Vorrei prenotare un posto sul treno per...
Non smoking/Smoking, please.	Non fumatori/Fumatori per favore.
Facing the front, please.	Nella direzione di marcia, per favore.
I want to book a sleeper to ...	Vorrei prenotare una cuccetta per...
When is the next train to ...?	A che ora è il prossimo treno per...?
Is there a supplement to pay?	Bisogna pagare un supplemento?
Do I need to change?	Devo cambiare?
Where do I change?	Dove devo cambiare?
Which platform does the train for ... leave from?	Da che binario parte il treno per...?
Is this the train for ...?	È questo il treno per...?
Excuse me, that's my seat.	Mi scusi ma quello è il mio posto.
I have a reservation.	Ho la prenotazione.
Is this seat free?	È libero questo posto?
Please let me know when we get to ...	Mi può avvertire quando arriviamo a...?

GETTING AROUND | IN VIAGGIO

Where is the buffet car?	Dov'è il vagone ristorante?
Where is coach number ...?	Dov'è la carrozza numero...?

Ferry | Viaggiare in traghetto

Is there a ferry to ...?	C'è un traghetto per...?
When is the next/first/last ferry to ...?	A che ora è il prossimo/il primo/l'ultimo traghetto per...?
How much is it for a car/camper with ... people?	Qual è la tariffa per una macchina/un camper con... persone?
Where does the boat leave from?	Da dove parte la nave?
How long does the crossing take?	Quanto dura la traversata?
Where is ...?	Dov'è...?
the restaurant	il ristorante
the bar	il bar
How do I get to the car deck?	Come si arriva al ponte per le auto?
Where is cabin number ...?	Dov'è la cabina numero...?
Do you have anything for seasickness?	Ha qualcosa contro il mal di mare?

Plane | Viaggiare in aereo

Where is ...?	Dov'è...?
the taxi rank	il parcheggio dei taxi
the bus stop	la fermata dell'autobus
the information office	il banco informazioni
Where do I check in for the flight to ...?	Dov'è il banco accettazione del volo per...?
Which gate for the flight to ...?	Qual è l'uscita del volo per...?

When is the latest I can check in?	A che ora chiude il check-in?
When does boarding begin?	Quando comincia l'imbarco?
Window/Aisle, please.	Finestrino/Corridoio per favore.
I've lost my boarding pass/ my ticket.	Ho perso la carta d'imbarco/il biglietto.
I'd like to change/cancel my flight.	Vorrei cambiare/annullare il biglietto.
Where is the luggage for the flight from …?	Dove arrivano i bagagli del volo da…?
My luggage hasn't arrived.	I miei bagagli non sono arrivati.

Local Public Transport | Trasporti urbani

How do I get to …?	Come si va a…?
Where is the nearest …?	Dov'è la… più vicina?
bus stop	*fermata dell'autobus*
tram stop	*fermata del tram*
underground station	*stazione della metropolitana*
Where is the bus station?	Dov'è la stazione degli autobus?
A ticket, please.	Un biglietto per favore.
To …	Per…
Is there a reduction …?	Ci sono riduzioni…?
for students	*per gli studenti*
for pensioners	*per i pensionati*
for children	*per i bambini*
for the unemployed	*per i disoccupati*
with this pass	*con questa tessera*
Do you have day tickets/ multi-journey tickets?	Avete biglietti giornalieri/ validi per più percorsi?

How does the ticket machine work?	Come funziona il distributore di biglietti?
Do you have a map of the underground?	Ha una cartina della metropolitana?
Please tell me when to get off.	Mi può dire quando devo scendere?
What is the next stop?	Qual è la prossima fermata?

Taxi | In taxi

Where can I get a taxi?	Dove posso trovare un taxi?
Call me a taxi, please.	Mi chiama un taxi, per favore?
Please order me a taxi for … o'clock.	Mi può prenotare un taxi per le…?
To the airport/station, please.	All'aeroporto/Alla stazione, per favore.
To the … hotel, please.	All'hotel…, per favore.
To this address, please.	A quest'indirizzo, per favore.
I'm in a hurry.	Ho fretta.
How much is it?	Quant'è?
I need a receipt.	Mi fa una ricevuta?
Keep the change.	Tenga pure il resto.
Stop here, please.	Si fermi qui, per favore.

ACCOMMODATION	TROVARE UNA SISTEMAZIONE
Camping	**Campeggio**
Is there a campsite here?	C'è un campeggio nelle vicinanze?
We'd like a site for ...	Vorremmo un posto...
a tent.	*tenda.*
a camper van.	*per il camper.*
a caravan.	*per la roulotte.*
We'd like to stay one night/ ... nights.	Ci fermiamo una notte/ ...notti.
How much is it per night?	Quanto costa a notte?
Where are ...?	Dove sono...?
the toilets	*i bagni*
the showers	*le docce*
Where is ...?	Dov'è...?
the shop	*lo spaccio*
the site office	*la direzione*
the restaurant	*il ristorante*
Can we camp here overnight?	Possiamo campeggiare qui per la notte?
Can we park here overnight?	Possiamo parcheggiare qui l'auto per la notte?
Self-Catering	**Appartamento**
Where do we get the key for the apartment/house?	Dove troviamo la chiave dell'appartamento/della casa?
Do we have to pay extra for electricity/gas?	L'elettricità/Il gas si paga a parte?
How does ... work?	Come funziona...?
the washing maching	*la lavatrice*
the cooker	*la cucina*
the heating	*il riscaldamento*
the water heater	*il boiler*

ACCOMMODATION	TROVARE UNA SISTEMAZIONE
Who do I contact if there are any problems?	A chi mi devo rivolgere in caso di problemi?
We need ...	Ci può dare...?
a second key.	*un'altra chiave*
more sheets.	*altre lenzuola*
more crockery.	*altre stoviglie*
The gas has run out.	È finita la bombola del gas.
There is no electricity.	Non c'è la corrente.
Do we have to clean the apartment/the house before we leave?	Dobbiamo pulire l'appartamento/la casa prima di partire?

Hotel — Albergo

Do you have a ... for tonight?	Ha una... per questa notte?
single room	*camera singola*
double room	*camera doppia*
room for ... people	*camera per...persone*
Do you have a room ...?	Ha una camera...?
with bath	*con bagno*
with shower	*con la doccia*
I want to stay for one night/ ... nights.	Mi fermo una notte/...notti.
I booked a room in the name of ...	Ho prenotato una camera a nome...
I'd like another room.	Mi può dare un'altra camera?
What time is breakfast?	A che ora è servita la colazione?
Can I have breakfast in my room?	Servite la colazione in camera?
Where is ...?	Dov'è...?
the restaurant	*il ristorante*
the bar	*il bar*

ACCOMMODATION	TROVARE UNA SISTEMAZIONE
the gym	*la palestra.*
the swimming pool	*la piscina*
I'd like an alarm call for tomorrow morning at ...	Mi può svegliare domani mattina alle...?
I'd like to get these things washed/cleaned.	Mi può far lavare/lavare a secco queste cose?
Please bring me ...	Mi può portare...?
... doesn't work.	...non funziona.
Room number ...	Camera numero...
Are there any messages for me?	Ci sono messaggi per me?

SHOPPING | FARE ACQUISTI

I'm looking for ...	Sto cercando...
I'd like ...	Vorrei...
Do you have ...?	Avete...?
Do you have this ...?	Ce l'avete...?
in another size	*in un'altra taglia*
in another colour	*in un altro colore*
I take size ...	Porto il...
My feet are a size 6.	Porto il 39 (di scarpe).
I'll take it.	Lo/La prendo.
Do you have anything else?	Ha qualcos'altro?
That's too expensive.	È troppo caro/cara.
I'm just looking.	Do solo un'occhiata.
Do you take ...?	Accettate...?
credit cards	*le carte di credito*
debit cards	*le carte di addebito*

Food Shopping | Fare la spesa

Where is the nearest ...?	Dov'è il/la... più vicino/a?
supermarket	*supermercato*
baker's	*panetteria*
butcher's	*macelleria*
grocer's	*negozio di alimentari*
Where is the market?	Dov'è il mercato?
When is the market on?	Che giorno è il mercato?
a kilo of ...	un chilo di...
a pound of ...	mezzo chilo di...
200 grams of ...	200 grammi di...
... slices of ...	...fette di...
a litre of ...	un litro di...
a bottle of ...	una bottiglia di...
a packet of ...	un pacchetto di...

Post Office	All'ufficio postale
Where is the nearest post office?	Dov'è l'ufficio postale più vicino?
When does the post office open?	A che ora apre la posta?
Where can I buy stamps?	Dove posso comprare dei francobolli?
I'd like … stamps for postcards/letters to Britain/the United States.	Vorrei… francobolli per cartolina/lettera per la Gran Bretagna/gli Stati Uniti.
I'd like to post/send …	Vorrei imbucare/spedire…
this letter.	*questa lettera.*
this parcel.	*questo pacchetto.*
by airmail/express mail/ registered mail	per via aerea/per posta celere/per raccomandata
Is there any mail for me?	C'è posta per me?
Where is the nearest postbox?	Dov'è la buca delle lettere più vicina?

Photos and Videos	Foto e video
A colour/black and white film, please.	Una pellicola a colori/in bianco e nero, per favore.
With twenty-four/thirty-six exposures.	Ventiquattro/trentasei pose.
Can I have a tape for this video camera, please?	Vorrei una cassetta per questa videocamera, per favore.
Can I have batteries for this camera, please?	Vorrei delle pile per questa macchina fotografica, per favore.
The camera is sticking.	Mi si è inceppata la macchina fotografica.

Can you develop this film, please?	Mi può sviluppare questa pellicola?
I'd like the photos ...	Vorrei le foto
matt.	*opache.*
glossy.	*lucide.*
ten by fifteen centimetres.	*dieci per quindici.*
When will the photos be ready?	Quando saranno pronte le foto?
How much do the photos cost?	Quanto costano le foto?
Could you take a photo of us, please?	Ci può fare una foto per favore?

Sightseeing	Giri turistici
Where is the tourist office?	Dov'è l'ufficio turistico?
Do you have any leaflets about …?	Avete degli opuscoli su…?
Are there any sightseeing tours of the town?	Ci sono visite guidate della città?
When is … open?	A che ora apre…?
the museum	*il museo*
the church	*la chiesa*
the castle	*il castello*
How much does it cost to get in?	Quanto costa il biglietto?
Are there any reductions …?	Ci sono riduzioni…?
for students	*per gli studenti*
for children	*per i bambini*
for pensioners	*per i pensionati*
for the unemployed	*per i disoccupati*
Is there a guided tour in English?	Ci sono visite guidate in inglese?
Can I take photos here?	Si possono fare foto qui?
Can I film here?	Si può filmare qui?

Entertainment	Spettacoli
What is there to do here?	Cosa c'è di interessante da fare qui?
Where can we …?	Dove si può…?
go dancing	*andare a ballare*
hear live music	*ascoltare musica dal vivo*
Where is there …?	Dov'è…?
a nice bar	*un locale simpatico*
a good club	*una buona discoteca*
What's on tonight …?	Cosa danno stasera…?
at the cinema	*al cinema*

LEISURE | TEMPO LIBERO

at the theatre	*a teatro*
at the opera	*all'opera*
at the concert hall	*all'auditorium*
Where can I buy tickets	Dove si possono comprare i
for ...?	biglietti per...?
the theatre	*il teatro*
the concert	*il concerto*
the opera	*l'opera*
the ballet	*il balletto*
How much is it to get in?	Quanto costa il biglietto?
I'd like a ticket/... tickets	Vorrei un biglietto/... biglietti
for ...	per...
Are there any reductions ...?	Ci sono riduzioni...?
for children	*per i bambini*
for pensioners	*per i pensionati*
for students	*per gli studenti*
for the unemployed	*per i disoccupati*

At the Beach | In spiaggia

Where is the nearest beach?	Dov'è la spiaggia più vicina?
Is it safe to swim here?	È pericoloso nuotare qui?
How deep is the water?	Quanto è profonda l'acqua?
Is there a lifeguard?	C'è un bagnino?
Where can you ...?	Dove si può...?
go surfing	*fare surf*
go waterskiing	*fare sci d'acqua*
go diving	*fare immersioni*
I'd like to hire ...	Vorrei noleggiare...
a deckchair.	*una sdraio.*
a sunshade.	*un ombrellone.*
a surfboard.	*una tavola da surf.*
a jetski®.	*un aquascooter.*
a rowing boat.	*una barca a remi.*
a pedal boat.	*un pedalò.*

Sport | Sport

Where can we ...?	Dove possiamo...?
play tennis/golf	*giocare a tennis/golf*
go swimming	*nuotare*
go riding	*andare a cavallo*
go fishing	*andare a pescare*
go paragliding	*fare parapendio*
How much is it per hour?	Quanto costa all'ora?
Where can I book a court?	Dove si può prenotare un campo da tennis?
Where can I hire rackets?	Dove si possono noleggiare delle racchette?
Where can I hire a rowing boat/a pedal boat?	Dove si può noleggiare una barca a remi/un pedalò?
Do you need a fishing permit?	Bisogna avere una licenza di pesca?

Skiing | Sciare

Where can I hire skiing equipment?	Dove si può noleggiare l'attrezzatura da sci?
I'd like to hire ...	Vorrei noleggiare...
downhill skis.	*degli sci (da discesa).*
cross-country skis.	*degli sci da fondo.*
ski boots.	*degli scarponi da sci.*
ski poles.	*delle racchette.*
Can you tighten my bindings, please?	Mi può stringere gli attacchi, per favore.
Where can I buy a ski pass?	Dove si compra lo ski pass?
I'd like a ski pass ...	Vorrei...
for a day.	*un giornaliero.*
for five days.	*uno ski pass per cinque giorni.*
for a week.	*un settimanale.*
How much is a ski pass?	Quanto costa uno ski pass?

When does the first/last chair-lift leave?	A che ora è la prima/l'ultima seggiovia?
Do you have a map of the ski runs?	Ha una piantina delle piste?
Where are the beginners' slopes?	Dove sono le piste per principianti?
How difficult is this slope?	È difficile questa pista?
Is there a ski school?	C'è una scuola di sci?
What's the weather forecast for today?	Come sono le previsioni del tempo per oggi?
What is the snow like?	Com'è la neve?
Is there a danger of avalanches?	C'è pericolo di valanghe?

English	Italian
A table for ... people, please.	Un tavolo per... persone, per favore.
The ... please.	Mi/Ci può portare...
menu	*il menù.*
wine list	*la carta dei vini.*
What do you recommend?	Cosa mi/ci consiglia?
Do you have ...?	Avete...?
any vegetarian dishes	*dei piatti vegetariani*
children's portions	*delle porzioni per bambini*
Does that contain ...?	Contiene...?
peanuts	*noccioline*
alcohol	*alcol*
Can you bring (more) ... please?	Mi può portare ancora..., per favore?
I'll have ...	Prendo...
The bill, please.	Il conto, per favore.
All together, please.	Un conto unico, per favore.
Separate bills, please.	Conti separati, per favore.
Keep the change.	Tenga pure il resto.
This isn't what I ordered.	Non è quello che avevo ordinato.
The bill is wrong.	C'è un errore nel conto.
The food is cold/too salty.	Il cibo è freddo/troppo salato.

TELEPHONE | AL TELEFONO

Where can I make a phone call?	Dove posso fare una telefonata?
Where is the nearest card phone?	Dov'è il telefono a scheda più vicino?
Where is the nearest coin box?	Dov'è il telefono a monete più vicino?
I'd like a twenty-five euro phone card.	Vorrei una scheda telefonica da venticinque euro.
I'd like some coins for the phone, please.	Mi potrebbe dare della monete per il telefono?
I'd like to make a reverse charge call.	Vorrei fare una telefonata a carico del destinatario.
Hello.	Pronto.
This is …	Sono…
Who's speaking, please?	Scusi, chi parla?
Can I speak to Mr/Ms …, please?	Posso parlare con il signor/la signora…?
Extension …, please.	Mi passa l'interno…, per favore?
I'll phone back later.	Richiamo più tardi.
Can you text me your answer?	Mi può mandare la risposta via SMS?
Where can I charge my mobile phone?	Dove posso ricaricare il telefonino?
I need a new battery.	Vorrei una batteria nuova.
Where can I buy a top-up card?	Dove posso comprare una scheda ricaricabile?
I can't get a network.	Non c'è campo.

Passport/Customs | Passaporti e dogana

Here is ...	Ecco...
my passport.	*il mio passaporto.*
my identity card.	*la mia carta d'identità.*
my driving licence.	*la mia patente.*
Here are my vehicle documents.	Ecco i documenti della mia macchina.
This is a present.	È un regalo.
This is for my own personal use.	È per uso personale.

At the Bank | In banca

Where can I change money?	Dove posso cambiare dei soldi?
Is there a bank/bureau de change here?	C'è una banca/un ufficio cambi da queste parti?
When is the bank open?	Che orari fa la banca?
I'd like ... euros.	Vorrei... euro.
I'd like to cash these traveller's cheques.	Vorrei cambiare questi traveller's cheque.
What's the commission?	Di quanto è la commissione?
Can I use my card to get cash?	Posso prelevare dei contanti con la carta di credito?
Is there a cash machine here?	C'è un Bancomat® qui vicino?
The cash machine swallowed my card.	Il Bancomat® mi ha mangiato la carta.

Repairs | Riparazioni

Where can I get this repaired?	Dove posso farlo/farla riparare?

PRACTICALITIES | CONSIGLI PRATICI

Can you repair …?	Mi può riparare…?
these shoes	*queste scarpe*
this watch	*questo orologio*
How much will the repairs cost?	Quanto costa la riparazione?

Emergency Services | Servizi di emergenza

Help!	Aiuto!
Fire!	Al fuoco!
Please call …	Per favore, chiami…
an ambulance.	*un'ambulanza.*
the fire brigade.	*i pompieri.*
the police.	*la polizia.*
I need to make an urgent phone call.	Devo fare una chiamata urgente.
I need an interpreter.	Ho bisogno di un interprete.
Where is the police station?	Dov'è il commissariato di polizia?
Where is the hospital?	Dov'è l'ospedale?
I want to report a theft.	Devo denunciare un furto.
…. has been stolen.	Mi hanno rubato…
There's been an accident.	C'è stato un incidente.
There are … people injured.	Ci sono… feriti.
I've been …	Mi hanno…
robbed.	*derubato.*
attacked.	*assalito.*
raped.	*violentato.*
I'd like to phone my embassy.	Vorrei chiamare la mia ambasciata.

Pharmacy	In farmacia
Where is the nearest pharmacy?	Dov'è la farmacia più vicina?
Which pharmacy provides emergency service?	Qual è la farmacia di turno?
I'd like something ...	Vorrei qualcosa...
for diarrhoea.	*contro la diarrea.*
for a temperature.	*per la febbre.*
for car sickness.	*contro il mal d'auto.*
for a headache.	*per il mal di testa.*
for a cold.	*per il raffreddore.*
I'd like ...	Vorrei...
plasters.	*dei cerotti.*
a bandage.	*una fascia.*
some paracetamol.	*del paracetamolo.*
I can't take ...	Non posso prendere...
aspirin.	*l'aspirina.*
penicillin.	*la penicillina.*
Is it safe to give to children?	Va bene per i bambini?

At the Doctor's	Dal dottore
I need a doctor.	Ho bisogno di un dottore.
Where is casualty?	Dov'è il pronto soccorso?
I have a pain here.	Ho un dolore qui.
I feel ...	Ho...
hot.	*caldo.*
cold.	*freddo.*
I feel sick.	Ho la nausea.
I feel dizzy.	Mi gira la testa.
I'm allergic to ...	Sono allergico/allergica a...
I am ...	Sono...
pregnant.	*incinta.*
diabetic.	*diabetico/diabetica.*

HEALTH | LA SALUTE

HIV-positive.	*sieropositivo/sieropositiva.*
I'm on this medication.	Sto prendendo questa medicina.
My blood group is ...	Il mio gruppo sanguigno è...

At the Hospital | In ospedale

Which ward is ... in?	In che reparto è...?
When are visiting hours?	Qual è l'orario di visita?
I'd like to speak to ...	Vorrei parlare con...
a doctor.	*un dottore.*
a nurse.	*un infermiere/un'infermiera*
When will I be discharged?	Quando mi dimettono?

At the Dentist's | Dal dentista

I need a dentist.	Ho bisogno di un dentista.
This tooth hurts.	Mi fa male questo dente.
One of my fillings has fallen out.	Mi è saltata un'otturazione.
I have an abscess.	Ho un ascesso.
Can you repair my dentures?	Mi può aggiustare la dentiera?
I need a receipt for the insurance.	Ho bisogno di una fattura per l'assicurazione.

Business Travel | Viaggi d'affari

I'd like to arrange a meeting with …	Vorrei organizzare una riunione con…
I have an appointment with Mr/Ms …	Ho un appuntamento con il signor/la signora…
Here is my card.	Ecco il mio biglietto da visita.
I work for …	Lavoro per…
How do I get to …?	Come si arriva…?
your office	al suo ufficio
Mr/Ms …'s office	all'ufficio del signor/della signora …
I need an interpreter.	Ho bisogno di un interprete.
May I use …?	Posso usare…?
your phone	il suo telefono
your computer	il suo computer
your desk	la sua scrivania

Disabled Travellers | Disabili

Is it possible to visit … with a wheelchair?	È possibile accedere alla visita del/della… per un disabile?
Where is the wheelchair-accessible entrance?	Dov'è l'accesso per i disabili?
Is your hotel accessible to wheelchairs?	Il vostro albergo è dotato di un accesso per disabili?
I need a room …	Ho bisogno di una camera…
on the ground floor.	al pianterreno.
with wheelchair access.	con un accesso per disabili.
Do you have a lift for wheelchairs?	Avete un ascensore per disabili?
Where is the disabled toilet?	Dov'è la toilette per i disabili?
Can you help me get on/off please?	Mi può aiutare a salire/scendere, per favore?

The tyre has burst.	Ho una gomma forata.
The battery is flat.	Ho la batteria scarica.

Travelling with children | In viaggio con i bambini

Is it OK to bring children here?	Si possono portare i bambini?
Is there a reduction for children?	Ci sono riduzioni per i bambini?
Do you have children's portions?	Avete delle porzioni per bambini?
Do you have ...?	Avete...?
a high chair	*un seggiolone*
a cot	*un lettino*
a child's seat	*un seggiolino*
Where can I change the baby?	Dove posso cambiare il bambino/la bambina?
Where can I breast-feed the baby?	Dove posso allattare?
Can you warm this up, please?	Me lo può scaldare per favore?
What is there for children to do?	Cosa c'è di interessante da fare per i bambini?
Where is the nearest playground?	Dov'è il parco giochi più vicino?
Is there a child-minding service?	C'è un servizio di baby sitter?

I'd like to make a complaint.	Vorrei fare un reclamo.
To whom can I complain?	A chi posso rivolgermi per un reclamo?
I'd like to speak to the manager, please.	Vorrei parlare con il direttore, per favore.
... doesn't work.	...non funziona.
The light	*La luce*
The heating	*Il riscaldamento*
The shower	*La doccia*
The room is ...	La camera è...
dirty.	*sporca.*
too small.	*troppo piccola.*
too cold.	*troppo fredda.*
Can you clean the room, please?	Può rifare la camera, per favore?
Can you turn down the TV/the radio, please?	Può abbassare il volume della televisione/della radio, per favore?
The food is ...	Il cibo è...
cold.	*freddo.*
too salty.	*troppo salato.*
This isn't what I ordered.	Questo non è quello che avevo ordinato.
We've been waiting for a very long time.	È da un bel po' che aspettiamo.
The bill is wrong.	C'è un errore nel conto.
I want my money back.	Rivoglio i miei soldi.
I'd like to exchange this.	Me lo/la potrebbe cambiare?
I'm not satisfied with this.	Non sono soddisfatto.